Forensic Focus 1

Forensic Psychotherapy
Crime, Psychodynamics and the Offender Patient

Editors:

Christopher Cordess
Professor of Forensic Psychiatry at the University of Sheffield
Honorary Consultant and Director of Research at Rampton Hospital

Murray Cox
Consultant Psychotherapist, Broadmoor Hospital

Forewords by
John Gunn, *Professor of Forensic Psychiatry, Institute of Psychiatry*
Richard Wells, *Chief Constable, South Yorkshire Police*

Jessica Kingsley Publishers
London and Philadelphia

First published in the United Kingdom in 1996 by
Jessica Kingsley Publishers Ltd
116 Pentonville Road
London N1 9JB, UK
and
400 Market Street, Suite 400
Philadelphia, PA19106, USA

Paperback edition 1998

Second impression 2000
Third impression 2002
Fourth impression 2004

Copyright © 1996 Jessica Kingsley Publishers

'Murderous Guilt' by Nicholas Treurniet was first published in
The Dutch Annual of Psychoanalysis 1993 edited by H. Groen-Prakken and A. Ladan
(Swets and Zeitlinger, Lisse, 1993.) Reproduced by kind permission.

British Library Cataloguing in Publication Data
Forensic Psychotherapy:Crime,
Psychodynamics and the Offender Patient. -
(Forensic Focus Series; no.1)
I. Cordess, Christopher II. Cox, Murray
III. Series
614.1

Library of Congress Cataloging in Publication Data
A CIP catalogue record for this book is available from the Library of Congress

ISBN 1 85302 634 4 pb

Printed and Bound in Great Britain by
Athenaeum Press, Gateshead and Tyne and Wear

Contents

Part I • Mainly Theory

Part II • Mainly Practice

Forensic Psychotherapy and its Neighbours   5

Training and Supervision – The Interface with Forensic Psychiatry

Research   507

The Creative Arts Therapies   543

Postscript
The Editors

Acknowledgements

One of the themes repeated in these pages is the fact that forensic psychotherapy always implies a corporate endeavour. No forensic psychotherapist can work in isolation. This applies, *a fortiori*, to those whose editorial task it has been to collate and integrate material from so many sources. First, our thanks are focused upon those patients and their therapists whose encounters furnish the substance of the numerous illustrative vignettes. Second, we are grateful to all who have written against the clock, and the constraints of space, to give us such a richly woven tapestry of theory and practice. Third, it is doubtful whether Jessica Kingsley and her colleagues could ever know the magnitude of the debt we owe them, although the very size of these volumes speaks volumes. Finally, mention must be made of Malcolm Smith of Karnac Books, who originally suggested that it was about time a book on Forensic Psychotherapy was written.

To all, our thanks.

That these final notes were written on Guy Fawkes Day may have some unconscious link to the possibility of threats to walled-off, closed institutions – no matter whether these are of the mind, of professional disciplines or of custodial establishments. On the other hand, Bonfire Night is also associated with the Catherine Wheel, and Saint Catherine is the patron saint of learning!

Christopher Cordess and Murray Cox
London
5 November 1994

Caveat

Substantial though this publication is, it has a relatively circumscribed frame of reference. This is not a text book embracing the wider field of forensic psychiatry. Thus it is taken for granted that, for the patients under discussion, forensic psychotherapy is one of the relevant treatments of choice. Important though forensic psychotherapy is in its own right, it only represents a fraction of an overall therapeutic policy which may legitimately apply to a forensic patient. When there are sound clinical indications, physical treatments, such as ECT, may be life-saving. For example, a patient may be so depressed that his psycho-motor retardation renders him inaccessible to dynamic psychotherapy, until appropriate medication has been prescribed for an adequate duration. Yet again, there are other general medical conditions, such as organic brain damage, hypertension or diabetes, which may have contributed to the pre-disposing/precipitating constellation of determinants originally leading to an individual entering the forensic field and becoming an 'offender patient'.

These introductory remarks are self-evident and patronizing to those who know the field well. Nevertheless, we hope that early establishment of such basic frames of reference will avoid subsequent misunderstanding and confusion.

By the same token, it will soon become apparent that our aim has been to present material which will be of relevance to those from a wide range of disciplines and at all levels of professional experience.

Before engaging with the first sentence of the book itself, it is to be stated unequivocally that any details which might render an individual patient recognizable or identifiable have been changed. We trust, however, that the psychodynamic significance of the clinical material and its illustrative potential are not thereby diminished.

Issues of confidentiality are of crucial importance in the forensic field. This cannot be emphasized too strongly, especially at a time when the communications explosion and the introduction of market forces into public health care systems threaten to blur the boundaries of who should know what about whom.

In the interest of gender presentation, brevity and cadence, as editors we have avoided the 'he/she', 'his/her' amalgam by using 'he' when individuals of either gender are implied. We would be equally happy writing 'she' to include 'he'. But, being male, this seems unnecessarily pedantic and absurd.

C.C. & M.C.

Foreword

John Gunn

It is a pleasure to me to welcome a book devoted to 'forensic psychotherapy'. As one of the editors says in one of his introductions, forensic psychotherapy is not a wholly felicitous term. Presumably this is because psychotherapy does not actually relate to the court of law ('the forum' of forensic). Presumably, too, it is because although psychiatry is getting specialized, is it not yet so specialized that it is legitimate to identify a special form of therapeutics called forensic psychotherapy. Nevertheless, the term is a useful one and many potential readers will rightly discern what they can expect between the covers of these volumes.

The treatment of mentally disordered people who offend has always and will always lean heavily on the talking treatments. Psychotherapy is an essential skill in any branch of psychiatry, and is particularly important for patients who have chronic problems and who are relating to the rest of society through unwelcome deeds, rather than through words. The term forensic psychotherapy also serves to remind mental health professionals that individuals with mental disorders who are offensive and prone to rejection need psychotherapy just as much as the better organized, better heeled members of society who tradition-ally make their way to the psychotherapist's chair or couch.

This book is written by professionals and enthusiasts with a wide range of skills, from psychoanalysis to occupational therapy, from law to social work, from psychology to dancing. One bias I have discerned is that most (but not all) writers seem to be talking about treatment within an institution. Perhaps this is inevitable as forensic psychiatry becomes the last repository of extended inpatient treatment, and furthermore there are groups of offender patients who can only be reached within an institution. Partly for that reason I want to highlight the few chapters that deal with offenders who live in the community. In many ways forensic psychiatry, with specialist hostels and sophisticated probation services has been a leader in community psychiatry, and pioneers such as Glover did most of their work in the outpatient clinic. It is important, therefore, to emphasize this aspect of psychotherapeutic potential, especially now that closer collaboration with police and probation services is becoming easier.

There is no danger in this book of an over-emphasis on what some people who work within the criminal justice system call 'the medical model'. This curious term, often used in a pejorative sense, seems to mean an over-emphasis on medical practitioners as therapists. This book acknowledges the obvious, that good treatment needs many skills (including exclusively medical ones such as pharmacotherapy) and these skills will always be delivered by a wide range of professionals. It is best that they work in harmony.

It is highly gratifying to see a chapter on research in this book. So often psychotherapy and research seem incompatible. As the authors of the chapter lament 'in an ideal world this chapter would review a large number of publications...but we do not yet live in that ideal world'. The chapter sets out many useful ideas for research in psychotherapy. Perhaps forensic psychotherapy can not only show that it is possible to treat the untreatable, but also that it is possible to research the unresearchable. Certainly a topic that tries to persist without a scientific basis is ultimately doomed to extinction.

There is another chapter which says it is a research chapter, but I found more difficulty with that one. Treurniet calls his detailed account of the psychoanalysis of a killer, scientific research. I wonder whether this is just a semantic problem, or whether there is something fundamental here which forensic psychotherapy needs to tackle. The chapter is interesting and the treatment enabled both the psychotherapist and the patient to acquire meaning for the killing; it seemed to provide a way for the patient to grow a little, perhaps become less guilt ridden, and thus find it easier when he was released. However, whilst this is a nice description of a piece of psychotherapy in action, it is not an example of scientific research. That is not to demean it or devalue it, it is simply to say that scientific research is a different enterprise with its own rules. Scientific research is not the only way we can understand the world, but it is a very powerful way and psychotherapy cannot afford to eschew it, nor, in my view, can it afford to make the error of thinking that all descriptive activities such as the careful recording of a psychoanalysis are necessarily the same thing as scientific research.

This book has something for everyone; a veritable bran tub. My hope is that it will make tongues wag, first in the clinic (that's what it is all about), but also in the corridors and in the committee rooms, so that the role of psychotherapy in forensic psychiatry can be more easily understood and appraised.

Foreword

Richard Wells

I am delighted to be able to offer a modest introduction to this seminal work edited by Christopher Cordess and Murray Cox, each in his own right a signal contributor to the corpus of knowledge and experience in forensic psychiatry.

Many readers in this specialist field may be provoked to ask: why on earth a foreword from a police officer?

The answer, for me, is fairly simple. Whereas once the world of psychiatry and psychotherapy was inward-looking and inclined to find its contentment and even verification in its own deliberations, these days this seems to be less and less the case. Perhaps it is because of the access to this specialist world provided by increasingly popular television documentary films; perhaps it is a result of society's becoming more questioning and challenging about itself; yet again, it may be in furtherance of a genuine spirit of partnership which appears to be growing in kindred professions, inspired by national strategies of trying to squeeze more product out of fewer resources.

Police officers encounter daily the world of the emotionally disturbed. Sometimes the degree of disturbance necessitates immediate care for and control of the patient, and officers, ill-equipped to make judgments on 'sectioning' despite the fact that the law suggests the opposite, call with relief upon the services of those who *are* so equipped.

Officers who are confronted, in their peace-keeping role or in their investigative role, with what to them are inexplicable horrors – either horrors of commission by individuals or horrors of omission by society – seek first practical assistance and then, often in the quiet of the aftermath, seek explanations, some sense of context in which their experience can be placed.

I do not suppose this to be a text book for police officers, for it is truly a specialist work, with a great deal of intricate and professional detail for the enrichment of each practitioner in the field of forensic psychotherapy. But it is a compendium which acknowledges, owes its origins to and complements the emergent spirit of partnership between parties within the criminal justice system.

There is something in this unique volume for all who are involved, whether at the core of forensic psychotherapy or, like me, at its periphery; whether interested in theory or practice, in understanding short of treatment or in understanding in order better to treat, there is an abundance of wisdom and experience captured in these pages.

In a hundred years, future practitioners – and, if they are so minded, social historians – will devour this text as offering a panoramic view of our contemporary society seen through the eyes of a wide variety of professional commentators.

One of the challenges for present readers will be to stand back sufficiently far to be able to glimpse that same broad perspective of our own communities, to ask ourselves what part we play, however small, in its betterment and to determine to widen that role through greater understanding and collaboration.

This work will provide both significantly greater appreciation of virtually every aspect of the field, and invaluable indicators to ways in which co-operative ventures might usefully be undertaken.

Preface
In and Out of the Mind

The Editors

'In and out of the mind' is a phrase which presented itself in early editorial discussions. It was intriguing because it had arisen simultaneously in separate settings. It occupies the key location which the opening words of a book always command for two reasons. First, in non-technical terms, it is in keeping with those vital polarities between inner and outer world phenomena, and between contents and container, which forensic psychotherapy ignores at its peril. This book is concerned with events in the inner world which destructively influence events in the outer world which, in turn, impinge upon the inner world of both assailant and victim. The forensic psychotherapist constantly weighs and re-weighs the impact of turbulence in one world as it precipitates turbulence in the other. This, subsequently, calls for the offender patient's tailor-made corrective emotional experience which it is hoped that psychotherapy can provide. With this end in view, the therapist's attention is never far from those energies and objects which are both 'in and out of the mind'.

It is important to underline the fact that the first paragraph refers to '*the* offender patient'. In other words, *individual* forensic psychotherapy pervades our subject and permeates both 'Mainly Theory' (Volume I) and 'Mainly Practice' (Volume II), to the extent that it seemed superfluous to include a separate chapter on Individual Psychotherapy.

The second source of 'In and out of the mind' is the title of a book by Ruth Padel (1992), a classicist, who is also at home in our field, her father, John Padel, being a psychoanalyst and Shakespeare scholar. The perspectival world of the classicist serves to re-frame current experience by setting it against earlier frames from history and larger frames from myth. Forensic therapeutic experience repeatedly testifies to the fact pointed out by Erikson (1959, p.13) that 'we cannot lift a case history out of history' – and forensic clinical histories are always embedded in the history, both 'in and out of the mind', of those who commit the criminal act and those who are their victims, whatever form this may take. Most psychotherapeutic processes can, with minor modifications, be regarded as ways of framing, de-framing and subsequently re-framing perception, emotion, experience and behaviour: the vicissitudes of transference development, differentiation and subsequent resolution can be thought of as the re-framing of affective location and attachment. We may link current preoccupation with clinical history, via trans-generational conflicts – and their resolution – to the ubiquitous and constant cosmos of myth. By way of illustration of this widest frame of reference, the first specific question posed in the present volumes is one which invites the reader to make an informed guess as to how many times the word *Oedipus* (or Oedipal) is likely to occur in a work of this size, without taking the short cut to the index pages! The very mention of *Oedipus* makes the point that timeless issues are also finely focused in the numerous clinical histories which forensic psychotherapy explores and these pages explicate. Padel (1992) writes as follows:

> '*When tragic poets write about what is inside people, they are also writing about what is outside,* as their culture represents it. *Outside explains inside, and vice versa.*' (p.11. Emphasis added)

It should come as no surprise that the second invited guest to join the theme of this preface is Sherlock Holmes, for the impact of myth and the work of the detective have close links to forensic dynamics. In *The Cardboard Box* (Conan Doyle 1893), Sherlock Holmes asks:

> 'What is the meaning of it, Watson?
> What object is served by this circle of misery and violence and fear?'
> (p.52)

Although there is a long tradition of the application of psychodynamic ideas to the understanding of the offender and his act, it is only in recent years that this body of experience and theory, and the treatments which have evolved from it, have been acknowledged as an essential ingredient within the hybrid speciality of Forensic Psychiatry. A main reason is the increasing recognition of the centrality of psychological trauma and victimization in the personal histories of offenders, together with recognition of the suffering of the victims of criminal acts and other traumata, and their psychological sequelae. Whether we are considering the individual offender or the offender within the context of the family, the group, the institution or broadly within society, forensic psychotherapy asks, along with Sherlock Holmes, 'What is the meaning of it... this circle of misery and violence and fear?' The answer may frequently be complex and is sometimes elusive. But, invariably, it contains elements of past neglect, or trauma – such as a major early loss (of parent or sibling, for example) – or of abuse and failures of parenting, with consequent failure to achieve full emotional and personality development. This may later be manifest in a restricted capacity for empathy, poor self-esteem and unusually disruptive attachments and relationships, which may all play a part in leading to offending behaviour. This is as true for the major mental illnesses as for the personality disorders and sexual deviations. Mental illness alone is rarely a sufficient explanation of later violent and offensive behaviour, since there is no clear association between mental illness, *per se*, and criminality, except in the case of the paranoid psychoses.

The work of the forensic psychotherapist is similar to that undertaken in generic psychotherapy but with the crucial additional task of understanding the psychological necessity and the meaning of the criminal act. Within the therapeutic relationship, psychotherapist and patient *together* seek to understand the whole situation – not only intellectually but also emotionally.

One of the turning points in man's view of his place in the world, and specifically a spur for future developments in theories of sexuality and aggression, was Darwin's publication of *The Origin of the Species* (1859) and later *The Descent of Man* (1871). Later in the century and around its turn there was a rapid development of the concept of the unconscious which had a considerable impact upon the dynamic understanding of deviant and criminal acts. Mention only has to be made of the dynamics of 'dissociative phenomena' to bring a range of clinical considerations into focus. Ellenberger (1970) shows how much Freud was indebted to numerous scientific and literary sources in the gradual elaboration of his theories of the unconscious and of the repression and expression of sexual (libidinal) and aggressive instincts.

The Freudian body of clinical and theoretical knowledge forms the basis from which contemporary forensic psychotherapy traces many of its origins. Although Freud wrote little specifically on criminality – the classic papers being 'Criminals from a sense of Guilt' (1916) and 'The Exceptions' (1916) – there are other texts of particular relevance, such as 'Three Essays on the Theory of Sexuality' (1905c), 'The Case of Schreber' (1911b), and 'Group Psychology and the Analysis of the Ego' (1921), to cite just a few.

Later, the development of 'object relations theory' provided a huge impetus to psychodynamic thinking in relation to the criminal and his act. It should be noted that in this technical sense as used here and throughout these volumes, 'object' refers to another person, an animal or a thing. In their different ways Klein, then Winnicott, Bowlby, Fairbairn and later Bion moved away from instinct theory and the *intra*-personal, and towards 'object' relatedness, that is, the *inter*-personal, inter-subjective and the social context. Some of the crucial theoretical concepts, which are fully addressed in this book, include those of 'internal objects' (or 'mental representations'), 'unconscious phantasy', the 'holding environment' and the 'container and contained'. Using these concepts, psychodynamic knowledge has been applied increasingly beyond the individual patient to the greater understanding of groups. Its relevance and application to both secure and open institutions has been a recent growth area (see 'Special Settings' in Volume II). The former includes regional secure units, prisons and Special Hospitals and the latter category embraces a wide range of different settings in addition to the Therapeutic Community.

Forensic psychotherapy consists of the adaptation and application of this psychoanalytic *corpus* of knowledge, in conjunction with related sister disciplines – such as the other psychotherapies, criminology, sociology, psychiatry and ethology. It necessarily contains elements of the interests of society and of an expectation of social adjustment. There is thus always the idea of a third party present. Moreover, a third party is usually present in fact, represented by one or more elements of the Criminal Justice System. The concretization of this third party, in terms of legal constraints, and its impact on the inherent dynamic processes, forms much of the substance of this work.

A cursory glance through these pages will immediately convey the impression of a wide variety of writing styles and modes of presentation. Not only was this inevitable, it was also encouraged. But lest we are accused of diminished editorial responsibility, it needs to be stated that each contributor was given free rein, within the minimum of inevitable editorial constraints, to write as he felt best. There is thus no enforced editorial imprint. When a book of over 1000 pages, with 66 chapters, has been written by an ensemble of more than 60 authors a certain degree of repetition and overlap is inevitable.

It is our hope and expectation that the confluence of diverse professional interests and theoretical positions has been allowed to begin to map out the boundaries surrounding the currently crystallizing discipline of forensic psychotherapy. The orchestration of the 'Mainly Theory' section is clear evidence that no single theoretical persuasion has a monopoly of explanatory truth. Critical eclecticism is of the essence. These pages also give clear evidence of the interdependence of theory and practice. 'Mainly Theory' invokes illustrative clinical vignettes, whilst 'Mainly Practice' is permeated by conceptual and theoretical issues.

There are certain axiomatic aspects of forensic psychotherapy which, although beyond question, still need to be made explicit. They could be regarded as 'ground-base' motifs which underlie the ensuing theme and its variations. We refer first to the relationship between the *criminal act* and the tantalizing search for an accurately fitting *therapeutic act*. Or should we speak of the *criminal process* to be reflected in a reversed yet isomorphic *therapeutic process*? Second, we underline the collaborative nature of forensic psychotherapy.

It is entirely fitting that the first chapter of Volume I should be devoted to the crucial issue of 'the criminal act and acting out'. Debate about the nature and duration of such an act is both heated and prolonged. Thus, in answer to the question 'How long does it take to commit a murder?' one patient replied 'A lifetime', although the lethal gunshot wound required increased pressure on the trigger for less than a second. But if the criminal act cannot easily be defined and isolated, how much more complicated is the endeavour to delineate the therapeutic act. Again, the self-positing question is 'does such a definable entity exist?' In these volumes the forensic therapeutic process is looked at by a wide range of experienced practitioners, who inevitably approach the theme from divergent vantage points.

The necessity for eclecticism is underscored by the fact that, despite the size of the present volumes, there is much that remains conjecture or rests upon the weight of 'clinical experience' which may be only slightly more reliable than hazardous. It is for this reason that, as editors, we attach such importance to the triple-authored chapter on research. We well understand that critics and reviewers will be searching for hard evidence as to the efficacy or otherwise of forensic psychotherapeutic practice. Even so, immediate existential imperatives also refuse to be silenced. When dealing with such awesome issues, frequently involving interpersonal violence, humane 'containment' and all that this implies can never be less than important: this ambiguous, bi-focal term refers both to the *concrete* containment within a secure environment and the *metaphorical* containment within a holding relationship. The offender patient often needs both at the same time.

The second ground-base of this theme and variations is the indubitable fact that forensic psychotherapy always implies a collaborative endeavour between a range of agencies and disciplines. Sometimes, it is involved in residential and/or custodial settings and sometimes it is practised in the wider community of the 'body politic'. No forensic psychotherapist can 'go it alone'. Ethical issues are inevitable and intrinsic to the whole field. Such topics as confidentiality, public safety, the dilemma between the premature release of a potentially dangerous offender, or the unnecessarily prolonged detention of a no-longer-dangerous detainee, are matters of daily deliberation.

However encompassing a text such as this may be, there are inevitably some areas which deserve more emphasis than they have received. These volumes are no exception. The significance of issues of gender, of the differential rate of criminality and the different responses of the criminal justice and healthcare systems to men and women are increasingly acknowledged. The social, political and psychological constructions which underlie such differences are complex. In Chapter II:15 Estela Welldon contrasts the male and female perversions, but forensic psychotherapy needs to address issues of gender more widely. Similarly, issues of race, of ethnic diversity, of refugees and exile, where they impinge upon criminality, are increasingly the focus for other related disciplines – forensic psychiatry, for example (Cope 1990; Department of Health 1992). This is another important area in forensic psychotherapy which requires greater exploration. We hope that both these themes will be the subjects of future volumes in the *Forensic Focus* series.

It was more by good fortune than deliberate foresight that the interesting dialectic emerged between the title of the first chapter, *The Criminal Act and Acting Out*, and that of the last, namely, *Dance Movement Therapy*. In psychodynamic circles mention is often made of 'movement' occurring during the session. This usually refers to intrapsychic movement. It is evidenced by a relinquishment of primitive defences and a growing capacity to enjoy creative living: this includes an augmented ability to be both self-critical and more self-controlled in some ways and less so in others. It is therefore something of a light relief to discover that movement therapy and the dance – literally that which involves whole body movement as well as an abandonment to creative body rhythms – invites us to 'take the floor' and see where the latent energy in the ideas presented in these pages may lead.

As editors, we hope that these volumes will suggest areas of expertise which should be the preserve of specialist forensic psychotherapists. A greater hope is that they will be a source of information and stimulus to those who work in related disciplines where society, the offender and particularly the victim try to come to terms with the implications of what Shakespeare described as 'the acting of a dreadful thing' (*Julius Caesar* II.1.63).

Sherlock Holmes and his question 'What is the meaning of it, Watson?' here join forces with those of antiquity in studying and attempting to modify issues which are 'in and out of the mind'.

PART I
Mainly Theory

Introduction

Christopher Cordess

'Forensic psychotherapy' is the not wholly felicitous term used to describe the psychodynamic treatment of offenders and victims. Offenders themselves have frequently been victims of earlier exploitation and trauma and, psychologically speaking, are commonly victims of their own criminal behaviour, whether they fully recognize it or not; victims and survivors may become offenders. The overlap is great and is increasingly recognized.

Crime statistics inform us that reported criminal activity increases year on year, and, for example, popular literature, film and the media attest to a preoccupation within our culture with the criminal, and especially with violence. Whilst crime *per se* is a man-made concept, its origins lie in such notions as transgression, evil, sin and wickedness (Midgely 1992) and are as old as history. Just as we largely define health by the absence of ill health, so it appears that we seek to define our experience of the 'good' by an absence of its negative; at least some of our interest in or fascination with crime can be attributed to this function.

The origins and evolution of the psychodynamic body of knowledge are part of the history of ideas. As such, psychodynamic ideas draw from a range of different sources; they change, develop and even now are moving on. Ellenberger (1970) describes the diverse ancestry of the concept of the 'unconscious' and of 'the first dynamic psychiatry' which grew rapidly during the nineteenth century. He further traces 'the dawn and rise of the *new* dynamic psychiatry' in this century, and the part played by its four great representatives – Janet, Freud, Adler and Jung.

This broad ancestry of psychodynamic theory in general is reflected in its contemporary application to the understanding of the criminal mind: it necessarily shares territory with many close and, one hopes, friendly neighbours. Thus, in Part I, alongside chapters on the central concepts of psychoanalytic theory and related forensic aspects, the reader will find contributions from many cognate and overlapping disciplines, and their incorporation and application to evolving psychodynamic theories of offending behaviour and treatment. We take as our cue Freud's (1925b) own view that 'in the case of children and young delinquents, and as a rule, criminals dominated by their instincts, the psychoanalytic method must be adapted to meet the need' (p.vii).

Exploration of the inter-relation of criminology with early concepts of the unconscious mind were also common in the nineteenth century. For example Freud (1916a) in his brief and classic paper 'Criminals from a sense of Guilt', records that 'a friend has since called my attention to the fact that the "criminal from a sense of guilt" was known to Nietzsche, too. The pre-existence of the feeling of guilt, and the utilization of a deed in order to rationalize this feeling glimmer before us in Zarathustra's sayings "Of the Pale Criminal"' (p.333) – which Nietzsche wrote in 1883. Ellenberger (1970) describes, too, the pre-Freudian concept of self-deception of consciousness by the unconscious and by emotional thinking. He writes that, 'the vicissitudes of instincts (their combinations, conflicts, displacements, sublimations, regressions and turnings against oneself), the energy load of representations, the self-destructive drives in man' (p.543), as well as the origins of conscience, of guilt feelings and morals were typically Neitzschean, and common to much German Romantic philosophy of the nineteenth century. The reader will find much in the following chapters of these and other roots and their development in contemporary psychodynamic thinking.

There is one concept of particular interest which provides a forerunner to much which is central to forensic psychotherapy – and indeed any dynamic psychotherapy – and that is the theme of 'The Pathogenic Secret' (Ellenberger 1966). The idea of the pathogenic effect which a guilty secret may exert over its bearer has been common in different civilisations throughout history: so, too, have related ideas of the healing action of group or individual confession. The concept was brought into the psychotherapeutic sphere largely by Moritz Benedict (1835–1920): its development can be traced, through early dynamic psychiatry as a consciously held secret, into the theories of Janet and Freud who first conceptualized it as an *unconsciously* known secret. For Freud it was classically one consequence of repression and 'splitting' from consciousness of unacceptable events and phantasies. The concept of splitting – of both the ego and the object – and of fragmentation of the mind were much developed by Klein (1946) and by later theorists, and have become central to our subject. The theme of the pathogenic secret provides a strong link with contemporary theories of trauma – and specifically of the emotional and psychological consequences of early neglect and physical and sexual abuse – and the later effects if the traumatic event (the 'secret') cannot be worked through. These include abnormalities and impoverishment of personality, a range of psychiatric disorders, a propensity to 'dissociative' states of mind, and most pertinently, later offensive and criminal behaviour. The idea of the pathogenic secret is a forerunner, too, of the whole debate and furore which surrounds 'recovered memory syndrome'. The concept of 'the secret' and of the clandestine – both conscious and unconscious – have centrality in psychodynamic theories of offending and therapeutic practice, and are a primary theme which is explored in many different ways in the following pages.

The range of different viewpoints which exist within contemporary psychodynamic thinking is perhaps nowhere better illustrated than in the theories of aggression and hostility, which lie at the heart of forensic psychotherapy. They provide a direct focus for a number of these chapters, but are a prominent theme, indirectly, in others; for example, in the chapters on 'Psychotic and Borderline Processes', and in 'Defence Mechanisms'. The harnessing of aggression is described, too, in the chapter on 'Personality and Sexual Development'. The creative use and management of aggression within the transference–countertransference relationship brings us to the very core of our subject.

The Criminal Act and Acting Out

Christopher Cordess & Arthur Hyatt Williams

In law there are two requirements for a criminal act: the *actus reus* – that is, the overt act or offensive conduct (which may include an omission) – and a *mens rea* – or guilty state of mind. The exceptions are the so-called crimes of strict liability. For pragmatic reasons the law generally places greater emphasis upon the cognitive aspects of mental state rather than the emotional, although clearly the two elements are intimately entwined. Thus different offences may require a range of different mental elements, from intentionality, for example 'malice aforethought' as in murder, to recklessness or negligence. Other common terms which can be the source of legal dispute include questions of whether an act was 'voluntary', or whether it was 'knowingly' committed and whether the subject can be judged mentally responsible.

For the forensic psychotherapist such questions are central but viewed from a different standpoint. For the psychotherapist the criminal act is seen as a consequence of a state of mind in which unconscious processes and unconscious phantasy, as well as conscious thought, may also be major components. What is the meaning of the act? is the recurrent question. The therapeutic process aims to elucidate the frequently multiple conscious and unconscious meanings, and to lend to it greater affective as well as cognitive understanding. The offender may thereby no longer wish to repeat his criminal acts and may achieve greater powers to desist: he may also become able to make both psychic and actual reparation.

Crime is a man-made construct and is relative within different societies at different times. For the psychotherapist there is an assumption that all of us from our earliest years, as well as later, 'commit crimes' within our unconscious and conscious minds which we do not necessarily, however, enact. Thought, fantasy (conscious) and phantasy (unconscious)[1] is free: the 'thought crime' of George Orwell, or adultery 'in the heart' of the New Testament have had no place, at least yet, within English law. Williams (1983) quotes Sir Edward Coke 'No man shall be examined upon secret thoughts of his heart, or of his secret opinion: but something ought to be objected against him what he hath spoken or done' (p.146).

The 'secret thoughts of his heart' and his emotional life are the primary focus of all psychodynamic psychotherapy, but forensic psychotherapy takes account also of past and future possible criminal acts. The personality of the patient and his way of being are the subject of mutual investigation by patient and therapist. The psychodynamic model assumes developmental continuities through stages of life built upon inherent (constitutional) capacities of the new born and dependent upon later progressive life experience ('object relations'). It places particular emphasis upon the developmental importance of the experience of the first and early years, so that early failure by the primary carer (usually the mother) or experience of trauma or abuse are predicted to have significant psychological effects in later life. It joins with Socrates, in its own particular way, in assuming that 'the unexamined life is not worth living' (Plato 1993, p.63). It is the theory of the unconscious and of the use of the transference and counter-transference inter-action within therapeutic relationships which give it its particularity.

All psychodynamic psychotherapy provides some sort of narrative to a life – as a particular type of biography or autobiography. There is debate (as in biography) about the degree to which this is an historically true narrative and the degree to which, instead, it can aspire only to be an emotionally true re-construction (Spence 1983). Strict historical truth is not necessary for the healing process to evolve. Forensic psychodynamic psychotherapy emphasises the criminal act (or acts) as an important focus within this narrative. To borrow from behavioural-cognitive terminology, the task is to examine as many as possible of the 'antecedents' to the act, the 'act' itself, and its 'consequences' in detail, both consciously, and for the psychodynamicist also in terms of unconscious forces and phantasy.

There have been, it should be said, some strident objections to the use of such narrative re-constructions in the understanding of the criminal mind and the criminal act, and to the drawing of deterministic and causal inference from the re-construction. Foucault (1979), for example, objects that (in his terminology) 'the *delinquent* is to be distinguished from the *offender* by the fact that it is not so much his act as his life that is relevant in characterising him' (p.251, emphasis added). This objection needs to be taken seriously; a variant of it is

---

1   The convention of the different spellings of fantasy/phantasy is used in this chapter to refer to conscious and unconscious representation respectively.

heard day-to-day, clinically, in the justifiable complaint of some offenders, as in, for example, 'I am not a rapist, but I am a man who committed a rape'. Foucault goes on to argue against a 'punitive technique...(which) reconstitutes all the sordid detail of a life in the form of biographical knowledge and a technique for correcting individual lives' (p.252). Actually it is the conjunction of criminology and psychiatric discourse which Foucault criticizes but the critique provides a significant counterpoint for the over-zealous, and to the coercive imposition of 'correctives' to offensive actions in the name of 'therapy' which may thereby follow. The Criminal Act – as other acts – is multi-determined, and is the consequence of many variables both in the external world and in the internal world of the mind.

Richman (1932, p.45) points us to some of the obvious but frequently neglected truths concerning some crime: first, the criminal cannot always give a reasonable explanation for his act: second, there is frequently a compulsive element to the behaviour, and third, criminals, when we meet them often do not, in fact, appear to be so aggressive as we expect and as they are commonly regarded by the general public, as a consequence of their act. For the forensic psychotherapist these are common observations which require investigation and understanding in each individual case.

How does the *actual* crime emerge from a conscious fantasy or unconscious phantasy? Does it directly short circuit into action or hesitate for a shorter or a longer time in a constellation of 'criminal impulses'? What psychic processes are involved in the different procedures? In an individual case, how much is the potential criminal consciously aware of what is going on inside his mind? And most important, from a therapeutic point of view, can the sequence be diverted into some less criminal outcome, or will it gather a more criminal nature (as in the mental 'rehearsal' of a crime) during the course of the progression from phantasy-to-impulse-to-action? Retrospectively, the pre-existing fantasy (or phantasy) is commonly found to have been present and to have crystallized in the mind long before the actual criminal act. Sometimes it is quite simple, like the children's story about Burglar Bill and Burglar Betty whose behaviour was based upon a greedy wish and need to get what they wanted by simply taking it. Sometimes it is recognized by the conscience of the subject as being wrong and while his reality sense battles with the impulse to act it out, the impulsive part of his mind demands that he should 'do it', whatever it is.

Freud (1911a) describes the interplay and opposition of the *pleasure principle* – that is, the desire for the direct discharge of impulses – and the *reality principle* – which may oppose such discharge. Translated into our own terms the question becomes: can this conflict – which may be conscious or unconscious – be kept in the mind, so that some 'mellowing in cask', so to speak, can occur whereby the outcome may be modified and the action (in this case the criminal act) not therefore necessarily follow? In certain circumstances, the conflict 'to be or not to be' is pre-loaded by earlier experiences and the way they have been handled in the mind. Commonly, traumatic sensitizing experience, repressed in the unconscious, may be reawakened and detonated by a subsequent similar experience. Unworked-through anger and resentment, for example, may explode in a way which is quite out of proportion to the contemporaneous provocation. There may be triggering factors such as alcohol or drug intoxication: or intoxicating substances may be taken intentionally – to give 'Dutch courage' – in order to make the commission of the criminal act possible. An opportunity for violence may be sought or provoked. In forensic practice one frequently meets people who routinely carry a lethal weapon, which is rationalized as 'for the purposes of self defence': underlying such rationalization there may be the thought or phantasy: 'if I am threatened, I can and I will kill'.

A prisoner patient in psychotherapy with one of the authors (HW), said, 'It all happens in my mind and I feel that I can contain it no longer, so I go out and do it: after that I feel better, and I can be kind to my victim, and I can face the consequences' (of the action). The action was the serial assault of pre-pubertal girls. It consisted of a token constriction of the throat with her scarf, then quickly releasing it, then touching, but never penetrating, her genitals with his penis. In this sequence, as it became understood during therapy, he reversed and re-enacted what had happened to him as a young boy at the hands of a pre-pubertal girl. Although the fantasy is partially enacted in this repeated sequence, shame, guilt and reparative wishes had so far intervened before the ultimate tragedy ensued. A similar – albeit more terrible – pattern may be seen in the case of a type of serial murderer. In those instances in which the victim does not die immediately as the perpetrator intended, then, when, for example, the victim recovers consciousness, the later actions may be basically reparative (Masters 1985). The surge of murderous intent has by then diminished for the time being.

Of course, some criminal acts are planned in full conscious awareness, and may be motivated, for example, by greed, revenge, envy or perverse sexual desire. Nevertheless, they will all, also, have less conscious elements. The elucidation of these elements and the opportunity to talk about them may enable the individual to have the luxury of prior consideration and a capacity for thinking about what he has a mind to do, and may thereby offer him the possibility of not having to carry it out.

The aim of helping the potential offender talk about his emotional state is captured, at its very simplest, by William Blake (1794)

'I was angry with my friend:
I told my wrath, my wrath did end.
I was angry with my foe:
I told it not, my wrath did grow.'

As already described, a previous, emotionally unbearable traumatic experience may erupt into offensive action if it has remained 'split off' and, psychologically speaking, has remained 'undigested' or 'unmetabolised'. When there are later psychological stresses – either external, like the loss of a loved one, or intrapsychic, such as depression or a paranoid illness – then the previously stable, internal dynamic situation may explode, so that the individual feels 'taken over'. Such a situation was described first in the psychiatric literature by Wertham (1949) as the 'Catathymic Crisis', which for the perpetrator at that moment appears to be 'the only way out'.

Such eruptions into action are sometimes loosely referred to as 'acting out', by an analogy to the specific use of the term 'acting out' (German: 'agieren') as used by Freud (1905a, 1914b). 'Acting out' referred originally to a clinical, psychoanalytic concept which was confined quite specifically to the psycho-analytic, treatment relationship. It was seen as a transference reaction, as a manifestation of resistance to it, and as a substitute for a failure of 'remember-ing', and being able to think within the analytic relationship. In the case of Dora (S. Freud, 1905a), the patient left treatment, according to Freud, as a way of taking her revenge on him transferentially, in a way that she felt that she had been deserted by a figure in her past. Later, Freud (1914b) writes of this phenomenon as '...the patient does not remember anything of what he has forgotten and repressed but acts it out. He reproduces it not as a memory but as an action; he repeats it, without, of course, knowing that he is repeating it...for instance, the patient does not say that he remembers that he used to be defiant and critical towards his parents' authority; instead he behaves that way to the doctor (therapist)' (p.150).

Premature departures from treatment are particularly familiar in the treat-ment of offender patients, and acting out may well be an accurate description of such occurrences. However, many authors have commented upon the imprecision and over-generalization which have accrued to the term: for example Blos (1966, quoted by Sandler *et al.* 1973, p.94) writes that the concept 'has by now been expanded to accommodate delinquent behaviour and all kinds of...pathology and impulsive actions'. The term 'acting out' has even been applied on the one hand to the actions of creative artists, and on the other to the whole range of offending behaviour, the addictions, to the conversion symptoms of hysteria, to the rituals of the obsessional and to psychotic states. When a term is used so widely it becomes devalued.

Put another way, if the term 'acting out' is to be used, there is a necessary subsidiary question to be asked 'an acting out of what?'. As applied to the criminal act committed by a person who is not in a therapeutic relationship, it is being used in its widest sense and refers to a motor action associated with conscious or unconscious fantasy or memory. When applied to the action – whether criminal or not – of a patient who is already in a therapeutic relationship, its specific meaning is that of the *actualization* of unconscious memory (for example, of a trauma) or phantasy which is not being contained within the transference. Rycroft (1979a) puts the matter characteristically simply, 'Since psychoanalysis is a "talking cure" carried out in a state of reflection, acting out is anti-therapeutic. Acting out is characteristic of psychopathy and behaviour disorders and reduces the accessibility of these conditions to psychoanalysis' (p.1). It is for this reason that forensic psychotherapy – although it traces its origins predominantly to the psychoanalytic body of experience and knowledge – is an applied discipline, which necessitates the incorporation of the points of view of many other related disciplines and the application of techniques of 'management', when acting out threatens to become unacceptably dangerous.

In addition, although a pejorative sense is not intrinsic to the concept, its usage has often amounted to a description of actions which others (frequently the therapist) condemn, and it has come to imply too great a judgmental quality. Whilst this may have a 'feel good' factor in it for the therapist, it is useless to the patient unless the meaning of the action can be understood by the therapist, and communicated to the patient so that he feels understood.

Freud made the distinction between acting out *within* the analytic (therapeutic) relationship, and acting out *outside* of it, but 'both forms are regarded as a consequence of the analytic work and the treatment situation' (Sandler *et al.* 1973, p.96). An obvious example of the former is that of a patient repeatedly missing his sessions or turning up late: an example of the latter is when a form of idealized relationship is preserved with the therapist, but the patient behaves dismissively and aggressively in his relationships with others, as a consequence of unconscious rejection of, and anger with, the therapist.

Extrapolating from the concepts of Klein, and Bion (1970), 'acting out' may encompass a 'breaking in' of the self as a container into psychosis or suicide, or alternatively 'breaking out' into offending behaviour.

Two other terms should be mentioned, for the sake of completeness. 'Acting in' is a term which has been coined to refer to non verbal enactment within the therapeutic session, for example psychosomatic manifestations of anxiety or aggression. It is a disputed and specialized concept and need not detain us here.

More important is that of 'acting out' in the countertransference – or, alternatively 'acting out *of* the countertransference'. This is a constant and ubiquitous danger in forensic psychotherapy. Put starkly, the patient may induce in the therapist – by projective identification – a range, for example, of antagonistic or seductive feelings which the therapist may act upon without conscious realization. Acting out of the countertransference – in fact, acting out *for* the patient – may merely repeat for the patient what he sadly already knows from past experience only too well. An obvious example is that the therapist may feel that he wishes to reject the patient who has had a lifetime of rejection: the patient repeatedly induces an impulse or desire to dismiss him and thereby, as it were, to fulfil his expectation. Alternatively, the feelings engendered by the patient may be more than the therapist can hold and the therapist may act out outside of the relationship with the patient, or he may himself break down. Alternatively, he may cut off emotionally from the patient, and, thereby, behave in an emotionally ruthless way. Put another way, the therapist may become 'blind' and 'deaf' to the criminal past and potential for the future. The task of finding a way of talking to the patient using the countertransferential experience, without succumbing to these alternatives, is part of the essence of forensic psychotherapy. The subject is more fully discussed in Chapter I:2.

The Criminal Act can tell us much about aspects of the internal (mental) world of the perpetrator, which frequently have remained unconscious and unknown to him consciously – until, that is, he is faced with the fact and the consequences of his act. The internal 'state of affairs' – to use a phrase of Fairbairn's (1951, p.170) – may be denied by the perpetrator in many different ways, both conscious and unconscious, but all with the common goal of 'not wishing to know'. For example, in the sexual perversions, say in the actions of paedophiles, there may be an *exquisite* requirement for replicated detail, with evidence of planning, but remarkably little conscious fantasy. Denial may be conscious and stark as in: 'I didn't do it', or it may be that there are a range of different levels of partly conscious or unconscious self-deception. Typically, the paedophile may maintain 'I really do love children' – a denial and reversal of hate and of his wish to damage; or, 'they wanted me to do it' – a clear projection of desire and responsibility. A very literal example of desperate (and only partial) self-deception was that of a patient treated by one of the authors (CC), who not only effectively emptied his mind of any thought or other form of mentation whilst he sexually abused his step-daughters, but also covered his eyes with a pillow during the act – for fear of seeing what he was doing. In fact the acts were ritualized, elaborate and unvarying.

Alternatively, denial may take the form of a genuine amnesia. For example, in something like a half of all murders and some other major violence (at least in Britain) there will be partial or total amnesia for the fateful act, as if the mind could not bear the stark and emotionally traumatic experience of it: in other cases there may be memory but little or no feeling. Part of the task of the psychotherapist will be to try to help the perpetrator know more, both cognitively and affectively, about his action.

Some criminal acts may be considered analogous to the dream in which the 'manifest' content (S. Freud 1900, 1901) is either a representation of the internal unconscious state of mind, or the consequence of a compromise between 'latent' content and defensive censoring. For example, one psychotic patient spoke of his act of murder not as something that had, tragically, *actually* happened, but rather as 'a dream' (more like a day-dream): upon being asked to tell the dream, he related the narrative sequence of his act in minute and (so far as corroboration allowed one to judge) exact detail.

Stoller (1979) makes a related but more general point when he writes that, 'In an episode of erotic excitement is packed an individual's life history, the resultant character structure, and the more varied and movable defences we call neurosis...a fine way to understand someone is by that person's typical erotic daydream (p.293). Later he says 'Daydreams – all, not just the erotic – are terribly revealing as their owners know' (p.294); it is the tragedy of the criminal that he may only know his possible 'day dreams' by his acts, as it were, after the fact.

Another analogy is that of 'play'. Klein (1927) writes of her experience in the analysis of children using her (then) very original play technique. By the use of tiny dolls, animals, cars, trains and so on, she could, she writes, 'enable the child to represent various persons – (for example,) mother, father, brothers and sisters – and by means of the toys to act all its most repressed unconscious material' (p.174). She describes the very violent, murderous – biting, cutting and mutilating – phantasies of the normal child revealed by this technique, as well as the feelings of guilt and the consequent reparative wishes which are engendered by them. Klein herself draws attention to the analogy between this evidence of children's unconscious phantasies and some 'very horrible crimes', enacted by adults: she cites Jack the Ripper and serial killers known indirectly to her from contemporary reports.

In this chapter we have placed the criminal act centre stage. The psychotherapist allows himself to forget the past, or current, criminal acts of his patients at his peril: 'I've put it all behind me, doctor', and 'I've turned over a new leaf'; or 'I'm starting a new life', are tempting but frequently omnipotent fantasies with which we can all sympathize. If based on denial, they can be catastrophic as a way of dealing with a traumatized and traumatizing history. However, it also needs to be said that the past criminal act should not be allowed to occupy the whole of the arena of the therapeutic relationship all of the time, and there are some patients at some stages of their treatment who invite the therapist to do this. A patient may feel a consuming guilt for his act(s) – for example, the killing of a child or a spouse, *or* an objectively relatively minor transgression but one which he feels is unforgivable and puts him beyond redemption or recovery. In these cases the therapeutic task will be to help the patient to gain perspective, to help him hold on to a feeling of hope, and to the possibility of making some form of reparation.

It is within the psychotherapeutic relationship and the interplay of transference and countertransference reaction that the 'criminal act' and offensive behaviour needs to be experienced for it to be understood, jointly, by therapist and patient.

Transference and Countertransference
General and Forensic Aspects

Nicholas Temple

INTRODUCTION

In this chapter I will outline how the concepts of transference and counter-transference are used in psychotherapy. These concepts provide a framework which allows us to understand the therapeutic relationship and its complex interaction with the patient's subjective conscious and unconscious mind (the 'internal world'). In the forensic field this framework is essential to understand the often very disturbed aspects of the internal world which are acted out in criminal behaviour. These disturbed aspects become part of the transference relationship and present the therapist with special difficulties in tolerating his responses.

In psychodynamic psychotherapy transference and countertransference are the main therapeutic tools and the most important means of making contact with the patient's unconscious mental life. This type of psychotherapy is defined by the use of the relationship with the therapist as a focus of the work and distinguishes it from other forms of therapy.

Transference not only occurs in therapeutic relationships but also appears in many human relationships, when a way of relating to a figure from the past is repeated in the present, with a person who may trigger the old pattern of relating to be re-enacted. It is essential for all psychiatrists to be aware of this tendency and to be able to recognize and understand it, even when it is inappropriate to take it up with the patient. This understanding can prevent the psychiatrist from re-enacting with the patient an unhelpful pattern of behaviour derived from the past. The psychiatrist's countertransference feelings may draw him more deeply into acting out with the patient or can be the means by which he can begin to understand what is happening.

Transference is part of everyday life, because we all live out scenarios from our own inner world. We repeat our own internal unresolved dialogues with the people we come across. Frequently, this enactment will involve the other party in a similar repetition of a past relationship. This is why people find they repeat the same pattern of relationship, for example in a marriage, even with a different partner. The power of the internal world and its tendency to repetition is greater than is commonly recognized. The re-enactment of relationships with internal figures will be accompanied by emotional qualities and anxieties which are characteristic of the past relationship.

The internal relationships reflect relationships with early and important figures which have been transformed into the inner objects. These figures are found again in the present and repetitive attempts are made to resolve the difficulties of the past in the present. All too often these attempts at resolution are based on a sense of grievance derived from experiences of neglect, which involve the preoccupation with justified revenge and the conviction that revenge can bring about a resolution. The preoccupation with revenge is rooted in a wish to punish the figure that has failed and will involve sadism towards that figure, who is felt to deserve cruelty. This form of transference can be the explanation for many crimes in which a chance victim becomes the focus for revengeful and cruel acting out.

Forensic psychotherapy presents many difficult therapeutic tasks. One of the central problems is the powerful countertransference that is set up as a response to the patient's transference. The predominance of sado-masochistic pathology makes this particularly difficult. In forensic psychotherapy a good understanding of transference and countertransference phenomena is vitally important. Anyone undertaking this work should have supervision from senior colleagues and peers and will need to have had personal therapy as part of their training.

TRANSFERENCE

Freud (1895) first noted the phenomenon of transference in Breuer's treatment of Anna O. The patient's intense erotic attachment led Breuer to discontinue the treatment with some alarm. Freud first gave the process the name 'Transference' in 'The interpretation of dreams' (1900). He began by regarding it as an instance of the displacement of affect from one idea to another and did not see it as a useful part of the therapeutic relationship, but rather as an obstacle to treatment. He thought it was a manifestation of resistance to the therapeutic process of making the unconscious conscious. Emotional events and relationships are repeated in the transference without their being remembered. He identified the transference as being based on the repetition compulsion, in which old patterns of conflict and relationships are repeated in an attempt to find a solution, where separation from the primary object does not occur. Later, he discovered that the transference was an essential tool of the analytical process, a valuable means of gaining access to an understanding of the patient's unconscious inner world. The patient's relationships to his original objects were recreated and brought to life with all their richness in the analytic relationship, and transferred onto the person of the analyst.

Strachey (1934), in examining the therapeutic action of psychoanalysis, showed that what is being transferred is not the real relationships of the child's past but the internal objects which are built up by projection and introjection and represent a psychic reality which is different from the historical truth of the individual's past.

Klein (1952) helped to extend understanding of the nature of transference and the processes which create it, particularly projective identification. She emphasized that total situations are transferred from the past. She also made it clear that many aspects of everyday life reported by the patient gave clues to the unconscious anxieties provoked by the transference situation. This view of the transference as having wide repercussions in the whole relationship with the analyst and in the patient's everyday life was further developed by Joseph (1985, p.47) who describes how the patient unconsciously acts on the analyst to feel things and to become drawn into acting out with them in order to communicate the inner world. She emphasizes how many of these experiences are beyond the use of words and they can only be discovered through the feelings aroused in the analyst through the experience of the countertransference. The countertransference, like the transference, was originally seen by Freud as an obstacle to analytic work. Its discovery led to Freud's requirement for personal therapy in training, on the grounds that the analyst's own emotional difficulties would have a distorting effect on his response to the transference. The countertransference can now be seen as essential to the analytic process – the analyst's feelings in the countertransference provide a powerful means of understanding the patient and of monitoring the changing state of the transference.

In the analytic and psychotherapeutic relationship the transference is intensified by the encouragement to regression. The offer of emotional help alone may be an invitation to regress. This has certainly been noted at the Cassel Hospital where admission for in-patient psychotherapy causes some patients to regress severely and destructively. Some of the techniques of psychoanalytical treatment such as the analyst's neutrality and the use of free association and the couch will reinforce regression. The transference is itself a form of regression. The projective processes involved are a primitive means of communication, which are of great importance in infancy and will be a major means of communication in a regressed patient. In criminal acts projective processes are central to the acting out and will give rise to strong emotional responses in those who are on the receiving end of the projections.

In the transference, early experiences are brought to life with a strong sense of immediacy. Freud observed that in psychoanalytic treatment the transference could reach a great intensity and become the focus of the patient's emotional life, creating the transference neurosis. Then the transference became the basis of a new set of symptoms focused on the relationship with the analyst. This neurosis intensifies with the deepening of the therapeutic work. The intense experience of the transference facilitates the therapeutic effect of interpretation because of the emotional involvement with the therapist.

When the transference becomes dominated by deluded or paranoid ideas and the therapist is viewed in a fixed and unchanging way for example as a persecutory figure, a psychotic transference has been formed. This can be a persistent and unchanging state which may make further psychotherapy impossible. There is a preoccupation with the therapist's neglect and lack of care and a determination to seek revenge. Sometimes this state will be preceded by an idealization of the psychotherapist. The patient loses contact with any benign aspect of his internal objects and negates the existence of good aspects of the therapeutic relationship. He becomes stuck in what Klein described as the paranoid schizoid position, where good and bad objects (internal representations) are totally split from each other.

The implication for all transference work is that the therapist becomes the subject of powerful emotional attitudes in the patient. The transference is brought about by active projective processes. The patient will project parts of his internal world onto the psychotherapist in a way that causes the psychotherapist to feel as if he were one of those internal figures. Introjection will also occur when the patient identifies strongly with the psychotherapist and internalizes aspects of his personality, rather as children identify with parents and adopt aspects of their character.

Melanie Klein's concept of projective identification is basic to understanding how the therapist can feel taken over by an aspect of the patient. Projective identification causes the therapist to feel invaded by experiences which belong to the patient's internal world. Klein (1932a) describes phantasies of attacking the inside of the mother's body and invading it. She developed the term Projective Identification to define this process. It is closely associated with the paranoid schizoid position, where there is a phantasy of the projection of split off parts of the subject's own self or even of his whole self into the mother's body. The split off parts of the self are seen as having been put into and having become part of the other person. Projective identification is a type of projection – the ejection of something bad into the outside world which the subject cannot tolerate in himself, with the result that part of the subject's self is projected. A danger of this process is that the patient's ego can be impoverished because projective identification deprives it of parts of itself, both good and bad, which are lost and cannot contribute to the ego's function.

The psychotherapist on the receiving end of projective identification is liable to experience complex countertransference feelings, which may appear in his mind without an immediate sense of where they originated from.

B, a professional man, was consciously unaware of guilt about his destructive sexual behaviour and delinquency. He was calm but concerned at the unfairness of the proceedings being taken against him. His psychotherapist, on the other hand, experienced a sense of intense moral disapproval about his behaviour. His own harsh, critical super ego seemed to have been projected into the psychotherapist, while he remained unaware of it, with the danger that the psychotherapist would become morally disapproving and unable to understand the patient's split off superego. The patient had frequently acted as if he was in defiance of an unfair authority and sometimes had set up cruel punishment for himself by having accidents or being passive in the face of danger, as if his severe conscience was an active force in him which remained unconscious or was projected into the external authorities against whom he had rebelled.

In working with a forensic patient where sado-masochism is often present, the therapist can have the experience through projective identification of feeling himself to be a sadistic figure, representing a cruel internal figure of the patient. The cruel figure will be a manifestation of the patient's own harsh superego, an internal conscience figure inclined to cruel judgment rather than fairness. This type of transference and its retaliatory countertransference response may explain the cruel treatment of sexual offenders and the inherent sadism of the culture of some penal institutions, where the cruel superego may be acted out by the authorities and the other prisoners. The transference can also involve the projection of a submissive, masochistic part of the patient, so that the therapist may, in identifying with this projection, become the victim of the patient's sadism. This can occur when a psychotherapist finds himself colluding with unreasonable demands, or placating criticism.

The transference involves the therapist deeply in the patient's projections and can easily become an overwhelming experience. In forensic work where the patient has a disturbed internal world, the bad early experiences in the distorted form which they now exist in the internal world will be recreated in the transference relationship and, by projection, experienced directly in the countertransference, sometimes by feelings which are difficult to contain. It can prove to be difficult for the therapist not to be drawn into acting out a retaliatory response to the transference and so to create a repetition of the patient's experience of primary relationships. The psychotherapist needs to be closely in touch with his countertransference to enable him to monitor the transference and to improve his understanding of the patient and his own reactions.

THE COUNTERTRANSFERENCE

Freud (1910b) described the countertransference as resulting from the patient's influence on the physician's unconscious feelings and he stressed the fact that no psychoanalyst goes further than his own complexes and internal resistances permit, emphasizing the psychoanalyst's part in creating the countertransference. It is from this conclusion that he developed the principle that all psychoanalysts must have personal analysis as part of their training. Freud's own self-analysis must have played a part in his understanding of this. Personal therapy or training analysis is essential to enable the psychoanalyst or psychotherapist to be able to understand his own unconscious difficulties and make allowance for them in studying his countertransference responses. The therapist must maintain constant attention to his self-analysis.

Carpy (1989) has pointed out that although Freud changed his views about the therapeutic value of the transference, he never realized the therapeutic value of countertransference. In fact, Carpy points out that Freud's use of the term (S. Freud 1910b) referred to the analyst's unconscious resistance against dealing with areas of the patient's psychopathology that the analyst found difficult. This is quite distinct from the present day use of the term where it is applied to all the conscious, pre-conscious and unconscious feelings which the analyst has towards the patient.

Heimann (1950) was the first to clarify this view when she defined countertransference as 'all the feelings which the analyst has towards the patient' and includes the unconscious in this, concluding that there is an important communication of the patient's unconscious to the analyst's unconscious in the transference–countertransference relationship.

Carpy underlines the point that modern usage can neglect these unconscious aspects of countertransference, yet if one of the main vehicles of the transference–countertransference interaction is projective identification, then a significant part of the countertransference is unconscious and this only becomes conscious as a result of the analyst's or psychotherapist's analytic work on his countertransference feelings.

Carpy has helpfully pointed out that although the countertransference may lead to an understanding of the transference which could be the basis of an interpretation, this may often be counter-productive, creating in the patient the feeling that the analyst is trying to force something at him. Since transference experiences are often completely split off and projected, the attempt to create the link again may be disturbing to the patient. Carpy describes the therapeutic value of a capacity to tolerate the countertransference, until such time as it may be possible to take it up interpretatively. The timing of the interpretation derived from the therapist's countertransference will depend on the patient's capacity to reintegrate something split off and projected. This is an important principle in forensic psychotherapy, where too early attempts to interpret or too intensive forms of psychotherapy can intensify paranoid feelings, with the breakdown of treatment. This has long been recognized at the Portman Clinic where most treatment is based on a once weekly approach.

The countertransference will be the means by which the transference can be understood and experienced by the therapist and is therefore an equally important therapeutic tool. If the countertransference experience too closely corresponds to the transference and the therapist consequently acts it out, it may not be possible for the interaction to be understood at a conscious level. Rather, there will be a re-enactment of the unconscious relationship, with neither patient nor therapist being able to be consciously aware of what is happening. There may well be a motive for the psychotherapist to join in the resistance against understanding which, as Strachey (1934) points out, can be painful and difficult for the analyst as well as the patient.

The significance of countertransference depends on the function of the psychotherapist in the treatment. The psychotherapist or psychoanalyst has two functions. First, he is the object of the unconscious processes and second, he observes and interprets these processes (Racker 1968). As Carpy points out, a third function is the capacity to contain or tolerate the countertransference. The countertransference can help or hinder the perception of unconscious processes. The psychotherapist's countertransference experience sheds light on the unconscious processes of the transference but it will also provoke emotional reactions which impair the psychotherapist's understanding and interpretative capacity. The countertransference may affect the psychotherapist's manner and behaviour which will in turn affect the patient's perception of him. Thus the countertransference by affecting the psychotherapist's understanding and behaviour influences the patient's further transference and affects the therapeutic process. This emphasizes the dynamic and changing nature of the transference–countertransference interaction despite its capacity to remain very stable over long periods.

The much greater understanding of projection and projective identification which has resulted from the work of Klein and others has led to a greater emphasis on the countertransference as a field in which the therapist can experience and understand the patient's internal world. Internal objects can be understood much more thoroughly through having been directly projected, when the therapist experiences them as if they were part of his own feelings or attitudes, although he subsequently understands them as originating in the patient.

The countertransference becomes an important method of understanding the patient's unconscious experience, which may be quite different from what he is aware of. The therapist can have powerful emotional experiences which derive directly from the countertransference and seem at odds with the patient's conscious presentation. A middle aged man described being left in hospital for a long period as a child. He described this without emotion, as an interesting historical event and he made an effort to remember what had happened. His psychotherapist felt overwhelmed by sadness and had difficulty in controlling tears. This part of the patient's emotional experience had been located in the psychotherapist.

There has been disagreement about the extension of the concept of countertransference. Some authors take the countertransference to include everything in the analyst's reaction liable to affect the treatment, while others restrict it to the more unconscious processes brought about in the analyst by the patient's transference. A broad definition of countertransference allows the total situation in the transference to be better understood since any reaction in the therapist is liable to have a bearing on the unconscious relationship between patient and analyst.

The countertransference can usefully be divided into two categories: first of all into reactions which relate to the analyst's own internal figures which may be projected onto the patient, for example when the patient becomes a conscience figure for the psychotherapist. This can be described as the analyst's transference to the patient, when the patient becomes a transference figure for the therapist and the patient represents a figure from the therapist's own internal world. This can become a source of difficulty in psychotherapy and can cause confusion, particularly if the therapist acts out and is unaware of his unconscious interaction with the patient. Second, when the psychotherapist experiences emotions or attitudes which he is aware derive from the patient's transference and do not belong to him. Frequently there will be a situation in which the therapist's own internal world does interact with the transference projections but the therapist is sufficiently aware of his difficulties to identify the interaction.

If the psychotherapist's countertransference is reinforced by his transference to the patient, a confusion develops which can become overwhelming. This can always occur because of the tendency of the patient's transference to find areas in the psychotherapist's unconscious which resonate to the projections.

At times the patient may have a transference attitude that does not powerfully affect the therapist, leaving him emotionally uninvolved but aware of a misperception on the part of the patient. This is more likely to occur when the psychotherapist has understood what is taking place.

The psychotherapist's own training therapy should help him to be more aware of these areas and more able to distinguish between projections from the patient and his own internal objects. The countertransference work will need to be maintained by continued self-analysis by the psychotherapist. Brenman Pick (1985) described the importance of carefully monitoring the countertransference and the need for the analyst to work through its interaction with the analyst's own defences and vulnerabilities. Helpful interpretative work would grow out of this process of working through, in which the analyst can begin to distinguish his own areas of disturbance from that which is projected by the patient and to see how the two may interact. One of the dangers for those undertaking psychotherapy who have had no personal therapy is that they are not well equipped to be able to study their own inner world, including areas of disturbance in themselves. They are thus handicapped in using countertransference experiences.

A young psychiatrist, who had had no personal therapy, had taken on a difficult patient in regular psychotherapy. The patient was demanding and critical of the ward staff. The psychiatrist had rather positive views of his therapeutic capacity, which he thought would be enhanced by his special understanding of the patient. He became over-involved with the patient, giving her sessions at her demand. Despite the increasing strain he remained convinced that he would make her better because of his conscious desire to help her. A situation developed which was similar to that described by Main (1957). The psychiatrist concealed his anxiety and incapacity to cope with the patient's hostility by placating her and regarding himself as an ideal caring figure, while allowing all the criticism to be directed at other members of the staff team.

The patient's tendency to split can be seen to match closely the psychiatrist's own tendency to avoid hostility and criticism by seeing himself as an ideal therapist. The patient's and the psychiatrist's defences and transference matched one another quite closely. It was observed that this patient had a powerful tendency to affect staff by getting them over-involved. Other staff were inclined to be dismissive and critical of the patient. As a consequence of the interaction with the psychiatrist, the patient's hostility could not be tackled in the psychotherapy. The patient became troubled when the psychiatrist wished to bring the treatment to an end because he was moving to another job. He considered taking the patient to his next job but was advised against this because of anxieties about his over-involvement. The patient was quite unprepared for the collapse of the ideal relationship and regressed, became disturbed and made a suicide attempt. Some of this reaction was rage at the disillusion with the therapist but it is likely that the patient experienced the psychotherapist as having retaliated against her hostility which was split off in their relationship and not able to be dealt with openly.

The patient's projections into the therapist will lead the therapist to feel strong emotions, derived from these projections, either directly from them or from the emotional reactions caused by them. If they do not strongly link to the analyst's own internal figures they will not create such a difficult unconscious reaction in the analyst. He may become aware that these reactions do not really belong in him and are the result of a projection from the patient. It will necessarily be a complex task for the analyst to sort out his own internal feelings and reactions to the patient from that which has been projected into him. For this reason he will need to examine his countertransference carefully (Pick 1985; Carpy 1989).

This capacity to accept and understand countertransference reactions lends strength to the therapist's therapeutic understanding and is of importance as a way of tolerating the patient's internal world. It is also a valuable therapeutic tool that allows the analyst both to experience and empathize with the patient's internal state. It is the basis for the beginning of accurate interpretive work.

Before an effective interpretation can be made the process of working through the countertransference experience will need to take place. Sometimes this is an unconscious process when the analyst suddenly feels he knows what is happening or knows what to say without having thought it through at a conscious level. On other occasions it requires a period of reflection before it is possible to make sense of the countertransference experience. Supervision and clinical discussion are important sources of help to enable the psychotherapist to identify and understand the countertransference experience.

Vignette

L was a volatile young woman who had sought help for homosexuality, delinquency and phobic states. When she was agitated she relieved herself of the overwhelming anxiety by making another person agitated and upset. She would often choose a minor official such as a ticket collector, a policeman or a taxi driver and proceed to make this individual feel angry, humiliated and confused. This had been the pattern of her relationship with her father whom she had always provoked in this way. When she achieved this she gained relief and felt calm and triumphant, feeling superior to the other person who was now agitated and aggressive, even though she was at risk of being physically attacked.

She was often anxious and uncertain on Monday after a weekend break. She started the session by being highly critical of the analyst and the work that had taken place. She impugned the analyst's ability and claimed a general weakness in the whole theoretical basis of psychoanalysis. It appeared that she had felt anxious about her dependency on the analyst and was made more aware of it by the break and needed to protect herself from this vulnerable state. Despite the predictability of this attack the analyst felt provoked and inclined to retaliate by strongly refuting what the patient was saying or even, when the pressure became very great, felt like kicking the patient out. It was necessary for the analyst to remain silent and not to attempt to interpret what was going on until he had regained a capacity to examine his countertransference response and to note what was being projected, including the strong irrational wish to counter-attack and kick out the persecuting, humiliating experience.

In the midst of an intense countertransference experience it may not be possible to respond until the pressure to act has been contained. After a period of reflection it becomes possible to recognize the projection and to understand what has happened. This requires a knowledge of the patient's experience; in the case of L, needing to rid herself of an overwhelming experience of anxiety and humiliation by a critical internal figure. The patient triumphantly identified with the critical superego and projected the vulnerable attacked version of herself into the psychotherapist. The psychotherapist can learn how intolerable this experience is for the patient, leading to its expulsion into the therapist. The therapist's countertransference experience helps to throw light on the superego's relationship with the self in this patient.

This pattern of transference projection can underlie the delinquent individual's relationship with the victim of his crime. The psychic function of the criminal act enables the criminal to free himself of persecution and humiliation and project this into the victim, while he has a sense of omnipotence and triumph, because he has rid himself of intolerable feelings.

The psychic relief obtained by projection is reinforced by the material gain which results from the crime. In sexual crimes such as rape, the sadistic excitement associated with that which is disturbing and humiliating to the victim is profoundly important to the perpetrator of the crime. It allows him to rid himself of a very disturbing internal experience. Sado-masochism is closely connected with this defensive mechanism and the sexual excitement involved. Sadism allows the projection of what is disturbing and upsetting into the victim and allows the sadistic person to feel omnipotent and sexually excited by the triumph.

The treatment of adolescent offenders demonstrates how common these defences are. The psychotherapist will often first encounter the projective defences in his experience of the countertransference during the assessment.

In violent individuals it is evident that the violent murderous attack occurs at a time when the patient is feeling intolerably persecuted and identified with the victim by projection of the persecuting figure. The attack on the victim would reverse the situation to the extent that the persecuting experience becomes located in the victim and the attacker becomes identified with the aggressive internal object.

Vignette

D, an eighteen-year-old boy, was walking home with a rather sexually provocative adolescent girl who lived next door to him and to whom he felt attracted. She insulted him sexually by using a word for the female genitalia when he tripped over in the gutter. This humiliation led to an explosive reaction in which he stabbed her many times, leaving her bleeding and near to death. In subsequent psychotherapy with this patient, it became clear that it was easy for D to experience ordinary comments or questions as being critical and persecuting, whereupon he became agitated and aggressive. He also experienced his forceful mother as mocking his sexuality. On several occasions it felt as if a violent incident could occur in the consulting room, after an interpretation from the psychotherapist which the patient experienced as an intrusive criticism which humiliated him and made him feel small.

The projective mechanisms that are involved in criminal offences are more extreme versions of the same processes which take place in any transference relationship between patient and therapist. The forensic psychotherapist needs to be skilled at understanding his countertransference reactions to be able to cope with encountering the internal world of the offender and to be able to contain the projections without acting out or retaliation, which can be liable to lead to an explosive situation.

The most difficult kind of countertransference reaction is that which remains unconscious, so that the therapist is not aware of his reaction to the transference, nor properly of the nature of transference itself. This may occur when the therapist feels satisfied or pleased with what is happening. A patient who creates a pleasant, conforming atmosphere and a good response to the therapy may be creating a false, compliant atmosphere, setting up a relationship which is supportive and avoids conflict. The seductiveness of this situation can result in a therapy which does not progress, or where perverse or destructive behaviour is hidden and not dealt with. When this occurs it is likely that the analyst is unconsciously involved in a collusion with the patient. An intense sense of anxiety about destructiveness can lead to this collusion. The therapist may wish to avoid dealing with an angry, disappointed, or paranoid patient. This can make the pleasure of a conforming, positive patient very rewarding, as an avoidance of these difficulties. The therapist's own capacity to cope with persecutory anxiety and criticism and to be able to make a judgment about what is a valid criticism and what is an accusation will be necessary if a collusive situation is to be avoided.

Where perverse sexual fantasies in the patient are involved it may be difficult to examine the analyst's own involvement and perverse excitement. The psychotherapist's unconscious interest in perversion can result in collusion with the patient's perverse excitement. As Chasseguet-Smirgel (1985) points out, we are all capable of perverse excitement and sadism. This can include the subtle perversion of the therapeutic relationship itself.

It is possible for the psychotherapist to become unconsciously the masochistic victim of a bullying or sadistic and perverse situation in the therapy. A perversion involves a sadistic attitude towards the object, who can respond in a retaliatory fashion, and so be sadistic in return to the patient or become masochistic and accept the role of victim. It is possible for the psychotherapist to act out in either of these ways. The talion principle is fundamental to the sado-masochistic state, where the principle of 'an eye for an eye and a tooth for a tooth' is dominant, as if only by full retaliation can the injury be undone.

One of the greatest difficulties is to intervene in the sado-masochistic relationship between the superego and the patient's self in a way which allows some form of mediation and fairness in this cruel exchange.

SOME PROBLEM AREAS IN THE TRANSFERENCE–COUNTERTRANSFERENCE INTERACTION FOR THE FORENSIC PSYCHOTHERAPIST

Many of the problems encountered in managing the transference–countertransference relationship and in using it constructively to further therapeutic work are common to forensic psychotherapy and all psychodynamic psychotherapy, but there are a number of areas in which the forensic psychotherapist is presented with particular difficulties because of the intensity of disturbance which is encountered in forensic patients and because of the particular type of primitive defences which are encountered. It may be helpful to consider some of these areas separately to clarify the problems which can be encountered in forensic work.

Severe Disturbance and Primitive Defences

The high degree of underlying disturbance which is defended against in delinquent and perverse acting out will inevitably be drawn into the therapeutic relationship and will be projected in the transference. There will be a tendency for more paranoid processes to be evident which will test the therapist's capacity to contain and understand this in the countertransference. The therapist is likely to be treated as a dangerous and persecuting figure who will need to be controlled. Inexperienced therapists find this difficult when their conscious intention is to be helpful. A recognition of this state will allow the therapist to be cautious in not interpreting too quickly or forcefully and not demanding too great an intensity of contact which may provoke uncontrolled reactions. The capacity to tolerate the countertransference as described by Carpy will be important, particularly in the early stages of the treatment, when a treatment alliance is being established. The treatment alliance will have to become sufficiently strong to contain the negative disturbed aspects of the transference.

Sadism and Masochism and Sexually Perverse Defences

The importance of the sadistic dynamic has already been emphasized. As Chasseguet-Smirgel (1985) has pointed out, perversions are 'temptation in the mind common to us all'. The perversion is based on sadism which, apart from triumphant and erotically exciting cruelty, aims to destroy the order and structure of differentiation. Differences are abolished and feelings of helplessness, smallness, inadequacy as well as absence, castration, death and loss are abolished. It is possible to see how effective an omnipotent defence sadism can be against a sense of loss or psychic pain. This is even more clear when it is organized into a sexual perversion so that the destruction of differentiation, the projection of weakness into another and sexual excitement are combined to avoid the individual's sense of vulnerability. When the psychotherapist enters into this situation and a transference relationship develops, he will feel the consequence of these primitive defensive structures; initially he may feel the victim of them, and then become identified with a wish to retaliate, thus acting out the countertransference. The therapist's experience of vulnerability in the countertransference can make the pressure to retaliate sadistically very strong, although to do this is to enter into the sado-masochistic exchange and to act out with the patient.

Vignette

P, a sixteen-year-old boy who had a strong sense of vulnerability about his masculinity, developed a paedophiliac perversion. He had a compulsion to control girls aged seven or eight to prevent them urinating and then finally to hold them when they became desperate and did urinate. He had imprisoned girls for this purpose. The control and sadistic excitement gave him great relief from his own sense of weakness. The fear engendered in the girls was essential to his excitement. He engendered a vicious retaliation from the police and parents, including castration threats which indicated the degree to which he projected an internal attacker while he was excited to identify with the same attacker in the perverse behaviour. In psychotherapy the same dynamic was recreated. The therapist felt controlled by the patient and yet to break free of the control seemed like an attack on the patient. It became clear that P's experience was of the therapist being a dangerous figure who had to be controlled in this way.

Acting Out

Patients in forensic psychotherapy are by definition strongly prone to dealing with conflict by acting out. Action is substituted for thinking or feeling because this would involve contact with painful experiences of humiliation, vulnerability or persecution. In acting out, the internal world and its internal objects are projected into the outside world, in such a way that others are forcibly recruited to play the parts of internal figures. One of the effects of acting out on the countertransference is for the therapist to be under pressure to join in the acting out and to take the part of one of the internal figures. This can result in a situation in which the therapist finds it very hard to contain his responses long enough to be able to understand the projective processes that are involved.

There are times when acting out in forensic patients needs to be contained by external structures such as institutional care, the police or probation officer. Inevitably prison is a container for acting out which becomes so dangerous as to force a containing reaction, even if an extreme one.

In the countertransference the therapist will need to be able to take acting out seriously, including the dangers of it, while avoiding retaliation. The therapist must take care that he is not drawn in to the cruel relationship between the patient's super ego and a more vulnerable part of the patient's self. Often acting out represents a defiant attack upon the threatening superego figure which is provoked to a punishing retaliation, as was the case with the patient P whose acting out led to such threatening retaliation. Acting-out has been addressed elsewhere, and specifically in Chapter I:1.

Rigid Defences and Resistance

The nature of the disturbance and the primitive internal world mean that there is a fear of a catastrophic reaction if the system of defences comes under threat. There may be the phantasy that the breakdown of defences will lead to an explosive state of extreme persecution, murder, violence or psychosis. The therapy can therefore be experienced as a dangerous threat to the psychic equilibrium.

The resistance will represent the forces which oppose change or understanding. It will certainly be present in the patient and the therapist as a pressure against understanding the transference–countertransference relationship.

Resistance is important in that it will protect the patient against the catastrophic breakdown of defences. The resistance will be directed against the therapeutic endeavour and will maintain the status quo. In depressed patients there can be an intense attachment to a sadistic superego figure which cannot be abandoned at any cost. The therapist will need to be able to cope with countertransference reactions to destructive blocking of the resistance, which can be seen as purely negative and it is easy to lose sight of the protective function of the resistance.

Negative Therapeutic Reaction

The negative therapeutic reaction is a particular example of a resistance against therapeutic progress which protects against the catastrophic risks of change. Phobic anxiety about contact with the therapist is a common situation in the delinquent and perverse patient. This leads to a state of affairs in which good contact established with the patient can itself lead to further worsening of the patient's state and acting out. The negative therapeutic reaction occurs where good progress leads to disturbance in defences and a violent worsening of the patient's state, restoring the equilibrium of the patient's defences. A negative therapeutic reaction can lead to a very confused countertransference experience for the psychotherapist, when progress and real contact with the patient lead to a worsening in the symptoms, implying a failure of the treatment. The negative therapeutic reaction can take the form of a new set of symptoms which block the progress of the therapeutic relationship.

Vignette

A borderline young woman, who entered psychoanalysis with a male analyst and began to engage in the treatment, developed an intense homosexual affair within a few months of beginning, which directed her away from the developing work in the analysis. During this period of sexual acting out, which included sado-masochistic behaviour with her partner, it was not possible for much work to be done in the analysis. She had once before had a homosexual affair in her life, when she left home to go to university and felt guilty about leaving her ill mother.

Timing of Interpretative Work

In considering the patient's reaction to involvement with the therapist, it has been observed that too rapid interpretation and involvement can lead the patient to become persecuted and to break off treatment. This will be because the analyst's involvement and interpretation are experienced as if they were an attempt to push something persecuting back into the patient. By this means the psychotherapist becomes an actively persecuting internal figure and this will lead to more forceful acting out, as if in an attempt to rid the individual of this disturbing experience.

Thus it will be important for the therapist to be able to judge rather carefully, by examining the patient's reactions, how much involvement and interpretation the patient can take on at that time. It will be a difficult judgment since it will be important to be able to interpret these persecutory anxieties, but in such a way that the patient feels that something is being contained rather than being forced at him.

Defence Mechanisms
General and Forensic Aspects

Anthony Bateman

INTRODUCTION

A central theme of psychotherapy is of division and conflict between internal wishes and external reality, producing inner tension and anxiety, which in turn necessitate adaptation and compromise to both internal need and external demand. Adaptation is made possible by defences – psychological configurations which minimize conflict, reduce tension, maintain intrapsychic equilibrium, regulate self-esteem and play a central role in dealing with anxiety whether arising from internal or external sources. If used inappropriately or excessively they distort perception, increase vulnerability, and may lead to incongruous or dangerous behaviour. This traditional view of defence as an internal moderator has been complemented by other formulations such as relational models in which defences are considered to operate between a vital experience of the self on the one hand and an insufficiently responsive environment on the other. The subjective sense of oneself is viewed as authentic and protected by defences rather than distorted; defences form part of an attempt to facilitate the development of a 'true' (Winnicott 1965) or 'nuclear' (Kohut 1984) self in balance with relational needs. Alvarez (1992) has taken this point further and sees some uses of defence as developmentally necessary. The boasting of a little boy becomes a powerful force in overcoming inferiority and attaining manhood; omnipotent and paranoid defences rather than being protective against inherent destructiveness or innate division and conflict are desperate but necessary attempts to overcome and recover from states of terror and despair.

By contrast Klein (1946) extended the psychopathological aspects of defence in her concepts of splitting of the object, projective identification, omnipotent control over objects, idealization and devaluation; her followers have extended these ideas further and now consider defences not so much as transient psychological processes but as combinations of psychological configurations that coalesce to form a rigid and inflexible system. These defence systems of the personality have been variously known as narcissistic organizations (Rosenfeld 1964), defence organizations (O'Shaugnessy 1981) and pathological organizations (Steiner 1982) and are invariably associated with powerful, controlling internal objects. Meltzer (1968) described a patient dominated by a 'foxy part' of the self that continually persuaded him of the attractions of grandiose and destructive aspects of relationships; Rosenfeld (1971) an internal 'mafia gang' that demanded emotional protection money from the good parts of the personality which then had to collude with the idealization of destructiveness and devaluation of love and law and order; Sohn (1985) the omnipotent self, formed by identification with an external object, which takes over the whole personality and splits off the weak and needy parts which are then incorporated as an omnipotent 'satellite' self or 'identificate', a composite of the arrogant parts of the self and those of the external object. One difficulty that needs working out with regard to these ideas of defence systems or styles is the limited number of defences involved, namely projection, projective and introjective identifications, idealization and devaluation, which contrasts with the distinct differences of the patients described and the complexity of their individual psychological functioning.

Bowlby reframed defences in terms of attachment theory and saw them not so much as reducing internal distress and disruption but as different patterns of attachment (Hamilton 1985). Secure attachment provides a positive primary defence whilst secondary or pathological defences retain closeness to rejecting or unreliable attachment figures. These 'avoidant' and 'ambivalent' strategies respectively can also be formulated as dilemmas (Ryle 1991) or in terms of intrapsychic processes. In avoidance the aggression may be seen as split off and the individual has no conscious knowledge of the need to be near the attachment figure, appearing aloof and distant, whilst in ambivalence, omnipotence and denial lead to clinging and uncontrolled demands.

The use of defensive structures as part of functioning social systems is well recognized and forms a major aspect of interventions in the organization of business as well as the Health Service (Jaques 1955; Trist and Bamforth 1951; Menzies Lyth 1988b; Hinshelwood 1987, 1994), and Prison Service (Hinshelwood 1993). The work of Bion has also been influential in the understanding of defensive systems in groups (Pines 1985a).

A further theoretical aspect of defences is their relationship to levels of development with some mechanisms being appropriate to earlier development and others to later stages. The excessive use of stage inappropriate mechanisms through regression, or their persistence to a later stage in an unmodified form may lead to the formation of psychiatric symptoms and a propensity to anti-social behaviour. Such ideas stem from Freud (S. Freud 1894b, 1896b, 1926) and although there is little confirmatory evidence to link particular defences with specific psychiatric diagnoses, there is empirical evidence to suggest a relationship with psychological adjustment and maturity. Vaillant (1971, 1977) has shown that there is a continuum of defences from normal or mature through to the distinctly pathological and that the use of theoretically more mature defences is correlated with successful life adjustments in work, relationships and medical history. The differentiation of defences into psychotic/immature, neurotic, and mature, functioning along a continuum from pathological to normal, forms a powerful theme within contempory psychodynamic theory linking specific aspects of childhood psychological functioning to emotional difficulties in adulthood if immature mechanisms persist or are used inappropriately. However, the use of immature or psychotic mechanisms is not in itself pathological, as under stress we may all resort to earlier tried and tested ways of dealing with anxiety and distress; it is their persistent use that is maladaptive.

In summary, there are five aspects of defence phenomena that need to be taken into account when formulating personality and character. These are:

(1) Defence as a way of deflecting and adapting to internal desires, feelings, and phantasies.

(2) Defence as part of a stable defensive style.

(3) Defensive interactions with the environment.

(4) Defence in the context of attachment patterns.

(5) Defence as primitive or mature developmental phenomena.

Turning now to forensic aspects of defence mechanisms, we can see that all the formulations of defence enumerated above are necessary in understanding criminal behaviour. Offenders are often unable to account for their criminal actions, feeling at the mercy of their emotions, which they experience as irrational and frightening. As emotional turmoil increases, phantasies become compelling, and pressure for action builds up; internal attempts at defensive adaptation occur; defences against intolerable emotion lead to stable defensive configurations forming a fixed part of character – a 'foxy' or 'mafia gang' controlling the personality and leading to sudden and dangerous behaviour; delinquent behaviour suggests the individual is trying to obtain a particular response from his environment which is perceived as hostile and threatening to his underlying self; violence is often encountered in the context of ambivalent attachments; and the presence of immature/psychotic mechanisms is pervasive.

Implicit in these formulations is the presence of innate, underlying emotional impulses causing anxiety which have to be controlled either by internal defence or by acting on the environment. Defences are seen as operating against the expression of aggressive instinct. The belief that humans are innately dangerous, tamed by up-bringing and social pressure, is a popular one in psychodynamic theory as well as in literature and religion. Melanie Klein especially emphasized the role of destructiveness in shaping the psychological development of the child. However, there has also been emphasis on the astonishing capacity of humans to be socially orientated (Montagu 1979) or object related (Fairbairn 1952b). In essence, there is conflict between unconscious aggression and destructive phantasy of an individual and his relational needs and experience of social pressures. In mental health an individual's internal needs and phantasies are in equilibrium with external pressures and social mores whereas in criminal behaviour the balance is lost. When internal defences fail the individual is only left with action. Criminal behaviour itself becomes a defence, often trying to stabilize a mind in emotional turmoil. What then are the ways in which an individual utilizes defences to maintain intrapsychic equilibrium?

Repression, the pushing back of unacceptable wishes from consciousness, is the primary mechanism of defence, ensuring that wishes incompatible with reality remain unconscious or disguised. The intrinsic tendency of repressed wishes and impulses to return to consciousness – the return of the repressed – means that tension and anxiety remain and an array of other defences are mobilized to alleviate the resulting conflict, reduce tension and stabilize the personality, but at the cost of distorting internal reality. Repression is best seen as primarily dealing with the internal world, whereas many of the defences mobilized as a result of its failure are interactional, for example projection, splitting and projective identification. All operate outside the realm of consciousness. To complicate matters further, those that are primarily related to external experience, such as denial, are sometimes conceived of differently, especially within experimental and social psychology, and are conceptualized as coping mechanisms (Lazarus, Averill and Opton 1974). In contrast to the unconscious nature of defence mechanisms, coping mechanisms are supposedly conscious, but this distinction has also been questioned (Murphy 1962; Haan 1963). First, a number of everyday coping activities occur automatically, much like a reflex, whilst a refusal to listen to something or the denial of particular feelings may be conscious. Second, changes in the external world may evoke unacceptable affects which are dealt with through the mobilization of the mechanisms of defence. Third, the perceived danger of an external threat requires internal assessment, which is itself dependent on unconscious antecedents, and so there can be no clear distinction between internal and external conflict, with the two interacting in a complex way (Bond 1992). Coping strategies can be taught and further developed into cognitive-behavioural strategies as well as operationally defined. Unconscious defence phenomena can also be operationally defined, although this is not an easy task (see Vaillant 1992 for summary). Horowitz *et al.* (1990) have attempted to link up mechanisms of defence with cognitive psychology; they see defences as the outcome of cognitive control processes which sequence ideas and join meanings together. Thus too rigorous a distinction between mechanisms of defence and coping strategies or too great an emphasis on either aspect, misses elements of the whole picture. Defence and coping mechanisms are related phenomena and yet exemplify the great but unnecessary divide between psychodynamic psychiatry and experimental psychology.

TYPES OF DEFENCE

Immature Mechanisms

In forensic psychotherapy an understanding of immature mechanisms is essential if treatment is to be informed and appropriate. the most important are splitting, projection, projective identification, manic denial and omnipotence.

Splitting

Splitting is most often used to refer to a division of the object into good and bad. A child, in her mind, will split her mother into two separate persons, the bad, frustrating mother whom she hates and the good, idealized mother whom she loves. By mentally keeping the good and bad mother strictly separate, the ambivalent conflict between loving and hating her mother who is, in reality one and the same person, and a mixture of good and bad, can be avoided. This developmental aspect to splitting persists throughout life in the widespread tendency to split the world into good and bad, right and wrong, black and white, heaven and hell and profoundly affects our attitudes not only to individuals but also to social institutions and political, religious and other organizations. It enables an individual to regard others as being one-dimensional rather than characterized by a myriad of human characteristics.

Vignette

A 25-year-old man, living at home with his parents, violently attacked his father with a carving knife, stabbing him in the groin. When interviewed, it transpired that following puberty he had become withdrawn, self-contained, and shy, and rarely went out. He looked after his disabled mother, seeing her as an 'angel' who was ill-treated by his father who seemed to embody all that was bad – 'someone who gets in the way'. In fact the stabbing had occurred at a moment when his father had been showing some tenderness to his wife and their son had come into the room telling him to 'take his dirty hands off her'. The son's love for his mother had been sexualized, split off within his mind and represented as a black and white view of his mother and father. His father came to represent the sexual split of parts of himself and it was these aspects that he attacked in trying to castrate his father.

Splitting is often associated with projection and projective identification.

Projection and Projective Identification

We commonly attribute our more difficult and unacceptable feelings to others, sometimes blaming those who are close to us for our own short-comings. This externalization, the outward limb of projection, allows us to disown responsibility and to see problems as belongings to others rather than ourselves; but if our unwanted impulses and feelings boomerang back and result in a feeling of being under constant attack, the projection has gone full circle and leads to anxiety or, if extreme, paranoid delusions.

Identification is the process by which our self-representation is built up and modified during development and is distinct from imitation, which is a conscious process of copying. The little boy who copies his father is simply imitating, but if his internal image of himself is then changed and this later becomes transformed into a personality characteristic identification has occurred. Piaget (1954) referred to these aspects of learning as accommodation and assimilation respectively.

Projective identification combines aspects of projection and identification thereby emphasizing a dynamic process. It is often considered to be a concept that has developed in three stages (Sandler 1987, p.20):

(1) It was originally cast in terms of a one body system taking place in phantasy within the intra-psychic realm (Klein 1946), the projection and identification taking place within the individual's mind.

(2) In the second phase of development, the concept became a phenomenon with an interactional or two-body context with the phantasy being enacted with someone else.

Vignette

A patient with a borderline personality disorder cared for her new-born baby in an exemplary fashion. However, as her baby grew, she began to feel that he needed more and more affection and care, and was looking at her resentfully whenever she tried to do something for herself. She started to punish him and became so frightened by her wish to hurt him that she left him on the steps of a hospital. The love that she herself desired was projected into her baby who was then cared for in the way she wished to be cared for herself. As this process faltered she felt increasingly threatened by her child and envious of all he had received seeing him only as emphasizing her deprivation.

Heimann (1950), Grinberg (1962) and Racker (1968) developed this second stage concept of projective identification within the treatment situation to involve the helper's identification with the self or object representations in the patient's unconscious phantasies thereby linking it with countertransference.

(3) In the third stage of the evolution of the concept, parts of the self are actually conceived of as being put into the external object (Bion 1955). In this form of projective identification, whole aspects of the ego are split off and projected into another person, animal or inanimate object who then represents and becomes identified with the split off parts; attempts are then made to control these split off parts of the self by asserting control over the other person. Sandler (1987) takes the view that control over the object is important – 'what one wants to get rid of in oneself can be disposed of by projective identification, and through controlling the object one can then gain the unconscious illusion that one is controlling the unwanted and projected aspect of the self' (p.5). He sees the process as one of 'role responsiveness' in which there is a creation and actualization of a phantasy in which each individual has a particular role. This gives projective identification a communicative component as it may evoke unspoken feelings in the recipient who may process them and give them back in a modified, less persecuting form – a process known as introjective identification. Inevitably, processing may fail and instead of the interactional element being positive, the relationship becomes a vehicle through which aggressive, sadistic, violent, or other phantasies are acted out. This is in contrast to projection, in which the recipient of the unacceptable feelings may be unaware of his role; the paranoid individual may project malevolent intentions onto all sorts of people with whom he never comes in contact, such as KGB, Freemasons and politicians. In projective identification the projections go 'into' the object, whilst projection only takes them 'onto' the object – the 'into' versus 'onto' debate.

Vignette

Two young men, one of whom was sexually experienced with both men and women, spent most evenings together trying to 'pull' women. Neither individual went 'prowling', as they called it, alone. One evening, following rejection by a woman in a local pub, they lay in wait. As she left, they bundled her into a car, took her to a warehouse and tied her up. Whilst one raped her, the other masturbated. Afterwards, the boasting of the rapist led to their arrest and subsequent imprisonment. The joint activity was the result of a mutually satisfying projective system. The rapist carried in him the aggressive sexual needs of the other. In phantasy his accomplice identified with the victim, wishing to be aggressively dominated by his friend. Indeed his friend taunted him as a sexual weakling. The rapist had projected his own underlying feelings of sexual inadequacy into his friend.

Recently there has been much discussion as to whether the term projective identification should be used for all those instances described above or restricted to those occasions when the recipient is himself emotionally affected. A restricted use of the term would have the advantage of precision and clarity but it would gently limit its usefulness, and projective identification is best seen as an umbrella term. Spillius (1994) suggests the use of adjectives such as 'evocatory' to describe the type in which the recipient is put under pressure to respond according to the projector's phantasy. In the example above each young man evoked a particular role for the other. A further sub-type may be normal projective identification which, like splitting, has useful developmental aspects and forms part of the basis of human empathy. It is wrong to see it as solely a primitive mental mechanism representing severe underlying pathology.

It has already been mentioned that when mechanisms coalesce they form defensive styles. Of particular importance in forensic psychotherapy are the manic defences in which omnipotence, projective identification, denial, idealization, and splitting come together. They specifically attack reality and are characterized by a triad of feelings – triumph, control and contempt. These feelings aim to diminish need of and dependency on someone who is valued in order to avoid the experience of loss, yearning and guilt. Sometimes the need is projected and seen outside the self. This may be the case in some paedophiles who believe they are showing necessary paternal affection to the children with whom they become involved. In phantasy the paedophile omnipotently 'becomes' the child and through his phantasy during masturbation magically repairs his own earlier trauma. He idealizes the relationship, believing it to be beneficial to the child, feeling safe in dependency which can be controlled.

Other individuals enter a grandiose world through their omnipotence in which they believe their wishes are others' commands.

Vignette

One such patient was referred via a magistrates court where he had been charged with theft of pornographic magazines. At assessment he outlined his own conditions of treatment which included being seen in a specific hospital. When this was questioned he became angry and dismissed the psychiatrist as a fool. Later he contacted the Purchasing Authority demanding to be referred to the hospital of his own choice even though they had no department of psychiatry or psychotherapy. His sole reason for being seen in the hospital was that he liked the style of the building. He expected his psychiatrist to see him in surroundings that befitted his importance. The reasons behind his odd request became clearer when he eventually relented and came into treatment in a day hospital setting. His father, said to be an Hungarian soldier, had left home before he was born and he was brought up by his mother with whom he shared a bed until he was fifteen. His relationship with his mother was infused with ambivalence. On the one hand he wished to be free of her and had moved into a bedsit nearby but, on the other, he found himself needing her – he neglected himself enough for her to have to visit him every day to bring food. On occasions he had attacked her by throwing the food at her. His brittle compromise was to buy pornographic magazines of older women, and masturbate whilst spitting onto the pages. He also visited prostitutes who humiliated him whilst dancing in front of him naked until he threw them onto the floor, triumphing over their control, and buggering them.

This man was as much a victim as a victimizer. His overly close relationship with his mother, in the absence of a father who could intervene, had left him with an omnipotent structure in which either he controlled or was controlled. The sexualization, resulting from a simultaneous arousal and abhorrence of incestuous wishes, became encapsulated in enactments with prostitutes and the use of pornography. He was enraptured and tempted by their seductions before taking recourse to identification with a powerful fantasy father who saved him from their control. Inevitably, he brought this to treatment, experiencing the refusal of being seen at a hospital of his choice as a humiliation. He tried to sabotage treatment many times, complaining to the hospital managers and threatening to sue. Need and dependency were experienced as annihilatory, a final surrender. Tolerance on the part of the staff, along with an understanding of his fight to avoid dependency led to some improvement.

It is not only immature mechanisms that are important in the understanding of offenders. Other mechanisms may play a part and one aim of treatment is to help an individual move from the use of immature mechanisms to more mature ways of dealing with underlying turmoil.

Neurotic and Mature Mechanisms

Neurotic mechanisms are common in healthy individuals as well as those with neurotic disorders, and in persons dealing with stressful situations. They may appear as quirks to the observer, for example the individual who persistently approaches things from an intellectual point of view, rationalizing life and his actions. Offenders may use particular neurotic mechanisms such as 'reaction formation' and 'identification with the aggressor', to stabilize themselves in relation to someone else and it is only when the relationship is threatened, usually by a loss, impending separation, or rejection, that breakdown may occur. The possibility of a sudden criminal act should not be overlooked in these individuals as it may range from a petty crime to a sudden outburst of violence. Mature mechanisms, such as sublimation and humour, integrate reality, interpersonal relationships and private feelings. In general, the use of mature mechanisms is absent in criminality since the offender finds a solution in more immature ways of reacting.

Reaction Formation and Identification with the Aggressor

If an individual takes a psychological attitude which is diametrically opposed to his wish or desire it is known as a reaction formation. Reaction formations develop during latency and bridge to more mature defences such as sublimation which make up whole aspects of character. Reaction formations may be highly specific, such as loving someone whom one hates, despising someone one feels dependent on, or caring for someone else when one wishes to be cared for oneself, or more generalized, in which case they form part of a character trait. The personality traits of conscientiousness, shame and self-distrust may be examples of this when they are associated with obsessional personality and obsessional neurosis. Reaction formations alter the structure of the ego in a permanent way so that the defence is not simply used when the danger threatens but is used as if the danger is always present.

Vignette

A quietly spoken and timid patient was a successful lawyer who argued his cases in court forcefully and intelligently but often used fraudulent tactics to obtain information and to win. He justified his activities on the basis that he was looking after his clients, which was in part a rationalization as he enjoyed seeing his adversaries squirm. It became apparent that his sadistic wishes were covered by a successful professional attitude and a quiet, unassuming manner. Inevitably, this clouded his marital and social life. The psychodynamic background to this defence is described below.

Although Freud (1920) had alluded to identification with the aggressor, and Ferenczi (1932) had used the term to describe the behaviour of a child to an adult in which there was a total submission of the child to the adult's aggression and a resulting internalization of profound feelings of guilt, it was Anna Freud (1936) who described the mechanism in detail and linked it to the early formation of the superego. Identification with the aggressor has links with both reaction formation, in that there is a reversal of affects, and identification.

Vignette

Returning to the lawyer, we can see an example of an identification with the aggressor. When he was a small boy his father used to dominate the household and often threaten, humiliate and beat him. Prior to being beaten he would run away to his room whilst his increasingly angry father chased him. After the chase the little boy would suddenly go quiet and bend over and his father would then beat him, whilst he remained completely silent and entered a dissociated state. At this moment, the boy had dis-identified with his self-representation and identified with his father (the aggressor) who was going to beat his naughty bad body. In adult life, he himself continued the identification with the abusive father by taking illegal drugs and cutting himself, thereby allowing both the abuser and the abused to continue living out their interaction through his mind and body and through his behaviour in court. He also challenged authority, often breaking the law himself, and continually risked being caught.

Identification with the aggressor is particularly important in theories of child abuse in which there may be a cross-generational cycle with the abused in one generation becoming the abuser in the next.

The mature mechanisms of defence, namely sublimation and humour, allow partial expression of underlying wishes and desires in a socially acceptable way whilst simultaneously enriching society. In sublimation, wishes are channelled rather than dammed or diverted; aggressive urges may find expression in games and sport; feelings are acknowledged, modified and directed towards significant goals; narcissistic needs may be fulfilled by becoming a successful stage actor. Our basest and deepest desires as well as our aspirations and ambitions are contained within our culture and gain expression through carnival, drama, music, poetry and within societies' highest ideals. Humour allows us to share emotion without discomfort, to regress without embarrassment, to play games with freedom, to laugh with impunity and relax with pleasure; it is involving rather than excluding and may at times allow what it too terrible to be borne.

Vaillant and Drake (1985) and Vaillant, Bond and Vaillant (1986) have demonstrated that mature defences have a higher adaptive value than all others and Perry and Cooper (1989) have shown how immature mechanisms of defence are associated with psychological symptoms, personal distress, poor social functioning, and delinquent behaviour. Psychotherapy encourages psychological development and therefore a shift from the use of immature or neurotic mechanisms to those of maturity. Psychotherapeutic treatment may allow the offender to move from distress to psychological health and to develop more mature ways of coping with turmoil and expressing his need.

I · 4

Related Disciplines

Introduction

Christopher Cordess

It is emphasized throughout these volumes that forensic psychotherapy, whilst having a basis in applied psychoanalysis, also shares ground with many related and overlapping disciplines.

It is in the tension *between* the similarities and the differences that much of the stimulus to thinking lies. Thus, for example, as cognitive science comes increasingly to acknowledge a form of *the unconscious* (albeit different from the 'systematic unconscious' and the 'descriptive' and 'dynamic' unconscious of classical Freud (see Power and Brewin 1991)) so *some* cognitive–behavioural approaches (section (ii)) come to share *some* common ground with dynamic psychotherapy. Also, the development of cognitive–analytic therapy (Ryle 1991) offers new points of view, at the same time as psychoanalytic ideas of the unconscious, for example of the place of repression, are modifying.

Similarly, the comparatively young science of ethology (section (iv)) offers psychodynamic theories challenging new data and ideas which have been taken up for example, in attachment theory, and in the understanding of aggression and violence.

Hermeneutics (section (iii)) is defined by the OED as 'the art or science of interpretation', which definition itself raises that old but significant chestnut of where to place dynamic psychotherapy within the contemporary 'arts' and 'science' divide. That debate is for another place but is touched on here: 'interpretation' in its many manifestations, and 'communication, speech and language' (section (vi)) are clearly central to much of the content of this volume.

Dynamic psychotherapy began with an emphasis upon the psychology of the individual, with a predominantly intra-subjective focus; later developments have stressed and incorporated the inter-personal, and have been applied to the wider family, group and corporative perspective. Systems theory (vii) and contemporary sociology and criminology (v), start as it were from the other end, from a social rather than an individual standpoint. These two latter sections describe the possible interactions at the interface of these different emphases.

In this chapter only a selection of related disciplines can be represented. We believe, however, that they provide a broad and stimulating canvas in which the reader will be able to find his own preferred landmarks and points of interest.

The Cognitive–Behavioural Approach

Derek Perkins

INTRODUCTION

Cognitive–behavioural psychotherapy (CBP) is a branch of psychotherapy which has its origins in the phenomena of classical and operant conditioning which were first studied in Russia and the USA respectively.

In what follows the terms 'therapist' and 'patient' will be used to cover the range of other variations commonly used in the psychotherapy literature.

LEARNING THEORY

In classical conditioning, the repeated presentation of a conditioned stimulus (e.g. a bell) at the same time as an unconditioned stimulus (e.g. food) eventually elicits a conditioned response (salivation) to the bell (conditioned stimulus) just as the unconditioned stimulus (food) elicits an unconditioned response (salivation).

In operant conditioning, an action (e.g. asking a question) which is followed by a rewarding consequence (e.g. interest and praise) makes the action more likely to occur in the future (positive reinforcement). When the action is not followed by positive reinforcement, its repetition is less likely (extinction). When the action is followed by an unpleasant consequence such as ridicule its future occurrence is likely to be suppressed (punishment).

Behavioural science expressions such as reinforcement, extinction and punishment are technical terms with precise definitions. It is important to be clear in clinical discourse whether these and other terms (e.g. negative reinforcement, shaping and generalization) are being used in their (precise) scientific sense or in their non-scientific (imprecise) sense.

The term 'punishment', for example, is often used in its unscientific sense to mean something which the therapist presumes will be unpleasant for the patient, for example verbal confrontation. In the scientific sense, it can only be ascertained that punishment is operating if repeated use of the supposed punishing stimulus actually reduces the behaviour it follows.

BEHAVIOUR THERAPY

Early therapeutic uses of these principles in behaviour therapy, for irrational fears and avoidance of situations, drew from what was known as the two factor model of fear. If avoidance of a situation had developed through previously experienced pain in that situation (classical conditioning) and, subsequently, if avoidance of similar situations was then reinforced by anxiety relief at avoiding the situation (operant conditioning), a maladaptive or neurotic pattern of behaviour could develop.

Clinical applications of behaviour therapy seek to break these learned maladaptive behaviour patterns (e.g. fear of social situations) by a process of deconditioning the conditioned response of fear and avoidance. For example, in the method of systematic desensitization the patient gradually learns within therapy sessions to associate calmness and relaxation with a hierarchy of potentially anxiety-arousing images (systematic desensitization in imagination) or real life situations (systematic desensitization *in vivo*).

Relaxation is achieved and the patient thinks about meeting one close friend whilst remaining calm, and then moves on to the next level of the hierarchy whilst maintaining this relaxation. Eventually, the patient would be able to tolerate the top of the hierarchy (e.g. entering a social situation comprising friends and strangers) whilst maintaining relaxation, which would be incompatible with the previously experienced fear and avoidance.

Other methods of deconditioning were developed by behaviour therapists, such as flooding treatment for phobias, exposure treatment for obsessional disorders, and aversive treatment for dangerous maladaptive behaviours.

COGNITIVE–BEHAVIOURAL PSYCHOTHERAPY

Progress in behaviour therapy suggested that analyses confined only to behaviour patterns in their environmental context was inadequate to achieve successful results for some problems, and that the cognitive, emotional and physiological responses of the patient would also need to be taken into account.

Techniques such as self-efficacy and self-control were developed, based on the finding of Bandura (1977, 1986) that patients' perceptions of their ability to handle situations can help bring about behaviour change. Seligman (1975), Meichenbaum (1977) and Beck (1970, 1976) developed other cognitive techniques for treating patients' negative automatic thoughts, often rooted in childhood, and which can be associated with behaviour problems such as depression, dysfunctional sexual relationships and criminal behaviour.

The main features of cognitive behavioural psychotherapy (CBP) are:

(1) an agreed contract with the patient on the problem behaviours to be reduced or eliminated and the desired behaviours to be strengthened or established

(2) an historical analysis of the development or non-development of these behaviours

(3) a functional analysis of the patient's current problems, including a comprehensive description of the antecedents ('triggers') of the problem behaviour and its consequences for the client ('reinforcers')

(4) the design of a programme of intervention for the specific features of the patient's maladaptive learning, informed by the above functional analysis, aimed at achieving the patient's legitimate goals, and

(5) a recognition that the therapeutic process is itself a social learning situation subject to reinforcement contingencies within therapy sessions and within the patient's legal and social circumstances.

In this work the therapist's own *mores* will play a part: most therapists will not, for example, work towards goals aimed at the patient continuing to perpetrate child abuse. However, these *mores* are explicit and negotiated at the contract stage.

It is also inherent in this approach that, although therapy goals are specified and progress toward them monitored, the patient's initial appraisal of what he or she wishes to achieve may change as a result of therapy and this review and redirection needs to be accommodated. The patient who begins with a goal of stopping child sexual abuse and establishing an adult heterosexual relationship may come to view as more appropriate a goal of achieving adult homosexual relationships.

The clinical practice of CBP requires an overview of the patient in his or her total context. This means the context of personal history, the context of the environment(s) within which problem behaviours have arisen, the context of his or her current circumstances and the context of the therapeutic relationship.

All forms of psychotherapy recognize that problems of human behaviour do not just spontaneously arise. They are the product of a personal history of family, peer group and other social relationships, through which developments or failures to develop occur within the educational, occupational, social and sexual spheres of life.

CBP views these developments within a learning framework, in which personal assets, deficits and problems, first elicited by early environment, are then shaped or extinguished by subsequent events. The interaction between classical and operant conditioning is seen as the mechanism whereby these developments occur.

FORENSIC COGNITIVE–BEHAVIOURAL PSYCHOTHERAPY

In the context of anti-social behaviour, research has shown that certain features of early environment such as disrupted early relationships, inconsistency of care and general poverty can predispose to subsequent anti-social behaviour. These features are, however, not uncommon and it is also not uncommon for young persons to pass through a phase of anti-social behaviour, peaking in the mid teens, which subsequently diminishes or disappears (see Feldman 1977).

Persistent delinquency is less common, and less common still is persistent anti-social behaviour which has its expression in physical aggression towards other people. It is this kind of behaviour which is typically the focus of forensic psychotherapy.

At a global level, researchers have shown that persistent interpersonal aggression has a number of markers in childhood and adolescence. For example, Burgess *et al.* (1986) found that the perpetrators of sexual homicide tended to have childhoods characterized by low levels of adult supervision or inappropriately high demands placed upon them.

The significance of this finding seemed to be that this early social context set the scene for traumatic or abusive events, which in turn set in motion maladaptive learning and hostile acting out. Personality traits such as interpersonal hostility or secretive introversion gradually became established, which increased the likelihood of fixed and aggressive behaviour patterns.

For the individual aggressor, a process of personal development might arise thus: inadequate early social environment and lack of social competence results in inappropriate approaches to other children which are ridiculed (punishment), making such approaches less likely to recur. Aggressive responses terminate the ridicule temporarily (negative reinforcement), making the use of aggressive retaliation more likely in the future. Ruminations about revenge lead the individual to feel powerful (positive reinforcement) and to wish to repeat the experience in imagination or perhaps in reality.

Later, in adolescence, masturbation to distorted media images of women leads to an association between these images of women and orgasm (classical conditioning). Inappropriate approaches to girls or women results in rebuff (punishment) but watching, and then following women leads to the reactivation of ideas about revenge and feeling powerful (positive reinforcement) and provides imagery for future masturbation (positive reinforcement).

As opportunities for pro-social behaviour and sexual relationships diminish, the individual's repertoire of thinking, feeling and behaving becomes progressively more fixed on ruminating about being different, of having 'the right for pleasure', of anticipating sexual pleasure from following and assaulting women, and from the sense of power that this creates. A feedback loop is set in place in which the individual's repertoire results in negative reactions from others, a decrease in self-esteem and/or an increase in self-justifying thoughts, with further escalation in dangerousness.

This kind of analysis, originally confined just to observable behaviour, was subsequently extended in forensic CBP to include 'internal behaviours' such as thoughts, feelings and physiological responses, about which the patient's self-report (supported by such other data that may be available) then becomes of major importance. The way in which a patient's 'chains' of cognitions, feelings and behaviours link together and interact with the environment to produce aggression vary from individual to individual.

For example, some people feel angry over one event and then ruminate upon other similar events before acting aggressively. Others begin ruminating about a situation, then feel depressed and hopeless and then seek compensation in the thrill of aggression. Knowledge of these individualized chains of reactions is helpful in structuring the sequence and intensity of therapy with the patient.

Assessment

Where the therapist is dealing with patient problems for which the patient is highly motivated to receive help and to cooperate with the therapist, self-reports (systematically recorded in interviews, diaries and rating sheets etc.) will prove helpful in understanding how problem behaviours are being triggered off and maintained, as well as monitoring how therapy is progressing.

However, where the patient may be experiencing mixed motivation about cooperating in treatment, as is often the case in forensic settings, there may be greater need for caution in the use of self-reported information. This is not to minimize the importance of such data, but to underline the fact that greater sophistication is required in addressing the questions of reliability and validity for such unobservable behaviour.

This can be achieved by checking the reliability of information provided on different occasions (and under different conditions) and by different sources (e.g. the patient, friends or relatives, and other professionals). Psychometric assessments with norms for different populations and with built in detection of 'faking good' or 'faking bad' can also help clarify the picture. So, too, can methods of assessment which are difficult to fake such as role play assessments of social skills or psychophysiological assessments of sexual interest.

Inherent in this process is the fact that patient disclosures can themselves been seen as pieces of behaviour which are subject to the influence of conditioning principles. Hence, those who work with offenders soon come to realize that client disclosures about aggressive impulses or deviant sexual interests will soon dry up if the client is 'punished' but anxiety-provoking or anger-provoking confrontations about his or her behaviour.

THERAPY

Clearly, important therapeutic goals for forensic patients are likely to be to work with the therapist on reducing or eliminating antisocial propensities and achieving other related goals such as enhanced self-esteem, a successful job and a satisfactory sexual relationship. Within the CBP paradigm this needs to be carefully structured so as to facilitate an experience of gradual progress towards agreed goals.

Gratifying as dramatic bursts of therapeutic progress can be for both patient and therapist, CBP accepts that progress will often be a gradual process. The patient will typically achieve change in one area of functioning (e.g. improved social skills) before moving on to the next (e.g. overcoming fear of rejection) and then another (e.g. managing anger non-aggressively).

The sequencing of these interventions tends to be determined by some compromise between the logical course of action suggested by the functional analysis (e.g. work on victim empathy before social/sexual relationship skills) and the patient's own wishes and insights (e.g. the patient may see the need for, and be motivated to gain sexual relationship skills but be unmotivated to work on victim empathy, which he or she may not yet see as a problem). In community-based treatment, the tackling of issues in this patient-directed way can be more of a problem than in secure settings: social/sexual skills without victim empathy is a greater potential danger in the community than in a secure hospital.

The Therapy Process

Since many forensic patients have not actively chosen therapy, there can be considerable potential for change in the fact that external contingencies are operating on the patient, such as a forthcoming court appearance or consideration for eligibility for parole. However, for the therapist to wield these contingencies at the patient in a threatening way can be punishing and counterproductive.

Equally, though, to collude with the patient in suggesting that these contingencies are unimportant or unreal is equally counterproductive. A calm recognition that the contingencies are present and that the therapist and patient can work together to create the best outcome for the patient within the legal and social influences that are acting upon him or her is a good starting point.

Theoretically, a dilemma can arise where the patient reacts in a way which prevents him achieving his own objectives, for example ruminating over past misfortunes (which the patient might maintain is an acceptable thing to do) where evidence exists that such ruminations tend to result in an escalation to aggressive urges (which the patient accepts are in need of change).

This dilemma can perhaps be best expressed as 'how to help the patient do what is best for himself despite himself?' Within the principle of working towards the patient's own goals, the therapist has several possible strategies. One is to use rational argument and persuasion with the patient about what he should be doing in order to meet his therapy goals: this is a simple idea but one which patients often say has not been used.

Within this process, conditioning principles will continue to operate. Patients are more likely to change their own ideas if these changes are positively reinforced. Setting out the advantages for the patient that the change will bring about and the disadvantage that not changing will create can help. Encouraging the patient to come up with his own suggestions and then reinforcing those for which most evidence exists of their likely efficacy is more likely to be effective than arguing with the patient that the therapist knows best. Reducing the tension in the situation by allowing the patient to make decisions at his own pace (but in recognition of the external contingencies which are operating) can be a powerful influence for the patient to move through self-imposed barriers to his own progress.

Specific Interventions

Within this therapist–patient interaction specific interventions are devised to address each aspect of the patient's problem. For example, a patient who is violent partly through a lack of skill in dealing with confrontations might receive a structured programme of training in which increasingly difficult interpersonal situations are role played and discussed. Feedback might include videotape replay, discussions with the therapist or the comments of others if in a group therapy situation.

There may also be skills or responses which the patient exhibits which contribute to his violence and which may usefully be redirected. For example, the patient who derives a sense of power partly from the planning and physical exertion inherent in his nocturnal prowling in search of a victim may learn to redirect this pleasurable side of his offending into a legitimate channel, such as sport.

For other problem behaviours, there may need to be an elimination or suppression of a particular repertoire. It is difficult to envisage, for example, a legitimate means of redirecting the sadistic sexual arousal of a serial rapist in a way which will not leave the risk of reoffending still present. For such repertoires, aversive conditioning techniques may be helpful. Contrary to what is sometimes supposed, the level of aversive stimulation required should not be high as this will interfere with the patient's learning process. It is sufficient for the unwanted behaviour to be followed by stimulation which is just sufficiently unpleasant that the patient would wish it to stop.

A good example of this is the technique of satiation used with sex offenders (see Marshall, Laws and Barbaree 1990). In this technique the offender masturbates to orgasm but then, unlike his usual practice, he continues to masturbate to his deviant imagery beyond the point of orgasm. The frustration and boredom which results is a punishing outcome, which eventually contaminates the arousing properties of the deviant imagery and makes the use of this deviant imagery less probable in the future. Despite the somewhat contra-intuitive feel to this procedure, follow up data does suggest that it is one of the most effective means of reducing deviant sexual arousability and helping sex offenders avoid relapse.

CONCLUSION

The key features of cognitive behavioural psychotherapy (CBP) with forensic patients are:

- the explicit nature of the contract with the patient on behaviours for reduction or strengthening
- a comprehensive assessment of the patient's history
- a comprehensive analysis of the antecedents and consequences of the patient's problem behaviour and desired alternatives
- the importance of a collaborative and positive relationship between therapist and patient in which the undesirability of his/her problem behaviour is recognized
- recognition of, and working with the legal and societal contingencies operating on the patient

- the use of conditioning principles to maintain and extend the patient's motivation for change and cooperation with the process of uncovering the facts necessary to understand and modify his or her behaviour, and

- the construction of specific therapy programmes to bring about the necessary changes in behaviour, thinking and feelings necessary to achieve the patient's therapy goals.

Hermeneutics

Anton Mooij

In a general sense, the primary aim of forensic psychotherapy is to treat the mental or personality disorder of a criminal by psychotherapeutic means, in order to diminish the chance of his or her reoffending as a result of that disorder. When put like that, forensic psychotherapy seems to be a category of psychotherapy: psychotherapy in so far as it is applied to a certain well-defined group of clients, namely criminals.

PRIMACY OF THE ACT

The above representation is not, of course, in fact wrong, but in principle it is. Forensic psychotherapy is not merely a sub-division of general psychotherapy – although it is that too; its forensic emphasis lends the psychotherapy a character of its own that results from the central position of the act. Indeed, the criminal act forms the basis of forensic psychotherapy the aim of which, as we have seen, is to prevent a repetition of this or a similar act. This means that not only a certain type of act, namely a criminal act, lies at the heart of forensic psychotherapy, but the concept of action itself. This may, however, be interpreted in several ways. Within the context of forensic psychotherapy we are not concerned with the appearance of the act, but with what it says or expresses. This double aspect distinguishes forensic psychotherapy – in this sense – from behavioural therapy on the one hand and experiential therapy on the other (Rogers 1961). In behavioural therapy, the primary emphasis is on externally observable behaviour, while experiential psychotherapy emphasizes experience or emotion. Forensic psychotherapy may look to both approaches, but will always have an emphasis of its own. For it is concerned with neither external behaviour nor with introspective, internal experience, but with the way in which behaviour expresses meaning. The emphasis lies both on behaviour and on meaning.

The central position of the act and its expressive nature forms a specific characteristic of forensic psychotherapy, but does not constitute its exclusive domain. Rather the opposite: an emphasis on the expressive nature of action places forensic psychotherapy within the broad field of hermeneutics, a wide philosophical school of thought that originated with such thinkers as Schleiermacher and Dilthey and was further developed by, for example, Heidegger and Gadamer. Initially, Dilthey was concerned with the interpretation of texts, but widened his field to include the interpretation of action and non-textual, cultural products. Heidegger broadened the field even further to include not only texts, acts and cultural products, but human existence itself, regarding it as a form of understanding, a form of designing possibilities from within a given situation. Finally, Gadamer narrowed the focus further by pointing to the historicity of understanding, resulting in a specific concept of experience as something that occurs within a context of prejudices. We shall take a closer look at Dilthey, Heidegger and Gadamer in the following paragraphs.

THE INNER AND THE OUTER: DILTHEY

From a general point of view, hermeneutics occupies a position somewhere between positivism on the one hand and phenomenology on the other. Hermeneutics is concerned neither with the outer nature of things, as is positivism, nor with the inner nature as is phenomenology. Rather, there is a third, hermeneutic, perspective that lies between the objectivism of positivism and the concern with the subjective of phenomenology. The specific hermeneutic approach concerns the way in which the inner is expressed in the outer: the importance that is attached to the outer links hermeneutics with positive science, the emphasis on the inner forms a protection against far-reaching positivism and a link with phenomenology.

The inner itself can be divided into different types. The early Dilthey was concerned with the inner, mental state of an actor. He maintained that we cannot observe the pure mental state of another – anger or anxiety, for example – but we can observe their expression in gestures, attitude and so forth. Moreover, we have experienced ourselves what it is to be angry or anxious and therefore we can determine anger or anxiety from their expression because we know from experience what they are. The early Dilthey regards this subjective state of, for example, anger or despair, as the inner factor. In his later work there is a shift from the inner factor conceived as a subjective state, to a general entity such as the mind, the state of an era, a culture. There is a shift in emphasis from the 'subjective' to the 'objective' mind (Hodges 1952). This is the mind or mentality that is expressed in a certain culture or in a cultural product, society or group behaviour. This change with regard to determining the inner factor does not mean that there is a change in scheme. Indeed, the same scheme can also be found among philosophers who do not advertise themselves as hermeneuticists, but nevertheless can be so regarded on the basis of this general theme, such as Wittgenstein and the representatives of the Anglo-Saxon philosophy of action (Wittgenstein 1953; Melden 1961). The knowledge of the inner through the outer, and the mutual dependency of both, is also one of Wittgenstein's central themes. The theme of the outer that expresses the inner and of the inner that is expressed in the outer was, however, first expounded by Dilthey as a specifically hermeneutic theme.

THE NATURE OF HERMENEUTIC RELATIONSHIPS

Unravelling such relationships is neither purely descriptive nor explanatory. To qualify behaviour as an expression of anger or anxiety is more than simply to describe that behaviour, it is to add something: the behaviour is placed in a broader context. This contextual addition, however, does not concern causal, but expressive relationships. There is no causal relationship because the inner state (anger, intent) cannot be seen as a causal antecedent of the outer consequences. Exactly because the act cannot be seen as the external result of intent or meaning, the relationship between the act (the outer) and intent, meaning or mental condition (the inner) must be regarded as an internal relationship. Such internal, hermeneutic relationships therefore differ essentially from external, causal relationships. As a result, a basic strategy of hermeneutics is to regard relationships that are presented externally as being nevertheless internal relationships. The primacy of the expressive relationship within the hermeneutic perspective therefore leads to a strategy of internalization (Mooij 1991, pp.50, 60–62).

In its turn, this hermeneutic strategy is important to forensic psychotherapy, because it is here that patients are so often inclined to externalize the determination of their behaviour. The neurotic is inclined to internalize the determination of his behaviour – seen as guilt – and to localize it within himself as a subject. The criminal (whose structure might be narcissistic, antisocial or borderline), however, is inclined to externalize phenomena – although this does not rule out the possibility of free-floating feelings of guilt. Appropriation therefore, is a central concept of hermeneutics; it is also central to forensic psychotherapy (Schafer 1983, pp.241–9).

THROWNNESS AND PROJECTION: HEIDEGGER

Appropriation in operation does not concern the sphere of incidental action alone. What happens in appropriation is that what is apparently external and experienced as alien, is recognized as internal. In general, this refers to the situation in which we find ourselves, that we have not chosen and in which we have, therefore, to use one of Heiddeger's expressions, been thrown (Heidegger 1962, p.135). Thrownness means that there is an element of contingency in the fact that we are where we are. It also means that the situation in which we find ourselves but did not choose to be in makes us what we are because we can never be without any situation. Lacan, who has elaborated on Heidegger here, gives a specific meaning to thrownness by seeing the situation in which we find ourselves from birth as a part of a symbolic order (Lacan 1977, pp.65–68). The symbolic order is made up of the language and its structure, the narrative network, the symbolic system of rules and norms that makes speaking, telling and acting possible. The symbolic order surrounds us as alien, but also offers markers for building our own identity.

Existence is not only thrown, a thrownness that we may or may not appropriate, it is also a projection (Heidegger 1962, p.145). Man is not simply determined by a given situation and cultural order, he is not pinned down by it: man is able to transcend the given order. Therefore human existence can be described, again in Heidegger's terms, as a potentiality for 'being in itself' (p.143). We are in a given situation, but there is always the possibility of somehow interpreting it. From this perspective, we are never completely knocked out by a situation, but always somehow able to look at it, think about it, process it emotionally and therefore transcend it, precisely because human existence is a thrown potentiality for being (p.144).

The final question here is that of responsibility. In the projection of one's own life, one is in charge because certain possibilities are realized while others are not and one can be called to account for that choice and that realization. However, this responsibility is already present at the level of appropriation of thrownness, namely the possibility of accepting as one's own the situation into which one has been thrown. This even refers to one's own past, in so far as it is disturbed. This is congruent with what Freud (1909) calls 'choice of neurosis', according to which a subject may choose and agree with his own neurosis or disturbance, however intangible this may be (pp.153–250). This is a moment of choice – although it need not occur within a moment and may be prolonged over a certain period of time – in which a person may choose a certain disturbance, rather than another which, considering the given situation, would also have been possible, allowing for a certain degree of health.

The emphasis on the idea of appropriation, and on one's own responsibility, within the hermeneutic perspective, give it special importance for forensic psychotherapy, because the criminal is more inclined than the average neurotic patient to refuse responsibility not only for incidental acts but for his life as a whole. This may form a trap for the psychotherapist, who could be tempted to go along with the patient's story in which the situation into which the patient is thrown (parents, environment, culture, society) will be blamed for shortcomings in his own life.

In the sense of countertransference, the therapist's reaction here may also be one of adopting a contradictory attitude: drawing the patient's attention to missed opportunities and generally approaching him in an aggressive manner. Psychotherapeutic discourse has scope for both approaches: identifying with the patient by pointing an accusing finger at the situation or another person; or identifying with another person and pointing an accusing finger at the patient because he failed to make use of opportunities. The hermeneutic perspective may serve as a corrective by neither excusing nor accusing, but by posing the question of the patient's responsibility for his own problem.

EXPERIENCE: GADAMER

An emphasis on appropriation and responsibility, however, does not give an activist tinge to hermeneutics; rather this is linked to their antithesis: experience. This point was already raised by Dilthey. The outer expresses the inner, that is experienced itself. The dimension of experience is therefore essentially linked to the hermeneutic project. As hermeneutics developed further, Gadamer in particular drew attention to this aspect. It is partly concerned with the interpreter (or psychotherapist), who must approach the experiences that the patient evokes with an open mind. He will not achieve understanding by leaving his own experiences behind, but he will achieve objectivity by introducing his own subjectivity and prejudice (Gadamer 1985, pp.245–67). By introducing these, the therapist becomes vulnerable and relinquishes the position in which he knows all, in which he is the all-knowing teller of the patient's life-story (Lacan 1986, pp.230–43).[1] By correlation, the status of what the client says is raised because he is afforded a hermeneutic 'right' in accordance with which he is regarded as an intentional subject, responsible for what he says, to whom no one can attribute anything without his permission. The other must open his mind to whatever the text (or expression) expresses as the truth (Gadamer 1985, pp.333–45).

However, if it is not only the psychotherapist but also the patient who is able to introduce his own prejudices, thereby rendering his own horizon debatable, there will be scope for what Gadamer has called a 'fusing of horizons'. Both horizons come together partially: the patient takes over (part

---

1 Lacan's concept of a 'subject who is supposed to know.'

of) the psychotherapist's perspective, while the psychotherapist adjusts his view of the patient. This gives hermeneutics its own concept of experience that emphasizes its dynamic nature. Experience is not something one possesses, rather it is a specific attitude: that of openness (Gadamer 1985, pp.323–4). This concept of experience seems to have special significance for forensic psychotherapy. In the forensic context, decisions about the patient are often taken in which the other appears as the almighty other with no shortcomings. In the life histories of such patients, others are often almighty figures who have no respect for the patient's ownness. A therapeutic situation in which the other in the figure of the psychotherapist is emphatically not an all-knowing figure, but a person who is willing to be instructed by the patient's experiences, is of special significance in a forensic setting.

FINITENESS

The dialectics of experience, however, both in and outside of therapy, never end in comprehensive knowledge. In part experiences complement each other, for example because they are confirmed by others (the other). But life also provides what one may call negative experiences that cannot be integrated or placed within a framework (Gadamer 1985, p.320). If all goes well, such negative, traumatic experiences will lead to acceptance of the limits to human planning and looking ahead, and therefore also to acceptance of the ever continuing situatedness of human existence and of experience itself. According to Gadamer, such negative experiences lead to the ultimate hermeneutic experience: the experience of finiteness. This means that in the end the hermeneutic experience is not the appropriation of ever new points of view, but rather a disappropriation, in the sense of relinquishing one's own perspectives and desires and accepting one's own limitations and, as a result, the acquisition of radical openness (pp.148–9).

In so far as current hermeneutics are the hermeneutics of finiteness, this aspect too appears to be of special significance for psychotherapy, because its 'eventual aim is, as far as possible, the acceptance of one's own limitations, limits and finiteness. In so far as crime is concerned with a failure to recognize one's own limits, and therefore also those of the other (the victim), the theme of finiteness in the modern hermeneutics of finiteness, is of special significance for the whole of forensic psychiatry. The direct practical significance of the hermeneutic approach is, of course limited: it does not offer technical rules but rather it offers a framework within which it makes sense to place forensic psychotherapy in all of its aspects. And it does offer a specific framework for that form of psychotherapy that concerns itself with the problems that the limitations and finiteness of man present to everyone, and certainly to the criminal.

CONCLUSION

The central themes of hermeneutics are the mutual involvement of the inner and the outer with the internal link between them, a view of human existence as a thrown projection, a dynamic concept of experience, and openness towards the negative experiences of finiteness and death. Transposed within the framework of forensic psychotherapy, this leads to an emphasis on a strategy of internalization, on appropriation and responsibility. Activism, however, is avoided by stressing the limitations of the psychotherapist who is led and restricted by his own horizon or prejudices, and by stressing the significance of negative experiences and therefore also the significance of the finiteness and limitations of human existence as such.

Ethology

Digby Tantam

Ethology, the science of animal behaviour, has demonstrated a previously unsuspected complexity of behavioural organization throughout the animal kingdom. Behavioural patterns are, like organs, subject to evolutionary forces and are sufficiently stable to be traced from one species to another, in much the same way that anatomical features such as wing shape or pectoral bones can be traced. This suggests a close link between behaviour and heritability. Experimental evidence suggests that what is inherited is a population of neurones with receptors to one or more transmitters in common. Thus fight–flight behaviour is elicited by stimulation of the amygdala and the septum, which are receptive to gamma-aminobutyric acid (GABA) and benzodiazepines, and modulated by neuropeptides such as cholecystokinin (CCK). Comparable effects are elicited by stimulating these neurones in rats, monkeys, and probably all other mammals. The use of characteristic animal behaviours to model human states, and the manipulation of these models by novel drugs is one of the growth areas of ethology and psychiatry.

Desmond Morris' (1969) *The Naked Ape* remains a remarkable *tour de force* of primatology but I suspect that remarkably few psychiatrists would have it on their reading list. It no longer seems as likely as it once did that ethology will be a key to human behaviour. There may be two reasons for this attitude. The first is that it has always proved easy to underestimate the complexity of animal behaviour, and it has been equally hard to resist the temptation to apply simplified animal models to human behaviour. Thus Lorenz, one of the founders of scientific ethology, in his excellent book *On Aggression* (1966) reminds readers that aggression towards conspecifics serves important functions, not least the dispersal of territorial animals across a wide range. Elsewhere in the book he says that carnivorous animals have strong inhibitions against attacking conspecifics and bemoans the fact that man, as an omnivore, lacks these inhibitions. Lorenz cites the big cats specifically. These are, however, a particularly difficult species to study in the wild and Lorenz may have based his observations on captive animals, always an unreliable source of evidence. In fact, a recent study of Indian tigers has shown that juvenile tigers do disperse beyond the territory of the parents but in the process acquire wounds which indicate that dispersal is attended by fighting, presumably with their parents and siblings. *Homo sapiens* is neither the worst nor the best of animal species.

Ethology may also have been brought down by the fall in behaviourism and the rise in cognitivism. It is true that attempts to introduce cognition into animal studies have largely been a failure (Ristau 1991). However ethology is not inimical to cognitive science. Nor is it deterministic like behaviourism. It is recognized that the elementary behavioural sequences ('displays') which ethologists describe are rarely exhibited in pure culture in natural settings. Animal – and human – behaviour is always the result of the activation of several motivational systems simultaneously. These may produce conflicting behaviours, or behaviours which alternate according to the intensity of the evoking stimulus or the arousal of the animal (a typical example of this is approach–avoidance behaviour, in which an animal first approaches and then flees a strange or threatening object or animal). Ethology is not therefore concerned with 'instincts' – the fixed action patterns of the instinct psychology – but with dispositions to engage in particular action sequences, dispositions which rarely if ever manifest themselves fully in the intact animal and in a normal environment. In man, and probably in the higher primates, behaviour is also influenced by cognitive factors. Psychoanalysts will note that this distinction between cognition and behavioural disposition is comparable to that between conscious and unconscious motivation.

AGGRESSION AND SUBMISSION

Predators have developed behavioural sequences that culminate in a lethal attack on a prey animal. Prey have developed behavioural repertoires designed first to elude and, if this fails, to respond to an attack by a predator. The behaviour of the predator towards the prey is not associated with marked expressive display or signs of emotional arousal, and is therefore unlike the behaviour of conspecifics engaged in violent conflict. The terms 'aggression' or 'agonistic display' are therefore usually restricted to conspecific conflict and that is how I shall use them.

Aggression is bound up with three motivational systems: dominance; response to threat; and sexuality.

Dominance

Dominance is a means of structuring social groups of animals. Dominance ranks are also apparent in human groups, and are often institutionalized, as in some occupational titles. Animal species differ in the extent and importance of ranks, and that is also true of human societies. Primates have distinct, albeit overlapping, male and female rank orders. Male ranks are heavily influenced by success in conflicts, but this is less true of female rankings. Human dominance differs from the primate situation in that there are multiple criteria for ranking. A duke may be a major, and a commoner a general, and both may have lower status than a pop-star. Human ranks may be informal ('power'), legitimated but obtained through individual effort ('status'), or legitimated and hereditary ('class'). Moreover, dominance in one behaviour setting may not hold good in another. The person who dominates in the boardroom may not be dominant in the bedroom.

Dominance is a means of peaceably allocating scarce resources. High ranking individuals (known by primatologists as 'alphas') have their choice of food, water, or sexual partner and subdominant animals wait. Dominance is established and maintained by aggression, or by the threat of it, but the normal state of affairs is that dominance is not challenged. In a group with a stable rank order, competition for scarce resources can be managed without conflict. Dominant animals may, in fact, be less overtly aggressive than subdominant primates. Rank in primate groups changes as dominant animals age or become incapable for other reasons, or when newcomers arrive. They may also change as a result of the development of coalitions between subdominant animals, or with the dominant animal of the other sex. Kin animals may be more likely to form coalitions with each other. Coalitions may make subdominant animals strong enough to attack, and replace, a dominant animal. Observations of chimpanzees in the wild and observations of large chimpanzee and bonobo colonies show that *coups* of this kind may be the cause of severe violence or even killing (Waal 1989).

Raleigh, McGuire, Brammer and Yuwiler (1984) have shown that dominant rhesus monkeys are biochemically different from non-dominant primates, having lower levels of circulating cortisol and higher levels of brain serotonin. Animals which have ceased to be dominant, or which are removed from the social group, show a fall in brain serotonin. This is of particular interest because depression, a state which some say is associated with depleted serotonin, and impulsive aggression or self-harm, for which there is also evidence of serotonin influence, have been linked with social disintegration or social marginalization. Price (1992) has speculated that the function of depression is to minimize intra-group tension as a result of dominance changes. Depression, he suggests, incapacitates the humbled animal, and therefore stabilizes the *status quo*.

Fight–Flight

Aggression is also a response to threat, part of what Cannon (1927) famously called the fight/flight system. Whether or not threat produces aggression is likely to depend on the level of threat, and whether escape is possible. Kalin (1993) has performed a series of experiments examining the response of rhesus monkeys to a combination of separation anxiety – a young animal being moved to a cage on its own – and danger – an experimenter standing outside the cage. Kalin *et al.* (1991) showed that if the experimenter did not look at the monkey, the monkey adopted an inhibited fear response of immobility and concealment. However, if the experimenter stared at the monkey, this triggered an attack response in which there was a blend of fear displays, aggressive vocalizations, rushes towards the experimenter and shaking the bars of the cage. Since these animals were caged, escape was impossible but it was possible for the animal to avoid drawing attention to itself by 'freezing' (a common behavioural response to fear). Attack followed, Kalin suggests, because the animal could neither hide nor escape.

Animals may be unable to escape for social as well as physical reasons. Mother animals may refuse to separate from their young and so, if both are attacked and the young are unable to escape, may attack the attacker.

Sexuality

In many animal species overt sexual activity is a blend of mating and aggression. Sexual activity may also be a powerful inhibitor of aggression. Waal (1989) argues that primate species vary on the rigidity of their dominance hierarchies, and on the extent of their sexual expression. Pygmy chimpanzees, or bonobos, are highly sexually active, both heterosexually and homosexually. Sex in bonobos appears to act as a tension reliever, and is used to inhibit aggression by more dominant animals, being used along with other submission gestures. Acceptance of sexual invitation terminates hostilities

PREDATION

Although the distinction between predation and aggressive killing is well established in primate groups, primates of other species may be preyed upon and conspecifics belonging to other groups may also be attacked. In other species the recognition of in-group and out-group may be much less clear cut. Carnivorous rodents, for example, prey on the young of their own species and may eat their own young. Certain monkeys will also kill their young, although this may be a population control mechanism. Chimpanzees will attack and kill members of another chimpanzee group and strange monkeys introduced in a group will also attack and kill group members. Examples of 'child abuse' in primate colonies that have been studied suggest that monkey infants are at particular risk of attack, although probably not of predation from other monkeys within their group. It is not clear what motivates these attacks, but it may lie in infant monkeys' ignorance of the dominance hierarchy and unwitting challenges to it. Infant monkey abuse is more likely to occur when their parent is less watchful. It has also been shown that mothers who become more anxious at their separation from their infant are less likely to have children that come to harm.

THREAT AND APPEASEMENT

Management of Aggression in Animals

In order to avoid physical fights many animal species have evolved threat displays in which the possibility of aggression is signalled. The angry facial expression is one such threatening display. Other signals include intention movements – the first few movements in a behavioural sequence which are repeated without the whole behavioural sequence being activated. Chopping movements with the hands, or clenching the fist are examples of intention movements. Animals initiating a behavioural sequence may also show redirected behaviour in which the behaviour is directed away from the current target to another more neutral one. Banging the table is an example. Aggression may also be diverted into displacement behaviours. Drumming one's fingers on the table, brushing lint off one's coat or shuffling papers are all examples.

Many primate species have combined these *formes frustes* of aggression into specialized threat displays, and have developed appeasement displays alongside them. A major element of most appeasement displays is a display which is in some obvious way the opposite of the aggression display. Appeasing animals make themselves small by crouching down and by allowing their feathers or fur to lie flat. Threatening animals stare. Appeasing animals drop their gaze. The bow or the curtsey are both appeasing gestures. In the angry face brows come together and knit, nostrils become clenched, brows come down and 'knit', the lips thin and, if the person is very angry, part to reveal the teeth. The sad face – the eyebrows elevated, mouth turned down at the corners and tightly shut is in some ways the opposite of the angry face.

The possibility of agonistic encounters is increased by crowding but, when rhesus monkeys are deliberately crowded, aggression does not much increase. There is, however, a marked increase in the use of appeasement gestures, suggesting that appeasement serves an important function in stabilizing primate groups.

THE IMPLICATIONS FOR HUMAN ETHOLOGY

As animals are more exhaustively studied, it becomes apparent that their behaviour is always a blend of elementary behavioural types and that this blend allows for complex motivation. In social primates at least, animal behaviour cannot be understood without evoking concepts such as peacemaking, reconciliation, and appeasement which have previously seemed to be exclusively human. Similarly identification of the in- and the out-group, and therefore who is prey and who is not, has similarities to the type of identification which underpins human relationships. It may be time to rediscover ethology as a valid source of insights into the human condition.

Criminology
A Cautious Neighbour

Elaine Player

Contemporary British criminology incorporates a wide range of academic disciplines and a diverse subject matter. Historically it has claimed to be an empirical and scientific undertaking which yields a specific type of discourse about crime and criminality that can be distinguished from those produced by moral philosophers, theologians and lawyers. It has recently been argued that modern criminology has developed by combining two quite separate fields of inquiry: first, the 'Lombrosian project' which has attempted to create a scientific explanation of the causes of crime, unswervingly abiding by the positivist assumption that criminals possess discernibly different characteristics from non-criminals; and second, the 'governmental project' which has focused inquiry upon the administration of criminal justice and the development of penal policy (Garland 1994). According to David Garland, criminology is 'orientated towards a scientific goal but also towards an institutional field, towards a theoretical project but also towards an administrative task' (p.27). Yet, regardless of whether criminology is wearing its administrative or theoretical hat, it retains an empirical interest in forensic psychotherapy and, more generally, in the psychological treatment of crime and criminality. For the theoretician the practice of psychotherapy potentially unearths clinical information from which broader characterizations or typologies might be constructed. For those concerned with the administration of the criminal process, forensic psychotherapy offers treatment as part of a wide array of diversionary and sentencing strategies designed to manage and control crime in society. It is perhaps curious, therefore, that the level of communication between the disciplines, and the extent of joint enterprise, is so limited.

HISTORICAL LINKS

The distant relationship which now exists between criminology and psychotherapy has not always prevailed. During the first half of the twentieth century
criminology was dominated by psychological and psychiatric investigations
into the causes of crime, all of which emphasized the need to understand the
individual character of the offender and develop specialized programmes of
treatment. Much of the early research was undertaken by prison doctors, since
during the first two decades of the century there were no specialized research
units either in the Home Office or in the universities. Hamblin Smith, a
psychiatrically trained prison doctor, was an early proponent of psychoanalysis,
which he used both to assess the personality of the offender and as a means
of treatment (Smith 1922). Similarly, Dr Grace Pailethorpe, who had previously
worked with Smith in psychoanalytically investigating female offenders in
Birmingham, published a study of female prisoners in Holloway in which she
advocated psychoanalytic treatment as a means of correcting the women's
behaviour (Pailethorpe 1932). At this time interest in psychological treatments
was growing amongst the medical profession generally, and new out-patient
clinics such as the Tavistock and the Maudsley were established. In 1932 the
Institute for the Scientific Treatment of Delinquency (renamed the Institute for
the Study and Treatment of Delinquency (ISTD) in 1948) was founded and
the following year it opened its own clinic, which subsequently became the
Portman Clinic (Saville and Rumney 1992). The involvement of practitioners
working outside the penal system was important in that it introduced a new
emphasis into criminological theory. Although research continued to rely upon
the clinical exploration of individual psycho-pathology, it introduced a new
concern with crime *prevention*, whereby individuals could be treated before
their mental conflict led them into criminal activities.

Psychoanalytic approaches to the treatment of criminal behaviour were
perhaps too radical and esoteric to appeal to the pragmatic conservatism of
British politicians and civil servants of the 1930s. Instead, the work of W.
Norwood East, another prison doctor and subsequently a Prison Commis-
sioner, reflected the psychological approach to crime which proved most
influential in shaping official policy up to World War II (East 1936; East and
Hubert 1939). East was particularly concerned with the mundane problems of
the criminal justice practitioner and advocated a more cautious policy of
intervention, which acknowledged that only a minority of offenders were
psychologically abnormal and that research and experimentation were needed
to determine the parameters of this population and to identify effective
programmes of treatment. The influential legacy of this period of psychological
thought is evidenced by the continued existence of HMP Grendon, a therapeutic prison established in 1962 to give effect to East and Hubert's recommendation, made some 23 years previously, that an experimental institution

should be set up to offer psychological treatment to specific groups of abnormal offenders within the prison population (see Genders and Player 1995).

Up until World War II criminology in Britain was dominated by a medico-psychological model which concentrated upon the pathology of the individual offender and was specifically directed towards the development of a correctionalist penal policy. Garland notes that this is hardly surprising given that the key authors of criminological research had been 'virtually without exception, practitioners working in the state penal system or else in the network of clinics and hospitals which had grown up around it' (Garland 1994, p.54). The development of criminology as an academic discipline and its migration into the university began in the mid-1930s. Intellectual influences from abroad started to take hold, in particular the emergent sociological perspectives of American criminology. These progressively challenged biological and psychological theories and emphasized the need to explain the causes of crime in terms of social, rather than individual, pathology. Indeed, some sociologists disputed the concept of pathology altogether, arguing that crime can serve positive functions for society and that criminal behaviour may be a 'normal' response to certain situations (Davis 1937; Miller 1958). The importance of the social environment in determining who commits offences, and where and why offences are committed, came to dominate criminological debates and was variously explained in terms of 'social disorganisation' (Shaw and McKay 1942), 'anomie' (Merton 1938), 'differential association' (Sutherland and Cressey 1960) and 'sub-cultural conflict' (Cohen 1955). In common with the earlier medico-psychological perspectives, however, these theories upheld the basic principles of positivism: namely, that criminals could be differentiated from non-criminals by scientific means, and that these differentiating factors determined a person's criminality and placed it beyond their control. Social positivism thus established that crime is a result of flawed social conditions, caused by poverty, inequality and deprivation. Its policy agenda has thus focused upon the need to tackle these 'root causes' by social welfare interventions that largely address educational provision, employment opportunities, housing conditions and urban planning.

In the second half of the twentieth century British criminology has mounted a critical attack upon its positivist heritage. Modern political concerns about rising crime rates, and the apparent failure of social welfare programmes to rehabilitate offenders, has led to a resurgence of interest in eighteenth and early nineteenth century classical theories (Beccaria 1764; Bentham 1838) which portrayed the criminal as a rational and moral actor, freely choosing crime in pursuit of his or her own interests. Yet positivism is far from dead; the basic tenets of a positivist science have survived and remain a major component of contemporary criminology. Young (1994) has argued that the modern discipline of criminology essentially embodies the incessant competition between two equally abstract images of humanity: on one side, the individual who is granted 'free will, rationality and unfettered moral choice'; on the other, the non-rational actor who is determined by internal or external forces over which he or she has no control (p.69). Young characterizes criminology in the 1990s as encompassing four major paradigms: 'left idealism; the new administrative criminology; and realism of the right and of the left' (p.80). Each of these are rooted within distinct theoretical traditions and each points to contrasting strategies of criminal justice. More specifically, each of these approaches has implications for the nature of the relationship which can currently exist between criminology and forensic psychotherapy.

LEFT IDEALISM

For the left idealists crime is caused by the material inequalities of a class-based society. Within such a society, individual consciousness is structured by a series of institutions which, by means of persuasion and coercion, uphold and promote a dominant ideology that perpetuates certain conceptions of what is 'normal' and 'abnormal', 'good' and 'bad', 'desirable' and 'undesirable'. Far from reflecting an absolute natural order, these definitions are socially con-structed and function to perpetuate the existing social order. Thus, from this perspective, the criminal justice system serves those who are in dominant and powerful positions in society by criminalizing, and thereby repressing, those who are poor and dispossesed. In so doing it diverts attention from the 'crimes of the powerful' and from the irrationalities and injustices of the existing social institutions (Reiman 1979). In short, the role of the criminal justice system is to maintain order – a specific type of order – rather than to control crime, and the task of the left idealist criminologist is to expose this duplicity and lay bare the true purpose and functioning of the criminal justice agencies.

   This strand of criminological thinking has little room to accommodate forensic psychotherapy, locating it within the ideological machine of state control: the velvet glove of treatment concealing the iron fist of repression. The introduction of therapeutic programmes, staffed by the 'caring professions', which individualize and pathologize the causes of crime and promote solutions which address the dysfunctioning of the individual, are seen as a potent means by which attention is diverted from the true dynamics of criminal behaviour and the inevitable failure of the state to control crime. Only by transforming the economic and social institutions which destine specific groups in society to poverty and criminalization can the problem of crime be addressed. The correctionalist role of psychotherapy is, at best, limited to an unspecified, yet inevitably small, number of mentally disordered offenders. However, within the left idealist perspective it is possible to envisage a more radical role for forensic psychotherapy. This would be to provide offenders with insight into their own behaviour, and how it relates to their position in the social order, and thereby serve as a conciousness raising exercise which would foment political pressure for social change.

LEFT REALIST CRIMINOLOGY

The left realists criticize their idealist colleagues for failing to take adequate account of the lived realities of crime. The realists do not deny that the causes of crime are rooted within the structural inequalities of society, but they challenge the mechanistic notion that absolute levels of poverty and deprivation automatically lead to criminal behaviour. Crime is not simply created by powerful interest groups labelling as criminal the collective protest of those who are surplus to the needs of the capitalist enterprise. This type of analysis, they argue, contradicts reality in at least two important respects. First, it fails to recognize the degree of consensus and cooperation which exists across class lines in defining and policing the moral and legal boundaries of society. Although the majority of people in prison are working class, so too are their victims, who turn to the state to uphold the law and punish those who offend against them. The condemnation of murder, rape and other violent and sexual assaults is not restricted to any particular sector of society. Second, the left realists claim that the idealist approach distorts reality by overstating the collective nature of crime:

> 'The truth is that the majority of crime is an individualistic response: it does not have to be individualised by the powers that be.' (Young 1994, p.86)

They are criticized for their myopic tendency to focus on relatively rare instances of collective protest, such as the inner city riots of the 1980s, and to ignore the ways in which social conditions can foster individual, anti-social outcomes.

For the left realists the social context of crime must be understood as extending beyond a static analysis of the overarching social structure, to encompass an understanding of how individuals actually experience their structural location. Crime is thus conceived not as an inevitable consequence of an *absolute* level of material impoverishment but as a response to a sense of *relative* deprivation. Left realism thus emphasizes the subjective as well as the objective realities of the social context. The major cause of crime is 'when people experience a level of unfairness in their allocation of resources and turn to individualistic means to attempt to right this condition. It is an unjust reaction to the experience of injustice' (Young 1994, p.108). Certain social circumstances, such as unemployment and poor housing conditions, are seen as facilitating criminal behaviour not in a mechanistic way, which determines human action and denies the individual moral choice, but in a way which objectively restricts the options an individual actually has and shapes his or her subjective perception of what are available and appropriate courses of action. Emphasis upon the subjective experience of the offender, and the individualistic nature of the 'solution' that he or she chooses, thus enables crime to be seen as a category of conduct which occurs across all sectors of society rather than being the sole preserve of the poor and underprivileged.

The correlations that have been identified between crime and certain biological factors have not been ignored by the left realists, although they unconditionally reject the notion that crime is physiologically determined. Instead, they argue that it is the cultural meanings that attach to particular biological facts, rather than the facts themselves, which are the important predictors of criminal behaviour. For example, the significance of sex and age derive from the way in which gender and youth are conceptualized in given social situations, and not from a biological predisposition which is fixed and independent of time and place.

The intellectual foundations of left realism are not antithetical to psychotherapeutic analyses that attempt to understand how and why particular individuals behave as they do in particular circumstances. Similarly, although psychotherapeutic programmes are not a central plank of the left realist policy agenda, they are not necessarily inimical to its purpose. Left realists recognize that the control of crime requires a multi-faceted programme of social change that attacks, at a macro and micro level, the underlying causes of social injustice. Innovations to develop employment opportunities and decent housing conditions must aim not only to redistribute material wealth and power, but to build a sense of social cohesion and communal identity that undermine selfish individualism and foster a regard for community interests. Psychotherapeutic interventions that enable offenders to understand how they have arrived at the situation they are in, and which facilitate an awareness of the consequences of their anti-social behaviour for their victims, can be compatibly accommodated within the left realist perspective. It is, however, an accommodation hedged by conditions. The first is that psychotherapeutic programmes can only operate in conjunction with broader strategies of social transformation. Psychotherapy which aims to persuade offenders to reappraise their behaviour in the absence of major structural change is guilty of the charge levelled against it by the left idealists. This alleges that forensic psychotherapy enforces a particular conception of social reality and advocates a rehabilitative programme for the offender which protects and perpetuates the injustices of the existing social order. The second condition is that psychotherapeutic interventions must explicitly acknowledge that psychological characteristics do not single-handedly determine criminal behaviour, but are themselves created, at least in part, by material conditions which combine to shape individuals' perceptions of their situation and inform their behavioural choices.

ADMINISTRATIVE CRIMINOLOGY

This is arguably the dominant paradigm in modern British criminology (Rock 1988; Young 1988). Much of the research within this tradition has emanated from the Home Office's own research and planning unit and from academic criminologists who have been funded directly by the Home Office to carry out specific 'external' projects. The major emphasis of this work has been to address immediate policy questions concerning the control of crime and the cost effectiveness of the criminal justice process. Little, if any, effort has been devoted to exploring the root motivational causes of offending, since these are deemed to be of limited value in providing practical solutions to the 'crime problem' (Clarke 1980). Criminal behaviour is perceived not as reflecting an 'abnormal' predisposition on the part of the offender but as a 'normal' opportunistic response to certain situations which present possibilities for crime. The theoretical foundations of this approach are to be found in Travis Hirschi's control theory, which argues that the key question for criminologists is not why certain people offend, but why certain people refrain from doing so: it is conformity, not deviance, that requires explanation. He postulates that crime is caused where there is an absence of controlling factors which impose constraints upon an individual's behaviour and where certain courses of action are promoted over others. In other words, criminal conduct is likely to arise where an opportunity for crime exists and where there is a lack of controls which restrain and limit an individual's behaviour.

The approach to criminal justice policy which has been adopted by administrative criminologists has largely focused upon situational crime pre-vention schemes, which aim to control crime by reducing the structural opportunities for criminal activities. For example, the development of Neigh-bourhood Watch and the introduction of video cameras into public places are designed to deter offenders by increasing surveillance, and the installation of more sophisticated security devices in the home and on vehicles provide physical barriers which make crime more difficult to commit. From this perspective, social conditions are deemed to be of significance in understanding the causes of crime to the extent that they create the situational opportunities for crime to occur. The offender is depicted as a rational actor, making decisions based upon his or her perceptions of the available options. The positivist assumption that certain social factors predispose or motivate individuals to commit crime is largely rejected, as is the idea that a clear distinction can be drawn between the social or personal characteristics of criminals and non-criminals.

Within the administrative paradigm criminology is at its most empirical and pragmatic. Its purpose is to find answers, or at least temporary solutions, to pressing problems of crime control. The flawed nature of the earlier positivist approaches is seen to be demonstrated by the failure of their assumptions to be supported by empirical evidence and by the inability of their criminal justice policies to reduce the level of crime in society. Social utilitarian policies which attempt to control crime by means of deterrent, rehabilitative and incapacitative sentencing strategies have also failed to be proven effective (Martinson 1974; Tarling 1979). The feasibility of the criminal justice system effectively controlling the levels of crime in society has also been thrown into doubt by the evidence revealed in successive sweeps of the British Crime Survey which shows that only a small proportion of criminal offences come to official recognition and that, of these, only a minority result in prosecution and conviction (Mayhew, Maung and Mirlees-Black 1993). The Home Office cohort study has also revealed that criminal behaviour is far more widespread than previously imagined (Home Office 1989), and growing awareness of 'white collar crime' and, in particular, the crimes of powerful organizations in relation to health and safety in the workplace, environmental pollution and fraudulent business practices, indicate still further the inadequacy of conceiving of crime as an activity engaged in by a narrow and 'abnormal' sector of society.

Alongside these empirical and pragmatic criticisms are a series of moral and ethical arguments which claim that utilitarian criminal justice policies not only fail to achieve their own stated objectives, but also violate individual rights and basic principles of justice. The high degree of discretion accorded to criminal justice decision makers and the wide variation and inconsistency in the sentences meted out to persons found guilty of similar types of offence, have been denounced as fundamentally unjust. Individual offenders, it is argued, must be protected against the subjugation of their rights to broader social purposes. State punishment should be limited by the concept of 'just deserts', that is, guided by retributivist principles which ensure that individuals are treated in accordance with the seriousness of their offence.

The methodology of forensic psychotherapy, with its traditional emphasis upon clinical evaluation and case studies, contrasts sharply with the uncompromising empiricism of the administrative paradigm. However, it would be misleading to suggest that it is impossible for administrative criminology to accommodate forensic psychotherapy within its criminal justice framework. The administrative perspective does not deny the existence of individual pathology as a cause of criminal behaviour. Rather, it argues that this has been greatly exaggerated and extended beyond the limits of empirical validity. It is recognized that, aside from those crimes which are manifestly irrational and represent symptoms of a diagnosable mental disorder, there are other forms of criminal behaviour which demonstrate careful planning and execution but which are informed or driven by distorted patterns of reasoning. Cornish and Clark (1986), for example, acknowledge 'the operation of pathological motives acting in concert with rational means to secure irrational ends' (p.3). Similarly, proponents of a 'just deserts' approach to sentencing recognize the need to 'fine tune' sentences to accommodate the needs of individual offenders (Ashworth 1989, von Hirsch 1976). Rehabilitative and therapeutic programmes are viewed as having a definite, even if somewhat limited, role to play, so long as their degree of intervention is in proportion to the seriousness of the offence committed. However, the ways in which administrative criminology contributes to the development of criminal justice policy make it likely that any development or continuation of therapeutic initiatives would be subject to rigorous empirical evaluation in relation to their effectiveness and efficiency in achieving prescribed objectives. As mentioned earlier, the methodological foundations of psychotherapy do not fit comfortably within a paradigm which relies so heavily upon empirical measurements to establish validity.

RIGHT REALIST CRIMINOLOGY

Right realism has flourished in American criminology but has arguably gained little hold amongst British academics (see Rock 1994). Its influence in relation to debates about criminal justice policy, however, has not been so inconsequential. For the right realist the core task of criminology is to consider how the level of crime in society could most effectively be controlled. Its leading exponent is the American criminologist James Q Wilson, who has attacked the bedrock of liberal penal policies by repudiating the simplistic equation between poverty and crime. He points out (1985) that in the 1960s crime rates in the United States soared, despite unprecedented levels of prosperity and the initiation of a vast range of expensive welfare programmes designed to strike at the heart of social inequality and deprivation. Wilson acknowledges that the causes of crime may be many and varied, but he suggests that the long-term, upward trend in crime rates can be accounted for by three primary factors. First, demographic changes which increase the numbers of young males in society, in other words those 'most likely to be temperamentally aggressive and to have short time horizons' (Wilson and Herrnstein 1985, p.437). Second, variations occurring over time in the benefits and costs associated with criminal behaviour, in particular the increased opportunities for crime and the decreased risks of getting caught and suffering severe penalties. And finally, cultural changes which reduce the 'level and intensity of society's investment (via families, schools, churches and the mass media) in inculcating an internalized commitment to self-control', deferred gratification and a willingness to conform to social rules (p.437). Wilson (1985, p.253) acknowledges that much of what encourages crime in the United States reflects the competitive and individualistic culture of American society and that 'marginal improvements' in crime control, rather than the utopian goals of liberal criminal justice policies, are the realistic targets. Formal criminal justice policies, however, have only a limited role to play. Of far greater significance are the informal mechanisms of social control and, in particular, methods of child rearing, which inculcate a commitment to the social order. According to Wilson and Herrnstein, the early conditioning a child receives from his or her family enables certain rules to be internalized, facilitating the development of self-control, which can be reinforced and developed in the school, the work place and the local community. High crime areas are, by definition, those in which informal processes of social control have broken down, hence the primary role of the police and other criminal justice agencies must be to resuscitate effective methods of control by the community. However, the 'realism' of this perspective insists that there are some high crime neighbourhoods, typically those accommodating members of the 'underclass', that have deteriorated beyond repair. Police resources must, therefore, be concentrated 'where public order is deteriorating but not unreclaimable' (Wilson and Kelling 1982, p.38). Social utility becomes the guiding principle when dealing with high risk repeat offenders, who are to be targeted by the police and given disproportionately long incapacitative sentences in order to inhibit the spread of social malaise and protect the *status quo*. Priority is thus awarded to the maintenance of order and social control rather than to liberal concepts of justice. The protection of the public against crime and, by definition, the conservation of the social order, is given greater importance than the rules of due process and equal protection of individual rights.

In order for therapeutic programmes to be incorporated into a right realist policy agenda certain conditions would have to be met. The primary requirement would be that the programme promoted conformity to established values and codes of behaviour and directly inhibited conduct which deviated from this path. Given the aetiological assumptions of right realism, and the priority accorded to social utility over individual rights, therapy could be orientated toward preventive as well as curative goals, embracing those individuals considered to be in high risk categories who have yet to become involved in criminal activities. Obvious targets would be children deemed to be suffering from 'defective parenting' who require compensatory interventions to enable appropriate forms of social learning to take place. However, it is unlikely that psychotherapeutic methods would play a major role in the delivery of these therapeutic goals. Rehabilitative approaches which rely upon methods of behavioural conditioning would be more consistent with the ambition of right realism to foster a commitment to specific social rules and conformity to particular codes of conduct. Psychotherapeutic approaches tend to be considerably less prescriptive, striving principally to enable the individual to understand and appreciate the rich tapestry of life's choices, rather than imposing a specific and predetermined 'solution'. Regardless of methodology, however, the survival of any therapeutic endeavour within the right realist perspective would depend upon its ability to demonstrate at least a 'marginal gain' in the control of crime.

CONCLUSION

Criminology is a broad church, incorporating a wide range of different schools and disciplines. Its distillation here into four separate sociological paradigms is not the only way in which it can be depicted, but it does provide a conceptualization that acknowledges the diversity of criminological theory and practice whilst still enabling a generalized analysis of its relationship with psychotherapy. It has been noted that, despite an overlap of subject matter, criminology and forensic psychotherapy have tended to keep a respectful distance from one another. The previous discussion has endeavoured to explain how criminology variously approaches its field of study and how this can shape the contours of its relationship with psychotherapy. In this concluding section it is perhaps time to attempt a general synthesis of the major stumbling blocks criminology faces in bridging the gap which exists between itself and forensic psychotherapy.

Modern criminology is wary of positivist analyses and is particularly uncomfortable with those that individualize the causes of crime and associate criminal behaviour with personal pathology. Recent research has consistently emphasized the ubiquitous nature of criminality and has presented the criminal as a rational actor who has made a series of 'normal' adaptations to particular social environments. Few, if any, criminologists would dispute that there are some offenders whose anti-social behaviour is directly related to their psycho-pathology, and that psychotherapeutic and other psychological treatments might be appropriate and beneficial in these cases. The question is whether forensic psychotherapy has any theoretical or practical relevance for those who fall outside of this narrow band.

If it is accepted that the theory and practice of psychotherapy does not assume in all cases that the offender is acting irrationally, or is entirely determined by distorted psychological processes, then a second problem confronts the criminologist. This refers to the dilemmas of incorporating psychotherapeutic treatments within criminal justice policy. The criminal justice system coordinates a range of state punishments which are, by definition, coercive and non-negotiable. Is it possible, then, for psychotherapy to operate in this context whilst still enabling voluntary participation in treatment? In principle, the criminal justice system should not force offenders to receive or cooperate with treatment, unless they have been dealt with under specific conditions of the Mental Health Act 1983 and have thus passed into the care of the health services. Therapeutic programmes within the criminal justice system can only operate ethically with the consent of the offender. But, in a setting where the state arrogates power to itself and disenfranchises the offender, can such consent be regarded as voluntary? What pressures are offenders under to conform to a recommendation that they receive treatment? In a custodial setting these questions are particularly pertinent, especially in a system, such as the British, which incorporates indeterminate sentences and discretionary parole. But even in a non-custodial setting an offender's consent to treatment may be circumscribed by the real or imagined threat of more severe penalties being imposed in the event of his or her refusal to cooperate.

If therapeutic programmes were removed from the arena of state punishment then issues of consent would undoubtedly become less problematic. However, if all opportunities for treatment were to become totally separate from the formal process of punishment, and thereby located outside of the criminal justice system, a rather different set of problems might arise. These would focus largely upon definitions of eligibility. In particular, who should be the recipients of such opportunities: those whose psychological state is deemed to be most in need of treatment; those defined as most likely to benefit from any such intervention; or those assessed as representing the greatest risk of serious harm to the public? If it is the latter, then should treatment be extended to those whose behaviour has yet to constitute a criminal offence? A question is also raised about who should be responsible for making each of these assessments and what system of public accountability should exist to oversee such decision making.

The role of the state and the legitimate extent of its power to control and manage its citizenry has been a focus of concern in contemporary criminological debates. Evolving from the work of Michel Foucault (1979) it has been argued that the net of state control has spread insidiously across the population as methods of supervision and surveillance have increasingly superseded other more visible forms of punishment (Cohen 1979). The development of psychotherapeutic measures within the criminal justice system may be seen to epitomize the growth and intensification of such regulation by the state. Their control is described as potentially more intrusive and complete than traditional 'techniques' of restraint, embracing the ways in which individuals think as well as the ways in which they act. Yet their coercive nature has been shrouded by the identification of such programmes with the welfare of offenders and the humanitarian endeavours of the caring professions. Such invisibility, it is suggested, masks their true identity and purpose and thus places them beyond public scrutiny and accountability.

Finally, from the point of view of public policy, criminology can be seen to have played a role in exposing aspects of social 'malaise' which contribute to and encourage delinquent and criminal behaviour. Criminal justice programmes that start from the perspective of correcting individual pathologies are suspect, irrespective of their benefit to the persons concerned, because of their potential to divert attention and resources away from necessary social reform. Thus, it can be seen that, for criminology, there are a series of pitfalls which inhibit its relationship with forensic psychotherapy. A pre-requisite for bridging the gap that currently exists must be a less rigid adherence on the part of criminology to its distrust of the individualism inherent in forensic psychotherapy. But, in turn, there must be a corresponding flexibility on the part of forensic psychotherapy to acknowledge social, economic and political factors as relevant criteria in understanding the why, where and how of criminal behaviour.

Communication, Speech and Language

Jennifer France

COMMUNICATION

Disorders of communication, speech, language and hearing greatly reduce intelligibility of communication and limit communicative exchanges of thoughts and feelings. This is often met with intolerance, ridicule and rejection leading to isolation, hostility and anger, engendering feelings of low self-esteem and self-confidence, worthlessness and uselessness. Successful communication is the setting up and maintainance of full interactions of utterance and response which achieves mutually acceptable outcomes. People communicate in varied ways – for example, a look can kill, vocal tone can mean the opposite of what is being said and a touch can sometimes say more than a look or words – and effective communication can be more how something is said rather than what is said. We know that people are different when alone and when in groups and have different standards of approach according to the setting and those who are present.

There are a great number of human activities that cannot be avoided, according to Phillips (1984); just as there are few people who can avoid talking during the course of a day, there is no way to avoid being evaluated on the way we talk. Phillips believes that it is through talk that way we convey our personalities and that speaking well is usually associated with effective living as speech connects us with other human beings whom we try to influence in order that our daily lives are improved. People who are not able to communicate well experience a number of problems; communication can therefore be both the cause and cure of many emotional impairments.

Speech is the central component from which people may develop satisfactory social relationships as a result of effective communication. Many people believe that they need no training or education in an activity that they assume they perform quite well every day, but a variety of indicators reveal that our communicating needs are not always necessarily being met. It seems that seven per cent of the normal adult population experience serious difficulties in social behaviour (Argyle 1981) and therefore skill in communicating is not something that should be taken for granted. With all the communication devices available, it is almost impossible not to communicate. If you tried not to communicate, your accompanying behaviour alone would communicate your negative choice (Gleason 1992).

As good communication skills are a pre-condition for successful participation in most forms of psychotherapy it is important to understand the impact of disorders of communication, speech and language, by studying the complexities of their development and use in the normal context of every day life.

SPEECH

Speech is a complex physiological act which results in the production of sound waves involving the integration of neurological, physiological and anatomical systems (Grundy 1989). Speech is unique to man and its individuality manifests in several ways: for example, it requires only one person, a choice can be made whether to speak or not, what to say and how to say it. The speaker's assessment of the listener's state has a lot to do with what he says; just as speakers are free to ignore their listener, so too can others speak to destroy a conversation, as for example in some schizophrenic exchanges in which we know that conversational goals are not always being shared.

Speech has been defined as a system of communication in which thoughts are expressed and understood by using acoustic symbols (Espir and Rose 1976). These acoustic symbols are produced by the vibrations of the vocal cords situated in the larynx (which produces the vocal note), from which the vowels are formed (phonation). This is caused by the flow of air (respiration) and given final form by movement of the lips, tongue, alveolar ridge, hard and soft palates and pharynx, producing the consonants (articulation). The study of this sound system of language is phonology. Otswald (1963) states that normal human speech consists of two simultaneous sets of cues, the articulated sound patterns that convey semantically meaningful material, that is, words, phrases and sentences, and the discriminable qualitative features of the voice itself. As we listen to a person produce connected discourse Alpert (1981) states that we can make valid assessment as to the certain fixed or adherent characteristics of the speaker such as sex, age and education and a number of other factors. The experienced ear helps us to make remarkably skilful subjective evaluations of speakers from the speech they produce. The pragmatic criterion for communication competence is the appropriateness of speech used in context and this requires co-operation and emphasizes the usefulness and effectiveness of form and the accountability procedures practised by speakers in negotiating their different scenes. The analytical criteria for evaluating linguistic competence can be based on a sentence's grammatical structure (syntax), its semantic content and the pragmatics or appropriateness of speech in context (Dore 1986).

VOICE

The voice is an expression of who we are and how we feel and this includes both its tone and timbre. Newham (1993) also observes that there are vocal changes in therapy such as regression from adult to child's voice, as when describing childhood experiences and the child's ability to assume a mature adult voice when reflecting adult words. The voice can be an important indicator of both physiological and psychological well being or ill health.

As previously described, voice is the result of breath under pressure from the lungs causing the approximated vocal cords to perform the rhythmic excursions of separation and closure. The alternate expression and rarefaction of the stream of air particles thus created is responsible for the sound waves which determine the fundamental pitch of the vocal note produced (Greene 1975). Scherer and Scherer (1981) are of the opinion that voice can be affected by personality variables, fundamental frequency, vocal energy, or intensity and energy in the voice's spectrum and these qualities are experienced by observers mainly as pitch, loudness and voice quality.

Speech and language therapists also recognize acoustic features of voice production (Fawcus 1986) in terms of pitch, intonation, intensity and quality (as well as the variables involved) in the development of voice disorders by attempting to describe the causes as functional or organic. Three conditions can affect phonation, according to Fawcus: the first is when the vocal folds show structural abnormalities; the second when the folds appear normal but demonstrate a disturbance of movement patterns; and the third when there is no apparent organic impairment of structure or function.

Variations in the normal 'healthy' voice will be observed during times of stress, anxiety, happiness, sadness, anger, denial and regression, and also in those who suffer profound hearing loss and in transsexualism. A voice disorder exists according to Aronson (1980) when quality, pitch, and loudness or flexibility differs from the voice of others of similar age, sex and cultural group.

The offender patient's vocal quality varies from within normal limits to no audible voice at all (aphonia) or, when apparently 'sounding' normal, that is without any obvious voice pathology, some patients will vocalize above or below their own normal pitch, others will vocalize using only partial voice, producing a husky, creaky, rough sound aided by considerable muscular tension of the neck and shoulders, and a few use inappropriate vocal volume either too loud or too soft, usually the latter. These vocal signs are significant and an indicator of personal distress or progress, most of which will resolve spontaneously during the course of psychotherapy. In some cases voice therapy may be needed to assist the production of a healthy voice.

LANGUAGE AND ITS ACQUISITION

Language is the most important tool of communication (Foss and Hakes 1978). It permits people to communicate tremendous ranges of attitudes and information, biases and truths. We don't really think much about language, we just use it. A native speaker of a language knows a great deal about his language that he is never taught, implying that learning the words of, for example, English script requires knowledge about the structure of words and that this is acquired through exposure.

According to Bolinger (1975), acquiring a language calls for three things: a pre-disposition; a pre-existing language system and a competence. The attainment of language is life-long and therefore learning never ceases (p.3). Bolinger emphasizes that language is never completely learned, that it is an enormously complex system and that the rate of learning a language diminishes rapidly so that well before adolescence it seems almost to have come to a stop (p.8). The learning curve starts at near infinity and ends by plunging rapidly towards zero.

The development of normal speech and language is also determined by appropriate sensory, motor and intellectual development and psychomotor maturation of the infant in an environment offering adequate communication. The quality of personal language that evolves during speech development is dependant not only upon the day-to-day experiences of life but upon the quantity, quality and style of language used in the domestic, social and educational environments and, overall, the child's use of language is thought to reflect that of his mother's verbal style (Gleason 1992). Obler (1992) informs us that language development of early childhood and even late childhood is different from that of adulthood since there is probably a core language all children learn, whereas the special language registers and skills of adulthood are relatively optional; only people who need them and find themselves exposed to them have a chance to acquire them. Much of adult language acquisition is not formally learned but is acquired in context; there are registers or styles of speech we need to acquire in our work and in our social relationships.

Mature language is efficient, and appropriate utterances are selected for psychosocial dynamics of the communication situation. Less mature language users are unable to select the appropriate code because they have a limited repertoire of the language form, and this is demonstrated by many offender patients both in their daily lives and in psychotherapy. It is important to emphasize, therefore, that in late adolescence and adulthood we can still acquire language skills. Linguists know that there exists the potential for long-term acquisition of language and there is speculation that there are actual changes in brain substrate organization for language throughout older adulthood, as throughout the life-span (Obler 1992).

The complexity and time span involved in the development of language leads us to believe that something more than the imitation of the language of others plays an influential role. Carey (1978) states that by the age of six years a child may have learned over 14,000 words, and if vocabulary growth begins in earnest at 18 months then this works out to an average of nine new words a day or almost one word per waking hour! By the time the child has reached adolescence he should have developed his own speech style and be able to moderate his speech depending upon his listener. It is thought that working class children are supposed to have only one code and that is the restricted code, as it has been noticed that these children lack the flexibility of vocabulary and grammar to demonstrate modifications. De Villiers and de Villiers (1978) describe how these children fail to recognize the listener's needs and they have not recognized that certain groups require different forms of address. This is thought to be caused either by delayed development or lack of social and educational opportunities. Disorders of adolescence which usually begin in early childhood are often well established chronic conditions by the time the teenager comes to treatment for psychosocial problems. It is now thought that language acquisition must be considered in terms of development of communicative competence.

'I am no good with words
I know what I want to say,
but somehow the words don't come out right.'

Poor communicators in early childhood are associated with behavioural problems which may persist. Severe limitation of language is seen to lead to behaviour problems in several ways; for example, sometimes patients use precocious language which they don't completely understand (echoing) thereby giving the impression that they are more able than they really are, and abnormalities in language development tend to have far reaching effects on many other areas of development (Gath 1987). High rates of persisting social, emotional and behaviour problems in children attending clinics or special schools for language handicap have been recognized and a whole range of psychiatric problems are found (Paul and Caparulo 1983), just as severe disorder of language can produce disturbances of attention, activity and motor skills. The frequent association between language and/or speech disorders in psychotic disorders suggests that children with linguistic impairment are at risk for psychiatric pathology (Cantwell and Baker 1985), that children with language and or speech impediments have been reported to present increased frequency of psychiatric disorder, and that the prevalence of speech and language impairment is higher among children with psychiatric disorders. Older aggressive boys present with poor verbal skills (Camp 1966) and communication disorders can contribute to problems of deviant parent/child interactions which could enhance the usual stresses of growing up and make the child vulnerable (Kotsopoulos and Boodoosingh 1987).

Speech and language therapy research leads us to believe that parental mistreatment may lead to children having difficulty processing language and thence to language disorder. The required skills, in particular verbal skills, are known to deteriorate under stress and children with learning disorders have difficulty in interpreting social situations. This is highly relevant with regard to mentally disordered offender patients. Law and Conway (1992) also report that developmental sequelae, of which children's speech and language difficulties are a part, are likely to be associated with the experience of abuse and neglect and Rodeheffer and Martin (1976) specifically refer to these children's difficulties in attending to instructions, their hyper-vigilance, their fear of failure, and the passive aggressive behaviour which may occur during testing. Knowledge of these difficulties is as relevant for assessments of speech and language as for other forms of developmental assessments. Abused children can also experience a sense of overwhelming loss; there is no one to whom it is safe for them to turn and therefore no one with whom to trust that special forbidden language of abuse

'you see it all and can tell no one.'

It is this 'not telling' which endures throughout childhood into adult life and eventually into therapy. Sharing 'the secret' becomes more difficult with time and the fear of retribution lives on maintaining negative cognitions and limited expressive language usage. Thus, the creativity of content of language and the flexibility, fluidity and spontaneity of utterance can be affected by developmental delay and other forms of speech pathology as well as mental illness.

THE EFFECTS OF MENTAL DISORDER ON COMMUNICATION AND SPEECH

Most forms of mental disorder exhibit changes in all aspects of communication and speech behaviour demonstrating incongruency between verbal and non-verbal behaviour as well as the quality and quantity of interpersonal interaction. The resulting effect on communication is possibly governed not only by social isolation and reduced motivation but by perceptual changes caused by the disorder, such as reduced visual and auditory awareness. France (1991) suggests that speech disturbance can be divided into three possible areas for consideration: first, the communication and speech pathology evident prior to the onset of the illness and possibly maintained and exacerbated by the illness; second, communication and language disruptions/disorder caused predominantly by the illness; and finally, additional problems resulting from drug and physical treatments, organic conditions such as brain damage, epilepsy and learning and hearing disorders. There is now a school of thought that those who eventually develop major mental illness such as schizophrenia may well have experienced developmental problems in the past and that there is a possibility that the emerging mental illness may be of longer duration than previously thought. Perhaps there are links that can be traced back to childhood connecting the language delay of childhood with a thought disorder of the later developing mental illness. Could this early influence on normal language development be in some way responsible for the later communication problems, experienced by many, once the mental illness is established?

Until recently it was assumed that the left hemisphere was dominant for language and the right hemisphere had little if anything to do with language, but recent studies of various language and communication functions which have considered right hemisphere damage have found that although basic language areas such as phonology, lexicon and syntax are not impaired in patients with right hemisphere damage, the ability to use language appropriately in broader pragmatic senses may well be affected (Obler 1992).

It is thought that there is more to language than phonology, syntax and lexical/semantics and there is a large body of evidence which demonstrates that right hemisphere disordered patients can present with impairments in non-componential, non-literal and more complex features of language which are context bound, such as understanding jokes, stories and metaphors. The aspects of language which evidence suggests are disturbed by right hemisphere damage are lexical/semantic processing, high level language processing and prosody (Bryan 1989). Studies have shown that the communication competence of these patients can be impaired at the level of discourse and that successful discourse requires a firm grasp of the context. Pragmatics is concerned with the context of language usage and encompasses the way in which knowledge about this situation, the participants, the topic at hand, previous parts of conversation and social conventions are used in language all of which can be assessed with Bryan's (1989) *The Right Hemisphere Language Battery*. This assessment also concerns how the speaker uses contextual as well as verbal and non-verbal aspects of the message to express a desired intervention and it would appear that there may be important links here between these disorders and ongoing research into personality disorders, and schizophrenia.

A schizophrenic may tend to be unaware of the fact that human relations are multi-polar phenomena (Reusch and Bateson 1987), since his cognitive processes appear to be disrupted. There is reason to doubt that the patient desires to communicate in the normal sense, hence the resulting semantic/pragmatic difficulties. When working in a group setting with schizophrenic patients and using video recordings of the group it is interesting to note how fascinated and how observant the patients are regarding the communication performances of others and how they are less observant of their own behaviour. They remark particularly on the immobile postures of others, their limited gestures, expressionless faces and boring/flat voices. These same patients later notice change and progress on the video and tend to be more observant regarding their own performance once they are used to working with video recording in therapy.

Barch and Berenbaum (1994) explored the relationships between information processing and language in order to further the understanding of language disturbances in psychiatric patients. The results of their study indicated that certain facets of information processing are associated with at least some of the language disturbances found in schizophrenia and they recommend further research.

LINGUISTIC COMPETENCE AND PSYCHOTHERAPY

Good communication skills are a precondition for successful participation in most forms of psychotherapy. The ability to engage in and benefit from psychotherapy also necessitates the ownership of sophisticated linguistic skills, from which, during therapy emerge the accompanying paralinguistic skills supporting the evidence of developing psychological well being and personal maturity. Communication problems experienced by mentally disordered offender patients are similar to other non-offenders suffering from mental illnesses, particularly if the onset of the illness was during the adolescent years and therefore before the acquisition of adult language and communication skills. During the assessment process we may learn that present communication problems reflect long traumatic histories of deprivation, separation, neglect and abuse, and when these histories are compounded with the communication problems accompanying major mental illness, it is not surprising that our patients are initially ill equipped to benefit from most forms of psychotherapy.

> 'I've never been one for talking
> I've always bottled things up,
> Other people have their worries
> I shouldn't burden them with mine.'

> 'There was never anyone to listen.'

'People never believed me,
they listened but they didn't hear.'

'I couldn't talk about *these* things to anyone I *knew*.'

Linguistic imbalance in group psychotherapy is not only a handicap to individual patients but to the group as a whole. It is known that the development of language skills in a group is a slow process and that supplementary support and treatment to assist the development of linguistic competence is necessary in some cases. Patients themselves report that language deficiencies in individual therapy can exert pressures that initially inhibits development. A specialized vocabulary is needed to assist the descriptions of daily life (the here and now) to describe and rediscover the past and eventually to plan the future. The expression of grief and loss, past violence, abuse and neglect, and the ability to talk about the offence or offences and the time leading up to the offence demands a sophisticated vocabulary. Therapy offers the opportunity to encourage and rehearse some of the semantic/pragmatic difficulties which assist in the development of the psychotherapeutic dialogue. Long term effects of developmental language disorder can be partly redressed during psychotherapy; this is particularly relevant in the treatment of offender patients.

Speech and language therapy involvement in psychotherapy ranges from the use of cognitive and behavioural approaches, dramatherapy and psychodramatic techniques to supportive and psychodynamic psychotherapy. All these methods can be employed to stimulate communication competence and to improve vocal quality, expressive and receptive language development, with particular emphasis upon increasing the lexical store, and finally to enhance fluency of utterance.

Amongst the specialized battery of assessments and tests employed by speech and language therapists, to both diagnose the deficits and to promote the continuing development of language growth, are two additional therapeutic approaches. The first is personal construct psychotherapy which is based on George Kelly's theory that man continually attempts to predict and control his world and in order to do this he invents 'constructs' which are bi-polar, and it is through these constructs that he perceives events. It is presented as a completely formal stated theory: it accounts for all human behaviour, it makes philosophical assumptions explicit and it is concerned primarily with 'the person'. It is dependent upon language and therefore offers an extremely useful method of assessment of how the patient sees his world and his place in it. The second approach is that of neurolinguistic programming which is a model of human behaviour and communication which draws from the knowledge of psychodynamics and behavioural theories. It is concerned with the identification of both conscious and unconscious patterns in communication and behaviour and how they interact in the process of change (Dilts *et al.* 1980).

Li and Greenewich (1991) state that the task of the psychotherapist is to reach out for a common language to share with the patient, to express feelings, to form experiences and ultimately to reclaim a sense of self, and that this comes about through a shared language, and the single most important feature within the psychotherapeutic space is the freedom for communication of which talk is the most dominant feature. Psychopathology is defined by Reusch and Bateson (1987) in terms of disturbance of communication and they state that rehabilitation can only be carried out within the context of a social situation, and that therapeutically effective agents contained in psychotherapy are to be found in communication. Psychotherapy can then be used primarily as an attempt to improve the patient's communication.

Schank (1990) believes that we need to tell someone a story that describes our experience because the process of creating the story also creates the memory structure that will contain the gist of the story for the rest of our lives. Seeing similarities between these stories can lead us to recognize patterns of behaviour that will repeat themselves. Some people need to hear themselves played back to themselves so that the therapist becomes their memory, thus helping in some sense to provide some insight to their behaviour by simply employing a different indexing scheme from that of the patient. The stories we tell each other we also tell ourselves (a statement of ownership) and this in turn stimulates memory. In a group setting this can assist in the recalling of a story for another patient and is helped by the choice of echoed words and phrases from others. In a secure setting without a time limit and where open-ended psychotherapy can continue for years, the frustration for the patient of repeating 'the story' many times gives the therapist the opportunity to observe changing prosodic features. During the repetition of stories we may become aware of only few language changes, the style of the story may stay the same, but the subtle changes in prosodic features such as pitch, volume, stress and fluency of utterance highlight the patient's emotional contact between his 'story' and its ownership. We witness the emergence of remorse and developing empathy towards victims and others through changes in verbal and non-verbal expression, assisting the therapists to record progress.

Whilst sharing childhood memories in therapy we hear of the regression to childhood emphasized by recognition of defective early speech patterns, articulatory mispronunciations and occasionally, when under considerable stress, there will be a re-emergence of a dialect or accent which has hitherto been disguised or modified. Other forms of early speech pathology can also be unconsciously re-experienced by the patient and therefore detected by the therapists as genuineness; conversely, fluent speech styles can be used to destroy, camouflage or mislead.

Towards the end of psychotherapy a patient reported that she was now 'worth' something and was not now prepared to allow people to 'belittle' her or 'bring her down'.

'I want to be *me*

I've got my identity back.'

In the early days of therapy she was frightened of 'talking too much' and remembered how she was eventually able to talk using her drawings.

'I didn't know how to talk.'

By describing her drawings she was able to experiment with her own language, she found that it was 'safe' to use and a relief once she knew how she could trust both herself and her therapist. Her developing self-confidence, self-esteem and linguistic competence has not only

'given me insight into myself,

it helps me see what I am worth'

but has helped reduce behaviours of self-abuse and aggression towards others.

Systems Theory

Arnon Bentovim

INTRODUCTION

The term 'systemic approach' encompasses what is more commonly known as a family therapy approach. The development of the systemic notion aims to ensure that issues which involve the individual also extend their concern to the family and the social context in a single conceptual framework. Therapeutic work which flows from this approach includes the consideration of all involved with the problem. Systems thinking encompasses three different issues:

(1) A philosophy of observation to include the context as well as the object of concern.

(2) An approach to treating problems in families and those concerned with them.

(3) A number of methods of treatment.

Thus although problem behaviour, particularly offending, has to be considered as the responsibility of the individual who commits the criminal act, their offending behaviour as a problem needs to be understood in context. It is important to consider the offending individual and the intimate relationship which exists between that individual and other family members, their current and past history and their relationships within the wider social network of which a family and the individual is a part.

Identified problems, for example offending behaviour, need to be defined not only by the act but also by the way acts are socially constructed. A violent act is defined differently by the perpetrating individual, the victim, the family households of each, the extended family and institutions with whom household members have daily contact – whether this be educational, health, social services or the criminal justice context. The definitions of what is offending behaviour change over time: for example, the growth and recognition of phenomena such as child sexual abuse and the decriminalization of some consenting sexual behaviour (eg. homosexual acts), and the shift in ages of consent.

THE DEVELOPMENT OF SYSTEMIC APPROACHES

The concepts that underlie the collective title of general systems theory were originally developed by Von Bertalanffy (1962) in response to dissatisfaction with the reductionist tradition which saw events as cause and effect chains. Such thinking is embedded, for example, in psychodynamic models which see past events predicting future ways of relating. The alternative model was to study the pattern and form of the organization of biological systems, the family being seen as such a system (Jackson and Weakland 1961; Watzlawick, Beavin, and Jackson 1969). Observations of the family relied on the notion that a system was defined as an organized arrangement of elements consisting of a network of interdependent coordinated parts that function as a unit (Von Bertalanffy 1962). The particular family, therefore, develops characteristic patterns and core ways of being and relating. Such patterns are carried forward in life into subsequent social contexts by family members (Main, Kayman and Cassidy 1985). Clinicians attempted to analyze such patterns by seeing the whole family together, including the referred individual; they observed what went on between family members, and tried to understand how this related to presenting problems; they then attempted to convey their understanding in such a way that it could be used by the family to change what were perceived as unhelpful ways of relating.

An interest in treatment of the family as a group was stimulated by studies of communication patterns in families containing a schizophrenic member (Bateson, Jackson, Haley, and Weakland 1956; Lidz 1973). Several research groups began to examine the role of family factors in the genesis of schizophrenia and of various psychiatric disorders of childhood.

A focus on violence and offending behaviour in systemic approaches was introduced by Minuchin (1974) and his colleagues. They introduced the *structural* approach to family therapy. This work originated from the awareness that mental health problems and delinquent behaviour in children were sometimes more associated with major social stress, for example poverty, poor environment and immigration, than they necessarily were with the early history of family members. Families were helped to develop communication and social skills, and action techniques were introduced – such as the enactment of a conflict, or an emotional entanglement – in order to help the family find a new resolution to the problem presented. The therapist was directive and controlling: there was immediate supervision available to him through the use of the one-way screen, and immediate communication to the therapist to help him intensify his effect in promoting change within the family. Such approaches were introduced to help restructure a family whose rigid patterns were playing an important part in both triggering and maintaining destructive behavioural patterns (see Minuchin *et al.* 1975).

Other models of systemic thinking include *strategic* approaches (Watzlawick, Beavin and Jackson 1967, 1969; Watzlawick, Weakland and Fish 1974): this model assumes that complaints or symptoms arise as a result of failure to deal adequately with critical life transitions or stressful life events. The dysfunctional response and the solution which fails is the problem. So that, for example, inappropriate punishment for a perceived misdemeanour triggers off further aggressive responses which then become an escalating problem.

Therapeutic work thus focuses on the many solutions that have been tried (unsuccessfully) to resolve a difficulty: exceptions to the pattern of failure are sought no matter how small they are. This has led to a current school of 'solution focused' therapy which attempts to discover the exception to the normal problematic pattern (de Shazer *et al.* 1986).

The power and relevance of the symptom and its relationship to the way that systems patterns maintain the symptom, and the way the symptom in turn regulates the family and social system has been an important focus of systemic thinking. Hayley (1963, 1971, 1977) and Madanes (1991) have acknowledged the importance and power of the symptom and the part it plays in stabilizing family life. In this model, offending behaviour would thus be seen not only as a product of the complex set of relationships which impact upon and affect the development of the individual, but also, as a symptom – which may play a major role, and impact upon, individual and family life and social context – and have both a modifying and stabilizing role. Such an analysis has now extended to examination of offending behaviour in relation to such contemporary issues as feminist thinking about the gender structure in society, multi-ethnic perspectives, and the nature of the narrative structure of social discourse and relationships.

In recent years the split between psychodynamic and systemic ways of thinking have been bridged. Bentovim and Kinston (1991) have shown how traumatic and stressful events experienced by individuals in their family of origin, or in the current family, can have an organizing effect on current relationships, problem formation and problem maintenance. A powerful bridge between psychodynamic and systemic thinking is also provided by the Milan associates (Palazzoli, Boscolo, Cecchin and Prata 1978, 1980), who attempt to link an understanding of the unconscious processes which control family relationships over time with a systemic approach to changing the hidden rules in the family's patterns of communication. All behaviours are seen as working to preserve stability and coherence. The Milan group developed a highly organized and influential way of working; they use an observing team behind a one-way mirror, and have developed a variety of ways of practice which include careful formulation and generation of hypotheses to explain the problem and then, as it were, *in vivo* testing. The hypotheses are explored using a variety of questioning techniques which recognize, and attempt to challenge, the mutual influences and control which members of the family exert both on each other and on the therapists. A position of neutrality is adopted by the therapist, who asks, for example, questions of each member of the family: invariably he gets different answers – which can then be further explored to

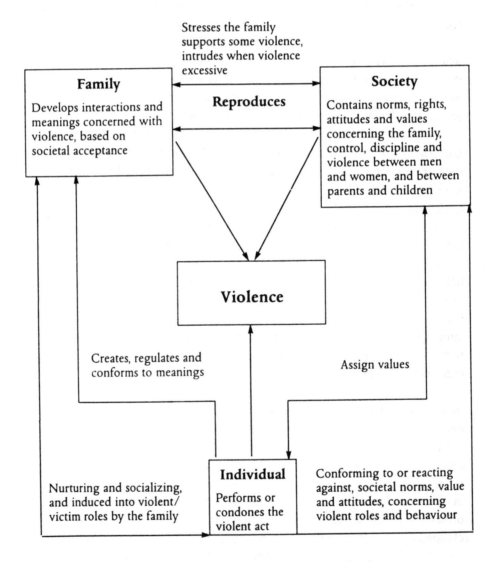

Figure 1 Relationships between the individual, family and society and violence

construct a total picture. The observing team helps the therapist in the room to explore the different ways in which a problem could be viewed by different family members and the way they are connected.

VIOLENCE AS A PARADIGM OF OFFENDING BEHAVIOUR

Figure 1 demonstrates a systemic approach which considers the relationships between the individual, the family, society and violence. This figure shows that all three agencies are concerned with the initiation and maintenance of violent interaction. Violence is placed in the centre to emphasize that it does not uniquely belong to any single setting, but can be seen as the property of each.

Society – which has a core of culture and a surface of behavioural conventions – contains a set of norms, rights, attitudes and values concerning what is deemed 'appropriate' violence, and what may be committed against whom and in what circumstances. Society legitimizes violence and approves the violence or 'discipline' of family members in its proper place. The family in turn becomes the setting of a violent act. Violent interactions and roles thus emerge as an integral aspect of this process and, in turn, create and regulate meanings within the family, and feedback to reinforce them. Individuals are nurtured, socialized and induced into violent or victim roles by the family: the individual then performs or condones the violent act and in turn creates, regulates and conforms to the family beliefs and meaning systems, and takes these into society.

Society stresses the importance of the family and supports a degree of expected violence/discipline: it will only intrude when violence is excessive, or when it defines violent or offending behaviours as unacceptable. Such definitions are influenced by complex, changing, and socially constructed processes. Privacy is a characteristic of the family as an institution: therefore, society cannot act unless there is sufficient communication to draw acts to the attention of those who can provide either social control, or therapeutic work to ameliorate such patterns. Society assigns values to individuals who in turn conform to – or react against – societal norms, values and attitudes concerning violent roles and behaviour. Until recently there has been an extraordinary lack of social consequence for aggression of all types. A 'blind eye' is turned, for example in domestic violence, and women may be blamed if they meet violence with violence, since such actions breach traditional societal norms and expectations. The woman who cannot escape from the violent home, and cannot protect her child, is often more the focus of condemnation than the man who perpetrates the violence. Only recently has there been a public debate, in terms of legal and moral responsibility, about the woman whose only perceived escape has been to kill the man who abuses her.

SYSTEMIC THINKING AND PATTERNS

People living in close proximity set up patterns of interaction with each other which have been shown to be made up of relatively stable 'items' which build up into sequences and patterns of behaviour (Kinston and Bentovim 1990). These 'items' involve family members in dyadic, triadic or whole family patterns of relating. They are often inter-generationally shaped, and – through inter-subjective responses – a set of complementary or symmetrical meanings comes to delineate the reality for individuals of their family contexts. A set of coherent myths and scripts (Byng-Hall 1986) emerge which can be general, for example 'ill luck has always dogged the Browns' or 'the Smiths have been an argumentative lot for generations' or 'John takes after his father, he's got the same eyes and he's a bad lot just like him'. Families thus replicate or recreate such scripts or meaning patterns, or they can attempt to reverse or overcome them, and mount a struggle to overcome their 'fate'.

A number of descriptive terms and 'domains' have been introduced to help to describe such family patterns (Bentovim and Kinston 1991). They include the *affective* life of the family; the *communication patterns* of the family; the *boundaries* which encompass the family as a whole and the way that they divide individuals from one another; the *alliances* between family members; the *adaptability* of the family and the *stability* of *organization and competence* for family tasks. A model is described which sees family contexts as functioning in a graded way from (1) an *optimal* level, (2) an *adequate* level, (3) a *dysfunctional* level, to (4) *breakdown* level.

It is also possible to describe larger institutions – such as hostels, or hospitals – where individuals (including ourselves) are in living or working relationships with each other using similar terms.

Optimal patterns of relationships in families or organizations occur where the nature and strength of relationships between family members is constructive and appropriate to their respective ages and roles. An *adequate family* or organization would be one where there are satisfactory relationships but with greater closeness or distance between some family members than others. A *dysfunctional family* or organization is one in which the patterns show serious discord or distance between members, and shifting or over-exclusive alignments. It is noted that children in such families repeatedly detour parental tensional conflicts. *Breakdown in a family* or an organization is shown by serious deficiencies. Family patterns show marked splits, scapegoating and severe triangulation where parents achieve closeness through attacking a third family member, or there is isolation of all family members.

Using such concepts it is possible (1) to delineate what is specific about the family/organization through the observation of concrete items of interaction; (2) to understand the meaning of the particular family's interaction by using the multi-generational family history to deepen understanding – which enables the therapist to make a more complete holistic formulation; (3) to provide a complete account of the family/organization in context; (4) to predict – on the basis of clinical and research knowledge – what the family/organization might become if therapeutic interventions were to be successful.

CHARACTERISTICS ASSOCIATED WITH OFFENDING BEHAVIOUR

The importance of looking at the systemic characteristics associated with offending behaviour lies in an examination of 'the pattern which connects' (Bateson 1973). The distinction between a model of 'cause and effect' needs to be expanded. If the factors associated with criminality are examined, it is noted significantly frequently that the individual has often become caught up in a series of relationships into which he or she has been inducted, and which will remain as future 'working models' of relationships.

Studies of juvenile delinquency repeatedly note the association with factors such as neglect, lack of parental supervision or failure to exert discipline. A further association is a lack of active parental responsiveness to children's antisocial acts, and a consequent failure of the individual to develop a self-regulating pattern towards a more socially responsible position. There may be deviant family values, such as drug and alcohol abuse, and the modelling of antisocial behaviour by parents. Such experiences can have a deep influence on subsequent behavioural responses and relationships both within future families and the wider society. A family climate of pronounced discord, conflict, abuse and family violence in turn induces a set of meanings and realities for a young person which will propel that person into a re-enactment and repetition of such patterns themselves.

There has been considerable recent interest in the development of protective factors which will interrupt such patterns. The following factors are noted to have a protective effect in ameliorating negative modelling and the stressful impact of 'negative living contexts'; educational opportunity; positive peer group influence; positive effort by teachers and the expectation of achievement; the intervention of community agencies; living in neighbourhoods of low delinquency; elements of family cohesiveness and consistency and development of at least some positive relationships with some family members.

PATTERNS OF TRAUMATIC STRESS AND OFFENDING BEHAVIOUR

Highly dysfunctional and breakdown level family/organizational patterns and beliefs are often related to major stress. Such stress may be defined as a 'disorganizing event' and can arise within the current family/systemic context, or may have origins in the past but still exert an effect on current functioning. If stressful events are of sufficient severity they can become traumatic and have long-standing 'traumatogenic' effects. It has been shown that such events can have an organizing effect on both individual and family relationships over lengthy periods and result in a 'trauma organised system' (Bentovim 1992b). The notion of 'problem-determined' or 'problem-organized' systems was introduced by Anderson, Goolishan and Windermans (1986). They based their thinking upon systemic/constructivist views concerning the way that communication about problems itself creates a system, that is, a problem-determined or problem-organized system. This is paralleled in the way in which highly traumatic events, interactions, and responses to violent offending acts come to 'organize' the reality and the perceptions of those participating – including the professionals. Through such processes the responsibility of the abuser is minimized, and the victim or some characteristic of the victim is seen as adequate 'cause' of the abuse. Responsibility is not placed where it belongs.

Helplessness is associated with the dynamic/systemic effect of powerlessness, with feelings of 'invasion' and psychic pain, and the absence of protection from the environment.

Individuals who are caught up within such systems feel a sense of grievance and a desire for revenge which are characteristic of those involved in offending behaviours. The systemic approach to therapeutic work attempts not only to develop an understanding of the offending individual in terms of the factors which have led to his offending, but also the context in which he or she is currently living and the influence of others in triggering and maintaining offending patterns. It will concern itself, too, with the effect of the individual and his offending behaviour on his family and social context. This requires a number of levels of assessment and analysis. An assessment of dangerousness not only requires an assessment of the individual, but also those in the living and social context who may have a significant role in the triggering and maintenance of such patterns.

Gurman, Krisken and Prusoff (1986) have identified the ingredients common to all models of systemic therapy, whether with individuals, families, groups, or within organizations. These include (1) helping to change the perception of the problem by all those in the systems; (2) modification of communication between individuals and within families and organizations; (3) the creation of alternative modes of problem solving; (4) modification of the degree of distress, or anger associated with symptomatic behaviour; and (5) a modification of the breakdown/dysfunctional modes of family functioning.

Because of the powerfully organizing effect of serious offending, particularly within the family, there has been a modification of thinking and technique. Instead of working with the family group from the outset, working with the family is now regarded as an aim to be achieved through individual, sub-system or group work.

Research on systemic approaches (Gurman *et al.* 1986) has demonstrated the effectiveness and power of systemic therapeutic interventions and their value, for instance, in the modification of offending behaviour, for example within family contexts (Bentovim *et al.* 1988).

Personality and Sexual Development, Psychopathology and Offending

Peter Fonagy & Mary Target

AN OVERVIEW OF PSYCHOANALYTIC THEORIES

Scope of the Chapter

There are no psychoanalytic theories of crime. Crime is a legal or sociological, not a psychoanalytic, construct. Psychoanalytic theory therefore considers criminality under the heading of character or personality disorder. Each psychoanalytic theory takes a different approach to explaining how individuals who are more likely to come to be considered as criminals may have developed that way. Thus criminality may be linked to different character pathologies within different psychoanalytic frameworks and all such frameworks contain somewhat distinct formulations of each character pathology. We will consider some major psychoanalytic theories of two forms of character disturbance most commonly linked to criminality: narcissistic personality disorder and borderline personality disorder. Reviewing all these ideas falls beyond the scope of this chapter. Here our focus will be on psychoanalytic theories of personality rooted in theories of psychosocial development.

Antisocial personality disorder is seen in most psychoanalytic traditions (e.g. ego-psychology) as a combination of extremes of particular personality types: individuals who are selfish, grandiose, lacking in empathy and identity (narcissistic), or are impulsive, violent, self-harming, socially maladapted, emotionally labile (borderline) personalities. This chapter provides a selective review of certain psychoanalytic theories, including classical and ego psychological models, and US object relational approaches to such personality disorders and the implications for the understanding of criminal behaviour are explored. Other psychoanalytic models are considered elsewhere in these volumes.

Freud's (1905c) psycho-sexual theory of development was revolutionary in presenting a predominantly developmental view of adult psychopathology, in that he begun to construct an understanding of adult disturbances in terms of infantile and early childhood experience. The details of the model were etched in by Karl Abraham (1927) who identified specific links between character formation, neurosis and psychosis on the one hand and instinctual development on the other. Contemporary followers of Freud proposed alternative foci for clinical study, but all were based on developmental formulations: Adler's (1916) focus was on the child's feelings of inferiority as the roots of the adult's striving for power and maturity; the Hungarian analyst Ferenczi (1913) outlined the vicissitudes of the child's development of a sense of reality and the simultaneous sacrifice of fantasized omnipotence; Rank's (1924) focus was at an even earlier stage, that of the birth trauma, which in his view underpinned all subsequent human conflicts, defences and strivings; even Karl Jung's (1916) model may be considered a developmental one, if in a somewhat negative sense, in that he proposed true maturity and mental health to lie in the giving up of the 'child-self'.

More recent psychoanalytic theories continue to follow a strictly developmental motif. Anna Freud (1936) provided a developmental model of ego defences and later (1966) a comprehensive model of psychopathology based on the dimensions of normal and abnormal personality development. Melanie Klein (1935, 1936), influenced by Ferenczi and Abraham, was a pioneer in linking interpersonal relationships to instinctual developmental factors to provide a radically different perspective, both on severe mental disorders and on child development. Meanwhile, in the US Heinz Hartmann (1939) with Kris and Lowenstein (Hartmann, Kris and Loewenstein 1946) provided an alternative, equally developmentally oriented framework, focusing on the evolution of mental structures necessary for adaptation, and elaborated on the common developmental conflicts between mental structures in early childhood. Margaret Mahler (1979) and her colleagues (Mahler, Pine and Bergman 1975) provided psychoanalysts in the North American tradition with a dynamic map of the first three years of life, and ample opportunities for tracing the developmental origins of disorders. Fairbairn (1952a) traced the development of object seeking from immature to mature dependence; Jacobson (1964) explored the development of representations of self and other. Kernberg (1975) drew on previous work by Klein, Hartmann and Jacobson to furnish a developmental model of borderline and narcissistic disturbances; Kohut (1971, 1977) constructed a model of narcissistic disturbances based on presumed deficits of early parenting.

Unfortunately, early theories have not been supplanted by later formulations and most psychoanalytic writers assume that a number of explanatory frameworks are necessary in order to comprehensively account for the relationship of development and psychopathology (see Sandler 1983). So-called neurotic psychopathology is presumed to originate in later childhood at a time when there is self–other differentiation and when the various agencies of the mind (id, ego, superego) have been firmly established. The structural frame of reference (Arlow and Brenner 1964; Sandler, Dare and Holder 1982) is most commonly used in developmental accounts of these disorders. Personality or character disorders, as well as most non-neurotic psychiatric disorders, are most commonly looked at in frameworks developed subsequent to structural theory (e.g. borderline personality disorder, narcissistic personality disorder, schizoid personality disorder). Here, a variety of theoretical frameworks are available, including the structural, most of which point to developmental pathology arising at a point in time when psychic structures are still in formation (see, for example Kohut 1971; Modell 1985).

PSYCHOANALYTIC MODELS OF DEVELOPMENT

Freud's Model of Development

Major Shifts in Freud's Thinking

Freud and Breuer (1895) initially believed that he had discovered the aetiology of neurosis in the actual event of childhood seduction. In this conception the interpersonal event of the early trauma was represented in a distorted form in the neurotic symptom. For example, a child of eight with hysterical blindness may have achieved relative internal safety by 'shutting his eyes' to the memory of having witnessed his mother's rape. This model posited no mental apparatus, it reflected the physical conversion of energy. For example, he wrote in 1894: 'Where physical sexual tension accumulates – anxiety neurosis.' (S. Freud 1894a, p.192).

The turning away from his seduction hypothesis in favour of his second model, emphasizing fantasy driven by a biological drive state, discredited psychoanalytic theory as a social theory of development. It led Freud (1905c) to attempt to explain all actions in terms of the failure of the child's mental apparatus to deal adequately with the pressures of a maturationally predetermined sequence of drive states. Adult psychopathologies, as well as dreaming, jokes and parapraxes, were seen as the revisiting of unresolved childhood conflicts over sexuality (Freud 1900, 1901, 1905b). For example, he saw anxiety as arising from the failure of repression of unacceptable sexual wishes (Freud 1905c, p.224).

The fundamental influence of the social environment again found a preeminent place in the emerging analytic theory with the third major shift in Freud's thinking (Freud 1920, 1923, 1926), This new structural theory was to survive long after Freud because of the compelling fit with clinical observational data in the dual instinct theory (Freud 1920). For example, the significance for psychopathology of the child's struggle with innate destructive and self-destructive forces was finally fully recognized. At this time, Freud (1926) also revised his view of anxiety from being a biologically determined epiphenomenal experience associated with inhibited drives, to a psychological state linked to the perception of internal (instinctual or moral) or external danger. The danger situation was specified as the fear of helplessness resulting from loss (loss of the mother, her esteem, loss of a body-part or loss of self-regard). This revision restored adaptation to the external world as an essential part of the psychoanalytic account, and recast the theory into more cognitive terms (Schafer 1983). Freud nevertheless retains the concept of a more primitive form of anxiety which arises in an involuntary automatic way 'whenever a danger situation analogous to birth' had established itself (Freud 1926, p.162). It is this automatic pervasive anxiety and the associated state of overwhelming helplessness which is warded off with the help of 'signal anxiety' which prompts the ego to limit the threat of a basic danger situation (see Yorke, Kennedy and Wiseberg 1981).

This final revision in Freud's thinking provided a developmental framework based around the tripartite structural schema of id, ego and superego (Freud 1923, 1933, 1940). The hypothesis that conflicts within the human mind are chiefly organized around three themes (wish versus moral injunction, wish versus reality and internal reality versus external reality) has had extraordinary explanatory power. In particular, the ego's capacity to create defences which organize characterological and symptomatic constructions as part of the developmental process, became the cornerstone of psychoanalytic theorization and clinical work in the US (Hartmann *et al.* 1946) and Britain (Freud 1936).

The limitations of Freud's developmental model are manifold, and the subsequent elaboration of psychoanalytic theorization is testament to the cultural context-dependent nature of psychological theory and the need of subsequent theorists to make their own contributions to the culture or context in which they live. Perhaps the most important post-Freudian contributions have been in the domains of the cultural and social context of development; the significance of early childhood experiences; the developmental significance of the real behaviour of the real parents; the role of dependency, attachment and safety in development alongside the role of instinctual drives; the synthesizing function of the self; the importance of the non-conflictual aspects of development. Many of these shortcomings were pointed out by Freud's contemporaries who frequently moved away from organized psychoanalysis under a cloud, at least so far as Freud was concerned. Their association with these themes may have delayed general consideration of them within mainstream psychoanalysis. For example, Jung's rejection of libido theory drew attention away from the undoubted advances he made in the understanding of narcissism and his development of a theory of the self throughout the life cycle (Jung 1912, 1916, 1923).

Freud's Views of Crime and Criminal Tendencies

Freud never concerned himself specifically with criminal behaviour. His views, however, continue to exert a significant influence on psychoanalytic thinking in this area. In 1908 he wrote:

> 'Our civilization is built upon the suppression of instincts... Each individual has surrendered some part of his possessions – some part of the sense of omnipotence or of the aggressive or vindictive inclinations in his personality... The man who, in consequence of his unyielding constitution, cannot fall in with this suppression of instinct, becomes a "criminal", an "outlaw" in the face of society – unless his social position or his exceptional capacities enable him to impose upon it as a great man, a "hero".' (1908a, p.187)

Thus, Freud's view of criminal tendencies contains many of the components which were to be emphasized by many post-Freudian psychoanalytic thinkers. He considers constitutional predisposition to be a critical factor in the development of criminality. He sees weakness of repression to be the primary cause along with a failure to renounce infantile omnipotence. He sees untamed aggression as central but remains sensitive to the proximity of criminality and personality disorders, such as a narcissistic personality (the 'hero') which is further stressed in his paper *On Narcissism* where he links sociopathy with excessive narcissism. He explains the common fascination with the 'criminal' as an almost envious stance taken by us with their 'blissful' state of mind which allows them to adopt libidinal positions which we have been forced to abandon.

Perhaps somewhat less valuable are Freud's attempts at classification of criminality. In his paper on character types encountered in the course of psychoanalytic work (S. Freud 1916c) he traces all crimes to either incest or parricide. His argument for this is less than compelling and has largely been abandoned by later writers. In the course of the same review, he distinguishes psychopathy (guiltless crime) from criminals whose actions arise out of a sense of guilt (conscious or unconscious). The latter group, he feels, commit their acts to relieve their vague sense of inner torment by deliberately creating situations where punishment will be inevitable – a manifestation of unconscious guilt. The psychopath he feels 'develops no moral institutions' (p.333) – later he termed these 'psychical structures' (S. Freud 1925b, p.275) – which would prevent them from entering the world of crime.

Classical psychoanalysis was already sensitive to the most critical aspects of understanding delinquency. Karl Abraham in 1925 suggested that 'impostrous' antisocial tendencies could be understood as long term consequences of 'psychological undernourishment' during childhood (p.304). Abraham felt that the lack of love which characterized the early childhood of such individuals undermined their capacity for object relationships, causing a regressive enhancement of their narcissism and a lifelong hatred of the other. The limitations in their capacity to form relationships critically undermined their ability to enter and resolve the challenges of the Oedipal stage, leaving them vulnerable in all future social relationships. The absence of successful Oedipal resolution explained their failure to make lasting bonds, their remaining self-centred, their excessive need for admiration, bragging, fraudulence, perverse chaotic sexuality, and chronic tendency to disappoint and betray others.

Freud was pessimistic about the usefulness of psychoanalysis as a treatment method for criminals. The superego was seen by him as an essential component of successful psychoanalytic treatment. This view has been largely borne out by later developments and most current psychoanalytic forensic clinicians would accept that the psychoanalytic treatment of such individuals requires significant modifications of technique which permit the evolution of psychic structures which are developmentally compromised in individuals with criminal tendencies. Freud's lack of experience with this group prevented him from making appropriate recommendations about the nature of these modifications and the development of the entire forensic field within psychoanalysis suffered as a consequence.

The Structural Approach

The Structural Approach to Development

HARTMAN'S EGO PSYCHOLOGY MODEL

Freud's model was refined and advanced in the ego psychology of Heinz Hartmann and his colleagues. Hartmann (1939) demonstrated how psychoanalysts frequently used the developmental point of view in an oversimplified and reductionist way. His concept of the 'change of function' (p.25) highlighted how behaviour originating at one point in development may serve an entirely different function later on. The internalization of parental injunction may, through the mechanism of reaction formation, lead the child to adopt a stance repudiating the anal wish to mess and soil through excessive cleanliness and orderliness. The same behaviour in the adult may serve quite different functions and is likely to be independent, to have achieved secondary autonomy (Hartmann 1950), from the original wish. The failure to recognize this has been termed the 'genetic fallacy' (Hartmann 1955, p.221). Similarly, the persistence of dependent behaviour in adulthood cannot be treated as if it were a simple repetition of the individual's early relationship with the mother.

Sandler and Dare (1970) point out that whereas the infant's first year of life may be considered as characterized by oral dependency, such longings are likely to occur at any phase at times of stress, when the child wishes to have what he fantasizes was true earlier. Adult behaviours are invariably seen as having multiple functions (Brenner 1959, 1979; Waelder 1930).

Hartmann's admonition continues to be relevant. The identification of what are presumed to be primitive modes of mental functioning in individuals with severe personality disorders (e.g. Kernberg 1975, 1984; Kohut 1977) is often regarded as evidence for the persistence or regressive recurrence of early pathogenic developmental experiences. Yet, even if splitting or identity diffusion were representative of early modes of thought (an issue which is in any case highly controversial, see Westen 1990), their reemergence in adult mental functioning may be linked to later or persistent trauma. The structural view of development, perhaps more than any other psychoanalytic developmental framework, attempts to take a holistic view of the developmental process, resisting the temptation to identify particular, especially early, critical periods (Tyson and Tyson 1990).

Following Anna Freud (1936), Hartmann, Kris and Lowenstein (1946) postulated an initial undifferentiated matrix which contains the individual's endowment and from which both the id and the ego originate. They also introduced the concept of an 'average expectable environment', which affirmed the importance of the parental contribution to development, and outlined a scheme for the phase specific maturation of autonomous, conflict-free ego functions, accommodating both environmental and maturational influences upon personality development. They described the self as gradually differentiating from the world during the first half of the first year, and the gradual evolution of the child's relationship to his or her own body and objects in the second half, as the influence of the reality principle is increasingly felt. In the second year, an ego–id differentiation phase emerges, marked by ambivalence, as the reality principle begins to assert its influence over the pleasure principle. The final phase is that of superego differentiation as a consequence of social influences, identification with parental values and the resolution of the oedipal conflict. Rapaport (1950), suggested a stage theory of the development of thinking which commences in hallucinatory wish fulfilment through the drive organization of memories, primitive modes of ideation and the conceptual organization of memories, until finally the capacity for abstract thought is attained.

Structural Model of Psychopathology
GENERAL FEATURES OF THE MODEL
Within the structural model, neurosis and psychosis of adult life are seen as arising when an individual's urge for drive gratification reverts from an age

appropriate mode of satisfaction to a formerly outgrown infantile mode. Such regressions are brought about by psychic conflict which the ego is incapable of resolving. The id's regression and the associated revival of infantile urges intensifies the clash with parts of the personality that have maintained a mature level of functioning and intense internal conflict is the outcome. The ego's failure to manage such conflict – the intensification of guilt and superego pressure, the intensification of drive demands as a consequence of the regression, and the greater inappropriateness of these demands in terms of age appropriate adaptation to the external world – leads to the formation of symptoms.

Symptoms are compromises, reflecting the ego's manifold attempts to restore inner equilibrium between the unacceptable drive representations and the opposing agencies of ego and superego. In other cases, it may be the regression of the ego owing to psychological and organic causes which is reflected in the pathology. In psychosis, the ego is seen as being threatened by complete dissolution. Essential ego functions may resume modes of functioning characteristic of early childhood and come to be dominated by irrational, magical thought and a failure to control impulses. Thus, whilst mental health is seen as the harmonious interaction between psychic agencies that function at age appropriate levels, mental ill health is seen as the result of the ego's attempt to reconcile developmentally contradictory impulses and aims. The pathogenic sequence is perceived as follows: (1) frustration; (2) regression; (3) internal incompatibility; (4) signal anxiety; (5) defence by regression; (6) return of the repressed; and (7) compromise formation and symptomatic disorders.

Symptomatic disorders are not the invariable developmental consequences of childhood fixations. Within the classical structural model, inhibition is seen as a powerful, albeit potentially quite crippling, way of reducing conflict between the psychic agencies. At extreme levels, inhibitions are seen as characteristic of personality disorders (Freud 1926). For example, an individual who avoids any kind of human contact which might stimulate drives and their associated affects, may be seen as schizoid in personality type. Sexual inadequacy (erectile dysfunction) may be seen as the inhibition of the expression of the sexual drive. Inhibitions may apply to the ego (see A. Freud 1936), whereby an ego function which has become psychically painful may be abandoned. Ego restrictions of this kind would be exemplified by someone whose conflicts over competitiveness would cause them to withdraw from sports activities and invest their energies elsewhere, for example in writing. Restriction of affect may occur with individuals who experience emotion as highly threatening.

STRUCTURAL MODEL OF BORDERLINE AND ANTISOCIAL PERSONALITY DISORDER

Individuals with borderline personality disorder were initially described in the psychoanalytic literature as patients who are unlikely to do well in classical psychoanalysis and frequently reacted adversely to it (Deutsch 1942; Stern

1938). The issue of modification of classical technique was also raised at an early stage (Schmideberg 1947). Knight (1953) was the first to propose a comprehensive developmental model of the disorder in terms of ego functions impaired by traumatic development. Among the ego functions he considered were: 'integration, concept formation, judgment, realistic planning, and defending against eruption into conscious thinking of id impulses and their fantasy elaborations' (p.6). Erikson (1956, 1959a), in his epigenetic sequence of identity formation described the syndrome of identity diffusion, which he saw as reflecting deficiencies in a sustained sense of self-sameness, temporal continuity of self-experience, and a feeling of affiliation with a social group of reference. Jacobson (1953, 1954, 1964) drew attention to how these individuals, at times, experience their mental functions and bodily organs not as belonging to them, but as objects which they wish to expel. They may also attach their mental and body self to external objects. She saw them as retaining an 'adolescent fluidity of moods' (1964, p.159).

Aichhorn (1935) was the first psychoanalyst seriously to concern himself with delinquent individuals and his techniques for addressing their problems were both imaginative and effective. His etiological formulations, however, were even more influential, perhaps because these were strongly endorsed by Freud himself (Freud 1925b). He proposed a dual deficit model. He posited a failure of progression from the pleasure principle to the reality principle in conjunction with a malformation of the superego in his developmental account of the disorder. This accounts for lack of impulse control in delinquent individuals, as longings for immediate gratification persist and remain unquestioned. Excessive strictness and overindulgence were both seen as causes of the child's failure to renounce the pleasure principle. His ideological notions stressed deprivation as not only impeding the renunciation of the pleasure principle but also disrupting the internalization of parental norms. This and the internalization of poor parental norms (in delinquent families) were put forward as explanations of superego dysfunction.

The two central components of Aichhorn's model (the dominance of the pleasure principle and an underdeveloped superego) were retained in most ego-psychological writings on antisocial personality (Friedlander 1945). The relative emphasis given to these two components and the type of early object relationships to which they may be traced differentiates later authors from this tradition. Models remain remarkably similar and etiological speculations seem more a function of the particular clinical population studied than genuine differences in the perception of the nature of the problem.

Aichhorn's revolutionary approach to treatment included a phase of 'seducing' the patient into the treatment process. Aichhorn believed that in order to renounce their narcissistic position and give up the pleasure principle in favour of the reality principle, delinquent individuals had to establish an idealizing relationship with their therapist. To establish a relationship which would compensate for the loss of narcissistic cathexis, the therapist had to be able indulge the patient and compromise traditional psychoanalytic technique.

Reich (1933) proposed a new structural conceptual framework for understanding personality types which he described as 'instinct ridden'. Following Freud, he proposed that in normal personality structure, the superego is able to elicit compliance from the ego, or at least to force the ego to make adaptations to these demands. By contrast, in instinct ridden personalities, Reich suggested that the ego kept the superego at a distance, causing it to be isolated and therefore unable to prevent the individual yielding to an impulse. Reich was clear that this did not mean that conscience (or superego) did not exist in such individuals; thus they might well manifest remorse or guilt in real, and at times overwhelming ways. Nevertheless, at moments of great instinctual temptations, the superego was isolated and therefore was unable to exert its inhibitory influence. A similar idea of partial or functional absence of superego restrictions is contained in Alexander's (1930) concept of the neurotic character.

Fenichel (1945) emphasized that the superego was not absent in these individuals, but pathological; not just isolated by the ego but also 'bribed' by satisfaction of some kind of ideal requirement or punishment. He felt that the pathological superego reflected the contradictions and ambivalences of the child in his relation to the primary objects. The early ambivalences of object relationships manifested in the tendencies of such people to fluctuate between rebellion and ingratiation, charm and seduction, followed by betrayal and revenge. Objectively, the early environment of antisocial individuals was seen by Fenichel as loveless, inconsistent and subject to frequent and radical change. Reciprocal object relations could not evolve under these circumstances; the Oedipus complex was not properly entered or resolved; its solutions were disorganized and weak. Hoffer (1949) explains this in terms of the child's idealization of the father, disavowing his true feelings, internalizing him as idealized, and identifying with his lies, deceptions, and even violence.

Further understanding of the nature and source of the structural deficits which may underpin criminality was provided by Phylis Greenacre (1945). The patients she describes are impulsive, affectively labile, have superficial relationships, manifest perversions, and show a characteristic incapacity to learn from past experience. Consequently, they are commonly highly self-destructive, abuse drugs and alcohol, and are trapped in various vicious cycles of provocativeness followed by punishment. Greenacre was the first explicitly to pinpoint the common failure of such individuals to distinguish signifier from signified, intentions from deeds, 'the substitution of the symbol of gesture or word for the accomplished act' (p.167).

Greenacre's formulation was in terms of assuming that such individuals had commonly experienced parenting from highly narcissistic figures who could not tolerate imperfections in their children, which they disguised or concealed in various ways. They were narcissistic extensions of the parents' fragile self structure, which would have been intolerably challenged by misbehaviour on the child's part. Being narcissistic extensions of the parent increased the child's frustration and aggression and intensified their need for a separate identity. The parents' determination to deny the reality of the child's vulnerabilities, led to a distorted sense of reality, making the child manipulative and opportunistic in wishing to create 'good' impressions. The externalization of their intense aggression, in combination with a lack of a solid paternal introject (usually because father was absent from the child's life for prolonged periods) leads to the creation in the mental world of such individuals persecutory external figures of ferocious strength and intensity, from which they spend their lives escaping, both in fantasy and in reality. Greenacre here describes something very close to the primitive and intense guilt, which is also pointed to by Kleinian writers, and is in contrast to classical phenomenological descriptions emphasizing the absence of guilt in antisocial individuals. Thus the apparent absence of guilt in antisocial personality is the ego's adaptation to an over-whelmingly intense and totally intolerable and destructive unconscious primitive guilt. Greenacre identifies a further important root for the intensity of these feelings. She suggests that the child internalizes the parents' shame and guilt concerning the child, who identifies with these feelings and attempts to rid himself of them by rebelling against them. Schmideberg (1949) also viewed the toughness of even the most hardened criminals as highly defensive, and acknowledged that the state of being free from guilt may be more apparent then real.

Friedlander (1945) should be credited with being the first to put forward a transactional model of antisocial personality. Along with other ego-psychologists, he suggests that the mother's inconsistent attitude to the child's instinctual life, augmented by violent emotional outbursts, undermines the renunciation of the pleasure principle and weakens the internalization of the superego. In an imaginative description of family interactional patterns, he points out that not only are attempts at the internalization of subsequent authority figures compromised by the failure to create a coherent structure in the child's mind around which parental demands may be organized, but also, under these circumstances subsequent punishments will not serve to 'strengthen the superego' (the person will not learn from punishment) because such aversive experiences fall outside the realm of morality and are experienced either as instinctual gratifications or as representing frustrations of gratifications, creating further hostility without the possibility of corrective emotional experience. This formulation raises important questions concerning the value of a penal system as the primary method for attempting to correct antisocial behaviour.

Kurt Eissler's (1949, 1950) contribution was primarily in providing a psychodynamic descriptive summary of the common features of antisocial personalities. He identified ten features which represent somewhat of a mixture of theoretical constructions and phenomenological descriptions: (1) predominantly narcissistic orientation (selfish motives); (2) paranoid view of world; (3) excessive sensitivity to displeasure; (4) an alloplastic tendency; (5) outward directed aggression; (6) weak and inconsistent system of values; (7) infant-like omnipotence alternating with feelings of helplessness; (8) an addiction to novelty (sensation seeking); (9) subtle body image disturbances; (10) concreteness of thinking and value systems and lack of capacity to benefit from experience.

Eissler's model of these abnormalities is also rooted in less then expectable early environments. Injury to omnipotent feelings in childhood which may take the form of a traumatic betrayal of the child, just at the time that he is ready to give up infantile omnipotence in favour of idealized relationships with adults, is regarded as the key to the mistrustful, evasive, defensively thrill seeking behaviour of such individuals. Most interesting in Eissler's formulation is his description of the delinquent's attitude to the new. In his view, the object relations experiences of such individuals lead them to be wary of novelty and, not surprisingly, they show a tendency to describe as new and exciting situations and experiences which they have encountered many times before. This adaptation to trauma by the creation of false novelty actually prevents them from genuinely encountering new circumstances and creates a substantial obstacle to treatment. In his treatment model, causing genuine surprise to such individuals in the course of therapy has an important place.

Johnson and Szurek (1952) moved away from the notion of generalized superego weakness and tackled the phenomenological problem presented by observing guilt in antisocial personalities by suggesting that superego lacunae (lack of superego in certain circumscribed areas) was the nature of the superego pathology. Such gaps in the superego were thought to occur because of the parents' unconscious wish to act out forbidden impulses; the child is unconsciously encouraged by the parents to act in amoral ways, but consciously discouraged from doing this. Their ideas in many respects resemble systemic formulations based on family therapy. They suggest that the child may be scapegoated, unconsciously chosen by the parents to act out their prohibited wishes and then punished severely for doing so, depending on the severity of the parents' superego structure. The child is thus presented with a potentially unresolvable dilemma: either he remains totally inhibited or he becomes particularly clever in actualizing the parents' unconscious fantasies. Maybe it is not surprising that antisocial individuals can at times appear very inactive, as if their intentionality were pervasively inhibited. The superficial charm and manipulative skills of antisocial personalities would be understood as deriving from the clever strategies required of them to satisfy unconscious parental demands whilst avoiding manifest injunctions on such behaviour.

Lampl-de-Groot (1949) suggested that the balance of the superego and the ego ideal explained why certain individuals became neurotically depressed, whilst others became antisocial. The former corresponds to a severe superego and strong ego ideal, whereas the latter is a consequence of a menacing superego and a weak ego ideal. Singer (1975) proposed a tripartite synthesis of the ego-psychology model identifying: (1) drive disturbances (stealing as acquiring an aggrandized penis to undo hidden feelings of being small, impotent, castrated and worthless); (2) disturbances of ego functions (heightened sensitivity to displeasure, disturbed reality testing, inability to delay action by fantasy); and (3) superego defects (the superego is corruptible (Alexander 1930), isolated (Greenacre 1945; Reich 1933), and riddled with lacunae (Johnson and Szurek 1952).

More Recent Psychoanalytic Contributions

Anna Freud's Model

That development is both cumulative and epigenetic (i.e. each developmental phase is constructed upon the previous one) is a fundamental tenet of all psychoanalytic developmental models. Anna Freud (1966) was one of the first coherently to adopt a developmental perspective on psychopathology, a precedent which is widely acknowledged by today's leading developmentalists (Cicchetti 1990; Emde 1988b; Sroufe 1990). She argued that psychological disorder could be most effectively studied in its process of developmental evolution and asserted that it was the profile or pattern amongst strands (lines) in development that best captured the nature of risks the individual child faced.

Anna Freud (1966) stresses that, for children, the degree of inner equilibrium compatible with normality is very hard to establish, as the forces that determine the child's development are external as well as internal, and to a marked degree outside the child's control. The child needs to integrate his constitutional potential, the influences emanating from the parental environment, and the expected vicissitudes associated with the gradual structuralization of personality. When one or other of these aspects of development depart from the expectable, disturbances of equilibrium are bound to occur and healthy development is jeopardized.

Anna Freud views such developmental disharmonies (deviations and asynchronies) as a background for psychopathology. Developmental pathology is, however, seen as separate and to some degree independent of the symptomatic pathology of Hartmann's structural model. For example, a simple insight-oriented treatment method is unlikely to be able to tackle the psychological difficulties faced by such a child (see A. Freud 1974, 1983; Kennedy and Yorke 1980). Treatment directed toward developmental assistance may, however, help to correct developmental discrepancies. Minor degrees of disharmony are ubiquitous (Yorke, Wiseberg and Freeman 1989, p.26). Gross disharmony, however, may in itself constitute pathology as well as being the focus of later neurotic development. In general terms, disharmony is seen as a 'fertile breeding ground' (A. Freud 1981, p.109) for later neurosis and more severe psychopathology, and the major constituent of non-neurotic developmental disturbances of the personality (personality disorders).

Anna Freud agrees with structural theorists in regarding severe personality disorders as reflecting structural deficits such as defects in reality testing, the dominance of primitive defences, limited capacities for anxiety tolerance, poor superego development. She explains these as developmental disturbances (deviations or disharmonies). For example, Yorke *et al.* (1989), suggest that the inadequate response by the mother to an infant's instinctual needs creates dangers and external conflict. Such disharmony of need and external environment will be most intensely felt when structuralization is not yet ready to sustain the pressures caused by the internal and external stresses thus created. Ego development will suffer because the internalizing and identificatory processes will be specifically threatened. Object constancy, for example, may not develop if the early relationship with the mother is disrupted by trauma. The failure to achieve structured compromise produces the labile character of borderline and other personality disturbances. Narcissistic character disorder is seen as rooted in early emotional deprivation which compromises the process by which objects (representations of people) are invested with instinctual energy. The individual attempts to identify with the frustrating and disappointing object, providing a focus for libidinal cathexis that heightens narcissism and cathexis of the self (ego-centrism).

Anna Freud, in her contribution to a Festschrift for August Aichhorn (1949), provided a developmental model of antisocial personality. She dates the critical experiences as taking place during the first year of the child's life when an absent, neglectful or ambivalent mother fails to provide steady libidinal satisfaction for the child. This prevents the natural progression of the child's interests moving away from his body needs and genuine interest in the object never develops so that the slightest disappointment is likely to lead to withdrawal from the object and a re-cathexis of the self and its body. Thus the primacy of body needs over object relationships is by-and-large retained. Destructiveness and criminality is a consequence of the failure of libidinal development to reach a stage where aggressive impulses are successfully bound. The child becomes destructive and later develops criminal tendencies.

Anna Freud distinguished the above form of deeply rooted criminal tendency from a less malignant form, where delinquent behaviours result from unconscious displacements of conflicts (pre-Oedipal and Oedipal) from the family setting to the outside world. This kind of behaviour is common in school-aged children and shows a far greater tendency to resolve spontaneously and respond to psychotherapeutic intervention. The child, for example, may act out primal-scene-related fantasies and get into difficulties at school for aggressive sexual behaviour, the root of which is not a flawed character structure but simply neurotic conflict. Other forms of neurotic delinquency may arise if a child's sexual behaviour (e.g. phallic masturbation) is frustrated by overly strict parental constraints on sexuality. The ego's adaptive activities may then be overwhelmed by sexual content. The recognition of this duality of delinquent behaviour is consistent with longitudinal, prospective studies of delinquency and is more sophisticated then many other psychoanalytic notions which tend towards homogenizing delinquent behaviour. However, the distinction suggested by Anna Freud has never been operationalized and is therefore of unknown relevance to the long term outcome of this problem.

The British Independent Group's Contributions to Understanding Personality Disorder

The key contribution by Fairbairn (1944) was the proposition that early trauma of great severity is stored in memories which are 'frozen' or dissociated from a person's central ego or functional self. This conception steps beyond the classical psychoanalytic notion of repression in developmental accounts of psychopathology. The classical model of pathogenesis (conflict → repression → reactivation of conflict → neurotic compromise) is still seen to apply to conflicts which reach the Oedipal (3–4 year) level. The Independent model applies to disorders of the self, thought to arise out of traumatic events before that age. Although their clinical formulations apply particularly to narcissistic and borderline personality disorders, the notion of multiple self representations is of profound importance in all domains of psychoanalysis. For example, the Independent approach to dream interpretation differs from the classical position, in seeing dreams as communication patterns between different parts of the self (see Bollas 1987; Rycroft 1966; Rycroft, 1979b).

Schizoid personality (Fairbairn 1940, 1952a) arises out of the infantile experience that love is destructive for the mother and therefore has to be inhibited along with all intimacy. In schizoid states the ego is so split that the individual may be mystified about himself and is transiently disturbed about reality (finding the familiar in the unfamiliar and *vice versa*). These individuals resist perceiving others as whole persons and substitute bodily for emotional contacts. They hide their love and to protect themselves from others' love, they will erect defences designed to distance others, seeming indifferent, rude or even hateful. Loving is dangerous and intimate relationships can only be maintained by retaining a part of the self which remains uninvolved. Often, since the enjoyment of love relationships is forbidden to them, they may give themselves over to the pleasure of hating and destruction. Fairbairn (1952a) differentiates depressive disorder from schizoid conditions in that it derives from later in infancy and is rooted in the infant's feeling that his aggression was destructive towards the object and has to be defended against (e.g. turned against the self).

Winnicott (1956, 1963) uses his formulation of the *false self* to elaborate a theory of antisocial behaviour, particularly in children (Winnicott 1956). He sees antisocial behaviour as starting in the environment's failure to adjust to the child, but its continuation to be ensured by an essentially 'reparative' function; it is an expression of hope, an attempt by the child to restore his situation to a pre-traumatic one. The outrageousness of the antisocial act is a cry of help, 'failing to find it, it seeks it elsewhere, when hopeful'. With development, the original symbolic meaning of the anti-social act is lost and it is replaced by secondary gain (economic gain replaces the symbolic possession of love from stolen goods).

In the case of destructive behaviour, 'the child is seeking that amount of environmental stability which will stand the strain resulting from impulsive behaviour' (p.310). This represents a search for lost environmental provision, an attitude of humanity, without which the individual feels no freedom to act or get excited. Therapeutically, Winnicott's insight is critical. The natural response to outrageous behaviour is outrage, and an expression of hope for a humane response is met with further deprivation and thus hope quickly withers away. The appropriate treatment is not psychoanalysis but an attempt on the part of the therapist to meet and match 'the moment of hope' (p.309) of the patient.

Kernberg's Integration of the Object Relations and Structural Schools

Kernberg, an analyst with a Kleinian training, writing and practising in the environment of ego psychology, achieved a remarkable level of integration between these two, quite possibly epistemologically inconsistent (see Greenberg and Mitchell 1983) developmental frameworks (see Kernberg 1975, 1976b, 1980, 1984, 1987). In Kernberg's theory of development, affects serve as the primary motivational system (Kernberg 1983). He suggests that combinations of a self representation, an object representation and an affect state linking them are the essential units of psychic structure. He sees affects as coming to be organized into libidinal and aggressive drives, always *vis à vis* interactions with a human object. To put this differently, he treats drives as hypothetical constructs manifested in mental representations and affects; these representations are of the self and object linked by some dominant affect state. The object is not just a vehicle for drive gratification, and the major psychic structures (id, ego, superego) are seen as internalizations of object representations and self–object relationships under the influence of various emotional states. The characteristics of internalization depend upon the affects active at the time. A superego may be harsh because of a prevailing affect of anger and criticism.

Kernberg (1976b) describes the concept of self-image as a component of the process of internalization. It is one of three components (the others being object representations and dispositions to affective states). There are also three processes of internalization: introjection, identification and ego identity, which correspond roughly to developmental processes involving the acquisition of experiences and behaviours which reflect an individual's self-image as well as his object representation.

His model of early development is based on reconstructions from the treatment of severely disturbed adults which are strongly influenced by Kleinian theory. It is less concerned with the child's real experience and focuses on the force of introjects and fantasies. Kernberg (1976b, 1980, 1984) is also strongly influenced by the work of Jacobson (1964) and proposes a three stage developmental theory associated with a theory of character pathology based on developmental failure.

Kernberg differs from other proponents of object relations theory such as Klein, Fairbairn, or Mahler, in that he focuses less on any particular time at which the currently dominant pathogenic conflicts and structural organization of the personality may have originated, and more on the current state of the patient's ideation. He accepts that subsequent development makes any one-to-one link between current state and the past risky. He sidesteps the distinction between Oedipal or pre-Oedipal problems which characterizes much of structural psychoanalytic writing. He believes that all levels of disturbance are more complex in severe personality disturbance but exist across the entire spectrum of psychopathology.

Here, the tolerance of ambivalence characteristic of higher level neurotic object relationships is replaced by a defensive disintegration of the representation of self and objects into libidinally and aggressively invested part object relations. Instead of the more realistic and readily comprehensible relationship patterns of neurotic personalities, he finds highly unrealistic, sharply idealized or (through aggression) highly persecutory self and object representations. These cannot be traced back to actual or fantasized relationships in the past, as he believes they do not correspond to any real relationship.

What Kernberg sees as activated in these patients are, for example, highly idealized part object relations formed under the impact of diffuse, overwhelming emotional states of an ecstatic nature, or equally overwhelming but terrifying and painful emotional states which signal the activation of aggressive or persecutory relations between self and the object. As the object relations are very poorly integrated, the reversals of the enactment of self and other representations may be very rapid. This can make relationships with such individuals confusing and even chaotic. For example, love and hate may exist in a dissociated way side by side; several object relations may be condensed into single images, and so forth. He identifies the central problem of borderline patients as the activation of primitive, overwhelming part-object relations which continuously alternate.

In contrast, the problem in the case of psychosis is the blurring of boundaries between self and object representation. Here, the protective quality of the defensive object relation fails because the confusion between self and object blurs the origin of the intolerable impulse. This is therefore reactivated without the protection of the defensive relationship pattern into which it was cast. Such patients will be frequently overwhelmed in any kind of intimate relationship.

For Kernberg (1967, 1977), the root cause of borderline states is the intensity of destructive and aggressive impulses, and the relative weakness of ego structures available to handle them. The good introjects are repeatedly threatened with destruction by the predominance of negative, hostile images and impulses which are necessary to achieve stability. Kernberg sees the borderline individual as using developmentally early defences in an attempt to separate contradictory images of self and others. This is necessary to protect positive images from being overwhelmed by negative and hostile ones. The wish to protect the object from destruction with only the most rudimentary psychic mechanisms at its disposal leads to the defensive fragmentation of self and object representations. Manifestations of the borderline condition there-fore represent a continuation of an unresolved infantile conflict state. The defences of borderline individuals centre on the splitting (defensive separation) of contradictory self and object representations in order to forestall the terror associated with ambivalence. Splitting causes others to be perceived as either 'all good' or 'all bad' with the result that attitudes to them may rapidly shift between extremes. Primitive idealization, also a consequence of splitting, protects the individual from the 'all bad' objects through creating an omnipo-tent object in fantasy which is the container of grandiose identifications. Projective identification is seen by Kernberg as a by-product of the absence of self–object differentiation; the individual using this defence is left with a sense of empathy with the object of projection as well as a need to control him/her. The use of primitive denial ensures that the individual can totally disregard his experience of 'good' feelings toward the object when 'bad' feelings dominate his consciousness. Splitting also results in a 'diffuse sense of identity' which is characterized by a confused internal representation of the 'real' object, and an unintegrated primitive superego which sets unattainable ideals and internalized persecutory images. Since representations of the self are organized in a parallel fashion with those of others, splitting also leads to

'extreme and repetitive oscillation between contradictory self concepts...the patient, lacking in a stable sense of self or other, continually experiences the self in shifting positions with potentially sharp discontinuities – as victim or victimiser, as dominant or submissive, and so on.' (Kernberg, Selzer, Koenigsberg, Carr, and Appelbaum 1989, p.28).

Kernberg (1987) illustrates how the self-destructiveness, self-mutilating behaviour and suicidal gestures tend to coincide with intense attacks of rage towards the object. They can serve to re-establish control over the environment by evoking guilt feelings, or express unconscious guilt over the success of a deepening relationship. In some patients self-destructiveness occurs because their self-image becomes 'infiltrated' with aggression, so that they experience increased self-esteem and a confirmation of their grandiosity in self-mutilation or masochistic sexual perversions. The caring professions can respond only with despair to these patients' obvious sense of triumph in their victory over pain and death. Their efforts seem futile to the patient, who at an unconscious level experiences a sense of being in control over death. Self-mutilation, such as cutting, may also protect from the identity diffusion (derealization) which is a constant threat to the fragmented internal world of the borderline individual.

Kernberg (1970) groups together borderline and schizoid personality disorders, viewing both these as lower level character organizations (see also Kernberg 1967). The overlap is to some extent substantiated by empirical investigations demonstrating co-morbidity between the two conditions (Plakum, Burkhardt and Muller 1985) as well as overlaps in pathological psychic mechanisms (Grinker, Werble and Drye 1968; Gunderson 1985).

Kernberg (1975, 1976a, 1984, 1989) believes that patients with antisocial personality disorder usually have underlying borderline personality organizations. Because superego integration is minimal at this level and sadistic forerunners are easily projected outwards, there is deficient guilt, lack of goals, inauthenticity and erratic potential for sublimation. The function of the ego to synthesize libidinal and aggressive derivatives is impaired, leading to pregenital aggression, erratic work record and lack of goals and direction in life. The ego is not clearly differentiated from the ego ideal, and from the superego, leading to a chaotic mixture of shameful and exalted images of the self, deficient guilt, magical thinking and repetitive and contradictory behaviours. Primitive defences and poor object constancy leads to paranoid attitudes, unstable self-concept, superficial concern with others, and a lack of genuine empathy.

Antisocial behaviour occurs in most severe personality disorders because of the common underlying personality organization but is best treated as a sub-category of narcissistic personality (Kernberg 1970, 1971). The narcissistic features are invariably strong (self-centredness, grandiosity, and lack of concern for others). Superego pathology is more evident in these individuals and is behaviourally manifest in an absence of loyalty, guilt, anticipatory anxiety, and an incapacity to learn from prior experience. Kernberg (1989) takes the DSM-III-R approach to the diagnosis of antisocial personality disorder to task for concentrating on behavioural indicators at the expense of internal object relations, thus potentially blurring important distinctions between different character constellations. He distinguishes four groups of individuals: (1) those suffering from 'pathological self-love' who are thus self-centred, exhibitionistic, overambitious, and suffer from severe bouts of inferiority alternating with grandiosity; (2) those whose internal object relations are pathological and who thus manifest greed, envy, defences against envy, entitlement, appropriation of others' ideas and property, lack of concern for others and the predominance of exploitative relations with others; (3) those whose basic ego state is characterized by chronic emptiness, stimulus hunger, and a diffuse sense of the meaninglessness of life; (4) severe superego pathology, manifesting in a deficit of depressive position type sadness, and absence of guilt feelings and he also mentions the important component of an absence of self reflection in these individuals.

Kernberg saw narcissistic pathology as rooted in experiences of a rejecting primary caregiver who was cold but who was the only available source of comfort. The child inevitably falls back on the grandiose self. The child's rage reaction to protect the grandiose self is projected onto the parents who are then perceived as even less likely to meet his needs, and the child is increasingly restricted to the grandiose self for soothing and comfort. The term 'grandiose self' is one also used by Kohut (1968), but in a different way from Kernberg. For Kernberg, this aspect of the self contains the admired aspects of the child, the compensatory fantasies about the self as all-powerful, and a fantasized image of a loving and understanding caregiver. The needy parts of the individual remain dissociated from experience. The grandiose self differentiates narcissistic personality from borderline disorder. Whereas both manifest a predominance of splitting over repression (unlike obsessional or hysterical personalities which he sees as being organized around repression, (Kernberg 1984), narcissistic personalities have a cohesive, albeit highly pathological self.

Kernberg (1989) makes a helpful distinction between individuals with passive and active superego pathology; whereas the former is more likely to commit crimes of lying, swindling, forgery or prostitution, the latter is more likely to commit violent crimes, assault, robbery, and murder. Individuals with narcissistic pathology are more likely to present with passive antisocial behaviours, show some guilt and demonstrate sublimatory capacities. Malignantly narcissistic individuals are closer to the active type of Kernberg's antisocial personality schema, in so far as they are likely to manifest ego-syntonic aggression or sadism, or triumphant kinds of self-mutilation or suicidal attempts, and a strong paranoid orientation. Both should, in Kernberg's view, be carefully distinguished from reactions to abnormal environments, which may be neurotic or even normal adjustments (dyssocial reactions) and may emerge in studies of sub-groups where criminal behaviour is highly prevalent, and socially accepted.

The Attachment Theory Model of Bowlby

The infant comes into the world predisposed to participate in social interactions. The British psychoanalyst, John Bowlby (1969, 1973, 1980) was the first to give central place to the child's biological proclivity to form attachments, to initiate, maintain and terminate interactions with the caregiver and use him/her as a 'secure base' for exploration and self-enhancement. Bowlby's (1958, 1969) critical contribution was his focus on the infant's need for unbroken (secure) early attachment to the mother. The child who does not have such provision is likely to show signs of *partial deprivation* – excessive need for love or for revenge, gross guilt and depression – or *complete deprivation* – listlessness, quiet unresponsiveness and retardation of development. Later there are signs of superficiality, want of real feeling, lack of concentration, deceit and compulsive thieving (Bowlby 1951). Later Bowlby (1973) placed these reactions into a framework of reactions to separation: protest → despair → detachment.

Bowlby's attachment theory is unlike most other psychoanalytic developmental formulations in that it is, for the most part, prospective (Bowlby 1969). Laboratory investigations such as those of Brazelton and colleagues provided important support for Bowlby in demonstrating the innate social disposition of the infant, and the adverse consequences if expectations of social responsiveness from the caretaker are not met (see Brazelton 1973, 1982; Brazelton and Als 1979; Brazelton, Tronick, Adamson, Als and Wise 1975; Tronick, Als, Adamson, Wise and Brazelton 1978). He is also most bold in claiming that the infantile roots of pathology lie in *actual* realistically-based fears.

Bowlby (1973) takes a Balint–Fairbairn (as opposed to a Kleinian) approach to frustration and aggression. He maintains that anger may have survival value in alerting the parent who has withdrawn attention. However, when loss has become permanent and the parent is irrecoverable, the anger has no function yet may persist and even intensify in the absence of appropriate feedback mechanisms.

Bowlby (1969, 1973) suggests that disruption in the functioning of the attachment system will interfere with the child's developing capacities for regulating his behaviour, emotions and arousal. He argues that since children have many of their first experiences of emotional states (intense anger and anxiety, as well as love and happiness) in the context of their early attachment relationships, the quality of these relationships will determine their capacity for self-regulation at times of high stress. Insecurely attached children should therefore be more vulnerable to emotional and behavioural disregulation, and have fewer opportunities to elaborate the capacity to regulate emotional experiences, than secure ones (see also Ainsworth, Blehar, Waters and Wall 1978). Further, Bowlby (1973, 1980) maintains that secure attachment will generate internal working models of relationships characterized by an expectation of emotional as well as physical support, leading to positive self-concept and confidence in the availability and responsiveness of the other. Insensitive parenting will give rise to insecure models of relationships, characterized by lack of trust in the other and a self-representation as unworthy and undeserving of love and affection (see also Bretherton 1985; Cummings and Cicchetti 1990; Main, Kaplan and Cassidy 1985).

Broadly speaking, Bowlby's prediction that insecure attachments are associated with various later difficulties has been borne out by empirical research. Insecurely attached children appear to be more likely to experience fluctuating and unpredictable affective states, including intensely negative emotions such as excessive sadness and anger (Berlin 1993; Cassidy 1993). Insecure attachments are associated with maladaptive functioning in other contexts (Crittenden 1988; Field 1989), with problems of emotional disregulation (Kobak and Sceery 1988; Sroufe 1983), heightened sensitivity to stress (Lewis, Feiring, McGuffog and Jaskir 1984; Sroufe and Fleeson 1986; Sroufe and Rutter 1984), pervasive anxiety and distress (Grossmann et al. 1985) problems in interpersonal relationships (Erickson, Sroufe and Egeland 1985; Pastor 1981; Sroufe 1983), internalizing (Campbell 1987; Erickson et al. 1985) and externalizing (Armsden and Greenberg 1987; Lewis et al. 1984) disorders.

The issue of the continuity of psychological attributes across developmental stages has come to dominate debate within developmental psychology (Emde 1988a; Kagan 1984; Rutter 1987). Attachment research demonstrated that there are marked continuities in children's security of attachment, maintained probably by the stable quality of the parent–child relationship (Grossmann et al. 1985; Main et al. 1985; Sroufe 1985). There is no assumption of linear continuity (e.g. an overly dependent preschooler emerging from a very clinging infant, or an aggressive child emerging from an infant with many tantrums). Rather, Bowlby's theory assumes complex developmental relationships: for example an affectively dependent infant becoming a self-reliant schoolboy, a prediction which has been confirmed by research (Sroufe 1983).

In 1969, Bowlby identified three psychological states associated with the disruption of early attachment in the first three years of life. Following on from the acute distress of the protest state, the despair state is characterized by preoccupation, withdrawal and hopelessness. Most pertinent, from our viewpoint, is Bowlby's third state, which is thought to follow prolonged separation, that of detachment. Detachment represents an apparent recovery from protest and despair, but there is no resumption of normal attachment behaviour following the refinding of the object. The infant is apathetic, and may totally inhibit bonding. There is an intensification of interest in physical objects, and a self-absorption which is only thinly disguised by superficial sociability.

In 1946, Bowlby (1946) linked affectionless psychopathy to the absence of a maternal object and to a biological predisposition. The term 'affectionless' is perhaps unfortunate in the light of the common clinical experience that emotional detachment from others in the past and present does not stop psychopathic characters from repeatedly and aggressively engaging with others (Meloy 1992). In primary psychopathy (Hare and Cox 1987; Meloy 1988b), the violence is predatory; it is planned, purposeful and apparently emotionless. By contrast, affective violence is not predatory; rather it is a reaction to a perceived threat and is accompanied by heightened emotional (autonomic) arousal (Meloy 1988a). The attachment system may be involved in both predatory and affective acts of violence; while in the former case the individual seeks the object and the purpose of such proximity seeking is primarily destructive, in the latter case proximity triggers an intense defensive reaction of a violent kind.

Although a significant proportion of individuals with criminal records meet diagnostic criteria for borderline or narcissistic personality disorder, it would be foolhardy to claim any kind of isomorphism between borderline personality disorder (BPD), as defined phenomenologically, and criminal acts. From an attachment theory perspective, we may, however, identify commonalities at the level of psychic mechanism between individuals in the two groups. Recently, Meloy (1992) made a systematic attempt to link the object relations theory approach to BPD to a wide variety of violent criminal behaviour. For example, he explored cases of ego-dystonic, sudden violent acts which appear to be impulsive rage reactions without a prodromal period. These acts would be exemplified by Intermittent Explosive Disorder whose typical victim is a spouse, lover, boyfriend or girlfriend (American Psychiatric Association 1987; Felthous *et al.* 1991) or more chronic obsessive preoccupations with the future victim where depression, helplessness, and a conscious sense of tension build up over a period of months and years to be 'released' by a violent act. A small scale controlled study showed sudden murderers to be apparently ambivalently attached to dominant mothers and to experience their fathers as rejecting, negative and hostile (Weiss, Lamberti and Blackman 1960). The fragmentation of the self-structure through splitting and projective identification makes such individuals vulnerable to injuries to the perception of the self (criticisms, insults, belittling rejection), which are common precipitants of the violent act (Blackman, Weiss and Lamberti 1963). Ruotolo (1968) came to the same conclusion in a clinical investigation of five sudden murderers. Some authors stress the symbolic meaning of either the violent act or the victim (Revitch and Schlesinger 1978, 1981; Wertham 1966). The violent act is directed against a split-off part of the self with which the individual is projectively identified. Rather than pursuing Meloy's excellent analysis, I would like to explore the applicability of our own attachment theory formulations of BPD to certain types of criminal behaviour.

Gacono and Meloy (1992) used the Rorschach to investigate sixty DSM-III-R Antisocial Personality Disorder prisoners of both psychopathic and nonpsychopathic type. Antisocial personality disorder was associated with pathological narcissism and omnipotence. Narcissism was allied with lack of affectional relatedness (indicated in the Rorschach by low mean and frequency of texture responses); with a relatively high number of 'hard', non-human or part-human objects; a failure to represent whole people. Evaluative comments were predominantly negative, idealization was rare and predominantly directed towards non-human objects. These tendencies were stronger in psychopathic than in non-psychopathic individuals.

Gacono, Meloy and Berg (1992) extended these findings to an outpatient sample of narcissistic and borderline personality disorder individuals. Compared to these groups, psychopaths showed minimal capacity for either attachment or anxiety. Non-psychopathic antisocial personality disorder individuals tended to be more anxious and easily provoked into feeling threatened than psychopathic individuals with the same diagnosis.

In a further study, Weber, Meloy and Gacono (1992) studied adolescents with conduct disorders, with dysthymic inpatients as a comparison group. Conduct-disordered adolescents manifest emotional detachment and devaluation observed in the prison population of psychopaths, but to a lesser degree. Conduct disordered adolescents showed very weak desire for relationships compared to depressed adolescents, and were indifferent to people as whole, real, and meaningful individuals. In line with Deutsch and Erickson's (1989) findings that undersocialized conduct-disordered adolescents had disrupted early life and attachment experiences, the study found socialized delinquents could be less severely affected on these measures. These findings may be interpreted as psychometric evidence for disturbance of attachment relationships in at least some conduct-disordered adolescents.

Bruhn and Davidow (1983) demonstrated that the earliest childhood memories reported by delinquents could be distinguished from a matched non-delinquent sample of youngsters. One of the strongest distinguishing features was the way other people were represented in the early memory. Delinquents recalled them in terms of whether they helped or hindered their activities but not as three-dimensional characters. The non-delinquents were much more likely to embellish their portraits of others by recalling personality traits and other distinguishing characteristics.

Davidow and Bruhn (1990) replicated this study with 71 delinquents matched with 71 non-delinquents under control on age, SES, and family constellation. Particularly striking was the amount of description of the other.

The majority of delinquents gave minimal or moderate descriptions, whereas non-delinquents tended to give extensive portraits of the other. In a similar vein, parents were recalled as not available to help, offering minimal assistance or as causing injury. Davidow and Bruhn note a qualitative difference in the description of the other person: in the delinquent individual the description tends to be self-referred as well as negative (e.g. 'he was mean to me'). In the control group, the other person is described as a separate human being (e.g. 'my father was jumpy and nervous').

Interestingly, considerable epidemiological research related to attachment theory formulations of criminal behaviour has been carried out in the context of large-scale studies inspired by social control theory. Social control theory (Durkheim 1951; Hirschi 1969; Kornhauser 1978) proposes that crime and deviance will result when an individual's bond to society is weak or broken. In Hirschi's (1969) formulation, there are four elements to the social bond: attachment, commitment, involvement, and belief. Attachment refers to affective ties with parents, schools and friends. Changes across the course of life that strengthen the individual's bond to institutions of social control will reduce criminality, whereas transitions which weaken the bond will be associated with increases in deviance.

Although in these large-scale studies measures of attachment tend to be superficial, the results are in line with the assumption that criminality involves disturbance of attachment processes. For example, marriage is likely to reduce criminality if the individual is strongly (securely) attached to his/her spouse. In Sampson and Laub's (1990) re-analysis of the Glueck's data of 800 individuals in both delinquent and non-delinquent childhood groups those who had weak ties to work and family were far more likely to engage in crime and deviance. Adolescent delinquents and matched controls were both more likely to show adult antisocial behaviour if their attachment to their spouse, occupational commitment, or job stability were weak. Over three-quarters of the delinquent group with adult criminal records had weak attachments to their spouse. Attachments made a highly significant independent contribution to the prediction of criminal activity, even when a history of prior convictions had been controlled for, and amongst married men this was stronger than either job stability or occupational commitment.

Shoham et al. (1987) were able to distinguish impulsive or planned violence in a population of prisoners on the basis of attachment to the family. Individuals who appeared to be attached to their family were more likely to be impulsively violent. Lack of punishment in childhood was strongly associated with planned violence.

Marcos, Bahr and Johnson (1986) reported a questionnaire study of over 2600 adolescents and found that self-reported drug use was most highly correlated with drug-using friends, although parental attachment and religious attachment also contributed to explanations and life time drug use. Judith Brook and others (Brook, Whiteman, Brook and Gordon 1981, 1984; Brook, Whiteman and Gordon 1983; Brook, Whiteman, Gordon and Brook, 1984; Brook, Whiteman, Gordon and Brook 1985; Norem-Hebeisen, Johnson, Anderson and Johnson 1984) in a series of studies offered convincing evidence indicating that aspects of mutual attachment may insulate young people from drug use. Brook, Whiteman and Finch (1993) looked at drug use over a ten year period in 400 children in order to identify the reason why attachment may provide a protective function. In this longitudinal study she was able to show that earlier child aggression appeared directly to influence drug use, lead to adolescent unconventionality, and difficulty in *later* attachment relationships, which in turn lead the young person to drug abuse. The study offered clearer results indicating that earlier aggression decreases the likelihood of later attachment for women. Weak parent–child attachment (measured by question-naire) at 13–18 years was seen to lead to unconventionality (rebelliousness, lack of responsibility, intolerance of deviance), which in its turn led to drug use. Aggression (assessed on the basis of maternal reports, included anger, non-compliance, temper tantrums, aggression with siblings), was a powerful predictor of low attachment, and to a lesser extent of unconventionality and drug use. This suggests that parent–child attachment has an important recip-rocal role. Aggression, as we have seen, may be the outcome of inadequate early attachment relationships but may also cause a weakening of the parent–child bond, and in this way contributes in an important way to the development of deviance.

Only a handful of studies have succeeded in linking traditional work on attachment with these large-scale epidemiological findings concerning the ecology of crime. For example, Shaw and Vondra (1993) demonstrated that risk factors normally considered to be related to delinquency and criminality (e.g. parental criminality, over-crowding, quality of relationship with a signifi-cant other), were more commonly observed together in families of insecure infants. These challenging findings suggest that infant security and risk factors considered relevant to the child's choice of a deviant developmental trajectory may be inter-related. At the present state of knowledge it is not possible to determine which may be of primary significance.

Even were there more such studies, the logic of the link between large-scale epidemiological investigation and the single-case orientation of clinical work is not entirely clear from an epistemological viewpoint. Very often, the bare facts of epidemiological associations are precisely that. For example, the influence of marital relationships on criminality will be hard to understand until measures of marital quality are better able to tap the meaning of the relationship to the individual, rather than just overt signs of difficulty such as marital conflict. From a clinical point of view, we know that an individual may

have an extremely strong attachment to a fraught, sado-masochistic relationship. Measures such as the Adult Attachment Interview will need to be
developed for all important current relationships if the impact of adult
attachment relationships on criminality are to be appropriately assessed.

Stern's Approach to Infant Development and a Possible Alternative Formulation of Criminality

Stern's (1985) book represents a milestone in psychoanalytic theorization
concerning development. He challenges many of the ideas of previous approaches to developmental schemas. His work is distinguished by being
normative rather than pathomorphic and prospective rather than retrospective.
His focus is the reorganization of subjective perspectives on self and other as
these occur with the emergence of new maturational capacities.

His model uses four different senses of self, each with an associated domain
of relatedness: (1) 'The sense of emergent self' involves the process of the self
coming into being and forming connections (from birth to two months of age);
(2) 'the sense of core self' (from between two and six months of age) and 'the
domain of core relatedness' is based on a single organizing subjective perspective and a coherent *physical self*; (3) the 'sense of *subjective self*' and the 'domain
of intersubjective relatedness' (between seven and fifteen months) emerges with
the discovery of subjective mental states beyond physical events; (4) the sense
of 'verbal self' which forms after 15 months.

The capacities underlying the sense of subjective self include a number of
clinically extremely relevant mental functions, which have only been elaborated
by developmental researchers over the past 10 years. Its earliest manifestation
may be an understanding of the mental state of attention which is evident in
normal infants from about nine months of age in the monitoring of the gaze
of the mother (Butterworth 1991; Scaife and Bruner 1975), and through
gestures such as protodeclarative pointing (Bates *et al.* 1979). That infants
apprehend the intentions and motives of others is evident in gaze monitoring,
as they appear not only to check where someone is looking, but also how the
person is *evaluating* what they see, as is clear in the phenomena of social
referencing (Sorce, Emde, Campos and Klinnert 1985). Such emotional communication can be conveyed through the face or the voice by a parent or
familiar caretaker, and it can regulate behaviour towards an object, a location
or a person (Boccia and Campos 1989; Camras and Sachs 1991). In protodeclarative pointing, children appear to use the pointing gesture as a comment
on a topic of interest, concern or fun (Baron-Cohen 1991; Tomasello 1988).
Phillips, Baron-Cohen and Rutter (1992) found that normal 9–18-month-old
toddlers respond to an ambiguous action of an adult by instantly looking at
the adult's eye, but do so on only a minority of occasions when the adult's
action is not ambiguous. Thus infants from this stage appear to sense the

congruence or lack of congruence between their own state and that of another person.

The sense of verbal self and the domain of verbal relatedness represents a move to a stage where oneself and other people can be represented as storehouses of knowledge and experience. This experience may be shared, which involves the ability to objectify the self, to reflect upon mental contents and to use language to communicate. Baron-Cohen (1993), identifies six different classes of mental states of which the developing child comes to have an appreciation at different moments.

(1) Understanding beliefs, particularly understanding that a belief may be false was considered by Dennett (1978) as a litmus test of the child's capacity to develop an understanding that people have minds and mental states, and that mental states relate to behaviour. Wimmer and Perner (1983) designed a famous false belief test in which the child's (true) belief and the child's awareness of someone else's different (false) belief were contrasted. They showed that around three to four years of age, normal children pass such a test.

(2) Desire is often regarded as the other key mental state of folk psychology (Dennett 1978). Together, belief and desire explain most behaviour. For normal children, desire is understood earlier than belief. Wellman (1993) shows that desire is understood by most normal two-year-olds. The oppositional behaviour of two-year-olds may be interpreted not as a desire to establish separateness (see Mahler *et al.* 1975), but as evidence of their growing awareness of the frustrating difference between their own and their parents' desires (Wellman 1990).

(3) Understanding knowledge appears to be easier than understanding belief for normal children (Wellman 1990). This may be because knowledge is true belief, and misrepresentation (which involves false belief), is not involved.

(4) Understanding pretence is regarded by some psychoanalytic workers as the earliest, and perhaps most important, developmental achievement on the way to symbolization (Fónagy and Fonagy, in press). Understanding that something can be something while at the same time knowing that identity to be inappropriate (e.g. that a chair is a tank), is a crucial characteristic of mental functioning at the level of meta-representations (Leslie 1987). This can be argued to be one of the roots of language, as well as of artistic capacity (Fonagy and Fonagy, in preparation). The moment at which true pretence arises is a controversial issue, some developmentalists finding evidence for pretence in the second year (Leslie 1987),

whilst others see genuine pretence as evident only in three- and four-year-olds (Lillard 1993).

(5) Understanding perception appears easier than appreciation of the other mental states previously considered. Whereas belief, knowledge, desire and pretence are all *opaque*, that is, inferred rather than observed perception applied to the physical world. Flavell, Everett, Croft and Flavell (1981) report that understanding of perception is well within the ability of normal two-year-olds, who can readily judge if someone saw something or not. Until three to four years of age they cannot master the more complex task of how something will appear to someone from a different perspective.

(6) The development of an understanding of emotion is perhaps the most relevant form of understanding of mental states for clinical psychoanalysis. Harris (1994) reviewed empirical work on the child's understanding of emotion. Early in the first year of life, infants begin to respond selectively and appropriately to the emotional expression of the caretaker. Infants of ten weeks manifest affective states appropriately, but not by mimicking of the mother's expression (Fernald 1992; Haviland and Lelwica 1987). Infants also expect the caretaker 'to be emotionally responsive to their own expressive signals' (Murray and Trevarthen 1985) and have no similar expectations of mobile but non-human stimuli (Ellsworth, Muir and Hains 1993). The child also understands the intentional nature of emotional states – the fact that they convey an appraisal of objects or persons in the child's environment (Boccia and Campos 1989).

Infants of depressed mothers 'expect' less emotional responsiveness and therefore gaze less at their mother (see, for example, Cohn *et al.* 1986). Infants generalize this expectation toward the stranger (Field *et al.* 1988). There is evidence that the effect is cumulative and it shapes the behaviour of strangers interacting with the infant who behave less positively towards him or her (Cohn, Campbell, Matias and Hopkins 1990; Field *et al.* 1988).

Infants also understand anger in the caregiver and respond to it by crying, looking angry or just watching their mother in an expressionless fashion (Haviland and Lelwica 1987). Toddlers understand affect between others such as covert tension between the parents or overt conflict (Cummings, Zahn-Wax-ler and Radke-Yarrow 1981, 1984). Laboratory observations indicate that a simulated quarrel is most likely to be associated with a freezing response with subsequent aggression, and to sensitize children to further similar experiences (Cummings, Iannotti and Zahn-Waxler 1985). Children appear to understand quarrels differently; whilst for some it serves as a licence to engage in hostile behaviour, for others it is a stimulus that arouses solicitous concern. Children assimilate such exchanges into larger causal schemata encoding general assumptions about how quarrels arise, who is to blame and how one may avoid and ameliorate the experience (Harris 1994).

Two- to three-year-olds appropriately distinguish among and can name various emotional states, and appear to understand the equivalence between their own states and those of other people (Bretherton, Fritz, Zahn-Waxler and Ridgeway 1986; Brown and Dunn 1991; Dunn, Bretherton and Munn 1987). Wellman, Harris, Banerjee and Sinclair (in preparation), report that children up to four years of age almost invariably explain emotion in terms of an intentional target, a person or a physical object at which the emotion is aimed.

Stern's starting point is the 'emergent moment' which is the subjective integration of all aspects of lived experience that takes its input from emotions, behaviours, sensations and all other aspects of the internal and external world. The emergent moment is seen as deriving from schematic representations of various types: event representations or scripts, semantic representations or conceptual schemas, perceptual schemas, and sensory-motor representations. He adds to these two further, clinically highly relevant, modes of representation: 'feeling shapes' and 'proto-narrative envelopes'. These schemata form a network which he terms 'the schema-of-a-way-of-being-with' (see also Horowitz 1991; Kernberg 1976a).

The 'schema-of-a-way-of-being-with' is conceptualized by Stern from the assumed subjective point of view of the infant who is in interaction with the caregiver. The infant's experiences across a number of domains are organized around a motive and a goal, and in this sense echoes Freud's (1905c) original formulation of drives and object relationships in the Three Essays. The goals which organize these moments are not only biological, they include object relatedness, affect states, and states of self-esteem and safety, as well as physical need gratification, be it hunger, thirst, sexuality or aggression. The representation will contain a proto-plot with an agent, an action, an instrumentality and a context which are all necessary elements for the comprehension of human behaviour (see Bruner 1990).

Although Stern (1994, 1985) implies many links to pathological states he does not propose a comprehensive model of psychopathology. A number of workers, equally committed to integrating findings from developmental research with clinical goals, have proposed models, loosely based on Stern's developmental approach (Fonagy, Edgcumbe, Moran, Kennedy and Target 1993; Fonagy and Moran 1991). Work with case records at the Anna Freud Centre (Fonagy and Target 1994; Fonagy and Target, in press; Target and Fonagy 1994a, 1994b), in conjunction with research on the determinants of early relationships (Fonagy, Steele and Steele 1991a; Fonagy, Steele, Moran, Steele and Higgitt, 1991b; Steele, Steele and Fonagy, in preparation; in press) has led to an extension of certain psychoanalytic assumptions concerning the nature of psychic change in child analysis (Fonagy and Moran 1991). In these papers we delineated two models of the psychoanalytic treatment of mental disturbance. The first (the synthetic model) describes the mechanism by which the patient is helped to recover threatening ideas and feelings which have been repudiated or distorted in the course of development as a result of conflict and defence. The second model (the mental process model) draws attention to the therapeutic effects of engaging previously inhibited mental processes within the psychoanalytic encounter. This engagement tends to occur primarily through patient and analyst focusing on the thoughts and feelings of each person, and how the child understands these. The two models entail distinctions between two types of pathology, requiring two types of analytic work, with different predicted rates of change.

The notion of unutilized mental processes offers a conceptual bridge between psychoanalytic work with children and advances in cognitive science; it also stresses the therapeutic value of a mentalizing or reflective capacity, which independently emerged as important in the parent–child attachment relationship. Furthermore, it offers a theoretical explanation of a long-established clinical finding, that children with marked developmental or personality disturbances require longer treatment, with modifications of classical psychodynamic technique (e.g. A. Freud 1966). This theoretical basis leads us to predict that there will be clear differences in technique, levels of change, and rates of change depending on the depth of personality disturbance in a child.

This approach may be exemplified with some ideas about the role of inhibition of mental functioning in borderline personality disorder (Fonagy 1991; Fonagy et al. 1993). The theoretical ideas outlined above, concerning a connection between disturbed attachment, inhibition of mental processes and personality pathology, are being examined in a study of BPD. The hypothesis is that an early and sustained history of trauma and abuse in these individuals would be associated with inhibition of their capacity to envisage mental states (reflective self-function). This has been supported by both a cross-sectional and a longitudinal investigation. Patients who met Gunderson's criteria for BPD were rated as having lower reflective self-function than control groups of patients with non-psychotic psychiatric disorders of equal severity. The inpatient psychotherapeutic treatment of BPD patients was associated with an improvement in reflective self-function in all cases who showed substantial symptom reductions in response to the treatment. These findings offer preliminary support for the hypotheses that (1) part of the disturbance of BPD patients may be understood in terms of a deficit of mentalizing functions, and (2) that these functions are inaccessible to such patients, but may be recovered in the course of psychotherapeutic treatment.

There is considerable evidence which supports the possibility of conflict-induced deficits in the functioning of mental processes which normally evolve through constitutionally determined developmental pathways (or, to use Waddington's (1966) term are 'canalised'). Adlam-Hill and Harris (1988), for example, compared nine-year-old boys attending ordinary schools with boys of the same age attending schools for the emotionally disturbed. Members of the latter group frequently failed to distinguish real from apparent emotion, implying that the disturbed family environment which characterized most of these children in some way impeded the normal development of the capacity to understand how and in what situation feelings could be hidden. They were particularly unlikely to see any need for concealing feelings if the other person's feelings were at stake. Mary Main (1993), from an attachment theory perspective, found evidence that ambivalently attached children, who are most likely to have had experiences of emotional entanglement with their primary caregiver, are also most likely to deny the inherent privacy of mental state. Main argues that such children continue to assume that their caregivers have access to their innermost selves, and that they themselves can read the thoughts of an attachment figure. From a broader psychoanalytic perspective, we would claim that the child defensively inhibits his capacity to accept the mental separateness of the mother because to do so would entail the pain of experiencing her incomprehension of his feelings, beliefs and desires (Fonagy et al., in press).

Evidence is also accumulating that suggests that these fundamental cognitive processes underlying the understanding of mental states are far more vulnerable to the vicissitudes of environmental experiences than previously thought. There is evidence to suggest that the development of the capacities underlying the false belief task may be enhanced by the proximity of a sibling (see Jenkins and Astington 1993; Perner, Ruffman and Leekam, in press). Close interaction with a sibling who is of a similar age enhances the child's understanding of mental states. Preliminary data from our own prospective study, as well as data reported by Main (1993), is consistent with the view that a secure attachment to a caregiver enhances the child's capacity to explore the mind of that person and facilitates the evolution of emotional self-awareness and a theory of mind.

Following the philosopher, Davidson (1983), and psychoanalytic exponents of his work (see Cavell 1988a, 1988b, 1991), we believe that getting to know our own minds is a process of familiarizing ourselves with the mind of another. The child perceives and eventually comes to recognize himself in his caregiver's perception of him. We believe that the development of the self entails the internalization not of the object, good or bad, as classical object relations theory posits, but rather, that it is the caregiver's image of the intentional infant which comes to be internalized and comes to constitute the core of the child's mentalizing self. Incoherent perception of the child's mental state therefore places the child's self-development at risk. Accurate perception of the child as a psychological being is particularly critical when the caregiver's own history of deprivation places her at risk of recapitulating her own adverse early relationship experiences with her child (Fonagy *et al.* 1993).

An inhibition of the capacity to envision the state of mind of the other may be assumed to disable the normal aversive emotional reaction which we experience when we observe distress in others, particularly when the distress was caused by ourselves. The development of moral behaviour may crucially depend on this negative emotional state, without which the distinction between conventional and moral behaviour (Turiel 1983) may never be established.

Blair (1992) examined the attributions made by criminals diagnosed as showing antisocial personality disorder (APD) and other criminals without a diagnosis. He compared their responses to a number of stories which could normally be expected to evoke guilt, happiness, sadness, or embarrassment in the protagonists. The happiness story concerned an individual winning the pools, the sadness story a person coming last in a competition, the embarrassment stories involved three forms of audience condition (no audience, passive audience or negative audience) with the embarrassing acts being, for instance, dropping a tray of food. The guilt stories were also divided into three groups: person harm (a man punches another man), object harm (a man smashes up public property), and unintentional harm (to either property or person). Differences emerged both in the intentional and unintentional person harm stories: in both cases, APD individuals made fewer guilt attributions and more indifferent attributions than other criminals. Both groups made fewer guilt and more indifferent attributions than normal controls. Attributions of happiness and sadness emotions were not different between the groups.

This study, despite its small sample, offers support for the contention that certain criminals lack the capacity to envision the state of mind of victims' distress. On the basis of the investigations of BPD we are inclined to assume that these difficulties arise because of failures of the primary attachment relationships. We have some preliminary evidence that is consistent with this point of view.

There are a number of research teams working with prison populations using the Adult Attachment Interview (AAI). We have almost completed a small study of prison hospital patients with a matched group of psychiatric controls. There were 22 male patients in the prison sample, mean age 27.6 years. Eleven had been sentenced by the end of the study; the remainder were on remand. A further five patients were convicted subsequently. Their crimes ranged from attempted burglary, theft, damage to property, taking and driving away, handling stolen goods, obtaining property and services by deception, gross indecency, possession and intent to supply heroin, importation of drugs, grievous bodily harm, malicious wounding, multiple armed robbery, kidnapping, rape, murder. They were interviewed using Structured Clinical Interview for DSM-III-R (SCID I and II) structured interviews to obtain DSM-III-R diagnoses. They all had at least one Axis-I disorder (80% three or more diagnoses) and 91 per cent had at least one Axis-II diagnosis (American Psychiatric Association 1987). Fifty per cent had a DSM diagnosis of border-line personality disorder. The average GAF score for the group was 47. These patients were individually matched with patients from a sample of non-psy-chotic inpatients.

Although we have not completed the analyses of our data, a number of striking correspondences have emerged between a subgroup of these 22 criminals and the borderline patients in our psychiatric sample. In this sub-group, entangled classifications were also the most common; extreme depriva-tions in childhood were commonly and convincingly reported, and these mostly involved severe physical abuse at the hands of borderline or psychotic parents. The interviews were marked by incoherence and a notable lack of an 'intentional stance' towards both attachment objects and the self.

The offenders could be divided into two groups on the basis of the patterns of AAI ratings: those in Group 1 were predominantly classified as Dismissing, Entangled–Preoccupied or Autonomous, had Reflective Self Function (RSF) ratings higher than the median and were unlikely to be classified Unre-solved/Disorganized or Cannot Classify. Group 2 subjects matched the bor-derline diagnoses in terms of AAI, although not all of them met DSM diagnostic criteria. They tended to be classified Entangled–Preoccupied or Cannot Classify, none were designated Autonomous, and all but two scored above five on the lack of resolution of trauma scales, they scored below the median on coherence of mind and reflective self function, and had histories of abuse. This group could also be differentiated in terms of the crimes they committed. The index offenses of prisoners in Group 1 were predominantly crimes against property, whereas those of prisoners in Group 2 were largely serious, violent assaults including rapes and a murder associated with pathological jealousy.

This is only a pilot investigation, but the results are promising to the extent that they link the AAI narratives to index crimes. Naturally, a likely alternative account to the one proposed here is that it was these crimes which caused the disorganization of the attachment system, and which permeated the interviews of Group 2. The less serious offenses may have made less impact on the representation of relationships.

We propose that crimes are often committed by individuals with inadequate mentalizing capacities, as part of their pathological attempt at adaptation to a social environment where mentalization is essential. We assume that these individuals did not have access to meaningful attachment relationships which would have provided them with the intersubjective basis for developing a metacognitive capacity capable of organizing and coordinating their internal working models of relationships. The disavowal of the capacity to represent mental states (momentary or permanent) may be a key component of crime against the person. Thus, violence against another may not be possible unless the mental state of the other is insufficiently clearly represented for this to block the violent act. Violence is a solution to psychological conflict because of the inadequacy of the mental representation of the mental world in the minds of these individuals. Their metacognitive capacity is limited, and they experience ideas and feelings in physical, often bodily, terms.

This, of course, opens a whole avenue to adaptation. Unpalatable ideas may be felt to be removed by destroying the physical object which embodies that idea. We have proposed (Fonagy, Target and Moran 1993) that aggression is a defence to safeguard the self from thoughts and fantasies which it does not have the representational capacity to protect itself against through mental manipulation. Similarly, aggression in disruptive children is an adaptation to the activation of discordant internal working models by a caregiver, through disruption of the relationship. In more severe disorders, this defence might come to be integrated within the working model of relationships, thus aggression may become a part of self-assertion. The violent act is, we suggest, aimed at destroying symbolic representation (Fonagy and Target, in press b). The assault on the perpetrator's fragile sense of self has to be removed. As one murderer put it: 'Either he or I must die, something has to give' (Meloy 1992, p.58).

Psychotic and Borderline Processes

Patrick Gallwey

INTRODUCTION

The overlapping of badness and madness creates a domain of popular and deep anxiety. The really bad, serial killers and the like, provoke fascination and are usually perceived as mad, yet the fear of unleashed savagery compels retribution and punishment. It is unlikely, if the violence has been extreme and especially if there is more than one victim, that a plea of diminished responsibility to murder due to an abnormality of mind will be achieved by the killer. This is true even when, as in the case of the serial killer Sutcliffe, there is clear evidence of psychosis. Madness has been a defence against crime from the middle ages but the universal belief in the untamed ferocity of human nature finds affirmation and celebration in such rare individual atrocities. The tradition that humans are instinctively antisocial and, without dire threats of punishment, likely to run wild, inspires the punitive element in most religions and is the central philosophical plank of criminal jurisprudence. It seems to have inspired Freud to write his three essays on sexuality (1905c) and to continue the idea in the concept of the id (1923) and is taken for granted by many educated people. It has been seriously challenged by some social anthropologists (Montagu 1979) and an alternative to instinctual hedonism has been put forward by the object relation theorists of the British School of psychoanalysis following Fairbairn (1944) and in a more complex way by Klein (Klein 1957). Freud's belief in unstructured pleasure seeking drives, looking for gratification with any object as a utensil and only socialized with difficulty by repression, is still held unquestioningly by many analysts. Klein (1946), whose ideas opened up the psychoanalytic study of psychosis, was less pessimistic than Freud in so far as she believed that the infant was quite naturally capable of forming a loving relationship with the mother from the beginning. However, as we shall examine later she believed this primary bonding was reliant upon omnipotent phantasy and threatened by innate destructiveness. She linked this destructiveness to Freud's belief in inborn passivity, which he named the death instinct (S. Freud 1920), a theoretical move that is too much for many analysts, but her thinking over the question of inborn envy is in line with Freud's gloomy view of human instinct (Klein 1957).

It is also broadly the case that most psychoanalytic theories of early mental life view it as dominated by omnipotent phantasy, with an infant who is either totally out of touch with reality or only grasping a very modified and grandiose form of it. Psychosis tends to be seen as a regression to these primitive omnipotent states of mind. Thus, in the main, psychoanalysis views human nature in its unmodified early aspect as mad, bad and selfish; the psychological equivalent of original sin. This is not a very encouraging start, I'm afraid, for anyone turning to psychoanalysis for guidance as to where goodness can be discovered in those who are both psychotic and maladjusted.

Something of a paradox is experienced by those working with patients who have endured very great abuse, neglect and childhood suffering, as have many criminals: what impresses most is how well they have managed and not so much how evil they have become. It is quite extraordinary how brave is the childhood spirit that can survive the extremes of abuse with some hope and sanity intact and keep going in spite of crippling damage during crucial periods of development. Criminals become known for the suffering they cause but what has led them to become the way they are or to any awareness of the goodness they have managed to retain is usually lost in the outrage that they understandably create. In fact, to mention such realities is to risk the charge of being 'soft on crime' and to provoke a bluster of enthusiasm for even harsher punishments, as if to add more suffering to the appalling equation will somehow put things right. There appears to be a universal need to confine criminals to a domain of punishment from which we exclude ourselves. In spite of reliable research that demonstrates how crime is the outcome of early prolonged disruption to the basic necessities of nurturing (West 1982), offenders continue as popular moral scapegoats, particularly so for politicians on the look out for votes: so that recently members of the government have recommended more punishment and less understanding and have, apparently seriously, suggested that the fear of hell should once more be instilled in children as an antidote to maladjustment!

Bad behaviour is, of course, a major cause of widespread misery and it is understandable why many people have a fantasy that it can be completely banished. That this is also an apparently informed idea is more serious because, as a consequence, the very social harmfulness of crime is never properly tackled. Empirical research into the causes of crime is ignored and many psychoanalysts and those who follow still view criminal behaviour as a simple expression of instinctual aggression. In spite of the work of Bowlby (1973) and Winnicott (1984), and partly because of the problems of undertaking long term detailed psychoanalytic research with criminals, psychoanalytic writing on the psychopathology of bad behaviour tends to stick to simple adaptions of standard theory.

Although crime is a relatively neglected area of psychoanalytic theory making, this is not true of psychosis and borderline states, the theory and practice of which have been extensively developed, particularly in the UK, the USA and in South America. However, I want in this chapter to approach the subject of psychotic and borderline states, and crime, from a somewhat different perspective. I hope this perspective does justice to the fact that, in their different ways, psychosis and criminal behaviour represent a grievous failure in the quite amazing capacity for social interdependency and altruism in human nature that is taken for granted by the mentally well. In order to do this I shall advance a theory of normal development which I hope adds a fresh dimension to current theories of psychosis and of crime. First I shall give a short and incomplete account of the way psychoanalysts have viewed the question of madness.

THE PSYCHOANALYTIC APPROACH TO THE PSYCHOSES

Perhaps the first serious psychoanalytic contribution to psychosis was made by Freud in his paper 'Mourning and Melancholia' (1917). In a previous paper (1911b) he had postulated that a case of paranoid psychosis was a reaction formation to unconscious homosexual wishes – the case of Schreber. Unlike the paper 'Mourning and Melancholia' which derived from direct observations of patients in depressive psychosis, this paper was purely speculative and he had never met the patient he wrote so much about. He had already, in his work on narcissism (1914a), included psychosis as one of the ways in which withdrawal of the object relating instincts into the self could be manifested. However, it was not until 'Mourning and Melancholia' that he put forward a theory based on direct clinical observation to explain the manifestations of a psychotic condition. Freud believed that the melancholic was demonstrating a pathological identification between the self and the dependent object. However, he then went on to make a move which is very characteristic of psychoanalytic thinking, to formulate this as the return to an earlier stage of normal development, rather than seeing it as pathology *per se*, so that the illness becomes essentially a maturational regression. The pathological identification that Freud believed explained melancholic states became a variant of a universal mechanism in which the relinquishment, under the impact of reality, of being the central object of the parent's love, was achieved through an omnipotent phantasy of incorporating the abandoned object cathexis into the ego and setting up the object there as part of the structure of the self. Freud believed that every abandoned object cathexis was managed in this way, and that object relationships with the parents in particular, especially the father, resulted in the incorporation of the object into the ego, thereby creating a super-ego, representing the internal seat of conscience and morality (Freud 1923). Although it is perfectly reasonable to construct a link between the excessive self-reproach of the melancholic with the less self-torturing conscience of a normal individual, Freud's thinking results in an omnipotent phantasy coming into play as part and parcel of normal human development. Depressive illness and everyday moral self-regulation becomes part of a continuum. Psychopathology lies simply in the extent and quality of depressive activity.

The development of a psychoanalytic approach to psychotic states took an enormous move forward as a result of the theories of Melanie Klein. Like Freud, she relied on introjective identification (an omnipotent phantasy involving the oral incorporation of the object into the self) as a normal developmental process, most importantly and most fundamentally when the good and loving aspects of the mother's breast are taken in to form the foundation of the primitive ego. She formed her ideas on ego development whilst she was working clinically with disturbed children using her special play technique (Klein 1932b). She noticed that, after her child patients made aggressive attacks during play, there would be a marked increase in paranoid anxiety in relation to the object that had been the target of the aggression. Detailed observation of the play of these disturbed children and imaginative construction of the phantasies that could be presumed to be represented in the play, led her to conclude that, in order to protect the ego from the anxiety created by aggression, the aggressive aspect of the self would be split and projected into the object that was felt to be responsible for the violent feelings. This created an object that contained the projected part of the self, now experienced as part of the identity of the object and therefore disowned and disassociated. The self was divested completely and omnipotently of the aggressive aspect of the self, so what remained was an idealized self in unconscious introjective identification with an ideal object. This good internal object was continually re-experienced in the giving and non-frustrating aspects of the external nurturing breast. The frustrating aspects of the mother would be perceived as one and the same as the intrapsychic bad, persecutory object (Klein 1957).

Klein, like Freud, assumed these highly omnipotent mechanisms to be part and parcel of normal development. The original introjective identification of the good breast, seen as fundamental to the coherence of the ego, places omnipotence not only at the heart of normality, but as a *sine qua non* for the development of sanity. Although this is not finally achieved until the other omnipotent mechanisms of splitting and projective identification are finally relinquished – in the depressive position – nevertheless, the introjected good object remains as the sheet anchor of ego coherence and growth. Should the depressive position not be traversed then the ego will remain flawed by the splitting and there is a persistent paranoia. The seeds of psychosis have then been sown.

The identification of the self with an ideal object has been described by Rosenfeld (1971) as libidinal narcissism since the confusion between the self and the object obliterates the real difference between the self and the other, a proper perception of which is essential to dependent object relating. Klein saw this consequence of her theories upon the nature of the ego: in discussing the oceanic feeling she expressed the view that full contact with the world of goodness and beauty is essentially narcissistic and based upon the fundamental union of the self with the good breast which is the source of all such experience.

Like Freud's, Klein's theories maintain a continuum between mental illness and normal states of mind. Whereas the continuum for Freud is between depressive illness and normal human conscience, for Klein it is between paranoid and schizoid states and the universal tendency in human nature towards persecutory anxiety and a paranoid outlook on life, embodied in self-righteous xenophobia, supported by stereotypical mythologies of good- ness and evil. She was also able to explain some features of normal mourning and combined these with the paranoid element characteristic of many depres- sive states of mind including, of course, depressive illness (Klein 1935).

Klein's theories have been very influential in the UK, not only on those who follow her theories closely but also on those analysts who have worked more independently, such as Winnicott and Balint (Rayner 1991). There have been two main consequences: (1) the psychotic elements in apparently neurotic states of mind became analyzable and (2) a number of analysts in this country, notably Bion, Rosenfeld and Segal, have used these theories in the clinical approach to the treatment of psychosis.

It would be impossible, in the space available, to summarize the richness of much of this work, but I will select one or two key features of the work of Bion, Rosenfeld and Segal. I wish to highlight their points of departure from Klein which I feel are valuable in advancing our understanding of the enormous shift that occurs when individuals move from non-psychotic to psychotic states of mind, or live out on others the equivalent of destructive phantasies.

Both Bion and Segal have made contributions in relation to the develop- ment of psychotic thinking. Segal (1957), in an important paper, examines the concrete thinking to be found in psychosis. She suggests that in normal development, 'symbols' arise because of the gradual ability of the infant to recognize the difference between the self and the object and to form a bridge between the two. This perception of separateness requires the management of separation anxiety: if this proves intolerable, it will be obliterated by projective identification, producing a phantasy of 'oneness'. If this occurs, then instead of the creation of symbols which represent the thing symbolized, the symbol becomes a thing in itself – what Segal calls a symbolic equation. This gives rise to the concrete thinking characteristic of many psychotic states of mind.

Bion, on the other hand, in his extensive writing on the development of thinking and disorders of thought in psychotic states, asserts a quite different emphasis. He suggests that the development of normal thinking is reliant upon the same mechanism – of projective identification – and that it is a universal primitive form of communication between the infant and the mother. He postulates that, in a process he called reverie, the mother accepts the projective identifications of the infant – such as the fear that a part of itself is dying, and through a process he calls alpha function, alters that fear so that the infant can re-introject the now manageable part of itself (Bion 1961b, 1962). He suggests that this activity is a form of thinking carried out on behalf of the infant by the mother who is able to act as a container for unmanageable fears that the infant cannot process. Here Bion is extending to projective identification the healthy role that Klein saw in introjective identification, namely an omnipotent phantasy acting as a process to establish healthy mental functioning. Bion's theories on the development of normal thinking are, of course, in direct opposition to Segal's. Whereas Segal uses projective identification to explain the failure in the development of normal thought, Bion uses it as a mechanism for its formation. This disparity never seems to have been fully reconciled among Kleinians. Segal (1991) recognized the problem and suggested a mental space in which symbols could begin within Bion's concept of the mother as a container. She is plainly uneasy, however, at the issue of the confusion of identities which is a defining characteristic of projective identification, and fails eventually really to resolve the contradiction in their ideas.

In my view Segal's original understanding of the negative role of this process on symbol formation was much more helpful than Bion's because it keeps splitting and projective identification as a mechanism essentially leading to pathology, whereas in Bion's work, the mechanism is used to account for normal as well as abnormal states of mind.

Rosenfeld (1987), who worked extensively with actively psychotic patients, gave accounts of both projective identification and introjective identification producing narcissistic states in which the difference between the self and objects in the world were destroyed by the obliteration of separateness and individual differences. He became more and more of the view that it was important, in the analysis of borderline states and psychotic individuals, to try and help the patient recognize the dependent part of themselves, which often emerges in the analytic material as a child part of the patient. The dependent self is the sane part of the self, which could be attacked by other aspects of the self that are unable to manage the impact of reality and so seek a grandiose refuge in omnipotent phantasy. In a key paper (Rosenfeld 1971) he describes the malignant narcissism of certain borderline states and how essential it is to alert the patient to the fight going on within themselves, between different aspects of their personality, as well as to the attacks upon the dependent object. In these gravely ill patients he attempted to help the patient rescue the dependent part of themselves, which was often trapped in fearful omnipotent confusion. He also, in his later work, expressed the view that early dislocations in nurturing, in which the dependent self had been unable to thrive, were recreated in the illness and within the transference. In treating such ill patients, these early impasses to development needed to be understood by a close examination of the counter-transference. He believed that many obstacles in the treatment of disturbed patients, particularly senses of frustration and hopelessness in the analyst, were potentially very fruitful areas of study since they derive from the early dislocations in development, so that if they can be understood then the patient can be helped to get better (Rosenfeld 1987). In this part of his work there is less emphasis on envy, as the central variant causing grave pathology, than exists in the work of Klein and Bion.

Envy is an important concept because it introduces the innate element into the genesis of psychopathology. It can result in greed or refusal to take in good experiences, with unconscious violent attacks upon the source of them. Since it is essentially anti-life and anti-reality, it has great explanatory value for borderline, perverse and psychotic states of mind and has proved enormously important in the analysis of destructive forces within the individual's personality. In Rosenfeld's work, however, one finds another dimension entering his thinking and he persuaded those he supervised not to rely on the consolation of envy in their patients as a way of explaining the lack of progress in the analysis but to examine their own emotions and difficulties in perception which could be standing in the way of releasing the patient from some perennial impasse within their inner world. It seems to me that the emphasis by Rosenfeld on identifying the normal dependent part of the self as the sane element within the personality offers another way of understanding the basis for mental health in terms of a primitive part of the self which is not dominated by omnipotence. The development of psycho-pathology can then be understood as any interference with this essential healthy dependent function and not as a simple persistence of the primitive or a regression to omnipotent levels of development.

Fairbairn (1951), who was also concerned with the impact of schizoid mechanisms in the development of mental disorder, held a different view from Freud and Klein, insofar as he saw instinct as essentially adaptive. He pointed out there could not be an instinct that did not have a goal and the goal was always some form of attachment to an object. This has always seemed to me a very sensible view because it is difficult to understand how human beings could have developed in the extraordinarily successful way they have if this were not the case. The idea that madness and badness are the essence of human nature and require curbing and modifying by benign parents in a controlling and civilizing society, makes the question of how civilizing restraint on the supposedly uncivilized passions could have come about in the first place. I find it more satisfactory to adopt a model of mental health which does not rely on omnipotent phantasy and which does justice to the importance of human interdependency on the one hand and the features of adaptability and inventiveness on the other.

AN APPROACH TO THE PSYCHOSES VIA A THEORY OF MENTAL HEALTH

The model that I use is a modification of some of the ideas of Fairbairn, Kohut, Bion, Segal and Rosenfeld and having at its root Freud's inspired revelations. It seems to me very sensible to see instinctual patterns of behaviour, and their counterpart in mental life, as essentially object seeking, as Fairbairn (1951) maintained. However, he does not go into much detail about how the self as an object in its own right comes into being. Kohut (1971) has attempted this in his views on narcissism which, although sometimes difficult to follow, nevertheless highlight the importance of a relationship between the mother and the child which, if lacking in some essential ingredient of exclusivity, can result in a persistent unconscious and partly conscious hunger for such a state of affairs. This leads, of course, to a very unrealistic set of expectations of the world and much destructive reaction formation. Kohut's ideas have been taken as an alternative to the more destructive theory of narcissism stressed by the Kleinians, post-Kleinians and by Kernberg. It seems to me, however, that they begin an account of early mental development which does justice to the realities of infantile behaviour and need, in the way that Bowlby (1969) puts forward in his views on attachment, but within a frame of reference that can be integrated with established analytical models of the mind. In my model of mental health I have tried to incorporate Bowlby's observation of children and Rosenfeld's description of the dependent part of the self as a foundation of sanity from which thinking and other mental development can grow, from an instinctual starting point that is based on the observation of children and infants as developed by Bowlby.

Bion (1962) describes the concept of an object, such as the good breast, coming about as a result of the successful realization of the instinctual preconceptions of such an object. For him the realization of preconceptions form basic prototypic objects whose functions, when introjected, enable the mobile linking together of simple elements of experience in a way that leads eventually to the capacity to think. However, his theories rest very much on the successful conceptualization of the object and the introjection of some of its aspects, such as the primitive nipple and penis, to form a basis for the self's ability to link with the object externally and to link primitive thoughts together internally, again relying on the omnipotent mechanism of introjective and projective identification as the basis for these healthy achievements. If one applies the same formula, however, to a preconception not only of the object but of the self in a dependent relationship with the object, which is after all the biological reality, then one can suppose that, where nurturing is successful in so far as primary bonding is encouraged to occur, then the self will realize not only pre-conceptions of the nurturing objects but also those aspects of its self which have responded to the good nurturing. The capacity for the progressive development of ego function including primitive thinking will then depend on the realization of the innate potential within the self and not on an omnipotent phantasy of acquisition of the object or its functions.

Using this model of development, the self is progressively realized, hand in hand with progressive realization of different aspects and functions of the object. This will result eventually in a dual concept of a complete self in a dependent and interdependent relationship with complete objects, in which the omnipotent mechanisms of splitting with projective and introjective identification have played no direct part. *Primary identification* is a good way of describing this development of healthy and entirely realistic achievement. The omnipotent mechanisms of splitting with projective or introjective identification may have played a part in protecting the early identifications that have been realized from destabilization in the face of excessive stress, but in my view, since they are essentially secondary phantasies (see below) they will not be available until at least some degree of primary conceptualization of self and object have been achieved.

The very first 'elementary concepts' are in all probability the building bricks of whole object identifications but already in their early form will have the separate duality described above. I use the term 'e-concept' to distinguish them from the whole object concepts which form eventually the primary identifications of self and dependent object (e-concepts can be inferred from the nature of pathological part objects that cannot be integrated, found in the analysis of many psychotic patients). The early dual primary concepts will, of course, include the reality of separateness and create the necessary conditions for the development of symbols to bridge the gap between the self and the dependent objects – a gap which has both functional and spacio-temporal realities. It is these realities which are the source of early and later healthy conflict in terms of frustration of need, fears of loss, of being left behind and dying and, intertwined with all this, problems of aggression, jealousy and envy. Anxiety is essentially a response to a threat, real or perceived, to the safety of the self and or the dependent objects. This is true in whatever stage of development the threat occurs.

I take the view that there are pre-conceptions needing realization to form primary concepts, appropriate to all stages of instinctual development, although the later in life they occur the more difficult they will be to distinguish from learned configurations. The early linking instincts take the form of *prospecting functions, holding on functions* and *substantive functions*, all of which are innately present in mutually realizable forms both in the infant and in the nurturing parents; particular, of course, the mother in her feeding capacity.

Prospective functions on the infant's side are connected with searching for the object of need and on the nurturing mother's side by alertness to these needs. Prospective functions, when successful, give a sense of optimism and trust in existence, a sense of potency, a sense of being in a safe space and a belief that home can be located. The ability to conceptualize the absent object is a consequence of having first been able to find it. This promotes the toleration of separation and the early enjoyment of independence. The eventual development of the logical constant of negation is laid down when abstract thinking becomes possible.

Sight, hearing and smell are all utilized in prospective functions and when their realization is faulty then the conceptualizations that are eventually made, rather than being benign and containing a loving valiancy, will be marked by fear, anger, suspicion and despair. Trust, optimism and potency will be absent. The inability to conceptualize the absent object will at its worst result in a basic confusion of identity or, if separateness is achieved, then the ability to tolerate absence will be very reduced. A pessimistic voyeurism replaces hopeful searching and the fear of evil eyes, of spying and being spied upon dominates a world in which the location of safety is never clear.

Holding on is the next function and depends upon the mutual holding functions of the infant and the parents. The instinctual behaviour of infants in grasping with the hands and mouth and the complementary need in mothers to hold and be held by their infant results in a sense of boundary – the psychic skin as described by Bick (1968). Good experiences in this domain will result in a sense of being well contained by the object and being well contained in one's own skin. Shape, size, a sense of proportion and the affirmation of difference are conceptualized. The conditions for the logical connectives of conjunction and disjunction are laid down as well as the capacity for attention, concentration and the belief in the existence of choice. Bion's (1962) description of the contact barrier, allowing some thoughts to be held in mind while others are kept as a penumbra of associations, would also derive from successful holding on. Clearly, when holding on is faulty, these positive qualities are lost. A fear of contact and an inability to contain emotions together with an excessive fear of falling to pieces will occur. Dysmorphobias, inability to tolerate boundaries, claustrophobic entrapment and confusion with a cold mechanical cruel object are the most serious outcomes.

Substantive linking is the final stage in a progressive series of linking activity in which a sense of substance of the object and a sense of fullness within the self, is achieved through the exchange of warmth, food and love. Belief in the achievement of reward, of happiness, of creative outcome and the specificity of cause and effect are achieved and will make possible the logical connectives of material implication and material equivalence when the capacity for abstract thought is acquired. The eventual capacity for deductive reasoning is inspired by the completion of the total process. Clearly, its faulty realization will result in problems connected with emptiness, a sense of poverty, a lack of depth in emotion or a sense of being full of hate and fear. More serious defects are confusion with an empty object or an inability to have a sense of meaning other than being in a black hole. Added to the previous failures a desperate autism is heralded. The capacity to think will be profoundly affected and show itself through difficulties in learning to talk, to read or to write. The popular label of dyslexia includes many whose difficulties are due to failure in primary linking. Such thought disorders spring from the failed or faulty achievement of primary separateness and are therefore more intractable than similar ones that are the outcome of the obliteration of separateness due to secondary narcissistic confusion between self and object as the result of projective or introjective identifications.

However, when the development progresses reasonably well, then at a very early state in neonatal life, an inchoate concept of the self will be achieved in a safe dependent relationship with a nurturing object and this irreducible dual concept (the primary identifications) will form the basis of all ego functioning and later development. It seems to me to be equivalent to the central ego of Fairbairn and it represents the sort of early integration that Klein mentions in her later work. In my model, once this essentially dual object has been successfully conceptualized, from what can be described as primary phantasies (the instinctual preconceptions), then the way is open for the development of secondary phantasies which will give rise to imagination and thinking and the provision of mental buffers against stress.

SECONDARY PHANTASY

Secondary phantasies are the outcome of separateness to which the self is heir, once the primary identifications of self and other have been achieved. The difference between the self and the dependent object – the psychological and physical gap – will be a primitive perception. It has two aspects: a spacio-temporal one in which absence impinges, and a functional one of differences in need. Secondary phantasy forms the psychological bridge that keeps the self in touch with the object internally both during its absence and during the vicissitudes of attachment.

Secondary phantasies will begin as simple memories and anticipations. Their emotional content will be a reflection of the way the primary identifications were acquired, complicated by the emotional experience of the spacio-temporal and functional gaps. This in turn will determine the extent to which the realities of experience will be altered by secondary phantasies to maintain comfort and ultimately avoid the anxiety of threat to the ego.

Shortage of space prevents a full discussion of the role of secondary phantasy, as I envisage it, but certainly Freud's understanding of dreams as wish fulfilment and the preservers of sleep, which have become known as ego defences (A. Freud 1936) describe something of what I have in mind. However ego defences have traditionally been somewhat over defined into rather rigid categories. The imagined alterations in the realities of dependency both remembered, perceived and foreseen that I discern in my patients, whose purpose is to reduce stress and maintain psychic equilibrium, are only classifiable by *the degree of omnipotent detachment from the primary dependent object*. I have called this the psychosynthetic activity of secondary phantasy. I believe this can be achieved, even from the beginning, without such a fundamental alteration as will obliterate the link with the dependent object.

Loss of this link can come about as a result of flights into grandiosity so that the self wanders too far from the dependent link or by splitting and projective identification in which the functional link is broken. These more omnipotent defences are reserved for extreme states of stress, when less profound alterations of reality, which do not involve the complete loss of contact with the dependent object, have failed to achieve the sense of safety that the ego requires. The maintenance of the link between the self and the dependent objects is reflected in secondary phantasy as an acknowledgment of the truths of interdependency and combined with the constraints of reality on attempts to realize psychosynthetic phantasies in the world, and provides the human relevance to invention, discovery and the development of social institutions. This contact with interdependent truths is the essence of all creative activity and I have called it the psychopoetic function of secondary phantasy. Psychosynthesis and psychopoesis, although appearing to work in different directions are really different components of the same mental function so that at any one time the configuration of experience will have a truth factor that reflects the extent to which the truth can be tolerated without undue threat to the ego. The pull away from reality or towards it is reflected in a highly changeable and active internal world of phantasy, affecting and being affected by the interaction with the external world. If the primary identifications have been adequately realized, then the potential for logical reasoning will have been laid down. There is, after all, only one set of absolute truths and that is in the irreducible realities contained in the primary concepts. However, provided the preconception of the way the primary identifications have been realized has itself become a concept, then abstract reasoning can occur with the concept of absolute truth values being included as part of psychosynthetic activity. This results ultimately in the development of logical reasoning and mathematics. Experimental science follows on as the attempt to realize absolute truth values in the external world and as a result is only indirectly relevant to human happiness and need, contributing as much danger to mankind as comfort and safety. The real world of interdependent existence is essentially artistic and will, in health, tolerate and exploit the lack of formal truth value in most statements, will gain meaning from degrees of ambiguity, extra meaning from metaphor and thrive on the emotional subtleties of non-verbal communication. The mistake of academic psychology and much sociology is not to have recognized the artificial domain of their chosen methodology.

To lose relevance in an attempt to hang on to certainty is too high a price to pay and although psychiatry has wandered down that path, the real needs of patients have kept most clinicians alive to the elusiveness of human reality. By and large they use scientific method as an aid to patient care and not as a way of seeking personal existential reassurance. The contrary argument that they have attempted to define such a reality is well developed by Foucault (1988). He makes important points, for the attempt to impose strict truth value on interpersonal thinking is the characteristic of theocracies and political tyrannies and usually results in appalling state criminality and cruelty through the imposition of conformity to institutional 'goodness', which is precisely the argument of the antipsychiatry movement.

However let us not digress further. When things have gone well enough, the fortunate individual will be heir to strong primary identifications and a mobile repertoire of secondary phantasy, will be able to buffer stress while coming to terms with its meaning and through psychopoetic adjustment to an acceptable truth take, via thinking, adaptive or adventurous action. Provided the link with the primary concepts is maintained, such a process, however socially eccentric it may be, will have relevance to the interdependent needs of the group in which it occurs and integrate the individual socially at the same time. This is the hallmark of sanity and positive social participation.

Failure to realize the dual primary concept of self and object necessary for the definition of separateness, or primary identifications that are so faulty that secondary phantasy fails, occasionally or habitually, to maintain the dependent link between the self and the dependent objects, will result in insanity or behaviour unmodified by secondary phantasy. We will look at each of these possibilities and the different outcomes in turn.

AUTISTIC ENTRAPMENT

If there is a profound failure in the realization of the primary preconceptions then the inchoate self will remain trapped inside an unidentified object and no proper realization of the self or dependent object can come about. Within this autistic domain there will be confusion, great terror and much rage, with an increasing despair and helplessness. This state of affairs is functionally equivalent to the sorts of confusion arising from profound projective or introjective identification of the self with the dependent object that occurs in later severe narcissism. However, in this primitive confusional state the situation is not reversible unless the realization of the vital preconceptions is brought about in sufficient time for the deficit to be overcome. If this is too long delayed then, even if later realizations succeed in providing sufficient concepts of self and object to equip a functioning ego, there will remain an autistic area that will be a source of very great vulnerability and disturbance. If the failure in realization is sufficiently prolonged, a frank autistic state occurs with a child trapped inside an ill-defined object unable to construct secondary phantasies and therefore unable to play, explore the world, develop or properly communicate.

However, when the failures are less prolonged and extensive, then autistic elements derived from faulty e-concepts (the equivalent of Bion's beta elements) which cannot be integrated into the ego, remain as highly anxiety provoking impenetrable defects in ego structure. These will be experienced as fearful black objects or as an ubiquitous nameless dread. Since they contain no concept of separateness, there is no spacio-temporal or functional gap to bridge, hence symbol formation is absent or rudimentary. Autistic elements cannot therefore be incorporated into secondary phantasy and are not dreamable or thinkable. They give rise to night terrors rather than nightmares. If they do appear in dreams or in fantasy then they are often experienced as black infestations or a fierce feeling of nameless dread. Sometimes some degree of separateness has been achieved and they emerge then as bits of the self confused with bits of the object, or perhaps as terrifying faces with horrific eyes. Such objects can also come about as a result of fragmentary splitting and projective identification (see Bion 1962 on bizarre objects). If at all possible the two need to be distinguished from each other, since the latter derive from the fragmentation of achieved primary objects, whereas the former result from primary failure and are therefore more anterior and more malignant.

Autistic elements will always pose a threat to the ego, but the degree of potential destabilization will depend upon the quantity and content of the autistic distress and the effectiveness of the ego defences against the anxiety. Space prevents a very full discussion of the various possibilities and in any case the connection between the clinical conditions that are explained by this model and the presumptions of causation are very far from established. However three broad categories can be postulated.

(1) An ego which is able to seal off autistic lacunae, which in themselves do not contain an extra threat from violent experiences, and in such a way that there is no very great immediate persistent anxiety. This encapsulation will be achieved by splitting and is presumably possible because the subsequent achievement of the dual primary identifications is sufficiently good to enable such efficient omnipotent psycho-synthesis to be mobilized. When this is less good, then bouts of neurotic anxiety, obsessional thinking or disorders of mood are a pronounced feature and indicate a hard pressed psychosynthesis due to a leaking of the autistic elements.

The resultant personality structure will be incomplete, so artificial, over controlled, false personality characteristics are likely. The potential for psychotic illness is always present and occurs when the encapsulation fails. This may come about as the result of significant stressful life events, particularly those that interfere with the realization of more adult preconceptions such as genital sexual conceptualization or child rearing. These later preconceptions may themselves produce internal changes that awaken the unrelinguished drives of the autistic domain. Perhaps the cause of schizophrenia is the release of overwhelming autistic anxiety which progressively undermines an ego that is already fundamentally flawed within each element of its total structure by the original failure in primary identification. Such a pathological situation could well arise from an innate deficit in linking functions of the self, operating psychologically at all crucial stages of primary developmental opportunity and having specific counterparts in neuro-physiological abnormalities. Once the sealed off early deficiency becomes released, the functioning ego can only be rescued from catatonic annihilation by elaborate grandiose psychosynthetic defences of splitting and projection, giving the first rank symptoms of schizophrenia.

When the primary autism is not so invasive then the illness is likely to be more transient as in many schizo-affective conditions, or self-limiting as in severe disorders of mood.

(2) The same encapsulated arrangement of the primary autism but with a contents that carries the sequelae of violent life-threatening experiences. The failure in primary linking is always life-threatening since, in order to survive as a going proposition, the self needs to realize its own identity within the concept of the dual dependent identifications. Hence the malignant anxiety of autistic entrapment. This failure usually comes about through passive deficiency in the response of the mother or in failures in the drive for attachment in the infant.

Where there is an aggressive or violent component to this failure on the part of the environment then the sense of catastrophic and violent threat carried within the autistic experience will be that much the greater. Then, when the encapsulation fails, there is no possibility of psycho-synthesis protecting the ego, so that not even psychotic phantasies, however grandiose, can come to the rescue. Violence and anxiety are lived out in catastrophic behaviour that may be unrestrained or homicidal.

Sometimes, when the encapsulation is not so complete, so that there is a small degree of leaking of autistic anxiety, the self will have some psychosynthetic way of handling this. Since the contents of the primary narcissism are not capable of symbol formation in their own right, this management will involve splitting and projective identification of the unintegratable elements or their organization, often through sexual deviant behaviour, into a collusive relationship. When the destructive and violent elements are too strong, then only extreme varieties of collusion or frank criminal abusive behaviour results. A more complete account of these varieties of borderline psychopathology can be found elsewhere (Gallwey 1985). In that contribution I used Bion's formulation of beta-elements which arise in his theory from splitting and projective identification and the arguments therefore need to be reformulated within the terms of the model of psychopathology that I have come to prefer and have set out here.

(3) Where there is an autistic deficit of varying proportions and content which has not been sealed off by an ego capable of efficient psycho-synthetic activity. In this state of affairs the individual will demonstrate a life long disturbance with the characteristic history of night terrors, early behavioural problems, hyperkinesis, repetitive destructive play, unsatisfactory early interpersonal relating and the likelihood of self-medication with psycho-active drugs in the face of persistent and ubiquitous anxiety. If the parental environment has been more passively or subtly disordered than is the case in many delinquent histories, then the individual may be less behaviourally disturbed but more isolated and enclosed, with severe difficulties in communication and achievement. Individuals who have failed to encapsulate their autistic elements are likely to meet diagnostic requirements of borderline or other similar varieties of personality disorder within the standard psychiatric nosologies.

We will now discuss briefly the other situation, namely a significant but lesser degree of interference in the realization of the primary preconception of self and dependent object which I term dysmorphia.

DYSMORPHIA

Since no nurturing can be ideal and since there is a good deal of variation in the extent of innate passivity, there will always be some unevenness in the path to the achievement of the primary identifications leading to individual personality variations and vulnerabilities, broadly compatible with mental health. However, past a certain point these types of deficit will give rise to significant problems which at their worst will not be sharply distinct from those produced by autistic entrapment. The important difference is that these deficits will not have prevented the realization of the primary preconceptions of self and dependent object, so that separateness has been achieved, with a functional and spacio-temporal gap in which secondary phantasy can begin to develop. The specific nature of the disruption to the primary identifications, which I have termed dysmorphia, is reflected therefore in the nature and content of the secondary phantasies. If the dysmorphia is severe enough it will produce active psychopathology or significant vulnerability that affects mental health and social adjustment. The ways in which this occurs are complex but, as has been indicated, the steps in linking between the self and the dependent object of prospecting, holding on and substantive contact, variously contribute to the final distortion in the primary identifications with the emotional distress that accompanies this.

The term dysmorphia is intended to cover both the structural and emotional distortions. It results in disturbances in identity and body image, basic reduction in existential confidence, feelings of impotence and inadequacy, diminished capacity to tolerate separation and general vulnerability to stress both from life events and in accomplishing later developmental realizations. Secondary phantasy is affected and will reflect the specific nature of the problems over linking as described above. Psychosynthesis will predominate over psychopoesis because of the degree of anxiety with which the ego has to cope. There will be a greater pressure towards grandiosity with severe stretching of the link with the dependent object as well as a tendency toward the more omnipotent defences of splitting with projective and introjective identification.

When the nurturing environment continues to be neglectful or abusive, secondary phantasy formation will be extremely impoverished. Problems in connection with learning and an inability not only to manage stress but to engage with the external world in a creatively imaginative way, will result in the development of a personality disordered way of life. As I have discussed elsewhere (Gallwey 1991) much compulsive delinquency is due to an impoverishment of psychosynthetic capacity, including the more omnipotent psychotic defences, resulting in the individual manipulating the external world in order to bring about the sort of rearrangement in reality that would otherwise have been achieved through the operation of psychosynthesis. Criminal acts, criminal sub-cultures and prison society reflect this mixture of entrenched, often ruthless, manipulation of others, that is tainted with grandiose wish fulfilment and the realization of nightmare.

Some other criminal activity, together with a great deal of non-criminal maladjustment, is due to the attempt to realize secondary phantasies, not as psychopoetic thinking resulting in inventive exploration of the world, but in the service of secondary phantasies which carry cruel and revengeful feelings which have lost the dependent link with a nurturing object. Such phantasies are usually grandiose or represent an attempt to realise a narcissistic rearrangement of the dependent realities based on splitting and projective identification (Rosenfeld 1971). I disagree with Rosenfeld in relation to those who present as libidinal narcissists, who in my experience have a malignant narcissistic aspect somewhere in a split off realm, often projectively identified in an object by whom they seem to be cruelly victimized. They often suffer from depressive illness and if this split suddenly closes, the eruption of violence can be homicidal. The persistence of severe splitting with projective or introjective identification results in manifestations of psychosis, borderline states or destructive behaviour close to that which has been described above in the discussion on primary autism.

In fact, from an immediate point of view the origins of the clinical states and the nature of the core psychopathology may be impossible to elucidate. The presence of an encapsulated autistic area is suggested when persistent severe anxiety, increase in psychotic symptomatology or destructive acting out accompanies an apparently successful psychotherapeutic working alliance.

This takes us to the therapeutic consequences of this model of psychosis and mental health.

THE PSYCHOTHERAPEUTIC STRATEGIES

It is always unsatisfactory to advance modifications of psychoanalytic theory without bringing substantial clinical examples and this chapter suffers from that shortcoming. Indeed, the same is even more the case when describing therapeutic issues. However, the demands of space are such that only a bare outline of the treatment implications of the model set out above can be undertaken.

I shall confine myself to two main issues. The first is the question of therapeutic goals and the second some very general implications for technique that arise from the model of psychopathology that has been advanced.

From what I have said regarding the profound nature of the various psychopathologies in borderline conditions, in psychotic states and their associated maladjustments, it will be realized that to rectify the defects is in most cases an unrealistic goal. Before attempting psychotherapy, an assessment of the vulnerability of the ego to being overwhelmed by destructive anxiety and the very great unfulfilled needs that lie within areas of severe ego dysmorphia or autistic confusion must be carefully made.

Anyone who presents in a borderline or psychotic state and is reliant on drugs or alcohol, has a history of significant behavioural problems, or who has been abused or severely neglected in childhood must have a very full period of appraisal before psychotherapy is attempted. A separate assessment should be undertaken by the prospective therapist, who should never rely completely on the opinion of the referring agency, whoever they may be. The therapist will have to carry the direct pressures and anxiety of the therapeutic relationship, so it is vital to sit down with the patient and try to get some idea of what one is in for. Careful history taking is all important not only in relation to childhood and presenting problems but also the extent and severity of failures to cope, especially attempts at suicide, other episodes of self-harm, criminal or violent behaviour, reliance on intoxicants, the quality of supportive relationships, as well as the course, severity and chronicity of any mental illness.

Many patients in forensic psychiatry will be extensively traumatized and the risk of making their situation much worse by over expectation or a failure to provide adequate support for the frailty of their egos is a very real one.

Many will have massive dependency problems and a great burden of anxiety, with which they may have managed to cope in one way or another. It is very unwise to involve such individuals in a treatment in which the dependent transference or the core pathology is gathered, unless one is ready to try to carry on when the inevitably demanding angry acting out behaviour arrives. Otherwise it will be impossible to see the treatment through to a reasonable conclusion. Many tragedies involving both therapists and patients have come about because the therapist, having come under pressure from severe disturbance in the patient or aggressive demanding behaviour, capitulates quite suddenly, leaving their patient in a much worse state than they were before the ill-conceived psychotherapy was begun. Many patients who have disorders of the type described in this chapter may require, during crucial phases, a managing psychiatrist or supportive mental health team. This should ideally be set up before the work begins if the depth of the disorder can be foreseen. Many such ill patients will of course already be in an institution, so that integration of the treatment with the multi-disciplinary team can occur. Even when such precautions are undertaken, the anxiety and pressures of working with this group of patients is very considerable, so that adequate supervision and a level of training that gives some chance of effective work is imperative.

What then can be put forward as psychologically beneficial for this group within the framework of the sort of psychotherapy that is available at the present time?

First and foremost comes the importance of a down-to-earth appreciation of the extent of the patient's problems, measured against the extent of the therapist's ignorance of what it's all about. It is much better to stick to conveying those realities with an attitude of real concern for what the patient is up against, than to use the situation as a vehicle for one's own set of theoretical preconvictions or need to enjoy making inventive formulations. The patient, who will be in real need of understanding, will have either to accept them as a kind of religious duty or face the added anxiety of being blamed for undue resistance when things get worse. Disturbed and ill patients benefit from someone sharing their sense of being in the grip of a force that threatens their identity, safety or capacity to think. They fear madness and fear they will never get better or recover their lost personality strengths. To have the opportunity to share these kind of anxieties with a psychotherapist and not to have to put on a brave face or find refuge in denial may be more enhancing of recovery than attempting more detailed explorative work. The acceptance of the role of neuroleptic drugs goes hand in hand with this approach as does the need to understand the staff group reactions to one's patient, which may be a formidable task in non-therapeutic environments such as prisons.

However, there is always the chance of a more detailed understanding of severe pathology and if this can be achieved, it can be of lasting benefit.

In the model of primary linking, the functions of prospecting, holding on and substantive experience will be conveyed in the transference through the various expressions of secondary phantasy, both in psychosynthetic and psychopoetic response to the dependent relationship with the therapist. This supplies a real opportunity to lessen the deficit in the primary identifications, particularly if the disordered linking problems can be picked up, when their sensitive interpretation may rectify quite specifically the dysmorphia that has been their consequence. Obviously, a patient's sense of a lively prospecting therapist who enables them to feel psychologically held in a substantive way will depend upon the sensitivity and skill of the therapist and on the frequency of the sessions. Achievement of inroads into autistic entrapment is hard and requires interpretations that demonstrate an understanding of the fear of becoming lost and trapped in confusion. When the patient decompensates into an autistic state, the fact that they will have lost the capacity to link thoughts together or to conceptualize an individual object as a constant entity will make ordinary interpretive work impossible. Under these circumstances contact can sometimes be made by simply interpreting the nature of the problem and why that has arisen; by saying, for instance, how the patient feels that objects and people seem to change all the time and how they feel trapped and muddled with what should be outside them.

With less autistic patients the study of difficulties in following what the patient is trying to say may reveal subtle disorders of thought. Particular attention to the nature of muddles in the construction of logical statements can then be related to specific problems in the linking functions. For instance, those who have failed to achieve satisfactory holding on may be at times very hard to follow even when they are apparently describing everyday occurrences.

Instead of seeing this as resistance or asking for clarification it is worthwhile trying to see what it is that is missing, what logical connective, say an 'if' or 'but', would help to make sense of what they are trying to formulate. This can then be related to feeling unheld or even dropped. I have found this analysis of problems in comprehension a sensitive route to making contact with specific misfortunes in primary linking and a valuable way of freeing obstacles to progress. The advantage of working in this rather detailed way with those who have been emotionally deprived is that, when affinity of thought is achieved, the patient experiences a duality of linking within the terms of the analytic functions that will to some extent reproduce the kind of physico-emotional experience that they missed out on at an earlier stage. This greatly reduces their clamour for more direct reassurance and greatly enhances the therapeutic alliance.

The length of the treatment is another important factor and the time constraints need to be made clear from the outset. Again one is reminded of the importance of having some idea of what is a reasonably realistic goal and integrating a psychotherapeutic approach with general psychiatric care (Jackson 1991). As he describes, psychoanalytic understanding of the psychotic world of ill patients is a powerful aid to their treatment and management. Such understanding should, of course, include other approaches such as well-conceived cognitive strategies, which may be more appropriate with disturbed patients than attempting transference-based or other interpretive approaches. A specific approach to the omnipotence of psychotic experience (Chadwick *et al.* 1994) is the kind of well thought out cognitive therapy that needs to be developed. Group treatment in these cases may be very valuable (Cox 1976) and provides a very good opportunity to make contact with disguised pathology through the study of the group's difficulties in communicating with each other along the lines mentioned above.

In setting out these thoughts and modifications to theory I do want to stress that they represent the conclusions reached in direct clinical work with patients both as a psychoanalyst and clinical psychiatrist. The model derives from the work of the major psychoanalytic theorists and represents an attempt to integrate and reconcile a variety of different theoretical positions which, because of the problems of refutation unique to psychoanalysis, tend toward the dogmatic.

It will be recognized that the model makes redundant the concept of the id and diminishes the depressive position as a distinct developmental requirement by substituting a more continual 'depressive' pull towards reality in the psychopoetic function of secondary phantasy. All instincts become ego instincts and, although essentially self-preservative, are also social in so far as the preservation of the self is inextricably connected with innate interdependent capacity. Death instinct is maintained not as an instinct *per se* but as a specific innate deficiency in the range of primary linking functions which serve the instinctual preconceptions of a primary object relationship. Primary phantasy as the mental counterpart of instinct (Isaac 1952) forms the central thesis of this model. The metapsychology of super-ego formation is taken out of omnipotent phantasy so that conscience becomes the resultant of fortunate experiences of acquiring basic identifications within the framework of a good dependency.

I hope the model has some meaning and usefulness for those working in this perplexing and poorly understood field of human misery.

Theories of Aggression and Violence

Felicity de Zulueta

INTRODUCTION

The terms aggression and violence are often used interchangeably. However, whereas aggression is understood by ethologists and biologists as a normal form of social behaviour we share with other animals, its manifestations should not to be confused with violence, which is essentially human and relates more to the meaning we give to a destructive form of interpersonal or even personal behaviour. For example, a man kills another: this can be interpreted as a 'bestial' act of violence and 'the inevitable manifestation of our instinctual drives' or, as a 'legitimate act of courage in the defence of the nation', or as 'necessary for the preservation of law and order'.

These different interpretations depend upon how individuals perceive themselves and the world they live in: they are related not only to people's personal experience but also to the social and cultural matrix to which they belong.

Whatever form violence takes, the fact that humans resort to such behaviour suggests that there is a thinking subject doing something to another who, from the observer's point of view, would be defined as 'human', be it an infant in the case of abuse, a woman in the case of rape, a man in the case of murder.

But how do those who commit acts of violence perceive their victims? What is going on in the minds of those who torture and kill? What is the victim in the eyes of his or her tormentor at that moment? And what drives the attacker to this cruel behaviour?

Some of the answers to these important questions lie in the close study of the effects of loss, abuse and psychological trauma on the attachment relationships of both children and adults. What emerges most clearly from this research is that the individual can only exist in relation to the 'other': this finding is crucial to our understanding of human violence. One could go further and say that is the denial of our intrinsic biological and psychological need for the 'other' that may partly explain the length of time that it has taken to begin to understand the origins of human violence.

Indeed, the more we explore the subject of human destructiveness, the more we realize that what is at stake is not so much a scientific enquiry regarding its origins but more a philosophical and religious debate about human nature. This is an old debate in the West, dating back to the fourth century AD. At that time, some early Christians, such as Julian of Eclanum, believed that if humans die or suffer it is because they belong to nature and are mortal beings. However, Augustine rejected this view: how could the plight of sick or deformed children be explained if it were not due to the fact that 'sin' was transmitted from parents to children. By blaming mankind (and sexuality in particular), Augustine gave a meaning to human suffering and evil at a time when plagues and wars were ravaging Europe. His belief won the day: Julian of Eclanum and his followers were excommunicated and the myth of 'original sin' is still with us, manifest in the current belief that mankind is intrinsically violent and driven by what Freud (1920) called the 'death instinct'. The latter not only reflects a traditional view in the continuous debate regarding human nature but also humanity's desperate struggle to give a meaning to pain, violence and death. This need to feel guilty in the face of disaster is a way of making sense of the incomprehensible and of regaining some sense of control when faced with total helplessness: victims of trauma, incest or abuse all tend to cling to the belief that they are in some way to blame for what happened to them (de Zulueta 1993, pp.11–12). Fairbairn described this need to feel guilty as the 'moral defence' (1952b, pp.65–68). The abused child would rather see himself as 'bad' in order to make the parents 'good'. At the level of his internal object relations, he will cling to his 'bad rejecting objects' with resulting destructive behaviour.

> 'What Freud describes under the category of the "death instinct" would thus appear to represent for the most part masochistic relationships with internalised bad objects. A sadistic relationship with an internalised bad object would also present the appearance of a "death instinct".' (Fairbairn 1952b, p.79)

For Fairbairn there is no need to postulate a 'death instinct' to describe sadistic or masochistic behaviour: it can be explained in terms of the individual's object relatedness.

However, what needs to be taken into account in this debate is that there is, underlying the belief in the human species' innate destructiveness, the assumption that individual gratification is what drives mankind: such a view presupposes that the individual's need for the other is essentially materialistic.

This fits with our Western cultural premise concerning the central importance of the individual in relation to society. This assumption, shared by Freud (and many of his followers including Klein (1930) and Kernberg (1976a)), ethologists (Lorenz 1966) and sociobiologists (Wilson 1978), is that we operate as individuals with innate drives, including aggressive drives, that need to be discharged: the 'other' is essentially an outlet for the individual's gratification. Not only does this simplistic approach fail to address recent findings regarding the aetiology of human destructiveness but it precludes further thinking regarding the importance of the relationship which exists between the perpetrator and his or her victim and the sociocultural context in which this relationship is being acted out.

As we have seen with Fairbairn, there are also psychoanalysts who hold the opposite view, based upon the assumption that we are essentially 'object seeking'; that is, relationship seeking (Fairbairn 1952b; Kohut 1977; Suttie 1935). This view implies that outside relations are what lead to frustration, self-destruction and violence because we are essentially social animals (Zulueta 1993, pp.64–77). This approach could be seen to represent the opposite view of human nature, the view that human beings are essentially loving, like Jean Jacques Rousseau's 'noble savage'.

These beliefs reflect two profoundly incompatible visions of life and of the fundamental nature of human experience (Greenberg and Mitchell 1983, p.406). Neither opinion can really help us understand the origins of human violence unless it is backed by scientific research evidence. This will remain the focus of the rest of this chapter.

Paradoxically, it is because of current interest in the study and treatment of victims of human violence such as war, concentration camps, child abuse and rape, that we are beginning to realize just how much human beings depend upon their attachments to one another. Trauma has, in fact, been defined as 'the sudden cessation of human interaction' (Lindemann 1944).

These findings come as no surprise to those involved in the study of attachment behaviour in early childhood and it is to their findings that we need to turn first in order to understand the aetiology of human destructiveness.

THE IMPORTANCE OF ATTACHMENT BEHAVIOUR IN THE UNDERSTANDING OF HUMAN VIOLENCE

We are indebted to the British psychoanalyst, John Bowlby (1988, p.81) and to his American colleagues for having made us aware of a hitherto unrecognized and yet crucial reciprocal relationship which appears to exist between our need for the 'other' and our destructive behaviour.

What is now clear is that human beings, like all mammals, are born with an innate predisposition to form intense attachments to their primary caregivers (not necessarily their mothers), and then to their secondary caregivers. The vast literature in the field of attachment has been reviewed elsewhere (Zulueta 1993, p.43–77), and I will attempt to present here some of the most relevant findings in terms of our interest in forensic psychotherapy. The separation studies (with the sequential response of protest, despair and denial) carried out on primate infants and their mothers reveal that:

(1) Attachment behaviour has a psychobiological substrate.

(2) It is a form of behaviour partly mediated by opiates – so much so that one researcher describes social bonding as an 'opiate addiction' (Panksepp, Siviy and Normansell 1985, p.25). Indeed the distress symptoms produced by separation are similar to those seen in narcotic withdrawal states and they involve aggressive behaviour. This implies that emotions are at the root of social bonding: pleasure is the outcome of attachment mediated by endogenous opiates. Separation produces distress and aggression. These findings lead us to postulate that the mechanisms underlying love and hate may be reciprocally related.

Developmentally, the process of attachment is achieved through a complex process of psychobiological attunement between the infant and caregiver (Stern 1985, p.140–42). This allows the infant's early physiological and hormonal systems to be regulated by her primary caregiver, functions that the infant gradually acquires as she develops. Hofer (1984) maintains that it is the presence of internalized 'biologic' regulators within the interaction that determine the infant's response after separation.

For example, if bonnet macaque monkeys are obliged to forage for food rather than receiving it *ad libitum*, the mother–infant relationship becomes more tense with increased maternal rejection and increased infant independence. When separated from their mothers, these infants show the normal 'protest' behaviour of the acute phase but become markedly depressed in the second week of separation. This does not occur in their usual environment (Rosenblum and Sunderland 1982).

This study, amongst others, shows how the nature of the mother–infant relationship prior to separation can have important effects on how the infant behaves after separation. Hofer suggests that this response is linked to the presence of the internal 'biologic' regulators which, if disrupted through deprivation or trauma, can produce an altered response to separation or loss. He also thinks that such regulators are important throughout life.

Harlow's research on maternally deprived rhesus monkeys produced, amongst other abnormalities, grossly inappropriate aggressive behaviour (Harlow and Mears 1979). For some researchers, this is attributed to the reciprocal manifestation of a damaged attachment system.

These physiological changes are accompanied by parallel psychological and behavioural developments arising from the interaction between mother and infant which lead to the development of the self and the internalization of 'working models' or 'object-relations'. Hofer (1984) suggests that the 'biologic' regulators are precursors of these mental representations or 'psychologic' regulators: the latter may well allow us to endure temporary separations without full scale bereavement responses (p.192).

The complex process of psychobiological attunement between the infant and her caregiver is to be replayed throughout the individual's subsequent relationships and is at the heart of her attachment to others. This implies that any disruption of this essential developmental process leads to serious long term effects both at a physiological and psychological level. Thus the trauma of loss, deprivation or abuse (whether physical, emotional or sexual) can all have longstanding effects on the individual's capacity to form satisfactory relationships, her sense of self and, in particular, her potential for violent behaviour. Satisfactory attachments, which are essential for our emotional well-being, are dependent on our capacity to become attuned to the 'other'. Ainsworth, Blehar, Waters and Wall (1978) in the USA have shown that the 'securely' attached one-year-old infant (as determined by the Social Isolation Test) of a 'good enough mother' has the self-confidence and the capacity to form satisfactory relationships: the 'other' for such an individual is perceived and treated as another human being whose needs can be empathized with and attended to.

On the other hand, the insecurely attached infant, who has been emotion-ally deprived or abused, has little self-confidence and tends to relate to others with hostility. Such an infant shows an unexpected response to their mother on her return in the Strange Situation Test: she avoids interacting with her caregiver whilst remaining in fairly close proximity to her. Although the child appears to be emotionally detached, her heartbeat indicates that she is highly aroused.

This 'avoidant' (or Group-A) behaviour appears to arise when an infant is placed in an intolerable conflicting situation by her caregiver. Usually, threats of any sort arouse in the infant a tendency to withdraw from the frightening object and make close contact with her caregiver. However, what if mother is both threatening and forbids contact, as the mothers of these infants tend to do? The infant can displace her attention elsewhere and thereby 'cut herself off' from feeling both angry and fearful in relation to her mother, on whom she totally depends: she has learnt to dissociate in order to preserve her love object and her 'secure base'. This form of defence is very common in all victims of psychological trauma.

Such an 'avoidant' response is found in 20–25 per cent of one-year-old infants in the USA, whilst 63 per cent are securely attached (Group-B). The remaining 12 per cent are also insecurely attached: they display anxious behaviour in relation to their mother as a result of her inconsistent behaviour and behave in an ambivalent manner upon her return in the Strange Situation Test (Group-C).

The study of attachment relations is beginning to provide important evidence as to the links between the infant's attachment patterns, the formation of internal working models (or object relations) and the development of the self.

One such study is of particular interest: nineteen pairs of children aged four to five years old were observed at play.

In those pairs where one or both partners were Group-A children, there was victimization: in five of these pairs one partner continuously victimized the other, both verbally and physically. In these couples the abuser had an 'avoidant' attachment response in the Strange Situation Test and the victim was also insecurely attached (Group-A and Group-C). Securely attached children were neither abusers nor victims (Troy and Sroufe 1987).

These findings are important for our understanding of human violence and its links with Group-A attachment responses. They also help us to understand how object relations are internalized: the fact that a Group-A child can be either victim or victimiser suggests that it is the relationship, the self in relation to the 'other', which is internalized. What researchers have also noted in particular is the high stability in the infant's reunion behaviour with mother. This stability is explained by the fact that, once established, patterns of attachment tend to be self perpetuating. This allows the individual to preserve a sense of continuity in terms of his or her sense of self. For this to be achieved, perceptual and cognitive distortions have to play an important part in the maintenance of the Self: we tend to perceive the world as we need to see it.

An example of this kind of cognitive distortion is provided by Frodi's (1985) study on the effects of infant crying on caregivers (p.363). The baby's cry is always aversive, producing a similar effect to that of being repeatedly insulted or being given an electric shock. The effects are even more marked if the subjects watching the video were told that the baby was either 'premature' or 'difficult' when, in fact, the child was normal. A smiling baby elicits a positive reaction for most people. However, for abusive mothers both smiling and crying appears to be aversive.

The same observation has been made with abused children who, faced with a crying peer, will respond negatively and may even hit the other child (Main and George 1985). This response could be attributed to the fact that 'avoidant' children may find the crying unbearable because it could remind them of their own pain and, possibly, of the way their caregivers dealt with it, too.

Conclusion

What these studies on attachment behaviour appear to show is that deprivation in all its different manifestations results in attunement failure and that the resulting *avoidant* child grows up with little self-confidence and perceives the 'other' much as she perceives herself to be, as a dehumanized being, or, as 'part object'.

Such insecurity has important implications in terms of self for it results in a desperate need to have some sense of control over the 'other' who thus becomes an object of exploitation or abuse and is perceived as a dehumanized other. Indeed, the loss of an important relationship to the self – otherwise described as self object failure – in an insecure personality is tantamount to an attack on the self, with all that this entails in terms of destructive narcissistic rage and the associated cognitive and physiological manifestations mentioned above. One last finding that is of particular relevance for psychotherapists working with those who abuse and victimize is that it is not so much the experience of rejection and trauma that determines how secure people feel as adults, but the capacity they have to gain access to the information about their childhood and how coherently they can organize such information. This could be seen as an important function of the therapeutic experience, which should aim at providing a 'good enough' attachment relationship to help the patient rediscover that which was helplessly endured and then defensively 'split off' in order to survive.

THE IMPORTANCE OF PSYCHOLOGICAL TRAUMA IN THE UNDERSTANDING OF HUMAN VIOLENCE

If psychological trauma is defined as 'the sudden uncontrollable disruption of affiliative bonds' (Lindemann 1944), it is no coincidence that there is considerable overlap between attachment disorders and psychological trauma: those are the result of a disruption to the attachment system. Both lead to disruption of the attachment system with all that this implies in terms of psychological defences, biological manifestations and violence.

Freud (1896a) was one of the first to suggest the possibility that what was then called hysteria was the outcome of child sexual abuse in childhood. His findings and theories were rejected by the psychiatric establishment, and later by Freud himself.

Nearly one hundred years later many psychiatrists are still doubtful about the role of sexual abuse or chronic psychological trauma in the aetiology of psychiatric disorders. However, there are studies which do show strong links between sexual abuse, borderline personality disorders and eating disorders (Brown and Anderson 1991; Herman, Perry and Van der Kolk 1989; Mullen *et al.* 1993), as well as between sexual abuse and perversions (Welldon 1988).

The long term effects of psychological trauma or post traumatic stress disorder (PTSD) are no longer denied. This syndrome recognizes the wounding of the human psyche during states of terrifying helplessness. It took a devastating war and the defeat of a world power for the importance of psychological trauma to be recognized again. PTSD essentially recognizes a biphasic response to traumatic events involving, on the one hand, the reliving of these events in some form or another and, on the other hand, a sense of numbness and reduced responsiveness to the outside world.

Dissociation and Re-Enactment

Traumatized people find themselves reliving their traumatic experience mainly through intrusive thoughts in the form of visual flashbacks, nightmares, or recurrent memories, or through the actual re-enactment of the event. In the latter, the subject may play the role of victim or victimizer. It is this particular consequence of psychological trauma that is a major cause of violence, one that is all too often neglected but which can be at the root of what appears as cold or unprovoked violence occurring many years after the original trauma. In such individuals, damage to the attachment system and to the self results in intense rage that is often split off from consciousness.

Vignette

'In 1968, a Vietnam veteran lit a cigarette which led to the murder of his buddy by the Vietcong. On the anniversary of this death, for the next eighteen years, he carried out an 'armed robbery' by putting a finger in his pocket and carrying out a 'holdup' in order to elicit police gunfire. His unconscious re-enactment only came to an end when he discovered its meaning.' (Van der Kolk, 1989, p.391)

What is most striking in the study of psychological trauma is to discover how the psychobiological effects of trauma often remain hidden by the human psyche's vast repertoire of defences. Painful memories are lost to consciousness as the individual literally dissociates himself from feelings or thoughts that are too disturbing to acknowledge. This is how abused children and trauma victims cope with the unspeakable pain of their past. It is only when these dissociated feelings are triggered back into consciousness by an internal or external stimulus that the dissociated rage and its accompanying perceptions are brought back into action (although not necessarily into consciousness), often to recreate the very pain to which the victim was subjected, either in himself or in the 'other', as we see happening with parents who abuse their children as they were abused or with 'battered wives' who recreate their childhood abuse with their male partners.

Repetition Compulsion

As a result of the failure to integrate the traumatic experience into declarative memory, trauma can become organized at a sensory or somatic level which is difficult to change (Van der Kolk 1994). As a result, the traumatized individual is likely to be exposed repeatedly to states of high arousal which cannot be handled because of an associated inability to modulate such experiences, both biologically and psychologically. Indeed, victims of chronic trauma cannot use symbols and fantasy to cope with their feelings and therefore tend to act rather than think. This state of mind is what has been termed alexythimia.

Links between social bonding and opiate addiction have also been confirmed in men suffering from PTSD.

Vignette
'A group of eight Vietnam veterans suffering from PTSD were exposed to a fifteen minute clip of a Vietnam war film: seven of the men showed a 30% reduction in perception of pain and were found to have released the equivalent of 8 mg of morphine.' (Pitman, Van der Kolk, Scott and Greenberg 1990)

As Van der Kolk (1994) points out, one of the functions of the mother–infant attachment relation is to modulate physiological arousal in the infant. When subject to deprivation, these infants appear to develop less opioid receptors and therefore need higher levels of endogenous opiate secretion to feel soothed. They may then resort to all kinds of addictive behaviour including compulsive re-exposure.

In childhood victims of sexual abuse who suffer from prolonged and repeated trauma, otherwise known as complex PTSD (Herman 1992, p.119), this tendency to re-enact the abuse is further reinforced by another defence, which is that of perversion (Welldon 1988). These victims sexualize their attachment relations just as their abusing parents did. The resulting ritualized form of behaviour defends the individual against overwhelming feelings of pain and loss of control.

Vignette
A young woman who has been both physically and sexually abused in childhood cannot bear the feelings which emerge at the end of her therapy: terrified of her own rage and dependency, she fends off these feelings by becoming an omnipotent seducer whose central aim is both fusion with and control of her object-therapist in the service of her threatened self.

One of the main findings in PTSD sufferers and child abuse victims is the sense of guilt which these people feel and which also compounds the need to repeat the trauma. Identifying with the aggressor gives the child victim a sense of control and power that is desperately needed. But, such an identification with the abusing parent also implies a belief that the child is 'wicked' and needs to be punished. As Fairbairn (1952b) points out, the abused child will cling to this belief in his own badness because in becoming 'bad' such a child also makes his objects of attachment 'good' and this gives him a part to play in his downfall, hence the term 'moral defence' (pp.65–67).

For the developing child this leads to splitting of the caregiver into idealized good and bad rejecting part objects and a clinging to the paranoid schizoid position seen very clearly in borderline personality disorders.

Thus, both child and adult victims of psychological trauma hold onto this need to feel bad and therefore in some way responsible rather than totally helpless. This moral defence could be seen to have found its cultural equivalent in the myth of original sin. As Freud was to admit, the death instinct may well serve the same function. he wrote: 'It may well be that this belief in the internal necessity of dying is only another of those illusions which we have created to bear the burden of existence' (1920, p.39).

IMPLICATIONS FOR FORENSIC PSYCHOTHERAPY

The Therapist's Need to Deny the Reality of the Trauma and the Dangers of Re-Enactment

Working with the victims of psychological trauma makes people realize that we all need to hang on to a belief that we are both invulnerable and have some control over our lives. The meaning we give to the world about us is terribly important. The helplessness experienced by those who have been traumatized, whether perpetrators or victims or both, can really threaten these 'secret psychoses' or normal delusional beliefs of everyday existence.

This threat, in addition to the pain, rage and violence these patients communicate, either directly or through massive projective identification, makes it even more likely that those involved with the treatment of traumatized individuals will seek to deny the reality of their patients' experience. This therapeutic denial is made more likely if the therapist relies on a psychoanalytic theory and/or personal psychoanalysis that does not acknowledge the reality of trauma and the dangers of re-enactment. In such cases, repetition of the denied abuse in the therapeutic setting becomes quite likely, particularly with victims of child sexual abuse. It was Foulkes (1964) who pointed out that the psychoanalytic encounter can so easily be used by therapists as a way of dealing with their own needs and trauma: 'the psychoanalyst really defends himself by psychoanalysing others' (p.151). This can lead to therapists developing their own unconscious identifications with their patients, making them even more vulnerable to the effects of projective identification and re-enactment.

Thus, both therapists and patients can get caught up in either the unconscious re-enactment of their patients' perverse defences, with all the excitement this engenders, or in a re-enactment of the psychological trauma itself. The result is a perversion of the therapist's professional's relationship, much as takes place between abusive caregivers and their children.

Importance of Supervision

These observations make it absolutely essential for all involved in the psychotherapeutic treatment of forensic patients to have some form of supervision, a space to think about what is happening, or not happening, in the therapeutic relationship, a place to be supported, confronted and held, through what can be an overwhelming experience for both the therapist and the patient.

Also, if violence is to be understood as the reciprocal manifestation of attachment gone wrong, the treatment of those who resort to socially destructive behaviour requires a capacity to give as well as the humility to know when therapy itself may simply not suffice to give a patient a 'good enough attachment experience' to let go of the need to be 'bad'. It may well be in some patients' interests to remain 'bad'.

CONCLUSION

The crucial importance of attachment as a major motivational system in our species and of its reciprocal links with violence is only just beginning to be recognized (de Zulueta 1993, pp.41–75). What is now being suggested, as a result of studies on attachment and psychological trauma, is that there are at least two dimensions involved in the manifestation of human violence. The first stems from the neurophysiological underpinnings of the attachment system and their profound disruption as a result of trauma and abuse.

The second arises from the self in the form of narcissistic rage derived from a matrix of internalized early attachment relationships bolstered by powerful psychological defence mechanisms such as denial, dissociation, splitting, projection and projective identification, all commonly used when dealing with trauma and abuse.

In other words, if love and hate are reciprocally related, affiliative and destructive behaviour are the different manifestations of the same underlying attachment system and its psychological representations at the level of the self. These conclusions are not easy to hold onto when working in the field of forensic psychotherapy. When treating patients whom society has labelled as 'evil' and whose perverse and cruel activities cannot fail to engender feelings of horror and fear in all of us, it is hard to believe that we all share the same ceaseless need for the 'other'. But, as Bowlby (1988) reminds us: 'human infants are pre-programmed to develop in a socially co-operative way: whether they do or not turns to high degree on how they are treated' (p.9). In other words the forensic patient does to his objects what was once done unto him.

The Origins of Rage and Aggression

Neville Symington

INTRODUCTION

It is a mistake to think that psychoanalysis has one theory. Psychoanalysis is a clinical methodology that encompasses a wide range of theories. Nowhere is this more evident than when psychoanalysts start to discuss the cause of aggression. At its most simple there are two theories. The first states that aggression arises when a human being's basic needs are frustrated. This theory is based upon the homeostatic theory of motivation, which states that the organism has a built-in tendency to equilibrium, to homeostasis; when inner tension arises the organism is programmed to reduce that tension through incorporating food, water or finding an object that will satisfy a sexual need. Aggression arises when one of these needs is frustrated. Aggression is therefore a reaction to frustration. The other theory states that aggression is a basic instinct in man. Those who hold the latter theory say that man is a savage creature by nature, but those who follow the former state that man is essentially benign and only becomes savage when frustrated of his basic biological needs. I believe that both theories are wrong. The homeostatic theory is wrong because it fails to account adequately for certain areas of human experience such as a person's love of beauty, the individual who dies for his country, and, emotional and mental satisfactions in favour of which an individual will be prepared to sacrifice pleasures associated with the homeostatic theory. Although there must be few analysts today who hold the homeostatic theory, there are many who hold what is in fact one of its consequences: that aggression arises through frustration of a basic biological need. Some would extend this to include frustration of emotional needs. The theory that man is innately aggressive does not give sufficient account of the transformations of instinct which have progressively taken place in the evolution of mankind. I want therefore to put forward another theory and to do this I will start from a piece of experience and its interpretation.

Vignette

In the early 1970s I worked as a psychotherapist at HM Prison Grendon, near Aylesbury, England. Grendon is a psychiatric prison, and group therapy is the treatment of choice (Parker 1970). I was also associated at this time with an organization whose goal was the social rehabilitation of prisoners. It was the philosophy of this organization that rehabilitation started from the day that a man first went to prison. For this purpose then I went one day to interview a man who had just been remanded in custody at Wandsworth Prison. This young man had entered the house next door to where he lived, where he found the ten-year-old girl, Isabella. He pulled her by the hair around the top landing and then dragged her screaming down the stairs. When he got her to the ground floor he raped her and then killed her by bashing her head against a wall.

I was shown into the interview room by the prison officer and I sat on a wooden upright chair with the prisoner opposite me and a bare wooden table between us. He spoke in an affectionate manner towards me; he was nervous and looked very young. He looked bewildered, as if he had been catapulted into this world from another planet. After explaining to him the purpose of my visit and asking him for the date of his trial, and he giving me some details about his legal representation, I set about asking him about his crime. He had known Isabella quite well, I gathered. The problem arose when it came to the day of the crime. He remembered that he had gone on his bicycle down to the greengrocer. He had come back and he had seen Isabella in the garden and he had gone to play with her and then there had been an accident. I pressed him to tell me exactly what had happened. 'We were playing along the stairs', he told me, 'and then Isabella screamed.'

'What made her scream?'

'She was hurt.'

'Can you remember what happened?'

'It wouldn't have happened if her mother had been there. She should have come back. Young children should not be left on their own. You never know what might happen to them.'

He then wandered off as if in a dream. He started to talk about Isabella's mother, Josephine:

'We used to be together, you see.'

'You mean you were having an affair?'

He smiled with embarrassment and apparent guilt. I pressed him to talk but he remained silent. I tried to talk of other things. At one moment he murmured,

'Isabella saw us.'

'Is that what made you attack her?'

'Hair. Oh heavens – stairs.' He then murmured:

'Accident – Oh no!'

He was now only semi-talking to me. I had the impression that some visual images were flashing across the 'memory screen' and he was giving his reaction to them. At this point in the conversation a very strange thing happened to me: I fell asleep, or at least I would have done so had I not struggled with all my might against it. It was in the morning. I was sitting on a hard wooden upright chair. He commented:

'What, sleepy?' and he smiled again with embarrassment.

It was as if an anaesthetic slug had been fired into me. I struggled on with the interview but all my energy was directed towards keeping awake. The interview came to an end. I returned for a second interview about a week later. Again when we talked of his crime he went into his 'memory screen' mode and I was overcome with sleepiness.

A week after the second interview he went on trial at the Old Bailey, was found guilty and received a very long prison sentence. A few days later a prison officer opened up his cell in the morning and found that he had hanged himself.

I will give you my reconstruction of these events. The facts were that he had committed the crime of which he was accused. When I was interviewing him I don't think that he was consciously suppressing knowledge or lying to me. I think a part of his mind had blanked out his crime and just the odd flashes came back to him but not what he had done himself. My conjecture is that subsequent to the trial a memory of what he had done came back to him and that is was as a consequence that he hanged himself.

DISCUSSION

In a psychoanalytic treatment the analyst represents a part of the patient's mind which I have termed the *embryo mind*. Speaking generally, we know the mind's enormous potential. The human race has been blessed with Plato, Michaelangelo, Shakespeare, Mozart, Kant, Marx, Einstein and hosts of others too numerous to name. We all know the heights of which the mind is capable. It is my experience as a psychoanalyst that many minds have a latent potential capable of considerable creative emotional work. This is the emotional correlate of what Vygotsky named the *proximal zone*. He meant by this that part of the mind which is capable of further cognitive development. The *embryo mind* is the *proximal zone* but applied to the emotional sphere of the mind. It is the *embryo mind* that the analyst represents. The phenomenon of the analyst as external representative of this inner capacity of mind is called the *transference*. My mind was knocked for six when I was interviewing this violent prisoner. On the basis of my *countertransference* I am led to infer that his *embryo mind* was being violently smothered by a part of the mind which is known in psycho-analytic discourse as the *archaic superego*. I have found a model of the mind where different parts are, in relation to other parts of the mind, indispensable for understanding the emotional phenomena I encounter in clinical work. So my own personal experience of being slugged by an anaesthetic dart in itself leads to the inference that his *embryo mind* is being violently attacked. This inference receives confirming evidence in view of the fact that the memory of what he has done to Isabella has been almost entirely obliterated. This paralleled the fact that my mind was not entirely knocked out – a small part remained struggling.

There are three main aspects of this constellation of physical and mental action:

(1) A savage tyrant part of the mind – the *archaic superego* – is attacking the part of the mind with all the creative potential – the *embryo mind* – with the result that events of great importance are wiped out.

(2) The young man attacks with great brutality a ten-year-old girl.

(3) In interview with the young man an analyst's mind is nearly knocked unconscious.

Number Two is an infamous public event; Number Three is a personal private event passing between two people; Number One, however, is an entirely private inner drama. Now I want to trace things in the following manner.

The hypothesis is that the murderer blotted out the memory of what he had done because he felt so appallingly guilty. As you can imagine it was a crime which was reported in the media and sent ripples of shocked outrage through the public community. The world at large experienced the horror which the criminal himself could not experience. It is a phenomenon often observed in clinical psychoanalysis that what is not experienced by the agent himself is projected outwards and experienced in the wider community. The only person who had no conscious horror of the event was the man who perpetrated it. My hypothesis is that to allow himself to know what he had done caused an insupportable guilt. It was guilt, therefore, that led him to blot out the memory of what he had done. The anaesthetizing of my mind was the external correlate of this blotting out of the memory of his crime and the source of this attack on my mind was the very same guilt. My further hypothesis is that the emotional origin of that savage attack upon Isabella was also guilt.

Guilt is a feeling consequent upon an action. Guilt only makes sense if it was within the field of possibility for me not to do the action which produces the guilt. What I am saying, then, is that in the murderer there was a prior guilt that led to the killing of Isabella; that there was enormous guilt about the slaughter going on in his own mind. When he killed Isabella he had entirely surrendered himself into the power of that part of his mind which Melanie Klein (1975) first named the *archaic superego*.

The guilt about the inner situation is so great that it impels him to dramatize it in the outer world. When the inner drama is catapulted into the outer world an actual killing occurs and the man is caught and sentenced to prison. Punishment is society's revenge against the perpetrator of the crime but it is also the medicine of healing. This is, paradoxically I believe, the driving motive behind the crime. This is illustrated most clearly in Dostoievsky's (1870) *Crime and Punishment*. The novel opens with Raskolnikov brutally axing the old woman to death. The main portion of the book describes Raskolnikov's doubt: 'Shall I or shan't I confess?' He finally does confess and is sent off to hard labour in Siberia. The reader understands, however, that through the relationship with Sonia the punishment is the first step towards recovering a sane mind. With my murderer at the moment at which recovery might have started he killed himself.

CONCLUSION

Guilt may be the instigator of violent outbursts of the sort I have tried to describe. In such outbursts aggression – which is a natural endowment of human beings – is used destructively rather than constructively. I have sketched the activity in the mind, using an example, that produces this guilt. To go into how these activities in the mind originated would take us into another area of inquiry. What I am stating is that it is guilt, a guilt which is not conscious, which accounts for these sudden outbursts of violent rage. This process was first described in the psychoanalytic literature by Freud (1916a).

To return to where I started, these violent outbursts of murderous rage neither occur because a biological need has become frustrated nor because aggression is innate in man. The problem is in whose service the aggression is being employed. It is when it is employed against the potential capacities of the mind that guilt arises. A person does not feel guilt unless there was an alternative activity open to him. The origin of some violence lies in guilt. This means that an inner unconscious decision has been made. That the origin of violence is to be found in the ego rather than in an instinctual urge means that it is a personal construction in which it is possible to find meaning. There is, therefore, some hope because the possibility of constructing things differently is always there. The more we understand guilt and the way it comes about in the mind the more chance we have of arriving at measures which are prophylactic against the eruption of violence in our society. It is to this I believe that we should address ourselves.

Murderous Guilt

Nikolaas Treurniet

INTRODUCTION

Scientific research into the psychoanalytic process is difficult to conduct with any degree of methodological soundness. After all, the basic observations are not public, nor, usually, are the ways in which observations are arranged, deduced and summarized – in order either to develop or test hypotheses. The clinical retrospection by which post factum causes are deduced from consequences produces circular thinking (Wallerstein 1991). Conversely, the psychoanalytic process is often disturbed in an unacceptable manner when basic observations are made public in a methodologically responsible way, although this is viewed rather differently from the way it used to be (Weiss and Sampson 1986). These restrictions severely limit research. Ever since countertransference has become a respected concept, justifiable doubt has arisen about the analyst's ability to give an 'objective' report on what happens in an analysis. As in the law there is good reason for applying *unus testis nullus testis* – one witness is no witness; more than one person is necessary to make argumentation credible: a *tertium comparationis*, an objective correlative. Through our knowledge of child development we do know how important the triangular relationship is for the development of the sense of reality. So the more witnesses there are, the better. In every analysis the danger of a *folie à deux* is very much present. Hence the vital importance of supervision, consultations with colleagues, clinical study-groups and so forth. In the Netherlands, Verhage (1994), in particular, has rigorously formulated and applied this principle to clinical practice. This chapter will describe one particular aspect of such an application: the exploration of unconscious determinants of a crime. (See also category (4) in the next section.)

FRAMEWORK OF THE RESEARCH

The analysis – forty-five minutes five times a week – took place in a residential setting, the Van Mesdag Clinic in Groningen for delinquent patients placed in government custody. At the time the analysand, a man, was twenty-seven years old. His crime was murder. The analyst wrote a report after each session on the day itself, but never during the session. The reports, covering twenty sessions each (known as one period), were sent to four different commentators who, independently of one another, sent in their written comments divided into specific categories, to a central registration point, to which no one but the leader of the project, Verhage, had access – not even the analyst himself. Once every six months, that is, after each five or six periods, the commentaries were sent to all members of the project group. The analyst produced a synopsis of these, setting out the agreements as well as the differences, after which this material was discussed for one whole day. This discussion was recorded on tape, typed out and then sent to all the participants. The analyst was supervised at a frequency of once a month. The supervisor did not write commentaries himself, but did attend the six-monthly discussion and contributed to it. The categories by which the commentators judged the material were as follows:

(1)   *Transference neurosis.* How do you perceive the patient in the real situation? What is most important in the process of transference neurosis? Which actual factors, as opposed to the analytic technique (e.g. the residential setting or other artefacts or external influences), have influenced the process and so altered the material?

(2)   *Structure.* Which change in the defence mechanisms, other ego functions and/or object relations do you find important during this period? Likewise for drive organisation and superego/ego-ideal formation.

(3)   *Technique.* Which interventions by the analyst have brought about changes in the material and/or influenced the process?

(4)   *Crime.* Has anything during this period helped in your opinion, to 'explain' the patient's crime or at least to make it more explicable?

(5)   *In the realm of speculation.* What interpretation or behaviour on the part of the analyst would you have omitted or vice versa: What kind of influence would this or could this have had on the analytical process and what are your arguments for this?

Each of these categories was subdivided into factual commentary on the one hand and speculations, hypotheses and predictions on the other.

The team of commentators consisted of two women and two men. Both women were very experienced analysts from Amsterdam (Jeanne Lampl-de Groot and Bets Frijling-Schreuder). Both men were from Groningen, one of them being a very experienced analyst indeed, with considerable experience in forensic psychiatry (Hein Goudsmit), while the other had extensive experience of psychotherapy with delinquents in the Van Mesdag Clinic (Koos Reicher).

THE CRIME

The following is taken from the law authorities' records. During a stay in Sweden, when he was twenty-two, the patient, along with a Dutch friend, K, who was a couple of years younger, killed another Dutch boy, F. The patient's friend, K, lured F to the house where the murder took place on the pretext that F's girlfriend, who had been raped shortly before (by someone who plays no further part in this account) would be there. *En route* they talked a little, in the front room, they 'smoked' a bit and after a while F was bound hand and foot with a rope. K took the initiative and the victim allowed it all without protest, even when he was gagged with a scarf. Then they went to the back room, where the victim's hands were briefly untied and he was tied to a post with his hands behind his back. After some hesitation and 'discussion' amongst themselves K started to undress F. Now F began to use his voice. He said he would not take the matter any further if they set him free instantly. This was fatal. Now the patient started to interfere. Probably to shut F up, he hit him on the head several times with the handle of a knife, after which F collapsed and fainted. The patient and K put a rope around his neck and tightened it vigorously. After that K cut one of F's wrists in such a way that his hand was effectively severed. Then the patient stabbed the victim in the neck, back and arm with a knife, penetrating his heart, lungs and carotid artery. According to the autopsy it was highly probable that F had by then already died from strangulation.

CASE HISTORY

The following is derived from biographical notes taken by staff at the Van Mesdag Clinic. The patient is the youngest of six children. His parents' marriage took place in 1932 and was known to be happy. The mother, born in 1906, died in August 1948, just after the patient's fourth birthday. She had the strongest personality in the family and was the binding element in it. She is characterized as a nice, calm woman who was not afraid to assert herself either. She came from a farming family. The patient's father, born in 1889, had worked as a deck-hand on a sand-dredger and after his wife's death took a steady job as a factory worker. His children described him as fanatically religious; he was totally absorbed by his Roman Catholic faith.

After the mother's death he was completely unable to care for the family, especially in an emotional sense. He spent a lot of time with his children, but was more like one of them, and this applies especially to his attitude towards the patient. He allowed himself to be belittled at home and also by official bodies. The children felt themselves to be at the mercy of outsiders. When interviewed, the father was experienced as a friendly but gloomy person who saw himself as having been knocked about by life. That, in a sense, was true: because of his father's alcoholism he was brought up in a foster-home and after the death of his (motherly) wife he was totally at loss. The children appreciated him, but also found him very difficult: for instance when something was bothering him, he would sulk and shut himself off, creating a tense and intolerable atmosphere.

The patient's life history clearly shows the extent to which his mother's illness and the very changeable circumstances of his upbringing, had had a disruptive effect on his emotional development. The very early years were probably adequate, but little is known: in last year of her life the mother was in a hospital far from home for four weeks. A mastectomy took place there. Subsequently she came home for four weeks, after which she had to return for a biopsy. She was at home, ill, for seven months after that, presumably in bed most of the time. Since she was increasingly bedridden, contact between the analysand and his mother took place more and more in her bed. Thus he was involved with her physical decline and – finally – her destruction. Because of the pleuritis carcinomatosa (the spread of cancer to the chest wall), the direct cause of death, she had serious difficulty in breathing. For the child it seemed that his mother was crushed, killed. This did not even happen at home, so it became very mysterious.

At the time of mother's death the family structure was as follows: the father was fifty years old, then came a son of fifteen, then four daughters of fourteen, eleven, ten and eight respectively, and last the patient, who was four years old at the time. From the children's point of view connections within the family were continually disrupted, because the domestic help from the Roman Catholic family-care centre changed so often. Little more is known about the patient as a toddler and during latency except that he had enuresis until he was seven, that he repeated his first year at primary school, probably because he was not yet ready for school, and that he was intensely afraid of the dark. The latter was exacerbated by his solitary confinement in the cellar, where his sisters often put him when they were sick of his provocations. The patient invited punishment a good deal, even more so as he grew older. At thirteen he was put in a Roman Catholic reform school by order of the court because of his behavioural problems. After that some minor offences followed; nothing serious, but enough to result in punishment time and time again.

Before the analysis started one of the research's commentators (Reicher) produced a survey of the existing reports, in which he also wrote down a number of suppositions, a summary of which follows.

The mother left home at twelve to become a housemaid. The father's youth was difficult due to his father's alcoholism and he ended up in a foster-home. The couple had to get married when she was twenty-six and he was thirty-four years of age. The eldest son, the 'reason' for the marriage, got himself into a lot of trouble when he was young, for theft amongst other things. He frequently got a telling-off from his father and often a hiding too in the presence of the analysand. It is said that the mother protected the children from the father time and time again. She was the axis, the driving force of the family. In relation to the mother, the father was not so much a father as a child along with the other children, something which the mother possibly encouraged. In 1944 there was talk of another pregnancy, although this was contra-indicated because of the mother's known kidney trouble. The analysand, the child of this pregnancy, was named after the father's alcohol-addicted father. The mother fell ill when the analysand was not even three. He was seen as mother's favourite. Before her death the mother made father promise to be sure to take care of the analysand.

After mother's death the father was at loss for long spells at a time: very touchy and emotional and rarely at home. He was completely absorbed by his own sorrow and abandoned his children literally as well as emotionally. Despite help from neighbours, social services and so forth, the family was completely disturbed. It seems not impossible that the father had to cover up feelings of hate towards his youngest son – whom he could have seen as a contributory cause of the mother's illness and subsequent death, since the pregnancy was contra-indicated – by depression and feelings of guilt about the death of his wife. He was tied to the defence of his anger particularly, because he was the one responsible for the pregnancy and he had made his vows to the mother. It was the eldest daughter who was really the apple of her father's eye – she was also named after him – but the analysand was the father's link to the deceased. In short, ambivalence in abundance: he was too concerned, could not miss him and often had to try to show his love, all of which made him corruptible and ready for manipulation. The only area in which the father appeared firm was the Roman Catholic faith. It was only here that he set anything of a dependable example. He was, however, always referring to the inimitable figure of Christ, a completely unattainable ideal, an example, surely, of the fanaticism which the father demonstrated and demanded.

Based on the anamnestic data and the material of the first three months of analysis, the study-group arrived at the hypothesis that there was a very close relation between the crime, on the one hand, and the trauma of the experiences surrounding the process of dying of the mother on the other. Unconscious feelings of guilt especially, were seen as having a decisive, motivating role. This I call the central hypothesis central in relation to category (4) (understanding the crime), a crime powered by feelings of guilt, as the title indicates.

THE 'MATERIAL'

In the following review of the research material only one question will be considered: 'In your opinion has anything occurred which clarifies or 'explains' the crime committed by this patient or at least makes it more explicable?' A certain artificiality is inevitable here. It is hard to answer the question satisfactorily without taking into account the whole analytic process. However, this goes far beyond the scope of this chapter, which will have to remain a broad description only of the analysis in all categories, (1), (2), (3) and also (5). And even this restricted review cannot be complete. To include all the material obtained by each commentator on category (4) alone would require more that the total space allotted to me. I have therefore restricted myself to those sessions that were considered most relevant to the crime's 'explicability' by the largest number of commentators. The number of the session is indicated in brackets.

In (5) the analysand casually mentions that as a child he already knew he would murder someone one day. He gives as his motive: I am such a weak boy, I never count as one of the real boys, I am too scared to play soccer. A few days later (7) he recalls a terrifying dream from his past: *he was walking in a corridor while there was a heavy storm outside; large frog-like monsters pressed themselves against the windows and he was scared to death that the windows would give way and the monsters would hurt him.* He believes this was connected with the fact that his guinea-pig had lost so much weight. When it dies, much later in the analysis (532), it becomes clear how much of an unconscious substitute for the mother the guinea-pig was. In (9) he describes how he used to do sadistic things to animals, like throwing frogs in the fire or burying creatures alive and how terribly guilty he felt afterwards. In subsequent sessions he describes in detail his current safeguard against 'such sadistic things': the inexorably strict religion of Jehovah's Witness which enables him 'to fight the seven-headed monster' (18).

In (24) he produces memories of his violent jealousy of Katja, his eldest sister and father's favourite. Father took her to town on Saturdays and the analysand was not allowed to go with them, but he blackmailed his father by following him and being given money to go away. His thieving and general misbehaviour really started when he was six years old. He had bought twenty roosters for five cents each and sold them again for twice the amount. His brother objected to it, but his father said he could keep the money because he had earned it fair and square. However, when the analysand had raised five more young roosters on oat-waste from the flour-mill nearby, his father took them and – in the presence of the analysand, who was aghast – chopped their heads off one by one. They would, after all, be so tasty for Christmas.

Not long after that, the father also smashed the skull of the analysand's rabbit. This is followed by the story of a sheep-dog he looked after but tormented as well. The analysand became furious when the dog was afraid of him. Whenever possible he took the dog inside, near the fire, but his father and his brother made him put it outside again. Finally it caught pneumonia and died. In (26) what has been bothering him all week becomes clear: he has a headache and is irritable and hypersensitive to noise because he masturbated four days ago. 'So punishment does come!' It then becomes evident that his hypersensitivity to sound has to do with his fantasies when masturbating: each sound feels like a whiplash; so whiplashing is what it is all about.

During the following sessions he talks with increasing shame of his masturbation problems. He has masochistic fantasies when he masturbates. He loves to look at a book about Mina, the Goddess of the Whip, while he is at it. He also constructed a box with nails attached and into it so that as he lay on his back the nails would scratch his chest. As he did this, in his fantasy he was split, both actively sadistic and at the same time enjoying along with the passive other, whom he also was. In the same session (43) he recalls that he loved it when his father helped him do a wee-wee and stroked his little penis in doing so. In (56) he describes a terribly frightening event during his detention in the Roman Catholic reform school. He was sexually abused by a much older boy and nearly choked with fear when he was forced. Later on he mutually masturbated with a friend, which was no problem at all. It was a big problem however, to lie in bed with another boy and be affectionate: that is what he finds most shameful of all, being affectionate. In (66) he casually mentions that his father went to Australia for a year to visit his sister Katja, who had emigrated there. 'Strangely enough it was just before I turned twenty-one and left for Sweden. It was a shame for Dad, because when he returned, I had just committed that murder. He had written to me from the ship, telling me that he had bought an expensive bottle of wine for us to drink together.'

In (74) he establishes that he is terribly split; it is like a cycle: after the debauchery of filth, the masturbation, comes a longing for eternal peace, but before long that becomes boring. Then in (75) there is a remark about the murder. The first time he consciously and clearly thought: 'I am going to kill someone', was when he was eighteen. The immediate cause was a poster which said that you always should do what you plan to do. He knew he would go through with it as soon as he became of age, for then he could really be held responsible, then he could really be punished. They could not prove anything in Sweden; after all he did have a watertight alibi, and when that became obvious, he confessed voluntarily. However, this was on a Saturday so the judge had to come all the way from his weekend cottage to Stockholm. Fearing the judge's reproachful eyes, he didn't at first want to admit to his active role in the murder. He says he has longed for punishment all his life, to be in a cell and be taken care of, and be especially ascetic as a deliverance from his atrocious inner fantasies: hence his becoming a Jehovah's Witness.

One memory (89), dating from when he was eleven, begins a period involving not only much associative material, but also actions during and outside the analysis, in which magical thought is central. At that time he had taken his big brother's razor-blade and said to a girl at school: 'How about me cutting your hand?' She laughed and he cut her. She bled severely and the patient got a terrible fright. He had not imagined that such a thing could really have an effect. A complete series of punishments followed. He continues pushing away reality during the next hour and tries to scare me with magic: 'The Holy Ghost is a sort of instrument and could also make you drop dead just like that.' He expresses a similar idea in (124) when he tells me that at a tin-factory, where he used to work, he was terribly afraid he would jump into the boiling lead just like that, as if drawn towards it by an invisible hand in order to prove he was invulnerable.

He raises the subject of his mother in (130). She had a Swedish name – the reason he started to learn Swedish as his first foreign language. So he had good reason to go to Sweden as soon as he became of age. His mother was so fond of him and she minded so much that she was dying, leaving him behind when he was so little and so young. He tells me that after her death he became increasingly troublesome to his sisters; they had to feed him and he soiled his trousers. Then the idea occurs to him that, by doing this, he might have been trying to say: I am so young again that mother will have to return. 'And maybe I went to Sweden to recover her, or part of her' (131). Shortly after this he admits to me with shame that he painted blood on his body with red paint, drew wounds on his arms and torso and subsequently masturbated while looking in the mirror (143).

Then in (164) he speaks his conviction: 'Fortunately I am invulnerable; reality does not exist for me and so there are no consequences; somehow I have always known that the murder I committed would go unpunished, even before I did it. Committing a murder is different for me from when other people do it'. The same magical grandiosity continues, not only in his thoughts, but also in his behaviour in the clinic, provoking increasingly severe punishment. In (178) he brings a stamp with the Queen's head on it along to the session and tears it to pieces. Jokingly he says she will probably die now, or might die if he were to send her a lot of those torn-up stamps, because she would grow nervous and have a heart-attack, just as his father did. In (184) he explains that his fantasies are really much worse than his actions. He is only really wicked when he masturbates and fantasizes torture and triumph. In (186) he says that he really believes in magic: if he were to make a doll in someone's image and stick pins into it, the person would actually die. 'If I really wanted to, I could do magic, but I don't want to, things might get out of hand.' Then, for the first time, I am able to show him a link with the feeling he might have had as a child, when his mother became ill: it was as if, when he became so angry with mother for being ill, things got out of hand. And the more ill she became, the angrier he grew, and the angrier he grew, the more ill she became: he made her ill by his anger.

In (223) he starts to ask himself why, in a relationship with another person, he absolutely cannot tolerate it if he is not the only one who counts for them and is not absolutely in control. He also says it is very true that he cannot endure jealousy. So he wonders whether or not he felt terribly deprived by his mother's illness and death. Then suddenly he remembers what he was thinking just before he committed the murder: I am going to prison and I want to go to prison. At that moment the idea comes to him: I have killed mother and I want her back, that is why I want to be somewhere where I feel totally secure. But this is also the punishment and penalty for the murder I have committed. In (233) he talks of his experiences with Jack London's book *The Call of the Wild*. He tells the story with a growing intensity of feeling, interrupting himself from time to time in order to laugh it off. The more moved he is, the more he must call it sentimental. The story boils down to this: a man rescues a dog from certain death. After this the dog is absolutely faithful to the man and willing to prove it in the most absurd ways, until one day in spring the mating-call of a wolf is heard. The dog goes to the wolf for one night only and that very night his owner is murdered by Indians. When the dog returns, it is so sad and angry, that it attacks the Indians, savaging two to death, at which the others flee. After that he became the terror of the Indians; he grows to twice the size of a normal dog, but nevertheless every year he returns to the scene of the crime to have a little cry.

In my interpretation I make it clear to the analysand that his own feelings would have been something like this: When strange men – the doctors – took his mother away, his revenge was: I am going to become twice my size and be the terror of the neighbourhood; I have become a dangerous murderer, and I had to do this in order to revenge my mother. After discussing this the analysand becomes so emotional that, for the first time during his analysis, he has to swallow his tears and ten minutes before the end of the session he asks if it is not time yet. We are getting too close to home and that, too, is something for discussion. For the last ten minutes he cries silently, saying nothing.

In (243) it turns out that he feels less and less at home with the Jehovah's Witnesses: increasingly he cannot be a martyr with them and it looks as though in committing murder that was one of his aims. In (293) he voices the feeling that Holland is really a very pleasant country, far more tolerant than others and why not? He goes on to say that he does in a way appreciate analysis. And, regarding the Jehovah's Witnesses, I should not assume that their way of life is terribly orthodox. Sometimes things are very cosy, but...aren't they all a little neurotic if they need such a strict religion? Then he says that he never ever relaxes with a book, it is always the Bible, or the other extreme, comic-books. The last time he could really read a book at ease was in jail in Sweden: 'Raskolnikov,[1] a crime out of guilt and his mother went along to Siberia with him when he was convicted' (his very own words!).

He talks about his masochistic fantasies and actions in more detail in (324). He wants to seduce people to approach him in a sexually sadistic manner. In this way the other person is tied to him by feelings of guilt towards him, and so must pay the penalty by spoiling, cherishing and pampering him. At the same time all this has to remain unreal and so it is done under the influence of hashish. It is really a kind of game, a strange, unreal scenario. I then make the connection with the ultimate goal of it all, the cherishing and spoiling he has to earn by punishment and torture. The unreality seems to indicate that it is about a memory or event from the past, one that must push out the reality of the present: I can only have mother back if I have done to myself as I have done to her. I am able to show him how he also seeks punishment in all sorts of other areas, not just the sexual one, and how he confuses reality and fantasy. So his fantasized murder of his mother is more real than the actual murder of F, his victim.

Surprised, he says that he now understands why he had always consciously known that he would commit murder one day; unconsciously its purpose was to make him the murderer he already was. Only when the real murder had been committed could he be punished for his fantasy murder. To him (and to me) an important part of his masochistic fantasies now becomes understandable. It is like a game of make-believe in which the unbearable reality of his mother's death is

---

1   The protagonist of Dostoievski's (1870) *Crime and Punishment*.

'solved' and 'repaired' by reversing it. The unbearable reality – 'I have destroyed you and so have lost you' – has been made into a reversible game: 'By having you destroy, hurt and punish me, I will have my dear mother back and I'll be cherished and spoiled.'

For the first time without being prompted he says in (344): 'I am really just a very small, angry child, stamping my feet in rage. I cannot even stand it when I do not know my physics book by heart after leafing through it once.' I then suggest to him that his fantasy is that he might always have had his way if his mother had stayed alive. He ends the session by saying that Narcissus must not only have been in love with himself; he must have found himself unendurable as well.

Shortly after this more discoveries come to the surface. Just before the end of one hour (345) he says he has been having very strange fantasies lately. He has created a new sculpture with all sorts of round shapes and he fantasizes that he is small and walks amongst these round shapes as if they were the whole world. In (353) he tells me he has produced a new piece of work in creative therapy. It is a sort of hidden tit, he says, and done so well, that the creative therapist says it is professional. He could go to art school, though he does not want to – having to make all those baroque little objects; what does he want with them anyway? This sounds languid and bored and the way he says it seems to me flat, empty and sad. He is much more open in the next session (354) and talks about his feelings of hopelessness. He firmly believes in the teachings of the Jehovah's Witnesses, but really dislikes their gatherings: he cannot belong any more, he is too wicked: he is being put under more and more pressure, sometimes he can take a little break from his conscience by smoking some hashish, but it does not really help. In fact it is a situation with no possible solution: on the one hand he wants his firm belief in the strict doctrine, but on the other hand, being a murderer, a homosexual and somebody who masturbates, he is bound to be cast aside.

Of course, the more real the murder becomes, the more doomed he is. He says he pondered on it yesterday, but immediately after forgot what it was. It is very hard for him to fall asleep at the moment and most of all he likes to listen to Beethoven's violin concerto. He can follow and retain the part of the violin so well that it is as if his mother is singing to him. He does realize more and more that he committed the murder out of helplessness and a longing for shelter and punishment. Soon he wants to show me his sculptures, but without playing the childish game of me having to admire him; no, he has got something to say with these, he just does not know what. One is a breast in a kind of cover. It is very immaculate and smooth, not even interrupted by a nipple; in contrast the cover is rough. He is saying literally: 'This is my tit, I am looking for something within myself.'

He starts the next session (355) by telling me he is feeling so empty again. I suggest to him that he is looking for an ideal in the perfect breast, something in his own person which ought to be there and which is a substitute, or should be, for the religion of the Jehovah's Witness. It is the only thing that can make him full again. However, this religion is also his death-sentence, making it impossible for him to stay alive. Yet because of his need for punishment it is the only solution to his deep feeling of guilt: by sacrificing himself, he in a sense revives his mother. By creating a perfect breast, he magically repairs the mother's breast he destroyed, and by entrusting himself to the mighty, immaculate and perfect Jehovah, he at least keeps all this secure. He is literally saying: 'The Jehovah's Witness religion is my mother, it is also the perfect tit which is my only salvation'. It is as crystal-clear, logical, smooth, perfect and purified as the breast he has created. His problem is, of course, self-destruction; the necessity to recover repair and maintain the mother-Jehovah-breast: to save himself he has to destroy himself. Because this too is so unbearable, he desperately seeks help in hashish, in art and in the analysis.

When we have discussed this he says it is exactly how he feels and asks how such a thing could have happened. Then we discuss the fact that a three-year-old is almost bound to feel he is the cause of all the bad things that happen to him – the more so because it gives him the feeling that he at least has some influence on events. If he were really to feel how helpless he is, it would be so unbearably frightening that he could only feel panic and that would be unendurable. So it becomes clear to him that the normal process of gradually being disillusioned, yet still feeling safe was badly upset for him, because everything went too far too fast, especially since this was at a time when his mother was the complete source of all perfection, and consequently of all good feelings about the self. Besides that, his father did not prove such a good candidate for this role later on because, even though he loved his father, he did not think him strong.

It is very apparent that when neither analysis, nor sculpting, nor his Jehovah's Witness belief provide him with that perfection, he withdraws into his own perfect make-believe world: hashish, megalomania, not giving a shit about anything, using and ridiculing people – yet it does not really satisfy him. The analysand then says that this is his biggest problem: everything has to be so passionate, so extreme, so total; if only he could stand it when this is not so; what does he have to do to be able to live with the feeling that the perfect breast is nowhere to be found?

In fact, he cannot live without a religion or a faith; every human being has religious feelings and all other religions are inferior to the beliefs of the Jehovah's Witnesses, to him this is the implacable, logical, unavoidable truth. He cannot really abandon this wonderful ideal; he could never become a Catholic again, he sees that as ostentation and fraud. Here I make the connection with his father; after all he was fanatically Catholic, but he was exposed by the analysand, even before the mother's death, as someone with little backbone, who wanted all the attention for himself.

It is a few months later when next he approaches the subject of his crime. Then the father is discussed a little more thoroughly. In (420) he raises the subject of father being suspicious and stingy. Father had been afraid the cashbox would be stolen. The analysand himself advised him to enjoy the money while he still could, to spend it all, not save it. It was he who suggested that father should go to Australia and visit Katja...'and when he came back I was in jail!' He says he thinks he was furious that father actually followed his suggestion; you see, father should have said: no, no way, I am saving all that money for you and furthermore I do not want to go to Australia at all, because I do not want to be away from you for one single day. Could the murder not also have been a revenge for this? He goes onto say that the summer holidays will be coming shortly and that he really does not begrudge me them. I point out that he had said something along those lines to his father too. After a silence, he says ominously that the world will have gone to blazes in a couple of years anyhow, the end is near, but people are blind and do not see that as yet. Here his feelings of revenge towards me surface, and I tell him so.

In (438) he says that he still strongly believes that he can go on living only when he has suffered the death penalty. This is nonsense of course, but only then will he have done penance and be able to continue. He says that now he can understand why he started believing so rigidly and fanatically: the code of the Jehovah's Witness is as tough and inhuman as his own strict conscience. He did feel better for it for some time, rather blameless and 'endearing again', but he could not live with it, because that whole religion was a sort of death-penalty. 'Now I find it hard to believe I did not masturbate in the first one-and-a-half years that I belonged to that group.' In (439) he starts to recall his father's heart-attack. In fact he has always had the fantasy that he was responsible for it because he was always such a handful. 'I must have been a nail in his coffin.' Father was such a strange man, so weak and easily manipulated. He recalls his crying-spell 'which lasted a week' in the Roman Catholic reform school, after his father had written to him that he found it hard to go on living without his mother. It appears he then got the feeling that his father was only interested in his own sorrow and not in his, yet he also felt he should be a replacement for his mother to him. Otherwise his father would be miserable, which in turn made him feel guilty: he had the feeling, after all, it was because of him that mother had died.

In (468) he says: 'I never told you exactly what happened during the murder; it was really a game. Only, it got totally out of hand.' From the start it was an unreal affair to him, something like a game of torture: we are going to play at it, it is not for real. It would not be fun if it were not a game, because then he would not be in charge. K, his fellow offender, and the patient were going to wait for F, the victim. The patient left everything to K, telling him: you think up something. Throughout, K was the active one, except for one moment – more about that later. To lure F, K thought up the story about a girl waiting for him and kept on talking. The patient followed his lead in this very unreal atmosphere. Upstairs in the warehouse the analysand went to stand by the window and looked out. F let himself be tied up by K, after which K asked the analysand for a knife – which he had on him – which he wanted so as to cut F's clothes to undress him. When F protested, K began calling him rude names and using worse and worse threats, for example, we are going to kill you. This made the analysand very scared – after all, this had to remain a game – and he snapped at K to stop for heaven's sake. F started to scream with fear and at that moment the analysand just could not take it any longer and hit F on the head with the handle of the knife. But that was only to silence him, because he could not stand the shouting and F's fear any longer. Then pandemonium broke out. 'However silly this may sound, I can't hurt a fly. I couldn't bear F's fear. Suddenly it wasn't a game anymore and I had to shut him up by hitting him on the head. After that F said groggily: 'I won't report this to the police if you untie me now.' Then we really got scared. It was as though the damage had already been done, could not be reversed and must be brought to a halt.' F was strangled by both of them and when he was already dead, the patient stabbed him in the back. During this account the analysand becomes more and more emotional. Tears of bitter regret run down his cheeks, as he says: 'It all got so terribly out of hand.'

In (532) he describes how his guinea-pig died. It was awful, the animal's breathing became more and more difficult and the analysand felt utterly powerless. At first he was furious with the vet, who could do nothing, but then he realized that it felt like a murder: if you die young, it is like a violent death. Others don't lift a finger, so they are really murderers, because they ought to be able to do something about it! In (537) he starts talking about his masturbation fantasies again. It is nicest when he is tortured by his sisters, all four of them, and sometimes his brother may join in, but his father has no part in it at all. He is eliminated, he says laughingly, but there are always onlookers. After a silence he says that there is something else too. It serves his sisters right that there are onlookers, so others can see what is happening. After another silence he says with shame that there is something else which is also essential: Maria Z (a girl he met and fell in love with at the Jehovah's Witnesses and who has the same Christian name as his mother and his favourite sister) is among the onlookers and watches him being tortured.

In (603) this fantasy changes: now he is nailed to a cross and the last event of his life is that his mother jerks him off and his sisters look on in admiration. There are still many spectators present. Yesterday, he continues, he walked around a jumble-sale (he is allowed to leave the clinic unaccompanied for a short while) and saw a crucifix for sale for thirty-five guilders. He said to the salesman: 'That's far too expensive man, it is not even worth ten guilders.' I suggested to him that Jesus was very important in his family home and that must sometimes have made him furious, because his mother, like his father, was a fanatic follower of Jesus. After all, Jesus was the good, pure favourite who had renounced all sexuality. He, on the other hand, like all little boys, was proud of his penis, and showed it to his mother but, as with his sisters, he always drew a blank. Maybe his masturbation fantasy is reparation for all of these intolerable injuries; he has eliminated father and is also punished by crucifixion for this mortal sin.

During the next session (604) he describes how a woman tried to chat him up in town, but then obviously waited for him to show some interest. Now he finds that unthinkable, intolerable: he cannot be actively masculine as long as he feels women are after his penis, because they do not have one themselves. Then he suddenly remembers how he restlessly wandered to the graveyard and had a strange impulse to pull a dove off a gravestone. Maybe he was a bit jealous of mother's dove: Jesus. Very much ashamed he goes on to tell me his latest masturbation fantasy: yesterday he looked at himself in a mirror, posing this way and that, getting more and more excited, working himself up slowly, for if he came too soon it would not be fun anymore, would it? However, the important thing was that he saw his own erection in the mirror, yes, that his whole body was actually a kind of erection. At that moment he fantasized that he was his mother who was looking at him, while he was being tortured, consequently he was Jesus and at that very moment he came.

DISCUSSION

I will rest the discussion mainly upon the central hypothesis contained in the title: crime resulting from guilt. However, I would like to call attention to a certain artificiality, namely that only material thought of by the commentators and the analyst as relevant to the crime, has been included. Everything relating to the process, structure, transference–countertransference continuum and technique has been purposely omitted. Despite this restriction, a clear development is visible. It is also important to realize that isolating the dependent variable, often desirable in scientific research, can only be an illusion in the field of psychoanalysis. It can clearly be deduced from this material, that feelings of guilt about the actual murder could be a cover for feelings about the fantasized murder of the mother or father. But the reverse could also be true: at any given time remorse, regret and sorrow for this crime suddenly appear intensely from behind feelings of guilt about what had been done to mother or father. So cause and effect cannot be clearly separated here: they are interdependent. Feelings that are a consequence of the crime mingle with feelings that have a causal significance. The two are in interaction and, moreover, can ward one another off, according to where the pain is least unbearable. As long as one is aware that mutual interaction by plural determinants – hence multicausality – is in operation here, one can avoid having expectations which are too great. This chapter is no more than a description of a description which all participants have tried with great care and determination to make objective by exploring different points of view.

I will now briefly summarize the material chronologically in order to show that during the analysis a development has occurred, which clarifies the meaning of the crime and also affects that part of the analytic process which the restrictions permit us to consider.

From the very beginning of the analysis it is clear how intensely a combination of sadism, grandiosity, defective sense of reality and magical thought dominates the analysand's present as well as his past behaviour. The father's behaviour with the young roosters, his own with the frogs and the sheepdog (7, 9, 24), the rapes he suffered at the Roman Catholic reform school (56) explain nothing of course, but they do indicate that danger and seduction were in the air. The wounding of the young girl (89) proves that something was thoroughly wrong at an early stage. Note his genuine surprise that this act had consequences which shows how strongly he already had to deny his own ability voluntarily to do something evil by the age of eleven. He implies something similar when he talks about his inclination to jump into the boiling lead (124).

In the analysis his masturbation fantasies play a large part in falsifying reality. They continue to be about gaining power over others, usually by making them feel guilty, and more intrapsychically, by his double identification during masturbation – by scratching his skin with nails (43), or simulating wounds with red paint (143) for example. In the not directly sexual field this is coupled to magical denial in various areas, the most common element being that fantasies are more real than actions, especially that the fantasized murder is worse than the real one. During the course of treatment the need for martyrdom also emerges as central, later becoming increasingly defined as a crucifixion ritual, in which the mother, especially, plays an important part. Then we gradually gain much clearer insight into the meaning of this fantasy-world, suggesting that this was his only 'solution' to his extreme helplessness during the mother's illness and death.

At the start of the analysis our patient indicates that even as a child he knew that he would murder somebody one day (5). He rationalizes this in various ways: 'because he was such a weak boy' or 'because you should always do what you plan to do' (75), but by then the importance of punishment is showing through his bravado: he knew he would do it as soon as he had really come of age and so was truly responsible. Meanwhile he has told me the trigger for the murder at that particular time: the fact that father left him to go to his hated sister in Australia. In (130) and (131) the reason for his stay in Sweden becomes apparent: to recover something of mother. In (164) he announces that there are no consequences for him, he has always known he would not be punished (to him this means not executed) for the murder he has committed. In fact this was an important resistance in the analysis: I am a murderer, I am in paradise being cared for in the clinic and getting psychoanalysis into the bargain; you see, the laws of reality do not apply to me; that is why I need to be a Jehovah's Witness; at least that is real, because it is strict! In (233) the connection is made with feelings he remembers about the doctors who took and destroyed his loved (and hated) mother. In (243) his fantasies of martyrdom appear and his longing to be persecuted for noble reasons. Then in (293) he arrives at the insight that the need to be a Jehovah's Witness is an aspect of his neurosis and he ends with Raskolnikow. After he has been able to understand the function the masochistic fantasies have for him in (342) – the regaining of mother – there is rapid progress (344, 345, 353, 354, 355): insight into the repair function of his impossible ideal, the faith of the Jehovah's Witness and the perfect breast, the magic repair both of mother's breast and of his own world that he destroyed.

After the deep guilt related to his mother has become at least partially conscious and been worked through, the subject of the father is raised. In (420, 438, 439) his fear of having been a nail in his father's coffin, because of his father's heart-attack which he witnessed as a child, comes into focus, and through it he is able to make the connection with his anger about father's egocentricity. Only then, after repressed feelings of guilt about his mother and father have surfaced, do very real experiences connected with the crime appear

(468). This could, of course, only happen after the other meanings he gave to the crime had been 'soaked off'. After this his central masturbation fantasy (which is ideal) surfaces (603, 604): he is his mother, who looks at him and he experiences orgasm at the moment when, as Jesus, he is tortured and his father has been totally put aside. I will leave the dynamic meaning of this fantasy there; for further theoretical understanding I refer to Chasseguet-Smirgel's (1974) work on the relation between idealization and perversion.

EPILOGUE

A little more about what happened to the analysand. After three full years of analysis the government custody order was lifted and he could leave the clinic a free man (except for some ambulant support by rehabilitation officers). As often happens with patients who leave the clinic, he terminated the analysis, probably because, while there, he had found a homosexual partner, with whom he went to live. The analysand had a strong feeling that his partner would not put up with his continuing his analysis. The partner agreed to it only if it could become 'joint therapy'; which was something the analysand absolutely did not want. They did go and live together in a village, managing on the income the analysand made from his drawings and paintings. In 1980, six years after the termination of the analysis, I visited them. The relationship was stable, his work was quite satisfying and provided a regular enough income. In the autumn of 1991 I made contact again and to my shock learned that the analysand had died of a brain-tumor some years earlier. I had a long conversation with the patient's partner about the period after 1980. It emerged during that talk that the theme of guilt had remained important. It was a comfort to the analysand that, in a sense, he did not out-survive his mother, for he died a few days before he reached the age at which she had died. According to the partner they talked a lot about the idea of substitute guilt, which after all was very relevant to Jesus. Even though the analysis was by no means 'finished' at the time of termination, something had changed: before his admission the patient had never had a steady job situation, nor a steady relationship; afterwards he did. Structurally the superego had changed: feelings of guilt were not murderous anymore.

CONCLUSION

Conclusions drawn from a research project like this are bound to be very subjective. It has value for me not only because it is by intersubjectivity that we can take a small step towards objectifying the suppositions we have about a patient, but also because it is extremely instructive. This way of describing and discussing the psychoanalytic process has also activated quite another process in all participants: one could call this learning process one of 'relative controversy'. In a contribution to the 'Kohut controversy.' I have described it as follows:

> Ultimately, the only possible realistic answer to these different ways of looking at the situation is a close cooperation on a practical, clinical and technical level between expert members of 'opposing' groups. Frans Verhage developed and implemented such a process in Holland. This method involves a situation where a specialist analyst writes a daily or weekly report on an analysis which is then given to four or five experienced analysts whose theoretical standpoints differ as much as possible and who note down each month their comments and prognoses independently from one another. It would be conceivable that experienced advocates of self-psychology and of classical analysis would thus be able to supervise or instruct one another. (1985, p.939)

It is no coincidence that the 'controversial discussions' between the Kleinians and the Freudians in London during the 1940s (King and Steiner 1991) not only did not cause a break – which alone is extremely rare in the world of psychoanalysis – but also created a 'middle group', with people like Winnicott, Balint, Heimann and Bollas, to name but a few. The continual discourse and teamwork of a study group, which has been busying itself with the same clinical material for a long time, makes it extremely productive.

From Practice to Psychodynamic Theories of Delinquency in Adolescence

Donald Campbell

INTRODUCTION

Anxiety motivates us to develop theory in an effort to understand puzzling and disturbing phenomena. I am using the word 'Theory' in its broadest sense as 'supposition explaining something...' (*The Concise Oxford Dictionary*). In this chapter I will consider those psychodynamic theories which have furthered my understanding of individual delinquent adolescents as I worked with them in youth clubs and in individual and group psychotherapy. I believe these theories can also be applied to work with delinquent adolescents undertaken by youth workers, probation officers, teachers, social workers, education welfare officers, nurses, residential workers, art therapists, psychotherapists, psychologists, and psychiatrists.

Vignette – an encounter with Max
In the early 1960s I ran a youth club for adolescents in Manhattan. One of my regulars was a sixteen-year-old boy I will call Max. Max, a veteran delinquent, was a failure both at school and with his peer group, which is why he played the superior tough guy role around the fourteen-year-old club members. He entertained and intimidated the younger children with tales of petty crime and vivid accounts of his exploits in gang warfare. Then, via the grapevine, I heard that Max had failed his driver's test.

Much to my surprise, Max came to the club that week. Half way through the evening a terrified girl ran over to me shouting that Max had a gun. I didn't move, although my first thought was to get out of the way, duck behind a pillar, or better yet exit unnoticed through a side door. However, a crowd was already cautiously edging up to me while Max flashed a nickel-plated revolver at Mary Lou, a sexually provocative girl who had always brushed him off. Mary Lou put on a brave face as she backed into a corner. I was now embarrassed by my thoughts and angry that these teenagers were expecting me to deal with the situation.

Max then turned and approached me. He was tense and giddy with excitement. His face was flushed as he waved the gun at me and said, 'Hey, Campbell, how do you like my piece?' I paused for a moment, obviously groping for what to say, and then told him that he was frightening the kids with his revolver so why not come to my office and show it to me there. In the heat of the moment, at an intuitive level, I had sensed that Max was also frightened. He wanted to appear in control, while also needing me to contain him without leaving him defenceless and humiliated.

Since delinquent activity always involves a second party it is, as such, antisocial. Whether the delinquent behaviour is aimed at a person's mind (such as lying or trying to deceive), someone's body (as in causing grievous bodily harm, assault or murder) or their property (by burglary, arson, theft or shoplifting), it is always unsettling for the victim. Delinquent actions do not necessarily disturb, at least consciously, the perpetrator. It is the disturbance, or what Winnicott (1956) called the 'nuisance value' in the antisocial symptom which compels the environment to manage the offender.

It was the impact of Max's delinquent behaviour upon me which motivated me to look for theories which would help me make sense of how he made me feel and react. Theories which emphasized the defensive function of delinquent behaviour were most useful in this respect.

THE DEFENSIVE FUNCTION OF DELINQUENT BEHAVIOUR

Williams (1982), following Melanie Klein, draws attention to delinquents who evacuate into others by means of projective identification feelings such as anger, envy, confusion, fear and excitement which have become intolerable. The delinquent act is the vehicle by which the adolescent projects these unwanted states of mind into others (victims, authority figures, parents, professionals, by-standers, accomplices, etc.). Delinquent behaviour also supports other defence mechanisms, such as denial, splitting, reversal, passive into active, and identification with the aggressor. *It is the reliance upon action to project painful thoughts and feelings outside of himself and into the environment that is the fundamental characteristic of the delinquent's psychological defences* (Campbell 1989).

When Max brandished his gun, he succeeded in splitting off his fear of women and his anxiety about being mocked for failing his driving test and projecting these into the crowd. Everyone in the youth club was frightened. I felt tense and backed away from Max. Max turned his passive experience of being failed by the driving instructor into an active one by dominating the group with his gun. In this way, he reversed the trauma of his failed test and Mary Lou's previous rejections. He was not able to handle the car, but he could control an entire crowd. He was no longer looked down upon by the boys of his age who had their driver's licences. Mary Lou could not brush him off. Max was not frightened about being able to cope, but I was.

However, this tendency to project internal conflict into others generates a vicious, self-fulfilling prophecy. As pain builds up inside, the delinquent projects it out and others become disturbed and retaliate in obvious or subtle ways to get back at the delinquent (instead of trying to control or understand him). This confirms the delinquent's expectation that others will relate to him as he did to them; that is, in a delinquent way. The antisocial child now feels persecuted, not by something inside that he feels unable to deal with, but by another person or institution, a tangible something, that he can actively, sado-masochistically engage. I will return to this dynamic later, but first I want to consider theories which seek to understand how the adolescent's past and present may contribute to his delinquent behaviour.

EARLY DEVELOPMENTAL INFLUENCES

The normal infant is unaware of the needs and rights of others. The child is preoccupied with itself and the task of ridding its body of bad feelings and maintaining good ones. In this way the infant achieves a sense of safety and pleasure. When the child feels hungry, or too hot, or too cold, it relies upon actions (e.g. it squirms, screams or cries) to get rid of discomfort and pain. When these involuntary reactions of nerves and muscles are perceived correctly as signals and the mother responds appropriately, the child's needs are met. As these 'dialogues' are repeated with satisfactory results, the child stores the good feelings away in his memory along with the links between discomfort, physical reaction, and disappearance of pain.

However, when the mother is repeatedly unable, for whatever reason, to respond early enough with enough of what is needed, more and more activity is required of the child as the pain persists and his own resources threaten to collapse. There are also insufficient memory traces of good feelings to support fantasies which might postpone his need for gratification. In fact, his inner world is full of memories of pain that wasn't relieved, phantasies that persecute him, and feelings of helplessness. Bad memories, like awful feelings, are expelled by *actions* which are used to project bad memories/conscious fantasies and unconscious phantasies, just as activity was the first reflexive response to physical discomfort.

Later, during the separation and individuation stage of development which we refer to as toddlerhood, the child is involved in negotiating a solution to what Glasser (1979) refers to as the Core Complex. As the child begins to move away from the mother, anxieties about abandonment experienced as threats to survival are aroused. These primitive anxieties about survival revive in the child a wish to return to an earlier fusional state of intimacy with mother which provided safety and relief from fears of abandonment. However, for the toddler who is also individuating itself from the mother, the prospect of fulfilling the wish to merge with mother carries with it another anxiety about survival; anxiety associated with loss of self–object boundaries and loss of one's separate identity by being engulfed or taken over by the mother.

In normal development the good enough mother recognizes when her child needs to be separate and independent and when it needs to be comforted and contained and, thereby, helps the child to separate and move into the world as a unique individual at its own pace and in its own time. However, narcissistic mothers may have difficulty in accurately tuning in to their child and reading its behaviour as cues for an appropriate response. The narcissistic mother is more likely to relate to the child on the basis of her own needs, that is to hold the child when the mother herself needs to be held and to leave the child on its own when she needs to be separate. Consequently, the child of a narcissistic mother often experiences her as providing too much too soon, or too little too late. As a result, the child is left with mounting anxieties about being engulfed or trapped by a mother who is holding the child when it wants to be separate, or terrified of being abandoned when the mother is rejecting or unavailable at a time when the child needs to be fed and comforted.

These twin annihilation anxieties of abandonment and engulfment which make up the Core Complex mobilize self-preservative aggression which aims to negate any threat to physical or psychological survival. Psychological survival includes the child's separate and independent identity, its sense of well being, self-esteem, and is dependent on such factors as safety, biological needs and good enough relationships. For the toddler the threat to its survival and its mother are indistinguishable. Consequently, the child is in a bind. The child cannot afford to eliminate the object which is threatening its survival, because it is the same object upon which it is dependent for its survival.

Glasser (1979) draws attention to a resolution to this dilemma which involves the child changing the aim of its aggression from eliminating the threat, that is, getting rid of mother, to controlling her by sexualizing the aggression. Aggression becomes sexualized (sadism) when pleasure is derived from making the victim suffer and watching the victim. Anxiety about survival is replaced by pleasure in 'torture' and relief that the object can be controlled. The fundamental difference between these two types of aggression is the relation to the object. It is paramount in the use of sadistic aggression that the object not be destroyed but be preserved in order to be seen to suffer. The dangerous mother and the life-sustaining mother, who are experienced as one and the same mother by the child, is not eliminated, but controlled.

Delinquent activity can be characterized by its aim as either self-preservative or sadistic. Adolescents who repeatedly engage in self-preservative delinquent activity are more likely to have weaker controls over their impulses and more unstable personalities than those who perpetrate sadistic delinquent acts. An example of self-preservative delinquency can be found in the following incident which I have described more fully elsewhere (Campbell 1994):

Vignette

One Friday afternoon a handsome, blond seventeen-year-old boy of average height and build who I will call Stan was chatting with some friends. Grummond, an intimidating bully, insinuated that Stan was homosexual. Stan took it all silently but was hurt and fuming. Two days later Grummond again insulted him, and Stan hit him on the head with a hammer, again and again. He was quickly restrained by a number of his friends, although he struggled to inflict more injury on Grummond. Initially, Stan was on a manic high, feeling exhilarated and triumphant. He recognized that he felt absolutely no regret or guilt about what he had done to Grummond but was soon overcome by shame and self-hatred 'for not doing the job properly and finishing him off'. For Stan, the person and the threat were synonymous. While Grummond existed he posed a threat. Stan's violence was essentially self-preservative and, as such, served a defensive function.

Max's use of the gun to threaten and intimidate is an example of sadistic aggression. He controlled the crowd and clearly derived pleasure from Mary Lou's terror. His aim was not to get rid of Mary Lou, but to make her suffer. As the object of a sadistic delinquent act Mary Lou was less at risk than Grummond, who was the object of a self-preservative attack.

Delinquent behaviour does not appear out of the blue when a child reaches adolescence, but is preceded by a pre-delinquent period (A. Freud 1966) which reflects a reliance upon action as a primary mode of dealing with internal conflict. The persistence of a tendency to action-oriented solutions beyond the pre-school years undermines the *capacity to think* about how one might contribute to one's failures and painful feelings.

The potential for delinquent adaptation to conflict can be observed in children who have not achieved an age-appropriate level of social adaptation;

children who behave anti-socially, over-react to stress, viciously attack other children or animals, or damage property. Aichorn (1935) considered such behaviour as evidence of 'latent disasociality'. Another example would be the development of a playful, provoking, self-willed attitude of a toddler into a quarrelsome and acquisitive youngster who tends to make hostile rather than friendly relationships by the time he or she enters school. It is the persistence of a dis-social phase from a time when it was age-appropriate into later phases of development where it is clearly inappropriate (A. Freud 1966) that provides a warning signal for those who are concerned about the development of an antisocial tendency.

The delinquent's body is not only the instrument of its projection but also the medium through which he or she is gratified. We can see signs of pre-delinquent dependence upon bodily excitement in the play of young children. Winnicott (1958) reminds us

> 'that the play of a child is not happy when complicated by body excitement with their physical climaxes...a deprived child with the anti-social tendency, or any child with marked manic defence restlessness, is unable to enjoy play because the body becomes physically involved. Physical climax is needed and every parent knows the moment when nothing brings an exciting game to an end except a smack which provides a false climax but a useful one.' (p.419)

The 'short sharp shock' for delinquents advocated by some politicians is an institutionalization of the parental smack of the child which stops an exciting game while exposing the adult's failure to understand its meaning. Discharge of anxiety through action also by-passes the perpetrator's self-observation and leaves him unaware of the conflicts which produced the need to act out in the first place.

Delinquent behaviour is an enactment of an internal conflict which becomes intolerable and can no longer be dealt with internally. Whatever has precipitated the current emotional crisis for the delinquent, it is likely to be linked to traumatic, perhaps now unconscious, events of childhood over which the child had no control.

Vignette
Helen was referred to the Portman Clinic[1] after her mother discovered she had stolen jewellery from the mother of two children she had been working

---

1   The Portman Clinic is an out-patient National Health Service Trust facility which offers psychoanalytically-oriented assessment, treatment and management to patients of any age and both sexes who are delinquent or suffer from a sexual deviation.

for as an au pair. Helen had been stealing from her own mother and shops for as long as she could remember.

Helen's father was away on business so much that he felt like a stranger to her. While she was extremely possessive and protective of the older sister, mother handed over the care of Helen to a succession of nannies, some good and some bad, but all, in the end, were found to be inadequate by mother and abruptly sacked. Mother also kept the family isolated from the rest of the village behind the walls of the grandest house in the area. Helen put on a cheery face, and denied the deprivation she had experienced. Her 'solution' was to identify with her mother's possessiveness and, in this way, she managed to feel close to her mother without being smothered by her as she felt her older sister had been. Helen's stealing from other mothers, or taking objects associated with her own mother, appeared to serve at least two functions: it was the means by which Helen displaced her enormous rage toward her mother onto mother substitutes who were, like Helen herself, forced to suffer the loss of something valued; it also enabled her to reverse the experience of deprivation and loss which she couldn't control by actively taking from another mother figure what she could not get from her own mother.

Donald Winnicott (1956) held the view that where an antisocial tendency exists there has been what he called 'a true deprivation'; that is to say, there has been something good and positive in the child's experience up to a certain date that was then withdrawn. The withdrawal extended over a period of time which was really too long for the child to keep alive a memory of the good experience. Winnicott always believed that lack of hope was the basic feature of the deprived child. However, it is during the antisocial time that the child is actually expressing hope because it believes that the environment is there to be contacted and will respond, albeit in a punitive way.

Helen's stealing represented, on one level, her search for something that was good and had been lost. She was trying to take back a mother upon whom she still believed she had a child-like claim. However, Helen's attempt to master the deprivation of her childhood by stealing also served to defend against properly mourning the loss of the good experience that Winnicott referred to. Helen invited her mother to discover her delinquency by leaving the stolen jewellery on top of her chest of drawers in order to provoke containment and restraint. Helen, like other delinquents, unconsciously wishes that her mother (or those authorities who represent mother) would take care of her in an attempt finally to master the relationship that originally she could not control to her satisfaction.

Stan's mother had been depressed and unable to hold him during his early years. He still yearned for his mother and recognized that her early unavailability was somehow linked to his failure to develop a secure masculine identity and stable relationships with women in adolescence. After stomping on the face of a 'yuppie' who insinuated that he was a homosexual, Stan rushed home and bitterly reminded his mother that when he was young she became 'mad, dead, and couldn't leave the house' (Campbell 1994).

ADOLESCENCE

Usually, during the phase of development which precedes puberty, which we refer to as latency, Oedipal wishes to have a sexual relationship with the parent of the opposite sex and get rid of the parent of the same sex are repressed. However, the physiological and hormonal changes which take place during puberty and initiate the adolescent process thrust the sexual and physical body into the forefront of the adolescent's mental life. With the emerging appearance of a man or woman, the adolescent can, for the first time, enact what he or she could only wish for previously. After puberty the adolescent has the capacity to impregnate or bear children and the potential strength to convert into reality any wish to kill the rival parent. The newly developed sexual maturity heightens wishes and anxieties about sexuality and puts pressure on the adolescent's defenses aimed at maintaining the incest barrier. *In this developmental context the boy and girl face the fundamental tasks of adolescence: assuming ownership of a sexually potent body, that is separate from their parents, in the context of heterosexual relationships with non-incestuous objects.*

Delinquency in adolescence represents a developmental breakdown, a failure to complete the tasks of adolescence. It is the pain associated with the awareness of the failure to integrate genital sexuality and heterosexual relationships outside the family that motivates many adolescents to search for excitement in delinquency. The physical excitement experienced by the delinquent is linked to their emerging sexuality. In my view, the adolescent's delinquent act, whether it be motivated by self-preservative or sadistic aims, is the fulfilment of a sexual fantasy and, as such, it generates sexual excitement which momentarily blocks out internal distress. Max's immediate distress grew out of his failure to pass his driving test.

Menzies (1969) has drawn attention to the adolescent's use of inanimate objects (such as motor cycles) to compensate for feelings of inadequacy about their sexual organs and their sexual functioning. The automobile is often a representation of the driver's phallic potency, particularly so for teenagers in car-conscious America. Getting your driver's licence at sixteen is a rite of passage in America; the equivalent of a tribal initiation into manhood. It is a public, even official, recognition of potency. The ability to control this powerful object representing the adolescent's wished for genitality reassures against anxiety that he or she may lose control of his sexual impulses or be unable to satisfy or be satisfied by a sexual partner.

The pain of Max's failure to pass his driver's test, symbolic of the task of adolescence, was wiped out when he dominated the sexually provocative Mary Lou. His gun, flushed complexion, and tense body betrayed the sexual nature of his excitement. Max no longer felt humiliated or weak, but potent and powerful.

While Helen and Stan illustrate the influence of early deprivation on later delinquent behaviour, Roger is an example of a delinquent 'solution' to Oedipal conflicts as they are revived during adolescence.

Vignette

Roger, a diffident, passive sixteen-year-old, had been exposing his genitals to women for six months but had only recently been apprehended by the police for the first time. He said that the excitement and fear associated with risk was the strongest feeling. A smile slipped out when Roger described the 'surprised' look on the woman's face. Roger did not know why he did it. Exhibiting himself did not, in any way, fit the image he had of himself. But, then, he was not sure who he was anyway. He admitted that he would rather not think about exposing himself and thought he would never do it again now that he had been caught.

When he exposed himself Roger explained that he was in a state of mental confusion, at war within himself and cut off from everything around him which was outside a three yard cube. The war inside was described as one part of himself trying to stop another part from exposing himself. He seemed disassociated from both. Only the fear of being caught ever restrained him. However, when his 'defenses were down' or when he was 'a little drunk' he felt out of control and unable to stop himself. At no time did Roger convey any concern for the women he had exposed himself to.

Roger started 'flashing' shortly after his eighteen-year-old brother's girlfriend Caroline moved in to live with the family and share a bed with his brother. Roger told me that the occasion that resulted in his being arrested was unlike all the others because he exposed himself from a window in his parent's bedroom (while his mother was away) to women passing by on the pavement.

His father, a high-ranking police officer, had little time for Roger and appears to have been dominated by his ambitious and unpredictable mother. There were rows and a chronic state of tension between his parents. Mother returned to pursue a high powered career in advertising when Roger was six months old and left him in the care of au pairs. Roger gave me the impression that he grew up with a narcissistic mother who was withdrawn and preoccupied at times and close and intimate at other times. Roger said that she relates to the whole family via 'emotional blackmail'. He would wait for her to come home from work and study her face to see what sort of mood she was in so that he could determine whether she was approachable or not. If he got it wrong or tried to confront her, she would verbally attack him for his insensitivity towards her and then become sullen and withdrawn.

Mother's reaction to Roger telling her about his offence illustrates the intrusive, seductive dimension to their relationship. Mother was lying in bed with the curtains drawn. Roger sat on the bed, told her what he had done, and they 'cuddled'. She then reported that she told Roger that perhaps he had his father's physiology. His father wakes up every morning with an erection. If Roger had the same physiology, his mother said, it must be difficult for him to cope with his erections. After all, his father had herself right there every morning, but Roger had no-one.

Recently, Roger had become more concerned about his inability 'to get beyond friendships with girls'. Roger confirmed my view that his relationship with his mother and the tension between his parents may well have contributed to his difficulties in developing sexual relationships with girls. He agreed that he felt more despairing when he compared himself with his brother who was sleeping with his girlfriend, Caroline, and was particularly upset when she moved in. He felt crowded out of his own house. All this left him feeling depressed and sorry for himself. After all he went through growing up in his family, after all the hassles from stupid and insensitive teachers at school, why should he have to contend with the police and court? All he could think of was, 'Why me?'.

As early as 1916 Freud (S. Freud 1916c) remarked upon children who were naughty on purpose to provoke punishment and were then contented after being punished. He believed that these misdeeds were motivated by an unconscious sense of guilt arising from repressed Oedipal wishes to kill father and have sex with mother. Both the guilt and its source were unconscious. The adolescent who is overwhelmed by guilt arising from the revival of Oedipal fantasies may commit delinquent acts in order to attach the guilt to something conscious and find some temporary relief when he is caught.

Freud's theory is useful in understanding why Roger moved into his parent's bedroom in order to exhibit himself after months of exposing himself on the streets without being apprehended. It would appear that the incestuous excitement aroused by being sexually active in his parent's bedroom also increased his guilt and anxiety about being able to control himself as he moved closer to his parents. Roger's revenge and triumph over his Oedipal rival are evident in his violating the parental bedroom, exposing his father's ineffectual defence of the incest barrier to his police colleagues and the court, and shaming his law enforcement father who raised a son who committed a crime. The sadistic gratification derived from his encounters with women is also evident in Roger's pleasure in the 'surprise' the woman registers in response to the sudden exposure of his penis. Roger unconsciously behaved in such a way as to ensure that law and order would be brought into the parental bedroom and that his Oedipal guilt would be punished.

Roger also brings to mind Freud's (1916c) paper about those characters who feel they are justified in no longer submitting to any disagreeable reality. They feel they are *exceptions* because they have already suffered enough, unjustly so, during their childhoods. I believe Roger sees himself as an exception. The process of taking responsibility for his exhibitionism, acknowledging that he committed an offence and facing up to the reality of that image of himself, and then thinking through, albeit with a professional's help, why he did it, represents a disagreeable reality for which he would like to claim an exemption because he has already suffered enough.

SEXUAL EXCITEMENT AND DELINQUENT BEHAVIOUR

Stoller (1976), identifies three components of both a conscious and an unconscious sexual fantasy which can be applied to the fantasies and phantasies underlying delinquent behaviour: mastery, risk and excitement. Helen and Stan demonstrate the use that can be made of delinquent behaviour to master childhood traumas and compensate for early deprivation. The element of risk is introduced to the sexual fantasy and phantasy and, therefore, to the enactment of it, in order to heighten the excitement between the fear of repetition of the original trauma and the hope of mastering it and achieving a pleasurable outcome. Roger was conscious of the paramount importance of excitement generated by risk in his exhibitionism. Sexual excitement, so evident in Max's behaviour, is the product of an oscillation between the *slight* possibility of failure and the anticipation of *very probable* triumph. When Max pulled out his gun he knew he was holding all the cards.

Limentani (1984-85) builds upon Stoller's observations to distinguish two types of excitement: primary and secondary excitement. In his paper, *Toward a Unified Conception of the Origins of Sexual and Social Deviancy in Young Persons*, Limentani maintains that original primary excitement was stimulated by early phantasies and traumatic experiences which were felt to be entirely outside the individual's control. Later in life, a memory of both the pain and helplessness implicit in these early traumas, fantasies and phantasies has to be avoided at all costs. For this purpose the individual develops a sexual fantasy with an implicit or explicit revenge motif, and the capacity to enact it in a delinquent way, thus generating secondary excitement. Secondary excitement is brought on deliberately by the delinquent himself when he fantasizes about a delinquent act. The fantasy underlying a delinquent act functions in much the same way as a masturbation fantasy. However, the underlying Oedipal and pre-Oedipal aspects of the phantasy motivating the delinquent act are sufficiently repressed so that childhood wishes and anxieties are no longer conscious.

FROM PSYCHODYNAMIC THEORIES TO PRACTICE

Those who have worked with delinquents like Roger will be familiar with the difficulty in perceiving the sexual phantasies fulfilled by delinquent behaviour and the obstacles in the way of enabling the individual to accept these fantasies. Limentani (1984–85) reminds us of the frequency with which

'...the suggestion of aggression and hostility being inherent in the socially or sexually devient act will be utterly denied. The denial, of course, will be supported by the absence of guilt and of any motivation; in practice most offenders will show little interest in finding why they have acted in a certain way. They will, on the other hand, show readiness to take punishment if necessary so that the episode can be forgotten.' (p.396)

The danger for the therapeutically minded is to collude with the delinquent's wish to forget the offence. Preoccupation with punishment not only obscures attempts to understand what motivates the delinquent activity, but may actually gratify the underlying sexual fantasy when, for instance, it has a strong sado-masochistic element.

If the delinquent episode can be 'forgotten', the underlying sexual fantasy can be protected and a recourse to secondary excitement is preserved. Any threat to this capacity to generate secondary excitement must be resisted fiercely because the delinquent fears he will be defenceless against primitive anxieties about his survival. It is the wish for sexual excitement through the delinquent act which accounts for the compulsive and repetitive character of some delinquent activity. The chronic offender is erotically bound to his antisocial behaviour.

The professional's awareness of the existence of an underlying sexual fantasy may alert them to the likelihood that, consciously or unconsciously, a delinquent will see them as playing a role in it. Max clearly wanted me to play a role in the drama he created. I did not know at the time what part he wanted me to play, but I had just enough sense and fear to take Max seriously. I had heard that he had failed his driver's test and knew he would feel humiliated. Somewhere I also realized that what he had in his hand was something which was more than a gun to him. Later, I learned from Max that beneath his conscious fantasy of intimidation was a less conscious homosexual wish to submit to my potency so that he might bolster his flagging masculinity. He gratified this latter wish by acquiescing to my invitation to come into my office.

However, a male adolescent's wish to submit passively to another man may well be accompanied by fears, often unconscious, of losing his masculinity.

The delinquent is likely to draw the practioner into playing a role which will enable the adolescent: (1) to extract revenge for parental failure and, paradoxically, (2) to attract containment or punishment of adolescent sexual impulses which are experienced as dangerous or arouse guilt, and (3) to compel gratification of unconscious unacceptable infantile wishes to be taken over by some person or institution representing a longed-for nuturing and protective mother and supportive, boundary setting father.

Once the environment responds, the delinquent experiences relief, but only momentarily. Soon he becomes anxious again about repeating his or her childhood experience of being abused by his environment. The revival of these primitive anxieties about physical and psychological survival signals the need to generate secondary excitement to block them out. Although this vicious cycle of delinquent behaviour will be repeated by many adolescents, psychodynamic theories which shed light on the meaning of the delinquent act in the context of the adolescent's background and his thoughts and feelings about himself in the present can increase our effectiveness in containing, managing and treating those adolescents who cross our professional paths.

A Group-Analytic Perspective
From the Speech of Hands
to the Language of Words

John Schlapobersky

'Psychotherapy is identical with the process of communication itself.'
(Foulkes 1964 p.112)

'There was speech in their dumbness, language in their very gesture.'
(Shakespeare, *The Winter's Tale*, V.2.13)

'There is a sense of enclosure and division which is engendered by walls of any kind and anywhere, whether physical or invisible. All of us build walls which, though invisible, are nonetheless tangible; for the walls of fear, silence and prejudice, convention and religion are just as impregnable as the great stone walls man has thrown up through the centuries.'
(Walker (1994) *Remember Walls*, p.1)

FORENSIC PARAMETERS IN GROUP ANALYSIS
When More Means Less: A Central Paradox in the Use of Group Methods

Group analysis is a clinical and theoretical discipline that originates in the work of S.H. Foulkes, a psychoanalyst who came to the UK from Germany in the 1930s (Pines 1981b). Over the last 55 years its clinical application – group-analytic psychotherapy – has been developed with different populations and in many settings, including the forensic field (Pines 1981a). My task in this chapter is a discussion of its theory for the light it might shed on the nature of deviance, criminality and violence, and to consider what insights of a general kind we can cull from group analysis that will be of general relevance to the emerging discipline of forensic psychotherapy. Group analysis stands at the interface between sociology and psychology. Within psychology it bridges two traditions, the depth psychologies that begin with Freud, and the positivistic tradition that includes developmental and social psychology (Farr 1990). So the discipline is well-placed by its location to provide a meeting ground for social theorists – whether in criminology, sociology or law – and for practitioners working in the field, including doctors, prison officers, psychologists, therapists and lawyers.

I will make an assumption and then pose a question to open the enquiry. The assumption is that group methods can provide a powerful psychotherapy with beneficial results in a wide range of forensic applications. I make this assumption in order to be spared the task – and, in a brief chapter, the valuable space – of justifying and validating the use of group methods. I want to be able to concentrate here on why group methods work and what we can learn from the fact that they do, that will be of general relevance to the two fields of criminology and psychotherapy that come together in this volume.

For those who question this fact – that group methods 'work' (in any of the different meanings of this word) – I would refer readers to Welldon's chapter on group work (II:6) and to a number of other sources. Caddick's surveys show that 'the Probation Service is the agency most actively involved in the practice of groupwork in Britain today' (1991, p.198), and that 'the use of groups in the Probation Service – particularly in direct work with offenders – is now probably more extensive and more varied than it has ever been' (Brown and Caddick 1993, p.2). A recent report for the Department of Health and Home Office confirms the many studies of therapeutic communities and their small groups which have 'shown the most promising results of any form of treatment for psychopathy' (Department of Health 1994a, p.16). At Special Hospitals such as Broadmoor (Cox 1976, 1990b) and Rampton (Kennard 1993), in prisons such as Grendon (Cullen 1994) and Barlinnie (Boyle 1994), the use of groups in forensic psychotherapy has established credibility for a principle of positive intervention with populations previously thought untreatable, creating movement in both directions across the most impervious boundaries in society.

Most studies indicate that when members of a deviant population are aggregated, their deviant characteristics are aggravated. Research into the dissemination and consolidation of criminality within a prison sub-culture leaves no doubt about this. Therapeutic groups, on the other hand, work in the other direction and what is of general interest is how and why they should do so. Let us imagine eight men with long criminal histories in prison who meet regularly for no directed purpose other than that of talking. How can this exchange hope to make any of them less dishonest? Or, in a Special Hospital, how does the regular exchange amongst eight people with histories of violent offences against others, make any of them less dangerous? The central paradox in the use of group methods in psychotherapy is that *exposure to one's own problem, as it is experienced in the life of someone else, can bring about change of an unforeseen and unexpected kind with far-reaching consequences.* I shall try to consider why this should be so, taking as my reference point the curriculum of a group-analytic training programme and assessing the relevance of its theory to the concerns of a forensic psychotherapist.

The Group-Analytic Frame: The Timeless and the Timed

In therapeutic group analysis a varied or homogeneous group of people with needs or problems of one kind or another, meets on a regular basis with the therapist responsible for the selection. All present will have been chosen by the therapist. They will themselves have chosen to participate and will be expected to justify their continuing presence in the group by reliable attendance. Even within the forensic field there are too many variations in the principles of selection, organization, frequency and pattern of meetings to set them out here. I am concerned with the common principles that will be found in the many different applications. These inform the *setting*; the *therapist* who is referred to as the *conductor* in group analysis; the *therapeutic method*; the *shared experience in the group* referred to as the *matrix* in group analysis; and the *language of the group* (Foulkes and Anthony 1965; Foulkes 1975).

Once a group is assembled no instructions are given to its members beyond the therapist's encouragement that they talk as freely as possible about whatever comes to mind. What ensues is called *free-floating discussion*, the group equivalent of free association (Foulkes 1975; Schlapobersky 1993). Therapy in the group is born out of ordinary language in the free exchange of its members. It occupies the cultural domain of all shared, conversational experience in which people struggle with meaning – in congregational life, in the confessional, in theatre, narrative or poetry – and as such it calls on principles through which:

> 'The depths of the mind are reached and touched by simpler words that speak in images and metaphors…a universal, timeless language, pre-dating contemporary ideas…that touches the heart, the ancient seat of the emotions; (and) that speaks to the soul.' (Pines, in Cox and Theilgaard 1987, p.xxiv)

There are accounts that go back the genesis of story-telling, of people who have found points of renewal in the lower depths and have risen to live in ordinary society, or to flee from it, speaking of the uncomfortable truths of their experience. Theirs is an occasional and exceptional experience. Joseph's prophetic dreams in prison and Jonah's experience in the belly of a whale are some biblical illustrations. Sophocles' *Oedipus*, Gorky's *Lower Depths* and Victor Hugo's *Les Misérables* are three of the many in the literary world.

In group analysis we utilize a set of clinical principles that governs the setting, the therapist, the therapeutic method, the group matrix and its language to take what is occasional and exceptional and turn it into a programme that can open the world of ordinary society to many who would otherwise live and die on its margins. To do so we must move from the timeless to the timed, from universal cultural experiences to an exacting methodology summarized by Cox as the structured use of time, depth and mutuality (Cox 1978b). The method begins with Freud who:

> 'Made it possible for therapists and patients to engage in...forms of transformational dialogue that had never existed before. He showed therapists how to do things with words to help revise radically their patients' hitherto fixed, unconsciously directed constructions of both subjective experience and action in the world...Freud's clinical dialogue alters in crucial ways the analysand's consciously narrated presentation of the self and its history among people by destabilizing, deconstructing, and defamiliarizing it.' (Schaffer 1992, p.156)

These transformational principles are given a group context where, instead of being deployed by one therapist in relation to one patient's monologue, they become the property of the group as a whole. Here they operate through any one of three different forms of speech that arise in the matrix of every group. First, in the most basic form, they are addressed to the monologue of the group's individual members, along the lines Schaffer describes above. Second, in a more advanced form, these transformational principles become part of a dialogue between individuals in the group or between sub-groups representing polarized aspects of the group's life. In the emerging dialogue we begin to see some exchange between these opposites. And third, in the most advanced form, they become part of a discourse in the group as a whole in which each member is a contributing participant. Here there is no single or exclusive narrative line, no individual or polarized contributors and the group's exploration is open and diffuse. It proceeds as a chain reaction of associated experiences that can include words, images, feelings, laughter or tears. To understand a group working in this way we should have to consider the texture of the discourse rather than the text of its narrative. We would need to pay attention to context as well as content; ground as well as figure; and group atmosphere as well as the dynamics of the individual. This is the form Cox and Theilgaard refer to as omniference, in which:

'All-carry-all (including the therapist) temporarily, until each individual can claim responsibility for his own actions, and acknowledge the balance of those internal and external forces which helped to mould him into the person he is.' (Cox and Theilgaard 1994, p.358)

In the process of any well-functioning group there is a steady progression that begins with monologue in the individual's first encounter with themselves. It moves to dialogue in the discovery of the other, and then to discourse as each individual's multiple inner objects are externalized and encountered in the group. The group-analytic approach is distinguished from other group methods in that neither of the two earlier speech forms are disregarded. On the contrary, both monologue and dialogue are encompassed by and integral to group-analytic experience. Free-floating discussion allows a pattern of exchange to move freely between these different speech forms and:

'Through this movement – from monologue through dialogue to discourse and back again – the group-analytic method comes into its own, creating an arena in which the dialectic between the psyche and the social world helps to refashion both.' (Schlapobersky 1993, p.212)

Now, modifying Schaffer's description above to take account of the group context, I shall illustrate in what follows a progression in group development from constructive to deconstructive and finally reconstructive experience, each of which introduces the possibility of change at a different and more fundamental level. In a well-functioning therapy group all three modes are operative and the group moves between them as it does between the different patterns of speech described above. When the struggle with meaning – the timeless – is given a bounded and well-structured clinical framework, language can work to generate mutative metaphors that come in a moment but that can last a lifetime. At such a moment, as Cox and Theilgaard (1987) describe, 'A sense of mystery, astonishment, and uniqueness…transcends any desciptive technicalities' (p.17). Moments of this kind can arise through monologue, dialogue or discourse in which therapeutic transformation is close to its more timeless cultural forms. Monologue is like a soliloquy; dialogue – the resolution of opposites – is like Plato's dialectic; and discourse is like the work of an ancient Greek chorus.

Pure Culture and Extreme Experience

'Offender patients will have been involved in disturbed and disturbing social relations ranging from committing petty offences to such catastrophic out-cropping of violence as the savage dismemberment of a homosexual partner.' (Cox 1978b, p.267)

The index offence usually determines the setting in which treatment takes place and consequently the populations from which groups will be selected are relatively homogeneous (Murphy 1993). In any event, a population that has known extreme experience – as protagonist or as victim – can only realistically be worked with in homogeneous groups (Schlapobersky and Bamber 1989). Group analysis had its very genesis in providing therapy for the 'pure culture' of combat neurosis amongst servicemen during World War II. However, the pooling of experience at the extremities of human deviation might readily be expected to aggravate its aberrant features, as we have already noted. Foulkes (1964) poses the question thus: 'If they all deviate…from what is in any given community considered healthy or normal, how can they possibly be of use to each other therapeutically?' The answer he provides, is that *collectively they constitute the very norm from which, individually, they deviate* (pp.297–8). This recognition serves as the touchstone for group analysis.

To use it as a touchstone a therapist composes a group in which he fosters a therapeutic culture that is drawn from the personalities and personal resources of the group's membership and it is this that becomes normative and normalizing. 'Deviants agree collectively between them upon the very same basic values held by their own community', Foulkes suggests (Foulkes 1964, pp.297–8), and it is this underlying humanity in any deviant sub-group that becomes its most potent therapeutic resource leading, in due course, to a group culture that is both healing and normalizing. As Pines describes it, the members of a group, to receive help, have to create the structure that provides it and in doing so undergo change (Pines 1985b, p.26). 'Criminal impulses are in everyone…the manifest trio – criminal–society–judge – are the personifications of three elements present in everyone…the id, the ego and the superego.' Criminality 'enacts on an external stage what takes place internally in the mind of everyone' (Foulkes 1990, p.120). The group's therapeutic culture now provides the stage for the personification of these elements in the shared experience of its members. The drama of each individual's inner conflicts is given an audience amongst others who will recognize its different elements and, as the destructive and sometimes bizarre experience of different members is decoded amongst others who not only recognize it but find it in themselves – or find themselves in it – isolation is broken down, new emotional outlets are constructed and a new sense of self can begin to emerge.

CLINICAL PRINCIPLES

The Setting

The therapist supplies, creates and maintains the setting throughout the group's life. This will differ depending on the wider system in which the group is located, calling for one role from the therapist if, for example, it is an out-patients' group where a secretary or receptionist is the only other important person on the boundary; and a much more active liaison role if it is located in a hospital or prison where negotiations with ward and custodial staff are an integral part of the therapist's administrative task (Kennard 1993). This is a continuing and fundamental part of therapy and will involve protection of the group's external boundaries and careful attention to its internal boundaries such as meeting times, including punctual beginnings and endings, the predictable frequency of its meetings and breaks, and the general guarantee of a stable background against which the instability of individual members can become the foreground for the group's attention.

Every aspect of the group's life, including absences, departures, late attendances and extra-group communication in terms of letters, telephone calls and messages, referred to generically as boundary events, are open for discussion and enquiry (Foulkes 1975; Pines, Hearst and Behr 1982). Boundary events are interpreted for the meaning they might hold for the life of the group as a whole. This is a task initiated by but not confined to the therapist and, as the analytic frame and the events that break its boundaries become topics for discussion, the setting itself – to which each member is seen to contribute – acquires a capacity to hold its individual members and contain their anxieties and insecurities. For a forensic population the issue of containment is of great importance, as is the discovery – by people who may have no belief in themselves as responsible members – that they can take responsibility for themselves and expect responsibility from others. The group is thus responsible not only for the nurture, acceptance and security of its members – in a sense for their 'mothering' – but also for their containment, the setting of limits and the maintenance of consistent authority – for their 'fathering'. The therapist will invariably have to lead the way in modelling both roles for the group's members, but the evolution of a therapeutic culture will see individuals taking up these roles and the emergence of some capacity in the group as a whole to develop and maintain its norms from the standpoints of both 'mothering' and 'fathering'. Mark (1993) describes the maintenance of the setting in an applied group-analytic therapeutic community for offenders as follows:

'Tolerating deviant behaviour to a sufficient degree to allow it to be examined in a safe setting was the most difficult aspect of the work. Allowing damaged, often violent men and women to feel safe enough to rage against the boundary and the restrictions, and to internalize an understanding of how better to deal with 'authority' in the outside world was a constant challenge. The principle of reality confrontation was crucial in this task, emphasizing straight and open communication, so difficult with often highly manipulative, boundary-testing clients.' (p.24)

And in a Special Hospital Cox describes the setting as follows:

> 'Within the security of a custodial setting, an offender patient said: "I'm shielded, in here." The defence of a "secure setting" allowed his personal dynamic defences to be slowly and safely relinquished. Changed defences and an opening of latent capacities followed his deepening awareness of corporate life and this was commensurate with enhanced self-esteem.' (Cox 1978b, p.273)

The Therapist

The therapist is referred to as the group conductor, a leadership role in which he is both the group's therapist and one of its members (Foulkes 1964; Foulkes and Anthony 1965). In the former capacity his responsibilities include the selection of its members and the maintenance of its setting as described above. As one of the group's members he participates with some lattitude for free expression of his own, modelling a capacity for open and direct communication whilst – at the same time – maintaining a neutral, analytic stance and withholding personal material (Pines, Hearst and Behr 1982). The question of whether the therapist speaks directly from his own experience of the group at one point or makes an interpretation at another is a matter for clinical judgement but is often determined by the group itself which will call upon him for a varied range of responses to differing situations (Kennard, Roberts and Winter 1993). The importance of the therapist's firmness in his administrative role, and his accessibility and responsiveness in personal terms, allows what Cox calls 'a partial regression in the service of his patient's regression' (1978b, p.265). If 'the executive aspects of the therapist's personality retain a firm hold...on reality', it gives the therapist 'an executive, stabilising autonomy' that then allows him a 'para-regression' in which 'he shares the perceptual perspective and affective thrust of his patient's world', by 'sinking into his patient's social construction of reality' on a controlled and temporary basis (pp.264, 265). If this duality can be developed, the therapist can 'come alongside' individual members in the group and 'be welcomed' in this proximity; members will, at the same, time move towards his therapeutic position as they take an increasingly responsible part in the maintenance of the group's culture and norms.

It is in this area that a profoundly reparative process is engendered as the therapist's emotional proximity earns him members' trust; and their responsibility in the group earns them his trust. This example gives some sense of it:

Vignette

A group with a stable population but still in its early months had recently been joined by two new members. During a session the therapist gave notice of his forthcoming absence – an event which would normally be dealt with by an arrangement for group to meet without him. On this occasion there was some question whether it might be safer if the session were cancelled altogether. Amongst the established membership there was indignation about the imposition of two new members and, in the two new members, there was anxiety about being left to the care of the others who were jealous and resentful about their arrival. The anxiety abated to some extent when the therapist placed himself – in what he said – close to the experience of both sub-groups. People were only able to make a decision to attend in the therapist's absence when he assured the newcomers that he was confident he could entrust them to the others and had every confidence all would be well without him. In the event a constructive meeting took place in which people spent most of their time discussing the therapist! In due course a new-found sense of trust emerged that proved a landmark for the group's progress. People attributed it to the fact that the therapist had entrusted them with one another.

The therapist is trustee for the group; he is entrusted by the group; and, most important, he is there to trust the group so that they can come to trust themselves. This is a subtle and demanding role in any of the applications of group analysis. With a forensic population it is all the more important and is charged with special difficulty. Cox suggests that 'there is no more exacting therapeutic task than that of conducting group psychotherapy with borderline patients (which includes)…many offender patients with histories involving serious crimes of violence' (Cox 1978b, p.271) and he regards trust as the key consideration. In his 1990 S.H. Foulkes Annual Lecture he states:

> 'There is this pull of the primordial, not as a destiny but as a starting point in the therapy. There is this primordial, shared humanity…only when the trust is there, deep, deep down, then we're able to get up to a level where analysis is tolerable.' (Cox 1993a)

It is for reasons of this kind that a practitioner could not hope to learn the application of the method from its theory. Group analysis makes great demands on its practitioners for whom training and, especially, reliable supervision are absolutely essential. Those interested in its use would gain most by either joining a small group as a member or by enrolling on one of the group-analytic courses that provides an experiential group as part of the training.

Therapeutic Method

Moving up now to the level at which analysis is tolerable, the conductor's first aim is to facilitate members' participation which, as discussed above, often takes the form of serial monologue. Out of this monologue arise the capacities to talk and to listen – capacities which are often undeveloped or even non-existent at the outset of therapy (Pines, Hearst and Behr 1982). From talking and listening comes self-disclosure and from self-disclosure identification which in due course leads to dialogue. So the conductor must give place to monologue whilst, at the same time, cultivating dialogue – the exchange between members or sub-groups – and, ultimately, promoting discourse. In order to do any of this he needs an understanding of the group's dynamics in terms of its structure, process and content (de Maré 1972).

(1) Structure

The notion of structure describes the more enduring aspects of any group's makeup, the 'architecture' of its interpersonal relations, conceptualized first in terms of the setting and its boundaries as described above; and then conceptualized in the triangular bond between each individual, the conductor and the group as a whole. If we imagine a group of eight individuals and consider the bond between each individual, the conductor and the group as a whole, we can see why the breadth and complexity of this network is referred to as a matrix. Each of its members experiences a relationship between themselves and all the other members in a complex *relational field* that will undergo change in terms of alliances, sub-groups and polarizations. Whatever its size or variability, attention to structure will provide a secure and reliable bounded space between the group's principal psychological 'objects' – that is, each individual member, the conductor and the group as a whole.

(2) Process

The notion of process describes the fluid and dynamic fluctuations of emotion and experience based on the key concept of resonance, the unconscious communication of emotion. The group provides its members with a wide field of meaning – a *semantic field* – which is explored as they mirror one another's experience, find their emotions amplified by association with one another and find condensed, in sometimes highly aroused, cathartic experiences, moments charged with meaning and significance.

(3) Content

The group matrix is the 'operational basis of all relationships and communications' (Foulkes 1964, p.118). The matrix has a relational field that is understood through its structural elements, and a semantic field that is understood through its process. These different ways of understanding the matrix are not conflicting but complementary, just as the physics of light supports both wave and the particle theories.

The matrix is analyzed at four different levels, each of which arises through the interplay of its semantic and relational fields. These are: the current or social level; the transference level; the projective level and the primordial or archaic level. The manifest content of a group's life takes place at the current or social level in the course of free-floating discussion which produces an area of mutual exchange and understanding – what Foulkes calls the common zone (1964, p.112) – in which people first come to understand each other. It is dominated by accounts of members' problems, reflections, recollections and feelings, located in the past, the present (in the group) and the outside world. Analysis of this current level – in which everyone participates – sees the emergence of deeper latent content at the second, transference level in which people in the group come to stand for or represent the internalized 'whole objects' of one another's childhoods – their mothers, fathers, siblings and others. The pathology of family failure which is so ubiquitous in a borderline or forensic population emerges as the latent or unconscious content of the group's life. And then, as the group's experience deepens, the transference level is in turn analyzed and beneath it is found a third level comprised of 'part-objects', the more regressed elements which members hold, carry, project or reflect as parts of their own and one another's earliest experience – their rage, need, dependency, sexuality or malice. And finally, at the fourth, primordial level there are the archetypes of primitive experience, the objects and emotions of primary process in dreams, psychotic experience or primitive enactments (Schlapobersky 1993).

Vignette

A man had been in a therapy group for some three years. When he began his marriage had just broken up after he discovered his wife's infidelity. At the time he was sometimes hypomanic and often frightened of his rage. He was now coming to terms with this history, making peace with his ex-wife, doing a good job raising their children who still lived with her and putting his business on its feet. He would often bring the group a clear picture of this emerging sense of resolution, but none was clearer than this dream. He recounted it as he came in one day. He was at sea and there was no way to stay afloat. Eventually he sank to the bottom where a terrifying monster was waiting to attack him. He turned and ran 'til he could go no further. The monster was still pursuing him so he turned to face it and taught it how to sing.

Here, the primordial level provides imagery that records a benevolent transformation. Its redeeming quality needs no interpretation. It arises directly from the fourth level but the work of transformation engaged the group at each level of its experience over a lengthy period of time in which the assurance of its setting and the reliability of its conductor played a crucial part.

THE MATRIX OF SHARED EXPERIENCE

The Language of the Group

Therapists new to the group-analytic method are sometimes at a loss as to how the opening moments of a group should be conducted, particularly if it is composed of a homogeneous population that has known extreme experience of any kind. But the convening frame itself can provide an illuminating point of departure. The group's members may have lost all they hold most precious – their self-respect, their liberty, the lives of their loved ones – but what is still present and available amongst them in the room is the capacity to be of use to others just like themselves. The therapist's language, used in this way, can provide a statement of confidence at the beginning of what may prove to be a long journey. Thereafter, everything that happens in the group, and everything within its purview, is considered a kind of language, a communicative system made up of signs and symbols which will in many cases need decoding. The quest for meaning will discover 'speech in their dumbness, (and) language in their very gesture' (*The Winter's Tale*, V.2.13).

Free-floating discussion proceeds through an interplay between narrative and drama, story and exchange, reconstruction and encounter. As already described, all verbal activity takes the form of monologue, dialogue or discourse. Each of these speech forms will be expressed either as narrative, in which a story is recounted, or as drama in an immediate encounter or event. Cox and Theilgaard describe how:

> 'Repression enables us to forget…so that our memory fails and so does narrative continuity…repressive forces which cause narrative failure, to the extent that a patient is unable to tell that part of his story of which he needs to speak, *can be faced and transformed within therapeutic space*.' (Cox and Theilgaard 1994, pp.24–5)

In their account transformation comes from the prompter who intervenes 'when narrative flow is at the brink of failure' (Cox and Theilgaard 1993, p.8). This is how they describe the key role of the therapist. In group analysis prompting is the prerogative of the group as a whole in which we find 'reciprocal prompters' who might take up an issue in its dramatic form – as it arises in the here and now of the group – and turn it into a narrative reconstruction. This in turn can give rise to other associations that might in due course bring the experience back to something immediate and dramatic in the room. The language of a group, however, is much more complex and varied than the words of its members. It will encompass gesture, behaviour, body-language and other non-verbal communication, and actions that convey feelings when emotions have no words. Here is an example:

Vignette

Christine and Steve are both in their early thirties, the two borderline members of a long-standing group. Their social backgrounds and presenting problems differ but they have related personality problems. She has a boyfriend but, whilst they enjoy trust and affection, she allows virtually no sexual contact and suffers from a disorder of desire. Steve's only sexual experience was a mechanical affair with another man some years ago. He has worked in the group to free himself from long-standing cocaine and alcohol addiction but, despite this progress, hard won over the years, members of the group know nothing about his sexuality or orientation. Christine and Steve often serve each other as reciprocal prompters, drawing each other into more open participation in the group, pulling the enquiry back to early memories of tormenting fathers, and even populating one another's dreams.

One evening Steve had been active during a confrontation with another woman. Christine, too, had played an unusually active part. In the closing minutes of the session she declined the invitation to share a dream – it was something she had referred to but not yet recounted. She was pleased to be saved by the bell. People recognized the contrast between her availability to others and her own defensive secrecy. She entered others' experience, but allowed no-one to enter hers. The therapist took up this language and linked it to her relationship with the boyfriend outside the group. In the group she would not let people in, psychologically, just as at home she would not let her boyfriend in sexually. She found the connection helpful and, with others' assistance struggled to find words common to both areas that would explain how she felt. 'Intrusion; invasion; no room…' Steve interrupted to change the subject and conclude some unfinished business with the woman he had been talking to earlier. The group rounded on him over this and for the first time Christine was distressed at being interrupted. She cried and accused him of selfishness. The therapist suggested that Steve's interruption was a protective act to save Christine from an examination of her own sexuality, which he – Steve – could not tolerate because his own sexuality was still such a secret. Like Christine, he entered others' experience in the group but allowed no-one to enter his.

Steve's interruption represented narrative failure. He broke the thread of a meaningful enquiry and used the act of prompting defensively to protect a collusive alliance. Christine's experience was reversed as she found the therapist helpful and her customary ally destructive. The work of the group illustrates the concepts of *location, translation and interpretation*, each of which has precise clinical significance in group analysis (Foulkes and Anthony 1965). A core conflict – Christine and Steve's borderline defences – is *located* in the group, *translated* from the obscure language of defensive behaviour into a form understandable to all and finally an *interpretation* is constructed drawing on group process that sheds new light on the problem as it arises in the world outside.

There is a correspondence between the form taken by defensive behaviour in the group, the character defence in the individual's personality structure and its manifestation as a sexual problem in their relationships. The defence, the pathology it gives rise to in the outside world and the behaviour it is responsible for in the group are all regarded as analogues of one another. They are isomorphic and consequently change at any level will produce change at every other level. If, at the current or social level of the group, Christine can let people in, the likelihood is that she will find it easier to let her boyfriend in. An exploration of the transference level in the group will help her understand why, until now, she needed to keep people out and this will resolve at least some of her pain about sexual and emotional abuse in her family of origin. An exploration of the projective level will help her understand and resolve the splitting and fragmentation that separate affection from sexuality. And at the primordial level we have a dream – shared with the group – in which she is crushed by an enormous wave at the sea's edge as she asks it whether she can share something beautiful with someone she loves. The many sessions spent exploring the meaning of the dream have provided her – and the other members of the group – with an understanding of the archaic fears that sex might overwhelm love-ties felt to be fragile.

Forensic Applications: Constructive, Deconstructive and Reconstructive Experience

'Offending' or 'offence-related behaviour' is analyzed by its significance in the interpersonal domain. The offence is construed as a a person's attack on, or a perverse affirmation of, their links with others. Our understanding of schizoid and psychopathic personalities provide polarities at opposite extremes of the spectrum of psychopathology, between which the small group does its work. Psychopathic offenders – a group of sexual offenders for example, who rationalize that their victims enjoyed the experience – inhabit a social world of one in which others are not understood to have selves like their own. The group helps to extend subjectivity from the privacy of the self to encompass the lived realities of others. At the other pole, in the case of a borderline offender with a schizoid personality, for example, whose disavowed anger emerges in violent episodes which are then dissociated, periods of quiescence are a disembodiment of the self. The offender might attend the group regularly, but with no access to the emotions of the person who committed the offence. The group can help to locate their violent impulses, uncouple the impulse from the action and thus give access to real emotions which, once contained and expressed in reflective language, can be owned, understood and resolved. The schizoid has no real links with others; the psychopath has no others with whom to have links. In the interchange of a group the self emerges as a social object; and social objects – other people – are recognized as other selves for the first time. In a group, the self, the person, becomes an object in the social world of others and, in the course of interacting with these others, the individual becomes – for the first time – a continuous object to and for themselves. People can begin to recognize the sound of their own voices, uncover the continuing threat of their own aggression and discover the truth about their own inner injuries and needs.

CONCLUSION

Forensic Applications: From the Speech of Hands to the Language of Words

> 'Speak hands for me!' (*Julius Caesar* III.1.78)

In this quotation from *Julius Caesar* we hear Casca's rage as he leads the assassins in the first strike. The hands that speak tell a story of political intrigue and republican outrage in ancient Rome. The story is followed in all political use of terror. In the case of offender patients with borderline personalities, the dreams that erupt as actions tell stories about different orders of experience. It is primary process rather than political rage that erupts in primitive enactment. As Foulkes (1990) puts it, 'The neurotic acts in his dreams whilst the criminal dreams in his actions' (p.20). The aim of the therapist is to help patients find words that speak rather than hands, so that the dream-like quality of primary process, and the impulses or compulsions through which it has been expressed, can be uncoupled from action and explored in the relative safety of reflective language in a process sometimes referred to as negative elaboration. The elaboration of negative emotions including hostility, anger, despair, loss and envy becomes a major part of the group's work as it provides 'psychic space for perspective, negotiation, recognition, acceptance and verbalization of hurt and anger… Feeling and sharing the past and the present makes it accessible…(as) Internalized, persecutory, vengeful monologues are brought into dialogue.' (Pines 1992, pp.152–153). Cox writes that:

> 'During the early stages of his life in the group the offender patient may hide beneath the label of formal mental illness… Progressive disclosure of hitherto ego-alien material is facilitated… During the affective flow and sequential progression towards deeper disclosure…[we see the] Development of retrospective responsibility [which] is intimately linked with the development of insight and the capacity to sustain emotional disclosure [which] frequently runs parallel to the gradual demisting of focal amnesia for the traumatic episode…' (Cox 1978b, p.272)

Writing about the language of words, Cox and Theilgaard describe how:

> 'Forensic patients, when attempting to relive their offences and to to pluck their rooted sorrows from the memory, use phrases whose poetic purchase on the memory is as embedded as their psychic pain was, until released in language. For example, a patient whose victim's head had been crushed by an immense boulder, said:

> > "His face was squashed like an apple…and terribly disfigured"

> …forensic group psychotherapy often has the task of enabling patients to come to terms with the sequelae and aftermath of assaults involving massive mutilation. But what tends to hold the group's attention is the "terrible disfigurement" rather than "being squashed like an apple"…

> …in the presence of such a phrase and such feelings, the paedophile cannot retreat, neither can the arsonist nor the poisoner. All have caused disfigurement of one sort or another. All are kept in the active current of the group matrix, facing their personal homologue of the crushed face that was "squashed like an apple". Yet their painful confrontation with self becomes confluent as their life-streams converge under the bridge of "terrible disfigurement".

> Their lingering distraction persists until psychological work is complete, and they have come to terms with all that happened between the first motion and the acting of a dreadful thing.' (Cox and Theilgaard 1994, pp.357–8)

Acknowledgements

I should like to acknowledge the assistance received in the preparation of this chapter from Murray Cox, co-editor of these volumes; and from David Kennard, Chairman of the Group Work Co-ordinating Committee, Rampton Hospital. I should also like to acknowledge the access allowed me to the theoretical papers of two graduates on the Qualifying Course of the Institute of Group Analysis. They are Peter Mark, Student Unit Supervisor, Inner London Probation Service and Dennis Murphy, Consultant Forensic Psychiatrist, St. Thomas' Hospital.

A Psychodramatic Perspective

Jinnie Jefferies

Psychodrama was conceived by J. L. Moreno whose interest in philosophy and theatre led to the development of a method of group psychotherapy that used theatrical format to incorporate his existential beliefs.

As a therapeutic method it employs action methods to encourage the expression of repressed emotions and to introduce the possibility of change by correcting the maladaptive learning that has taken place. It helps the offender patient, within the context of the group, to find new ways of perceiving and reacting to past and present life experiences and to understand how he has projected negative feelings and transferred his inner world onto other persons and situations.

Vignette

Alan, by his own admission, raped a woman rather than deal with his feelings towards his mother, his childhood and his own inadequacies. Faced with his victim in a psychodrama session he told her, 'I hate myself for what I have done to you. The only person I wanted to hurt was my Mum. God knows what was going through my head that night because I don't.'

A classical psychodrama consists of three stages: the warm up, the enactment and the sharing.

THE WARM UP

This increases a sense of trust and group membership through techniques that encourage interactions between the group members. It stimulates the creativity and spontaneity of group members and helps them to focus on personal issues. The offender patient whose work will be the focus of the enactment is selected by other group members who feel sympathetic to the issue presented. In this way he works for the group, carrying the group concern, as well as for himself.

THE ENACTMENT

In the enactment stage the offender patient, with the support of group members and the therapist, explores the issues heightened by the warm up process. In psychodrama there is no script; the drama is spontaneous, created in the moment by the protagonist, group members and the director (therapist). Because psychodrama is intrinsically an action method the protagonist is encouraged to move quickly into the drama, creating the space in which events took place and an experience of re-experiencing rather than re-telling. The physical setting of scenes and their portrayal evokes memories and emotions associated with the space and counters the distortions and evasive manoeuvres that may be introduced by verbal disclosure (Meloy 1988, p.310).

The characters the offender patient places on the psychodrama stage are part of his internal world. The choice of certain group members to play these parts, 'auxiliary egos', is determined by complex factors which Moreno defines as 'tele' (the two-way flow between people). I suggest they are also determined by transference reactions towards other group members. Playing the role of an 'auxilary ego' can in itself be therapeutic, often providing the offender patient with an opportunity to develop roles not hitherto experienced or to discover aspects of himself that he has chosen to deny. The process also helps the offender patient to develop some understanding and empathy for another's position: 'Playing the role of George's Mum made me think of how it must have been like for my Mum', is not an uncommon comment.

Central to the understanding of psychodrama as a method of treatment is the theory of 'role'. Moreno defined role as:

> 'the functioning form the individual assumes in the specific moment he reacts to a specific situation in which other persons or objects are involved. The form is created by past experiences and the cultural patterns of society in which he lives... Every role is a fusion of private and collective elements.' (Moreno 1962 in Fox 1987, p.62)

Whereas the concept of role is usually employed to describe complexes of behaviour limited to a social dimension, psychodramatic role theory carries the concept through all dimensions of life beginning at birth and continuing through the lifetime of the individual. The total of all roles in which a person interacts is his role repetoire, and it is from this complex that the personality develops. Like other role theorists Moreno believed that the self arises out of social interactions with others. Application of psychodrama role theory requires two sets of skills, identification and intervention.

Vignette

Roy presented two scenes in the early part of his psychodrama; in the visiting room where his girlfriend boasted of her sexual exploits with other men and the scene of his offence where the prostitute he had murdered had laughed at his inability to have an erection. The context for him was the same, a situation in which a woman had left him feeling humiliated, and defenceless. His behavioural response was one of anger.

Roy was helped to see how the present situation and his offence held memory traces of past experiences, how his actions were influenced by distorted belief systems and negative feelings associated with these early experiences. Roy's mother had both humiliated and hurt him emotionally as a small child, and he grew up believing that he could not trust women, that they were out to repeat his earlier experiences with mother. They consequently became the object of his angry feelings.

If one is to intervene in the process whereby offender patients redirect their repressed feelings onto others who trigger them again by their attitudes or actions then these emotions need an arena for expression. The psychodrama stage provides just that by creating the 'as if' principle (Vaihinger 1924). George, the offender patient, holds the role of 'rejecting father', for the protagonist; Anna, the probation officer, the role of 'humiliating mother'; as such the action transcends the limitations of reality, allowing repressed emotions to be accessed and expressed. The affectionless character who has learnt to cut off from his emotions is helped through the psychodrama process to contact them again and the psychopath is encouraged to express his feelings verbally rather than move into physical action.

It is as important for the offender patient to understand his own actions and motivation as to understand those of others. Roy needed to differentiate between anger at mother from present anger at self for maintaining patterns developed in the past and transferred onto his victim. 'Self criticism of one's own actions can only follow if these actions are accessible or reportable' (Sarbin 1954, p.236).

Finally, Roy was given an opportunity to explore new ways of dealing with the situation with his girlfriend by bringing together both the affective and cognitive elements of the enactment sequence in order to integrate the work that had taken place.

THE SHARING

In the final stage of the psychodrama process, protagonist and group members come together to share the ways in which they identify with the protagonist's psychodrama. It is not a time for interpretation or comment about what has taken place, for the protagonist will need time fully to internalize and integrate the process. The sharing stage allows the protagonist to feel once again integrated with the group and allows other offender patients to share their own powerful feelings and thoughts, which will have emerged from either participating in the psychodrama or observing the action. Sharing also serves the purpose of focusing on future psychodramatic work.

ROLE REVERSAL AND DOUBLING

Much has been written about the inability of the psychopath to take another's perspective, his lack of empathy (Gough 1948). The psychodramatic techniques of 'role reversal' and 'doubling' develops the ability to see a situation from the other's perspective.

Vignette

John had wanted to take revenge on his own father, whom he described as cold and unapproachable, with little time and energy for him. Having berated him in his psychodrama for all that he had not given, John was asked to reverse roles with his father (a technique requiring the protagonist to experience the interaction from the other pole) whilst another offender patient held John's role. In the role of father, John achieved for himself a clearer understanding of his father's position, struggling for explanations and feelings of which he had hitherto, as son, had little or no awareness. Following this session John told his father of his work in psychodrama and what he had discovered from reversing roles with him. John's willingness to look at the relationship from his father's position opened up an interchange between them that had not previously existed. His father began to talk about his feelings of inadequacy and resentment in his marriage and his job. It also enabled John to share with his father his own angry feelings of past events that had been displaced onto his innocent victim. The technique is frequently used to increase the offender patient's awareness of the consequences of his criminal actions on his victim.

The 'double' expresses thoughts and feelings that the protagonist is repressing or censoring in the psychodrama. These thoughts may be accepted by the protagonist or rejected as incorrect. The process develops an empathetic bond between protagonist and double.

ROLE RECIPROCITY

The offender patient often presents himself as a helpless victim of past experiences and present relationships. He waits for things to change and of course they do not. His way of releasing the frustration and tension of feeling so powerless is to find another kind of power through his antisocial behaviour. The concept of role reciprocity which occupies a key position in psychodrama theory and practice firmly embeds the notion of roles in the arena of interpersonal relations and neatly distributes responsibility for the existence of the interaction. By remaining the passive victim of what he perceived to be true, staying with the relationship in his head rather than confronting the relationship in reality, John had to take part responsibility for the barren years that existed between himself and his father.

If both parties of an interaction bear some responsibility for its maintenance, it follows that both also have some power to halt or alter it. Taking an active part in dealing with his internal and external relationships can be both freeing and empowering for the offender patient.

Vignette

Alan in his psychodrama dealt with his internalized mother–son relationship in which he had previously seen himself as the 'helpless victim' and her as the 'aggressive abuser'. Within the session he was encouraged to express his negative feelings and to find some understanding of her actions. It was a moving moment when he knelt at her psychodramatic grave, placing a flower on the imaginary gravestone, stating 'I love and forgive you'.

In psychodrama, altering the perceptions and challenging the belief component of role is all important. A new way of construing the problem brings its own solutions.

WORK WITH POTENTIALLY VIOLENT PATIENTS

Kernberg (1992) emphasizes the dangerous violence inherent in paronoid attitudes of some offender patients which makes it difficult to work within the ordinary psychotherapeutic approaches. These approaches rely on the therapeutic relationship to represent symbolically the client's internal world – a world full of destructive feelings that places the therapist at considerable risk.

Psychodrama is also concerned with the client's symbolic representation of his external and internal reality but the representation takes a different route through the enactment itself, relying on 'auxiliaries' and 'scene setting' to represent time and place. 'Psychodrama lays out fantasy in three dimensions, and relieves the therapist of the task of becoming everything to the protagonist'

(Williams 1989, p.159). In psychodrama, the re-living of past events is re-enacted on the psychodrama stage. The therapist's interpretations are expressed through the psychodramatic interventions themselves.

The therapist in psychodrama intentionally adopts a more active approach and, when transference reactions do occur, attempts to resolve rather than interpret them.

Vignette

Dave was referred to the psychodrama programme for his violent paranoid behaviour. His mother had suffered from severe schizophrenia and had played with his emotions unmercifully. I was for him his manipulating untrustworthy mother who, in the midst of his emotional vulnerability, would cast my blow. Choosing not to work with Dave's transference reactions, we agreed that he would ask for clarification or share with me and the group when he perceived my actions to be manipulative or potentially harmful. In this way I became a little less like his mother and he less like the helpless son.

Eventually, we explored his relationship with his mother, how the acted out role of mother (held by an 'auxiliary' and not by me) was not only based in history but was part of Dave's reality. The aim was, as in all therapy, to get Dave to reincorporate those aspects he had projected onto mother and others and to see that not only was he vulnerable and helpless, as was his mother in her illness, but also manipulative and potentially harmful. The content of his psychodrama work was full of emotional intensity. In order to create a safe enough environment for all (including myself) it was crucial that I did not encourage transference reactions and resolved those that did exist before we began so that I could work alongside him, as director and facilitator rather than someone who was perceived as out to play 'mind games'.

There is a frequent anxiety amongst offender patients as to whether the group, the protagonist and 'auxiliaries' can survive the emotions that need to be expressed.

Vignette

No one wanted to volunteer to play the role of Jim's violent and abusive uncle, fearful of his own safety in the face of Jim's negative feelings. When Jim came to the psychodrama session stating his need to work, it was obvious that the protagonist and the group were in different places. It took several weeks before there was enough group cohesiveness, trust in the method and myself to consider how his work could be undertaken.

Eventually Jim was provided with a laundry bag of dirty underclothes and an old cupboard which symbolically represented the coffin of his uncle, in reality now dead, but internally very much alive. The auxiliary who had been playing uncle was asked to step aside and Jim was directed to focus his aggressive feelings onto the cupboard.

The psychodramatist relies heavily on psychodramatic techniques to control the action. Should a offender patient be experiencing intense and perhaps violent feelings towards the 'auxiliary' who is playing the role of a significant other, he is asked to reverse roles. Role reversal defuses the intensity of the feelings. Mattresses are used to wrap up and protect 'auxiliaries' from the expression of repressed, hostile feelings; 'batokas' are used instead of fists and the rule that no one is allowed to be hurt in psychodrama is strictly adhered to. When the aggressive feelings seem too much for the protagonist to deal with himself, 'doubles' act as advocates, or the aggressive feelings may be sculpted and explored in a less emotionally provocative manner.

CONCLUSION

More often than not angry outburst are followed by tears. Aggression for many offender patients has been the only form of survival and meaning. To go beyond the despair over what they have done to others to their own personal despair is a journey to be taken cautiously. It is essential to use one's professional judgement as to how much, and at what moment to go further. Not to do so puts all at risk.

Like other psychotherapies, psychodrama (through dramatic representation of self, one's behaviour, beliefs and feelings) is based on the knowledge that a person has the ability to be self-correcting when given accurate information about his behaviour. This is no less so for the offender patient than it is for any human being

PART II
Mainly Practice

Introduction

Murray Cox

When discussing psychodynamics and the offender patient under the rubric of forensic psychotherapy, it is rarely necessary to refer to specific aspects of mental health legislation or the criminal justice system, although apart from those broad distinctions as to whether the patient is an ambulant 'out-patient' – either on a voluntary basis or on probation – the subject of legal detention in a secure setting (Special Hospital or RSU) or serving a custodial prison sentence need to be drawn. This is in marked contrast to the literature dealing with Forensic Psychiatry, where various national provisions of the law impinge upon the legal 'disposal' of the patient. It is then clearly necessary to consider local constraints and freedoms relevant to statutory requirements.

Forensic psychotherapy, closely linked as it inevitably is to the wider professional field of forensic psychiatry, is concerned with dynamic issues at a different level and of another *genre*. Inner world phenomena, unconscious motivation, object relationships and other intrapsychic and interpersonal dynamic processes constitute the fabric woven, unwoven and rewoven within therapeutic space. The progressive re-patterning of relationship possibilities within the therapeutic process is catalysed by analysis, synthesis and integration. All this takes place within the ambient circumstances of a geographical location, and is influenced by the emotional and ethical climates which, for better or worse, impinge upon the therapeutic undertakings.

It is the wide range of applications of such dynamic systems that demands the extended consideration undertaken in Volume II, which is devoted to 'Mainly Practice'. And the 'practice' in question covers a huge terrain.

A brief survey of the individual chapter headings in this second volume leads to a kaleidoscopic impression of numerous detailed issues – each calling for expanded consideration – yet all firmly enclosed within the secure perimeter of 'Practice'. It is impossible to say that one topic is more important than another and to give a brief run through of the themes to be discussed is to usurp the function of a contents page.

Perhaps a more distanced overview would be provided by considering the titles of the ensuing sections. These are: Forensic Psychotherapy and its Neighbours, Central Issues, Training and Supervision – The Interface with Forensic Psychiatry, Special Challenges, Special Settings, Research and The Creative Arts Therapies. Even so, we could scarcely fare better than by looking at the chapter titles themselves. There seems to be a 'Clapham Junction'[1] of ideas and practice where so many lines of thought and action converge, communicate and diverge, *en route* to distant destinations. We find ourselves back at the ground-base, mentioned in the preface, where the essential reciprocal relationship between inner and outer phenomena, and contents and context, was emphasized. The sheer inter-relatedness of the material illustrates the amalgam of such a diversity of disciplines. One could take any couple of chapters at random (how about 4 and 14, or 11 and 29?) and discover how close is the link and how well woven the conceptual fabric which they represent, because all approach the central focus of Forensic Psychotherapy in Practice from differing vantage points. Only a metaphor has the carrying capacity to bring together so wide a field. Only an image can convey such condensed substance without reductive diminishment.

When searching for an appropriate image, I found myself thinking about a group therapy session with psychotic patients in Broadmoor. It had taken place a week or two before Christmas when we were all informed and/or reminded that 'It will soon be Christmas in Broadmoor!' I wondered whether my informant thought that this Christmas experience could be confined within the hospital walls. '*Just* in Broadmoor?', I asked, and was assured that this was indeed the case. '…Yes – just in Broadmoor'. A few days later I was speaking about such things to a gathering in Trinity College, Cambridge. The then Master (Sir Andrew Huxley, President of the Royal Society) explained that the issue raised by the patient, as to whether a universal phenomenon, such as 'Christmas',[2] could also be circumscribed and localized, was precisely in step with one of the major current concerns of theoretical physics: namely, 'the relationship between that which is universal and that which is localized everywhere'. I was told that this was still an undecided issue and one which elicited considerable conceptual heat! Here, in microcosm, is one of the perennial fascinations of forensic psychotherapy. We constantly discover that the events in question disturb entrenched traditional explanatory frameworks: unconscious motivation is not necessarily enough, repressed infantile sexuality

---

1 Said to be the biggest railway junction in the world.
2 By strange synchronicity, on the very day when the final proof of this page arrived, I read an invitation to visit a psychiatric hospital in Bethlehem.

may not be relevant – but neither are organic factors or sociological constraints necessarily determinative. Precise and technically 'correct' psychoanalytic interpretations do not thereby drain the material of the possible relevance of other meanings. Conceptually, we are kept on our toes, so that 'Mainly Practice' is a daily visitor to its neighbour 'Mainly Theory'. Indeed, the last chapter reminds us of the necessity of ensuring that both staff and patients are kept on their toes. But this is centre stage in dance therapy, carrying both concrete and metaphorical veracity.

So it is that the disturbed patient continues to jolt the therapist's pseudo-safety of an unyielding 'fixed position'. The concrete and the symbolic are placed in a tension-arc of relevance. We find psychotic patients echoing, if not preceding – major theoretical and conceptual controversies which are not only linked to their own clinical predicament and the related therapeutic implications, but to wider issues of freedom and security, safety and danger, certainty and risk, precise location and ubiquity. To hear two arsonists discussing fire-setting mobilizes the therapist's discriminating attentiveness to such crucial matters as the relationship between psychopathology and prognosis, theory and practice:

> 'I knew someone who could move things with her eyes. She lit fires by just looking at them. ...It wasn't like that for me. I used matches and petrol. It isn't every day you kill someone. Just every now and then.'

The 'Christmas in Broadmoor' vignette, in which the disclosures of a psychotic offender patient are congruous with the considered reflections of the philosopher and scientist, is a capacious metaphor for conveying the rich tapestry of linked topics which we are now to encounter – in Mainly Practice. Theory and Practice, the general and the particular, are inextricable. Mainly Theory and Mainly Practice are interdependent.

It could never be 'Mainly Christmas' in Broadmoor or Christmas in 'Mainly Broadmoor'. It would be just as insular to write solely from an out-patient or an in-patient perspective. This second volume is, mainly, about the 'why', 'where', 'what', 'when', 'how' and 'with whom' of Practice. This is why we present an eclectic *ensemble* of contributions which delineate difference and span division.

Murality

Murality refers to the essence of a wall, the quality of 'wallness'. It is a concept which comes already laden with forensic implication. It carries both concrete and metaphorical relevance and may denote structural quality or dynamic defences. It obviously refers overtly to the secure perimeter surrounding a custodial institution, yet it is also adjectival to the boundaries of partition between cultures, disciplines, departments, units and individuals. It is intrinsic to the assessment of the intrapsychic defensive organization of each patient, because the establishment of effective defences often depends upon the measure of the containing capacity of the personality. Such a capacious metaphor invites consideration from several dimensions. These include duration – is it permanent or temporary? – permeability, resistance, elasticity, and friability. Within both the concrete and the metaphorical frame, it can be historic, mythic or fictive. Is it total or partial? It has not been mentioned in connection with the different range of forensic contexts because, without pursuing the analogy too far, it is actually built into the structure of virtually every forensic discussion. Murality as an 'over-arching' concept – in both senses – was clearly evident some years ago, when I used to conduct a group of probation officers whose clients were awaiting trial and might become 'lifers'. The sessions took place 'within' the wall of H M Prison Brixton; not outside the secure perimeter, nor inside it, but actually intra-murally, in an office *within the wall itself*. Boundary issues of every kind were always on the agenda. *Murality* was a fact of professional life.

It assumes great importance in inter-disciplinary deliberations between work in the forensic field and other disciplines, particularly when psychother- apy undertaken in conventional settings is not usually concerned with secure perimeters and therefore tends to regard murality as a dynamic intra-psychic and inter-personal concept. It is an interesting word which has to do with boundaries which separate man from man or enclose man with man, either individually or in groups. It is exemplified in its metaphorical mode in words spoken by King Lear which have extensive social and defensive implications:

> 'Plate sin with gold,
> And the strong lance of justice hurtless breaks;
> Arm it in rags, a pygmy's straw does pierce it.' (IV.6.163)

Forensic Psychotherapy
and its Neighbours

Expectations and Ethics

Adrian Grounds

EXPECTATIONS OF PSYCHOTHERAPY

Conventionally, psychotherapy is based on a voluntary agreement between therapist and patient. The patient's suitability for psychotherapy is assessed, arrangements for the proposed work are privately discussed and agreed between therapist and patient, and the treatment takes place in a confidential setting. The nature of the treatment, and the fact that it is being undertaken, may not be known to others with an interest in the patient's welfare, such as relatives, employers, friends and colleagues. Other clinicians may know that the work is taking place and may have initiated the referral, but details of what is emerging in the treatment will not be known to them. Agencies representing wider public interests, such as social services, the probation service and courts, are unlikely to have any knowledge or investment in the nature and outcome of the treatment. It is strictly a private matter.

The patient also has a high degree of autonomy and control in decisions about whether to embark upon, continue and terminate the treatment. Such issues would be negotiated privately between therapist and patient, confidentiality would be maintained, and the interests of external agencies are unlikely to enter this private space of decision making.

Care would also be taken in the assessment process to ensure that the patient was able to cope with the demands of the proposed psychotherapy without engaging in destructive or dangerous acting out; and the therapist needs to be confident that the setting and boundaries of the therapy sessions will be respected. Histories of seriously disturbed and criminal behaviour may be regarded as contra-indications to psychotherapy in many cases. Malan (1979), for example, cites what he describes as 'a fundamental law of psychotherapeutic forecasting', namely that, 'In intensive psychotherapy, a therapist always runs the risk of making a patient as disturbed as she (or he) has ever been in the past, or more so' (p.220), although he acknowledges that the principle is not true for all patients.

Most clinical work in forensic psychiatry takes place in a quite different context of expectations and relationships with other agencies. Forensic psychotherapy has to to deal with the tension between the conventional expectations of psychotherapy and the wider responsibilities of forensic psychiatry services.

EXPECTATIONS OF FORENSIC PSYCHIATRY

One of the key tasks of forensic psychiatric services in assessing and treating mentally disordered offenders is combining the interests of the welfare of the individual patient with public safety and protection. Assessments may be carried out at the request of third parties, such as courts and legal representatives, who should be provided with honest, objective opinions about diagnosis, prognosis and risk (in so far as the latter is a matter for clinical judgement). Assessments are carried out on the basis of the patient knowing the purposes of the assessment, and to whom it will be disclosed. Whilst, as a matter of principle, treatment should always be provided in the least restrictive alternative setting, considerations of risk and public safety will require some patients to be treated in secure conditions, ranging from low security hospital care for a brief period, to maximum security hospital conditions for long periods of time. In many cases treatment and supervision are also provided within a statutory framework that gives the State and Judicial bodies the powers to discharge from and recall to hospital, and to require regular reporting on patients under supervision.

An offender with mental disorder may be diverted to the care of psychiatric services at various stages of criminal proceedings; and orders for psychiatric treatment (e.g. in England and Wales the hospital order and the probation order with a condition of treatment), may be imposed as alternatives to normal custodial and non-custodial sentences. However, when psychiatric treatment is chosen as a social response to crime, the treatment decision by the court may carry with it expectations that the medical disposal is compatible with other public and criminal justice interests. Treatment may be expected to meet other utilitarian sentencing objectives, such as public protection and deterrence, as well as rehabilitation. The framework of care provided for the individual patient in forensic psychiatric services will take account of these concerns in the specific arrangements that are made for supervision, information sharing and the use of statutory powers, in each particular case. Those working in the services know that major failures of social protection – a patient escaping from a Special

Hospital, a sex offender on a psychiatric probation order committing a further offence, or a patient released from a secure hospital committing serious violence – are likely to lead to an understandable public outcry.

EXPECTATIONS OF FORENSIC PSYCHOTHERAPY

The context in which forensic psychotherapy takes place differs from that which applies to most conventional psychotherapy. The interests of the public and criminal justice agencies may be more prominent, and they have to be recognized and taken into account. The setting of forensic psychotherapy is thus more complex, and more likely to be characterized by competing interests, than psychotherapy with non-offenders. The expectations that apply to conventional psychotherapy and to forensic psychiatry are combined, and the framework of psychotherapeutic treatment with offenders needs to be carefully planned so as to ensure as far as is practicable that integrity of the therapeutic space is maintained, whilst also maintaining close links with other components of the patient's care and treatment, proper concerns for public safety, and a realistic appreciation of the risks, benefits and limits of the treatment.

Whether the psychotherapy is to be carried out with an individual or group in an outpatient clinic, open hospital or secure hospital setting, a variety of practical and ethical issues need to be considered. Some of the main issues are briefly summarized below.

Reporting and Treatment Roles

In the USA there is a stronger tradition than in the UK of separating assessment and treatment roles in forensic psychiatry. Indeed, Stone (1994) has recently argued that, whenever a forensic assessment turns into a therapeutic encounter, this should preclude the psychiatrist from giving testimony in legal proceedings. Separating the roles of preparing court reports and providing treatment may be particularly desirable in forensic psychotherapy, so that the therapist's role does not become confused, and the therapist can concentrate on the treatment relationship.

The separation of roles is applicable both to initial assessment, when reports are prepared for courts and treatment recommendations are made, and to subsequent reporting, for example, in England and Wales to the Home Office and to Mental Health Review Tribunals in the case of patients under restriction orders. However, the separation of roles does not negate the need for briefing and liaison between the psychotherapist and the reporting clinician, so as to ensure that there is a shared appraisal of the patient's needs, an agreement about the nature and objectives of treatment, prognosis and the overall management plan.

Relationships with Other Clinical Professionals

Psychotherapists treating offender patients will often need to work in close partnership with other clinical staff involved with the patient's care. The respective roles of those involved need to be defined and agreed. The psychotherapist may expect back-up and containment to be provided for the patient by clinical colleagues and, conversely, the clinical team may expect the psychotherapist to keep them appraised of the patient's progress, and to alert them to significant evidence of deterioration or risk that emerges in the psychotherapeutic work.

The psychotherapist can also play a useful role in ensuring that other staff have some psychodynamic understanding of the patient's difficulties and the ways in which the patient's psychopathology is represented in their behaviour and relationships with clinical team members. It is particularly important that there is recognition of any pathological patterns of relationship that re-enact earlier difficulties from the patient's past; and the danger of becoming drawn into repeating earlier destructive patterns of relationship needs to be guarded against.

Confidentiality and Information Sharing

At the outset of treatment there should be agreement between the therapist and clinicians, and a clear understanding on the part of the patient, about the nature and limits of confidentiality that will apply to the psychotherapy. Sharing of general information concerning the patient's progress is likely to be uncontentious, but the problem of disclosing information if significant risk to others emerges may cause greater difficulty. Sometimes the patient may undertake to convey important information of this kind themselves, or may consent to disclosure.

However, on occasions it may be necessary for the therapist to report concerns irrespective of the patient's wishes. The possibility of this, and the likely threshold for disclosure need to be discussed with and understood by the patient before treatment starts. Reporting of concern to clinical colleagues is likely to be necessary when it is considered that the patient might be at serious, acute risk to themselves, or may pose serious risk of harm to others. There is a particular obligation to report concerns if it is thought that children may be at risk from the patient.

Responsibility to Third Parties

In general, clinicians may be justified in breaching clinical confidentiality in exceptional circumstances when there is an overriding public interest; for example, if it is necessary to prevent a grave offence being committed (British Medical Association 1984; General Medical Council 1987; Royal College of

Psychiatrists 1985). In the UK there is not the same legal duty to warn third parties that was established in the USA in the case of *Tarasoff* (see Stone 1984; Appelbaum 1994). The *Tarasoff* case concerned a student at the University of California who in 1969, in the course of psychotherapy, led his therapist to become concerned that he might harm a young woman, Tatiana Tarasoff, who had rejected him. The university police were asked to detain the student pending arrangements for psychiatric commitment. The police accepted the student's assurances that he would not harm Tatiana Tarasoff and let him go. Two months later he killed her. Her parents sued, and in 1974 the California Supreme Court held that the therapist had a duty to warn identifiable potential victims. In 1976 in a further, definitive judgement on the case the duty to warn was replaced by a broader duty on therapists to take reasonable steps to protect potential victims when a patient presents a serious danger of violence to them. Other States subsequently adopted similar duties to protect third parties, although with considerable variation (Appelbaum 1994; Weiner and Wettstein 1993).

Although the legal duty enshrined in the *Tarasoff* case does not apply in the same way in the UK, it is nonetheless good practice when drawing up a treatment programme which includes psychotherapy for an offender, to consider in the light of the patient's history whether there are potential victims and contexts of risk for the future. If there are, there should be a policy about thresholds and procedures for warning and advising third parties, should this become necessary.

Appelbaum (1994) describes the widespread concern expressed by psychiatrists in the aftermath of the *Tarasoff* case that the duty to protect third parties would pose an insuperable barrier to therapeutic relationships and would deter patients from undertaking treatment. He notes, however, that these fears turned out to be exaggerated; warning third parties when necessary was already part of established good clinical practice, and the case probably did not have the effect of deterring patients from treatment that had been anticipated.

Coercion

As noted above, forensic psychotherapy tends to be practised in a context of close working partnerships with other clinical colleagues, and prominent awareness of the roles and expectations of criminal justice and other agencies. In some cases the treatment is carried out within a statutory framework of detention in hospital or supervision in the community. It needs to be recognized that this context may impose powerful pressures on patients to accept assessment and treatment, and to demonstrate progress. For example, for a defendant in court proceedings, treatment may be an alternative to a prison sentence, and for a patient detained in a maximum security hospital on an indeterminate restriction order, progress under treatment is a pathway towards release.

Evidence of work on their offending behaviour may influence recommendations for parole of longer term prisoners.

These pressures may make clinical assessment of motivation and psychological change difficult, and the pressures may also have a coercive effect on
offenders, influencing them towards reluctant or ambivalent acceptance of
treatment. Clinical professionals and others can add to this when they emphasize that treatment is necessary if the offender is to be helped to achieve their
ultimate goals; for example, liberty, return to their families and children, and
resuming their occupations. In conventional psychotherapy, the patient's circumstances need not be adversely affected if treatment is refused, but in the
context of forensic psychotherapy there may be damaging consequences for
the patient if treatment is not accepted, and the prospective patient has to weigh
up the possible risks of increased deprivation of liberty and other personal
losses that could result from treatment refusal. Some of the problems and
dilemmas patients experience in relation to psychotherapeutic treatment in
maximum security hospitals are well described by Dell and Robertson (1988).
To some degree, these tensions are unavoidable when treatment is carried out
in secure settings and under court orders, but efforts should be made to ensure
as far as possible before orders are made that the dilemmas are openly discussed,
genuine motivation is assessed and the patient and clinical team can agree on
and work towards shared therapeutic objectives.

The Nature of Treatment

The context of social and criminal justice expectations in which forensic
psychotherapy is conducted may introduce other subtle and important influences on how the nature of treatment is understood. Psychotherapeutic work
with offenders focuses on achieving psychological understanding of their
offences and offending behaviour. It has been noted elsewhere that there are
illuminating parallels between this therapeutic task – in which the patient is
seeking salvation from his or her past, and psychological understanding of the
complex relationships between therapist, offender and victim is sought – and
the central themes in Christian theological doctrines of salvation (Cox and
Grounds 1991). However, the point of practical importance is that psychological treatment of offenders may be seen by the public, social and criminal justice
agencies, and sometimes by clinicians, as having a moral purpose, and the
concept of treatment may be used to describe what is actually a moral
enterprise.

This characteristic of psychiatric treatment has long been recognized and
features prominently in the work of Foucault (1967), but it is particularly
significant in forensic work. Psychiatrists are used to employing a broader
notion of treatment than that which applies in other branches of medicine.
Treatment in psychiatry does not only embrace a narrow conception of

ameliorating symptoms and disabilities of specific medical illnesses, it also embraces psychotherapy, and for people with learning disability, social training and education. However, in forensic psychiatry and psychotherapy, where the focus is on criminal behaviour, the practical goals of treatment may be more concerned with the offender's attitudes and values. What is sought is awareness of the experience of victims, acceptance of responsibility for the offending behaviour, and responses of recognition and remorse instead of avoidance and denial of what has been done. These expectations tend to be especially prominent in the treatment of sexual offenders. Altered attitudes and responses to the offending are seen as manifestations of the intra-psychic change that is the target of psychotherapy.

Whilst such changes are clearly desirable and necessary, it has to be recognized that what is being described in the name of treatment is essentially a moral enterprise of inducing repentance (in the proper sense of the term), and it is work that lies outside the conventional boundaries of what we ordinarily mean by medical treatment. The use by clinicians of persuasion, influence and power over patients in advocating this work, needs to be tempered with professional humility and self-questioning. An awareness should be maintained of the potential abuses of professional power and of the clinical role that can occur when therapists move into this non medical territory of social and moral judgement.

Maintaining Therapeutic Relationships

As a matter of professional ethics, the maintenance of professional boundaries and a strictly therapeutic relationship between therapist and patient are essential. The guidance of the General Medical Council (1987) about the maintenance of professional relationships is as applicable to forensic psycho-therapy as other branches of clinical practice. Breaches of this principle resulting in sexual relationships between therapists and patients are more extensively discussed in North American than British psychiatric literature (see, for example, Hankins, Vera, Barnard and Helkov 1994; Pope and Bouhoutsos 1986; Stone 1984).

In the psychotherapeutic treatment of offender patients, powerful pressures on the therapeutic relationship can arise for psychodynamic reasons. Forensic patients are particularly likely to have suffered deprivation, cruelty and other forms of victimization in early life and they can induce powerful reparative motivation in others. Patients with borderline psychopathology who charac-teristically oscillate between extreme idealization and extreme denigration of therapists can pose immense demands on those treating them (Shapiro 1978). When the psychotherapist works in close partnership with other clinical colleagues, there is also the danger of splitting amongst those involved in the patient's care. The divisions that may develop between those who are made to feel they have privileged understanding of the patient's difficulties, and those who adopt a firmer, more detached approach, and thus become critical of their more sympathetic and indulgent colleagues, were well described in a classic paper by Main (1957). Psychotherapists and their colleagues need to maintain a shared, self-critical awareness of such phenomena in their difficult task.

CONCLUSION

The above provides only a brief selection of some key practical issues in relation to forensic psychotherapy. More comprehensive, general accounts of ethical issues in psychotherapy and forensic psychiatry are given by Gunn and Taylor (1993), Karasu (1981), Rappeport (1981), and Rosner and Weinstock (1990).

A Legal Perspective

Stephen Tumim

The title of this paper presents me with a problem. As a lawyer I might usefully discuss the special problems of the relationship between the law and the psychiatrically ill offender. Such problems would be likely to centre on matters to do with human rights under the law, personal responsibility and legal intervention and the legal minefield surrounding the issue of personal freedom and the enforced intervention of the medical profession upon those who are mentally ill.

Important as these issues are, they are not the centre of my attention. For although I am a lawyer and a judge, for the past seven years I have been HM Chief Inspector of Prisons for England and Wales, providing independent advice to the Home Secretary of the day on the state of prisons and, in particular, on the ways in which prisoners within them are treated. I am, therefore, a lawyer who sees offenders living out part of their lives in custody. Among these people are those who suffer from mental illness or abnormality, for whom some treatment programmes are offered within prison. The success of any programme for prisoners must depend upon the policies in force which govern the purposes of custody, and the strategic decisions which are in place to fulfil these purposes.

The prison system is divided into fifteen areas, each containing upwards of eight establishments. An Area Manager provides the link between each establishment and the Headquarters of the Prison Service Agency in London. The quality of regimes on offer in each establishment is largely dependent on the quality of the Governor in post, and the facilities on offer in the establishment. There is little continuity of regime between different establishments except, for example, when a prisoner is moved from closed to open conditions. So, if education or work opportunities at one place allow a prisoner to develop skills or qualifications, these may be jeopardized if a decision is made to move the prisoner to another establishment. Similarly with treatment programmes. Prisoners on specialist courses of therapy, such as Sex Offender Treatment Programmes, will on completion (and if other arrangements are not made for them), revert to the normal regimes for their category. Sentence Planning is an attempt to structure a prisoner's sentence so as to allow a progression, but such planning is largely limited to the options available within the prison to which he is sent.

There is one prison establishment in the system which is designed to offer psychotherapeutic support to the majority of prisoners in its care. Selection to Grendon Underwood prison is based on the willingness of the prisoner to participate in programmes of therapy, which largely comprise the regime of the prison. Selection to the main regime is undertaken in a preliminary assessment course. If successful, the prisoner moves on to specialist wings and engages in groupwork and other forms of related activity on a daily basis.

The legal basis of the custodial experience is satisfied if the prison service holds a prisoner securely in custody in conditions which are considered adequate by the courts. There are no statutory standards, but prisoners may, and have, sought judicial review or have appealed to the European Court of Human Rights, to gain judgements on the legality of the conditions in which they are held. Over and above any legal requirement the Prison Service Agency 'Statement of Purpose' (HMSO 1995) makes clear that there is more to custody than humane containment:

> 'Her Majesty's Prison Service serves the public by keeping in custody those committed by the courts.

> Our duty is to look after them with humanity and help them lead law-abiding and useful lives in custody and after release.'

This admirably concise statement makes clear that prisons have a useful role to play in dealing with offenders. I take it to mean that prison regimes have to be constructive, and directed where applicable to preparing the prisoner for release. I take it to mean that prison staff have to work with outside agencies in order to assist the passage of the prisoner from custody to community. However, if it is to work properly, it must also mean that the Prison Service organizes its business to allow for sustained and planned regimes for prisoners throughout their sentence.

Those in prison form not one, but several, distinct populations. There are prisoners on remand, short sentence prisoners, those serving long sentences, vulnerable prisoners, young prisoners and female prisoners. I wish to see a system which recognizes that each of these groups (my list is not exhaustive) requires a specialist regime. Normally the front line of work with the prisoner will be the prison officer. I see this person as being trained for the specific population before working with it, and I see specialist help, in the form of teachers, instructors and counsellors.

A prisoner entering Grendon Underwood is placed on an assessment course which is used to decide whether he should embark upon a therapeutic programme. If he is not successful on this course, he returns to an ordinary prison. If he fails while on therapy, he runs the risk of returning to an ordinary prison. At the end of his therapeutic course, if he is on a long sentence, he may also return to an ordinary prison. The same is true of prisons that run specialist education or work programmes. When they come to an end, the prisoner returns to normal prison life.

What is this 'normal' state? The prisoner might move to another prison with a dynamic regime, or not be so lucky. There are good prisons and bad. Too often, on my inspections, I come across establishments where the atmosphere is one of low standards bordering on idleness. In the system as it is presently structured, even the best prisons cannot provide the service of which they are capable. There has to be a systematic approach to regimes, which allows the system as a whole to give purpose to the contributions of each establishment.

The psychotherapist working with the offender patient in custody is operating within an environment which may well impede any progress that the therapy is designed to assist. Is the objective of such therapy to reconcile the offender to his circumstances, or something more? It seems to me that prison regimes should be about the development of constructive lifestyles both in custody and after it. If psychotherapy has a part to play in the custodial setting, then its practitioners will need to work with other professionals to establish the most appropriate regimes into which their specialized programmes might be fitted, and the most appropriate regimes which should follow.

Custody is a situation in which individuals lose much of the control over their lives. Therapeutic programmes are surely partly about helping patients to regain control over a life that is awry. If such programmes have a place in prison regimes, the working practices of those who provide them will have to involve inter-disciplinary work and the recognition that full control cannot immediately return to the prisoner. This places the practitioner in a difficult position. If the regime available to a prisoner who has undergone a treatment programme is limited and lacking direction, the programme may turn out to be damaging. A new sense of understanding, self-perception and purpose may be dashed by an indifferent system. I suggest that the purposes of custody must be identified by those who impose it, otherwise the duty of care implied by the Statement of Purpose referred to above may be jeopardized.

A Police Perspective

Barrie Irving

INTRODUCTION

Policing and psychodynamic theory and practice touch indirectly in a number of ways, although there is very little empirical evidence about police views on these subjects. These points of contact provide some indications of what those views might be.

The latest and most direct contact between forensic clinical practitioners and police has been promoted by the growing popularity of offender profiling among senior investigating officers. Clinical practice in the field of forensic psychology and psychiatry provides insights about criminal behaviour which can be of direct value in the conduct of police investigations. Clinical psychologists and psychiatrists are now collaborating with criminal investigation departments on offender profiling; trying to predict offender behaviour; linking unsolved crimes and advising on investigation tactics. This work is being evaluated for the police service by the Home Office and there is already some evaluative evidence from the United States (Pinizotto and Finkel 1990).

The rapid development of profiling in the UK, following precedents set by the US Federal Bureau of Investigation, has thrown up a number of methodological and ethical issues. These have been illustrated dramatically in the case of R v Stagg in which the police investigation, which involved an undercover police officer befriending the accused, was directed by a clinical psychologist. The evidence so obtained was not admitted in court, the police were censured and the accused was acquitted (Cohen 1994).

The application of psychodynamic theory can affect public order and its maintenance. While it is more common for psychotherapists to think in terms of the individual client's quality of life, clinical effort can have a wider social impact if the antisocial behaviour of individuals is contained, reduced or eliminated. In this context, it is useful to explore relations between the police and therapeutic institutions such as drug addiction treatment centres and mental hospitals. These institutions play a part in mitigating public manifestations of certain kinds of disordered and antisocial behaviour with which the police usually have to deal. Police attitudes towards these institutions help to define the probable status of psychodynamic theory and practice in the police culture.

The police themselves are consumers of psychotherapy. Police officers suffer the same emotional trauma and chronic stress as other occupational groups. Where stress, trauma or mental illness lead to deviant behaviour, officers may themselves need psychotherapy to enable them to continue their work. While the service has been slow to recognize this need, and even now would not necessarily see the counselling and psychotherapy that it makes available to officers as forensic in character, the clinical treatment of officers is an important point of contact between the service and the psychotherapy profession. Attitudes generated in this context are likely to affect police attitudes to psychotherapy more generally.

Finally, we can consider police attitudes to the causes of crime; job satisfaction depends in part on job-holders feeling a sense of purpose. Police officers working to convict offenders so that they are appropriately punished by the courts may be expected to develop ideas about what causes crime and what means therefore exist for controlling it. This may affect policing practice by altering the balance between law enforcement policing tactics and preventative, therapeutic and conciliation approaches.

This chapter will briefly review these four points of contact between policing and psychodynamic theory and its applications and attempt to draw some tentative conclusions about future development.

OFFENDER PROFILING: DEPLOYING CLINICAL INSIGHTS IN CRIMINAL INVESTIGATIONS

Offender profiling was 'formerly the stock-in-trade of whodunnit writers whose fictional detectives transformed crime scene facts into a portrait of the perpetrator' (Pinizotto and Finkel 1990). After a rapid rise in popularity over the last decade, the technique has recently aroused considerable controversy (Casey 1994).

We are concerned here with one branch of profiling. The technique has two groups of proponents, one empirical and statistical in its approach (Canter and Heritage 1989), the other psychodynamic, admitting the possibility of unconscious motivation. The debate about the relative merits of the two schools is not relevant in this context; what *is* relevant is the way in which the psychodynamic approach creates a link between that body of theory and practice and criminal investigation. The Home Office is currently reviewing police use of profiling and although the research is as yet unpublished, it has already identified the range of 'experts' operating in the field. The majority have a psychodynamic background.

The general approach of the clinician operating as a profiler can be characterized as follows: experience in both forensic psychotherapy and psychiatry, which provides the practitioner with a wealth of case history material. From this material the able clinician can draw inferences about the dynamics of given types of criminal behaviour – links may be established between characteristics of offenders and characteristics of their behaviour at the scenes of their crimes. Close contact with classes of offender in a clinical setting and opportunities for observation in prison or secure unit help establish patterns of thought and details of behavioural style. These kinds of data can lead to the establishment of hypothetical causal connections between types of criminal behaviour and types of criminal personality structure. It is a short step to applying the outputs of this process to new unsolved cases at the instigation of detectives.

Senior investigating officers have to establish lines of inquiry and define priorities. If suspects emerge, a strategy for handling them has to be evolved. In all of these endeavours speculation about the behaviour, personality and demographic characteristics of the offender plays a vital part. Detectives have always used their own experience in this speculative process; it is natural that they should seek to form working alliances with other professionals who have similar opportunities to study offenders and offences. The process of asking for and receiving interdisciplinary advice of this kind will build up mutual respect and awareness of each others' knowledge base.

However, these benefits are balanced by some inevitable costs. The causal links and psychodynamic descriptions which the clinician makes available to an investigation are prone to error (Kirby 1994). Both the clinician's original observations and the process of logical inference based on them may have been faulty. Or valid deductions from previous experience may be misapplied to a new case which, if all the evidence had been available, would have been recognized as belonging to a different class of case. In addition, because advice is being given across a disciplinary boundary, what the psychologist or psychiatrist says is not necessarily what the police officer hears. The police do not have the expertise to distinguish between a profiler's statements in terms of their reliability and validity. This places a heavy onus on the profiler to couch advice in very careful terms and insist on reviewing the way in which it is used.

If these potential costs are not recognized, a useful inter-professional alliance may be jeopardized. The current Home Office evaluation will, when published, do much to stabilize relations between the police and forensic psychologists and psychiatrists in this field.

POLICE RELATIONS WITH PSYCHOTHERAPEUTIC INSTITUTIONS

Psychotherapy clients may offend, some of them regularly or habitually, and this brings those who care for them or treat them into direct contact with the police.

Clinicians working for mental health institutions located close to police stations may have regular or institutionalized contact with the police in respect of the Police and Criminal Evidence Act and the protection of vulnerable prisoners. However, all mental health institutions have a proportion of patients/clients who will provoke police concern or action because of their behaviour, and this will lead to intermittent contact between police, psychiatrists and psychologists.

Police behaviour towards those with florid psychiatric conditions is generally appropriate; police officers usually make reasonable assessments of extreme psychiatric conditions but, not surprisingly, find it difficult to identify mental illness or learning disability in more ambiguous cases (Bean et al. 1991; Tully and Cahill 1984). A clinical assessment of suspects passing through a police station has confirmed a high incidence of cases exhibiting signs of mental illness and/or learning disability (Gudjonsson, Clare, Ruther and Pearse 1993; Gudjonsson 1994).

In coping with the revolving door phenomenon in which psychiatric patients become criminal suspects, only to be reclassified as psychiatric cases, police have been undersupplied with appropriate medical expertise. A review of the training and practice of forensic medical examiners (Police Surgeons) has shown that relevant psychiatric expertise is in short supply. The ethical position of Forensic Medical Examiners is also frequently ambiguous: they can appear to be treating prisoners when in fact they are present in police station as consultants to the police (Savage, Moon, Bradshaw and Twigg 1991; Savage, Kelly, Moon and Bradshaw 1993). It is a provision of the Police and Criminal Evidence Act that vulnerable suspects in police stations should have an 'appropriate adult' present to safeguard their interests. Bean and Nemitz (1994) have shown that this provision of the Act is hardly ever used in practice.

In the light of the dearth of professional psychiatric help available to police stations, it was suggested to the Royal Commission on Criminal Justice by the Royal College of Psychiatrists that community psychiatric nurses might usefully act as a resource to police stations by liaising with mental health professionals (MacKeith 1994, personal communication). In addition, the police service is now grappling with two reports on the mentally ill in the criminal justice system which call for better training and procedures (Etheridge 1994).

However, it is with reference to drug treatment centres that policing and clinical psychology and psychiatry are most liable to conflict. When clients are engaged in psychotherapy it is essential that clinicians and other staff maintain trust with them. Clients may be on maintenance doses or drug substitutes. They may well be still in contact with drug users and dealers. It follows that these clients are a potential source of criminal intelligence for the police and using them as such or creating the conditions in which individuals might turn informer puts trust relations with clinic staff at risk if they are suspected of providing the police with information. The effective running of such institutions therefore demands sympathetic action by the police at all levels. This has not always been forthcoming. The reasons are complex. On the police side, the sectional interests of detectives with the clear target of increasing detections for drug offences can override more sophisticated and broader objectives set for the force as a whole. However, therapeutic institutions are also capable of being abused and manipulated by their clients who can use them as a front, the better to continue both dealing and abusing. In practice, although many drug treatment centres and their local police may not be on the best of terms, it has been argued by a recent Home Office report that both need each other. The clinics cannot operate effectively unless the rule of law prevails, and the police cannot single-handedly deal with the problems of drug abuse through law enforcement. The difficulties of forming and maintaining inter-agency alliances in this area are described in detail with recommendations for reform in the forthcoming report of the Advisory Council on the Misuse of Drugs subcommittee on the Criminal Justice System (ACMD 1994).

Best policing practice as exemplified by developments in policing drug abuse in Southwark (Southwark Arrest Referral pilot project monitoring group 1991) emphasizes using arrest as a springboard for treatment. In this narrow area at least, police officers dealing with drug abuse have come to see themselves as intermediaries between the drug abuse/youth culture and treatment institutions. As treatment will necessarily involve teaching self control and coping mechanisms via a range of psychotherapeutic techniques, police are already involved in deploying forensic psychotherapy, although as yet they may not fully appreciate their role in the community mental health system.

A particular issue has arisen in the fields of marital violence and child abuse where police officers work closely with mental health professionals. Joint training for social workers and police officers has been effective in increasing empathy and understanding (Fletcher and Newland 1989), but this can cause role confusion: therapeutic and conciliation methods and procedures may conflict with the need to collect legally admissible testimony (Bannister and Print 1989).

POLICE STRESS AND THE COUNSELLING REVOLUTION

Until the early 1980s police officers who suffered emotional disturbances as a result of traumatic experience on duty were expected to cope, seek help from their GP or, in serious prolonged cases, seek a medical retirement. The idea that the police service should itself provide any specialist counselling or therapeutic help ran counter to traditional police culture (Cooper, Davidson and Robinson 1982; Gudjonsson and Adlam 1983). However, reacting to rising demand from the service, the Association of Chief Police Officers set up a working party on police stress and its alleviation in 1981 and this eventually gave rise to the formation of a central stress unit to advise on counselling and therapy services (Brown and Campbell 1994).

Following a number of obviously traumatic incidents, including the mis-taken shooting of Stephen Waldorf in 1983 and the Zeebrugge ferry and Hillsborough stadium disasters in 1987, post-traumatic stress counsellors and therapists offered a variety of services to police forces (Brown and Campbell 1994). Such services have quickly become an established part of the police response to disasters and traumatic incidents.

The original heavy accent on traumatic experience in the causation of occupational stress in police officers (Manolias and Hyatt-Williams 1986) is, however, somewhat misplaced. Alexander, Walker, Innes and Irving (1993) have shown that certain aspects of police personnel management are a more important source of police stress reaction than traumatic incidents. Indeed, the kind of incidents classified by clinicians as potentially traumatic (sudden death, risk of fatal injury, shooting, disasters) are often seen by police officers as positive aspects of their job which create professional excitement and pride rather than stress.

Alexander demonstrates that stressed officers tend to look to food, drink, smoking and defensive routines at home rather than professional help to cope with the kind of stresses induced by routine police work, but this inevitably reflects a traditional police cultural view which may well be changed by management reforms over the last ten years as well as the introduction of counselling and therapeutic services at force and divisional level (Eades 1987; Brown and Campbell 1994).

Provision of such services has thrown up important managerial and ethical problems associated with confidentiality. Should such counselling services be set up so that the contents of all sessions are unavailable to police management even if they provide evidence of criminal activity, negligence or misconduct (actual or potential) (Butler 1987)? In general, officers cannot be offered guarantees of complete confidentiality by counsellors working inside the police service. This necessarily reduces the value of such services for those who want to discuss particularly sensitive topics (Irving and Dunighan 1993; Wright, in press).

The Police and Criminal Evidence Act 1984 and the reform of rape investigation (Blair 1985) did much to raise police officers' awareness of psychodynamic and mental health issues. In the last twenty years there has been a dramatic increase in the number of officers studying psychology and related subjects at first degree level. Workload, public criticism of policing and increasing street violence have all conspired to make police managers more aware of stress levels and their symptoms – absenteeism and poor work performance. These conditions have generated a steady growth in police welfare services aimed at officers' mental health. We would expect this internal cultural change to be reflected in police attitudes to such services in society at large.

POLICE VIEWS ON THE CAUSES OF CRIME

Empirical study of police officers' attitudes to crime and punishment has not in general focused on causes of crime (Reiner 1992; Fielding and Fielding 1991). However, an enterprising and useful small-scale study in the Metropolitan Police District (Hunt 1994) provides some interesting insights.

In a concise review of crime causation theory, Hunt identifies the main strands in the biological, psychological, sociological and economic literature.

Relative support for these four classes of theory was assessed with a detailed attitude questionnaire. Factor analysis revealed that police attitudes do not conform to the most obvious divisions in the literature. Economic and biological causation factors did emerge as separate and distinct, but the hypothesized sociological and psychological factors split four ways. Sociological causation of crime is seen by police officers as dividing into a social relations paradigm and a self-esteem factor.

Three psychological causal paradigms are suggested by Hunt's analysis:

- the individual's level of helplessness induced either by socioeconomic or biological factors
- lack of ability to control mood and/or behaviour
- the effects of alcohol.

Although few significant differences by background variables were observed in support of these paradigms, younger officers were significantly less inclined to support biological theories of crime causation.

In general the study is useful in describing the extent to which officers support a psychodynamic view of the causes of crime. Psychological factors were supported on average by 43 per cent of the random sample of 420 officers, compared with 13 per cent support for biological factors. While 27 per cent supported economic causes, these economic variables are clearly mediated through the individual's inability to exercise self-control and the failure of pro-social learning (Staub 1978).

In so far as forensic psychodynamic understanding seems relevant to such issues as self-control, pro-social learning, assertiveness, empathy and acting out, it can be seen as addressing what most police officers in the sample saw as the causes of criminal behaviour. It should be emphasized that this sample was taken in a particularly crime-prone area of London where other studies would suggest police cynicism (Lester and Butler 1978) and authoritarianism (Coleman and Gorman 1982) might be at their most prevalent.

CONCLUSION

This chapter has reviewed four topics which indirectly throw light on police attitudes to the development of forensic psychodynamic theory and practice in the criminal justice system. We have seen that detectives have adopted a positive attitude to using the insights of clinical work with offenders. However, this field of experimentation has thrown up ethical and methodological issues which must be dealt with to safeguard ongoing collaboration between police and clinicians. It is expected that a forthcoming publication on Home Office evaluation of profiling will help in this direction.

With the police adopting increasingly sophisticated views of mental illness, handicap and drug abuse, attitudes to working with therapeutic institutions of all kinds and those specializing in drug abuse in particular are becoming steadily more sympathetic. The extent to which police and mental health practitioners are aware of some common purpose seems to be increasing. Important experiments in collaboration can now be identified.

Changing police attitudes to providing counselling and therapy services to officers stressed by their duties demonstrate that police management now values the contribution such services can make to police performance.

Finally, there is some direct evidence which supports the view that police officers conceive of the causation of crime in a way which endorses forensic psychodynamic insights.

A Probation Perspective

Deirdre Sutton-Smith

INTRODUCTION

As a probation officer, working in the Criminal Justice System, I meet offenders to help them identify and recover from the traumatizing experiences which are a legacy of an unsatisfactory 'facilitating environment' in infancy and child-hood. The court decides on the aggravating and mitigating circumstances which determine the seriousness of the offending and therefore the appropriate sentence. I assess whether defendants can, with or without assistance, complete a community-based sentence and control their antisocial behaviour.

Historically, the probation service has viewed the offender as carrying the disturbances and injustices of the wider community or culture in which he lives. His (or her) offending is a symptom of a disturbance which concerns a whole network of people. Foulkes (1964) assumed '...that the individual patient and even the nature of his disturbance is only a symptom of conflicts and tensions within his group' (p.291). People have always lived in groups and it is a central tenet of group-analytic theory that the problems of individuals should not be tackled in isolation but rather in relation to their social community.

In his introduction to *The Maturational Processes and the Facilitating Environment* Winnicott (1965) contends 'that the anti-social tendency is a reaction to deprivation, not a result of privation...' (p.10). For a child to experience deprivation in terms of the loss of a good-enough facilitating environment – which is the point of origin of the antisocial tendency – Winnicott argues that the child once had the experience of relationships with primary carers who adjusted appropriately to the essential differing needs of the child. Winnicott suggests that it is the failure of the home to continue to provide a good-enough holding and facilitating environment that has led to our clients' difficulties. The majority of probation service clients have suffered and are still experiencing deprivation, and they have little hope of improving their situation whilst they have not yet fully negotiated the normal maturational stages of development. Their antisocial behaviour is both a communication about their early deprivation, and a symptom of it, a symptom that can quickly become a compulsive and habitual way of behaving, with its own secondary gains, including a sense of belonging – albeit to a criminal sub-culture. It is often tempting to become embroiled in tackling the evidence of this deprivation at the expense of tackling the underlying reasons for the development of the antisocial tendency.

The courts and the parole board, together with the society that they represent, have the expectation that a period under statutory supervision in the community will reduce the risk that an individual will re-offend. The offender's impulse is to avoid getting in touch with his or her pain and despair by passing the problem on to another. The task of the probation officer is to make maximum use of his 'facilitating environment' in order to allow previously 'acted out' offending behaviour to be 'acted into' and contained within the relationship between offender and caseworker. It is my view that the probation officer's success or failure will depend on the use that he makes of the setting, that is, the Criminal Justice System as a whole, in which he works.

I see my primary task as providing a setting – in other words a facilitating environment – which adapts sufficiently to the differing needs of each individual in a way that holds that individual in a relationship. Within this relationship he can begin to identify the origins of the antisocial tendency and negotiate the missing developmental stages of maturation. To this end, I am assisted by the contract between the court and/or parole board and the offender; that is, the conditions of the order that authorizes my contact with each client of the agency. The client is held within the conditions of that order, and held in a relationship with me as caseworker. This relationship then becomes the container for much of the client's despair and hopelessness – often in the form of an aggressive verbal assault detailing my inadequacies or failure to 'help' and the threat of being held responsible for the offence that will inevitably follow. For example, I feel wretched saying 'No' to a barefooted client who demands money and claims that I am forcing him to steal if this is not forthcoming – and relieved when he is seen by a colleague outside the building reclaiming his shoes from a companion's bag. At other times the relationship contains the hope that family and community links can be sought and reality becomes less persecutory.

In 'Delinquency as a Sign of Hope', addressed to the Borstal Assistant Governors' Conference in 1967, Winnicott (1986, p.90) describes the antisocial act as an attempt by the offender to get back behind the moment of deprivation in the hope of finding the lost sense of containment and holding. By contrast Meyerson (1975), in his paper 'Adolescence and Delinquency' equates delinquency with 'failed hope' – the delinquent act providing an 'artificial emotional fix' to alleviate the intolerable feelings of hopelessness, inadequacy and despair (p.36). It is an attempt by the offender to make contact with another person in order to achieve a sense of belonging 'at any price' – even when this sense of belonging is gained through a 'secret' (or stolen) relationship with the victim. Meyerson acknowledges that the delinquent act does embody some hope, albeit hope of apprehension and containment – with its inevitable contact with others.

OFFENDING AS A COMMUNICATION

The courts and the probation service deal with each offender separately, although his offending behaviour has placed him in a group which can include offending peers, victim(s), police, sentencers, the probation service and the prison service. The dynamics of his relationships within the particular group that the offender has 'sought to join' is, in my experience, significant and communicates something about his unconscious reasons for offending.

DETECTING DYNAMIC CLUES

Sometimes an offender provides us with clues from his first contact with us. A young man with few previous convictions was returned to court for failing to complete his community service order. I was asked to prepare a pre-sentence report for the court, but he failed to keep the appointment that I offered, although my letter indicated this was the only available time before his next court appearance. Repeated telephone calls and an attendance in person persuaded my secretary to offer him another appointment. Having worked hard to achieve this 'second chance' he arrived nearly thirty minutes late. Interested by my strong antagonism towards an individual I had not yet met, I saw him for the thirty remaining minutes of the session. I found myself wanting to impress on this young man how much probation service time he had wasted as he continued to fail to attend as requested. Instead, I asked who had treated him the way that I experienced him treating my colleagues and myself. After a pause, whilst he registered surprise at my question, he answered – 'My Dad'. He went on to share how, after his parents separated, he would wait Saturday after Saturday for his father's pre-arranged access visits – always to be disappointed because his father frequently neither arrived nor telephoned, or at best was very late. In the space of that thirty minutes this young man decided he would like to be different from his father and he asked for the opportunity to keep his word and complete his community service order. My pre-sentence report to the court allowed the magistrate to understand the underlying reasons for this young man's antisocial behaviour and he was given the chance to complete the community service order which, I learnt later, he did satisfactorily.

NEEDING A GROUP TO DECIPHER THE CLUES

By comparison, it was not until he had been held captive for seven of a fourteen-year sentence and was attending a monthly group that a colleague and I held in a prison, that we made sense of another client's need to be in such a situation. He told fellow group members how he had lost his job, lapsed on the repayments for his car, and decided importing drugs was the sole solution to his predicament. He saw this as a financial decision, but others perceived it as his fear of losing face. He repeatedly told the group how at visiting times he and his family were humiliated by prison officers. It was when other group members accused him of holding back in the group, as if he was laughing at their struggle to tackle the underlying reasons for their difficulties, that he told us that at the time of his circumcision when aged seven he had been terrified (there were no 'drugs' in those days). When eventually caught and held by his 'captors' he screamed out to his father – who had 'laughed in his face'. It was only by recreating the experience of being captured, held and humiliated – both within the prison and within the relationships in the group – that he was able to get in touch with this experience.

PRE-SENTENCE TENSION: HOPE VERSUS DESPAIR

Most probation service referrals come from the courts in the form of a request for a pre-sentence report on a defendant. At this moment the defendant is held by the court in a time-warp between offence and sentence. It is a time when the defendant is most likely to be in touch with feelings of despair –symbolized by the fear of imprisonment, and feelings of hope – symbolized by the possibility of leniency. When the defendant's offending has become compulsive, my assessment must include a view as to whether he has the capacity to be held in a therapeutic alliance within the boundaries of a probation order. The ultimate boundary of a probation order is the threat of a return to court for failure to comply with the condition to attend appointments. Such an order can contain additional requirements such as residence at a hostel, psychiatric treatment, attendance at a day centre or a therapeutic group. Those defendants whose offending places themselves or others at risk may need the holding experience of imprisonment before they can feel safe enough to engage in a relationship that can contain the emotional conflicts and tensions they have been expressing through their offending.

'GETTING HOLD' OF THE CLIENT

When the same colleague and I were working with offender addict clients (individuals whose offending pre-dated their addiction) we found them pre-occupied with the task of *getting hold* of their drug supply. We had great difficulty *getting hold* of them. When they did attend appointments they frequently flooded the session with the horror of their predicament and left us experiencing their despair and fear of falling apart. As one client explained, 'Being without drugs *is* like being without a skin.'. We saw our first task as trying to provide a containing environment where the possibility of hope could be experienced, acknowledged and pursued – hope that being without drugs only *feels* like being without a skin. We asked the court to extend the period of time between offence and sentence, with its possibility of hope and despair, to enable defendants to legalize their drug supply. The court offered those that did so the opportunity of the sentence of a probation order and we offered them a place in a weekly therapeutic group.

Our facilitating environment therefore included the court and the medical services. We then tried to establish a sense of belonging to the setting where we worked in order to encourage that sense of group membership and level of relatedness with others which is essential to individual health. Our probation service assistant provided a weekly 'surgery' for group members who needed practical help with welfare issues. Our group room was off the main reception area, so members were able to join us without seeking help from reception staff. A colleague who offered assistance to an early arriver was told 'No thanks, I'm a group member'. Group members' level of contact with our office increased as they became more involved in the group and began to depend on themselves and other resources rather than escaping behind a wall of opiates. Reception, secretarial staff and colleagues contributed to our 'setting' by reminding the caller of the date and time of the next group. This helped clients who had become accustomed to obtaining 'instant' relief in the form of an escape from reality to learn to hold on until the next session.

It is Foulkes' view (1964, p.282) that delinquents and addicts are amongst those groups which are 'better treated in "special problem" groups of their own'. The various cultures and values of a community are always passed on from generation to generation and offenders share the same values as their home communities. Foulkes (1948) suggests that '…collectively they (group members) constitute the very norm from which, individually, they deviate' (p.29).

THE INNER STRUGGLE: GRATITUDE VERSUS OUTRAGE

As our group continued to meet, the atmosphere fluctuated between hope and despair: hope that they could recover a sense of inner security, and despair as those responsible for the security of others (the police) continued to treat them as suspects. Moments of emotional contact alternated with flights of panic. There was considerable splitting between the 'caring' probation service and the 'persecutory' court, despite the fact that group members who re-offended were viewed by the court to be taking flight from the group and were helped to retain their place there. The magistrates' assistance in *holding* these offenders in their commitment to the group included a request from one magistrate for a progress report. The group member concerned struggled with feelings of gratitude at being understood and outrage at the intrusion into his life. His outburst of 'Who does he think he is – my father?' made him reflect on his wholly inadequate experience of being fathered.

It is my contention that the offender unconsciously commits an antisocial act when the time is right, that is when he experiences either a sense of hope or is in flight from feelings of despair. He also selects the time when he is at risk of being 'caught in the act'. He is then caught up in the Criminal Justice System where hope and despair are symbolized by freedom and imprisonment. The court has the power to have the convicted offender held either in prison or in the community under the terms of a probation order. My task then is to make maximum use of the setting, that is, the Criminal Justice System as a whole, to hold the offender in a relationship. It is in the context of his relationships within this new grouping that he will re-enact those internalized dynamics of his family group which led to the development of the antisocial tendency. Only then does he have the opportunity of recovering from his early experiences of deprivation and developing the capacity to live in a state of healthy relatedness – healthy belonging – with his fellow human-beings.

Note

The views presented in this paper are those of the author, and do not necessarily reflect those of the Inner London Probation Service

Central Issues

II · 5

Psychodynamic Approaches to Assessment

A Forensic Psychiatric Interactional Perspective

Hjalmar Van Marle

INTRODUCTION

Forensic psychiatric assessment never takes place in value-free circumstances. Much is at stake for the person in question. The circumstances in which the examination takes place is of great influence, especially when strongly characterized by the aspect of detention. The more detailed the examination, and the longer it takes, the more differentiated and specific data will come to light. The examination is particularly aimed at determining the propensity of the examined person for behaving in a particular way, behaviour which will not often occur in his case or in the case of others and certainly not at the moment at which the examination takes place. Forensic psychiatrists should be alert to these factors, which play their part from the very beginning. In this chapter, methods of examination, their indications, the diagnosis and ethical questions will be dealt with successively, with the emphasis on their interaction with the personality of the examined person.

METHOD

The forensic psychiatric examination can be carried out in various ways: (1) by one assessor (mono-disciplinary) or by more assessors (multi-disciplinary), (2) a standard psychological and psychiatric examination or a more detailed, specifically functionally-directed examination, and (3) ambulantly or clinically. All these methods of examination have their own advantages but at the same their limitations. That is why the indication leading to the examination is decisive for the choice.

When the examination concerns the state of health, short-term risks and possible indications for treatment, then a mono-disciplinary approach by a forensic psychiatrist will suffice. However, if it concerns the question of the degree of accountability, long-term recidivism risks, and a lengthy hospital treatment after a period of imprisonment, then a multi-disciplinary approach will lead to an essential improvement of the data on the grounds of which a decision must be based (Van Marle 1986, 1992; Webster and Menzies 1987). These data are collected so as to be able to make a long-term behavioural assessment, extrapolating from the present to the past but also into the future. Therefore, it is necessary to detect and study personality-ingrained recurring behavioural patterns. A combination of a psychiatric diagnosis and psychological examination of the characteristics of the personality is consequently to be preferred. Whether this takes the form of the standard examination or an extended form, with a neurological or neuropsychological examination to show functional disorders, will be determined by how the question can best be answered. For example, does the patient suffer from a described neurological illness, or a diffuse neuropsychological disorder?

The difference between ambulant and clinical examination is fundamental. These forms of examination yield completely different types of data and consequently, different reference points for decision making. An ambulant report is often drawn up after a private interview with the psychiatrist in a consulting room. The person in question speaks, while no further observations are obtained that give information about the person's behaviour in interactions other than with the assessor. Provided the person cooperates adequately, this method of examination, supplemented with anamnestical data about the personality, at least produces a picture of the person in question. The interactions between the assessor and the examined person during the examination itself may offer the opportunity of verifying personal characteristics, that is, relational patterns that have surfaced from the person's preceding experiences. New assumptions cannot be checked practically, though. Each interview is limited in time and is relatively short. It is therefore difficult to form an opinion in context about such personality factors as immunity to stress, impulse manifestation tendencies and fear tolerance, so that predictions about future behaviour cannot be supported by observational data. So, the predictive quality of these interviews relates to the period immediately following it. As a result, in the case of a forensic question with substantial consequences for the person concerned, a clinical examination is to be preferred.

THE SETTING FOR CLINICAL OBSERVATION

General mental hospitals and the psychiatric hospitals that belong to university hospitals sometimes carry out observations on behalf of forensic psychiatric assessment. The conditions for observation are not satisfactory, nor is there sufficient security and personnel for a systematic and controlled observation, to determine the complicated question of the degree of accountability and the long-term prognoses, such as a long detention period. Often the observation in these hospitals takes place in ordinary non-security psychiatric departments, carried out by frequently changing staff who are less experienced because they are not specialists. This will probably change with the introduction of forensic psychiatric departments in the mental hospitals, as a result of which the increase in expertise and in the quality of consistent observational circumstances will be possible. In Holland, because those under hospital orders are distributed over state mental hospitals, forensic psychiatric observation in hospitals is mainly carried out in the Penitentiair Selectie Centrum in The Hague, in the Pieter Baan Centrum (see Bluglass and Bowden 1990, p.1341) and in the Dr. F.S. Meijers Instituut (these last two in Utrecht).

Forensic psychiatric reports which are made in Holland with the help of clinical observations, are but a small part (a little over 10%) of all forensic psychiatric criminal writings (Van Marle 1993), since the opportunity for observation is limited. So, specific guidelines should be drawn up for those observations that are carried out clinically.

These guidelines are partly of a diagnostic nature as regards content, and partly methodological. In the case of forensic writing it concerns the clinical psychiatric diagnosis in its own right less than the relationship between the (possible) disorder and the charge, on the basis of which the degree of accountability and the consequent recidivism risks can be determined. The nature of the disorder is then essential, since in the case of one clear psychological disorder the will-power may be decreased considerably, dependent on the intrapsychological power play and on the situation. Methodological criteria are those in which the method of observation is not so much based on the demand for diagnostics but rather on the demand for unity within the variety of data.

Primarily, diagnostic indications are:

(1) The assumption of disorders in the offender, especially in those cases where the relational effects of the inadequate development or a pathological disorder must be mapped out, if some clarification is to surface regarding the motives in relation to the charge.

(2) Serious offences, in cases where either a lengthy detention period or hospital orders are possible. In those cases it is of great interest both for society and for the person in question if after an adequate diagnosis the lawful detention is executed in a prison or in a state

mental hospital where there is the possibility of treatment (Van Marle 1993).

(3) Those offences, which at first are incomprehensible *casu quo bizarre*, as a result of which there is the assumption of a serious psychological disorder.

(4) Serious aggressive and sexually-aggressive offences because of the risk of recidivism.

(5) Offences committed in groups, because in these cases the degree of mutual manipulation possibly plays a role.

(6) Offences aimed at an acquaintance, with a long history.

(7) Offences within an incest network, because in this network unintentional loyalties, self-interest and an unbalanced psychological development often form a very specific inter-play.

(8) Serial offences which show a progression in seriousness; especially in the case of young delinquents, where frustrating the recurring tendency leads to an important decrease in recidivism.

Methodological indications are:

(1) Evaluating a patient during a certain period, who has been examined at various times. Instead of the accumulation of interviews, so characteristic of an ambulant examination, now the data obtained ambulantly can be contrasted with the results obtained in stable and continuing clinical circumstances.

(2) Persons whose motivation fluctuates to cooperate with an examination and therefore, during interviews, a strongly varying and even incoherent pattern could emerge in their cases.

(3) Besides the continuity in the diagnosis, it is also possible to motivate the person in question to treatment during the observation period, especially to make him familiar with his own wishes to change, or to give him insight into the nature of his disorder.

(4) The denying suspect, because by reason of the lack of his account of what happened at the moment of the offence, an investigation into the degree of accountability is invalidated. The relation between a possible disorder and the charge cannot be made clear. By daily observing the various moods and behavioural patterns of the person in question, the more subtle nuances in the habitual behavioural pattern are found, so that in this way – without going into any furnishing of proof, though – the charge can be considered more clearly in the context of the personality data.

(5) Evaluations of earlier clinical reports, for example when the person in question spent a couple of years in a (state) mental hospital, with the related doctors' reports. The statutory evaluation of six years' hospital orders, or twice as long, should in fact be carried out clinically right away. A prediction of dangerousness, is only possible once he has been removed from his familiar milieu in the state mental hospital, and he has tried to adapt himself to a department which is unfamiliar to him, more neutral and not immediately aimed at treatment. Changes in the personality caused by hospital orders will surely surface in a more differentiated manner in the constantly fluctuating circumstances of clinical observation.

(6) Diagnosis to decide on the indication for a further treatment and a possible selection for a certain hospital. In this context one should think of finding out about and formulating indications for treatment leading to hospital orders with treatment, or the psychodynamic diagnosis for a more detailed forensic treatment purpose within the general mental health care system, or the specific approach in the case of hospital orders with medical treatment. Indicating and selecting in this way is aimed at reaching the ultimate goal, prevention of recidivism, using the least drastic means.

DIAGNOSTICS

In forensic psychiatric diagnostics the following aspects, about which information must be provided, can be distinguished. Preceding the forensic question of the link between disorder and recent, possibly criminal, behaviour, the question should be answered whether it is a matter of disorder, or (under Dutch law) an inadequate development or a pathological disorder of the mental faculties. These indications are the legally binding criteria for the existence of an illness which will consequently lead to some sort of statutory regulation. Formulating the answer to that question can best scientifically be dealt with in combination with the use of diagnostics in earlier or future psychiatric reports on the same person and others. That is the reason why there is much to say in favour of classifying this diagnosis in accordance with accepted standards, for example that of the Diagnostic and Statistical Manual (American Psychiatric Press 1980).

A psychiatrically classified diagnosis in its own right is, however, not sufficient to describe the ego-strength of the person, nor are the relevant interactions that have played a role in the development of the disorder or the offence committed. Also regarding this point, the various axes of the DSM-III and IV can at least partly help us in determining the degree of social adaptation and the degree of stress that is normally in the person in question. However, the nature of the object relations with others and the possible tension or aggression which this entails, the person's imaginative powers and the person's psychodynamics will not yet have surfaced. These aspects of the personality are essential though, for the determination of the degree of accountability, an indication for intensive psychotherapy or for a clinical psychotherapeutic treatment. That is why these points should be treated explicitly and classified, and be registered in the report.

Then it is necessary to establish a connection with relevant events from the person's earlier experiences and to give a psychodynamic interpretation to it, that is, an emotional meaning. 'Relevant' means that, on the basis of repeatedly recurring behaviour, certain behavioural patterns can emerge which are linked up with the presentation of the question in the report. This recurring pattern occurred during the greater part of the person's life and consequently determined it. Clinical observation is by far the best method to verify hypotheses about behaviour to be expected, hypotheses which have been formed on the basis of the person's life story, and on that person's actual behaviour in the observation department. Because of their great influence on the (conscious and unconscious) motives and conflicts, the sexual and aggressional development should be given separate and standardized attention on the one hand when inventorying the data of the person's social milieu, and it should also, on the other hand, be given attention in the case of an individual examination.

The reason for the report, such as the indication for treatment or determining the degree of accountability, entails with it that the person's experienced degree of suffering and the motivation to cooperate in a therapy or the committing of the offence, will be registered in detail. The decisive moment that triggered the occurrence of the complaints or the offence is especially of importance in the person's subjective reality perception. In that way it then becomes clear whether, and if so, to what extent, certain situational factors have influenced an already existing increased psychological sensitivity or disorder, and if that combination led to to a decreased psychological aversion and a possible impulse breakthrough. The relation to possible victims might be highly revealing for specific relational problems. Systematically collecting details is essential in this respect, to map out the development of the final picture and its intrapsychological dynamics, as if it were a scenario.

Then the entire dynamics of intrapsychological and situative factors is summed up in a psychodynamic construct which logically should lead to the answering of the original presentation of the question.

REFUSAL AND DENIAL

When the examined person refuses to cooperate in the examination, it is hard to form any insight into the relation between the personality (with possible disorders) and the charge. It is the assignment, that question (with the consequent conclusion about the degree of accountability), which requires the assessor to speak freely with the examined person about his experiences and moods at the moment of the offence. Some refuse on the grounds of a disorder in their ability to make judgements, as a result of which they cannot comprehend the intentions and consequences of such an examination. Examples of these are syndromes in which paranoiac delusions occur and other disorders of reality perception. We can say that persons suffering from the latter syndromes refuse on account of pathological motives and so cannot be held responsible for this refusal. They are not in a position to decide freely whether or not to cooperate in such an examination. So in the case of these 'pathological refusers' the examination can take place in the usual way, including the investigation of the social background of relatives, acquaintances, and so forth.

Other refusers are persons who refuse for opportunist reasons, fearing hospital orders, for example. It is no use talking with them about themselves and about the purpose of the forensic examination. However, a report can be made about their stay in the observation department or about impressions of interviews (ambulantly obtained). Although interpretations for the purpose of finding out about the presence of a disorder and its link with the charge are of necessity virtually impossible, a factual report of the person's daily activities and of his behaviour towards the assessors, enables the judge still to observe over the assessor's shoulder and to form his own opinion. In those cases in which somebody refuses to cooperate, collecting other data will not always be possible through questioning others and questioning the person about his life story (hetero- and auto-anamnesis), since he will be able to influence these others or prevent their cooperation.

In the case of a denying suspect we are in fact confronted with the same problem. It is impossible to speak about the offence in the case of the relation between offence and offender; after all, the examined person claims not to know anything about this. However, what is possible, is to carry out a psychiatric and a psychological examination in the approved manner. The existence or absence of illnesses can be determined. Clearly, the forensic psychiatrist cannot be asked the required question: 'can this person possibly have committed the offence?', since he is not involved in the furnishing of proof. Moreover, this question presupposes a precision in predictions for one person, which is not sensible. In principle anybody may commit any crime.

PREDICTION

Clinical examination *pro Justice* takes place in the same milieu twenty-four hours a day, in this case, the clinical observation department and its staff. As has been mentioned, this offers other possibilities for examination: clinically reporting has its own indications and results. Because here it is a continuing process, the examined person need not be changing his relations with relevant others, so that the contact will gain somewhat more depth. Specific, personality-linked interactions will come to light, transference phenomena can be specified and contra-transferences can be recognized. Superficial assimilation processes will soon become visible and worn, because they are constantly being tested in a balanced observation milieu. It is also possible to make visible which 'spontaneous' choice the examined person will make in relation to the persons with whom he socializes. Recurring patterns, choice of relations and socializing with other persons at the same time, will, generally speaking, substantially contribute to a reconstructive insight into the relation between the suspect and the offence of which he is accused. In this examination it is rather the constant value of the personality characteristics that surfaces and at the same time what its quality is in the continuing process of socializing daily with others. In this way also the possibilities for alternative behaviour become clear, respectively the incapacity for such behaviour. Determining the tendency for decompensation in a certain situation is of essential importance to assess future functioning under stress situations, both in society and during a clinical treatment.

From the above it is evident that it will be extremely difficult to predict somebody's behaviour on the basis of an ambulant examination during an intramural forensic psychiatric treatment, especially if there are a number of years of imprisonment between the examination and the treatment. If we want to determine the long-term recidivism risks and the behaviour during a later clinical treatment, a clinical examination will be necessary to find out about, to lay down and to generalize the situational factors (Appelbaum and Gutheil 1991; Kirkland Gable 1986; Monohan 1984). Unfortunately, it is not known whether continuing research took place to confirm this expectation.

ETHICS

It is not medical principles, but legal principles which determine the areas of attention of the forensic psychiatrists and psychologists, namely: examination, reporting and legally enforced nursing and treatment. Accordingly, in all these territories the question has non-medical consequences. A number of questions about legal criteria must be answered. In his advice for the jurist, the forensic psychiatrist selects what is, and what is not relevant for the answer, and then answers the questions put forward. The questioner is not supposed to have any doubts about the answer, or to be forced to frame his own answer just on the basis of the data provided. But psychiatrists and assessors do continue to work by their own methods and techniques. In that way they offer favourable conditions for a private interview with the jurist in the consultation room of a remand centre and create a balanced observation milieu in a psychiatric hospital or observation department and they try to decrease the individual recidivism risks with the use of modern methods of treatment.

During the examination *pro Justice* the psychiatrist remains a doctor and his activities are medical, whereas the integral part of the doctor–patient relationship, professional secrecy, is not relevant here. The interrogator is, metaphorically, always looking over the psychiatrist's shoulder and that constitutes the relationship. As a consequence, the examined person can never demand that the assessor observe his medical professional secrecy. Naturally, he should be told this at the beginning of the first interview. A psychotherapeutical relation is absolutely out of the question. That is why in the case of ambulant treatment and in forensic psychiatric hospitals, psychotherapists and behavioural psychiatrists must be clearly distinguished, in other words, the distinction must be made between those who offer treatment under professional secrecy and those who report on the possible changes in the behaviour of the patient.

Although the doctor–patient relationship is essentially changed by the necessity for these reports to others, another medical principle remains prominent, namely using specific expertise in such a way that the examined person or patient will not harmed by it. This medical approach is completely in accordance with the Dutch legal principle that the suspect may not be forced to contribute to his conviction. The forensic psychiatrist is not to provide legal evidence, but to give independent advice. This implies that the assessor must treat his client in such a way that, wherever possible, he will not be tempted to cause himself harm by uncontrollably giving evidence, self-incriminations, and so forth. If, despite this, such should happen, then the assessor must refer the examined person to his legal adviser immediately.

The usual respect of the doctor for his patient must continue to exist as well. This, however, does not mean that, incidentally, the assessor would not be allowed to use confronting interview techniques to form a picture of the patient's reaction, similar to the somatic physician who literally puts his finger on the sore spot. Since a lot depends on the forensic psychiatric examination, namely a judgement on the mental state and the following punishments or measures, the examined person must be well-informed in advance of the limiting conditions of the examination.

A Clinical Psychological Perspective

Alice Theilgaard

INTRODUCTION

The development of experimental psychology in the latter half of the nineteenth century formed the foundation for psychological testing. The world's first psychology laboratory was established in Leipzig by Wilhelm Wundt in 1875, and it became a meeting place for psychiatrists and psychologists. The German psychiatrist Emil Kraepelin was among the guests, and he became inspired to develop the basic features of the psychiatric diagnostic system. Psychologists responsible for the research on which foundation the test-method developed came from many quarters. James McKeen Cattell from the USA, Charles E. Spearman from Great Britain, and Alfred Binet from France, to mention but a few of the most prominent.

The early experimental psychology had physiology and physics as its model. Gustav Fechner studied psychophysic problems as early as 1860, and the goal was to find general laws regarding perception, memory and thinking. After the elaboration of behavioural norms the attention was focused on individual differences, variations in behaviour, and the first 'mental test' was constructed in 1890 by James Cattell. In 1905 Alfred Binet, in cooperation with Thomas Simon, published the first attempt to assess intelligence quantitatively. From then on the development of cognitive tests progressed rapidly, encouraged by their practical use. The assessment of personality – either in the form of inventories or of projective techniques – made their appearance much later.

METHODOLOGY

In the traditional view of the testing procedure 'objectivity' was stressed as one of the advantages. But psychology is in the same epistemological situation as any other branch of science: all are dependent on direct observation in order to obtain basic data. Thus it follows that they cannot be 'objective' in the proper meaning of the word: observer-independent. It is more correct to speak of 'degrees of subjectivity'. One of the assets of testing is that methodology helps to discipline subjectivity.

The scientific climate which prevailed around the début of the 'mental tests' was fertile for a so-called objective psychology, behaviourism and learning-process theories being the most fecund. The method followed that of classical experimental psychology, in which the individual is made the object of strict laboratory-like exploration. Only data which could be registered unequivocally, measured exactly and expressed quantitatively was of interest. The procedure is nomothetic, that is to say it consisted of extensive investigations of the occurence of isolated phenomena in selected populations. Test scores are treated statistically and stochastic predictions are made on the basis of normative studies.

The humanistic background for the development of psychological tests is constituted by Gestalt psychology, psychoanalysis and related holistic and organismic personality-theories. The procedure of choice is idiographic, that is to say it consists of intensive, often prolonged investigations of the individual. Predictions are based on interpretations and not on statistical processing of observational data. Case records form the dominant way of presenting data.

The schematic survey opposite will serve to elucidate the characteristics of the two methods (Østergaard et al. 1993, p.30).

Clinical psychologists traditionally work according to the idiographic method, aiming to give prognostic evaluations based on their knowledge of the personality of the individual and the interplay of situational factors. The idiographic method does not imply that predictions rest on intuitive-speculative estimates. They are founded on logical, inductive principles and based on empirical observations. This does not necessarily involve an opposition to the nomothetic method, which tries to establish laws on statistical grounds. Both methods are often applied in research (Theilgaard 1984). Idiographic procedures serve to create ideas and formulate hypotheses, and the application of nomothetic procedures secure information of the validity of such hypotheses.

In contrast to the clinical examination, the test situation searches a more circumscribed field because of carefully chosen prior test selection.

Like clinical observations, test data do not contain single, certain pathognonomic signs, for example, thought disturbances are not confined to schizophrenic patients. The particular data have to be weighed against each other

NATURAL SCIENCE

Identified with 'statistical method'

Extensive research

METHOD: nomothetic

Many probands, often cross section-studies, momentary impressions.

Isolation of single features reduction to 'key phenomena'

Observation of behaviour, registration of outer phenomena.

Measurement, quantification.

Objectivity emphasized, the role of the examiner tends to be eliminated.

Clinical examination: Cognitive tests, dexterity-measurements, questionnaires, inventories, structured interviews.

The ideal: 'The good test'.

EXPLANATION: actuarial

Generalizations rest on calculation of probability.

Stochastic connections are transferred to causal connections.

THEORY

Learning-process-trends

Mosaic psychology

Association psychology

Reflexology

Stimulus-reaction theory

Factor-theory

Behaviourism

HUMANISTIC TRADITION

Identified with 'clinical method'

Intensive research

METHOD: idiographic

Few probands (casuistics), often longitudinal studies, developmental investigations.

Elucidation of broad connections, complex personality features, interactional processes.

Introspection, registration of phenomenological data.

Descriptive, qualitative assessment. Subjectivity tolerated, the intuition of the examiner tends to be utilized.

Clinical investigation:

Projective tests, free association, play observation, unstructured interviews.

The ideal: 'The good psychologist'

EXPLANATION: hermeneutic

Generalizations rest on interpretations, and psychological phenomena are seen as finalistic

Hermeneutical experienced connections are transferred to causal connections.

THEORY

Dynamic-psychological trends

Gestalt psychology

Holistic theories

Organismic theories

Bio-social theories

Field theories

Personality theories

Humanistic psychology

Psychoanalysis

and to be related to information concerning the patient's motivation, social situation and life-history.

Only with a holistic description, which also elucidates personality resources, can a nuanced clarification of diagnostic and prognostic features become possible. It may be said that the reliability of the examiner's interpretation is enhanced, the more frequent the variable in question is manifest, the more experience and insight in general psychology and psychopathology the psychologist possesses, the more the examiner is able to discipline his subjectivity. It is the psychologist's training in observation and analysis that leads to reliable results, not a strict adherence to mechanical and standardized practices.

THE RATIONALE FOR PSYCHOLOGICAL ASSESSMENT OF THE OFFENDER PATIENT

The purpose of psychological assessment is to deepen the knowledge and understanding of the personality. Thorough and nuanced descriptions, based on the results of a varied test-battery, enhance the possibilities for refined psychiatric diagnosis, thereby providing more reliable grounding in the choice of optimal treatment. It has been claimed that clinical psychologists should desist from using a psychiatric diagnostic system, and allow the personality description to be their sole professional constribution. A psychiatric diagnosis contains aspects which cannot be weighted equally in every individual case. There are ethological, descriptive, therapeutic and prognostic variables. Diagnosis is a model tending to simplify complex dynamic data. Simplification always occurs at the expense of something, and the more the weight is laid on the 'typical' in contrast to the 'specific', the more the hypothetical aspects are increased. This does not imply that clinical psychologists should refrain from making diagnoses. If the features of resemblance which are implicit in the classification are ignored, years of clinical experience would be precluded. But the prognostic evaluation can be made more precise if the diagnostic classification is complemented by a description of the idiosyncratic features of the individual, such as those furnished by psychological test-reports.

In the forensic setting the rationale for using psychological tests has several tributaries; namely, psychological, medical, and juridical. To the primary diagnostic indications given by van Marle in the preceding chapter, the following may be added from a psychological perspective.

It should be in the interests of the patient to obtain as valid as possible a description of his personality, including both the pathological and healthy features, in order to ensure that disorders – such as organic brain damage or psychosis – are not overlooked. Nevertheless, his motivation for participating in interviews and testing may fluctuate.

Individuals with character disorders often exhibit 'that glib and oily art to speak and purpose not' (*King Lear* I.1.223). They thus parry the questions or answer with nugatory or insignificant clichés.

Psychological tests – especially those with projective qualities – have the advantage, compared to the interview, that it is not so easy to discern the consequences of one's reactions. Accordingly, psychopathic manipulation (Cox 1994) and manoeuvering will be more difficult to carry out. On the other hand the 'non-transparency' of the tests will be a disadvantage where a paranoid patient is concerned. It is always a challenge to the tester to get a paranoid person to cooperate, regardless of type of test.

Refusal to participate in a psychological examination – which is different from clinical denial – belongs, in my opinion, to the field of Human Rights. It is my experience that very few patients refuse to cooperate, if the purpose of the testing is explained and good contact is made. Assisting in promoting the motivation for engaging in the tests is the *Aufforderungscharacter* (Lewin), 'request-character', inherent in the task.

The question of exemption from punishment due to psychosis and related states brings reality-testing into focus. Psychological tests, especially those of a projective nature, are often instrumental in establishing accurate data about an individual's perception of the inner and the outer world.

The very moment a psychotic individual is charged with a criminal offence, the question of his accountability is of crucial importance. In many countries, including, for example Denmark, the law operates with two conditions for exemption: (1) insanity (or related states) (2) unaccountability. Danish penal legislation §16,1 states:

'Persons who at the time of the criminal act are unaccountable due to insanity or states equal to insanity or feeblemindedness in higher degree, will not be punished.'

In the McNaughton rules formulated by The House of Lords in 1843 the most important sentence is

'that to establish a defence on the grounds of insanity it must be clearly proved that, at the time of the committing of the act, the party accused was labouring under such a defect of reason, from disease of the mind, as not to know the nature and quality of the act he was doing; or, if he did know it, that he did not know he was doing what was wrong.'

These rules have been modified, but the basic tenets hold. The Norwegian penal legislation has this simplified version:

'An act is not punishable, when the perpetrator at the time of the act was insane or unconscious' (!)

Here the basis for the juridical decision is a clear medical evaluation. When the concept of 'accountability' has been preserved, the purpose might have been to emphasize that 'impunity' is first and foremost a juridical matter.' (Lunn and Kramp 1985)

Whereas manifest psychotic individuals rarely present problems with regard to accountability, with incipient schizophrenics, pseudoneurotics, borderlines with micropsychotic episodes, syndromes where paranoid delusions occasionally occur, not to speak of the whole range of 'related states' such as post-ictal epilepsy and other organic brain damage cases, hypoglycaemic twilight states, and diverse transitory abnormal psychic states – to name but a few – it can be difficult to decide whether or not reality-testing is compromised. In these matters the undertaking of projective testing is advantageous on account of the 'subclinical' attributes inherent in the semi-structured material.

> *By the way in which he organizes and interprets the material, the patient unconsciously leaves an imprint of his personality. Among other features, the microcosmos of the Rorschach gives clues about the patient's hold of reality.*

Neuropsychological tests, which have been refined (Luria 1966; Lezak 1983) during recent decades, are in keeping with technical means of brain-mapping. They are obviously of great importance in cases where there is the slightest suspicion of organic factors as a cause for unaccountability.

THE TEST BATTERY

Diagnostic assessment, using a battery of tests comprising both cognitive and projective techniques, is imperative if the examiner intends to do more than merely ascribe a nosological category to the patient. In forensic cases where the question of detention or hospital prevails, it is of utmost importance that the assessor aims at giving as broad and psychodynamic a description of the complexities of the personality as possible. 'Human beings, sick or well, cannot be described only by the name of a nosological category' (Rapaport, Gill and Schafer 1967, p.523). Likewise, an individual cannot be adequately described by a test profile or the sum of rating-scale items.

> *Although personality-features may be inferred from cognitive tests, and cognitive functions from projective ones, both categories are necessary if a full picture of the personality is to be obtained. For example, individuals with borderline pathology might exhibit thought disorder in projective tests, such as Rorschach, yet manifest relatively normal performance on more structured tests, such as the Wechsler Adult Intelligence Scale (WAIS).*

The chosen combination of tests will depend upon the specific problem presented. A fixed test battery has the advantage that it facilitates the comparability of patient and patient and test–retest results from the same patient. But, in order to cover the possible range of dysfunctions, a fixed battery runs the risk of being too extensive and unnecessarily time-consuming. Flexibility with regard to selection of tests is also called for when unexpected findings appear during the testing, such as the suspicion of organic dysfunction, which has hitherto not declared itself.

COGNITIVE TESTS

The broad field of psychometric testing pertaining to attention, perception, memory and intelligence also includes neuropsychological testing, which tends to become specialized. In the forensic setting it is not only an advantage, but *an absolute requirement*, that the psychologist has neuropsychological experience and is skilled in administering such tests. It is always essential to bear in mind that organic pathology might be a contributory factor in the overall clinical picture.

NEUROPSYCHOLOGICAL TESTS

The purpose of the neuropsychological sequential procedure is to map out disturbances of higher mental functions including sensomotoric, visual, acoustic and kinaesthetic perception, sense of time, linguistic factors (language spoken, written, read) and the higher intellectual processes such as thinking, abstraction, concept-formation.

The aim of this branch of clinical psychology is to elucidate the relation between the central nervous system and the psychological processes. It became established almost simultaneously in East and West Europe around 1940, although it should be noted that as early as during World War I Kurt Goldstein (1878–1965) examined and treated soldiers from a neuropsychological point of view. His early work gave inspiration to the development of neuropsychology in Soviet Union with Lev Vygotsky and Alexander Luria as the most prominent practitioners. In the English speaking countries D O Hebb was the first to use the designation neuropsychology as a subtitle to his book, published in 1949, *The Organization of Behaviour: A Neuropsychological Theory*.

In *Higher Cortical Functions in Man* (1966) Luria expounds his approach (also described by Christensen, 1975). It is not a case of narrow localization of mental processes, but of an organization of cooperating ones, each of which performs its specific role.

'Higher human mental functions are complex reflex processes, social in origin, mediate in structure and conscious and voluntary in mode of function'. (Luria 1966, p.32)

The neuropsychological examination accordingly starts as a stepwise survey of essential functions. The primary tests are relatively standardized but adapted to the individual's primary functional level. Based on qualitative analysis – concerning not only whether a problem is solved but also the way in which it is solved – the psychologist makes hypotheses regarding possible neuropsy-chological symptoms. This builds up to a new test programme, selected to disclose defects in more detail. This technique allows for an analysis of the structural dynamics. Reliability of the results is ensured by syndrome analysis.

Luria's test material essentially consists of paper-and-pencil tests and of different visual and tactile equipment, yet all are of a nature allowing bedside administration. Recent technical advances have introduced scanners and EEG apparatus serving brain-mapping procedures. This has, however, not rendered neuropsychological examination superfluous.

Alongside Luria's qualitative, dynamic approach a second field of neurop-sychology developed inspired by Paul Meehl's (1954) book, *Clinical Versus Statistical Prediction*.

Meehl undertook to compare the two forms of prediction: statistical and clinical. He analyzed about twenty investigations from different fields, such as the effects of psychotherapy and recidivism of criminality. He showed that routine administration of statistical procedures gave as correct predictions as clinical observations. But – as Østergaard *et al.* (1993, p.31) points out – the comparisons merely included predictions based on the same data, thereby excluding the advantage of the clinical method, which gained information of observations lying outside the areas specifically covered by the quantitative tests.

The debate is still ongoing. But instead of 'locking and bolting' (to use a Danish idiom) the discussion as Meehl did with his antithetical viewpoint, it is more fruitful to regard the two methods as being complementary. Nomotheti-cal conclusions are not valid for the single individual, and idiographic state-ments cannot account for groups of individuals.

The question of whether a quantitative or qualitative processing of psycho-logical test-data is to be preferred has to be weighed against the purpose of the investigation. In forensic settings, where a thorough personality description is called for, the dynamic approach is preferable. It is only when working with simple, well-defined psychological entities that a quantitative processing is expedient. Not all psychological phenomena can be reduced and fragmented to allow for quantification without losing their meaning. And as mentioned previously, the objective aspect of testing is often exaggerated or illusory. An example is a recent Danish investigation applying neuropsychological tests computerized to the extent that even the test-instructions were mediated by the computer! Among the many variables examined, the highest significance was found when the differences of results related to the various psychologists participating in the investigations were compared. Even in such a seemingly objective test-situation, the interplay between psychologist and patient cannot be ignored.

INTELLIGENCE TESTS

The construction of intelligence tests is not based on a general accepted theory of intelligence. Since the days of Cicero there have been popular-psychological ideas about intelligence, but the attempt to define the concept scientifically has either been too vague and all-embracing, or too narrow and specific. None the less, intelligence research represents a field within psychology with far-reaching practical consequences. The introduction of the intelligence quotient involved a conceptual drifting toward an identification with intelligence. In this respect a literally applied, quantitative intelligence test result runs the risk of becoming stigmatizing.

Intelligence tests, which have gained the greatest international recognition, were developed by the psychologist David Wechsler (1939, 1981) at Bellevue Hospital, New York. They are pragmatic and include types of tasks, which have previously been applied by other test-constructors. The first adult version appeared in 1939, and the latest revised edition WAIS-R (Wechsler Adult Intelligence Scale – Revised) was launched in 1981. The WAIS consists of eleven subtests: six verbal and five performance tests, measuring varied functions such as attention, comprehension, abstraction, proficiency in arithmetic, visual-spatial analysis, and so forth. Each subtest has its own norm, and it is thus possible to ascertain how an individual's score is placed within each type of test in comparison with a group representative of the population. Wechsler's test lends itself to differentiated analysis of intellectual disturbances, functional as well as organic. The points for the different subtests can be converted to a verbal IQ and a performance IQ, respectively. The sum of the points makes the basis for calculation of the total IQ. In my mind, this need not be regarded with that exaggerated awe with which the IQ is sometimes invested.

An individual is better served by having his cognitive functions described with due deference to qualitative features than by a single number, which may be incorrectly perceived as a perfect objective measure of an exact magnitude. Intelligence is a complex concept. Non-intellectual factors such as motivation, curiosity, perseverance, stamina, and goal-directedness are important to consider when assessing cognitive functions. The advantage of a broad functional analysis is evident when it comes to estimating actual capacities and potential resources.

The subtest-profile mirrors the inner structure of the intellectual functioning and may provide diagnostic pointers.

J C Raven's *Progressive Matrices* (1948) is a non-verbal intelligence test inspired by Charles Spearman's (1863–1945) mathematically-based theory of intelligence, with its concepts of general and specific factors. The Raven test consists of sixty problems distributed in five series of increasing difficulty. The obtained score is converted to an age-associated percentile, placing the result in relation to a standardized population. Raven's Matrices deal with a delineated area: the capacity for abstraction in the sense of making analogical inferences and developing logical thinking. It has its advantages in cases where verbal difficulties and/or socio-cultural differences are in evidence.

PSYCHOMETRIC PERSONALITY TESTS

The first attempts to systematize personality descriptions were made during World War I, and the technique chosen was the questionnaire method. Questions about behaviour, attitudes, emotions, and so forth were selected and combined in different ways depending on what specific features were the focus of interest. It is concerned with reported behaviour rather than observed behaviour.

A variation of this technique is the inventory method, building on a series of written items formulated as personal statements. The proband rates, whether or not he finds the statement fitting. The number of items may be considerable, and they are often divided in various scales representing different psychological variables. As in the Wechsler tests the scaled scores may be transferred to weighted values, making possible the construction of a personality profile.

A critical point regarding the composition of these questionnaires and inventories is the solidity and validity of the criteria forming the grounds for the questions or statements. In some cases they are based on intuition, more or less influenced by various personality-theories. In other instances the items are selected among a great number of questions put to standardized groups with known characteristics, for example psychopathological symptoms. Correlation analysis finally decides which questions are most apt to characterize the various groups.

The test which without comparison has been applied most extensively is *The Minnesota Multiphasic Personality Inventory* (MMPI) construed by the psychologist S R Hathaway and the psychiatrist J C McKinley (1942). A collection of 550 questions was empirically tried out on normal and psychiatric populations, resulting in the establishment of different scales relating to psychiatric diagnoses: depression, schizophrenia, paranoia, hysteria, sociopathy, and so forth. Apart from the diagnostic scales, a number of control scales are built into the test to increase its reliability, for example an error-score and a lie-score. With this empirical procedure the troublesome question – often presenting itself with this method – 'Does the individual tell the truth?' will not have to be considered. The answers to the test is looked upon as verbal behaviour correlated to certain personality characteristica.

In contrast to the MMPI, the personality scale developed by H J Eysenck (1975) attempts to isolate by factor analysis the smallest possible number of personality types. Based on extensive studies, three main dimensions present themselves: introversion–extraversion, neuroticism, psychoticism.

Among the more recent inventories the *Millon Clinical Multiaxial Inventory* (MCMI) is of special interest, because it is in accordance with the amplification of the Axis II in DSM-III (see Millon 1981, p.105). It consists of 175 statements distributed to twenty scales, partly mirroring normal personality variables, partly pathological features.

'Personality,' as Millon uses the term, refers 'to the pattern of deeply embedded and broadly exhibited cognitive, affective and overt behavioral traits that emerge from a complex biological-environmental formative matrix' (Millon and Everly 1985, p.5). Normality and abnormality are conceived of as relative concepts, representing points along a continuum rather than discrete categories. The latter viewpoint is inherent in many of the rating scales representing an over simplistic conception of personality:

> 'Rating Scales have the advantage that they are quantifiable and easy to administer, but the disadvantage that the individual disappears behind the diagnosis. The salient features of the personality vanish behind the clichés. A one-sided application of rating scales runs the risk that the account of the personality imitates or is coloured by the statements contained in the rating list, resulting in limitations of descriptions.' (Theilgaard 1993, p.212.)

A reduction of behaviour to scores inevitably diminishes information.

Another possible shortcoming of rating scales is the equal weighing of answers regardless of their meaning and importance. In Beck's depression scale (1967) the final score consists of the total number of points in the answering of 21 questions. A statement like 'My appetite is much worse now' counts as much as 'I would like to kill myself' (!)

In order to enhance the 'objectivity', the scale-maker often recommends as much rigidity in procedure as possible which, in my view, reduces the clinical value of the assessment. From an epistemological point of view – stressing the importance of meaning – the clinical application of the diagnostic process depends upon empathy and understanding. And these are qualities called for in the hermeneutic method.

PROJECTIVE TESTS

If the personality is viewed as 'a structured, dynamically functioning whole, in which the particular psychological variables constitute integrated parts without independent existence' (Theilgaard 1985, p.104) projective tests are likely to be the chosen method.

The projective technique adds experiential, phenomenological and object-relational dimensions to the assessment.

> 'Emphasis is placed on the clinically based methodology, on the means for capturing the complexity and unique nature of clinical phenomena,

and on a qualitative approach to data collection and analysis that allows
the data to maintain their clinical richness.' (Lerner 1991, p.151.)

This underlines the value of the empathic, intuitive skills of trained psychologists.

Among the projective tests, the Rorschach test is the best known – popularly
named as 'The ink-blot test'. It was described in 1921 by the Swiss psychiatrist
Hermann Rorschach in his work *Psychodiagnostik*, to be followed up by a vast
amount of research and literature coming from different disciplines: psychology, psychiatry, anthropology, literary criticism, all representing diverse theoretical schools. The very idea that vaguely structured material – ten cards with
symmetrical ink blots – may serve as a medium for expressing structuring
principles of perception characteristic of the individual, is not new. Hamlet was
there before us: 'Do you see yonder cloud that's almost in shape of a camel?'
(III.2.366).

Rorschach himself spoke of 'accidental forms'. Being semi-structured, the
inkblots provide a wider range of projective possibilities (Theilgaard 1992,
p.170) than perceptual structuring of the real world. The miniature Rorschach
universe does not deal with questions to which there are unequivocal answers.
The principle of the tests rest on the fact that the individual shows a certain
degree of continuity regarding cognitive style from one situation to another.
The more vague the stimuli, the more will the structuring principles of the
personality be in force, and they will be reflected in the interpretation of the
test material. The responses are registered verbatim and later scored accoring
to various qualities: localization, level of form, colour, movement, factual
content and so forth.

Foremost among the grounds upon which the psychologist's interpretation
is based, is the premise that personality is not compartmentalized, but should
be regarded within a holistic, dynamic frame of thinking, that is, all psychological processes are conceived as interrelated and in constant interplay. A single
score should be evaluated with respect to the total configuration of which it is
a part, and no one-to-one relationship between a score and a specific psychological process exists. Each response has perceptual, associative, communicative
apsects and may also carry impulsive, emotional, defensive and adaptive
implications.

In a forensic setting when the aim is to give a differentiated picture of the
personality, and to highlight individual features of special interest for the
understanding of motives of the criminal act, then the Rorschach must be
considered invaluable, provided the test results are processed by an experienced
and knowledgeable tester. A forensic assessor is aware that the offender patient
is not always keen to be informative and may be reluctant to reveal things about
himself. Another asset of projective tests is to be welcomed: The subject cannot

prepare ready-made answers. The response has to be created 'on the spot'. There are neither clichés nor conventional answers to hide behind.

The Rorschach test has also proved its usefulness when the possibility of organic brain damage enters the picture. As a supplement to a neuropsychological test battery, it may reveal features of coping strategies and resources aside from the 'organic signs', first described by Piotrowski (1936), later by Delay, Pichot, Lemperière and Perse (1955) and several others.

The Rorschach test has been the subject of criticism. It has been blamed for being 'atheoretical', and this statement calls for comment. It is correct that Rorschach himself did not advance a theory to frame his empirical research. But subsequent personality theorists from several quarters: experimental and developmental psychology, psychoanalysis (including Jungians), existentialistic, and phenomenological psychology have given the test a solid theoretical anchoring.

Within the last decades the reliability and validity problems of the Rorschach test have been attacked by the American psychologist J E Exner, who has made comparative studies of the traditional Rorschach-systems (Exner 1969). As a consequence of his extensive work, a new scoring-system *The Comprehensive System* (Exner 1974) integrates the empirically best founded elements from the five hitherto most used scoring systems. He standardized the procedure, developed a computer programme, and undertook extensive reliability investigations. Another merit of Exner's work is his collection of protocols from large groups of normal children and adults, stratified with regard to sex, socio-economic status and geographical location. Such material from a normal population will diminish the objection that the Rorschach test is biassed toward psychopathology. It is, however, worth drawing attention to the fact that *being 'subclinical' the Rorschach may convey latent conflicts*. To my mind this is more an asset than a disadvantage, provided that the tester does not assume that potential liabilities are actual. They must be substantiated by an inner consistency of the test-data, by findings from other cognitive and projective tests or from interviews.

The Thematic Apperception Test (TAT)

Christiana Morgan and Henry Murray (1935) constructed the TAT which is also widely used. It consists of 30 pictures, depicting people in different situations. All are meaningful but ambiguous, with potential for mirroring the individual's needs, expectations, attitudes, mood, conflicts, and such personality structuring factors as cognitive style, defence mechanisms and integrating functions (see Bellak 1986).

Since the TAT has its strength in giving information about motives, attitudes, defence mechanisms, and aspirations, it serves as a useful supplement

to the Rorschach. The same precautions mentioned in relation to the administration of the Rorschach apply to the TAT.

INTERVIEW TECHNIQUES

These are among the tools of the clinical psychologist when it comes to giving
a psychodynamic assessment of the personality. The Karolinska Psychodynamic Profile (KAPP) interview will serve as a paradigm (Weinryb and Rössel
1991).

The KAPP interview is based on psychoanalytic theory in general and on
Otto Kernberg's structural interviewing (1984) in particular. The KAPP
interview is not a diagnostic instrument in a psychiatric sense, and it cannot
be juxtaposed with psychological tests. Yet it can add to a description of
personality or psychopathology. It also serves as a rating instrument, but not
as a rating scale. It has a satisfactory validity and with practice a good inter-rater
reliability. The 18 subscales are ordinate scales, where the distance between the
various steps is not assumed to be of equal size. The scales are graduated from
relative normality to increasing degrees of disturbance.

The structure of the KAPP interview is so relatively free that the interview
takes the shape of a dialogue. As far as possible it is left to the patient to take
the initiative and tell his story. Subscales 1, 2 and 3 describe essentially
interpersonal relations; subscales 4, 5, 6 and 7 mirror more specific aspects of
personality as frustration tolerance, impulse control, regression, handling of
aggression *(all evidently very important to assess in forensic cases)*. Subscales 8 and
9 describe differentiation of affects, 10, 11 and 12 deal with body image and
the meaning of the body for self-esteem. Subscale 13 and 14 describe sexual
function and satisfaction, 15, 16 and 17 reflect ideas of social sense and social
meaning and, finally, subscale 18 refers to a superordinate description of
personality. The manual gives instructive examples of scoring but, as mentioned
previously, a proper use of the instrument requires practice, clinical experience,
and a thorough knowledge of psychoanalytic theory and psychiatric nosology.

THE PSYCHOLOGICAL TEST REPORT

As Bellak (1959) points out 'the problems of communicating the data derived
from psychological testing are inherent in the tools, in the concepts and in the
organization of the report itself' (p.76). Very little systematic attention has been
paid to the presentation of the psychological report. The diagnostic formulations advanced by the psychiatrist and the psychologist, respectively, will often
build on data acquired from diverse abstraction- and influence-levels, and the
theoretical frames of reference may also be different. Obviously, this does not
facilitate communication *per se*, but the advantages of different vocational

training, theoretical background, and selection of methods far outweigh the drawbacks. Cross-disciplinary cooperation also offers the challenge that mutual insight and integration of the two disciplines' theoretical models and concepts is necessary, if understanding is to be secured. This does not imply that psychological jargon and technical terms should be used. As Lerner (1991) recommends: 'avoid mechanistic phrases...explicate more abstract concepts, and – with a sprinkling of illustrative test responses – remain emphatically close to the patient's subjective experience' (p.13).

The organization of the report should not only be dictated by the clinical issues that prompted the request for the investigation, but also by the findings that arose in the course of testing. In general, one may say that projective techniques usually probe deeper personality levels than the initial psychiatric interview. Cox and Theilgaard (1994, p.364) explore the scope of the 'depth' of projective interview in their consideration of Depth Activated Aesthetic Imaging. In this way the psychologist's dynamic assessment may aquire material which is sometimes difficult to elicit and not readily apparent otherwise.

Everything which may be used can also be misused. When the psychologist feels that the laboriously prepared report does not have the intended influence on the clinical process, whether it concerns diagnosis or treatment strategies, several influences may be at work: the attitude and lack of clinical experience of the receiver of the report, inadequate referral or limited opportunities to utilize the information of the report in a clinical context, and finally an incomplete, kaleidoscopic or otherwise badly drawn up test report. Confusion is further compounded by oscillation from: 'on the one hand' to 'on the other', or jumping from content to structure analysis, from a description of cognitive functions via emotions and defence mechanisms back to intelligence level and ego-strength plus catathymic areas, all without mediating links. Some reports are so non-specific in their descriptions that individual characteristics are lost among generalities.

The psychologist's task includes both data-collection and data-interpretation. Due to personal insecurity or lack of experience some may cling to concrete test findings and remain non-commital.

Sometimes the psychologist wants to illustrate the more or less abstract account with direct quotations of the testee's associations or statements. If the quotations are well chosen, they may give life and depth to an otherwise dry report. This may also involve a risk. The psychologist makes his inferences on the basis of normative frames of references and clinical experience. But this background knowledge is not always shared by the receiver of the report, and, therefore, a detached quotation, however convincing it may seem to the psychologist, may give the reader other associations. In such a case the psychologist runs the risk of being accused of 'wild analysis' and having his interpretations refuted. The use of quotations may also raise the suspicion that the psychologist made far-reaching conclusions purely on the basis of the quotation alone.

The pointing out of draw-backs has first and foremost served to draw attention to questions of interprofessional concern. In what way can the communication between psychiatrist and psychologist be improved? In the case of the offender patient, where not only clinical but also juridical consequences are at stake, it is absolutely necessary to secure as valid an assessment as possible. To that purpose the psychiatric interview and the psychological testing complement each other, provided that reciprocal respect exists. In matters as complicated as those presented by the forensic patient, a cross disciplinary approach in assessment is not a counsel of perfection, it is a working necessity.

Group-Analytic Psychotherapy in an Out-Patient Setting

Estela V. Welldon

INTRODUCTION

Group-analytic psychotherapy is frequently the best form of treatment, not only for severely disturbed perverse patients but also for sexual abusers and sexually abused patients. Group-analytic therapy breaks through patterns of self-deception, fraud, secrecy and collusion present in and essential for social and sexual deviancy. In this chapter I shall only summarize the most relevant points and discuss in more detail two specific issues. First, the emergence of erotization and sexualization against the therapeutic alliance and, second, work undertaken with victims and perpetrators of sexual abuse in the same thera-peutic group. Other aspects of group therapy with forensic patients have been dealt with elsewhere (Welldon 1982, 1984, 1992, 1994).

There is often an overlap between deviant sexual behaviour and antisocial acts, particularly in the case of incest perpetrators, who have often themselves been incest victims. Such is the degree of identification with the aggressor demanded by their 'psychic survival'. The socio-family microcosm of a group also affords a much better understanding of prevailing problems, which are deeply related to violence and antisocial actions occurring within socio-family dynamics.

Forensic psychotherapy involves three interested parties – the therapist, the patient and society's criminal justice system (de Smit 1992). Treatment of the forensic patient population should ideally be carried out within the National Health Service, not within the private sector, since forensic psychotherapy has to be considered in the overall context of health care for people involved in the criminal justice process. There is an inevitable, and indeed necessary, conflict of values (Harding 1992) with those of the criminal justice system. For example, society views sex offenders and their victims in distinct and reflex ways. Whereas the treatment of victims is encouraged and everyone is concerned about their welfare, the same does not apply to the offenders, who are believed to be the products of 'evil forces'. Lip service is paid to the fact that victims could easily become perpetrators but emotional responses tend to be biased. Victims are left without the benefit of being fully understood, since it is generally assumed that they are devoid of any negative, hostile feelings. The healthy expression of these feelings is not allowed and this suppression easily leads to revenge. The most exaggerated and distorted forms of hate and love are unquestionably present in both perpetrators and victims of sexual abuse and openly expressed when placed together in group therapy.

Another social stereotype casts women as victims and men as perpetrators. When men are sexual abusers many different agencies, social and medical, intervene and very soon the police are called in. By contrast, the female 'offender' finds it very difficult to get a hearing (Welldon 1988).

THE FORENSIC PATIENT

Most forensic patients have deeply disturbed backgrounds. Some have criminal records and very low self-esteem, which is often covered by a facade of cockiness and arrogance; their impulse control is minimal and they are suspicious and filled with hate towards people in authority. Some rebellious and violent ex-convicts have long histories of crime against property and persons. Others who may refer themselves are often insecure, inadequate and ashamed people. They enact their pathological sexual deviancy, such as exhibitionism, paedophilia or voyeurism, in a very secretive manner so that only their victims know about their behaviour. Some patients have a great capacity for expressing anger, yet seem shy and awkward in showing tenderness or love to anybody.

Forensic patients are often deviant both sexually and socially. Exhibitionism, for example, is a criminal activity by definition, whereas fetishism is not. Some patients who indulge in these activities may never have been caught. This is a secret or secretive population who apparently lead normal lives in both work and domestic situations. However, the links between criminal actions such as 'breaking and entering' and sexual deviations are not always obvious, at least not until the unconscious motivation is revealed. This connection has been noticed by many psychoanalytic writers, such as Zilboorg (1955), Glover (1944), and notably in young persons by Limentani (1984).

In short, the sources of referral are various and the type of people who become patients even more so. But, if understanding is to occur, all patients must be treated according to a rigorous professional code in which the offender is understood whilst the crime is not condoned. This process must begin with a comprehensive assessment of the patient.

Psychodynamic Assessment Prior to Group-Analytic Psychotherapy

The patient should be clear from the outset about the reasons for the assessment interviews. This is particularly important since the procedure could easily be taken as yet another legalistic encounter. In the initial period of treatment, beginning with the first interview, it is especially important to follow firm guidelines. Never make a patient wait beyond the appointment time – neither earlier nor later – earlier will be felt as seduction; later as a sense of neglect, repeating the experience of 'nobody caring'. These diagnostic meetings should be conducted at irregular intervals in order to avoid the intensity of the emergence of transference. The meetings are not as structured as psychotherapy sessions: there is some flexibility but the timing is always to be preserved rigorously. The approach needs to combine silence and direct questioning so that the patient can feel allowed to talk freely about difficult and, at times, painful predicaments while also being expected to give, in answer to questions, more details for further clarification.

The clinician must not let the patient involve him in anti-therapeutic manoeuvring, such as laughing at a patient's joke. Such jokes are frequently made at the expense of the patient's own self-esteem. No sooner has the therapist laughed than a sudden realization emerges that he or she is laughing *at* the patient and not *with* the patient. It is a serious mistake, into which inexperienced therapists fall in their attempt to appear friendly and nonjudgmental.

During the assessment sessions, there are often attempts to recreate the original injurious, traumatic situation as experienced by the patient. Frequently, this will have been experienced as being treated as a 'part-object', and becomes vividly alive in the transference.

Boundaries are crucial to establish a sense of differentiation, in which 'them' and 'us' create a sense of order and justice which can be rightly acknowledged.

Setting and surroundings are important, especially as the forensic patient has usually had previous experience of the judicial system, having been caught, detected and judged. In his dealing with the psychotherapist, he is prone to feel judged, charged, persecuted and subject to prejudice. If the diagnostician is not well trained, a new confrontation could easily be experienced by the prospective patient as a further condemnation of his or her illegal action. At times the action is symptomatic, when the offender knows it is wrong but finds himself unable to resist it. At other times the action is an enactment which the person is not willing to admit is odd or wrong. This action has sometimes been unconsciously committed, in an attempt to obtain a response from society to his individual predicament; the action takes over, and society focuses its attention on the action and not on the person who has committed it, until, of course, it comes to condemnation. Therefore, it is of basic importance to 'see' and to 'acknowledge' the person in his or her totality.

As infants, these adult patients experienced a sense of having been 'messed about' in crucial circumstances in which both psychological and biological survival were at stake. In other words they were *actually* – in reality, not only in fantasy – at the mercy of others. These traumatic, continuous and inconsistent attitudes towards them have effectively interfered with the process of individuation and separation. There is a basic lack of trust towards the significant carer, which accompanies them throughout their lives. Some psychopathological features are evident and can be understood in the light of the early background. They use over-sexualization in the same way, as a way of dealing with an enormous sense of inadequacy and inner insecurity.

It is obvious that all these different survival mechanisms and ways of functioning will appear intermittently when the defences are down. Then alarm and the old feelings re-emerge and put the person concerned on the alert. Defence mechanisms go in waves and when a situation of closeness is about to be achieved the person withdraws in horror. Such people loathe any new scenario which might involve or develop into trust. Thus the therapist could appear as a tyrannical and despotic paternal figure, who is only there to satisfy his or her own whims.

Because of their fears of intimacy in a one-to-one situation, these patients form a strong transference to the Clinic as an institution. The institution treating them can become as, or more, important than the therapist himself. A safe and containing atmosphere in which the patients feel secure and acknowledged from the moment of their arrival is essential. In short, the assessment is to be carried out like any other assessment but, if anything, with even greater care and sensitivity.

It appears that our patients are very much in need of the three structures: fellow patients, therapist, and institution. All are deeply related in their mental representations, which constitute a process of triangulation. They are indispensable for the effective running of a group therapy programme.

The forensic psychotherapist should feel safe and securely contained in caring and unobtrusive surroundings. Institutions should provide such structures to protect the therapists from the inherent anxiety produced by working with forensic patients. These patients act out sadistic and intrusive attacks on therapists and on their treatment in many different ways, including attacking their capacity to think: this leaves therapists confused and unable to offer adequate interpretations.

Money matters are important both in concrete and in symbolic terms. This is obvious with patients whose day-to-day living is provided by their own or close associates' delinquent or perverse actions. A frequent problem is the offer or 'pushing' of a gift which could at times render the therapist a receiver of stolen goods. The therapists' and patients' knowledge that the State is paying for treatment is very important. It reinforces both parties in the contractual agreement on which the therapy is based. The therapists are protected from blackmail and the patients feel neither exploited nor able to exploit anybody about money matters.

The psychotherapist must listen to the patient carefully, without interrupting, however difficult or painful the material may be. Some supposedly 'unusual' or 'rare' predicaments are not truly unusual: the so-called rarity is often due to the clinician's inability to listen because of the psychic pain involved. This is frequently the case with incestuous relationships. Most of these patients' material can be profoundly disturbing; at times it feels like 'dealing with dynamite'. If unprepared, the therapist can become irate, as if he or she were being 'taken for a ride', and indeed the patient often tries to be in total control of the situation. In other instances, patients succeed in making their therapists become their partners in their perversions.

Selection Criteria for Psychotherapy

It is important to make a basic distinction between offenders who are mentally disordered and those who are not. Some offenders have a professional orientation towards their criminal activities. They calculate the consequences, going so far as to engage in a cost-benefit planning of their actions, involving such matters as how many months or years in prison they are prepared to risk. In other words, such offenders may not differ in important psychological traits from ordinary careerists.

The psychodynamic assessment involves a wide understanding of all other factors concerning the individual in question; his psychological growth, his family – taking it back at least three generations, his own sub-culture, and other circumstances. The psychotherapist needs to investigate the 'crimes' in detail, especially the sequence of events leading up to the action as well as the offender's reaction to it. This can give clues to early traumatic experiences and to the unconscious ways in which an individual tries to resolve conflicts resulting from these experiences.

It is important to record how the patient interacts with the clinician and the changes observed during the series of meetings. At times it is useful to make a 'trial' interpretation to elicit the patient's capacity to make use of it, and his capacity for insight. In order to assess treatability for psychotherapy accurately in these patients, we must develop new concepts related to their situation. For example, if a criminal action is committed clumsily so that the person is especially susceptible to detection we can see that the action has become the equivalent of a neurotic symptom. If the offender expresses fears of a custodial sentence this may indicate that now is a good time to start treatment, since he is susceptible, however much under duress. He is now ready to own his psychopathology and this may denote an incipient capacity for insight. From the therapeutic standpoint, it is not unfortunate that a patient has to face prosecution: it is unfortunate, however, that just when he is ready for treatment he may instead have to face punishment.

Group-Analytic Psychotherapy

We have thought carefully about how to improve selection criteria. For example, given that such people present serious personality disorders and are unable to form relationships, it was obvious that some were more suitable than others for group treatment. It is necessary to be aware of the importance of certain factors in their personalities, family structure and living circumstances. For instance, the family root influence is crucial. Patients who have been subjected to an intense, suffocating relationship with one parent would be suitable candidates for group therapy. Often these people are still subjugated to an over-possessive mother, who does not allow them to develop any independence or individuation. Others would leave home only to find them-selves extremely isolated. In the group, with the help of fellow patients, they begin to express openly some rebellious, anti-authority feelings and eventually some self-assertion.

On the other hand, those whose psychopathology is rooted in the absence of an adequate parental attachment – including amongst others those fostered, those with major psychiatric problems in adoptions, evacuations and other upheavals, and those with particularly large and chaotic families, would be more likely to find the group threatening, frightening and destructive. Serious criminal patterns are not reasons in themselves for exclusion providing the delinquency does not preclude the personal disclosures required for therapeutic progress. The one diagnosis we have found not to respond to this form of treatment is voyeurism. Group sessions are used by these patients as a captive audience for the concrete acting-out for their perversion without the intricacies of inner changes associated with the acting-out in the sessions. Their inclusion in these groups has deleterious effects on the other members and hinders the development of trust and cohesiveness in the group process.

Before effective group therapy can begin, preparation of members is necessary on an individual basis. A vital aspect of the treatment is the introductory work of engaging with prospective group patients. Their inability to tolerate time-lapses, and the likelihood of experiencing reality-testing work as provocation, establishes the need for brief, irregular, and low-key introduc-tory sessions without interpretations, from which nutritious and holding experiences might then be transferred to the group. There, the emerging sense of commitment, belonging and responsibility – in respecting rules, for example – would continue with the holding aspect of the work.

Assessment of patients' present living circumstances are crucial. There are those who could benefit from group therapy but are involved in the criminal world. If they talk about of their own or their spouse's criminal activities, the confidentiality rule is impossible to sustain.

Extreme secretiveness, such as in sexual abuse for victims and perpetrators, is most frequently found to respond positively to group psychotherapy.

Violent behaviour seems better contained and even better understood within the framework of group therapy. Freud (1916c) points out that the mechanism of identification is a basic one in group formation. He elaborates the way in which identification not only helps to further positive feelings within the group but also helps in limiting aggressiveness, since there is a general tendency to spare those with whom one is identified. The presence of other participants, who may notice hostility before it is expressed openly (often against the therapist), gives the group a capacity to confront violent behaviour and to deal with it openly and honestly. Multiple transference provides patients with the possibility of more than just one target for their anger (cf. one-to-one therapy), which they find highly reassuring.

The amount of fear, rejection and humiliation which such patients experience when confronted with their 'secrets' in a group therapy session is difficult to convey. It is not unusual for them to deal with their enormous fears of being rejected by conjuring up an image of a nagging or possessive mother who has been experienced as both frightening and contemptuous. They will tend to gang up with each other, creating an atmosphere of unhealthy solidarity with the main object of assigning that image to the therapist. The therapist may be trapped into situations, such as being seen as a sadistic policeman who every time they talk about their problems tries to moralize, condemn or put them away; or a nagging mother who uses the group to question every patient in a persistent and repetitive way about their illegal actions, expecting them to conform to society's norms. The therapist has to be skilful in dealing with such interactions between patients from the outset. If collusion appears to develop between members this will create further anxieties, because patients are aware that covering-up brings frustrations when the therapist does not intervene properly by offering adequate interpretations. Unless unhealthy expectations can be clarified quickly as part of transference interpretations, the therapist and his expertise is likely to be immobilized.

Separation anxieties can easily produce most dangerous acting out. Therapists' holidays are very distressing for group members since they feel neglected, abandoned and uncared for, just as they did when they were infants. There are often, however, signals in the sessions leading up to holidays that 'something is going on'. It is important to recognize these clues, for they form part of this constellation or syndrome responsible for 'acting out' behaviour. It may be seen as the erotization of the group process as a resistance to the therapeutic process (Welldon 1982).

In an attempt to deny their intense oral needs and subsequent depression, the group starts operating or functioning through one of its members in a somewhat manic fashion, listening to him talk in an erotic way about sexually perverse material (although seeming to involve an Oedipal phenomenon, this actually corresponds to earlier phases of development). The patient goes on and on talking about his or her sexual predicament with extreme richness of details in a very repetitive fashion. To start with this might be thought to denote great trust in the group, but the fact that a particular patient talks with such freedom and so openly about actions of which he had previously felt so ashamed, should make the therapist suspicious. It soon becomes obvious that the patient is using the therapeutic situation, the group session itself, as the partner to his perversion. In other words, by describing his criminal and sexual offences in such detail, the patient is trying to seduce and excite the other members, thereby getting an enormous amount of sexual gratification. The point is that in such a case the patients have forgotten that they have come together for the manifest purpose of psychotherapy. The time and the place for therapy has now become the time and place for the perversion itself. Sometimes the patients might talk about weekly expeditions either shoplifting or 'cottaging' the lavatories to seek homosexual experiences. That particular group member is using the weekly session in a symbolic fashion as a lavatory to be rid of all the dirt he feels inside himself but in so doing the group is now taking on a cathartic purpose, and not a therapeutic one. On all these occasions a climate of excitement is created by giving great richness of material.

At other times a violent threat is cast upon the group by one very angry member. This creates a situation of fear mixed with excitement, about which our patients feel so vulnerable. The patient might not now do any acting-out in the traditional sense of the word, he might not indulge any more in actions outside the group, but what he is doing is a repetition of the act itself in talking about it here. From my own experience of dealing with these sorts of patients in group therapy, this particular phenomenon appears in the middle phases of the group process with patients who have been rather quiet and secretive about their actions in the initial phases. As mentioned earlier it seems that a traumatic situation usually linked with separation anxieties triggers off the erotization.

Clinical Material

Paul

Paul had referred himself for treatment because of heterosexual paedophilia – from the start he created a strong dependency on me as he had with his mother, in a very oral fashion, his fantasy being to be fed on demand by an ever-available breast represented by the group.

When the dates for the first summer holidays were announced almost two months in advance – everyone had been informed at the outset about official holidays – Paul was shocked; he had assumed that I was accessible at all times, living in at the Clinic. A good deal of interpretive work was done about separation anxieties, but it was dangerously apparent that Paul was unable to accept the reality of the coming holidays. He began to behave like a deserted child. At one session Paul was able for the first time to talk in detail about what exactly took place between him and the little girls involved in his actions. He did 'warn' us that he had disgusted his father in Court by telling how he pursued the girls in the playground.

I noticed that at the time the whole group had become mesmerized by this account. There were no interruptions, no confrontations, no questioning. There was not only silence, but the whole atmosphere was charged with electricity; by this I mean that everybody was very excited, actually sexually aroused, so this patient had succeeded in turning the whole group into a 'child' which he could molest. He was exercising the situation for his own pleasure. Now he did not need to seduce the children outside in the 'playground', he had the group and in a symbolic way he was displaying his perversion to a most satisfactory degree for his own sexual gratification. The group was behaving like the child described by him, obtaining sexual pleasure with full consent; he claimed he did not force, but only seduced the child.

Susan

Another example; Susan, a stripteaser-prostitute, who revealed herself very little indeed in the first few sessions. After a few months just before the Easter holidays, in a slow and determined fashion, she began to 'show bits of herself' in a provocative and seductive manner. For example, she spoke of her difficulties in having a one-to-one relationship, her contempt of men not being as competent or capable as she was expecting them to be, her fears of commitment, her close association with her daughter aged nine, her sense of boredom, her skill in mastering men, and eventually in a most histrionic manner she talked about the way she seduced men for financial profit. By then the group was behaving like a dirty old man, unable to question or to confront her but only too willing to give her all the attention and whatever *she* wanted out of the situation. As we see, they are all repetitive manoeuvres to engulf the group in a situation where no change is possible, being stuck in the same pattern.

Miriam

At other times a climate of fear and threat is present, again creating an enormous amount of excitement, as in the case of Miriam, who to start with was rather antagonistic towards me and later developed the most sadistic attacks on me, trying to belittle my function and denigrate my technique. She took a 'special interest' in Jason, a young member of the group who had no sexual experience with girls. Jason was very rigid. He used to come dressed in black leather with plenty of chains, and sit up immobile on his chair. After a few months of treatment he began to have explosive outbursts, first with another member who happened to be a homosexual paedophiliac. So we got to know for the first time of the traumatic experience he had gone through as a child in boarding school, being seduced by a teacher. Slowly these aggressive outbursts began to be replaced by situations in which he could cry, showing all his vulnerability. He had always felt very deprived and had become the child of the group. It was then that he began to get plenty of sympathy from Miriam. He was utterly dependent on me and used to take my interpretations very seriously; Miriam felt very angry with me and in sexual competition for Jason, especially since the holidays were approaching. Later on we learnt that on two occasions she had followed him to his bed-sitter and forced her way in there, trying to seduce him. This acting-out outside the sessions was to do with her attempting to be a sexual therapist for him in intense rivalry with me. He was very frightened and came to the group to explain it.

Erotization facilitates the process of acting-in and this easily leads to acting-out. The acting-out usually takes the form of pairing, either homosexual or heterosexual. One of the group members feels in open rivalry and competition with the therapist's authority. They see the therapist as ineffectual, uncaring, deserting and passive and this makes them operate in a very active and seductive manner, becoming the alternative radical therapist which makes them feel strong and powerful. They usually choose an inexperienced and insecure partner. The acting-out takes place frequently at the same time as the missed session. Following it they come back to the group and eventually they reveal their secret acting-out with the perverse hope of a renewed process of attempted erotization of the group.

This phenomenon can prove to extremely difficult to contain, even with accurate interpretations. The conductor has to be very much aware of that, because sometimes the environment is charged with so much eroticism that it is very difficult to be able to make an interpretation which will cut through what is going on right there.

Group members will try in many other ways to make the therapist part of the perversions in which they are involved. After all, why is the therapist interested in this bizarre behaviour? Is he or she getting some satisfaction out of it, thereby playing the willing partner to their perverse activities or fantasies? They tend to talk a lot about their 'willing victims', especially with exhibitionist and paedophiliac patients.

As we can see, all these different attempts to pervert the group therapy strongly indicate their own need to be denigrated. They are also implying their hopelessness and helplessness, in which they are not expecting anyone to understand them and to help them in the process of growing up. This is the ideal time for interpretations dealing with their infantile needs and their intense fears of being left alone.

GROUP THERAPY FOR SEXUAL ABUSE

These patients tend to feel unique in individual treatment and usually succeed in making the therapist feel not only protective but also possessive about them. In some cases, this may provoke feelings of collusion in the therapist who may feel cornered or blackmailed by the confidentiality clause. At other times, the therapist might feel either like the consenting child or the seductive parent in the incest situation. Either way therapy – meaning internal change – is in real jeopardy. The group setting makes more difficult this transferential–counter-transferential process to take place. Group members must open up and overcome the taboo of secrecy. This is because trust must lie with the peers, not just with the therapist.

Sometimes such patients present problems related to violence and secrecy in the family, as in the case of incest where the father or mother has been the perpetrator of sexual abuse. Alternatively, in the case of adult women, an undetected early history of incest accounts for a wide spectrum of problems, from chronic psychosomatic symptoms to a very high incidence of prostitution. These are unconsciously related to those early traumatic events.

Female patients with a history of early incest may behave from the very start in the group as 'ideal assistants' to the therapist. Even those who have never been familiar with unconscious processes seem to discover immediately appropriate ways in which to 'help' the therapist–mother–father keep the group-family together. Fellow patients often react with surprise and bewilder-ment, and later with competitiveness. When interpretations are made to the effect that the newcomer is repeating a pathological pattern learnt early in life, fellow patients seem relieved by this understanding but it is then the turn of the 'helper' to be filled with rage at this interpretation. After all, she is 'doing her best'; why is she being so 'harshly criticized'?

Treatment for Victims and Perpetrators

Group treatment for the victims and perpetrators of incest offers unexpected qualities of containment and insight which are virtually impossible in a one-to-one situation. Perpetrators become deeply aware of the extensive consequences of their actions when confronted by other members who correspond to their victims' mirror reflections and they can see how unable they are to see themselves as separate human beings, but only as parts of their parental figures. For example, all members experience a powerful sense of belonging to the group. During the treatment period the capacity for self-assertion, emotional growth, independence and individuation are some of the characteristics that patients gain. They see themselves and others developing into respected individuals with self-esteem which is acknowledged by others and by themselves. They are not only allowed but encouraged openly to express anger and frustration which has been kept hidden for lengthy periods. This encouragement comes especially from other 'old' members who have gone through similar predicaments.

Group Clinical Material

I shall first offer some clinical material from a group setting. This includes transferential and countertransferential responses which I hope will give some flavour of the mechanisms operating in these types of patients. Second, I shall describe some of the contrasting responses to paternal and maternal incest. I shall then speculate about the unconscious motivations underlying this contrast.

A group was formed in early 1981 containing not only women victims and men perpetrators of incest, but also women perpetrators and men who had been sexually abused. The experience with this particular group afforded us all, therapist and group members, many new understandings of the complexities of abuse, although we are still far from understanding everything. For example, we have learnt that in such mixed groups male perpetrators become aware that their actions are not just limited to physical effects but also inflict deep psychological wounds on their victims. It is also clear that victims, who may at the start be quiet and compliant, have much anger to express, anger that they have never felt able to display before. This is fundamental for them in achieving any real change. Anger is expressed in two different ways – first in a straightforward manner leading to self-assertion; second, in a vengeful way in which the person is still intertwined with the original relationship. So when the victim claims she can now express anger against the perpetrator, but this is in a twisted and vengeful way, we can see that she is still a partner in the old incestuous process.

The group

Keith referred himself for treatment after the disclosure of his incestuous relationship with his stepdaughter. I saw him for several diagnostic interviews. These were beset with complications as all the different agencies involved demanded information about his activities. I was placed in a double-bind situation, first because of his demands for immediate treatment and second because of his request for complete confidentiality. I began to feel more and more cornered and blackmailed into giving him treatment in the utmost confidentiality, which actually in this particular case meant 'secrecy'. I became deeply aware of the transference–countertransference issues involved in 'incest with a consenting child'. These were very powerful feelings. At times I would feel like the child keeping quiet about it all; at other times, I would feel like the controlling and exploitative parental figure. After a great deal of careful thought I decided to offer him group therapy, a suggestion which first surprised and then enraged him. I gave him time to think about it, and tried to explain to him clearly why this would be the most suitable therapy for him: secrecy between parent and child is a key pathological trait in incest, which in group therapy becomes no longer available. Everything is open to everyone. A few weeks later it was my turn to be surprised when he accepted my recommendation.

When he was admitted to the group, Fiona reacted with the most anger to Keith's admission of incest. She had many rows with Keith and felt incensed with him because she saw a mirror image of herself in him, in her relationship with her daughter and also with her father. Keith confronted her with the inconsistency between her alleged wish to change jobs and her feeble attempts to do so; by now it was obvious that she was still a practising prostitute. Keith himself was a conscientious worker, had kept his job and has been promoted several times. Fiona, on the other hand, confronted Keith with his erotic feelings towards his stepdaughter. He has been able to take this in, or let's say he has swallowed these confrontations which involve much truth.

By April 1982, Fiona had started a series of clerical jobs in which she usually got into terrible rows with women in authority. All this had to do with her idealization–denigration of me, not only for Fiona but also for everyone in the group. They were confronted with great expectations of and dependency on the mother figure, but simultaneously with fears that I would be inadequate in dealing with all their demands, as had happened with their real mothers. This was interpreted in transferential terms which involved the whole group since this experience was shared by all. In one session, Fiona caused much alarm when she mentioned how much she had regressed in her relationship with her daughter, to such an extent, indeed, that in accordance with the group members' suggestion I took the unprecedented action of suggesting the referral of her daughter for treatment to a Child Guidance Clinic. The draft of this referral letter was left on the table, in the centre of the group, where all communications about patients and outside agents are shown. (Letter writing is very much part of the culture of our groups where patients write to absent members, requests for reports are also prepared with the contribution of all members. This creates a sense of responsibility and group members own up to their own changes and psychological maturation.) Fiona was at first very distressed by this, but was later able to come to terms with it as being the best solution. The other patients appeared to be contained and held by this action, with which they had all agreed. From then on Fiona began to appear more reassured, far less resistant and more insightful. She had experienced me and the group as caring and supportive in her feelings of inadequacy in dealing with her functioning as a mother. In so doing, she had used projective identification with me as an omnipotent mother, who was supposed to deal with all problems within the group, even the outside ones.

Everyone in the group had some lesson to learn from my lack of resources to deal with everyone's problems solely by treatment within the group. This was acknowledged by my requesting help from the outside, which was promptly implemented. I was not aware that this experience had been so deeply felt until we eventually learnt that Keith had followed suit and had himself referred his stepdaughter to the same place for treatment. We got to know about this two years later when Keith confronted Fiona about her folly in wanting to stop her daughter's therapy. He told her that he knew all the processes, since he had thought it such a good idea that he had taken his stepdaughter for treatment. Obviously there was a degree of identification and role model in operation which could have never occurred in individual treatment.

The group dynamics became even more complicated with the arrival of Patricia in January 1984. Patricia was a victim of incest which had taken place between the ages of eleven and twenty-one. She joined the group at the age of thirty-six after referral from her GP when, for the first time in her life, she admitted first to herself and then to him her repressed or 'forgotten' history of incest. Although an experienced doctor in psychosomatic problems, he had for fifteen years felt puzzled at not being able to understand the causes for her extensive and serious psychosomatic complaints.

As soon as Patricia joined the group she started behaving as the 'ideal' assistant to the therapist, even though she had never previously been in any kind of psychotherapeutic treatment. She fulfilled perfectly the role of the incest victim who tries to 'keep the family together'. This produced much aggravation amongst most members but especially in Fiona, who in her adult life had 'chosen' the 'prostitution solution' as opposed to the psychosomatic one. Together with Myra she was the only remaining member of the original group. She now experienced enormous pressure to become the 'grown up' adult member of the group.

In a subsequent session, there was a very active confrontation between Patricia and Fiona in which both were 'assessed' by other members who thought Patricia to be by far the more mature of the two, despite her recent admission. All sorts of interpretations on my part about Patricia's re-enactment of her early behaviour seemed to be of no avail. Fiona threatened to leave the group and wrote several letters to the effect that she felt hurt and humiliated by the others 'misunderstanding' her maternal role. Eventually, and on subsequent occasions, she returned to the group. (Incidentally she left after five years of group treatment in a healthy way, after she had obtained a very good professional position and her daughter was continuing treatment for her own problems.)

Group members clung to the belief that Patricia was the most assured member and quite healthy, such was their wish for a 'healthy incest' which could have no damaging effects on the victims. However, at a later session Patricia appeared to be distressed and distraught. She then proceeded to tell us how the evening before she had been 'prevented' from watching a TV programme on incest, due to her father's telephone call at exactly the time of this programme. He had talked for an hour, the duration of this particular TV programme. Now it was Keith's turn to become aware of the deep implications that incest had for Patricia when he confronted her with her submission and her acceptance of the situation, with her inability to stop her father and with her lack of assertiveness in not being able even to ask him to phone her an hour later.

A similar situation occurred a few weeks later when she was in tears telling us of her extreme humiliation in her recent visit to her parents, who knew of her decision to be a vegetarian. She had already told her mother clearly about this and had reaffirmed it before spending the weekend with them. So she was amazed when confronted on Saturday morning with her father having cooked 'especially' for her breakfast an enormous amount of sausages and bacon, which she reluctantly but acquiescently ate. However, it looked as if father had 'read' some inner changes on her part, because he angrily 'questioned her about being in some sort of nonsense or therapy'.

Whereas previously Keith and Patricia had been unable to make any connection, even refusing eye contact, they were now in open confrontation with one another. Keith indignantly questioned her inabilities to assert herself and her compulsion to give in to her father's requests. Suddenly and quite unexpectedly, a complete understanding of their own respective roles and of the implications was available to us all. We all became aware that incest is much larger than life, that its power is not only physical, sexual, or erotic. This secret union provides both partners with a 'uniqueness' which it is almost impossible to describe. It gives as much as it takes away. No one was able to resist the realization of Patricia's suffering despite her maturity, helpfulness and 'insight'. Fiona now learnt about Patricia's real predicament, and indeed she became very caring and helpful to her in a realistic manner and was able to see the chronic disabilities that incest had inflicted on Patricia.

Patricia was at first completely unable to assert herself in any direction. She was compliant with any wish of her father's and of her mother's too. In the group treatment she began to assert herself very slowly and in a very determined fashion, but only after an initial period of being extremely compliant to the therapist in order to keep the 'family' together. Eventually, she began to express anger. This took place with another group member when she was able to scream at him and tell him to 'sod off'. She and everyone else were extremely surprised at this and we all experienced a sense of achievement at her ability to express anger.

However, the reaction of the group members and myself was completely different when a few months later we saw her looking extremely elated, with a sense of triumph emerging from her of which we were all very aware as soon as she entered the group. Interestingly enough, nobody felt very at ease with this feeling and somebody asked the reason for her feeling so triumphant. Her answer was, 'The bastard got what he deserved'. At that point everybody knew who she was talking about but nobody knew what she was referring to. Then she said, 'The bloody bastard just got to know that his testicles will be removed because he has cancer of the testicles. Isn't that wonderful?'

A few members attempted a smile but most people felt extremely worried about her. Then I had to offer her an interpretation dealing with her inability to separate herself from the person who had committed incest with her, and in a way she was still part of it in that she was not being completely separate. She was now strongly expressing the need for revenge. We all know that the expression of anger is therapeutic and a healthy sign, but the wish for revenge is a unhealthy trait which poisons the person who suffers from it and everybody around her too. This situation revealed how much the victims cling to the perpetrators like an enemy.

They react in a rebellious way when I am on holiday and make me feel that I shouldn't be away since they need me so much. A similar situation takes place whenever I take new members into the group. It is so cosy and closed that everyone feels reluctant to take new admissions. There is always a fantasy present among group members that if they stay long enough the 'ideal' one-to-one situation will come to pass. Perhaps this is an important reason for patients tending to stay for long periods while sometimes being very jolly and at other times angry and full of threats of leaving abruptly. They want to be thought the most special one or the only child. Animosity, rivalry, open hostility and even murderous feelings towards their siblings emerge on different conscious and unconscious levels. These are often more vividly experienced just before arrivals into the group. Sometimes a 'group dream' is produced which contains powerful aggression towards the newcomers. On one occasion, just before new patients were admitted, a member of the group had a dream in which he and a female patient were terrorists in an airport, each carrying hand-grenades. Then there was a big explosion and he ended up with her head on his lap while his head was somewhere inside her body. Here we see the analogy of the airport – a place of arrivals and departures; and the intertwining of mind and body.

These patients' psychopathology involves shame, manic defenses and primitive defensive mechanisms such as denial, projection and splitting. This tends to divide the helping professions, creating sides for either child or perpetrator and making them forget the neutral stance often necessary to understand the whole family dynamics.

The patients are fearful that the therapist, in a one-to-one situation, will lose control, and that he or she will fall prey to their own seduction, the outcome of which is both hoped for and dreaded. Their underlying anxiety is associated with tremendous fears of separation and being discarded by parental figures if they do not comply with their inappropriate demands. I consider this to be yet another indication in favour of group therapy in which they are confronted with a reality testing from their co-equals, in which the power of being so favoured and unique has to be worked through in a group situation, a bit like the family, although it operates on very different dynamics. There is a generation gap in their real and emotional lives in which role reversal has occurred and the group interaction offers a completely different experience.

The group

In October 1987 when Patricia and Kevin were still members of the group, several new patients were admitted. One of them, Erica, provoked an enormous amount of trouble during her two-year stay in the group. She was a victim of maternal incest. Her reason for referral was her compulsion to 'flash' to people in authority, expecting a shocked response from them. Whereas in general her perversion seemed to be the exact counterpart of the male flasher, this was not actually so since male flashers usually flash to strangers and to the other gender. Erica, on the other hand, very much confined her flashing to women whom she had invested with so-called 'maternal' qualities. I was warned of her 'dangerousness' which had to do with her pestering doctors to an alarming degree, such as getting into their houses and consulting rooms and making phone calls to them at all hours of the day and night.

During her stay in the group, Erica inflicted on us all much suffering, pain, helplessness and hopelessness. She projected a strong quality of pervasiveness which we learnt was characteristic of victims of maternal incest. Victims of maternal incest operate altogether rather differently from victims of paternal incest. This has been corroborated by many other patients, male and female, in treatment at the Clinic.

Erica began by being rather seductive towards the therapist. This seductive maneuvering had a hostile–sadistic characteristic different from the compliant, acquiescent attitude found in victims of paternal incest. The seductiveness operated in a very nagging and cloying way which began to escalate to physical proportions. She wanted to be the best of them all and began to make attempts to sit on my lap. She would get into the room first to make certain to sit next to me, and then she would push her chair nearer and nearer to me. The other group members would try to demonstrate in different ways how to deal with this impossible situation and to function effectively as a group. This proved to be more and more difficult as the weeks went by, because of her increasing demands and her complete inability to do any sharing with the other group members and her firm determination to be almost one with me.

This situation became a challenge in which group members tried different devices to deal with Erica's continuous, unacceptable demands. The last device adopted was to have two different members of the group sitting on either side of me, almost like bodyguards protecting me from her. The interesting thing about this was that Erica was a very small, slightly-built woman, who actually had by then changed her pathology from being a flasher to being anorexic; almost trying to disappear before my eyes but being very much present in other ways. She was now considered to be the most dangerous person; this very innocuous, benign-looking little girl had to be constrained by two men assigned to protect me from her ferocious attacks. An extraordinary feature was that they were perpetrators of incest towards their own daughters. At that point it occurred to me, 'Here I am being protected by two men who are perpetrators of incest from someone who has been a victim of maternal incest.'

Groups can give us quite a range of potential solutions and outcomes that in themselves appear superficially to be wild and quite crazy from any rational point of view.

Workers of all disciplines involved in cases of incest frequently find it difficult to maintain a detached professional stance. They tend to take sides, usually becoming emotionally bound to the victims. In addition, or alternatively, they feel punitive towards the perpetrators. In their distress, they lose their understanding of the dynamics of what is happening. For example, they sometimes become so indignant that they fail to see that victims who become perpetrators experience a conscious or unconscious desire to take revenge for the pain inflicted upon them. These victim-perpetrators believe they are creating a situation in which justice is satisfied. Actually, however, they are identifying with their aggressors. In somewhat similar ways, the professional workers often identify with the victims. Supervision has an important role in clarifying these issues, thus enabling therapists to avoid such pitfalls.

Group psychotherapy offers particular advantages as a treatment option for victims of sexual abuse, since secrecy and isolation are replaced by disclosure within the containing atmosphere of the group. The threat of intimacy and the phantasied risks of seduction/exploitation are reduced for both patients and therapists. The power of the group as a whole acts both as auxiliary ego in strengthening individuals as they confront past pain and abuse, and as superego in moderating the sadistic need for revenge which fuels their innate capacity for perpetrating abuse in their turn.

CONCLUSION

Group analysis has considerable potential in the field of forensic psychotherapy. Small groups reflect the disordered early family experiences of forensic patients, but can also offer not only containment but enlightenment to both victims and perpetrators of abuse. The group functions also as a microcosm of society, and thus provides an opportunity for group members constantly to re-negotiate and develop further a sense of social responsibility, and to understand the consequences of anti-social actions. The capacity to interpose *thought* between impulse and action must be the aim of forensic psychotherapy. Achievement of such insight and understanding of the unconscious motivations can free the forensic patient from the tyranny of having no choice. The participation in group psychotherapy by forensic patients may contribute to freeing society from the damage which results from forensic psychopathology.

Acknowledgements

I am grateful to Dr. Pamela Ashurst for her valuable professional contributions to this chapter.

Supportive and Interpretive Psychotherapy in Diverse Contexts

Murray Cox

INTRODUCTION

The opening to this chapter is paradoxical. It reinforces the emphasis, already established in 'In and Out of the Mind' (I.1), that although context and content are discrete, they cannot be considered in isolation. Context influences content, never more so than during those vital moments when therapist and patient first meet.

The initial interview is always important and the *primordial* movement of emotional contact can have far-reaching consequences. Although this holds true for all therapeutic endeavours, it is of particular significance in forensic work. This partly reflects the patient's personality structure, and is partly due to the psychological and physical context.

This chapter deals with two sets of variables. There is the continuum between interpretive and supportive psychotherapy, on the one hand, and the impact of the wide range of contexts in which such work is undertaken, on the other.

The establishment of Empathic Contact is a major priority. It commands an extensive bibliography[1]. Many forensic patients are initially and erroneously regarded as being empathy-resistant. A further error is to presume that lack of an initial ability to trust – an attitude so often based on experiencing the repeated failure of human 'reliability' – implies that the patient is therefore also

---

1 See Cox and Theilgaard 1994, pp. 234, 236 for Empathy and Modes of Contact

treatment-resistant. No matter whether the long-term therapeutic aim is analytic psychotherapy for the sadistic narcissist, or supportive psychotherapy for the virtually defenceless psychotic, the moment and context of contact can be crucial. Mutual trust is then on trial.

It has been found that the *aesthetic imperative* (Cox and Theilgaard 1987, p.26; 1994, p.35) frequently facilitates unthreatening *aesthetic access* to the inner world of those fragile patients who fear and thus withdraw from human proximity, especially when the context of the initial encounter is less than auspicious. The word 'aesthetic' is here used in Bateson's (1979) sense: 'By aesthetic I mean responsive to the pattern which connects' (p.17). It is the therapist's discernment of this connecting pattern upon which so much hinges. Thus a successful initial interview may lead to sufficient empathic bonding for subsequent supportive or interpretive therapy to take place, in spite of the 'alien' context of a prison cell, a hospital corridor or a laundry room!

Prior consideration will be given to a brief survey of those dimensions in which all psychotherapeutic work, and the supervision thereof, can be structured. It opens with a statement about the ubiquity of the development of transference and countertransference phenomena. This is not the venue to discuss the pros and cons of individual, small group or therapeutic community approaches. There is always some optimal pivotal point in the support–interpretive spectrum which will be determined by the prevailing needs of the patient and the setting in which he is seen. For example, group psychotherapy may formally be designated as supportive or confrontational. Yet there is inevitably a dynamic 'mix'. Thus, an apt, well timed dream interpretation is felt to be supportive, because attentive discernment has led to a deeper understanding of self. The patient could not do this 'unaided' – without the therapist's 'support'; or, in the case of group therapy, without the buoyancy of the group matrix. In other words, to say that interpretive therapy is taking place (i.e., primitive defences are being relinquished) does not imply that the patient is not simultaneously experiencing support.

THE UBIQUITY OF TRANSFERENCE AND
COUNTERTRANSFERENCE PHENOMENA

The fulcrum of interpretive psychotherapy has to do with the restoration and relocation of feelings, attitudes and thoughts which were transiently and anachronistically invested in the therapist. These are the essential components of transference phenomena. The therapeutic process is concerned with their development, interpretation and, in due course, resolution at the right time and in the cadence of the right affective key.

The cardinal distinction between the interpretive, or analytic mode, and the supportive mode of psychotherapy is the way in which transference phenomena are dealt with. They are inevitable indications of a developmental phase of therapy. In supportive therapy, negative transference phenomena are considered to be contaminants, or unwanted side-effects, which should be minimized where possible and, ideally, avoided. Space does not permit justification or the presentation of theoretical and clinical evidence in support of what must, reluctantly, be presented as a 'given'.[2] Even so, it is impossible to enter into any meaningful exploration of the inter-relationship between interpretive and supportive psychotherapy in forensic contexts without reference to transference phenomena. This is because one of the crucial distinctions between generic psychotherapy and forensic psychotherapy is that in the latter there are *auxiliary recipients of transference phenomena.* Once again, anachronistic and inappropriate affect transient relocation is the key. During forensic psychotherapy it is not uncommon to find that the patient's perspectival world (Poole 1972, p.90) has been so 'tilted' that a victim is invested at the crucial 'material time' with fantasized features of the object to be destroyed. For example, feelings originally felt, but unexpressed, towards a previously persecuting father may have been transiently relocated in the conventional stereotype of the innocent victim ('the little old man at the bus-stop'). He may have been killed because he was present and available in the relevant *'now'* of the patient's released aggression, whereas the absent or long-dead father, the primal 'target', was not. During subsequent psychotherapy, the therapist, himself, may temporarily become the recipient of such hitherto buried affect, so that feelings expressed which had resulted in a dead man at the bus-stop, and originally evoked by and 'targeted' upon the father, may once again be resurrected and worked through in the patient's relation to the therapist. Exactly how the therapist's countertransference response to both primary (the father) and secondary (the man at the bus-stop) anachronistic relocations is dealt with is tangential to our current theme, although it is central as a topic to be repeatedly explored in supervision (see Chapter II:13).

NECESSARY DIMENSIONS FOR THIS EXPLORATION

The relationship between interpretive and supportive psychotherapy can best be considered under the headings of the following dimensions which impinge upon every kind of psychotherapeutic endeavour. These are well documented (Cox 1978b) and will not be considered in detail here. Each is itself multi-dimensional and many faceted, although, fortunately, they can be succinctly stated; namely, Time, Depth and Mutuality. It is one of the particular emphases of forensic work that the importance of the context can never be ignored. This is in marked contrast to some of the pioneer psychoanalytic and psychothera-

---

2   Chapter I:2 (Nicholas Temple) is devoted to these fundamental dynamic issues.

peutic literature in which the 'outer' world received relatively little attention, because it was the 'inner' world that counted.

It is interesting to note how a forensic focus gives an added emphasis to many issues which are familiar in generic psychotherapy. Thus attention will always be upon intrapsychic phenomena, interpersonal phenomena and trans-generational existential issues. This third focal point, augmented through dramatic distance and the aesthetic imperative, is brought out so clearly in the poignant encounter described by Shakespeare between 'A son that has killed his father' and 'A father that has killed his son'. In the ensuing couplet he presents us with the juxtaposition and intermingling of ethical and forensic engagement which war situations so often expose:

> 'I'll bear thee hence; and let them fight that will,
> For I have murdered where I should not kill.'

(III Henry VI II.5.121)

However brief this survey, the dimension of Time and its relevance to the reactivated past is particularly important in all forensic psychotherapy. For many patients, previous experience has led to the development of disabling symptoms or a diminished sense of resilience and self-esteem. In the forensic world the consequences may be catastrophic. It is then not merely a question of a reduction of self-esteem as a symptom, but possibly also of criminal acts, such as arson or homicide. Interdisciplinary debate centres on the relationship between previous potentiality, past precipitants and present pathology which subsequently lead to explosive action at 'the material time': the *now* of the moment of attack, the criminal act.

There is an interesting semantic parallel between the title of a paper by Treurniet (1993, p.888) and a question asked in the Heidelberg Catechism, compiled in 1562. The former asks 'What is psychoanalysis *now*?' and the latter asks 'What doth it help thee *now*, that thou believest all this?' (emphasis added). So often forensic psychotherapy has to deal with the immediacy of the prevailing present – even though it may have been 'a present in the past'. This is Treurniet's closing sentence: 'Finally, the dialectics of insight and relation are theoretically clarified through the clinical concepts of background and foreground, which are clinically bound to the concrete psychoanalytical situation and form a tool to distinguish the two types of transference [explored in the paper], resistance and conflict'. Once again, his reference to 'background and foreground' is of widespread forensic relevance. The narcissistic psychopath, far from merging into the background, needs to merge into the foreground until he dominates and *is* the foreground of collective attention.

Previous exemplification (Cox 1978b) of a 'Heidelberg' predicament seems relevant here:

'However sophisticated his professional training may have been, a Heidelberg type of confrontation may face, say, a probation officer whose client says

Would you like to see photographs of my victim?

The probation officer finds he is asking himself

How does it help you now that you 'believe' or know all this?

about appropriate handling of such a situation or just what controlled emotional involvement means in these circumstances. Morbid curiosity might provoke a desire to see the photographs; nausea at the prospect of a mutilated body might cause revulsion. This could lead the client to feel that if his probation officer was revolted by what he did, he would therefore be revolted by the client himself. A circle of diminishing disclosure and increasing distance...might ensue.' (p.81)

Such a Heidelberg predicament refers to a paradigmatic forensic contextual predicament. It leads us into a concentrated statement about interpretive and supportive psychotherapy. This very concentration runs the risk of making the passage seem more assertive than is intended. Reflective unhurried conversation about these issues would certainly render it less dogmatic and more equivocal.

CONFRONTATION AND SUPPORT: A CONTINUUM

Neither confrontation nor support exists in pure culture. Their inextricability and reciprocity contribute to the complex affective multi-modal exchange between the forensic patient and the therapist.

The writer knows little enough about the mechanics of the gear-box, yet he is aware that when an 'automatic' gear-box is fitted, the driver's attention is not diverted from his 'primary dirigible preoccupation' – to adapt Winnicott. Differential 'diagnosis' between interpretive and supportive psychotherapy is fraught with theoretical and logistic debate, but it cannot be avoided here. At the outset the author's view – and it is a personal perspective – needs to be made clear: namely, that there is a 'continuum', a spectrum, with polarization only in extreme positions. Interpretive therapy would never have reached the end of the first 50-minute hour was it not for an attuned empathic holding ethos, albeit unspoken and virtually gesture-free. Supportive therapy, *per contra*, may continuously and slowly allow the patient to retrieve hitherto threatening and therefore denied aspects of his own experience, so that he 'confronts himself' as his capacity to endure increases. *The optimal structuring of Time, Depth and Mutuality is of the essence.*

SUPPORT

There is prolonged and heated controversy as to whether 'supportive psycho-therapy' can be labelled 'therapeutic' in any sense whatever. By definition, supportive psychotherapy is usually regarded as a process in which the patient's precarious and fragile defences are buttressed and reinforced. Few who have worked in a conventional psychiatric hospital with chronic schizophrenic patients, or with those whose self-esteem is so virtually non-existent that they can seriously say 'it will be a long time before I am well enough to be a patient', will doubt the necessity of supportive endeavours. Indeed, Werman (1984) has written a monograph entirely devoted to this topic. Much of the main-stream work undertaken by the corporate team efforts, by colleagues of several linked disciplines, involving every kind of supportive activity, including medication, is to this end. It is often life-enhancing and suicide-preventing. It seems ironic and cynical to debate whether such clinical humanitarian engagement should be deprived of the appellation 'therapy'. Certainly, many patients and their relatives are grateful for work of this nature. Derogatory debate and disdain towards collaborative 'support' usually come from those far removed from 'chronic' wards of long-stay patients – or the risky ferocity of front-line forensic encounters.

CONFRONTATION

Interpretive psychotherapy, on the other hand, which is variously called analytic or confrontational, through the development, interpretation and resolution of transference phenomena seeks to free the patient from the restrictive legacy of the past. This means that anachronistic experience is relocated in its rightful place within the patient's developmental line. Such interpretive therapy aims to help the patient relinquish primitive defences, establish object-constancy, free gyroscopic introjects from encrusting impedi-ment so that, ultimately, he is enabled to live and love with less anxiety and greater enjoyment.

The word 'confrontation' calls for a note of clarification. In this realm of discourse such 'confrontation' does not imply a fierce 'confrontation' between therapist and patient. On the contrary, it implies that the therapist endeavours to facilitate a patient's confrontation with himself. It is the patient's primitive defences which are to be relinquished, rather than those of the therapist.

TWO PREVALENT PARADOXES

1. Conducting sustained long-term supportive psychotherapy for the chronic psychiatric patient – including the chronic forensic patient – is one of the most finely honed clinical skills that a therapist can acquire. It could be said that in

these circumstances he is learning to use the minimum effective dose of his own personality, to use Balintesque language, which can maintain the dilapidated ramparts of the patient's ineffective defensive organization. That such a therapeutic endeavour should sometimes be regarded as work appropriate for a registrar or other young trainee, who is present, by definition, only on an interim basis, constitutes a misjudgment of clinical priorities.

2. There is an in-built inherent buoyancy and dynamic source of inductive energy in interpretive psychotherapy which is absent from supportive endeavours. The whole cosmos of psychoanalytic theory endorses this, even though there are innumerable pitfalls and complications awaiting the uninitiated or the inadequately supervised. But, all in all, the very process of activating and subsequently moderating endopsychic instabilities evokes the collaborative energy of both therapist and patient. There is a sense of 'work to be done' and on-going 'work in progress'.

Supportive work has no such in-built energy. 'Successful' interpretive and supportive psychotherapy are both exceedingly complicated, densely laminated enterprises needing every personality resource and professional skill that the therapist can muster. For this reasons it is absurd, and borders on the unethical, to regard supportive psychotherapy as an activity which is scarcely worthy of the name 'therapy'. Furthermore, this undertaking can be exceedingly risky if wrongly structured – and is not for a junior colleague at the outset of a professional career.

THE RISKS OF INADEQUATE FORMULATION OF SUPPORTIVE INITIATIVES

If these issues are relevant in generic psychotherapy, how much more *gravitas* is implicit in this debate when forensic psychotherapy is under consideration. Consider, a male chronic schizophrenic who has killed. He subsequently announces during a therapeutic 'supportive discussion' with a young female doctor that he has recently been dreaming about his index offence, but that the victim (also a woman with a Welsh accent) 'is now beginning to look and speak like you, doctor. But I know I am seeing you to talk about my injections.' Such material is the substance of forensic supervision. Human exchange of this order is trivialized and diminished when the debate as to whether supportive psychotherapy can be regarded as psychodynamically legitimate, or authentically therapeutic, is in the air. Mention only has to be made of transference psychosis, victim substitution, a residual endopsychic enclave of still-ready-to-murder hate, which is just beginning to 'leak' into a therapeutic session, to see how potentially deep is such material and how dangerous can be the consequences if psychological mishandling takes place.

DIVERSE FORENSIC CONTEXTS

The two ensuing diagrams succinctly illustrate the contextual setting in which forensic therapeutic encounter may occur. They also depict the importance of the point in the developing chronology of the offender patient's transit through the criminal justice system and/or health care system.

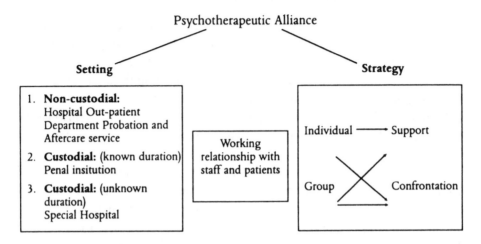

Figure 1 Settings for the Psychotherapeutic Alliance (Cox 1974, p.6)

Figure 1 has itself an in-built time-marker. It will be noted that under the heading 'custodial' there is the known duration of time spent in a penal institution and the unknown duration of time within a Special Hospital. The paper (originally published in 1974) makes no reference to a Regional Secure Unit (RSU). Had this diagram been drawn today an RSU would certainly have been one of the main settings to be discussed.

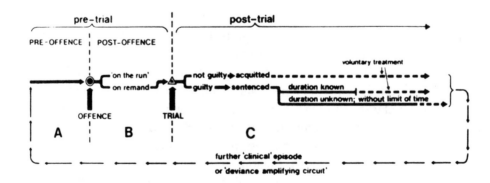

Figure 2 Time and the Therapeutic Encounter (Cox 1979, p.318)

Figure 2 serves to illustrate the point at which the individual patient's psychological developmental line merges with his forensic progress. With the realism of extended experience, it also indicates his 'season' ticket for the same journey on account of a 'further clinical episode' or participation in a 'deviance amplifying circuit'.

Taken in conjunction, these diagrams obviate the need for further description. They emphasize the perennial importance of considering the impact of the context, in which therapy is conducted, upon the open endedness of a without-limit-of-time setting or the restrictive determinacy of a known duration. Both factors inevitably impinge upon the nature of the therapeutic process itself. This re-emphasizes the constant relevance of the structuring of all psychotherapeutic endeavours in terms of the dimensions of Time, Depth and Mutuality – and their impact upon the context in which therapy is itself conducted.

THE SCOPE OF METAPHOR IN FORENSIC PSYCHOTHERAPY

Metaphor can be *mutative* – which is to say that it can 'clothe' and 'flesh out' psychoanalytic interpretations indicated on conventional grounds. Metaphor can also be stabilizing and affirmative. It may be purely descriptive.[3]

There are many facets to the contribution of the mutative metaphor to forensic psychotherapy. Indeed, much of the original work (Cox and Theilgaard 1987) was 'discovered' in forensic settings. The word 'discovered' is used deliberately, as it was a phenomenon which presented itself through a process of un-covering, rather than one which was, so to speak, devised. Such work has wide forensic ramifications and overall relevance. It points to the value of the *autogenous interpretation* and the therapist's discretionary option of either remaining within the metaphor or relinquishing it in a moment of interactive confrontation or support. The metaphor also allows parallel themes to be developed simultaneously, thus enabling him to remain upstream of foreclosure. A vignette may illustrate this:

Vignette
A female patient in a Broadmoor group was re-living a pleasant early childhood memory. ...'I was about five years old, proudly wearing my new Wellington boots and bravely walking into the little stream in the village. There was a kind of fear and excitement as the water level rose and when

---

3   For example, in reply to the question 'Could you tell me something about your family?', a patient replied 'My parents are a couple of walking islands'. This is phenomenological shorthand of a high order.

it went over my boots and round my feet I had a funny squashy and excited feeling. I wanted to go on and I was afraid. Just at that moment two large eels came down the stream. I was frightened and tried to run back to the bank but I could not move fast enough... Murray, is this why I am afraid of penises?'

Such an autogenous interpretation has many benefits. It inevitably takes place at the right time for the patient to link her fear of penises, her fascination with sexually excited dogs, doubts about her own gender and the 'penetrating' aspects of her index offences. This example is 'upstream' in a double sense, illustrating the intricacy of mutative potential.

NON-MUTATIVE METAPHOR KEEPS OPTIONS OPEN

A vignette illustrating metaphor's facilitation of parallel themes – so that the therapist appears to be talking of two things at once, is exemplified in this short segment of dialogue:

Vignette
A female patient was describing a fierce, punitive father who would punish her whenever she made a mistake in her homework and an over house-proud mother whose one concern seemed to be that, of all crimes, the bringing of dog-shit into the house was the most serious in the calendar. At one juncture the patient was comparing her mother and her father. Each had assets and liabilities. When talking about her proclivity to make mistakes and the ominous consequences of bringing dog-shit into the house, the therapist made a comment which kept his response upstream of foreclosure, so that the patient could readily have presumed that he was commenting on either situation. Having been informed of the fear of retribution from both mother and father, he observed:

'Yes...it's so easy to put your foot in it.'

This simple use of metaphor was in fact the opposite of mutative. It deliberately changed nothing so that the patient's affective emphasis could be followed. Endopsychic mutation ensued precisely because the therapist 'spoke' of both worlds simultaneously – 'to put your foot in it' retained the double referent of making mistakes and treading in dog-shit. The patient could no longer fail to discriminate *between* fear of mother and fear of father. In this way the patient's affective choice-point was put under the spotlight.

The use of mutative metaphor within a forensic focus is a fascinating theme, but well beyond the scope of this chapter (see Cox and Theilgaard 1987).

STABILIZING METAPHOR

Supportive, non-threatening affirmative language can be richly endowed with metaphor. There is no particular 'forensic' quality to it. Psychological support, against widespread threats to self-esteem in times of narcissistic depletion: bereavement, dislocation, illness, unemployment – indeed every kind of loss, or anticipated loss, culminating in the eventual certainty of *Exeunt All*, may well call for stabilizing therapeutic initiatives.

SOME ASPECTS OF INTERPRETIVE AND SUPPORTIVE PSYCHOTHERAPY ARE INEXTRICABLE

By way of conclusion, we return to the opening comments about the initial interview and the necessity of adequate empathy and affective support, without which interpretive psychotherapy would never be able to start. A motivated forensic patient is as essential as is motivation in all psychotherapy. Nevertheless, there are some inbuilt reluctances to trust. This is because, since childhood, repeated life experience has so often informed the forensic patient that those in authority are likely to be unreliable or only 'interested' as a passport to subsequent abuse. It is for this reason that interpretive forensic psychotherapy inevitably depends upon adequate initial affective purchase. The 'hold' in the early moments and days of such therapeutic exploration is bound to depend upon a degree of empathic understanding. Volumes have been written on the theme of empathy but the brief definition given by Kohut (1959) who describes empathy as 'vicarious introspection' comes close to the heart of the matter. It is appropriate that this chapter on interpretive and supportive psychotherapy in diverse contexts should end with the theme of 'vicarious introspection'. The capacity to look inside on behalf of another is a therapeutic attribute which cannot be overvalued. Likewise, its growth in the patient is a *sine qua non*. He may then reach the point of establishing anachronistic vicarious empathy with his victim. Only then, can he begin to understand the inner life of the original 'other', for whom the victim so often served as an understudy and recipient of 'fatal' (because 'attacked') projective identifications.

This brief concluding paragraph reaffirms that supportive and interpretive psychotherapy are as interwoven as the dimensions in which they can be safely explored; namely, Time, Depth and Mutuality.

The Multi-Disciplinary Team

Introduction

Christopher Cordess

The multi-disciplinary team (MDT) has been defined as 'a group of colleagues acknowledging a common involvement in the care and treatment of a particular patient (Royal Commission on the National Health Service 1979). It sounds deceptively simple: a colleague, by contrast (when team work was going particularly badly), described it as 'like walking on broken glass'.

With the increase in knowledge and with the development of sub-specialities it becomes increasingly unrealistic for any single clinician to think that he can know all the relevant information, or that, single-handed, he can provide the necessary clinical care. Even individual psychodynamic psychotherapy on an out-patient – or private – basis will have involved a referring agent and should include some form of ongoing supervision.

Collaboration between disciplines is especially important in the treatment of the offender patient. As previously emphasized in the Preface, and elsewhere, no forensic psychotherapist should, or can responsibly, 'go it alone': on the contrary, there are many benefits, for both patient and staff, which accrue from cohesive and effective team work. For example, Glover (1960) has written of the benefits of the so-called 'distributed transference' which allows a sharing of the countertransferential burden, and allows a team – when it works well – to be of greater support and help to some patients than any one individual therapist.

However, the subject of the MDT is not necessarily one which generates wide enthusiasm or excitement; rather, dissatisfaction is frequently expressed about how teams operate and a range of criticisms are to be heard. The issues raised by inter-disciplinary and multi-disciplinary work are, indeed, frequently painful and potentially divisive, involving as they do our place within an ensemble or group. Matters of hierarchy, status, leadership, and power – and its abuse – and the necessary demarcation and maintenance of personal and professional boundaries are not easy: they require much thought, effort, and continuing vigilance if the team is to function optimally as an integrated whole. Regular and dedicated times for the pooling and sharing of information between all staff who are part of the therapeutic team are indispensable to the maintenance of an effective team effort. This should be part of all good clinical practice and therefore is a suitable subject for the 'audit' which is required of us in the current British system of health care. The tendency for destructive 'splitting' and its possible consequences within the team is described in different ways in the following chapters: the need for a scapegoat within the MDT and the wider institution will be well known to us all.

The MDT has a variable constitution according to the setting – whether in-patient or that of community care – and according to the needs of the particular patient. The conceptualization of team work and practice differ in specifically psychotherapeutic services, for example, the Portman Clinic or the Therapeutic Community (e.g. the Henderson Hospital) from mainstream forensic psychiatry and probation: inter-agency team work – so necessary in forensic practice – brings its own particular challenges. They are described in detail elsewhere in this volume.

Team work and the workings of the MDT have been studied particularly in rehabilitative psychiatry, with which forensic psychiatry and 'the psychotherapies' share many common tasks and goals. The diversity of patients' needs, their long-term care (where indicated), the necessity of working with them not only individually but also in their wider contexts of family, and in different social and occupational settings, requires the skills of a number of professionals and have been well described by Watts and Bennett (1991). However, there has been little discussion of the specialized function of the MDT within forensic psychiatry and forensic psychotherapy and even less written from the specifically clinical point of view on the subject.

In this chapter five core disciplines drawn from two different forensic psychiatry services are directly represented, but many others could have been invited. The presence in such a team structure of the core disciplines is essential: without their contributions important aspects of the patient will remain unaddressed. Where there is a designated psychotherapist he will usually have wider responsibilities to other parts of the institution than a single team, but he may attend meetings such as case conferences and ward rounds. The efficient working of the MDT relies on many others, too: for example, clinically speaking, secretarial and administrative staff will be in the background, but they play a fundamental role in marshalling and maintaining the functional boundaries of the team.

This is an important subject which has received far too little attention in the forensic literature. We hope that this 'team' presentation will stimulate the discussion, investigation and innovation that the subject deserves.

The Nurse

Michael Killian & Nick Clark

INTRODUCTION

> 'When a prison is a psychiatric hospital, the frontline staff personnel are the nurses who deal with the patients on a continuing basis. Inmates may view nursing staff as part of a much-hated system and use them as a "dumping ground for their hostility."' (Cheek and Miller quoted in MacDonald and Grogin 1991, p.19)

From its origins in the system of the Victorian asylums and of 'lunatic attendants', psychiatric nursing has evolved in the shadow of the medical profession, retaining, however, a 'general nursing' orientation.

The 'open door' policy of the 1960s and the associated move towards community care benefited all but the 'difficult to manage' patient and mentally ill offender: unsuited to psychiatric wards in district general hospitals or the new psychiatric day hospitals (where they exist), some were eventually to find themselves neglected and unsupervised in the community, remanded to prison, or more rarely in conditions of maximum security in Special Hospitals.

Consequent upon the Butler Report (1975), regional secure units (RSUs) were built to provide a rehabilitative environment in conditions of medium security. Psychiatric nurses rather than prison architecture were envisaged as providing the main security barrier. 'The intention was for the building design to support nursing staff, who are the main security barrier' (Snowden 1990, p.1383).

It may be argued that this security role has become something of a 'bogey' for our society, whose perceptions of the profession may involve images of men in white coats or prison uniforms performing a mainly custodial task. The images are reinforced by a media ever willing to exaggerate society's views by focusing almost exclusively on the sensational, dramatic and sometimes catastrophic actions and aspects of mentally ill offenders.

SECURITY AND PHYSICAL CONTAINMENT

The exchange of physical boundaries for the security provided by the relationships that patients develop with nurses places a large demand upon nursing staff: they have to provide both emotional and practical (physical) containment, whilst allowing at the same time for optimum conditions of therapeutic interaction. One of the difficulties, for example, is highlighted by the carrying of keys which lock off areas of wards to patients and controls their movement through the institution. This in itself provides a dynamic that most nurses have to work out for themselves, in order to find the right balance for them between the custodial and their more clinical role. There is rarely open discussion of dilemmas – for example what it means for nurses forcibly to lock up in seclusion a person with whom they have established a close relationship, often over a period of years.

In considering how nurses working in regional secure hospitals provide a relatively successful degree of security within a comparatively fragile structure, it may be appropriate to emphasize that on occasions patients attack other patients and staff, yet few break the comparatively fragile physical structure. Windows and doors could be broken with relative ease, yet the majority of patients do not try to 'break out' but rather remain within their location. Those who escape invariably return either with the assistance of outside agencies or under their own steam. Many find it difficult to cope outside the institution for both emotional and psychological reasons and for lack of practical provision. One may consider the nurse's role as providing a sense of containment, aspects of which are to tolerate a level of behaviour and distress which would not be tolerated outside the institution and yet still maintain a therapeutic stance. It is difficult enough to tolerate face-to-face contact with psychotic communication, and frequently aggressive, disturbed or threatening behaviour for fifty minutes or less; it is very demanding to be exposed to it or the threat of it for a nursing shift of seven and a half hours or more.

Some patients become rapidly disturbed when frustrated because they cannot satisfy their physical or emotional needs and cannot communicate what they want. They may be calmed by sympathetic listening and a firm but emotionally containing attitude: more rarely it requires that the necessary physical control and restraint be employed. In the latter case there is frequently a shared sense of relief for nurses, fellow patients on the ward and the patient himself at the ability of staff to 'contain' the behaviour in whatever way required. The patient's anxiety may be of becoming completely out of control, which may be extraordinarily alarming. Patients will on occasion talk of being very frightened by their awful potential as they feel themselves losing self-control. At the same time they may recognize that they need literal physical containment: a physical 'auxiliary ego'.

> 'Violence was a method of reducing anxiety. One of the residents became anxious and stressed in communal and stimulating environments; as a result he hit out wildly and unpredictably to relieve these feelings. Many patients used violence as a coping mechanism to combat feelings of helplessness and to control others. But, at the same time, violent patients are considered to be frightened by their own hostile urges and fear of losing control. It can therefore be argued that potentially violent patients want staff to contain their violence in a safe manner and also require clear boundaries.' (Benson and Den 1992)

NURTURING

There is a large expectation of nurses that they should be nurturing as well as able to exert 'control'. It is this nurturing part which, for example at times when a patient isn't responding to treatment in the expected way, can lead the nurse to feel in an invidious position, like a mother in a department store. If the children become out of control and she physically chastises them, others 'tut' in disapproval. Alternatively, if she tolerates their behaviour and tries to negotiate, then others are equally disapproving of the mother's perceived inability to control the children. The nurse in this situation becomes acutely aware of how people carry with them their own internal 'institutions', families and codes of behaviour, which they project onto others.

Nurses often feel a lack of understanding and tolerance on the part of other clinical disciplines of their difficulties with particular patients. Patients will often take their frustrations out on nurses, and nurses can give in to institutional pressure to be a 'good' nurse in the eyes of others, a sort of 'ideal' mother, rather than a 'good enough' nurse. For example, it is not unknown for patients to be difficult and demanding day-to-day with the nursing staff and then to present themselves quite differently to the consultant upon his arrival on the ward. Injury to nurses may be institutionally tolerated, whereas violence to other disciplines is taken more seriously. Some responsibility for this remains with nurses, some with the wider institution.

PROFESSIONAL ROLE DEFINITION

One may ask the question: why is it taken for granted that nurses provide the physical security in secure institutions? The responsibility for ensuring the acts of violence or threat are monitored as well as making sure that effective responses ensue is left to the nurses. In the Christopher Clunis report, for example, it is documented that nursing notes had recordings of violence, while such records were mostly absent from other notes.

In their study of comparative levels of stress within psychiatric nursing, Lyons, Tarbuck and Williams (1992) found that regional secure unit nurses identified one main area of stress – that of professional role definition – and ambiguity within the 'therapy versus security' dichotomy. We seek to combine two aspects of care – security and therapy – whilst the present configuration of institutional care separates them.

Splits between multi-disciplinary teams (MDTs), or possibly between those who provide continuity of care and those who provide clinical treatment may not be confronted and resolved. The dysfunctioning family must function at some level for it to remain the same. Nurses may be seen as the (unappreciated) mother in the family, with the removed powerful (psychiatrist) father remaining disengaged and aloof. We suggest that this replicates the families in which many patients will have grown up, and that this structuring of the health professionals is a response to the massive projections of the patients.

It is argued that the present structure both encourages and facilitates splitting by creating a bewildering and confusing world around our patients. The temptation is then to avoid confronting the issues involved. The difficulty of remaining emotionally close to the suffering experienced by patients becomes too great and defensive strategies are adopted, initially by individuals and eventually by groups of staff. Anxiety among nurses may then be reduced by a concentration on the 'efficient' running of the ward, focusing on the physical tasks such as escorting patients to and from therapies and other security-orientated work.

The hierarchy of career advancement in nursing quickly allows individuals to reduce contact with patients in favour of administrative tasks. The youngest and most junior staff with the least training or experience remain in most contact with patients. They may find refuge in practical tasks and in security matters, rather than being able to bear continued engagement with distressed and disturbing individuals: responsibility is avoided and transferred to other senior members of staff or members of the MDT. Nurses may then become excluded from the decision-making process which contributes in turn to the danger of the nurses' essential part in the team work becoming marginalized, with consequent demoralization. Nurses can feel deskilled, too, during MDT meetings, despite the fact that often they have the greatest experience of the patient: they may feel that they are not empowered with the same professional and coded language to achieve their aims of shared professional participation.

CONCLUSION

In considering the nurse's perspective we have chosen to focus mainly on the issue of security and the difficulty involved in its reconciliation with other, perhaps more acknowledged, therapeutic roles. Having presented images of a confused role it is perhaps not surprising to discover that within the clearly defined perimeter fence of a regional secure unit, boundaries are often blurred. The intense isolation caused by mental illness and its associated physical incarceration, can often result in nurses being used by forensic patients as 'surrogate friends'. It is perhaps one of the most difficult experiences to terminate a relationship with an excessively dependent patient, without leaving him or her emotionally wounded.

An example that best illustrates this concerns an attempt by nursing staff to limit a male patient's contact with a female nurse from another ward, this limitation being perceived by the patient as evidence of 'jealousy', on the part of the staff involved, of his relationship with that nurse.

Different aspects of the nurse's blurred role are often polarized with startling clarity by particular patients, whose capacity to engage feelings in the recipient is greater perhaps, than that of many a trained therapist. The nature of nursing with its prolonged patient contact can often give certain patients an opportunity to engage with latent conflicts within the nurse. This can then arouse intense countertransference feelings. Intensified by keys and other emblems of security, these feelings often only become evident in certain situations, predominantly unique to nursing. Where nurses are obliged to force patients physically to take prescribed medication against their will or where a decision is taken to lock a patient in a room, as in 'seclusion', it becomes painfully apparent to nurses that they are perceived by the patient involved as being in either a good or bad 'camp'.

To accompany a patient on 'escorted leave' outside the perimeters of the unit is another situation almost entirely unique to nursing. In various social settings the boundaries between friendship and professional relationship are constantly re-defined. As the patient gradually integrates into the social world outside the hospital, renewing contact with family and acquaintances, the accompanying nurse is often introduced as a 'friend', as he or she struggles internally to acquire an outward reconciliation of conflicting roles. It can also be said that true friendships do sometimes develop.

However, in our opinion, the occupational mandate given to nurses to access the private lives of their patients together with the opportunity this gives for the projection of unwanted aspects of ourselves into the patient group, suggest that the greatest challenge to nursing is the prevention of the development of unhealthy and ultimately destructive symbiotic relationships. This challenge can only be met by a comprehensive clinical supervision structure. Perhaps then the true nature of the nurse–patient relationship will be better illuminated as increasingly meaningful contact is made with the inner world of our patients.

The Occupational Therapist

Elizabeth Flannigan

INTRODUCTION

The underlying philosophy of occupational therapy is based on the belief that performance of an activity which has purpose and meaning to the individual promotes learning, adaptation and change (American Occupational Therapy Association 1979).

Unique to the practice of occupational therapy is the analysis, selection and adaptation of an activity which, when reduced to its component parts, meets the needs of the individual. The overall aim is to enable the individual to learn, relearn and maintain activities of daily living.

In the 1950s and 1960s the work of Azima and Azima (1959), and Fidler and Fidler (1963), developed the psychoanalytic theory into a psychodynamic approach within occupational therapy. As a result, many therapists became highly skilled in the use of projective media (art, music and pottery) in analytic group psychotherapy, but in doing so everyday problems of the disabled individual trying to adapt and cope in their daily lives became secondary (Kielhofner 1989). Occupational therapists struggled with role diffusion and a loss of identity and in the 1970s, occupational therapy, under the guidance of Dr Mary Reilly returned to its initial premise and concepts.

However, the profession has retained some common themes with psychotherapy:

- 'belief in people's potential to effect change in themselves and others

- catering for different levels of intensity of treatment according to the needs of the client

- opportunities for intrapersonal and interpersonal learning

- acknowledgement that change in feeling leads to change in behaviour and adaptation to life
- promoting individual responsibility while concurrently providing emotional support.' (Blair 1990, p. 197)

OCCUPATIONAL THERAPY AND THE FORENSIC PATIENT

For the forensic patient, many basic life skills have never existed or have been lost due to institutionalization (Freeman 1982). His motivation may be low, due to his involuntary internment, and symptomatic of a mental illness. He experiences a loss of autonomy and responsibility for himself and it is the task of the occupational therapist to work in conjunction with the patient to establish a group programme that not only meets his needs but has purpose and meaning to him.

By involvement in occupational therapy individual sessions, and groups – for example cooking, gardening, communication – the patient develops and maintains life skills and gradually accepts responsibility for himself and his actions.

The forensic occupational therapist needs to be aware of issues of security, and assessment of the patient's potential danger to himself and others is ongoing within groups. The occupational therapist has the opportunity, for example (1) when trust has been established, to introduce the use of knives in a cooking group, and (2) to observe an individual's interaction and tolerance with others.

Working in day-to-day, hour-to-hour proximity with the forensic patient is taxing and can be disturbing. Supervision and peer discussion is important in maintaining staff motivation and enthusiasm for the work.

GROUPWORK

It is of primary importance that the occupational therapist focus on enabling the forensic patient to develop adequate life skills so that he may live within the community. However, nothing is in isolation and the occupational therapist is aware of the principles of group dynamics and the frame of references applied. Unless the occupational therapist has specialized in psychotherapy training, the approach used within a group is supportive rather than explorative.

The functional group approach (Howe and Schwartzburg 1986) uses activity to help patients learn about their environment. The therapist uses activity and group dynamic principles to focus on the here and now learning experience, to empower the group, to facilitate the participation of individuals, to build on individual and group strengths, and to bring about change.

PERSONAL EXPERIENCES AND VIEWS

Motivation

One of the occupational therapist's core skills is the ability to maintain her own motivation and motivate both staff and patients. My level of motivation is constantly challenged and, as a whole, motivation can enter a downward spiral within a forensic unit. Within occupational therapy it is important to be aware of this, so that if patients actively or passively challenge a group the occupational therapist maintains her level of commitment to the group and continues to prepare properly for the activity.

Naming of a Group

The forensic patient is frequently resistant to groupwork and all professions have to advocate the need for active rehabilitation to the patient in an united way. The name of a group may be very significant for the patients referred to it. For example, within this occupational therapy department we organized a social skills group. This title may seem innocuous, but to the patients who were required to attend, the very name suggested to others that they had difficulties in this area. The shame involved with this increased patients' level of resistance and their denial of any needs within this area. Perhaps calling it an expressions group may have eased this.

The Multi-Disciplinary Team (MDT)

Working as part of the MDT provides support for any work I do with individuals and assists in encouraging patients to participate in a rehabilitative programme. A team approach when it works well gives the patient clear boundaries and discourages splitting.

It is important for the occupational therapist to feed back the patient's progress and quality of participation within the groups rather than merely the number of groups he attends. There appears to be a general tendency for staff to see that a patient is occupied, thus giving the impression that staff have fulfilled their job. It is irrelevant how many groups the patient attends; what is important is whether he actively participates within the group and whether he can structure his free time.

Supervision

Supervision and support for staff is important in maintaining morale and ensuring a good standard of work. Within this department staff receive regular weekly supervision. In addition, monthly supervision of our groups is provided by a psychotherapist. Although we do not always agree with the interpretations, he enables us to focus on the group dynamics and promotes discussion that continues long after the supervision has finished. It has proved to be a good forum for team building.

Respect for Occupational Therapy Groups

Unfortunately, occupational therapy is still seen today by some as 'occupying the patient' and the groups are not seen to have any other function. This can be substantiated by the lack of respect given to the groups by other professionals. For example, I have experienced staff interrupting a group activity either to remove a patient, borrow something, or just to observe. Does this happen in a psychotherapy group? I think not.

Activity as a Catalytic Agent

I believe that activity acts as a catalytic agent. Patients absorbed in an activity tend to relax and are more likely to reveal or discuss issues concerning them. In other words, when the emphasis on talking is removed they are more likely to talk. When this happens it is, of course, difficult and not always appropriate to explore every issue they may bring up, but it is important to support the patient. This information can be invaluable to the MDT, enabling them to evaluate a patient's progress and possibly indicate a patient's readiness for individual psychotherapy.

It is essential that the occupational therapist is aware that certain activities may trigger memories that may disturb the patient. For example, I run a gardening group. The aims focus on assessing and developing concentration, interaction, team-work and stamina. After a particularly bad summer of trying to combat the weeds in the garden one patient said 'Let's get into the garden and strangle those weeds' whilst at the same time carrying out the action of strangling with his hands. He looked down at his hands and froze. At this point he appeared to connect with his index offence of strangling.

Nothing in Isolation

A patient attends different groups to meet his individual needs. Progress in one area invariably leads to progress in other areas. For example, one patient I worked with usually dealt with others in a verbally aggressive manner. In role-playing groups he would always manage to turn his role into an aggressive one. He was referred to an assertiveness group. It was observed during this time by the therapists running the other groups he attended that his behaviour gradually became assertive rather than aggressive. This work was complemented by his involvement in individual psychotherapy. Feedback within the MDT was, of course, crucial to this success.

One-to-One

A patient's needs can not always be catered for within a group setting. Occupational therapists see patients individually to establish rapport; identify needs and goals; formulate group programmes and review treatment and feedback on progress. Relaxation skills, cooking assessments and gradual reintegration into the community by using public transport and community facilities are examples where specific needs can only be met properly with individual support.

The occupational therapist needs to be aware that the patient she escorts to community facilities such as the gym, a cafe or the library may have experienced or imagined such outings with friends, family or spouse. It is crucial that the occupational therapist maintains therapist–patient boundaries and is aware of the role she may play in a patient's fantasies.

CONCLUSION

The forensic patient must have access to both occupational therapy and psychotherapy. The occupational therapist is able to provide support and have awareness of the psychodynamic issues that may arise for a patient. Ultimately, however, our main role is to equip the forensic patient with the practical life skills necessary to live independently in the community.

The Social Worker

Martin Wrench

INTRODUCTION

As a forensic social worker I have been fortunate to work in a service where I have been involved with patients in a range of settings: in a medium secure unit, with patients on open wards, and with out-patients. The last setting has included participation in a Sex Offender Clinic. I have, therefore, been a member of a number of multi-disciplinary teams operating within one service, each with its own primary objective and challenges. The different contexts create different expectations of the social worker and in this section I shall describe both the key tasks of the social worker within a forensic setting and also convey how the social worker's role in the team may be experienced.

FORENSIC SOCIAL WORK IN A SECURE SETTING

Although it is not the social worker's sole prerogative, it is nonetheless primarily the social worker's task to locate patients in a social context that takes account of their family background, their significant relationships and social network and which considers such diverse issues as race, gender, religion and culture. In the medium secure setting in which I work this is achieved through involvement in the initial assessment of a patients both prior to admission and during the first few months of admission. During this stage I interview the patients and their families and write a report detailing the following: the patient's social history, significant relationships, understanding of his or her current circumstances and any hopes and aims the patient may have for the future. At a later stage my involvement with patients might include working with them and their families, writing Mental Health Review Tribunal reports, seeking accommodation, liaising with funding authorities and exploring with them in individual sessions the implications of a move to the community. These and other endeavours serve to complement the work of other colleagues by contributing to the team's understanding of how social factors may have affected the patient in the past and what likely impact they may have on the patient's future.

In addition to contributing to the team's understanding of the patient and the patient's future needs, the social worker is also required to demonstrate a capacity for independent judgement that should enable the social worker, where necessary, to express in ward rounds, case conferences or Mental Health Review Tribunal reports views that may be at variance with other colleagues. Indeed, social workers are required at times to act independently. This is generally in relation to statutory duties as, for example, when acting as an Approved Social Worker. However, in a broader sense, it is the social worker's experience of patients and how they function outside of clinical settings that equips him or her with the capacity to offer a perspective that is distinct from that of other disciplines.

Until recently social workers working within forensic settings have been employed by local authorities and not by health authorities. Although this is no longer universally the case, social workers still tend to be viewed as standing somewhat outside the system and this can contribute as much to their marginalization as it can to their influence or relative independence within the team. At its most extreme, marginalization is expressed by viewing the social worker as there to perform solely practical tasks such as sorting out benefits and liaising with external agencies in the search for accommodation. This may result in the social worker devaluing the practical aspects of the role which may, in fact, be of paramount importance to the patient, while feeling envious of those colleagues with more clearly prescribed treatment roles and the power and 'mystique' that is attributed to them.

What needs to be understood and acknowledged (and it is the social worker's duty to make this evident to the team) is that social workers have considerable experience of working with their clients in a range of contexts. This work includes visiting hostels, day centres, drop-ins and visiting patients in their family homes. Such experience provides unique insights and understanding specific to the social work role which equip the social worker with the ability to envisage how a patient might manage the transfer from maximum or medium security to the community and the services and supports he or she might require. In addition, the social worker's knowledge and understanding of the patient and his or her environment will assist the team's understanding of any further risks the patient might pose.

I have had experience of restricted patients elevating the social work role above other team members, with the exception of the responsible medical officer, (RMO), particularly in the latter stages of their stay in medium security, because they have come to view me and the RMO as the key players in their transfer to the community. One patient who had been conditionally discharged by a Mental Health Review Tribunal, against the team's clinical judgement became contemptuous of the nursing staff and junior doctors because he believed they were of no further consequence to him. This behaviour had to be addressed in concrete terms by my seeing the patient jointly with his key nurse for a number of sessions. This helped to avoid further splitting and to reinforce the role of the team as a whole in plans for his discharge. Whilst such behaviour is certainly indicative of the patient's psychopathology, it also illustrates the fact that, depending on the stage of the patient's in-patient care, the social worker's role may assume greater or lesser significance to the team and to the patient. At its most positive the social worker's presence in the team conveys hope to the patient of contact with the external world and of a future life within it and it is my aim during a patient's stay to enable the patient and the team to work towards a realistic appraisal of the issues that may confront the patient in the community and how they might be managed.

The relatively closed environment of a secure unit can be a constraining influence on creative social work practice and the exercise of independent judgement. In common with other staff, the social worker may feel hemmed in physically, and rigid hierarchies may be more evident than in more open settings; this is partly attributable to environmental factors such as air locks. The outside world is less actual and accessible, not only for the patients but also for the staff. Other constraints include the need for decisions to be ratified by the Home Office and the impulse to seek safety in the team in a setting where individual workers may feel threatened or persecuted by patients at one extreme, or risk being idealized and split off by patients at the other. It is, however, necessary as a social worker to retain one's individual perspective and contribute something of an outsider's view as well as a view of the outside; not to do so would be to fail the team and the patient.

FORENSIC SOCIAL WORK IN THE COMMUNITY

Working with forensic patients in the community poses different challenges: the social worker and the community psychiatric nurse (CPN), have a key role in retaining contact with a group of patients who may feel they have been ill-served by both the criminal justice system and general psychiatry. The work itself involves frequent contact with the patient, his or her family, day centres, hostel staff, the police and probation. Although conditionally discharged restricted patients are likely to have committed far more serious offences than other community patients they are, in certain respects, easier to manage in the community than those patients who may have committed relatively minor offences but over whom one has no statutory control. I have had the experience of being the only worker in the team to have known patients over a number of years and thereby to have gained a detailed knowledge and understanding of them which was not available to medical colleagues who may see patients infrequently for clinical appointments. Sometimes lengthy contact with the client and the family is required before the client has recognized any benefit from my interventions. In the case of a young Afro-Caribbean man, sessions with his family, which he only infrequently attended, enabled the family members, particularly the mother, to overcome their guilt about wanting the patient to move away from the family home into his own accommodation. Once the family's anxieties about how he might be cared for had been addressed, the patient did move to his own accommodation and although he has had occasional relapses requiring re-admission to hospital, he has attained a measure of independence that he would have been unlikely to achieve otherwise.

Long and intensive involvement with patients is far from exclusive to social workers, but it is not uncommon for a social worker to have had more regular on-going contact with a patient in a range of settings than his or her colleagues. The attraction of social work with such clients lies for me in its mundane quality, rooted as it is in the client's every day life and circumstances. Maintaining contact with such clients requires tenacity and a capacity for 'creative plodding', to borrow a term from a colleague, which may include extensive liaison with community agencies. The reward lies in seeing apparently grossly disordered and difficult-to-manage patients develop a degree of order and enjoyment from their lives, resulting in less frequent brushes with the criminal justice system as they become engaged in work training and other constructive activities.

The social supervision of conditionally discharged restricted patients requires the forensic social worker to work in a manner similar to probation officers' work with life sentence parolees. The task is to act both as an enabler, assisting the client to re-establish himself in the community, and as an agent of social control who needs to consider any possible threats the client may pose to public safety. The enabling role comes readily to social workers but the need to ask intrusive questions about the client's relationships and activities is rather less familiar. I have made it my practice to explain clearly to restricted patients the dual nature of the social supervisor's role and my need to work closely with other professionals including the RMO, the CPN and hostel staff.

I have also worked with sex offenders as part of a small team in the department that runs a weekly clinic and have been involved in the assessment and treatment of sex offenders, both individually and as the co-leader of a group. I have found working with my colleagues, a psychiatrist, psychologist, a CPN and a probation officer very rewarding, primarily because we are a close-knit team where mutual respect has developed through working jointly.

We do joint assessments, co-lead groups and we provide training. The key determinant, in my view, of being able to work effectively with sex offenders (besides a sound knowledge base) is a capacity to manage one's response to deviance and perversion in others in a way that is neither unduly punitive nor condoning, neither unduly voyeuristic nor prurient. The ability to maintain a balanced perspective contributes to the team's effectiveness and morale. Although issues of hierarchy pertain, as in other multi-disciplinary settings, they are, for a range of reasons, including the considerable contribution made by psychologists and probation officers in work with sex offenders, less inclined to be reinforced by adherence to a predominantly medical model.

The experience of applying my social work skills in a variety of settings within one service has enhanced not only my awareness of the extent to which team dynamics are dependent on the environment in which the team is operating but has also made me very aware of gaps in service provision for mentally disordered offenders. The Reed Committee report proposed a seamless service that would ensure both good in-patient and good community care for forensic patients; it placed a high premium on inter-agency working. What is evident to me is that the development of medium secure provisions for mentally disordered offenders, which is expanding to some extent, if not to anything like the level recommended by Reed, is not matched by increased community resources or inter-agency cooperation. As a social worker, it is becoming increasingly difficult to find appropriate resources for forensic patients, and my understanding of the client and what he or she needs in order to succeed in the community is not matched by what is available for them. At the same time, negotiating with funding authorities is becoming a more complex and less certain process. The effect in the long term could be to undermine the social worker's role and credibility within the team. While clearly it is essential that more community based resources are committed to this client group, their current paucity serves to sharpen social worker's negotiating skills, which are a crucial part of any social worker's armoury as someone whose task it is to mediate between the world of the institution (and its often arcane practices) and the external world.

CONCLUSION

The forensic social worker's role is a potentially varied one, ranging from performing practical tasks to offering treatment through counselling, group work or family therapy and otherwise aiding the rehabilitation process and providing support and supervision for clients in the community. Working within a predominantly medical setting where hierarchies are often strongly reinforced may result in the social worker feeling marginalized and unheard, particularly where his or her role is not clearly statutorily defined, or where other disciplines have an equal or greater claim to providing treatment interventions. The social worker has some responsibility to assert his or her capacity to counsel patients and their families in those areas where he or she may have specific training and expertise, for example in working with victims of sexual abuse, in family therapy or group work. Social workers also have a duty to assert their views in ward rounds and Mental Health Review Tribunal reports in order to ensure that the patients are understood within their social and cultural context and that they and their families are represented and heard and not simply pathologized. Central to the social worker's role, hampered though it may be by insufficient resources, is the need to convey to the patient a sense of an achievable future that relates to their needs but is realistic, attainable and has the support of the team.

The Psychologist

Maggie Hilton

INTRODUCTION

At their best, multi-disciplinary teams provide a forum for sharing skills and generating, through discussion, the best possible decisions about patient care. However, all members of such teams are likely sometimes to experience frustration that their views are being ignored, boredom when what is being discussed bears little relationship to their own perspective on what is important, and disappointment that their expertise is being undermined or inappropriately used. Psychologists and social workers are most prone to resentment at the emphasis on the medical model rather than psychological and sociological perspectives, whilst the frustration of nurses is more likely to be aroused by others failing to appreciate the significance of their day-to-day experience of the patient.

All psychologists will have witnessed the misapplication of psychological techniques by staff who discount, or are unaware of, the theoretical bases underpinning successful treatment. This is particularly common when punishment, justified as a behavioural intervention, serves to express countertransference reactions in staff, rather than addressing a patient's needs. Attempts to advise or intervene in such circumstances are often resisted, being interpreted as the psychologist being too precious or protective of their skills.

The roots of such tensions are historical: psychology encompasses a substantial body of scientifically derived knowledge aiding our understanding and interpretation of both normal and abnormal behaviour. The success of clinical psychologists in utilizing this knowledge to improve health care has created particular dynamics in team working. Initially, clinical psychologists functioned as technicians, developing and administering psychometric techniques to aid assessment and diagnosis. As the profession developed, acceptance of psychologists having a specific role in providing therapies based on learning theories extended to include the use of a wide range of psychological models including cognitive therapies, psychoanalytical psychotherapy, gestalt and transactional analysis. Psychological methods are also relevant in understanding team functioning and in relation to organizational issues, such as the management of change and service evaluation. The variety of potential roles, as well as the psychologist's ability to function independently, providing care in a wide range of settings and problem areas, has often been resented. In some cases, such innovation has been seen as a threat, needing to be controlled or taken over, rather than as a unique contribution to the team's work. When such attitudes apply, psychologists may feel that the roles expected of them by other team members constrain their ability to use their skills most effectively in contributing to patient care.

THE CLINICAL ROLE

Psychological assessment, including examination of mood, thoughts, feelings, behaviour, personality and organic functioning is particularly valued by other staff. Functional analysis which embraces not only data on problem behaviours, its antecedents and what maintains it, but also information on all aspects of personal history and functioning, can contribute to the team's planning of care programmes for individuals, identifying goals as well as barriers to treatment. The primary focus is on the anti-social behaviour itself and understanding how it has arisen and what is motivating and maintaining self-destructiveness and destructiveness to others. This will necessitate a very broad assessment incorporating personality features underlying the offending.

Neuropsychological and personality assessment can further aid understanding of the origins and nature of a patient's difficulties. Tests may identify specific learning difficulties or types of brain damage which have resulted in behavioural disorder, including offending. The Repertory Grid Technique (see Beail 1988) can provide unique information on a person's cognitions in relation to themselves and others that can prove invaluable in planning and evaluating treatment. Similarly, the Minnesota Multiphasic Personality Inventory (MMPI) (Graham 1990) can corroborate impressions gained from clinical interviews and observation, and projective techniques, such as the Object Relations Technique (Phillipson 1973), can facilitate dynamic understanding.

The primary role of psychologists working in forensic services, however, is concerned with the management and treatment of behavioural disorder, particularly aggression and sexual deviation. New approaches to personality disorder are being developed, including techniques aimed at influencing anti-social behaviour directly, by skills training and behavioural interventions, and via cognitive strategies (Beck and Freeman 1990; Blackburn 1993). Similarly, relapse prevention techniques, developed for use in addiction, are now being applied to sexual deviation and offending in general (Pithers 1990). Furthermore, there is a growing body of knowledge to help patients with treatment resistant psychotic symptoms, (Birchwood and Tarrier 1994). The art of successful treatment in the forensic field,however, goes beyond mere understanding of theories and techniques, necessitating a creative ability to work eclectically and tailor interventions to the individual's complex and changing needs.

Assessment and treatment interventions are generally what most teams expect of psychologists. The recommendation that, because of a national shortage of psychology manpower, psychologists should act as consultants to other staff carrying out direct interventions (Manpower Planning Advisory Group (MPAG) 1990), is much more contentious: it raises anxieties about psychologists encroaching on other people's territory or inappropriately controlling their work. Similarly, many teams are reluctant to use the psychologist's research and occupational psychology skills to aid understanding and support effective team functioning (e.g. Dunne, 1994).

EXAMPLES OF CLINICAL INTERVENTIONS

At its best, team work enables the skills of all members to be utilized to their maximum effect for the benefit of patients. This implies that different combinations of staff will work together, depending on identified needs. For instance, individual work with sex offenders is generally carried out by a single professional, generally a psychologist, whereas group treatments are likely to include other professions, in order to utilize the generic skills of care workers as well as to provide training opportunities. Inpatient work, on the other hand, is always multi-disciplinary.

Psychologists often work with nurses when specific behaviour is problematic. A common problem is a patient's refusal to get up or go to occupational therapy, leading to resentment in other patients and staff and missed opportunities for rehabilitation. Several approaches could be taken to influence such behaviour, depending on the reasons for refusal and the patient's personality. One such case involved a patient suffering from personality difficulties manifested by a range of difficult and demanding behaviours and complicated by occasional psychotic episodes. Psychological assessment suggested that a programme based on punishment would merely intensify his resentment and difficult behaviour. It was also suggested that he was unlikely to change his behaviour unless he felt that there was something to be gained by this. A programme was drawn up with the patient and staff, involving specifically chosen reinforcers, not generally available, to be given for compliance with particular staff requirements. That is, the patient's desire to have special privileges was incorporated rather than confronted. Such programmes, however, never run smoothly and the psychologist needed to be available to staff at all times to deal with teething problems. In this instance, the patient began aggressively demanding rewards while failing to comply with the programme. It was suggested to the patient that the programme would need to be stopped as it appeared to be disturbing him. Because of wanting the privileges that had been negotiated, the patient agreed to continue and his behaviour settled. Such programmes need to be continually modified according to the patient's behaviour, personality and rehabilitation goals. This illustrates a fairly traditional psychology role.

Good multi-disciplinary work on an outpatient basis implies that staff feel supported by others in managing very difficult patients in the community. Psychologists often work individually with patients, but at times will require the help and support of other team members, in joint work, in providing greater security, or in facilitating admission to hospital should this prove necessary. A case example involved a young man who had a strong compulsion to harm children, which he had great difficulty resisting. The level of risk was very high, and previous inpatient care involving a range of different techniques had failed to have a significant impact. Further inpatient care was not considered to be appropriate and outpatient care by an individual was felt to be too risky, because of the need for close monitoring and potential crisis management. It was agreed, therefore, that initially the psychiatrist and psychologist should work on the case together, seeing the patient individually. The psychiatrist's primary roles were to monitor mental state, provide medication where appropriate, and contribute to decision making, while the psychologist provided active psychological treatment. This initially focused on providing the patient with a framework for understanding the origins of his desire to attack children. Multiple techniques were used: most important, links between the compulsion to harm children and specific attributions, beliefs and feelings arising from the patient's abusive childhood experiences were identified by discussion and imagery of past abuse, and worked with, both cognitively and dynamically. In order to increase self control, the patient was recommended certain literature relevant to understanding and managing his distressing and dangerous urges. In addition, anxiety management techniques were used, and practical suggestions given for reducing the risk of attacks. The ability to combine a number of theoretical approaches is perhaps the essence of what psychologists uniquely offer to teams (MPAG 1990).

A further case involved a 40-year-old man, seen solely by a psychologist, with serious problems of aggression, rape fantasies and alcohol abuse. A history of emotional neglect at home, and sexual abuse at school had resulted in anti-social behaviour fuelled by a sense of being different from and rejected by others. A growing sense of isolation during adolescence developed into a long standing pattern of alcohol abuse and gratuitous violence. Previous attempts to stop drinking had been unsuccessful, but there was considerable motivation to change. In particular, the patient had become alarmed at the level of violence he was capable of, and frightened of losing his only longstanding relationship. Initially, a cognitive behavioural approach was used to tackle his alcohol abuse. Despite his level of motivation to change, there was considerable reluctance to accept the need for complete abstinence from alcohol until many relapses, involving extremely dangerous behaviour, allowed a recognition of how destructive any drinking was in his life. Cognitive distortions maintaining anti-social attitudes and behaviour were explored and challenged. An important aspect was to locate the origin of distorted beliefs in negative childhood experiences. Equally important was to understand the transference issues acted out during therapy as well as to safeguard the therapist from aggression from the patient at particular stages in treatment.

To produce lasting change, such therapy needs to continue over a considerable period because of the many levels of disturbance present.

CONCLUSION

Forensic patients present particularly complex problems necessitating expertise and flexibility in using a wide range of interventions. Substance abuse, self-harm, poor self-esteem, aggression, sexual perversion and other features of destructiveness to the self or others interact in complex ways. The above cases, albeit offering a simplified account of complex therapeutic interventions, illustrate ways in which clinical psychology's broad theoretical bases offer approaches that contribute effectively to good multi-disciplinary care. An understanding of dynamic issues, including the intense dependency needs commonly experienced by such patients, underpin the art of successfully applying psychological methods in forensic settings. Transference and countertransference issues need to be understood, even if not directly worked with, and the possibility of dangerous acting out in reaction to breaks in treatment anticipated and planned for.

Multi-disciplinary support and backup can be invaluable in facilitating safe and effective psychological therapy with such patients. However, primitive defences including splitting, projection and projective identification, as well as high levels of persecutory anxiety commonly operating within forensic patients can also operate within staff groups, as was so aptly described by Tom Main in his landmark paper 'The Ailment' in 1957. Constant vigilance, including staff support and supervision, can ensure that multi-disciplinary working fulfils its promise rather than succumbing to the common pitfalls identified by Main more than a third of a century ago.

The Psychiatrist

Christopher Cordess

THE ROLE OF THE FORENSIC PSYCHIATRIST

The role and responsibilities of the forensic psychiatrist or responsible medical officer (RMO) share much common ground with that of the general psychiatrist but include, in addition, certain specialized and statutory functions. A document outlining the responsibilties of consultants within the National Health Service and private practice is in preparation by the Royal College of Psychiatrists, and includes a section on working within the multi-disciplinary team (Royal College of Psychiatrists 1995, pp.8–10).

In Britain, the Royal College of Psychiatrists oversees the training requirements of psychiatrists, including specialist forensic psychiatrists – the latter through The Joint Committee on Higher Psychiatric Training (JCHPT). To be appointed as a consultant in forensic psychiatry it is necessary to spend a recommended period of four years and a minimum of three years in a Senior Registrar or equivalent academic post. The aims and objectives of this training have been seen by the Royal College of Psychiatrists as:

(1) *Assessment*

At the competion of training in forensic psychiatry, the trainee should have competence in the following areas:

(a) Assessment of behavioural abnormalities.

(b) Assessment of risk and dangerousness.

(c) The writing of reports for courts and others, e.g. Mental Health Review Tribunals.

(2) *Knowledge*

    (a) A knowledge of mental health legislation and relevant knowledge of criminal and civil law.

    (b) Knowledge of the range of services available for the mentally disordered offender and how to use them.

(3) *Therapeutic skills*

    (a) Understanding and using security as a means of control and treatment.

    (b) The treatment of chronic disorders, especially where behavioural problems are exhibited, e.g. severe psychosis and personality disorder.

    (c) Skill in psychological treatments for behavioural disorder, particularly psychotherapy.

(JCHPT 1995, pp.40–41).

The trained forensic psychiatrist should, so the requirements read,

> 'be able to take full clinical and managerial charge of forensic clinical services in several settings including out-patients, in-patients, security and juvenile services. In addition, the forensic psychiatrist should have expert knowledge of all the relevant literature, be able to teach the skills of forensic psychiatry to junior medical and paramedical staff and be able to conduct research.' (JCHPT 1995, p.41)

Reference is made, too, to liaison with the prison medical service and to the crucial relationships of the psychiatrist and other members of the MDT with other psychiatric services (general psychiatry, substance abuse, learning disability and child and adolescent services, especially). Add to this list the increasing requirement for general management and entrepreneurial skills – necessary accomplishments in many areas of the newly introduced marketplace of the National Health Service – and 'The Psychiatrist' of the title may be seen to be expected to become a veritable 'Jack of all trades': the hazards are clear. In the struggle to avoid the dissatisfaction and ineffectiveness of becoming 'the master of none', there is a danger that yet more sub-specialities are spawned, with increasing fragmentation of service delivery to the patient.

    Also, the Royal College of Psychiatrists issues 'Guidelines for regional advisors on consultant posts in forensic psychiatry'. This document makes explicit reference to the necessity for MDT work, and, in addition to the core disciplines, recommends access to a liaison probation officer. It also states that 'it is important that the operational policy for forensic psychiatric services should be agreed by, and be acceptable to, members of the MDT' (Royal College of Psychiatrists 1991, p.232). Another document produced by the

Forensic Psychiatry Specialist Section Executive Committee, Royal College of Psychiatrists (1995) outlines the role, responsibilities and work of the Consultant forensic psychiatrist, with particular emphasis on the multi-disciplinary team.

It will be clear from these education and training schedules and from the guidelines that – as has been emphasized throughout this text – there is always a third force present in the clinical interaction between the offender patient and the clinician, in the form of the Criminal Justice System as representative of the interests of society. Whereas in other clinical situations such responsibility towards society is implicit but in the background, in forensic psychiatry it is intrinsic to the speciality. The focus placed by the legal system, the courts and the Home Office upon the responsible medical officer and medical 'expert' necessarily affects the way he functions within the MDT. However, although this relationship with the law predetermines certain functions and roles, it leaves many other areas potentially free for development by the team.

It is also true that all consultant psychiatrists, including forensic psychiatrists, are increasingly bound by 'guidelines' and codes of practice which have taken on the status of 'requirements' in many cases: this status is the source of considerable current disagreement and debate. For example, the Care Programme Approach (CPA) the Supervision Register, and now the proposed Supervised Discharge and 'tiered' CPA (for an overview, see Department of Health 1994b) and the rival proposals for a Community Supervision Order and the new role of a 'Community Responsible Medical Officer' place, and are likely to place, new and added responsibilities upon psychiatrists and upon the 'key worker', as well as others.

There has been debate in forensic and other psychiatric specialities, about who the leader of the team should be and how he should be chosen. The major issues of contention have been summarized by Rowbottom and Hey (1978) and Cockburn (1989). However, leadership can be specific to task and there is no necessary assumption that leadership roles should be held predominantly by the psychiatrist, as appears generally to be the case. Also, the introduction of the 'key worker' system, whereby each qualified member of staff is allocated a coordinating responsibility for one patient, can change the nature and quality of team discussion. For example, Fewtrell and Toms (1985) compared the usual structure of the psychiatrist-led ward round, with a ward round format which combined the key worker system and an interview by that key worker of the patient during the meeting. This new type of ward round 'produced a swing away from medical and diagnostic issues to more discussion on domestic and social matters' (Thomas 1994).

THE PSYCHIATRIST AS PSYCHOTHERAPIST

Since the subject matter of this book is that of the theoretical and practical inter-relationship of psychotherapy and other forensic disciplines – and the many different expressions of that relationship – I will first summarize the different ways in which the psychotherapist may work in a hospital setting. I shall then examine specifically how the forensic psychiatrist who is also a psychotherapist may bring his psychotherapeutic function into the MDT, and will allow myself some selective, personal reflections.

Hobbs (1990) has eloquently delineated the ways in which a psychotherapist may bring his expertise to bear in general psychiatry, in-patient settings. More specifically, Macphail and Cox (1973) describe four possible *modus operandi* for the psychotherapist within the specialised environment of a British maximum security Special Hospital, but they have general applicability.

'(a) Theoretically, he could function as a "purist", working alone, seeing only patients, and having no communication with other staff within the hospital, thereby aiming to preserve the "classical" and more usual therapeutic relationship available to the, non-forensic, voluntary patient. He would allow himself to play no part in the life of the hospital.

(b) He could follow the practice of psychotherapists in some general psychiatric hospitals and see no patients at all. His time would be spent supervising other members of staff.

(c) He could be available for contact with all levels of staff – treating patients referred to him by the RMO, and regarding the issues that this practice brings to light as part of the material to be examined in therapy.

Finally, (d) he could take over total care of the patients, acting, in effect as a specialized RMO.' (pp.14–15)

This latter is the role that I adopt. For the purposes of this section, at least, I am not entirely typical of the consultant forensic psychiatrist within the MDT, since I, also, bring to the role my training and experience as a psychoanalyst.

Whereas, in Britain, few psychoanalysts are employed as consultant *general* psychiatrists, there are, relatively speaking, a greater proportion of psychoanalysts/psychotherapists who work within *forensic* psychiatry in this way. The first was Patrick Gallwey at St George's Hospital, London, and others have followed.

There would appear from this perspective to be a particular affinity between forensic psychiatric and psychoanalytic thinking and practice, which continues to be represented too by the psychotherapeutic interests and wish to train amongst those in the training grades of forensic psychiatry. There are several possible reasons provided by the 'external' conditions of forensic practice: (1) forensic patients are detained as in-patients, and are then followed up as out-patients, for periods of several years: they frequently have time on their hands – whilst rehabilitation or 'change' – a prime aim of psychotherapy – is expected of them (2) we treat fewer patients than the general services; we get to know them very well and may develop intense relationships which offer the possibility of the use of transference–countertransference interaction for the promotion of change. Although it was customary for psychodynamic psychotherapists to assume that the 'acting out' offender patient and those suffering from the psychoses could not, and did not, make such therapeutic relationships, this is now understood not to be the case. The intensity and duration of the staff relationships with the patient in in-patient settings, and subsequent compulsory and then voluntary treatment alliances, make this compellingly clear. To give one example from my own practice: a patient was compulsorily admitted to hospital from prison in a florid psychotic state after the attempted murder of his parents. He was initially aggressively antagonistic to treatment and then for about a year was opposed to therapeutic interventions, including family therapy. Now, five years on, he lives in his own flat and has close relationships with members of the MDT. He is now a voluntary patient and has complained that I do not see him often enough.

Cox (1983), who works according to category (c) above, has described the mutual contribution which the psychodynamic psychotherapist and the forensic psychiatrist can make to each other's work, invoking the metaphor of the 'double harness'. The question arises, however, whether one person can justify working in his own 'double harness', attempting to juggle and balance both roles, without the 'double harness' tying him up or causing strangulation. Is there some omnipotence one must ask, in attempting to combine these roles, and may the consequence not be an impoverishment of one's role in each discipline? Kraemer (1988), for example, writes of the impossibility in his view of combining statutory responsibility and psychotherapeutic potency and efficacy (specifically, in this case, when working with abusive families), and makes a powerful case for a division of labour – between administrative and psychotherapeutic functions – when working with any offender. The psychotherapist, he says, needs to feel free to

> 'take leaps in the dark if real discoveries are to be made. Further, therapists have the privilege of inactivity when in doubt, yet action is just what is required when a child (in his specific example) is in danger.' (p.251)

This is the purist's view (a less extreme version of (a), above) and from one perspective, at least, is indisputable. However, it is rarely the case, except in a few highly specialized centres, that psychotherapeutic treatment is offered to offenders by highly trained psychotherapists or analysts.

The further question arises: does this hybrid creature – forensic psychiatrist and psychotherapist – and his practice (which I represent) have life and a future, or – in this world of increasing sub-specialization – can the species look forward only to extinction? My own view, tentatively, is that he does have a place, and that the advantages of dual training and dual role provide a creative space between the two disciplines – and provide at the very least *one* model for the future.

Within the regional secure unit in which I work the patients suffer predominantly from the functional psychoses, but also frequently have a wide spectrum of previous or residual personality disorders: they have frequently suffered extremes of emotional as well as material deprivation (Gunn and Taylor 1993). It is the nurses and occupational therapists who have by far the greatest direct face-to-face patient contact and bear the brunt of what this brings: it would clearly be quite impossible for me or the registrar or senior registrar to fulfil our functions without the full cooperation of nursing and other colleagues, whereas, conceivably, they can get on with their job, at least for a while, without us. In this sense I 'consult' to my MDT colleagues, who have greater direct patient contact, and provide – at first hand, as the RMO – what I hope is an 'added' quality of psychotherapeutic understanding to the clinical work of the team.

The criminal act, and psychotic or other symptomatology and what they communicate, may be able to be understood in a psychodynamic way, making use of one's knowledge of the unconscious, so as to help staff in their day-to-day management of the seriously mentally ill offender patient. Only later does attention turn to specific psychotherapeutic interventions. There are many ways, too, in which the members of the MDT may form different dyads so as to work with the families of patients (Cordess 1992) or in groups, both in in-patient and out-patient settings.

In a general psychiatric setting, the experience, distilled knowledge and understanding – garnered from many years spent working psychodynamically on a psychiatric ward for functionally psychotic patients – is comprehensively, and movingly, described by Jackson and Williams (1994). I attempt to work in a related way. In my experience, my MDT colleagues greatly value the opportunity for their routine, but nonetheless, exceptional, and intense, day-to-day experience of disturbing and dangerous psychotic patients – broadly, their countertransference – to be heard: they welcome suggestions of how they might attempt to 'be' with a particular patient, and how they might then respond. Individual staff members find that their anxiety in their own work can be made more tolerable if the consultant listens with a psychodynamic 'third ear'. 'Acting out' by the patient may become more palatable – because understandable – and need not necessarily lead to a restrictive or punitive response.

The main forum for the interchange of these experiences and ideas, for in-patients, is the weekly ward round where the patient's progress may be discussed, and where he may be invited to attend. Although this can sometimes be a persecutory experience for the patients, and has uncomfortable overtones of Charcot's 'displays' at the turn of the century, it is more often experienced by them as supportive, and has many advantages. It is, for example, the one time during the week when the communications of the patient are heard simultaneously by all the members of the MDT, and this frequently proves to have an integrative effect.

The attempt to fulfil the 'dual role' presents many challenges. To take but one example, the *status* of one's psychodynamic understanding needs continually to be questioned and there are few hiding places – and nor should there be – within the MDT and wider institution. Questions include: (1) the status of the clinical data on which psychodynamic hypothesis are made, (2) the degree of unconscious determinism which can be allowed in understanding the patient and his offensive acts, and, (3) the fact that the psychodynamic method of 'enumerative inductivism' – finding examples consistent with a proposition – has clear methodological weakness. 'It is, at most', writes Fonagy (1993),

> 'an educational device and not a method of scientific scrutiny. It has been discredited in many fields of social science because of its lack of power to eliminate false positive observations.' (p.577)

This statement puts its finger on a central problem for the psychodynamic method and its evaluation. Such large questions are beyond the scope of this account. My point is that working in 'dual harness', combining two roles, as previously described, confronts one uncomfortably but stimulatingly with such epistemological but very practical, day-to-day, dilemmas.

The different levels of inter-relations between psychotherapy and forensic psychiatry – but also the range of other disciplines involved with the offender patient – raise crucial questions. They are brought to a focus, now, as the Royal College of Psychiatrists examines how best to fulfil its requirement of at least some psychodynamic psychotherapeutic knowledge and skill for *all* psychiatric registrars, and, specifically, how to provide it as a part of *all* Senior Registrar forensic psychiatric training. For example, there is an increasing recognition of the desperate need for specialist psychotherapy provision in settings of maximum security (Department of Health 1992a). Also, there has been a necessary developmental stage within psychiatric training for sub-specialities to establish their separate identities. There is considerable pressure now, however, particularly from Senior Registrars in training, to have the freedom to have experience across the sub-speciality divides. This includes not only psychotherapeutic experience, but an intermingling of many sub-specialities within psychiatry including child and adolescent psychiatry, learning disability, substance abuse – all of which have a central place within forensic clinical practice.

There has been a long divorce within British psychiatry – if indeed there were ever any marriages – between the 'biological' and related 'medical' model, and that of the psychoanalytic and psychodynamic. This has not, however, been the case in all English-speaking countries: for example Australian trained psychiatrists frequently find this 'split' and polarization alien and absurd. One version of it has been well caricatured as

'the intense and sometimes comically strident...schism between the believers in psychotherapy and the adherents of pharmacotherapy – which resembles the medical quarrels of the eighteenth century (to bleed or not to bleed?)...' (Styron 1991, p.11)

Although such contrary positions remain sometimes entrenched, there seems to be some evidence that they are becoming less so, and that survival in a particular professional view point (which, one hopes, will change over time in any one individual) no longer requires the vilification of those in the other 'camp'. In Britain, it appears that within forensic psychiatry at least, some integration has occurred and that such a coming together is seen as a necessity for all good clinical practice.

The Inter-Disciplinary Network and the Internal World of the Offender

Richard Davies

'...the Child is looking for something, somewhere and failing to find it seeks elsewhere, when hopeful.' (Winnicott 1956, p.306)

'...when the environment does not understand the inner significance of antisocial behaviour, such behaviour is likely to become aggravated.' (Limentani 1966, p.277)

INTRODUCTION

The view is taken that professionals who deal with offenders are not free agents but potential actors who have been assigned roles in the individual offender's own re-enactment of their internal world drama. The professionals have the choice not to perform but they can only make this choice when they have a good idea of what the role is they are trying to avoid. Until they can work this out they are likely to be drawn into the play, unwittingly and therefore not unwillingly. Because of the latter, if the pressure to play is not anticipated then the professional will believe he is in a role of his choosing. Unfortunately, initially, only a preview of the plot is available in the somewhat cryptic form of the offence. If this is misunderstood then further opportunities to 'preview' may arise through further offences but the behaviour may become worse. As long as the offending continues there is some hope, albeit diminishing, for the professional and thus for the offender whose internal drama is the subject for modification.

If some initial sense is made of the 'assigned' role then time may be given to understand more and further clues may be provided for encouragement. At the same time pressure will continue to be applied to play the assigned role. That is to say, accompanying the hope, conveyed through the offence will also be an attack on hope.

It is also important to comment that it is not only the offender's internal drama that professionals are called upon to enact but also those more explicit scripts of their own organizations and central government. They will also be under pressure from themselves to re-enact their own dramas. Thus for example a professional who was adopted, may experience great difficulties in working with a client who has just lost a parent. The professionals I refer to throughout have 'clients', 'patients', 'suspects', 'defendants' and 'prisoners'. For convenience I have settled on 'client' and also for convenience, the masculine pronoun 'he'.

CASE EXAMPLE

The following is an instance of how various professionals responded to a dangerous man who had been released from prison. It is an extreme case in terms of level of disturbance, chosen for what I believe to be its clear illustrative value. It is not, however, atypical, in my view, of how professionals can often respond. It is an actual case disguised sufficiently to protect confidentiality without detracting from the significant points. I have tried to outline the case as simply as possible.

This is a case in which I was asked to offer some consultation to a probation officer. I was also provided retrospectively with some detailed information by others who had been involved.

Vignette

A forty-three-year-old man was released from prison following a long sentence for committing two particularly vicious rapes of middle aged women. He was only at liberty for twenty hours before he raped again. This time it was a pregnant woman who subsequently lost her child. He then went on to commit a violent sexual assault on an eleven-year-old girl. He was arrested with little difficulty shortly after and went on to serve another long sentence.

All the women lived alone. He had observed that the girl had been alone for some time in a park for some hours before he attacked her.

On the first occasion he was released with nowhere to live and had gone to his elderly mother who had refused to let him live with her.

Because he had been considered too dangerous to release any earlier than was absolutely necessary, he was therefore deprived of the statutory parole supervision he would have had if released earlier. Following the second sentence he was again released at the latest possible date and therefore again without statutory supervision. However, a female probation officer, who recognized the high risk, took a serious interest in him and recognizing his dangerousness, organized a placement in a hostel which catered for ex-prisoners. She agreed to provide liaison support. She did this against some pressure from her authority who were concerned with the organizational priority for the many cases of statutory supervision.

It was recognized that it was not very realistic to expect such a man to 'survive' for very long outside prison and that the likelihood was that he would have to commit further offences. Nevertheless, an attempt to do something was seen as preferable to standing by and waiting for more rapes. There was an element of hope in that the man was worried about further violence and had, in fact, asked if he could stay in prison. It was useful that he was willing to cooperate with the arrangements made by the probation officer and perhaps hoped that the hostel would have a prison-like regime.

The important details in his history were that he was the middle child of three. His father abandoned the family soon after the third child, a sister, was born. He reported no memory of his father. Mother remarried and two more girls arrived. This marriage also collapsed and mother raised the five children on her own. He described his mother as having been harsh and violent towards him and he had been frightened of her. He felt particularly picked on by her while felt his elder brother was treated well.

He reported that since adolescence his sexual experiences had been largely homosexual. He was afraid of making normal advances to women because he thought they would reject and ridicule him.

The hostel accepted him in the knowledge that he was dangerous, particularly to women, and so arranged that he would be carefully monitored by the manager and deputy, both males. Female staff were to have minimal contact with him. It was known that he had withdrawn from group treatment in prison as he could not handle it and this was taken as an indication that he would require careful supportive management but without intensive counselling. The wish and the anxiety to know what he was thinking and feeling and where he was going, had to be resisted on the basis that it might provoke him to leave, or worse, provoke him into action. It would be difficult to resist the wish to know because the anxiety about him would be very high, both in relation to staff safety and that of the community.

The need for a constant awareness of his violence and to 'hold on to the anxiety' and contain this on his behalf without expecting any fundamental change was central to the plan.

Within a week of the man's arrival the hostel manager had to go on extended sick leave and the deputy took over his role and became quickly entrenched in administration, thus considerably diminishing his monitoring role in relation to this man. The remaining staff members, who were all female, perhaps feeling that they had no option, agreed that one of them would offer him counselling on the basis that this might provide him with a positive experience of a woman. Somehow the original plan had already been perverted.

The probation officer was not told of the above sequence of events. Soon after, the man was seen by a hostel staff member standing outside a school near the hostel at the time children were due to leave. The male deputy dealt with it appropriately by telling the man he had been seen and warned him against going near the school. However, this worker then became inaccessible again. It was later learned that the man continued to hang around schools and had been seen speaking to children.

As time went on his contact with the female worker increased, mainly at her instigation. Because the framework of support had collapsed, this worker could not safely acknowledge her anxiety and later reported that she had found herself saying to the man that he was good looking and sexy and that he could easily find a girlfriend. The man had then asked her if she would like to be his girlfriend. Without the proper support which would have helped her withdraw, this worker compensated for that lack by falling into the role of both victim and tormentor. She was the 'victim' by putting herself in that situation and the 'tormentor' by appearing from this man's point of view to offer something and then to withdraw it. She began to see progress that didn't exist in the man. She talked with him alone at night in the hostel for long periods, often with no other staff members in the vicinity. She claimed that she did not feel afraid and felt sure that he would not be violent towards her. She later admitted that she had forgotten he had committed rape and remembered his offence as 'an assault' of some kind. Something serious had clearly happened to her capacity to think and to remember and also to the minds of the rest of staff who had failed to notice what was happening.

Further events occurred which I shall just state in brief for clarity.

The probation officer saw the problem and tried to help the staff look at the dangerous position in which they had placed themselves and also the community they were seeking to protect. The female worker withdrew and the male worker came back into the picture. At the same time, however, the probation officer was also offering the man appointments at her office at night and then after she saw him walked alone to a dark car park. The man expressed fears of his compulsion to rape. The fact that he could say this, was a measure of the degree to which he did feel held in the minds of others. He must have felt that he was being taken more seriously than ever before in his life. Paradoxically, it became even more difficult to 'hold him in mind' as so much anxiety was created. Extra male staff were urgently requested and the management committee provided agency staff, for twenty-four hours. Subsequently, the client received a letter from the management committee warning him that he was disrupting the hostel and costing them money and if he did not behave he would have to leave.

The client then began to express suicidal feelings which seemed easier for the staff to address than his rape warning. He was referred to a telephone counselling service who suggested he find a prostitute as an outlet for his aggression.

Around this time it was discovered that a female prison visitor who had seen him frequently during his sentence had renewed contact with him without the knowledge of her organization. She invited him to her house where he hit her several times and then begged her to call the police. She refused and tried to persuade him to talk. He complained of feeling suicidal and ran to the local Samaritans who talked with him for several hours. Although he told them what he had done they could not help him to go to the police because no crime had been reported. He left and immediately took an overdose. He was admitted to hospital where they recorded that he was extremely depressed and at risk of suicide. They discharged him the next day. He returned to the hostel where he appeared very angry and frustrated. The probation officer referred him to a medium secure unit for assessment.

In spite of threats and protests the client attended an assessment interview at the secure unit. He explained that he had been out armed with a knife on the previous evening, had visited a prostitute and, unable to get an erection, had taken an overdose. He was admitted as a voluntary patient discharging himself shortly after. Later he was detained under the Mental Health Act and put on the 'observation' ward and absconded. He rang a radio station confessing to rapes which he couldn't possibly have committed. The police tracked him down and arrested him but released him soon after as a 'crank.' Eventually, after further absconsions and the complications of a lapsed order, he was eventually referred to a special hospital.

SOME OBSERVATIONS ON THE ABOVE

(1) If the probation officer had not struggled against her own organization at the outset there would have been no 'plan' and I believe violent sexual offences would have quickly occurred.

(2) The 'available' men disappeared very quickly, not to be replaced.

(3) None of the women protected themselves properly and each, including the volunteer, attempted to draw him into the kind of close working relationship which had been contraindicated.

(4) Until the final event, all the institutions that exist to take disturbed people seriously (police, hospitals, prisons, secure units) let him go.

(5) With the important exception of (1) where the probation officer struggled usefully with her own organization and also with the hostel, the notion of a 'couple' was barely viable in all cases where a thinking pair was vital. Potential 'couples' would have been: the hostel and its management committee; the other workers and their female colleague; the volunteer and her 'parent' organization; the Police and the Health Service.

COMMENT

If this case should be viewed simply as a case management example of a violent man, then it should be viewed as 'successful' even though some of the participants could not be swayed from the unrealistic idea that they had failed miserably to rehabilitate this man.

DISCUSSION

In the following discussion I shall explore the above observations and through looking at some of the questions that might be raised in relation to these I will go on to propose a model for the way we think about our work with offenders.

Consequences and Intentions

A legitimate starting point would be to question whether there is anything to discuss. One might say that the man had served his sentence and should be allowed to put his 'past behind him'. However, the reported behaviour outside the schools and his attack on the volunteer, showed clearly that his 'past' was not 'behind him' and he had also confirmed this when he asked not to be released because he was afraid of his own violence.

One might say that the events described above 'just happen' and, given the circumstances, all the various professionals were effective in helping to avoid further serious offences. I would agree with the latter but not the former as there was an identifiable pattern which merits further investigation as it certainly was not random. The central characteristic of the pattern was that the seriousness of this case had forced the key people to think out a clear plan in advance and that this had been repeatedly contravened; moreover and more important, there was no conscious acknowledgement by staff or the management committee of this contravention. How could they not notice? Had something happened to their thinking?

To focus on the detail. What, for example, is my aim in mentioning that the men in the hostel 'disappeared' What am I suggesting? That the warden went off deliberately to avoid this man; that he wasn't really ill and the deputy also arranged for his own reasons to avoid the man? That they and the management committee left their female colleagues in a dangerous position deliberately? That was the consequence of their action but not the intention.

Am I perhaps saying that the offender somehow made them go away to leave him alone with women?

What am I saying about the women? That they deliberately put themselves at risk by not demanding greater security from the management or failing that by walking out? Given the initial warnings about very limited contact am I suggesting that the female worker who tried to engage him in a counselling relationship was therefore, in a masochistic way, deliberately trying to provoke sadistic violence? From the offender's point of view the only experience available to him was the latter. Action could have been a consequence but this would not have been the intention.

Was the volunteer asking to be raped? Was she masochistically provoking him to give in to the impulses he was desperately seeking to contain? This was not the intention but was to a limited extent a consequence.

How is a prison supposed to keep somebody in when they have finished their sentence? Nevertheless, the man felt abandoned by a system one day that up to the previous day had said he was too dangerous to release.

Later at the secure unit: how is a psychiatrist supposed to detain somebody under the mental health act when there are no florid symptoms? What are the police supposed to do with a man who confesses to rapes that he patently did not commit?

Blame: Management, Workers, Government

Develop New Procedures

Why was there such a discrepancy between what was agreed and the way people acted?

Any understanding needs to go beyond the above concerns which focus on the professionals. If we maintain our focus on professionals we concentrate only on what they 'did' what they could or should have 'done' and either conclude that they did their best or we criticize them or their management. We then suggest regular supervision, with which few people would disagree. Equally, we may criticize the volunteer or her supervisor, and forget that a volunteer is somebody we ask to befriend; can we now ask her to un-befriend? We could blame government for poor resources such that in residential provision in particular the most inexperienced unqualified staff are often asked to look after the most seriously disturbed people in our society.

This is not by way of making a political point but to suggest that the offender will always have an ready applicant in his drama for the assigned role of abandoning or neglectful parent where economics are concerned.[1]

If something serious had occurred, as was entirely possible, there would have been an enquiry which would have produced guidelines about vigilance and alarm systems but would not have touched upon the internal attack on the capacity to remain vigilant. An enquiry would probably also make recommendations for greater communication and liaison in the professional network. The notion of a professional network is something which I propose to discuss later in the chapter.

Blame The Offender

The offender is also a suspect in the search for an explanation of the way professionals find themselves behaving in a way they either dislike or for feeling something they would like to disown.

A familiar phrase 'He is manipulative' is often used (see Cox 1994 on manipulation). It can be used to describe a clearly discernible way of relating as part of an overall assessment. The phrase can also be used in a pejorative way which appears to attribute blame to the offender for making the professional feel manipulated such that 'he stops me from thinking straight and gets me to do things for him'; 'He gets people to collude with him and they get sucked in…he is very powerful' is a complaint which I have frequently heard. The offender stands accused of a further 'offence'.

A more sophisticated sort of blaming occurs where the concept of 'splitting' is sometimes used to describe something that the client does to two or more professionals to stop them working together. The client also is held responsible for 'projecting his feelings into' people and making them feel 'angry' or 'antagonistic' or 'untrusting'. 'Projective identification' and 'mirroring' are also terms frequently used or misused in the hope that they can explain the experience of this complicated phenomenon.

The Powerful Offender

Gradually you may find yourself hearing about a seemingly very powerful individual who is apparently capable of getting people to do what he wants and is able to transplant his unwanted feelings into others. If he really is this powerful, however, we have to ask why does he bother to offend?

If we turn to the professionals we hear of how they cannot think, or of how they feel impelled to do, say or feel things they later wished they hadn't. They may squabble amongst themselves and feel highly critical of each other and may refuse to speak to one another. In other words, professionals can often

---

1   For example the recent closure of Peper Harow School in Surrey, a major therapeutic community for adolescents with disturbances.

appear to be quite helpless and powerless and may retrospectively describe themselves in these terms. When they 'discover' what has happened they may blame the client and sometimes may even complain to him for what he has 'done' to them.

Yet while we know that this phenomenon occurs, how do we come to think of somebody such as this man as being so psychologically powerful when we know how frightened he was of his violence and how his principal means of relating to the world was through futile acts of violence to women and children and through brief homosexual encounters with men? He would probably agree that it was because he felt powerless on release from prison that he accepted the help offered.

Initially the professionals in this case would certainly have seen themselves as behaving as though they were in charge. Yet to the observer, the professionals in the hostel and elsewhere behaved 'as if' they were powerless and 'as if' the client was in charge. However, the staff in the hostel were only able to begin to observe this phenomena for themselves after the probation officer had pointed it out. We would have had an even more difficult task convincing the police, the volunteer and the secure unit staff that something had inhibited their capacity to think. For example in the case of the police, a computer check would have told them that they had a rapist and not a crank. However, the suggestion that they had unwittingly become embroiled in a re-enactment of an unconscious drama would doubtless have met with great resistance.

If our clients seem manipulative or as though they are deliberately trying to 'sabotage' the professional it is a facet of *their* problem that we are witnessing which would be useful to try and understand both from a treatment and a management point of view. However, the 'sabotaging' effect, which I prefer to think of more in terms of pressure to take on the assigned role, is rarely obvious from the perspective of the 'actors', as in the case example. If, however, it can be assumed that this pressure will always be present from the start then it makes it possible to observe one's own feelings and reactions in relation to the subject.

What I am saying is that if 'blame' were to be pursued – for the professionals' unwanted acts and feelings – it is not the offender who is to blame but his unconscious internal world.

The Internal World

I have left discussion of the internal world until last because in my firm opinion it is absolutely necessary for professionals in a network to work through external world considerations and preoccupations. These are not just 'resistances' to understanding and change, such as in the psychoanalytic situation, these considerations are valid and often crucial, but without some understanding of the internal world dimension they may often be useless. For example the provision of alarm systems and other procedures in case of attack are important. However, the professional, like the probation officer, who is temporarily unable to inform herself of danger, and sees a violent person alone in an environment containing these systems, renders them useless because there will be nobody to respond. From the point of view of working with the offender, failure to recognize the internal world communication, intuitively or cognitively, will just mean repetition of the offending. In cases of dangerousness such as this the consequences of repetition are likely to be very serious for the community as well as the offender.

The example I have given is one in which a glimpse of the internal world drama is made manifest first through the offences and then again reproduced in the external network. If we think of the client as the 'powerless' child whose internal experience is that of a sadistic mother who keeps him there to hurt him, then we have a view of somebody who, when with the female worker or the volunteer feels, powerless, wondering what they are wanting to do with him. From the re-emerging violent feelings which he describes, we can surmise that he believes they want to hurt him. When the defence, which the child would have had to employ against his rage, fails him as an adult, he attempts to reverse the position through his sadistic attacks on women; he was in this dilemma when he hit the volunteer. We might speculate that his homosexual feelings and encounters were a frail, developmentally later, defence against his violent and sado-masochistic wishes towards women and against their sadism towards him. We might also speculate that in attacking a pregnant woman and later a child he was attempting to remove an object by which he possibly felt displaced in his mother's affections. There is also a hint that he may have felt that he was held responsible for his father's departure from the family if we can regard as evidence that something was reflected in the management committee's accusing behaviour towards him. What the latter highlighted, which is an extension of my central theme, was that acting out that is misunderstood can be met with an equivalent kind of 'acting out' in the network; that is, in this case, the experience of blame is repeated.

With regard to the father, we may think of him as non-existent and therefore, non-thinking. He may not even have been experienced as absent. We can see the evidence of this abandonment or absence throughout; from the prison system that knowingly releases a dangerous man; from the hostel staff and their management as well as the absence of 'security' at the secure unit and by the police.

As I have already discussed earlier we also saw external evidence of the absence of an 'internal' couple that would be capable of getting together and thinking about his urgent needs. The absence of the father to rescue him from mother is repeated when there was no 'father' to 'rescue' him (and thus the victims) while he was committing the offences. I am referring to his preparation for the offences where he carefully ensures nobody is available to stop him.

My model is simplistic. It is based on the limited evidence gained from offences, the way the man related to the professionals and the way they related to him; in addition, there was a scant history. The model does not include any evidence of positive experiences which we could assume he did have if only for his demonstrated capacity to be worried about himself on leaving prison and his willingness to try and cooperate with a plan for his management. This would allow us to enquire about the older brother or other potentially 'hopeful' figures whom the professional could come to represent for him.

The Network

I feel that some discussion of the term 'network' is necessary as I think it is a misleading and unhelpful concept. It is common sense and obvious good practice that professionals should liaise where appropriate. However, as I have shown in this case, people do not always communicate and work together even when it seems essential. Why in the above example didn't the women say to the men or the men say to the women 'let's talk, something is going wrong here'?

Chambers dictionary defines 'network' as 'any structure in the form of a net:...a system of lines...groups of persons constituting a widely spread organization and having a common purpose'.

There is certainly no structure and no widespread organization in what I would call a fairly haphazardly assembled loose temporary collection of individuals which typically form what is called the network.

Professionals come onto the scene piecemeal and different disciplines share little common purpose. They may all agree that offending is undesirable but after that they may have widely differing objectives which may inhibit liaison when this is indicated. Welldon (1994, p.470) draws our attention to the differences between the interests of law and psychiatry and also between forensic psychotherapy in general and the criminal justice system. Even within the newly emerging philosophical umbrella of forensic psychotherapy there will be differing objectives between some of its component disciplines. For example the dramatherapist's primary concern may be that of the offender's welfare while the probation officer may have to put the community first. In general professionals working in parallel need to liaise frequently but I have addressed in my example how difficulties occur in this apparently ordinary situation. I conclude therefore that the concept of 'professional network' as it is commonly used and the lack of liaison therein is just another 'suspect' in the search for an explanation of the phenomena that I have been describing.

Perhaps the term 'offender network' could develop some meaning if it is used to describe the troupe of potential actors for the pre-assigned roles which were cast within the internal world of the offender. This would be a 'network' owned and controlled by the offender with a common purpose to make the external world conform to the internal world. The offence-preview suggests something hopeful but this is obscured in the main drama as it is often hidden by the main plot as well as by confusing sub-plots. Ideally, from the 'hopeful' perspective the 'offender-network' would never recruit any actual players. In other words, as each professional becomes involved they immediately begin the process of identifying the allotted role(s) and resisting them.

As a way of using this concept: in the case example the 'offender-network' roles could have been anticipated more clearly, which might then have strengthened those who did share a common purpose to work together.

CONCLUSION

I have used an example with some extreme features to illustrate as clearly as possible the dynamic process between the offender and the professionals who encounter him. In my example the professionals actually appeared to take on the ascribed 'roles' in the internal drama of the offender. This occurs frequently in my experience in cases of serious disturbance. In less 'serious' cases the effects are more subtle but less difficult to resist if the 'offender-network' roles as I have called them can be identified and pre-empted.

II · 10

From Our Own Correspondent

The United States

John L. Young

An insanity acquittee came in for her routine visit with the inter-disciplinary forensic team preparing its required status report on her mental condition. Her therapist, a social worker, came in with her. This was not particularly unusual, but the visit was unique for the presence of the attending psychiatrist who had recently assumed responsibility for the patient's medication management. Clearly an able and caring practitioner, he wanted to know as much as he could find out about his patient's legal status and all of its potential implications as they could affect her treatment and his own liability. Although he knew the essential points from his own experience and from discussion with the therapist, he insisted on making certain that he understood much more. He peppered the forensic team members with probing and incisive questions for the better part of an hour until he was fully satisfied, and he seemed greatly relieved once it was clear that he could provide services for this patient according to his usual practice routines without worrying that unpleasant surprises would arise from her status as an insanity acquittee.

Although they formed a team providing competent and comprehensive treatment to a forensic patient, neither the social worker nor the psychiatrist considered himself to be a forensic psychotherapist. Nor did either appear to have any interest in doing so. The social worker had already learned to minimize any forensic implications in his work, and the psychiatrist seemed eager to follow that example as best he could despite the broader scope of his responsibility. This attitude is not unusual. In fact the term *forensic psychotherapy* sounds strange to North American ears.

It is instructive in this regard to compare two recent textbooks of forensic psychiatry, one from each side of the Atlantic. The North American text,

Principles and Practice of Forensic Psychiatry, edited by Dr. Richard Rosner (1994), offers in its index two references to psychotherapy. The first refers to the chapter by Dr. Robert I. Simon (pp.146–153) covering the boundaries of psychotherapy in general. The other is to Dr. Kenneth Tardiff's chapter (pp. 438–443), 'Violence: Causes and Nonpsychopharmacological Treatment'. This title might lead one to expect a discussion of forensic psychotherapy, but there is only a single paragraph, containing no references. It opens, 'Long-term psychotherapy can be useful for violent patients who are nonpsychotic and primarily have personality disorders or intermittent explosive disorders,' and briefly notes the use of couples therapy for spouse abuse. There is no mention of group therapy. Although one of the book's sections is entitled 'Forensic Evaluation and Treatment in the Criminal Justice System,' it contains very little about treatment and less about psychotherapy.

In marked contrast, the predominantly European text, *Forensic Psychiatry: Clinical, Legal, and Ethical Issues,* edited by Professors John Gunn and Pamela J. Taylor (1993), offers over twenty index citations under psychotherapy. It contains extended sections describing the use of psychotherapy in the treatment of forensic patients. There is also a convincing advocacy of this use of psychotherapy, along with information on how to match various kinds of forensic patients and different types of psychotherapy.

These two current and deservedly respected texts present an opportunity to contrast the work of leading writers in North America with those in Europe. Striking as it is, the contrast is limited by its emphasis on psychiatry. What, then, about psychology, social work, and nursing? In North America, a sizeable and thriving division of the American Psychological Association is available to forensically interested psychologists. The Board of Professional Psychology determines educational standards and offers examinations leading to a highly respected board certification. The two-year-old International Association of Forensic Nurses, now at well over 500 members, continues to experience rapid growth. The National Organization of Forensic Social Work began in 1982 and has some 200 members.

Each of the professional forensic organizations places a defining emphasis on applying the member's knowledge and skills to legal matters. The principal psychiatric body further declares that this is done for legal purposes. This body is the American Academy of Psychiatry and the Law, founded in 1969 and currently numbering over 1500 psychiatrists. Each group's self-description does of course mention the role of treatment, including psychotherapy, but clearly not as a major concern. Statements of purpose, for example, place far more emphasis on assessment, research, education, and consultation. The standards for forensic psychiatry fellowship programs by the Joint Committee on Accreditation of Fellowship Programs in Forensic Psychiatry (1982) call for 15–25 hours per week of supervised clinical experience, but quite clearly emphasize assessment, report writing, and testimony rather than forensic psychotherapy or treatment in general.

Although American forensic psychiatry as an organized discipline can be traced back to 1948 (Rosner 1989), it is the formative influence of the late Seymour Pollack (1974) that appears to have cast the discipline-defining die so strongly in the direction of providing psychiatric assessment on legal questions for legal purposes. Pollack relied heavily on Isaac Ray's pioneering 1838 work, *A Treatise on the Medical Jurisprudence of Insanity*, which interestingly enough figured heavily in Daniel McNaghten's defence five years later (Quen 1974). Pollack (1974) marked out a clear separation between forensic psychiatry as concerned primarily 'with the ends and values of civil and criminal justice, rather than concerned with the therapeutic objectives and values of the medical system' (p.2). One does well to keep clearly in mind the early influence of this fundamental distinction when trying to understand the contemporary direction towards assessment rather than treatment of the four forensic mental health disciplines in North America. It also accounts for both clinicians' discomfort with their patient's forensic status in the opening vignette.

There are strong themes in North American psychiatric and psychotherapeutic practice in general that might well explain forensic psychotherapy's failure to thrive on this continent. Writing about the corrections setting, Weinstock (1989), for example, invokes the well-known and typical American pragmatism that has generated widespread impatience with psychotherapy in general as unproven and expensive. He correctly points out that its efficacy is merely difficult to prove, and would be both ethically and technically problematic to study in a dangerous population. Moreover, as a group, American clinicians are especially vigilant about double agentry problems. Therapists worry about being or being perceived as jailers, and now may even have to begin worrying about being pressured to testify in ways that may hasten a death penalty verdict (Weinstock 1994). Mandatory reporting requirements are spreading, and especially affect child therapists (Anderson *et al.* 1993). Finally, most forensic practitioners do maintain separate non-forensic psychotherapy practices (Simon 1994).

Browne *et al.* (1993) have eloquently generalized the widespread 'collective anger' described by Reid (1985) that is felt both by therapists and by society at large towards the forensic patient population, especially its antisocial members. Americans, however, seem to have a more fully developed pessimism about therapy for this population, a belief that is supported by research for some of the same reasons that make efficacy so difficult to study in general. Nonetheless there remain good reasons for optimism (Reid 1985; Nelson and Berger 1988).

There are further problems for forensic psychotherapy that appear unique to North America, or at least more influential here than in Europe. Perhaps the most influential is a rapidly rising sensitivity to cost. There is also the very strong influence of drug abuse among the mentally ill, the so-called 'dually diagnosed' (Rappeport and Oglesby 1993). In addition, recent accelerations in the recognition of patients' rights has extended to include, even for most forensic patients, a right to refuse unwanted treatment. Thus the atmosphere in many facilities offers little to encourage patients to persevere through the inevitable challenges of effective psychotherapy. All too often, forensic patients are unable to engage in psychotherapy as an indirect consequence of having exercised their right to refuse antipsychotic or antidepressant medication. Finally, a Canadian psychologist (Quinsey 1988) has found that treatability itself is not generally well assessed, a surprising finding in view of the general emphasis on assessments described above.

Despite these factors, it is heartening to note that a recent survey of public sector mental hospitals documented 58 per cent claiming to make use of individual psychotherapy and 30 per cent using group psychotherapy for forensic patients (Heilbrun et al. 1992). Clearly the conditions are in place in North America for the development of forensic psychotherapy as a distinct discipline. More precisely, it is a subspecialty within a subspecialty. It involves the determining and practicing of psychotherapy appropriate to forensic patients; it requires identifiable forensic skills, including especially the ability to assess whether therapy will or will not be helpful for forensic as well as clinical purposes. The forensic psychotherapist must shape and/or supervise the shaping of the work so that it can proceed effectively within a legally determined context.

As a clinical scientific discipline, forensic psychotherapy also must address a variety of important research questions. Some of these become obvious as a result of reflecting on the scene in North America. For example, in keeping with the pragmatic American style, there is a large family of questions regarding efficacy, to which, incidentally, a large part of the forensic population readily lends itself because of their inevitably long stay. What characterizes antisocial personality-disordered patients who are helped by psychotherapy; what characterizes the successful therapy itself? How should successful outcome best be identified, defined, measured? How can therapists avoid making their patients more effective criminals thanks to their effective treatment?

We have yet much to learn about the impact of the forensic context on therapy; doing so will be generally useful since no psychotherapy is free of its context. Weinstock (1989) points out that the prison environment encourages ego weakness, paranoia, and sealing over, all qualities opposed to the goals of psychotherapy. He adds that at the same time the prison environment may also discourage such qualities as truthfulness and initiative, associated with therapeutic progress, and further points out that the prison system may even exploit therapeutic success when it does such things as encourage a more trusting inmate-patient to inform on his peers.

Forensic psychotherapy is a rich source for broader research on questions regarding countertransference and for the many continuing research issues in group therapy, especially inpatient groups with specialized purposes such as coming to terms with one's legal status, gaining impulse control, learning communication skills, and assertiveness training.

The probability that conventional psychotherapy will diminish under continuing efforts to cut costs may herald a strong future in North America for forensic psychotherapy. The normal ebb and flow of social trends indicates that at some time there will be an upswing in the practice of psychotherapy, forensic and otherwise. Whatever the future brings, attention to our European colleagues' work in forensic psychotherapy now will greatly benefit our patients and ourselves.

Australia
'Terra Australis Incognita'

Stephen Freiberg

In order to balance the globe, the geographer Ptolemy, in about 150 AD, speculated that there was a large mass of land stretching across much of the south of the world. This was the 'Unknown South Land', Australia. Freud, too, speculated about the existence of the unseen mass of the unconscious, balancing the conscious mind. The metaphor may be extended further to the world of forensic psychotherapy as much of it still remains uncharted. Although this field is a rapidly growing discipline, in Australia it is still evolving and research remains 'fragmentary' (Cordner *et al.* 1992).

One of the important issues facing Australia today is the move towards becoming a republic. This involves both cutting our ties with England and coming to terms with our convict and colonial past. Each state is currently debating issues under its own legal system. New South Wales (NSW), the most highly populated state, with the largest prison population, addresses the problems of drug use and trafficking, while Queensland deals with corruption and Tasmania debates its pre-war laws criminalizing homosexuality between consenting adults in private. (Recently, a Tasmanian parliamentarian demanded that offenders be transported back to England!) As a result, each state's prison system differs with respect to its prison population, its inherent problems and resources. The basis of this essay is the writer's experience as a prison psychiatrist and psychotherapist working with male prisoners in NSW prisons.

Currently, the NSW prison population is approximately 6500, an increase of almost 80 per cent since 1985. In addition, 15,000 prisoners pass through the gaol each year serving sentences of various lengths.

The state's annual law and order budget was $1800[1] million in 1991, third after education and health. For instance, a maximum security prisoner cost the government $120 per day in 1991, an increase of 70 per cent since 1985. These costs increased at a rate greater than that of inflation over this period.

Despite politicians' claims that we are in the midst of a 'crime wave', statistics do not validate this. In NSW since 1991, there has been a significant decrease in armed robberies, fraud and car theft, while murder, sexual assault, drug trafficking have remained the same. Only malicious property damage and theft have increased. Both government and opposition are paralyzed by a fear of the public's perception that they are 'soft' on crime, especially with a state election on the horizon. The NSW government passed a 'Truth-in-Sentencing' Bill in 1989 which forced judges to impose sentences which were effectively heavier than in the past. This bill, condemned by barristers, civil-liberties groups and the press has effectively increased the length of sentences by 50 per cent, as a result of which prisoners in NSW serve far longer sentences than elsewhere in Australia or in other western countries. This has led to the phenomenon of 'Judge-Shopping' (see Totaro 1994): delays and adjournments are used to obtain hearings before 'lenient' judges, as it has been proven that some judges are three time more likely to send offenders to gaol. On the whole, an 'out-of-sight, out-of-mind' attitude existed with respect to prisoners. One of the greatest catalysts for change was the Royal Commission into Aboriginal Deaths in Custody (1991). They commented:

> 'The whole regime of prisoners in every prison system in Australia urgently needs to be re-examined. If the purpose of a health system is...to deliver services where they are most needed, then the case for general improvement of prison medical and psychiatric services is absolutely overwhelming.' (Cordiner 1991, p.814)

NSW responded with a quiet but steady reform of prison management. The system slowly changed from a reactive, centrally-controlled organisation with rigid rules, to a more pro-active, locally-managed organization where initiative and responsibility were encouraged.

Most Australian prisons were constructed over a century ago. These stand in stark contrast to the newest privately-run prisons with state-of-the-art electronically controlled security. As in many countries, the subject of privately-run prisons have been a controversial one.

A unique social world exists in these closed institutions which skews all presentation and management of psychological distress and psychiatric disorders. Goffman (1961) described the world of total institutions where there was a sharp social division between 'the keepers' and 'the kept'. The prison has its

---

1   Australian dollars.

own complex set of unwritten rules, both for staff and for prisoners. For instance, when a prisoner enters gaol, he must face an informal trial by peers. Sex offenders and child molesters are considered the 'lowest', and are openly scapegoated and attacked by other prisoners. A pecking order develops and deep tensions are played out in often incomprehensible violence. Prisoners can sometimes wait a long time to settle an old score. As Freud (1914b) believed, they will inflict the same or even greater cruelty than they have endured in the past.

In the 1980s the NSW Department of Health implemented a policy of deinstitutionalization and closure of public psychiatric hospitals. As a result, psychotic and developmentally delayed patients drifted into the prison system. They formed some of the 'weaker' members of the prisoner group who are often tolerated, nurtured and protected. Dentler and Erikson (1959) hypothesized that these group members introduce emotional qualities which the population (lacking women and children) could not otherwise afford.

In the prison 'the kept' are dependent on 'the keepers' to dispense both minor privileges and relatively severe punishments. The former are apt to occupy the inmates concern and attention, while the later force him to play a regressed, child-like role. Many prisoners try to 'play it cool' so as to keep out of trouble. They may even be 'converted' into the perfect, model inmate. However, some consciously seek trouble. The 'black sheep' of the family and society becoming the 'black sheep' of the prison. They often gain a sense of pride and status from this 'negative identity' (Erikson 1963). 'Lifers' often become group leaders and friction is evident between rival groups. An escalation of tension may be seen in dangerous games of brinkmanship (Byron 1976) or fights where esteem, dignity and status are at stake (Geertz 1973).

Sykes (1958) hypothesized that the deprivations suffered by prisoners are aimed at attacking their self-esteem. These include deprivations of liberty, possessions, services, autonomy, security and heterosexual relationships.

Objects play important and highly symbolic roles in the prison world. Wedding rings, photos and letters become concrete representations of loved and lost persons. Recently, violent and destructive riots occurred after the Minister of Corrections, against all advice, ordered the removal of personal property from prisoners' cells.

Like violence, sexuality is a part of the prison world, although its existence is denied or minimized. Homosexual relationships, both transient and long-term are part of prison life, as is the overtly flamboyant and often promiscuous behaviour of the transsexual prisoner. Rape is common but under-reported; in a recent survey, twenty-five per cent of male prisoners claimed that they had been sexually assaulted in NSW prisons (Slee 1994).

Condoms are still illegal in NSW prisons, despite repeated calls for their introduction by medical experts. Each state prison authority has reacted differently to the AIDS crisis. In NSW, HIV-positive prisoners are now fully integrated into the general prison population. Other states have partial or full-segregation policies which have been successfully challenged in the courts. A recent case of a prison officer seroconverting following a needle attack by an HIV-positive prisoner has highlighted the anxiety and vulnerability of all prison staff.

Although all prisoners are confronted with the difficulties of life behind bars some groups, such as aboriginals, have unique problems. Although they number only 1.5 per cent of the Australian population aboriginals constitute 15 per cent of the total prison population. For example, in NSW, an aboriginal juvenile has a 21 times greater chance of being incarcerated than a white juvenile; in Western Australia the rate is 48 times higher.

The Royal Commission into Aboriginal Deaths in Custody found an overall prison suicide rate of 1 per cent, while aboriginals had an 11 per cent prison death rate. In 1992, the Federal Government granted $450 million to implement the Royal Commission's 339 recommendations. Tragically, new statistics show that the deaths in custody continue to increase, and the Federal Social Justice Commissioner blames 'bureaucratic inaction' for the continuing deaths (Chamberlin 1994).

In the confined environment, a complex interdependence develops in the relationships between the officers and the prisoners. This contrasts with the public's perception that the institution has absolute control over the prisoners. For example, the authority of guards can be corrupted by friendship, reciprocity and default in their relationships with prioners (Glaser and Fry 1987). Rule infringements and 'trouble' can be overlooked by both: for the prisoner trouble spells punishment, while for the officer it means more paperwork.

A study by Holland et al. (1976) showed an intriguing similarity between the personality profiles of prison officers and prisoners. They speculated that this may enable the officers to function in, and possibly also find enjoyable, roles that others might find distasteful or impossible to play. On the negative side, however, these same personality characteristics might be expected to predispose officers to take advantage of, or exploit inmates. Recent media reports claimed that 10 per cent of prison officers had a previous criminal record. One of the most famous NSW prisoners in recent times was a previous Minister of Corrections who was gaoled on corruption charges.

The NSW Prison Medical Service and the Department of Corrections often view problems from different and at times conflicting perspectives. Winnicott's (1963a) comments regarding adolescents in hospital care are applicable to the prisons:

> 'Not only do the care- and the therapy-personnel become jealous of each
> other, each unable to see the other's value, but also some patients tend
> to foster a split between the two groups. There is often a reflection here

of the tensions between the patient's parents, and we see in displaced form the patient's fear of allowing the parents to come together (in the unconscious fantasy system).' (p.245)

To complicate matters, the Department of Corrections has repeatedly battled with the Department of Health to take over financial control and administrative responsibility for the Prison Medical Service.

Until recently only a small number of doctors, specialists and psychiatrists worked in the NSW Prison Medical Service, with little if any contact with other public or private health systems. Prison doctors frequently see prisoners who present with insomnia and depressive symptoms. In the 1970s benzodiazepines were widely prescribed, and these were replaced by antidepressants in the 1980s. With continuing problems of abuse, misuse, trading of medications and overdoses, a trend towards using sedating antihistamines has emerged. Of the many causes of insomnia, the disruption in a primary relationship is the most important factor causing increased vulnerability at nights (Ellis 1991).

Pharmacotherapy in the prison is greatly influenced by transference distortions. The transference may be positive (with the physician seen as responsive, empathic or validating) or negative (the physician perceived as withholding, sadistic, uncaring or unwilling to help). Countertransference may also be expressed in giving or withholding medications (Gutheil 1982).

Self-injury and suicide attempts elicit the most rapid response from all prison staff. Winchel and Stanley (1991) estimated that self injury occurs in 2–7 per cent of prisoners. Power and Spencer (1987) found that it was more likely to be motivated by avoidance of expected confrontation with other inmates, manipulative intent and emotional upset rather than by psychiatric disturbance. Rieger's study (1971) found that serious suicide attempts followed the recent loss of a loved one, and Schwartz *et al.* (1974) believed that suicidality was a means of coercing nurturance from others.

Prisoners often choose unstable and unpredictable methods of suicide, such as cell arson and attempted hanging. Smialek and Spitz (1978) suggested that there was a high probability of unintentional death from hanging as only two kilograms of pressure is required to obstruct cerebral blood flow, and the adult head weighs about three kilograms.

Self-mutilation takes on bizarre forms in the prison, including deep lacerations to arms, legs, achilles tendons, carving words into one's skin, eye-injuries and body-piercing. Graff and Mallin (1967) hypothesized that as the patients' psychopathology was at a preverbal level, so their relief is sought through 'physical preverbal messages'.

Cooper *et al.* (1991) published their discussion paper on the prevention of suicides and attempted suicides in NSW prisons. They addressed the need to develop strategies in order to prevent costly liability claims against the government for failure in their duty-of-care.

Following the Royal Commission and with ongoing media attention many prison staff reacted very anxiously to threatened or attempted suicides. Psychiatrists and other staff may be 'blackmailed by these disasters' and this may compromise their care for other prisoners (Winnicott 1963a, p.245).

In prisons, 'almost all of psychiatry's problems are raised to a higher power' (Weinstein 1989, p.1094). In addition to this, 'psychiatrists practising in such facilities attempt to provide adequate services under the most difficult working circumstances, with inadequate professional recognition, renumeration and, perhaps most burdensome of all, in the midst of frequently deplorable conditions' (American Psychiatric Association 1989, p.1244).

The NSW Prison Medical Service is responsible for all the health needs of its prisoners. To improve the service, the psychiatric department should be developed in two specific areas: a medicolegal assessment service and a treatment service. The assessment service needs to respond to various external agencies (courts, tribunals, parole board) requesting reports at all stages from arrest to release. For example, a 'clumsy' crime highly suggestive of a neurotic wish to be punished (Adler 1982) could be referred to out-patient psychotherapy and diverted from the prison system. The anxiety and drama of the court process (Lennings 1988) could be used as a potentially positive 'psychotherapeutic experience ' (Gzudner and Muelle 1987). In the prison, when control is established and flight is not possible, the frustration and confusion of outpatient assessment of sociopathic disorders is diminished (Vaillant 1975).

The prison treatment service needs to be 'locally' organized into teams which manage all problems in the different prisons. For example, remand prisoners in maximum security present different problems to those in minimum security on a day-release program. In New South Wales a highly specialized unit houses Crown witnesses. Unlike all other prisons, it is designed to keep others out. In this unit, all prisoners are known only by coded numbers, and names are never used.

A comprehensive range of psychological and psychiatric services should be offered, using multi-disciplinary teams with appropriate supervision and staffing levels determined by what is essential to ensure access. For more difficult problems, such as the chronically suicidal prisoner, and the life-sentence prisoner, more highly specialized services must be available (Litman 1989). These include long-term individual and group psychotherapies. (In Australia, capital punishment does not exist.)

In an era of increasing accountability, the patient/therapist dyad is being replaced by the patient/therapist/court triad. Consequently, methods for ongoing assessment of treatment efficacy need to be established so as to ascertain quality assurance, justify funding and further service development, without interfering with the therapy.

Countertransference issues are very important in the treatment of prisoners. Symington (1980) described the responses aroused by the psychopath as collusion, disbelief and condemnation. Lion and Pasternak (1973) remind us that countertransference to violent patients may interfere with effective management, while identification and counter-identification with the patient may occur (Nadelson 1977).

No matter how thoroughly trained and experienced a therapist may be, there is no guarantee that the therapist will be able to bear all the patient's feelings, or as Cox (1983) stated, be at ease in the presence of patients who have savagely mutilated, dismembered or murdered others.

Changes in legal and penological practice are usually made for political reasons (Ellard 1988), and the punishment ethic still seems to dominate in New South Wales prisons where the rehabilitation ethic should. New and creative methods of disciplining and treating offenders need to be developed. For instance, a pilot program for young offenders in which they have to face their victims in a community conference has had excellent results. In Wagga Wagga, a rural centre in NSW, ninety per cent of young offenders subjected to the Youth Conference Scheme did not reoffend. In comparison to this, seventy per cent of young offenders who were involved in the normal judicial procedures reoffend (*Sydney Morning Herald* 1994).

While psychiatrists are returning to work in prisons and drug and alcohol services, proper training and support structures are in their infancy. In NSW no specialized forensic outpatient service exists. Offenders can only obtain treatment at public facilities after release from prison if they have 'dual' or 'triple' diagnosis. Sadly, Scott's comments in 1960 are still relevant today: 'Much devoted work in institutions is thrown away through lack of aftercare' (p.1645).

Toch (1979) reminded us that although prisons are stressful, they need not be wasteful or destructive. 'There are experiences in prison that are pleasurable, constructive, healing and growth-promoting. It may not be easy, but it is not impossible to make the prison experience a more fruitful one for many prisoners'. As Parsifal is told before he enters the Grail Castle in Wagner's opera:

> 'You see my son
> Time here becomes space.' (I.1)

Purchasing and Providing
Forensic Psychotherapy in the Marketplace

Dilys Jones

INTRODUCTION

Forensic psychotherapists play a large part in the overall work of many clinical teams, although they themselves are small in number (Reed Committee 1992a). Therapists may be medically trained or have come from a variety of other backgrounds. The value of the therapist working as part of the clinical team is well appreciated by its members. The preparation of a diagnostic formulation for discussion within the team can greatly aid the understanding of why offences occurred.

Patients value highly the opportunity to develop a good therapeutic relationship with their therapist, to feel that they are being listened to and understood, and to be able to acknowledge that they have developed greater insights into their behaviour and feelings. This forms the basis of working with mentally disordered offenders (Scott 1977). Generally, and in tandem with the other aspects of the individual treatment programme, progress is enabled leading to the eventual transfer or discharge of the patient from the secure setting. Although the value of the therapist is well recognized by fellow professionals, with the move to general management and Trusts within the National Health Service (NHS) reforms, it has now become necessary to demonstrate the efficacy and appropriateness of such an approach to managers, who have the ultimate responsibility for dispersal of funding.

Since the introduction of the National Health Service and Community Care Act (1990), NHS Trusts now provide most of the services in the NHS (Department of Health 1992b). Trusts, one of the main planks of the new legislation, were introduced as part of an internal market for the NHS. District health authorities now have the role of 'purchasers' or 'commissioners', and Trusts (and directly managed units – those facilities not yet granted Trust status, but still directly managed by the district health authority) have the role of 'providers'.

The Department of Health allocates funding to district health authorities on the basis of weighted capitation for the catchment area population. Funds are thus limited: the reforms were intended, amongst other objectives, to provide a focus on value for money, placing greater emphasis on outcomes and quality, and to provide services based on the assessment of needs of the population (Department of Health Press Release 1990). There is thus now the requirement, as for all branches of medicine, for forensic psychotherapy professionals to be able to define and measure the needs for provision of the service, audit the service provided, showing what the outcome, or health gain, for the population is (Department of Health 1989). The significance of this is that without such measurements being available, purchasers may decide to spend their limited funds elsewhere. This chapter examines these issues in relation to forensic psychotherapy, as well as identifying possible threats and opportunities in the 'marketplace' created by the NHS changes.

FORENSIC PSYCHOTHERAPY AS PART OF FORENSIC PSYCHIATRY

As a specialism (i.e. psychotherapy with mentally disordered offenders and those with similar needs), forensic psychotherapy is practised in Special Hospitals, regional secure units, specialist units such as the Henderson Hospital, prisons with specialist regimes and in out-patient as well as other community settings, for example probation hostels. As part of a range of treatments offered to offender patients, it caters for a relatively small group of patients, who are, nevertheless a significant and important group by virtue of the complexity of problems and issues with which they present. They are a resource-intensive group. As a group, they have recently been the focus of a major review of health and social services (Reed 1992b).

The Reed Committee (1992a) recommended that training opportunities for psychotherapy with mentally disordered offenders should be increased and that the development of such training should be based initially on units which currently have psychotherapists working with these or similar patients.

PERFORMANCE MEASUREMENT

An examination of the research and current thinking in the literature reveals that performance indicators are a well-established feature of management in the public sector. The measurement of results continues to be at the centre of the initiative to make public sector managers more accountable. Public sector managers are finding the use of indicators of positive benefit in the complex task of improving quality of service and value for money. A key area is in measuring how objectives are being met. Results can then be fed back into the system to improve services and define superior strategies. It is necessary to make very clear the distinction between three frequently used words in this area: economy, efficiency and effectiveness.

'Economy is defined as input minimisation – purchasing the inputs for the organisation at the lowest possible cost. Efficiency is defined as the improvement of the ratio between inputs and outputs. Effectiveness is defined in an objective orientated way. Thus effectiveness is measured by answering the question how far do the final outcomes or impacts of the policy match the objectives of the policy? The definition focuses on outcomes and impacts rather than outputs'. (Open University 1990)

Effectiveness is very much more difficult to measure than efficiency, as outcomes (or health gains) are dependent on a variety of factors, all of which need consideration and analysis with respect to the outcome.

With reference to any branch of health care, including forensic psychotherapy, it is not only managers but clinicians who need indicators to help them assess the effectiveness of their contribution to the health care of the population they serve. The White Paper 'Working for Patients' (Department of Health 1989) asked district health authorities to

'concentrate on ensuring that the health needs of the population for which they are responsible are met; that their population has access to a comprehensive range of high quality, value for money services; and on setting targets for and monitoring the performance of those management units for which they continue to have responsibility'. (p.6)

An indicator is defined (Jenkins 1990) as a 'measure that summarises information relevant to a particular phenomenon, or is a reasonable proxy for such a measure' (p.500). Indicators need to measure what they are supposed to measure and provide the same answer if measured by different people in similar circumstances (Cook and Campbell 1976). Indicators should also be able to measure the change required and reflect changes specifically in the situation concerned (World Health Organisation 1981).

Health care could be considered in terms of structure, process or outcome (Donabedian 1966). Structure (or input) is concerned with the amount and type of resources available, for example, finance, buildings, bed numbers and staffing levels (Standing Medical Advisory Committee 1990). Process relates to the volume and nature of activity by the staff in providing care. The outcome is the effects of the health care on the health status of the patients (or the population) in terms of changes in functioning, illness or even death. In psychiatry, the level of social functioning is an important outcome. It is reasonably easy to measure input/structure and also process. However, in terms of effectiveness it is outcome measures which are of great interest and which provide the greatest challenge in achieving. Research (Taylor *et al.* 1989; Department of Health 1991b) has shown that measures of structure and process are not a good substitute for outcome and the former two bear little relationship to the latter. Outcome measures or effectiveness measures are significantly superior because they reflect *all* the influences on health status, and not just the effect of the particular services under study (Schroeder 1987), but as noted above are considerably more difficult to establish.

With reference to the individual consumer, patient satisfaction is also an important aspect of the outcome of health care. Research (Conrad 1985) indicates that 'compliance with the treatment programme depends very much on the effect of the treatment on the patient's feelings of wellbeing' (pp.29–37). The feelings of wellbeing of the staff involved in managing the patients are also of importance. Working in a frustrating, ineffective environment has 'knock-on' effects for staff as well as patients and any system of performance assessment needs to take account of this, using the results to help improve the working environment.

There are a large number of agencies, both within the criminal justice network and the NHS and the social services, which are involved in the management of mentally disordered offenders. In order to aid local planning, delivery and monitoring of services, both through individual agency line accountability and on a multi-agency basis, performance and health outcome indicators need to be developed, for use both nationally and locally. This will enable targets to be set and performance assessed. Systems need to be in place to collect the information, to digest it and to disseminate it as appropriate.

At present, most health care data is collected on indicators of process. Outcome measures need to be developed.

AUDIT

The process of medical audit has been defined as 'the systematic critical analysis of the quality of medical care, including procedures used for diagnosis and treatment, the use of resources and the resulting outcome and quality of life for the patient' (Department of Health 1989, p.3). Audit is gradually becoming a regular activity in psychiatric practice and this includes psychotherapy. It is a means of review, by peers, of medical activity and its inputs, process and outcomes. The results can be examined, and constructive changes made to clinical practice and/or services as a result. It is a means of improving effectiveness of services to patients and, if used properly, is a powerful tool. In psychotherapy, as in other areas of clinical practice, it provides the opportunity for clinicians to monitor their practice – not to do so is no longer regarded as acceptable or justifiable (Parry 1992). It is not only medical audit but clinical audit which is of importance (National Health Service Management Executive (NHSME) 1994).

It is perhaps not surprising that, given the large amount of direct public expenditure on mental health services – some £2 billion in 1990 (Blom-Cooper and Murphy 1991) – the Department of Health has well developed policies and guidance on the inclusion of audit in every day practice (NHSME 1994). It is important that, with limited resources available, what is available is managed in the most effective way possible. In many hospitals it has been recognized that the successful development of effective health care resource management is not possible without the full involvement of the medical profession. The full range of possible roles and influences of doctors in the whole area of resource management is well documented (e.g. Mumford 1989).

In terms of forensic psychotherapy, audit can be used to demonstrate the effectiveness of it as a treatment. It is also important, that having justified an approach clinically, 'purchasers' or 'commissioners' have the ability to identify the 'current pattern of health care, identify the need for and options for change (including new services) and monitor the effects of their actions on the health of local people' (NHSME 1991, p.5).

Demonstrating that a treatment works and that there is a demand for it may not always lead to the logical conclusion that those who need it should have access to it, however. Dolan and Norton (1991) correctly predicted that the new contracting system 'would reduce referrals to specialist units, particularly supra-regional units such as the Henderson Hospital' (p.745). This was essentially because units such as the Henderson are largely dependent on funding from extra-contractual referrals.

The core treatment offered by the Henderson Hospital for its severely personality disordered patients (50% of whom have criminal convictions) is psychotherapy and it functions as a therapeutic community. Dolan and Norton had anticipated that for units such as the Henderson, dependent for a large part of its income on extra-contractual referrals (ECRs), purchasers would decline to fund such referrals. This despite the fact that in the guidelines for ECRs (Department of Health 1991a), it is clear that DHAs should not challenge the GP's choice of provider unless it can be shown that the proposed referral is wholly unjustified on clinical grounds or where an alternative referral would be equally efficacious for the patient, taking into account the patient's wishes. This proved to be the case, with only 36 per cent of ECRs being agreed. They later argued that this was false economy: not only were those who were turned down in this way more likely to fall into the criminal justice system, but along the way society would pick up a much larger bill. As Dolan and Norton (1991) said 'Although the delay in responding to ECR requests undoubtedly saves money for the individual funding authority concerned, the cost to the nation as a whole does not disappear' (p.747), personality disordered patients being high users of psychiatric, social work, probation and other criminal justice agencies. Menzies, Dolan and Norton (1993) demonstrated that refusing to fund such treatment is a false economy. The benefits accrued by the treatment offered at the Henderson resulted in fewer convictions and rehospitalizations following it – after four years the savings would have outweighed the costs of funding admissions to the Henderson.

The threat to the Henderson Hospital in terms of closure was averted by the South West Thames Regional Health Authority stepping in to secure future funding. However, it is of concern that a service with proved effectiveness and a demonstrable clinical demand for its services was under threat because of the NHS contracting system. Clearly, these sorts of problems apply to all such supra-regional units. Of help also was recent government policy; Circular EL (90)190 (NHSMR 1990) (and its successor EL (92)6 (NHSME 1991)) 'Services for mentally disordered offenders and difficult to manage patients' drew attention to the need for regional general managers to ensure that service provision for this group was at least maintained at current levels. In addition, the Reed Committee recommended that regional health authorities should, in conjunction with other agencies, ensure that there is a regular assessment of needs of their residents for secure provision (Jones and Dean 1992). This was carried out (NHSME April 1992) under the aegis of EL (92)24 and again subsequently.

RESULTS OF AUDIT IN PSYCHOTHERAPY

As with many other branches of medicine, psychotherapists are starting to audit their work. Standards used to set the framework are those devised from Royal College guidelines, service specifications which can be laid out in contracts between purchaser and providers (NHSME 1993), and derived from other sources such as research, audit results and other professional guidelines.

Denman (1994) describes a review of tapes of psychotherapy sessions which resulted in a 'comparatively large effect on organisational thinking' (p.82). As a result of deficits noted, the assessment progress was re-evaluated and re-emphasized, and a system was established to enable identification of personal strengths and weaknesses of student therapists, with a more formal training course and supervision.

Andrews (1993) identifies possible concerns about funding long-term dynamic psychotherapy as not only does it as yet lack formal demonstration of its efficiency but its is very expensive and he states that there is concern about the safety: '10% of mental health professionals report that their own therapy harmed them, the number of patients harmed who do not complain might be considerable' (p.448). The shorter, more focused psychotherapies have been subject to greater evaluation than the longer term therapies and few would argue about their efficacy (Drugs and Therapeutics Bulletin 1993). Greater doubt has been cast on the value of the longer term therapies, although evaluation in some areas has shown positive benefits as noted above (Menzies, Dolan and Norton 1993). Nonetheless, there are many patients who report enormous help from such therapy and further work is required to develop measures of quality, outcome and patient satisfaction in this area. It should be remembered that there are many other areas in medicine where practitioners are in a similar position; that is, treatments require further evaluation. Nonetheless it is possible to argue that removing such a treatment is unethical, particularly where it may be the only treatment available. Holmes (1994) and Marks (1994) provide an up-to-date review of evaluation in this area.

THE MARKETPLACE

Holmes (1991) predicted that the introduction of market forces 'may paradoxically, have the effect of raising the status and morale of psychotherapy, since it is what many patients want...' (p.151). Forensic psychiatry is a growing specialty and it has already been noted that the need for more forensic psychotherapists has been identified (Reed 1992a).

In the 'jargon' of the marketplace, any strategy to develop the specialty locally needs to follow careful analysis of local and national conditions, including a 'SWOT' analysis. (This refers to the Strengths, Weaknesses, Opportunities and Threats facing the specialty.) There is generally an increasing awareness of the need for service development for forensic psychiatry, including forensic psychotherapy – recent assessments of need (NHSME 1992) have identified clear market need. In addition, the Health Care Service for Prisoners has become a purchaser rather than a provider of services to prisoners and this too should in theory widen the market. The Reed Committee (1992b) recommended that Regional Secure Unit beds should increase, initially to the target set by the Glancy Committee in 1975 and then to a target nationally of 1500. There is thus considerable opportunity for development.

Purchasers will need to be assured of the efficacy, and a weakness is the lack of the data as yet in this respect. Providers need to commence evaluation of their work, particularly in respect of developing outcome indicators.

It will be important also to develop 'care pathways' which outline to purchasers how forensic psychotherapy is an integral part of the overall treatment process. A care pathway is essentially a brief and lucid step-by-step account of what a patient undergoes during his or her period of care.

A Chief Executive of a Hospital Trust stated at a conference recently that he had not understood what exactly happened in hospital to a patient with a broken leg until he had seen the care pathway the patient would undergo. Once he had understood, he could support and influence issues related to the care, and help to develop means by which purchasers could be attracted to use the services, that is, 'market' them. The value of this is that by packaging and pricing a product (in this case forensic psychotherapy) and publicizing it, all those who wish to purchase it are made aware of it and of its benefits. Purchasers can then include it in their plans, and the funds generated by increased demand can be re-invested in developing the service further.

Doctors and therapists have to remember that they have a separate working ideology and language from that of managers. The current system where managers have control of resources both as purchasers and providers is likely to be with us for the foreseeable future. It is important that both groups understand each other; psychotherapists should be able to utilize their skills of empathy to considerable advantage in this respect! Developing a shared vision for the future direction of services, learning how to aid managers effectively in formulating carers' aims and objectives into a Business Plan for the hospital and a marketing strategy are important aspects for the new way of working and essential if there is to be further development. This means that therapists and doctors have to work hand-in-hand with managers – each group after all has common objectives in that they are working towards higher quality services for patients, although each has different working ideologies. A significant barrier to progress in many areas has been the widely reported 'power struggles' between doctors and managers. Others have found a collaborative approach of greater benefit to patients' service development (Jones and Franey, in preparation). As with all other aspects of healthcare, costing of the service needs to take place so that purchasers can be billed appropriately. As well as providing services in a variety of settings, for example prisons, probation hostels and out-patients, it is likely that attractive packages can be developed for teaching and family purposes. All in all, there are exciting opportunities for the development of these services for the mentally disordered offender.

Training and Supervision –
The Interface with Forensic Psychiatry

Introduction

Murray Cox

The introduction to this volume drew attention to the interesting philosophical distinction between that which is universal and that which is localized everywhere. This dialectic surfaces in a particularly acute form when it comes to issues relating to training and supervision in forensic psychotherapy. There are indeed universal issues, such as the impact of unconscious motivation behind both the criminal act and its exploration within transference-intensified therapeutic work. Other universal considerations involve the relationship between the impingement of external security upon the internal security of all those involved within the 'holding environment', no matter whether this is concrete (literally, made of concrete), metaphorical, or both. Nevertheless, the relevance of that which is localized everywhere – such as the structuring of time, depth and mutuality, becomes endowed with a different focal emphasis, depending upon the containing location, the patient population and precise therapeutic intent. The very number of contributors to these volumes is a tacit statement that, even within this new and relatively circumscribed field, there already exists a wide range of expertise which, fortunately, can be called upon.

It is impossible to imagine a therapist who would be deeply experienced in the kind of out-patient work for which the Portman Clinic stands, as well as being equally at home in secure settings, where the conditions in which therapy is undertaken differ in so many ways. It is for these reasons that training and supervision will inevitably involve rotational placements, so that adequate experience can be gained in a variety of settings. Here we run into a seeming impasse. There is an inherent paradox which the trainer and the trainee never fully resolve. The dilemma can be stated succinctly. In essence, the trainee forensic psychotherapist needs the possibility of long-term relationships with patients, so that he can – at first hand – learn of the vicissitudes of transference–countertransference turbulence. He also needs to appreciate the impact of superimposed exigencies – such as the augmentation of affect induced by anniversary re-activation of index offences, court appearances – and the like. But, in addition, experience of therapy in a wide range of settings – from the most 'open' to the most 'secure' – which must imply frequent rotation in the short term, is an integral component of comprehensive training.

The trainee will come to learn of the importance of distinguishing between narrative and historical truth (Spence 1982) and the significance of narrative polish, through which parts of the story which 'don't quite fit' are 'smoothed out' and rounded off. Spence writes:

> 'What starts out (in the clinical encounter) as a discontinuity or a lack of closure or a failure to make sense is inevitably smoothed over by the narrative tradition with the result that...it...[acquires] a narrative polish that makes it look unexceptional.' (p.26)

It is not only the narcissistic patient who adorns (a word so close to 'adores' – and one which is often equally appropriate) his history in order to create a more striking impact, but it may also be the defence lawyer who presents a 'polished' story in order to make a stronger point in mitigation. Furthermore, there is sometimes a temptation for the forensic clinician himself to want to change an emphasis, so that the story 'fits' more accurately into an inferred underlying theoretical 'explanatory' formulation. One of the constant challenges about forensic psychopathology is that so often such formulations *do not quite fit* the clinical facts. They explain *almost* everything. The therapist is called upon to assess the differential weighting of factors which may be internal, internalized, external or externalized when seeking to achieve a balanced appraisal.

Anxiety is experienced by all those who work in the forensic field. Errors in diagnosis and prognosis have such ominous societal sequelae, that the self-esteem of individual practitioners and the institutions which they represent, is ever at stake. Nevertheless, although those who attempt to treat psychopathic patients with narcissistic personalities will never die of an over-dose of gratitude, there is a certain resilience in the corporate awareness that no forensic psychotherapist can 'go it alone'. He will always be grateful for the experience of those who are, metaphorically, in the same boat. The importance of interdisciplinary collaborative support is a *sine qua non*.

Beyond the perimeter of training and supervision will be the questions asked by society as a whole, on the efficacy of the whole endeavour. This is why research in forensic psychotherapy is urgently needed. I have little doubt that the chapter on the topic (Chapter II:25) may well be the one to which certain reviewers will first turn. Spence – a psychoanalyst and a professor of psychiatry – sounds a cautionary note when he refers to the 'non-trivial consequence' of 'the way in which the psychoanalytic establishment tends to downplay research' (1994, p.25). In future, both training and supervision will have a far more focused eye on relevant research implications.

Forensic psychotherapy training will seek to integrate relevant aspects of the established training trajectory of forensic psychiatry. It is interesting to see how the chapters by the clinical tutors from these respective fields deal with those issues which are generic and those which have a more focal preserve.

The current explosion in continuing professional development will, in the future, exert considerable pressure upon the first generation of trainees to qualify as consultant forensic psychotherapists.

And what of supervision? Denman (1994) furnishes an up-to-date overview of 'training and supervision in psychotherapy'. Even though he does not specifically address forensic problems, he touches crucial concerns when referring to 'the anxiety-promoting nature of the topics which need to be covered by trainee therapists' (p.237) and the trainee in forensic psychotherapy will know of additional forensic-specific issues. In a study of 'psychotherapy supervisors judged to be excellent teachers', Shanfield *et al.* (1993) showed that 'supervisors with high ratings allowed the resident's story about the encounter with the patient to develop. They consistently tracked the most immediate aspects of the resident's affectively charged concerns. Most of their comments were directed towards helping the resident further understand the patient and were specific to the material presented in the session' (p.1081). It is also salutory to note that 'technical terms or jargon were used sparingly'. These comments could be directly translocated to the realm of forensic psychotherapy supervision. Certainly, consistent tracking of the most immediate aspect of the therapist's affectively charged concerns is intrinsic to the process.

Following the section on supervision, a trainee forensic psychiatrist describes the disturbing impact of the account of a savagely attacked victim. This is an experience from which no professional working in the forensic field can be immune. How it is possible to retain professional poise and discretional distance, in the face of such phenomena, is of the essence of training and supervision. There are immense psychological demands made upon those at the clinical front-line, such that the ancient question 'Who is sufficient for these things?' is not misplaced.

It is no accident that this section ends with a chapter on burnout. Compassion fatigue, diminution of diagnostic acumen, blurring of boundaries and displacement of dynamic discernment are hazards to which those in forensic psychotherapy may be particularly prone. The possibility of chaotic disorganization due to fear of the patient and other threats to self-esteem from many sources make staff support mandatory. Such feelings are often intensified by a sense of helplessness engendered by the weight of the clinical load, the duration and uncertain outcome of prolonged therapeutic commitment and the public opprobrium when things go wrong.

It is to these important topics that we now turn.

II · 12

Training

The Psychotherapist and Clinical Tutor

Estela V. Welldon

INTRODUCTION

The integration of forensic psychiatry and psychoanalytic psychotherapy has produced a new discipline, forensic psychotherapy whose aim is the psychodynamic understanding of the offender and his consequent treatment, regardless of the seriousness of the offence. The purpose is not to condone the crime or excuse the offender but, on the contrary, is to help him acknowledge responsibility for his acts and thus save both him and society from further crimes. The more we understand about the criminal mind the more possible it becomes to take positive preventive action which should lead to better management and the implementation of more cost effective treatment of offender patients (Welldon 1994).

In such an enterprise the mutual trust and complete cooperation of both forensic psychiatry and related disciplines, and psychodynamic psychotherapy is required. Also, it must be noted that forensic psychotherapy goes beyond the dyadic relationship between patient and psychotherapist: it is a triangular situation – patient, psychotherapist, and society (de Smit 1992).

In this chapter I shall give a personal account of (1) the history and the work of the Portman Clinic and the foundation of the International Association of Forensic Psychotherapy (IAFP), and then describe (2) the course in forensic psychotherapy of which I am the Director.

BRIEF HISTORY OF THE PORTMAN CLINIC

The Portman Clinic in the UK has been in the forefront of forensic psychotherapy throughout its history, which dates back to 1931, when a small group of men and women met in London and established the Institute for the

Scientific (later, Study and) Treatment of Delinquency (ISTD) to promote a better way of dealing with criminals than putting them in prison.

From the start, the founding members aimed to:

- initiate and promote scientific research into the causes and prevention of crime
- establish observation centres and clinics for the diagnosis and treatment of delinquency and crime
- coordinate and consolidate existing scientific work
- secure cooperation between all bodies engaged in similar work in all parts of the world, and ultimately to promote an international organization
- assist and advise through the judiciary hospitals and government departments
- promote educational and training facilities
- promote discussion within and educate the opinion of, the general public by means of publications, lectures and so forth.

These idealistic and hopeful goals from sixty years ago were in fact adopted in 1991 by the International Association of Forensic Psychotherapy. Not many of the original aims had flourished and it is interesting to speculate upon the reasons for this 'failure to thrive' (Pilgrim 1987).

Of course, we should be aware not only of the lack of 'voice' but also of the absence of hearing. Scepticism about the application of psychodynamic theory and treatment to the offender patients has been common. Eastman (1993), for example, has noted that 'in a specialty where there is an extraordinary level of psychopathology, as well as of childhood deprivation and abuse, it seems extraordinary that the (forensic establishment) has paid so little attention to psychopathological understanding and psychotherapy' (p.28).

Throughout the history of the original Institute and then the Portman Clinic, clinical work has always been the main concern, to the extent that the promotion of ideas and training were neglected or even ignored: so much was this the case that it was commonly assumed that the clinic was 'private'. Highly trained professional staff devoted their working time to the provision of psychoanalytic psychotherapy but failed to recognize the growth of a new discipline. The provision of proper training for junior practitioners was neglected and there was accordingly no natural reproduction in out-patient clinics elsewhere. However, some degree of internal consolidation had been necessary before any plans for expansion could effectively be developed. This was especially so since the outside world was cautious and suspicious when faced with the idea of an offender having an 'internal' (mental) world.

Such had been the stigma attached to contact with criminals that it had been difficult to find a landlord who would rent premises to the Institute in the 1920s and 1930s. For some years, the medical staff saw patients in their own private rooms, and the Institute was housed under one roof for the first time in May 1937. In 1948, with the National Health Service Act, a division of the old ISTD was decided upon: the Portman Clinic became part of the National Health Service (NHS), concentrating on the treatment of offenders: the Institute for the Study and Treatment of Delinquency (ISTD) continued under that title (now housed at King's College, London) taking responsibility for research and the expansion of training programmes. Scientific cooperation between the two had been assured, and it was hoped that, despite the split, the Clinic would become a model of its kind undertaking specialist teaching, experimental work and clinical research. These hopes have only been partly realized. Why?

In my view, mechanisms of projective identification are used by those professionals working with 'fringe' patients, within a 'fringe' framework, in a society which operates with splits about 'good and evil forces'. At times of stress when staff members, in their intense commitment to their work, experience lack of support from those outside, they obtain a sense of solidarity by experiencing the 'outside' as failing to understand and threatening – actually as the 'bad' ones, for example, ready to close them down. There is also some identification with the patients anti-authority feelings and rebelliousness.

Consequently, an ethos developed at the Portman Clinic where there was a cosy, safe, small family atmosphere in which there was felt to be comfort in the uniqueness of providing optimal psychotherapeutic services: this was rarely challenged from the outside world. The Clinic did not need to face the difficulties which are now encountered in trying to promote a wider influence outside the small institution. This feeling of safety and closeness led to the enormous ambivalence and internal tension which characterized both the creation of the Course in Forensic Psychotherapy (1990) and the founding of the IAFP (1991). Both, in different ways, have exerted some pressure on the Portman Clinic to change, by opening their doors to the training of a wider membership.

The founding of the course and the resulting suspiciousness and conflict within the Clinic were born also out of insecurity and arrogance. This insecurity related to fears of invasion from outside, revealed by the sentiment of 'they will take over': the arrogance was reflected by feelings and expressions of 'they will never understand', or 'they will corrupt our purity of work'. This again reflects the deep splitting processes which characterize the nature of our work, requiring as it does the amalgamation of the positivist stance of forensic psychiatry with the understanding and compassion which psychoanalytic psychotherapy can provide.

The obvious need that has been revealed by this course has been recognized both nationally and internationally and this, in turn, led to the founding of the International Association for Forensic Psychotherapy in 1991.

HISTORY OF THE COURSE IN FORENSIC PSYCHOTHERAPY

In 1988, I was appointed Clinical Tutor at the Portman Clinic, an appointment automatically attached to the BPMF (British Post-Graduate Medication Federation), University of London. I approached the Director of the BPMF, Professor M Peckham, with an idea I had harboured for over twenty years, of creating a multi-disciplinary psychodynamic training course for all those who work in different forensic settings. This had always been thought, by both sides (i.e., psychodynamic and forensic), to be a quixotic, unrealistic and impractical suggestion. In fact the idea of integrating both fields met with derision. 'How could soft-wet psychoanalytic psychotherapy ever blend with hard, sceptical, cynical "real" world forensic psychiatry?'

It was fortunate that Professor Peckham was not a psychiatrist, but a professor of oncology as well as an artist. In other words, he was the epitome of one who bridged the 'two worlds' of science and art. It also helped that he was not at all familiar with the different divisions within the psychiatric world, and lived in blissful ignorance of the assumptions or prejudices associated with the various factions. To him, not only did the idea of such a course make a lot of sense but he was amazed that it did not already exist. In the half hour available for our meeting, we were able to reach an agreement for the creation of the course, as well as design a steering committee with professionals from both the psychotherapeutic and forensic worlds. Later the advisory group was formed, comprised of senior professional, National Health staff as well as senior members of the judiciary. The BPMF took charge of the administration and academic approval of the course, and a faculty of Portman Clinic staff and other consultants was to be in charge of the actual teaching and syllabus. Both were under the scrutiny of the steering committee and advisory group. There were many changes under the wise, effective and neutral leadership of Professor Peckham who continued in his role as director until the course was consolidated. A tacit awareness emerged that the Portman Clinic had to 'open up', and to trust that the intermarriage of disciplines would work – however difficult it was to accept other opinions and ways of thinking and working. There was no other possibility of forcing the issues: adaptation and discussion were the only ways.

THE DIPLOMA COURSE

A one-day-a-week, one-year course on forensic psychotherapy (the first of its kind in the world) was set up in 1990 under the aegis of the BPMF in association with the Portman Clinic. This multi-disciplinary national course, for professionals working in the forensic field, has now been running success-fully for four years: in September 1993 it was extended to a two-year course and given BPMF Diploma status. There is an organizing committee composed of consultants in both the psychotherapy and forensic psychiatry fields as well as an advisory committee composed of senior professionals from the legal, judicial, media, medical and mental health fields.

The underlying philosophy of the course is that forensic psychotherapists must be properly trained in order to be able to respond adequately to the difficult predicaments of both private and public dimensions. They have to be equipped with insight into their own internal world and motivations, thus the need for personal therapy. It can be all too easy to respond unwittingly and automatically to unlawful situations: a 'normal' reaction might be a very natural reaction but can also amount to an abdication of professional responsibility.

The Diploma course aims to increase a candidate's understanding of the psychodynamic considerations underlying offending behaviour. Students learn how to:

- assess offenders according to basic psychodynamic principles
- assist professionals within the criminal and the family justice systems by their professional reports to the civil and criminal courts
- assess dangerousness
- improve the functioning of agencies offering services to offenders and, where appropriate, their victims and their families
- assess the cost effectiveness of such treatment programmes.

Coursework comprises the supervised psychotherapy of at least one forensic patient; interdisciplinary discussion of clinical work in a range of different settings; reading and lectures on theoretical and clinical topics; and personal experience in psychoanalytic psychotherapy.

The syllabus consists of basic developmental and psychodynamic theories including individual, group and family psychotherapies and their adaptation to the forensic field, plus knowledge of basic psychoanalytic techniques adapted to psychotherapy and to the forensic patient within community, residential, or prison service establishments. All trainees undertake personal therapy; this is regarded as essential for the student himself as well as part of his learning experience.

Participants

There were fifteen trainees in the first year course and the numbers have grown in subsequent years: the combination of homogeneity in professional interest with heterogeneity in experience and background has proved to be successful.

Year 1

Requirements of the Course

Apart from the usual requirements of attendance and academic work (including written papers), there are two other basic requirements which remain a vital part of the life of the course. As already described, one is for the trainee to have personal therapy while attending the course – either individual or group. The requirement for personal therapy was initially objected to by a minority of steering group members. However, in response to the students' course evaluation questionnaire after the first year there was overwhelming support expressed for the need for personal therapy as an intrinsic part of the personal and training experience. Not only did they acknowledge its personal value, they felt that such an experience is essential for the understanding of their own work with forensic patients.

The other requirement is to have a forensic patient in weekly supervised dynamic psychotherapy. Our assumption that the first requirement would be difficult to achieve, proved to be wrong: it was the second requirement that caused more problems than had been at first envisaged: it was difficult to find patients. Such difficulties, however, provided valuable information about the trainees' places of work as well as their fellow workers' attitudes about their attendance at the course. Co-operation and support from colleagues and superiors has come to be seen as vital. At times it has seemed that competition and rivalry has predominated instead. We have since become aware, however, that the presence of one or more trainees from the same institution, either at the same time or subsequently, facilitates the trainees' emotional and practical entry in the course.

Structure of the Day

The day begins with a *discussion group* in which all trainees present clinical cases and clinical dilemmas from their own place of work, the aim being the acknowledgement and recognition of their various professional perspectives. Different professional approaches are presented, discussed and scrutinized. The students familiarize themselves with, and are expected to respect, the viewpoints of others so that they do not tend towards the common practice of discarding, dismissing or denigrating the ways others work. They are able to examine their own working scheme and thus explore how best to interact with one another. As a result, a network system is created. It is important that the faculty member convening this meeting changes periodically since they invariably need to learn much themselves about other forensic institutions.

Lunch follows in which students feel free to discuss their own experiences with one another. *Supervision* in groups of three or four with supervisors who are Portman staff begins the afternoon. It is important that these small groups contain students from different professional backgrounds and work settings. The more heterogeneous they are, the more successful integration there is.

The *afternoon lecture* is given by faculty members who may or may not be Portman Clinic staff.

A *plenary session* ends the working day. This is unstructured and convened by the course director, who also chairs the earlier lecture. It is difficult to convey what happens here: there are many silences, containing different qualities of meaning, for example frustration, dissatisfaction, contentment, and reflection. At other times the students express a longing for 'guidance', 'directives' and an 'agenda'. There are switches between the need for interpretations and the complete rejection of the idea of being an experiential group and becoming 'patients'. Many of the characteristic phenomena of the therapeutic group occur: comments of how good it is to have some time to think together; rivalries; conflicts; attempts at scapegoating; pairing; projection of unwanted parts of the self into others, or other institutions; rebelliousness against authority (especially against the Portman Clinic who are 'unable to understand the hardships of their own forensic settings'), denial, mourning, grief, idealization of the training as well as feeling de-skilled by it; even the composition of poems. These are a few of the themes the students have to face, to talk about, and they get variously angry, or at times sad. Altogether, the plenary provides an intense experience of sharing powerful emotions: the suggestion often made during the first term that this plenary session should be dropped as unnecessary has proved to be traceable to the intense anxieties contained within these meetings.

Staff Meetings

The staff members meet regularly to discuss different issues related to week-to-week events. During students' lunch time the teaching staff meets to discuss the happenings of the previous week, supervision issues, aspects of the lecture, the plenary and the discussion group of the day. Our interaction is rich and makes us see not only the interwoven connections between students but also our own patterns and structures – which offer insights regarding our own splitting and projection: for example, our own disagreements about structures are at times taken up unwittingly, and concretely, by our trainees. We are in a constant process of learning and many changes have been implemented since we first started. The survival and success of the Course has largely depended upon the faculty members from the Portman Clinic who have generously given of their time and tremendous efforts. At times, it has been difficult for them too, to envisage this 'cross fertilization', and its achievement is due to their consistent trust in this exciting new venture.

During the initial year of the foundation of the course, the composition of the student group included not only professionals from both forensic and psychotherapeutic worlds, but also those working privately in their own rooms as psychotherapists.

Some forensic professionals were in possession of minimal basic psychodynamic understanding and had no experience of personal therapy, whilst some psychotherapists had no forensic experience at all. We learned how problematic this 'mix' was for students and faculty members alike. Portman staff members had little, if any, background in dealing first hand with some of the forensic settings of the students: conversely, some forensic colleagues considered it unnecessary for trainees to undergo personal therapy. Paranoid anxieties were generated with each person wanting to demonstrate the merits of their position. The difficulties encountered are described by Williams (1991). Prejudices and assumptions ran high and were fuelled by everybody's lack of experience in the first year. During the first term the different groups disowned, consciously or unconsciously, parts of their own working situations which they projected onto the other group. During the plenary services there were jokes representing either 'wet' or 'hard' responses according to which 'group' someone belonged to. Sarcastic and cynical remarks were the rule when the 'forensic team' attacked the 'psychotherapeutic team' for their gullibility, softness and lack of awareness of the conditions in which they themselves were working. The 'psychotherapeutic team' counter-attacked with subtle but sadistic interpretations showing lack of sensitivity, and over-simplicity. At this time, the faculty members, according to trainees, were 'faultless' and beyond criticism, except for some few and apparently innocent remarks about the staff being rather 'nannyish'. In brief, the students' responses resembled those observed by Hinshelwood (1994) when he writes of his own experiences working as a psychotherapist within the social defence system of a prison. I am indebted to his clear insights in this extremely difficult and painful area.

At the beginning of the academic year students meeting for the first time feel insecure and inadequate and they try to compete from their own position. For a long time those from the same place sit together and then regrouping takes place. Students working in forensic settings show off their toughness and reality sense in dealing with all sorts of terrible crimes and predicaments. They are not aware of being used as 'protective containers' by the psychotherapeutic team, who may experience them as devoid of a capacity for empathy and compassion. On the other hand, members of the psychotherapy team appear to be rather naive and act as irritating and nagging 'do-gooders'. Both groups feel deskilled in their own areas of expertise, and it takes a while for them to find, not only their voice, but also an empathetic hearing. This only happens when they are ready to look at their own areas of 'not knowing' what to do with the forensic patient. As a matter of fact, both groups experience all these mixed feelings of harshness and compassion but they are split into the different factions in order to avoid facing confusion. During the second and third term both faculty and trainees begin to work more effectively together with some degree of integration and reparation.

Development of the Trainees' and Faculty Members Attitude in the Life of the Course

We have observed that the trainees' attitudes has changed during the second and third years of the first year course as a result of changes both in the composition of the trainees group and our own role. The fact that the trainees all now work in forensic settings facilitates the understanding of the specific difficulties encountered in the functioning of their work. Earlier mechanisms of projection and splitting – which expressed splits in the patient population – were no longer available. Similarly, there are no easy targets for the derision and contempt to be projected into 'the other student population' as had been available in the initial year of the course.

The split between 'hard' and 'soft' had worked so effectively that our own faculty members had been left almost beyond criticism or fault. Indeed, the faculty members were on the contrary understanding and rather tolerant of the divisions. This began to change when the composition of the trainees' group became more homogeneously forensic. To start with, the supervisors who had previously been seen as 'soft', 'humane' and 'wet' became suddenly and unexpectedly seen as 'hard and brutal, judgmental, tough and controlling'. Faculty members began to notice 'tremendous' changes occurring in their students and a sense of pride and achievement began to emerge. They, themselves, began to change their own stance from being somewhat analytically omnipotent to being more understanding of the hard, difficult circumstances of the forensic setting.

It is only possible as the year progresses for trainees to start introjecting and to acknowledge their own 'bad bits' and thus to make sense of the requirement for personal therapy. They also become aware of the tremendous limitations of their work and how much more they need to know. In other words, a little knowledge leads to a thirst for further training. Goals become more limited and more realistically based, a realization which is of great importance when we bear in mind the considerable difficulties of offering psychotherapy to our patient population.

Year 2

Only candidates who have successfully completed Year 1 are eligible to apply for a place on Year 2 of the Diploma course; in other words, progression is not automatic. The criteria for such a move include a sense of commitment to working with forensic patients; an ability to engage patients in therapy and to reflect on progress; a capacity for written work with the clear and coherent expression of ideas; commitment to personal therapy and capacity for insight in his or her self-assessment.

Since forensic psychotherapy cannot be the heroic effort of one worker, but rather the integrated work of a team, the Year 2 group needs to be selected in such a way as to facilitate candidates' collaboration and to increase their knowledge of, and insight into, other professionals' expertise and the diversity of forensic settings.

The Year 2 course is based on a half-day in which candidates are allocated in small groups to a supervisor and candidates can either bring to supervision an individual patient or a group: it is becoming clear that group therapy is at times the best and most cost effective treatment for patients. The candidate is continuously assessed and he or she is also required to produce a theoretical paper at the end of the final term of about 5000 words relating to his or her individual patient or group. This is expected to include an investigation of relevant theoretical issues as well as clinical material. On successful completion of Years I and II the participants are awarded the BPMF Diploma in Forensic Psychotherapy.

The first years of the development of the course have been described by Cordess, Riley and Welldon (1994).

My own role as a founder course director has also developed and changed over time. In our third year I ceased supervising a small group, since this was experienced by the faculty members as implying that the trainees in my supervision group were 'favoured' – so increasing splitting mechanisms. On reflection, after this change was introduced, I realized that boundary issues for both students and staff had been at stake. It appeared that my role was actually much more one of container of anxieties for both groups.

As a direct result of achieving the Diploma status, many changes were implemented. I hope that I have given an accurate history, and that I have been just to everybody concerned, in this description of the creation and development of a training in forensic psychotherapy. There have been difficulties but these have been outweighed by the long-term advantages and great rewards encountered in establishing what I believe to be a new model of training for disciplines who have been traditionally ambivalent if not hostile towards psychoanalytic psychotherapy.

SUMMARY

The history is sketched of a small out-patient NHS Clinic with highly trained staff which over the years has provided a resource of practice, experience and teaching. It is now involved more actively in offering postgraduate training to professionals of various disciplines working in the public sector, which has been known to be resistant, and sometimes cynical, to the psychodynamic therapeutic approach. Specific difficulties have included opposition to the requirement of personal therapy and conflicts arising in supervision from the contrasting therapeutic approaches of the base work place and the training centre. Despite this, the BPMF course in association with the Portman Clinic is developing and flourishing and, one hopes, provides a model for other countries to follow. The view has been expressed that Forensic Psychotherapy is an 'evolving species' (Adshead 1991). All those involved from the beginning are extremely proud of this achievement and are deeply grateful to all those who have cooperated and worked hard in this venture.

Someone might have once said 'So what's all that about: mixing up the hard and the wet together? Please, I don't want to be part of it. Can you imagine forensic psychiatrists admitting to any unconscious motivations? This sounds bizarre'. Well, not any more, I am happy to say.

Acknowledgements

The author is grateful to the Portman Clinic, to all Faculty members, members of the Advisory Group and to Wendy Riley, from the BPMF, for the continuous support, great efficiency, personal commitment and consistent solidarity demonstrated throughout the years of the course.

The author is also indebted to Professor Michael Peckham for his vision, unique understanding and support.

She also wishes to thank Dr Cleo Van Velsen for her valuable professional contributions and editorial help.

The Psychiatrist and Clinical Tutor

Clive Meux

INTRODUCTION

The ability to understand and communicate effectively with patients and colleagues underpins good and safe psychiatric and forensic psychiatric care. Some are better than others at such understanding and communication but all must endeavour to improve these talents. Offering formalized training in forensic psychotherapy is in its infancy but its development is vital and should both directly and indirectly improve necessary skills. The Royal College of Psychiatrists Forensic Psychiatry Special Advisory Committee (FPSAC) to the Joint Committee on Higher Psychiatric Training (JCHPT) has stated that the 'development of psychotherapeutic skills for treatment and management is essential for training in forensic psychiatry' (JCHPT 1990, p.1). Forensic psychiatric trainees are apparently keen for relevant psychotherapy experience (Adshead 1991). Psychiatric training in the UK has a well established pattern of progress involving increasing clinical and theoretical experience, increasing clinical responsibility and examinations involving written, clinical and oral sections. The adequacy of such training depends upon good supervision, teaching and clinical opportunities and is monitored and accredited by the Royal College of Psychiatrists. Many other disciplines also have well structured and independently accredited training. A trainee's experience of psychotherapy can be variable in both general training and sub-specialty higher training. The precise structure of psychotherapy experience for trainee psychiatrists can be debated (e.g. Mohl *et al.* 1990). The psychiatrist and clinical tutor must be aware of all current relevant training guidelines and contemporary psychiatric teaching issues so that he can appropriately inform both trainer and trainee colleagues. The clinical tutor must facilitate training, both theoretical and clinical, in a way that interests and benefits the trainee, trainer and, directly or indirectly, the patient.

TRAINING RESPONSIBILITIES

The clinical tutor as a consultant forensic psychiatrist has numerous professional responsibilities in relation to his patients, the public and professional colleagues, including both junior and experienced, medical and non medical and managers.

(1) Training Responsibilities and the Trainee

It is important that the education which is provided is broad and non-patronizing. To facilitate any teaching it is important to enthuse the trainee and the trainer and this is helped if the individuals are appropriately matched. High quality guidance and supervision must be provided and consideration must be given to the trainee's career needs. The trainee must be informed of all the training opportunities available, including both clinical (e.g. different settings, supervision) and theoretical (e.g. courses, lectures).

(2) Training Responsibilities and the Patient

Training must never be performed at the expense of patient care and relevant ethical issues cannot be forgotten. Training should benefit the patient either directly, via specific therapeutic involvement, or indirectly by increasing the skills of an individual who will subsequently treat, effectively, many future patients. It is, of course, very important that any patient understands the quality of any therapeutic contact that they are receiving. The issue of informed consent, particularly in forensic psychiatry and in secure settings is complex. However, it is certainly important that any patient is informed of any trainee's role and responsibility in their care and should be reassured of the trainee's supervision and the facilities for the ongoing longer-term care of the patient when any trainee has departed. Trainees often enter a patient's life, become involved in a number of powerful interpersonal issues and then depart to continue their training elsewhere. Such losses need to be carefully dealt with, particularly in patients who are often already vulnerable to loss as a result of past experiences. The apparently important effects on patients of the loss of carers in the forensic psychiatric setting has been described (Persaud and Meux 1994).

(3) Training Responsibilities and Other Professional Colleagues

It is important that training does not hamper overall clinical care but facilitates and expands it, allowing for reflective development. The importance of training and teaching in improving the quality of care must be emphasized. Such improved quality of care and the recognition that a training centre is a centre of excellence must be emphasized to those colleagues who have influence over financial resources so that training is perceived as an investment for the future and something which improves the therapeutic and professional environment rather than as an unnecessary irritant.

(4) Training Responsibilities and the Public

Any training must not increase the risk of harm to others. A public awareness that a particular hospital is a training hospital should be facilitated. Indeed, it should be realized that such status is a recognition of the high quality of that hospital. When the public, or relatives, realize that patients are having contact with trainees, they will need to be reassured that good supervision is provided and that all relevant safety issues have been appropriately considered.

GUIDELINES FOR TRAINING

The FPSAC to the JCHPT of the Royal College of Psychiatrists has produced a guidance document (FPSAC 1990) which lists both essential and desirable experience for psychotherapy training for senior registrars in forensic psychiatry. It states:

'Essential Experience

1) Experience in exploring and understanding the interaction between inpatients and other staff, especially the role of anxiety, grandiose excitement and paranoid build-up in the mobilisation of violence.

2) Experience in the design and operation of behavioural programmes aimed at lessening violence and antisocial behaviour as well as relaxation and anger control techniques.

3) An understanding of the issues involved in individual or group psychotherapy of inpatients and the problems that can result from such special treatments for inpatients and staff.

4) The development of an ability to formulate psychopathology and assess psychological needs in terms sufficiently sophisticated to do justice to individual cases but to be understandable to co-workers within a multidisciplinary framework.

5) The psychotherapy and monitoring of at least one Restricted case, preferable on Conditional Discharge in the community.

6) At least one ongoing case in out-patient, time-limited psychotherapy.

7) An understanding of the social and psychological structure of penal establishments with a special emphasis on the role of the prison hospital.

8) Supervision of others, e.g. juniors or probation officers, attempting psychological support with clients.

Desirable Experience

1) To take a group of sexual offenders for a specific purpose, e.g. the exploration and development of appropriate remorse, the exploration of triggers to offending behaviour, the development of self-support groups, etc.

2) To take a victim support group.

3) Family work with those in which an individual member of the family has become violent or maladjusted.

4) To take a psychotherapy group or individual case within the prison setting.'

Although the above guidelines refer specifically to higher psychiatric training in forensic psychiatry, their principles could be generalized to trainees, both medical and non medical, at all levels, if the experience and supervision is individualized to training needs and facilities. Of course, any training in forensic psychotherapy should be in the context of a broader experience and not occur in isolation. Broader guidelines for forensic psychiatry training are available from the Royal College of Psychiatrists (Joint Committee on Higher Psychiatric Training 1990). Initially, simpler forensic psychotherapeutic skills can be developed and consolidated before more complex issues are tackled in training. Training and education must surely be an integral part of all professional life and forensic psychotherapeutic issues should be an integral part of any programme of continuing professional development in forensic psychiatry; even the trainers must maintain their own ongoing training.

TRAINING OPPORTUNITIES – CLINICAL

All clinical training must be safe and appropriately supervised. Training opportunities should be as broad as possible and rare but important facilities may need to be shared by various training organizers. The trainee should be exposed to patients of all ages, both sexes and different cultures. Therapeutic contact must occur with patients from different diagnostic groups, including patients with psychoses as well as personality-disordered and neurotic patients. It is often important for a trainee to obtain a longitudinal view of a patient's progress and therefore following a patient through their treatment is important even if this means maintaining contact after the trainee has moved to a different training area. Trainees must be be exposed to patients who have committed different types of offences.

Clinical training opportunities should occur in a multi-disciplinary setting and in different treatment areas, including out-patient clinics (including contact with victims and Restricted cases), hostels and in-patient hospital units. The in-patient experience should include care in a therapeutic community setting if possible and also in conditions of low, medium and maximum hospital security. One particular ward which has been popular as a training environment where psychotherapeutic principles are used in maximum hospital security has been described (Grounds et al. 1987; Brett 1992) and is outlined in Chapter II:26 of this volume. The trainee should in addition be exposed to psycho-therapeutic issues in the custodial setting (e.g. in HMP Grendon, other special units and more normal prison settings) and experience would ideally include contact with adolescent patients – and those with learning disabilities if possible. The importance of understanding dynamics within institutions cannot be underestimated.

Clinical training opportunities should include the possibility to improve interview skills, provide individual supportive psychotherapy and, at least, a period of short-term (6–12 months) individual supervised interpretive psycho-therapy. Some experience of individual cognitive/behavioural therapy, including the exploration of psychosexual issues is of significant use.

Some experience of group psychotherapy, both dynamic and cognitive/be-havioural, preferably by regular attendance at an appropriate therapy group in the presence of an experienced therapist is necessary. Some involvement with family therapeutic work and the creative therapies would also be beneficial.

TRAINING OPPORTUNITIES – THEORETICAL

The trainee must be exposed to clinical seminars where patients cases are discussed. Such seminars would usually involve consultant forensic psychia-trists, consultant psychotherapists and a broad group of trainees, plus others preferably from a number of disciplines. Didactic teaching in forensic psycho-therapeutic issues should also be offered through seminars and lecturers. A Journal Club attended by the trainee can include discussion of forensic psychotherapeutic research and review papers. The trainee should also be encouraged to attend relevant conferences, both national and international, such as those organized by the International Association of Forensic Psycho-therapy and attend training courses in forensic psychiatry and forensic psychotherapy. Examples of such courses include the Diploma in Forensic Psychiatry course organized by the Institute of Psychiatry at the University of London which includes forensic psychotherapeutic aspects, and the Forensic Psychotherapy course organized by the Portman Clinic (Cordess, Riley and Welldon 1994) which offers useful and specifically psychotherapeutic experience and can also lead to a diploma in forensic psychotherapy.

Research seminars attended by the trainee can include forensic psychotherapeutic issues and consideration of both past research in the field and current issues. All trainees must be involved in some form of research work and the possibility for developing research in the field of forensic psychotherapy should always be considered and appropriately encouraged.

The theoretical aspects of forensic psychotherapy should be covered as broadly as possible, indeed, the curriculum for this is covered by the contents of these volumes! Trainees must be provided with appropriate reading lists in forensic psychiatry which should include forensic psychotherapy sections. Trainees must also have access to appropriate computer research facilities and relevant texts enabling them to develop both national and international perspectives.

The debate surrounding the treatability (including psychotherapeutic treatability) of personality-disordered patients is important. The trainee should be helped to understand the debate and the associated clinical and legal implications (e.g. Gallwey 1992).

Clinical and theoretical training opportunities should develop the individual's communication and treatment skills and therefore allow the trainee to himself become a trainer with abilities to effectively supervise and teach others.

SUPERVISION AND LEARNING

It is vital that high quality supervision is available to the trainee and, indeed, to all those involved in forensic psychotherapy. Because of the nature of the issues involved, forensic psychotherapy can be very stressful to the therapist. The supervisor should be an experienced individual who himself understands broad forensic psychiatric issues, including the practicalities and restraints of the 'system' within which they and the trainees are working. Supervision may be provided by consultant psychotherapists or consultant forensic psychiatrists, the clinical tutor or colleagues of other disciplines (e.g. psychologists). It is important that all trainees have access to an appropriate consultant psychotherapist who can advise, in consultation with a patient's consultant forensic psychiatrist and other carers, on the allocation of the trainee to a particular patient or group of patients and on their supervision, having considered the treatment environment and the trainee's and patient's qualities. Psychotherapy is a powerful treatment and without adequate supervision can have negative effects or even be dangerous (Crown 1983), particularly in the field of forensic psychiatry. It is important that any supervision includes both clinical and theoretical issues.

During forensic psychotherapeutic supervision a number of issues are likely to be discussed with the trainee, including:

(1) *Transference issues*, which are likely to feature highly. Many forensic psychiatric patients have significant past victim experiences and this often features in the transference relationship.

(2) *The choice of treatment styles*, which may be varied.

(3) *The placement of the psychotherapeutic treatment in the broader context*; for example, the effects of the ward milieu and any medication that the patient is receiving may well facilitate or hamper a psycho-therapeutic relationship.

(4) *Issues of confidentiality* and the secondary life of any information divulged during psychotherapy. This is likely to be a particularly sensitive issue in the field of forensic psychiatry.

(5) *The importance of psychotherapy as both an assessment and treatment tool* as a greater understanding of the patient develops.

(6) *The role of information* developed through psychotherapy in the vital area of risk assessment.

(7) *Issues involving the trainee gaining greater insight into themselves*, both professionally and personally, during forensic psychotherapy. Such insight will, one hopes, be highlighted by the trainee's better psychodynamic understanding of:

 (i) Relevant countertransference issues.

 (ii) Group dynamics including within patient groups, ward groups, clinical teams and institutions.

 (iii) Difficulties which arise with patients and colleagues.

 (iv) The important role of defence mechanisms.

 (v) Important issues in personality development.

 (vi) Violent acts, offending behaviour and its causes.

 (vii) The effects of victim experiences.

 (viii) Relevant psychopathology, including psychosexual pathology.

CONCLUSION

Collaboration between forensic psychiatry and forensic psychotherapy is important, and, of necessity, intimate (Cox 1983). Training in forensic psychotherapy is very important as both part of the broader training of professionals in the field of forensic psychiatry and for the specific development of future forensic psychotherapists. I have offered, without apology, a personal and medically-based view of training issues in forensic psychotherapy. My perspective has primarily been the training which can be offered to trainee forensic psychiatrists although I wish to emphasize that the principles can be applied to trainees of other disciplines. In addition, training in forensic psychotherapy should be offered to general psychotherapists and training in forensic psychiatry should be offered to general psychiatrists.

In principle, there are many similarities between a patient and his therapist and a trainee and his trainer. There must be commitment on both sides of the relationship which itself needs to succeed and be professional. Treatment and training, like therapy, must be individualized and must take account of past experiences, current issues and future possibilities. In both relationships, successful development depends on careful and appropriate guidance, the use of an agreed approach, objectivity and good supervision.

There is currently great competition for financial resources within the Health Service. The cost-effectiveness of psychotherapeutic treatments may be debated but training, including in forensic psychotherapy, is a great general investment for the future of good patient care and must be both protected and, realistically, justified. Training not only develops the trainees but also the trainers and the treatment environment. Teaching and learning are two-way processes and they must surely benefit all involved including, most important, our patients.

A Supervisor's View

Murray Cox

INTRODUCTION: SUPERVISION – *A SINE QUA NON*

The first thing to say about supervision is that it is, or should be, *sine qua non* of all forensic therapeutic undertakings. Whereas a similar claim is legitimately appropriate for generic non-forensic initiatives, it assumes enhanced *gravitas* in the forensic field. This is because there is always the possibility of the malignant development of unrecognized countertransference distortion, neurosis and – fortunately very rarely – even psychosis. But when homicide and/or serious suicidal attempts precede therapy, and are frequently prime motives for referral, the 'containing' institution needs to be doubly sure that supervision arrangements are 'in place' before the therapeutic wheels begin to turn. It is obvious that this should be so, but under the pressure of crisis-minimization logistics, it sometimes happens that a patient has 'started therapy' before supervision arrangements have crystallized. It is more than semantic finesse to claim that supervision – or *supravision* – should be intrinsic to the *infrastructure* for all therapeutic planning. It is essential for all therapeutic staff, including the supervisor himself.

A FUNDAMENTAL RISK

At the heart of all analytic therapy there is a point of incipient weakness and potential instability. It is implicit when the therapist is on the 'receiving end' of a patient's free-associations. The moment when 'Tell me *anything* that comes into your mind' – or any of the numerous paraphrases or silent gestures making the same invitation – is operative, there is then an implicit assumption that the

listener can equally well *hear everything*. Freedom to tell anything is linked to
the potential to hear everthing.

   In the forensic field more than any other – apart from work with torture
victims – there is an augmented possibility that the patient may need to disclose
material involving, say, savage mutilation or sadistic dismembering, which even
the best-trained therapist may find difficult to receive, particularly when
attempting to adopt the traditional psychoanalytic psychological posture of
'hovering attentiveness'. We then find ourselves recalling Macbeth's words:

> 'Take any shape but that.'
>
> (*Macbeth*, III.4.101)

which is to say, I can hear anything but 'that', when 'that' comes too close to
an experience I have endured or which I dread. Such issues arise during training
and, *par excellence*, during forensic supervision. One patient said that she needed
nurses to ask certain questions, indicating that they were ready to hear the
answers she needed to give.

LEVELS OF PRESENTATION

Strenuous discrimination is necessary when it comes to choosing the level at
which to pitch the discussion of supervision. While it is theoretically sound to
present a coherent overview of relevant theory, at the same time it is important
not to avoid facing those existential predicaments in which the therapist (or
the supervisor) may find himself, by retreating behind a defensive shield of
technical terms. We need to remember that no matter whether the forensic
psychotherapist feels at home under a Freudian, a Kleinian or a Jungian
umbrella, or one belonging to their descendants, all have to endure the same
psychological storms. As do existentialists and Foulkesians – although the latter
might seek collective refuge beneath a giant group umbrella.

   The capaciousness of this metaphor obviates our getting side-tracked into
relatively trivial concerns when the supervision process itself is the prime
consideration. We are thus free to concentrate upon the central issues of formal
psychotherapy supervision. Our attention will be firmly upon the relationship
between patient and therapist, as it is echoed, reflected upon and re-presented
in the presence of therapist and supervisor. Nevertheless, this chapter may also
throw light upon some of the complexities and perplexities of 'appropriate'
human exchange in the informal, often unexpected and explosive 'happenings'
involving primary psychiatric nurses and their patients. Supervision of such
'front line' forensic activities should be no 'optional extra' in a well run secure
setting.

The single most important development in the organized supervision of Forensic Psychotherapy was the inception in 1990 of the Day Release Course conducted at the Portman Clinic[1] in London. It takes place under the aegis of the British Postgraduate Medical Federation (Course Director, Estela Welldon). In 1994 a two-year Diploma course was launched. Prior to this, the supervision systematically conducted in several centres by individual therapists, was inevitably deprived of the collective impetus achieved at the Portman Clinic.

SUPERVISION: A WORD WITH SEVERAL CONNOTATIONS

Reference needs to be made to the dual connotation of 'group supervision' – which may imply a supervision group in which several individual therapists collectively explore individual therapy sessions, or the supervision process as it applies to group psychotherapy (see Sharpe 1994). A clarifying disclaimer is called for at this early stage, because the word 'supervision' also has two distinct connotational frames, even within the relatively small field of forensic psychiatry. Thus Prins (1990) writes:

> 'From time to time, general psychiatrists are asked to supervise offender patients who have been conditionally discharged into the community either by direction of the Home Secretary or by a Mental Health Review Tribunal (Mental Health Act 1983, Section 42(2) and 73(2)(4b)).' (p.157, emphasis added)

This chapter is *not* concerned with supervision of this genre. It is perfectly true that such formal psychiatric 'supervision' will often involve the delicate handling of psychodynamic quicksands and such complex issues might be appropriately discussed in a 'psychotherapy supervision' session. But the formal legal supervision is not our prime concern at this point. At the time of writing (Spring 1994) correspondence is taking place between The Secretary of State for Health and the President of the Royal College of Psychiatrists on 'Supervision Registers' (Caldicott 1994, p.385). The debate is about 'supervision' in the community as described by Prins.

This chapter focuses upon various aspects of the psychotherapy supervision process which is both a necessary part of the training of the forensic psychotherapist, as well as the never ending learning-about-self and learning-about-life. It may include formal peer review as well as being intrinsic to the sometimes frustrating, sometimes gratifying, continuous growth in the acquisition of psychotherapeutic skills. Nevertheless, even after temporarily disown-

---

1   Although therapy directly undertaken at the Portman Clinic is restricted to out-patient work, the teaching staff on the course represent forensic psychotherapy conducted in varying degrees of security.

ing the important professional task of 'supervising offender patients…in the community' the trainee forensic psychotherapist may still find himself involved in a dual supervision process in both dynamic forensic psychotherapy and forensic psychiatry. The latter will include experience of assessing forensic patients, writing court reports, attending court and learning of the opportunities and pitfalls of giving evidence under cross examination, as well as growing increasingly familiar with the various locations where forensic patients may be seen. The setting ranges from a conventional out-patient consultation via the open ward of a district general hospital to a variety of secure settings, from the police cell to the regional secure unit (RSU), the prison and the Special Hospital.

Exactly how the dynamic interchange between patient and therapist is influenced by the presence or lack of a secure setting is one of the constant variables under scrutiny during forensic psychotherapy supervision sessions. This is so, even though the topics under discussion such as transference, countertransference, apposite interpretation or the judicious use of the extended or extra session – depending on ambient circumstances – may sound so conventional and orthodox, that a third party listening to an account might be forgiven for forgetting that such therapy was taking place in a secure setting. But for those involved in such therapy, and those hearing it re-located and re-presented in a supervision session, will not be able to forget the proximity of alarm bells, the presence of unbreakable glass or such fundamental details that known arsonists do not carry lighters or matches in those early days of therapeutic exploration before trust can be taken on trust. Recalling the opening phase of therapy, a patient whose index offence was arson, who had just returned a nurse's lighter after lighting a cigarette said 'In the early days I wouldn't have given it back' to which the nurse replied 'In the early days I wouldn't have lent it to you!'

The orientation of this chapter is best served by giving an overview of the dynamic supervision process.

THE NATURE OF THE DYNAMIC SUPERVISION PROCESS

Each parent discipline has a well-established developmental line of professional training, with appropriately prescribed institution-related minimal requirements for subsequent professional recognition. For obvious reasons, psychoanalysis and forensic psychiatry – being such distinct and well differentiated areas of expertise, adopt widely different frames of reference when it comes to such issues as duration and location of 'patient contact'. Reduced to its simplest terms, it is clear that psychoanalytic training inevitably demands sustained, frequent and regular professional involvement with the same patient (or group of patients) in the same setting for many years, whereas the training requirements for the forensic psychiatrist, just described, differ in virtually every parameter.

There would be certain didactic value in printing this chapter adopting the style of those modern diaries which are described as having 'two weeks to an opening'. Written with 'two disciplines to an opening', it would prompt critical thought if, say, the left hand page were devoted to psychoanalytic aspects and the right hand page to forensic aspects of these prevailing concerns of forensic psychotherapy which call for recognition from both parental fields. Both are important. Neither has a monopoly.

Reference has recently been made to bridging issues and it is perhaps useful to recall that from an etymological point of view, a bridge – that which carries one across – is the Greek origin of the word *metaphor*.

The word *mutative* is firmly embedded in a seminal psychoanalytic paper by Strachey (1934) who described 'the nature of the therapeutic action of psycho-analysis' invoking the concept of the mutative interpretation – that is to say, the interpretation which changes things. When describing the dynamics of the therapeutic process, Cox and Theilgaard (1987) linked these two crucial words and referred to the place of mutative metaphors in psychotherapy and the supervision thereof. This affords a further link to those studies of the process of supervision undertaken by Szecsödy (1990). He writes of 'supervision: a didactic or mutative situation' (p.245) '...thus it is important to differentiate supervision according to the trainee's interests, which are to increase knowledge and skill, on the one hand, and to acquire a profession on the other' (p.245). Ehlers (1991, p.49) repeatedly stresses the importance of ensuring that the supervision stimulates the creativity and mental maturation of the supervisee, which may not ensue if too great an emphasis is placed on the didactic regulation of supervision.

Ever since the early work of Ekstein and Wallerstein (1958) and Fleming and Benedek (1964) various models or metaphors for the supervision process have been adopted. Each has inherent strengths and weaknesses. For example, both the 'hydraulic' model and the 'cultivating' model have been described. The former, although grandiose and naive in many ways, implies that the supervisor 'pours' a certain quantity of this distilled essence of therapeutic experience in carefully controlled measures into a willing receiving vessel – the supervisee. The latter model suggests that the psychotherapy process is regarded as carrying some of the positive attributes of gardening. This much more sophisticated metaphorical model considers such phenomena as preparation, timing, removing injurious impediments and, *above all, waiting* and not trying to hasten the process of assimilation, growth and subsequent flowering of the necessary skills.

It is when we move to the second page of our 'two disciplines to an opening'
diary that we are suddenly aware how incongruous this present discussion
seems when set alongside the demands made on the trainee forensic psychiatrist. He is needing to learn about the relevance of various aspects of the Mental
Health Act, the need for the necessary bi-lingual skills of converting clinical
psychiatric terminology into that appropriate when facing cross questioning as
an expert witness in, say, issues such as adequate evidence for diminished
responsibility.

Nevertheless, despite the considerable polemic about the relevance of
appropriate models of supervision, the traditional 'apprentice' model which is
ubiquitous in general medicine has much to commend it. In spite of the
inevitable play upon words, surgical analogies are often clear cut. The trainee
surgeon learns as an apprentice. He watches an experienced practitioner at work
and then gradually assists in the proceedings with greater involvement as
experience and skill develop. Ultimately, he assumes the mantle himself and
independently – after adequate supervision and recognition – undertakes
surgery in his own name. There is copious literature on the nature and process
of psychotherapy supervision on the one hand, and virtually non-existent
literature on how the supervision process in forensic psychiatry is undertaken,
although there are clear statements of the issues needing to be faced (see II:12:ii
(Clive Meux)). But both disciplines depend upon the trainee learning how to
become most effectively himself in the presence of both the supervisor and the
patient. Over time, the trainee gradually works more autonomously as he comes
to distinguish between his 'internal support that is autonomous and separate
from the internalized supervisor' (Casement 1985, p.24); although he will
never outgrow the need for peer group supervision.

In *The Quiet Profession* Anne Alonso (1985) has not only described various
aspects of the process of psychotherapy supervision, she has also written about
the supervisor himself/herself; indeed the subtitle is *Supervisors of Psychotherapy*.
Under the heading 'What do supervisors do?' she explores the following issues:
didactic teaching; imparting an appropriate attitude towards patients; expanding the affective capacity of the therapist; developing the capacity to work in
the metaphor of the transference; supporting the therapist.

THE DISTINCTIVE CHARACTER OF FORENSIC
PSYCHOTHERAPY SUPERVISION

It can reasonably be claimed that the arena in which forensic psychotherapy is
undertaken demands all that is expected of generic dynamic psychotherapy
with the crucial codicil that the highest discriminatory attention is also paid
to the context. This is important because it links the here-and-now of present
dynamic engagement with the there-and-then of the past dynamic engagement

in which the criminal act took place. Both are considered against those previous interpersonal constellations in which personal patterns of responding developed. This means that scrupulous attention must be paid to the trainee's acquisition of an adequate understanding of intra-psychic developmental lines, in addition to a matching sociologically-orientated appreciation of inter-personal dynamics, together with an over-arching appreciation of the existential nuances of the present therapeutic moment. Some psychoanalytic literature gives the impression that a clear appreciation of *intra-psychic dynamics* vastly outweighs the relevance of *inter-personal dynamics*, as though those untrained in psychoanalysis had better settle for clear inter-personal understanding and leave intra-psychic discernment to those fully trained in such matters. The forensic psychotherapist will pay equal attention to both processes and never diminish the significance of inter-personal 'activity'. This may be homicidal in intent and effect, even though prompted and brought into effect through the process of projective identification. Fortunately, object relations theory bridges the dynamic understanding of both intra-psychic and inter-personal processes.

The forensic psychotherapist will be involved in the patient's projective field and will be the recipient of many transference displacements of affect. Thus his countertransference response to the patient's reactivated externalized hostility means that he will come to learn how to distinguish between counter-transference distortion and prudential fear. As this chapter is entitled 'a supervisor's view' I regard this as providing tacit permission for a comment in the first person. In my view, *the skill of disentangling countertransference phenomena and prudential fear is one of the most important components of developing professional expertise which a forensic psychotherapist can ever attain.* It is certainly an issue which makes its presence felt in many supervision sessions in one way or another.

We have now shed both general psychiatric 'supervision' of offender patients and conventional supervision in forensic psychiatry which, say, a senior registrar, will receive from the clinical tutor and/or the consultant with whom he is currently working. This frees us to concentrate upon the central issues of forensic psychotherapy supervision. This is a huge theme and justifies considered attention to certain generic issues. Even so, the material from supervision sessions is so kaleidoscopic and multi-faceted that it could rapidly become psychologically indigestible if too much detail is given. On the other hand, the avoidance of relevant detail deprives the reader of necessary substance. Once again, refuge will be taken in the capaciousness of illustrative metaphor and a selection of crucial vignettes which carry teaching potential.

THE SUPERVISOR'S PERSPECTIVAL WORLD

There is inevitably an amalgam of personal experience, professional training and a gradually crystallizing *weltanschauung* which contributes to the peculiarly unrepeatable 'presence' of the supervisor with which the supervisee will become increasingly familiar. The same blending of experience and behaviour leading to a recognizable cognitive style and the ability to use theory, symbol and metaphor will also say much about the inner world of the supervisor to the therapist, and the inner world of the therapist to the supervisor. Together, they will be exploring these very matters as they impinge upon the sequential disclosure of the patient's inner world phenomena. Rarely – although it is of the greatest significance when it occurs – is forensic psychotherapy concerned with such matters in relationship to the terminal interweaving of affective disclosure between patient and victim. It is, however, familiar in forensic psychotherapeutic practice that the death of the victim is never the death of the retrospective fantasy of the patient, who may only be able to affectively breath again because of the prolonged working through during many therapeutic sessions. Repeated reference to what the victim said 'as the knife went in' can absorb much therapeutic time until the patient's responsibility for the killing is unwaveringly claimed.

> *The central dynamic issue of forensic psychotherapy is in keeping with that of generic psychoanalytically orientated psychotherapy. A clear understanding of the developmental line, the blocks thereto, and the deviations therefrom, point to areas to be studied under 'high magnification' in the supervision session.*

Particular attention is given to those areas of the patient's experience, coming to light as the unconscious becomes conscious, which the therapist is unable to 'receive' because *his* defences block reception. Indeed, one way of viewing the dynamic task of psychotherapy is to consider how far it can, as it were, free the patient to rejoin his own developmental path and liberate those creative energies which integrated living and loving can both evoke and require. Much therefore depends on what the therapist is free enough to hear without diversionary retreat.

Of particular relevance in forensic psychiatry, is the indubitable significance of the forensic 'event'. The offence has always implied the eruption into activity of hitherto[2] fantasized catastrophe, of one sort or another – be it arson, theft or one of the many savage faces of offences against the person. For this reason forensic supervision often mirrors forensic therapy which mirrors the primary forensic event itself. This, in turn, may mirror a previous episode – often years before, in childhood – when the present assailant was, himself, a victim. Thus, in addition to the universal relevance of developmental issues there are often

---

2   'Hitherto' may imply years of 'planning' or micro-seconds prior to an explosive crisis.

heightened existential nuances and imaginal impressions etched on the memory of the supervisor – the therapist – the patient – and, if he lives, the victim.

Such is the wide panorama of issues which is likely to arise, colour and permeate forensic supervision. As his experience grows they will influence the supervisor's perspectival world. In order to give a measure of containment to so wide a field, there follows a series of pragmatic pointers to some of the major topics which may arise.

SOME PRAGMATIC POINTERS

1. Forensic psychotherapy is always 'on location'. Borrowing this phrase from the film-maker, it is always important to describe the context and setting in which psychotherapy is conducted. Although the issue is obvious, it is often neglected when forensic psychotherapy sessions are presented to a supervision group.

2. That the supervisee feels safe enough to trust the supervision process is *an essential ingredient of effective supervision*. (The words given added emphasis come from a paper by Watts and Morgan (1994, p.14).) An implicit distinction is drawn between supervision and 'effective supervision'! This ironic comment draws attention to the fact that developed and sustained post-basic trust is essential if the supervision process is to live up to its name. Whenever there is a hint that the supervisee is deficient in theoretical knowledge there is inevitably a fall in self-esteem in an already precarious situation, so that many kinds of defensive and avoidance manoeuvres intervene. The trainee then retreats from psychological proximity and any kind of mutuality with a supervisor who threatens. As with so many of these issues, they are present in a generic psychotherapy forum but are brought into disturbingly acute focus in a forensic setting. By this I mean that the patient, say, of whom the therapist feels afraid, has already acquired the status of being a forensic patient precisely because in previous fear-engendering situations injury and maybe death ensued to those who were afraid. The threatening supervision session is as great a distortion of what is meant to be a supportive process as a 'staff support group' in which participants are afraid to admit that they need support. In spite of a certain catechetical ambience, it is a reasonable question for self-enquiry which should be an ever present issue in the supervisor's mind: 'would this session qualify as 'effective supervision', and if not, why not?'

3. The psychological maturity of a supervision group is often indicated by the willingness of the participants to present cases they would not have hitherto 'dared' to present for supervision. There is an enigmatic aspect of a self-unfulfilling prophecy here. Plainly, a supervision group originally set up to consider cases the participants would not dare to bring to supervision would scarcely get off the ground. Nevertheless, at the other end of the spectrum is the supervision arena in which only 'successful' or 'textbook' therapeutic dilemmas would be presented, so that the worries which genuinely beset the therapist in the early hours of the morning are not mentioned – at least not mentioned in the public forum, but only in the confidentiality of 'a brief word' elsewhere. Both therapists and supervisors are inevitably aware of this gossamer-thin dividing line between the presentation of the difficult patient who really disturbs the personal world of the therapist, rather than the 'difficult but safely managed' patient who carries acceptable and interesting theoretical challenges and does not disturb the therapist other than perhaps sending him to the library.

   Sharpe (1994) explores issues implicit in the supervision of analytic groups. All the topics raised are relevant to group forensic psychotherapy which is the chosen mode for many forensic patients whose offences are so often evidential of previously disturbed group experiences.

4. THERAPY – SUPERVISION – DIDACTIC TEACHING constitutes a well known tripartite juxtaposition which can also be considered in a triangular configuration.

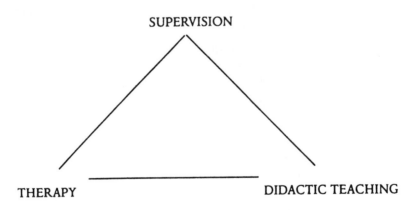

However much uncontaminated supervision is the central fulcrum of the supervision process, there are existential moments when a supervisee's need of supportive defence buttressing or analytic defence diminishing self-scrutiny are 'in the air'. In the exigency of the moment a prudential decision on the supervisor's part may be to suggest that the issue is perhaps best brought up in therapy. Nevertheless, in such a moment, it would be inhuman not be manifestly supportive when a supervisee is decompensating and afraid of the patient he is due to see in the next therapy session. On the other hand, deflection from the prime purpose of supervision can also be made in the direction of seminar-worthy didactic material. This may in fact be a *bone fide* turn of events and should then be treated as such, always bearing in mind that it is more likely to be a retreat from affective disturbance contoured and sculpted by prevailing countertransference dynamics.

5. That the supervision sessions mirror the therapeutic session is universal in both generic dynamic psychotherapy and forensic psychotherapy. It therefore does not qualify for elaboration here – though to forget its existence and prevailing relevance implies lack of supervisory vigilance.

6. 'Almost unmentionable thoughts.' Kraemer (1992) underlines the importance of 'direct attention to clinical experience. By this I mean hearing about the work the trainee has been doing in some detail – asking question like: what was it like being with that patient? what did he actually say? what did you actually say? what almost unmentionable thoughts did you have about his problem? and so on' (p.2). We might almost put the word 'almost' in italics. Because there is such an important distinction between that which is *almost* unmentionable and that which *is* unmentionable. This is of course a highly individually tailored aspect of psychotherapy and supervision. It leads us to the vast field of *deictic stress* and *intonational surge* – both terms referring to the emphasis of the spoken word and the gushing forth, or the verbally constipated chunks of poorly formed language which are intermittently 'released'.

To take an extremely simple example, we could consider a member of a psychotherapeutic group referred on account of 'blushing all over'. When a second patient joins the group who also has complaints of blushing, a transcript of the words of the former patient could convey two entirely different meanings. There is a vast difference between 'It's blushing all over. Again.' and 'It's blushing, all over again'. Likewise, from a forensic arena when a patient refers to 'the last victim I killed' and this brief utterance is set before and behind with silence, it is – at the material time – difficult to know whether the meaning was likely to imply something like 'I tortured the first three victims, the last victim I killed'. Or 'the last victim I killed was strangled, the others were drowned'. (For extended consideration of *deictic stress* see Cox and Theilgaard 1994, p.157).

7. *The ubiquitous influence of the limits of language.* One of the many benefits of conducting psychotherapy supervision in a country where the first language is not English brings home the ubiquitous and indubitable fact that the deepest feelings cannot be expressed in language. How often in a supervision group in Denmark or Norway has the point been reached where it is said 'you cannot really say that with the full weight of implied feeling in Danish, Norwegian...or English'. It then dawns on all those present that feelings of such a depth cannot be expressed in *any* language. Non-verbal communication then stands in its own light.

8. Because of the paucity of the spoken word to convey the finest laminations of meaning and expression, the greater the intensity of the affect the greater is the significance of non-verbal communication. It is one of the ironic aspects of psychoanalysis that so little attention is paid to non-verbal communication evident in facial expression and in particular the depth of eye contact, when it is the mode of dynamic psychology which claims to place greatest emphasis on non-verbal communication. However understandable is the precedent which explains the prevailing psychoanalytic analyst–analysand configuration ('I cannot put up with being stared at by other people for eight hours a day, (or more)' S. Freud (1913, p.134)), it is still a great loss in forensic psychotherapy when such crucial non-verbal clues to inner world phenomena may be, literally, 'overlooked' because they cannot be seen. To cite as one example a patient whose disclosure was perhaps one of the most soul-searing I have ever witnessed. His victim had been crushed and disfigured almost beyond recognition, though he was still alive. The patient – after many years psychotherapy – was scarcely able to say that which he knew could be contained no longer:

'I decided to finish it off. It became a kind of mercy killing.'

In this instance the longed-for acceptance, 'spoken' by the pain in the patient's eyes, depended upon receptive eye contact if he was to utter what he felt. This micro-vignette carries ramifications implying bodily configuration, mutuality and permeability at the transference–countertransference threshold.

9. *Therapeutic Questioning 'Against the Grain'*. This unusual phrase has been used to ensure its retention in the supervisee's memory. The patient is often relieved to be asked 'what was the worst part?...it is clear that you were upset by the whole thing, but what upset you *most?*'. Questioning of this kind is so often in contra-flow to virtually all benevolent counselling endeavours. It goes 'against the grain'. There is a need to retreat from the past. The ethos being that 'those awful experiences are now in the past and we are looking to the future, to your life outside, to a new life'...and the like. But if this has happened at the wrong phase of therapy, that is to say when there is still deeply disturbing material which has not been safely reached, formulated, ventilated, understood and integrated with other conscious aspects of the personality, the patient may be left with an insidious endopsychic enclave like an unexploded bomb. This might erupt and cause further disturbance at some unpredictable time in the future. Such interrogative movement is in the direction which appears to be counter to the patient's well-being and can be construed, by the uninformed, as merely stirring and 'looking for trouble' when things are best left to settle. Nothing could be further from 'informed' psychodynamic understanding – when such 'informing' comes from the subsequent histories of patients whose therapy sessions never reached 'the worst part'.

10. *The pain of self-exploration for the patient may also evoke painful identifications within the therapist.* Decompensation and lowering of the therapist's self-esteem may be evoked because he has not faced his own depths to the degree and with the intensity at which his patient is currently struggling. Shakespeare makes this point clearly when Banquo, who braces himself for a forensic exploration, refers not to 'your naked frailties' but '*our* naked frailties'.

> 'And when we have our naked frailties hid,
> That suffer in exposure, let us meet,
> And question this most bloody piece of work,
> To know it further.'
>   (*Macbeth* II.3.124)

11. The psychotic is the spokesman for all patients who demand that the therapist and supervisor are constantly alert to the possibility that *the perspectival world of the other may call for transient, yet partial, perceptual reframing by the therapist.* In other words, there can be a surprising or shocking quality to a psychotic utterance which jolts the too-set-in-his-ways therapist into renewed attentiveness. One simple vignette illustrates this point so clearly that further

elaboration is unnecessary. Such a patient, Mary, meets me in a hospital corridor:

MARY: 'That clock's wrong.'

MURRAY: 'I don't think so, Mary,' *(looking at my watch)* 'it *is* two o'clock.'

MARY: 'Oh, I know the time's right. It's the clock that's wrong. It's the wrong shape. The figures aren't in a circle.'[3]

The very mention of the psychotic patient opens a window onto a broad expanse of changed meaning, concrete thinking, catatonic hyper-location and neologism. The psychotherapy of the psychoses is professional territory in which forensic psychotherapists have a particular contribution to make to the wider world of generic psychotherapy. This is because concrete thinking so often leads to the most disturbed and bizarre offences against the person. Indeed, as far as understanding and unravelling psychopathology is concerned, they probably posit the greatest demands upon therapy and hence upon forensic supervision. The incipient fear of being sucked into a psychotic patient's inner world, only to discover that the therapist's executive discretion has been lost, can assail even the advanced supervisee. Such predicaments explored and rendered safe, carry convincing evidence that the supervision process is no academic or 'paper' exercise.

The recognition of disguised meaning in fragmentary psychotic utterance is one of the most subtle and absorbing aspects of forensic psychotherapy (Cox 1995b).

12. *Compromise with Chaos: Time, Depth and Mutuality.* There is always the possibility of chaos within the personality of the patient, which may activate temporary mirroring within the personality of the therapist or the supervisor, as well as in the therapeutic or supervision space in which they encounter each other. The dimensions in which both the therapeutic and the supervision process can be most usefully structured are those constituting the broad categories of Time, Depth and Mutuality (see Cox 1978b). Understanding these dimensions is one of the essential components of the supervision process, because it augments the possibility of an appropriate

---

3 She explained that when 11, 12 and 1 are on the same horizontal line you cannot easily see what the hands are doing. Then followed an intensely condensed, sexually-laden associative stream, of reference to 'wandering hands', private parts and things that should never take place.

therapeutic and theoretical grip on processes which so frequently prove elusive. They have been repeatedly put to the test in generic psychotherapy and still found to have fail-safe, working value in that particular arena where the sharpest discriminatory attentiveness and affective sensitivity is called for, namely, forensic psychotherapy.

13. *The relationship with the parent institution is an issue which impinges upon the supervision process in many ways.* Psychotherapy supervision may be part of a formal training programme, linked to an established training institute, or it may be part of the on-going daily life of monitored clinical endeavours undertaken in 'the institution' as a place of work. It can, of course, be both.

14. *The Mutative Potential of the dynamic image as an Alternative Response to Thwarted Therapeutic Initiatives.* This important theme often indicates a constructive way forward when resistance has reached an uninterpretable impasse. Cox and Theilgaard (1987, p.xiii) cite Bachelard's words as the *fons et origo* of such energizing initiatives: 'But the image has touched the depths before it stirs the surface'. The inherent energy implicit in imagery can be tapped and allowed to mobilize areas of mutative potential within the patient, the therapist and the 'seized up' supervisor.

15. *The Maintenance of Hovering Attentiveness: The Vital Balance* Applying Menninger's (1963) phrase 'the Vital Balance' to the supervision process, it can be taken to refer to the supervisor's hovering attentiveness to the therapist which mirrors the therapist's attention to the patient. This is, of course, a counsel of perfection which is sometimes close to practice and sometimes far from it when personal emotional poverty or distraction prevail.

A diagram can convey in an instant those interactive processes which would otherwise call for extended verbal description.

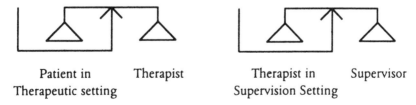

| Patient in | Therapist | Therapist in | Supervisor |
| Therapeutic setting | | Supervision Setting | |

Figure 1 Optimal Hovering Balance

Distorted Balance when the therapist (A) or supervisor (B) experience emotional poverty (e.g. loneliness) in their personal lives and are thus 'over-involved' or 'married' to their work (see Figure 2). They seem to be highly motivated (arriving early and leaving late) but are actually working *too* hard!

A   B

Figure 2 Personal Emotional Poverty

Distorted Balance when therapist (A) or supervisor (B) experience undue emotional distraction (severe family illness, divorce, bereavement etc.) in their personal lives and are thus 'under-involved' and unable to offer the therapeutic/supervision process anything approaching the necessary hovering attentiveness (see Figure 3). They 'do their hours' and 'honour their obligations', but their soul is not in the work. In forensic work this configuration can also arise if the patient's index offence comes too close to the personal experience of the therapist.

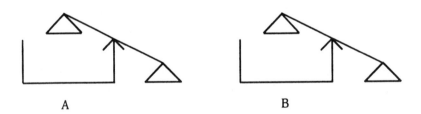

A   B

Figure 3 Personal Emotional Distraction

In practice, it is not difficult to discern when a therapist is over-involved or under-involved, although he may be unaware of it until it comes to light during supervision.

16. *The supervisor's need for supervision.* The supervisor, himself, needs the opportunity to have his work monitored. His responsibility is such that there can be ominous consequences if his balanced 'hovering attentiveness' becomes skewed or his clinical discernment distorted.

Exactly how this *meta-supervision* is arranged will inevitably depend upon ambient circumstances and the availability of experienced colleagues. More often than not, *peer-supervision* – sometimes known as *intervision* – is the realistic nature of things.

Supervision always calls for a measure of *professional distance* between the emotional and physical 'setting' of the work being supervised and the actual 'location' of meta-supervision.

There is, however, another dimension of distance which is of particular value to the forensic psychotherapist. I refer to the *inter-disciplinary distance* furnished by the fact that he tends to be healthily out-numbered by his peer group of forensic psychiatrists! I, personally, receive most help from the supportive challenge constantly offered by experienced forensic psychiatrists. They are unlikely to be persuaded by dynamic terminology such as 'the internalization of a toxic introject', on the one hand, or existential emphases on the 'thrown-ness of human existence' on the other. It is those dynamic processes which carry survival value in the face of forensic challenge, and yet still manage to convey something about the intricacies of the inner world of the patient, the therapist and their interaction which the therapist learns to trust. How far the supervisor is incorporated as the 'third party', available as a recipient of transferred affect and energy, should be under constant scrutiny.

Technical phrases can be helpful when the auto-supervisor is operating and one feels isolated, as far as peer contact is concerned. Thus increasing forensic experience has a way of augmenting a therapist's 'gyroscopic supervisory introjects' which tend to keep him on course in the face of storms, or suspiciously calm seas which may prove treacherous.

Peer group supervision with other forensic psychotherapists is a rare consummation, devoutly to be wished. The other source of invaluable 'correctives' is the primary nurse who knows the patient as a person – a person in the predicament of the current moment – better than anyone else. The primary nurse tends to have his finger on the patient's psychological pulse and becomes highly skilled in detecting future irregularities. How this meshes with the psychotherapist's concerns serves as a dynamic touchstone in monitoring the supervisor's supervision.

WHEN PROFESSIONAL DISORIENTATION THREATENS

The Six Horsemen of the Apocalypse:
The Withdrawal of Therapeutic Presence

The subtitle of this section stands in such stark contrast to all that precedes it, that the reader is jolted into asking 'What is this doing here?' This is clearly written in a different mode and thus carries implications of a hidden agenda in another key.

It is included in the chapter on supervision in counterpoint to the plethora of theoretical concepts and technical terms which are entirely appropriate in a work of this nature. Nevertheless, there is also the risk that they may, on occasion, serve as a cloak for spurious certainty which camouflages anxiety and ontological insecurity. It is important that, somewhere in this volume, the fundamental existential question is raised: 'What do you do when there is nothing you can do?' The experience is heightened by a volatile combination of anxiety and conceptual confusion. Furthermore, it is paradoxically reassuring to the trainee, to discover that his supervisor also knows how it feels to be standing on ground which is rapidly becoming *terra infirma* (a *lapsus typi* from times past, which referred to *terror in firma*, stated the position so clearly).

Responding to the Threat of Disorientation and Dislocation

The therapist may be aware of an increasing sense of foreboding, when it dawns upon him that the patient is approaching material which he will personally find disturbing. It may be fortuitous – although this makes it none the less painful – that *the arena of anguish* which the patient needs to explore is in the same psychologically contoured landscape of personal predicament as that assailing the therapist. In other words, there is a matching resonance in terms of that which is, at best, disturbing and, at worst, intolerable. It then becomes exceedingly difficult for the therapist to maintain his attitude of hovering attentiveness. The exigency of the situation leads to the possibility of receptive resistance, dispersal of discernment and even thematic re-routing. The latter is, by definition, exactly contrary to the basic tenets of free-association and signals the withdrawal of therapeutic presence.

Because none are immune from trauma of this kind, and no professional training can obviate its capricious development, I thought it would be helpful to step briefly over the threshold of personal presentation at this point. I do so, knowing that such an idiosyncratic statement is inevitably 'tailor made'. But, even so, it might encourage the trainee to explore what makes him 'tick', and usually 'survive', in the face of threats to his self-esteem. Moreover, such a window of supervisor transparency would offer a glimpse of what is taking place within a senior colleague in the face of incipient dislocation.

Masterson (1976, p.38) has a masterful description of the intensity of feelings and the hold they have 'over the patient's entire life'. His reference to the Horsemen of the Apocalypse is helpful to us here. He writes of the intensity, the immediacy and the primacy which ego-alien feelings hold over *the patient's entire life* (emphasis added). It is my suggestion that the therapist's life – *although rarely his entire life* – may be similarly afflicted. The therapist, himself, may be no stranger to the sudden clouding of a hitherto well conducted session, when a cloud – no bigger than a man's hand – appears on the patient's horizon of disclosure and seems to be heading towards him.

'The scene begins to cloud.' (*Love's Labour's Lost* V.2.712)

At times such as these, reference to 'countertransference distortion' may itself be a defensive reduction, which denies the existential pervasiveness of the dread known by those 'for whom the ground may fail to come'; at least the trusted ground of professional *terra firma*. What did Masterson actually say?

> 'The six psychiatric horsemen of the apocalypse – depression, anger, fear, guilt, passivity and helplessness, and emptiness and void – vie in their emotional sway and destructiveness with the social upheaval and destructiveness of the original four horsemen – famine, war, flood, and pestilence. *Technical words are too abstract to convey the intensity and immediacy* of these feelings *and* therefore *the primacy they hold* over the patient's entire life.' (emphasis added)

I have previously stated that it felt retreatist not to refer to a personal *weltanschauung* in relation to these imponderables (Cox 1978b, p.97; Cox and Theilgaard 1994, p.376). What actually goes on – what has survival value when a therapist feels isolated at the clinical front-line? What does the therapist do when there is nothing he can do? If his gyroscopic introjects are living up to their 'job specification', what should they be enabling him to do in terms of intra-psychic and inter-personal navigation when the threat of disorientation and dislocation is in the air?

This is the Janusian dilemma. Looked at from one side, it appears to be a theoretical philosophical and psychodynamic theme which would be suitable for a dissertation. Looked at from the other side – particularly when involved in therapeutic space with an explosive aggressive psychopath, this has more of the immediacy of knowing how to respond in those crucial seconds before a potential car crash or when fire sweeps through an adjacent corridor. (This reminds me of a seminar I once conducted in which one participant was studying for a PhD on the psychopathology of arson and another was a prison officer who had personally rescued five inmates who had set their cells on fire and barricaded the door. The fascinating dialectic which pervaded the entire session was fuelled by the fire of speculation as to who actually knew most about the useful things to know about fire! There was no doubt that each participant valued highly the contribution of the other.)

Forensic Framing and Re-Framing

The ensuing resumé of a personal *Via Integrata* – at least the 1995 formulation thereof – is inevitably tentative, provisional and partial. Yet it is bound to provoke the reader into thinking what he would formulate under the same heading.

In the psychoanalytic world, the word 'fixation' implies points of arrest at some location on a developmental line and therefore denotes pathology and even predicts likely reception areas for regressive retreats. How different is the significance of the word 'fixation' in the world of navigation, where the possibility of taking a 'fix' allows precise location and orientation to take place. It is in this second sense that I now use the term, for in this way potential dislocation is averted, and disorientation ceases. What are those reliable landmarks, in the territory of adjacent disciplines, from which trustworthy bearings can be taken?

In my experience, such threats of being lost or dislocated occur when there is a misalignment between my formulation of the patient's predicament – in traditional psychodynamic terms – and its theological homologue.[4]

For me, it is this other frame of reference which, like the surveyor's fixation on a certain landmark, allows comprehensive re-framing to correct the de-framing experience and avert incipient disorganization. Self-esteem regulation, which is so intimately related to man's progressive self-definition and re-definition, is congruous with the re-defining nature of the psychotherapeutic process. It is often acutely focused in the theological implications of forensic psychotherapy (Cox 1973a, 1993b; Cox and Grounds 1991).

As a bridge between psychotherapy and theology, a passage by Ramsey (1964) is apposite:

'He writes: "The only distinctive function theology can or need claim is that of being the guardian and spokesman of insight and mystery." Psychotherapy is frequently held to be the guardian of insight, but it is impoverished if it cannot co-exist with mystery. The ability to tolerate mystery, ambiguity and uncertainty alongside psychic determinism is linked to the therapist's *weltanschauung* and how he construes the nature of his task.' (Cox 1978b, p.101)

---

4   This sentence invites the reader to consider what his 'equivalent' sentence would be. MC

Space does not permit adequate development of this theme. But it is so important that to exclude it from the chapter would be tantamount to a denial of trying to face what goes on in the depths of a therapy session, when the therapist, himself, finds the going difficult. We therefore have to make another conceptual leap and in so doing we run the risk of ending up in the arms of another 'pack' of technical terms!

In predicaments such as this, a phrase of Hölderlin's serves as a reinforcing psychological hand-hold:

'But where there is danger, there grows also what saves.' (Heidegger 1971)

An alternative translation offers us 'Where there is danger, there flourishes that which saves'. This carries the implication that it is only in the experience of danger that that which can 'save' is discerned as being what it is. Gilkey (1979) has written 'Our present is saturated with possibilities' (p.80) and one of the consequences of anxiety is that it diminishes horizons, intensifies tunnel-vision and reduces possibility.

'The greater story which encompasses the story of [our] life.' (Dunne 1973, p.50)

The *eschaton* (Greek) refers to the 'final things' namely, death, judgement, heaven, hell - *eschatology* being 'the science of the four last things'. The way in which these things seem to impinge upon and within therapeutic space can be existential. That is to say, they do so along the trajectory established by C H Dodd (see Vidler 1950, p.105) who formulated the concept of *realized eschatology*. This implies that the final things are here and now. Through our decisions, in the options of the present moment, we are continuously being judged. Closely linked to this dynamic perception is the relationship between *Immanence* and *Transcendence*, which intersect at a nodal point within therapeutic space where patient and therapist meet. In doing so, they maintain the fine-tuning, by patient and therapist alike, to 'the pattern which connects', Bateson's (1979) definition of *Aesthetic* (p.17). What concerns us now is the relationship between events as points in the Time-Series and events which have Permanent Significance (Taylor 1956, p.1).

The Eternal Now – The Unfolding Present

If we imagine a moving cursor on a computer screen we can think of it as representing the present moment. It is a 'now' which continues to move as time presses the advance key. Let us further imagine it progressing to the right, in the direction of time, between two arrows

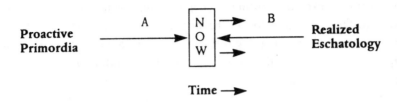

Arrow 'A' is pointing forwards from the past, representing *Proactive Primordia* and arrow 'B' points backwards from the future, representing *Realized Eschatology*. The former implies that all the events in the past, both conscious and unconscious, are impinging upon the present moment – where the cursor lies. In psychodynamic terms, this conveys the inevitable thrust of psychic determinism. At the same time, the latter represents the potential future which is pulled back into the existential present, so that we are continuously in the presence of ultimates. 'Final things' always confront us where we are and continue in the progressive *NOW* of the present moment – *The Eternal Now* (Tillich 1963).

Chronos and Kairos

The Greek word *Chronos* is carried in all our words to do with time and the developmental process, such as chronology and chronic. On the other hand, the word *Kairos* refers to the right moment – in psychoanalytic terms the *mutative interpretation* (Strachey 1934) occurs at the *Kairotic moment*, at the patient's point of urgency (Cox 1978b, p.157). It is self-evident that the timing of the criminal act at the intersection of *Chronos* and *Kairos* is an issue of crucial forensic relevance, as is the impact of unresolved transgenerational dynamic energy, whereby what never reaches kairotic potential in one generation may erupt with disastrous consequences in the next (see also Cullmann 1951).

Current Conceptual Challenges

I have been involved in a collaborative study of the implication of 'the larger story' and the sense of escalating therapeutic poverty when such contact is lost (Cox and Theilgaard 1987). The 'points of urgency' are not only those of the patient (Strachey 1934) but may be those of the therapist too. There is indeed a challenging work of integration waiting to be attempted. It has something to do with the conceptual link between in-depth psychoanalytic engagement and existential theological implications.[5] For example, the *mutative interpretation*

---

5   Professor John Macquarrie is the theologian who has written most about existentialism. *Existentialism* (Macquarrie 1972) is a good point of access to his work.

(Strachey 1934) occurs at 'the patient's point of urgency'. Here we are currently considering the therapist's point of urgency and endeavouring to set it in context of the relationship between *Chronos* and *Kairos*. The next challenge is the integration of the concepts of the *developmental line* (A. Freud 1966, p.62) and the *redemptive line* (Cullmann 1951) of events which are mutatively operative. It may be ectopic to present such intellectual issues under the heading of 'Six Horsemen of the Apocalypse'! But I suggest that it is this very lack of a sufficiently all-embracing frame of reference which ultimately, and intimately, leads to the therapist's sense of impotence and incremental anxiety. It seems to me that, to adopt Gilkey's phrase, the clinico–theological–forensic interface is 'saturated with possibility'. There is a prospect of exciting new levels of conceptual coherence which interdisciplinary exploration now offer.

What One Can and Cannot Do for Oneself

This is the crux and the precise wording needs to be maintained. The psychotherapeutic process can be defined as 'one in which the patient is *enabled* to do for himself, what he *cannot do on his own*' (Cox 1978b, p.4). The classical *Forensic theory* of the Atonement emphasizes the fact that 'Christ did for us *what we cannot do for ourselves*' (Taylor 1956, p.72, emphasis added).[6] It should be noted that to the definition of therapy is added 'the therapist does not do it for him, but he cannot do it without the therapist'. This conceptual linking has both converging and diverging implications, depending upon the source of enabling energy. The common ground is that whatever needs to be done cannot be done 'solo'. Grace is the dynamic in the theological frame of reference, whereas the prolonged working through of transferred feelings, attitudes and energies, which distort perception of current relationships, is energized by the inherent momentum of the therapeutic process itself. And its momentum is released in therapeutic space where patient and therapist meet.

Setting these affirmations side by side is revealing and thought provoking: 'He is enabled to do for himself, what he cannot do on his own. The therapist does not do it for him, but he cannot do it without the therapist'....'He did for us what we cannot do for ourselves.' At the deepest level we are here touching upon that which the therapist and the patient, as an *ensemble*, cannot by definition do independently and yet *together* can find the necessary mobilizing energy.

Charles Wesley refers to the creativity implicit in 'Forever beginning what never shall end' and those involved in forensic therapeutic space for whom 'without limit of time' is not an unfamiliar term, may see this initiative for what it is. Thomson and Kahn (1970) write 'As the capacity to endure increases –

---

6   I think the first time I heard the word 'forensic' was during a theology supervision session.

so [the patient] is given more to endure' (p.67). Sometimes the forensic therapist is called upon to endure, not only the patient's experience of being at the destructive 'receiving end' of the Six Horsemen of the Apocalypse, but also with being with the offender patient who is coming to terms with the implications that he is just such an apocalyptic agent. *This imposes a greater strain on the therapist's identity-retaining energy than is usually the case in generic psychotherapy.* It is not only the working through of the passive experience of having been tortured, it is being with the patient while he comes to terms with being the destructive torturer in person.

En passant, it should be emphasized that such issues are both intensified and, simultaneously, made more tolerable within the context of group analytic forensic psychotherapy. There is no doubt that there is a corporate quality of 'all being in the same boat'. All, including the therapist, are carried by all. This is a vital constructive and sustaining energy which, in my view, is entirely congruous with a theological frame of reference. It has been defined as the process of *Omniference* (Cox 1993a, p.6).

Eschatology and Forensic Dynamics

I am indebted to Professor Langdon Gilkey for the thought-provoking statement 'The *eschaton* is equidistant from every point of history', although I cannot recall its precise location in his extensive theological and philosophical writings. It is probably to be found in *Naming the Whirlwind* (1969), *Reaping the Whirlwind* (1976) or *Message and Existence* (1979). This implies that the *eschaton* is also equidistant from every point of clinical history, remembering that Erikson (1959b) stated that 'we cannot lift a case history out of history' (p.13). We have already come across this phrase in the preface 'In and out of the mind'. The *eschaton* must therefore be equidistant from every point of a therapeutic session, including the therapist's point of urgency. The stabilizing anchorage within another frame of reference, of which the *eschaton* can be an emblem, can offer the therapist an endorsing validation that where he senses professional 'danger' there may also flourish that which saves.

It is perhaps prudent to return to more conventional concerns, such as the place of projective-identification as a defence underlying many forensic incidents, and identification-with-the-aggressor as a dynamic which should always be explored. These processes are of a different order from those we have just been considering, but they need to be integrated if the totality of the constellation is to be understood. There is a fascinating and almost magnetic philosophical pull between von Balthasar's Christology, Eschatology and Forensic Dynamics when we read 'Jesus being dead with the dead...entering into solidarity from within with those who refuse all solidarity' (see Kehl and Löser 1982, pp.44–45). I find myself wondering how therapists of a range of persuasions would formulate a sentence trying to describe what follows. It is almost beyond words yet, somehow, it has to be expressed. During deep phases of analytic psychotherapy a deadness may settle in, so that, for a while, the therapist too may be dead with the dead parts of the patient, which gradually come to life when frozen introjects (Giovacchini 1979, p.29) thaw out. Issues of this kind have been explored in relation to the amending imagination and the therapeutic process (Cox and Theilgaard 1994). The aesthetic imperative (Cox and Theilgaard 1987, p.26) invokes a rich mantle of meaning. Nevertheless, it seems that the implications of being dead with the dead and entering into solidarity with those who refuse all solidarity suggest many parallels with aspects of forensic psychotherapy in which the 'quick and the dead' carry a connotational amalgam. Activity, passivity, what one has to do for one's self, and what one has to let happen, have a way of concentrating the mind wonderfully *en route* to the sombre significance which a job specification might imply as being 'all in a day's therapeutic work' in a forensic setting.

This brief excursion in a personal *weltanschauung* may provoke others to have a throw with their matching thought-provoking boomerangs. Such issues need exploration and airing. Although, fortunately, they rarely lead to agreement. But it was with this end in view, and in response to peer pressure to attempt to describe such things, that we saw the Six Horsemen of the Apocalypse on the horizon – and did our best to move towards them.

*   *   *   *

Without a break, attention now moves from this broad survey of the dynamics of supervision to focus upon the response of a trainee to her first forensic encounter. The vignette in the following chapter is by Ann Stanley, who, as a registrar in forensic psychiatry, found herself professionally involved in issues 'beyond the usual range of professional human experience', to adapt the wording of DSM-III. This thought-provoking dialectic is best served by the simple juxtaposition of these serial pragmatic pointers and the first forensic encounter which ensues. This, by definition, is *not* formal psychotherapy. But the *primordiality of its capacity to disturb* gives the material a *frisson* with which all are familiar, and whose personal parallel all can recall.

The Impact of the First Forensic Encounter
A Trainee's View

Ann Stanley

INTRODUCTION

This chapter is based on events which transpired on the first working day of my first registrar appointment. It was Monday 3rd August 1992 – a day I will never forget.

A registrar appointed to a training post in forensic psychiatry receives no advance intimation of the emotional demands of a job which is likely to stretch his or her defence mechanisms to the limit. At the Reaside Clinic in Birmingham, junior and senior trainees are fortunate in being members of a weekly supervision group. This lasts for an hour and is conducted by an experienced psychotherapist. He has no other input into the clinic, thereby reducing any conflict between management and therapy. Furthermore, his expertise is in general dynamic psychotherapy, so that we explore issues other than those usually regarded as 'forensic'.

The usual format of the sessions is that a trainee brings to the group the psychodynamic aspects of a case which has interested or challenged him. There is a brief presentation of the salient features. The trainee then explains his dilemma. A discussion follows considering the psychodynamic, forensic or legal aspects. The issues raised here are primarily those confronting a trainee endeavouring to tolerate the intolerable for the purposes of writing a court report. Nevertheless, the initial encounter is the same as that of the assessment interview for psychotherapy, which may involve listening to material which can be so upsetting that the listener does not find it easy to concentrate. In *The Roots of Crime* Glover (1960, p.149) refers to '*the psychopaths's assaults on [the*

psychiatrist's] most cherished possession, namely his capacity to heal (original emphasis). Learning how to endure such assaults without retreating, or denying their
existence, seems to be inherent in the training process. This concentrated theme
covers much that the young forensic psychiatrist tries to assimilate. He feels
that both his capacity to heal and his capacity to hear may be repeatedly
challenged, to the extent that the developing rudimentary skills often lead to
the experience of being deskilled.

The importance of the supervision session came to the fore recently. The
following vignette was first presented by a senior registrar who had seen the
patient with a view to writing a report. It had been considered with particular
attention to the recommendations regarding diminished responsibility. Although the discussion had been carried out at a safe emotional distance from
the 'machinations' of the man's mind, the 'vile' nature of the crime had led to
a wide spectrum of responses. (These non-technical words, despite their
'Tabloid' associations, have been deliberately used because they do convey the
nauseating horror which pervaded the group. The early impact had not been
sanitized by technical terms.)

Vignette

A young man was charged and later convicted of murder. He had taken
a girl back to an empty flat. There, during anal intercourse she
involuntarily defaecated on him. He had lost his self-control and beat
her, probably unconscious, dragged her into the bathroom, strangled her
with the light cord, and sadistically sexually killed her. He then attempted
to destroy the body, stole items from her handbag and placed one of her
family photographs on her body. Then he left and went to the local
maternity hospital to be present at the birth of his own child.

In court, it was shown how the sequence of events was pieced together from
forensic evidence and the patient's mental state. The cold reading of the facts
resurrected all the original emotions with even greater vividness. Imagination
was transformed into stark reality by photographs of the scene. There was the
realization that the casual initial telling always implies that there is 'another
story...which the patient can only blurt out fitfully and partially – if he can
tell it at all' (Cox and Theilgaard 1987, p.4).

Discussion of the issues at the end of that day did little to soothe the
emotions raised.

The following day the supervision session took place. The group of doctors,
both male and female, consisted of a mixture of those who had been present
at the original presentation and those for whom it was new. The debate during
the session was based on the history as outlined above. It was not concerned
with the events but with the emotions that it engendered in those who had

seen him and those who had not. These were varied. There was a strong feeling of anger that the issues were brought for consideration. There was also a feeling of guilty, voyeuristic enjoyment at the level of the tabloid newspaper sensational headlines, disgust that anyone could so treat another human being, and of identification with the victim. Above all came the realization that the nature of the material had brought staff emotions out into the open. Barriers came down and the issues were discussed in a constructive manner for two consecutive sessions. At the end of the group there was the open admission that, for professionals to function, they must have limits to their defence and coping mechanisms which will, on occasion, be reached. We came to realize that there was a great need for a safety-net to explore our own emotions. As we present in the group we are presenting part of ourselves. Our own restrictions may increase those of the patient. Cox (1978b, p.148) explores these issues under the heading 'The Therapist Speaks'. Carers are often unaware of their own vulnerabilities, and may work in a culture which is not receptive for discussion of the powerful negative feelings so generated (Watts and Morgan 1994).

A few weeks later we considered the structure and purpose of future sessions. All the trainees felt that the opportunity to explore their own emotions and coping mechanisms in a non-threatening and controlled environment was an invaluable part of our experience of forensic psychiatric training.

As trainees, it is important to learn where the boundaries of our defence systems lie and to recognize that there will, occasionally, be cases that penetrate the armour of even the most experienced. To admit this is an essential part of the trainee's learning experience. Prins (1990, p.160) talks of 'ambivalent investment', stating that there are three elements involved: coming to terms with the feelings of horror that the crime may raise, the burden of responsibility for both the public and the offender, and the need for things to go well. Denial may occur in both professional and offender. The patient has a vital role as teacher. One has to come to be aware of one's own blind spots and what sounds our inner 'alarm bells'. Cox (1992b, p.31) cites a vignette in which the customary 'alarm bell' in a secure setting serves as a metaphoric model of the 'internal alarm' for both therapist and patient. We must learn that, within human limits, the capacity to be at ease with everything that the patient needs to disclose is as much to do with personal experience as with formal training. This aspect is rarely given adequate emphasis in forensic psychiatric training.

The need for further exploration of the emotions raised in the sessions led to the advice of a Broadmoor psychotherapist being sought. At this point I made contact with Murray Cox. During our initial discussion on the telephone and in subsequent correspondence I tried to describe the issues we had to face both individually and collectively. Amongst these was the fear that we might be unduly sensitive and that our defence mechanisms, which had been almost breached by the nature of the material, were in some way less effective than those of others. We explored the fact that academic interest may, itself, be a defence mechanism. Further discussion led to the realization that such feelings were frequent among workers in forensic settings and that the vital issue was learning how to respond to our innate responses. I could see that in forensic psychotherapy supervision this would be an important focus. The necessity for an adequate conceptual and dynamic framework for dealing with these very difficult issues was immediately apparent; the nature of the material means that this will be highly individual. For the beginner, it may be hard to admit to himself and to colleagues that the limits of effective defences have been reached. There is always the fear of being or appearing deskilled. I could begin to see that, with increasing clinical experience, there could also come a greater willingness to admit to the powerful feelings so generated and thus learn how to use them. But this was certainly not clear to me on day one of my first forensic placement!

Postscript

It will be clear that the fundamental issues raised by Ann Stanley confront all who undertake forensic psychotherapy. All are caught between the Scylla of voyeuristic hyper-involvement on one hand and the Charybdis of hyper-defended professional 'distance' on the other. Seniority and long experience do not confer affective immunity in such matters. All have feet of clay and continue to need supervision, as well as the inherent challenge which peer-support, and the support which peer-challenge, provide. Such issues are never outgrown.

M.C. Editor

The Risks of Burnout

Adrian West

'We begin with penalties:
The cost of seriousness will be death.' (Porter 1978, p.30)

'I am so exhausted by work and lack of recreation...' (S. Freud 1908b, p.107)

'To help...(one) must study the nature of the emotional burden which the psychiatrist bears in doing his work... However much he loves his patients he cannot avoid hating them and fearing them, and the better he knows this the less will hate and fear be the motive determining what he does to his patients.' (Winnicott 1949, p.69)

INTRODUCTION

The patient has an Indian ink mark under one of his eyes, the unconscious symbol of a permanent tear, and a rage which, he says, is the only thing that keeps him going. I listen to his violence and mayhem, and after he has told me that he would feel so much better if he hit someone today, he bridles and says, 'You'll get tired before me'. If at such a moment, 'there is [for the therapist] a certain choice between responding and not responding to fear,' just as there is also a decision available 'not to amplify fantasies about the patient's past offences and potential for violence' (Karban and West 1994, p.142) in order to hold the patient there, then it must be assumed that a fairly optimal set of conditions about the state of the therapist and the holding institution pertains. The reality is that often our best efforts are thwarted by deficiencies in both. This chapter will briefly explore some of the personal consequences of attempting to work in such extreme settings: that is with difficult patients in difficult institutions.

Burnout is a term first used by Freudenberger (1974) to describe the emotional exhaustion he experienced in his work as a mental health professional. It describes the negative physiological, emotional and psychological effects on an individual of prolonged stress, when in a dynamic relationship, the demands of the environment are perceived by the individual as exceeding his or her resources. (Lazarus 1966, 1981; Freudenberger 1989; Edelwich and Brodsky 1980). Nowadays the term has become so overused and applied to so many contexts, describing both a process and an end state, that it has become almost meaningless. However it is defined, it generally results in a decrease in effective functioning or productivity in a committed activity (Brown 1983), and is often seen as a precursor to more serious impairment (Jenkins 1989).

Maslach's (1982) definition states that its main features are, 'physical and/or emotional exhaustion, a negative depersonalised attitude towards others, and negative responses towards one's self and one's level of personal accomplishment'. These three dimensions of emotional exhaustion, depersonalization and reduced personal accomplishment are included as measures within the Maslach Burnout Inventory (Maslach and Jackson 1986). Burnout is used, more generally, in this chapter to signify the states of disillusionment and depression which are possible consequences of the stresses inherent in psychotherapeutic work, however that is defined, with offender patients (Margison 1987). Such negative states will effect the equilibrium, productivity and growth of the therapist and are seen to result from the dynamic interaction between the therapist, the patient and the institution.

THE THERAPIST

Many mental health professionals, some without any formal training and some without even supervision, involve themselves in 'psychotherapy' with offender patients. The negative consequences of this involvement often reflect their level of training and self awareness.

The Therapist's Training

Mollon (1989), aware of inadequacies in the general training of clinical psychologists, remarks 'Clinical psychology trainings do not on the whole prepare the trainee for the fact that they may have to face people's emotional pain, overwhelming trauma and despair, and that the client may generate very powerful interactional pressures which can be very disturbing and incapacitating to the inexperienced clinician' (p.9). He distinguishes between 'learning from experience' in the apprenticeship mode which characterizes medicine and psychotherapy and 'learning from research' which he believes characterizes clinical psychology. A fundamental problem with this latter approach is that, 'it does not recognise authority based on experience but rather assesses the value of an opinion in terms of the cleverness of the research strategy; it can foster a tendency to learn from the literature rather than personally from teachers' (p.8). Instead of completing an apprentice's journey with the required time to learn and grow and 'acquire gradually an authentic professional identity based on skills and understanding, developed bit by bit through struggle and some emotional pain' (p.10) the trainee too soon becomes the autonomous, omnipotent professional walking confidently around the unit, but inwardly feeling fraudulent (Mollon 1989).

The point is that clinical psychologists are not alone in experiencing inadequate training in clinical skills, especially within the complexities of the forensic setting. If the development of professional and clinical competence is dependent on increasing self-awareness so that the therapist becomes more clear about how his attitudes, beliefs, past history and relationships influence how he solves problems and deals with other people, then there has to be a willingness to listen to those whose experience of life has made them, one hopes, wiser and so qualified to be commentators and mentors. This kind of development often entails more than supervision but is likely to be resisted even when it is obvious that a detached intellectual stance with its associated cognitive behavioural techniques 'may contain elements of a manic defence against mental pain' (Mollon 1989, p.9).

The Therapist's Self-Awareness

Cox (1983) recognizes that however thoroughly trained the therapist may be, there is no guarantee that he will be able to tolerate the patient's feelings. He says, 'it is here that the therapist's Weltanschauung is called upon. This takes us into a vast philosophical field which, for many,... is also a theological one' (p.96). (Here Thomas Merton's (1955) exhortation seems particularly pertinent to burnout: 'Therefore in order to give Him glory we must be quiet and humble and poor in all that we suffer, so as not to add to our sufferings the burden of a useless and exaggerated sensibility' (p.82).) Lewis (1961) had also said, 'Nobody in psychiatry can do without a philosophical background, but very often it is an implicit and not an explicit one' (p.585). Thus stated, but applied to forensic psychotherapy, in order to write this chapter, one intention had been to ask those who chose to involve themselves in the dynamic explication and treatment of such complex misery, what general philosophies had helped them sustain the commitment to work with offender patients. It was perhaps a naive hope from someone obviously near the beginning of a career to ask the elders to be so intensely personal, because these answers have not been forthcoming. Indeed, in giving his own personal account, Cox (1973c) says 'It is not for me at this time to ask other therapists how their world view influences their inner world, which inevitably comes close to that of the patients, with whom they share therapeutic space'.

It seems clear that, as well as formal training, there is no alternative but some journey to be gone through where we will begin to make discoveries for ourselves out of our own experiences and then be prepared to relearn them. It is as the retired psychiatrist, who was very familiar with the workings of the Special Hospitals said to me as a trainee, 'Young man, you'll be a lot older before you leave this hospital'. Whilst it has to be acknowledged that neither formal education nor the help of a guiding mentor can prepare one enough for some of the encounters and conscious/unconscious reactions experienced when working with serious offenders, openness to reflect on that experience should make the initiate therapist that better prepared.

Hill (1970) in considering the contribution of psychoanalysis to psychiatry stated, 'The therapist's understanding and capacity to know another's experience is based on his knowledge of his own...we can only know others "on the inside" by an act of identification; we can only know them on the outside, by acts of perception' (p.614). It is in this way that, 'The therapist faces himself as he faces his patient' (Cox 1978b). Thus the mindful struggle to know oneself because of what flourishes from what patients expose in the therapist becomes the basic cost and benefit of such work: 'Therefore the therapist is re-exposed to his own earlier experience which might include destructive hate, engulfing love, or a sense of dereliction, way-outlessness or chaos...it means that the therapist must be able to tolerate his own murderousness, sexuality or the threat of non-being'.

Margison (1987) states how, 'normally defences associated with a professional role keep these experiences at bay' (p.115). He also refers to how 'key events' in settings of intense personal threat and intense work pressure are able to reactivate highly defended areas based on 'early relationships'. 'These intense feelings are experienced as shameful, representing as they do "un-owned" aspects of the self. The difficulty in accepting such feelings is compounded by their occurrence in a setting where a "professional", competent persona is being maintained' (p.115).

Jung (1946) had previously also identified this process and recognized the therapist's fear, if not of fusion, of at least contagion:

> 'The patient, by bringing an activated unconscious content to bear upon the doctor, constellates the corresponding unconscious material in him, owing to the inductive effect which always emanates from projections in greater or lesser degree. Doctor and patient thus find themselves in a relationship founded on mutual unconsciousness'. (p.176)

Jung also anticipated the therapist's resistance to this fact by adding,

> 'One is naturally loathe to admit that one could be affected in the most personal way by just any patient. But the more unconsciously this

happens, the more the doctor will be tempted to adopt an "apotropaic" attitude…yet this lack of insight is an ill counsellor, for the unconscious infection brings with it the therapeutic possibility – which should not be under estimated – of the illness being transferred to the doctor. We must suppose as a matter of course that the doctor is the better able to make the constellated contents conscious, otherwise it would only lead to mutual imprisonment in the same state of unconsciousness'. (p.176)

To know that you have been violated in fantasy by a patient is a heavy enough burden, but to feel oneself as the patient is often too intolerable. Kottler (1986) notes that it was Freud who first suggested that therapists submit themselves for further treatment every five years because of the regressive effects caused by constant contact with patients.

The Therapist's Isolation

Psychotherapeutic work is lonely. The therapist often spends hours at a time in the company of patients with whom his or her relationships are supposedly purely professional despite the intensity of emotions that they sometimes encapsulate (Jenkins 1989). Moreover, 'Psychotherapists are often constrained in their ability to share their work with others by the confines of confidentiality' (Jenkins 1989, p.134). This professional isolation is a source of serious risk to the therapist and his own personal world:

Bennet (1987), discussing the doctor–patient relationship in clinical medicine, noted how, 'Traditionally, it is a relationship in which one person reveals all and the other does not have to reveal anything. Furthermore, the one who reveals nothing can switch the relationship on and off at will, so that he has closeness when he feels like it and solitude when he does not' (p.76). Bennet notes that this kind of doctor can come, in effect, to live through his patient, finding the clinical relationship more agreeable than the turmoil of family life. However, there are serious dangers inherent in such living at second hand:

'The power which the doctor has in these circumstances is in danger of being used to nourish him emotionally, even feeding his fantasies, sexual and otherwise, so that he has an interest in maintaining a close and dependent relationship with his patient'. (p.76)

That this can have a deadening effect on a doctor's personal and family life is also clear from Bowlby (1988) who reminds us that 'a person's whole emotional life – the underlying tone of how he feels – is determined by the state of (these) long-term, committed relationships, namely his relationship with a sexual partner, relationships with parents, and relationships with offspring' (p.80) Bowlby, perhaps alluding to the effects of these relationships on the therapist's potential stated,

'As long as they are running smoothly he is content; when they are threatened he is anxious and perhaps angry; when he has endangered them by his own actions he feels guilty; when they are broken he feels sad; and when they are resumed he is joyful'. (p.80)

It is a developmental fact that people's relationships will change and that those changes will affect the potential of the therapist. Even so there is often an expectation that the therapist must every day have the equanimity of an enlightened religious, and there is stress in deceit. Genet (1990) refers to, '[the] effort you had to make – blindly so to speak, in the darkness of the body – in order to look always the same to others and to yourself' (p.122).

THE PATIENT

On Recognizing Negative Feelings Towards the Patient

Bowlby (1988) said that in providing the patient with a secure base, 'the therapist strives to be reliable, attentive, and sympathetically responsive to his patient's explorations and, so far as he can, to see and feel the world through his patient's eyes, namely to be empathic' (p.140). It requires some honesty to admit that the sympathy and acceptance of the therapist might be compromised from the outset. There is often a tendency by therapists to depersonalize the victim of an offence by referring usually only to 'the victim' which contrasts, say, with the way police officers often refer to a murder victim by their first name. But somewhere in the background are the victims and somewhere within us there is a rage and a vengeance motive towards the wrong doer (Bromberg 1948) which can influence our own attempts as therapists to help offenders revalue their own lives. Most patients have often been rejected by their parents, their families, their communities and ultimately themselves because of what they have done. Whilst we obviously accept as an essential article of faith that therapeutic work is not about rejecting but accepting them, we still have to deal with the powerful and sometimes natural urge to reject (Karban and West 1994). It is a recognition of this vengeance motive and urge to reject which should begin to illumine those other 'little, deeply based emotions [which]…constitute a powerful influence to stimulate or retard a psychologically oriented treatment programme for wrong doers' (Bromberg 1948, p.52).

Bromberg (1948) believed that unconscious feelings dominate attitudes towards criminals. He stated, 'the normal individual expels his own hostile tendencies from consciousness, transforms them into community mores and heaps them on a scapegoat – the criminal' (p.52). More recently Mollon (1988) referred to 'a primal and universal incestuous fantasy about which we all unconsciously feel anxiety and guilt' (p.19). Mollon's (1988) statement, 'Unconsciously we are all abusers' (p.19), has echoes of Laing's (1967), 'we are all murders and prostitutes' (p.7). Such unconscious motivations, if ignored, will continue to impede our therapeutic efforts. As Bromberg (1948) has said, '…it is a primary task of psychiatric criminology to expose the resulting reaction formations which have interfered with successful management of anti-social elements in our society' (p.107). Thus, it might well be that sexual offenders are unlikely to be willing or motivated patients for individual psychotherapy; it might well be a long time before the unconscious life of such a patient begins to surface; unlike other patients he is not likely to need to impress the analyst by being a good patient and bringing useful materials, but it is probably even more important then not to collude with the patient's own rejection of himself.

Watts and Morgan (1994), in discussing the management of suicide risk, remind us how unconscious countertranference hate may give rise to well rationalized but destructive acting out by carers. Unless there is some recognition of hateful feelings towards certain patients, these feelings will be sublimated or projected elsewhere. 'Knowing which patients provoke these feelings and how staff deal with the feelings is crucial to understanding the alienation process' (p.12). They identify two components of countertransference hate: whilst malicious feelings might be harder to tolerate for the carer, they still imply a preservation of the relationship with the patient. 'The aversive impulse', on the other hand, 'tempts the carer to abandon the patient…(alienation on the ward, premature discharge, transfer) which has lethal potential' (p.13). This work has an urgent relevance for 'those patients who are hard to like' in forensic settings.

On the Effects of Listening to Violence

Those therapists that work with patients who have a bizarre fantasy life are kept constantly on the alert (Cox 1990a) since such fantasies are sometimes used as a means of rehearsal for at least a future offence and even a future killing. 'It is not surprising that it is at the threshold over which aggressive fantasy becomes aggressive activity that the therapist need forensic reorientation and reassurance' (Cox 1983, p.91). Sometimes the need for the mentor with forensic experience can appear all too urgent. It is not only the patient's feelings and fantasies that are often difficult to bear; the actual details of what they disclose can have unexpected effects, especially when they permeate the therapist's dreams. Nor does that detail need to be of gross mutilations or 'basic crimes' (Cox 1990a) to be so disturbing. Often it is the seemingly minor details that can get fixed in the mind: 'She walked towards the window and she said, "But I haven't done anything". It was just an ordinary day and then it turned into a nightmare etc…' Mahoney (1991) is very accurate when he says, 'Just as Milton Erickson could assure a departing client that "my voice will go with you" (Rosen 1982), the practitioner can be equally assured that aspects of client's life experiences will remain (and "go with") him or her' (p.357).

Abel (1983) observed how, 'the recounting and exploring of the details of such violent fantasies and atrocious acts in effect serve to surround the therapist in an emotional world of violence on top of violence'. It is no surprise that it can be very exhausting to be alert, awake, and receptive to such malevolent introjects. It has been noted how the therapist becomes invested with many assumptive roles (e.g. inadequate father, rival sister, impatient lover), 'which must co-exist alongside the firmly reality-based knowledge of the meeting of man with man, and this takes its toll upon the therapist's identity-retaining energy. It would be strange if psychotherapy was not tiring. Mining, teaching, shopping are tiring, and there is no reason why the activity of the therapist should be less so' (Cox 1973c, p.167).

On the Effects of Anxiety

Menninger (1990) states how 'the intensity of the effective interaction between the patient and the therapist sets the stage for anxiety-provoking situations in both' (p.232). He notes how the psychotherapist may use a sense of anxiety in the therapy process to signal an area that merits special attention and consideration. He cites Cox (1974):

'All psychotherapists experience anxiety and it is as much part of their professional equipment as is the surgeon's manual dexterity, and likewise, it must be used in the best way, at the best time... His (the therapist's) anxiety enables him to gauge how much of the intolerable elements within himself the patient can begin to tolerate at a particular stage in his treatment'. However, the therapist is aware that too much anxiety renders him over controlling and therapeutically impotent whereas too little anxiety borders on psychopathy.' (pp.15–16)

On Being Frightened

Working in extreme settings entails the likelihood of being very frightened not only in fantasy but in reality and, however rare, it is a dangerous kind of omnipotent defence to presume otherwise in the face of such potential unpredictability, even in a hospital or clinic setting. It is worth remarking here that it was an experience in a hospital that taught me how loud and how fast the human heart can beat. Slater's (1986) brief description of working conditions for the psychiatrist at St Quentin is a powerful even if extreme reminder. Defending oneself, however manically, against an atmosphere of fear can be exhausting. Coid (1991) has observed how most assaults on doctors and nurses occur in the early stages of their careers which reflects lack of experience as well as more contact with patients. He advises that 'unless junior members of staff are clear about the direction in which they are going, and about the overall management policy for such [aggressive] patients, their work will become increasingly stressful and demoralising and it will be difficult and unsafe for them to work with this group of patients' (pp.97–98). His chapter, 'Interviewing the Aggressive Patient', offers some very useful advice and strategies for handling potentially violent clients. It is also grounded in good sense: 'It is often forgotten that many aggressive patients are actually frightened themselves and that their aggression stems from overwhelming feelings of passivity and helplessness, with imagined fear of the destruction of their own self esteem and sometimes their own physical selves' (p.98).

Karban and West (1994) talk about, 'not amplifying the fear,' recognizing that in some instances, 'there is a certain choice between responding and not responding to fear. "I know it is there, but I try not to add to it..."' (p.142) Here, it is also worth repeating what Cox refers to as, 'the vital necessity of distinguishing between countertransference phenomena and prudential fear' (1983, p.93). In a recent assessment interview when the young powerful patient, enraged at his recent transfer from prison to Special Hospital shouted, 'The only reaction is over reaction,' the fact that anxiety can interfere with one's voice, never mind the interpretation, was adequately demonstrated. As Cox (1983) indicates, 'interpretation is not everywhere and at all times necessarily safely indicated' (see also Madden et al. 1976; Bernstein 1981; Jenkins 1989).

On the Effects of Mood

Mindful of the effects of mood on the way we perceive patients, Dumont (1993) reminds us that researchers in social cognition have shown for example that, 'when one is in a "bad mood", one is more prone to hear and encode material that is consistent with that mood than material that inspires optimism' (Bower 1981; Isen 1984) (p.199). Thus, it becomes more evident how depression and disillusionment can lead to an increase in denigrating and cynical remarks about patients. Notwithstanding the mechanisms of projective identification, 'vigilance must be exercised...in the measure that we sense ourselves under the influence of intense mood' (Dumont 1993, p.200).

The Effects of Working with Sex Offenders

In a survey of twenty-four therapists who had been working with sex offenders, Farrenkopf (1992) observed the following progression in their reactions to this type of work.

After the initial shock 'of encountering sex offenders on such a close up, personal level' a feeling of increased vulnerability and increased vigilance is often seen. Subsequently, in the next phase of professional 'mission' which includes hopes for the effectiveness of therapy, 'therapists exercise emotional repression and desensitisation'. This phase, according to Farrenkopf (1992), might last from one to five years. During the next phase these repressed emotions, feelings of anger, intolerance of 'criminal thinking errors' and a more confrontative attitude begin to appear. 'The therapist becomes less allied with the offender client and identifies more with the victim and society at large' (p.221). Anger and intolerance can culminate in a sense of resentment and thoughts of the futility of treatment. Those therapists who regain their work motivation and 'therapeutic compassion' did so by adopting, 'a more detached attitude, lower their expectations, philosophically tolerating the human dark side'. This kind of attitude adjustment was seen as a prominent survival technique by twenty-five per cent of the respondents surveyed and referred to 'a realistic detachment from client outcome or client change' (p.222), a process called 'detached concern' by Maslach (1982). Farrenkopf 1992). The fact that it is difficult to marry that detached concern with the potential of some offender patients signifies another stressor, namely that of carrying the burden of a patient's potential as if his whole future behaviour depended solely on one's intervention.

THE INSTITUTION

On Facing a Negative Work Setting

As Foucault (1965) argued, mental hospital and prison institutions, offer a mirror of what society values and devalues. A fuller discussion of the socio-logical perspective on institutions is beyond the scope of this chapter and is adequately reviewed elsewhere (Jones and Fowles 1984; Perucci 1974). However, we who face the inertia of the system are not blind to its effects on patients, and it is stressful to have to justify one's working existence in an institution that others see as necessarily repressive and punitive. It is often all too evident, as Szajnberg (1990) points out how

'The mental institution, with its too complex bureaucratic organisation, puts the patient in a position of busily figuring out the external bureaucratic organisation, rather than reflecting on his or her inner structure. Bettleheim captured this sad paradox – the patient, too disturbed to function in a complex world outside the hospital, is placed in a hospital world that is often more complex.' (p.33)

Szajnberg used Bettleheim's model of successful analysis to force the individual within an institution to ask himself what he contributed to his misery. In a successful analysis the first step that the patient often takes is reciting what evils have been done unto him by others (mother, father, siblings, and so forth). In the second step the patient says, 'Look what has become of me because of what evils have been done unto me.' In unsuccessful analysis or in parlour discussions of analysis these are the only two steps taken repeatedly, look what has been done to me because of that. Bettleheim suggests that there is an important third step to successful analysis, that is one that fosters the individuals autonomy: 'Look at what I have contributed to the outcome of my inner life' (pp.35–36).

Mittler (1984) referring to the effects of institutions on patients, notes how, 'the dead weight of the institutional routine [can] soon lead to boredom, apathy, loss of initiative and institutional neurosis, as richly described in the novel *One Flew Over the Cuckoo's Nest* as in any of the classical research studies' (p.221). Ten years on, the present reality on some special hospital wards at least does not seem so different. Wing (1993) commenting on his three hospital study of the 1960s reminds us that, 'one of the key factors in the initial superiority of the environment at Netherne was the degree to which patients were encouraged to keep active' (p.449). He also states that the reports of the various Commissions of Inquiry, 'are necessary reading for those who wish to promote good practice and avoid conditions in which neglect and cruelty can occur' (p.449). He refers to work by Mechanic (1968) and Cummings and Cummings (1956) which can elucidate some of the mechanisms whereby, 'a sub culture that suppressed dissent was being allowed to grow and flourish without being exposed to the ethos or control of the organisation more generally' (p.449). (See also Dell 1992.) Indeed, some professionals have chosen to leave forensic settings altogether, seeing the institutional abuses as so deeply entrenched that their own personal and professional survival can only continue if they go elsewhere. Clearly, the need to investigate more intensively the reasons why our penal and therapeutic institutions continue to fail those they detain, whilst at the same time working as a member of these systems, constitutes another significant stressor. At the same time, we need to be alert to the possibility that we will inevitably be drawn into the dynamic process of institutional resistance where whatever the effect of an intervention in one direction there will likely be another effect which will only serve to preserve the system's homeostasis (Milne 1984).

Gallwey (1992) discussing the psychotherapy of psychopathic disorder warns us that, 'Outcome in psychotherapy is very much bound up with the enthusiasm and skills of therapists, and if these are shaky, patients may be made worse' (p.168). He believes that, 'the key is to fit patients to therapists and to provide adequate supervision' (p.168). Whatever the perspective on transference, account must be taken of the effect of the therapist on the patient (Gallwey 1992) and *vice versa*. He also recognizes that little can be achieved, 'when there are splits within the staff group, so that attention to that common and distressing reality must precede any attempts at explorative psychotherapy, particularly with dangerous or borderline psychotic individuals' (p.168).

Hobbs (1990) advocates that the psychotherapist as consultant to an in patient psychiatric unit is in a position, because of his detachment and analytic stance, to identify and expose some of the obstructive and destructive processes which can be generated by difficult patients as well as by some staff (Menzies 1959; Main 1957). These defensive manoeuvres employed by staff against anxiety can become institutionalized and limit the emotional availability of staff. Such defences 'constitute a formidable challenge to the consultant, and will not go away (any more than will the individual defences) simply because challenged. The consultant may need to work steadily with a staff group, over long periods, to expose such processes to collective scrutiny, interpretation and modification' (Hobbs 1990, p.10). In the case of the Special Hospitals at least, where anxiety is even more intense and the resulting defensive processes more entrenched, the consultant will need to be prepared to work long and steadily indeed. 'His contribution to the maintenance of morale and therapeutic optimism in the unit will depend on his capacity to know when to be supportive and when to confront' (Hobbs 1990, p.11).

CONCLUSION

This chapter sets out some of the sources of disillusionment and depression which can develop during psychotherapeutic work with offender patients. Throughout, the requirement of supervision and training has been emphasized as a necessity. Of course an extensive literature exists on coping mechanisms, but it is up to each practitioner to ask whether his own mechanisms are active and nurturing or escapist and destructive (see for example Leiter 1991). It is, however, a shared responsibility that we continue to explore the meaning of the effects of such work:

> 'The doctor knows – or at least he should know – that he did not choose this career by chance; and the psychotherapist in particular should clearly understand that psychic infections, however superfluous they seem to him, are in fact the predestined concomitants of his work, and thus fully in accord with the instinctive disposition of his own life. This realisation also gives him the right attitude to his patient. The patient then means something to him personally, and this provides the most favourable basis for treatment.' (Jung 1946, p.177)

Special Challenges

II · 15

Sex Offending and Perversions

Collaborative Strategies for Sex Offenders in Secure Settings

Peter Lewis & Derek Perkins

SEXUAL OFFENDING

There has been a dramatic change in public attitudes towards sexual offending over the last twenty years. The influence of the women's movement in raising public awareness (see Herman 1990) plus increased attention to sex offending within the police, judicial and penal systems have played their part.

Treatment programmes for sex offenders tend to be directed primarily towards adult male perpetrators of child sexual abuse, both within and outside family settings, and adult male sexual aggressors against women. Sexual abuse perpetrated by women and young people is also becoming increasingly recognized. However, treatment in secure settings tends to be primarily concerned with adult male offenders, and it is on this group that this chapter focuses.

The primary purpose of sex offender treatment is to reduce levels of victimization in society. Second, treatment should aim to help the offender to live as free and satisfying a life as possible. Within these two broad principles, treatment initiatives can be considered in the various parts of the system through which sex offenders pass, including the prison, probation and social services, as well as the psychiatric and psychological services, which are increasingly called upon to become involved in such work.

COLLABORATIVE STRATEGIES WITH SEX OFFENDERS

One of the authors (PSL) has practised as psychodynamic psychotherapist at Broadmoor Hospital for over twenty years and has learned that whilst psychodynamic psychotherapy can play an important part in the treatment of the sex offender it cannot be the sole mode of treatment since there are defects and deficiencies in the development of thinking, feeling and behaviour which frequently require additional complementary and supplementary therapeutic and educational inputs to enhance changes in the areas of cognition, emotion and conation.

The other author (DEP) is a forensic clinical psychologist who has worked with sex offenders for over twenty years in a predominantly behavioural, and latterly cognitive-behavioural way, in prison, in the community, often in conjunction with forensic psychiatric and probation colleagues, and over the last eight years in Broadmoor Hospital.

We have both come firmly to the view that collaborative strategies in the context of multi-disciplinary work, with psychiatric, psychological, nursing, social work, occupational and educational input, are imperative in the diagnosis, clarification and resolution of the difficulties that underlie sexual aggression.

TREATMENT IN SECURE SETTINGS

The extent to which society deals with sex offenders by custody varies according to the offence committed. Most men convicted of rape can expect to receive a custodial sentence, whilst most of those convicted for indecent exposure will receive a non-custodial disposal. However, if sexual offences which would not normally receive a custodial disposal persist, the courts may eventually resort to custodial disposals in order to protect the public (Howard League 1985).

Approximately one per cent of indictable offences known to the police are sexual and about five per cent of the prison population are sex offenders. Imprisonment alone appears ineffective in helping most offenders change their behaviour. In some cases it makes matters worse, for example by exposing offenders to people with even more deviant attitudes and interests than their own.

A small minority of convicted sexual offenders are classified as mentally disordered (usually psychopathic disorder) under the terms of the Mental Health Act 1983 and may as a result be hospitalized in a regional secure unit, which provides treatment in medium security, or indeterminately in a Special Hospital, which provides treatment in maximum security. Even the most uncooperative sex offender in a secure psychiatric hospital will generally come to see that unless his problems are addressed he will not progress.

ASSESSMENT ISSUES

The identification of persons who could be classified as sex offenders may be hidden under the heading of homicide or manslaughter or even on occasions under the heading of arson or burglary. The context of offending requires clarification (see McGrath 1976).

For effective treatment, the early identification of psychosexual pathology is essential. The complexity of psycho-socio-sexual difficulties requires a comprehensive family history including patterns of reward and sanction, details of earlier childhood difficulties and behavioural patterns, together with full details of the offending behaviour from the offender and from independent sources such as depositions.

A clear narrative description obtained as soon as possible after offending will inform the treatment process more effectively than if left until later, when it might be subject to rationalization and retrospective falsification. Attendance at the trial might be helpful in this respect. Other current information such as newspaper articles may convey aspects of the victim's distress and the degree of public outrage which may be of value in later therapeutic interventions, particularly those related to issues of denial and victim empathy.

It is often possible to have direct contact with those involved with the offender at the time of the index offence as well as seeing the offender's usual living conditions and environment. This can provide a useful picture of the mode of life and relevant factors such as proximity to schools, or playgrounds. Interviews with relatives can also be helpful but may be a delicate issue, particularly where family members are also victims.

A family history, extending to grandparents and significant others, should be taken. Dysfunctional family features such as rigidity, secrecy, isolation, denial, can alert to the likelihood of important sexual features somewhere within the family. The history of offending may reveal a repetitive pattern of abusive relationships and loose intra-family boundaries.

Within the family setting it is important to understand the relationship of the offender to both the mother and the father. Many individuals might not have clear recollections of these relationships because of their experience of being taken into care. Elicitation of the memories of relationships, friendships or lack of them 'in care' can reveal pointers to the origins of egocentricity, impulsivity, promiscuity or other aberrant behaviours.

The pattern of general offending and alcohol/drug taking is also often relevant. Burglaries might have been the excuse to enter the house when there had been a fantasy of rape in mind. Acts of aggression towards women or children may conceal sexual motivation. Theft of garments might also raise the suspicion of underlying sexual motivation. It is now well established that a history of both sexual and violent offences, and a pattern of victimizing both males and females is indicative of increased risk of re-offending.

The developmental history of the socialization process requires investigation, particularly family and peer group relationships, and early sexual awareness, interests and experiences. An essential part of this history should contain:

(1) Sexual orientation.

(2) The origins of the offender's sexual knowledge,

(3) The presence or absence of sexual abuse.

(4) The offender's first awareness of his sexuality.

(5) Age at which the offender first observed or heard about other persons' sexual behaviour.

(6) The first awareness of some degree of sexual arousal and the context in which this took place.

(7) The first awareness of erections and nocturnal emissions.

(8) The age of first solitary masturbation and experience of orgasm. The context and content of this experience.

(9) The first sexual experience with another person, and who that person was.

(10) The first onset of sexual fantasies, their progression over time and the current content of sexual fantasy.

(11) The experience of exposure to pornography and whether pornography is incorporated into the offender's personal sexual life.

Assessment of the 'index offence' attempts to obtain as comprehensive a description as possible of all the factors which may illuminate motivational dynamics. These include the environmental, social and behavioural context and antecedent patterns of the behaviour leading to the offence. This information may also inform later decisions about eventual placement on discharge, taking into account environmental stresses and the potential for re-offending.

The occupational history may have a bearing in patterns of sexual offending, for example whether there was contact with women or children may be important. Types of leisure activity which might have brought the offender into contact with potential victims should also be elicited, for example organizing youth groups or babysitting circles.

Following admission to hospital or prison, the relationship between the offender and the nurse or prison officer, respectively, allows information concerning the offender's personality and sexuality to be understood. Careful observation when carrying out routine duties often reveals traits within the offender relevant to offending behaviour, including styles of behaviour such as bullying, the capacity for coercion or the lack of assertion. The routine compilation of a property list or the observation of the offender's room can reveal personal possessions and literature which indicate problems of sexual adjustment.

Contact and discussion between the offender and care staff, both informally and in the more formal setting of group work, together with observations on how, and with whom he associates on the ward/wing and at social gatherings, increases the ability of staff to answer questions such as:

(1) What is the offender's perception of any previous treatment he has received?

(2) Is there any indication that the offender has been sexually abused and by whom?

(3) What appear to be the offender's sexual preferences?

(4) What are the offender's current sexual activities?

(5) What sort of sexual material does the patient seem interested in?

(6) Are there unusual features past or present which may help with treatment?

TREATMENT ISSUES

Early therapeutic work with sex offenders tended to emphasize understanding how the sex offender's behaviour had developed and gave therapeutic predominance to insight-developing psychotherapy. Later work, recognizing the limitations in this approach, focused more on identifying and modifying current behaviour patterns, referred to as 'cycles of offending'. Each approach on its own has limited effectiveness. Treatment incorporating both approaches is the most likely path to success.

Feldman (1977) distinguished between factors related to offence acquisition, in childhood and adolescence, and offence maintenance, within the offender's current environment. Information is required on both the acquisition and maintenance phases of offending. Factors which lead to the acquisition of sex offending may be quite different from those which maintain subsequent cycles of offending.

Early behavioural treatment of sex offenders tended to be too simplistic, often focusing exclusively on either deviant sexual orientation or inadequate social skills. Whilst both of these issues are relevant to many offenders, each alone will be insufficient to set up a comprehensive behavioural treatment programme.

It is important that sex offender treatment is both:

comprehensive – bringing together all (acquisition and maintenance) factors responsible for the offender's behaviour, and setting in motion an appropriately tailored set of effective interventions to deal with these, and

relevant – to offending behaviour. Each treatment target should be related to the analysis of the offender's case. Unless a particular deficiency, such as a lack of social skills, is instrumental in the offending cycle (e.g. by handicapping achievement of consenting adult relationships), then it may be not only irrelevant to treat it, but counter-productive to do so: a sadistically-orientated but socially inhibited indecent assaulter could become 'treated' to become a more socially confident rapist.

For an understanding of the factors maintaining an offender's behaviour, the method of 'multi-modal functional analysis' is particularly relevant – the A-B-C method. The offender's offence behaviour (B) is analyzed in terms of its immediate antecedents (A) and its consequences (C). This highlights the *functions* that the offending fulfils for the offender, eg revenge or relieving stress, on the various *multi-modal* levels of his functioning, which require treatment.

For sex offenders, particularly relevant *multi-modal* aspects of functioning are:

- *behavioural*, i.e., what the offender and others were doing at the time of the offence
- *cognitive*, i.e., thoughts (or 'self talk') in the offender's mind before, during and after the offending
- *attitudinal*, i.e., what attitudes held by the offender were in the forefront of his mind at the time of his offending
- *emotional*, i.e., how the offender was feeling before, during and after his offending – angry, depressed etc.
- *physical condition*, i.e., the physical state of the offender at the time of his offending, eg affected by drink, drugs, hunger or lack of sleep
- *personal relationships*, i.e., how the offender was relating to other people before and after his offending
- *sexual interests*, i.e., whether the offender is more (or less) sexually aroused by the offence behaviour as compared with any alternative consenting adult sexual behaviour,
- *opportunities* for offending inherent in his lifestyle or which he might create for himself.

In addition to its use within a functional analysis, multi-modal analysis is also useful as a linking system between information from the developmental history (acquisition phase) and the cycle of offending (maintenance phase). Some themes in the acquisition phase, for example habitually hostile appraisals of others' motives, may also be relevant in the maintenance of offending, for example feeling 'put down' by, and vengeful towards women before committing offences.

Antecedents and consequences of offending, on the various levels of multi-modal analysis, each represent a potential focus for therapeutic input. 'Vicious circles' can be identified, for example an offence antecedent of social isolation might also become an offence consequence. Breaking such vicious circles can be an important therapeutic objective.

Information for such assessments can be gathered by a combination of:

(1) Documentary evidence already on record, for example school records, previous psychiatric reports and deposition material such as witness statements.

(2) Information from interviewing the offender, using various techniques developed for the purpose of gaining the offender's cooperation, eliciting information and counteracting denial and minimisation.

(3) Psychological tests, a variety of which have been developed to assess functions such as intelligence, personality, attitudes and current skills or states such as social skills and anger, and

(4) Psychophysiological assessments of the offender's physical responses to various kinds of sexual and aggressive stimuli.

(5) Observation of the offender's behaviour and interactions by the various members of the multi-disciplinary treatment team treating the offender.

TREATMENT TECHNIQUES

The ultimate aim of most reported work on sex offender treatment is a reduction in the dangerousness and/or frequency of sex offending after treatment compared with that which would have pertained without treatment. We now consider some therapeutic techniques under the three broad headings:

Psychodynamic

Cognitive–behavioural

Medication

Psychodynamic Approach

Psychotherapy for the sex offender tends to be eclectic, but retains an emphasis on psychic determinism, the significance of unconscious motivation, and the importance of the degree to which an individual has the capacity to form and sustain successful object-relationships (the capacity to relate to other persons with warmth, concern, respect and affection).

The psychodynamic task is complicated, many layered and prolonged. In both group and individual sessions the therapist pays careful attention to the structuring of time, depth and mutuality in order to facilitate the process of disclosure. In the task of reaching a psychological understanding of what happened, how it happened and for what reason it happened the patient has to recognize and own aspects of the self that are distanced and hidden (see Cox 1979).

Group therapy is an important and essential contributory treatment modality for the sex offender. There are distinct advantages because it amplifies the phenomenon of universality ('we are all in the same boat'). This contributes significantly to the reduction of denial, a characteristic of the sex offender.

Psychodynamic psychotherapy allows for the 'working through' of significant issues many times over and enables the offender to see how the characteristics of his behaviour are manifest in many areas of his life. Work done in psychodynamic psychotherapy links with those issues which are embraced under the term 'multi-modal analysis', offering an opportunity for thorough, repeated discussion.

The phenomenon of 'resonance' whereby the discussion of a particular experience for one offender activates thoughts previously withheld or not yet recollected by another offender permits discussion of individual styles of behaviour and will inevitably address the styles of offending.

The analysis and synthesis of previous life events enables the offender to learn by his and others' experience: the process allows and facilitates what is unconscious and unremembered to become conscious and remembered, helping to prevent the repetitious behaviour which is often motivated by unconscious drives.

Psychodynamic psychotherapy also requires the offender to develop the capacity to think, not only of his own needs but of the effects that each individual's actions have on other persons, as well as developing a capacity for concern for the other, especially when the offender examines his relationship to his victim whom he had previously treated as a 'thing' rather than as a person.

Studies in object relationships imply that individuals are constantly reworking old relationships. The role and relevance that they have had in the current and recent past behaviour can be understood.

Frequently revealed in therapy is that offenders' primary relationships, that is, relationships with parents, frequently the mother, are often disappointing and rejecting. This has led to an unexpressed anger and rage in childhood years. This becomes repressed and unconscious, and primes the individual with a wish for revenge for the rejecting process and towards the rejecting individual. In adult life the offender frequently reacts within his adult relationships or desired relationships with degrees of failure. This leads to a reactivation of the feelings of rejection, an upsurge of repressed revenge which motivates a wish for some retribution in the present for past hurts. The relative 'inferiority' which the individual feels at this time in relationship to a female person causes him to wish to reverse this reality and restore his 'masculine superiority'. This frequently culminates in the act of offending in which the female person is humiliated and the offender feels vindicated and superior. Frequently, offenders have experienced significant physical and/or sexual abuse from parental figures which 'models' a trend to aggressive, inconsiderate, unempathic behaviour which is then re-enacted in later adult life. (see Lewis 1990, 1991b).

Concomitant with the exposition of these psychodynamics underlying the offences comes a degree of rationalization based on many cognitive distortions which reinforce the offender's view of events. Subsequently, the realization that the primary carer, that is, the mother, did not intentionally, deliberately or maliciously behave in the hurtful way which the offender perceives them to have behaved, allows for rapprochement, whereby the offender begins to understand the difficulties that existed for the carer and the consequent deficiencies that occurred in the primary relationship. Thus, the offender no longer blames his early relationships and allows a forgiving process to take place. The relinquishment of the blaming tendency facilitates assumption of personal responsibility.

The offender begins to examine the idea of negotiating new relationships as new in their own right, avoiding the repetition of the previous maladaptive behaviour which caused him to see most women and act towards them as if they were the female persons of his previous experience. These phenomena would have continually reactivated the offending behaviour.

The individual discovers the importance of learning about his own 'self' (see Cox 1973b). The development of awareness of other persons is discovered to be important in relationships. The awareness that these persons cannot be treated like objects facilitates the discussion of empathy for the victim. Thus future relationships may be carried on at a more 'personal' level rather than at a level which disregards the humanity of the other person.

Group psychotherapy affords the 'public acknowledgement' of the offence behaviour. Because the other persons in the group are accepting of the individual, this facilitates the individual's experience of shame. Shame enables the individual offender to have a heightened awareness of the future consequences of his actions. The group acts as a vehicle for acceptance, understanding and caring which aids the corrective emotional experience. The containing atmosphere allows the individual to redefine himself as a person with more options (see Lewis 1991a).

Out of the group may spring ideas on which more specific individual treatment initiatives may be based, whether these be behavioural or cognitive.

Because unconscious motivation becomes recognized consciously during the treatment process, unremembered phenomena become accessible, for use in dynamic and cognitive–behavioural therapy. In this way psychodynamic psychotherapy can be seen as complementary to other initiatives and allows these ideas to be worked through repetitively.

Cognitive–Behavioural Approach

The cognitive–behavioural approach to the treatment of sex offenders focuses on current patterns of sex offending behaviour which are seen as the interaction between previously learned responses, in childhood and adolescence, and current environmental contingencies, such as social stressors or risks of apprehension.

The specific treatment techniques employed with institutionalized sex offenders can be broadly categorized in terms of the goals they seek to achieve, as follows:

(1) Increasing motivation and decreasing denial

It is well established that sex offenders often show limited motivation to change deviant behaviour, thinking and sexual orientation. Linked to this, there may be denial of the facts of their offending ('I only committed one offence'), denial of their responsibility ('she provoked me') and denial of its serious consequences ('she'll soon get over it').

Techniques have been developed to enable the therapist to negotiate with, and persuade the offender to reconsider this position and see the full benefits of engaging in therapy (see Perkins 1991). Sometimes referred to as motivational interviewing, such techniques are central to engaging with, and maintaining ongoing commitment from the offender as he passes through the institution.

(2) Modifying deviant sexual interests

Treatment at the level of sexual interests involves decreasing deviant, and increasing non-deviant interests. Identifying which offenders require such interventions in order to avoid future offending is one of the most important decisions in planning treatment. Some offenders are primarily aroused by the content of their offending, fantasizing and masturbating about it in private. Others are, however, primarily aroused by non-offending sexual scenarios but offend due to a lack of confidence, skill and opportunity for consenting sexual relationships.

Successful outcomes in modifying sexual interests have been reported for variations of aversion therapy, in which visual or auditory material depicting or prompting deviant images is systematically paired with unpleasant consequences; satiation therapy in which the offender masturbates to orgasm over non-deviant imagery but then continues masturbating to deviant material over a lengthy period of time; and orgasmic reconditioning in which the offender systematically replaces deviant for non-deviant imagery during masturbation (see Marshall, Laws and Barbaree 1990; Perkins 1991).

(3) Developing appropriate socio-sexual behaviour

Both group and individual social skills training for sexual offenders has been reported. Rehearsal of, and feedback on role-played social interactions relevant to the offender's behaviour patterns together with coaching and modelling by the therapists are the central features of this approach. Sex education has also been used in both the prison and hospital settings by a number of workers who have noted the lack of sexual knowledge of many sex offenders (see Grounds et al., 1987).

(4) Modifying deviant or distorted attitudes, beliefs and thinking

Sex offenders often display anti-social attitudes or distorted cognitions which pre-date and contribute to the development of their offending behaviour ('If I don't take what I want in this life, I'll never get any pleasure') and/or serve to reinforce offending behaviour ('Women are only after my money and deserve to be used for my sexual gratification'). Programmes of systematically assessing and challenging these distorted ideas have proved to be an important component to behaviour change.

(5) Enhancing victim empathy

For some sex offenders, the persistence of their offending is attributable in part to their lack of understanding of what offending means for victims or a lack of concern about these effects. In the case of the former, therapy aimed at putting the offender 'in the victim's shoes', including reading/hearing/seeing the victim perspective through books, tapes or role playing can be effective.

(6) Relapse prevention

Sex offenders leaving treatment programmes often put themselves into risky situations through a combination of general life style deficiencies (living in situations high in anxiety and stress but low in legal pleasures and satisfactions) and engaging in what are termed 'seemingly irrelevant decisions' or SIDs ('I'll take a short cut through the park – and playground – to save money on the bus fares'). These SIDs, about which the offender may have only partial insight, lead him closer and closer to situations in which self-control over sex offending is reduced and offences recur.

Sex offender treatment programmes are increasingly recognizing the need to build relapse prevention into therapy, well in advance of its termination and ideally at the point at which the offender has begun to recognize that he has a problem and is becoming committed to the idea of tackling it. A combination of awareness raising and skills training techniques to help the offender avoid SIDs and high risk situations can be helpful in preventing relapse (see Laws 1990).

Anti-libidinal Medication

Most sex offenders commit their offences for motives other than just sexual gratification, and simply reducing the libido for these offenders will not necessarily be sufficient to control their offending. Although anti-libidinal medication early in the treatment process may be helpful in dampening down the offender's sexual urges, it can also cause the offender to continue denying the full range of his problems. Because his sexual interests and urges have become suppressed, it can lead the offender to believe that the problem no longer exists.

In summary, medication can be useful in suppressing sexual urges where these are central to the offending behaviour, but can, depending on the individual offender, either increase or decrease his accessibility to alternative interventions. The main problems with this procedure are ethical (where the procedure is irreversible or where there is a high probability of unwanted side effects such as thrombosis).

MULTI-DISCIPLINARY COLLABORATION

There is a broad range of therapies relevant to the sex offender including counselling, dynamic and cognitive–behavioural therapies, provided individually or in groups, by staff from within the medical, nursing, psychology, social work and rehabilitation disciplines.

At Broadmoor Hospital, staff providing treatment for sex offender patients do so within the context of each patient's multi-disciplinary treatment plan, coordinated by the Consultant Forensic Psychiatrist. The three main parameters within which treatment services at Broadmoor Hospital are contained are, therefore:

(1) The type of treatment.

(2) The profession/discipline of the therapist.

(3) The level of competence/experience of the therapist in the particular type of treatment.

This can be diagrammatically represented as follows.

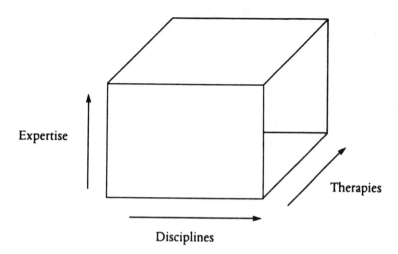

A comprehensive programme of sex offender assessment and treatment run along broadly cognitive-behavioural lines and involving different professional groups has now been operating within the British prison system since 1990 and is currently being evaluated.

At Grendon Prison a form of therapy, called psychoeducational therapy addresses the cognitive and affective domains in the hope that this will lead to recognition of inconsistencies, denying attitudes, contradictions, patterns of psychosexual responses, unprofitable forms of emotional reaction, susceptibilities and lead to challenges of cognitive disorders. This therapy is aimed at being reconstructive, learning by recognising maladaptive response patterns in the hope that there will be reversal of deviant and repetitive behaviours, providing insight into subconscious conflicts decoding subliminal messages, confronting attitudes or avoidance, denial and negativism.

Although psychoeducational therapy combined with psychodynamic psychotherapy is a new technique used in Grendon, the therapeutic milieu of a therapeutic community coupled with regular group therapy has been a significant approach to sexual offenders since the early 1960s in the United Kingdom. This psychoeducational therapy gives a much more specific breakdown of the necessary issues that are required to be addressed with the sexual offender and does prevent the significant avoidance mechanisms which sexual offenders practice both to deceive themselves and others.

Quayle (1989) at Broadmoor reports, in the context of multi-disciplinary working, on the use of a series of groups for young adult male patients diagnosed as suffering from 'psychopathic disorder', many of whom have committed sex offences or sexually motivated acts of violence. Patients progress, from basic social skills training groups, into groups, in which they take part in exercises like 'family sculpting' (to uncover and work on past family relationships) and reverse role-playing (in which they come to see their past offending behaviour through the eyes of their victims).

STAFF ISSUES

Any interaction with sexual offenders may induce complex feelings in members of the treatment team. Frequently, powerful feelings of revulsion and anger occur when hearing of distasteful acts committed by the offender. If staff are not adequately supervised and supported, it is possible that these strong, induced feelings may cause actions to be taken which are counterproductive to the progress of therapy, at the professional level, and, if unrecognized, may give rise to some significant stress symptoms, at the personal level.

It should be emphasized that these transferential and countertransferential reactions do not solely occur in the psychodynamic interaction but in interventions of any therapeutic kind. Thus, there are important implications for close collaboration, sensitivity and awareness so that all members of the multidisciplinary team can provide a supportive context where these evoked feelings can be recognised, understood and accepted. These feelings may be based on prejudice or on reactivation of uncomfortable/unpleasant scenarios in the therapists' life experiences.

Among the methods which may be helpful in dealing with this are:

(1) regular peer group meetings to air and share feelings about the work,

(2) access to specialist supervision/consultancy dealing with treatment techniques and processes,

(3) joining multi-disciplinary 'special interest' groups on the treatment of sexual offenders within and between agencies

(4) developing and promoting practise guidelines derived from clinical experience in working with sex offenders.

CONCLUSION

The themes developed in the chapter echo and develop the conclusions of a multi-disciplinary working party on sex offenders assessment and treatment at Broadmoor Hospital which had representatives from the disciplines of social work, nursing, dynamic psychotherapy and clinical psychology (Lewis *et al.*, 1992). We acknowledge the contributions of our colleagues on the Working Party whose informed discussion and contribution enabled us to bring together our ideas of collaborative services for the sex offender.

Amongst the key recommendations which we have discussed in this chapter are:

- The need for early identification of sexually related offending.

- The need to address offender denial.

- The need to stress the offender's active engagement in therapy.

- The need to address the full range of problems and needs presented by the sex offender.

- The need to anticipate future difficulties by way of a specific relapse prevention programmes.

- The need to ensure multi-disciplinary collaboration in offender assessment and treatment within the institution

- The need to ensure appropriate therapist support and supervision.

- The need to ensure that no sex offender will be recommended for transfer or discharge from the hospital without successful and active participation in assessment and treatment.

- The need for subsequent coordination with after-care facilities.

The Out-Patient Treatment
of the Sex Offender

Friedemann Pfäfflin

VARIATIONS OF SEX OFFENCES AND TREATMENTS

The title of this chapter might foster the notion that sex offenders constitute a relatively homogeneous class of people. However, the only common denominator they share is that they are judged socially and/or legally as persons who have broken laws or other social norms concerning sexual behaviour. There is a great variety in what is judged a sexual offence, depending on what kind of norms are applied; for example, statistical, moral, health-related, or legal norms.

These norms may change within very short periods of time. The following examples illustrate this. According to statistical norms, auto-fellatio, albeit not a legal offence, is a deviant behaviour, because there are only three in 10,000 men who practice it (or rather, are able to perform it, because, just as with other acrobatics, it requests continuous training from early childhood onwards). Masturbation was, for a long period, one of the most severe sins, whereas today it is rather felt unusual if somebody has never practised it. Adultery, most probably a widespread behaviour even in times when it used to be a crime, was cancelled from the German Penal Code in the early 1970s, as was bestiality. Homosexual behaviour between adult men is now accepted as an alternative mode of life, while fifty years ago, in this country, it could cost a life sentence or even death penalty. For transsexuals, formerly not differentiated from homosexuals and legally treated in a similar way, a number of European countries have passed laws legalizing sex-change, and the European Court for Human Rights in Strasbourg in 1992 even sentenced France to financial compensation for a French citizen who had been denied a legal sex-change by

French authorities, having had sex reassignment surgery abroad. This should be kept in mind when considering psychological and medical treatment measures for sex offenders.

Apart from the historical variation, there is also a wide range as to the damage that is caused by sexual offences. There are violent sexual behaviours that are harmful to others, and some of them are not even condemned by the law (e.g. in the German Penal Code, rape is defined as coercive *extra*-marital intercourse, and the law does not protect spouses in the same manner as it does other women); and there are other behaviours which, according to the law, are 'crimes against sexual self-determination' (e.g. exhibitionism), yet do not have sustained negative effects on prospective victims.

For the most part, sex offenders are usually seen by psychiatrists (and very few psychotherapists) in the context of the criminal justice system, when they are evaluated for the court. Once sentenced to imprisonment – depending on their previous legal history and the severity of their offence – they have almost no chance of getting treatment in prison. If the offender is judged by the court as not fully responsible for his act according to criteria defined in the Penal Code, and/or if he is expected to remain dangerous to others, the court may transfer him to a psychiatric institution. The kind of treatment he will get there mainly depends on the philosophy of the director of such an institution and the training of the doctor in charge of the patient. There are tremendous regional, inter- and intra-institutional differences in the availability of psychotherapy. Only in less severe cases, such as exhibitionism, or first convictions for other sexual offences in less severe cases, will the perpetrator be granted probation, and psychotherapeutic and other medical treatment measures then may be the first choice of prospective interventions. The judges thus play the key role when it comes to paving the way for psychotherapy.

Psychotherapy cannot guarantee public safety. For many years the courts preferred more drastic treatment measures as alternatives to imprisonment, the most archaic of these being *surgical castration*. It is estimated that this was performed in Nazi-Germany on approximately 3000 sex offenders, mainly involuntarily by court order. It was quasi-voluntary for homosexuals. After the war, so called voluntary castration for all kinds of sex offenders was continued. Although applying for and getting it was not a guarantee, it was often a prerequisite for being released from prison or detention in a psychiatric ward. When, in 1969, a new castration law was passed with stricter regulations, this practice was increasingly abandoned, and it is now applied only in extremely rare cases. This is certainly due to a shift of attitudes towards more liberal views, but it should not be forgotten that the decline of surgical castration was parallelled with the introduction and widespread application of *anti-androgens*, namely cyproterone-acetate (Androcur, produced by Schering), a drug which reversibly suppresses testicular function and the intake of which (injection of a depot) allows control. This drug has less feminizing side-effects compared to other hormones, but it was not cleared by the Federal Drug Administration (FDA), so that in Anglo-American countries *other hormones* (e.g. medroxy-pro-gesterone-acetate, Provera) as well as various psychopharmacological substances are preferred. (In August 1994 cyproterone was implicated in the causation of liver cancer in experimental animals, and this is now under scrutiny by the Federal Bureau for Drug Admission in Germany.) Although there are almost no controlled studies on the preventive effects of Androcur as regards the frequency of relapses, and although it is generally agreed that it should only be given in combination with psychotherapy, courts and many doctors tend to rely more on the drug than on verbal (psychotherapeutic) interventions. Misuse and blind application are common. As an aside it may be mentioned that in the 1960s and 1970s even *stereotactic brain surgery* was carried out as an experiment on about seventy patients in different German institutions, but this was abandoned soon after the German Society for Sex Research had protested (Schmidt and Schorsch 1981).

Today it is generally agreed that psychotherapy is of paramount significance for the rehabilitation of sex offenders. Psychiatric experts in court often recommend psychotherapy, and judges willingly join that recommendation or even include in their sentences mandatory psychotherapy. Due to the high recidivism rate of sex offenders, such recommendations, however, have lost much of their value, and scepticism as to the effectiveness of psychotherapy is gaining ground. When investigating the background of this development one is confronted with difficulties on the sides of all parties involved: patients, therapists, juridical system and society. Before discussing details of treatment, it seems, therefore, necessary to discuss obstacles which prevent the very onset of treatment.

OBSTACLES FOR GETTING STARTED

When reading psychoanalytic literature and case studies one is impressed by the enthusiasm with which the authors focus on the perverse phantasies of their patients, interpret and understand the function of such phantasies for the patients' psychic equilibrium and stability. In contrast, they hesitate to take patients into treatment once the threshold between phantasies and acted-out behaviour has been overstepped. Such deeds frighten. They may be seen as signs of lack of impulse-control, and most psychotherapists have little or no experience with such patients. Obviously, it is often difficult for a sex offender to find a psychotherapist who is willing to start therapy under a court order. Sex offences, understood by therapists as acting out inner conflicts, do not recommend these patients who ostensibly do not experience these conflicts intra-psychically or, at least, did not have enough motivation to seek psychotherapy before having committed the offence. Some psychotherapists will not accept such patients, and they doubt their motivation when they come only under pressure of feared or actual sanctions or when they are sent by the court. They assume that the combination of momentary pleasure and offensive act precludes the offensive behaviour from being accessible to change by insight because the pleasure experienced will reinforce the patient's longing for its repetition and, finally, they might fear for the reputation of their private practice and that they will be sued if the therapy fails. They do not want to be involved in court cases, do not want to give expert witness, do not want to be instrumentalized, either by courts, or by patients. In their view, psychotherapy has to concentrate on the intra-psychic world of the patient, and every direct intervention would be incompatible with that aim.

Patients, on the other hand, often also feel uneasy when 'sentenced' to therapy. Much more than from the sexual deviation they consciously may suffer from the social consequences of having been caught (e.g. social exposure, loss of job and partner). What they seek primarily is practical help. They may see the therapist as a representative of the institutions condemning or persecuting them, especially in cases where they experience their sexual deviant behaviour ego-syntonically, which is often so with paedophiles, and they may meet the therapist with great mistrust.

Therapists should reflect their own prejudices as well as try to understand the patient's reservations against therapy. It is no use, when the therapist teams up with the patient against the court or society, or when he plays down or denies the fact that patient and therapist are dependant on outside forces. Nor should the therapist blame the patient for lack of motivation, or ignore the patient's scepticism by acting out social control in the guise of therapy by, for instance, devoting himself to rigorous removal of the symptom using equally strict techniques. Instead, he should open a space for the patient, allowing the opportunity of conjointly exploring the patient's distress. To create motivation for treatment will thus in many cases in itself be an important achievement in therapeutic work.

PRINCIPLES OF PSYCHOTHERAPY

The *somatic treatments* for sex offenders mentioned above (castration, stereotactic brain surgery, hormonal and anti-androgens) are based on a monocausal conception of sexual deviancy. The same is true for the early models of *behavioural therapy*, namely the one-dimensional therapy studies which focused exclusively on the removal of the deviant behaviour without considering its etiology or meaning. Various techniques were applied to pursue that aim, for example symptom-focused methods (e.g. aversive conditioning, shame aversion therapy, covert sensitization, negative exercise, biofeedback, self-management methods). Other techniques did not exclusively focus on the deviant behaviour but aimed at developing additional skills simultaneously (e.g. conditioning sexual arousability with nondeviant stimuli, systematic desensitization of social and sexual anxieties and increasing social skills, sex therapy, and couple therapy). The dissatisfaction with the results of most of these studies led to the development of a multi-dimensional behavioural approach in which two or more areas of disturbance were examined and tackled with corresponding techniques.

Reducing sexual deviations to deviant sexual arousability and tracing back their origin to the incidental coupling of sexual arousal to neutral stimuli is certainly too simple a model. Not exploring the meaning and function of paraphilic symptoms handicaps the definition of appropriate therapy goals and is an invitation arbitrarily to apply therapeutic techniques in order to reduce deviant behaviour.

On the other hand, psychoanalytic theory and *psychodynamic therapy* have drawn most of their insights from highly selected patients with sexual deviant phantasies who, usually, were treated for their distress with their perversions, but not for delinquent behaviour. Such phantasies will pass away once their function for the individual's psychological equilibrium has been properly understood and alternative models for solving inner conflicts have been developed.

Important contributions to the psychodynamic theory of deviations are Stoller's (1975, 1979) writings *Perversion: The Erotic Form of Hatred*, and *Sexual Excitement*, which emphasize that perverse rituals can be seen as re-enactments of childhood traumata undertaken in an attempt to transform tragedy into triumph (Money 1986). In patients who have already drawn satisfaction from acting out deviant phantasies, understanding and interpreting may, however, not be enough, and analysts may have overemphasized for a long time the meaning of deviant phantasies and behaviours while neglecting the development of techniques promoting change.

Instead of playing off the behavioural against the psychodynamic approach, or *vice versa*, it seems much more useful to integrate both approaches according to the increasing tendency towards a convergence of therapeutic methods which is documented in the results of psychotherapy research (Bergin and Garfield 1994). There is evidence of the need for an interlinking of empathic, interpreting, confronting, supportive and active-directive procedures with varied emphases, depending on the specific problems involved, provided this is backed up by a carefully considered therapeutic theory.

THREE CASES FOR ILLUSTRATION

The traumata forming the background of the sexual deviant acting out may be manifold and very diverse, even in cases with similar behaviour as seen from a juridical point of view. The symptomatic behaviour therefore may serve very different defences, the purposes of which are sometimes first experienced in the patient–therapist interaction before the specific biographical backgrounds are detected. To illustrate this, three cases, legally judged as exhibitionism, are presented.

Vignette – the first patient

The first patient was a twenty-five-year-old man who had been seen flitting around the neighbourhood at night without any clothes on. Eventually he was arrested by the police, taken to court for exhibitionism and ordered to undergo therapy. He was more a flasher than an exhibitionist. He was a big strong man, very muscular, bearded, a carpenter by trade, an imposing physical presence, yet when he talked I had the impression that he was hardly there, his voice was so quiet and what he told me about himself seemed so unimportant. By and large, he said, he led a quite normal life.

He was the youngest of four sons and still lived with his Iranian parents, who rigidly maintained their national traditions despite having lived abroad for more than twenty years. The family was run along strictly hierarchical lines. Each brother was under the thumb of the next elder one, with the eldest under the father's thumb; the mother ruled the roost, and when in doubt there was an uncle in Iran who had the last word. Everything was decided from above, what and how one should eat, where one sat at the table, what clothes one wore, and what job one took, and even whether and how each member of the family was allowed to take part in conversations.

The patient told me all this without the slightest hint of complaint or a suggestion that it might be a problem. It all seemed absolutely normal to him, just as his regular nightly excursions without clothes seemed completely inexplicable. He had no idea why I was interested in finding out about his family; this in turn was hard for me to grasp, and we talked at cross-purposes, uneasily linked only by the court's instructions and my pledge to treat him. I felt irritated and helpless, and found it hard to concentrate on what he was saying during the sessions. I regretted having taken on the case. My mind tended to wander until I finally found myself imagining the patient slipping out into the night, year in, year out, summer and winter, and sliding naked through the streets and across the parks. I imagined him shivering, his feet freezing in the snow, or the warm summer wind stroking his skin, gently caressing him. Having mentioned his naked trips in our first conversation he never talked about them again, and simply recounted daily events in a factual tone. For me, the sessions were a long drawn-out misery which I only survived with the help of these phantasies.

In our setting, the situation at home was reversed; the patient tied me down with his repetitive, apparently inconsequential remarks. It felt like being smothered in rubbish, endless trivia and accounts of good behaviour; the only way I could save my skin was by fleeing into the phantasy to join his nightly excursions naked under the stars, where I could breeze freely, be myself and actually experience pain and pleasure. His special way of behaving became intelligible, feelable. In a sense he put me through what he had suffered at home for years and what he had again undergone at the hands of the court that sent him to me. It was some time before I could communicate this to him and before he could listen without feeling I wanted to rob him of his only refuge from his suffocating family.

Vignette – the second patient

The second patient, a thirty-year-old medical student who was in his twentieth semester and still had not passed his preliminary examinations, only came to the notice of the courts after spending years with a whole series of therapists. He was brought into court for exhibitionism on five occasions, always in the same shopping arcade and always in front of the same woman. I was asked to make an assessment of him.

This description of him – a medical student in the twentieth semester (wow, that's pretty impressive) who still hasn't passed his prelims (good heavens, what a disgrace) – captures something of the bewildering mixture of magnificence and disparagement which this patient experienced and conveyed. Both aspects coloured our first encounter: the patient, armed with a hat and a stick like a dandy, came forty minutes late, did not remove his coat or sit down, waved his stick about wildly and declared in a supercilious tone that he did not have the slightest inclination to talk to me. He had run through practically all therapy programmes in the city and used up all the therapists available. None of them wanted to have anything more to do with him, not even write a report on him.

The way he entered into a new relationship was always the same: the patient introduced himself to the new therapist and assured him that he was the only person capable of helping him; at last he had found what he was looking for; all the other therapists were a dead loss and 'arseholes'. Despite all the scorn he exuded there was something fascinating and charming about him; all the therapists must have fallen prey to this approach and he despised them all the more for accepting him. He was particularly damning about the women psychologists whom he had been able to charm into varying the therapy setting: prolonged sessions, meeting outside the practice, and so on.

He was equally biting about a doctor whose group therapy he had joined and who proved unable to prevent him from showing off his penis to the other members of the group. He had managed to provoke other therapists to react sadistically: they tried out shame aversion on him by instructing him to exhibit his genitals in front of women psychology students who had been instructed how to react. Nothing helped. His triumphant response to this degradation was to change therapists again and gleefully tell them what an 'arsehole' the therapist had been who had tried this out on him.

His story revealed that as a child he had often been a voyeur and that from early puberty onwards he had taken to showing off his penis. He experienced life as a series of sexualized encounters and seemed unable to conceive any way of behaving which was not exhibitionist. He recalled a scene in childhood when his grandmother fled screaming from the room when she saw his erect penis, it was so huge and beautiful. For the previous fifteen years he had exposed himself five to ten times a day, always in different places without being caught. Occasionally he had managed to attract a woman and have intercourse with her. He had had dozens of sexual encounters but never saw a woman again.

He had gone into therapy not because he regarded showing off his penis as a problem but because he noticed that his sexual compulsions left him no time for an ordinary life. After all these therapies had failed he had finally landed with an experienced psychotherapist who refused to be taken in by him but equally felt no urge to punish him, the two reactions he knew all too well from his own family. Working with the therapist over a period of two years gave him the most reliable contact he had ever had, not too intimate, not too off-hand, and this enabled him to turn his attention for the first time to matters other than his sexual obsessions. It also had an effect on his symptom: he no longer exhibited in front of any woman in any part of town but sought women he liked in his neighbourhood and tried repeatedly to approach them; this was when he was arrested. Therapy had weakened his defence.

Vignette – the third patient

The third patient was a thirty-six-year-old man, also a carpenter, married, with a seven-year-old son. From time to time he was overcome by a deep urge to expose his penis; this was always accompanied by a profound feeling of guilt. These impulses seemed to suddenly overwhelm him, striking him quite out of the blue. One day he tried to stop two sixteen-year-old girls who had twice ridden past him on their bicycles; he felt an irresistible urge to rape them. The girls screamed, pulled themselves free and got away. The patient, whom the police had failed to catch, went to his general practitioner and was sent to me for treatment.

Apart from the information given here, he hardly managed to say anything about himself. Mostly he was completely silent, sat and stared at the floor or looked awkwardly past me. But he came regularly, once a week. I was extremely active and kept trying to find ways to get a conversation going. At the very most we spent ten or fifteen of the fifty-minute sessions actually talking to each other.

In the course of several years I gradually found out a little about his current situation, his unhappy marriage to a woman who was five years older and had physical disabilities making any sexual activity painful and unpleasant to her. On the surface the patient could accept this but he could not work out any alternatives. He gave me the impression of seething with frustration, full of pent-up rage, although outwardly he seemed calm and under control. He also talked about how difficult he found it to relate to his son and his colleagues at work. The way we sat facing each other in silence, gazing at or past each other was often extremely tense and aggressive. My attempts to put this into words brought no change of the situation, and I was often very angry with the patient who would not let me approach him.

This tension became intelligible only after I found out that he had grown up in crowded barracks where several families lived in extremely close quarters. He shared one room with his parents and his sister. There were quarrels and fights everywhere, not just in his family but, perfectly audible through the thin walls, in all the neighbouring families too, who assaulted one another verbally and physically, so that he felt utterly helpless and frightened for his own life and the lives of others. When he was as old as his son now was, his mother insisted on divorce and refused to let his father come back into the home.

He told me all this in disconnected fragments, usually just after a bout of exhibitionism, luckily without being caught by the police. Sometimes his father used to come by on a motorcycle, apparently to get a glimpse of his children; he would stop on the opposite side of the street and look up at their window. The boy's gaze met his, but there was no way of saying anything or waving, for his mother immediately noticed, marched over and intervened by pulling down the blind in front of his nose. The patient's comment on this loss of his father was: 'and that was the end of it'. But of course it wasn't. On the contrary, he harboured an immense and overpowering hatred of his mother, to whom he would have liked to 'show it', but did not dare to because of her threatening behaviour. Having told me this, the patient dreamed of splitting his mother's head with an axe. He was appalled and extremely perturbed, and felt a strong urge to exhibit his penis again. Shocked by what he had experienced in the dream, he spontaneously said he preferred to carry on being an exhibitionist.

The cases show that it is rarely possible to name a single event to which the patient reacts in erotic triumph, and even where it may be possible it may take a long time to discover that event or, at least, a screen memory of it. In addition these cases show that the meaning and function of the symptom may first be revealed by modes of the patient's acting-in within the therapeutic relationship, and sometimes by acting out outside this relationship. Very aggressive sexual deviancy is therefore hard, or even impossible, to treat in an out-patient setting. From the therapist's viewpoint these three legally similar cases are very different: with the nocturnal wanderer, therapy has to concentrate almost exclusively on narcissistic aspects, whether and how he could literally feel and be aware of himself as an individual. With the second, the dandy, it was a matter of how to enter into and maintain relationships, and with the third how to cope with immense rage; his exhibitionist behaviour protected him from doing anything worse, such as raping or murdering a woman.

RESEARCH

Reports on psychodynamic out-patient therapy with sex offenders up until now has mainly been described in single case studies. Considering the longstanding tradition of psychodynamic therapies, there is a deplorable lack of controlled studies of out-patient treatments. The latest edition of the *Handbook of Psychotherapy and Behavior Change* (Bergin and Garfield 1994) does not even touch this important field. One large sample of sex offenders was treated in an out-patient programme at the Department of Sex Research of the Psychiatric University Clinic of Hamburg, Germany (Schorsch *et al.* 1990). The team there started off with an attempt to apply a manualized programme mainly based on behaviour therapy techniques, but soon learned that this was not enough to cope with the complex phenomena and dynamics of sex offences and it incorporated more and more psychodynamic theory and supervision into its work. The results from Hamburg clearly demonstrate that patients need not be primarily motivated for therapy and even patients coming into treatment under court order can be treated successfully.

Research on risk assessment is now being conducted in large scale multi-centre studies (Monahan and Steadman 1994). Although it is stressed that managing risk as well as assessing risk must be the goal of such research, the focus of research still lies on the development of better diagnostic and prognostic instruments and on outcome research. There is not yet one multi-centre study of the treatment of sex offenders. The sophisticated methods of psychotherapy process research which have been developed during the last twenty years have not yet been applied to therapies with sex offenders (Pfäfflin, in press). There is still a lot to be done.

Contrasts in Male and Female Sexual Perversions

Estela V. Welldon

Until recently perversions have been thought of almost exclusively in relation to men. In this chapter I shall discuss this and later I shall develop my own views on the conceptualization of female sexual perversion, a field still unknown and unexplored. My views are based in the clinical work done at the Portman Clinic for the last twenty-five years.

Perversion is an accepted clinical condition in which the person afflicted does not feel free to obtain sexual genital gratification through intimate contact with another person. Instead he or she feels 'taken over' by a compulsive activity which is subjectively experienced as inexplicable and 'bizarre' but provides a release of unbearable and increasing sexual anxiety. This activity usually involves an unconscious desire to harm others or him- or herself. In this usage perversion is a technical, psychoanalytic term, and carries no moral connotations. It is preferable to use perversion rather than deviation, since the latter implies only a statistical abnormality.

By definition, perversion embraces some specific and characteristic features which correspond to a dysfunction of the sexual component of personality development. In some cases perversions may be encapsulated from the rest of the personality so that the person appears superficially to the outside world as completely normal. This is because perversion involves a deep split between genital mature sexuality as a living, or loving, force, and what appears to be sexual, but in fact corresponds to much more primitive stages of development, which are pervasively dominated by pregenitality. Achievement of intimacy with another partner through sexual intercourse – the norm – is replaced in perversion by release from increasing sexual anxiety through a bizarre action or situation which is in itself inexplicable not only to others but also to the person himself (Welldon 1988).

The 'inexplicable' action gets rid of sexual anxiety which contains aggression and an unconscious wish to hurt the other person. This overrides any desire to make use of sexual tension for the creation of intimacy in loving a partner. Therefore, those suffering from perversion make hate instead of making love.

Perversion is different from a classical neurotic or psychotic condition, although the three terms have been interlinked in the history of psychoanalytic thinking. Freud's famous axiom (1905c): 'Neuroses are the negative of perversion', was later taken up by Glover (1933) who, under the influence of Klein, suggested that perversions were the negative of psychosis. This view was supported by Mrs Klein's followers who saw perversion as a defence against psychosis. Etchegoyen (1970) considers perversion to be as much a defence against psychosis as its cause, and considers that on occasions it may be the psychosis itself. Steiner (1993a) argues that 'psychotic omnipotence is precisely what makes the enactment of perversion more likely and considers more dangerous'.

Gillespie (1940, 1956, 1964) supported Sachs's view (1923) that the splitting of the ego is the result of the conflict between the ego and the id, and considered the activity of the superego to be a fundamental mechanism in perversion. Gillespie (1956) thus supported the Kleinian viewpoint as the above mechanism is of paramount importance in understanding the association of perversion with psychosis. Mrs Klein's (1932a) theories centred on the relationships between mother and baby in the first year of life and Greenacre (1968) and Sperling (1959) have also acknowledged the importance of a disturbed relationship between mother and baby in the creation of perversions. The nature of this early relationship and the better understanding of the dynamics of the ego thus started to replace instinct theory in the understanding of perversions. Pre-Oedipal factors and the role of early disturbances in the mother–child relationship are also stressed by McDougall (1984), and Coen (1985). Mahler (1963) examines symbiosis and separation/individuation stages in normal infant development and proposes that their failure can result in perversion.

Khan's (1979) view is that perversions have a specific structure of their own related to an inability to establish a sense of intimacy. Stoller (1975) furthers this view and attaches major importance to the pervert's need to hurt, humiliate and hate the object. Chasseguet-Smirgel (1983), Greenacre (1968) and Arlow (1971) highlight the role of sadism and control of aggression in perversion. Kernberg (1991) describes perversion as 'the recruitment of love in the service of aggression – the consequence of a predominance of hatred over love' (p.153).

THE CLASSIFICATION OF PERVERSION

Freud (1905c) using instinct-theory, classified sexual perversions into two groups, according to the sexual object (e.g. paedophilia) or its aim (e.g. sado-masochism). The International Classification of Diseases (ICD) (1978) follows Freud's classification: 'The sexual activity of affected persons is directed primarily either towards people not of the opposite sex, oᵢ towards sexual acts not associated with coitus normally or towards coitus performed under abnormal circumstances' (p.40).

The DSM III-R-(American Psychiatric Association 1987) uses the term paraphilia (*para:* deviation; *philia:* attraction): 'Arousal in response to sexual objects and situations that are not part of normative arousal-activity patterns and that in varying degrees may interfere with the capacity for reciprocal, affectionate sexual activity' (p.279). Note here that despite the inclusion of the quality of the relationship, no attempt is made to give a developmental perspective. With regard to female perversion DSM-III states: 'Paraphilias are practically never diagnosed in females, but some cases have been reported'

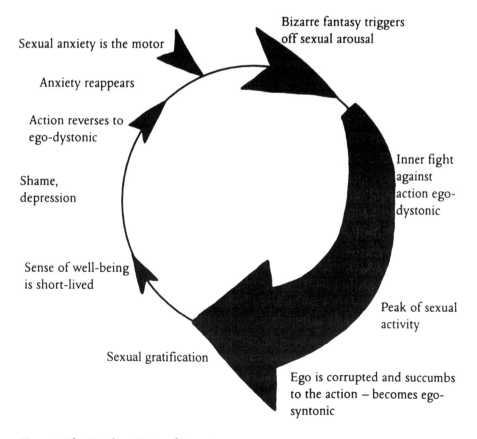

Figure 1. The Circular Motion of Perversion

(p.281). In the new DSM-IV (1994) it is asserted that '...Except for sexual masochism, where the sex ratio is estimated to be 20 males for each female, the other paraphilias are almost never diagnosed in females, although some cases have been reported' (p.524).

Overall, the diagnosis of female perversions has been lacking. It is as though our society has feared to reach a deeper understanding, perhaps because women are seen as being incapable of committing perversions.

These observations are illustrated in the following example.

A man aged forty-one wrote a self-referral letter: 'I'm in complete despair over my compulsive behaviour in which I feel compelled to exhibit my genitals to women and to obtain a response from them which frees me from awful states of anxiety. I became aware of this at the age of eleven and since then I have been able to perform these actions with much care and premeditation which have prevented my detection. However, in the last few months I've noticed that I take more and more risks, as for example, doing these at the train station near my home, at the same time and even to the same woman, or from my car, all situations in which I could be easily identified. I'm forty-one, married, with four children and with a very responsible job. I'm aware that all my personal and professional achievements are in jeopardy but I feel unable to stop myself from this irrational behaviour, the more dangers I encounter the more sexual pleasure I get out of it. Please help me.'

MENTAL MECHANISMS

In perversion, sexual anxiety appears as a result of conflict between the id and the superego, in which the id titillates the ego with the bizarre fantasy. The id puts pressure on the ego to be partly, or temporarily, corrupted by its increasing needs (see Figure 1).

The ego, supported by the superego, fights against the acting out of the fantasy since it is felt to be incompatible with the ego's sense of integrity. Thus anxiety increases, and immediate action is demanded. Eventually, under the increasing pressure from the id, the ego is corrupted and succumbs to the 'acting-out'. The action has become temporarily ego-syntonic, thus allowing the perversion to take place. The goal, which is the release of hostile sexual anxiety, is essential. The hostility is related to revenge for an early trauma associated with early gender humiliation and/or tremendous fears of not being in control when facing the imagined loss of the most important person (primary object). However, the sense of well-being achieved is of short duration. It is immediately afterwards superseded by feelings of guilt, self-disgust, shame and depression. The 'acting out' is again experienced as ego-dystonic, and the circular motion starts up once more.

Other aims involved in the perverse acts are the regulation of self-esteem (Rosen 1979) and the taking of risks (Stoller 1975), in which there may be success or failure. Success constitutes a shocked response from the victim reassuring the pervert of his dangerousness; failure arises from a repetition of the early humiliation.

HOW TO DIAGNOSE A PERVERSION

The following psychodynamic and phenomenological features of the patient's personality structure should be present:

- A compulsive and repetitive action which is subjectively experienced as bizarre, and is incomprehensible but which provides for the release of sexual anxiety.

- The patient is only too painfully aware of the compulsion to repeat the action, but is oblivious to the hostility which causes it: he is deeply unconscious of who he hates and on whom he wants to take revenge. The symbolic unconscious links become apparent during psychodynamic therapy.

- Fantasies about bizarre or perverse actions are not enough to qualify as perversion. True sexual perversion always involves the use of the body. The 'body barrier' means that the individual must use the body for the perverse action. Characteristically there is a complete restriction in the choice of a sexual scenario which usually has a fixed and repetitive 'script'.

- There is inability to have a whole 'object-relationship', but instead there is a 'part-object relationship'. I use the word 'object' as opposed to subject, and a part-object relationship when the individual finds it impossible to see the other person or 'object' as a whole and complete separate being.

Such people have extreme fears of being 'trapped' and need to be in complete control, which accounts for the emotional interference in the achievement of a loving and sexual relationship. Instead, they experience hostility and humiliation which they direct towards their partner or themselves.

This accounts for the dehumanizing quality that characterizes the view of sexual objects in the relationships of those suffering from perversions.

PSYCHOGENESIS

Early emotional deprivation in both sexes may include a history of the following: neglect, abandonment, a symbiotic relationship with mother, humiliation of gender identity, physical abuse, sexual abuse, wrong gender

assignment at birth, being cross-dressed during infancy, absence of acknowledgment of generational differences and victims becoming perpetrators. All
may occur, either singly or in any combination, although the most frequent
combination is that of seduction and neglect. In turn all these traumas could
be thought of as the consequences of a the three generational process. Ashurst
and Hall (1989) describe the link between the after-effects of childhood sexual
abuse in a woman and the propensity she might develop in engaging in
sado-masochism as 'she is unable to assert herself because she feels that, since
her boundaries have already been breached, she must satisfy any man's sexual
needs'. Hence, one of the long term consequences of being sexually abused as
a child for a girl could be to engage in sado-masochistic practices which could
also involve women. These, in their own turn, could be one of the precursors
in becoming an abuser.

Rascovsky and Rascovsky (1968) in their now classical study on filicide
called our attention to the frequent and serious injuries inflicted upon the infant
by parental acting out and regarded these factors as responsible for 'an increase
in born hostility and envy and consequently responsible for adult acting out
and psychopathic behaviour' (p.390).

The Three-Generational Process

This process has been partly explored in the extensive work written about the
defence mechanism known as identification with the aggressor; also called the
Stockholm syndrome or the trauma hypothesis. Stoller (1991) writes '...It is
common knowledge that battered children grow up to be battering parents,
that paedophiles were sexually molested boys, and that serial rapists were often
victims of forced or exploitive erotic abuse in boyhood'. Clinically, it is known
that incest is transmitted intergenerationally; that is, carried across generations.
Incestuous mothers are unable to facilitate individuation and separation in their
offspring. In order to understand the dynamic mechanisms which have been
in operation, perpetuating themselves in the successive generations, it is
important to consider the three generations prior to that of the patient. In so
doing it may be possible to break the cycle. We are more familiar with the
long-term consequences of paternal incest than with those associated with
maternal incest victims. My hypothesis is that the victims of paternal incest
tend to react in a 'victim'-like way, that is, passive and compliant, whereas the
maternal-incest victims react in explosive, sudden and unexpected outbursts of
violence, likened to those experienced in serial killers whose previous personalities were rather quiet and withdrawn.

From being victims people may become victimizers. They perpetrate against
others the victimization and humiliation which was previously inflicted on
them. They treat their victims in the same way they themselves felt treated,
usually by their mothers, in other words, as part-objects who are there only to

satisfy whims and bizarre expectations. Such apparent sexual acting-out is a manic defence which contains much hostility and revenge and defends against formidable fears related to the threat of losing mother. The outside part-object target is, symbolically speaking, the mother.

The person suffering from perversion has been prevented from achieving sexual emotional maturity, that is genital sexuality, because he or she felt humiliated in his or her own sense of gender identity (masculinity or femininity). These early traumas are partly responsible for a faulty libidinal development, and later on, for difficulties in forming satisfactory heterosexual relationships.

Paedophiliac patients are usually attracted to children of a fixed age range. During evaluations they go to extremes to demonstrate how much they care for the child involved and how much love and tenderness they have given to that child in a very 'special' relationship. But this proves to be false since as soon as that particular child grows beyond the preferential age barrier he or she is immediately replaced by another which belongs to the 'suitable' age which arouses the patient sexually. Incidentally, this fact is crucial in establishing a differential diagnosis between paedophiliacs and incest perpetrators. The latter tend to stick with a particular child until he or she grows and leaves home or the family dynamics change to such extent that disclosure occurs. In paedophilia, there is arrested libidinal development with a marked fixation to the mother–baby unit and a longing to merge with mother, with whom a symbiotic relationship had been established; all early characteristics as already mentioned in perversion. Thus incest is associated with present and actual family dynamics rather than with more internalized and individual ones.

Vignette

A man of twenty-five was referred for a consultation on account of his strong sexual impulses towards children of both sexes between the ages of eight and ten. He had been actively engaging in sexually assaultive acts with various children over a period of five years but had never been detected. He would pick the children up in the Charing Cross area of London, offer them cash, and have sexual intercourse with them. His victims were usually boys and he would anally penetrate them. He was very scared of the police and deeply worried at the prospect of being sent to prison. Although he was aware that his actions were wrong, he was unable to stop himself. He had been aware of his sexual attraction to children from the age of twelve and had never experienced any sexual attraction to women or men of his own age. He felt backward in social circumstances and unable to envisage a one-to-one situation: this being painfully apparent during a difficult one-hour interview. He showed no capacity for insight in spite of his realization of his need for help. He was not motivated to look into the reasons for his sexual attraction and violent actions towards children and displayed no concern about the children themselves. He was the first child in a family of three boys. There were constant rows and physical violence at home. Father was constantly drunk and began to sexually abuse him from the age of seven and his mother never noticed anything. She was deeply depressed by expecting a girl which never arrived, and continued to harbour vengeful fantasies against all men, since she had herself been victim of paternal incest.

This example gives evidence not only of the victim becoming perpetrator but also of the different dynamics and personality structures which exist between paedophiles and incest perpetrators.

CONCEPTUALIZATION OF FEMALE PERVERSION

Experience at the Portman Clinic has shown that female perversion exists but that there is an important distinction between male and female sexual perversions. In both men and women the reproductive functions and organs are used for perversion; the man uses the penis to carry out his perverse activities, while the woman uses her whole body, since her female reproductive-sexual organs are more widely spread. Their different psychopathology originates from the female body and its inherent attributes, including fecundity.

As early as 1968 Rascovsky and Rascovsky noted that the neglect of this area in psychoanalytical literature could be regarded as: 'an aspect of the universal resistance to acknowledging the *mother's* filicide drives, undoubtedly the most dreaded and uncanny truth for us to face' (p.390).

The psychopathologies most frequently associated with women are syndromes of self-injury associated with biological/hormonal disorders affecting the reproductive functioning. For example, anorexia nervosa, bulimia, and forms of self-mutilation, where the absence or presence of the menses can act as indicators of the severity of the condition; self-abuse; some forms of prostitution and the sexual and physical abuse of children, including incest with children of both sexes. Victims can experience an addiction to trauma that induces self-destructiveness. The main differences between a male and female perverse action lies in the object. Whereas in men the act is directed at an outside part-object, in women it is usually directed against themselves, either against their bodies, or against objects which they see as their own creations, that is, their babies. In both cases, bodies and babies are treated as dehumanized part-objects (Welldon 1988).

Vignette

A patient was referred for a psychiatric assessment because of violent behaviour directed towards her second child. Her first pregnancy had come as a surprise to her but she felt the need to go ahead with it, because in this way she felt she was taking out insurance against the dread of being alone. The child could become utterly dependent on her and be totally under her control. When this first child arrived, she was overcome by feelings of repulsion and revulsion against her baby. She felt ready to kick it, but after reflection she decided that in order to overcome these horrid feelings she would fix in her mind the idea of the baby being part of herself. Despite the fact that she hated it, she surprised herself by finding thoughts and actions against her baby sexually exciting and eventually it became her source for sexual gratification. Some days she would choose her right arm as being the baby, and at other times it would be one of her legs. In this way she felt able to master her impulses to beat up her first child. Later, unable to do the same with her second baby, she asserted, 'There is no more room in my body for a second one, all has been used up by the first one'.

A strong quality of dehumanization and the reduction of object to part-object, which are features in perversion are present here. However, also present are a quality of concern escalating to alarm and a strong wish to understand in order to stop the destructive actions.

The literature in this area is scarce. Female fetishism is an exception, though still considered to be the *exact* equivalent of the male counterpart (Zavitzianos 1971, 1982; Raphling 1989). Such a view is seriously challenged by Gamman and Makinen (1994) in a more recent and comprehensive study which provides a new theoretical representation of female desire, although their definition of female perversion is not the classical one.

Many psychoanalytic authors refer to the mothering process in the production of future perverts. Most agree that the mother–child relationship is of paramount importance in understanding the genesis of perversion but the acknowledgement of the perversion of motherhood is absent. Furthermore, little is said about the *real* pathology of those mothers and one is left uncertain as to whether the authors considered the 'cruel', 'sadistic' mother to be a fantasy of their patients or an accurate assessment of these mothers.

It is difficult to believe that practitioners have never had access to women whose pathology included that of being unable to fulfil their mothering functioning adequately. After all, the study of the life history of our patients shows evidence that there are women who treat their infants as fetishes and part-objects, whose function is merely or entirely to be used or abused as dehumanized parts of the mother's narcissistic self.

Perhaps this selective blindness or deafness is still part of our own atavistic needs *always* to interpret the woman's 'fulfilled' capacity for procreation as a healthy and mature part of the ideal ego, that is, associated with improvement. Did practitioners ever hear any women talk, in the most despondent and despairing ways, of 'bizarre' needs they experience toward their children? Furthermore, did they ever hear women's designs to get impregnated not out of love but out of hate. For example those women who are consumed by a desire for revenge on their male partners for humiliation suffered. The need to get impregnated is at times clearly stated as 'just to teach the bastard to commit himself and from now on to treat me with respect as the mother of his child'. Were the practitioners trapped themselves in a countertransferential response which included a denial of a mother in distress over her abused child? From the work of Greenacre we have learnt of the basic separation and individuation which indicates the ambivalent nature of the maternal response to a new baby. Winnicott (1949) described how mothers can 'hate' their babies. Hermann (1936) made the first reference to a 'pregenital mother' and was the first psychoanalyst to observe sadomasochistic phenomena in the mother–child relationship with the two primary opposite components of the libido co-existing.

Such basic themes are later elaborated by authors such as Mahler (1963) with her work on symbiosis and separation/individuation stages in normal infant development and their failure resulting in perversion. Socarides (1988) describes 'the urge to regress to a pre-Oedipal fixation in which there is a desire for, and a dread of, merging with the mother in order to reinstate the primitive mother–child unity'. Glasser (1979) discusses the 'core complex', in which there is a deep-seated and pervasive longing for an intense and most intimate closeness to another person, amounting to a 'merging', a 'state of oneness', 'a blissful union'. This is never realized, partly because whenever such a person has the opportunity to be emotionally close to another, he experiences a threat to his identity and withdraws. Related to this, Stoller (1991) emphasizes the dynamics of humiliation in 'symbiosis' or 'merging anxiety' where the consequences of maternal attitudes could be devastating in the future life of the pervert. In comparing the erotic differences between men and women Stoller (1991) asserts: '…men's propensity for fetishizing – that fundamental dynamic of perversion – (is) in contrast to the opposite desire in women for relationship, intimacy and constancy' (pp.44–5). Well said, but if women fail to obtain these wonderful 'feminine' qualities in their relationships they could fall into perverse behaviour. Fantasies of revenge against their partners could then materialize in motherhood using their children as dehumanized, fetishistic objects over whom they have complete control.

Greif and Montgomery's (1991) description of the masochist's 'pregenital mother' as: 'The woman swallows up the man and the man must annihilate the woman' is almost identical to my own definition of 'perverted' motherhood, which gives rise to perversogenic traits in the offspring. The function of motherhood as a perversion is clearly identifiable in their clinical material concerning maternal incest and the attempted murder of children by their mothers.

Cooper (1991) makes an important contribution in acknowledging the existence of a 'trauma core' as 'the experience of terrifying passivity in relation to the preoedipal mother perceived as dangerously malignant, malicious, and all-powerful, arousing sensations of awe and uncanny' (p.23) and three accompanying fantasies, all related to a sadistic preoedipal mother, in many if not all perversions. Even though Cooper is so aware of the crucial element of power the mother holds and also of the dehumanizing factor being more essential than aggression, he then disappointingly says: 'It may be that it is women's perversions, not their superegos, as Freud thought, that lack crispness and definition because of their attenuated castration anxiety. In switching to the conventional ideas regarding female perversions as equivalent to male ones, he is missing the whole point of women using motherhood as a vehicle for their own perversions' (p.30). For Cooper 'the perverse exhibiting woman uses her capacity to excite a male by the sight of her breast or body to overcome her own sense of smallness and unfemininity compared to her mother, as well as to demonstrate the greater power of her breast or whole body compared to the male penis' (p.31). If he had in mind woman's unique inherent attributes, including specifically her capacity to be pregnant and her functioning as a mother he may have arrived at similar findings to mine. However, he still works from the point of view of *assumed* superiority based on phallic centricity. He gets very close when he writes: 'The fetishistic object is not a phallus but a breast' (as a matter of fact, both girls and boys have had first hand experience of breast as opposed to the penis). And then, even closer when he says: 'one can raise the question whether fantasies of the huge breast do not underlie the fantasies of the phallus in fetishism' (p.31). Kaplan (1991) redefines female perversion as a 'psychological strategy' failing to fulfil the criteria of perversion as clinically defined. She also (1991b) uses much ingenuity in depicting the interesting phenomenon of women masquerading as women. However, once again the real and painful issues of dealing with female perversions resulting from perverted motherhood are absent. In her assertion that 'the extent of the clinical and theoretical neglect of perversions in females has become apparent' (p.133) she fails to acknowledge my own seminal work on the subject. Kaplan's thesis is that perversions 'are as much pathology of gender-role identity as pathologies of sexuality' (p.128) and that 'what makes a perversion a perversion is a mental strategy that employs some social gender stereotypes of masculinity and femininity in a manner that deceives the onlooker about the unconscious meanings of the behaviour she or he is observing' (p.128). Kaplan doesn't agree with my hypothesis that there are different psycho-biological processes functioning in men and women (Welldon 1988) which are responsible for the differences between perversions in the two genders. In not being aware of this possibility, Kaplan misses the most valid evidence for her thesis; that is, women can use heterosexual intercourse as a scenario for her revenge in her wish to become pregnant by the man she hates – making hate instead of making love. The onlooker, together with most of humanity, could certainly be deceived by the general assumption that woman's pregnancy is the evidence of her being in a blissful state of mental health. As a matter of fact she is able to harbour and produce a future perversion by using both her own social gender stereotype and her gender-role identity.

Rascovsky and Rascovsky (1968) asserted that the maternal persecutory objects within the affected child introjects are very much connected with the actual parents and not just fantasied ones.

It seems apt here to adopt the model proposed by Fonagy and others for understanding the early environment in the development of borderline individuals (Fonagy 1989, 1991; Fonagy and Higgit 1990, 1992; Fonagy and Moran 1991). Following a Kleinian framework they stress the state of deficit which arises as an adaptation to early deprivation and intrapsychic conflict, but in contrast to other Kleinian authors they see 'the root of borderline (pervert) disturbance in the child's, generally accurate, perception of the caregiving figure as harbouring hostile and ultimately destructive thoughts about the child' (Fonagy and Higgit 1992, p.26). The infant, usually between the age two and four, protects himself against the violence and neglect of the 'primary caregiver' (mother) by withdrawing and making himself unable to think since there is so much real pain. This obviously impairs his capacity to develop any sense of trust or to establish intimate relationships. Thus the existence of perverted motherhood is acknowledged when the process of individuation/separation is not only actively impaired but also finds maternal libidinal rewards. Masterson and Rinsley (1975) describe this quality of mothering as alternating and withdrawing at the time of separation/individuation: The infant is left at mother's mercy, unable to individuate, separate or go through genital libidinal development. 'Psychic survival' (McDougall 1992) of the future pervert is ensured by erotization of the hostility and characteristic rigidity. This particular feature is poignantly described by Milton (1994) when writing of the link between severe childhood physical abuse and frank perversion in women. She refers to a serious aspect of the victim's plight being her corruption in early life through extreme stimulation of her own hatred and destructiveness, which then becomes eroticized in her identification with the aggressor, again as a means of psychic survival.

This follows my own hypothesis that motherhood is sometimes chosen for unconscious perverse reasons:

'the woman would know that in achieving motherhood she is automatically achieving the role of master, that of being in charge, in complete control of another being who has to submit himself or herself not only emotionally but also biologically to the mother's demands, however inappropriate they may be.' (Welldon 1988, p.81)

Some of the psychodynamic principles operating in perversion appear in females when they become mothers. A woman's capacity for getting pregnant and containing the baby within her own body provides her with some of the same emotional characteristics in her object-relationships as are found in exaggerated and highly distorted forms in perverse relationships. These include the desire and intention to engulf the other person, to dehumanize the object, to intrude into, to invade, to be in complete control of and to merge with the other.

Perverse motherhood is the product of emotional instability and inadequate individuation over at least three generations. It is the end product of serial abuse or chronic infantile neglect.

Vignette

Another woman patient was referred because of exhibitionism. She told me that her compulsion to 'flash' occurred when she became attached to a person whom she invested with idealized 'maternal' qualities. She wanted to get closer, to be noticed and to be taken care of by that particular person but she also wanted a shocked response from her 'victims'. She carefully planned the 'appropriate' clothing to wear when she was to meet the individual which consisted of an overcoat covering only a little vest in order to respond readily to her urges. She knew this was 'wrong' and that she would be rejected but she could not stop herself. It is interesting to note that, even when her exhibitionism could superficially appear to be the equivalent of a male counterpart's, this is not so. It is well-known that male exhibitionists have the compulsion to 'flash' only to women – and women who are unknown to them – while this patient suffered from this compulsion only with other women to whom she felt a close attachment. This clinical finding is confirmed by Richards (1989) when she describes a woman's perversion which consisted of her repeatedly and compulsively making obscene phone calls to her mother and other female protective figures. This is yet another remarkable difference between the genders.

Another woman wrote:

'...My feelings of arousal in certain situations with my eighteen-month-old son, started a couple of weeks ago. I have touched him twice in response to those feelings. After having spoken to my husband, the Psychiatric Social Worker (PSW) and the National Society for the Prevention of Cruelty to

Children (NSPCC) I have been jolted out of it. I now recognize when I am aroused, but I will not act on those feelings inappropriately. When he is toddling around I feel that he is my son, my baby and I love him as such. I would not hurt him physically and I do not want to hurt him psychologically either. I have resorted to my own old adolescent ways of cutting myself and at times I eat myself sick.

'I am writing to you in desperation. I need help. I am an adult, thirty-year-old woman, with three children presently in care and one due, within the next few weeks, which it also looks as though I am going to lose.

'I desperately want my children back, but also recognize that this is difficult because of my own abuse as a child and in many ways through my adult life. Hence my daughter being sexually abused by one of my abusers when she was younger.

'I am now at the stage where I am experiencing flash-backs, nightmares, awful depression. I can't bear to be touched by my partner – I also recognize that my relationship cannot continue as it is – I don't even know if I want it any more, but I seem to be addicted to it somehow.

'I know that somewhere I have to find the help I need, and see it through not only for my children, but also for myself so that I can feel like a person, a human being and not one of society's rejects.

'I hope and pray that you can help me.

'PS I was sexually abused by three different people from the age of two to twelve years, then raped at the age of seventeen years. My mother was physically abusing me at this time too.'

These examples undoubtedly demonstrate that some women who have problems in adequately caring for their children can clearly communicate their desperate need for help. The last letter is from a patient who was charged with aiding and abetting sexual abuse. She had taken her daughter to be babysat by her own stepfather who had previously abused her as a child. A high degree of unconscious identification with her own daughter is present. There is also present a sense of self-loathing which is confirmed by her sado-masochistic relations and her brutal treatment of her own body. The abuse is simultaneously active and unconscious; in other words she is quite unaware of her own participation in the process, because the original trauma (her own abuse) had been buried away and only emerged into consciousness when she became aware of her own daughter's abuse.

This patient was placed in a therapeutic group and only there was she able to look into her own 'abusing' behaviour when supported by others with similar histories. She did not feel judged by others; indeed, she experienced the constant confrontation and 'taking in' of her own sense of responsibility

Table 1. Phenomenological psychopathological features of male and female perversions

Male Perversions	Female Perversions
(1) Aimed at an outside 'object' or person.	(1) Aimed at themselves or at 'objects' of their own creation.
(2) Onset: usually at an early age.	(2) Onset at variable stages, with earlier psychopathology such as self-abuse, promiscuity and sado-masochistic relationships.
(3) Inflexibility and habitual chronicity in the action.	(3) More flexibility than their male counterparts.
(4) Lack of freedom in the object-choice.	(4) Some degree of changeability in the object-choice.
(5) No emotional or physical attachment to the object or 'part-object'.	(5) Some degree of emotional or physical attachment.
(6) The action does not usually involve heterosexual intercourse.	(6) The action frequently involves heterosexual intercourse for fantasy purposes and as a means to produce the perverse scenario.
(7) Interference at all times with all other areas, including volition, thought processes and affects.	(7) Interference at times of emotional crisis with other areas including volition, thought processes and affects.
(8) Desire to harm others, sometimes not obviously apparent to himself.	(8) Desire to harm themselves and/or their babies.
(9) Persist through life.	(9) Appear and fade away at different stages of life.
(10) Unrelated or not significantly related to present stress conditions.	(10) Significantly related to other distress conditions.
(11) Lack of concern of consequences inflicted on their victims.	(11) Awareness of the consequences inflicted on their victims.
(12) Poor Prognosis.	(12) Variable prognosis.

as enlightening and extremely helpful. Her own capacity for internal and constant change provided the others with reassurance about their own capacity to give positive things. Cohesiveness, connection, identification and mutuality emerged in the group affiliation which she was able to comprehend and which helped her to make internal changes which were reflected in her capacity to take on positive criticism and to trust others at times of need and conflict.

A comprehensive and thorough study of self-mutilation in female remanded prisoners has been completed by Wilkens and Coid (1991) and by Coid (1992). Although the psychopathology of the women was different from the patient population of the Portman Clinic these were similar findings concerning early emotional deprivation in the family; abnormal psychosexual development and 'polymorphous perversity'. They also surveyed the preceding affective and emotional disturbance and the external present stresses. They concluded that self-mutilation was experienced as a symptom relief mechanism accompanied by 'great pleasure or excitement'. These encompassed patients who obtained sexual arousal and orgasmic release. I have also encountered women who have subjected their bodies to the most painful and dangerous practices such as bonding and self-hanging, as a way of controlling their mounting desires to attack their own offspring. They also admit sexual gratification achieved through these practices.

All the women seen at the Clinic are aware, not only of the suffering they can cause to others but also of that they inflict on themselves. Their histories are consistently characterized by exposure to early, repeated and serious traumatic incidents of emotional and bodily abuse by their caregivers.

As opposed to men, women are usually physically and emotionally attached (negatively or positively) to the 'objects' of their abuse, that is their own bodies or babies.

It may be helpful here to summarize the differences between male and female perversions (see Table 1).

The onset of female perversion can appear at any developmental stage and it is usually triggered off by surrounding circumstances which are acting as facilitators of the perversion. In other words, they are usually stress related. The origins for the disturbance can go back as early as their birth, for example if the gender of the new baby was not welcome to her family at times this can even be a source of great disappointment. Obviously this will seriously affect the relationship between mother and baby girl.

Some of these differences are independently corroborated by Matthews (1993) and Bentovim (1993). Bentovim speculates about the reasons why women make up a small proportion of abusers despite the fact that girls are abused four or five times more commonly than boys. He postulates that during their socialization girls tend to internalize their response to abusive experiences, developing low sense of self-esteem, and symptoms such as self-mutilation and anorexia nervosa, whereas abused boys externalize and project their experiences of abuse.

Women seem to suffer more from their own abusing actions, to be more aware of the deep psychological wounds and long-term consequences they produce, to take more responsibility for them and to ask for professional help which, as unfortunately observed, is not easily available.

These differing characteristics of perversions in women, namely a degree of responsibility, the experience of psychic pain, the flexibility in their 'choice' of perversion and the degree of attachment displayed in female perversions which is absent in their male counterparts, may account for better prognostic appraisals in women.

Detection by police is rare except in cases in which the mother is alleged to have aided and abetted sexual abuse perpetrated by the father. In the case of single mothers, outside agencies are sometimes quite unaware of the degree of suffering involved. At other times, women's self-reporting is prevented by some legal agencies who want to keep the children at home regardless of the emotional and physical costs.

CONCLUSION

New awareness and deeper insights into women's psychopathologies are available and should be used in a positive way to promote further understanding and prevention of the particular conditions here described. Perversion is, of course, intertwined with the politics of power; women have access to domestic power where men have access to public power, but unfortunately there is not space here to develop this argument.

More adequate resources should be available to provide appropriately for mothers and babies. The goal is to prevent further abuses of domestic power which cause much pain, suffering and distress to both mothers and babies in the short term and to society in general in the longer term. We should aim to promote a close cooperation between all those professionals who care for either mothers and/or babies in order to secure both accurate diagnosis and adequate provisions.

Acknowledgements

The author is indebted to Drs. Pamela Ashurst and Cleo Van Velsen for their generosity in giving valuable suggestions, encouragement and editorial help in the preparation of this manuscript.

The Trauma Organized System of Working with Family Violence

Arnon Bentovim

INTRODUCTION

In recent years there has been a major concern about the inequalities and violations which are an inherent part of family life. From a feminist gender-based perspective, violence, incest and other forms of family violence are not seen as a symptom of a malfunctioning family, but as the expression of societal views about women and children as appropriate objects for abuse and violence.

This chapter builds on the systemic approach described in chapter I:4:vii. It attempts to integrate factors known about family violence and to develop a meaningful contemporary approach to both assessment and treatment, which includes individual and family issues in a societal context.

EXPLANATORY MODELS TO DESCRIBE VIOLENT AND ABUSIVE FAMILIES

The cycle of violence – the inter-generational transmission of violence – is advanced as an important factor on the basis of the following findings. The more parents are violent to children, the more violent those children are to siblings. The more violent husbands are to wives, the more violent the wife is towards her children. Violence experienced as a child, in the form of 'benign' abuse, is repeated a generation later. The degree of subsequent violence depends on intensity and length of victimization. Although this 'trickle-down' model is generally true, it is also the case that a man who is violent to his marital partner will be disproportionately more violent to his children, than is the partner (Gelles 1987). A variety of explanations focus on the individual (i.e., psychopathological explanations) the social context (i.e., socio-cultural or ecological explanations) or 'interactional' (i.e., social interactional explanations).

Psychopathological Explanations

These link the inability to control violent impulses towards partners or children, with that person having a pervasive sense of discontent, anger, and irritability. These basic attitudes are seen to arise from individual scars, for example, from abuse and deprivation, which affect the ability to relate. A good deal of empirical research has been carried out to test this model, with limited confirmations, – for example abusers are more likely to be impulsive, immature, and prone to depression. Such explanations pay insufficient attention to the processes that individuals become caught in – situational/contextual variables, ways of coping, and styles of attribution that may be more helpful in understanding which individual will abuse, who, where, and when.

Socio-Cultural Models – Ecological Explanations

These put forward the view that human behaviour should be studied in context. It is asserted that social and economic deprivation transforms predisposed high-risk individuals into abusers, and that violence is an attempt to control stressful events. Normal parents, it is argued, may be socialized into abusive practice through interactions with cultural, community, and family influences, for example harsh punishment in childhood, and patriarchal societal views which are seen as normative. Unemployment and limited occupational opportunities are all seen as stressors, which lead to abusive action.

But these factors are also not predictive of who will abuse and when, and recent research has indicated that when individuals who have been abused in childhood are followed up into adulthood, they do not inevitably abuse children more frequently than other parents – although they are significantly more likely to be arrested for criminal activities. Other research indicates that there is a three to five times risk of an individual who has been abused in childhood, abusing his or her own child, compared to those who have not been abused (Straus and Kantor 1987).

But one immediately has to ask what the factors are that protect those individuals who develop a more positive attitude to children, reversing their own abusive experience. Other research that has followed vulnerable individuals into adulthood has indicated that positive parenting is to do with availability of some positive relationship during childhood, which may include a psychotherapeutic experience (Egeland 1988).

Social-Interactional Explanations

These focus on the interactional processes between parent and child within the specific familial context, and also within the context of larger social structures, in seeking an explanation as to why some parents abuse.

Research findings do support some interactional differences in families where abuse occurs compared with non-abusive families of similar social backgrounds. The important differences are the presence of reciprocation of aversive behaviour, reinforcement of inappropriate behaviour, ineffective use of punishment, negative emotional response, and arousal towards children. Stable, global negative attributions exist about children and partners who are subsequently victimized, which predispose to grievance and anger. Such explanations involve a dynamic interplay among the individual, the family, and society. It can be stated with some confidence that violence – whether physical, sexual or emotional – is the result of an interaction within a system which seldom provides alternative solutions or restraints.

Dobash and Dobash (1979), two of the strongest proponents of a feminist gender-based view of family violence, describe women in society as 'appropriate victims' of family violence and seen as deserving of blame and punishment. In general, physical punishment in the bringing up of children is still widely accepted. Although attempts in Scandinavia to construct a view that children should not be hit have shown some evidence of success, there is a broadly accepted view that within families it is permissible, or even proper, to hit people one loves, for more powerful people to hit less powerful people, and to use hitting to achieve some end or goal.

In this context sexual violence is an act perpetrated not as a mutual act freely enjoyed by partners who can consent, but as an act initiated for the satisfaction of one individual without the consent of a partner, or with a partner who by reason of age or understanding could not give consent.

There is an implicit view in society that sex can occur without consent, that more powerful people can demand sexual favours from the less powerful, and that sexuality may be used to achieve ends or goals, such as power or control. Similarly, emotional abuse, denigration, disqualification, criticism, and hostility may each similarly be used with those who are loved, with the less powerful, and to achieve ends or goals.

Weakness, vulnerability, and dependency are central unifying and common features of all types of family violence, and until recently there has been an extraordinary lack of social response within the family to aggression of any type. Sociological investigators conclude that the benefits of aggression, even including the injury to the victim, often outweigh the cost. The history of recognition of different forms of family violence attest to this. There is a far higher profile of concern about abused children in the media since the Maria Colwell case in the 1970s, and far lower for the often horrendous physical violence and injury seen in wife battering. Indeed, it is only currently that the crime of rape in marriage has been recognized.

The earlier chapter on a systemic approach argued that major psychopathology in family violence is associated with the development of a *trauma organized system*. This grew out of the traumagenic experiences for parents in their families of origin, the recreation and re-enactment within the current family and the recurrence and perpetuation of such patterns, through the addictive secrecy surrounding patterns of violence.

TRAUMA ORGANIZED SYSTEMS – AN ACCOUNT OF FAMILY VIOLENCE PATTERNS

Physical and Emotional Abuse

Physical and emotional abuse and neglect represent extreme abnormalities of parenting and are defined as active physically or emotionally violent acts, or a passive failure to protect and provide adequate care. Therefore a major deficiency of attachment behaviour occurs between parents and children, and such patterns are an integral component of the trauma organized system. There is a great deal of confirmatory evidence that attachment patterns between parents and children where abuse occurs are highly insecure (Egeland and Sroufe 1981; Crittenden 1988). Empirical investigations with adults who were abused as children are now defining the way that these patterns originate and develop, and their specific effects on relationship patterns.

Avoidant Patterns

Avoidant attachment patterns in families are characterized by parents who are rejecting in their response to their infants, and aversive and wooden in their contact with them. Their infants are avoidant of contact when attempts are made to pick them up and play with them. Minimal emotional responses are shown following separation; the infants avoid contact on reunion and remain guarded. They seem to have developed what we described as a 'shell' of apparent indifference and self-sufficiency (Bentovim and Kinston 1991) which persists. Being treated as a thing, the 'world' in turn is treated as a thing and as of no importance; models are created that are 'closed' to new information, and such patterns can persist through childhood into adult life (Crittenden 1988).

Re-Enacting or Reversing Patterns

The second type of insecure attachment is more 'active' in form: anger, neglect, coercion, clinging, or rejection are the characteristic behavioural patterns observed. Parents are observed to be either intrusive with their infants or rejecting towards them. Infants are intensely ambivalent on separation and can be angry on reunion or cling.

Children who earlier showed an inconsistent mixture of anger and neglect respond with coercive behaviour to others in pre-school settings. They may be sullen and oppositional and their 'closed' model of the world – in which are perceived constant threats and hostility – is countered by the use of power-orientated responses. They are later perceived as aggressive, miserable children showing conduct difficulties, taking their identity by re-enacting their aggressive experiences (George and Main 1979).

Parents who perpetuate angry or neglectful patterns of parenting reveal that they remain enmeshed in and preoccupied with the past. They are full of anger and resentment, and are seen to be re-enacting or re-experiencing their traumatic or stressful experiences in relation to their children. To such parents, normal children's behaviour is perceived, interpreted, and attributed as being intrinsically negative and out of control – abusive – and creates a feeling of threat for the parent. Punishment is justified to gain some measure of control; there is an increased perception of the child as being bad and deserving further punishment. Rejection and negative interaction patterns become reflexive and can relieve the parents' tension, and may even feel momentarily invigorating. There can be a reversal of roles, the abused becoming the abuser.

Disorganized Patterns

The third pattern is the recently described 'disorganized' pattern of attachment. This is characterized by confusion, distress, fluctuating anger, and misery. Parents seem to be living out their own unresolved stressful and traumatic experiences to an even greater degree. Typically, traumatic-stress or loss responses predominate. Instead of anger and resentment – which could be seen as a structured, organized form of 'survival' through 'reversing' abusive contexts – traumatic-confusion reactions continue and children cling or are dazed, distressed.

SEXUAL ABUSE

Sexual abuse is defined as coercive sexual activities to which the victim cannot give consent due to age or dependent role, and which break social taboos. The trauma organized system of sexual abuse results from the victimizing action on the part of the abuser. 'Sexualization' is the traumatic response characteristic of the individual who is not giving consent or cannot give consent.

A review of what is known about the 'victimizing processes' involved in sexual abuse (Bentovim and Davenport 1992) include two major factors which underlie the behaviours and action of the perpetrator. These are (1) the substitution of sexual responses for normal affectionate contacts, the 'sexualization of inter-personal relationships' and (2) the use of sexual victimizing responses to assert power and control over the other, the 'sexualization of subordination'.

It is important to note that whereas physical abuse and neglect is perpetuated by men and women, men and boys are responsible for 95 per cent of child sexual abuse. A significant number of such individuals have themselves been sexually, physically or emotionally abused, and an examination of the effects of abuse in the long term on boys may help understand the origin of victimizing behaviour.

The traumatic sexualization characteristic of sexual abuse and the powerlessness of sexual, physical, and emotional abuse have profound effects on the identity and meaning system of the individual. There are major differences in the way abusive activities are processed by boys and girls. Flash-backs and memories of abusive acts may be responded to actively by boys, through identification with the abuser, leading to sexualizing and abusing others. Girls more commonly respond in a more 'victim' mode.

Acting in boys, the trauma-organizing dynamic of powerlessness stimulates an aggressive dominating response. This goes hand-in-hand with the sexualization response to find someone who literally can take over their own traumatized self-representation; someone who reminds them of their powerlessness and can be made to feel it instead. Finding emotional closeness through sexuality to compensate for rejection is another commonly reported experience. Focusing on someone younger and less powerful acts as a source of sexual satisfaction, assertion of power, and emotional closeness. The sense of powerlessness – sexual, emotional, and physical – is briefly but addictively overcome and bears the seeds of repetition and re-enaction. Other organizing traumatic dynamics, betrayal and stigmatization also operate for boys in terms of seeking out partners to 'divert themselves' of their self-image by humiliating and initiating others, perversely treating the others as 'things', as they, themselves, had been. This becomes instituted as part of the cycle, and there are ample models in societal views of the appropriateness of women and children as victims.

Girls adopt a more internalizing mode as a result of their sexualization and powerlessness. They feel that the abuse must be their fault, reinforced by the adults' justifications that children like 'sexual' attention. Girls develop highly negative self-attributes which they struggle to deal with by self-mutilation, anorectic patterns, clinging to their abuser – even 'falling in love' or finding unsuitable partners or adopting promiscuous roles, which then justifies the abuser – or develop 'multiple-personalities' with false selves to gain some degree of control.

The most difficult aspect of traumatic-sexualization sequelae are to 'bring forth' the sexual responses in the child. A sexual reaction frequently makes the child feel that she initiated the traumatizing action and the other must have known she would respond. It is a great relief when this can be broached in a girls' therapeutic group. They can then realize that they are physiologically sexually responsive beings and that the abuser's actions and their responses are not on the same level.

Sexual Abuse and Interlocking Roles

There is considerable controversy about the 'interlocking' roles in sexual abuse. Men may justify their abusive actions by blaming their partners' 'failures' for their sexually abusive orientations. Do they 'find' vulnerable partners, or are they found by partners who have themselves been abused? Is there a complementary fit of perpetrator and victim? Alternatively, do men with abusive orientations choose vulnerable partners or single mothers with children of particular ages, and organize their partners' and children's victim roles?

Our own recently completed research (Monck *et al.* 1991) revealed that a considerable proportion (43%) of the mothers of children who were abused had themselves been abused; also twenty or thirty per cent of those men who abused subsequently admitted to having been abused in childhood. Both the abusers and the mothers had very mixed care in childhood, and many men and women had few good memories of their childhood. Over a third of the mothers could not bring themselves to believe that their children had been abused by their partner, and they supported the parent who denied responsibility. Indeed, only about nine per cent of the abusers properly took responsibility for their abuse.

Traumatic effects on children are related not only to how extensively they have been abused, for example abuse with penetration, but also whether they were believed, supported, and warmly nurtured by their caring parent. Older girls were less likely to be believed, and are more likely to be rejected and blamed. Such responses deepen traumatic effects already caused by being directly abused, creating yet more vulnerable young people and, in turn, parents.

ABUSE WITHIN PARTNERSHIPS

To Be a Battered Wife

To be a battered wife is defined as one who receives deliberate, severe, and repeated injury from her husband, involving punching with a closed fist, and more severe forms of violence.

Rape in partnerships can occur either as one aspect of a violent response or as a result of perverse sexual orientation.

Goldner, Penn, Sheinberg and Walker (1990) have recently described an attempt to make sense of the processes involved in violence between men and women. They felt that the development of gender differences represented a key. They pointed out that gender perceptions and the development of self-perceptions occur at the same developmental phase. They felt that the primary identity of the child is co-created from a series of conflict-layered internal self-representations for boys and girls.

'Gender self-representations' and responses to the traumatic experiences results in differential abusive responses in boys and girls. Through such abusive enactments, boys 'divest' themselves of traumatic responses and hand them on. Girls take a more passive identification, see themselves as responsible, punish themselves, and take on victim roles.

Goldner and her colleagues point out that boys are familiar with the process of constructing themselves from 'negatives' (i.e., what they are not; not being the mother, not being the victim) and taking on the exact opposite role. For boys and men, the threat is being reminded of powerlessness, a powerlessness which triggers violent modes of controlling.

These are only limited examples of the violence that can occur within family contexts. There is concern about violence and sexual abuse between siblings, the contentious issue of whether husbands can be battered by wives and the status of such actions, the abuse of the elderly and its association with taking revenge for traumatic experiences in childhood, when the once powerful parent is seen as powerless with a reversal of roles.

THERAPEUTIC WORK WITH VIOLENT FAMILIES – BREAKING THE DENIAL PROCESS

The essence of trauma organized systems is that they are focused on action, not on talking or thinking. Victimizing activities are justified by construing some action or aspect of the victim as causal and justifying abusive action, whether physical, sexual or emotional. The impulses to hit, to be sexual or to criticize are felt to be overwhelming, out of the victimizer's control, 'stronger' than (s)he is himself (or herself), described as a reflex response, with no time for thought.

Attributing the cause to the victim – as justifying punishment, sexual action, hurt – then justifies the loss of control and disinhibition of violent action. This scenario, of course, becomes a repetitive one and shapes the attitudes and responses of victimizer and victim. Thus building into what White, linked to Brunner's views on action and meaning, described as a 'dominant story' (White 1989) and we described as common and inter-subjective meanings (Kinston and Bentovim 1980). The dominant story emerges from 'internalizing conversations', which victimizer and victim alike develop to make some sense of earlier and current experiences. Similarly, individuals in the context who might take a protective role develop their own 'story' influenced by their own experiences and by the victimizer or victim.

The victimizer blots out and deletes his actions as forcefully as the traumatized individuals and avoids thinking, talking, or being reminded of his or her abuse as if the reality of action is negated. This is essential to avoid guilt and a sense of responsibility, and an alternative story is developed, for example never to abuse again, or even to think that it did not happen. Yet the context that arouses the abusive action remains; the urge may be felt as addictive, arousing a sense of helplessness to control the impulse. Punishment may be expected, yet arousal and action recurs; relief follows briefly, which maintains the abusive impulse. If discovered, the abuser reconstructs his own reality to feel a victim of society, a victim of his uncontrolled impulses, a victim of the child who describes his abusive action, a victim of the professional who gets the child to speak. He rapidly engages others in his construction – and there are many in the extended family, or the media, who are willing to be recruited to believe his word against the weak word of women and children, who are seen as 'incapable of truth'.

Externalizing Conversations

To counter these organizing stories it is necessary to engage in externalizing conversations between the therapist and the individual or family. This generates what White and Epston (1989) have described as counter- or anti-language. Problems are objectified, put outside the self through hypothetical questions, future questions, circular questions, the use of 'dolls' of the self rather than the self, the objectification of the abusive or victim self.

There is then the possibility of developing an alternative and preferred knowledge separate from the 'dominant' stories that constitute their lives and are constructed from traumatizing and traumatic responses. Alternative stories have to be constructed which separate the individual from the activities in which he or she has been enmeshed.

The very common picture of denial of abusive actions can be dealt with in the following way to challenge deletion and denial in the frequent situation where a parent denies his sexual abuse of a daughter and states that his daughter is a liar or has had ideas implanted in her mind. The following creates an alternative story to justify the deletion:

> 'Would it be better not to know, because, if the Court believed your daughter, could a man who did not know he had abused a child ever be trusted?'

> 'Do you feel a man who abused children could ever be trusted?'

'If there is a grain of truth, could you as a man undertake a mission to develop a more caring, respectful view of children, or would it be impossible to live with yourself?'

These questions help test whether the individual has the strength to face the reality of his actions and construct the stark truth of his actions and their origin. As another approach, an alternative story may be mobilized to spare the child from having to subscribe to a story of blame and self-regard.

Abusive individuals are frequently only ever able to admit to a small proportion of the reality of their abusive activities as so many of them are deleted, to avoid guilt, fear of retaliation, and punishment. 'Externalizing' or objectifying can be used with great effect in helping abusers think about the violent, inconsiderate, uncaring individual who takes them over and who needs controlling. Once this 'external' story is accepted, the individual can take the step of creating a story that includes the origins of these actions, rather than excluding them.

The victim can be helped to think of abuse as something being put into them, taking them over, making them remember, think, or try to run away from situations in which it may be met again. This also helps victims and perpetrators to take control, actualize and develop their caring or competent self to develop an alternative story of control. They may need to discover the 'unique outcomes' that represent the times they respond differently, develop a different conversation, learn to acknowledge, value and develop their resources, not denigrate and feel powerless to resist endless repetition.

ASSESSMENT FOR TREATMENT

The first step of treatment is to explore the extent of violent action within the family context. This ensures that a victim is protected, and that through breaking the taboo of silence there can be an open acknowledgement by family members of what has happened within the family, which factors have initiated abusive action, and which factors are maintaining it.

In this first phase, one of the major decisions to be taken is how best to ensure the protection of a child – or an adult – victim of abuse. Is there a natural protector within the family; for example, can a non-abusive parent understand and believe sufficiently to be able to protect against further abusive action? Does the abuser take sufficient responsibility for his or her action to enable appropriate statutory services to work with families on a voluntary basis? Is there a need for appropriate statutory action (e.g. prosecution, or civil actions) to exclude an abusive partner or parent from the home? Does a child have to be removed for his or her own safety?

Whilst the taboo of secrecy is being challenged, therapists cannot work alone since by definition therapeutic agencies do not have the statutory authority to be able to take the sort of action that will ensure a child's protection. It is essential that there be a link between the therapeutic agency and the statutory agency which has sufficient authority to ensure that action can be taken on behalf of victim or perpetrator.

To assess these issues requires the combination of family and individual interviews. A child living in an abusive atmosphere will not speak about his or her experiences in the presence of a family member who is part of that system. Even though a non-abusive parent can often be of assistance to a child in beginning to share his or her experiences, that parent may unwittingly be part of the trauma organized system. Thus, despite themselves, they may give the child a cue which may be silencing. The partner subject to intimidation and abuse cannot trust an abusive partner not to become aggrieved and punitive when revealing the extent of abusive interaction. Externalizing techniques are often necessary to help the traumatized victim begin to share experiences rather than continue to be organized into silence.

There are a number of areas that need to be explored to help decide which family member can be helped, where the victimized member needs to live, and what the longer term prospects are, for example for rehabilitation of a child to a seriously abusive family, or for a partnership to have some prospect of stable outcome.

Responsibility for the Abuse

The first key issue, when confronted with a failure to provide adequate care or with serious abuse, is how much responsibility the individual takes for the state of the child; or partner, where this is relevant. How aware are such individuals that they need to change, and make some major shift in their behaviour or relationship, to ensure, future safety and protection of a child or partner?

An extension of the issue of responsibility for direct abusive action is the attitude of the other parent in child abuse. Often the trauma organized system means that not only is a child abused, but a partner is intimidated or threatened into the dominating story. A parent might frequently telephone a child in care saying that unless she changes her story the father will commit suicide, or that he cannot tolerate life without a partner. It is very difficult to be certain of a 'protective' parent maintaining a caring stance in the face of the pressure of her own needs, or those of a powerful partner.

The Ability to Put the Needs of the Victim First

The second major issue is the ability of family members to put the needs of the victim first, to show an appropriate degree of warmth rather than an attitude which blames and scapegoats the child. There would need to be further exploration to know whether there was a genuine warmth which could be brought out between mother and daughter, in order to assess whether there was sufficient care and concern for the child to remain with its mother.

In partner abuse, the issue of the extended family response may be an important determinant as to whether a victim of marital abuse can find protection and support from an extended family, or will be criticized, blamed, and almost driven back into the arms of the abusive partner who shows contrition, shame and guilt.

Recognition of the Need for Help for Long-Standing Problems

The third issue is the degree of recognition by the victimizer that he or she has a need of help for long-standing personal, marital, or relationship problems, drug, alcohol abuse. Likewise for psychiatric illness, versus denial that such problems may be present, or a gross minimization of their severity and relevance. If the individual victimizer is taking little or no responsibility for the abuse, he or she will be unlikely to acknowledge the presence of personal factors that may in addition play a major role in violent, or abusive actions.

Such issues as long-standing alcoholic problems may only come to light when, for instance, a family attends a day or residential centre and the extent of individual and inter-personal problems is revealed. The notion of a therapeutic trial to assess whether parents are able to acknowledge and begin to reverse such long-standing problems may be a helpful approach to the assessment of treatability, particularly during the early stages following recognition of severe family-violence patterns.

Such assessments need to be multi-modal, looking at individual, parental, and family functioning: the use of day and residential settings where families can attend are very helpful in finding out whether trauma organized systems are modifiable or whether they have such a hold on individuals that, for instance, children must be removed. The longer-term follow-up for seriously abused children rehabilitated to their own families indicates the very high risk of recurrent physical and emotional abuse. Review of a variety of research indicates reabuse rates of between 30 per cent and 60 per cent.

Asen, George, Piper, and Stevens (1989) used an assessment period to decide whether rehabilitation was a possibility in serious abuse. They felt that 30 per cent of serious-abuse cases have trauma organized systems of such severity that they cannot be resolved within the time-frame for the children. In our own work with severely sexually abused children, just over a third of mothers were unable to believe or develop a story that their children had been abused. Therefore, rehabilitation of children to those families could not be contemplated.

POTENTIAL FOR CHANGE OBSERVED

During a period of assessment it is essential to observe whether parents can take responsibility not only in word, through development of an appropriate story, but also in deed, by demonstrating a different form of response to the child over a period of time. The major test is whether this change can occur within a child's time-frame. A particular stress for professionals is the situation where a parent, subjected to past and current violence, cannot develop an alternative story and positive way of being quickly enough to nurture the child.

In partner abuse, the issue is how much a man can not only acknowledge the degree of abuse but also how much he is able to work with an agency to confront his abusive actions. During this period it may be helpful to have joint meetings with partners, as it is with families, to maintain the momentum of breaking the taboo about abusive action. However, it is unlikely that it would be possible to explore either the traumatic effects on the individual child or adult, or the extensiveness of abusive actions, abusive fantasies, or abusive cycles, whilst the partner is present.

When considering child sexual abuse, there is a need, during the assessment period, for interviews with children alone, children with their protective parent, protective parents alone, the abuser alone, the abuser and partner, and the whole family context.

As a result of such assessments, it becomes possible to see whether attachment patterns are rigidly fixed in aversive or highly ambivalent patterns, or whether there is a potential for change. Is there a potential for such a positive attachment within the family, or has it to be sought outside?

Cooperation with Professionals

To reverse trauma organized systems requires the collaboration of a therapeutic agency and a protection agency. In the case of a child this needs to be the child-protection agency, and in spouse abuse it may well be the police or a women's refuge which can lay down the rules for adequate and continuing protection. Although many families would like a therapeutic agency to be the only one they are in contact with, basically therapeutic agencies cannot protect. Only a protection agency has the statutory power to take action and to empower the therapeutic agency to do the work necessary to achieve the reversal of traumatic effects.

Collaborative work between therapeutic agencies and family members can influence the authority and is a powerful tool which helps to achieve a painful goal, namely talking about abusive experiences for the victim, talking about abusive actions for the victimiser, and the parental acknowledgement of what has actually happened in the place of setting a protective role. There can be an insistence on the need to develop an alternative model of relationships, to convince the court!

An important aspect of cooperation is the availability of therapeutic agencies, and of appropriate settings, for parents to be able to do the work and achieve change. Insufficient residential and day settings are available, and it is essential that treatment agencies work closely with protection agencies to create a network of therapeutic settings where work can be done with families where violence occurs.

The role of group work for offenders, whether against children or partners, is an essential development, as is group work for children and for mothers and the use of family network approaches to bring together statutory agencies and therapeutic agencies to be able to assess safety and change. Protection work with children is now embedded in a complex structure of case conferences and a variety of statutory agencies with differing views about working together. Family members need therapeutic advocates who will undertake to do work even with serious abuse situations as an essential component of the whole structure.

Assessment of Attitudes to Family Violence

When assessing treatability or potential for work, we have found it helpful to rate trauma organized systems as hopeful, doubtful, or hopeless.

Hopeful Situations

Hopeful situations are those where family members are able to acknowledge their role, or their responsibilities for the state of a child or partner. In such situations the victim is not blamed excessively but is seen as having been subject to an abusive act, and care is recognized as being essential. Other family members may need to recognize their own role in abuse and failure to care, even though they may be not directly responsible. Abusive individuals need to be willing to work on their problems, and the life experiences that they have had that have played a part in bringing about the victimizer status. There needs to be appropriate agency support and a therapeutic plan with a sufficient degree of co-operativeness to feel that there is a good prospect of change.

Doubtful Situations

Doubtful situations are those in which there is a degree of uncertainty as to whether victimizers are taking proper responsibility for the state of the victims. There may be a denial of the extent of the involvement, the victim may be attributed as having continuing responsibility for his or her own abuse, and there may be no revision of the original attribution. There may be a relative lack of support from other family members. The need of the partners for each other may be so great that the danger of re-abuse – which may then require a period of separation – cannot be confronted. There may be a limited perception for the need to change, and a discrepancy between the perceived needs of family members for help and their own willingness to acknowledge this.

Cooperation between parents and professionals my be limited, and there may be a considerable sense of doubt about commitment to change, even though resources are available to provide therapeutic input and maintain appropriate protection. It may well be that in these cases a variety of statutory instruments may be necessary to ensure protection. Almost inevitably, these may well arouse further anger and a bringing together of family members to minimize abusive interactions and to blame professionals.

Hopeless Situations

These are situations where the degree of harm to the victim is totally denied, even when there is a professional consensus that violence has been committed. There may be a denial that abuse has occurred, professionals may be accused of putting the idea or story into a child or a partner's head, and even the interviewers may be blamed. Other explanations and stories may be offered for fractures and bruising, and there may be a considerable coming together of family members, both nuclear and extended, to feel that the professionals are to blame rather than the family members.

There may be a failure to acknowledge problems of alcoholism, psychiatric illness, long histories of violence, or other major problems. Specific resources such as residential settings may be absent, or there may be insufficient taking of responsibility to make the use of such resources justifiable.

Typically, co-operation with professionals may have broken down. There may be such stories of anger and grievance and feelings of being blamed and scapegoated that it is impossible to create the sort of alliance which leads to a sense of trust and makes protection possible. Full use of the statutory processes may be essential to protect a child in such family contexts. It is likely that there will be considerable battling over such issues, with recruiting of other professionals to create a massive trauma organized system, to obliterate the traumatic actions within the family itself. Recruiting representatives in an adversarial court context for a father, a mother, a child, the local authority, the guardian of the child, even for a therapeutic agency, may complicate the most fiercely contended of cases.

THE TREATMENT PROCESS IN ORGANIZED SYSTEMS OF FAMILY VIOLENCE

Basic Issues

There has to be work with each individual involved in the trauma organized system, as well as the system as a whole. Basically this involves work with the victim and work with the victimizer.

Work with the Victim

There are two processes which have to be addressed:

(1) Emotional Processing

(2) Cognitive Processing

Emotional Processing refers to work with the processes set in train by a traumatic event, for example the intrusive thoughts and re-experiencing; the avoidance phenomena of blanking out, deleting; and the arousal component which connects with anxiety, fear, and fight/flight feelings. These processes need to be dealt with, which means being acknowledged, talked about, rehearsed in various ways in a supportive context. Instead of the reinforcement of fear, there needs to be re-experiencing in a context where support can be given, where integration can occur, and a new reality and alternative story can emerge that can overcome the reality organized by the traumatic processes. Thus traumatic responses need to be 'deconstructed' and appropriately protective responses constructed.

Cognitive Processing describes the process by which explanations for the event, and its effect on ways of seeing and experiencing and giving meaning to relationships, can be reviewed. A 'reality' and set of expectations can be developed that do not put the individual at risk. The extent of treatment necessary will depend on the severity and extensiveness of the traumatic action of the traumatic effect.

Work with the Victimizer/Abuser

A second core component is work with the abuser. If work with the victim entails detailed exploration, and sharing, of experiences, in a facilitative, supportive environment, then the analogous process with the victimizer is a detailed examination of his or her abusive action. This needs to be carried out in a context of support and validation, rather than criticism. This then allows that individual to confront the way the abuse controls his life, and those close to him. He needs to examine the rationalizations, minimizations, and denials that surround the detailed abusive process, the sense of arousal, the transformation of anger to aggression whether physical, sexual, or emotional; the action itself in considerable detail, the feelings that accompany and follow the abusive action; the processing of the event, deletions, excitement, fantasies, the guilt, shame, arousal, and the re-emergence of abusive wishes and actions.

There are, of course, variations in terms of whether the major violence is physical, sexual, or emotional; whether violent actions have become part of an addictive cycle, whether violent interactions involve more than one individual, within or outside the family. Abusive actions must thus be deconstructed and constructed so that caring, safe ways of relating can be developed, and can emerge. There is a similar need to be aware of emotional and cognitive processing of traumatizing, victimizing behaviour.

Putting the Work in Context

Although work with victimizing and victim responses are the core elements for the individual, it is necessary to confront the fact that these elements may have to be dealt with in each individual. The 'victim' may need help to avoid future abusive behaviour, for example in boys who may develop an abusive orientation as a defensive style. Victimizers construct their abuse on their own powerlessness. There is a current consensus among therapists that work on victimizers' own abuse experiences needs to follow the 'deconstruction' of their abusive behaviour, rather than preceding it. This then avoids the construction of further grievance and justification of abuse which can follow discussion of their own traumatic experiences.

There is an advantage for this work with individuals to occur in various contexts: with peers to counter feelings of aloneness and uniqueness, and for cross confrontation and support; with individuals to face experiences both as abuser and victim which feel 'beyond' sharing; and within the family to acknowledge, share, accept responsibility, and give and receive support.

Work also needs to be done in the family and social context to clarify the nature and extent of abusive action and effect, and the protective capacity of those individuals not directly involved in traumatizing and victim actions. It is helpful to think of this work as a number of stages.

The first stage includes the discovery and breaking of the taboo of silence, when what may have been a long-standing violent pattern is revealed. During this phase the necessary assessment process has to be elaborated, to determine how the abusive violent pattern can be stopped, how the individual victimized can be supported; whether the individual responsible for abusive actions can take responsibility, and whether there is a potential to work on the processes described previously. It is helpful to be able to acknowledge in the total family context that an abusive act has occurred, and to make a beginning to the open taking of responsibility, facing the minimizations and rationalizations, acknowledging the hurt, beginning the process of understanding the origin of the abuse, and viewing the factors that have maintained silence, facilitated abusive actions or secrecy.

The second stage is work undertaken when protection can be guaranteed to the victim, and a setting provided for the detailed work with all individual and family contexts. From the assessment period it will become clear whether a child can be protected and supported by a member of the family, or whether the child will need to be placed in a foster home or a therapeutic setting to initiate the work process. It may also become clear whether a couple can make a contract of safety, as described by Goldner and her colleagues, or whether a period of separation is needed; again the issue of responsibility – the acknowledgement of an abusing role – is an important part of this.

A variety of different ways of achieving emotional and cognitive re-processing need to be initiated relating to the particular set of problems and abusive patterns that are being re-enacted. Any of the following may be necessary:

- Individual work, or work with in group individuals with similar traumatic experiences
- Work with individuals who have perpetrated similar violent acts
- Work with parents whose partners have abused their children
- Subsystem work, for instance to re-build or build a relationship between a care-taking parent and child that has been either damaged by abuse or has never been sufficiently strong.

Where there is violence between a couple, a combination of individual and marital work may be called for. Whole family sessions to help integrate share new modes of seeing self and others will be necessary during this phase.

The third stage is rehabilitation. This can be initiated once the processing during separation and in separate contexts has been achieved. It may then be possible to test whether a child can live within the original family context or whether a couple can live safely together. During this phase there is a maximum need for whole family work; contexts need to be considered to assess whether this should be on a day, or residential basis, or whether clinic attendance is sufficient.

The fourth stage is creating a new family context where it has proved impossible to achieve goals of providing adequate protection and a stage for the processing of victim and victimizing behaviour. For a child, a new family context may need to be confirmed. The child in foster care may require permanent adoption placement; other children may require longer periods of work within the therapeutic settings and the day and residential communities. This is necessary to help the child process his or her experiences sufficiently to be able to live within family contexts without enacting and re-enacting abusive patterns.

The incidence of abuse within foster and other caring contexts may be high, depending on the vulnerability of the child to re-enact, or the vulnerability of care-takers to the responses of particular children. The re-enactment by partners, through interlocking choices of partners with similar characteristics, is an additional risk associated with being involved with violent interactions, whether as child or partner.

The Issue of Social Control

Social control is one of the most difficult issues in planning and carrying through treatment in cases of family violence. Without a mandate to carry through the treatment processes delineated earlier it is unlikely that treatment will be persisted with. Considerable resistance may need to be overcome to achieve the core essentials of emotional and cognitive processing for both victims and victimizers and a whole family context. Conversations about painful experiences and shameful actions have to occur against a background of a pull to denial, silence, and re-enactment rather than talking through.

Protection as the Key Principle

The principle that we have always used in the child abuse treatment pro-grammes is that, without a specific aim, it is unlikely that painful issues will be confronted. It could be argued that, once a child or family member becomes involved with a treatment programme this in turn will create its own motiva-tion. This is certainly an important factor, but inevitably the family has to get to the door. This means that therapeutic work must be a key to a child returning home, partners re-uniting, a parent having contact with a child.

The model developed has taken the protective agency as the key agency to be reported to by both family and therapeutic agency. We insist that all therapeutic work involving more than one person – for example a meeting between a mother and children, a meeting between father and mother – should also include the protective agency built in as a constant validating pressure. It is a possible to say to a family member that 'although I as a therapist could trust a partner or a parent, the issue is not what is going to convince me, but what will convince the social worker assigned to the protective role, and through her to her senior, and hence to the court standing as a societal force'.

Can Therapy be Effective in an Open System?

The question may arise as to whether therapy that takes place in such a closely monitored and reporting context can be effective. Will there be real sharing, or only empty compliance and role-playing?

It is helpful to have a number of different therapeutic contexts going on in parallel – for example as regular review meetings between professionals and family members, family members seen by different people in different settings – and an open network of communication. This very rapidly ensures that issues that are not being faced in one context can be picked up and brought back. The trauma organized system which attempts to silence, delete, and punctuate reality in particular ways, will be challenged and opened up if there are sufficient contexts and appropriate professionals to know family members, where they live, and how they relate.

Therapeutic Sequences

Abusers

In work with abusing individuals it is helpful to have a sequence of issues that have to be confronted and dealt with in an open way. It is useful to indicate that there is a programme which includes defining the cycle of abuse, defining attitudes towards children and women, understanding victim responses, and looking at their own victimization. At each of these steps there is almost inevitably a resistance to looking at such issues in detail.

Victims

With victims there may also be major issues with social control and therapeutic work, in the sense that on-going protection may be necessary. Often there is a tremendous wish not to be involved in therapeutic work. In family contexts there might be pressure to deny that abuse has occurred, to minimize and trivialize abusive experiences. A reality may be created in which the child has to agree that there are no problems, that there is no current distress, that that is all in the past. It may be argued that bringing up the subject is just prolonging the agony and reminding the child of what he or she wishes to forget. The child may need to be asked whether he or she is always able to avoid thinking about past experiences, is never upset by a person who looks like or reminds them the victimizer, that situations, places, are never reminders, that there are never flash-backs or moments between sleep and wake when memories surge back.

A positive out-going style of therapeutic work is essential; involvement in a series of different ways of approaching matters – for example through the use of videotapes, tasks, role-plays, art work, written work – are all necessary to engage children in the process.

Peer group experiences – bringing together children of similar ages, stages, and experiences are helpful in reducing difference and in giving support. Themes that share details of experiences, understanding reasons, future scripts, self protection, assertiveness are all helpful in the processing of trauma.

Families

A variety of different approaches to integrating the individual and group work can be used. There is a current debate about what issues are appropriate to work with in which context. Structural approaches are helpful in subsystem work to help a mother and traumatized child to learn to replace silence with conversations. Experiential methods, for example sculpting, can keep track of the origins of traumatizing relationships and the influence of new siblings or partners or relationships. Such methods can explore past and current patterns and a variety of new future possibilities.

Reflecting teams, co-therapy and network approaches all have their place in looking at processes that involve the multiple groups of various professionals and family members. However, conflict resolution by proxy needs to be kept in mind – for example the re-enactment of 'victim'-creating, by coming together, seeing our professional or family members as the 'enemy', and recruiting others against them.

Can Therapist be Agents of Social Control and Therapy, and *Vice Versa?*

Can the role of therapist also include that of both a social control and a protection agent? This seems to be problematic. Although there is a major need for therapeutic authority to be able to confront and deal with issues in which there may be considerable pressure towards deletion and denial, it does seem problematic for the therapist who may not have the powers or the authority, to provide a protective service as well.

The therapist needs to keep in mind a face towards the family, and a face towards the community which sanctions his professionalism.

Working with Adolescent Delinquents

Peter Wilson & Graeme Farquharson

INTRODUCTION

It is in the nature of delinquency that there exists the necessity to circumvent the accepted conventions and rules of society and confound those who uphold them. This is not necessarily a moral imperative – there is often no deliberate or conscious intent to be bad. Rather the necessity is driven by a combination of internal forces and external circumstances to produce a fundamental inability or refusal to live within the confines of a shared social reality. Delinquency is by definition a failure – a failure of duty – to meet the legal and moral requirements of the prevailing social order.

The task of social adaptation is, of course, problematic for all and central in the path of child and adolescent development. From the beginning the individual is confronted with constraints and demands that frustrate and prohibit and impinge upon the sensibilities of the self. The success and the ease with which the individual can live within this realm of conflict is necessarily dependent on a wide range of factors, both genetic and environmental. Much depends upon the quality of an individual's life as an infant and young child.

The extent of delinquency varies considerably and it may be that delinquent tendencies are integral in the process of social adaptation. This is especially the case in adolescence which is characteristically a time of experimentation, of risk taking, of testing boundaries and general rebellion. Most adolescents, at one time or other, engage in delinquent activity; for the most part, it is petty and episodic. A small proportion, however, persist in their delinquency, engaging compulsively in often extreme activities, destructive both to themselves and others. These are disturbed young people who require intensive therapy, preferably in a day or residential treatment centre. This chapter focuses primarily on these young people – the persistent offenders, with significant characterological problems.

CHILD AND ADOLESCENT DEVELOPMENT AND DELINQUENCY

The primary experience of being well nourished and contained within a secure and loving environment is basic to the laying of a foundation of trust and positive expectancy of the world. Later experiences of feeling safe and held in an environment that is reliable, within clear understood limits, are crucial to the development of self-esteem and the formation of ideals and conscience. These experiences form the rudiments of a capacity to achieve adequate self-control and a readiness to participate and adapt in a social context.

Where these early positive life experiences do not prevail, the consequences are unlikely to be favourable for positive social adaptation. Children who have been subjected to various forms of maltreatment – whether it be neglect, deprivation, physical or sexual abuse – have to contend with the physical sensations and emotional experiences of hunger and pain that, unmitigated as they may be by any benign experience, become overwhelming and traumatic. Their fears remain at quite a primitive level, that of annihilation and self-dissolution; they lack sufficient parental support and guidance to build or fortify the capacity to defend adequately against such fears. They grow up as vulnerable people, fearful and wary with a deep sense of grievance and vengeance. Their preoccupations are necessarily narcissistic and they have little interest or willingness to meet the requirements of what is predominantly perceived to be a depriving hostile world.

The impact of these early experiences sustains itself through later childhood and into adolescence and adult life. In adolescence in particular, the impressions and sensations of that early period reawaken with especial intensity, as pubertal maturation and new cognitive abilities sharpen awareness. The key developmental tasks of adolescence – achieving ownership of one's body and establishing separation/individuation – raise many issues about control, adequacy and independence (Blos 1967; Laufer and Laufer 1984). Adolescence is a period characteristically filled with anxieties about the force of bodily pressures, of sexual and aggressive fantasies, and of the new and unprecedented experience of being alone. These anxieties are ordinarily manageable, given favourable enough circumstances during adolescence and on the basis of good early experience. They become significantly problematic, however, where these conditions do not prevail and where early experiences have been traumatic.

There can be no doubt, for example, that adolescents growing up in conditions of poverty and unemployment and in communities where there are entrenched criminal sub-cultures are more likely to behave in a delinquent way than others growing up in less disadvantageous and different socio-economic circumstances. Similarly, teenagers living in families in which there is a high level of discord or violence will have greater difficulty in dealing with their own developmental anxieties of adolescence than those living in more stable families. The situation is made the worse for those who enter into adolescence – whether in its normal turbulence or the additional disorder that may surround it – with memories of past terrors and limited resources to deal with its conflicts and challenges. Adolescent anxieties compound the early terrors of childhood, with the result that many vulnerable adolescents panic in the face of uncertainty and perceived threat and either withdraw or act out impulsively to master their anxiety.

Adolescents, for example, whose early attachments to their parents were not secure and whose childhoods were subjected to significant experiences of loss or separation, are more likely to find the adolescent task of separation/individuation especially taxing (Parkes, Stevenson-Hinde and Marris 1991; Holmes 1993). Much disruptive and delinquent behaviour amongst teenagers can be understood as an attempt to make some dramatic mark upon the environment in order to register contact and ensure involvement. The essential endeavour is to fill a sense of void, inherent in the adolescent separation process, that arouses fears of loss and abandonment (Greenberg 1975). Paradoxically, the gaining of such contact and involvement invariably arouses passive fears of becoming overly dependent – which in turn can lead to further disruptive or delinquent activity to achieve distance. Relationships are thus subject to chronic circular movements which give rise to agitated, disruptive and delinquent behaviour (Glasser 1979). Characteristically, such young people are unable to regulate inter-personal distance in the usual ways.

Vignette

A fourteen-year-old boy, with no real memory of his natural parents, was regularly 'at war' with his foster parents. Despite their obvious commitment and love for him, he was quite unable to make use of this and could only respond by stealing from them and drinking alcohol ostentatiously in front of them. At such moments he would castigate them that they only 'loved' him because they 'had' to; at other times he would physically embrace them, to their obvious discomfort, in the manner of a small child. These extreme oscillations continued to the point where the adults could no longer tolerate them and he was admitted into residential treatment, where he proceeded to reenact his entire social repertoire, most notably this too-distant/too-close pattern with care-giving adults.

There are two further major damaging effects of early disturbed experience on the adolescent's ability to negotiate the basic tasks of adolescence. One relates to the issue of self-control; the other to self-cohesion. The capacity to control impulse and tolerate frustration is of particular relevance for many who engage in delinquent activity. This can be significantly impaired as a result of early environmental failure to contain the child's anxiety and to provide necessary structure and boundary to the child's existence. The exposure of the child to incomprehensible and frightening experiences and the absence of consistency in limit setting seriously interferes with the process of internalizing controls and fortifies the later tendency in adolescence towards enactment rather than containment of feeling. The lack of a self-regulating capacity – based on an established internalized sense of containment – is a critical factor in the causation of delinquency – and in turn can heighten the adolescent's fear of loss of control and limitlessness (Gallwey 1991).

The issue of self-cohesion is of central importance in adolescence. This relates to the question of identity and the extent to which the adolescent feels and believes himself to be a coherent, distinct and valued human being. The origins of this again reside in the early caring relationship in which the child not only feels secure and nourished but basically affirmed and cherished. Where this basic sense of affirmation is, for what ever reason, lacking, the child can be left unsure of his value and easily threatened by rebuke or criticism. In defence against such narcissistic vulnerability the child resorts to grandiose compensatory fantasies and in adolescence holds on to an inflated view of him or herself to ward off characteristically developmental feelings of helplessness and confusion. The challenging of such fantasies may well be experienced by the adolescent as an affront and attack on his sense of dignity and value. He may well react with defensive rage (Kohut 1972) in various forms of destructive and violent activity in order to restore a sense of omnipotence, however illusory.

THE DELINQUENT OUTCOME

The combined influence of disturbing early childhood experiences and adolescent turmoil does not in itself produce a delinquent outcome. Many children show remarkable resilience in the face of family and social adversity (Kolvin *et al.* 1990), whilst others may emerge from comparable experiences in psychotic or borderline states. Socio-economic conditions and cultural factors play a significant part in determining outcome. Nevertheless, there are many young people whose history is such as to predispose them to a delinquent life. Early experiences of neglect and abuse, inordinate fear and resentment, limited internalized controls, impaired coping capacities and mistrust in others are basic ingredients that characterize the past experiences of many delinquents and complicate their adolescence.

These experiences produce an attitude and an expectation of the outside world that is fundamentally hostile, defensive and untrusting. Other people are seen as unreliable, uncaring, ungiving, frustrating and ultimately persecutory. There is a fundamental lack of faith and a deep and abiding resentment that leads to contempt for others. The delinquent act is essentially an act of rebuke and revenge. It represents an attack on socially accepted convention and its purpose is to defy and oppose those who represent it – those who have failed to adequately provide or have caused suffering. Paradoxically, the delinquent act is one of despair and of hope; despair, of ever achieving direct gratification or acknowledgement; yet hope, in the possibility that, through the doing of the act, something good will come of it. Winnicott (1984) referred to the 'anti-social tendency' as a reaction to deprivation, a testing of the environment, as a way of 'staking a claim' on what had hitherto been withheld. 'The problem children, because of their nuisance value, had produced a public opinion that would support provision for them which in fact catered for their needs' (p.60). He saw delinquency as indicating that 'some hope remains', in the sense that it calls the external environment to attention in the absence of an appropriate internal response. The implication of this for the responsible adults, be they family or therapeutic workers, is to be alert to even the most obscure communications, for when these are missed the only remaining options for the young delinquent is to 'up the ante' with even more compelling behaviour.

The specific form of delinquency that is adopted to express this range of feeling varies considerably according to different personality structures. At one end of the spectrum there are those adolescents who are impulse driven, with limited capacity for self control and unable to regulate their behaviour either to the requirements of the external world or to their own internalized notions of good and bad. Their tendency is to grab and take, to hit out indiscriminately, and to act seemingly without thought or regard for the consequences. Their difficulty in telling the truth is as much a reflection of their confusion between the distinction between fantasy and reality as it is of any clear intent to deceive. At the other end, there are those adolescents whose personalities are more organized and structured and whose behaviour is more deliberate and planned. Their delinquency is at a more sophisticated level, with greater emphasis on deception, manipulation and trickery. Their overriding purpose is to seduce and get round those who stand in their way, to defy them through concealment and duplicity and effectively undermine and destroy trust and relatedness.

There are clearly many gradations and mixtures between these two extremes. Some young delinquents have a poorly developed moral sense or one that is confused, inconsistent or fashioned according to a particular subcultural set of norms. Others have a clear comprehension of established notions of right and wrong but an inability to heed or comply with moral constraints. What is characteristic of all is their lack of basic trust in other people and an inability or unwillingness to meet conventional demands and requirements. What is ever present is a pervasive resentment and hostility, sometimes overt and defiant, sometimes covert and resistant – and this ultimately is destructive, both to the self and to others. The degree of destructiveness varies according to the narcissistic vulnerability of the individual. The more abused, maltreated and neglected the adolescents have been as children, the more helpless, frightened and sensitive to criticism they are likely to be in their adolescence and the greater their propensity to react defensively in narcissistic and violent acts. The corollary of this is that, at every turn, they will seek to draw the therapist or worker into their internal world and their personal view of events in order to 'agree' that the behaviour is not only understandable, but is justifiable.

Vignette

A tall, well built seventeen-year-old adolescent boy spent most of his early months in a therapeutic community in self-imposed isolation from everybody else. He refused to comply with many of the rules of the community – not getting up on time, cleaning his room, or eating with the rest of the group. He did not see why he should be required to do any of these things – and he expected the staff to go along with him and make an exception of him. His attitude to the community was determinedly indifferent; his manner was belligerent and menacing. To give full expression to all of this he had tattooed onto his forehead a four letter obscene word.

As he became more accustomed to the community so he became increasingly frightening. He seemed consumed by a towering splenetic rage which sprayed quite indiscriminately over whomever was close at hand. His behaviour at times was appallingly destructive – smashing furniture, fighting sadistically and also harming his own body through cigarette burning. This – together with his disdain for any gestures of human interest and the menace of his tattoo – all cohered in the service of his effort to impose control on his immediate environment; and to compel others to experience on his behalf the vulnerability which lay at the core of his personality and which was intolerable to him.

Endeavours to reach him and engage in therapeutic work with him met with extreme resistance. He was extremely touchy if anybody made any comment about him or indeed showed any interest in him. He made it abundantly clear that he did not care about himself or anybody else. The situation remained static for several months until one day in a community meeting he was suddenly and rather unexpectedly confronted by another resident, slightly older than himself. This boy found the right tone and the right moment to say 'That word on your forehead – is that about you or is that about me?' This simple statement seemed to confound him for a moment. He seemed perplexed and discomforted and instead of his usual angry and dismissive response he sat in silence and seemed for the first time able to show something of his vulnerability. He had encountered someone who had refused to accept his projection but who did not feel the need to force it back summarily.

THERAPEUTIC WORK WITH DELINQUENT YOUNG PEOPLE: GENERAL CONSIDERATIONS

The socially expected purpose of working with delinquents is essentially to stop them breaking the law. The less explicit but necessary purpose is to enable them to gain some further understanding of themselves and their predicament and to acquire skills and techniques to assist them to develop more socially acceptable and personally fulfilling lives. This is fundamentally a therapeutic task and in this chapter, all those engaged in this endeavour – whether they are qualified psychotherapists, psychiatrists, youth workers, residential treatment workers – are referred to as 'therapists'.

Both purposes meet with entrenched resistances from the delinquent – resistances that emanate from both the nature of the delinquency and from the nature of adolescence itself. A major problem resides in the area of motivation. Many delinquents do not of themselves see the need for change in themselves and have limited capacity to work towards it. As Eissler (1967) has put it 'The technical difficulty in treating a delinquent arises from his total lack of desire to change. His symptoms are painful not to him but to others in his environment. He has no need or motive to reveal to the analyst what is going on in him. Furthermore, he sees the analyst as a representative of that society against which his aggressions are directed and therefore meets him with distrust and fear' (p.230). This applies particularly to impulse ridden delinquents whose limited self-control, primitive defences of denial and projection, and lack of self-observation militate considerably against any effective therapeutic work being carried out. Equally, more sophisticated delinquents are loathe to give up a life style, that as far as they are concerned, serves them well enough and, at least in part, benefits them, for example financially.

In addition there are substantial resistances to any form of therapeutic scrutiny or enquiry which are specific to adolescence. The adolescent is keen to preserve both his privacy and his independence and is set to defend against any hint of being taken over or regulated. Parental or adult understanding, as much as it may be sought, is often experienced as intrusive and controlling. Many adolescents, too, find it hard to tolerate tension or frustration, or cope with the revival of painful thoughts and memories. They often have difficulty in articulating their ideas and in comprehending the therapeutic endeavour.

It is not to be unexpected that in the face of such resistances, considerable pessimism prevails about the effectiveness of any therapeutic work with delinquent young people. Many adults are dismissive and punitive in their attitude to young adolescents. Others take a more sanguine view, expressed perhaps most simply by Winnicott (1966, 1971a) who concluded that there 'is only one cure for adolescence and that is the passage of time...we hold on playing for time instead of offering distractions and cures' (1966, p.79). This is of equal relevance to young delinquents, the majority of whom do not go on to persistent criminal activity in their adult life. The dangers of intervention both judicial and therapeutic have been discussed by various writers and best summarized by Sheldrick (1985): 'Our present state of knowledge suggests that we should leave delinquents alone whenever possible and that we only intervene in the lives of those who persist in offending, particularly if this of a violent nature' (p.745).

In psychiatric literature the general conclusion to be drawn from research findings is that delinquent young people, or more broadly those with various forms of character disorders, are best treated with a combination of educational, vocational and practical social skills training, with additional focused problem-solving counselling (Sheldrick 1985). The predominant emphasis throughout is on behavioural and cognitive approaches with considerable skepticism expressed about the efficacy of psychoanalytic insight directed therapy. Increasingly, however, there would seem to be a need for a both a structured and an exploratory approach, partically in cases where more severe forms of character pathology exist; and for further research into different forms of application of individual and group psychoanalytic work.

Clearly, in working with delinquent young people, there is no one set way of conducting affairs. Delinquent youths do not form a homogeneous group and the range of their delinquent activities is wide – stealing, burglary, vandalism, taking and driving away, drug dealing, various forms of violent and sexual assaults and so forth. Considerable variation exists regarding the severity and frequency of these activities and whether or not they are carried out alone or in groups. Any therapeutic approach needs to be geared according to a clear evaluation of these variables, plus an assessment of the personal history and family circumstances of the adolescent concerned and of his own personal coping resources. There is evidence to suggest that, for the majority of young delinquents, various diversionary programmes and youth work activities in the community (NACRO 1988; Jones 1987) as well as family and individual therapy and Child and Family Consultation clinics and Child Psychiatric Departments, can be helpful in dealing with those engaged in relatively minor delinquency. There is also much that can be done to prevent the development of crime and anti-social behaviour through improving the economic and housing circumstances of poor families, offering 'free pre-school early intervention programmes' (Farrington 1985, p.15) and to teaching child-rearing practices to young parents.

Major difficulties prevail, however, in the task of working with persistent young offenders who engage repetitively in extreme acts of delinquency and whose general anti-social behaviour and attitude seems impervious to the normal range of sanctions. The popular and indeed professional temptation is to write these young people off, to see them only in terms of evil or untreatability. Whereas research evidence is certainly not encouraging, certain clinical experiences, particularly based on work carried out in intensive day or residential treatment settings, suggest that significant modifications can be made in delinquent behaviour and that improvements gained in general emotional and psychological development can have a substantial ameliorating effect on delinquent tendencies.

A critical issue that needs to be further addressed in how to approach the persistent young offender concerns the nature of the motivation to change. Whilst it is accepted that at one level there is a lack of conscious wish to change, there is also in most young offenders a depth of suffering and vulnerability that is essentially intolerable for them to bear and in need of attention and care. This is in fact a significant source of potential motivation; the wish for things to be different from how they actually are. Many young offenders are ashamed of their limitations and failures in relationships. They are painfully conscious of their intellectual, academic and vocational under-achievements and many do feel quite genuinely bad about the things that they do, albeit that this may be a feeling that they can not always sustain. There is in the majority of troubled adolescent delinquents an almost desperate desire – notwithstanding all their apparent indifference and bravado – to find a way of living a different life. 'I just want to be ordinary' is not an uncharacteristic expression of many so-called diehard offenders. Their difficulty is that they cannot find the way; they cannot stop themselves from persisting in their delinquency. Many are driven compulsively to do things that both attack the properties and bodies of other people and punish themselves. Because of their life experiences throughout childhood and adolescence, they are extremely wary of the offer of any help and fearful of the dependency that may be involved. They are caught between powerful longings to be cared for, yet intense feelings of hostility to those who may provide care. Truth, too, is something they cannot easily hold onto – whether it be because out of panic or fear, they lose touch with reality or because they simply cannot bear to face their current or past difficulties.

THE ATTITUDE OF THE THERAPIST

An appreciation of this complexity in the delinquent's motivation for change is essential to the therapeutic task of working with delinquents. Equally, the motivation of the therapist to work with the young delinquent is crucial. Without a genuine interest in adolescence, a compassion for the suffering beneath the delinquency and a clear personal relationship to criminality in general, there is little likelihood that any effective work on the part of the therapist will be accomplished. There are no therapists who have a neutral attitude towards young people; all have attitudes, influenced largely by their experience of their own adolescence or of their own adolescent children. Equally, most therapists have memories of delinquent activities or thoughts: and have their own personal issues in relationship to authority. These are of key importance in determining the therapeutic attitude to delinquent behaviour; whether it be broadly indulgent or punitive. There is as much danger in over-identifying with the delinquents activities as there is in censoring them. Intending therapists should also bear in mind that they will spend much time revisiting their own adolescence – both the experiences which they enjoyed and those which felt almost intolerable.

In working with delinquent young people, the most demanding challenge is to establish a working alliance, that is, a relationship in which the young person can share concern and curiosity about him or herself with the therapist and explore together the possibility of change. This fundamentally depends on the therapist's appreciation of the young person's difficulties and fears and his or her capacity to mobilize the adolescent's underlying need to be relieved of these difficulties and wish to be different. This is, of course, no easy task and takes time. It can occur in an individual counselling or therapeutic setting but, with more disturbed persistent offenders, it is more likely to be facilitated in a setting in which contact is more continuous and built around everyday life activities such as in day centres or residential treatment centres. In these settings, there is also the greater opportunity for group work, which, under supervision, has considerable therapeutic potential. The importance of the views, attitudes, expectations and insights of peers cannot be emphasized enough in influencing adolescent and delinquent behaviour.

In many of the evaluations of effective psychotherapeutic work with delinquents, the most significant factor is often the characteristics of the therapist – on qualities such as warmth, firmness, high expectations of the young person (Sinclair and Clarke 1982; Traux and Carkhoff 1967). Implicit in this is the therapists positive regard for the adolescent, his or her own sense of integrity and authority and belief in the possibility of change. The actual manner in which the therapist approaches the delinquent clearly depends on individual differences. Some may, for example, adopt a forceful approach, presenting themselves as larger than life and omnipotent – as a way of capturing the imagination and curiosity of the young and resistant young person. This has been suggested for example by Miller (1983) and Eissler (1967), drawing on the early work of Aichhorn (1935). The essential purpose here is to forge an alliance, built on the adolescent's need for someone to take command and offer clear guidance. On the basis of this need, the possibility exists for the delinquent to identify with the therapist's standards and ideals and lays the basis of the adolescent's motivation for further development. It is probable that there is an element of this approach in most work with delinquent adolescents both to overcome their initial resistance and to meet that part of them that is seeking to be held and contained. In certain circumstances, such as in therapeutic communities, it can be cultivated under the sway of a charismatic leader. There are considerable dangers inherent in such an approach, however. Apart from the inevitable disillusionment that must ensue and the fears of passive submission that are aroused, there have been examples of grotesque abuse and exploitation of adolescents by such leaders, most notably in the case of Frank Beck (Kirkwood 1993). The alternative means of building a working alliance is to proceed in a much less dramatic way, working alongside rather than 'above' the adolescent, showing both a consistent interest, yet caution in forcing the pace or demanding a commitment. The danger of this approach is that the therapeutic activity fails to draw the interest of the delinquent and is not concrete, specific or purposeful enough. It has the advantage, however, of proceeding at the delinquent's own pace, respecting his or her privacy and fear of dependency. It is an approach that requires considerable flexibility on the part of the therapist as well as both honesty and a sense of humour.

Whatever approach is taken, a working alliance needs to build on a gradual process of developing mutual trust between the therapist and the delinquent. This is necessarily a treacherous task – not only for the young delinquent but for the therapist who has to persevere often in the knowledge that the delinquent is continuing his or her delinquent activities. The therapist has to be clear in his or her attitude of acceptance of the adolescent as an individual, but not of the adolescent's delinquent activities – and he or she must be especially careful not to be conned or seduced either into believing the delinquent's acts are not occurring or into implicitly approving what is going on. He or she has to work with the familiar paradox of working with adolescents (Wilson 1991) – that 'the adolescent does not want to be understood and yet he does; that he wants licence and yet needs boundary'. The delinquent similarly both wants and does not want to be caught and found out. It is imperative, therefore, that the therapist, up to a point, can withstand 'acting out' and tolerate 'not knowing'.

Establishing and maintaining a working alliance is at the centre of all therapeutic work with delinquent adolescents. It fundamentally addresses the issue of trust and holds open the possibility of collaboration and of change. Within the context that it sets and according to its own particular rules and strengths, further therapeutic activity can proceed. Clearly, during the course of any on-going work, attention necessarily needs to be directed towards the behaviour of the adolescent, the nature of his past delinquency and the extent to which he may or may not be continuing his or her criminal activity. This must remain a central reference point for the therapy. To ignore it could be tantamount to condoning it.

DIFFERENTIAL APPROACHES

Behaviour and cognitive therapies may be useful with many adolescents working in a systematic way to reinforce socially acceptable behaviour, develop appropriate skills and clarify basic thinking that lays behind the delinquent activity and relationships involved. Such systematic approaches provide a useful structure and order to the therapeutic work whether in an individual or group context. They function in a practical way as a necessary form of containment for many delinquents who lack their own internal sense of order (Brown 1985; McAdam 1986).

The extent to which behaviour and cognitive work can be combined with more insight directed therapeutic activity varies according to the differences of individual therapists or therapeutic regimes. The fact of the matter is that delinquent adolescents who are persistent offenders need both a clear structure and guidance in their everyday lives and also the recognition and understanding of the emotional disturbance that drives their delinquency. In actuality, most therapists who are sensitive to the complex needs of such adolescents practise a mixture of different therapeutic techniques.

In order to address the underlying emotional forces and conflicts that lead to persistent delinquent behaviour, allowance needs to be made in any therapeutic endeavour for feelings and memories of past experience to be expressed and recalled. To some extent this can be provided for in individual and cognitive therapy sessions and in the ordinary course of day or residential treatment life. Much can be achieved through building on the working alliance; helping the young delinquent express his or her fears and share memories and make sense of how these have led him or her into difficulties with others and into trouble with the law. In this sense the therapeutic work has a crucial linking, integrative function.

Of greater impact in the way such feelings and memories can be expressed and understood is through the workings of the transference. By virtue of the intensity of past experience revived in adolescence and through the compulsive repetitive dynamic of the transference, adolescent delinquents inevitably bring into their helping relationship much of the nature of their earlier relationships and difficulties. In their attitude and behaviour to the therapist, they reenact what is familiar to them. As Freud made clear 'The patient does not remember anything of what he has forgotten and repressed, but acts it out. He reproduces it not as a memory but as an action. He repeats it, without of course knowing he is repeating it' (S. Freud 1914b). It is thus in the nature of transference that feelings are expressed through actual behavioural activities. This fits well with the adolescent's tendency to express him or herself through the language of action – and the disturbed young person needs to do something that establishes contact and registers what he or she is feeling.

In a therapeutic situation, for example, the delinquent adolescent does things that have a powerful effect on the therapist. According to his or her experience and character structure, he or she may please, delight, excite, seduce, attack, humiliate, provoke, manipulate or disappoint the therapist. Each of these activities is designed to provoke a response – at one level it may be to elicit care and support and, at another level, it may be to make the therapist respond in kind. There is, in other words, a strong compelling demand for the therapist to feel some of the key experiences that the young person has previously gone through – and an anticipation that the therapist will respond as other key figures have done so in the past – for example to abuse, to hit, and so forth. There is clearly a wide range of transference scenarios, differing according to the varied histories of different individuals. For example, a delinquent adolescent boy whose childhood has been characterized by domestic violence and physical abuse, lives through his adolescence with an underlying sense of terror and of his own helplessness and powerlessness in the face of people with authority and power. He approaches the therapist accordingly, convinced at some level that the therapist will hit and damage him. He is naturally defensive and on edge; and as a preemptive strike and to relieve his anxiety, he becomes aggressive to the therapist. The therapist is thus made to feel the powerlessness and the fear that the delinquent has gone through. He is also invited to repeat past patterns of relationships and become the abusive violent parent and hit the delinquent. The delinquent runs away and hides, he takes and drive away a car and breaks into a house – to escape, to get caught, further punished and to be abusive and so forth.

These kinds of transference reenactments make available therapeutic opportunities to understand the nature of individual disturbance and to find alternative outcomes. They are inevitable in one form or another, whether in an individual, group or community context and it is the fundamental task of a therapist to recognize their significance and to withstand them. The pressing invitation from within the transference is always for past experience to be repeated – for therapists, for example, to become the violators. The key therapeutic task is therefore not to join with this process, to resist all attempts to distort the actual current helping relationship and thereby to keep open the possibility of change. Much depends on therapists' actual behaviour, on their capacity to conduct themselves appropriately beyond the dictates of the transference. This behaviour, guided as it must be, by an understanding of the transference, constitutes in effect the most profound understanding of the delinquent's problems. Such behaviour is essentially interpretative and serves as a basis for verbal clarifications and interpretations.

Vignette

In a community meeting a seventeen-year-old girl was at the centre of everyone's attention. She sat in silence on the edge of the group and close to tears. Some of the other girls knew that something terrible had happened to her the night before but this could not yet be shared with the whole community. Everyone else in the meeting was apprehensive that something explosive was about to happen. The girl refused to speak despite numerous attempts to engage her; and she became increasingly tense. Eventually she rose from her seat, yelled abuse at everybody, raced across the room kicking furniture and tried to leave. Those in the group who knew her well – her close friends, both boys and girls, and her key workers – immediately clustered around her and tried to calm her. By now she was full of fury, insulting to everybody, including her friends and yelling at staff that they didn't care and did nothing anyway. She was for a while quite beside herself. Despite her verbal and physical attacks, her friends and staff stayed beside her, occasionally holding her, gently but firming both preventing her doing harm to herself and also from leaving the group.

Gradually she subsided and began to cry almost uncontrollably. Those around her continued to hold her, sensing increasingly that the 'fight' had gone out of her. They helped her back to her seat and sat with her. Eventually she began to speak. She talked of what she had done the previous night – going off grounds, against the rules, in the middle of the night to meet a man much older than herself whom she had recently met in town. She then fell silent again. As far as she was concerned that was all there was to it. No one said anything but she became increasingly angry and started to yell at two of the boys plus a staff member. She called them names, accusing them of not caring and of just being nosey for their own idle curiosity. One or two of her girl friends tried to console her, but she continued to shout and even directed some of her insults at them. One of the boys started yelling back at her that she was selfish and ungrateful – he wasn't going to waste any more of his time on her. Two other girls started talking and giggling with each each other and for a moment it looked as if the whole meeting would disband or lose interest in the girl.

One of the staff members, however, quietly said that he thought that behind this girl's anger was another story – that what had in fact happened the night before had not been at all enjoyable. At first the girl protested but again she suddenly broke down and cried; with renewed interest and comfort from the others in the group, she was encouraged to talk about what had happened. Gradually she spoke about how she had had sex with the man and how disgusted she had felt with herself. It was not something that she had wanted or intended – it had happened on impulse and she had felt confused. Now this morning her self-disgust was total. She spoke movingly about herself and in particular how she could see how she used sex, or allowed herself to be used sexually, whenever she felt lonely or depressed. Others in the group knew that she had been sexually abused as a child – as indeed they had been – and some of them talked of how easy it was to get rid of lousy feelings for a while through having sex. The meeting ended with the girl concluding that 'acting sex' got her nowhere, in fact, it did her no good at all. She finished by saying she felt a bit more 'together' now.

In this example therapeutic work was achieved through the whole community, staff and community alike, withstanding the pressure of her transferential wish to be abused and rejected. In her delinquent behaviour in the community and through her sexual acting out she had both risked and endured the experience of bring punished and abused. In bringing this experience into the community meeting, she sought both to share and understand her disgust and shame and to repeat a significant part of her life; her destructive and attacking behaviour was unconsciously designed to bring about the censure and dismissal of the group.

For a moment it looked like she might succeed in repeating a familiar pattern – but in the end those around her did not do as she implicitly required; instead, they stayed firm, they did not behave in a retaliatory way – they provided containment based on their understanding of her experience. In this situation the primary therapeutic task was to provide psychological containment – backed up in the face of her adolescent tendency to relieve tension through action – by physical holding. The sense of being both actually and psychologically 'held' by a wider group was an absolute prerequisite to that self-containment (feeling 'together') that is the mark of personal maturity.

This example also illustrates how therapists, and others concerned, can find themselves under fairly sustained attack. This attack may take many forms – violent assault, defiant and challenging behaviour, verbal ridicule and insults – and is invariably well targeted. Disturbed adolescents, as in the example, because of their own acute vulnerability, often sense or 'know' the vulnerability of others and quickly face therapists, for example, with their own fear of violence or unresolved adolescent uncertainties about authority and sexuality.

In the setting of an intensive day or residential treatment situation, where role distance is less than in conventional individual or group therapies, the effect of such attack can be quite relentless and debilitating. During phases when the pitch of such assault is particularly acute, the most important function for the therapist is simply to survive, to survive without rancour, and without abandoning the therapeutic stance. Such acts of survival go a very long way to creating the necessary experience for the young person to feel contained.

It is clearly essential that therapists, in order to carry out their task and preserve some sense of personal sanity, receive adequate supervision and staff support. They need the opportunity to understand their own countertransference. Young and relatively inexperienced therapists (who are most frequently placed in the front line of this kind of work) can especially be overwhelmed and find themselves getting drawn into unhelpful relationships with young delinquents.

CONCLUSION

Delinquency is not an uncommon feature of adolescence – it plays its part in the overall process of social adaptation and gives expression to many typical adolescent concerns. The extent and form of delinquency depends in large measure on the quality of childhood experiences, as well as the cultural and socio-economic circumstances in which the adolescent grows up. Favourable early childhood experiences build a foundation of trust and positive expectancy that bodes well for a later readiness to live within social constraints. Unfavourable early childhood experiences can have an opposite effect, creating attitudes of fear and resentment that lead to defiance and resistance to the requirements of the social order. In adolescence, much of this early experience is relived, exacerbating difficulties in coping with separation and individuation, in controlling impulse and dealing with frustration and personal humiliation. Delinquency in adolescence arises from these difficulties and ultimately is an expression of rebuke and revenge against a world perceived to be predominantly hostile and ungiving.

In order to deal with the complexity and variety of delinquent behaviour, therapeutic work needs to based on a clear assessment of the severity and form of behaviour as well as on the personal circumstances and coping capacities of the individual. On this basis it needs to incorporate a wide variety of approaches, including educational, vocational, social skills training, counselling and psychotherapy. There is a strong case for not intervening at all in many cases of delinquency; to focus on a range of interventions through various services in the community for those who are relatively more persistent and in difficulty; and to develop intensive day and residential treatment programmes for the most disturbed offenders.

Effective therapeutic work recognizes the need for both a structured and exploratory approach. Many delinquent young people need to live and work within clear and safe social structures, fortified by clear guidelines and sanctions. Behavioural and cognitive therapies have a significant role to play in this regard. Within this, young delinquents can benefit from an understanding of their past experiences and their links to current behaviour and offending. Crucial to the therapeutic task is the attitude of the therapist and the therapist's appreciation of the specific resistances to change, and to understanding of the young person, both as a delinquent and an adolescent.

The therapist needs to be clear about his or her own sexuality, past adolescent difficulties and attitudes towards authority and to criminality; the therapist also needs to be sensitive to the nature of the delinquent's ambivalent motivation to change and to the factors that have contributed to the delinquent life. On the basis of this understanding a working alliance can be developed, building trust and finding ways of addressing the underlying emotional and familial difficulties without denying the reality of the past and possible continuing delinquency. Further exploration may be inevitable and necessary, through the young person repeating past and painful feelings in the transference to the therapist. The ability to understand the nature of the transference, to withstand its emotional force and impact and to find ways of responding therapeutically so as not to repeat past experiences, is an essential requirement of the therapist. The need for establishing well structured therapeutic regimes that can support work of this kind, as well as the provision of good staff management, support and consultation cannot be emphasized enough.

The Antisocial Personality Disorder

Strategies for Psychotherapy

J. Stuart Whiteley

INTRODUCTION

The choice of the term *Anti-Social Personality Disorder* for a condition that has preoccupied diagnosticians for almost two centuries could be regarded as the failure of the medical categorizationists neatly to pigeon-hole the behaviour, or the triumph of common-sense in simply calling a spade a spade

There have obviously been those individuals who marched out of step with the rest of the company and thereby caused a certain havoc in the ranks, whether by accident or design, since man first began to gather in social groups, but the first attempts at medical labelling began in the early nineteenth century at a time when medicine was in a phase of discovery and medical men omnipotently sought to explain all human conditions in terms of ailments to be treated. Thus commenced the search for a suitable name and a medical aetiology for social behaviour which did not conform to the norms of contemporary society and which has led us through *moral insanity* (acquired disorder of the brain), *moral imbecility* (failure to develop), *psychopathic inferior* (genetic predisposition), *personality disorder* (early life psychological trauma), *sociopath* (environmental deprivation) and the more commonly used and more bluntly purgorative term – *psychopath*.

The term *psychopathic disorder* was first included in the Mental Health Act of the United Kingdom in 1959 as a category of mental disorder for which provision should be made in terms of specialist treatment facilities and for which legal powers were designated to enforce detention for treatment if necessary. The definition, however, was vague – a *persistent disorder or disability of mind, whether or not including significant impairment of intelligence, which results in abnormally aggressive or severely irresponsible conduct* – and whilst some regarded the inclusion in the Act as a step forward in recognizing that such behaviour was an entity for which treatment should be provided on humanitarian grounds, others regarded it as an infringement of civil liberties and very little use was made of the opportunity for either providing specialized treatment centres or enforcing treatment by the Mental Health legislation.

Peter Scott (1963), often seen as the father of English forensic psychiatry, abstracted four common clauses from the many definitions of psychopathic behaviour thus;

(1) The exclusion of subnormality or psychosis

(2) The long-standing duration

(3) The description of behaviour such as aggressive and irresponsible and

(4) A clause indicating that society was impelled to do something about it.

A subsequent revision of the Act retained the diagnostic category but added the rider to the effect that *compulsory detention should only be instituted if there was a prospect of benefit from treatment.*

The category of psychopathic disorder was not included in the Scottish version of the Act (1960) and no one seems to have suffered or been deprived as a consequence.

The term anti-social personality came into being as a separate category (it was previously included as sociopathic personality disturbance: anti-social reaction) in the American Psychiatric Association's *Diagnostic and Statistical Manual of Mental Disorders* (DSM-II) in 1968. It was an attempt to co-ordinate the DSM with the International Classification of Diseases (ICD) of the World Health Organisation (1968) and briefly described such individuals as *'unsocialised, incapable of loyalty, selfish, callous, irresponsible, impulsive, they feel no guilt and do not learn from experience. Frustration tolerance is low and they often rationalise behaviour.'* DSM-III-R (1987) then substantially revised and defined the diagnostic features and amended the term to *anti-social personality disorder.* Still further amendment is expected for the next revision of the DSM to bring the category even more into agreement with the World Health Organization's current International Classification of Diseases (ICD-10, 1989).

The considerable literature and debate concerning such attempts at definition and the further, less behaviourally inclined and more psychologically weighted, definitions such as the Minnesota Multiphasic Personality Inventory (MMPI). derivative of Blackburn (1975, 1986) and the Psychopathy Check-List of Hare (1985, 1991), is efficiently summarized and critically reviewed in the report of a working party set up jointly by the Department of Health and the Home Office (Dolan, B. and Coid 1993). Thus far the DSM definitions have laid more stress on the anti-social behavioural components of the disorder, whereas the ICD definitions have leaned more toward the personality trait aspects. One might venture the opinion that it is the latter abnormalities of personality that lead to the particular disorders of behaviour evidenced, but, as the many and varied attempts at descriptive definitions indicate, the condition sits uneasily astride the behavioural–psychological divide. Chessick (1969) writing of personality disorder states that 'these individuals seem to lie on the periphery of psychiatry, on the periphery of society, and on the periphery of penology' (p.264).

Kernberg (1967) holds the view that all clear-cut cases of *anti-social personality disorder* show an underlying borderline personality organization and much of the anti-social behaviour that they manifest can be seen in terms of their borderline state; the nearness to episodic psychotic ideation, resort to fantasy and the inability to tolerate anxiety, the tendency to utilize primitive psychological defense mechanisms (splitting and projective identification) and in particular the ever-present identity diffusion (see below).

The DSM-III, and the concept of *anti-social personality disorder* in general, has tended to stress the criminal behaviour of the individual, but not all such personalities are criminal in their anti-social activity. As Cleckley (1941) so vividly pointed out in *The Mask of Sanity*, these individuals may well be holding down such key professional roles as politicians, academics, writers, teachers – doctors even – whilst episodically acting in deviant ways. Such behaviour might include a cluster of socially unacceptable but non-criminal activities such as over indulgence in alcohol, sexual promiscuity or aberations, and irresponsibility in work, family or social interactions. It is difficult to measure changes in such behaviours, which are often maintained in a covert way, whereas the measure of criminal convictions and the decrease or not after a period in therapy is a statistic that is available and thus tends to be the yardstick of therapeutic outcome.

THE AETIOLOGY OF ANTI-SOCIAL PERSONALITY DISORDER

The long-standing search for definitive aetiological factors, whether physical or psychological, in personality disorder is well reviewed in several recent books and papers and it would be repetitive and space-consuming to reproduce the material here (Akhtar 1992; Dolan, B. and Coid 1993; Kernberg 1992; Tyrer and Stein 1993). Although the significance of some specific physical or psychological abnormalities can be recognized, no overall aetiological factor emerges as always present and inevitably followed by the disorder, and the search for such an agent is really the search for a solution to a worrying social problem.

An important contribution to the understanding of genetic, physiological, environmental, electro-physiological and psychological factors in the aetiology of psychopathic and anti-social personality disorders was made by international and multi-professional participants in an Advanced Study Institute sponsored by the Scientific Division of NATO (Hare and Schalling 1978). In particular, the inherited features of criminality, disorders of autonomic arousal leading to hyperactivity or excitement seeking, and the relationship to and origins of, neurotic patterns of behaviour were remarked upon. Subsequent advances in the neurobiological aspects of psychopathy reviewed by Dolan, M. (1994) take our understanding of the part that genetic and neurophysiological components may play a little (but not a lot) further, but nevertheless emphasize the need to consider the interaction between innate properties and social and psychological life-events in the development of behavioural and attitudinal abnormalities.

The more psychodynamic aspects of anti-social personality disorder are alluded to in the reviews already mentioned but receive less prominence than physical factors in most overviews. In the United States, however, Kernberg (1984, 1992) in particular has been a prolific researcher and writer on the psychodynamic aetiology and the psychotherapy of abnormal personalities and Akhtar (1992) has not only added a review of the development of psychodynamic thought on the subject but also succeeded in including psychoanalytic concepts of anti-social personality disorder within the descriptive definitions of the DSM-III-R in a most illuminating way.

The seemingly endless quest to pin down anti-social behaviours into a category by summation of the constituent parts (whether behavioural, psychological or physical) is not without its critics (Blackburn 1988, Lewis and Appleby 1988). Indeed, there remains a significant view not only in society in general but also amongst the psychiatric and psychology professions that personality disorders in general and psychopathic disorder in particular are not usefully retained as categories of mental disorder when the behaviour described is primarily anti-social or delinquent. There are even proposals that the terms should be abolished.[1] The *madness or badness* dichotomy of the nineteenth century is still perpetuated in thinly disguised form, yet even when such a debate was at its height in the early nineteenth century, Benjamin Rush (1812), who wrote insightfully about the condition of *moral insanity* although believing

---

[1] Recent correspondence in the *Psychiatric Bulletin* of the Royal College of Psychiatrists (1993, Vol. 17, 1994, Vols. 7 and 8) has advocated the abandonment of the term *personality disorder* as a diagnostic entity and one suggestion was to explain to the individual that he was to be treated for his particular disturbance of behaviour rather than being 'given the diagnosis of psychopath'. That may not be acceptable to the client either, however, and I recall the dismissive disparagement of the judgement of one previously encountered psychiatrist by a client whom we were assessing in a group interview (of staff and patients) at Henderson Hospital.
'He said I was impulsive and unable to control my temper. Me! After seeing me for ten minutes! I hit the bloody roof!.'

it to be organic and innate, raised the question of *'where disease ends and vice begins'* in this condition and that remains unclear.

However, increasing recognition of both the specific characteristics of the abnormal behaviour of such individuals and of their idiosyncratic attitudes to society and the frequent association with a variety of abnormal physical, environmental, psychological and genetic factors does support the point of view that *anti-social personality disorder* is a significant and proper diagnostic category. Tyrer, Casey and Ferguson write, in an excellent compilation of all aspects of personality disorder (Tyrer and Stein, 1993) that 'the concept of personality disorder is not likely to disappear from psychiatry despite its critics and once it is accepted universally there will be no need to give a nervous laugh or act as though the subject is a parenthetical appendage whenever it is mentioned' (p.12).

CLINICAL APPRAISAL

Clinical diagnosis, like the practice of psychotherapy, is an art which largely comprises skilled listening. The contribution of the diagnostic manuals and symptom definition tables referred to above is that they incline us to the recognition of the patterns of speech and behaviour and mental attitudes of the client provided that we give him or her space in which to interact rather than just subject the other to a battery of questions and investigative processes.

For the clinical practitioner faced with a client for assessment it is probably more likely that, rather than some clear-cut factor emerging, a combination of the many pre-disposing factors combine at some crucial time in the individual's psychological and social development to put a metaphorical spoke in the wheel and throw the process out of balance.

Vignette

Phil, born out of wedlock (genetic factor?) in the Glasgow Gorbals (environmental factor?) was brought up in the old-fashioned total institution where no concept of 'good-enough-mothering' had been heard of (psychological factor?). He also had a crippled arm from infantile poliomyelitis (medical factor?) and each day relied upon his one friend to tie his shoelaces before they went to primary school.

One morning, at the age of five or six, his friend was in too much of a hurry to do his duty. 'I remember that day as if it was yesterday', recounted the bitter, aggressive, solitary, thieving Phil some twenty years later. 'I never relied on anyone again, I went my own way.'

He turned his back on society, living on the actual and the emotional fringes of normality, stole what he needed for the immediate present, exploited to the limit the aid agencies, hospitals, prisons and hostels but always with the lingering doubt about relationships that drove him to seek out the helpers, attach himself to a 'friend' and then make steadily increasing demands until finally the friend or aid agency had to cry 'enough'.

Then he would react with explosive anger – as he had proved yet again that no-one was to be trusted – and retreat back into his underworld.

It seemed that he may have survived all the early traumas of deprivation and handicap, albeit with some residual vulnerability, until just at that *crucial time* in the social learning curve for a child, when he was to move from an egocentric position with his own world and needs around him into a world of others which demanded an adjustment in order to integrate with their egocentric worlds. Then, the extra enabling input that he needed was missing and his developmental progress crashed.

In making an assessment of the extent or presence of the diagnostic criteria for *anti-social personality disorder* one would look for evidence of:

(1) the social and environmental disturbance in the past history going back into childhood and

(2) the particular qualities of the attitudinal and behavioural dysfunction in the present which might be linked with the above.

PAST HISTORY

A social history profile of patients with personality disorder admitted to Henderson Hospital included a high proportion of individuals from a broken parental home, incidents of physical or sexual abuse in childhood, periods in residential child care, school truancy and a history of functioning below achievement expectations in school and at work. Conflict with the law, failure to make or sustain stable relationships, such as a marriage, and repetitive admissions to both psychiatric and penal institutions was almost universal (Whiteley 1970).

Robins (1966) in her long-term study of behaviourally disturbed children who became anti-social personalities in adult life, and which study contributed largely to the adoption of the diagnostic category of *anti-social personality disorder* in the United States, cited the following features: a failure to conform to social norms in the absence of serious mental defect and comprising behaviour which was callous or reckless and featuring lying, stealing, truancy, sexual promiscuity, drug or alcohol dependence, failure to maintain work, marriage or social relationships. The onset was usually before fifteen years of age and never after eighteen years.

In forty-four per cent of men the onset was discernible before the age of eight with lying, stealing or classroom disturbance and in fifty-five per cent of females the onset was between fourteen and eighteen years with sexual disturbance. The incidence in males was four times that in females.

Parental psycho-pathological disturbance was seen twice as often in the fathers as compared with the normal population and even for females the paternal pathology was seen as most crucial. After the age of thirty the more flagrant anti-social behaviour diminished, but within the narrower confines of the family the behaviour continued to be destructive. Death by violence, through suicide or as victims of assault was frequent.

Thus the myth of the 'burnout' of psychopathic behaviour[2] in middle-life which is often represented in text-books is set aside and one should be alerted to the increasing despair and danger of self-destructive behaviour with the passage of time.

Disturbance of personal, family and environmental interactions in early life can create the psychosocial dysfunction of later life which amounts to *anti-social personality disorder*, but this not an inevitable consequence, as many accounts of a normal life story emerging from appalling early life experiences will tell us. Bowlby in his initial paper on 'Forty-four juvenile thieves' (Bowlby 1944) seemed to direct attention to maternal deprivation as a key factor in the development of delinquency. Later modifications by himself and others brought this more into perspective, but nevertheless drew attention to the need for a secure early attachment to reduce the potential vulnerability to psychological and social breakdown in later life. Failures of attachment, either through absent parents or because of traumatic early relationships, feature highly in the histories of anti-social personalities. Failure of the first attachments then make succeeding personal and social attachments at best vulnerable and, at worst, further attachments are avoided at all cost leading to the social isolation of the individual.

PRESENT BEHAVIOUR

Robins (1966) also included in her description of the client with *anti-social personality disorder* that he or she often felt that others were hostile, and frequently expressed feelings of boredom. The feeling of boredom and the search for excitement often encountered may be linked with a physiological state of low autonomic arousal, even though the latter's connection with psychological function is unclear (Dolan 1994) Offences may be committed or violence provoked out of a physiological need to precipitate an adrenalin-like surge in order to feel alive, or out of a psychological need to be acknowledged by others and signified by society as an individual who exists and has to be reckoned with.

---

2 Compare this with the non-myth of staff 'burnout'. Chapter II:14. (M.C. Editor).

On the other hand, there are those who are in a constant state of heightened arousal and excitation and also commit acts of violence against the self or others in order to achieve a sense of release from the tension. In psychological profiles of patients referred to Henderson Hospital under a general diagnostic label of psychopath or sociopath, O'Brien (Copas, O'Brien, Roberts and Whiteley 1984) demonstrated both the weak ego-structure common to all clients but also that the disorder of personality could manifest itself in different typologies. One had the highly anxious individual with inwardly directed hostility comprising a more neurotic pattern and with a high incidence of psychiatric hospitalizations and, at the opposite pole, the non-anxious individual with outwardly-directed hostility comprising a more psychopathic pattern and with a high incidence of criminality. There were mixed categories in between these but it was interesting to see that all made a positive reponse to treatment when compared with an untreated group. The mixed category with high anxiety and outwardly-directed hostility (which perhaps comes nearest to the pure border-line personality definition) had the lowest response to treatment but – it is important to note – without treatment this group had virtually no chance of a positive outcome or personality change.

The feeling that others are hostile results partly from the social isolation and failure to integrate with society and partly out of the individual's defective interpretation of the behaviour of others in regard to himself.

In any check-list of *anti-social personality disorder* I would include:

1. The inability of this individual to see himself and his behaviour from another's point of view and the unawareness on his part that his behaviour could be seen as abnormal. The sociologist Gough (1947) described this as a deficiency in role-playing behaviour. The individual with *anti-social personality disorder* cannot put himself in another person's shoes and recognize what it would be like to be the recipient of his behaviour. Rush, in 1812, made a similar observation when he wrote that such individuals (with what was then termed *moral insanity*) 'cannot describe anything as it has appeared to other people'.

Cleckley, whose celebrated book *The Mask of Sanity* (1941) was the major influence in the United States in drawing attention to what was then named *psychopathic personality* called the condition a *semantic psychosis*; that is a disorder of understanding which he, nevertheless, considered to be a physical disorder of brain function. Johns and Quay (1962) more graphically described this conceptual dysfunction in terms of 'he knows the words but not the music'.

Vignette

Joe wrote to Henderson Hospital from a remand prison seeking hospital admission rather than imprisonment. He had on a previous occasion been referred for treatment by a probation officer after appearing in court and been offered admission to which the court agreed but he then failed to attend for treatment saying that he 'had learned his lesson now and did not need treatment'. He was thus at liberty and before long committed a further offence for which he was now facing sentencing. His letter of application read as follows: 'There does not seem to be an obvious reason for my repeated lawbreaking. I really want to lead the **** life of going to work, coming home, kissing the girl, having tea, watching the telly or working on the car, game of football at the week-end, the things all my friends seem to do, but all I am doing at the moment is slopping out, stomping around an exercise yard and generally wasting away.'

*The word I have temporarily set aside****and which he actually wrote was 'drab'. In this instance he knew the music but not the words!*

2. The phenomenon of *identity diffusion* is present in all severe personality disorders (Akhtar 1992). Living thus, on the fringes of society, uncertain of how he stands in relation to others and of what is expected of him and what he should expect of others, he becomes a social isolate. On the one hand he is wishing to be a part of society whilst on the other hand fearing too close an attachment lest it prove to be a repetition of earlier and traumatic failures of attachment which have left him with no stable model of social behaviour to follow. Like everyone else, he needs recognition of his existence and acknowledgement of his worth but, unable to establish a role in society, his social isolation can amount to a fear of not even existing. Some of the dramatic or chaotic disturbance he creates may therefore serve the purpose simply of getting himself and his existence acknowledged by others whilst also giving himself the confirmation of his existence through the autonomic arousal referred to earlier.

Vignette

Linda contacted us from prison to describe why she had smashed up the reflector mirrors of the police cars in the police station yard. This was not her first physical encounter with the police, whom she had assaulted for no particular reason on previous occasions, except perhaps that they represented some form of established authority and stability with a consistent response. 'I thought everything I did and thought was not real,' she wrote, 'that I was not real, almost as though I did not exist so I could never affect anyone – because I was not real. No one could possibly take me seriously because I was not real.'

Robins (1966), in her check-list of symptoms in the anti-social personality, cites vagrancy as one of the major features. In the search to be an entity and to establish an identity (and thus be a part of society) the anti-social personality will wander from town to town, leaving a bag in Glasgow and claiming a grand-mother in Bristol and once having had a job in Leeds, as if to try to establish that he comes from Glasgow or Bristol or Leeds and thus can be expected to have all the qualities of a person from Glasgow or Bristol or Leeds. There is also a kind of psycho-social vagrancy as he wanders through personalities, names and characterizations.

He is a Hell's Angel for a while, then when next seen may be a Born-again Christian or a Hari-Krishna devotee. All of these will be social groupings which will have their distinctive uniformity of dress, regular meeting places, consistent styles of behaving and mannerisms of speech. They offer a role to be acted out and a ready-made identity to wear. That the latter never quite fits is evidenced by the way he still fails to fit into the new grouping and has to move on again. Names and appearances are changed, less as a criminal alias but more as a means of making others take notice. Thus, John Jones became St. John Jones and when that failed to achieve much of an effect he appeared in group therapy sessions, Kojak-style, with all his hair shaved off. John Bottomley who felt he was out of step with society became John Graye and when that failed to change how he was perceived by others he became Jake Zed Mangle-Wurzel and adopted the career of an eccentric which has gained him a prominent role in his local community, frequent visits from media personnel – and academics seeking to research his personality – and a certain content although he is painfully and insightfully aware that his new identity is a defence against the lurking despair and social isolation that lies beneath the surface.

Identity diffusion and the inability to integrate with and be accepted by society can be seen as primarily arising out of the failure of early attachment to key parental figures so as to acquire from them models of social interaction and intimacy. In the course of normal development other attachment opportunities then follow and each adds to the growing social and personal awareness of the individual; immediate family members, the extended family, friends, school and the accepted *mores* of society all contribute to the process. Attachment gives identity through recognition and acknowledgement of one's existence and for those with no clear image of their own identity the search for an alternative identity leads into the societal and psychic vagrancy alluded to above.

STRATEGIES FOR PSYCHOTHERAPY

The conclusion of Dolan and Coid's (1993) meticulous review of the treatment and research studies on psychopathic and anti-social personalities was that the majority of such studies were so flawed as to be unreliable and that there is still no evidence that such psychopaths can or cannot be successfully treated. All methods of treatment (including physical and pharmacological) were reviewed and therapeutic community treatment emerges as the approach which has shown the most promising results in terms of psychological and behavioural change during treatment, and significant improvements following treatment in life-history variables (recidivism, re-hospitalization etc.) Higgitt and Fonargy (1992), reviewing the psychotherapy of personality disorders, also state that 'there is a great deal of clinical evidence to support the value of therapeutic communities in the psychotherapy of such individuals' (p.36).

Individual psychotherapy of the client with *anti-social personality disorder* is a daunting task. For the patient with *anti-social personality disorder* the one-to-one and face-to-face situation with the therapist can be threatening. The transference and countertransference interactions are intense. Projective identification, manipulation and resistances, both conscious and unconscious, can undermine the therapy and the therapist. Higgitt and Fonargy indicate that the therapist is in nearly as great a danger of being draw into acting-out in the course of treatment as is the patient because of the ability of these patients to sense and home in on the vulnerability of the therapist. They may simultaneously hold feelings that the therapist can provide relief for them but that he is also the cause of their suffering; he is both omnipotent and yet inadequate. Kernberg (1992) makes the point that the emotional burden that this type of client places on the therapist may require the therapist to spend time outside the treatment hours working through his own feelings of countertransference and that to be so preoccupied with these difficult individuals between treatment hours may be a healthy process and not neurotic.

Supportive psychotherapy in which there is both a holding and a limit-setting function has shown better results than interpretive therapy. The patient's inability to persist with an intensive and disturbing treatment process also lends some weight to a short term and targeted approach from which both therapist and client can withdraw with honour, as it were, at an agreed time and with some progress made if not a *'cure'* achieved. The inability to persist with therapy was also illustrated in a *Day Care* setting (Karterud *et al.* 1992) where, despite positive results from those who stayed with therapy, there was a greater early drop-out from therapy than from an in-patient unit run on similar therapeutic community lines.

Higgitt and Fonargy (1992) conclude with some recommendations on the psychotherapy of personality disorder which stress that the aim of the psychotherapy may as often be the reduction of suicide risk rather than a fundamental change of personality and that therapist commitment and empathy are of special significance in dealing with such individuals. Focus on the here and now of current relationships is advocated.

In *out-patient group psychotherapy* the anti-social personality feels similarly threatened by the group members with whom he cannot empathize and who increase his feelings of social isolation. He sets himself up in rivalrous conflict with the group conductor, greedily demands attention and becomes paranoid if attention is diverted from him. This may then lead to aggressive or threatening behaviour and an early drop-out from the group or a provoked dismissal. It is not surprising, therefore, that the *therapeutic community* can offer the best modality for psychotherapy of *anti-social personality disorder*. Such a setting provides the aura of excitement and drama that the patient seeks. The boundaries and limit-setting initially, and the caring peer-group eventually, provide the necessary holding, whilst for the therapist the team approach, including involvement of other patients with whom the client can make empathic associations, lessens the stresses on the therapist.

If the dysfunctional behaviour of *anti-social personality disorder* is seen as having its roots in early experiences and understood in those terms, a psychotherapeutic strategy utilizing the *potential space* (Winnicott 1971a) and amorphous body of the therapeutic community can be formulated which addresses the failure of attachment and its consequences in a way that provides a corrective emotional experience. The opportunity for regression to the earlier traumatic failures of attachment and the possibility of working through these in a safe and supportive setting then provide the optimum conditions for a positive outcome (Whiteley 1994)

Psychoanalytic Psychotherapy

Hjalmar Van Marle

CONFIDENTIALITY

For the patient, an important source of attraction of psychotherapy is to be found in the confidentiality of which he is assured. He will be trying to form a unique relationship with his psychotherapist. In this relationship he can also express the deeper layers of his emotional life. The therapist's decision as to whether to opt for an assurance of confidentiality or not during the psychotherapy should, in my opinion, depend upon the final aim of the treatment. By guaranteeing confidentiality in advance, a refuge is deliberately created where, basically, the patient's imagination is not limited – in contrast to his behaviour which is limited in matters such as time-keeping and refraining from aggressive behaviour. As a result the possibility for early childhood behaviour is stimulated, and this can subsequently become an integral part of the treatment. By lifting confidentiality and – as a practical result – allowing the psychotherapist to participate in the team treating the patient, the uniqueness of this one-to-one relation becomes superficial, and sessions comparable to a conversation with any other member of the team, without the psychotherapist's specific therapeutic activity. If the patient is assured of confidentiality, he regresses far more, because he feels unobserved. Completely different data can be discussed, so that psychotherapy is another and additional form of influence in relation to other forms of treatment.

When the choice is for a primarily supportive approach in psychotherapy or in a psychotherapeutic community, then the dimension of the strictest confidentiality will not be necessary and will even be counterproductive, because it interferes with the formation of social adaptation mechanisms. The fact is that the ever-present possibility of regressing to early childhood behaviour will be frustrated by the latter, since at first no reason for change arises. What remains important is confidentiality, which means that the patient dares to speak freely and dares to test his intimate mental life with his psychotherapist. In my opinion, confidentiality is essential in treatment primarily aimed at insight, in which closely related social skills functioning as defence must be circumvented to get to the essence of the symptoms, in this case the risk of the offence.

TRANSFERENCE

The primary motive resulting from the dyadic perception of patients with antisocial personality disorders, is claiming the care of the psychotherapist, to the exclusion of all others. In the patient's experience it is his 'own' psychotherapy; to put it more boldly: it is part of himself, with both real characteristics (his place, his appointment) and those to which he gives form (the personality of the psychotherapist) with the help of his imagination.

From the very start we see three important transference configurations for the psychotherapist which can best be described in Kohut's (1971) terms. Which of the three is dominant depends on the therapeutic setting and the patient's regression level. Those patients able to work within the transference (see also the section on forming the therapeutic relationship, later), have at some point in their development experienced what a positive relationship means and want it back again.

Such a relationship in the patient's inner life will in most cases offer the solution. The three forms of transference are:

(1) *Total attachment to the psychotherapist ('merger')*: not being able to do without him, only able to think about him and what he or she would do, and accordingly act like that. But also the other way around: in the patient's perception the psychotherapist acts in a way the patient expects him to act. When in reality this appears not to be the case, it may lead to great disappointments and even to furiously breaking off the relation.

(2) *Alter-ego transference*: the patient feels equal, that is to say, more an individual and more detached from the psychotherapist and imitates him. In the department he becomes a co-therapist of the sociotherapists. He will be differentiating and experimenting more in his behaviour. However, he has no identity of his own at all yet.

(3) *Mirror transference*: the patient now sees his psychotherapist more like a therapist; in other words he is no longer exclusively experienced as the product of his own needs. There is a greater distance. But then, it must be the ideal psychotherapist, with all his attention focused on the patient; he must particularly listen, understand him

and first and foremost approve of him. The psychotherapist becomes a mirror reflecting the patient's narcissism on himself, preferably even enlarged.

Idealizing transferences cannot last forever. Especially when a change for the better in the patient occurs, everyday reality will present itself: the psychotherapist appears to be a human being after all. The seemingly small disappointments upset the patient a lot, though. The confidence which originally flowers is interrupted by moments of distrust. These conflicting feelings, and also the increasing ability to form his own identity, constitute the conditions for the appearance of another transference configuration, namely the devaluing transference on the therapist. Psychotherapy is still followed, but with much disdain, as if it were taking place more in the interest of the psychotherapist than for the patient's sake. The latter will constantly try to prove that it is he who understands himself best, and that he is totally in control of the situation. By opposing his therapist he climbs the ladder of his own ranking.

This devaluing transference, in my opinion comparable with Kohut's grandiose transferences (1971), may also present itself as a primary motive during the diagnosis, during which the person concerned tries to prove that he is even the master of the psychotherapist and can make him believe his vision of what is really the matter. This is often deliberately rationalized by the patient who says that he wishes to find out whether there is still something wrong with him – in fact he doesn't think there is.

Whatever criterion constitutes the basis of the application for treatment, an attempt to the realization of an idealizing or devaluing object relation, it is of importance that the psychotherapy does not take place in the vacuum of the hospital, since then it is totally separated from the treatment reality of the clinic. The patient and the psychotherapist must not be linked to each other in isolation. They will in this situation lose too much contact with reality (of the hospital environment) so that they cannot keep a sufficient distance between each other. When there are grounds for psychoanalytical psychotherapy, it is of great importance that during the diagnosis the patient should have shown himself able to have managed to build up, if only minimal, relations in the department with the assessors assigned to him.

THE WORKING ALLIANCE

When discussing the psychotherapeutic relation in its own right, it is sensible to understand the differences between working alliance (De Blécourt et al. 1981) and transference. Greenson's concept (1967) 'working alliance', indicates that, despite all sorts of frustrations during the therapy, the patient still has the power to maintain the relation with his psychotherapist and to benefit from it. This presupposes some fundamental confidence in the non-destructive presence of this therapist: the examined person can feel at ease. The working alliance is based on certainty and security, which feelings have been acquired by the fundamental confidence the person in question once developed in relation with the mothering person. Accordingly, the working alliance has other roots than the transference methods during which unconsciously, impulses and desires are being relived in a therapeutic relationship (Laplanche and Pontalis 1973).

So the working alliance is the confidence in the psychotherapist that he can handle the patient and can work with his therapy and can retain it. The transference to the therapist may also develop into expectation, hope and drive for cooperation, but this should not be mixed up with the working alliance. For the origins are based on precisely unfulfilled wishes towards one of the parent figures and the urge for these wishes to be fulfilled by means of all sorts of conscious or unconscious acting out of this intrapsychic neurotic conflict. Besides a fundamental ability to form a relation of confidence, the working alliance is based on a deliberate insight to opt for the treatment.

A 'working alliance', as defined, is mostly not present with the patients mentioned above. In their cases there need not necessarily be an already existing confidence in the relationship with the psychotherapist – partly based on their own life experience. The first contact with the psychotherapist is triggered by transference motives or external interests, such as being prepared to cooperate. This implies that then the psychotherapist can not rely on the existence of a working alliance. If he wants to bring about a therapeutic relationship then he will have to actively anticipate the patient's transference, a patient who is primarily looking for a 'self-object', an extension of himself. This is an important difference with the psychotherapy and psychoanalysis carried out elsewhere. During the therapy the distance in the relation with the silent, expecting psychotherapist is not possible with the group discussed here. After all, the need to accept psychotherapy is based on certain early-childhood relation forms that do not put up with a purely expectant attitude of the therapist: this is seen as a lack of commitment. That is why in hospital psychotherapy also other parameters play a role, such as getting a cup of coffee or at the patient's request being present at an evaluation discussion by the psychotherapist.

Can these patients nevertheless take advantage of insight-giving psychotherapy? As regards patients who have been diagnosed as development psychopaths, on the basis of his reference list Frosch (1983) arrives at the conclusion that there is in fact only a chance of success if the treatment is started in an intramural setting. He is more optimistic for borderline (also serious) patients, although he is of the opinion that these patients need a high degree of structure too. Although the structure of the treatment situation is of importance for receiving all kinds of acting-out patterns, regarding the result of the treatment, achieving a therapeutic alliance in case of personality disorders is essential (Gerstly *et al.* 1989).

After all, the problem with personality disorders is that the separation-individuation has not been negotiated successfully. This implies that no consistency in self-perception has been achieved because the person does not experience the other as a unity with well balanced good and bad qualities. Therefore he cannot see himself as a unity with good and bad aspects experienced by the other person, but as a person who reacts upon the purposes of others. In these cases the transferences to the psychotherapist are very violent. On top of that the working alliance is difficult to form and is at the same time fragile. If there is some sort of suffering pressure involved, this may have a motivating effect on the formation of the working alliance. It is exactly this which is often absent in the personality disorder because, as we have seen, the problem is externalized to the outside world. Whether or not the patient still expects something from his therapist is a very important criterion since, in my experience, those patients who neither want any relationship with someone else, nor even want to involve anyone in their defence constellation, have a bad prognosis not only for ambulant but also for clinical treatment. The people who consequently fall by the wayside are especially those suffering from process psychosis, in which autism plays a leading part.

Forming the Therapeutic Relationship

When the criterion for establishing the working alliance is 'to want to do something with someone', this implies that there is some awareness of the other. In the cases of a disorder in the individuation, this can, however, be not more than sensing and using somebody else's qualities as a part object. The patient would like to use his therapist as an extension of his own imagination. The therapist is used to give shape to the narcissistic transferences. A breaking away from the mother–child dyad has not taken place because during one of the substages of early childhood development the optimal distance from the mothering parent figure was lacking. This insufficient mother–child relation could not adequately take care of the child in the various relations during its development; in other words, to provide a basis for the child to develop a 'narcissistic tie' (Lampl de Groot 1975) with the mother. When this internalization of an adequate, protective structure has failed, in fact no narcissistic identification tie has been established which is strong enough to maintain the relationship with the therapist when fierce emotions arise during the treatment. Where there is no security offered by the internalization of positive, motherly feelings, a further defence constellation will consequently have to provide the necessary structure in the world of experience.

So in the case of these disorders there is no question of establishing a working alliance to retain motivation of the treatment in difficult times. Therefore at that moment the therapeutic environment is being used for its qualities as a 'holding environment' (Winnicott 1960). This is the second reason why psychotherapy is not introduced at the start of the treatment in the hospital. First of all there must be some attachment in the living-quarters because else it cannot hold, like a container, the tensions stirred up by the psychotherapy and afterwards give it back again to the patient in a modified form. Similarly, in individual psychotherapy it is first essential to explain and discuss only all kinds of conflicting (somewhat ambivalent) feelings for a considerable period of time, before proceeding to interpreting unconscious data. With this self-explanatory and clarifying attitude, the possibility is created in the reality to come to a relation with the psychotherapist based on confidence which is supposed to bear and to handle the frustrations during the continuation of the treatment.

Another aspect at the beginning of the therapy is the question of whether the person concerned will indeed be trying to start real contacts with the psychotherapist, *casu quo* to make attempts to be liked. During the diagnosis it is of great importance to know whether there have been people who could have worked up sympathy for the patient in question. From a prognostic point of view, this 'Work of Conquest' (Balint 1968) is a favourable sign for us: it shows that preverbally the person concerned has a notion of the other as a person to become attached to and is willing to try to acquire this attachment. This is not automatically a drive for an individualized equal relation form, but rather the pre-Oedipal motivated symbiotic attachment, the 'anxious attachment' (Bowlby 1973). In such cases the patient shows that once in his life, at an early childhood level, he experienced a start to a satisfactory relationship. The verification of this observation will have to be effected on the basis of the person's life story. It shows that, despite everything, the patient has not given up the hope of his individuality being recognized by another person. The psychotherapist will consciously have to satisfy the patient's primary need for a relationship. If, however, the patient wants to form a symbiotic relationship once again and to organize it in accordance with his needs, then at best a symbiotic-like relationship may be expected from the psychotherapist – symbiotic-like in the meaning of a clear 'as if' quality. This also forms the difference between malign and benign regression (Balint 1968) in psychotherapy, in which in the first case the patient and the psychotherapist get involved in a symbiotic tie to such an extent that any further progress in the therapeutic process is out of the question. In this case the patient and the therapist have found each other in their mutual needs – and the external reality of the therapy – namely the growth of the personality structure is then lost. Benign regression can be compared with Abelin's remarks (1971) on the role of the father, who rather as a third person offers an escape route based on the child's symbiotic expectation and the primary caring person. The psychotherapist reflects, clarifies, and interprets the relationship of the patient with the offender. Weekly supervision and intervision, combined with a good education, are the conditions the hospital consequently demands from its psychotherapists.

RESISTANCE

In the psychotherapeutic setting, the psychotherapist's reliability (especially its preverbal effects, such as time, place, attitude) and his empathy (which is completely different from the concept of understanding, namely the recognition of the patient's subjective reality perception) stir up the sparkle of hope within the patient, that he may succeed in finding security with others while retaining a sense of self-respect. Thus all kinds of intense early childhood desires are being activated. In the absence of a working alliance the therapeutic process will at first have to be born entirely by the patient's transferences to the therapist. Therefore it is essential that aspects of the transference hindering the continuation of the therapy should be discussed with the patient as soon as they occur. Mostly concerned here are long-lasting early childhood transferences or their acting out.

The realization of the transference will, in contrast to the treatment of neurotic patients, occur very quickly and is actually present from the start as a result of the very weak ego-strength with personality disorders. The intensity of the feelings and also the perversions in the reality will quickly increase under the influence of the therapeutic process so that acting out or enacting will quickly occur. It is therefore important that the part of the patient's ego whose function is to keep firmly in touch with reality, continues to function so and will not be overwhelmed. For the creation of a greater confidence (and so less fear) there must be continuity in the agreements, constancy in the attitudes of the therapist, and also certainty in his reactions. In this way then the therapist is able to bring about 'holding' (see also Kernberg 1984) as a result of which the affects caused can be restricted in time, place and person so that they turn out to be less overwhelming and threatening. Besides it is also of importance to support the reality-directed part of the patient's ego, by being a clear identification figure for him. Thus in an 'exemplary' way the therapist can find out with the patient why and how the patient put his feelings into action, or disentangle with him his ambivalent attitudes towards a certain situation.

In my opinion it is not possible to bring a supportive (in other words assisting) psychotherapy to a favourable conclusion with these patients. The acceptance and support of the rather more healthy ego-functions is not sufficient for the patient to cause the ego-strength to increase for a longer period of time. On the one hand this is not surprising, since with personality disorders, generally speaking, in certain fields, in average situations, a satisfactory adaptation is achieved, so that supporting this would not be necessary any more. On the other hand it is not possible to get through the 'vertical split' (Kohut 1971) using a supportive attitude: in such an interview the pathological defence mechanisms remain hidden, split from, the social adaptation. Even if these defence mechanisms do occur in the here and now, they cannot be supported because of their pathological contents, but they must be understood, explained and interpreted to the present situation. The therapist must be an advocate of the reality, and an ally, as it were an auxiliary ego in the service of the reality check. An experience always characteristic for the patient is when in the here and now of the therapy, the perversions of the picture of the therapist, developed as a reaction of the subjects talked about, are directly recognized and the link is made with what has been said and what the patient experienced. If this is successful then the patient will react in a relieved way. This can also be read in the literature by Giovacchini (1979) and Kernberg (1984; Kernberg *et al.* 1972).

Part of the therapist's earlier mentioned 'holding' attitude is also that he does not allow himself to be frightened by the patient's fears and regressive transference phenomena. Experience shows us that these patients will quickly regress because of their small ego-strength; on the other hand this regression can also quickly be reduced when met with an adequate, cognitive and emotional reception. In the hospital milieu, especially with these patients, it is important to allow regression, and not to permit them to regress too quickly to an unworkable level but neither give them too much support lest regression does not occur at all, with the result that one cannot work on the relevant affects. In the beginning of the therapy regression is only allowed in certain situations and to such an extent that it must always be manageable for the patient himself. Yet it should not be prevented either, since then the patient will not benefit from this therapy at all.

The above parameters can technically and methodically be applied well and particularly in the beginning of the therapy they will have to be used. During the continuation of the therapy the rather cognitively possible interpretations of the here and now remain important because they shed a clarifying light, so that the patient does not feel surprised by all kinds of threatening emotions unknown to him. The therapy itself remains a game of allowing regression to take place, on the one hand by offering explanations, but also on the other hand by interpreting more and more unconscious data towards the power-play within the personality structure and towards the early childhood genesis of the disorder.

The defence mechanism of 'splitting' that has been used so far, in which the psychotherapist is respectively the only good and the only bad relation, is decreasing in importance. The patient increasingly accepts that his therapist has both 'good' and 'bad' sides, so that the quality of his reality check increases. One may say that because of the presence of a reliable relationship, namely with the psychotherapist, after everything which has taken place, the patient is able to develop the ability of object constancy. This then leads to self-constancy. The patient is also able to discern within himself the good and bad qualities, without this leading to a panic reaction or to acting ambivalently. Neither does the patient experience himself as absolutely white or absolutely black, as a result of which the frustration tolerance and the impulse control will increase considerably. Only when achieving self-esteem do the primitive defence mechanisms retreat to the background. From this moment onwards the therapeutic process shows similarities with the course of psychotherapy in ambulant practice.

Finally it should be mentioned that the above, which is put here in psychopathological terminology, is often denied using rationalizations that are very difficult to refute, since it would otherwise entail great fears of intrusion and destruction. In the case of rationalizations it is, however, of minor importance if they are correct (for they mostly are), but rather whether with this explanation everything is explained. To pose the question of whether everything is explained, it will appear that emotional life with its unconscious dynamics cannot be denied and is one reality among others. It is the psychotherapist's task to explain this to his client in such a way that he can act accordingly.

CONCLUSION

The early childhood transference phenomena that have been described here, encountered during my psychotherapeutic experience in hospital settings, namely the 'Dr. S. van Mesdagkliniek' in Groningen and the 'Dr. H. van der Hoevenkliniek' in Utrecht. These are both maximum security hospitals for those legally detained at the Government's pleasure. The 'holding environment' (Winnicott 1960) these hospitals offer enable both the psychotherapist and the patient to feel safe in each other's environment; since the security ensured by the working relations will frustrate escalations and hidden agendas.

However, on the other hand, because psychotherapy has found its proper place along side treatment activities in the hospital, the result of the psychotherapy as an isolated enterprise cannot possibly be evaluated. Experience has shown that patients who registered for treatment voluntarily show great therapy loyalty and in most cases do not terminate prematurely.

Psychotherapeutic Work with Victims of Trauma

Gwen Adshead & Cleo van Velsen

INTRODUCTION

No study of offenders is complete without a discussion of their victims. In the psychotherapeutic treatment of offenders, connections between the status of victim and offender remains a central question both intra- and extra psychically. It is known that those who have suffered severe victimization may inflict further suffering on others, but we struggle to understand the precise mechanisms involved.

In this chapter we will offer an outline of some current psychodynamic theories in relation to trauma, and the treatment of traumatic reactions. In addition, a number of particular issues linking victimology and offending will be discussed. The first is the distinction between the traumatic effects of disaster and those of victimization. In disasters, the trauma is caused by an impersonal agent, whereas victimization implies a trauma arising out of a relationship between victim and offender. As one popular film title put it, 'this time, it's personal'. Second, we will highlight the tendency for views of trauma to dissolve into polarizations; victim/offender, victim/survivor, innocence/blame. Such polarizations are defences that do not reflect reality, and undermine thinking in an area where thinking is already impaired. Third, it will be argued that it is often difficult to listen to accounts of traumatic experiences, leading to either a sentimental identification with victims, or a social avoidance of the reality of trauma; on the battlefield, in the home, in dangerous jobs, after disasters. Whatever the limitations of the post-traumatic stress disorder (PTSD) diagnosis, it has been important as a means of validating

traumatic experience. Finally, we will attempt to link the study of victimology
with studies of offenders, and their treatment.

THE CONCEPT OF TRAUMA: WHAT HAPPENS TO THE MIND?

It will not be possible in this chapter to review the entire history of the concept
of post-traumatic stress, nor all the relevant psychotherapeutic literature. Most
workers in the field acknowledge that it was Freud who first described the
psychological impact of an external trauma almost 100 years ago (in relation
to seduction theory; S. Freud 1895). The word 'trauma' is derived from the
Greek, meaning to wound or pierce, and Freud postulated that traumatic events
pierced the 'protective shield' that normally protects the ego from being
overwhelmed by intolerable stimuli (S. Freud 1920). The protective shield
manages the arousal excited by internal and external stimuli; but when the
arousal becomes unmanageable, this can cause 'disturbance on a large scale',
and 'set in motion every defensive measure'. Of particular importance was the
defence of 'repetition-compulsion', whereby the ego seeks mastery over the
intolerable arousal by re-experiencing it. Such repetition, Freud described as
alternating with periods of denial of the trauma.

Seventy years later, Horowitz (Horowitz and Becker 1972) postulated
exactly the same mechanism. Although heavily influenced by analytic theory,
Horowitz couched his account of post-traumatic responses in terms from
cognitive psychology, and information processing. He argued that survivors of
trauma respond with attempts to 'process' the event by alternating denial, and
avoidance of thinking, with intrusive re-experiencing of the trauma, often in
the form of flashbacks in the daytime, and nightmares during sleep. His model
is the basis of the criteria for Post-Traumatic Stress Disorder (PTSD) which
first appeared in DSM-III in 1980 (American Psychiatric Association 1980),
and has remained in later versions (DSM-I, DSM-III-R; American Psychiatric
Association 1987, 1994). Thus the essential elements of PTSD, in its modern
form, are almost exactly as Freud described them, and this is thought-provoking, especially when considering the claim that PTSD is a 'new' disease
concept.

Since Freud's first account of the psychological effects of trauma, the
concept of post-traumatic neurosis has continued to develop. Freud himself
elaborated it by suggesting that it was the helplessness of the ego which was
the essence of the traumatic experience. Conscious anxiety was a signal of the
possible danger of repetition; an early description of the hyperarousal which
is also recognized as one of the criteria for PTSD (American Psychiatric
Association 1994). The importance of helplessness was also recognized as
pathological by Seligmann (1975), especially in those situations where the
organism cannot escape. The notion of 'learned helplessness' in relation to

chronic trauma has been taken up by other workers, and is considered to be a particularly traumatizing aspect of child abuse, domestic violence and the experience of being a prisoner of war (Walker 1979; Herman 1992).

Although Freud rejected the notion of seduction as the actual, rather than fantasized, basis of all neurosis (S. Freud 1925a), he did not alter his account of trauma *per se*, and his views were also greatly affected by the massive loss of life caused by the 1914–1918 war (cf. 'Mourning and Melancholia', S. Freud 1917; 'Beyond the Pleasure Principle', S. Freud 1920). It is therefore untrue to say that Freud did not accept an objective reality of external trauma. Certainly he and the first generation of psychoanalysts became more interested in the role of fantasy, infantile conflicts and psychic trauma, leading to the relative paucity of investigation into external trauma. Ferenczi (1931, 1933) was an exception, emphasizing the importance of actual traumatic events, and the necessity in treatment of recovering lost and split off parts of the traumatic experience. In the 1940s, especially in the United States of America, there was a resurgence of interest in external trauma. Kardiner (1941), for example, placed more emphasis on the actual event or stressor, describing what he called 'ego contraction and disorganization' which lead to symptoms of numbing, disintegration and intrusion. Lindemann's classic paper on grief (1944) described the reactions of those who survived a major fire, and informed the later classic work by Parkes on bereavement (1972). The first Holocaust survivors were also describing their experiences, and struggling to make sense of what exactly had happened to them. Analysts working with Holocaust survivors noted the importance of regression and projective mechanisms as a means of survival (Krystal 1968; De Wind 1972; Auerhahn and Laub 1984). Bruno Bettelheim made use of analytic formulations to survive his own experiences in Dachau, and his early descriptions of this process became *The Informed Heart* (1960). This attempt to understand the thoughts and behaviours of victims of the camp, the guards who inflicted such suffering, and the relationship between victims and perpetrators, is important reading for forensic psychotherapists, and indeed, all those who work in custodial institutions. In the United Kingdom, an important consequence of the World War II was the development of group therapeutic approaches for the treatment of war neurosis by Bion and others (T. Main 1981), which has significance in relation to the treatment of PTSD.

There has been division between those workers who emphasize the importance of the stressor, and those who emphasize the importance of individual characteristics. In the last thirty years, attention to traumatic stress responses has been mainly in response to wars (Vietnam, the Falklands and more latterly the Gulf; see O'Brien 1994) or civilian disasters (Buffalo Creek, the Australian bush fires of 1983, the sinking of a British ferry off the Belgian coast). This work has emphasized the importance of the stressor as pathogenic

(Green 1993). More recently however, there has been an attempt to integrate such accounts with a developmental perspective, with questions about the life long effects of early trauma, and the importance of vulnerability and resilience factors in the *individual* (Herman 1992; McFarlane 1988; Rutter 1985; Werner 1989). Sandler, Dreher and Drews (1991) have argued that it may be helpful to understand a process of 'traumatization', where the traumatic event causes an internal adaptation which *may or may not be pathological or pathogenic* (emphasis added).

Brett (1993) has described two psychodynamic models of traumatic stress responses, following different types of trauma. The first draws on Freud's original description regarding re-experiencing as primary. The second derives from the work of Kardiner and Krystal, and describes the individual's 'massive adaptive failure' to the stressor as primary. Brett suggests that the former model may be more appropriate for less severe traumata than the latter, which was developed from work with Holocaust survivors.

What does seem to be common to all models is the importance of the subjective meaning that the individual gives to a traumatic event and its aftermath, and early childhood experience is likely to be relevant to this process. Children who are insecurely attached to their mothers as a result of early losses or deprivation show an decreased ability to access memories spontaneously, or think abstractly about loss (T. Main 1993). Children who have survived severe victimization make perceptual errors, and appear to show decreased ability to symbolise (Piaget 1962; Terr 1991). This work from cognitive psychology is resonant with psychodynamic accounts of impaired capacity to symbolize after trauma. An early account is given by Segal (1951) in her discussions of theories of symbolism. Garland (1991) draws on Bion's notion of an internal container, which is necessary for the digestion of intolerable affects, and for transforming the unthinkable into the thinkable.

Working through trauma is an essential aspect of growth and development. All of us have areas of weakness or vulnerability. However, the particular effects of victimization in early life may affect and distort the developing personality over a period of time, with subsequent long-term effects upon the individual and their relationships. Victimization implies a relationship between the offender and the victim, however brief or distorted.

If an adult has escaped victimization or serious trauma in childhood, it is likely that he may be better to able to withstand the shattering effects of a disaster, or victimization in adulthood. It is likely that those individuals who have suffered severe victimization and/or loss in childhood will be particularly vulnerable to the effects of later trauma in adulthood. Some recent research appears to confirm that early childhood abuse does increase the risk of developing PTSD after trauma later (Bremner *et al.* 1993). With specific relevance to forensic settings, de Zulueta (1993) has attempted to link attachment theory, trauma and violence, and suggested that violent behaviour is itself a post-traumatic stress response (of the most maladaptive kind).

PEOPLE AT RISK: SEVERE CHILDHOOD TRAUMA AND LATER PTSD

The human animal spends longer in a dependent and vulnerable state than any other mammal, or non-human primate. It is part of normal development for children to be exposed to traumas, particularly of separation and loss, for example, characterized by inadequate soothing or containment of arousal. This has consequent effects on the relationship between caregiver and infant (as described by Bowlby 1969). More severe and extreme trauma has more profoundly pathogenic effects. Hopper (1991) has suggested that it is the threat of annihilation that is essentially traumatic; this view echoes those studies of trauma in adulthood which make it clear that the development of PTSD in adults after disasters is more likely in those situations where the individual believes he is going to die (Green 1993).

Specifically, the infant or child may suffer more qualitatively and quantitatively serious trauma in the external world, such as physical or sexual assaults. This is characterized not only by the present threat of psychic annihilation, but also the real risk of physical annihilation and harm, at a time when the body/mind distinction is incomplete. If pace Freud (1923), the ego is a bodily ego, then threats to bodily integrity also threaten ego integrity.

One impact of the trauma is to disrupt the defences of the developing personality, superceding them with other defences, some of which are more primitive. The most significant defences associated with trauma are:

(1) **Denial,** where the reality of the trauma is not recognized or admitted by the individual.

(2) **Dissociation,** where perceptual consciousness is reduced in order to escape the full impact of the trauma. Children have an increased capacity for dissociation. Dissociation is recognised as an important post-traumatic mechanism in adults (Putnam 1990; Spiegel 1990), with a distinct neurophysiological basis, resulting in patchy amnesia and periods of 'blankness'. It has been suggested that individuals who adopt chronic dissociative states in childhood are at risk of severe personality distortion, or even of developing multiple personalities (Putnam 1990). Although this latter notion has been greeted with scepticism in the UK (Fahy 1988; Merskey 1992), it is clear that dissociation does occur with real effects upon consciousness. In psychodynamic terms, it is possible to link this defence with Bion's theories of thinking (Bion 1967).

(3) **Splitting** involves a polarization whereby the good and bad aspects of oneself or others are kept totally separate. In this way, the discomfort of

ambivalence (and the traumatic reality) is minimized. This is an important mechanism for victims of abuse in childhood, who are attempting to understand how someone they love (good) can hurt them (bad). Not only does splitting ('he is good, I am bad') offer an explanation, it also protects the family relationship for the child. This polarization is linked to idealization and denigration, which can have profound implications for future therapists. Another consequence of splitting may be concreteness of thinking, impairing fantasy life (Pines 1986).

Splitting is a defence against reality which affects the capacity to think. This impairs developmental progress, forcing the child to remain cognitively and affectively 'stuck' in the traumatic time. This facilitates repetition-compulsion, and makes action rather than thought more likely in times of anxiety. This is highly relevant to the background of some offenders' behaviour.

(4) **Projection and projective identification** is a process whereby unacceptable feelings are unconsciously located in others. Garland (1991) suggests that it is a mechanism whereby survivors of trauma non-verbally communicate intolerable feelings of helplessness and terror to others. Rage, and desire for vengeance, may also be projected, especially by victims, so that their intolerable anger is not recognized. Aided by splitting mechanisms, this may lead to a situation where such affects are not recognized by others, or indeed by the victim himself (Catherall 1991). One result may be an internalization as a sense of grievance which cannot be resolved (van Velsen 1990).

(5) **Identification with the aggressor.** By identifying with the aggressor, the victim makes the aggressor part of himself, and renders his victimization bearable. This also protects the aggressor as 'good', as described above. Identification may result in actually acting like the aggressor, or simply thinking like them. Bettelheim (1960) described this process in the concentration camps when certain prisoners identified with the guards. Children who have been victimized may act violently to other children, or show little sympathy for other children's distress (Main and George 1985; Otnow Lewis 1992).

Perverse Solutions

Although not classically seen as a post-traumatic phenomenon, it is suggested that a consideration of perverse mechanisms may be relevant here. Perversion involves the enlisting of the body into a defence of ego integrity. Classically, perversions have been seen in terms of sexual behaviour. Recent writers have postulated that there may be perverse mechanisms operative in thinking; for example as a defence against depression, loss and rage. For example, a woman abandoned by her father as a child has a memory of being on her knees before him, begging him not to leave. Now in adulthood, she experiences masochistic sexual fantasies in which she is intensely sexually aroused when on her knees before a man, begging him not to go. By sexualizing the trauma, she can protect herself against the loss of her father as well as organizing her aggression. There is thus a simultaneous avowal and disavowal of reality. Welldon (1988) has noted the common histories of abuse in those women who display perverse sexual behaviour, and makes the point that such behaviour relieves physical arousal, at least temporarily. Steiner (1992), drawing on Money-Kyrle's theory of the basic facts of life, has suggested that perverse mechanisms are involved in the construction of a 'psychic retreat', to be found in borderline, schizoid and narcissistic personalities. Such retreats may be thought of as one attempt to manage trauma.

Essential to perverse behaviour are defences against thinking (such as dissociation, splitting and projection), compulsive repetition, and the recruitment of the body (or someone else's) as a means of relieving tension and arousal (again cf. S. Freud 1923: the ego is a bodily ego). Deliberate self-harming behaviours (DSH) may be understood as perverse solutions in this context. Very common in those who were severely abused in childhood, such behaviour is repetitive and involves the body in a maladaptive way. Dissociation and splitting are common antecedents to such acts, and relief of tension is commonly described afterwards, and is often cited as a reason for such actions. Indeed, neurophysiological studies of self-cutters suggest that this perverse behaviour results in the release of endogenous opiates which provide an internal sense of ease (Coid, Alloio and Rees 1983).

The defences described above occur in the context of the developing personality and the impact differs from trauma that occurs in the adult, where established defences are shattered and replaced by more primitive ones. In both cases there is interaction with a range of affects for example loss, guilt, shame, rage and helplessness. Rebuilding shattered defences and restoring links are psychological tasks which are difficult enough for non-vulnerable adults who have survived disasters or victimization (Garland 1991).

This task is made considerably harder if the individual has vulnerabilities from severe trauma and victimization in childhood. However, such vulnerabilities may be affected by other factors; for example, exposure to non-victimizing adults, education, peer relationships, and chance. Thus it is impossible to say with certainty that the victimized child will become a disturbed adult, although one can say it is more likely if:

(1) the victimization is chronic

(2) the victimization is severe, in terms of physical force or injury (Browne and Finkelhor 1986; Mullen *et al.* 1993)

(3) the abuser is in a parental role (Herman, Russell and Trocki 1987; Russell 1986)

(4) there is no access to any other supporting adult (Werner 1989)

(5) there is no access to education (Mullen *et al.* 1993)

(6) the child is not believed (Browne and Finkelhor 1986; Conte and Schuerman 1987)

There is good research evidence that abuse in childhood is bad for one's long-term mental health. Survivors of childhood abuse are over-represented in psychiatric in-patient and out-patient wards compared with community samples (Carmen, Rieker and Mills, 1984; Bryer, Nelson and Miller 1987). This is true for both males and females. Histories of child abuse are particularly over-represented in patients with histories of deliberate self-harm, and diagnoses of borderline personality disorder (BPD) (Herman, Perry and van der Kolk 1989; van der Kolk, Perry and Herman, 1991). Community studies suggest that the experience of being sexually abused in childhood does increase the risk of developing a psychiatric illness in adulthood (Bifulco, Brown and Adler 1991; Mullen *et al.* 1993). What is less well understood are the protective factors which operate, and more studies are required on non-clinical samples.

As previously suggested, childhood victimization may result in a personality organization which is vulnerable to trauma in adulthood. Herman (1992) suggests that such a personality organisation is very similar to that described by the DSM category 'Borderline personality disorder' (BPD). She postulates, therefore, that it might be more appropriate to see BPD as a chronic post-traumatic phenomenon. Similarly, Gunderson and Sabo (1993) note similarities between the characteristics of BPD and PTSD; other authors have suggested that they may be synonymous (Burges Watson 1989; Lonie 1993). Other authors are more sceptical, citing the differences between the two disorders (Finkelhor 1993).

Any 'personality disorder' label acquires a pejorative ring because the diagnosis suggests inherent and unalterable flaws in the person with the label (Lewis and Appleby 1988), so that many mental health professionals are reluctant to see such people as patients at all. If those suffering from major personality disorders were seen to have a condition with an external, traumatic aetiology, it would be more difficult to exclude them from the traditional illness discourse, and the sympathy that patients usually receive. It would also mean that personality disorder would have to become a major focus of psychiatric services, treatment and research, in the same way as the psychotic disorders, and might compete with them for scarce resources.

PSYCHODYNAMIC TREATMENT OF RESPONSES TO DISASTER AND VICTIMIZATION

As suggested above, there are different types of traumatic event. We may distinguish, as Freud did, between trauma and danger (S. Freud, cited in Khan 1986). We have suggested that it may be helpful to distinguish between trauma caused by disasters, and trauma caused by victimization, where there is a relationship, however brief or distorted between the victim and the offender. We have also suggested that the adult exposed to trauma may respond in a number of ways depending on:

(1) His previous experience of victimization, especially if this took place in childhood.

(2) His experience of this particular trauma, and the meaning and attributions he ascribes to it.

(3) His degree of exposure to the trauma.

(4) The extent of his losses as a result of the trauma.

(5) The particular type of trauma.

   Green (1993) reviews the risk factors for PTSD which are related to the stressor itself. Any life threatening situation, in which the victim perceives that he is going to die, increases the risk of PTSD. Witnessing atrocities to other living things or grotesque imagery (usually mutilated bodies) increases risk; thus fires and aircrashes are types of disaster that particularly cause PTSD. Finally, it is clear that personal victimization (such as criminal assault) causes more PTSD than impersonal disasters. The effects of being victimized by another are worse than the effects of other crimes or disasters (Kilpatrick *et al.* 1989).

(6) His experience of support received after the trauma is over.

   This is an area which requires more research. Clinically, it appears that there is a small group of people whose chief complaint after a trauma is that they did not feel cared for by those who are perceived as having a duty to do so. This comes up in occupational settings, and may or may not be related to early experiences (de Zulueta 1993).

Therefore treatment of post-traumatic responses can only be initiated after a careful assessment of the individual's problems, since the relative contribution of each factor described above needs to be assessed. Two other caveats are required. The first is that, after any trauma, there are those who do not seem to suffer any psychological distress at all (Green *et al.* 1990; Feinstein 1993). Whether this is a good thing or a bad cannot be asserted. The other is that there is a period of normal distress after any trauma, in which all the 'symptoms' of PTSD are present, in other words, PTSD as a diagnosis probably represents a chronic distortion and prolongation of a normal process of recovery. Thus most people after a trauma will make a full recovery psychologically. This may be painful at times, and require support (just as a bone fracture requires pain relief and splinting during recovery). However, recovery is the norm. Those who still have symptoms at six to twelve months plus, are likely to be those for whom one of the six factors described above are operating. Lindy (1993) describes a special 'configuration' of the traumatic event for such survivors, which includes 'the multiplicity of stressors...multiple interacting affect states...[and] expectable compensatory fantasies' (p.805).

Treatment hinges crucially on the ego capacity of the person before the trauma. In someone with PTSD with a previously well functioning ego, whose current symptoms may be attributable to a particularly grotesque experience, supportive psychotherapy involving behavioural strategies such as exposure and cognitive therapy may be useful. For example, a patient with previously good psychological health and well integrated psychic functioning, developed PTSD after witnessing the murder of her husband in a particularly grotesque way. Treatment included bereavement work and a small degree of exposure therapy. Cognitive–behavioural, and some brief dynamic strategies may be more appropriate where the trauma was short-lived, occurred in one discrete episode, and where the patient has good pre-traumatic ego function (Richards and Rose 1991; Horowitz 1990).

Where patients do not respond to such strategies, it is likely that there is another dimension to their traumatic experience such as an unresolved loss from childhood, or some other area of repressed material which has been made more conscious by unconscious resonance with the traumatic event. This may be better addressed by psychodynamic psychotherapy. Psychodynamic work may be thought to be the treatment of choice in the first instance if the trauma is particularly severe or chronic, or in cases of victimization where the abusive relationship is part of the trauma. Use may be made of the transference to understand the patient's responses to his aggressor, both at the time of the trauma and subsequently. Psychodynamic work may also be more appropriate where the patient adopts a psychosomatic solution to his distress (Lindy, Green and Grace 1992).

Brief and long-term psychodynamic therapy, both group and individual, have been offered to victims of trauma (Dye and Roth 1991; Garland 1991; Horowitz 1973; Koller, Marmar and Kanas 1992; Lifton 1973; Lindy 1986, 1993; Marmar 1991; Marmar and Freeman 1988; Roth, Dye and Lebowitz 1988). A controlled study, comparing brief psychotherapy with systematic desensitization and hypnotherapy for traumatic bereavement, with waiting list controls, showed improvement for all treatment modalities (Brom, Kleber and

Defares 1989). Of the three, dynamic psychotherapy had more impact on avoidance symptoms, which are associated with chronicity.

Brief psychotherapy may be particularly useful for those who do not feel cared for, and for whom this is a crucial post-traumatic issue. Brief group therapies have been offered to both war veterans and rape victims, with reported good effect (Dye and Roth 1991; Koller, Marmar and Kanas 1992; Marmar 1991). It may be important for post-traumatic groups to have a task (Garland 1991). As expected, the brief psychotherapies are thought to be unsuitable for those who have suffered childhood trauma or who are unable to contain arousal without acting out (Marmar 1991). In such cases, longer term psychoanalytic psychotherapy may be more helpful.

Both Lindy (1986, 1993) and Marmar (1991) have described focal psychoanalytic psychotherapy for survivors, pointing out the necessary modifications in technique. In the *opening phase*, it is necessary for the therapist to express empathy, explain PTSD and link current symptoms with the trauma. It may be important to allow early grandiosity or idealization of the therapist, as a means of dealing with narcissistic regression. In the *middle phase* there may be more emphasis on the transference–countertransference matrix. Even here, the interaction between therapist and patient may reflect transference phenomena from the trauma, rather than the early past, and traumatic interpretations are important (Lindy 1986, 1989). The *termination phase* allows for integration of pre-traumatic and current material, as well as an opportunity to work through issues of loss and mourning. Marmar notes that early support for the patient facilitates the patients moves from rage to mourning, especially in those patients with pre-traumatic vulnerability (Marmar and Freeman 1988).

Patients who require psychodynamic psychotherapy may have more severe symptoms of PTSD. Co-morbidity with other psychiatric disorders (especially substance abuse and depression) is very common, and psychiatric support may be necessary. Krystal (1988) emphasizes the importance of careful choice of treatment for patients, particularly those who are alexithymic. He suggest that such patients are unable to think about affects, and therefore may be unable to face the reality of destruction and loss which is entailed in 'getting better'. Garland (1991) has emphasized the importance of restoring symbolic functioning, so that patients are able to think, and progress to achieve the depressive position, where losses and traumas can be mourned. Both authors imply that there may be some patients who cannot tolerate such treatment, and for this group, cognitive behavioural strategies may be a better solution.

PARTICULAR DIFFICULTIES IN WORKING WITH SURVIVORS OF TRAUMA

Work in the transference with those who have been victims of violence may be difficult for both therapist and patient (Lindy 1989, 1993). Much of the difficulty lies in the impairment of fantasy and symbol formation (Garland 1991; Pines 1986), so that language is lost or diminished. In patients who lack the words to describe their state of mind, the therapist's countertransference may be a powerful indicator of the patient's internal state (Sinason 1992). It may also be an obstacle to progress. Sinason's work with mentally handicapped adults who have been abused resonates with general trauma work; one might argue that those people without a learning disability who survive trauma have, nevertheless, been rendered 'handicapped' by their traumatic experiences.

Thus countertransferential reactions are an important part of the therapeutic process, and should be looked for and monitored in supervision. This is both for information, and as resistance to the push to act out in the countertransference, which is basic to the method. It is our experience that working with those who have been victimized is difficult work, and supervision is essential. An example which is often overlooked is the patient's rage. The sense of loss, sadness and vulnerability which is conscious and acceptable, may mask an unconscious rage which, in the early stages of treatment, is likely to be acted out. Although acts of deliberate self-harm or sabotage of therapy are most common, in more damaged groups of people, violence towards carers (particularly the therapist) is not uncommon (Adshead 1994, in press). More subtle acting out may take place in relation to the setting, and keeping of boundaries, and in this respect, the therapist may become collusive if care is not taken.

Particular problems may occur in the psychodynamic treatment of the victim of sexual assault (Notman and Nadelson 1976; Rose 1986; Schuker 1979), especially when the perpetrator was a trusted adult. The angry projections of the victim may be internalized by the therapist and re-projected in a countertransferential reaction of blame for the victim or disbelief of their account. This allows the victim to deny their rage, and also puts the therapist in the role of abuser. The therapist then may be drawn unconsciously to a re-enactment of abuse, and boundary violations are common. These often begin as small violations, but may go on to cross body boundaries. *The strength of the compulsion to re-enact the trauma in the therapeutic space cannot be over emphasized.* Although these difficulties have been noted most commonly in relation to sexual assault, there are similar problems in all cases where there has been victimization (van Velsen 1990). Other common problems are related to over-identification with the patient, or the induction of paralysing guilt, rendering the therapist ineffectual.

Even when the individual appears to have recovered from the trauma, there may be an area of permanent vulnerability to later life events. After a trauma, between twenty and thirty per cent of the population exposed will develop chronic PTSD. This group are unlikely to make further progress (Green *et al.* 1990). The task of the psychotherapist then may be to assist the patient to 'get on with it', rather than 'get over it' (Garland 1991); a model of living with disability, rather than cure. Tragically, such individuals are not immune from further disasters and losses, and will need special help should they occur. As well as the victim themselves, families and employers may need education and advice about chronic PTSD.

For some, the experience of a major trauma with massive loss of life, and/or multiple grotesque imagery may provoke a major existential crisis, the understanding of which may take a lifetime. In this context, it is important to consider the wider realm which influences a victim's recovery; his culture, his religion, his immediate family and social group and the wider social group (Morris and Silove 1992). Major personality change is recognized as a sequel of trauma in adulthood (Epstein 1990). While this is generally discussed in negative terms, it is possible for some survivors of trauma to achieve a positive understanding of their experience. Some have radically restructured their lives, in a way which they regard as positive.

Finally, it is important to mention crisis intervention and psychological debriefing. This is not strictly treatment (Mitchell 1983), but rather an educational and supportive intervention, which aims to promote psychological recovery after trauma, and prevent the development of PTSD, and other chronic disorders. Psychological debriefing shares some elements with behavioural treatment of PTSD, with an emphasis on early cognitive processing, and exposure to the experience in narrative in a supported setting. The efficacy of such interventions has not been proven; what is clear is that the majority of survivors of trauma say that they find them helpful (Robinson and Mitchell 1993).

In summary then, different types of trauma may suggest different types of treatment, depending on the individual's previous history and experience. Psychodynamic psychotherapy, brief and long term, individual and group, has an essential place in the therapeutic repertoire. This is particularly so for those survivors of trauma in adulthood who have had experiences of early childhood victimization.

VICTIMIZATION AND LATER VIOLENCE: A FORENSIC PERSPECTIVE

There is not space to review here the considerable literature discussing the so-called 'cycle of violence'. Since the 1960s and the recognition of childhood abuse by parents, workers have sought for connections between early experiences of being a victim of violence, and later acting as a perpetrator of violence.

Many of the defences discussed in (2) above have been suggested as possible factors in the commission of violence, and have been so described.

Two questions present themselves: do violent people have histories of trauma? And do traumatized people act violently? The answer to the first is clearly affirmative. Coid (1992) in a paper based on his study of psychopathically disordered offenders in a Special Hospital found that eighty per cent of them had histories of physical deprivation and abuse, either physical or sexual. Although child abuse and neglect is common in the community, it is not occurring in eighty per cent of the population. This high level of adversity has been found in other studies of criminal populations (Collins and Bailey 1990; Dutton and Hart 1991). By comparison, studies of sexual abuse in the community in the UK suggest that eight to twelve per cent of the population have been so abused (Baker and Duncan 1985; Bifulco, Brown and Adler 1991). Comparable studies of physical abuse do not seem to be available, but current National Society for the Prevention of Cruelty to Children (NSPCC) figures suggest that physical abuse and neglect occurs in twenty to thirty per cent of children (NSPCC 1994). It appears that child abuse is the experience of the minority in the community, but apparently the experience of the majority in Special Hospitals. Studies of offenders in prisons and probation programmes also repeatedly find that thirty to fifty per cent of them have been abused; this is particularly true of sexual offenders (Finkelhor 1986).

Clearly, retrospective analyses cannot prove causality, and the models of childhood trauma we have outlined above make it clear that childhood abuse is not a strict determinant of later functioning. However, the proportions of abuse histories in offending populations are striking, and justify other types of research such as prospective studies.

Prospective studies can address the second question; whether traumatized people act violently as part of a post-traumatic response. Studies of the behaviour of abused children suggest that abused children are more likely to act aggressively towards their peers (Otnow Lewis 1992). Abused children show less empathy towards the distress of other children (Main and George 1985). Harsh parental attitudes and a lack of love are strong predictors of later delinquency in boys (McCord 1984; West 1973). Sexually abused adolescents may act out sexually towards other children (Otnow Lewis 1992). Deprivation and abuse make childhood diagnoses of conduct disorder more likely in boys; Robins' classic follow up work on conduct disordered children suggests that such children are at high risk of becoming 'conduct disordered' adults (Robins 1966).

Finally, Widom and colleagues have shown, in prospective follow-up studies of abused children, that childhood abuse and neglect does slightly increase the risk of arrest in adulthood, and of developing anti-social personality disorder (Luntz and Widom 1994; Widom and Ames 1994). However, in relation to arrest in adulthood, this effect is strongest only for those sexually abused women who are later arrested for soliciting and prostitution, rather than crimes of violence. Physical abuse in childhood does increase the risk of arrest for violence in adulthood, but this effect was small.

These findings perhaps support Widom's previously expressed scepticism about the strength of the 'cycle of violence' argument (Widom 1989, 1991). The chief difficulties are that abuse and neglect are not well defined and may have separate and distinguishable negative effects in adulthood. Accounts of later acting out may have to depend on criminal records, which are notoriously incomplete, especially in relation to behaviours such as child abuse and domestic violence, where reporting and conviction rates are low. It seems possible at this point only to say that a small proportion of those who are abused and neglected in childhood may go on to be violent in adulthood, and research is needed into the risk and protective factors that operate. It is plausible to speculate that the worse the abuse in childhood, the higher the risk (cf. Miller 1983); but this *is* speculation.

It may be relevant to consider the literature on violence committed by those who have been traumatized as adults. Much of this research was stimulated by work with Vietnam veterans who sought to use PTSD as a defence against criminal charges (Sparr and Atkinson 1986). Reports conflict as to whether Vietnam veterans really are more at risk of acting criminally because of PTSD (Boman 1987; Marciniak 1986; Shaw, Churchill, Noyes and Loeffelholz 1987). What is clear is that individuals with PTSD are likely to be highly aroused, irritable and abusing substances, all of which are recognized risk factors for dangerousness (Monahan 1992). Outbursts of anger are recognized symptoms of both PTSD and BPD. Anecdotally, most clinicians are aware that traumatized adults are more likely to get into fights, at home, at work and in the street than they were prior to their experiences.

Finally, we refer to the use of perverse defences in offending individuals. Such defences are extremely common in those who offend against children, or in a compulsive manner, usually sexually (Welldon 1988). The origin of such defences is likely to be traumatic, as we suggested earlier; the question is then whether some individuals manage to sublimate such defences, and if so, how. More work is needed into an understanding of the development of perverse defences against pain. A first step may be to acknowledge that victims of trauma are not only sad, vulnerable and grieving; they may also be angry and dangerous.

CONCLUSION

Many questions about the effects of traumatic events remain; this chapter can only introduce the reader to the topic, and key areas of debate. One of the most important relates to the differences between trauma in childhood as compared with adulthood in terms of the long-term effects. Another relates to the relative contributions of risk and protective factors. Although the PTSD diagnosis in its current form does not begin to address these issues, it is an important formulation in terms of the validation of trauma as pathogenic.

In antiquity, the victim was necessary as a sacrifice for the welfare of the whole community. Idealization of victim status was widespread, as a defence against the reality of suffering, tragedy or sadism. The use of psychic splitting as a defence against trauma is still widespread and found in social groups wider than the victims of trauma themselves. In particular, the law and the media find it very difficult to conceptualize victims and offenders as anything but separate, distinct and antagonistic. Even at a cultural level, the victim is still simultaneously revered and denigrated (Hughes 1993).

As we have suggested in our final section, the truth is much more uncomfortable. Many victims of violence experience feelings of rage and violence, and many perpetrators experience real grief and loss. In the genesis of interpersonal violence, the relationship between the victim and offender, real or fantasized, is crucial.

From Abused to Abuser

Valerie Sinason

'The apple does not fall far from the tree' (Old Proverb)

'Eskimo fucks bear
Bear undresses eskimo
slow, with tender fangs.
Bear eats eskimo for food
Eskimo carves bear in stone'

(The Meaning of the Journey, Jeni Couzyn
House of Changes, Heinemann 1978)

INTRODUCTION

Most people have to face a range of difficult experiences. How we cope with them depends on the inter-relationship between our own unique temperament (Kagan 1994), external environment and internal world. Folk wisdom often holds the view that, regardless of specific trauma, the apple does not fall far from the tree: children end up in a roughly similar position to their parents.

Certainly, as far as sexual trauma is concerned, researchers (Gomes-Schwartz, Horowitz and Carderelli 1990) are aware that negative maternal response heightens the consequences of trauma whilst a positive response minimizes it. Similarly, children from families with pre-existing pathological relationships (Conte and Schuerman 1987) are more adversely affected by abuse. Where abuse victims are already emotionally disturbed, hostile questioning (Vizard 1987) can cause further damage and the interface between clinical and legal needs requires serious attention (Vizard 1993).

Although internal or external circumstances can ameliorate or exacerbate the trauma, clinicians (Bentovim 1992a) agree that there are a variety of negative consequences to childhood sexual abuse and that initial apparent adaptation does not rule out a reawakening of trauma at a different developmental stage. However, in addition to acknowledging the impact of environment (internal and external) clinicians also have to deal with the transformational power of certain kinds of encounters, that due to internal or external timing, nature or context cause dramatic radical change.

I am therefore going to focus on the nature of the encounter that occurs for the minority of abuse victims who go on to become abusers. In examining some of the issues involved in abuse victims (with or without a learning disability) becoming abusers it is very important to state that whilst a highly significant number of those who abuse were abused, a surprisingly large thirteen out of every fourteen who are abused do not repeat their abuse directly (Browne, K. 1993). However, the one in fourteen who do repeat their abuse are responsible for a highly significant percentage of sexual offences.

This is not surprising. Sexual abuse goes through the body and the mind of the victim creating a double tragedy. Not only does the victim have to bear the despair, perversion and sadism of the abuser but also the internal fantasies and bodily responses that the trauma evoked. Most of the abused patients I have treated found mentioning orgasm during abuse as the most shameful fact. I have found it useful to speak of 'involuntary' orgasm, as the body's way of accommodating intrusion for the purpose of survival. For some who become abusers there is a need to transmit the same complex sequence of pain followed by pleasure, seduction by betrayal. The original hurt can ossify into a mental masturbatory fantasy script that is compulsively repeated either through abusing (Watkins and Bentovim 1992) or perversion (Rosen 1979).

TRANSFORMATIONAL ENCOUNTERS

'Cut is the branch that might have grown full straight'

(Marlowe, *Dr Faustus.*)

A sixteen-year-old girl was referred as a result of self-mutilation several months after a summer holiday in which she was anally raped by a school teacher. Her mother believed her disclosure immediately and was the one to call the police but her father found the particular nature of the rape intolerable and initially disbelieved her. There was clear medical evidence, however, and the police were satisfied that a conviction would follow (as it did). In addition to self- mutilation, there were concerns that since the abuse she was behaving in a worrying way with her little brother, especially when changing his nappies. She was also dressing very provocatively – 'like a tart' – her father wrote.

At the first meeting she tottered in wearing a skin-tight jumper, micro mini skirt, patterned black tights and high heels. In a rather bruised dirty hand she held a cigarette, dropping ash contemptuously onto my floor. After closing the door she viciously ground the heel of her stiletto shoe into the cigarette butt.

Her body and body movements painfully came to my attention fractionally before her pale face, runny makeup and long dishevelled hair. The whole impact was to draw my attention to a state of dissociation in which her body existed separately, needed to seduce in order to be valued but also showing its devaluation. As Cox (1978a) points out 'if the therapist had to rely entirely upon the spoken word, his therapeutic potential would be drastically reduced... Whole body and part body language both contribute to non verbal communication which in turn contributes to the totality of communication' (p.19).

'What you looking at?' she asked aggressively as she sat on the chair. I was aware that her angry tone was like a war cry, an exhalatory sound designed to cover up the psychic and physical discomfort she was experiencing at the moment of placing her buttocks on the chair.

I said it must be hard coming here for the first time with all the painful things that had happened to her and perhaps she did not know what she would like me to see or look at with her yet. She relaxed and took off one of her shoes, curling her leg underneath her to make extra cushioning. Then looking at me with a mixture of hope and aggression she threw off her second shoe, aiming at my side. It made a loud noise when hitting the ground that satisfied her. In the one act of throwing those phallic shoes in my direction she was showing her vulnerability and her anger, herself as abuse victim and abuser. Her shoes, whilst not used as fetish objects by her, nevertheless revealed in the rest of her treatment the quality of a fetish, an object which reinforces a part of the body that feels vulnerable or inadequate.

Looking at the sharp high heels of her discarded shoes I said, with a smile, perhaps she did not need all her weapons now she knew me a little bit better. She giggled 'Fuck you!' (Sinason 1989) and then burst out laughing at the verbal significance of her reply. She sat upright, tossing her hair away from her face and looked at me with interest. I said I agreed with her understanding that those shoes were like an aggressive penis coming at me to fuck me and perhaps too she wanted me to know what it felt like to be ground down in shit – like a cigarette butt stabbed with a stiletto heel. We both looked down at the phallic shoes and the mashed-up cigarette end. My eyes then went to her grubby bruised hand and I realised that the marks on her hand and arm were the result of picking at herself, using her fingernails like a stiletto heel in her skin, like an aggressive penis piercing an anus.

She saw where my eyes had gone and her tone became angry again. 'You're looking again'. This time I was more direct. I said it was really hard because she wanted me to see all the holes she had made in herself. She wanted to be like him and be the one who made the holes in the wrong place and stuck something hard in where it had no right to go. But she also felt like a dirty exposed hole that anyone could look at or poke.

She broke into a burst of sobs, avoiding the box of tissues on the table in order to wipe her nose and eyes across her bruised arms. Then she started to speak. 'I kept hanging about, hanging about him', she whispered. 'It was hot weather. I had this skimpy top and shorts'. 'You wanted him to notice you', I agreed. There was a pause. She looked at me sharply for a moment and said 'Yes'. There was a long silence. She shifted her position on the seat looking in some discomfort. Very softly I said 'Perhaps you wanted him to look at you, admire you or even touch you but not do that'.

She sat bolt upright looking me straight in the eyes. 'I never, never, never wanted anyone to do that. Not even me with my own fucking finger. You've got to know that. I did want the other stuff. But the bastard did that. And you know what the worst thing is, he made me like it. I can't get it out of my mind. And I could kill him for that because if he hadn't done it I wouldn't know I could like it.' That impassioned cry represents, for me, one of the transformational tragedies of some acts of abuse. The act, for a mixture of conscious and unconscious reasons, sets in motion a dynamic would that have otherwise remained asleep. (See Sinason 1993 for a similar dynamic involving a woman with severe learning disability.)

Later work revealed her Oedipal problems with a father who was conspicuously emotionally absent for her and a consequent heightened displaced longing for her class teacher's attention. Her father's close physical attention to her little brother, including nappy changing, was the masturbatory image that was excited in her mind by the trauma of anal rape. By transforming an event of rape into a familial scene of toilet-training she was trying to make the trauma more bearable but the Oedipal ramifications excited further guilt. Her attempts to take over the nappy changing of her brother were checked by her observant parents and she turned to self-mutilation instead. Here, too, there is an abuse victim and an abuser but they inhabit the same body instead of two different ones (Sinason 1988a). I am not intending to explore here the particular consequences of anal abuse (see Meltzer 1993; Shengold

1988) but briefly to delineate within a single assessment session the fluidity of movement between abuse and abusing.

Rotten Apple, Rotten Tree

Andrew (not his real name), aged twenty-one, had attempted to strangle and molest several babies. He always selected a baby left in a pram outside a shop whilst the mother was busy inside. He would undo the baby's clothes to get to the nappy, would touch the baby's genitals as well as the nappy and would then place his hands round the baby's neck until the baby became blue in the face. However, he would take just enough time so that a passer-by, the shop-keeper or the mother would have a chance to notice that the baby was in danger. Placed in a secure unit he became sexually involved with several men and was found enacting scenarios of bondage and other sado-masochistic activities with more vulnerable residents as well making giant nappies as fetish objects for himself and others.

In the first two instances the fact that he had a learning disability led to the erroneous belief that his actions were innocent. Indeed, Booth and Grogan (1990) found that of sexual offenders with a learning disability in the North West region the majority lived in the parental home. It is a matter of concern that whilst deviant sexual behaviour is similar in those with or without learning disabilities, the former is less likely to reach the courts or treatment (Breen and Turk 1991)

When I went to visit Andrew for a therapeutic assessment to consider whether he would be suitable for group therapy it was a cold winter's day. I found a nervous young man, inappropriately dressed in shorts and a T shirt, pacing up and down like an overgrown infant school boy. He was talking about wanting to see babies. I commented that perhaps he was worried that I was only interested in talking about babies to him. He looked interested and relaxed for a moment. I said he may have not felt like seeing me, a stranger. Who would he have liked to see today?

'My mum' he said emphatically. 'You miss your Mum?' 'Yes.' He sat down next to me, staring desperately and intently. I considered that seeing me, a woman whom he knew was there to think about his problems, had stirred up a longing for a mother, but I did not know what kind of a mother yet.

I said I had never met his Mum and this was the first time I was meeting him. He nodded. I asked what sort of Mum he had. 'She is a nice Mum.' I said he was very lucky and he smiled for the first time. 'Is she nice the way she talks to you?' 'Yes. My mum is very nice the way she talks to me.' 'What about when you were little?' I asked. 'Can you remember when you were very little? Was she nice to you then?' There was a painfully false smile on his face (Sinason 1993) as he repeated 'My mum was lovely to me when I was little. She was a lovely Mum, a nice Mum.' 'Was she nice when she gave you food?' I asked. 'Very nice.' 'Was she nice when she played with you?' 'Very nice. Lovely.' 'Was she nice when you needed to go to the toilet?'

'My mum was very nice when I needed to go to the toilet. My mum loved changing my nappies, she did. My mum loved changing my nappies. She loved changing my nappies. She changed my nappies all day she did.' He went on and on, his face distorted by the current involuntary awakening of an old memory. Later in the session he described a strange man telling him off for picking an apple from a tree when he was little. 'And it was only a rotten apple and a rotting tree. All the apples had worm. I had worms.'

It did indeed turn out that his mother had sexually abused him in his early childhood, initially using the everyday-task of nappy changing as the means for sexual access and gratification as Estela Welldon has so clearly described (1988). Using the further excuse of his learning disability in order to keep him in nappies until the age of seven she then lost interest in him, moving her attention to a younger sibling. For Andrew, a baby represented the true object of maternal love and desire whilst to grow up meant to be sexually and emotionally rejected.

Without a father or any male figure to protect him Andrew was drawn into a corrupted attachment from which he was finally brutally ejected. After a miserable withdrawn childhood in which he did badly in school the sexual awakening of adolescence posed enormous problems for him. In identification with his mother he found babies were the object of his erotic delight but out of shame concerning his own abuse, which he linked with his disability, and hatred for the normal babies, who stirred up memories of his abuse as well as underlining his disability, he found himself obsessed with the longing to both touch and kill.

He described the way he sought babies who were made available to him by their mothers' negligence. In wanting to kill, but not killing, I considered he was repeating the inhibited infanticidal impulses of his mother towards him as well as his wish that by killing a disowned part of himself he might be able to be reborn.

In other words, the worrying abuser pattern in this deprived traumatized twenty-one-year-old accurately repeated or re-enacted the abuse he had experienced in early childhood. The child is indeed father to the man. Many young men with learning disabilities or mental handicap are referred for violent disturbed sexual behaviour when their mothers unconsciously excite and stimulate them. As one commented, 'It's like the dolls inside the dolls. They want to come out but if they do they will not be inside a mummy and they won't have a mummy' (Sinason 1989). Glasser (1979) explores the impact of such over-attentive yet neglectful maternal behaviour in the formation of perversions.

From Abuse to Abuser as a Result of Maternal Pseudo-Incest in Non-Learning Disabled Latency Boys

Over the last decade I have treated a number of latency-aged boys referred because of their excessive physical and sexual violence in school to both other children and to staff. They had been excluded, even from schools for disturbed children, as their level of aggression was unmanageable. These boys had three initial things in common in the referral letters; their level of violence, their lack of a father who either lived with them or provided any consistent attachment (Rosen 1979) and their use of bad language. Meeting with the boys or observing them in the playground revealed a very specific and poignant use of bad language – the term 'mother-fucker'.

Everything else about the boys – their academic levels, class, race and religion was different. After six months or so in once-weekly psychoanalytic psychotherapy they began to improve. They concentrated better at school and their violence decreased.

Then, with great difficulty, often after a destructive act in the classroom or the therapy room, they blurted out that they share a bed with their mothers at night. They take care to say 'share a bed' instead of 'sleep with' as the sexual connotation is so powerful in the latter. Some have got their own bedroom but their mothers insist they share the double bed. Others do not even have their own bedroom and give up on all friendships from shame at what another child would realize if they saw they had no bedroom of their own.

CLINICAL ILLUSTRATIONS

What the Mothers Say

Here is a story. It was told to me initially by three different single mothers from three different cultures who each slept with her eleven-year-old son. Since then I have heard it from many more and colleagues have added their examples.

There is this son of around eleven they all have. He is terrified at night, they say. He cannot sleep until she takes him to her bed or moves in with him, they say. They stress initially they do not like it. They want a proper night's sleep. They hate being woken up by his nightmares. 'I am so tired', they all say. 'I just let him go to sleep with me and then I get a better rest'. 'It's the culture', they say. 'I haven't got enough rooms' they say. But something stays wrong.

All those sons were referred for therapy because of physical and sexual violence, difficulty in learning or sexualized inappropriate behaviour.

Vignette 1

Lisa was black, working class and twenty-seven. She gave birth to Leroy at the age of sixteen. She had come to this country in her teens. 'In my culture', she said, 'children can share your bed until their teens. You take them to your bed and they can comfort you if you are lonely or you can comfort them if they are frightened of bad dreams.'

Leroy, in individual therapy, says 'I was asleep in my bed and my mum came in. She said I had to go to the toilet so I wouldn't wet the bed. Then she tells me to come back to her bed. She won't let me be on my own. She said I was frightened to sleep on my own because I didn't have a daddy with us but she was frightened, not me. Once when I leaned over in my sleep I woke up lying across her breasts and I felt excited and frightened. Why doesn't she let me sleep in my own bed.'

After three months Lisa said 'He is my child, mine. He came out of my body and he's mine. I don't care what he says about it. He's not a man, he's my child.'

Vignette 2

Mona is thirty, white and working class. She has two daughters and one son, Jake. 'In my family, everyone shared beds. We had to. We didn't have the space otherwise. And that's how it is for me too. If you don't like it get social services to rehouse me. I have three kids, me and two rooms. Tell me how to manage that…' A gentle question reveals that the two girls have separate beds in one large room whilst Jake shares his mother's bed.

Jake says 'My mum wants to kill me in my bed. She keeps sticking a leg or an arm over me in her sleep. It hurts me. My sisters have got a bed each in the big room but I have to share my mum's bed. I can't invite any friends over. They would say "where do you sleep?" and I would be so embarassed.'

Vignette 3

Penny is thirty-seven white and middle class. Her son Peter has a learning disability. 'I believe we separate children too early. My friends do the same as me. If our children need to sleep with us they can. Some cultures are much better at childrearing than us. They carry their young around with them and never separate until the child wants to. When you have a child like mine who is not going to grow up properly he needs even more time.'

Peter cries 'I want a dad. Then my dad could tuck me in. My mum keeps sleeping with me. She won't let me be alone. I can sleep by myself. I am not a baby. There is not much room and in my sleep I made a big wall in the bed.'

After several months another layer comes through – far more painful. I will not even separate out the identities of the mothers because they are all telling a similar story. We leave the realms of culture and kindness and find a very specific abuse – the emotional abuse of the sons by the mothers and the earlier abuse of the mothers when they were children.

- I am the mother. He came out of me so he is mine. Nothing else is mine. He is not a man. He is just a child...

- he's got a better willy than his dad.

- a little prick. You should see him try and hide his erection in the morning as if it mattered.

- in my country anyone could sleep with you if they were lonely – I was lent out to my grandma, my grandad and my uncles – so why shouldn't I have that comfort too.

- he thinks he is grown up the little bastard – looks just like his father – he'll turn out just as bad

- my mother slept with me when she was depressed. She didn't wash. Her bed stunk. He's lucky. I always wash at night.

- if he turned that thing on me in the night I'll cut it off – he's a little boy – he's my baby

In all these cases the child is a no-thing not a person. Estela Welldon (1988) comments 'mothers who display perverse tendencies towards their offspring do so within the first two years of their children's life'. The baby becomes the sexual toy, the missing penis. For a man the perverse act is against another, for the woman it is her own part-object, herself or her child.

Vignette

Tim was referred to a specialist unit after violent sexual attacks on female staff members. He was tall and strong for his age and his punches and kicks were already very damaging. He was hyperactive, unable to learn and highly eroticized. Despite therapy his sexual and physical violence to female staff members continued and the unit was considering excluding him. One session, after six months in therapy, he started making a double bed with the cushions and blankets. He flung himself down on the right side of the bed and punched ferociously at the empty space on the left screaming 'Mother-fucker, mother-fucker'. Then he burst into tears (something I had never seen) and started kicking a locked cupboard so hard it splintered. I said he had made a double bed and it sounded as if it was for him and a mother and this made him feel angry and excited.

He stopped kicking the door and stood still with his back to me – frozen with tension. I said he was not allowed to kick my cupboard and suggested he sat on the chair. With his eyes covered he shuffled to the chair and sat down making a loud humming noise.

I waited a moment until he stopped. I said he was pleased I did not want my cupboard broken into and perhaps that allowed him to hope that I did not want to break into his space. He burst into loud sobs – kicked the pillows on the 'mother' side of the bed violently and shouted 'she makes me sleep in her bed at night'. After we spent several weeks exploring his collusion with this as well as his fear of abandonment he said he could not stop it – his mother had to first – she was the grown-up. He asked me to see her with him.

Tina, his mother, was very keen to come. We decided to try a new pattern in which I would see Tim by himself, then with his mother and finally his mother for fifteen minutes on her own. After several sessions I considered it possible to raise the subject directly. I asked Tim if he was still sleeping with his mother. He nodded. I asked if it was worrying him. Again he nodded. 'But Tim, you don't talk about it to me' said his Mum. I said perhaps it was hard to speak about it to her when it was something she had found hard to help him with. I then directly asked. 'Is he still coming in your bed?' 'Yes' she said, 'At 2am after I wake him up to go to the toilet.' I asked what was so hard at getting him back in his own bed. 'I am just so tired at 2am' she said like an innocent child. I said that was very hard then because a little boy Tim got in her bed and a young man Tim felt very excited and worried about it. 'He certainly is a young man,' agreed mother. 'He is eleven now. I only think it is sexual for him because he is older now. His willy has grown too.'

I said that was why it was even more important for her to help him stop. Tim had his head down looking serious. I said there were some things Mum was brave about. 'What?' asked Tim. 'Going on the corkscrew in Alton towers' They both roared with laughter. I said I could never do that. 'Even my gran can do that' said Tim. I said 'Well your mum and gran can do something I can't. But I can say you shouldn't sleep with your mum.'

Mum and son looked much happier. 'I can go on the corkscrew' said Mum, 'but I am no good at helping him sleep on his own.' I said that was something we needed to work on.

I then said it was time for Tim to go down.

When Mother and I had fifteen minutes on our own I spoke to her again about bedsharing. 'He is a young man', she mused, 'I don't think of him as a little boy – to think it worries him – why the sexy little beast'. She smiled flirtatiously.

After six months Tim was still sleeping in her bed. What finally moved him was the advent of a new boyfriend. Suddenly Tim was a useless appendage. 'Move your ugly bum' she would say to him. 'You need more muscles on your tummy.' Suddenly he was no longer a sexual object. He was intrusively clung to and intrusively abandoned. His violence continues.

ATTACHMENT AND IDENTIFICATION

How does it happen that the one in fourteen who repeat their abuse are responsible for the largest number of sexual offences? A two-year-old boy, David, reached up to touch a china clown in his family's living room. 'No!' shouted his mother, 'Naughty! You're not to touch it!.' A month later the same little boy, playing in the same room began to reach his hand towards the same ornament. With his arm mid-way up he suddenly shouted 'No! Naughty!' He then kicked his teddy bear. 'Naughty Rupert! No!' A child shows how by identification with his parents and through his attachment to them he takes in aspects of their behaviour, both positive and negative, into himself. Children cannot help but take inside themselves aspects of their parents' real behaviour and language.

In an average home a child receives and transmits both loving, hating and ambivalent communications. There is a balance. Where David was spoken to sharply he could not tolerate the experience and needed to mentally and physically pass it on to his teddy bear. It is not surprising that Andrew, with a constant experience of abuse, could not resist trying to pass on his experience to babies. (For further examples see Sinason 1988a.)

In 1893 Freud was aware that 'the psychical trauma (of abuse) – or more precisely the memory of the trauma – acts like a foreign body which long after its entry must continue to be regarded as an agent that is still at work' (p.6). In 1932 Melanie Klein (1932c) suggested that the internal pressure to stop abuse can be so powerful that the guilt and anxiety actually increase desire. This followed Freud's awareness that for some individuals feelings of guilt could be so unbearable that they would need to seek out a crime to commit in order to relieve internal pressure. Any of these processes lead to dangerous and destructive cycles of repetition.

Short-term counselling or group work can reduce feelings of stigma and isolation and allow for grief and anger, but individual psychoanalytical psychotherapy or psychoanalysis is the only treatment that can deal with the internal damage fully. Children who have been abused once by a stranger and are in an understanding home environment will take a long time to recover from their ordeal but it is possible. However, children who have been abused violently or lovingly by a parent or step-parent over many occasions have been internally corrupted to a devastating degree. Short-term work can help them say what has happened and allow them to express anger and mourning for their lost innocence and lost healthy life. However, tackling the intricate weavings of corruption and mad defences is a longer, necessary and painful task.

Special Settings

The Setting
General Considerations

J. H. Scheffer

INTRODUCTION

The offence, the delinquent act, a transgression of boundaries, is that which distinguishes the patient in forensic psychotherapy from the neurotic patient who is motivated by complaints; this is the fundamental determinant for the setting in which this therapy may take place. The fact that there is a victim or victims implies the presence of a third person or party, which is equally fundamental to the setting. Here this third party takes shape (in part practically and in part symbolically) in the criminal justice system representing society, in officials responsible for the assessment of dangerousness, in the prison sentence or hospital order under which the patient is offered treatment, in the bodies controlling dangerousness and its possible reduction during the course of treatment and, finally, in the institution, prison or hospital to which the patient is confined or in the juridical order or condition under which treatment on an out-patient basis is made available. The setting in which forensic psychotherapy takes place thus always involves a triangular situation with a specific psychological dynamism. The triangle of therapist, patient and third party can be seen as the symbolic repetition of the original mother–father–child relationship and this has, for instance, consequences for transference. Given the physical boundaries created by the confinement this situation determines the space or sphere that is to contain the therapeutical process. It equally provides, in a metaphysical sense, for the primary sphere, the potential space in therapy as meant by Winnicott (Mooij 1982; Winnicott 1980), which allows for the optimal development of a 'holding environment'.

The *physical surroundings* may be a prison – perhaps a special prison – a forensic psychiatric institution or hospital, forensic units in psychiatric hospitals, correctional facilities for youth such as Borstal, or out-patient services, either in the domain of the Department of Justice or in that of Mental Health.

Whilst the different characteristics of these facilities logically influence the above mentioned space, the development of the potential space is further dependent on the rules that apply to the psychotherapeutic situation. The set of agreements and rules which constitute psychotherapy may be called the framework and will ultimately function as the proverbial backbone of psychotherapies. The establishment of this framework is often a complex matter, some negotiating may be necessary if not unavoidable and this will often yield a compromise between what is theoretically necessary and what is practically possible with a specific patient in a specific case. Symbolic aspects play an important role in this; it is also of relevance whether the institution is oriented more towards the individual or towards a group.

A further fundamental aspect is the therapist's approach to the aspect of delinquency: is he principally seeking to treat, facilitate change in the personality of the individual who is sitting opposite him or does he only aim at reducing this person's tendency to commit or repeat the same or similar offences; that is, when such a tendency has been established (or, at least has not been ruled out). Diagnostic criteria immediately come into this. Furthermore, the country and culture in which one is living and working have to be taken into consideration since they will reflect a general viewpoint of their society upon delinquency. Are offenders, generally, looked upon as criminals or as patients? Is there, consequently, a nuance in the view of an offender's personality, which may include a mental disturbance and a possible connection with the offence (large or small) which may lead to a differentiated conclusion about accountability – the degree to which he is considered responsible for the offence? If so, some indication criteria for psychotherapy are likely to have been considered in the assessment-stage.

The fact that limitations in the setting are the most frequent obstacles in forensic psychotherapy is a truism.

DIAGNOSIS

Superficially, it might be argued that the severity of the offence should determine the degree of physical restriction in the setting. However, a hermeneutical viewpoint upon the offence, as expressed by Mooij in Chapter I:4:iii may yield different factors. When the notion of psychic conflict is brought into consideration factors such as the localization of conflict in time will contribute to the diagnostic appraisal of the severity and complexity of the underlying disturbance or defective development. It may be of a primitive kind, for instance in the sense of abandonment during the earliest developmental phases, or more mature such as an unresolved oedipal conflict leading to a constant testing of authority.

Are we dealing with a single or multiple form of disturbance, for instance a psychosis or, often drug-induced, psychotic episode with or without an underlying character disorder? In the first case it may have been a matter of an off-set balance with an acute moment, which theoretically may only require a small amount of insight and a few psychogenic measures; in the second case it is a chronic matter requiring long-term treatment, a process of clarifying conflict and working through of the pathological traits – if this is feasible at all – social education and readjustment, to name but a few measures. Psychiatric assessment and diagnosis and, preferably, psychodynamic diagnosis is a necessary prerequisite.

If the presence of some form of psychic conflict is determined – or hypothesized – more can be said about possible therapeutical measures indicated in general, and psychotherapeutic ones in particular. By conflicts is meant here, for instance, the (true) identity of the father, the as yet unadmitted sexual inclination, the question of the identity of the offender as a replacement child, stagnation of a mourning-process or the failure to attain independence from the family of origin, often with defence against unconscious hatred towards one or both parents.

The same applies to the patient's capacities: intellectual, affective, conative and social, and for his limitations, which may ultimately come down to defect (in some perhaps even of an organic nature), but will generally concern limited intellectual and social skills. Of great importance is the presence or absence of significant others to the patient outside the institution, in the sense of providing contact with the outside reality, which includes training of alternative ways of behaving.

ONE PSYCHOTHERAPY?

Considering the setting of psychotherapy proper we may first want to establish the level at which psychotherapy should take place. Is there in the individual concerned a capacity for insight and similarly for affective growth, at least *in statu nascendi*, or are these capacities limited or lacking altogether? The first category can be considered a favourable condition for insight-oriented, psychodynamic psychotherapy, perhaps in some cases even psychoanalysis proper may be indicated. The second category may require (ego-)supportive measures and stimulation of the development of new faculties with the dynamics of conflict, keeping in mind present capacities and environmental aspects.

The quality of the dialogue between psychiatry and the law is of importance here to the extent that it should be clear how dangerousness in this particular patient should be defined. From the strict standpoint of a psychodynamic therapeutic process in which the therapeutical relationship is the vehicle of this process, any meeting on a regular basis between therapist and patient that doesn't meet these characteristics is not to be called psychotherapy.

On the other hand, these contacts may develop into psychotherapy proper – and they may not, but still be considered valuable – which might favour a definition of forensic psychotherapy which is not too restrictive.

The question of motivation is immediately linked to this. At the outset motivation may consist of nothing more than the wish not to find oneself in custody or in front of the judges' bench again; indeed motivation, here to be called 'extrinsic', may never, consciously or admitted by the patient, develop beyond this point. This will be the case in a fair number of patients with the diagnosis of character neurosis or personality disorder and in most perversions and psychoses. In spite of an unfavourable diagnosis, however, one can never be absolutely sure that no advance will be made in such a contact and that some insight into a causal chain leading to offending can be obtained. Much may also depend on the setting as a whole and its attitude towards psychotherapy. The traditional prison warden may be rather suspicious of psychodynamic insights, especially when they may concern his contacts with the prisoners. At the same time he will be perfectly aware of the prisoner's condition when he is 'working through' his offence.

RULES

Where rules are constitutional to psychotherapy (Mooij 1982), they equally form part of the forensic setting and will help to provide a sphere in which a primary process may develop. However, partly as a consequence of the way in which rules may be experienced by the patient, not all basic rules will always be applicable unaltered. Whether they are or not will depend on the capacities and limitations of the patient as well as the environment. Thus the basic rule that one say everything that comes to mind may have to be altered to saying as much as possible, but even this may not succeed without a certain amount of activity, help, explanation, and active interest in the patient by the therapist. Also, whilst regular appointments are fundamental, they may often be missed or forgotten, psychotherapy sessions being one of the few occasions by which anger and frustration can be acted out without this having immediate consequences. Similarly, three-quarters of an hour's duration may be the standard duration of the sessions, but to stop at the exact time may quite often, at least in the beginning stages (and indeed, one may never progress much beyond this) be experienced as a sadistic move which hence has to be avoided. Some patients complain that they have always just warmed up when the clock strikes and for those a longer session, at least from time to time may be the answer.

Whereas the answer to the question 'for how long?' may be 'we have got all the time we need', in those situations where duration of stay in the institute depends on the disappearance of dangerousness, this answer may similarly have a threatening quality because of the patient being unable to imagine anything – even life – 'within' an unlimited time-frame. The agreements that are made about rules should in general be much more tailor-made than with the neurotic patient. At the same time the therapist should be fully aware of the consequences of concessions or adaptations to the framework as a whole. If a leniency of five minutes to finish the last sentence is given it should not lead to a 'five more minutes' hour. The next point, the purpose of therapy, what should be aimed for, may or may not be made explicit. It may, for instance, vary from the acquisition of insight into the patient's problems or into the causes of his offending to the alteration of behaviour in certain stressful circumstances.

In addition, it may be necessary to add rules, or make exceptions to existing rules. This concerns in particular the aspect of confidentiality, where exceptions have to be made for the situation when the therapist gets the impression from the patient that he has become a threat to either the life of others or of himself. In this case one will, having verified the danger with the patient, inform others so that appropriate steps may be taken. The rationale of this exception is explained with reference to the presence of two individuals, therapist and patient as constitutional to therapy, which in the case of suicide or homicide would no longer exist. The question whether or not the third party should be informed about progress in therapy has similar aspects which are dealt with in the clinical psychotherapy situation. The fact that the maintentance of confidentiality is also expected on the part of the patient may be met with uneasiness by someone coming from an environment where the notion of privacy is virtually non-existent. Dealing with it in this sense may be totally new to him and it may therefore be a restrictive factor in group-psychotherapy within an institution: the patient may feel himself unable to keep things to himself and may discuss contents of the therapy with his fellow-patients for fear of breaking group-loyalty, as he sees it, on his unit. This is in contrast to the out-patient setting, which usually lacks these strong loyalty aspects, and may yield a potentially much greater deepening of the therapeutic process.

Finally, it has to be remarked that, given the fact that the personal aspects as operative in psychotherapies cannot be quantified, the person of the therapist him- or herself may be of vital importance in therapy and, hence, at the initial contact and during negotiating a contract. The ability to deal with this situation with confidence, the impression that the therapist is well prepared for any eventuality that might arise at this stage may make or break a therapy. It is underscored by the realization that there will always be anxiety in the patient which may lead to a mock-adaptation to therapy on the one hand or rejection on the other if confidence is lacking.

CLINICAL PSYCHOTHERAPY

Treatment of offenders may take place in a clinical psychotherapy setting – which may be described as a unit or ward where patients' behaviour and interaction is looked upon and interpreted psychodynamically. Literature about clinical psychotherapy is abundant (this setting is dealt with in detail in other chapters) and will not be dealt with here. The forensic setting may be basically much the same as that for the 'neurotic' and only be different in the aim of treatment: reduction of dangerousness (through resolution of conflict) and the emphasis upon the maintenance of safety, outwardly and inwardly. It is essential that a sense of 'relational safety' develop, which involves a fair notion of the emotional condition of all individual patients and the group as a whole, with a psychodynamic viewpoint to support this. An optimal atmosphere for the unit personnel or socio-therapists can only be reached if there is a maximum openness and free discussion of one's feelings (fear, love) evoked in contact with the patients is possible; the psychotherapist's contribution may be very valuable here. The ability to deal with aggressive or threatening behaviour, and the anxiety-tolerance is an equally important prerequisite. Finally, the question of whether unit staff or guards act in extreme circumstances has to be looked into.

The way in which unit and institution as a whole are organized may vary. The position of the psychotherapist may range from a full team membership to a relative outsidership with advantages and disadvantages for both. Closeness to the team may interfere with the necessary therapeutical neutrality, whereas absolute non-involvement may run the risk of psychotherapy being looked upon as a white elephant. Again, the question of confidentiality in psychotherapy is an essential one, whilst any indication of a leak may result in much more damage than stalemate in just one therapy. The involvement of the ward psychiatrist who may function as a filter or semi-permeable wall between ward-team and psychotherapist(s) may be a solution. He may be able to get his own impression about the ongoing intrapsychic process and its possible effect upon behaviour on the ward and reciprocally. Consequently, he will also be a vital person in the determination of the remaining dangerousness, which question principally should not be put to the psychotherapist. (By the same token one should avoid doing psychotherapy with patients whose dangerousness one has assessed beforehand, or allowing an assessment to slip into therapy. Should one decide to try to do so anyway there should be maximum information and freedom for the prospective patient to refuse.) The fact that a court-session for re-evaluation of dangerousness often involves a three-month standstill of psychotherapy has to be taken as it comes. When, however, the insight gained in psychotherapy fails to have any effect upon the patients' behaviour on the ward, indications for psychotherapy should be re-assessed.

The situation in which there is a psychotherapy committee, where cases are diagnozed, psychodynamically, indications for psychotherapy given, where matching takes place, intervision and supervision are provided and follow-up of cases is discussed may be considered optimal for forensic psychotherapy. In addition to that the psychiatrist, having a low threshold as a doctor, may 'deliver' many patients for psychotherapy whose psychosomatic complaints made them make their first step towards insight. A change from extrinsic to intrinsic motivation usually takes place gradually during psychotherapy.

When, however, the insight gained in psychotherapy fails to have any effect upon the patient's behaviour on the ward, indication for psychotherapy should be re-assessed. Finally, the importance of the institution as a whole, not as the much-criticized total institution (Goffman) but preferably as a transference-figure, mostly motherly but at times fatherly, has to be taken into account and at times interpreted as such. The same may go for the juridical title under which treatment takes place, which for many patients may feel as though this has been tattooed on their forehead. The discussion of this aspect may both yield vital information about the therapeutical process and be of prime significance for insight in one's dangerousness with increased possibilities for working through.

THE PERSON OF THE PSYCHOTHERAPIST

Forensic patients are not easy clients. This statement may appear a truism but it nevertheless requires explanation. Because of the nature of the pathological traits in many, which is a consequence of a limited or almost absent ability to be empathic, they are inclined to act out rather than experience feelings which therapy may bring about. They will include those in the primary sphere such as fear of abandonment, annihilation and deep depression. In the therapeutic relationship the therapist should be able to withstand the strong appeals which are made upon him. He should be prepared for this from the first moment in the first encounter when the patient, out of fear of insecurity, may immediately try to put the setting 'full-force' to the test and with it, the therapist. This testing may take very different shapes, ranging from direct aggression and accusation – for instance that one is simply a collaborator of the Criminal Justice System – to an idealized transference 'I have chosen you because I was told you are the best' with the aim of restricting the manoeuverability of the therapist. It is clear that unconscious fears, of rapprochement, of dependency, or of feelings of smallness appearing – will almost always be at the bottom of this testing. The basic assumption here is that, man being gregarious, in every individual there is always the wish to belong to – to return to – the human herd in a conflict free way.

Similarly, the classic transparency of the therapist may often be contraindicated, being experienced as unnatural and giving rise to much more suspicion than can be counteracted by the correct therapeutic attitude and interpretation. This has of course everything to do with the limited, or sometimes near absent ability for fantasizing and imagining. One should be prepared to do much more explaining and do this over again, than is customary in the neurotic realm. Any information, however, one is for this reason inclined to provide should be carefully scrutinized for its possible effects upon the process; this includes attention to the aspect of safety.

If progress in one's patient can only be measured in millimetres – which is often the case – one should realize that this is never insignificant; often tiny shifts and changes may together eventually be just enough to swing the balance of reoffending the other way.

Day Hospital Treatment for Borderline Patients

Anthony Bateman

INTRODUCTION

Over the last twenty years there has been a rapid development of day hospitals within general psychiatric services. This increase has arisen out of attempts to alleviate pressure on in-patient beds, offer an alternative to in-patient treatment, reduce costs and provide long-term rehabilitation in the context of inadequate day care provision. However, Wilkinson (1984) and Vaughan (1983) have highlighted the lack of knowledge and scanty research about efficacy. The expansion of day hospital care within general psychiatric services has not been matched by a similar process in the forensic services where specialist day hospital treatment is at best rudimentary. Forensic services tend to utilize expensive specialist in-patient units for acute or long-term treatment followed by out-patient attendance. Thus, broadly speaking, there is a gap between intensive in-patient treatment, often under medium-secure conditions, and rehabilitation in the community. A day hospital service can address this gap, forming part of a continuum from in-patient to out-patient treatment. More important, day hospitals offer an alternative to in-patient treatment for many patients, especially if criminal behaviour is associated with severe personality disorder. They are part of a community network involving the prison service, probation service and their often time limited day units, and courts.

Through this network, treatment of severe personality disorder and criminal behaviour can be integrated and tailored to an individual's needs without dislocation from the local community. This brief chapter will address the place of intensive psychotherapeutic treatment in a day hospital setting for patients with severe personality disorder, especially borderline personality disorder (BPD). Descriptively (American Psychiatric Association 1994), patients suffering from BPD show, 'stable instability' comprising intense but unstable personal relationships; self-destructiveness often involving attempted suicide, self-mutilation, drug abuse, and criminal behaviour; constant efforts to avoid real or imagined abandonment; chronic dysphoria such as anger, boredom, and emptiness; transient psychotic episodes or cognitive distortions; impulsivity; poor social adaptation; and identity disturbance.

BACKGROUND

Kernberg (1984) has been one of the most vigorous proponents of long-term, in-patient treatment for severe personality disorders. He suggests that in-patient treatment gives optimal containment to explore the patient's primitive object relations in the here and now of the transference and countertransference within an on-going group process. Tucker et al. (1987), in a descriptive study, have reported favourably on the outcome of such a process, and overall in-patient psychotherapeutic treatment for severe personality disorder, including those with emotionally unstable (borderline and impulsive) and dissocial (amoral, antisocial, asocial, psychopathic, and sociopathic) is reasonably well established (Copas, O'Brien, Roberts and Whitley 1984; Dolan, Evans and Wilson 1992b; Rosser et al. 1987; Whitely 1970). However, evidence for the efficacy of day hospital treatment, instead of or as a way of circumventing in-patient treatment, is accruing. Dick and Woof (1986) followed up patients treated in a psychotherapeutically-orientated day hospital and showed that the majority of patients reduced their dependence on psychiatric services following treatment. However, a sub-group, identified as borderline personality disorder, seemed to become more reliant on support.

In contrast Vaglum et al. (1990) and Mehlum et al. (1991), following up ninety-seven patients for two to five years after treatment in a day hospital specializing in intensive psychotherapeutic intervention, found patients with BPD showed moderate symptom reduction and good global outcome, but schizotypal patients retained poor global function although improving symptomatically. Karterud et al. (1992) investigated the containment function of a day hospital milieu for decompensated patients with personality disorders and found global outcome was good for Cluster C personality disorders (avoidant, dependant, and passive-aggressive) (American Psychiatric Association 1994), moderate for BPD, and limited for schizotypal patients. Of particular importance was the low rate of suicide in all these studies.

CONTAINMENT

A decisive factor in recommending in-patient or day hospital treatment for severe personality disorder is the degree of 'containment' needed. In contrast to custodial containment, psychological containment is an elusive concept. In psychodynamic theory, containment as part of treatment relies on Bion's (1962) concept of the mother as a container for the infant's projected feelings such as pain, fear of death, envy, and hatred. These are detoxified by the nurturing breast, and then returned in such a way that the infant gets back good feelings of being held and understood rather than the original bad projections. In this way the infant makes sense of his experiences and introjects an object that is capable of bearing and allaying anxiety.

In a day hospital setting this is represented by the 'listening', tolerant staff, therapeutic milieu and the ability of the team to make sense of confusion, create order from chaos, and turn action into understanding. The impulsive or violent offender has no such experience and as an adult rarely induces others to empathize. Consequently, he continually fails to develop an internal object that supports, understands and cares. Development of a capacity to tolerate frustration is needed if persistent offending is to be halted. In a day hospital setting this can develop through the 'doing' and 'being' functions of the staff team.

DOING AND BEING

Winnicott (1971b) writes about the capacity to be, or 'being', and contrasts it with an active manner of object relating or 'doing'. He equates 'being' with the object with the more receptive female element and 'doing' something to the object with the more active male element, both elements being potentially present in every man and every woman. Wolff (1971) has put it differently as 'being with' and 'doing to'. Wolff suggests that 'being with' involves a high degree of empathy and sensitivity to what the patient is experiencing. The therapist must be able to grasp the deeper meaning of the patient's verbal and also, and especially, of his non-verbal communications. He seeks the significance of what it means when the patient is silent, goes to sleep, becomes restless or reacts with actions rather than words. In contrast, 'doing to' is more concerned with outward behaviour rather than with its inner meaning and correspondingly in this mode the therapist uses his critical and intellectual functions more than his intuition and feeling functions.

In any psychotherapeutic work it is helpful to think of 'being with' the patient as essential to promote growth by providing space and time which frees and facilitates the patient's own potential for growth and development. In contrast, doing something to the patient, like giving an injunction, commenting on his behaviour, or making interpretations, relates more to the therapeutic functions. If 'doing to' is overdone it may deprive the patient of discovering his own answers and solutions and thus interfere with his developmental process. In contrast, too much 'being with' may neglect the use of effective therapeutic treatment to diminish symptoms and alleviate distress. This balance alters in any treatment and the art of dynamic therapy consists of finding the right balance between 'being with' and 'doing to'. In fact the 'doing to' functions very often require a well-established 'being with' relationship before they become effective. Balancing 'doing to' and 'being with' is the key to day hospital treatment of BPD.

In balancing 'doing to' and 'being with', a creatively functioning parental couple is formed which is essential in the treatment of patients with severe personality disorder, BPD, and psychosis. Their internal representation of a creatively functioning couple, like their sense of self, is fragile and may be distorted, lost or destroyed. The formation of a couple pushes the patient towards an oedipal formation. Triangulation ensures the relationship does not become over-gratifying, collusive, and over-involved, or distant, rejecting, and remote. The couple needs to be kept alive in the mind of the therapist, within the therapeutic relationship, with the staff group, and throughout the community network of which the day hospital is but a part. Maintenance of the couple by the staff team creates a transitional space (Winnicott 1951) which helps the patient tolerate anxiety, impulsivity, rage, and fear of abandonment, especially overnight and at weekends.

THE BORDERLINE DILEMMA

'Doing' and 'being' as treatment modalities represent two poles that are at the centre of theorizing about BPD; these are the conflict and deficit models, respectively. Some authors emphasize conflict as a central psychopathological theme whilst others stress deficit, each advocating different treatment approaches.

Both conflict and deficit models identify similar features that are important in the psychopathology of the borderline patient, namely difficulties with intimacy and aggression, problems of ego function, and the contribution of the environment, but put a different emphasis on their understanding and role in clinical practice. In the conflict model (Kernberg 1984) aggression plays a primary role as a driving force in the psychopathology of the borderline. In the deficit view (Kohut 1977, 1984), aggression is secondary to environmental failure, a protest against an unresponsive mother, or a way of holding onto an object through hatred in the absence of the capacity to love.

The ego is seen to be weak from both viewpoints. Conflict theorists see it as being unable to contain aggressive impulses, leading to poor impulse control and incapacity to cope with anxiety. Primitive defence mechanisms are brought into play including splitting, projection, projective identification, omnipotence and devaluation (see Chapter I:3). Deficit theory emphasizes the inability of the ego to soothe and calm the self. As a result, borderlines turn to others, forming over-dependent relationships, or alternatively become addicted to drugs, involved in compulsive, often deviant sexual activity, and engaged in recurrent self-destructive acts such as overdosing and self-laceration.

The degree of importance attached to the role of the environment in the development of BPD differs between the approaches. Kohut and Winnicott, and the deficit model, emphazise the importance of environment, and focus on the mother's attunement, her capacity to create a transitional space, and her ability to supply self-object needs in the development of a stable sense of self. In contrast, an emphasis on conflict and the importance of aggression tends to underplay the effect of the environment on the development of the self.

These theoretical polarities are often reflected, in practice, in rigid out-patient treatment regimes but in this author's view, treatment in a day hospital needs to take into account both approaches if a cohesive team is to be maintained and if treatment is to be successful.

TREATMENT

Although the theoretical polarities emphasize different areas of borderline function, all are agreed that because of the chaotic nature of the borderline's life, stability has to be maintained via external sources. In out-patient treatment this will include careful attention to consistent appointment times, ending sessions on time, making a clear contract and so on. In a day hospital setting the establishment of a coherent staff team who form a close therapeutic alliance between themselves and the patient is particularly important. All borderline patients engender powerful countertransference enactments in staff which, if enacted, lead to a breakdown in treatment. The staff need to ensure their programme allows time for mutual professional discussion about patients and groups.

Countertransference is a key therapeutic tool in BPD. The staff will be cast in the role of rescuers and attackers and must be able to recognize both roles as a distortion of reality. When the inevitable muddles occur the staff have to disentangle their own contributions from those of the patients. This can only be done if adequate support is given through supervision, adequate training, mutual respect for others' views and thoughtful listening. Dynamically, a supervisor acts as a 'third object' (Bateman 1995), much like a father may with a mother and new baby, who helps each staff member and the staff group get close enough, but not too close to the patient, and yet far enough away, but not too far, to think and intervene appropriately. Only then can projections be 'detoxified' and returned in a modified form to the patient rather than ricocheting around different staff members (Main 1957).

Conflict models require a focus on interpretation, a 'doing' function, whilst deficit approaches emphasize empathy, the creation of a holding environment and validation – 'being' functions. In a day hospital setting it is necessary to develop a balanced treatment programme otherwise splitting (see Chapter I:3) between different members of a staff team occurs with some advocating 'doing' even to the extent of discharging a patient and others promoting 'being' to the extent of tolerating damaging behaviour. This split reflects the theoretical divide. Conflict theorists accuse the deficit group of creating a collusive relationship in which real aggression is denied, mirroring the maternal deprivation in childhood which led to the development of a false self and an inhibition of autonomy. Deficit proponents believe too much emphasis on aggression and negative transference compounds the fragility of the already fragile self-esteem of the borderline patient. A pure approach on either side can cause severe difficulties. Too great an emphasis on deficit may lead to regression, dependency, and escalating demands; excessive interpretation, using the conflict model, may leave the patient angry and confused and liable to drop out of treatment. The evidence suggests that both conflict and deficit, 'doing' and 'being' in treatment, are important in the development and treatment of BPD.

A stable treatment framework is established, not only by cohesion of the staff team but also through agreed rules. Limits have to be set but they must not be so rigorous as to alienate those patients they are supposed to help. Some therapeutic communities form rigorous rules which, if broken, lead to discharge. The problem with such an approach is first, its denial of the unconscious force motivating behaviours such as self-laceration and overdosing, and, second, the danger of discharging patients for the very reason they have come for treatment. However, patients must be expected to come on time, show a commitment to all the therapies offered, agree to minimize their self-harm, refrain from drugs and alcohol, and not harbour secrets, especially about relationships with other patients.

In summary, a day hospital programme for borderline patients needs to combine an atmosphere of 'being' with an attitude of 'doing'. There are many ways in which this can be done. Individual sessions may be mixed with group work, active techniques with dynamic understanding, large group process with small group therapy. Treatment needs to be flexible rather than coercive, sensitive rather than rigid, permissive instead of directive, and thoughtful rather than reflexive.

Our day hospital programme consists of individual and group work within a structured five day week. Morning sessions are devoted to analytically-orientated group psychotherapy with small groups being held on three mornings a week and a large group of all day hospital patients twice a week. In the afternoons the group work is orientated around an activity or topic. Art therapy, psychodrama, and music and dance therapy are used. Those patients with eating disorders have a special group centred on eating behaviour and diet. One individual session is offered each week. Patients are expected to attend each day unless working towards leaving. In between sessions patients have access to pottery, art materials, and their own cooking facilities. Peer group support is encouraged during these times. Staff share all information about patients with each other including any material from individual sessions. This is important as the staff are often seen as parental figures and need to be experienced by patients as talking to each other and working out difficulties jointly. In this way creatively functioning couples are formed in many different guises: between different staff members, in the inter-relationship of active therapy and analytic therapy, between individual and group therapy, and between staff and patients.

The day hospital functions somewhere between the external and internal worlds just as it is located between in-patient and out-patient care. It is a transitional space in which creativity and therapeutic success may take place. The staff maintain this transitional space through a process of containment and boundary setting thereby allowing the patient to begin to differentiate his own intermediate area between the subjective and that which is objectively perceived. Only then can similarity and difference be explored, reality testing be fully developed, the links between the internal and external be established and, finally, illusion and disillusionment be worked through.

The Personality-Disordered Forensic Patient and the Therapeutic Community

Kingsley Norton

'RICK: You played it for her; you can play it for me...play it.

SAM   Yes, boss.

You must remember this,
A kiss is just a kiss,
A sigh is just a sigh.
The fundamental things apply
As time goes by...'

('Casablanca' 1942)

INTRODUCTION

Individual personality-disordered forensic patients although differing from one another in many respects share certain similarities, including countless examples of how they break or misapply fundamental rules. In no other treatment setting is this more clearly observable than in the in-patient setting of the residential therapeutic community. In part, the clarity results from the highly structured nature of the therapeutic community environment. Its tightly kept boundaries, especially time boundaries, are analogous to those of the traditional psychoanalytic session, and the therapeutic community yields many opportunities for patients to encounter rules and their enforcement, to break them and to experience the consequences of their rule-breaking. Clarity also results from the extended period of observation which is afforded by virtue of the twenty-four hour per day treatment which incorporates the collaborative vigilance of staff and patients. Such an approach, of course, relies upon adequate communication between the two groups.

What becomes apparent in the living–learning environment of the therapeutic community (Jones 1952) is the pervasiveness of forensic patients' maladaptive attitudes and behaviour, as it were polluting virtually all areas of their psychosocial function. Paradoxically, the environment with its implicit demand that patients become active members of the community and, in effect, also therapists to their fellow patients, reveals islands of healthy, adaptive functioning which can serve as anchor points for subsequent personality development.

Formative years of neglect and abuse will have favoured and spawned in forensic patients a deep mistrust of any who purport to care or help them and a rejecting, withholding or openly hostile response from staff will be expected. To an extent such a response is also wished for from caring professionals, since it holds little or no novelty value to the patient hence little anxiety (the usual defences being erected to deal with it). Alongside this, however, is a craving for care and recognition from others, especially those authority figures who represent caring and protection.

Potential carers, in their work with personality-disordered forensic patients, repeatedly have the authenticity of their care and concern tested via various strategies, ranging from straightforward physical or verbal assault, through subtler forms of rejection of care (such as failure to follow professional medical advice), to excessive or scandalous demands for care. All these scenarios provide opportunities for the patient to witness carers' reactions to such provocation and the resultant findings contribute to an evaluation of how genuine is the care and support on offer. Because these testing strategies tax carers there is a tendency for the latter to react, unthinkingly, in a way which provides the patients with their own expected rejecting response, as when staff respond to aggression with aggression, borne out of professional and personal frustration or reject the 'excessive' demands since they are judged inappropriate to the particular context. Alternatively, staff may deny the existence of patients' aggression (overt or covert) and try to meet the inappropriate demands. When staff either inappropriately reject or comply with patients' demands for care, the opportunity to foster personality development is lost since the patient is not exposed to any new experience. Familiar responses elicit no fresh thinking and thus patients will not be able to learn from this experience.

Avoiding the above pitfalls, enough of the time, and recognizing such testing phenomena for what they are, namely, rudimentary attempts to make meaningful contact or secure attachment, is one of the tasks of staff in a therapeutic community. The aim is to avoid the development of infantile dependent or exciting sado-masochistic styles of relationship but to foster more maturely dependent, psychologically differentiated and sober styles of relating.

Forensic patients exhibit and deploy a great energy and pressure to short circuit, undermine and overwhelm conventional boundaries and the resilience of these, and, as important, the manner in which the integrity of them is upheld, is crucial to the creation of an environment which challenges patients' attitudes while aiming to provide support and understanding. Henderson Hospital is used in this chapter as an example of a therapeutic community proper (Clark 1987) for the treatment of personality disordered adults which has been researched not only in terms of process but of outcome (Copas, O'Brien, Roberts and Whiteley 1983; Dolan, Evans and Wilson 1992b; Whiteley 1970).

PERVERTED CARING

The therapeutic community relies on the utilization of the total human resources of the community and not just that of the staff (Jones 1952). This means that it is primarily the resident group who provide support and care for residents who are acutely disturbed or distressed (see below – Responding to Crisis). It takes various forms according to the nature of the upset, the relationship of the individual(s) to the rest of the community, the potential genuine resources available and the time of day or night. The caring and supportive resources of the community are thus inevitably limited. They are also constrained in particular ways, especially by forensic patients, and this is exemplified at all levels within the therapeutic community – personal, inter-personal and inter-systems. The following clinical example reveals the distortions resulting in perverted caring and support at the level of interpersonal relationships.

Vignette

For two months resident members of the community provided nightly support to Ann, one of the female members (patients at Henderson are known as residents) who suffered extreme night terrors. Whilst still asleep, she would be disturbed by nightmares of her childhood abuse and would beat herself up. The community's resources were steadily depleted as the nightly vigils kept outside her room by shifts of fellow patients, two at a time for two hours, proved inadequate to curb her self-injury. After a time the solution of one resident per night, sleeping on her bedroom floor (all 29 residents have their own single rooms), who could awaken her at the first sign of disturbance or distress, proved more successful at preventing the self-harm.

At first sight the above solution seemed to provide a more reliable support system but, as time went by, only two stalwart male members of the community 'survived' the nightly ordeal and resultant sleep deprivation. Both had been seriously sexually traumatized in their formative years as had the resident being supported. One had been abused by a paedophile ring (which included a close relative) and the other had been seriously sexually abused whilst in prison and later required corrective surgery. Both the supporters had served prison sentences for serious convictions including violence against women. They also had problems with sleeping, involving recurrent nightmares thus being 'on call' served, at least to an extent, to distract them from their own nightly traumas.

Physical force was sometimes required to prevent Ann from self-injuring and the staff became increasingly concerned that some pathological repetition of her past abuse was being enacted under the apparent guise of genuine care and support. Attempts to voice this concern, however, were at best muted and the community as a whole seemed to have a need to condone the apparent action of the two male members even though the quality of, and motivation for, their care and concern was increasingly suspect. Their survival as carers, in the face of behaviour and distress which others could not withstand, appeared to give them an elevated caring status which silently impressed but also temporarily paralysed the rest of the community.

This perverted or distorted form of caring is characteristic of certain forensic patients wherein care is provided but always at a cost, usually of others (here the other members of the therapeutic community) who are denigrated for not providing care, either currently or in the past. In this example, the rest of the community felt emotionally bashed up by the caring couple.

It is as if this form of care is wielded as a weapon since it serves to silence or manipulate others. It is based primarily on a power motive rather than on love and reflects a counting or measuring mentality whereby caring amasses a kind of secret currency which is stored in the memory and later traded, as would be a concrete commodity, in exchange for favours or more tangible rewards which provide the trappings of power or status. It is used to achieve higher status and domination within the relevant social environment. (Of course, such behaviour is not only enacted within the therapeutic situation but outside with parents, partners, children, and others and is well-known in many institutional settings, especially prisons where hierarchies of inmates is often very evident.) The cared-for person also feels the weight of indebtedness to the carer.

The laborious aspect of this caring style was summed by up another female resident, Betty, in connection with a different male resident who had a forensic history. She commented 'Your energy wears me out!'. In this instance, 'energy' referred to the male resident's excessive 'caring' not only for other residents' emotional needs but for the general state of the unit which he incessantly tidied and cleaned.

Returning to the former clinical example, from what Ann had said during her daytime treatment sessions, the two men knew something of the nature of her sexual abuse and of the sexual favours she had been forced to bestow upon those who had previously abused her. It was only when the two male members had left the community that another version of this particular caring–cared for situation emerged.

Ann reported that one of them had attempted to take sexual advantage of her during and after their nightly vigils. He was saying to her, in effect, 'You gave it to them (who abused you); give it to me (who has cared for you)' – that is, Rick's drunken demand of sober Sam: 'You played it for her; you can play it for me... Play it!' Sam's reluctant and guilty capitulation is characteristic, any appeal to rationality being swamped – 'Yes, boss'. (N.B. This same interpersonal dynamic relationship is played out and resonates intrapsychically and results in, and reflects, a chronically impaired quality and style of caring for the self).

Such demands as above, which derive in an important way from intense envious feelings, are typical of many forensic patients and played out again and again in everyday situations as well as in their offending behaviour. They are at the core of much relevant psychopathology and represent, among others, the breaking of one of the fundamental things, concerning the passage of time and its experience – 'as time goes by' (see Bion 1961a; Winnicott 1963b). There is conflation of a request (for care, concern or simply sexual gratification as in the clinical example) with the expectation that the same will be withheld and, hence, the need for the coercion or threat which follows, 'Give it to me!'.

Stated thus, this paradoxical state of affairs – 'I know you won't give it to me, so, give it to me' – a conviction that what is wanted will be unforthcoming or withheld and yet is demanded nevertheless, can serve as a model for understanding much of the style of communication of forensic patients. The style applies to their contact with fellow patients, their therapists and in their offending and everyday lives. Correspondingly, the task of psychotherapy becomes one of teasing out the three conflated elements: (1) I want this; (2) you won't give it to me; (3) give it to me. This conflation, with the intrinsic distortion of time involved in such a compressed and contradictory state of affairs, does not allow for a simple articulation of the basic need – 'I want this' – which as a consequence may continue unrecognized as well as unarticulated. Nor is there time for a balanced or rational judgment of whether or not the desired response will be forthcoming, which thus remains an untested hypothesis. There is simply a firm conviction that the need will be unmet as it has always been or perceived to have been in the past. The urgency to resolve the inner tension, which mounts with the passage of time, results in the realization of an unrestrained impulse – a threat, gesture, violence or some other criminal act.

Together with the above may be the desire to experience a punitive and/or concrete response from the environment (which is better than no response), as when a forensic patient only experiences relief from mental torment once being 'banged up' and hearing the police cell door slam behind him or her – but this is temporary relief. The pain of the absence of a response is so painful, in part, because it is experienced as eternal.

Forensic patients' addiction to action and concrete solutions to their emotional conflicts and also their ambivalence and mistrust often compromises their treatment, whether as in-patients or out-patients, and this means that they experience little or no actual time to really question their own or others' attitudes and behaviour in the face of emotional conflict. Because of this there is difficulty in creating and maintaining a treatment alliance, which may require of the patient or resident delayed gratification of needs, especially during out-patient treatment, which necessarily requires survival between treatment sessions. The result is a strong, and sometimes overwhelming, tendency to pervert, challenge, distort or neutralize potentially therapeutic structures and processes so as to maintain the belief that genuine (i.e., depressive position) care does not exist. This is evident at every state of treatment.

Teasing out the conflated elements, *through actual external world encounters*, and in an external world time frame to allow for residents to truly test the hypothesis that there will be no individually responsive hence facilitating environment, can only be achieved, however, if a culture of enquiry is satisfactorily established within the therapeutic community (Main 1983; Norton 1992). Some of the ways in which the phenomena referred to above reveal themselves are described below, together with ways in which the rest of the community, but especially staff, can respond therapeutically rather than simply custodially and so facilitate the potential for change.

THERAPEUTIC OR PERVERTED PROCESSES AND STRUCTURES

What follows represent examples, at the inter-systems level, of how potentially therapeutic aspects of the community are misused, or used defensively, so as to avoid: the necessity to have a novel experience of a therapeutic environment; thinking and feelings; and personality development.

Selection

The selection of new residents is carried out in a group setting, as is all subsequent treatment. The selection panel comprises nine senior residents (greater than three months' stay) and three staff. At interview, powerful peer group processes are seen at work sometimes engendering a profound identification, between patients, as when an obviously scarred self-mutilator is interviewed by a group including similarly scarred individuals. The seeds of a treatment alliance, reflecting a more secure attachment to would-be carers than may have been possible before, can sometimes germinate at this stage. Unfortunately, there may be a blight at the seedling stage, with up to one quarter of residents leaving the community in their first month (Dolan, Evans and Wilson 1992b).

Overall, the more senior residents involved in the selection process experience genuine empowerment in performing this important function on behalf of the community, since the decision to accept is on the basis of a democratic vote by the selection panel. This is a new experience for those who have hitherto only experienced themselves as victims of abusing parents, the police, society. For some residents, however, the responsibility involved weighs all too heavily on their minds and some elect to abstain from what they experience as making (in fact only contributing to) such a decision, affecting another's life. Others admit to no doubts at all about a candidate's suitability but vote only for candidates who strongly resemble themselves in terms of life experience. In the end it is, and should be, like choosing like.

In the process of selecting new residents, which involves discussion by the whole selection panel, there is an opportunity for the residents and staff involved to consider what are the selection criteria for admission to Henderson. This 'professional' debate yields opportunities for residents to consider important criteria such as: the genuineness of motivation for psychological change; the nature of psychological mindedness; preparedness to accept confrontation from others; the potential or likely reactions to frustration; an assessment of dangerousness and so on. Asking such questions of others leads back to an enquiring self-examination and the close collaboration with staff, more or less as equals in such an important task, enhances the continuing engagement of the senior residents in the process of their own treatment and may also enhance self-esteem.

Settling In

There are a number of ways of settling into the therapeutic community and few residents achieve a gradual or smooth entry. At one extreme end, as typified by many residents with a forensic history, there is an adversarial stance with a challenging and denigrating of any evidence of 'structure' (for example, the content of the therapeutic programme, the community's rules, the need for punctuality and attendance of therapy sessions). They maintain a fixed view that staff are covertly authoritarian and a mistrust of the idea that residents are genuinely empowered to make decisions regarding important aspects of the life of the community, such as the selection and discharge of its members. They act as if they were compelled to reside at Henderson, whereas in fact all residents are members of the community in an entirely voluntary capacity.

This adversarial stance is particularly evident in those who have extensive experience of the penal system and who may have come straight from prison to Henderson. It is as if they do not attempt to question that the new environment might differ from other institutional settings and no time or space is permitted to frame the question that it might indeed be so. The resident 'knows' that Henderson is the same as every other past environment (even though there is a secret craving for it to be different) and every conscious effort is made to make this become a self-fulfilling prophecy; that is, that the apparent therapeutic environment which is only a mask for an abusive or neglectful one will be revealed as such. It is as if for these residents there is no genuine care but only variously camouflaged perverted forms of caring, as in the earlier clinical example.

At the other extreme, and interestingly also typified by forensic patients, there is an idealization of the structure and the view that treatment will inevitably be successful. This is associated with the residents' great need to absorb and rehearse, within hours or days of having been admitted, all the community's rules and this results in their becoming a caricature of staff or of those more senior residents for whom the structure has, in fact, come to symbolize something of importance. They move around in the community with an immature confidence and a false sense of certainty and apparent security.

Such new residents appear to avoid the ordinary anxiety of being a stranger in a new environment but, and as a consequence, the idealized view they hold of the community is fragile and readily fragments when non-ideal reality inevitably impinges. Given their views, they do not attempt to derive any real support from the community and so they refrain from testing out the extent to which the community might achieve their ideal requirements. These individuals tend to be liberal with advice to others (a thin veneer of caring) but reveal little of a personal kind themselves and do not take the risk of placing their trust in others. Rather, they require that the community runs like clockwork, that everything be black and white, and in spite of paying lip service to the power and resources of the resident group, they secretly expect that staff will take over, if and when necessary, in a crisis and be able to produce a perfect therapeutic result should they (the staff) wish to.

In some residents there is an oscillation, sometimes abrupt, between the adversarial and idealizing attitudes. In others there is no consistent pattern but the extreme positions are avoided. In others still there is a chaotic attachment with an inability to come to terms with the therapeutic programme and its ideology and the development of a pattern of unpunctuality, absenteeism and/or inappropriate behaviour, verbal and non-verbal, which may eventually end in pemature discharge.

Much of the therapeutic task which falls to staff is an attempt to introduce a middle ground between the two extreme stances, recognizing, stating and sometimes stressing the real strengths and weaknesses of the community and in this way, optimally, a therapeutic and stable disillusionment of new residents can be facilitated. Frequently, however, any disillusionment which results is experienced as sudden and catastrophic. Therefore, it may be at this stage that the new resident leaves the community without an authentic experience of the caring resources which can be available.

Remaining in Treatment

Remaining in treatment for forensic patients is problematic because of the impact of the implicit treatment contract which is to live by the therapeutic community's fundamental rules – no violence to self, others or property and no alcohol or drugs misuse. Breaking these rules, even as a response to emotional conflict or provocation, is the trademark of Henderson residents, especially those with a forensic history, and foregoing this places them under considerable emotional strain (against which, as above, strenuous defences are erected) from the day of admission since alternative, more adaptive, strategies with which to deal with the strain are under-developed or absent.

The treatment programme is highly structured with many different group settings available (see Appendix). These must all be attended unless prior absence is negotiated with the whole community and there is an emphasis both on the quality of such negotiation and on sensible forward planning. Many residents attempt to avoid confronting their difficulties by spurious or irrelevant excursions of one kind or another but the public forum of the daily community meeting, in which absence from groups must be negotiated, means that obvious manipulations, leading to avoidance of conflict or its creative resolution, are plain for all to see.

More than ten minutes missed from a given therapeutic group means that the whole session is considered as having missed, missing more than two groups in one week means that the whole community needs to vote democrati-cally on whether the resident continues his or her admission. This therefore concentrates the resident's mind and, optimally, enables a developing commit-ment to self and a disavowal of self-destructive or otherwise maladaptive attitudes and actions.

Very often, however, discussion in the community meeting avoids the relevant and difficult issue of confronting a resident with the effect their behaviour has had and it centres on the technicalities of the interpretation of a particular rule, for example whether the rule that residents should not exhibit threatening behaviour was actually broken. In the process, residents become polarized, often heatedly, over such an issue and what is lost sight of is the actual encounter so that the resident who has threatened another, or a member of staff, is not confronted about the maladaptive behaviour nor about the motivation for it nor about any failure to explore more adaptive strategies.

At other times, in response to a rule-breaker, the whole resident group may become harshly moralistic towards the resident concerned and, at such times, it is the task of the staff to mediate. Often in these cases the resident concerned has become the scapegoat of the community and, while having a part to play in this development, he or she does not truly merit the total weight of condemnation or rejection which is directed at him or her. Research evidence suggests that residents perceive themselves as less rule-breaking the longer they remain in treatment (Norris 1983).

Running the Community

The main meeting of the day (Monday to Saturday) is the community meeting which all residents and staff are due to attend and residents face a discharge vote for non-attendance. Domestic and housekeeping matters, for example washing up and cooking rotas, are organized. Distressed and/or rule-breaking members are questioned by the rest of the community and are supported and/or confronted, as appropriate. Democratic votes concerning residents' discharges from the community are taken in this forum. Both residents and staff are eligible to vote, one person one vote, and residents' greater numbers mean that were there to be block voting – staff versus residents – the latter have the greater say.

The community meeting is chaired in turn by three senior residents who have been elected by the community to the position of 'Top Three' for a month at a time. Their chairing style may be more or less conducive to a culture of enquiry, for example, permitting time for an experience of painful emotion and facilitating its verbal expression and examination rather than avoiding it. Distortion of the potentially therapeutic structure of this meeting, which has an agenda, may be more or less subtle. At a gross level there is often either too much or too little time allowed by the resident chairperson for a given agenda item so that either some important community items are not discussed at all or others discussed inadequately because too little time is allowed to discuss the particular conflict. Staff's efforts, mainly in the form of comments or questions (see later), are designed to punctuate the flow of the meeting, to clarify or summarize issues but, above all, to try to convey a meaningful psychosocial context to the issues discussed, since the community meeting is usually construed as a microcosm of the whole community. Such punctuation, ideally, has the effect of introducing time and space for important matters to be adequately discussed and not glossed over. Again the goal is to forge a middle road, thereby avoiding the mindless extremes of apathy or, alternatively, reckless activity.

Responding to Crisis

Meetings of the whole community are called in response to any important rule-breaking or marked distress, whether or not associated with rule-breaking.

This is regardless of the time of day or night and all residents must attend such 'referred meetings' or else themselves face a discharge vote for non-attendance. Sometimes the referred meeting is essentially for information sharing, for example, that a resident has left the community unexpectedly, impulsively leaving following confrontation and the ventilation of feelings arising out of this. Sometimes it is for confrontation of a resident and an examination of antecedents and consequences of acting out or other maladaptive behaviour. Such an immediate examination, there and then, maximizes the learning potential for all concerned. All, staff and residents, may then learn from their experience. Emotional and practical support for a disturbed or distressed resident is discussed and, where appropriate, organized in this setting. There is no routine one-to-one 'specialing' of disturbed or distressed residents by staff. The emphasis is on human rather than pharmacological support in the form of sedation. No psychotropic drugs are prescribed. There is no environmental manipulation as in seclusion. Support takes the form, at night, of residents sleeping together in a room (on their separate mattresses) or sitting in shifts outside the disturbed or distressed resident's room so that they are available for talking if necessary. In this way the community is able to contain many crisis situations which in other situations are dealt with so as to reward immature dependence. The case example of Ann, earlier in this chapter, is both unusual and extreme and clearly represents a distortion of the usual caring process.

Leaving

For residents coming up to a successful leaving of the community, usually representing a stay of around nine months (the maximum stay being of one year), there is a treatment group set up which aims to provide for the particular emotional and practical aspects of leaving. Many forensic patients have had an impoverished experience of leaving since they have often been expelled rather than leaving of their own accord (and usually with little notice) and because of this they have been unable to experience or integrate the range of emotions which regularly attends leaving people to whom they may have become attached, even if only ambivalently so. Thus it may be difficult to experience or show feelings of sadness or regret and, consequently, around the time of leaving there may be an apparent recurrence of their presenting action solutions including anti-social behaviours or other acting out, in the face of such unfamiliar and painful emotions.

In therapeutic terms, this behaviour needs to be construed as a surface phenomenon and not necessarily as a sign of deeper, and in spite of therapy, unchanged psychopathology. Being angry is often more comfortable for the resident, in the face of leaving, than feeling sad. Staff recognizing this should avoid becoming too condemnatory or provoked into anger, at least a simple anger which does not contain elements of understanding. They can serve as role models for residents who themselves singly, or as a group, can also convey a message to the resident who is leaving which is not simply condoning or condemning.

Rule-breaking around the time of leaving may be a way in which the resident attempts to re-establish a self-defeating and maladaptive pattern including being expelled as a way of leaving the community. However, sometimes the re-emergence of the former behavioural pattern represents a more conscious phenomenon than before and an attempt to compare and contrast the older with the new and changed status. It can also serve as a check that the resident has not become a 'Henderson clone' nor merely been indoctrinated. It demonstrates that his or her behaviour is indeed under better conscious control then previously.

Maintaining Boundaries

It is surprising that the therapeutic community's rules regarding no violence are not broken more often, given the individual violent histories of the residents (see Figure 1). One reason may be the fact that missing group sessions is registered early by the community since it is the elected position of two residents to record group attendances daily. In this way any trouble brewing may surface, albeit indirectly, at an early stage and verbal rather than more active behavioural expression can be encouraged. This policing of attendance at groups by the residents themselves provides for a more reliable and responsive environment which is experienced as less persecuting than might be the case were this function performed by staff. However, confrontation regarding absence, which takes place formally in the community meetings, is often avoided by residents and to some extent staff are forced (or at least may feel forced) into the vacuum which is left. Reinforcing the importance of such time boundaries can be therapeutic, depending on how it is carried out, and is often what has been absent during residents' formative years. The following represents a clear example of how forensic patients can operate so as to attempt to undermine time boundaries.

In the thrice-weekly small group meeting set up for new residents, where they are encouraged to ask questions about the treatment programme and also to voice any difficulties they have settling into such a strange environment as Henderson, the following conversation took place towards the end of the meeting.

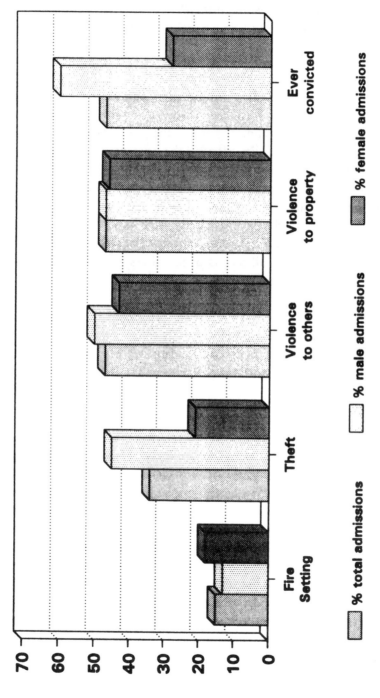

Figure 1. Anti-social behaviours: Henderson Hospital Admissions (N=66) (Source: Subjects referred April 91–August 92 (From data provided at referral))

GROUP FACILITATOR: It is twelve o'clock.

NEW RESIDENT: Is that it then?

GROUP FACILITATOR: That's it!

NEW RESIDENT: So, how do I go about borrowing £4 from the
                      community…

It is as if the words involved in the communication do not hold their conventional meanings. 'It is twelve o'clock', is, of course, an indirect or even obscure way of communicating the end of the group. The questioning of it is therefore quite justified. Having clarified the issue, or at least having appeared to do so, it makes no logical sense, however, for the new resident to proceed as if the state of affairs was other than that just established.

Many residents, such as in the above clinical example, live or more accurately survive in an unbounded world with little or no sense of ownership of time, place or person (including their own person). Consequently, they often feel disempowered in most or all sectors of their lives and experience this as the result of others' design and actions. This usually results in strong feelings of resentment (albeit variously defended against) and there may be a wish to retaliate in order to reverse the situation, the means to this end involving impulsive actions of one sort or another. The following example indicates the way in which, during treatment, one resident had begun to be able to curb such action solutions to emotional problems and to begin to inhabit his own time–space.

Vignette

Six months into his stay at Henderson a male resident, Derek, talked of a train journey undertaken at the weekend. The ticket collector, at the request of a fellow traveller, had requested that he turned down the volume of his personal stereo. Previously, the resident, who was a tough looking and robust man with a short haircut exposing a number of scars on his scalp, would simply have punched or threatened the individual without a second thought. Instead he merely glared, switched off the machine and took off the headset putting it on the table in front of him, albeit seething and feeling humiliated. Within a short time, so Derek claimed, he had calmed sufficiently to pick up the headset, re-adjust the volume (to a lower setting) and he resumed his listening. He felt proud of himself.

To have fought the ticket collector or his fellow traveller (or both) would have been anti-social, as would have been simply leaving the volume at the level it was. However, to have left the headset off, hearing none of his own music, would have been reactionary, in effect being dictated to by another and finding no time or space for himself or, if so, only for a wounded or martyred, grandiose self. Derek realized what an achievement it was to adjust the volume level to that requested and for himself still to be able to enjoy it – it had not become the other person's time or tune. It was very moving to hear Derek's account of the episode.

The abnormal experience of the passage of time (in those who have experienced insufficient psychological containment while growing up) may be difficult for a resident to express, particularly since words are often an under-used vehicle for communication and there is a belief that no-one will listen or understand. Elizabeth described feeling 'frighteningly calm', this feeling reliably preceding her frequent self-mutilation. Cutting herself allevi- ated, at least temporarily, the dreadful, timeless void of her internal world. Another resident painted, in vivid red, orange and black paint, a fiery message: 'There is too much noisy silence, so, shut the fuck up, why don't you'. This was displayed in the room where the community meetings take place six mornings per week and affected Frances, a new resident, who was able to identify with the sentiment, 'Shut the fuck up', this being her response to her own relentless internal thoughts. However, being presented with such a mirror to herself, so soon in her stay, she felt overwhelmed.

Many forensic patients veer uncomfortably from one extreme to another, from a state of being becalmed – in the doldrums – to being caught up in an unrelenting whirlwind of thoughts which they only know how to still by action solutions, for example, criminal acts, binge eating, self-mutilation, sexual activity and so on. They do not seem able to endure the passage of time when unaroused (Winnicott 1958).

USING AND ABUSING THE BODY

Both overt self-wounding and more covert self-neglect during the cause of physical illness form part of a somatizing defence against much mental anguish. This is often the case with forensic patients and the experience of physical pain may serve to distract from emotional difficulties. Turning aggression towards the self in this way can serve to remove them from the care and support of the total community, their pain being split off and compartmentalized with the community's medical and nursing staff who provide the 'GP' function for the hospital. Such behaviour by residents represents a subtle attack on the com- munity's structure, embodying a denial of the therapeutic resources of the whole community, residents and staff, and lodging the care giving capacity with staff by virtue of their professional roles.

Providing for the medical needs of forensic patients can be extremely taxing, since, in their minds, treatment is either present or absent and, if present, will be entirely successful because otherwise it is 'no f…ing use at all!'. If absent, this is experienced as being because it has been wilfully withheld by sadistic staff who secretly delight in the continued suffering of their charges. However, it has to be borne in mind that many forensic patients may not have the capacity to formulate a medical complaint because of their profound mistrust of staff and their expectation that they will not be listened to or, if heard, will be rejected, implying that their need is not genuine. This feeds low self-esteem and defences erected against humiliation often result in extreme anger and fury. There is also often a belief that physical illness represents a just reward for past (perceived) misdemeanours.

In therapeutic community treatment, it is an important therapeutic task to enable the relevant abnormal aspects of seeking and obtaining medical care to become grist to the therapeutic community's public mill rather than to be hived off in the one-to-one privacy of the 'surgery'. An aggressive attack on the structure creates a wound, the pain of which should be felt by staff and residents, not just staff. Open communication avoids the re-creation of abusive and secret relationships which characterize residents' past situations.

Even in the event of a genuine illness, there may not be a request for treatment or help not even a presented symptom but simply a demand for certification – a rubber stamping of the right to retire to bed and miss the therapeutic community programme without incurring the penalty of missed groups. The sick role, as in wider society, has high status and in the setting of the therapeutic community it is often used to communicate aggressive feelings, whose origins and aims are often confused.

Any attempt by staff to deliver a psychosomatic or holistic explanation of physical symptoms is usually experienced as intensely persecuting and reject-ing. There is little room in the resident's mind for such a view, as if an ailment cannot be both painful and also have a psychological cause. Staff are perceived as either for or against the resident, depending on their granting or not the privileges of the 'sick role'. Holding on to the (depressive position) emotional reality of a resident's medical condition, in the midst of all the negative emotion which may be engendered, is difficult even for experienced staff. This is especially so when there is a genuine and serious medical condition such as diabetes mellitus which itself gives rise to concern and when it is known that 'self-medication' has been used in the past as a means of self-destruction, for example, insulin overdosage. Mostly staff do manage to avoid hostile, retali-atory negative responses and such avoidance represents important modelling for the residents of how to care more maturely for one another and for themselves. However, in providing such mature care, staff often need to tolerate being depicted by residents as uncaring, malevolent members of a sub-human class.

THE FACILITATING ROLE OF THE STAFF

Even though all residents enter Henderson voluntarily and remain thus (that is there are no patients under Sections of the Mental Health Act or equivalent Court Orders which might militate against the rights and powers of the community to discharge its members) they may experience the placement as compulsory and react as if this indeed were the case. In such circumstances staff can find themselves unwittingly taking up an institutional stance more befitting that of gaoler. As a result they may be tempted to indicate the open door to residents but such an exhortation, as if to permit them to experience freedom of choice, may be tinged with retaliatory aggression and so be anti-therapeutic. Holding on to, and not directly or immediately expressing aggressive feelings of wanting to straightjacket or otherwise silence the resident can be hard work. Staff also need to be aware of other potential pitfalls, including becoming polarized in their views over issues, as in the following clinical example.

Vignette

A resident, Greg, painted a picture (in washable paint) on the wall of his room. The matter was brought to the community meeting by the chairperson questioning whether or not the behaviour constituted 'Damage to Property', which is a fundamental community rule which would carry with it automatic discharge, although with the possibility of reinstatement subject to permission from the community.

The community, staff and residents, became polarized on a discussion which hinged on the reversibility of the 'damage'. The meaning of the act for Greg could not be addressed in spite of an attempt by some staff to introduce this aspect into the discussion. In the following meeting, where staff alone reviewed the community meeting, fierce debate continued. Staff disagreed with one another over whether the painting of the picture had been a creative or defiling act. The staff sub-system was split.

To an extent, however, the recognition of evidence of the splitting processes, as it becomes enacted in the staff team, is beneficial since it points to otherwise hidden dynamics operating at the level of the individual resident and/or the community at large. Overall, of course, staff aim to minimize splitting and its destructive consequences, and effective communication is imperative if this is to be achieved. To this end there are meetings of the staff throughout the day. All staff attend the morning handover which is from the two night staff to all oncoming day staff (N.B. the same staff group cover both day and night shifts). Each group treatment session is followed by a review meeting involving all the staff concerned and there is a weekly peer group supervision, of staff by staff, as well as a weekly staff sensitivity group which is facilitated by an outside psychotherapist. Handover to the night staff is carried out in collaboration with day staff and two representatives of the resident group.

Sometimes rows break out in the staff team, as in the above clinical example involving Greg. Optimally this occurs during staff meetings rather than in between. Such disagreement often takes the form of: which staff member said what in the previous meeting; how it was intoned or should have been; who said too much; who said nothing but should have. It is possible for the staff structure to become unhelpfully rigid; individual members can be scapegoated and unhealthy subgroups can form – in fact the staff group, as a median group, is subject to, and falls victim to, all the pathological variations described in respect of patients (Bion 1961a). These formations are more likely to evolve when particular staff member(s) become involved with particular functions(s). An example would be always being the one(s) in community meetings to confront a particular issue, for example, the undesirability of sexual liaisons among the resident group; or being the staff member(s) who in staff groups attempts to keep the staff focused and task-orientated in their discussion of the business matters pertaining to the hospital. The effect of this can be to facilitate the abdication of responsibility for the particular aspects among the remaining staff and thereby lines of potential fracture or splitting are set up or reinforced.

The most effective staff interventions clinically are often simple and brief and addressed to such aspects as requests for a resident to speak louder or, alternatively, not to shout; or to indicate that it may be easier for all concerned to concentrate on the matter in hand if only one person speaks at a time. Sometimes, of course, staff need to resort to more formal or traditional interpretations including transference interpretations but, mercifully, these are few and far between, permitting thereby residents to step into this particular therapeutic breach for themselves. 'Community as Doctor' (Rapoport 1960) is a motto which still prevails, at least on a good day.

Refraining from a too active or directive style and exercising restraint in response to direct provocation are the stock-in-trade of therapeutic community work with forensic patients. Seldom easy, often frustrating but always a stimulating environment in which to work, it is chastening to hear from a resident that Henderson feels like a real home, especially on a day when staff question why on earth they are working there. Residents may need to be reminded, and to experience, that their anti-social behaviour is not synonymous with them and can be distinguished from them by others. In this way they have the opportunity to become other than forensic patients and marginalized people. Henderson is only one part of the treatment process for many patients and, at the end of treatment at Henderson, success may simply mean that forensic patients are now able to formulate an emotional (or medical) complaint with the healthy and reasonable expectation that a health care professional might respond without abuse or neglect and, ideally, with respect.

They may also be aware of their need for others with whom they can be intimate and in whom they can trust.

CONCLUSION

Rick, the most famous restaurateur in 'Casablanca', might have rationalized his demand of Sam to play for him 'As time goes by' by invoking an unaccustomed alcohol binge as the excuse. However, many of Rick's transactions in the film were less than legitimate (he does, after all, kill an SS Officer) and this style of relating to others might indeed have been habitual. In the end, however, he does a very noble thing. He gives up the woman he loves to a man whom he reluctantly admires. Such is the sad–happy ending of the film.

At Henderson Hospital personality-disordered residents with forensic histories do not all achieve such depressive position endings, and in this they are little different from non-forensic residents. They tend to experience difficulties at all stages of their treatment and this reflects, among others, profound ambivalence and mistrust in the face of any genuine care which is offered. Such care is only ever potentially present in the therapeutic community and residents with a forensic history struggle alongside fellow residents and staff to test the authenticity of the care and support that is available by various means, but particularly rejection and denigration. At the inter-systems level of the therapeutic community, such repeated testing reflects movement between basic assumption and work group function and, in the process, a personal level working through of hitherto partially understood dynamic aspects as they are enacted interpersonally on the wider stage of the therapeutic community.

Staff have a difficult role to play in the caring process and may need to remain healthily suspicious both of signs of psychological health and of distress in residents, keeping as far as possible an open mind. Sometimes a sigh is *not* just a sigh. At times, stern condemnation and rigid boundary setting is appropriate and staff should not shy away from this, as when a community rule has been broken by a resident who is popular and/or intimidating, whom the resident group avoids confronting. However, this needs to be with a sympathetic understanding of the resident's past, marked as it is by neglect or abuse or otherwise chaotic and erratic caretaking, since only in this way can the paranoid-schizoid position grip on relationships be loosened.

Ideally, the therapeutic community allows time for residents to reflect more maturely and rationally on their own motivation, their needs, the effect they have on others and for change to be possible as a result. Part of this may be the providing of care and the therapeutic community allows many choices for offering support and thereby making reparation, which in so concrete a form is not available in other treatment settings. Even this, however, is not without difficulty and envious feelings may surface in response to the recipient of care

Appendix 1: Weekly Programme

Time	Monday	Tuesday	Wednesday	Thursday	Friday	Saturday	Sunday
9.15 - 10.30 (45) am		"9.15"	Community Meeting				
10.30 (45) - 11.15 am			Morning Break				
11.00 -12.00 am	Small Groups	Cleaning & Reviews or Elections or Community Projects	Small Groups or Leavers Group	Welfare or Visitors or Probation	Small Groups		
12.00 - 1.30 am			LUNCH BREAK				
1.30 - 2.00 pm	Surgery	Surgery 2.00 - 2.10 pm	Cleaning				
2.30 -4.30 pm	Psychodrama or Art Therapy 2.30 -4.30 pm	Selection or Welfare/Housing or Community Work Project 2.30 -4.30 pm	Psychodrama or Art Therapy 2.30 - 4.30 pm	Work Groups (Art, Cookery or Gardening & Maintenance) 2.15 - 4.15 pm			
4.45 - 5.00 pm	Floor Meeting 4.45 - 5.00 pm	Tea 4.30 - 4.50 pm		Tea 4.15 - 4.35 pm			
		Women's Group 6.00 - 7.15 pm		Men's Group 6.00 - 7.15 pm			
7.00 - 9.00			COMMUNITY MEAL				
9.15 - 10.05 pm			Tens Group				Tens
10.15 - 11.00 pm			Summit Meeting				
11.00 pm			Night Round				Summit

Visitors Day - Thursday 9.15 am - 5.00 pm

(including care of self), hence a form of perverted caring and a corresponding distorting of the therapeutic structures and processes are seen to operate at all levels – personal, interpersonal and intersystems. Without doubt the effect on self-esteem that comes with such genuine reparative acts can be beneficial. For a substantial number the end of treatment at Henderson can mean 'the beginning of a beautiful friendship', with themselves as well as with others.

Acknowledgements

My thanks to Dr Bridget Dolan who provided Figure 1 and made helpful comments on an earlier draft of this chapter.

Psychodynamics and the Regional Secure Unit

Gabriel Kirtchuk & Harriet Haworth

BACKGROUND

Following the recommendations of the Glancy (1974) and Butler (1975) reports regional secure units (RSUs) were established to provide psychiatric care within conditions of medium security. Patients include those detailed under Part II (for ordinary patients) and Part III (for offender patients) of the Mental Health Act (1983): Part II patients are typically disruptive non-offenders; Part III patients, who make up the majority category of patients held in RSUs, have committed serious offences mostly of violence, including sexual violence and frequently homicide. Regional Secure Units are a National Health Service provision, but offender patients will frequently be under a Restriction Order and the Home Office retains the power over decisions of discharge.

Regional secure units across the country have many similarities but each has evolved independently and individually. This chapter recounts our experience within one such unit which opened eight years ago, but which continues to expand and change as the need for this sort of service provision is increasingly recognized. Patients are referred to the RSU from courts, prisons, Special Hospitals and occasionally District Hospitals. The majority of Part III patients have suffered from psychotic illness at the time of their 'index' offence but are not considered to need the maximum security of a Special Hospital. Traditionally, the criteria for admission to a Special Hospital were that the patient represented 'a serious and immediate danger' to others: nowadays, however, such a state of affairs no longer ensures a place in a Special Hospital and many such patients are admitted into and remain in RSUs.

The structure of this RSU comprises three wards: Acute, Rehabilitation, and Pre-discharge. Patients are admitted to the Acute ward which offers the highest level of security and the greatest nurse/patient ratio within the unit. Patients are reviewed continuously by the multi-disciplinary team over time to assess whether they can be accommodated on a ward providing less physical security, and in this way they move through the unit. There is an expectation that the overall length of stay in a Regional Secure Unit will be between 18 and 24 months, although many stay longer. The aim is that patients be placed in accommodation in the community or occasionally be transferred to a hospital of lesser security within this duration. Patients may be discharged from the RSU, either by the permission of the Home Office or by a Mental Health Review Tribunal.

THE ROLE OF THE PSYCHOTHERAPIST

This chapter considers the place of psychodynamic psychotherapy in support-ing the overall task of the institution. The challenge for the consultant psychotherapist consists in the application of psychodynamic principles and psychological understanding to individual patients and to the wider institution and thereby to contribute to the rehabilitation of very disturbed and disturbing patients and to the mental well being of staff (Menzies 1959).

The idea of appointing a consultant psychotherapist (CP) emerged from staff of different disciplines who had established psychotherapy groups within the unit for some years but without very much supervision. The proposal received the support of the medical director, management, and senior clinicians. The intention was to consolidate the existing work and to develop the psychotherapeutic culture of the institution.

During his or her stay in the RSU, each patient remains under the care of the same consultant forensic psychiatrist (Responsible Medical Officer (RMO)) and multi-disciplinary team: this includes the nursing team and primary nurse, an occupational therapist, a community psychiatric nurse, a psychologist, and a social worker. Thus there is a continuity of care as a patient moves from one ward to the next. Medico-legal responsibility is held by the consultant forensic psychiatrist. The various disciplines in the RSU respect hierarchical lines of management within disciplines. The consultant psychotherapist, in this model, does not carry any direct clinical responsibility for patients or for the manage-ment of staff, but contributes to the delineation of these structures by creating space to think about the different tasks and roles of each staff member. The exploration of matters relating to professional authority and boundaries are central to any psychiatric setting but are particularly relevant to forensic work where patients are detained for long periods, often contrary to their conscious wishes, and as a group are characterized, amongst other factors, by their transgression of society's accepted boundaries.

In forensic psychiatry patients often have very distorted concepts of authority. The multi-disciplinary team constantly evaluates the degree of restriction and security the patient requires. A balance is sought of working safely with a patient, both emotionally and physically, always bearing in mind, however, the potential damage the patient could inflict either upon himself, upon members of staff or upon the general public. The super-ego structure of our patients is frequently punitive and harsh both to themselves as well as others (Rosenfeld 1952). Alternatively, they may have an impaired sense of internal authority because the super-ego is fragmented and projected as, for example, in psychotic states: typically a patient who appears very passive might hear voices (auditory hallucinations) that command him to kill his family or rape nurses, thus effectively denying his own aggression by projecting a part of his violent mind externally, and this is then experienced as coming from without. Psychodynamic understanding in such a case aims to contribute towards the achievement of a more integrated, less punitive psychic organization: in such a case it does this alongside the prescription of anti-psychotic medication, and the provision of comprehensive nursing and other inter-disciplinary care (Cox 1983).

One of the functions of psychodynamic psychotherapy is to facilitate the understanding and the nature of a patient's relationships, and of how their primitive impulses and unconscious fantasies are expressed in their interactions with staff. There is a particular challenge in working with this group of patients who have actually enacted – sometimes horrifically – the most primitive violent and sexual fantasies: working in depth with forensic patients will inevitably put professionals in touch with parts of themselves that may be very disturbing. Unable to accept full responsibility for their offences, patients may blame their illness on staff, or anyone else, by projecting onto staff their internal persecutory objects. The staff and society at large are then felt to be withholding, frustrating and unwilling to supply what the patient needs, or frankly persecuting and punitive.

In response to these projections, staff may unconsciously become identified with the victims of the patients' offences and seek to limit potential attacks on themselves by various essentially unrealistic means: there may be different versions of denial of the unacceptable parts of the patient; for example, by working largely within a 'positive transference'. In a forensic context, the process of helping the patient to recover requires the staff to be able to withstand hearing unpleasant facts and facing the underlying aggressive fantasy. The ability of staff both physically and emotionally to 'contain' and understand the nature of a patients' fantasies, actions and anxieties is central to the psycho-dynamic aspects of this work. It is well documented (Jackson and Cawley 1992) that working closely with psychotic patients is disturbing for staff, since the therapist has to allow himself to accept and tolerate unwanted aspects of the patient which are split off and projected, at lest temporarily, into the professional. Alternatively, staff may 'shut off' and be unavailable for emotional interaction. This is the worst scenario, which may confirm for the patient his sense of his own unbearability, and is felt by him as a massive rejection. These processes, in which staff inevitably become embroiled, can be explored in supervision.

STAFF SUPPORT

The nature and frequency of contact with patients is determined by the core discipline to which a member of staff belongs. Junior nurses, for example, are exposed to relatively prolonged and unstructured periods of time with patients in the ward environment, in comparison with psychiatrists and psychologists, who may limit themselves to specific individual interviews. The CP has a function in supporting such staff by increasing their understanding of the day-to-day interactions which occur during their prolonged contact with patients.

Vignette 1

In weekly meetings with the CP, senior nurses described how, in their roles as ward managers, they had become removed from the clinical aspects of their work for which they had been specifically trained. They described how they found it increasingly difficult to relate to more junior nurses, who, in turn, were reluctant to divulge, to their managers, their experiences as key-workers to the patients. The junior nurses feared exposing the content of their work, preferring to regard the ward managers as people who were out of touch with their difficulties in managing patients on a daily basis. These natural fears and anxieties became 'split off' and projected into the managers who were then identified with a persecuting super-ego and were felt not to understand the work at the clinical 'coal-face'. This then impoverished the nurses' opportunities to obtain support from their seniors, and led to a demoralizing tendency in which the therapeutic role of the nurse became obscured behind an emphasis on security. The custodial aspects of the system were examined.

Although they were felt sometimes to assist in good clinical practice the custodian role was also felt to compromise the caring role of the nurse.

In discussing these processes with the ward managers, they were able to accept a much more benign and creative concept of their own authority. Understanding the negative aspects of their staffs' transference with the patients, particularly with regard to persecutory projections, allowed the ward managers to engage in a much more rewarding relationship with their juniors.

In this example, one of the key functions of the CP was to concentrate on the effects of the patients on nurses and how this was reflected within the hierarchy of the institution. Helping the ward managers differentiate the aspects of their jobs as administrators and as senior clinicians enabled them to integrate their dual functions.

Vignette 2

Supervision with the occupational therapists took place once a month: a member of the department was invited to present an example of her group work. As with nurses, occupational therapists are continuously exposed to contact with patients whilst other professionals are protected by working in offices and seeing patients by appointment.

At the time of the supervision group the RSU was undergoing considerable upheaval with a new extension of three wards being built on an adjacent site. A temporary six-foot high wooden fence had been erected which enclosed the site, whilst building work was under way. At the time of the planned expansion there was a temporary decrease in the number of the occupational therapy staff. One of the therapists brought to the supervision group a description of a project that she had initiated: it entailed organizing a group of patients to paint a mural on the new fence. The presenter described how she had taken a group of patients to measure the size of the fence which was to be painted. However, the patients had been unable to gauge the size of the fence and had instead engaged in increasingly grandiose discussions about what they would paint. In supervision this was seen as the patients defending against an anxiety of tackling a large project, possibly beyond their capacity.

The therapist was puzzled why an apparently straight-forward task could not be accomplished: why could the patients not agree on the size and area of the fence? The supervision group looked in more detailed at the actual experience of the task for these patients. It was seen that 'containment' is experienced by these patients at a very concrete and physical level: the walls and fences around the institution hold them together psychologically. In psychotic thinking there is a loss of the ability to symbolize (Segal 1957), so that a change in the physical boundary of the institution can trigger fears of psychotic fragmentation and loss of control. The anxieties provoked by working on the 'boundary' created a lot of uncertainty for these patients. However, the understanding of the meaning of the activity helped staff to measure the size of the psychological difficulties of the project.

PSYCHODYNAMIC PSYCHOTHERAPY GROUPS

In contrast to his role of staff support, the consultant psychotherapist also provides supervision of the four psychotherapy weekly groups which had been initiated some years previously, shortly after the opening of the unit. Thus they were established as part of the treatment of the majority of patients at some point in their stay in the RSU. Supervision provided an opportunity to examine processes within the groups and also looked at how psychotherapy contributed to the overall rehabilitation of patients. One of the aims of working with functionally ill psychotic offender patients is to reinforce and strengthen aspects of their minds which are unaffected by psychotic illness. Bion (1957) has described the differentiation of the psychotic from the non-psychotic part of the personality, and in the case of our patients the aim is to help the health part look after the psychotic and mentally ill part, for example, by acknowledging the need for medication or detecting the signs of early relapse. It is the acquisition of this kind of insight which allows for the creation of a treatment alliance, and which in turn allows consideration of transfer to lesser security. Psychotherapy groups can provide the forum for such a dialogue within the group and in turn can promote an 'internal dialogue' thereby – within the patients' own minds – providing an opportunity for patients to explore their index offences and contemplate their future outside a secure setting.

The safe setting for exploration and contact with murderous fantasies and, less prominently, sexual perversions, is achieved in a number of ways. First there is the physical security of the perimeter wall of the building and of the locked wards. There are alarm buttons in the therapy rooms, although one has yet to be activated during the course of a group therapy session, and patients have the reassurance of knowing that staff respond promptly to a signalled disturbance. Second, each group is run by a clinician experienced in psychodynamic work, in conjunction with a less experienced therapist who makes a commitment to run the group and to attend supervision on a weekly basis for a minimum of six months. This ensures a high level of skill and continuity for the group. Psychological containment and understanding for the therapists is maintained by all meeting as a large group each week with the consultant psychotherapist, when a session is presented in detail. In addition, each pair of therapists meets with the consultant every four weeks where a more private supervision can also address the dynamics between the therapists, alongside those within the group.

The regularity of supervision, including predictability of time and place of meeting, mirrors what we attempt to achieve for the patients in their therapeutic groups: this constancy has helped to maintain psychodynamic psychotherapy as a valued activity within the unit. The RMO refers patients to the groups so that patients are aware of a seal of authority and approval in committing themselves to what is predominantly a voluntary activity. However, the issue of choice for detained patients is acknowledged to be a complex one.

It has been found crucial to have all disciplines represented amongst the co-therapists so that psychotherapy is not viewed as an exclusive domain, either to be denigrated or envied. It is particularly difficult for nurses to maintain their weekly commitment to the group and to supervision, given the vagaries of shift work and the economic requirement to maintain minimum numbers of staff on the wards. Facilitation of nurses' attendance for this activity has to be made by ward managers and individual colleagues on the ward. Thus the impact of the psychotherapy process is felt at all levels and disciplines throughout the unit.

The majority of patients have committed offences when they were acutely psychotic: those guilty of homicide, for example, will consequently have been deemed to have had 'diminished responsibility' for their actions. This locates the offence within the illness, and accordingly a patient is considered to be less dangerous in the absence of florid psychosis. Whilst this is usually the case, it begs the question of why this particular patient killed that particular person when psychotic, whereas most mentally ill patients are neither violent nor offensive. The index offence – with its concomitant murderous impulses and actions – becomes split off from the current self, in the minds of both patients and staff who work with them. Whilst it is not possible for patients to be constantly in contact with the horror of their offences – since that would lead to an unbearable guilt, with its consequent despair and possible suicide, part of the psychotherapeutic function is to bring the patient into contact with these split-off parts of themselves, within a supportive setting, and thereby to encourage the acknowledgement of individual responsibility – whether diminished or not.

These issues have been conceptualized by Steiner (1993b, pp.116–130) in his account of Sophocles' Oedipus plays. In the account of *Oedipus the King*, Oedipus is able to accept responsibility for his crimes, namely, the killing of his father and marriage to his mother, with the consequent punishment: he blinds himself and is exiled from Thebes. By contrast, in *Oedipus at Colonus*, a later play chronologically, he is not able any longer to tolerate the guilt, and consequently turns to omnipotence and manic triumph. He becomes, in his own view, a holy man, the victim of circumstances, no longer aware of the truth of his actions. Steiner argues that Oedipus, his parents and the inhabitants of Thebes could have known the truth of Oedipus crimes before and after they were committed from the evidence available to them, but they choose to turn a blind eye. A vignette of one of our psychotherapy groups illustrates similarly the restricted capacity of an individual patient and the group as a whole to be in touch with, and tolerate, the emotional pain of the crimes they have committed.

The group consists of six male patients and two female therapists. The previous session had been cancelled. One patient, A, who came from a war-torn, violent country, began by saying that he had forgotten the name of therapist and insisted on knowing where the therapist came from since she had a foreign accent. The therapist felt interrogated, and almost compelled to answer, but was able to formulate an interpretation: she connected this pressure to know personal details with the cancellation of the previous session (where had she been?), particularly when the group had just begun, and how foreign all that felt. There followed a silence in which patients seemed to lose interest and to engage in a fragmented conversation. One of the therapists reflected on this and another patient, B, asked what were the aims of the group. C, another patient, said 'Well I think that we are supposed to talk about ourselves'. A, started to ask anxiously what they wanted to know about him. One of the therapists reflected upon how demanding and persecuting it must feel to talk about oneself when the group did not seem to be a safe place. After a moment of silence A began to talk again, but this time in a different mood saying 'I'm here because I killed my best friend, I lost my best friend'. D, another patient, who had not said anything so far said 'It can't be easy to say that'. C followed by saying 'Especially when you say your "best friend"'. Now A said 'I'm really sad about it, I really regret it, I wish I could set the clock back but I know I cannot'.

After a silence in which the group seemed to be engaged in a more thoughtful and reflective mood, A started again, saying 'I did it because of the voices, they made me do it, they made promises, they deceived me'. His mood changed, he became quite excited, and he began to talk about all the killings he had seen in his country of origin: he had seen men cutting babies' throats and dogs eating human flesh. The group responded by joining his excitement and engaged in a kind of morbid curiosity that had a manic flavour. Attempts by the therapists to make interpretations about the defensive nature of this manic flight were to no avail.

In this group a process of movement can be seen from a fragmented and paranoid atmosphere at the beginning to an account of one patient's index offence, which moves the whole group to a reflective mood. For a short time the group is more integrated and seems to be able to tolerate the pain involved. A realizes that he cannot put the clock back and he has to live with the consequences of his act. At this moment the guilt becomes unbearable; the responsibility and the aggressive fantasies are projected into internal and fragmented 'objects', that is, the 'voices', and then into the external world. The manic quality is expressed in the excited mood of the group and the content reflects the extent of their fantasies of the destruction, within a whole country, and within their whole world. For these patients, acknowledgement of their guilt is experienced as life-threatening, as if the quality of the violence in their fantasies have a massive, cruel and devastating effect. This fear of the annihilation of the internal world is what makes the guilt so difficult to acknowledge and sustain. It is the working through of these experiences that might enhance the patients' capacity to tolerate the more disturbing and destructive aspect of themselves and their offences.

The psychotherapy groups aim to find some measure of integration of the aggressive parts of the self in a way that is safe for both staff and patients to bear.

CONCLUSION

The role of psychodynamic psychotherapy in this setting is in supporting the overall task of the patients and staff within the RSU, namely the rehabilitation of disturbed, disturbing offender patients. More specifically, the contribution of psychotherapy is to the rehabilitation of the self, by increasing the patient's capacities to tolerate and own the disturbed parts of themselves. In all human relationships there is a constant process of affective projection and introjection but in this setting the content may frequently be psychotic and of fantasies of extreme violence. The acknowledgement and understanding of this complex inter-communication and dynamic interaction between patients and staff helps staff to maintain a meaningful emotional contact with their patients. In this chapter the work with nurses and occupational therapists illustrates this.

Group psychotherapy offers the possibility of looking in depth at patients' psychopathology, and provides a setting in which it is safe enough to explore the nature of their offences. It is paramount for psychotherapists to be aware of the risk of marginalization from the rest of the work of the institution, and to strive to be an integral part of it. Supervision is an essential ingredient, as it provides a setting wherein staff can explore and address the psychological effects of their patients upon them and of them upon their patients and the overall quality of their clinical work.

Psychodynamics
and The Special Hospital
'Road Blocks and Thought Blocks'

Murray Cox

INTRODUCTION

The terrain to be covered under this heading is so extensive that an introductory résumé could readily consume the allotted word-span, so that 'the thing itself' was never reached. Compression is therefore of the essence. The epigrammatic subtitle draws attention to the vast sweep of major issues which justifiably fall within the purview of this chapter. Every connotation of 'inner' and 'outer' world phenomena is relevant. None can be safely excluded. Conscious and unconscious energies jostle in stable-instability. Road blocks and escape 'procedures' are as essential variations on the theme as the psychological 'escapes' provided by thought blocks and other intrapsychic defence mechanisms. Brief reference will be made to several substantial concerns which cannot be entirely ignored, but which only receive passing mention.

Present Possibilities

Nevertheless, the briefest synopsis of this chapter could be the statement that every aspect of *murality* (p.3) is focally relevant to any consideration of psychodynamics and the Special Hospital. It is inevitable that, once the concrete nature of the containing perimeter has been acknowledged, it is the inter-personal aspects of murality which play such a decisive part in making – or marring – the possibility of a resiliently stable euthymic institution. It is for this reason that the original exploration of murality in relation to forensic psychotherapy was in connection with the amending imagination of the poet (Cox and Theilgaard 1994, p.353). For it is the poet whose laminated language and sensitivity to nuance enables him to call into existence things that were not there before. This is the process of *poiesis*. It is mentioned at this juncture for two strong reasons. First, the Special Hospital is on the brink of enormous structural changes in terms of management organization, directorate development and an overall increase in staff who, in keeping with *poiesis*, have been called into existence and were not there before. The question in the air is 'How much does the increase in hospital staff, who are *not directly* involved at the clinical front-line with patients, actually increase the efficacy, well-being and ethos of the daily life in the ward?' Second, does the recently imported management vocabulary which, by definition inevitably permeates the numerous daily formal and informal points of contact between staff, genuinely and appropriately offer new modes of contact? Or is this, at root, a hermeneutic exercise in which new terms are being used for well established processes, already familiar in another language.

Kirkegaard defined hope as 'a passion for what is possible' and a self-positing question pervades the hospital at the moment. Patients, staff and management are all asking themselves and each other 'What could come out of this?' A sense of exploration is in the air. 'What will the future bring?' is both an echo of an archaic question and a current one. No one knows exactly, but it is inevitably encouraging to hear that 'creative clinicians' were being appointed.

Homoeostasis and Defensive Strategy

An institution needs a sufficient number of flexible, dynamically 'moving parts' – not unlike a car engine – if it is to function efficiently and smoothly. It needs shock-absorbers, sources of energy and a driver familiar with the highway code. Once again, reference to road blocks and thought blocks aptly summarizes the extensive ground which needs to be covered.

In the same way that marriage has been described as a mutual projective system, so the division of the hospital community into management, staff and patients, is a potential tri-partite projective system. This, in itself, can serve as a shock-absorber for the hospital as a whole. Potentially destructive issues, which might rock the stability if there was no such structural division, can be contained and deflected. Senior, junior and middle-management add further laminations for re-routing responsibility and containing collision. Defensive organization may provide psychological by-passes, so that an individual or a department can claim 'this is not my (our) fault'. Nevertheless, by the same token, it is a poor outlook for the institution as a whole if no individual (or group) can say 'this is my (our) fault'. Lines which Shakespeare gives to Northumberland are self-referring to those activists who will recognize themselves:

> 'But I must go and meet with danger there,
> Or it will seek me in another place,
> And find me worse provided.' (*II Henry IV* II.3.48)

(How different are the cadences of this language from current administrative terminology which refers to 'quality control' but does not apply it to the quality of the language it controls. This hypothetical sentence has just crystallized in my mind 'Change facilitators are tasked with ensuring that on-stream packages are in place in order that prioritization can be actualized.') It may be a small point that far more references are made to hospital Complaints Procedures than to a Praise Procedure – which might mean congratulating the chef on the excellence of the curry or the gardeners on the well cut lawns and colourful flower beds. Relatively trivial though these matters may be, encouragement can never be unimportant. But we are considering wider and more sombre aspects of psychodynamics and the Special Hospital. After further reference to the three dynamic systems within the hospital, we shall study a series of significant signposts which can guide our consideration. But it needs to be re-emphasized that, throughout the ensuing discussion, a continuous entry in the margin is 'Do not forget that the hospital is poised at the brink of far-reaching readjustments'. The achievement of TRUST STATUS could not be a richer metaphor or more loaded with pragmatic *gravitas*.

Taking Shape

Just before we go to print, the first issue of the *Shaping British Psychiatry Journal* lies on my desk and the opening editorial refers to 'the implications and impact of the new forces shaping the development of mental health services' (1995). *'Shape'* is the ideal word for the purpose, being a substantive, and a verb which is both transitive and intransitive. It therefore may, or may not, 'take an object'. In a short essay of this kind, the symbolic condensation of poetic reference can sometimes stand in for paragraphs of technical description, so that in terms of the advantages and the potential risks of reshaping the institution – in this case, the Special Hospital – we listen acutely to the following poetic comments. Yeats (1971) referred to 'shaping joy', although he had previously written 'The wrong of unshapely things is a wrong too great to be told' (1950, p.62), whereas Macbeth recoiled when he saw the spectre of that which he had shaped, or rather unshaped:

> 'Take any shape but that...' (III.4.101)

We will shortly be considering some of the implications of restructuring, both of the architecture of the buildings and that of the management structures within the hospital. Much thoughtful preparation and planning lies behind such shaping initiatives. The importance of rapid, accurate communication at all levels, and between all disciplines within the hospital, as well as with the wider world of the public domain, has been emphasized in the recent appointment of a Public Relations Manager.

Everything mentioned thus far legitimately falls within the ambit of 'psychodynamics and the Special Hospital' but it is all at an 'external', executive, conscious, rational, 'left-brain' level. In other words, the 'shaping' in question deals with that which *can* be shaped, that is, line management, the establishment of multi-disciplinary teams and the like. Shaping, here, 'takes an object' – and carries an object relations imprint.

Somewhere in the system there must be a place for a psychological shock-absorber, a degree of slack in the management rope-line which can accommodate those inner disturbing shapings which lead us all, in one way or another, at one time or another, to cry to one spectre or another, 'Take any shape but that!' Unconscious forces cannot be shaped and internal object relationships defy order by management initiatives. It need scarcely be added that these matters cannot be exaggerated in a community such as a Special Hospital, in which all (patients, staff and management alike) are acutely aware of the psychological and physical 'wrong of unshapely things'. *Laus Deo*, there is much evidence of 'shaping joys' too.

Soni (1995a, p.2), for example, describes several different types of multi-disciplinary teams. Each will adopt its own shape, influence the shape the unit management is taking and call for its own mode of absorbing its self-generated tension, as well as shaping up to the demands of the hospital (Special or otherwise) as a whole. Soni's typology suggests the following categories: 'Network, Managed team, Integrative team, Coordinated team and Core team.' Each member will know of 'shaping joys', 'the wrong of unshapely things' and the haunting possibility of 'any shape but that…'

The unconscious forces which shape the individual's perspectival lens, through which he sees his peers, be they patients, staff or management, will have a decisive influence upon the *viable* and *visible* shape of the hospital as a whole. The psychotherapist, who needs to be attuned to both worlds, might be aphoristically described as an Object Relations Manager![1]

The Special Hospital runs the risk of developing defensive strategies which are based upon splitting and projective identifications. This is a composite process which initially appears to reduce institutional tension. The poised homoeostasis of communal life depends upon an optimal balance between three dynamic systems:

---

1 Although it would be strange to see an advertisement for such a post alongside that for the Public Relations Manager.

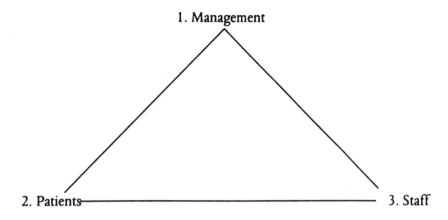

Corporate instability can ensue if 1, 2 and 3 are not 'tuned' to the same wavelengths and function as autonomous matrices. One of the traditional divisions of responsibility within Broadmoor has been reified in the shared clinical concerns of The Responsible Medical Officer (R.M.O.; Consultant Forensic Psychiatrist) and the Consultant Psychotherapist who work 'In Double Harness' (Macphail and Cox 1973; Cox 1983). This arrangement has served as an institutional way of diminishing the possibility of pathological splitting. *It adds to the tension-absorbing capacity of the hospital as a whole.*

SIGNIFICANT SIGNPOSTS

At first sight, the conceptual cosmos and discourse of psychoanalytic psychotherapy, which delineates intrapsychic energies, and the Special Hospital, one of the most extreme epiphanies of Goffman's (1961) 'total institutions', seem 'strange bed-fellows'. Nevertheless, each is often the object of uninformed criticism, suspicion and voyeuristic over-interest by those without first-hand knowledge of the qualities of life within psychotherapeutic space or within the secure perimeter. It is for this reason that a double measure of critical inquisitiveness is evident when the amalgam of psychotherapeutic space within a secure setting is under consideration. One of the objections to both psychoanalysis, and some aspects of Special Hospital ethos, is the affirmation that there is a measure of reasonable justification for saying that only those who 'know' from the 'inside' are qualified to comment, for better or worse.

A creative tension is implicit from the start when it comes to exploring the dynamics of a Special Hospital. It takes this form: only an outsider can give an over-all assessment of the *status quo*, yet only an insider can possibly know at first hand of the psychological air permeating the life of the hospital. Formal enquiries are always about events under the spot-light, and are inevitably deprived of the relatively uneventful, regular pulse of daily life.

It is self-evident that whoever undertakes to write on this theme will inevitably do so from the idiosyncratic vantage point of a personal perspectival world. But it could be argued that prolonged, intimate experience of psycho-therapeutic engagement both within the Special Hospital system, and in the wider world beyond the walls, might stand the best chance of yielding a balanced appraisal. In any event, such is the constellation of circumstance that finds a part-time consultant psychotherapist, who has worked in the without-limit-of-time setting for exactly a quarter of a century, setting out to write this chapter. It is understandable why philosophers and theologians emphasize that in order to influence a dynamic system, a fulcrum outside the system is essential (Brunner 1948) '[Man] loses that Archimedean fulcrum outside the world by which he really could move the world. By cutting himself loose from God, man precipitates himself into the world and becomes its prisoner.' (p.133)

Nevertheless, this engineering analogy fails to appreciate that life within the secure perimeter can only be known by those whose life is precisely there. In the same way, it is indisputable that intra-psychic life can only be known in its own terms, although it is easy to assume that an outsider is, for better or worse, less biased than an insider. By definition, the knowledge of the former is based upon officially available information and research, as well as upon unofficial 'leaks' which may see the world through glasses tinted by optimism and loyalty, or pessimism and malignant motivation. In a long-term institution, such as a Special Hospital, this kind of polarization is evident in both staff and patients alike. There are those who applaud and those who disdain.

Another important signpost to be studied points to 'Relevant levels of analysis'. In this instance the word 'analysis' carries a dual connotation. It refers to both psychoanalysis and the level of analytic commentary on the total life within the total institution. It would be easy to have several headings, of which the psychoanalytic contributions to hospital treatment would be one, set alongside sociological approaches and community psychiatry, de-institution-alization and trans-institutionalization. Attention could be paid to the history of management structures within the hospital – special attention being given to management strategy in the face of complaints and dealing with corporate tension. There is no doubt that the ethos and timbre of life is profoundly influenced when a hospital management team replaces long-established struc-tures of administration under the over-all aegis of a physician superintendent. Management teams and clinical teams will exhibit just as much defensive avoidance, in the face of threats to corporate self-esteem, as will a solitary superintendent when required to endure the unendurable. The mutual support of the collective 'we (the team) think' has no more certain a grip upon courageous veracity than does an individual who knows where the 'buck' stops. Assault may be verbal or physical, direct or oblique and it may originate from staff or patients within the institution or be launched from the wider world beyond the walls. Threats and the resorts to delegation and activation of complaints procedures do not remove anxiety from the body politic of a total institution. They merely relocate and distance the point of probable eruption. A clinical team cannot plough a straight furrow without a single guiding experienced eye on a proximate goal, in the same way that a severely regressed patient needs a primary nurse (parent) – a team of 'parents' can be too confusing. With the sure touch of metaphorical poetic precision Housman's commentary is disturbingly arresting:

> 'Is my team ploughing,
> That I was used to drive
> And hear the harness jingle
> When I was a man alive?'
>
> ('A Shropshire Lad.' *Collected Poems.* 1939, p.422)

There was a team, but the team was a 'driven' collaborative enterprise. Hospital policies imply sequences of action but no policy confers immunity from the Human Predicament. Deep psychic realities are active when fear is in the air.

Issues of this calibre could never be dealt with in appropriate detail within the confines of one chapter. Nonetheless, to fail to mention them amounts to neglect of topics of over-riding importance that impinge on all who are involved in the on-going life of the Special Hospital as patient, staff or administration.

We shall not be following the signpost pointing towards Polemic and High Drama. Daily life within the hospital is usually a far cry from the tabloid banner headlines about such exceedingly rare incidents as escapes, 'absconsions' or the high voltage scenario of hostage-taking. Indeed, one of the many faces of timelessness is the slow, plodding, seemingly uneventful routineness of things, perhaps more reminiscent of numerous entries in Columbus' journal when nothing seemed to happen: 'this day we sailed on' – with no destination in sight.

Nonetheless, when there is an occasional affective eruption – such as an assault, a suicide or a fire – the dynamic constellaton within the hospital changes abruptly. It is easy to understand why the analogy of a 'brush fire' springs to mind – as heightened anxiety and/or denial determine collective defences. Patients, staff and management are all inevitably involved in the ensuing realignments of solidarity. Theologians refer to such happenings as 'limit-situations' (Tracy 1981, p.4) and Shakespeare has so accurately caught the sense of potentially overwhelming adversity:

> 'When sorrows come, they come not single spies,
> But in battalions.'
>
> (*Hamlet: IV.5.78*)

It is at times like this that the psychotherapist's customary distance from 'high-profile' presence in the hospital gives him the freedom to move to the scene of the action. It would be more accurate to refer to the 'scene of inaction', because the prevailing ethos is so often one of silent, bewildered disbelief or a bland denial. Such endeavours also augment the tension-absorbing capacity of the hospital mentioned in the introduction.

Without fear of contradiction, because these are personal views, it can be said that forensic psychotherapy always involves attention to intrapsychic phenomena, interpersonal phenomena and the presence or absence of trans-generational existential obligations (Cox 1992a, p.253).

When drafting this chapter it was interesting to note how often phrases from everyday life kept cropping up, so much so that 'life within the hospital' almost became something reified and set apart. This is of course illogical and absurd, because the life of patients and staff is lived within the hospital and no technical terms could ever do justice to the thing itself. 'For better or worse' is another phrase expressing the Janusian polarity of long-term commitment with which this phrase is linked.

Psychoanalytic commentary on institutions is sometimes wrongly criticized for being what it is, namely, psycho*analytic*. Analytic emphases are bound to be analytic and reductive, in the same way that surgery cannot be anything but surgical. But the pejorative colouring persists if the most a psychodynamic appraisal can offer is a virtually ubiquitous, all purpose comment, 'This is defensive'.

There are many individual and communal responses to internal or external threats which are defensive and the analytic exploration of underlying dynamics is a *sine qua non*. Like all complex issues in the clinical field, 'a right judgment in all things' – using the words of an ancient collect – is a question of perceiving the pivotal point of optimal balance.

Professional anxiety abounds in all forensic endeavours. The research worker and the manager have anxieties of their own, which can be just as disturbing as those which beset the therapist (Cox 1974). The therapist's anxiety is often due to transference–countertransference factors which skew perceptual processes and thus cloud clinical discernment. *In extremis*, this can lead to a confusion of 'safety' and 'danger'. This is one of the many reasons why supervision is so important.

Such necessary enterprises as management or research are wrongly penalized if they are regarded as offering retreats to those individuals unable to face direct contact with patients. Management and research are essential in their own right. The hospital could not exist without management. And without research many current unknowns would remain unknown and future possibilities might not be able to declare their potential. Nevertheless, there is a grain of vocational truth in the fact that those who choose management or research are, by definition, not opting for direct, front-line patient contact 'in the trenches'. *Per contra*, it can easily be argued that to opt for a therapeutic career in inner world exploration of the sadistic psychopath is indicative of either sublimated voyeurism or displaced prurience. This is an issue of great depth, which involves an integration of many facets of the forensic therapist's *Weltanschauung* and inner world proclivities.

We now turn our attention to some key focal concerns.

KEY FOCAL CONCERNS

(1) The Individual, The Group and The Institution

Those psychodynamic issues now to be explored inevitably involve both the intrapsychic dynamics of patients and staff and the flux of small and large group processes which constitute the matrix of corporate hospital life. It is therefore impossible to ignore prevailing interactional and sociological perspectives. For example, such processes as differential association, deviance amplifying circuits and the prevailing relevance of controlling identity (Becker 1963, p.33) and ancillary identity (Matza 1969, p.160) may well have contributed to the final common pathway along which a patient became an offender-patient. The understanding of the impact of these processes may constitute a substantial component of psychotherapeutic working-through and un-doing which is an essential part of any forensic psychotherapeutic undertaking. It is the reversal, re-owning and reclamation of experience, temporarily banished through repression and projective identification, with which such therapy has to do. And it may 'do' it on an individual or a group basis, always bearing in mind that, although projective identification may only constitute a small fragment of the offender patient's life, it has often permanently distorted or indeed ended the life of the victim as a result of explosive acting out. Therefore, in addition to the working-through of such maladaptive behaviour, there is the added task of coming to terms with the guilt and exploring such reparative possibilities as there are.

(2) Self-Monitoring within the Institution: 'What *he* did' *versus* 'What *I* did'

Forensic assessment depends upon a finely poised prognostic balance between the objective 'what he did' and the subjective 'what I did' – appraisal by the patient. Such necessary concerns are a far cry from the emotive and prejudicial attitudes evident in the cynical pessimism of 'Never forget what he *did*' on one hand and naive un-grounded optimism on the other. Both extremes can be voiced by institutional staff and sour serious therapeutic endeavour, in which 'the aim of every moment of every session is to put the patient in touch with as much of his true feelings as he can bear' (Malan 1979, p.74). Nevertheless, however much the psychotherapist is disturbed by the comment 'never forget what he (the patient) did', this very issue, though framed differently, is likely to form the substance of those essential questions posited by the legal representatives of society who say 'Remembering what he did, can we be sure he will never do it again?'. We are then into the classic, utterly unanswerable ethical forensic dilemma. It is unethical to detain patients for ever. It is also unethical to allow them to leave the hospital *prematurely*. It is therefore vital never to lose sight of 'what he did'. Therapy is concerned to enable the patient himself to become what he can become in the undenied and unforgotten shadow of 'what I did'. The dialectic between 'what he did' and 'what I did' energizes the mutation from disowning, *via* transference and its resolution, to appropriation. This is the dynamic *sine qua non*. The existential tension between 'I can never forget what *I* did' and 'Never forget what *he* did' links corporate concern, the culture of the hospital community and *Koinonia* [an ancient New Testament Greek word for *togetherness*, recently adopted in the world of group analysis]. It is a philosophical exploration waiting to be undertaken.

(3) Some 'End of the road' aspects of Special Hospital Life

The end of the road *(ne plus ultra)* refers to both *location* and *duration*. If the 'end of the road', ethos applies to the hospital as a whole, it applies with particular force to all units where intensive care is called for. This realization was recently brought to mind on the publication of *Unimaginable Storms* (Jackson and Williams 1994). This book describes pioneering endeavours in running a ward for psychotic patients on psychoanalytic lines. In the foreword Steiner writes: 'it is sad that, on the author's retirement, under the pressure of conflicting ideologies, the hospital decided to close it down' (p.xv). It is a statement of the obvious, though it still needs to be made, that the ward in a Special Hospital where the most disturbed patients are treated could never be 'closed down'. It might be renamed and relocated, but there would always need to be such a ward in a Special Hospital where psychotherapeutic work was undertaken. For this reason, the forensic psychotherapist with this kind of experience may find he is working with impossible patients in which all sorts of impossible demands declare themselves, though it is beyond imagination that the need for such work should ever be curtailed on the grounds of expediency or finance.

There will always be disturbed patients and there will always be staff from several disciplines alongside them. It should therefore come as surprising that a photograph of Broadmoor Hospital in the correspondence columns of *The Independent* (11 April 1994, p.15) has the caption 'Broadmoor Hospital, where the staff needs security', as though this were unexpected. That the staff in Special Hospitals need both material and psychological security is as fundamental as the need to breath oxygen. This is because of exceptional demands made by working with psychopathic, unstable borderline and psychotic patients who are constantly distorting conventionally accepted frames of reference. They impose a continuous burden on the identity-retaining energy of the staff. This deep psychological need experienced by all staff, irrespective of discipline, is perhaps epitomized in the response of a schizophrenic offender patient to the question 'Why did you take a life?' Her answer is impossible to forget: 'I took a life because I needed one' (Cox 1982).

Here in microcosm is one of the key issues of forensic psychodynamics. During certain crucial phases of forensic psychotherapy, part of the therapist's personality is introjected by a patient. In this instance, previous experience of inadequate psychic life meant that she had killed for the very reason that she did not have a life and was desperate to acquire one: 'I took a life because I needed one'. It is scarcely surprising that adequate psychotherapy supervision assumes such major importance and that the lack of it is a source of staff anxiety. *There is the ever-present possibility of further explosive reactivation. In this instance, it is a primitive need to 'take a life' – because of a lack of significant existence,* which is frightening for the patient herself and the staff. This may be one of the components underlying the mixed resignation and fear expressed in the words 'never forget what he did'. In more technical terms, the patient's disclosure 'I took a life because I needed one' is as profound and disturbing an exemplification of Bollas' (1987) process of 'extractive introjection' as one could find. Bollas describes this process in these words: '[It] occurs when one person steals for a certain period of time (from a few seconds or minutes to a lifetime) an element of another individual's psychic life' (p.158). There is an ironic emphasis in his use of the word 'lifetime' when it is related to such forensic issues as are currently under discussion. He then continues with reference to 'intersubjective violence' which again places his comments at the centre of such forensic issues.

Freud's (1937) reference to psychoanalysis being one of those 'impossible professions' is of relevance here when we are considering impossible patients and the impossible-possibility of therapy. Yet endopsychic change does occur. Transference phenomena develop, are interpreted – in relation to both the therapist and the victim when relevant – and then recede. When this happens, it can thus be confidently stated that psychodynamic psychotherapy has indeed taken place.

(4) Psychiatric Defences Against Anxiety

This is another of those topics which could form a volume in its own right, indeed in the selected essays by Isobel Menzies Lyth (1988a) entitled *Containing Anxiety in Institutions*, it has already done so, though major forensic issues are not addressed. Its relevance as a forensic theme in connection with a Special Hospital, where many of the patients have committed homicide, can scarcely be exaggerated.[2] 'Containing anxiety in Special Hospitals, where all the patients have shown dangerous, violent or criminal propensities' could be the title of a much needed publication. Main (1977) on the other hand has looked at 'traditional psychiatric defences against close encounters with patients'. He writes

> 'the working distresses of psychiatrists are rarely fully conscious or owned openly, and (almost) never discussed as facts which merit scientific study. Rather they are suppressed, even repressed, as something we must rise above, some professionally shameful; subjectivity as a primary fact is rarely studied or valued because it is a menace to the idealized defence of objectivity. The doctor's strains are not however abolished by silence, merely hidden, and like the return of the repressed in neurosis they return in disguised forms, like pirates, sailing under flags of false objectivity and spurious science.' (p.462)

(5) 'Without-Limit-of-Time': the Dominant Determinant

This, again, is a relatively short section, but it is undoubtedly correctly titled 'the dominant determinant'. It is another 'end of the road' issue. It refers to the fact that patients in Special Hospitals are invariably detained preventatively until such time as they are no longer considered a risk to society. The 'without-limit-of-timeness' distinguishes, above all else, the dynamics within the Special Hospital from those within the prison. This would apply, even if there were (though there are not), matching therapeutic opportunities, trained staff and other favourable circumstances. That a patient is resident within a Special Hospital 'without-limit-of-time', colours all other considerations. The dimensions of Time, Depth and Mutuality are relevant in the structuring of all dynamic psychotherapy and supervision. But the 'without-limit-of-timeness' adds a different component to the ubiquitous significance of time and timing. So great is the force of this dimension that illustration seems superfluous. These things speak for themselves.

(6) The Threshold of Horror: A Partially Submerged Culture-Carrier

It can be said that the 'index offences' of most of the patients admitted to a Special Hospital involve experiences which either whet prurient preoccupation, or so horrify that psychological distancing, denial or distraction is the only possible response. Except, that is, for those thoroughly trained and currently supervised whose work finds them in the proximity of the patient, should he need to disclose such things. Indeed, thanks to the 'merciful function of repression', to use Bettelheim's expressive phrase, the patient, himself, is often

---

2   See Chapter II:26 p.x. for its importance in understanding prison dynamics. (M.C. Editor).

initially partially unaware of what he has done. It is only when the repression level rises, and the patient needs cautiously to explore such intrapsychic hitherto 'no go zones' that those in a therapeutic relationship with him find their personality resources tested. This is often almost to breaking point, and is sometimes beyond it.

Those whose task is safely distanced from the inner horrors of the patient's world can continue with undiminished efficiency. They can study patient populations as part of a research project, or they can attend to the hundred and one prevailing professional concerns which beset those in management. But those in direct patient contact, and it is often the most junior primary nurse, with very little previous psychotherapeutic training, are often literally on 'the receiving end' of that which the patient needs to disclose.

> 'But I have words,
> That would be howl'd out in the desert air,
> Where hearing should not latch them.'
>
> (*Macbeth* IV.3.193)

This last line has so elegantly caught the paradoxical quality of psychoanalytic psychotherapy. In some senses when the patient talks to the therapist he is, on reflection, talking to himself – where 'hearing should not latch [hold] them'. He is not 'heard' in the sense of being given a public 'hearing'. But all therapists, however fully trained, are human beings with feet of clay. It is for this reason that many will, in all honesty, say that they could not undertake forensic work for the precise reason that it stands the possibility of traversing their personal threshold of horror. This imposes an immense discriminatory burden on those who select staff to work in secure settings and undertake to teach and supervise them.

(7) What has not been said

In the same way that 'unvoiced narrative' is of interest to the psychotherapist, (Cox and Theilgaard 1994, p.128) so what has not been said in relation to such an important issue as psychodynamics and the Special Hospital can perhaps best be voiced by the psychotic patient. There is indeed an unquestionable and unquestioning power of intrapsychic penetration with which many psychotic utterances disturb the inner world of the therapist, the staff of all disciplines and those involved in management. We end this excursion into the inner world of the life of those within the Special Hospital with a statement – a conditional statement, not a question – from a psychotic patient to her psychotherapist:

> 'If you could talk to me the more human way, the night could come in properly.'

No attempt is currently made to explore the extensive range of significances of this comment on human encounter which has so many possible referents. One can imagine the manager, the nurse – indeed staff of any discipline or other patients – with whom this patient had to do, simply asking themselves what would have been different about the outcome of their last meeting with a patient had they spoken to him 'the more human way'. This is a disturbing confrontation because virtually every therapist faced with this challenge is perfectly well aware what he would have done differently – however slightly – had he responded 'the more human way'. Who can tell how the outcome would have been different? But it is on such small hinges as these that the large gates of the Special Hospital, and society's response to it, hang.

(8) 'The Other 23 Hours'

This phrase used by Stanton and Schwartz (1954, p.9) refers to all the time patients spend in a Special Hospital which is not in a formal therapy session – although it is now assumed that, because '24 hour care' is becoming the norm, the patient is permanently embedded in a therapeutic milieu. Recent studies of the therapeutic process emphasize the hitherto neglected life of the patient between formal 'therapy sessions' (see Cox 1995a).

(9) The Therapeutic Group

The therapeutic group never fails as a high-profile arena in which spontaneous interaction can be observed. Pathological responses may come to light which can be carefully hidden except in the unrehearsed explosive spontaneity of the group. Thus John, a patient who generally seemed to be 'doing very well', was sitting next to a woman in a mixed group who unexpectedly announced that she had cancer of the breast and was leaving Broadmoor that very day 'for treatment'. 'Are you dying?' was the insensitive, uncontrolled question asked by John whose index offence had involved killing, so that he could be 'close to death'. Thereby he had hoped to acquire vicarious familiarity with death – because of his own augmented fear of encountering the grim reaper. Such a man's continued dangerousness declared itself in a small therapeutic group. *However much the therapeutic efficacy of groups may be debated, there is no doubt of their potential as an arena for closely monitored interaction.* This is clearly evident in the vignette just given. In other words, even though a group may not necessarily be an agent of change, it always offers a forum where 'change' or hitherto hidden dynamics declare themselves.

(10) Staff 'Problems' that Cannot be Hung up with the Keys

A dangerous gulf can develop between the public image of a brightly-brochured, briskly managed institution and the unspoken depths, the undeclared dreams, nightmares and psychosomatic disturbance of the staff. Can an institution which inevitably depends on efficient management come close to drowning in hyper-conscious 'market' forces? Such a risk can be minimized by recognition of the importance of support and appreciation of psychological demands made upon the staff of a Special Hospital. Amos (8,11) refers to 'hunger but not for food and thirst but not for drink'. Staff who daily face patients, whose therapeutic task is to come to terms with their violence and fear as memory is restored, can be hungry – but not for food. They can be hungry for confidential supervision at an appropriate depth.

There is a traditional staff saying that 'Problems are hung up with our keys at the gate'. But dreams and nightmares cannot be so readily disposed of. 'Counselling' may be available to deal with 'staff problems' and such endeavours may be helpful with mortgages and removal expenses – but there remains a huge and darker purpose of the *corpus* of massed destructiveness and danger which is rarely ventilated. Because 'any man's death diminishes me'. How many staff have sought personal therapy, or elected to work elsewhere, because they are in constant touch with experience that bad 'dreams are made on', is not known. The impact on the inner world of those at the clinical front line is so often out of 'key' with those they meet after they have 'hung up their keys'. We recall 'Never forget what he did', and those who cannot forget may be defensively akin to those who forget too easily.

This is another major issue which can receive no more than passing mention here, but to ignore it would have been retreatist.

(11) Asylum within the Asylum

The final focal concern refers to implications about the role of the psychotherapist in a Special Hospital, in relation to those pervasive staff anxieties which cannot be hung up with the keys.

A balance needs to be maintained between the clinical distribution of psychotherapists on a traditional case-load basis, and provision made for those existential, unquantifiable crisis interventions that defy resource implications. Whenever there is a major incident – hostage, escape, fire, suicidal or homicidal attempt – staff of any discipline and at all levels need space for personal asylum, usually initiated by 'Can I have a word with you?'. Ideally, the need should have been anticipated, so that the anxious approach is superfluous.

In addition to such headline crises, there is the daily, weekly, yearly, limitless slow attrition of working with psychopaths, who relentlessly attack 'the therapist's most cherished possession, namely his capacity to heal' (Glover

1960, p.149). Continuous psychotic presence poses other demands for vigilance and takes its toll on staff energy. If no patients ever left Broadmoor, more rather than fewer therapists would be needed, as they would assume an increasingly de-fusing function for staff, patients and the hospital as a whole. Phases of Broadmoor's long history support this.

A reference to Road Blocks and Thought Blocks returns to the subtitle and closes the chapter. It serves as a healthy reminder that an intrapsychic, interpersonal and corporate iceberg has scarcely been tipped. The chaotic world of the psychotic may add to the narcissistic depletion of the staff. There are those whose task it is to be *primary* nurses to patients whose *primary* processes depend on borrowing (and thus draining) the inner life of the 'significant other'. Once again, life depletion cannot be hung up with the keys. So it is that the demands from the outer world add to those of the inner world, thus linking road blocks and thought blocks. This deliberately mixed metaphor conveys the enormity and variety of the terrain.

+ + + + +

A document on *High Security Psychiatric Services* (NHS Executive 1995) was published almost simultaneously with the printing of these volumes. It opens with a statement by John Bowis, Parliamentary Under Secretary of State for Health, in which he states:

> 'We have decided on a number of important changes in the organisation and funding of high security psychiatric services provided by the three special hospitals, Ashworth, Broadmoor and Rampton. The purpose is to integrate special hospital services more closely with mainstream mental health services whilst fully maintaining the protection of the public, staff and patients themselves.' (p.2)

However strongly these 'changes in funding and organisation' may be indicated, their meshing is of a different gauge from those complex transference issues involving the victim, the patient, the therapist, the hospital-as-a-whole and society, which are the prime concern of the forensic psychotherapist. Nevertheless, the psychodynamics within the Special Hospital are inevitably influenced by the way in which society – via government and popular opinion – values, or devalues, its endeavours. As for the individual, so for the Special Hospital, self-esteem regulation is of axiomatic significance.

An Integrated Modular Approach to Therapy in a Special Hospital Young Men's Unit

Marie Quayle, Jennifer France & Eric Wilkinson

The unit which specializes in the treatment of young 'psychopathic disorder' male patients in Broadmoor Hospital has been described in previous papers (Brett 1992; Grounds *et al.* 1987). The unit as originally described, Mendip Ward, was situated in the old building of Broadmoor Hospital. The present unit, Woodstock Ward, is a twenty-five bedded unit in the newer section, in which all patients have single room accommodation including washing and toilet facilities.

PATIENTS

Figure 1 gives a profile of the group of patients on Woodstock Ward on 1 August 1993.

It will be seen from Figure 1 that, although the majority of patients are classified as 'psychopathic disorder' a substantial number have the legal category 'mental illness'. These latter patients are judged to have severe emotional problems not dissimilar to personality-disordered patients in addition to mental illness and to be sufficiently stabilized on medication to be able to benefit at least to some extent from a cognitive–behavioural/interpretive approach geared mainly to personality-disordered patients. This mixing of legal classification is not primarily due to practical reasons such as a shortage of young psychopathic patients in Broadmoor, but rather to the philosophy of the ward, a belief that the two categories of patients benefit more from mutual contact than from segregation.

Figure 1: Woodstock Ward patients on 1/8/93 (n=25)

Age on 1.8.93 (Yrs)	Mean 25	Range 17–27	
Age of admission to Broadmoor (Yrs)	Mean 21	Range 16–27	
Legal Category	PD 16	MI 9	
Section	Hosp. Order 20	Prison Transfer 4	Section 3 1
Index Offences	Homicide 13	Other Violence 9	Sexual 20	Others 16
Length of stay in Broadmoor	<1 year 3	1–5 yrs 16	6–10 yrs 5	>10 yrs 1

Currently all the patients except one have been through the courts and have been convicted of one or more serious crimes. It will be seen that violent and sexual crimes predominate amongst this group of patients. Other crimes include arson, kidnapping, robbery and criminal damage.

The majority of patients in Woodstock Ward are transferred directly from the Admissions Ward, having been assessed over a period of three to six months. Others are transferred after a period of time in another ward since initially they are deemed unsuitable, for instance they are too disturbed to benefit from or contribute to the therapeutic regime of the ward. Some patients stay on Woodstock Ward until transfer from the hospital. Others are moved to another ward, for instance for specific pre-discharge work prior to leaving the hospital, because their age or therapeutic needs no longer match the particular therapeutic approach on Woodstock, or because they need more intensive nursing. Over the past five years twenty-nine patients have left the ward: nine to more intensive care, one back to prison, five to regional secure units and fourteen to other wards, with over half of these having since transferred to regional secure units.

STAFFING

The complement of nursing staff has increased from fifteen at the time of the original article (Grounds *et al.* 1987) to twenty-three in recent years, reflecting the increased commitment to therapy in Broadmoor. This allows six nurses on the two day shifts and two on the night shift. Members of other disciplines, who, unlike the nurses, do not work exclusively on Woodstock Ward, include a consultant forensic psychiatrist, clinical area manager, ward manager, senior registrar in forensic psychiatry, two clinical psychologists, a social worker, a consultant psychotherapist, a speech therapist/psychotherapist, a clinical nurse specialist and educational and rehabilitation therapy staff. The ward operates a primary nurse system and is a recognized training ward receiving Project 2000 students and other trainees. The multi-disciplinary clinical team meets weekly for case reviews and ward rounds and every three months there is a meeting of those involved in therapies to consider the need for new groups and which patients will be invited to join, and to review each patient's therapeutic input in terms of groups, individual therapy and other therapies such as family or couples sessions. Every six weeks there is a meeting of all patients with the Responsible Medical Officer (RMO) and other staff to resolve issues relating to the ward environment and suggest changes.

STRUCTURE OF THERAPY

Whilst there are opportunities on the ward for individual therapy or family or couples sessions, the predominant form of treatment in the unit is group therapy. At the time of writing five patients (20%) have individual therapy whilst twenty-two patients (88%) are members of at least one group, with thirteen patients (52%) taking part in two or more.

(1) GROUPWORK

The groups usually consist of four to eight patients and meet weekly, whenever possible with both male and female therapists and more than one discipline involved. There are usually six groups running at any one time, the particular approach and subject matter chosen to suit the needs of the patients at that time. There are two main types of group: unstructured, interpretive groups and structured, cognitive–behavioural groups. The majority of patients on the ward are members of both an unstructured and structured group.

(i) Unstructured Groups

The unstructured groups are either supportive or confrontative in approach. They are slow–open groups, membership changing according to patient need, and operate continuously with no set ending date.

The supportive group, called Current Affairs, is a useful beginning for patients new to group work and also caters for the more disabled patients who cannot sustain membership in more confrontative groups. It focuses on whatever issues the patients bring to the group, everyday as well as past concerns, or takes a topic of general interest, hence its name. When patients in this group are ready to address personal issues in more depth they are moved to one of the confrontative groups.

The confrontative groups are for patients who are already articulate or beginning to develop linguistic skills and are able to reflect on their past histories in some depth and be questioned and confronted by other group members, as well as the therapists. The two confrontative groups are categorized by both patients and staff as intermediate and higher level and membership is determined accordingly.

A mixed unstructured group for male and female patients has also taken place but at present is difficult to sustain as part of the stable group structure of the unit. The difficulty is due not only to the practical issues which can arise in having high security male patients on a female ward or *vice versa*, but primarily to problems of matching male and female patients' needs and group experience and a tendency for the group to become male dominated both in numbers and in approach.

(ii) Structured Groups

The structured groups focus on particular topics or areas of functioning and work through a programme over a period of several months with an ending, but not a fixed finishing time in advance, to allow the group to spend a shorter or longer time on topics according to the needs of patients. They are closed groups, membership changing only when the group ends.

Over the years a variety of structured groups have been run on the unit, with the possibility of new groups being added as the need arises. At the time of the first specific article focusing on the ward (Grounds *et al.* 1987) three structured groups were offered: sex education, social skills, including some assertiveness training, and anger management. Two further longer groups were introduced: an interpersonal relationships group, including sex education and work on relationships and sexual topics, and an actualization group, including self and sensory awareness, family issues, moral dilemmas and victim empathy. These latter groups were, in effect, complex groups containing several different topics and viewed by all as more demanding and higher level. The closed membership and length meant that some patients were excluded from joining these groups for a period of eighteen months or more. Thus it was decided to split these longer groups into separate modules with the possibility of change of membership at the end of each module.

The modular structure of groups offered at present on the ward can be described diagrammatically as in Figure 2. The modules can be placed along three strands: social, sexual and awareness/insight. Victim empathy is seen as the goal of each strand of development, to be attempted only after patients have participated in a number of groups. The awareness strand is to be extended shortly by the inclusion of an alcohol awareness group.

Figure 2. Structured Group Modules

	VICTIM EMPATHY	
ANGER MANAGEMENT	SEX MATTERS	MORAL AWARENESS
ASSERTIVENESS	INTERPERSONAL RELATIONSHIPS	FAMILY AWARENESS
SOCIAL SKILLS	SEX EDUCATION	SELF/ SENSORY AWARENESS
SOCIAL STRAND	SEXUAL STRAND	AWARENESS/ INSIGHT STRAND

The different modules in the structure can be described briefly as follows:

Social Skills

This is a typical 'micro' approach to shaping social behaviour, based on the model of Argyle and his colleagues (Argyle 1975; Trower, Bryant and Argyle 1978). This includes non-verbal, listening, vocal, verbal and conversational components, using role play and video feedback.

Assertiveness

This extends the approach used in social skills training to assertive behaviour but also teaches some assertive techniques such as broken record, fogging and negative enquiry (Smith 1975). It is often necessary with these young men to spend a considerable time demonstrating that assertive behaviour can be just as effective and a more acceptable approach than angry or aggressive behaviour.

Anger Management

This module can be adapted to suit those who readily express anger or those who suppress it. It is based on the behavioural–cognitive method, described by Novaco (1975, 1978) and includes the nature and functions of anger, relaxation training, monitoring and analysis of personal episodes of anger, identification of risk situations and replacement of negative by positive self-statements. The aim is not to remove anger entirely from the patients' repertoire, since it has positive functions and its suppression can lead to violent outbursts; rather the aim is to help the patient recognize and acknowledge his own anger and learn to use it in a constructive rather than destructive way.

Sex Education

This module uses slide and video material and covers all the basic factual information, including male and female physiology, sexual relationships, pregnancy, contraception, childbirth, sexual problems and sexually transmitted diseases.

Interpersonal Relationships

This module addresses the levels of intimacy and changes in relationships over time. It allows patients to analyze their own relationships on the ward as well as significant past peer relationships and interactions.

Sex Matters

The structure of this module focuses on the stages of emotional, sexual and social development and, using the parent–adult–child model of transactional analysis, ranges from issues of bonding, trust and gaining independence from parents, through gender identity and sexual preferences to adult and parent relationships.

Self and Sensory Awareness

This module includes trust, sensory awareness and relaxation exercises as well as exercises which enable the patient to assess his own presentation to others, how he is seen, and how he sees himself and others.

Family Awareness

This module focuses on relationships and roles in the patient's family and aims to help them achieve a more objective view of the family dynamics. Exercises include family trees, diagrams representing family groupings and hierarchies, sculpting a significant family memory and an empty chair 'conversation' with a family member, alive or dead.

Moral Awareness

This module traces the stages of moral development and how we reach difficult moral decisions. It includes a video exercise of a group decision with the opportunity to focus on the role each group member played in reaching the decision. It also includes discussion and debate of relevant moral dilemmas, following the method of Kohlberg (1964, 1971).

Victim Empathy

A major aim of this module is to help patients achieve an understanding of their own and other people's feelings and the appropriate expression of emotion. It aims to help patients focus in detail rather than avoid the reality of their offences and includes such exercises as drawing the location and talking or 'walking through' the offence, describing the offence from the victim's point of view and Gestalt 'two-chair' role reversal exercises where either the patient himself or the group as a whole takes on the role of the victim.

(2) OTHER THERAPIES AND WARD SETTING

The structure of group therapies takes place in the context of individual therapy, interpretive, cognitive–behavioural or counselling which is available for a minority of patients, and the immeasurably important supportive sessions with nurses, which are available to all patients and regularly made use of by the majority. Creative therapies are also available in the hospital and a five day workshop focusing on anger and aggressive behaviour, led by the Geese Theatre Company, was held recently for a group of patients and staff on Woodstock Ward. An evaluation of the effects of the workshop is currently under way.

This whole therapeutic structure is placed within the context of the hospital as a whole with the educational and work training opportunities, so important for such a relatively young group of patients, as well as opportunities for socialization, recreation, sport, rehabilitation and religion. Williams' (1993) reflections on rehabilitation in prisons could equally well apply to the Special Hospital setting: 'programmes directed at offending behaviour need to be integrated with programmes directed at other problem areas including work, education and relationships with authority and peers' (p.17).

(3) OUTCOME

A number of questionnaires and rating forms are used to assess progress in structured group modules and provide an objective component alongside the more subjective impressions of progress when therapists compile their report. In addition, patients are asked for feedback on their own progress and what they found helpful or difficult in groups. It is noticeable that the exercises which are judged most difficult are often also seen to be most helpful and that in many cases these are the non-verbal or 'different' verbal exercises.

The results of thirty-one patients on a sex knowledge questionnaire, completed before and after a sex education module, were analyzed to assess gains in knowledge. Results showed an overall significant increase in knowledge (mean increase from 52% to 71%; $p < 0.001$) but the greatest gain in the section dealing with female physiology (mean increase from 34% to 65%; $p < 0.001$). When results for sex offenders and non sex offenders were compared there were no significant differences before the group, contrary to a common assumption that sex offenders are more knowledgeable about sex or to their own frequent fear that they are inadequate in sexual knowledge. After the group, however, whilst both groups made significant increases in knowledge, the sex offenders were significantly better than the non sex offenders on overall percentage score ($p = 0.05$), on the sexual problems and diseases section ($p < 0.05$) and particularly on the female physiology section ($p < 0.005$). It seems likely that this reflects the particular relevance of this module to sex offenders.

An analysis of reports of thirty-five group members who had taken part in one or more of five structured group modules showed that 17 per cent left a group before completion because they felt unable or unwilling to continue. In some cases this occurs because the patient considers the module not relevant to him, but in the majority of cases the patient feels unable to undertake a particularly demanding group exercise at that time and group rules insist that all patients attempt (though not necessarily succeed in) all exercises. Using a simple rating scale of 0, 1, 2 to assess improvement, three per cent of patients scored 0 (very little or no noticeable improvement); thirty-seven per cent scored 1 (some improvement but could be better); forty-three per cent scored 2 (marked improvement).

As far as outcome of the overall ward regime is concerned, a detailed follow-up study of patients who have received treatment on the young person's unit has recently occurred and analysis of results is currently under way. It is hoped that the results of this study will allow the treatment regime to be refined.

(4) SINGLE CASE ILLUSTRATION

An example of one patient's progress through the ward is included here as an illustration of the different components of therapy, how they interact and how the whole therapeutic structure fits into the general hospital environment.

Vignette

The patient was one of very few who are admitted to a maximum security Special Hospital at age sixteen years, reflecting the seriousness with which his offence was viewed. When aged fifteen years, following an indecent assault on a teenage girl and two sexual approaches to mature women, he assaulted two middle aged women, in an isolated area, and raped and killed one of them whilst the other attempted to summon help. He was admitted to Broadmoor under Section 37,41 of the 1983 Mental Health Act with Home Office restrictions and with the classification of psychopathic personality disorder.

He was the fourth child of a relatively large family, with both brothers and sisters. His father's service in the Armed Forces during his early years meant a number of moves of house and school before the family finally settled in an old house in an isolated area when he was aged ten years. His early adolescence proved to be very stressful. He was unpopular at school and frequently truanted, a fact condoned or even encouraged by his parents since he was always willing to do housework, look after the younger children and run errands. There were mixed messages about sexuality in the family. He became aware of incestuous relationships involving various members of his family, and while those activities were apparently condoned, his own attempts at sexual experience within the family or with girlfriends were discovered, punished and ridiculed by the family, and he believed 'teasing' remarks made by his mother about his sexual inadequacy. His offences can be seen as a series of attempts to counter this self-doubt, with the final catastrophic attack which killed his victim as an explosion of anger against his parents, triggered by her innocent assumption of a 'maternal' role in an attempt to cope with a desperate situation.

This understanding of the dynamics underlying the patient's offence was arrived at very slowly. When admitted to Broadmoor he spent four months on the admissions unit before moving to the young men's unit. He quickly settled in, treating the hospital like a boarding school and indeed in later years admitting that Broadmoor was a home to him – a home which over the years has allowed him to recoup some of his earlier educational deficits, achieve both work and sports qualifications, and have a long and significant relationship with one of the women patients.

His behaviour during the first eight to nine years was very consistent but endeared him neither to patients nor staff. On the one hand he was polite, courteous, eager to please and helpful round the ward; on the other hand he tended to be sly and secretive, determined to have the last word in any discussions and to use other patients for his own advantage. This behaviour produced a situation which re-enacted his earlier unpopularity at school and his readiness to do chores, giving him a position of some control in the family.

During these years he took part in a variety of groups, structured and unstructured: a supportive and two confrontative interpretive groups, sex education, social skills, interpersonal relationships and the full actualization package. His progress in these groups was viewed in a markedly different way by himself and by others. For him progression through groups and from group to group appeared to be synonymous with progress, in much the same way perhaps that progression from class to class marks chronological advance through school, whether or not it results in educational achievement. It is worth noting that his offence and arrest occurred before the end of schooling and any testing of achievement via examinations. The unanimous view of group facilitators, however, was that, although always cooperative and eager to participate in groups, his progress in achieving either behavioural change or insight into his offence was very limited and that he had become increasingly skilled in retaining his defences, parrying confrontation and focusing on superficial, peripheral issues rather than significant, central ones. Having said that, it is worth noting that some significant 'revelations' did occur which were not fully recognized at the time by the therapists or indeed by the patient himself. One such was a drawing (Figure 3), completed during the family module of the actualization group, in which he represented his family as different plants, his mother being an ivy, clinging for support to his father, represented by a half standard apple tree, and encircling with her tendrils each member of the family with the exception of the patient who, standing apart from the rest of the group was 'pinned' by the end of a tendril rather than embraced by it. Later, in individual therapy, it became clear that this picture encapsulated the conflict in his perception of himself and his family: feeling different, unwanted, unloved, indeed belittled and ridiculed in the family, whilst at the same time feeling relied on, 'used' and trapped by his very attempt to gain acceptance by pleasing his parents.

The actualization group marked a further turning point for the patient, albeit a negative one. Following the role reversal exercises on victim empathy, he admitted that he was unable to feel remorse or empathy in the way some other group members clearly did. He was particularly impressed by one patient, who also had spent several years in Broadmoor before any noticeable change occurred, and this patient became his role model.

Figure 3

This admission of failure and the reasons given were capitalized on some time later when, following a full case review, he was removed from all group therapies and embarked on a treatment plan, involving an extensive assessment followed by a period of individual therapy with the psychologist, with regular support sessions with his primary nurse throughout. The aim was to attempt to establish whether an emotional 'vacuum' existed or whether feelings were present but not expressed or indeed suppressed/repressed. Assessment and therapy focussed initially on a variety of non-verbal or 'different' verbal exercises in an attempt to break through the sugar coated defence of words often repeated about his offence, devoid of feelings and indeed protecting him against them. Psychophysiological assessments included videoed material with sequences similar to his offence. An audio-taped account or 'thought track' of his offence spoken in the present tense, was compiled from his own account and statements by his victim's companion and played back to him. He drew a large scale plan of the area in which he lived and where all his offences occurred enabling him to talk through them in more detail. He also made an audio-taped account of his index offence spoken as though he were his victim. This last exercise, achieved with considerable difficulty, seemed to tip the balance, to break the log jam of emotions from the past. Perhaps it enabled him finally to encounter her, the woman he killed, as a real person and thus to separate her from all the feelings of self-loathing and of anger and resentment at his family which he had projected onto her. His use of individual sessions both with the psychologist and his primary nurse became more productive and enabled both him and the clinical team to gain an understanding of his offence.

He demonstrated this change when he rejoined an interpretive group, not only by his greater insight and genuine feeling when describing his offence and the circumstances which led to it, but by his markedly different presentation. Previously he had spoken in a soft, cajoling whisper with frequent pauses which controlled the contributions of other group members; on his return he was an active, spontaneous, confrontative group member at ease with himself and no longer trying to fit in with what he assumed would please the therapists. His greater insight was also apparent during a visit to the area where the offences were committed, involving 'walking through' them again in the actual setting. This brought him, not an anticipated cathartic rush of his own emotions at the time of his offence, but rather an encounter with the fear engendered by the loneliness of the place and the feelings of helplessness, hopelessness, and inability to change anything, which belonged not to him but to his victims.

To date the patient has been accepted at a regional secure unit and is awaiting a bed. He is still participating in relevant groupwork, is working in one of the most 'trusted' jobs in the hospital and has become a 'respected elder' in the patient community, a position he has long aspired to but achieved only in recent years.

DISCUSSION

A number of therapeutic or developmental models underpin the structure of therapy on Woodstock Ward. Maslow's (1954) hierarchy assumes that lower level needs must be satisfied before higher level needs can be addressed. This could describe the successful progression of a patient through Woodstock Ward and Broadmoor Hospital. Basic physiological and safety needs are satisfied when the patient is admitted to a secure hospital, allowing him to address interpersonal needs through discussion and skills training groups, social events and group living. Achievement needs can be met through educational and vocational services which provide opportunities not only to improve academic and practical skills but to enhance self-esteem and social relationships. Finally, self-actualization needs can be met in more demanding structured and unstructured groups and individual therapies, through which he can address and resolve past issues in order to achieve changes in the future.

Other models of progress also apply to the development sought through therapy. The progress from total denial to acceptance and empathy is outlined in the 'scala integrata' described by Cox (1986). Kohlberg's (1971) stages of moral reasoning describe the progression from the egocentric stages when decisions are based on personal punishment and gain to higher stages where living up to role expectations, considering the good of others and ethical principles are important factors. Yalom's (1970) curative factors specific to groupwork can all be realized in the more demanding and confrontative structured or unstructured groups, where patients are encouraged to leave the more dependent, 'What are you going to do for me?' roles and move into mature adult, 'I have to sort myself out', and altruistic parental, 'My experience may help you' roles. Painful earlier experiences which contributed to arrested emotional development can be re-addressed and re-enacted in a healing way.

Historically, the cognitive–behavioural and psychodynamic approaches to psychotherapy have developed in isolation from, if not in conflict with, each other. There have been voices, however, arguing that an integration of approaches can enhance understanding and the effectiveness of clinical work (e.g. Wachtel 1977). This integrative approach is deliberately fostered within and between the different group therapies on Woodstock Ward. There is a matching of patients in the hierarchy of groups, so that patients in the more straightforward educational and skills training groups are in the less confrontative unstructured groups, whilst patients in more sophisticated structured modules, requiring greater group experience and motivation, are placed in confrontative interpretive groups. This matching facilitates beneficial links between the two types of groups. For instance topics and exercises encountered in the cognitive–behavioural modules can stimulate memory and increase insight into other people's points of view, thus fostering the development of empathy and the re-structuring of perceptions of the past. This is worked through in greater detail in unstructured groups and the greater insight gained can then enhance later work in the structured group, the two groups thus working in parallel. Moreover Yalom (1970) notes that insight into developmental history is less useful than insight into current behavioural patterns and motivations underlying customary social interactions. Reflections on past experiences in the interpretive groups can be firmly anchored in the 'here and now' and less easily denied or distorted during specific exercises in structured groups when patients give feedback on their perceptions of each other.

Of particular importance in the structured modules, as noted in the single case illustration above, are the non-verbal or 'different' verbal exercises which tap skills other than those required, and often well rehearsed, in the 'talking' therapies. Initially, these exercises can meet with resistance or a high level of frustration since the reasoning behind them is not so immediately apparent. Perhaps because of this, they can break through defences and barriers and 'reach the part' other therapies do not – or not so immediately – reach. Trust exercises, presenting no problem for some, are achieved only with great difficulty by others. It is noticeable that in the latter case patient histories often reveal problems encountered in the early stages of security, acceptance and bonding. Diagrams and sculpting exercises illustrating the dynamics of their family from their own point of view and that of other family members, on the one hand can make them aware that their own family is not different from others and 'abnormal'; and on the other hand can lead to an appreciation of other people's viewpoint. This appreciation, together with specific exercises to gain access to the viewpoint of their victims, can lead to an acceptance of responsibility for their offences, together with remorse and empathy. It was noticeable in the 'empty chair' exercises when the whole group took on the role of a patient's victim, that some patients were able to gain access to the feelings of someone else's victim, whilst still blocking or diminishing the feelings of their own victim.

None of the group approaches used on Woodstock Ward is unique. Variations of the groups can be found in many settings, including non-secure settings. The fact that they are carried out in a secure hospital rather than a prison means that progress must be judged in terms of increased understanding and insight and changes in attitude and behaviour and cannot be linked merely to a date when discharge will occur. This requirement of change means that these groups for young psychopathically-disordered patients not only may but must become more confrontative as the patient progresses. Confrontation is made more feasible within the group setting by the knowledge of the supportive back-up of nurses always available on the wards.

The patients on Woodstock Ward have many differing deficits and needs; the hospital affords many differing opportunities to make good these deficits and increase their skills. The factor they share in common is their past offence(s) and dangerous behaviour which led them to require psychiatric treatment in conditions of maximum security. Therapy, if it is to be successful, must enable the patient gradually to address in more and more detail the circumstances of his offence, the various factors that led to it, the consequences for himself and others, and the implications for his present and future behaviour. This is a crucial aim of all therapy on Woodstock Ward but as the patient gradually progresses up the hierarchical ladder of structured and unstructured groups, it becomes an ever more integral and explicit component.

Acknowledgements

We are grateful to colleagues on Woodstock Ward for discussion and suggestions, to Assistant Psychologist, David Murphy for statistical analysis of questionnaire results and to Elaine McMahon for typing the manuscript.

The opinions expressed in this chapter are those of the authors and do not necessarily represent those of Broadmoor Hospital or the Special Hospitals Service Authority.

Changing Prisons
The Unconscious Dimension

R.D. Hinshelwood

INTRODUCTION

Prisons, like all other institutions, are swept by profoundly influential psychodynamics, some beneficial some otherwise. Thinking about prisons often fails to take into account this unconscious level of the institution. Consequently, deleterious effects occur for inmates; and consciously proposed changes in them, or in the prison, may be greatly impeded. Much has been written about the unconscious dynamics of institutions, but little notice, in *practice*, has been taken of what we now know.

A BACKGROUND THEORY

For some reason people aggregate in groups. Man is social and his personal identity is formed, and sustained, by his social relations. Fundamental problems of personal identity have their origins as well as solutions in the relations within and between social groups and institutions. Human beings need each other intensely. The individual's unconscious mind aggregates with others to contribute important features to the personality of an institution itself. A psychoanalytic view stems from Freud's paper on group psychology (S. Freud 1921). In this he considered the profound effects of falling in love and how it alters the identity of the lover. He (she) becomes so absorbed in his loved one that in certain respects aspects of his own personality appear to go missing – he often loses his appetite for instance; his aspirations narrow remarkably into a focus on his loved one and other interests atrophy; often his interests will

465

become merely those of his loved one. Such blissful states, we know, are usually (unhappily) short-lived. Freud was also interested in the way in which the subject of hypnosis when under trance will give up aspects of his personality to the hypnotist, notably his own will and determination. The hypnotist can come to possess the subject's control of mind and body. In such a relationship the person is only complete when in relation to the other person in whom part of his personality now seems to reside. To an extent all social relations are like this and we always need them to give ourselves a sense of completeness. This Platonic search for a completed self in others is a basic unconscious mortar that builds people into institutions.

> 'One of the primary cohesive elements binding individuals in institutionalized human association is that of defence against psychotic anxiety. In this sense individuals may be thought of as externalizing those impulses and internal objects that would otherwise give rise to psychotic anxiety, and pooling them in the life of the social institution... [This implies] that we would expect to find in group relationships manifestations of unreality, splitting, hostility, suspicion, and other forms of maladaptive behaviour.' (Jaques 1955, p.479)

In groups such as prisons, or total institutions as they are called, the individual seems to invest so much in the group he belongs to he can hardly be complete outside it. Then the individual is highly moulded (even constructed) by this continuing immersion in the institution. Consequently, a change in the institution itself means very severe disturbance to the individuals' sense of themselves which is constructed by the institution.

This approach was significantly elaborated by Elliott Jaques (1955) when he looked at how individuals use the institution unconsciously to protect themselves against their anxieties. Such problems in organizations were described by Isabel Menzies (1959) when she investigated a nursing service in a London Teaching Hospital. There are similar studies of many other institutions (Trist and Murray 1990) including a recent description of the psychological defensive aspects of a prison (Hinshelwood 1993). All these studies follow the following model. The work task creates specific *anxieties* that disturb the people engaged on the work to a greater or lesser extent. Individuals may seek to protect themselves against those anxieties – to make them unconscious – by using *psychological defences*. In the working institution those psychological defences may be supported by collective agreements to perform the work task in specific ways; and that will involve the development of certain *attitudes* to the work, often unrealistic, and certain work practices, called *defensive techniques*. This configuration of collective anxieties, with the unconscious organisation of collective attitudes and defensive techniques within the work practices is termed *the social defence system*.

THE SOCIAL DEFENCE SYSTEM OF THE PRISON

Writing about a different kind of institution, Spillius (1990) described an inherent conflict.

> 'The hospital provides services in the form of treatment and care intended to benefit but also to 'manage' the individual patient – i.e. to control the patient on behalf of society. The chief reason for admission to a mental hospital is that relatives and society cannot manage the patient... Since patient and society are in conflict and the hospital served both, the hospital has an intrinsic conflict within itself...it was often evaded or obscured by social defences.' (p.586–7)

The institutional contradiction, she claimed, was the source of personal anxieties which then gave rise to the *use of* the institution to support personal psychological defences against the anxieties.

How true is it of a prison? Is there conflict between its custodial function on behalf of an endangered society, and its caring, rehabilitative function for the individual inmates? If the staff are in such division *within* themselves, then various kinds of problems for the whole institution are likely to develop. A care-versus-toughness culture clash comes to exist within the prison itself (Hinshelwood 1993).

Such a divide is also a deep cleft in society in general. Indeed it is a conflict which is inherent in most ordinary citizens. We might well feel some sympathy with incarcerated human beings and at the same time feel outrage, even murderous, at their crimes. However, the 'offender' system expresses that cleft for the rest of society, and it does so in a specific way – by separating it out as distinct groups within the offender system. Even as ordinary citizens with mixed attitudes and feelings, when we go to work in the offender system we tend rapidly to form up in line with one or other of the working cultures we are part of. As psychotherapists and psychoanalysts we have our position within the system as proponents of the care side of the culture clash; though if we have ever had our car broken into we often smartly change sides. The clash within the offender system contains, as it were, the division and seemingly irreconcilable opposite stances within the individual in society at large.

The custodial attitude of control, assigning of blame, and punishment require a toughness of approach. And this is prominent in the prison. Not only the staff but inmates have similar tough attitudes. When individuals share collective attitudes it can be referred to as the *culture* of the group, and when the group is the members of a working institution then those collective attitudes are the 'working culture'. I shall use the terms 'culture' and 'working culture' in the senses just described.

The Social System

Crime is a social phenomenon – or, a social activity. Dealing with offenders is also a social activity (including catching them) and it is conducted within, and by, a social institution – the judicial/penal/probation/therapy system (the 'offender' system). This is a multi-faceted social institution and it is apparent that the working culture of attitudes varies with different groups in the prison. They are divided within themselves, and between themselves. There is a polarization of social attitudes to crime and the offender; polarized as either custody or care. Heated passions inform (or rather disinform) the debate between the two sides, and a person's attitudes are relative to his position within the offender system.

Psychotherapists have their own attitudes, *their* working culture, which contrasts strikingly with the dominant working culture of the prison. The psychotherapy lobby knows where it stands, and tends to be critical of custodial attitudes; just as those on the side of law and order are contemptuous of wishy-washy therapists.

Both sides do come together in a common view. Although they differ on what is wrong, they agree that the criminal relation between the individual offender and society is wrong and must be corrected. The prison appears to be a means of removing people who cause others to fear for themselves or their property, and to render them less menacing. However, the prison is not as it seems. Many people have observed with varying attitudes, from humour to head-shaking gravity, that the prison educates criminals; but there is no understanding of how it does so, nor how that could be challenged and changed. What it is (rather than what we all think it is) is a little society in itself. The prison has adapted to the offender.

I will review this functioning of the prison that is contributed by the unconscious aspects of the individuals, all of them: the offenders and the staff.

ILLUSTRATION OF THE CULTURE CLASH[1]

I worked two sessions a week in this male prison but after about two years I decided to give up the work because it seemed almost impossible to make psychotherapy effective there. At that time there were more psychotherapists in Wormwood Scrubbs than any other in the country, some of whom were very eminent and some had been working in the prison for many years. Despite that interesting investment, I found myself considerably frustrated in the work I wanted to do. I found that the prison officers had a particular view of the

---

1   Although these observations now date from a number of years ago, and may not completely reflect the present situation in all prisons, the point is to illustrate the general properties of a stable unconscious system of cultural attitudes.

psychotherapists, and indeed some psychotherapists shared that view. I was constantly warned by prison officers about certain patients I would be seeing. Those prisoners, I was told, would be wanting some particular privilege or concession. As a doctor, I had considerable authority in making requests on patients' behalf, and the prison officers were concerned that patients would coerce me to recommend a personal radio in their cell, night sedation, or some other indulgence. Clearly, the psychotherapist is an indulgent fellow, soft and acquiescing to the demands of these undeserving characters; the officers had to counteract that. They, pressed on me that prisoners are wily and trick their way into getting all sorts of things. Their job was to warn me of these tricks; without warnings I would be vulnerable to prisoners' trickery.

My perceived gullibility was part of a denigratory view of psychotherapists that was carried into practical aspects of the work. For instance there were times when I was told I could not see a patient because there were staff shortages and an officer could not be spared to go and fetch the patient from the wing. On two occasions, I was told innocently that they did not know where the prisoner was. And from time to time I would arrive to see a patient who had simply been moved off without warning to another prison since my last session with him. Many of my patients had similar expectations of me. They often implored special privileges which I could gain for them and which they tried to convince me they deserved because of the despair and depression which living in prison forced upon them. This picture of myself as indulgent and gullible and of my work as simply making life easier for suffering prisoners was not my view of myself or of psychotherapy. I was saddened that the view was widespread in a prison which employed more psychotherapists than any other. When I later thought and wrote about the prison I wondered what this view of psychotherapy meant? I concluded that it did have a meaning. Those sets of attitudes to psychotherapy form part of a culture, the prison culture, or rather the dominant culture of the prison, sustained by both prisoners and prison officers. The attitudes to psychotherapy were a by-product, but could give a clue to the whole cultural system. I understood it in terms of three groups within the prison: the prisoners, the prison officers, and other groups (such as the psychotherapists).

The Prisoners

The prisoners believed they must get whatever they could by trickery, from soft and gullible people. I quickly formed the impression of a major axis within the prison culture running between toughness and weakness. So many of the reports about life in the prison were refracted through a preoccupation with being tough: usually the prisoner I was seeing was tough, and it was the others who were weak. There were groups of prisoners who were regarded as weak – the Pakistanis for instance, or the sex offenders who the tough ones abused to demonstrate the toughness they idealize. The triumphant prowess which glowed in their faces when reporting this kind of activity was reflected in another area too. Invariably they claimed innocence of the crimes for which they had been convicted and thus occupied a triumphant position of righteous superiority over the police or whoever else had been responsible for 'framing' them. At the same time as they told me of their innocence they would also tell me success stories – of far more magnificent crimes that they had committed and got away with. I was confronted again and again with the contradiction of pained innocence plus prowess in committing crimes. Righteousness triumphed. It was clearly achieved by projecting weakness and guilt onto others. Prisoners identified with a powerful trickery, greatly superior to a sloppy honesty; brutality was prized above indulgence.

It is understandable how such cultural attitudes could grow up collectively and gain a persuasive conviction, forming the core of a dominant culture. As a reaction to their wrong-doing and culpability proclaimed publicly in court, they form a defensiveness against experiencing a crippling sense of weakness and helplessness of being imprisoned. Prisoners' fears and neediness[2] are immediately converted into a trickery that can assert a superiority and independence over the person of whom the demand is being made.

The Prison Officers

Turning to the prison officers, they seemed to have adopted a similar kind of cultural axis in their attitudes to their work – a toughness, bordering on brutality, deployed to meet that of the prisoners. The prison officers meet their prisoners neediness by triumphantly outsmarting and exposing their trickery. This leaves officers feeling one up or one jump ahead. They are tough in tracking down trickery. The officers need to contrive a continual sense of being in control and in command. This set of attitudes is equally understandable, related to the officers' predicament in having to contain for society people who have proved uncontrollable and uncontainable. Without their cultivated and defensive attitudes of being in control prison officers would be open to very considerable fear of the violence and criminality they have to deal with.

The Dominant Culture

On both sides of this dominant culture we find a collectively accepted set of cultural attitudes – one set for the prisoner and one for the prison officer. On both sides these sets of attitudes function as defensive methods to keep at bay

---

2 In this chapter I cannot address the internal states of terror and sadism, which so often contribute to an individual engaging in criminal acts (S. Freud 1916c; Klein 1927; Gallwey 1965).

serious anxieties – for the prisoner his guilt, helplessness and terror; for the prison officer the fear of violence. Both groups are driven to these one-sided attitudes by their deep personal anxieties that the individuals share. What makes the culture of brutality dominant is that the attitudes on both sides interlock. A joint system is co-operatively worked by the prisoners and the officers.

The Psychotherapists and the Non-Dominant Culture

Where do the psychotherapists fit in? We can now see the important place within this dominant culture for people who are identified as just those indulgent and weak persons that the prisoners and officers are reassuring themselves they are not. So, the relevance of psychotherapy in the prison is not what I had been trained to think it was. Instead, the jointly shared view saw psychotherapists weakly acquiescing to triumphant imperious demands. A non-dominant culture of sloppy weakness is a necessity for the dominant culture to survive. In fact it is not only the psychotherapists who are assigned to this role of personifying weakness. Other groups such as prison visitors, female staff, probation officers and those who work in the hospital wing are ready candidates for the role too. Amongst the disciplinary staff some who choose to work with certain prisoners, for example young offenders, are also recruited to the weak groups; as well as certain groups of prisoners – the sex offenders, or some ethnic groups.

My experiences as a psychotherapist came out of, and therefore indicated, the divisions in the working culture of the prison – and to a degree the reasons why such a division unwittingly and unconsciously arises and is maintained. They represent the *rejected* aspects of the prisoners or officers – weakness and indulgence, an opposite pole to the tough brutal attitudes of the dominant culture. Polarized in this way each set of attributes becomes one-dimensional. The offender system has split the two characteristics widely apart, one from the other; strength is idealized as toughness at one extreme, and concern is denigrated as weakness at the other. People at either pole actually *become* one or other of these one-dimensional roles in their professional identity; so polarized they barely recognize themselves at work; so tenacious they cannot change their conditions. All this is difficult for people in the system to recognize, unless they work part-time as I did.

Change

The difficulty in changing prison cultures is a common enough observation (e.g. Woolf and Tumin 1991). I have attempted to show how this derives from a grave difficulty arising from the conflict in the task of prisons. Separate working cultures arise that work against each other rather than struggle to come into some difficult integration; and that split is *needed* in order to efface certain unacceptable feeling states in both inmates and prison officers.

With this understanding of the deep reinforcement of personal and professional identity that the cultural system of attitudes provide, it is clear how problematic change is going to be. Any proposal for change first needs to consider underpinning personal identity which depends so heavily on the organization. New ways of providing support – at the conscious, and the unconscious levels – have to be designed. Without conscious design in that way there will inevitably be a runaway process of developing personal support from unconscious collective defensiveness.

It is difficult indeed to understand how staff can approach some greater degree of integration, especially when under pressure from two directions: first they are required by society at large to represent two sets of attitudes which publically have not been properly reconciled with each other; and second there is a powerful provocation from the inmates to sustain the dominance of the brutality over the contemptible 'soft' approach.

CONCLUSION – NEW SOCIAL DEFENCE SYSTEMS

There are various implications that arise from a recognition of the power of unconscious forces within the institution.

Alternative Social Defence Systems

Some prisons have experimented with very different systems, and have developed very different relations between the inmates and prison officers, and between the culture of custody and the culture of care. Notably Gunn, Robertson, Dell and Way (1978) reported objective measures of therapeutic achievement in prisons. They compared an ordinary one, Wormwood Scrubbs, with Grendon Underwood. The latter employs psychotherapy in a different way and the design of the whole prison came from the influence of psychotherapeutic ideas. In Grendon violence and conflict are channelled into therapeutic groups, thus to create very different structures of attitudes – in effect a different social defence system. At Wormwood Scrubbs psychotherapists are 'tacked on' to the traditional system. Gunn and his co-workers found that outcome as measured by comparative re-conviction rates was equivocal. However they report of Wormwood Scrubbs

'In so far as psychotherapy is intended to improve the patient's insight and thereby help him with his behaviour and personality problems, these results are disappointing, and very different from those achieved at Grendon.' (p.147)

In fact they assert that reconviction rates are much more to do with social factors on release and therefore out of the control of the prison. Instead,

> 'in our view, the appropriate criterion by which Grendon should be judged is whether or not it serves a useful therapeutic function. It is, after all, a prison. Its inmates, had they not been transferred to Grendon, would have served out their time in ordinary prisons. If its reconviction rate is no worse than that of other prisons, and it is also performing an effective therapeutic function, then Grendon can claim success.' (Gunn *et al.* 1978, p.123)

Thus other social defence systems manage the anxiety of prisoner and prison officer differently and are likely to have different outcomes – seemingly better ones. Therefore we could empirically test a variety of social defence systems. We could even attempt to design completely new ones.

One serious deficiency of the rigid social defence system I have described is that it not only acts against change in the prison but it also militates against personal change in the individuals. They are gathered fairly forcefully into defined roles and attitudes. This includes the inmates who need most to have an opportunity to change in themselves. In very powerful systems of this kind a kind of claustrophobia can develop.

Motive for Change

This consequence of an unconscious social defence system leads to a limitation on job satisfaction for staff. Without a careful design the one-dimensional interpretation of professional roles is not only protective of staff but also comes painfully to hamper their personal and professional identity. I do not mean merely the psychotherapists, or carers. It is equally true of the disciplinary staff as well. As part of an experiment to bring about a greater awareness of the prison officer's role, I held seminars to discuss relations between officers and inmates on the wings. It was very striking that when the officers came off their wing to discuss these things in what felt like a non-work setting they displayed a thoroughly sensitive understanding of the needs and suffering of many of the men in their charge. The prison officers were not in themselves particularly brutal people. They were merely required to reduce their sensitivity to invisibility when on the job.

The job limitation leads to resentment by the staff and even overt hostility towards the job. Expressed so often in displaced form as more brutal attitudes towards prisoners, it leads then to a potential vicious circle. The staff's hampered sense of themselves gives rise to expressions for changes in working conditions, as well as more obvious indicators of distress at work, such as absenteeism, attrition of numbers from the service, and frequent job moves. Often such frustration with the job is expressed in misdirected ways – for

instance for higher levels of staffing, when the need is really to understand
how resourceless the individuals may actually feel when on the job. Frequently
the demands for change meet a management that thinks merely in terms of
structural changes in the institution, not only the physical structure – more
secure prisons – but change in the structure of the organization. What may be
needed as well as change in structure is a change in the functioning that arises
from the rigid maladaptive cultural attitudes.

Nevertheless, there is within the limiting effects of a social defence system
a frustration that could be employed towards change – as well as towards the
freezing fear of it. Potentially, the frustration of a social defence system is the
energy for making changes and it counterbalances the *status quo* that comes
from fear of change which will inevitably, though unconsciously, undermine
the social system of psychological defences. To tip the balance towards change
it is necessary to understand the underlying anxieties and make new provision
for them, in some containing way.

Managing Change

In effecting change it is important to recognize, and then to apply a leverage
to, the unconscious psychodynamics that are revealed in this study. It is
necessary to intervene in the balance between frustration and the frightened
clinging to the defensive protection of the *status quo*. Whereas consciously it
makes sense to address the frustrating limitations of the social defence system;
unconsciously an alternative point of leverage is to address the anxieties
themselves which are protected against. This entails an institution, and specifically a management, that can allow staff to suffer their anxiety without
immediate relief; the pain of helplessness and the fear of violence need a
currency within the prison as much as brutality and competitive trickery. We
need consciously to forego technical tinkering with bits of the offender system
that avoid addressing the unconscious conflicts and suffering.

However, these conditions within a prison can only be partially met so long
as the wider social debate on the contradictions we demand from the prison
is neglected. Added increments of control and brutality demanded by political
expediency can only enhance the current extensive splitting of custody from
care. And in reaction to such political trends, sentimentalized demands for care
can only assist in extending and widening the split.

Acknowledgements

I want to thank Christopher Cordess for his consideration of this paper in draft form. There
are many people who have helped with the views that form a background to the paper
including, Isabel Menzies-Lyth, Elizabeth Spillius and Patrick Gallwey.

Exploring Shame in Special Settings
A Psychotherapeutic Study

James Gilligan

For the past twenty-five years, I have been able to engage in forensic psycho-therapy in two special 'maximum security' settings: prisons, and a forensic psychiatric hospital. My experience as Clinical Director of mental health services for the Massachusetts prison system, and Medical Director of the Massachusetts hospital for mentally disordered offenders at Bridgewater, has given me the opportunity to evaluate the comparative advantages and disad-vantages that those two different types of institutions offer for the practice of forensic psychotherapy (at least in our state); and to see if it might be possible, using those two settings as clinical 'laboratories,' to discover general principles about the causes and prevention of violent behaviour that could be applicable to violence wherever and in whatever form it occurs.

VIOLENCE, MYTH AND TRAGEDY

In order to understand the psychology of the violent men, and occasional women, whom I have encountered in those two settings, I have often found myself turning to mythic and tragic literature. Only the Greek tragedies and those of Shakespeare, the horrors described in Thucydides and the Bible, have

This chapter is an adaptation of the first of the two Erikson Lectures delivered by the author at Harvard University in 1991. A fuller exposition of the points made here can be found in the author's book, *Violence*, scheduled for publication in 1996 by the Putnam Publishing Group, New York; Weidenfeld and Nicolson, London; Mondadori Editore, Milan; Wilhelm Heyne Verlag, Munich; Bosch and Keuning, the Netherlands; and the China Times Publishing Co., Taipei.

seemed to me to map with fidelity the universe of human violence as I have seen it in the prisons and the prison mental hospital. It is only through thinking in terms of that literature that I have managed to find a way to mediate between ordinary sanity and humanity on the one hand, and unimaginable horror and monstrosity on the other. Compared to the tragedies I have seen and heard of on a daily basis, the abstractions of the 'social sciences' seem like pale imitations of reality, like the shadows on the wall of Plato's cave. In the worlds I have worked in, Oedipus is not a theory, or a 'complex'. I have *seen* Oedipus – a man who killed his father and then blinded himself, not on the stage and not in a textbook, but in real life. I have seen Medea – a woman who killed her own children in response to her husband's infatuation with another woman. I have seen Othello – a man who murdered his wife and then took his own life. I have seen Samson (the archetypal 'son of Sam'), and I have seen him many times – men who have brought the roof down on their own heads as the only means of expressing their boundless rage, when the whole world appeared to them as their enemy and they wanted to kill everyone, even, or perhaps especially, if it meant ending their own lives as well.

These experiences have led me to think that the classical myths and tragedies may have originated not so much as products of fantasy – as the symbolic, 'conscious' representation of fantasies that are unconscious in the minds of healthy people – but rather as attempts to describe and represent, to cope with and make sense of, indeed to survive, emotionally and mentally, the actual crimes and atrocities that people have inflicted on one another for as far back into history as our collective memories extend.

'In the beginning was the deed,' says Goethe, in *Faust*. He may well be right. In the violent men I have studied, the (violent) deed precedes the thought and the word. Much of the therapy we do with violent men consists of trying to facilitate their ability to think and talk about their thoughts and feelings before, and instead of, committing acts of impulsive, apparently 'senseless' violence. The blinding of Samson, Tiresias and the Cyclops, the blinding of Gloucester in *King Lear*, are not so much mythic 'fictions', as they are tragic depictions of real acts that real people commit in real life.

VIOLENCE AS RITUAL: THE SYMBOLISM OF VIOLENT BEHAVIOUR

I say that as a preface to my attempt to try to understand what could possibly have caused one particular act of violence that seemed to me to have pushed violence to the limit beyond which physical reality does not permit humans to go, just as it exemplifies the immemorial human propensity to push violence to the limit of what is physically possible. I am speaking of a 20-year-old man named Ross L, who was sentenced to prison because he had murdered a woman of his age, and in the process, also cut out her eyes and tongue (ostensibly so she could not identify him to the police if she lived).

His crime stood out for me not only for its brutality and its horror, for the extremest possible loss of that capacity for the most basic and normal human feelings that go to make up what we ordinarily mean when we speak of 'humanity' itself, that it seemed to represent; but also for its utter and total senselessness. If by some miracle she had lived, she still could have identified him, even without eyes or tongue, for she knew him. But in fact he had killed her, beyond any possibility of doubt, and dead men (and women) tell no tales; so why had he felt the need to add horror to horror by stabbing out her eyes and cutting her tongue apart as well? Doing this not only did not protect him from being discovered, it created even more evidence of his guilt for the murder. And of course murder itself is senseless and unnecessary; he did not 'have' to kill her in the first place. The only effect of his doing so (from the standpoint of his own 'rational self-interest') is that now he can look forward to spending the rest of his life in prison.

So why did he do what he did? His actions not only constituted the extremest possible violation of another person's humanity – they also seemed to me to represent a kind of individual version, in their irrationality and their violation of every canon of common sense and what we normally call self-interest, of the many collective atrocities which have occurred throughout the history of warfare and genocide; to pose a kind of parallel, on a microcosmic scale, to what those kinds of collective violence represent on a macrocosmic one. Those are among the reasons why the very extremity of both the violence and the irrationality contained in his crime seemed to me to imply the possibility that it might reveal, more clearly than a more limited or moderate act of violence could, the psychological forces that underlie all violence; so that if we could learn to understand the psycho-logic that underlay this man's crime, we might come upon factors common to all murders.

Only the importance of learning to understand what it is that causes people to behave in ways that are so inhuman, so that we can gain some better means of preventing such atrocities in the future, makes it possible to think further about this man and his motivation at all, or for such questioning to be more than an exercise in morbidity. But it is important to learn from the human beings who commit such crimes, and it is more important the more horrible the crimes. As Primo Levi wrote, referring to his descriptions of Auschwitz,

> 'It is neither easy nor agreeable to dredge this abyss of viciousness, and yet I think it must be done, because what could be perpetuated yesterday could be attempted again tomorrow, could overwhelm us and our children. One is tempted to turn away with a grimace and close one's mind: this is a temptation one must resist.' (Levi 1988, p.53)

When I began to ask myself what kind of person could have been capable of such atrocity, and what his real motivation could have been (for, as I have said, his ostensible purpose makes no sense at all), it occurred to me that his act had succeeded far beyond his purported intention: although the police caught him, the effect his crime had on the moral feelings of the people who then had to deal with him was that the sheer 'inhumanity' of his crime was so extreme that he had become to others barely, if at all, recognizable or identifiable as human, as a human being. It had become very difficult to see him as a person, in other words – his crime kept getting in the way, concealing him, so to speak. And it occurred to me that that elemental fact might be the first clue in my effort to understand what could have caused him to do what he did.

Reflecting further on this man, talking with him at more length, and seeing his utter absence of remorse or guilt feelings and his feeling not only of total innocence but of wounded innocence (despite the fact that he did not deny that he had committed the acts of which he was found guilty); his feeling that other people were treating him unfairly and picking on him and always had; his attribution to others of all responsibility for his problems; his feeling that all the justification he needed for his crime was that 'I didn't like the way she was looking at me' and 'I didn't want her talking about me'; his extreme sensitivity to insult; his boasting and grandiosity; his assumption that he was entitled to have special privileges; his reiterated threats that if he did not get what he wanted he would kill himself or us and that whatever he did would be our fault; his unwillingness to accept responsibility for anything that would make him 'look bad'; coupled with a repeated litany of complaints describing his constant, intolerable personal frustration and torment (all of which he attributed to his environment and the people in it, not to any inner conflict or dissatisfaction with himself), I began to realize that his crime makes all too much sense, when one grasps the special logic that lies behind it.

How can we go about learning to see what that logic is? I will start with Freud's insight that thoughts and fantasies are symbolic representations of actions, so that they can precede actions and serve as substitutes for them as well. But it is also true that actions are symbolic (pre-verbal) representations of thoughts. Thus, actions can precede and serve as substitutes for (conscious) thoughts. That is, if the behaviour is never interpreted or translated into words and ideas, actions can simply take the place of 'thinking' in terms of words.

The philosopher and literary critic Kenneth Burke (1966) wrote that in order to understand literature we must learn to interpret *Language as Symbolic Action*. I am suggesting that in order to understand violence we must reverse that procedure and learn to interpret *action as symbolic language* – with a 'symbolic logic', so to speak, of its own. Individuals or groups engaging in any given behaviour may or may not be able to state consciously what the meaning of their action is; or in other words, what thought the action can be described as having (in the medium of language). That is, they may not be able to translate a symbolic action, such as a ritual, into that other symbolic medium called language. Nevertheless, all behaviour is meaningful; all behaviour is the embodiment or enactment, the acting out, of a purpose or a wish; or, in a larger sense, of a wishful fantasy, a story, a personal or collective myth; a plot, scenario or narrative, and sometimes a dream, nightmare or delusion, that can also be expressed, by means of language, as a thought. (Actions also serve as a means of expressing the feelings associated with the thought, such as love or hate, sadness or fear, although again the symbolic medium is physical action rather than words.)

Freud taught us to see that people with disorders of character, whose psychopathology manifests itself in the form of abnormal, destructive, or life-threatening behaviour, act out in their behaviour the fantasies that normal and neurotic people experience only in their unconscious minds (such as in nightmares, or in the dreams of incest to which Plato refers). They can also be described as acting out the fantasies that psychotic people experience consciously in their delusions (which is one reason why it is appropriate to think of people with the most violence-producing character disorders as 'borderline' psychotic). To understand murder and the other forms of violent behaviour, then, we must learn to interpret that behaviour – that is, to translate its purpose or point of meaning into terms of words and thoughts – just as Freud began the process of learning how to interpret or translate or uncode the somatic symptoms of his hysterical patients as the symbolic speech by means of which they spoke through their bodies, so that the body itself, rather than language, became the medium of communication. It is time for us now to attempt to do the same with violence and to apply the same processes and principles to the understanding of violence as those that Freud also pioneered in the study of such non-verbal or non-logical modes of communication as compulsive behaviour, repetitive accidents, magical rituals, slips of the tongue, delusions, superstitions, myths, dreams, and so on.

In other words, to understand murder and the other forms of violence we must learn to understand what thought or fantasy the violent behaviour is the symbolic representation of, or the ritual enactment of; what it is 'saying', as that can be re-stated in words; and what unacceptable or threatening thought it represents the attempt, through the symbolism of action, to deny or ward off. Doing this is especially difficult in the case of many of the most violent people, because they are so oriented toward expressing their thoughts in the form of actions rather than words; in other words, their verbal inarticulateness prevents them from telling us in words what the thought is of which their behaviour was the symbolic expression.

But this task is important because regardless of whatever subjective, symbolic meaning violent behaviour has to the murderer, the objective consequence of it is not symbolic at all; it is all too literal and real. But it is also so senseless as to defy our efforts at comprehension through the usual means and the ordinary assumptions of rational thought, common sense and self-interest; and yet until we can learn to make sense of this senselessness, to comprehend this incomprehensible, how can we ever understand it? And if we cannot understand it, how can we ever prevent it? Understanding ultimately requires learning how to translate actions into words. My hope was that if we could learn to understand this one murder, then the same principles of interpretation could be applied to any given act of violence.

One clue as to what the thought was that was being expressed, or 'acted out', in this senseless and apparently unmotivated murder and mutilation, is that the more time I spent with Ross L, the clearer it became that his character – his habits and behaviour patterns, the moral value system in terms of which he justified his behaviour and goals – served as a defence against the threat of being treated with scorn and disrespect, of being perceived as a weakling, not a 'real man', someone who could be 'pushed around', laughed at, taken advantage of, and gossiped about. All of this suggested that he suffered from feelings of weakness, impotence, inferiority, and inadequacy as a man, and that as a result he might feel vulnerable and hyper-sensitive to any experience that would reflect that image of himself back to him. And as I talked with him further, he confirmed that he had indeed had such experiences, and he had indeed found them intolerable.

For example, before he reached puberty, he said, he was regularly beaten up and teased by other boys, who taunted him as 'a wimp, a punk, and a pussy'. 'Punk' is the derogatory homophobic prison slang term for the passive sex-object, or 'kid', of a more powerful man; and 'pussy' is, of course, the equally derogatory slang term for the female genitals. So he was being called an inadequate man, or non-man, in every possible way: as a wimp, he was a sissy, a Mr Milquetoast; as a punk, a homosexual; and as a pussy, not even male at all, but female.

When he was 13, however, he began drinking and taking street drugs (including cocaine), which he felt helped him to behave violently himself. That in turn bolstered his self-respect as a man. He boasted that he could rebuild the engine of any car within three hours. Mechanical expertise with cars was important to him, as it is to many teenage males, as a means of proving his adequacy as a man. But he committed his crime when he was without a car because he had been unable to pay the mechanic whom he had had to ask to rebuild its engine. The girl he murdered was a high school senior, a former classmate of his, to whom he had thus been forced to admit that he did not have either the money or the mechanical skills to have a car of his own, and upon whom he had had to depend for a ride on a cold night.

He also boasted of having become 'the Don Juan' of his hometown, a 'real stud' who had no trouble 'getting girls'. He claimed that he had not been hurt whenever he had been rejected by a girl, although he insisted that that had very seldom occurred. Despite this braggadocio, he was nevertheless sexually frustrated and unsuccessful enough to tell an acquaintance shortly before the crime that he wanted to get a woman, any woman, into a car, 'screw' her and then kill her and throw her out of the car. In the event, even raping proved to be beyond his abilities, so he 'only' killed and mutilated her. The task the police had in finding the murderer was made easier by the fact that he could not resist attempting to impress one of his acquaintances about how tough he was by boasting to him about the brutal crime he had just committed.

All of this suggests to me that the logic that underlay his murder and mutilation of another person was the emotional logic of the family of painful feelings called shame, humiliation, weakness, inferiority, incompetence, sexual and financial inadequacy – painful feelings which, when they become over-whelming because a person has no basis for self-respect, can be intolerable, and so devastating as to bring about the collapse of self-esteem and thus the death of the self. His behaviour, as we explore it further, can be seen as a desperate attempt – what could be more desperate? – to ward off these catastrophic experiences; and I will suggest that we cannot understand his grotesque crime without understanding the logic of shame.

We all know that shame motivates the wish for concealment, the wish not to be seen; the word itself comes from Old Germanic roots meaning to clothe or cover oneself[1] As Otto Frenichel (1945) put it '"I feel ashamed" means "I do not want to be *seen*."' (p.139) Darwin (1872) pointed out that 'Under a keen sense of shame there is a strong desire for concealment. ...An ashamed person can hardly endure to meet the gaze of those present...' (pp.320–21).

But Erik Erikson takes this common insight a step further, in a way that may help us to understand our murderer more deeply. 'Shame supposes,' Erikson (1963) says, 'that one is completely exposed and conscious of being looked at... One is visible and not ready to be visible; which is why we dream of shame as a situation in which we are stared at in a condition of incomplete dress... "with one's pants down." ...He who is ashamed would like to force the world not to look at him, not to notice his exposure. *He would like to destroy the eyes of the world*' (pp.252–53 emphasis added). Erikson quotes the folk song that the poet Carl Sandburg used to sing, about a murderer who is standing under the gallows waiting to be hanged, to illustrate this aspect of shame, and

---

1   Cf. the *Oxford English Dictionary*; Ernest Klein, *A Comprehensive Etymological Dictionary of the English Language*; Eric Partridge, *Origins: A Short Etymological Dictionary of the English Language* (1958); Carl Schneider, *Shame, Exposure and Privacy* (1977, pp.29–30).

the anger it stimulates toward the people in whose eyes one feels shamed (for one does feel shamed in other people's eyes):

> 'My name it is Sam Hall, it is Sam Hall,
> And I hate you one and all, one and all;
> *God damn your eyes!*'

All of which is less surprising when we reflect that, as Aristotle[2] realized long ago, '...we feel more shame about a thing if it is done openly, before all men's eyes. Hence the proverb, "*shame dwells in the eyes*"'. But not only the eyes – for as he also realized, we also feel more shame 'before those who are likely to tell everybody about you'; and since 'not telling others is as good as not believing you wrong', we can understand why preventing them from telling others about you, such as by preventing them from talking at all, is one of the oldest and most powerful ways of reducing one's risk of being shamed.

The psychoanalyst Leon Wurmser reached exactly the same conclusions more recently, when he wrote (1987) 'the eye is the organ of shame par excellence' (p.67). But not only the eye – for it is not only 'the punishing look, the scornful expression', but also 'the humiliating word, the derisive tone of voice and snickering, the rejecting gesture – ...sticking out the tongue – that signify shaming' (Wurmser 1981, p.79).[3]

The fear and anger and paranoia that shame provokes, and specifically toward eyes, is also captured in folk beliefs (and occasional individual delusions) about the 'Evil Eye' (Maloney 1976); although this anger can also, as in the case of this murderer, be directed toward the gossiping tongue that can repeat to others what the eye has seen.

I cannot see any way to understand or make sense of this man's mutilation of his victim, which is senseless from any rational standpoint, except by seeing it as the concrete, non-verbal expression of the following thought (which has the structure, like all unconscious thought, of magical thinking): 'If I destroy eyes I will destroy shame' – for one can only be shamed in the (evil) eyes of others. In other words, 'If I destroy eyes I cannot be shamed'; and 'if I destroy

---

2 '...*to en ophthalmois einai aido*', the eyes are the abode of shame. And, he added, 'For this reason we feel *most shame* before those who will always be with us and those who notice what we do, since in both cases *eyes are upon us*' (Aristotle, trans. and ed. Ross 1954). The proverb he refers to, '*aidos en ophthalmoisi gignetai teknon*', can be found in a fragment remaining from Euripides' lost play, *Cresphontes* (T.G.F. frag.457).

3 As long as shame is the operative emotion, these looks, this ridicule and gossip, are perceived as emanating from other people, who thus become the targets of the fear and rage that scorn and ridicule cause. It is only later, when people develop the capacity for feelings of guilt that, as Wurmser says, 'These physiognomic signs and signals may subsequently be duplicated metaphorically when the censor is introjected in the form of the "eye" and the "voice" of the conscience'.

tongues then I cannot be talked about, ridiculed or laughed at; my shamefulness cannot be revealed to others'.

Murder, in other words, is to behaviour what paranoia is to thought and hate is to feelings. That is, murder is the symbolic representation of a paranoid thought, but by means of actions rather than words, in people who are not necessarily delusional or psychotic, as those terms are conventionally defined. Violence toward others, then, can be seen as the behavioural equivalent of paranoia, or the behavioural version of it – its hypostasis, the translation into terms of physical reality of the waking dream (or nightmare) which paranoia represents in terms of words and thoughts.

But paranoia itself is simply the form of psychopathology that results when a person's ability to differentiate between feelings and facts is overwhelmed by feelings of shame, so that the feeling of being shamed is mistaken for a fact, and the individual develops the delusion that he is actually being shamed, or in other words, exposed and spied on and observed, held up to ridicule and scorn, criticism and scurrilous gossip. So we can also see murder, from the standpoint of the feelings that motivate or cause it, as the ultimate defence, the last resort, against being overwhelmed by shame and 'losing one's mind' by actually becoming paranoid – and experiencing, for example, such typical paranoid delusions as that one is being spied on, observed, hexed by an 'evil eye', gossiped about, ridiculed, accused of possessing such shame-provoking character traits as weakness, cowardice, impotence, homosexuality, sexual inadequacy, and so on.

People who are paranoid express these thoughts, and others of the same kind, in words; this murderer expressed the same thoughts (that he was vulnerable to being spied on and gossiped about as 'a wimp, a punk and a pussy', and that his victim would do those things to him if he did not take action to prevent her) not through the medium of words but through the medium of actions – the actions of destroying the eyes and tongue that could spy on him and gossip about him. The emotional logic that underlies this particular crime, then, which I called the logic of shame, takes the form of magical thinking that says, 'if I kill this person in this way, I will kill shame – I will be able to protect myself from being exposed and vulnerable to and potentially overwhelmed by the feeling of shame' (the 'objective correlative' of which consists of being observed and talked about).

My point here is not that violent people focus their hostility exclusively on eyes or tongues, for of course they do not.[4] Rather, I am attempting, by

---

4 For example, Samuel Edgerton (1985, p.132) mentions that in 1344 a man who insulted the City of Florence by kicking the Great Seal of the City with his muddy boot was sentenced by the Captain of Florence to have his foot cut off. In that case, the organ that committed the insult was the foot, so, according to the laws of what Freud called 'magical thinking', the shame could

analyzing a particularly extreme example of apparently unmotivated and irrational, senseless violence, to find symptoms that can serve as clues as to what is going on, and can help us to begin to make sense of the senseless so that we can improve our ability to prevent it. The fact that Ross L focused his attention and hostility on his victim's eyes and tongue is a valuable clue as to his corresponding preoccupation with, and morbid hypersensitivity to, the fear of being overwhelmed by shame and ridicule; and that at least suggests the plausibility of looking further to see if there is evidence that it might be that fear which ultimately motivated not only this particular murder, but all aggressive, apparently unprovoked violence. If Ross L is at all typical of other murderers, then we would have to conclude that the most dangerous men on earth are those who are afraid that they are wimps. Wars have been started for less.

THE SYMBOLISM OF SHAME AND VIOLENCE IN MYTH AND TRAGEDY

One clue that the emotional symbolism of this man's crime is not limited to him alone can be found in the frequent references to the violent destruction of eyes and tongues, in response to being shamed, in the Bible and Shakespeare. For example, what is the emotion (the motive) that leads Delilah to have Samson blinded? Of course, she and the other Philistines are already eager to avenge themselves on Samson for his past violence toward them; but why do they specifically want to blind him, as opposed to any of the many other ways they could have injured or even killed him once they were able to overpower him? Delilah tells us the answer to this question over and over again, uttering exactly the same reproach against Samson on three separate occasions (to make sure we don't miss the point?): 'Behold, thou hast mocked me' (in the King James version); or, as it is translated in the *New English Bible*: 'I see you have made a fool of me' (Judges 16.10, 13 and 15). To feel mocked, or made a fool of, is to feel shamed. The story teaches us that the most direct, literal and

---

be removed only by having the foot removed. Lest we imagine that we have evolved beyond such barbarism, it is worth remembering that within very recent decades, in both Denmark and many of the United States, the punishment for sex crimes (rape, incest, pedophilia), the essence of the offence in which is that they are among the most humiliating and shame-inducing acts a man can inflict on another person, consisted of castration; again, the offender is punished, or in other words, is humiliated himself, in the (sexual) organ with which he commits the (sexual) insult/assault. Thus, the shame of the rape victim is magically removed, by being transferred onto the rapist instead; the victim's shame, in this construction, can only be removed by having the rapist's penis removed, since his penis was the vehicle by which the victim was shamed.

'figurative' way to put an end to that feeling of shame is to blind the person in whose eyes one feels shamed – which of course is exactly what she does.

The Bible is full of images of eyes and tongues being plucked out or cut out in response to words or actions that expose someone to disrespect, insolence, haughtiness, boasting, or anything else that causes, or constitutes, shaming them. For example, what did the angels do to the men of Sodom who tried to rape (and thus dishonour) them? 'They smote the men that were at the door of the house with blindness' (*Genesis* 19.11). What happens to 'The eye that *mocketh* at his father, and *despiseth* to obey his mother [or, '*scorns* a mother's old age']'? 'The ravens of the valley pick it out, and the young eagles shall eat it' (*Proverbs* 30.17). The penalty for *mocking, despising* and *scorning* (three synonyms for '*shaming*') is to have one's eyes picked out and eaten. What happens to those who shame, insult or disrespect others by being proud and boastful toward them; who make fools of them by telling lies; who 'talk with smooth lip and double heart'? The Psalmist tells us that 'The Lord shall cut off all smooth [deceptive] lips, and the tongue that speaketh proud things [or 'talks to boastfully']' (Psalm 12). Similarly, the Psalmist prays to God, with reference to his enemies, 'Destroy, O Lord, and divide their tongues.' Why does the Palmist want God to destroy their tongues? 'Because of the voice of the enemy…: for they cast iniquity upon me [or 'they revile me,' or in other words, 'they denounce me with their abusive language']' (Psalm 55). The solution to the problem of being shamed verbally is written on the body: 'Destroy…and divide their tongues'.

Why there should be so much violence directed towards tongues and lips is less surprising when we read also how much destructive power is attributed to those organs. For example, we read in the Psalms, that 'Your slanderous tongue is sharp as a razor' (Psalm 52), we read of 'my persecutors…whose tongues are sharp swords' (Psalms 57), and so on.

This is, of course, poetry, not literal description. But what the poet does verbally, using one set of words and ideas as a symbol or metaphor for another, the violent person does literally and physically, using tongues and eyes as his symbol or metaphor for the same emotions and motives that the poet is speaking of – shame, pride, fear, hatred, and so on. It is precisely because the great poets have such an extraordinary ability to express, represent and evoke these emotions in words and, more specifically, in words that represent actions (such as cutting out eyes or tongues) which serve as 'objective correlatives' for these emotions, that we are able, with their help, to translate the actions of violent people into the words and ideas, emotions and motives, of which violent acts are the physical symbols.

Shakespeare, with his usual profound psychological insight, also understood that when people feel shamed by another person, when they feel inferior, envious, jealous, rejected, insulted, ridiculed or taunted, they feel an impulse to put out that person's eyes and tongue. For example, in *Antony and Cleopatra*, when a messenger exposes the Egyptian queen to feelings of shame and humiliation by informing her that her lover, Antony, has married another woman, Cleopatra attempts to diminish her feelings of shame by threatening to destroy the messenger's eyes: 'Hence, horrible villain, or I'll spurn ['kick'] thine eyes/Like balls before me' (II.v.63–64).

But these are only verbal threats. A much more gruesome scene appears in *King Lear*, when Edmund arranges to have his father, Gloucester, actually blinded. Why does Edmund do this? And especially, to his own father? Edmund explains his reason, quite explicitly: his father has shamed him; his father is the source of his feelings of shame. Gloucester has shamed Edmund by fathering him out of wedlock; Edmund is socially and legally a bastard. Edmund realizes that his bastardy constitutes, as he realizes the word itself implies, baseness and debasement; his father has made him base, of inferior or humble (humiliated) social and economic status, in a society that values 'legitimacy'. Shakespeare depicts Edmund's preoccupation with this theme:

> Why bastard? Wherefore base?
> When my dimensions are as well compact,
> My mind is generous, and my shape at true,
> As honest madam's issue? Why brand they us
> With base? with baseness? bastardy? base, base?
>
> (*King Lear*, I.2.6–10)

Furthermore, Gloucester has added shame by feeling ashamed of Edmund; that is, ashamed of having fathered a bastard. When Kent see Edmund with Gloucester and says 'Is not this your son, my lord?' Gloucester replies: 'His breeding, Sir, hath been at my charge: I have so often *blush'd* [i.e. *felt ashamed*] *to acknowledge him*, that now I am braz'd to't (I.i.8–11, emphasis added). Speaking of Edmund's bastardy, he says 'Do you smell a fault?', and adds 'yet...the whoreson must be acknowledg'd' (I.i.16–24). All this he says in front of Edmund – at the eventual cost of his eyes.

But eyes are not the only targets when people feel ashamed; tongues can be just as important. In *Troilus and Cressida*, for example, Ajax responds to the insults by which Thersites has been shaming him by threatening: '*I shall cut out your tongue*' (2.1.107). It appears that men who feel sufficiently shamed by another person's words (by their raillery, ridicule, gossip or slander) will be tempted to cut out that person's tongue, particularly if they do not feel articulate or witty enough to defend themselves adequately with words or non-violent actions of their own (which Ajax clearly does not). Verbal shame is the stimulus; cutting out the tongue is the expressive response. But it is also true that the man who already feels overwhelmed by shame (and that means, at the extreme, the paranoid person) does not have to be confronted by a Thersites in order to feel insulted and disrespected. The shame-driven person is quite capable of hearing shame – and may be incapable of hearing anything else – in even the most benign of words.

SHAME AND VIOLENCE IN AMERICAN PRISONS AND MENTAL HOSPITALS

If shaming people (i.e. insulting, ridiculing, and humiliating them) is such a powerful, and apparently universal, stimulus to violent behavior, then it is worth examining and reflecting on the practices that we as a society engage in in our prisons and mental hospitals, and asking whether we may be increasing the violence of the men sent to these institutions by subjecting them them to systematic and severe shaming.

It has been my observation that there is, for example, a particular kind of institutional ritual that is particularly well developed in the prisons of the United States, which constitutes what the sociologists Garfinkel (1956) and Goffman (1961) have called a 'successful degradation ceremony'. It is not called that by the prison authorities themselves, of course; they call it the 'booking', the process by which a new inmate is admitted (or initiated) into the world of the prison. I will describe some of the crucial features of this process, and relate it to the symbols we have just been discussing.

One of the most dramatic and central features of this 'total degradation ceremony' consists of stripping the inmate so that he is naked, in front of a group of officers, who then force him to bend over in an attitude of submission. He is then forced to spread the cheeks of his buttocks so that his anal orifice is completely exposed to the group. At that point one of the officers sticks a gloved finger into the man's anus – ostensibly to determine if the man is smuggling drugs into prison by secreting them there. I say 'ostensibly' because I know, from have talked with the superintendents of more than one prison in the past, that the whole admission ritual, including this part of the ceremony, is consciously and deliberately intended to terrify and humiliate the new inmate, by demonstrating to him the complete and total power the prison has over him, and to intimidate him into submitting absolutely to the institution and its officers. I should also emphasize, however, that that attitude is by no means universal among either superintendents or officers, and that many of them, quite appropriately, regard this ceremony as counterproductive and degrading to everyone involved, so that they refuse to permit or participate in such behaviour in their institutions.

What can one say about this practice? The symbolism is obvious: it is a kind of symbolic anal rape; it is a public humiliation; it is a total degradation ceremony; it is a massive assault on the manhood and the dignity of the new inmate. It is also a version of what ethologists call the 'presenting' ritual by which both animals and humans symbolize relations of dominance and submission. And it is a foretaste of the actual anal rapes to which many prison inmates will be subjected once they have been incarcerated among the others. With at least some inmates it achieves – in conjunction with the total incarceration experience – the intended aim of total degradation ceremonies, namely (as Garfinkel put it), the ritual destruction of the personality or manhood of the inmate, the death of his self, so that he becomes a 'non-person', a 'dead soul'.

But in addition to the above, it is worth remembering Freud's discovery that paranoia is precipitated by fears of homosexuality, so that whatever arouses, stimulates or intensifies those fears will only increase a person's level of paranoia. Being forced to strip naked in front of a group of other men, and having one's anus violated by one of them, could only increase the level of paranoia (i.e., fears of anal rape). I can only add that once one sees the intensity of the paranoia in prisons, and how that paranoia in turn stimulates the most extreme levels of violence among these already violent men, one understands why this admission ritual is absurdly and tragically counterproductive, if the purpose of sending a man to prison is to facilitate his becoming less violent. To put it another way, if the purpose of imprisonment were to socialize men to become as violent as possible – both while they are there, and after they return to the community – we could hardly find a more effective way to accomplish it, than through our present prison practices.

I do not mean that any one specific practice, this or any other, is 'the' cause of the violence these men commit, either in prison or on the outside. For most, they would not be in prison in the first place if they has not already committed some degree or other of anti-social behavior. But I am saying that certain practices stimulate these men's already existing potential for violence and their predisposition to engage in it, and only increase the likelihood that they will escalate their violence in the future to whatever is the maximum level for which they have the potential.

Needless to say, the attempt to alleviate the paranoia of these violent men by means of forensic psychotherapy, which is difficult, but nevertheless possible, under the best of circumstances, becomes much more difficult, if not impossible, as long as these and similar conditions continue. Or perhaps I should say rather that what is amazing is how possible it is to help some of these systematically degraded and brutalized individuals to become less paranoid and less violent, by means of psychotherapy that is sensitive to their need (a need they share with all of us) for pride, dignity, self-esteem, and self-respect – *despite* the conditions prevailing in most prisons in the United States!

In that regard, it is worth emphasizing that however inadequate the forensic psychiatric hospitals of the United States are as therapeutic facilities (and even the best of them, in my experience, leave an enormous amount to be desired), the best of them have at least established an atmosphere that is substantially more therapeutic, and more respectful of the dignity of those who are incarcerated in them, than the punitive and humiliating atmosphere that prevails in the world of the prison. The question that our American society seems not to have answered definitively yet is whether we are more interested in preventing future violence, by means of creating the conditions in which the psychopathology of these violent individuals can be effectively investigated, understood, and treated; or whether we prefer to indulge the impulse to get revenge on those who have violated the rights of others, regardless of the fact that that approach only stimulates further violence.

Consultation to the Institution

Jeannie Milligan

INTRODUCTION

Forensic psychotherapy staff confront, both consciously and unconsciously, particularly intense anxieties. Their patients by definition turn to action rather than thought, often unpredictably and frequently in an alarming fashion. As individuals, we use personal defences to help us bear the strain of the work, but we also need support for the roles we hold within our institutions, so that we can get on with our particular tasks effectively. However, just as our personal defences can become too rigid, so these potentially supportive organizational structures can turn into blocks or handicaps. These may be difficult to identify and work on from within the system, and hence when trouble is met or anticipated, an outside consultant may be employed to help. This chapter is based upon my observations and experience of working psychodynamically with forensic patients, and offering consultancy, at the Portman and Tavistock Clinics. Following the convention of the book, the consultant is designated as male. The term 'client' is used to denote the recipient of the consultancy service.

THE STUDY OF INSTITUTIONS

An institution is a structure, either temporary or permanent, organized to pursue a specific agreed aim. Responsibility is assigned, for those activities believed necessary in achieving this aim, to discrete roles. People considered suitable are then elected to take on those roles. Optimally, these people fulfil their tasks successfully, contributing to both the organization's aim and their personal satisfaction. However, much can interfere and undermine even the best arrangements, leading to inefficiency or failure.

The merits of understanding the complex dynamics of organizational life have been recognized since at least World War II. In particular, it became a subject of study by social scientists and by psychoanalysts. Some of the most acclaimed work is based on the application, in combination, of elements from both theoretical perspectives.

This approach makes particular reference to the powerful influence of unconscious processes on the execution of professional tasks as they are revealed in the subjective experience of the staff. Thus it lends itself well to application in institutions concerned with mental health problems, such as social work, probation, psychiatric and community services – what Miller calls 'people-processing institutions' (Miller 1993, pp.27–101). The scale and severity of emotional suffering which confronts staff often leave them feeling poorly equipped to help, or to deal with their own distress in response to the work. They are aware, too, of the expectations with which society invests them. The therapeutic task may be inextricably bound up with statutory requirements. Responsibility for this extremely worrying group of people is burdensome and, as Miller (1993) comments, when there is 'manifest mismatch between the needs and demands of the throughput, the pressure from the environment and the capacities of the staff to satisfy both constituencies', then 'powerful institutional defence mechanisms are necessary and inevitable'. He adds that 'such defences, like many drugs, only partly treat the ailment and also produce debilitating side effects' (p.97).

DISTINCTIVE FEATURES OF FORENSIC PSYCHOTHERAPY INSTITUTIONS

Since the pioneering study of hospital nurses by Menzies (1960), it has been recognized that defences against anxieties can be dysfunctional – and institutionalized – when confrontation with an intolerable amount of human pain is combined with an unmanageable sense of impotence to relieve it. It was noted then that levels of anxiety, and unconstructive defences against it, were directly in proportion to the degree of dependency arising between nurse and patient.

Forensic psychotherapy staff certainly face this phenomenon, but there are further complications added to it. The 'dependency' between patient and staff – and the associated ambivalence – are of a particular kind. For a start, the relationship may well be involuntary but even if it is not, the combination of being needed, and yet hated for being needed, is difficult. Staff inevitably re-evoke in their patients old fears, wishes, disappointments and rages which were unsatisfactorily resolved when directed against earlier dependency figures, especially the mother. Finding oneself to be the object of such intense feelings can drive staff towards 'going blank' to avoid discomfort. This shuts down on their emotional availability to patients. Such defensive manoeuvring may be counteracted if instead it is legitimate for staff to openly acknowledge feelings of uncertainty, fear or distaste. These experiences can then be considered as communications from patients about states of *their* inner world. Picking up disturbing emotional resonance gives staff the tools to help patients recognize it too.

It is this capacity to *think* which has not been previously available to patients when under extreme stress, and it is under those circumstances that they have tended to turn to *action* instead, when the build up of particular feelings has become unbearable. At the time of their offence, such patients might be described as being in the grip of particularly primitive feelings of which they are largely unconscious – for example, murderous hatred, overwhelming neediness, desperate humiliation, a terror of breakdown or death. It is, of course, all very well in theory for staff to know they will be targets for projection of these feelings. In practice, it may be hard to tolerate.

In the main, the plight of people who are physically or mentally ill engenders empathy for their pain in staff who are caring for them. This helps staff negotiate the less appealing aspects of the work. By comparison, the suffering of forensic patients confronts their carers with a most unpalatable kind of human frailty, that which leads to actively damaging others as well as the self. We would prefer not to recognize this potential for destruction in ourselves.

Thus, there is pressure amongst staff as well as patients to distance themselves from anxieties about underlying destructive impulses. Staff commonly find a means of avoiding this discomfort by retreating behind the defences readily available in their professional roles.

The result is a less coherent response to the needs of the patients on the one hand, and to the expectations of society on the other. The consultation model I describe focuses on:

(1) The ways in which staff are affected by, and contribute to, these defences.

(2) How this reflects the conflicts and pathology of the patients.

THE MODEL

As mentioned above, consultation of this kind makes use of two perspectives:

(1) Social Systems and Organizational Theory

An institution is seen as an open system. Rice (1969) describes how the survival of such a system depends on its exchange relationship with its environment. Terminology which Rice uses in the context of industry may be usefully applied to a forensic psychiatry setting, as when he states, 'Thus a manufacturing company imports raw materials, converts them and exports finished products (and waste)' (p.566). By analogy, 'helping services' attempt to engage offenders in therapeutic programmes. There will be some 'successes' leading to discharge, whilst some may need referral to alternative specialist provision. However, the behaviour of other offenders effectively excludes them and puts them in danger of being rejected as 'waste'.

Rice goes on to say that all transactions, even the intrapsychic transactions of the individual, have the characteristics of an intergroup process. As such, they involve multiple problems of boundary control of different task systems and different sentient systems and control of relations between task and sentient systems (p.580). It is these 'boundary control problems' which colour the inter-group dynamics of the institution and, thus, the way individuals perform their tasks. This has a direct effect on lines of accountability, the location of authority as distinct from power, and how choices are made about working practices. The principle tenet is that one part of the system should not be related to in isolation, but seen as part of the whole body.

(2) Ideas Drawn from Psychoanalysis about the Relationship between Anxiety and the Unconscious

Staff who work with psychological disturbance *consciously* recognize that it will be demanding and distressing, and may purposefully build into their organizational structures various means to address this, such as supervision or group meetings. It is more difficult to recognize ways in which good work is undermined by dynamics which operate *unconsciously* between different parts of the system, and between people in their various assigned roles.

In psychoanalytic psychotherapy, the transference and countertransference aspects of the relationship between therapist and patient are familiar and vital tools in understanding the nature of the patient's resistance and unconscious fears and desires. Similarly, in consulting to institutions, the experience in the here and now of communications (and blocks to them) between the consultant and the client gives a valuable clue to how the client responds to the underlying difficulties in the institution. Thus, while the consultant is not offering psychotherapy, he draws on theory and experience of such work with individuals and groups. As Halton (1994) describes, 'the psychoanalytically oriented consultant takes up a listening position on the boundary between conscious and unconscious meanings, and works simultaneously with problems at both levels. It may be some time before the consultant can pick up and make sense of these hidden references to issues of which the group itself is not aware' (p.12).

THEORETICAL REFERENCES

The model makes central use of Melanie Klein's ideas about the unconscious projection of unwanted feelings or parts of the self into another 'object' (Klein 1946). The intention may be simply to evacuate them, or it may be to locate them outside oneself so that they may there be attacked. Alternatively, the purpose may be to get certain feelings taken care of in a way that one feels one cannot do for oneself. To communicate something about the disturbing quality of these feelings carries with it the possibility that the other person may understand and even process them on one's behalf.

This links with the notions of reverie and containment as conceptualized by Bion (1962), referring to the way a mother optimally responds to her distressed baby. He describes an attentive state of mind in the mother which is receptive to unmanageable experiences of anxiety threatening the infant. If these frightening aspects can be allowed what Bion calls 'a sojourn in the psyche' of the mother, their painful and terrifying content may be modified. They are then more acceptable for the infant to receive back again. This therapeutic experience has a crucial role in enabling the infant to build up a repertoire of tolerance to otherwise overwhelming emotional states.

Another major contribution from the work of Bion is his description of the ways in which projective mechanisms operate within groups (Bion 1961a). He distinguishes between:

(1) 'Work group' functioning.

(2) 'Basic Assumption group' functioning.

When the first occurs, it is possible for the agreed tasks of the group to be constructively pursued. Different members of the group take up the various roles required according to their particular skills and position in the group. When the second type of functioning occurs, what Bion calls 'group mentality' operates. Group members become preoccupied with phantasies of a magical or omnipotent kind when they wish to avoid the painful effort required for seeking real solutions to real difficulties. Bion distinguishes three forms of this unconscious dynamic:

(i) Dependency – there is a belief shared by the group that they all depend on a particular person (often the leader) to meet their needs and wishes.

(ii) Flight/flight – there is a shared belief that a hostile force located outside the group must either be attacked or avoided.

(iii) Pairing – the group projects its hopes into the future that an as yet unknown person or event will produce the desired solution to the problem.

AIMS OF CONSULTATION

The focus is on the processes which occur in the organization as a whole, and on the particular parts being played by individuals or groups. Of course, personality traits do influence this, but it is not the consultant's job to engage with these. Rather, he provides the opportunity for the client to observe previously unrecognized processes, to identify which are 'anti-task' and to develop new ways of dealing with these.

In analogy with the function of psychotherapy for the patient, consultancy offers neutral ground away from the hurly-burly of work for staff to consider and articulate their experiences, including their – often secret – concerns and conflicts. Previously unrecognized difficulties will frequently reveal themselves as the consultant observes and describes the use (and misuse) the client makes of relationships with patients, colleagues and with the consultant himself in their meetings.

The 'neutrality' of consultancy aims to reduce the risk of the exercise being seen only as a means for the attribution of blame. To the extent to which the consultant is able to offer comments so that they can be accepted and digested by the client, the authority of the staff will be strengthened, not diminished. Rather, staff should be more or less free to collaborate with the consultant about what changes might constructively bring the pursuit of the primary task of the organization or sub-system back on line.

The general purposes of consultancy are:

(1) To identify dysfunction in the pursuit of the primary task of an individual role, sub-system, whole organization or collaborative enterprise between organizations.

(2) To examine how roles and functions become distorted or split off from others.

(3) To make that understanding available to the client in such a way that more effective methods of achieving shared aims may be developed, and that staff can manage their designated roles more autonomously.

Consultants may work singly, in couples or in teams. Intervention may be on a one-off basis for a short, defined period or designed as a long-term, semi-permanent support system. Consultation is commonly sought when an institution or a role-holder:

(1) Is facing change – whether defined negatively as imposed from outside or above, or viewed positively and actively sought from within.

(2) Feels paralysed in the achievement of an apparently desired change.

(3) Has experienced a crisis which is hard to understand and has disturbed the equilibrium.

APPLICATION

An 'essential user's guide' would include the following points. The consultant:

(1) is an external figure employed by the institution to undertake a specific task and is not more than a resource brought in for this purpose.

(2) should draw up a written contract at the start, clearly defining the aims and the terms (proposed length, frequency, fees and times). Lines of accountability should be clarified and support from the appropriate level of the hierarchy secured to reduce the risk that the project is undermined subsequently. Issues around confidentiality must be settled.

(3) should set aims for work which are realistic and not over-ambitious. This will mitigate the risk that he is heralded as the idealized saviour, or alienated as the hated critic, or defeated as the foolish dreamer of unattainable change.

(4) is an objective commentator offering working hypotheses based on his observations. He is not a teacher, or a manager, or a supervisor, though there may be pressure that he should behave like one of these at certain times.

(5) should hold a stance which is not didactic, but which encourages a 'work group' level of functioning while taking account of 'Basic Assumption' functioning when it occurs.

(6) should be aware not only of the projections directed towards him by the client, but any predisposition of his own to take them on.

(7) should report about the progress of the consultation to the appropriate level of the organization. If the consultation is long term, there should be regular reviews which properly feed back results to the original 'employer'. Actively involving those role holders serves as an important reminder that they hold the ultimate responsibility for the success or failure of the consultation project.

(8) should provide good evidence to senior management of why change is desirable if newly devised strategies are to be successfully implemented. Developments will be welcomed to the extent to which they are seen to benefit the system as a whole and not to undermine existing positions of power.

CONSULTATION AND FORENSIC PSYCHOTHERAPY

Forensic psychotherapy demands that special attention is paid to the relationship between:

(1) The internal, psychological world and

(2) the external, actual world.

The primary task is to help patients acquire understanding of the meaning of
their behaviour and to manage it better. Because these patients so frequently
take recourse to projective mechanisms, staff find themselves the recipients of
a bewildering range of unwelcome feelings, such as alarm, hostility, excitement
or profound depression. These are difficult experiences and there is always a
danger that staff will repeat this projective process and, as it were, pass the
feelings on elsewhere, in a state of denial as to their true impact. As previously
indicated, the risk is that important messages from the patient are overlooked.
Just as the aim of staff is to offer patients the means of metabolizing unbearable
feelings instead of expelling them, so in these circumstances the consultant
offers his client a model for working through painful realizations of what they
themselves are re-enacting.

I shall describe two examples to illustrate the application of this particular
model of consultancy, and the use it makes of the theoretical concepts referred
to above.

Vignette

Intra-organizational

A consultation was requested by staff at an outpatient psychiatric clinic
following a dangerous incident. The consultant was told that staff felt
variously angry, confused, guilty and frightened. They were aware that
something had gone badly wrong within the organization and wanted an
outsider's analysis to understand it. The story was as follows.

A female patient had been referred to the clinic for treatment. She had a
history of severe alcohol abuse, violent assault on lovers and had a year
previously thrown herself from a third storey window. Mr G, a senior
member of staff, assessed the patient, and considered her highly disturbed.
Nevertheless, he realized that because of this, she was unlikely to be offered
help anywhere else, and he thought she might benefit from 'supportive'
work. Ms X, who was newly appointed to the clinic, was asked to take on
the patient. Ms X was daunted by the challenge when she read the case
notes, but assumed that all staff were expected to undertake such patients
unquestioningly.

She began to see the patient weekly, and soon felt the relationship
became intense. It emerged that the patient's mother had abandoned the

family when the patient was one year old, and had re-entered her life ten years later, only to die two years subsequently. The patient had never talked to anyone about these traumatic separations, and appeared to value Ms X's help now in acknowledging how appallingly painful her early life had been. However, the more engaged the patient seemed to be with Ms X, the more often she became suddenly angry and dismissive. Ms X began to feel alarmed at this bizarre switch from good communication between them to extreme hostility and abuse. But, wondering about her anxiety, she imagined that other, more competent staff in the clinic would be untroubled by such a patient; perhaps she was making a fuss about nothing. So she put her anxiety down to inexperience rather than the possibility that there was good reason to be worried.

A holiday break was approaching and Ms X interpreted that this interruption to their contact might be upsetting for the patient. The patient said witheringly that she was looking forward to the free time to do much better things, and redoubled her criticisms. Ms X felt increasingly demoralized and began to look forward to having a break herself from this patient, who made her feel so inadequate. She felt guilty about this wish to escape and felt that it was not an admissible part of the professional neutrality she aspired to. So she pushed such thoughts out of her mind and soldiered on.

At the last appointment before the break, the patient arrived smelling of alcohol. She entered the room and immediately pushed Ms X over in her chair. She put her hands round Ms X's throat and shouted that she wanted to kill her. Fortunately, other staff were in earshot and intervened. The patient came to her senses, burst into tears and clung to Ms X, telling her she was the last person on earth she wanted to harm.

Everyone was shocked by this narrow escape from potential murder. Having gathered the facts, the consultant established which staff held what role in the overall task of providing treatment for this patient. He then met with Mr G, the assessor, Dr S, the clinic director and Ms X, the therapist. His hypothesis was that the links between these three roles had become disconnected. Meeting together allowed examination of the splits and their dangerous consequences.

In the discussion, the consultant observed that the issue of attributing blame felt present but all three staff avoided speaking about it. This implied a question about whether the assault was entirely the patient's fault. Had Ms X provoked or invited the attack? Should Mr G have refused to accept the patient in the first place, or worked with her himself? Had Dr S failed to ensure that Ms X was given adequate support? The phantasies about who had let down whom could be better understood when the consultant encouraged the three to talk openly about their experiences. His subsequent analysis of the dynamics was as follows.

The patient had clearly valued Ms X's skill in making sense of her distressed and her disturbed behaviour. The problem was that this very help put the patient in touch with her longing for the ever-present, all-giving helper/mother whom she had lost in childhood. Ms X then suddenly changed in the patient's experience and became a tormenting figure who reminded her of her painful deprivation. The patient found these contradictory experiences unbearable. Hence, at a conscious level, she could not be in touch with the fear, anger, or despair Mrs X suggested she might feel in the face of the impending break.

Instead, these feelings had been projected into Ms X, who initially *was* aware of feeling frightened, hopeless and upset to be so mistreated. However, she came to deny the strength of her countertransference response to the patient. She felt guilty about her powerful negative feelings, and kept 'secret' her wish to escape from parts of the patient's psyche she found repellent. She felt ashamed of her inexpertise and tried rather omnipotently to manage the situation alone instead of seeking help from colleagues. Thus she lost the opportunity to, for example, identify the patient's puzzling behaviour as a negative therapeutic reaction. Had she made such an interpretation, the patient might have felt better contained and the escalation might have been avoided. Mrs X had disabled herself from using her emotional responses as crucial indicators of the patient's state of mind. She had instead re-enacted the patient's tendency to deny or expel painful feelings.

This denial of the scale of the difficulties was mirrored in the systemic processes of the clinic itself. It emerged that Ms X was the least experienced member of staff. Yet there had been no appropriate anxiety about passing on to her a patient acknowledged as very difficult. Just as Ms X had convinced herself to view this frightening woman as 'any other patient', so the organization had considered Ms X as if she were like 'any other member of staff', overlooking her relative inexperience and, thereby, her extra vulnerability. Mr G was considered by his colleagues to be particularly skilled in making assessments. It was strange that, in this instance, he had failed to recognize the powerful impact this particular patient had. It emerged that he had felt touched by her plight, and guilty at the prospect of subjecting her to yet another rejection if he did not accept her for treatment. Nevertheless, her pathology was such that she was unlikely to benefit a great deal. He concluded that she did not merit the use of expensive senior staff expertise. Hence, the major problems in treating someone so disturbed became obscured, and then diminished. For example, it had been 'forgotten', until the consultant reminded the staff, that the patient had tried to kill herself by jumping out of a window. In addition, 'supportive' treatment had never been defined, so in reality no-one, including Ms X, knew what was being asked for.

It emerged that no new staff had joined the clinic for several years. The long-established existing group had grown used to its members working independently. There had been no need to question the effectiveness of this way of operating. However, when a system has become so familiar, there is bound to be resistance to change.

The arrival of Ms X challenged the status quo. For example, it raised the issue of diverting precious staff time to facilitate her development in the new post during the initial phase. Everyone was busy trying to meet the ever-increasing external demands on the clinic's resources. Dr S, who held overall responsibility for the functional life of the clinic and the deployment of its staff, was naturally preoccupied with these larger concerns. Thus, he 'overlooked' the need to make arrangements for the successful absorption of the new member, such as providing supervision.

The consultation helped the three staff concerned to understand the dynamics which had led to a dangerous incident. As a result, strategies were developed to minimize the risk of a re-occurrence. Regular supervision was arranged for Ms X. She resumed therapy with the patient, but stipulated that the session would be cancelled if the patient came having consumed alcohol. She changed the appointment time to the morning, and the room to one where other staff would always be at hand. Dr S set up a working party to re-examine policy on acceptance of patients, and to review provision for continued staff development.

Vignette

Inter-organizational

'Cover ups' and 'splits' in organizations can lead to one worker or one part of the institution being left holding all the anxiety, disconnected from, and unsupported by, other parts of the institution. In the last twenty years, there has been greater recognition of the dangers of splits that occur *between* institutions when they are collaborating in a joint enterprise. Some examples of this phenomenon have caused major public concern – for example, as exposed in the Cleveland Inquiry or the Orkney Report. The consultation model already described can be applied in these instances, with elaborations to take account of the greater systemic complexities: it offers some under-standing of how 'gaps' occur between organizations and why the use of projective mechanisms is resorted to.

Two organizations got into difficulties over their co-operative care of a seventeen-year-old boy. They sought help from a consultant who was told the following history.

The boy, Dave, was out for a walk in his village and met two thirteen-year-old girls whom he knew from school. The initial inconsequential exchanges between them turned into sexual banter. As the three of them became excited by this risqúe talk, Dave lured the girls into an abandoned hut. There, he drew a knife, threatened them and tried to rape them. After a struggle, the girls ran off and Dave was quickly arrested by the police. From the start, Dave admitted all charges brought against him and announced his intention to plead guilty. He was remanded in custody while awaiting trial. The psychiatrist preparing a report for the court was impressed by Dave and felt strongly that he could benefit from psychotherapy. This was confirmed by the psychotherapy clinic which assessed him, and it was hoped that he might be given the chance to address the 'out-of-the-blue' nature of his violent offence which Dave himself could not understand.

At this point, Dave's parents were seen by the probation officer preparing the social enquiry report. The parents referred to the incident as 'childish sexual exploration' and considered that, in any case, it was the girls' fault for leading on their son. They seemed incapable of recognizing the seriousness of Dave's behaviour. The effect of this minimization was so powerful that his mother successfully persuaded a judge in chambers to release the boy from custody on bail on the grounds that he did not like the food.

However, the trial judge was in no doubt as to the severity of Dave's offence. Dave was found guilty and he was admitted to a secure unit. The psychotherapy clinic offered Dave weekly treatment and much effort was made by staff there and at the secure unit to acquire the necessary Home Office approval and make complicated escort arrangements.

Knowing the dangers which so often arise when such institutions are not in good communication with each other, the clinic social worker, who held responsibility for inter-institutional liaison, recommended that regular meetings should be held between herself and Dave's key worker from the unit. The aim was that the two institutions responsible for Dave's care should maintain a link to support his treatment. While respecting the confidentiality of the psychotherapy, rather like two thoughtful parents, they would consider his general progress and address difficulties they encountered, either directly with him or between themselves. This was particularly important because Dave's real parents continued to be unconcerned, refusing to work with either the clinic or the unit. The professionals thought Dave's parents were letting him down drastically by failing to acknowledge the part of him that had committed a terrifying offence.

In addition, the staff recognized that, since psychotherapy is intended to stir things up, it can seem to those caring for the patient during the rest of the week to make their management task more difficult. Resentment and confusion then build up and they wanted to avoid this by regular discussions. However, Dave's behaviour was polite and deferential in the unit. Neither were there problems about his coming to psychotherapy – he was keen to come and settled to work readily. After several meetings, the key worker began to question whether, after all, they were really necessary in this case. Things were going smoothly, and attending meetings was an expensive use of staff time. The social worker emphasized the long-term value of their meetings, but the key worker began not attending them, always offering a plausible excuse. The workers became quite irritated with each other, each feeling that the other was messing them around and this led to even less communication. The situation drifted and, eventually, the social worker stopped making the arrangements.

Months went by, and the boy appeared to be a model resident in the unit. A request came from his parents for Dave to be given special leave to attend a family wedding. This was granted, albeit with a number of conditions attached about time and travel arrangements. Although the parents agreed to these conditions in advance, when the time came, they were blatantly disregarded. For example, Dave was returned to the unit two hours late, quite drunk, and having been driven by an unknown person rather than his father as specified. He was most upset about this, but because there were now no meetings between the two institutions, the incident was never presented for thoughtful examination.

The major summer holiday was approaching and Dave faced a long separation both from his psychotherapist, to whom by now he was very attached, and from the director of the secure unit, whose benign but firm authority he respected and frequently sought out. A week into this holiday, Dave was assisting a female member of staff in the store cupboard, a task she often asked him to do because he was so helpful and 'such a nice boy'. But on this occasion, he suddenly shut the door of the room, locked it and produced a knife which he had previously hidden. He menacingly told the woman to remove her shoes, which she, terrified, obediently did. He began to make sexual innuendoes, becoming more excited until the woman was able to gather her wits and tell him quietly but firmly that he had better put down the knife. Fortunately, Dave appeared to have been able to recognize and respond to a sensible authoritative, parental figure in his potential victim and stood aside while the woman unlocked the door and ran for safety.

The impact of this event on both institutions was profound. The analogy of the two parents now referred to acrimonious blame as to whose fault it was that their child should behave so horrendously. It was recognition of this breakdown in their collaboration which led to the appointment of a consultant to help them address the situation. The first question the consultant considered was why the agreement for joint meetings disintegrated. He wondered whether the arrangements had not been, or had not been *seen* to be, formally endorsed as important by the appropriate authority figures in the hierarchy of each institution. So he invited to the consultation meeting both the director of the secure unit and the psychiatrist who was 'case manager' for Dave in the psychotherapy clinic, to join the clinic social worker and Dave's key worker in the unit.

In the meeting, the secure unit staff conveyed their deep shock that the well-behaved boy they had believed Dave to be could turn into a senseless attacker. In their fright, they appeared to attribute the cause to his psychotherapy. The consultant suggested they wished to make the clinic responsible for the destructive aspects of Dave, which they, living with him on a daily basis, found too threatening and distasteful to bear in mind.

The psychotherapy clinic staff felt they were unrecognized for their efforts to help this boy come to terms with his primitive sadistic impulses. The consultant commented that their frustration had led them to withdraw from contact with the outside world into a position of isolation, focusing only on the internal world. Symbolically, the connection between these two worlds had been severed by the refusal of the two institutions to get together. Each had distanced itself from the other in order to retrieve some equilibrium in the face of the conflict in their relationship.

The consultant surmised that this split reflected the problem Dave himself had in relating the nature of his internal world to his external world of social relationships. The attitude of his parents offered him no help with this. He had been able to invest some hope in his psychotherapist and in the secure unit director. But when these two important authority figures were simultaneously absent, the pressure was too great and Dave feared he would be left alone at the mercy of his violent fantasies.

In abandoning their own agreed guidelines, the two institutions had come to behave like Dave's careless parents after the wedding. Now they, too, were letting him down by turning away from the uncomfortable recognition that the suffering, neglected boy who was doing so well in the eyes of both institutions was also a vicious sadist. Dave was provoked to remind everyone in a terrifying way that this was the case.

The staff were then able to acknowledge their guilt and regret about their inadequate attention. They were mobilized to re-establish regular joint meetings. The commitment to these reflected the return to proper levels of anxiety about Dave. It was underlined by the agreement of the clinic case manager and the unit director to attend.

CONCLUSION

In this chapter, I have described an approach to understanding particular pressures in forensic psychotherapy by reference to the powerful influence of unconscious processes on institutional systems and relationships.

The model is an application of the patient–therapist relationship. It addresses the dynamics which lead staff to re-enact psychically conflicts from their patient's internal world.

The risk of this occurring is inevitable because of the nature of the work. Awareness of the danger allows for more appropriate therapeutic responses to be developed.

Research

An Overview

Chris Evans, Jo-anne Carlyle & Bridget Dolan

INTRODUCTION

In an ideal world this chapter would review a large number of publications that would form a coherent body of forensic psychotherapy research. However, we believe that we do not yet live in that ideal world. We believe that the way forward is for forensic psychotherapists to consider the parentage of their discipline and to look anew at the variety of research methods open to it. Finally, we believe it is essential for forensic psychotherapists to think critically about the practicality of different methods and, in the light of applying their clinical wisdom, for them to research their own practice. We will attempt to explore these challenges to clinicians, in approximately that order.

WHAT'S IN A NAME?

For the purposes of this chapter we will define 'forensic psychotherapy' by the word 'psychotherapy' and by its clients. 'Forensic' psychotherapy clients are not only mentally disordered offenders, that is people found to have broken criminal laws, but also people who offend society less formally, whether by serious self-harm, by antisocial behaviours that may not be technically illegal, or through threats to break the law (by omission or commission). Definition by clientèle distances forensic psychotherapy research from general psychotherapy research since, at least in this country, paradigmatic forensic psychotherapy patients are probably 'sex offenders' and patients defined as 'psychopathically disordered' in the terms of the Mental Health Act of 1983. These are radically different from the undergraduates with minor neurotic problems and the depressed patients who form the paradigm client groups of general psychotherapy research. The difference is not only in the severity of the problems but also in criteria. Forensic psychotherapy patients are often defined by criminological or behavioural issues rather than by psychiatric, psychological or psychotherapeutic nosology: thus sex offenders are defined behaviourally and legally and even the concept of 'psychopathically disordered' within forensic psychiatry is a legal, not a psychiatric or psychological definition.

Just as the clients vary, so too psychotherapy is a broad church embracing a range of therapies based on communication between people (not restricted to verbal communication). However, for this chapter, we will limit our field to *psychoanalytically derived* 'talking cures'. We have chosen this focus because of our own sympathies and because the choice will highlight particular issues that can often be sidestepped in other theoretical models. There has been much criticism levelled at psychoanalytically-oriented treatment of offenders in the past – either because Freud's revised theory of childhood sexuality may have exacerbated societal blindness toward sexual offending against children (see e.g. Lerman 1988); or because of claims against the effectiveness of the therapy itself. These latter claims are interesting as it is not clear that there is more research support for other forensic psychotherapies than psychodynamic. It is also interesting as many psychodynamic psychotherapists argue, on the basis of their clinical experience and reading, that forensic patients' resistance to comprehensive and lasting change is generally proof against other psychotherapies. It would be good to see such claims and counterclaims resting in a unified framework for research. Behavioural and cognitive schools have undoubtedly contributed to our understanding of forensic patients and these approaches often have a part to play in treating individual patients at particular times. However, we have much sympathy for the strong psychodynamic position but are very well aware that claims on the basis of clinical wisdom and reading entirely within one theoretical tradition are not sufficient to convince practitioners of other schools, funding bodies, the arbiters in the criminal justice system, the public, nor forensic patients themselves. We hope that clinicians reading this chapter will feel challenged to consider how research methods might help them qualify and strengthen their claims. Although we will focus on psychodynamic methods, we believe that most of what follows will also apply to behavioural, cognitive, humanistic, and other forms of forensic psychotherapy.

Our definition has exposed the issue of definition by the clientèle. It also exposes the issues of intellectual ancestry.

The Inheritance from *Forensic*

'Forensic psychotherapy' is in no way a new discipline. It has a long history beginning with Freud himself. Although Freud's first work was on neuroses and hysteria, he very rapidly drew on the forensic arena, particularly for major developments in his metapsychology – the man who developed the talking cure was one of the first to recognize the difficulty of treating offenders and people with perversions; he was also among the first to appreciate just how clearly such work provides theoretical insights (S. Freud, 1910a, 1924). So two very early aspects of this history were that forensic psychotherapy is both difficult, often limited in impact, and also that it can expose theoretical issues with unusual clarity. Despite this early and promising start 'forensic psychotherapy' is only just beginning to emerge from its latency stage, as shown by the other work in this volume.

One aspect of 'forensic' which Freud did not develop much, although it was implicit in his concepts of the superego and in much of his anthropological writings, is that 'forensic' work usually involves a third party (society) in the therapy. This is in contrast to most psychotherapies which largely confine themselves to understanding of the patient and the therapist alone. This extension of the research field has many both practical and theoretical implications which we will address throughout the chapter.

The Inheritance from *Research*

Just as forensic psychotherapy has developed out of the traditions of psychoanalysis, so too forensic psychotherapy research draws on traditions of research. Questions of immediate parentage introduce the body of general psychotherapy research. However, it would appear that forensic psychotherapy research is something of a foundling. To play with this idea in a gendered manner, the absent father is general psychotherapy research as that discipline has often eschewed clinical let alone forensic clientèle, preferring to use the more malleable and experimentally controllable psychology undergraduate subjects. The absent mother is forensic psychotherapy itself as this has, symmetrically, often eschewed formal research methods.

However, the gendering of our putative parentage touches on the much more general question: 'hard' versus 'soft' science. Perhaps this is an issue of grandparentage or tribe: whether to ally our 'research' methods with those of the humanities; the almost religiously venerated natural sciences; or their hybrid progeny, the human or social sciences. This again has implications for the immediate relationship with general psychotherapy research but it also has major implications for the prestige of the new arena. General psychotherapy research has great respect for work deriving from the experimental tradition and has thereby commanded some respect. There *is* a tradition within general psychotherapy research which has leant more on humanities traditions but this has been largely confined to 'psychotherapy process research' (see below). This has, in line with most academic hierarchies in the second half of the twentieth century, tended to win less prestige than psychotherapy 'outcome' research. The latter has been strongly dominated by methods of the natural sciences: random allocation, placebo control comparison and group summary measures. The pressure to conduct forensic psychotherapy research within this latter paradigm will be stronger now, being driven not only by academic dominance of the natural science tradition, but also by the growing pressures for 'outcome' and even 'cost-benefit' studies to justify continued clinical funding.

It is no secret that these aspects of the natural science paradigm are radically different from the dominant traditions of most psychotherapies, particularly that of psychoanalysis. Psychoanalysis and formal aspects of psychotherapy trainings have generally espoused non-numerical descriptive data, leaning very heavily on discussions of observational data from treatment of individuals. The idea that the psychotherapies are not strongly aligned with natural science methods will be so familiar to most readers that their only surprise may be that we do not regard those methods as the only ones to be graced with the label of 'research'. In fact we will argue that there are many problems for the application of experimentalist methods to forensic patients and settings. Furthermore, attempting to use these methods can often push the research process inexorably into a posture antagonistic to psychodynamic clinical methods and theories. We will spend some time in this chapter exploring the possible structures offered in the experimentalist tradition as it is important to understand when and how these can be applied meaningfully. More prosaically, it is important to recognize the utility of, and to promote general psychotherapy research methods in the forensic area. Amongst other benefits, recognition of this overlap with general psychotherapy helps to counter the sense of isolation that often afflicts the forensic psychotherapy practitioner and researcher.

WHY DO FORENSIC PSYCHOTHERAPY RESEARCH AT ALL?

The role of *all* psychotherapy research must be to increase understanding of the mechanisms of change. In a determinist model, forensic psychotherapy research would involve monitoring all the moment by moment events of the therapeutic encounter together with simultaneous measurement of changes in the thinking, feeling and behaviour of the patient(s) and therapist(s). This would involve attention to the context of the patient, therapist, session, patient's family, institutional setting, and so forth. Of course psychotherapy research cannot capture even the overt behavioural components of all these elements for even one therapy. Furthermore, it cannot monitor in full the information that passes between patient and therapist at unconscious levels. Fortunately there is some clear evidence from the natural sciences and mathematics that such a determinist ideal is often unhelpful since it is unattainable. It *is* clear that psychotherapy research can begin to draw out observable and reportable patterns in therapies. Although it is recognized that the sheer complexity of the process means that we must select, and so, inevitably, diminish the therapeutic encounter.

At present we know so little about the mechanisms of change in forensic psychotherapy that it could be argued that we should only attempt exploratory 'pure' research. However, the distinction between pure and applied research is murky precisely because of the prescientific state of our knowledge. When most of the limited clinical services that do operate are publically funded, there is an obligation to provide research to explore at least the efficacy of the therapy process and to provide some summary measures of outcome. Just as political pressure from funding bodies could push the field toward premature outcome research, it is equally important that personal faith in practice should not push clinicians into ostrich-like opposition to all empirical exploration of therapy. Concentration solely upon outcome would be analogous to drug companies doing only formal, pre-licensing, clinical trials on all compounds they consider rather than winnowing possibilities through initial animal studies. At the same time we must accept that there is a need for both pure *and* applied research to be carried out by as many practitioners as possible in order that the public or third party funding should not rest on charismatic, professional, historical or magical grounds. All psychotherapies are at times construed as luxury goods and in the current political and economic climate there is an acute need for research to justify continued funding of clinical services, let alone the support of innovative work. The emotional pressures of these battles are never more charged than for forensic psychotherapy because of its almost total dependence on funding which so often comes from sceptical third parties who may have greater enthusiasm for moral panic, incarceration and retribution than for therapeutic work and understanding.

Despite the charged field, there is scope for clinician researchers to examine processes of change, to audit individual outcomes and to overview group summary outcome data. If this research is done well it can be done without loss of either integrity or credibility. Without minimizing the difficulties of doing such research in a 'good enough' way, it is also important to emphasize that it is not necessary for it to be 'perfect' (we would wish to challenge the idea that any psychotherapy research, perhaps any human sciences research could ever be 'perfect'). The recent saga of the threat to close the therapeutic community service for severe personality disorders at the Henderson Hospital may be an example of the way that various imperfect research projects can help political campaigns to prevent closure of a service.

Have We Hybrid Vigour? Is There a Comely Body of Forensic Psychotherapy Research?

By contrast with forensic psychotherapy research, forensic psychotherapy is an emerging discipline coming to form a whole comprised of sufficiently important parts that one can argue it has shaped the development of all psychodynamic theory. However, the existing pieces of 'forensic psychotherapy research' do not yet seem to constitute a vital whole. Like forensic psychotherapy, forensic psychotherapy research will develop through application of differing methodologies in a range of settings. However, review of the literature convinced us that it does not yet present a 'body' onto which new studies can be grafted to flesh out a comely overall form. This chapter will not attempt to draw together existing works to create the illusion of such a body. The heritage issues discussed have militated against the rapid development of a *deus ex machina*. In the rest of the chapter we will sketch out the diversity of research methods needed and give readers some tools to criticize constructively both existing work and their own ideas. Having established the scope of the area, we will explore the possible difficulties that may be encountered and offer ideas that may help people strengthen their chances of completing research. Our next step is to sketch out a skeleton for forensic psychotherapy research onto which studies can be hung.

HOW SHOULD THE AS YET UNLOVELY FRANKENSTEIN BODY OF FORENSIC PSYCHOTHERAPY RESEARCH BEST BE JOINTED?

A flexible skeleton will be developed by classification of research approaches. Our skeleton will finally take the form of two tables but invokes a number of distinctions that need to be thought about carefully. We have already touched on distinctions between process and outcome research and between pure and applied research and we have noted that general psychotherapy research takes a number of forms, not all distorted into the Procrustean bed of empiricism and experimentalism. For general psychotherapy we have suggested that there have been two dominant forms: the in-depth case analyses paradigmatic to psychoanalysis; and numerical empirical work rooted in the natural sciences. In general psychotherapy this dichotomy is often expressed as a contrast between case reports and 'research'; within general psychotherapy research, it is also sometimes expressed as a process/outcome dichotomy or as a qualitative/quantitative dichotomy.

In what follows we will draw very heavily on the natural science traditions of experimentation and of nomothetic, quantitative empiricism. We recognize that this paradigm can often push research, apparently inexorably, away from tenets central to both humanist and analytic traditions of psychotherapy.

However, we ask the worried reader to bear with us as an extensive exploration of the paradigm is the best way to appreciate not only its strengths, but also its limitations. Many of the dangers to humanist and analytical psychotherapies in the paradigm follow failure to appreciate that its pure form is simply inapplicable to psychotherapy. This leads to continuing protests that pure empirical defenses of forensic psychotherapy in the classical scientific tradition are not forthcoming. The other main class of threats from the paradigm arise from its misapplications or from misinterpretations of its results. By exploring the skeleton in detail we will present a classification of research approaches which we hope will counter polarization for or against research, and may also counter polarization for or against particular research methods.

Qualitative and Quantitative Methods

Some of the distinctions we will make to joint our proposed skeleton seem clear and unambiguous but others fall in grey areas. For example, the distinction between qualitative and quantitative appears clear until we have to decide where to place the joint. This revolves around whether any counting or numbers turns a project from qualitative to quantitative or whether it needs more than the introduction of numbers: a shift from studying a single individual to comparing across people, the assumption that some scaling is applicable to more than one individual. We have used an 'idiographic/nomothetic' distinction to capture this latter issue of whether concepts are considered unique to individuals (idiographic) or applicable across various people. Hence we will use the rather concrete definition that qualitative methods are those which do not employ numerical scales or counting. However, even that definition should probably be regarded as a dimension, a choice or intention of the researcher. This is clear as any qualitative description or event can in principle be made susceptible to counting or rating. For example, the data of the transcribed Adult Attachment Interview (AAI) (Main[1] 1991) are clearly qualitative but become quantitative if converted to an attachment classification used to describe the proportions of patients having different classifications in a particular psychotherapy sample.

At the most qualitative end, discourse analytic research methods might be seen either as joining the use of countertransference as a research tool in all clinical work or as matching the more cognitive monitoring of Glasser's 'core-complex' when that may be used as a clinical tool in regulating the distance between patient and therapist.

---

1 The AAI is a clinical style interview from which classifications of attachment style are determined. Interview transcripts are scored by trained raters (who have attained a high level of reliability in classifying transcripts).

Is There Such a Thing as Pure Descriptive Research?

After the distinction between quantitative and qualitative methods, perhaps the next contrast is that between pure descriptive work and comparative or correlational work.

Many qualitative research studies and case reports in the psychoanalytic tradition are criticized as 'purely descriptive'. Well, why not? Descriptive research is what it says: a description of a set of events. We have defined idiographic, qualitative descriptive research as analysis of non-numerical data strictly for descriptive purposes (since the idiographic qualifier implies that the findings are thought to be specific to the individual). Examples include simple narrative data, as employed in most case studies, or the use of transcriptions of the text of sessions. Quantitative descriptive research is any that employs numerical data, such as simple epidemiological description of forensic psycho-therapy clientèle in a particular setting, or work that enumerates certain events in therapy. Descriptive research serves a number of functions: to define the scope of the research area; to identify a range of questions that may then be explored further through comparative, correlational or true experimental methods; and to provide numerical parameters. These parameters particularly concern the homogeneity of a group, which may then indicate the sample sizes that are needed to gain greater precision in estimation or to move to compara-tive work which can provide usable answers to specific questions.

As with any other form of research, primary descriptive research can be subjected to meta-analysis in which results from a number of simple descriptive studies are pooled and explored to give increased precision over their individual descriptive estimates. Another possibility is to collate descriptive studies to use them for comparative or correlational meta-analyses. For example, one could use existing American and British descriptive reports to consider the question of whether American forensic psychotherapy samples are more often penal (than psychiatric) than British samples. This raises the issue of the implicit comparisons that almost always underpin people's usage of descriptive data: depression ratings of a highly specific sample of patients may constitute an overtly *descriptive* piece of research, but it becomes an implicitly *comparative* piece of research when it is read in terms of difference from an implied 'normal' sample. This latter sample may never have been formally collected, but is considered well known to the readership. Typical examples are instinctive comparisons with 'the patients *I* see' or 'people like me' or perhaps 'normal people (like me)'. Such comparisons are implicitly comparative or correlational.

Experimentation Versus Observation and Explanation Versus Understanding

There is often held to be a moral or aesthetic hierarchy of research, or of 'science', in which experimentation is the acme of perfection. Experimental control extends comparison or correlational analysis beyond its observational forms. The fundamental characteristics of experimental research, as opposed to the various forms of observational research, are that some components of the research situation are kept under tight control so that they are essentially invariate and thus unlikely to 'effect' any changes or differences. At the same time, one or more other aspects of the situation are varied deliberately by the researcher. If the deliberate variation is randomly allocated, then any association between values of that variable and other measures is either the result of chance sampling fluctuations or some explanatory relationship between the variables. Statistical hypothesis testing methods can make it possible to say how likely chance sampling variation was to have produced effects as big or bigger than those seen. In conventional inferential statistics, if this probability is lower than some preassigned probability value (generally 1 in 20, i.e. $p \leq 0.05$), then the null hypothesis (that the variables are unrelated) is rejected and the alternative hypothesis (that the experimental variable *is* systematically related to the other variables) is accepted. The strength of these designs and their congruence with inferential statistics, is that they provide 'explanations'. Experiments in the real world, particularly the real world of forensic psychotherapy research, are never so clean as this and rarely offer unequivocal guidance in the choice of explanations. However, the elegance and clarity of the strict experimental method is clear.

By contrast with experimental methods, observational methods, even when they reveal very strong associations between variables, always allow the possibility of many different explanations for the association. This arises as many extraneous or intervening variables which were neither controlled, nor manipulated, may have 'explained' the observed associations between variables. Glasser (1994)[2] argues that this preserves 'meaning' in research and others argue that a terminology of 'understandings' is more appropriate than a terminology of 'explanations' (Cooper and Cooper 1985; Graham 1967; Hill 1982). Many psychotherapists feel more comfortable with this terminology while others are adamant that an explanatory terminology is central to interpretation even if the grounds on which explanations have been derived are not those of experimentation. This distinction is often linked with the

---

2 One of the very few articles in the psychoanalytic forensic literature that describes in detail a research methodology.

separation between the natural sciences (seen to be rooted in experimentation, control, prediction and explanation) and the human or social sciences (rooted in observation and interpretation or understanding). However, the link is not as strong as it seems as many phenomena in the natural sciences are also beyond experimental control (consider astronomy). The real distinction between the natural and human sciences lies more in the practical separation of researcher and researched in the former. This separation enormously simplifies experimental manipulation where it is possible. This also leads to a mathematical exactness of the language expressed as an algebra of predictions and explanations. This in turn makes it possible to apply William of Occam's celebrated principle (Occam's razor): that the best theoretical explanation is that which invokes the smallest number of concepts for the same fit to the observed data or for the same internal coherence. Of course, many twentieth century natural sciences have themselves abandoned strong reductionist or positivist epistemologies; for example, this is true of particle physics, relativity physics, and many areas of mathematics since the work of people such as Church, Turing and Gödel. Although we believe that these developments call into question the strict separation of experimental and other research, experimental methods still undoubtedly have great advantages of clarity.

The philosophy of experimentation is so strongly linked with measurement and numbers that we are aware of no truly qualitative research based on experimentally manipulated situations. Most qualitative work is done in an hermeneutic tradition which is fiercely antipathetic to experimentation. Hence the cells G to I in Table 2 are actually empty in our experience to date. However, the inclusion of a qualitative data collection and analysis arm to most experimental studies in psychotherapy research would reap benefits. The nearest we know to date is a qualitative reflection on the process of doing research into biological problems (McFadyen and Altschuler 1990) although two reports from traditional general psychotherapy research studies are pertinent (Firth, Shapiro and Parry 1986; Parry, Shapiro and Firth 1986b).

Repeated Measures and Time as a Variable in the Model

Time is a very specific variable. Most of us accept that we live, for any practical purposes, in a world in which time is irreversible (at least in our conscious worlds). The distinction above between observational and experimental comparison and correlation actually turns on this irreversibility and the the ordering of random allocation of the experimentally controlled variable *preceding* measurement of the dependent or predicted variable in time. Since psychotherapy concerns the possibilities of change it too is deeply interested in the time dimension. It can be argued that any research which does not involve repeated measurements within an individual (or individuals: $n > 1'$) is of no use to psychotherapists since it cannot empirically address the possibility of change. This is a significant issue as group comparisons and cross-sectional data are sometimes interpreted or reported as evidence about change. However, the irreversible nature of time means that such studies are generally considered to have lesser power to address change question than studies involving repeated measures data.

As with so many contrasts we are discussing, the issue is not trivial. There is, of course, the vexed question of whether historical data collected at the same time as some current descriptor can form the basis for imputing a temporal relationship: the paradigm example is when data are collected about current psychopathology and about childhood histories and the relations between these variables *in a number of different people* are used to describe a correlation between childhood experiences and some adult state or trait. Such studies generally, but not always, show statistically significant positive correlations between negative childhood experiences and adult psychopathology. Of course such a study is vulnerable to all sorts of selection biases and the historical data may or may not be good quality. Self-report historical data is generally regarded as lower in quality than self-report about the present and lower than recorded historical reports. Hence a study with the above design which used original school reports for the information about the past is often regarded as providing a real time line on the data. Whatever the case of the quality of the data, it is clear that such studies have limited power to answer questions about whether a different childhood history would have had different adult consequences.

Whatever the practicalities, the assumptions of continuity and irreversibility of time do imply very different status to repeated and simultaneous data. A corollary is that time is often not treated as a variable amenable to exactly the same analyses as any other continuous variable: correlating depression against session number in a one year therapy is not like correlating depression with a working alliance measure over the same period precisely because the time measure can only go up, and only by one session at a time, whereas the working alliance measure can move in either direction and by any amount. There are statistical corollaries that turn on the difference between simple statistical correlation methods and 'time series analysis' methods but enough has been said about the special nature of time and repeated measures for the purposes of this chapter.

The Trade off Between Number of Objects, Breadth of, and Repeated Nature of, Data: Single Case ($n = 1$), $n > 1$ and Group Comparison Studies

The question of repeated measures is almost always linked practically with the number of variables measured and the number of independent objects on which data is collected. This follows from the rather obvious restrictions on our ability to generalize from a single datum about a single person at a single instant. These limitations mean that $n = 1$ studies will involve multiple descriptors. Many descriptors all in the one instant may be of interest as they may tell us that something is possible that we had previously considered impossible: the finding that a single person was simultaneously showing strong evidence of being in the paranoid-schizoid and in the depressive position would raise questions about the Kleinian theory of their complementary relationship. The example is, of course, absurd; a prosaic example might be the simultaneous observation of a weight of 4 stone (56lb, 25.4kg.) and a height of 6' 6" (1.98m.): this would raise rather more concern about that single person than a weight of 6st. 6lb. (90lb, 40.8kg.) and a height of 4' (1.22m.) even if it doesn't perhaps reshape our conceptual world.

Of course, if the descriptors about the person create a time line we can see them as creating a pattern of information about change, and interest in the data and our likely scope to generalize from it starts to increase. Data collected in a single psychiatric or psychodynamic assessment interview will contain at least two time lines (recalled history and current time in the sequence of conversation in the interview) turning them into multiple data on which observational relationships and sequences can emerge. Where data are collected from one person repeatedly over time they can be considered either as a purely descriptive study or else as a correlational study of the relation between the measure(s) and time, subject to the cautions noted above. Such studies are close to the classical methods of data collection in psychodynamic psychotherapy. Such data are also the meat of many types of qualitative research in which the relationships between data are explored purely linguistically.

At the other extreme from these 'repeated measures' data, the classical paradigm of much research has involved measurement of only one datum in each of a large number of people who are subdivided into groups. Such data collection, particularly when combined with experimental allocation to the groups, allows for tests of group differences. Intermediate between $n = 1$ repeated measures data and single measure, group comparison studies, are various studies involving $n > 1$ and repeated measures. The classic example is of 'cross-over' experimental studies which are sometimes possible in drug research into reversible drug effects on chronic conditions. The essential requirement of such studies is that it be plausible or even demonstrable that the effect of the first treatment ceases or has reached a plateau before the second treatment starts. While this may be plausible for the effect of a short term anxiolytic drug in chronic anxiety, it is difficult if not impossible to impose such designs convincingly on longer term or open-term dynamic psychotherapies. One attempt to do so was made by Shapiro and colleagues (Firth *et al.* 1986; Parry, Shapiro and Firth 1986a; Shapiro and Shapiro 1987) in a study utilizing a crossover design for exploratory (dynamic) and prescriptive (cognitive behavioural) psychotherapy for anxious or depressed white collar workers. This study served as a pilot for a much larger project and the methodology was abandoned for the second study.

The restrictions that group comparisons cannot address change, and that crossover trials are often difficult or impossible, taken with the similarity of $n = 1$ studies to clinical practice, would seem to suggest that $n = 1$, repeated measures designs should become the standard for psychotherapy research. Unfortunately, there is a problem here too which is that such designs do not lend themselves to experimental methods. This is less the case for cognitive and behavioural therapies than for dynamic therapies but 'multiple baseline' methods can be difficult to interpret even for those modalities.

The other crucial problem with $n = 1$ studies is that of generalization: if you find a certain profile over time, or a certain relationship between two variables over time in one patient what guarantee do you have that this can be generalized to another patient? By contrast, although group comparison methods without repeated measures may lack the attention to time and to individuality so central to psychodynamic theory, they do at least show up the level of interpersonal variation. So, although there is a logistic penalty in workload, these problems make multiple $n = 1$ studies or studies in which a number of patients are observed repeatedly over time the optimum for psychotherapy research. Until recently the logistic problem of workload and the change from the normal clinical focus were compounded by the problem that we did not have really adequate statistical methods for the proper handling of interpersonal and intrapersonal differences in multiple $n = 1$, repeated measures designs. That deficit has been corrected at least for statistical zealots (see below) by the development of hierarchical linear models (Bryk and Raudenbush 1987; Prosser, Rasbash and Goldstein 1991; Woodhouse, Rasbash, Goldstein and Yang 1992) and random regression coefficient models (Gibbons *et al.* 1993; Gibbons, Hedeker, Waternaux and Davis 1988) but it will be some time before these become widely and easily available in statistical packages and longer before a general readership could be expected to understand them without lengthy methodological explanation.

Generalizability, Extrapolation and Statistical Method

Discussion of the number of subjects in studies has already raised the question of generalization from study data to other subjects such as the patient you are going to see tomorrow. Psychodynamic psychotherapists vary in the extent to which they believe that a mechanistic model of internal structure or stored internal object relations is ubiquitous and in how much they believe this enables things to be generalized or extrapolated from one case to another. The central intention of experimental, and some observational, statistical methodology is to put generalization on a firm footing by drawing the research samples from random sampling of a defined population. Sample parameters can then be extrapolated to the population(s) from which the samples were taken with mathematically determinable precision of estimation ('confidence intervals') to test the plausibility of a given model of the population (the essence of statistical 'tests' or 'the frequentist sampling method of statistical inference' to give it its formal title). However, we know enough about the human psyche and we have enough respect for elementary ethical limits, to determine that people form anything but a definable population from which random samples can be constituted for most questions of interest to us. Hence the entire formal basis of generalization in experimentation is removed in all but the most psycho-therapeutically trivial of human subject research. Despite this, it is common-place to apply the methods of frequentist sampling statistics to comment on data from non-random samples in observational studies. This practice is only justified on the ground that it may be less prone to subjective bias and abuse than the available alternatives or guesswork and speculation. A stronger basis for generalization and extrapolation in research with human subjects is repli-cation in individuals or samples known to be *different* from the original in order that vulnerability of the results to known sample (and implicit population) differences can be explored.

Reviews of replicability across studies have tended to use an informal and subjective process and publication of such reviews has tended to be guided by the prestige of the author. However, as noted briefly already, assessment of generalizability across replications can be done systematically by methods known as 'meta-analyses'. In these reports, the results of a number of similar studies whose differences in method, treatment or sample are known, are subjected to quantitative comparisons to see how consistent the results are or how they appear to vary systematically with the parameters of the studies (observational, comparative or correlational research into other researches). Unfortunately, meta-analytic reports really cannot extract information that is not in the original studies and can do only a very little to extract better quality information from a collection of studies whose methods were poor. A number of meta-analytic studies, coming out both for and against, psychodynamic psychotherapies have spawned much discussion in literature in general psycho-therapy research and the time may be ripe for yet another of these (Barker, Funk and Kent-Houston 1988; Eysenck 1992; Jones, Cumming and Horowitz 1988; Shadish and Sweeney 1991; Shapiro and Shapiro 1977; Smith and Glass 1977; Telch 1981). However, forensic psychotherapy research is hardly at a stage at which formal meta-analysis of its ill-assorted limbs is possible. We are at the stage at which new researchers could learn from the experiences of the general psychotherapy research world in order to ensure that the primary studies will at least employ reasonable methods. We are also at the stage at which all researchers should understand the importance of including very careful description of how the sample was recruited, the setting, and as much descriptive information about the diversity of the sample as possible so that meta-analyses *will* be possible as the body of published studies expands.

Precision of Estimation, Statistical Power for Hypothesis Testing and n

As noted above, formal sampling at random from large populations of equiva-lent members underwrites traditional statistical hypothesis testing methods. It is important to explore these issues a little further as misinterpretation of 'non-significant' statistical findings is one of the misguided ways psychother-apy is criticized.

As noted above, in the sampling method of statistics, the probability of getting results as extreme as or more extreme than those seen in the sample is calculated from a model of random association and, if the probability is lower than a previously chosen criterion, typically 0.05, this is taken as an indication to reject that model and accept some alternative hypothesis that a systematic effect was in operation and caused the data to be as they were. Unfortunately, this method has been used to such an extent that it has become a sociosyntonic piece of overvalued, or frankly delusional thinking. This is not only because most of the requirements for the logic of the calculation are generally violated, but perhaps more important because the method is generally interpreted as a symmetrical one in which $p < 0.05$ *disproves* the null hypothesis supporting the alternative, so $p > 0.05$ disproves the alternative hypothesis supporting the null. This is just not true. Consider a study in which four people are given psychotherapy and four people are not, all are followed up for ten years to see if they relapse, two relapse in each group so $p > 0.05$. Surely no one would believe that this *disproves* the alternative hypothesis that psychotherapy given to some larger group can change the probability of relapse? Now what if the samples sizes were forty each and twenty relapse in each group? What about four hundred each with two hundred relapses per group? As you increase the sample size the 'statistical power' of the study increases. That is to say the the probability of rejecting the null model and accepting that therapy has some effect is increased. For the three examples given above, the power if psychotherapy given to very large numbers reduces the relapse rate from 50 per cent to 40 per cent has gone from 0.09 through 0.24 to 0.91. That is, the very large total sample ($n = 800$) gave a 91 per cent chance of finding a statistically significant result given a realistic and interesting effect of some therapy. Notice that not even this sample size, logistically almost impossible, actually gives the same probability of finding a significant result given a real difference as the 95% probability of finding a non-significant result if there really is no difference in relapse rate between psychotherapy and the comparison group. This illustrates the nonsense of treating non-significant results as *disproving* any systematic effects. Non-significant results should never be quoted without an estimate of the statistical power the study had to have found a realistically interesting result. It is essential to understand that if these methods are used, the sample size required to have a good chance of detecting a realistic advantage to psychotherapy is often large, sometimes logistically impossible. See (Ford *et al.* 1990) for a worked example of such a calculation based on a real exploratory study.

Table 1. Quantitative research designs

Research type	Measure(s) involved	Sample		
		$n = 1$ generally can be repeated measures over time	$n > 1$ with repeated measures on each individual over time	$n > 1$ not involving repeated measures over time
Pure descriptive	Categorical measure (counts and proportions)	1) Repeated classifications over time in one person counting proportions of classifications or of transitions.	2) Repeated classification of a number of people over time describing proportions or transitions.	3) Classification of a number of people each on only one occasion to give proportions by classification.
	Continuous measure (distributions, often summarised by location e.g. mean and spread e.g. s.d.)	4) Repeated rating of one or more variables in one person over time to give time profile.	5) Repeated ratings on each of a number of people to give profiles over time.	6) Ratings of a number of people each on only one occasion to give distribution of ratings.

Non-experiment al relational (comparative or correlational)	Categorical-categorical (*Chi squared and log-linear models*)	7) Counting occurrences of two or more variables in one person over time to find if there is any association between occurrence of one event and another.	8) Counting two or more variables in more than one person each observed repeatedly over time to find possible associations between occurrences.	9) Classifications of a number of people each classified only once on two or more variables to find possible associations between those variables.
	Continuous-categorical (*ANOVA and non-parametric equivalents*)	10) Repeated classificatory and rating measurements on one person over time to find association between the category and the rating (if any).	11) As for (10) but in more than one person to find any associations (which might be different in different people).	12) Measurement of a continuous variable once in each of a number of people from two or more groups to see if it is consistently different between the groups.
	Continuous-continuous (*Correlation and regression methods*)	13) Two continuous measurements from the same person taken repeatedly to see if they covary (move in a way that is apparently related).	14) Investigating relationship(s) between two or more continuous measures taken repeatedly on a number of patients.	15) Measurement of two or more continuous variables in a number of people each measured only once to see if there are associations beween variables.
Experimental relational (comparative or correlational)	Categorical-categorical (*Chi squared and log linear models*)	16) As for (7) but randomly allocating or determining at least one categorical variable.	17) As for (8) but randomly allocating or determining at least one categorical variable .	18) As for (9) but randomly allocating or determining at least one categorical variable.
	Continuous-categorical (*ANOVA and non-parametric equivalents*)	19) As for (10) but randomly allocating category (typically) or continuous variable (rare).	20) As for (11) but randomly allocating category (typically) or continuous variable (rare).	21) As for (12) but randomly allocating category (typically) or continuous variable (rare).
	Continuous-continuous (*Correlation and regression methods*)	22) As for (13) but randomly allocating one variable (rare).	23) As for (14) but randomly allocating one variable (rare).	24) As for (15) but randomly allocating one variable (rare).

WHAT SORT OF RESEARCH?

Table 1 gives a breakdown of research methods applicable to numerical
(quantitative) data. Examples relating to each box are then given. Although
many of these distinctions are not applicable to qualitative data the broad
pattern of rows and columns remains (see Table 2).

Table 2. Matrix of qualitative research designs

Research type	Measure(s) involved	Sample $n = 1$ (can be repeated measures over time)	$n > 1$ with repeated measures on each individual over time	$n > 1$ not involving repeated measures over time
Pure descriptive	Categorical	A) Description of one person (usually involving some indication of change or stability over time).	B) Descriptions of more than one person with temporal perspective.	C) Descriptions of a number of people not considered in terms of membership of subgroups.
Non-experimental relational	Categorical-categorical	D) Description of one person focussing on relationship(s) between two or more aspects over time.	E) Descriptions of a number of people focussing on relationship(s) between two or more aspects over time.	F) Descriptions of a number of people from two or more subgroups each described at only one point in time to explore subgroup differences.
Experimental relational	Categorical-categorical	G) Description of one person on some aspect(s) after (randomly) allocating them to different levels of some other aspect (rare).	H) Description of a number of people on some aspect(s) after (randomly) allocating them to different levels of some other aspect (rare).	I) Description of a number of people each at only one point in time and in two or more subgroups to which they have been (randomly) assigned (rare).

EXAMPLES OF DESCRIPTIVE FORENSIC PSYCHOTHERAPY RESEARCH (NUMBERS REFER TO BOXES OF TABLE 1)

(1) *Whether or not a patient refers to people abusing him or to his abusing other people (or neither or both) against session number.* This might be used to show a transition from: predominantly describing being abused; possibly through transitional periods of talking about both being abused and abusing; to a phase concentrating on his abusive index offences; to a period in which abuse was not a major issue; and a final phase in which transference experiences of the therapist's abuse of the patient was discussed. Improvements in this design might include rating the proportions of sessions in these modes, rating the intensity and nature of affects associated with them, noting therapist interventions, and so forth. A considerably more interesting design might be to see how often therapist attempts to focus on the relationship in the session were followed by each of these patterns, but that would move the design from descriptive to correlational (to box 7).

(2) *Psychotherapy assessment of the number of instances of splitting (assuming some rating of this that could be shown to have reasonable inter-observer reliability) present in a group of patients in standard interviews on admission and discharge from hospital.* It is arguable that the implied comparison between admission and discharge will involve a comparison and move this into box 8 but it could also be argued that the two interviews are likely to be different for so many reasons that it is only the descriptive data on the patterns of proportions and change that are of interest, not any comparison.

(3) *Use of an experimental Rorschach card that is seen to be associated with feminine archetypes, with 50 sexual offenders to determine the proportion who refuse to respond to the card.* Interpretation of such data will probably involve formal or informal comparisons with 'normative' or other clinical data.

(4) *Repeated measurement of a personal questionnaire item (e.g. 'My urge to shoplift is high after arguments') during psychotherapy for shoplifting.* As for box 1 it is immediately possible to see how any number of extensions to this basic design, all of which will involve correlations with other things, for example rating of tension with partner, might move this to a correlational issue belonging in box 13.

(5) *Repeated ratings of depression for a number of offender patients over the course of one year psychodynamic psychotherapy.* One might expect to find certain patterns, perhaps a rise then a fall in depression as defences were exposed and altered. The use of a number of patients

would provide some indication of the generality thus giving some more information from a nomothetic perspective than the equivalent study of one patient (box 4).

(6) *Empathy ratings for a number of offender patients at initial assessment.* Such simple descriptive data might be useful when deciding whether the empathy measure appeared likely to pick up variation across the client group and might therefore be useful in a comparative or correlational study either across subjects (box 12 and 15) or within a subject (boxes 10 and 13) or within a number of different subjects (boxes 11 and 14).

COMPARATIVE AND CORRELATIONAL RESEARCH

These approaches move research to overt examination of the relationships between variables. This subtable has often been rather strictly divided between approaches that compare different groups on continuous measures and those which look at correlations between continuous variables (with the former being linked with experimental methods). In line with this, the occasions when societal or natural processes provide comparative groups are often referred to as 'natural experiments' or 'quasi-experiments'. This polarization between group comparisons and correlations is almost entirely artificial. The element of experimental control is missing so causal interpretations of any of these boxes are dubious. Random sampling from populations is almost always missing as well, so application of sampling statistical methods, although common and arguably a useful corrective to wild speculation if done sensibly, cannot be interpreted in the formal ways that it can in true experiments.

EXAMPLES OF COMPARATIVE AND CORRELATIONAL FORENSIC PSYCHOTHERAPY RESEARCH (NUMBERS REFER TO CELLS OF TABLE 1)

(7) *The sessions of one sex offender undergoing weekly psychodynamic psychotherapy are recorded and rated. The therapists interventions are classified as interpretations or 'other', the next block of material (e.g. a speaking turn) from the patient are classified as 'rich information' or 'guarded/poor information' by a separate rater. Are interpretations more often followed by 'rich information' from patient than non-interpretative interventions?* This would raise a number of questions about the reliability of the classifications used and about the definition of a 'block' of material but it should be possible to establish reliable definitions (much qualitative research would probably be involved in that process). If so, the answer to the question is amenable to

time series analysis and probably would be expected to show a significant and strong association if the intention of interpretation is to make new material available to patient and therapist.

(8) *Numbers of spontaneous references to mother and spontaneous references to father are recorded for the each ten minute period of every session in the therapy described in (7) above and for nine other sex offender patients in other similar therapies with the same therapist.* This would allow relationships between the references to the parents to be discovered. Relationships with phase of the session and with session number could also be explored and the use of more than one patient allows some check on the generality of findings (although the number of patients is sufficiently small to make only simple descriptions of homogeneity or diversity sensible as estimation of generalizability from $n = 10$ is very low).

(9) *Projective tests with a categorical classification were given to a large sample of adolescents to see if any categories prospectively identified a subgroup of future offenders (see e.g. Lie 1994).* The prospective design of such a study eliminates selection and biased recall artefacts that would contaminate case-control retrospective designs. A very large number of adolescents would need to be tested to have high statistical power to detect relationships between test and future offending. The critical issue is the number who *do* end up offending so studies like this often concentrate on populations at risk, trading generality for statistical power. It is also important to recognize that there will be a group of offenders who escape conviction and so are 'wrongly' classified if the intention is to use the study to work out a target group for preventive interventions to minimize offending. Such problems are endemic and inescapable and their severity should be estimated by comparing the actual offending rates in the study group with published data about the likely prevalence of the offence in the population. 'Sensitivity' simulations can explore the impact of likely underestimation of offending on extrapolations from the study. Such problems should never be either dismissed or simply used to pour scorn on the utility of studies!

(10) *Ratings are made of the strength of the working alliance as a weekly psychotherapy proceeds and the sessions are classified as: 'on time' / 'late start' / 'left early' / 'didn't attend'. Time series methods are used to see if the working alliance in one session is systematically related to the category of the next.* A large number of sessions will be necessary to have much statistical power in this study and a number of complexities are hidden in the categories used but strong associations would give some support for the use of the working alliance measure.

(11) *The study described in (10) above is repeated for fifteen patients.* The extension to fifteen patients will strengthen the statistical power to detect weak associations if appropriate statistical methods are used and the sample of patients will provide some indication of the likely variety in associations.

(12) *The first ten sessions of therapy are used to rate working alliance for each of 40 patients classified as having a dissmissive attachment pattern on the Adult Attachment Interview (AAI), 40 patients classified as preoccupied/entangled and 40 patients classified as secure.* This is a classical group comparison design. Not finding a statistically significant effect might raise a few eyebrows but the power for a total *n* of 120 may not be all that high (it will depend on the reliability and variance in the working alliance ratings and on the strength of difference you expect to find between the groups). Remember how long it will take to get 120 patients through this study, even if you are only giving 15 session therapies. Will it be possible to get 40 forensic patients with secure classifications? You may wish to drop this group given this reservation but the contrast between that group and the other two may be the strongest effect you predict so that might lose you your best chance to find the effect you predict. Such are the choices you face if you consider statistical power seriously, so it is easy to see why it's widely ignored.

(13) *Proportion of a session rated to have been spent in the paranoid-schizoid position in Kleinian terms (%PS) compared with independent ratings of patient's level of sadness (PSad) immediately before and after the session by independent ward based observers. Carried out on each of the 24 sessions of a short-term psychodynamic therapy with a sex offender patient on a locked unit.* This would be a crude test of the rather crass hypothesis that observed sadness relates to being in the Kleinian depressive position and that it ought therefore to be negatively correlated with being in the PS position. This would only hold if you think that the shifts between positions take long enough for the ratings before and after the session to link with the rating of the internal object relationships from the session material.

(14) *As for (13) above but for fifteen patients rather than the one.* Here again the increase in numbers will test the replicability of the finding but provide only very weak estimation of the likely variation in a much larger number of sex offender patients.

(15) *Ratings of %PS and PSad are made for a single, standardized psychodynamic assessment interview for all of 50 patients on admissions to the unit described in (13) above.* This appears to address exactly the same issue as (13)

and (14) but note that although the result of this study will tell you something about the relationship between the two variables *across* people, it will tell you nothing about the psychodynamically interesting question of whether there is a dynamic relationship between these two things in any one individual over time. Only the two studies in boxes (13) and (14) can start to do that but this sort of study, which is commonly carried out by non-clinical researchers, is often misinterpreted as telling us something about psychodynamic variation over time. Clearly we need studies from the first and second columns of our table to do that. However, it is an unfortunate fact that the statistical methods appropriate for analysis of those first two columns definitely require support from, and early consultation with, statisticians if the results are to be analyzed correctly.

EXPERIMENTAL RESEARCH

As noted above, experimental research is the most rigorous and 'scientific' end of the research options shown in our table. This approach seeks to test hypotheses by manipulation of variables. This is generally difficult as full observation and control of all pertinent variables is complex. In research on human beings it is impossible to have *full* control over all parameters and even control of the main parameters of interest is often impossible. This is particularly true in psychotherapy research where the ethical implications of not offering an intervention thought to be helpful are great. In psychotherapy research there are, however, some questions for which experimental manipulation could be ethical, particularly questions for which strong bodies of belief do not currently exist or where the effects of *not* doing something may be tolerable in proportion to the value of the information to be gained from the research. These include: observations of changes in attachment patterns following specific psychotherapy interventions; changes in victim empathy following interventions; increases in therapist confidence and/or competence with supervision; and so forth. Despite these possibilities, the reader can see that many questions of great interest simply cannot be addressed if experimental control is considered a *sine qua non* for research.

EXAMPLES OF EXPERIMENTAL FORENSIC PSYCHOTHERAPY RESEARCH (NUMBERS REFER TO TABLE 1)

(16) *Random allocation of either a male or a female escort to take patient from ward to psychodynamic psychotherapy session (allocation not known by therapist and escort not seen by him or her). Related to whether or not the*

patient discussed sexual perversion in the session. It is difficult to see this proposed experiment as testing anything central to the theoretical basis of dynamic psychotherapy but if there were significant results it might be interesting to consider their implications for integrated working on wards. Also, there might be systemic ripples in response to knowledge of the experiment which might supply very interesting and important information for qualitative analysis.

(17) *Random allocation of cases supervised by twelve trainee psychotherapists to either group or individual supervision so that each therapist sees twenty patients, ten in group supervision and ten in individual supervision. Relating form of supervision to incidents on the wards after sessions.* This is an interesting study design as views of the relative benefits of group and individual supervision vary considerably and as they clearly carry different costs. The power to detect anything but a very large effect in this study would be very small and the study is still very large in relation to the personnel levels required so it would almost certainly have to be a multi-centre study.

(18) *Random allocation of sixty patients to ten sessions each of short term dynamic psychotherapy so that thirty patients receive therapy on the ward and thirty receive therapy off the ward. Relationship to early termination.* Again power to detect anything but large differences will be small and it might be better if numbers and severity of incidents could be used as some sort of continuous dependent measure or if the time element of the ten sessions could be reintroduced into the design. (Moving it toward boxes (21) or (17) respectively).

(19) *As in box (16), randomly allocating male or female escort but now relating this to rated proportion of the session spent in discussion of female objects.* The power to detect a relationship between this continuous measure and gender of the escort will be stronger than to detect a relationship with the dichotomous dependent measure of whether or not the patient discussed sexual perversion (box (16)) but the relationship might be seen as of lesser interest.

(20) *As in box (17), random allocation of forms of supervision (or perhaps presence or absence of any supervision) but looking at relationship with therapist ratings of stress in the therapy.* The intentions behind the experiment might need to be concealed from the therapists, if that were considered ethical, in order that any result will not be seen as simply an expression of the therapists' views on the supportiveness of supervision. This issue of 'expectancy effects' plagues issues of ethical consent. We felt it might be more acceptable for there to be some dishonesty in the explanation of an experiment to therapists,

given eventual disclosure and genuine options to discontinue, than it would have been to have comparable dishonesty in seeking consent from patients.

(21) *As in box (18), random allocation to on or off ward therapy but here related to rated depth of working alliance in the sessions (averaged over a number of sessions or perhaps based on just one session).* If a number of sessions are rated, reintroduction of the time element would move the design to box (20) but would probably provide much more interesting information as it would say something about the dynamic time course of the alliance. It might be that the early alliance is deeper in on ward therapy but that the late alliance is much deeper in off ward therapy. Such 'interaction' of the time and group effect cannot be detected if time is not analyzed.

(22) to (24) *Random allocation of therapist lateness against rated working alliance in, respectively, one therapist with one patient; many therapists and/or many patients again for a number of sessions; many therapists and/or many patients but only intervening on the fourth session for each therapy.* It seems to us difficult to imagine any feasible forensic psychotherapy research based on these boxes, so the designs we have suggested are deliberately unethical (in our eyes). Of course, without such studies, or perhaps more sophisticated ones in which the qualities of the material in the sessions is analyzed in relation to the randomized lateness, psychodynamic ideas about the symbolic importance of the boundary of the session and exploration of any therapist lateness will remain speculative in the eyes of strict experimentalists. Even in the natural sciences, where it may be quite feasible to allocate things to random values of continuous variables, for example allocating a steel bar to a series of randomly chosen temperatures while measuring its length, these methods are rare. These cells are included here for completeness but also to underline that it is the use of controlled allocation that separates experimental methods from observational ones, not the distinction between correlation and group comparison methods.

KEY ELEMENTS IN FORENSIC PSYCHOTHERAPY RESEARCH IN THE LIGHT OF OUR CLASSIFICATION

As noted there is currently little research on forensic psychotherapy and much of what does exist is outcome research based either on the outcome variable(s) of attitude change or else on recidivism. This brings us immediately to two of the important problems for forensic psychotherapy outcome research. First, the choice of a good outcome measure – attitude change, although obviously desirable, is not necessarily related to problem resolution. Similarly, the use of recidivism as an outcome measure, while at first sight very appealing, is notoriously unreliable (some of the reasons for these reliability and validity problems are discussed later in this chapter). A second problem is that most of the outcome research that has been done has used group outcome summary measures and so cannot tell us about specific factors that might have contributed to positive change, nor can it tell us about individual differences in outcome.

To overcome these limitations of group outcome research it has sometimes been complemented, in the general psychotherapy research literature, with process research. The following description has been used for process research:

> 'process research is the study of the interaction between the patient and therapist systems. The goal of process research is to identify the change processes in the interaction between these systems. Process research covers all of the behaviours and experiences of these systems, within and outside of treatment sessions, which pertain to the process of change.'
> (Greenberg and Pinsoff 1986)

Process research uses a variety of methodologies to explore the change process in psychotherapy and to facilitate our understanding of the therapeutic process and of the factors that are most effective in clinical work. Process research is applicable to all forms of psychotherapy and is most helpful in combination with outcome research and individual case analyses rather than group summary measures alone. The variables of process research are broadly distinguished from *input variables* – which are present before therapy and include: offence characteristics; personality structure; personal history; mental illness history; and so forth. Process variables are also distinguished from other variables which may change during the therapy, *extra-therapy variables* including: domestic circumstances; social support networks; life events. Finally, process variables are distinguished from *outcome variables* (Hill 1991[3], pp.85–118).

Clearly these distinctions between classes of variables and between outcome and process research is somewhat arbitrary since the psychotherapy process can be seen to be constituted of a series of mini-outcomes (Safran, Greenberg, and Rice 1988). Often the 'outcomes' of some research studies are really quite short-term punctuations in the longer course of the patients' problems. However, the distinction is undoubtedly a useful one and is of particular interest to forensic psychotherapy where there has been very little process research and where the phenomena of psychodynamic psychotherapy are so clear. Process research provides a great scope for development to be taken up both by

---

3   An easy to read guide to psychotherapy process research. Concentrates heavily on training raters.

clinicians prepared to do some research as well as by vocational psychotherapy researchers.

Hill (1991) describes seven types of behaviour that are pertinent to process research ranging from discrete short term behaviours to abstract long term behaviour: ancillary (e.g. speech dysfluency); verbal (e.g. therapist response mode); covert (e.g. therapist intentions, client reactions); content (e.g. content or discourse analysis); strategies (e.g. as used in particular therapeutic models); interpersonal manner (e.g. empathy); and therapeutic relationship.

In view of the limited attention paid to the process of psychotherapy in research with forensic patients, it is worth describing some of the methodologies that may be applicable. *Significant Events Methodology* (Elliott 1991;[4] Elliott and Shapiro 1988; Elliott and Shapiro 1992) collects data on significant events in therapy using a variant of Interpersonal Process Recall (Kagan 1975). Here the patient or therapist is asked to recall the moments in therapy that they judged to be most important and their recollection of these moments is then subject to intense analysis. The *therapeutic alliance* has been explored in many guises – working alliance, helping alliance, therapeutic bond, transference and countertransference and so forth. It attempts to describe the nature and impact of the therapist–client relationship. *Content and discourse analytic methods* (Luborsky and Crits-Christoph 1990; Potter and Wetherell 1987) take a rather different approach to process. The former might involve coding contents of sessions in a relatively nomothetic manner, the analysis of core conflictual material (Luborsky and Crits-Christoph 1990). The latter would be much less prestructured and might involve imputing less or no nomothetic equivalence in underlying dynamics in different patients therapies but would look for patterns of interest in the 'threads' of discourse. *The assimilation model* (Stiles *et al.* 1990;[5] Stiles, Shapiro and Firth-Cozens 1989) is a model that seeks to describe the assimilation of problematical experiences during the course of therapy and is applicable to an integrative model of therapy and one that expects the transfer of unconscious processes into the conscious realm. *Task analysis* (Greenberg 1983, 1986, 1992) aims to describe the processes by which client and therapist resolve particular cognitive-affective tasks over the course of the therapy through a checking of the goodness of fit of theoretical explanations by examination of empirical examples.

---

4   A comprehensive review of large and small scale psychotherapy research projects primarily in North America and Europe.
5   Paper describing the stages on assimilation during therapy. It has since been particularly applied to understanding the processes in integrative therapy.

CLINICAL AUDIT AS FORENSIC PSYCHOTHERAPY RESEARCH IN THE LIGHT OF OUR CLASSIFICATION

We have already made a number of references to the importance of service evaluation in forensic psychotherapy research particularly in the context of third party funding. There are increasing political pressures to justify interventions used, particularly in relation to more lengthy therapy. Audit is therefore an important part of forensic psychotherapy research if we wish to see the continuation of psychotherapy in forensic settings as this flies in the face of some increasingly powerful arguments for penal responses that focus more on containment and punishment.

Maxwell (1984) defines six dimensions of health care quality (see Table 3) that can be used to provide a richer understanding of what health services are delivering than the standard number-crunching exercise of how many people have been through the system.

Table 3. Maxwell's six dimensions of health care quality

Access to services	This might involve analysis of waiting times to assessment, waiting times to first session, evidence of selective bias in patients refused therapy or in those who declined or dropped out early. Qualitative analysis might involve things as simple as looking at the access for people with disabilities and the nature of the referral processes by which people reach the service.
Relevance to need (for the whole community)	This might involve analysis of the fit between the patients offered therapy and the patients who are perceived as most needing it. One might question a forensic psychotherapy service which was found to have drifted to seeing only patients who had not yet offended but presented worrying that they might.
Effectiveness (for individual patients)	This would involve various measures of outcome or of change during therapy. The problems involved in measuring effectiveness of routine forensic psychotherapy are legion but not to make any attempt can look cavalier to unsympathetic funding bodies.
Equity (fairness)	This returns to earlier issues of access and relevance but also raises questions such as about the continued monitoring for evidence of selective pressures leading to early terminations etc.
Social acceptability	This might involve: monitoring of the monitoring (ethical committee appraisals); evidence of the validity of consent to therapy if there are possible penal pressures (the recent public media experiences of the Gracewell clinic, though not apparently causal in its closure, may illustrate the importance of being able to show various strong measures of these issues for services taking patients on 'condition of treatment' probation orders). The details of how such monitoring might be set up are clearly not trivial but the penalties of not doing so might be very serious.

Table 3. Maxwell's six dimensions of health care quality (continued)

Efficiency and economy	Monitoring these parameters will involve evidence that the service is not wasteful. Particular attention to cancelled appointments and to delays leading to therapy sessions going unused will be one side of the assessment, the other may involve assessments of the costs of the patients to society before, and, ideally, after their treatment. Recent work at the Henderson Hospital illustrates this approach and is widely considered to have been influential in helping keep the service open simply because it put the very high costs of in-patient treatment into context even though it offered no evidence that the treatment *would* reduce costs (Menzies, Dolan and Norton 1993).

Parry (1992)[6] describes how these can be instituted in the context of other psychotherapy research in order to provide an audit function. Referring to Maxwell, she cites the criteria on which a service can be judged and suggests that three of the dimensions are particularly interesting to psychotherapy. 'Relevance to need' – is the service providing what the patient needs? This is a crucial question in the field of forensic psychotherapy where it is all too easy to make decisions about disposal (whether that be a question of treatment or punishment, or whether it be what type of treatment) on the basis of political pressure rather than on patient need. 'Effectiveness for individual patients' – does the treatment have a desired outcome. This is also an important question as the desired outcomes with forensic patients may be diverse and motivated by public, political or patient led interests – for example, they may be in terms of recidivism; reduction in seriousness of offending; improved psychological functioning; understanding of motivation for offence; and so forth. 'Efficiency and economy' – is the service being provided in a cost effective way? Forensic patients are already heavy users of public services, whether these be health service, social service, or Home Office, and it is therefore important to consider how efficiently funding can be used. This must be done with a long-term view as forensic patients are likely to continue to use services over a long period of time. It has been suggested that one positive outcome for therapy may be in helping patients become 'users' rather than 'abusers' of services. There are also implications for good quality evaluation of long-term therapy. Brief therapies are the order of the day; however, if an initially costly long-term therapy can be found to have better prognosis for future service use then long-term financial planning may indicate it should be provided. Parry also points out that

---

6   A detailed, sensible and useful article that helps to think about combining audit and psychother-
    apy research.

Maxwell's other dimensions of: 'equity'; 'access to services'; and 'social accept-ability' can be incorporated into service data collection by simply having accurate records of patients referred and seen.

ISSUES SPECIFIC TO, OR ACCENTUATED IN, FORENSIC PSYCHOTHERAPY RESEARCH

There are a number of key factors in carrying out good and ethical research, that take on added dimensions when applied to the forensic patient. These should be considered fully before embarking on research projects as problems in these areas form the bulk of the criticism of forensic research and forensic psychotherapy research.

Consent

Gaining full informed consent from any mentally disordered patient for participation in any research study is complex and problematical. However, a number of factors may impinge on consent from forensic psychotherapy patients. First, there are questions about the dynamics and motivations of patients detained involuntarily, sometimes under restriction orders giving the Home Office ultimate say in the patient's release on licence. Such patients may wish to be seen to cooperate both with clinical approaches and with research to ensure that any request for release on licence is seen positively. Second, there is the general concern about quality of consent of patients deemed to be suffering with a mental illness or with personality problems. Third, there are possibilities that long-term incarcerated patients may engage in research and therapy as a real and beneficial distraction but in a way that raises questions about the validity of their choice not to participate. Finally, there is the possibility that direct or covert pressure for consent may be applied to patients in total institutions.

Validity

In common with the issues affecting consent, there are issues about the validity of patients' self-reports: concern to be seen positively may lead to falsification or modification of information given; some mental illnesses may directly affect the validity of accounts; likewise, psychological processes endemic in some personality disorders, such as manipulativeness, may impair validity; third, patients who have long experience of services and institutions, such as many Special Hospital patients, often develop sophisticated psychological language and understanding which may engender a form of dialogue that restricts the true and fresh communication of their experiences; finally, the extreme nature of the experiences of some forensic patients is often difficult to believe. This may lead the patients not to expect to be believed and to develop an indifference to the way their views are received that may seriously bias the receipt of their reports. The recent debate about ritualistic and satanic abuse may be an example of the difficulties of accepting, or establishing, that some horrific experiences are true. The same may apply to gaining full descriptions not only of patients' own experiences of neglect and abuse, but also to descriptions of their offending or fantasies. Finally, and perhaps the least important of these problems, there is the possibility that patients may deliberately attempt to fake responses.

Setting

The setting in which forensic psychotherapy patients are seen is important, particularly if they are involuntary patients held under sections of the Mental Health Act of 1983. The setting may shape the experience of the therapy so markedly that extrapolation of results to similar work in other settings would be inappropriate. This is true both for the experience of a particular patient in some research, but it is also true of the way the dynamics and functioning of the institutions bears on the therapeutic practices. Cox (1986)[7] has described very clearly how dynamic psychotherapy work in the Special Hospitals involves psychological containment within highly secure physical and social containment. Clearly this is different from the nested containments of therapy within a medium or interim secure unit and radically different from the containments when forensic psychotherapy is done with patients in the community. Stable and secure social and support networks must be found if a patient is to engage in, and benefit from, dynamically-oriented psychotherapy. This may involve a secure base in the person's home or it may mean spending time in another setting. This is true of general psychotherapy patients but it is never more important than for forensic psychotherapy with patients who are not in secure settings. Clearly these issues will make generalization from work in one setting to work in another, potentially dubious if multiple containments and symbolic securities are critical variables in predicting change.

Follow-Up

The predictive value of psychotherapy research is only as long as its follow-up period. However, the problems of following up forensic psychotherapy patients are legion. They are often demographically members of a highly mobile population, and many have had, and continue to have, repeated prison

---

7 A classic article that addresses the duality 'holding' and 'containment' as relates to the forensic patient in high security.

sentences. Keeping track of patients, many of whom have strong reasons to become incognito, over periods of years is difficult and the factors that bias loss of follow-up are generally also those that are predictive of recidivism. These problems are exacerbated for single-handed psychodynamic researcher clinicians for whom contact with the patient after termination of therapy may fly against clinical theory and practice (this can also affect other treatments such as therapeutic communities where the community policy has been a very sharp cutting of links at discharge). These issues emphasize the importance for good research or collaboration or research assistant support for single-handed practitioners.

HOW TO SURVIVE AS A FORENSIC PSYCHOTHERAPY RESEARCHER – SUPPORT AND SERENDIPITY (AFTER HODGSON AND ROLLNICK 1989)

Doing research can be a particularly lonely activity, especially when it is being carried out by a lone clinical researcher as opposed to a larger research-based team. This is especially true for people working in forensic settings as, traditionally, forensic work has neither been popular nor integrated into the general sphere of psychotherapy for clinical research. Ensuring support in researching activities is therefore crucial. This can take a number of forms but the motto is 'Only connect'.

(1) Connect with existing work – court your local librarian. Ensure that you can get access to the journals that you need and become familiar with journals that may be of use to you. The references at the end of the chapter draw on general psychotherapy research as well as methodological and forensic areas. These may provide a new range of reading, however, it is not necessary to read everything, nor even the majority of things on this list before going further – *nil desperandum!*

(2) Connect with numbers if you can – statistics are the bane of some clinicians and psychotherapy researchers and the delight of others (the writers split into one phobic, one zealot and one who knows to whom to turn, when). If you are in the first category, remember that you are not a statistician and you need only sufficient understanding of statistics to be able to explain to a real statistician what your needs are. If you are a statistical zealot, it is important to ensure that you have some mechanism for orienting you to the real world as hours (days, weeks) of circumperambulation around statistical issues that do not answer your central research question are not in your interests – you too need to be able to talk to a real statistician.

(3) Connect with like-minded people – becoming involved with societies and special interest groups is important so as to maintain an awareness of current interests and practice in your particular field but also to

provide support from colleagues and a forum for new collaborators. Until recently there has been little specific to forensic psychotherapy and forensic psychotherapy research in their own rights. However, the recent setting up of the International Association of Forensic Psychotherapy provides an ideal forum and there are a number of less global organisations serving either psychotherapy research or forensic interests and participation in these groups can facilitate cross fertilization.

(4) Connect with reality – research is a complex activity, accept that your research project will take at least twice as long as you initially anticipate; would ideally require at least three times as many subjects as you are able to achieve; and will change its format at least four times before you finish it. Being realistic about these travails is important – strive for pragmatism balanced by a recognition that certain criteria must be fulfilled if your work is going to be useful (or publishable).

(5) Connect with serendipity – research is essentially a creative activity so, whilst it is important to be rigorous where possible, it is also important to allow yourself an open mind and an eye for discoveries that you may make by accident. We believe this nurturing of serendipity is the key feature of those who have changed psychotherapeutic history.

FURTHER READING

Barker, C. (1987) 'Interpersonal process recall in clinical training and research.' In F. Watts (ed) *New Directions in Clinical Psychology*. Leicester: British Psychological Society. *[IPR is the use of tape recording to stimulate memory of the process of thoughts and feelings – this article examines its use in clinical training.]*

Barkham, M. (1989) 'Research in individual therapy.' In W. Dryden (ed) *Individual Psychotherapy: A Handbook*. Second edition. Milton Keynes: Open University Press. *[A comprehensive article exploring methodology and conceptualizations for research in individual therapy.]*

Belsky, J. and Nezworski, T. (ed) (1988) *Clinical Implications of Attachment*. Hillsdale, NJ: Lawrence Erlbaum Associates.

Beutler, L. (1990) 'Introduction to the special series on advances in psychotherapy process research.' *Journal of Consulting and Clinical Psychology* 58, 3, 263–264. *[This reference really points you to one of the JCCP special series on psychotherapy research.]*

Beutler, L. and Crago, M. (1991) *Psychotherapy research. An international review of programmatic studies*. Washington DC: American Psychological Association. *[This is a comprehensive review of large and small scale programmes for psychotherapy research, primarily in North America and Europe. It is difficult to get hold of and might be offputting to 'new' researchers. However, it is extremely useful as a guide to who's in the psychotherapy research world.]*

Cordess, C. (1992) 'Pioneers in forensic psychiatry. Edward Glover (1888–1972): psychoanalysis and crime – a fragile legacy.' *The Journal of Forensic Psychiatry 3*, 3, 509–530.

Cordess, C., Riley, W. and Welldon, E. (1994) 'Psychodynamic forensic psychotherapy.' *Psychiatric Bulletin 18*, 88–90.

Dolan, B. and Coid, J. (1993) *Psychopathic and Antisocial Personality Disorders: Treatment and Research Issues*. London: Gaskell. *[A must for people researching into personality disorders. It will save you weeks of literature searching.]*

Everitt, B. (1987). 'Methodology for investigation: experimental research designs.' In S. Lindsay and G. Powell (eds) *A Handbook of Clinical Adult Psychology*. Aldershot: Gower.

Furby, L., Weinrott, M.R. and Blackshaw, L. (1989) 'Sex offender recidivism: a review.' *Psychological Bulletin 105*, 1, 3–20. *[A comprehensive and in many ways thorough paper offering a critique of the methodology of the literature. At times naive in its assumption that methodology of 'hard science' can be imposed on clinical work and bureacratic organizations.]*

Garfield, S.L. (1990) 'Issues and methods in psychotherapy process research.' *Journal of Consulting and Clinical Psychology 58*, 3, 273–280. *[An interesting article that provides a critique of psychotherapy process research.]*

George, C., Kaplan, N. and Main, M. (1984) 'Attachment Interview for Adults.' Unpublished manuscript. University of California, Berkeley.

Hill, C.E. (1990) 'Exploratory in-session process research in individual psychotherapy: a review.' *Journal of Consulting and Clinical Psychology 58*, 3, 288–294.

Hinshelwood, R.D. (1991) 'Psychodynamic formulation in assessment for psychotherapy.' *British Journal of Psychotherapy 8*, 2, 166–174.

Kendall, P.C. and Norton-Ford, J.D. (1982) 'Therapy outcome research methods.' In P.C. Kendall and J.N. Butcher (eds) *Handbook of Research Methods in Clinical Psychology.* New York: John Wiley and Sons Ltd.

Kraemer, H.C. (1981) 'Coping strategies in psychiatric clinical research.' *Journal of Clinical and Consulting Psychology 49*, 3, 309–319.

Lambert, M.J. (1989) 'The individual therapist's contribution to psychotherapy process and outcome.' *Clinical Psychology Review 9*, 469–485.

Luborsky, L., Barber, J.P. and Crits-Christoph, P. (1990) 'Theory based research for understanding the process of dynamic psychotherapy.' *Journal of Consulting and Clinical Psychology 58*, 3, 281–287.

Main, T.F. (1975) 'Some psychodynamics of large groups.' In L. Kreeger (ed) *The Large Group.* London: Constable.

Mancia, M. (1993) 'The absent father: His role in sexual deviations and in transference.' *International Journal of Psychoanalysis 74*, 941–949.

Marmar, C.R. (1990) 'Psychotherapy process research: progress, dilemmas, and future directions.' *Journal of Consulting and Clinical Psychology 58*, 3, 265–272. *[A positive appraisal of the achievements of psychotherapy process research to date.]*

Marshall, W.L. and. Barbaree, H.E. (1988) 'The long term evaluation of a behavioural treatment program for child molesters.' *Behaviour Research Therapy 26*, 6, 499–511. *[Recidivism data derived from various sources over a follow up period of 1–11 years. A cognitive behavioural paper that should be compared with the Furby paper.]*

Marshall, W.L., Ward, T., Jones, R., Johnston, P. and Barbaree, H.E. (1991) 'An optimistic evaluation of treatment outcome with sex offenders.' *Violence update 1*, 7. *[This is a direct response to the Furby paper and should be read with it. Much more hopeful (as the title would suggest) than the Furby article.]*

Meares, R. (1994) 'Psychotherapeutic treatments of severe personality disorder.' *Current Opinion in Psychiatry 7*, 245–248. *[An interesting overview with some useful references.]*

Orlinsky, D.E. (1989) 'Researchers' images of psychotherapy: their origins and influence on research.' *Clinical Psychology Review 9*, 413–442.

Patrick, M. (1993) 'Borderline Personality Disorder and the Mental representation of Early Social Experience.' In Contemporary Themes in Psychoanalytic Research – Public Lectures. 8th May 1993. London: British Psycho-analytic Society.

Peck, D. (198) 'Small *n* experimental designs in clinical research.' In F. Watts (eds) *New Directions in Clinical Psychology.* Leicester: BPS.

Rickman, J. (1932) 'The psychology of crime.' In *Selected Contributions to Psychoanalysis.* London: Hogarth Press and the Institute of Psychoanalysis.

Royal College of Psychiatrists (1994) *The Treatment of Perpetrators of Child Sexual Abuse.* (Council report No. CR31). London: Royal College of Psychiatrists.

Shapiro, D.A., Barkham, M., Hardy, G.E. and Morrison, L. (1990) 'The second Sheffield psychotherapy project: Rationale, design and preliminary outcome data.' *British Journal of Medical Psychology 63*, 2, 97–108.

Treurniet, N. (1993) 'What is psychoanalysis now?' *International Journal of Psycho-analysis 74*, 873–891.

Winnicott, D.W. (1992 (1956)) 'The antisocial tendency.' In *Through Paediatrics to Psychoanalysis – Collected Papers* (pp.306–315). London: Karnac Books and the Institute for Psychoanalysis.

Wolfe, B.E. and Goldfried, M.R. (1988) 'Research on psychotherapy integration: recommendations and conclusions from an N.I.M.H. workshop.' *Journal of Consulting and Clinical Psychology 56*, 3, 448–451.

Zilboorg, G. (1955) *The Pscyhology of the Criminal Act and Punuishment.* London: The Hogarth Press and the Institute of Psychoanalysis.

The Creative
Arts Therapies

Introduction

Murray Cox

True to its name, there exists a creative tension between the 'creative therapies' and the creation of an apposite all-embracing generic title which is wide enough to include what needs to be included, yet restricted enough to serve as a defining boundary. The matter is by no means settled. It can legitimately be claimed that there is a 'creative' component in all 'the psychotherapies', even though the term carries different connotations for each modality. Some opt for the 'creative arts therapies' and this is the chosen term to represent professions supplementary to medicine. Some prefer 'the expressive therapies', others opt for expressive therapy itself to be subsumed beneath 'The Creative Arts Therapies'. There are arguments in favour and against each of these options. What is not in doubt is that these therapeutic endeavours reinforce established mainstream therapeutic approaches. On occasion they may by-pass such approaches when they have become blocked, and often mark the first point of dynamic contact with a frightened preoccupied patient who has withdrawn from conventional therapeutic overtures.

There is always a *frisson* of the unfamiliar when the ethos of the creative therapies is set alongside time-honoured orthodoxy. There is something of the 'fringe' activity which takes place at the periphery – both in terms of priority and location – of a major arts festival. Yet it is common knowledge that very often the most creative initiatives arise exactly there. This is the stuff of *poiesis* – 'the calling into existence of that which was not there before' (Cox and Theilgaard 1987, p.23). It is this 'poetic' function in which novelty and the unexpected are found to generate the patient's own creativity and capacity to respond positively in unexpected ways. And it is this which is the hall-mark of the creative therapies. As such they do much to supplement orthodoxy, bringing a breath of fresher therapeutic air with them. The various chapters in this short section, when considered as a whole, show how much such therapies have to give to the patient and the life of the community in which he lives. The practitioners in these particular fields would be the first to emphasize how necessary is the link between these pioneer enterprises and established, well tried psychotherapeutic practice. Never more so than when the patients concerned are known to have 'dangerous, violent or criminal propensities' – to use words familiar in forensic circles.

There is a related issue which should find reference within these pages and this is the therapeutic value of 'Art in hospitals'. It is the subject of a review article by Miles (1994, p.161) which clearly conveys a familiar psychothera-peutic message about the significance of a 'Facilitating Environment'. This is an important topic *per se*. But its intrinsic relevance must not cloud the ensuing clear-cut presentation of the therapeutic creativity engendered by the creative arts therapies themselves.

An Art Therapist's 'Inside View'

Rein Innes

THE SETTING

The regional secure unit (RSU) in which I work is a purpose built secure environment for patients detained under the 1983 Mental Health Act. The building is set in the landscaped grounds of a large sprawling Victorian building until recently functioning as a psychiatric hospital. The RSU brochure includes secure psychiatric hospital and clinic as descriptions, the latter giving a certain anonymity to the low lying brick building now operating in its sixth year. The architecture is light and modern with no indication from the approach of its actual function. A high perimeter fence encloses a garden area for patients' use at the back of the building, the only obvious outer visible sign of security.

The forensic psychiatric service in the RSU covers the needs of three surrounding counties. The unit provides single accommodation with thirty-four beds on two locked mixed gender wards. Ward one receives all new patients who in time usually move on to ward two after the multi-disciplinary team (MDT) have agreed that the patient is ready to take responsibility and benefit from increased experiences in personal decision making.

The patients have access to rehabilitation facilities on both wards where they are encouraged to choose activities, therapies and interests in developing an individual daily programme which suits their needs. On ward two the emphasis is to prepare the patient for living as independent a lifestyle as he or she is capable of in the community. I will write more on these patients later in this chapter.

THE MULTI-DISCIPLINARY TEAM (MDT)

There are approximately eighty staff who work in various capacities in the RSU to cover twenty-four hour care. The demands in the patient group require unusually high staffing levels which in turn involves frequent inter-disciplinary interaction. When a group of people meet regularly over a long period of time they tend to form a shape which echoes that of a family interacting as a system. The MDT in the RSU where I work seems to function as a very large extended family. Each individual has an assigned role defined by their professional training or if untrained (i.e., nursing assistant), by their personal interest, their particular life and work experience and by the strength of personality.

Using the family as an analogy, the distinct disciplines in the MDT are similar to generational layers, the medical team holding supreme authority and responsibility, the parental figures. The nursing team represents another layer, the group with the most face-to-face contact with the patients while they are on duty. They are exposed to the nitty gritty of the patients' daily lives, including dealing with threatening or violent behaviour. Perhaps they are a bit like the loved cousins, aunts and uncles. The paramedic team (a term the team members feel uncomfortable with, but as yet no suitable replacement has been formulated) comprises two clinical psychologists, a physiotherapist, three occupational therapists, a wood technician/tutor, qualified dramatherapist/educational tutor who works seven hours a week and myself, art psychotherapist working sixteen hours a week. Individually we require a great deal of mobility, moving about the clinic as needs arise in the course of our work. We might generally represent the 'black sheep in the family', those family members who do not strictly conform to the usual way of doing things yet who are interesting because of that.

Inevitably a great deal of frustration arises as a result of (and in addition to) limited therapists' time. Once-weekly external supervision provides my main source of self-reflection in containing and understanding intrusive feelings and in clarifying boundaries. The use of time is mutable beyond specific ongoing commitments, allowing some leeway to organize assessment meetings and exchanges with other disciplines.

In working differently from other models of treatment, it is tempting to identify with the archetype 'the black sheep in the family', in my role as art therapist in the RSU. I endeavour to avoid colluding with the projection of being an 'idiosyncratic curiosity', in a context which is primarily geared to a medical model of treatment. This model is inclined to interpret the patients' behaviour and verbal communication literally rather than explore the metaphorical or symbolic content.

The main therapeutic activities I offer are a weekly clay group, a closed art therapy group and individual sessions.

I am bound to have an escort with me when I run the clay and art therapy groups and over the years I have learned how useful it is to have psychiatric nurses as my escort co-workers. This is not always practicable but where I can arrange this it would be my first option. Involving as a co-worker, a psychiatric nurse who is interested in exploring the creative process, means getting to know the nursing staff well enough to invite them to work closely with me. It is not so difficult to notice a person who is inquisitive and it is worth making this effort. The difference between having a co-worker who is interested as opposed to an escort who is there because they have to be makes all the difference to how the groups function and to the group's atmosphere. I expect this commitment to be not less than eight weeks and longer where possible, to allow the process of continuity and containment to develop into meaningful experiences for those involved.

The usefulness in having a psychiatric nurse as co-worker extends beyond the group setting and the immediate sense of support I may experience. Through her direct involvement in the group the nurse has the opportunity to enhance her existing understanding, in a conscious sense of the value of creative expression. Other co-workers might include medical, art therapy, occupational therapy, counselling and psychiatric nurse students who might pass through the group whilst on long work placements.

The experience others gain from being involved in the clay and art therapy groups can then be further used as a bridging mechanism between the art therapeutic model and other models of treatment in the unit. Most optimistically, the potential for a dynamic of dispersal of information from direct experience occurs. Within the framework of my limited time and access to members of the multi-disciplinary team this ripple effect contributes covertly towards a de-mythologising of the art therapeutic practice and process in the unit.

THE PATIENT

The majority of the people in the patient group I encounter from the two mixed gender wards in the RSU have committed a serious offence, or they have threatened to do so, whilst influenced by some kind of mental illness. Some patients are transferred from one of the special hospitals after the decision has been made that they are ready (well enough) to move on to a rehabilitation programme. Patients also come from the penal system, some directly from the courts and others from open psychiatric units or hospitals. The patient invariably arrives at the RSU in a state of bewilderment and shock. The new environment is likely to be utterly different from their previous experience.

Some patients may also be actively psychotic at the time of their admission. The staff to patient ratio in the unit is unusually high because of the dangerous

behaviour which some of the patients have exhibited and the emphasis is on
rehabilitation adopted by the unit. Therefore the actual staff/patient interaction
from all disciplines is likely to be far greater than the patient has been used to.

He will also arrive with varying degrees of defensive mechanisms, armour
serving and operating as a protection against external stimulus and inner
anxiety. The prescribing of medication by the medical team, for a large number
of patients, attempts to block out undesirable feelings and sensations. The effect
of medication seems to add to the prevalence of concrete thinking I have
observed in the individual patients I work with. Concrete thinking appears to
be a habitual way of responding; one of the aspects, perhaps, of long-term
emotional deprivation combined with a mental illness. This attitude appears to
serve a purpose; it has been and remains useful as an aid to survival in an
environment experienced internally and externally as hostile.

After the patient has adjusted to his new environment, usually after two to
three weeks, a member of staff who perceives art therapy as a beneficial method
of intervention will make the referral. I then have an assessment interview with
the patient which is conducted in a side room on the ward. From this point I
make a decision regarding the suitability of working either individually or in
a group setting.

PRIVACY

At all times in the unit I am able to be observed visually when I am with a
patient or running a group; we can be seen but not heard. The unit is designed
with large areas of windows with the intention of maximizing interspatial
visibility. The patients are able to be further observed in their bedrooms
through small windows in their doors and through a spy hole.

Every room contains an alarm button (I have not so far needed to use this).
The high degree of observation required because of the potential for acting
out negates the experience of privacy for the patient. The well patient is allowed
a greater degree of privacy, with less observation than the acutely disturbed/ill
patient. Conscious awareness of being observed emerges frequently as a theme
in the images and in the patients' verbal expression. Being too keenly observed
is experienced as an intrusion. This in turn may provoke a particular passive
compliance to suggestion, especially from stronger or authoritative figures.
Anxiety is then aroused which may outwardly manifest and be seen as the
patient becoming ill. A circular dynamic emerges, possibly reminiscent of some
patients' original early conflict. This leads me to think that privacy may be
synonymous with confidentiality.

CONFIDENTIALITY

Can the experience of confidentiality exist for the patients I work with? The 'absolute right to expect total confidentiality', which Casement (1985, p.224) describes in defining an essential ingredient in therapeutic relationship, does not and cannot exist in the RSU setting. By the nature of the index offence, combined with a mental health problem, already a great deal of personal information will have been gathered from various sources. In particular, detailed psychiatric reports describing the diagnosis and the patient's aetiology will be available for MDT staff to read. The patient also has the right of access to their notes. For those patients on restriction orders, the Home Office requires specific information about the individual's progress in their rehabilitation programme and details of their current state of mental health.

The patient knows that they have and will continue to be discussed at ward rounds and case conferences. They are also aware that I will sometimes be involved in the discussions. In these settings I will describe something of what happens during the art therapeutic interaction. I select carefully what I pass on or write down for others to read. Inherent in the process of selection and utterly paramount is the issue of dangerousness. In particular, where a patient's index offence was of a violent nature, or their current behaviour suggests a threat to other people, or to themselves, it seems necessary to develop a discreet vigilance in gauging an individual's capacity towards tolerating anxiety and frustration in deciding what I disclose. It is hard to disguise frustration and anxiety in the use of art materials, especially in the use of paint and clay where frustration is inevitably experienced.

Given that the patient knows that absolute confidentiality cannot exist, the idea of partial confidentiality is obviously a misnomer. Confidentiality either exists or it doesn't. Does this then mean such a thing as 'pockets' of confidentiality can exist and can be useful for the patients within certain professional settings in a RSU? This phenomenon does seem to happen without usurping professional boundaries or diminishing the quality of what is able to be meaningfully contributed to the MDT meetings or my working with the patients. This is one of the reasons why I rarely bring objects or pictures which the patients have made into the MDT setting.

THE 'PICTURE'

When we say 'I've got the picture' we mean an understanding, a grasping of certain circumstances and facts have fallen into place. The thing which was a quandary, which didn't make sense, begins to make sense within an existing framework; something unclear becomes revealed in a conscious sense; the bits begin to fit together. Yet, there is no literal picture or image being referred to in this context.

It is interesting here how the word 'picture' is associated with a mental image, a vivid impression which extends to a sense of knowing or comprehension. The experience begins to assume boundaries – edges to hold the comprehension, creating a distinction between the knowing and not knowing. The 'picture' is experienced internally as a visualized conception through the process of discovery and revelation and this takes time, it cannot be hurried. In the meaning of 'getting the picture' it seems there are dynamic parallels within the process of looking at and making real pictures and images in the art therapeutic setting. Of course, the difference is of there being an actual picture or object which emerges sooner or later in the art therapeutic space. The picture is literal and is referred to as such. It is outside, separate from the maker and has a unique usefulness because it is outside yet connected to the maker's inner world.

When self-consciousness diminishes, real time becomes suspended in brief moments or long periods; then the dropping into creative engagement similar to play can happen. In turn, the usual controlling factors of resistance and expectation can begin to lose potency. Ideally, there is not a goal or result to be achieved (thought there might be) and judgement is put aside as much as is consciously possible.

The meaning and value the picture or object comes to represent symbolically might emerge and become consciously clear. Yet it need not be known and perhaps is never consciously comprehended. The picture can act as mediator when it is imbued with personal meaning for the creator and this meaning not only exists but can be felt. The mobilizing of the feeling sense via creative engagement holds the potential for adding to and nurturing the undeveloped or damaged ego and of integrating conflicting feelings. The experience of wholeness and cohesion might be short lived and similar to the 'islands of clarity' described by Edward Podvoll in *The Seduction of Madness* (1990, p.5). Something has happened, a shift in being and it is forgotten, stops or is lost temporarily. So a return to being 'out of the picture' whilst the picture is being formed presents a paradox. It is when this tension in tolerating opposing forces of passivity and activity, the interplay of conscious and unconscious, that a person is able to engage in symbolic representation through their creative expression. They have begun to play.

There is a plethora of writing on the subject of play. These authors I have found most interesting and useful, and continue to do so, in my art therapy practice. Hanna Segal (1981), Rosemary Gordon (1971) and in particular the work of D W Winnicott (1971a) who has described the profound relationship between creativity and play in great detail. He says

'It is in playing and only in playing that the individual child or adult is able to be creative and to use the whole personality, and it is only in being creative that the individual discovers the self'. (Winnicott 1971a, p.63)

It is a tragedy that so many people have been forced or seduced through circumstances, when children, prematurely to relinquish their capacity to play. The people I work with are often such people, and they are likely to have formed a genuine suspicion of being spontaneous, founded on fear. When faced with the art materials and the possibility of exploring these imaginatively, most people I encounter appear to be self-conscious, as if they are thin skinned with good reason. They have not had the full experience of the mother as a 'protective shield' (Khan 1986, p.120) when dependent as children. Fearful and suspicious of losing control if they allow themselves to be spontaneous in a non-directive setting., for them appearing 'child like' means humiliation; not being 'good enough' – disappointment; 'not having an idea' – terror; 'becoming messy' signifies inner disintegration/contamination. The list is endless in what I hear people say in the initial stages of working creatively.

My aim is to establish as reliable and holding a framework as I can manage, given the vicissitudes of the RSU environment. Like all frameworks, nothing can be fleshed out or built on until this exists. Without doubt reliable holding is a pre-requisite for any trusting reciprocal relationship to begin, develop and for it to end well enough for something useful to emerge.

Dramatherapy

Sue Jennings

'Kind little walnut of a mother.'

> *Peer Gynt* Act 1 (Ibsen translated by Christopher Fry 1989)

'I think we should always look back on our own past with a sort of tender contempt. As long as the tenderness is there, but also please let some of the contempt be there...'

> Dennis Potter (interviewed by Melvyn Bragg 1994)

INTRODUCTION

Dramatherapy and its application in a variety of clinical, social and educational settings is an expanding field, and there are currently five post-graduate training programmes and two MAs in the UK (BADTh 1994). The generalist application of dramatherapy is discussed comprehensively in a variety of publications (BADTh 1994; Meldrum 1994; Jennings 1990), and its utility for people with mental health problems is both documented and researched (Mitchell 1994; Grainger 1990). By contrast there is a paucity of literature and research on the application of dramatherapy in forensic settings (Jennings, Orr and McGinley, in preparation), and to my knowledge there is still only a handful of dramatherapists working in prisons, Special Hospitals, secure units and with the probation service.

Nevertheless, dramatherapy has a unique role to contribute to prevention, therapeutic intervention and rehabilitation. It can stand in its own right as a primary therapy as well as being able to complement other aspects of a therapeutic programme. There are several models of dramatherapy which can be adapted appropriately to the particular needs of clients, (Meldrum 1994; Landy 1986) and which can be applied both with groups as well as individuals. It is important that dramatherapy is not confused with psychodrama (Chesner 1994), on the one hand or drama/theatre-in-education (Courtney 1981, 1987) on the other, even though they may share similar methods and structures.

DRAMATHERAPY AS DEVELOPMENT

Developmental dramatherapy is based on the hypothesis that all human beings 'are born dramatic' (Jennings 1993); that contrary to many developmental, cognitive and biological theories, people do not come into the world either as empty vessels or undifferentiated entities, or as a mass of instinctive responses. The observation of neonates shows that they are already socialized, being able to enter into 'an exchange of feelings' (Trevarthen and Logotheti 1989), and engage dramatically with significant adults (Courtney 1981; Jennings 1993). That is, they are able to respond mimetically through sound and movement to the people as well as the environment around them. Human dramatic development can be observed as passing through three stages of 'embodiment–projection–role' (EPR)' (Jennings 1990; Cattanach 1992).

Forensic Application

Many clients have developmental difficulties and are often functioning (behaviourally, emotionally, physically) at an inappropriate stage. Developmental dramatherapy can 're-stage' the client's embodiment–projection–role (EPR) within the dramatic scene. For example, preparing for the voyage of Odysseus (Jennings, in preparation (a)) enabled a 'warming-up' of the body which involved primary physical movement and coordination (see also Gordon 1981 for simple physical methods). Frequently I find that these groups of people need to re-experience imaginative playfulness through drama games and dramatic play (Hickson 1995) as a developmental step towards dramatherapy.

DRAMATHERAPY AS RITUAL

Dramatherapy and ritualization is an important model of working which enables people with chaotic lives to symbolize and structure their experiences. Symbolic rituals including rites-of-passage always have dramatic elements, and are primarily sensory experiences. The importance of the ritualization of experience is that it can be repeated and passed on. Even if individual performances may vary, we grasp the essential elements very quickly, so for example when we attend a wedding ritual for the first time, we very quickly grasp both the structure and our role. Dramatherapy groups may develop their own rituals, or various dramatized scenes and stories may need rituals such as the Greek chorus of Furies the *The Eumenides* or the Bergomask dance in *A Midsummer Night's Dream.*

Forensic Application

Crimes of killing and abuse are often 'ritualized' in destructive patterns, that is, there is a personalized attempt to create a meaningful ritual. However, this is not ritual in the accepted sense of the word because the action is underdistanced. That is, it expresses an immediate gratification of affect, although patterned and repeated, within which any symbolism remains personal. Ritual dramatherapy enables the participant to create 'dramatic distance' from his or her personal experience (Landy 1986, 1994) which leads to the structuring of shared symbolic material. Therefore participants can move from individual or gang destructive ritualization to the group performance of dramatic ritual which has shared meaning. For example, a group of severely disturbed prisoners who had all committed crimes against the body (mugging, rape, assault), surprised care-staff by being able to create a masked dance for the ball scene in *Romeo and Juliet* (Jennings and Landy, in preparation). The dance was ritualized with stylized gestures, greetings, bowing, which enabled physical distance on the one hand but appropriate touching on the other. Their dance contributed an important ritual to the total performance, and helped them structure their responses to a very disturbing story which had familiar themes.

DRAMATHERAPY AS THEATRE ART

Theatre art is primarily about dramatic performance whether through text or improvisation, within which an ensemble of actors rehearse and present the material. This process of creation is accepted as having a healing function (Mitchell 1992; Jennings 1992) for a witnessing audience (Cox 1992a) as well as for many of the performers. Dramatherapy recognizes the healing in aesthetic performance and enables client groups to participate in, rather than merely witness this process. The three primary threads in this process are:

(1) *Choice and development of role or character* (Landy 1994). The creation of a role/character by an actor is a total experience, that is, the character is a totality which gradually is inhabited by the performer. Often this process 'surprises the self'; the paradox of the dramatic distance is that it enables a person to come closer to hitherto unacknowledged or unrecognized facets of self. A client that has been 'beside themselves' with rage, may well be able to be 'within themselves' as a raging character.

(2) *Dramatic metaphors both scripted and spontaneous have the quality of shifting a person's experience in unexpected ways* (Cox and Theilgaard 1987). The dramatic metaphor usually brings about a physical and affective response when someone is taken unawares. Similar to the process in ritual, the person can be connected to the collective metaphor or symbol or image which has both individual as well as group meaning (Jennings and Minde 1993).

(3) Thematic material of individual scenes and the play as a whole (Jennings, in preparation, b). Great plays, stories and myths have themes with which most people can identify. The plays provide a structure within which people are secure to take risks. Most plays have ritual structures of introduction–exploration–resolution with various sub-plots and sub-texts. The ritual structure provides the foundation for risk-taking and exploration. However, it also provides a form of resolution. The play shows us the human dilemma and its many complexities (introduction), develops the themes in new and unexpected ways (exploration) and then moves towards reconciliation and compromise (resolution). Russell Davis (1992) describes three phases of a play: crisis (or challenge), exploration and reorganization. The play is not the life of the individual client, but a play where the individual client will find not only their own life but also an expanded perception of themselves in relation to others and the world.

Forensic Application

Role choice, dramatic metaphors and significant themes are all means through which it is possible to bring about change. 'Fixed roles' can be explored, the dramatic imagination can be developed, arrested endings can be completed and assumptions about stories and outcome can be challenged. For example, with one prisoner group, I was warned that their language 'is inappropriate' and there is a lot of swearing. I used *Shakespeare's Insults* (Hill and Ottchen 1991) to enable them to create a dramatic distance, and swear 'in character'. The build-up of tension before one very small man bellowed (for the first time) 'ear-wax!' at his partner brought the group to a halt. The fact that another group chose either to play Egeus or Oberon in a dramatherapeutic exploration of *A Midsummer Nights Dream* (Jennings, Orr and McGinley, in preparation) enabled in-depth work of violent male–female relationships to be explored within the character.

CONCLUSION

This is brief description of the main characteristics of dramatherapy and its potential in forensic settings. Dramatherapy, as an artistic therapy, engages clients in an aesthetic experience which dramatherapists believe is healing. Although its forensic application is currently limited, nevertheless, there is optimism regarding its beneficial outcomes:

'dramatherapy can allow patients to gain insight into their own emotions, to get back in touch with their feelings but to do this in a controlled and safe way.' (Dr M Orr, Consultant Forensic Psychiatrist, Broadmoor Dramatherapy Project)

There has been significant measurement of change in the recently evaluated Broadmoor Dramatherapy Project (McGinley 1994), which is now being evaluated using dramatherapeutic research methods innovated by Lahad (1992) through fairy-tales, and Landy (1994) by a taxonomy of roles.

Dramatherapy enables the 're-staging' of people's development that may have been distorted through early experience; the ritualization of chaotic life themes in order to structure and contain; the exploration of the totality of the character, often prompted by a dramatic metaphor, within the context of a significant theme.

'Excellent earth, don't be angry
That I trampled grass to no purpose.'
(*Peer Gynt* Act V)

Note

Some of these specific ideas for forensic dramatherapy have developed from two dramatherapy projects at Broadmoor Hospital using *A Midsummer Night's Dream* and *The Odyssey*; a self-image and mask programme at Wormwood Scrubs Prison and also with St Albans Probation Service; and a theatre of healing project with *Romeo and Juliet*, at Rikers, Prison New York. A third Broadmoor project with *Peer Gynt* is currently being planned.

Music Therapy

Helen Loth

INTRODUCTION

Music therapy uses music-making as a basis for communication in the development of a relationship between client and therapist. Both take an active part in the session by playing and listening. Clients are encouraged to use accessible musical instruments, mainly percussion, and their voices to explore the world of sound and to create a musical language of their own. By responding musically, the therapist is able to support and encourage this process.

There are different approaches to the use of music in therapy. Depending on the needs of the client and the orientation of the therapist, different aspects of the work may be emphasized. Musical improvisation, with therapist, client and group members, forms the basis of much music therapy work. How a person uses the instruments, the sounds they choose to make and the way they respond to others musically, reflects how they relate to the world. Music can also express something for which no words have yet been found. Songs, musical activities and recorded music may also be used in some approaches. The elements of communication, interaction and self-expression are key features of music therapy in all its settings.

MUSIC THERAPY IN THE FORENSIC SETTING

In the forensic setting, both group and individual music therapy is undertaken. This chapter discusses groups. The forensic music therapy group serves several functions. It provides a medium through which patients can engage in a group and a language with which they can express themselves and their inner worlds to a therapist who uses the same language. It can function on several levels, from dealing with issues which arise as a result of being in a secure setting, through looking at interpersonal behaviour, to gaining insight into the offending behaviour.

THE ROLE OF THE MUSICAL INSTRUMENTS

As a primarily non-verbal, action-oriented therapy music therapy is very often able to engage clients who do not readily respond to other treatment modalities. In contrast to purely verbal therapies, music therapy has a third element, musical instruments, through which clients who are less articulate, or who are withdrawn can enter into contact with the therapist and, in the group setting, with each other in a more indirect way. The physical action of playing and producing sound provides a way for clients to link their inner and outer worlds. For clients with limited insight or verbal skills, music therapy can offer a means for self-expression and exploration of feelings in a non-threatening and less intellectual manner.

THE MUSIC THERAPY GROUP

To illustrate some of the themes and uses of music therapy in the forensic setting, a brief summary of a group series will be presented.[1]

The group took place in an interim secure unit and ran for eight weekly hour-long sessions. The group was closed and consisted of the music therapist, an occupational therapist as co-therapist, and six clients. The clients were all male and were aged between twenty-three and thirty-nine. Index offences included indecent assault, grievous bodily harm (GBH), actual bodily harm (ABH), and murder. It took place in a room in which there were a large range of tuned and untuned percussion instruments, including drums, xylophone, metallophone, African and Latin American small percussion and a guitar. The patients had been selected by the therapists, and all had agreed to attend. The model of music therapy used was one of group improvisations, largely undirected, followed by discussion.

Vignette
The first session was characterized by a great sense of excitement. The group members began trying out the instruments as soon as they entered the room. After listening to a few group rules concerning times, and so forth, given by the therapist, the group began playing together enthusiastically. People continually changed instruments, gathered several each around them, telling

---

1   For a fuller description, see Loth 1994.

each other 'the drum's mine', and guarding their collections from each other. There was a strong sense of deprived children suddenly being given a huge bag full of toys and wanting to have all of them at once, not feeling safe in giving any up. Only after another two improvisations did they relax and share the instruments, feeling secure that their toys were not going to be taken away again.

An increasing sense of confidence and group ownership developed during the next two sessions. This was emphasized at the beginning of the third session by the therapists 'protecting' the group from the invasion of other patients of the unit, who had become interested and were now demanding their 'right' to attend also. In the first two sessions, the group's music had been very cohesive, characterized by a regular, shared beat and moderate tempo. The group members also said they did not want 'chaos'. By week three, there was enough safety in the group to allow for some relaxation of control. For the first time the music did not need a beat or harmonic structure. It became very free and changeable, fast and furious playing moving into slower rhythmic sections, and then breaking out into fast and arhythmic playing again. This flexibility allowed the development of a musical language, both group and individual, through which different aspects of the group could be expressed.

In the last few sessions, absences became a feature of the group, and the sense of cohesiveness began to break down. In the fifth session one group member refused to attend, signalling his withdrawal from all group activities in the unit. In the sixth session, another member was meeting with the Mental Health Act Commissioners to appeal against his Section and in the seventh, another was attending the court hearing into his case. The music of these sessions became more immediate and loud. There was a resistance to talking and to silences and the music became more of the focus of the session. By the last session, two members had left the unit and one had dropped out of the group. The music was rhythmic and fast, seeming to reflect a wish to end on a high note despite the sense of disintegration of the original group.

ENGAGEMENT

This sense of deprivation, often present with forensic patients, can lead to enthusiasm for something as enticing and novel as musical instruments. This enthusiasm and spontaneity helps to counter resistance to engaging in group work, as was shown in the initial session of this series.

IMPROVISATION

This model of music therapy has particular relevance to the forensic client group. The freedom of improvisation allows clients to participate on their own level and in their own way. Special skills do not have to be learned in order to do well in the group, a valuable aspect for clients with low self-esteem. Musical improvisation allows things to be expressed which cannot be articulated in words.

SELF-EXPRESSION

The music therapy group offers a context in which patients can admit to problems and begin to get in touch with their feelings through externalizing them in the music. The expression of the inner world is brought into the group and the interactions in the form of sound. This can then be discussed or further explored in the group's playing. This has value, regardless of whether clients show insight into their offence and remorse for it.

DENIAL

In this group, the music facilitated the acceptance of feelings associated with crimes which could not be acknowledged. There was much denial in the group; of offences, of responsibility for them, and of their seriousness. An outcome of this was the repression of feelings about the offences themselves, and about the situations the patients found themselves in, but did not feel responsible for. The admission of any 'difficult' feelings was very hard for them, and many clients did not have the emotional language to articulate them. This was illustrated in the later sessions referred to in the vignette on p.563.

Vignette
A group member could not acknowledge responsibility for his offence (the murder of his second wife, having served a prison sentence for the murder of his first wife), and had become depressed and suicidal whilst in prison. In the music therapy group he could not talk about his feelings or his offence, and would not admit to being anything other than 'all right'. As his court case approached, his playing increasingly contrasted with his denial of emotions, and was at times full of despair. He would sit hunched over his instrument, playing in a slow monotonous beat with little flexibility or responsiveness. This was acknowledged by the group in their music

which, by reflecting and supporting his, provided the containment and safety for him to begin to get in touch with and accept these vulnerable aspects of himself.

CATHARSIS

The cathartic release offered by the expression of tensions and feelings in a supportive musical environment is often cited by clients as the most valued aspect of the group for them. As one group member said *'it's the one chance in the week when we can really let go'*.

THE LAW

The intervention of the law in the lives of the clients was reflected and addressed within the group. All the clients were on different stages of their journey through the forensic and legal system. The absence of one group member through, for example, attending a court hearing, would lead those remaining to reflect on their own situations, and had a powerful effect on the group. Decisions received from the Home Office, such as the denial of parole often generated feelings of anger and frustration as well as a negative 'what's the point' attitude to therapy. When this happened, the group provided a useful container for these emotions, a safe place to deal with them where their admission and acting out did not result in further punishment.

CHOICE

The issue of choice, and the lack of it, seems ever present in the forensic setting, where most patients are resident against their will. The lack of choice in many aspects of life on the interim secure unit set up a feeling of resentment which characterized many of the groups and interactions which took place. Although given a choice, patients could never feel that their attendance in a group was entirely voluntary as they knew that cooperation with treatment was part of their progression to reduced secure status. In the music therapy group they could express their anger at having to attend, whilst participating in it. It provided a sufficiently constructive way of expressing their resentment to allow them to take part in the group. Sessions would often begin with loud, disorganized sounds, in which people were isolated, playing only for themselves. Once this had been acknowledged, the group could move on to other things.

CONCLUSION

Music therapy has a specific role to play in the forensic setting. It offers clients a different way to engage in therapy, by providing a creative, expressive and action-based medium in the form of musical improvisation. Whether it is the only therapy the client is engaged in, or it is complementing other more verbally-oriented therapies, the music can be a window into the internal world of the client.

Dance Movement Therapy

Jacqueline Blatt

As infants we explored our world through movement. Our sense of self, the extent of our own bodies, our relationships to others, our feelings of trust and security, and the development of our cognitive abilities were all experienced physically. These processes commenced *in utero* (Piontelli 1992) and continued through infancy. Much of the development which formed who we grew to become occurred prior to the time that we acquired verbal facility.

The acquisition of language reinforces symbolic thought and diminishes the preceding reliance on direct experience. Western society's reliance on verbal and later written communication forced a necessary transition on us as young children.

The body of knowledge required for full participation as members of our society is too vast to be acquired through direct experience. Western societies, therefore, emphasize verbal skills and competence in abstract reasoning. This does not mean that the previously developed skills in nonverbal communication and direct experiencing disappear. The foundation for all later stages of development is laid down nonverbally and our continuing use of nonverbal communication conveys to those trained in its interpretation and analysis, significant information about personality, decision making style, and emotional content (Davis and Dulicai 1992; Laban 1975; Lamb 1965; North 1975).

Dance movement therapy is a psychological treatment modality which relies primarily on nonverbal communication to explore the emotional, cognitive and behavioural issues of the patient and to accomplish therapeutic goals.

Dance movement therapy is based on four theoretical and clinical precepts;

(1) The use of movement to foster expression and stimulate communication between therapist and patient.

(2) The use of symbolic process.

(3) The inherent therapeutic effect of the creative process (Blatt 1991).

(4) An awareness that the personality is reflected in movement (North 1975).

Prisons are characterized by a high proportion of educationally disadvantaged, learning disabled, and emotionally disturbed individuals. Addiction and substance abuse are also found in a high percentage (Guy 1985). Inmates' poor impulse control frequently results in ill-considered antisocial behaviour.

Overcrowding, boredom, fear of abuse from other inmates and separation from the normal support of family and friends add to the stress levels that inmates must endure. This stress has the effect of exacerbating pre-existing emotional problems (Sykes 1958). These factors contribute greatly to the difficulty of maintaining order within authoritarian prisons. Restrictions on individual freedom and the emphasis on arbitrary and predictable routine that characterizes prison life foster an acceptance of and interest in reflection and self-expression.

Dance movement therapy is accessible for patients who have no previous artistic experience to communicate. The creative process in which the patients and therapist collaborate establishes a level of intimacy through which the patient can utilize the support of the therapist and the medium itself. The dance movement therapist can create an oasis in which the prisoner can feel safe enough from the tensions and fears of prison life to begin the work on intra-psychic issues through both verbal and movement means of expression (Blatt 1983).

Vignette

Simon was a white, Jewish, fifty-year-old male barber. He was of medium build. He walked into the therapy room with a two day growth of beard and a disheveled appearance. His concave chest suggested depression, while a rigidity of his torso indicated that he was alienated from his feelings. He was very talkative and engagingly manipulative. Simon was divorced with two children.

Simon was arrested for the sexual abuse of young adolescents having ensured his own discovery (Cox 1979). While in prison, Simon was referred for psychiatric treatment for situational disorders with severe depression as well as suicidal ideation.

Within the hierarchy that operates in prisons, individuals who have committed sexual crimes are at the bottom. This means that they are vulnerable to abuse from other inmates. Simon was first assessed in individual sessions to inform him of this vulnerability and to determine the extent to which he had acknowledged his exploitative nature.

During his dance movement therapy assessment, Simon expressed an elaborated and entrenched rationalization of his sexual abusive behaviour. He claimed that his acknowledged actions were done with consent and were of benefit to his victims. Simon's self-destructive tendencies were demonstrated when he knowingly and indiscriminately informed other inmates of the nature of his offence.

It was ironic that Simon was unable to express his emotions verbally despite his facility with language. He was, however, fully capable of exploring his emotional issues through movement. Simon's image of a 'wall' surfaced repeatedly during these nonverbal explorations. Throughout the dance movement therapy sessions, this metaphor described Simon's relationship to his fellow group members, his therapist and his own sensory feeling state. Further into the process of therapy, it emerged that the 'wall' was part of a long forgotten memory. In this recollection, Simon found himself crying in an abandoned house while curled up against a wall. This metaphor surfaced on a nonverbal level during a movement session. It permitted Simon to examine his previously inaccessible emotions without a verbal association.

During the session, Simon physically moved through this image. This process allowed him to recreate his experience on a sensory level bringing to conscious awareness his painful experience (Zwerling 1979). Simon cried for the first time when another group member mirrored this image of a lonely crouched figure leaning helplessly against the wall. He began to explore the significance of this memory, which was his initial step toward releasing his powerful control, revealing his sincere feelings, while communicating his pain and guilt to others. In this case dance movement therapy was the primary means by which the patient was able to defeat long held defences and gain access to his emotional life.

Within the prison walls, inmates may find the space to explore their inner worlds:

- because they are contained
- because they are hungry for stimulation
- because of the long stretch of time that prevails.

Dance movement therapy can be one of the psychological approaches to the treatment of these imprisoned patients.

A Final Reflection

Robert M. Hardy

At first sight it may seem odd to invite a Bishop to contribute a final reflection on such a detailed compendium as this, and I can only plead two responses to these understandable misgivings. The first is that I write from the perspective and experience of ten years as the Anglican Bishop to Prisons, alongside my normal diocesan duties. The Bishop to Prisons has no official or formal standing within the criminal justice system. He merely acts as the eyes and ears of the Archbishops of England and Wales (there are other senior clergy keeping the Methodist and Roman Catholic Churches informed) and as a kind of bridge between those who work in prisons and the general membership of the Church of England. That gives him a certain vantage point, for the dramatic extremities of the prison situation make it a useful environment from which to consider many aspects of care and response in the general area of criminal offending.

My second 'justification' is to point out that the prison is always the agency of the broader society, and a sometimes forgotten part of that society. Here I can do no better than to quote Andrew Coyle:

> 'Much of the attitude which society has about the prison reflects the reality that the old notion of exile is still very much alive. The high walls of the prison are intended to keep the community outside just as much as to keep the prisoners inside. There are fine words in the Woolf Report about the need to develop the notion of "community prison", and to encourage the prison the build up links with all relevant sectors of its local community. By and large there is a recognition within the prison system that this is necessary. But it has to be a two-way process. The community and its members have to accept the responsibility which they have towards the prisoner and the prison. The criminal who has broken the law and who is sent to prison, for however long or short a period,

remains a member of the community. Unlike the biblical scapegoat, he or she will return to the community, on completion of sentence. The community has an obligation to prepare both the prisoner and itself for that return.' (p.17)

For many, the experience of imprisonment is traumatic. It generates in individuals strong feelings of anxiety, self-pity and anger. Existing links with families and community life are put under enormous strain, and the movement and restlessness of the prison system have a disorienting effect on prisoners, severing relations sometimes for weeks on end, and often playing on an individual's worst imaginings. Prison itself is a stark and extreme environment. It is its own world, with harsh physical characteristics, sensory deprivation, enforced companionship and severe restrictions on normal social intercourse. The immature, the weak-willed, the mercurial and the violent are often thrown together, and the prison world quickly imposes its own particular customs and psychological character upon an individual. It is authoritarian, punitive, relentlessly regimented and often unpredictable. It also has its own ways and standards where evasiveness, deceit and pretentiousness can flourish, and the weak can be pushed aside and brutalized. Many prisoners come from deprived communities and families, with a long record of under-achievement and instability. Many have never experienced a secure, stable and supportive relationship. They are, therefore, vulnerable in the truest sense. They have never known regular employment, a settled routine or a secure home, and in consequence are often lost, damaged and resentful. Anyone working with them in whatever capacity or relationship finds him or herself under pressure, needing to call on a variety of skills and resources to sustain both balance and integrity, to bring healing and acceptance, and to create the possibility of something new.

Although the issues in this book are not exactly the same as those concerns facing a Prison Chaplain, there is certainly an overlap; and the same could be said of the Chaplain whose work brings him into close contact with those who are mentally disordered. The moral, ethical and spiritual issues raised by consideration of such topics as professional confidentiality, membership of clinical teams. and the place and nature of sacramental confession, emphasize the need for an extended exploration of these things in a future *Forensic Focus* publication – perhaps on 'Spirituality and Security'? However, I must return to the theme with which I am more familiar, by commenting on the literal and metaphorical phenomenon of imprisonment. These volumes have already explored both the theory and practice of many of the insights, challenges and skills required by those who work with prisoners and their victims, but it may be useful to draw these threads together and highlight some of the most significant features of forensic psychotherapy.

Arrest and committal to prison are de-humanizing experiences. They stereotype an individual and cause a good deal of pain, not to mention triggering a wide range of other emotions and responses. It is helpful at all stages, therefore, if the offender can experience some feeling of dignity and worth, and sense that help in coping with the loss of self-respect is available. Initial contacts here can be critical. Watchfulness is essential, and the communication of a sense of value is important. Many contacts in prison are transitory and informal, and the therapist, whatever his or her relationship with the prisoner, has to use a high degree of imagination and the rapid application of theory if these contacts are to be used and fruitful. Spontaneity, freedom and confidence are important here in the offering of pastoral care and support, not to mention the need for flexibility when circumstances change and the way forward is blocked. Often the irrational and intuitive responses of the therapist can further the relationship, but these need to come from considered reflection and a wide awareness of different possibilities.

Most offenders respond to a good listener, yet this process demands not only the skills of a competent interviewer, but also a sense that he or she is genuinely alongside the client. No one here can work with one particular psychodynamic theory. Indeed, a priority is to restore a sense of dignity – even arbitrariness – in the way people see and tell their histories. Again a balance has to be achieved between judgmental and accepting attitudes: when to be firm and when to accept.

Here the attitude towards truth is crucial to both parties. In society there is often a taboo about asking personal questions, but in prison straight questions can often be posed. Of course, truthful answers are not always forthcoming, but truth and freedom are connected and need to be explored in the reconstruction of the individual's story. Here, group experiences can often illuminate a way forward. Groups can lead individuals to take risks in self-disclosure, and even conflicts can be fruitful if handled well and resolved satisfactorily. Nor should one ever ignore the contribution to understanding of the creative arts – music and dance, drama and painting. For these can often pose the critical question, 'Who am I when I am not a criminal?'

Whilst it should be clear that many of the issued addressed by forensic psychotherapy have a theological dimension and interpretation, the response to them cannot be narrowly religious or even restricted to a specifically Christian approach. There is a whole area of multi-faith insight and dialogue here to be explored, particularly as the prison population is made up of a wide range of ethnic backgrounds.

What is clear is the need to develop a collective responsibility towards those who are convicted, using a multi-disciplinary approach, in the hope of creating both new insights and possibilities. There is a need for all involved in this work to submit themselves to continuing training and reflection, as well as further supervision and research. Above all, there is a need to keep the drawbridge down between the prison world and the wider community. No one has expressed this better than Bishop Rowan Williams in an address to Prison Chaplains in April 1994:

> '...just as the prisoner needs a ministry of truth-telling to assist him in putting him or her in touch with relations with positive potential, so there is a corresponding role in relation to those outside the institution, to put them in touch with the negative possibilities that the existence of a separated, enclosed penal institution makes it easier to forget. If those outside the prison can remember that the prison services the health of the whole social order, they may be less inclined to ignore justices and immunities in the conduct of the institution, more willing to see a continuity, however stretched, between desirable relations in the wider world and what happens within the prison walls. Prison can then be understood not as a dump for our negative and destructive elements...but as part of our recognition of social unwholeness and an expression of our willingness to work at it; this would in turn involve asking how the practices and structures of prison life could work towards reintegration into a constructive engagement with the wider community.'

Postscript

These volumes are brought to a close by redirecting attention to a recurring topic. The particular anxieties which beset the Forensic Psychotherapist have previously been linked (Cox 1974, p.16) to words from antiquity, whose timelessness ensures their perennial relevance:

'The psychotherapist experiences anxiety which may be a professional liability or an asset. The balanced polarity of therapeutic optimism and a simultaneous vigilance over the sombre issues of security and the possible recrudescence of violence has not been better expressed since St Augustine wrote: "If there is no joy, there is defect in us; if we feel wholly safe, we exult wrongly."'

Appendix

Forensic psychotherapy is the subject of new proposals and guidelines devised by the Royal College of Psychiatrists for service provision and higher specialist training in England and Wales.

It is to be proposed that

(1) There should be at least one full-time equivalent forensic psycho-therapist in each of the 14 (old administrative) regions of England and Wales, and each Special Hospital should have the equivalent of at least two such posts – local characteristics will dictate how many.

(2) There should be Senior Registrar posts established, whereby two years are spent in forensic psychiatry training and two years working in psychotherapy; attachment to units or departments which can offer specialist forensic psychotherapy experience, where feasible, will be encouraged.

These new service and training developments are currently confined to medically qualified personnel. However, it is intended that well-trained but non-medically qualified psychotherapists should be encouraged to seek posts and work in forensic settings. There is no shortage of need.

Christopher Cordess
May 1995

Bibliography

Abel, G. (1983) 'Preventing men from becoming rapists.' In G.S. Albee and H. Leitenberg (eds) *Promoting Sexual Responsibility and Preventing Sexual Problems.* Hanover, NH: University Press of New England.

Abelin, E.L. (1971) 'The role of the father in the separation-individuation process.' In J.B. McDewitt and C.F. Settlage (eds) *Separation-Individuation.* New York: International Universities Press.

Abraham, K. (1925) 'The history of an impostor in the light of psychoanalytic knowledge.' In K. Abraham *Clinical Papers and Essays on Psychoanalysis.* New York: Brunner/Mazel.

Abraham, K. (1927) *Selected Papers of Karl Abraham.* New York: Brunner/Mazel, 1979.

Ackerman, N.W. (1958) *The Psychodynamics of Family Life.* New York: Basic Books.

Adlam-Hill, S. and Harris, P.L. (1988) *Understanding of Display Rules for Emotion by Normal and Maladjusted Children.* Unpublished paper. Department of Experimental Psychology, University of Oxford.

Adler, A. (1916) *The Neurotic Constitution.* New York: Moffat Yard.

Adler, G. (1982) 'Recent psychoanalytic contributions to the understanding and treatment of criminal behaviour.' *International Journal of Offender Therapy and Comparative Criminology 26,* 281–287.

Adshead, G. (1991) 'The forensic psychotherapist: dying breed or evolving species?' *Psychiatric Bulletin 15,* 410–412.

Adshead, G. (in press) 'Damage: the relationship between abuse in childhood and adult violence.' *Behavioural Sciences and the Law 12,* 235–250.

Advisory Council on the Misuse of Drugs (1994) *Drug Misusers and the Criminal Justice System Part II: Police, Drug Misusers and the Community.* London: HMSO.

Aichhorn, A. (1925) *Wayward Youth.* Reprinted 1948 New York: Viking Press.

Ainsworth, M.D.S., Blehar, M.C., Waters, E. and Wall, S. (1978) *Patterns of Attachment: A Psychological Study of the Strange Situation.* Hillsdale, NJ: Lawrence Erlbaum Associates.

Akhtar, S. (1992) *Broken Structures Severe Personality Disorders and Their Treatment.* Northvale, NJ: Jason Aronson Inc.

Alexander, D.A., Walker, L.G, Innes, G. and Irving, B.L. (1993) *Police Stress at Work.* London: Police Foundation.

Alexander, F. (1930) 'The neurotic character.' *International Journal of Psycho-Analysis 11*, 292–311.

Alonso, A. (1985) *The Quiet Profession: Supervisors of Psychotherapy.* New York: MacMillan Publishing Company.

Alpert, M. (1981) 'Speech and disturbance of affect.' In J. Darby (ed) *Speech Evaluation in Psychiatry.* New York: Grune and Stratton.

Alvarez, A. (1992) *Live Company.* London: Routledge.

American Occupational Therapy Association (1979) 'The philosophical base of occupational therapy.' *American Journal of Occupational Therapy 33*, 12, 785.

American Psychiatric Association (1980) *Diagnostic and Statistical Manual, Third Edition.* Washington, DC: American Psychiatric Press.

American Psychiatric Association (1987) *Diagnostic and Statistical Manual of Mental Disorders, Third Edition - Revised.* Washington, DC: American Psychiatric Press.

American Psychiatric Association (1989) 'Position Statement on Psychiatric Services in Jails and Prisons'. *American Journal of Psychiatry 146*, 1244.

American Psychiatric Association (1994) *Diagnostic and Statistical Manual of Mental Disorders, Fourth Edition.* Washington, DC: American Psychiatric Press.

Anderson, E., Levine, M., Sharma, A., Ferretti, L., Steinberg, K. and Wallach, L. (1993) 'Coercive uses of mandatory reporting in therapeutic relationships.' *Behavioral Sciences and the Law 11*, 3, 335–345.

Anderson, H., Goolisham, H. and Winderman, L. (1986) 'Problem determined systems toward transformation in family therapy.' *Journal of Strategic and Systemic Therapies 5*, 14–19.

Andrews, G. (1993) 'The essential psychotherapies.' *British Journal of Psychiatry 162*, 447–451.

Appelbaum, P.S. (1994) *Almost a Revolution: Mental Health Law and the Limits of Change.* New York: Oxford University Press.

Appelbaum, P.S. and Gutheil, T.G. (1991) *Clinical Handbook of Psychiatry and Law.* Second edition. Baltimore, MD: Williams and Wilkins.

Argyle, M. (1975) *Bodily Communication.* London: Methuen.

Argyle, M. (1981) 'The contribution of social interaction research to social skills.' In J. Wine and M. Smye (eds) *Training in Social Competence.* New York: Guilford Press.

Aristotle, *Rhetoric,* II.vi.18–20 (1384a), translated and edited by W.D. Ross. Oxford: Oxford University Press, 1954.

Arlow, J.A. (1971) 'Character perversion.' In I.M. Marcus (ed) *Current in Psychoanalysis.* New York: International Universities Press.

Arlow, J.A., and Brenner, C. (1964) *Psychoanalytic Concepts and The Structural Theory.* New York: International Universities Press.

Armsden, G.C. and Greenberg, M.T. (1987) 'The inventory of parent and peer attachment: individual differences and their relationship to psychological well-being in adolescence.' *Journal of Youth and Adolescence 16*, 427–454.

Aronson, A.E. (1980) *Clinical Voice Disorders: An Interdisciplinary Approach.* New York: Thieme-Stratton.

Asen, K., George, B., Piper. R. and Stevens, A. (1989) 'A systems approach to child abuse: Management and treatment issues.' *Child Abuse and Neglect 13,* 45—58.

Ashurst, N. and Hall, P. (1989) *Understanding Women in Distress.* London: Tavistock and Routledge.

Ashworth, A. (1989) 'Criminal justice and deserved sentences'. *Criminal Law Review,* May, 340–55.

Association of Professional Music Therapists (1993) *An Introduction to Music Therapy.* Cambridge: Association of Professional Music Therapists.

Auerhahn, N.C. and Laub, C. (1984) 'Annihilation and restoration: post-traumatic memory as pathway and obstacle to recovery.' *International Review of Psychoanalysis 11,* 327–344.

Augustine, Sermon on Psalm 85,16. Patologia Latina; 37, 1090 (As quoted in Jean Mouroux, *The Christian Experience.* London: Sheed and Ward 1955.)

Azima, G. and Azima, J. (1959) 'Outline of a dynamic theory of occupational therapy.' *American Journal of Occupational Therapy 13,* 5.

BADTh[1] (1994) *Dramatherapy Information and Resource Pack.* Swanage: British Association for Dramatherapists.

Baker, A. and Duncan, S. (1985) 'Child sexual abuse in Great Britain.' *Child Abuse and Neglect 9,* 457–467.

Balint, M. (1968) *The Basic Fault.* London: Tavistock Publications.

von Balthasar, H.U. (1982) *The von Balthasar Reader.* Eds M. Kehl and W. Löser, translated by R.J. Daly and F. Lawrence. Edinburgh: T. and T. Clark.

Bandura, A. (1977) *Principles of Behaviour Modification.* New York: Holt, Rinehart and Winston.

Bandura, A. (1986) *Social Foundations of Thought and Action: A Social Cognitive Theory.* Englewood Cliffs, NJ: Prentice-Hall.

Bannister, A. and Print, B. (1989) *A Model for Assessment Interviews in Suspected Cases of Child Sexual Abuse.* NSPCC Occasional Papers series No.4. London: NSPCC.

Barch, D. and Berenbaum, H. (1994) 'The relationship between information processing and language reduction.' *Journal of Abnormal Psychology 103,* 2, 241–250.

Barker, C. (1987) 'Interpersonal process recall in clinical training and research.' In F. Watts (ed) *New Directions in Clinical Psychology.* Leicester: British Psychological Society.

---

1   British Association for Dramatherapists, 5 Sunnydale Villas, Durlston Road, Swanage, Dorset BH19 2HY.

Barker, S.L., Funk, S.C. and Kent-Houston, B. (1988) 'Psychological treatment versus nonspecific factors: A meta-analysis of conditions that engender comparable expectations for improvement.' *Clinical Psychology Review 8*, 579–594.

Barkham, M. (1989) 'Research in individual therapy.' In W. Dryden (ed) *Individual Psychotherapy: A Handbook.* Second edition. Milton Keynes: Open University Press.

Baron-Cohen, S. (1991) 'Precursors to a theory of mind: understanding attention in others'. In A. Whiten (eds) *Natural Theories of Mind: The Evolution, Development And Simulation of Second Order Mental Representations.* Oxford: Basil Blackwell.

Baron-Cohen, S. (1993) 'The development of a theory of mind: where would we be without the intentional stance.' In M. Rutter and D. Hay (eds) *Developmental Principles and Clinical Issues in Psychology and Psychiatry.* Oxford: Basil Blackwell.

Barratt, A., Trepper, T.S. and Fish, L.S. (1990) 'Feminist-informed family therapy for the treatment of intra-familial child sexual abuse.' *Journal of Family Psychology 4*, 151–166.

Bateman, A.W. (1995) 'The treatment of borderline patients in a day hospital setting.' *Psychoanalytic Psychotherapy 9*, 1.

Bates, E., Benigni, L., Bretherton, I., Camaioni, L. and Volterra, V. (1979) 'Cognition and communication from 9–13 months: correlational findings'. In E. Bates (ed) *The Emergence of Symbols: Cognition and Communication in Infancy.* New York: Academic Press.

Bateson, G. (1973) *Steps to an Ecology of Mind.* St Albans: Paladin.

Bateson, G. (1979) *Mind and Nature: A Necessary Unity.* London: Wildwood House.

Bateson, G., Jackson, D., Haley, J. and Weakland, J. (1956) 'Towards a theory of schizophrenia.' *Behavioral Science 1*, 251–64.

Beail, N. (1988) *Repertory Grid Techniques and Personal Constructs: Applications in Clinical and Educational Settings.* London: Croom Helm.

Bean, P. and Nemitz, T. (1994) *Out of Depth and Out of Sight.* Midland Centre for Criminology MENCAP Report. London: MENCAP.

Bean, P., Bingley, W., Bynoe, I., Faulkner, A., Ranaby, E. and Rogers, A. (1991) *Out of Harm's Way.* London: MIND Publication.

Beccaria, C. (1764) *Of Crimes and Punishments.* Reprinted 1963. Indiana: Bobbs Merill.

Beck, A.T. (1967) *Depression: Clinical, Experimental, and Theoretical Aspects.* New York: Hoeber.

Beck, A.T. (1970) 'Cognitive therapy: nature and relation to behaviour therapy.' *Behaviour Therapy 1*, 184–200.

Beck, A.T. (1976) *Cognitive Therapy and the Emotional Disorders.* New York: International Universities Press.

Beck, A.T. and Freeman, A. (1990) *Cognitive Therapy of Personality Disorders*. New York: Guilford.

Becker, H. (1963) *Outsiders*. New York: The Free Press of Glenco Inc.

Bellak, L. (1959) 'Psychological test reporting: a problem in communication between psychologists and psychiatrists.' *Journal of Nervous and Mental Disease* 129, 76.

Bellak, L. (1986) *The Thematic Apperception Test*. New York: Grune and Stratton.

Belsky, J. and Nezworski, T. (ed) (1988) *Clinical Implications of Attachment*. Hillsdale, NJ: Lawrence Erlbaum Associates.

Bennet, G.B. (1987) *The Wound and the Doctor*. London: Secker and Warburg.

Benson, S. and Den, A. (1992) 'Monitoring violence outbursts of aggression can cause considerable problems in psychiatric hospitals. Sally Benson and Anil Den 'describe how they addressed this issue in their unit.' *Nursing Times 88*, 41, 46.

Bentham, J. (1838) *The Works of Jeremy Bentham*. Reprinted 1962 (edited by J. Bowring). New York: Russell and Russell.

Bentovim, A. (1979) 'Theories of family interaction and techniques of intervention.' *Journal of Family Therapy 1*, 321–45.

Bentovim, A. (1992a) *Trauma-Organised Systems, Physical and Sexual Abuse in Families*. London: Karnac Books.

Bentovim, A. (1992b) 'Sexual abuse of children and adults.' In J. Harris and A. Craft (eds) *Proceedings from the Bild Regional Seminars/Royal Society of Medicine 1992 National Conference*. Bild Seminar Paper 4, London.

Bentovim, A. (1993) 'Why do adults sexually abuse children?' *British Medical Journal 307*, 144–145.

Bentovim, A. and Davenport, M. (1992) 'Resolving the trauma organised system of sexual abuse by confronting the abuser.' *Journal of Family Therapy 14*, 29—50.

Bentovim, A., Elton, A., Hilderbrand, J., Vizard, E. and Tranter, M. (1988) *Child Sexual Abuse within the Family*. London: Butterworth/Wright.

Bentovim, A. and Kinston, W. (1978) 'Brief focal family therapy when the child is the referred patient – I Clinical.' *Journal of Child Psychology Psychiatry* 1–12.

Bentovim, A. and Kinston, W. (1991) 'Focal family therapy – joining systems theory with psychodynamic understanding.' In A. Gurman and D. Kniskern (eds) *Handbook for Family Therapy Vol 2*. New York: Brunner/Mazel.

Bergin, A.E. and Garfield, S.L. (eds) (1994) *Handbook of Psychotherapy and Behavior Change*. Fourth edition. New York: John Wiley and Sons Ltd.

Berlin, L. (1993) 'Attachment and emotions in preschool children.' In J. Cassidy and L. Berlin, Co-Chairs of Symposium on Attachment and Emotion at the Meeting of the Society for Research in Child Development. New Orleans, Louisianna.

Bernstein, H.A. (1981) 'Survey of threats and assaults directed towards psychotherapists.' *American Journal of Psychotherapy 35*, 4, 542–549.

von Bertalanffy, L. (1962) 'General systems theory: a critical review.' *General Systems 7*, 1–20.

Bettelheim, B. (1960) *The Informed Heart.* London: Penguin Books.

Beutler, L. (1990) 'Introduction to the special series on advances in psychotherapy process research.' *Journal of Consulting and Clinical Psychology 58*, 3, 263–264.

Beutler, L. and Crago, M. (1991) *Psychotherapy research. An international review of programmatic studies.* Washington DC: American Psychological Association.

Bick, F. (1968) 'The experience of the skin in early object relations.' *International Journal of Psycho-analysis 49*, 484–486.

Bifulco, A., Brown, G. and Adler, Z. (1991) 'Early sexual abuse and clinical depression in adult life.' *British Journal of Psychiatry 159*, 115–122.

Bion, W.R. (1955) 'Language and the schizophrenic.' In M. Klein, P. Heimann and R. Money-Kyrle (eds) *New Directions of Psychoanalysis.* London: Tavistock Publications.

Bion, W.R. (1957) 'Differentiation of the psychotic from the non-psychotic personalities.' *International Journal of Psycho-Analysis 38*, 266–275.

Bion, W.R. (1961a) *Experiences in Groups.* London: Tavistock Publications.

Bion, W.R. (1961b) 'A theory of thinking.' *International Journal of Psycho-analysis 43*, 306–310.

Bion, W.R. (1962) *Learning from Experience.* London: Heinemann.

Bion, W.R. (1967) *Second thoughts.* Reprinted 1993. London: Karnac Books.

Bion, W.R. (1970) 'Container and Contained.' In W. Bion *Attention and Interpretation.* London: Maresfield Reprints.

Birchwood, M.J. and Tarrier, N. (1994) *The Psychological Management of Schizophrenia.* Chichester: John Wiley and Sons Ltd.

Blackburn, R. (1975) 'An empirical classification of psychopathic personality.' *British Journal of Psychiatry 127*, 456–460.

Blackburn, R. (1986) 'Patterns of personality deviation among violent offenders: replication and extension of taxonomy.' *British Journal of Criminology 26*, 254–269.

Blackburn, R. (1988) 'On moral judgements and personality disorders. The myth of psychopathic personality revisited.' *British Journal of Psychiatry 153*, 505–512.

Blackburn, R. (1993) 'Clinical programmes with psychopaths.' In K. Howells and C.R. Hollin (eds) *Clinical Approaches to the Mentally Disordered Offender.* Chichester: John Wiley and Sons Ltd.

Blackman, M., Weiss, J. and Lamberti, J. (1963) 'The sudden murderer III: clues to preventive interaction.' *Archives of General Psychiatry 8*, 289–294.

Blair, I. (1985) *Investigating Rape: A New Approach for Police.* London: The Police Foundation.

Blair, R.J.B. (1992) *The Development of Morality.* Unpublished doctoral thesis, University of London.

Blair, S. (1990) 'Occupational therapy and group psychotherapy.' In Creek (ed) *Occupational Therapy and Mental Health, Principles, Skills and Practice.* London: Churchill Livingstone.

Blake, W. (1794) 'A Poison Tree.' In W. Blake *Songs of Experience. A Selection of Poems and Letters.* Harmondsworth: Penguin Books.

Blatt, J. (1983) *The Development of the Arts Psychotherapy Program in the Philadelphia Prison Systems.* MA Thesis, unpublished. Hahnemann University.

Blatt, J. (1991) 'Dance movement therapy: inherent value of the creative process in psychotherapy'. In G. Wilson (ed) *Psychology and Performing Arts.* Amsterdam: Swets and Zeitlinger.

Blecourt, B. de, Beenen, F., Gomes-Spanjaar, C., Hommes, H., Verhage-Stins, L. and Verhage, F. (1981) 'Het samenwerkingsverbond ('working alliance') van patiënt en analyticus.' *T. Psychotherapie 7,* 6, 307–317.

Blom-Cooper, L. and Murphy, E. (1991) 'Mental Health Services and Resources.' *Psychiatric Bulletin 15,* 65–68.

Blos, P. (1966) 'Discussion.' In E. Rexford (ed) 'A developmental approach to problems of acting out'. *Monographs of the American Academy of Child Psychiatry, No. 1.*

Blos, P. (1967) 'The Second Individuation Process of Adolescence'. In *Psychoanalytic Study of the Child 22,* 162–186. New York: International Universities Press.

Bluglass, R. and Bowden, P. (1990) *Principles and Practice of Forensic Psychiatry.* London and Edinburgh: Churchill Livingstone.

Boccia, M. and Campos, J.J. (1989) 'Maternal emotional signals, social referencing, and infants' reactions to strangers.' *New Directions for Child Development 44,* 24–29.

Bograd, M. (1990) 'Why we need gender to understand human violence.' *Journal of Interpersonal Violence 5,* 132–135.

Bolinger, D. (1975) *Aspects of Language.* New York: Harcourt Brace.

Bollas, C. (1987) *The Shadow of the Object. Psychanalysis of the Unthought Known.* London: Free Association Books.

Boman, B. (1987) 'Antisocial behaviour and the combat veteran: a review (with special reference to the Vietnam conflict).' *Medicine and Law 6,* 173–187.

Bond, M. (1992) 'An empirical study of defensive styles: The Defense Style Questionnaire.' In G.E. Vaillant (ed) *Ego Mechanisms of Defence.* Washington, DC: American Psychiatric Press.

Bond, M., Gardner, S.T., Christian, J. *et al.* (1983) 'Empirical study of self-rated defence styles.' *Archives of General Psychiatry 40,* 333–38.

Booth, B. and Grogan, M. (1990) 'People with learning difficulties who sexually offend.' Community Resource Centre, Thameside General Hospital, Ashton Under Lyne, UK.

Bowen, M. (1966) 'The use of family theory in clinical practice.' *Comprehensive Psychiatry 7*, 345–73.

Bower, G. (1981) 'Mood and memory.' *American Psychologist 36*, 129–148.

Bowlby, J. (1944) 'Forty-four juvenile thieves: their characters and home life.' *International Journal of Psychoanalysis 25*, 1–57 and 207–228.

Bowlby, J. (1946) *Forty-Four Juvenile Thieves: Their Character and Homelife.* London: Ballière, Tyndall and Cox.

Bowlby, J. (1951) *Maternal Care and Mental Health.* Geneva: WHO.

Bowlby, J. (1958) 'The nature of the child's tie to his mother.' *International Journal of Psychoanalysis 39*, 350–373.

Bowlby, J. (1969) *Attachment and Loss, Vol. 1: Attachment.* London: Hogarth Press.

Bowlby, J. (1973) *Attachment and Loss, Vol 2: Separation.* London: Hogarth Press.

Bowlby, J. (1980) *Attachment and Loss, Vol. 3: Loss.* London: Hogarth Press.

Bowlby, J. (1988) *A Secure Base: Clinical Application of Attachment Theory.* London: Routledge.

Boyle, J. (1994) *Sense of Freedom.* London: Pan.

Brazelton, T.B. (1973) *Neonatal Behavioral Assessment Scale.* London: Spastics International Medical Publications.

Brazleton, T.B. (1982) 'Joint regulation of neonate parent behavior.' In E.Z. Tronick (eds) *Social Interchange in Infancy.* Baltimore: University Park Press.

Brazleton, T.B. and Als, H. (1979) 'Four early stages in the development of mother-infant interaction.' *The Psychoanalytic Study of the Child 34*, 349–369.

Brazleton, T.B., Tronick, E., Adamson, L., Als, H. and Wise, S. (1975) 'Early mother–infant reciprocity.' In *Parent–Infant Interaction: Ciba Foundation Symposium 33.* Amsterdam: Elsevier.

Breen, T. and Turk, V. (1991) 'Sexually Offending Behaviour by People with Learning Disabilities, Prevalence and Treatment.' Unpublished paper. Kent: University of Canterbury.

Bremner, J.D., Southwick, S., Johnson, D., Yehuda, R. and Charney, D. (1993) 'Child physical abuse and combat related PTSD in Vietnam veterans.' *American Journal of Psychiatry 150*, 235–239.

Brenner, C. (1959) 'The masochistic character: genesis and treatment.' *Journal of the American Psychoanalytic Association 7*, 197–226.

Brenner, C. (1979) The components of psychic conflict and its consequences in mental life. *Psychoanalytic Quarterly 48*, 547–567.

Bretherton, I. (1985) 'Attachment theory: retrospect and prospect.' In I. Bretherton and E. Waters (eds) 'Growing Points of Attachment Theory and Research.' *Monographs of the Society for Research in Child Development 50*, 1–2, Serial No. 209, 3–35.

Bretherton, I., Fritz, J., Zahn-Waxler, C. and Ridgeway, D. (1986) 'Learning to talk about emotions: a functionalist perspective.' *Child Development 57*, 529–548.

Brett, E. (1993) 'Psychoanalytic contributions to a theory of traumatic stress.' In J.P. Wilson and B. Raphael (eds) *International Handbook of Traumatic Stress Syndromes.* New York: Plenum Press.

Brett, T.R. (1992) 'The Woodstock Approach: one ward in Broadmoor Hospital for the treatment of personality disorder'. *Criminal Behaviour and Mental Health 2*, 152–158.

British Medical Association (1984) *The Handbook of Medical Ethics.* London: British Medical Association.

Brom, D., Kleber, R. and Defares, B. (1989) 'Brief psychotherapy for PTSD.' *Journal of Consulting and Clinical Psychology 57*, 607–612.

Bromberg, W. (1948) *Crime and the Mind: An Outline of Psychiatric Criminology.* Philadelphia: J.B. Lippincott Company.

Brook, J.S., Whiteman, M. and Finch, S. (1993) 'Role of mutual attachment in drug use: A longitudinal study.' *Journal of American Academy of Child and Adolescent Psychiatry 32*, 982–989.

Brook, J.S., Whiteman, M. and Gordon, A.S. (1983) 'Stages of drug use in adolescence: Personality, peer, and family correlates.' *Developmental Psychology 19*, 269–277.

Brook, J.S., Whiteman, M., Brook, D.W. and Gordon, A.S. (1981) 'Paternal determinants of male adolescent marijuana use.' *Developmental Psychology 17*, 841–847.

Brook, J.S., Whiteman, M., Brook, D.W. and Gordon, A.S. (1984) 'Paternal determinants of female adolescent's marijuana use.' *Developmental Psychology 20*, 1032–1043.

Brook, J.S., Whiteman, M., Gordon, A.S. and Brook, D.W. (1984) 'Identification with paternal attributes and its relationship to the son's personality and drug use.' *Developmental Psychology 20*, 1111–1119.

Brook, J.S., Whiteman, M., Gordon, A.S. and Brook, D.W. (1985) 'Father's influence on his daughter's marijuana use viewed in a mother and peer context.' *Advances in Alcohol and Substance Abuse 4*, 1–7.

Brown, A. and Caddick, B. (eds) (1993) *Groupwork with Offenders.* London: Whiting and Birch.

Brown, B. (1985) 'An application of social learning methods in a residential programme for young offenders'. *Journal of Adolescence 8*, 321–331.

Brown, D.L. (1983) 'Burnout or copout.' *American Journal of Nursing 83*, 1110.

Brown, G.W. and Anderson, B. (1991) 'Psychiatric morbidity in adult inpatients with childhood histories of sexual and physical abuse.' *American Journal of Psychiatry 148*, 55–61.

Brown, J.M. and Campbell, E.A. (1994) *Stress and Policing: Sources and Strategies.* Chichester: John Wiley and Sons Ltd.

Brown, J.R. and Dunn, J. (1991) '"You can cry, mum": the social and developmental implications of talk about internal states.' *British Journal of Developmental Psychology 9*, 237–257.

Browne, A. and Finkelhor, D. (1986) 'Impact of child sexual abuse: a review of the research.' *Psychological Bulletin 99*, 66–77.

Browne, F., Gudjonsson, G.H., Gunn, J., Rix, G., Sohn, L. and Taylor, P.J. (1993) 'Principles of treatment for the mentally disordered offender.' In J. Gunn and P.J. Taylor (eds) *Forensic Psychiatry: Clinical, Legal, and Ethical Issues.* Oxford: Butterworth-Heinemann.

Browne, K. (1993) 'Family violence and child abuse'. In C.J. Hobbs and J.M. Wynne (eds) *Bailliere's Clinical Paediatrics.* London: Baillière Tyndall.

Bruhn, A.R. and Davidow, S. (1983) 'Earliest memories and the dynamics of delinquency.' *Journal of Personality Assessment 47*, 476–482.

Bruner, J. (1990) *Acts of Meaning.* Cambridge, MA: Harvard University Press.

Brunner, E. (1948) *Christianity and Civilization.* Gifford Lectures, The University of St. Andrews. London: Nisbet and Co.

Bryan, K.L. (1989) *The Right Hemisphere Language Battery.* Kibworth: Far Communications Publishers.

Bryer, J.B., Nelson, B.A. and Miller, J.B. (1987) 'Childhood sexual and physical abuse as factors in adult psychiatric illness.' *American Journal of Psychiatry 144*, 1426–1430.

Bryk, A.S. and Raudenbush, S.W. (1987) 'Application of hierarchical linear models to assessing change.' *Psychological Bulletin 101*, 1, 147–158.

Burges Watson, P. (1989) 'A tormented mind.' *ANZ Journal of Psychiatry 23*, 97–102.

Burgess, A.W., Hartman, C., Ressler, R.K., Douglas, J.E. and McCormack, A. (1986) 'Sexual homicide: a motivational model.' *Journal of Interpersonal Violence 1*, 3, 251–272.

Burgess, R.L. and Conger, R. (1978) 'Family interactions in abusive, neglectful and normal families.' *Child Development 49* 1163–1173.

Burke, K. (1966) *Language as Symbolic Action.* Berkeley, CA: University of California Press.

Butler Report (1975) *The Report of the Committee on Mentally Abnormal Offenders.* London: HMSO. Cmnd 6244.

Butler, A. (1987) 'Strictly confidential.' *Police Review 95*, 4905, 580–581.

Butterworth, G.E. (1991) 'The ontogeny and phylogeny of joint visual attention.' In A. Whiten (eds) *Natural Theories of Mind.* Oxford: Basil Blackwell.

Byng-Hall, J. (1973) 'Family myths used as defence in conjoint family therapy.' *British Journal of Medical Psychology 46*, 239–50.

Byng-Hall, J. (1982) 'Dysfunction of feeling. experiential life of the family.' In A. Bentovim, G. Gorell-Barnes and A. Cooklin (eds) *Family Therapy: Complementary Frameworks of Theory and Practice.* New York: Academic Press.

Byng-Hall, J. (1986) 'Family scripts, the concept which can bridge child psychotherapy and family therapy thinking.' *Journal of Child Psychotherapy 12,* 3–13.

Byng-Hall, J. (1991) 'The application of attachment theory to understanding and treatment in family therapy.' In C.M. Parkes, J. Stephenson-Hinde and H.P Marr (eds) *Attachment Across a Life Cycle.* London: Routledge.

Byron, A.J. (1976) 'Underworld Games: A transactional view of Rackets.' *British Journal of Criminology 16,* 267–274.

Caddick, B. (1991) 'Using groups in working with offenders: a survey of groupwork in the probation services of England and Wales.' *Groupwork 4, 3,* 197–214.

Caldicott, F. (1994) 'Supervision register: the College's response.' *Psychiatric Bulletin 18,* 385–388.

Camp, B.W. (1966) 'WISC performance in acting out and delinquent children with and without EEC abnormalities.' *Journal of Consulting Psychology 30,* 350–353.

Campbell, A. (1987) 'Self-reported delinquency and home life: evidence from a sample of British girls.' *Journal of Youth and Adolescence 16,* 167–177.

Campbell, D. (1989) 'A psychoanalytic contribution to understanding delinquents at school.' *Journal of Educational Therapy 2, 4,* 50–65.

Campbell, D. (1994) 'A violent adolescent's ego ideal.' Read at the Anna Freud Centre, London.

Camras, L.A. and Sachs, V.B. (1991) 'Social referencing and caretaker expressive behavior in a day care setting.' *Infant Behavior and Development 14,* 27–36.

Cannon, W.B. (1927) 'The James-Lange theory of emotions: a critical examination and an alternative theory.' *American Journal of Psychology 48,* 1097–1111.

Canter, D. and Heritage, R. (1989) 'A multivariate model of sexual offence behaviour.' *The Journal of Forensic Psychiatry 1, 2,* 185–212.

Cantwell, D.P. and Baker, L. (1985) 'Speech and language development and disorder.' In M. Rutter and L. Hersov (eds) *Child and Adolescent Psychiatry.* Oxford: Blackwell.

Carey, S. (1978) 'The child as a word learner.' In M. Halle, J. Bresnan and G.A. Miller (eds) *Linguistic Theory and Psychological Reality.* Boston: MIT Press.

Carmen (Hilberman) E., Rieker, P.P. and Mills, T. (1984) 'Victims of violence and psychiatric illness.' *American Journal of Psychiatry 141,* 378–383.

Carpy, D.V. (1989) 'Tolerating the countertransference: a mutative process.' *International Journal of Psychoanalysis 70,* 287.

Carter, B. and McGoldrick, M. (1989) *The Changing Family Life Cycle: Framework for Family Therapy, second edition.* Boston: Allyn and Bacon.

Casement, P. (1985) *On Learning from the Patient.* London: Tavistock/Routledge.

Casey, C. (1994) 'Mind over matter.' *Police Review 102,* 5286, 22–24.

Cassidy, J. (1993) 'Emotion regulation within attachment relationships.' In J. Cassidy and L. Berlin, Co-Chairs of Symposium on Attachment and Emotion at the Symposium Conducted at the Meeting of the Society for Research in Child Development. New Orleans, Louisianna.

Catherall, D.R. (1991) 'Aggression and projective identification in the treatment of victims.' *Psychotherapy 28,* 145–149.

Cattanach, A. (1992) *Drama for People with Special Needs.* London: A and C Black.

Cavell, M. (1988a) 'Interpretation, psychoanalysis and the philosophy of mind.' *Journal of the American Psychoanalytic Association 36,* 859–879.

Cavell, M. (1988b) 'Solipsism and community: two concepts of mind in psychoanalysis.' *Psychoanalysis and Contemporary Thought 11,* 587–613.

Cavell, M. (1991) 'The subject of mind.' *International Journal of Psycho-Analysis 72,* 141–154.

Chadwick, P. (1994) 'The omnipotence of voices: a cognitive approach to auditory hallucinations.' *British Journal of Psychiatry, 164* 190–201.

Chamberlin, P. (1994) 'Custody deaths continue to rise.' *Sydney Morning Herald* 30 June.

Chasseguet-Smirgel, J. (1974) 'Perversion, idealization and sublimation.' *International Journal of Psychoanalysis 55,* 349–357.

Chasseguet-Smirgel, J. (1985) *Creativity and Perversion.* London: Free Association Books.

Chasseguet-Smirgel, J. and Grunberger, B. (1986) *Freud or Reich: Psychoanalysis and Illusion.* London: Free Association Books.

Chesner, A. (1994) 'Dramatherapy and psychodrama: similarities and differences.' In S. Jennings, A. Cattanach, S. Mitchell, A. Chesner and B. Meldrum (eds) *The Handbook of Dramatherapy.* London: Routledge.

Chessick, R. (1969) 'The borderline patient.' In S. Arieti (ed) *American Handbook of Psychiatry.* New York: Basic Books.

Christensen, A.L. (1975) *Luria's Neuropsychological Investigation.* Copenhagen: Munksgaard.

Cicchetti, D. (1990) 'An historical perspective on the discipline of developmental psychopathology.' In J. Rolf, A. Masten, D. Cicchetti, K. Nuechterlein, and S. Weintraub (eds) *Risk Protective Factors in the Development of Psychopathology.* New York: Cambridge University Press.

Clark, D.H. (1987) 'The therapeutic community.' Review article, *British Journal of Psychiatry 131,* 553–64.

Clarke, R. (1980) 'Situational crime prevention: theory and practice'. *British Journal of Criminology 20,* 2, 136–47.

Cleckley, H. (1941) *The Mask of Sanity*. St. Louis: Mosby.

Cockburn, J.J. (1989) 'Clinical decisions about patients. Management within multidisciplinary clinical teams.' *Psychiatric Bulletin 13*, 130–134.

Coen, S. (1985) 'Perversion as a solution to intrapsychic conflict.' *Journal of the American Psychiatric Association 33*, 17–57.

Cohen, A.K. (1955) *Delinquent Boys: the Culture of the Gang*. Chicago, IL: Free Press.

Cohen, N. (1994) 'Inside story: Rachel Nickell.' *Independent on Sunday*, 18 September.

Cohen, S. (1979) 'The punitive city: notes on the dispersal of social control.' *Contemporary Crises 3*, 339–63.

Cohn, J.F., Campbell, S.B., Matias, R. and Hopkins, J. (1990) 'Face-to-face interactions of postpartum depressed and nondepressed mother–infant pairs at 2 months.' *Developmental Psychology 26*, 15–23.

Cohn, J.F., Matias, R., Tronick, E.Z., Connell, D. and Lyons-Ruth, K. (1986) 'Face-to-face interactions of depressed mothers and their infants.' In E.Z. Tronick and T. Field (eds) *Maternal Depression and Infant Disturbance*. San Francisco, CA: Jossey-Bass.

Coid, J. (1991) 'Interviewing the aggressive patient.' In R. Corney (ed) *Developing Communication and Counselling Skills in Medicine*. London: Routledge.

Coid, J. (1992) 'DSM-III diagnoses in criminal psychopaths: the way forward.' *Criminal Behaviour and Mental Health 2*, 78–95.

Coid, J., Allolio, B. and Rees, L.H. (1983) 'Raised plasma metemkephalin in patients who habitually mutilate themselves.' *Lancet 2*, 545–546.

Coid, J., Wilkins, J., Coid, B., Everitt, B. and Matthews, J. (1992) 'Self mutilation in female remanded prisoners II.' *Criminal Behaviour and Mental Health 2*, 1–14.

Coleman, A. and Gorman, L. (1982) 'Conservatism, dogmatism and authoritarianism in British police officers.' *Sociology 16*, 11.

Collins, J.J. and Bailey, S. (1990) 'Traumatic stress disorder and violent behaviour.' *Journal of Traumatic Stress 3*, 203–220.

Conan Doyle, A. (1893) 'The cardboard box.' In A. Conan Doyle *The Memoirs of Sherlock Holmes*. Oxford: Oxford University Press 1993.

Conrad, P. (1985) 'The measuring of medications; another look at compliance.' *Social Science and Medicine 20*, 29–37.

Conte, J.R. and Schuerman, J.R. (1987) 'Factors associated with an increased impact of child sexual abuse.' *Child Abuse and Neglect 11*, 201–11.

Cook, T.D. and Campbell, D.T. (1976) 'The design and conduct of quasi experiments and true experiments in field settings.' In M.D. Dunnette (ed) *Handbook of Industrial and Organisational Psychotherapy*. Chicago, IL: Rand McNally.

Cooper A. (1991) 'The unconscious core of perversion.' In G. Fogel and W. Myers (eds) *Perversions and Near Perversions*. New Haven, CT: Yale University Press.

Cooper, C.L., Davidson, M.J. and Robinson, P. (1982) 'Stress among police detectives.' *Journal of Occupational Medicine 25*, 7, 30–36.

Cooper, D., Lillie, R. and Ritchie, G. (1991) *Discussion paper on the Prevention of Suicides and Attempted Suicides in the NSW Prison System.* Sydney: Department of Corrective Services.

Cooper, Z. and Cooper, P.J. (1985) 'A note on explanation and understanding in psychology.' *British Journal of Medical Psychology 58*, 19–24.

Copas, J.B., O'Brien, M., Roberts, J. and Whiteley, J.S. (1983) 'Treatment outcome in personality disorder: the effect of social psychological and behavioural variables.' *Personality and Individual Differences 5*, 565–73.

Cope, R. (1990) 'Psychiatry, ethnicity and crime.' In R. Bluglass and P. Bowden (eds) *Principles and Practice of Forensic Psychiatry.* London: Churchill Livingstone.

Cordess, C. (1992) 'Family therapy with psychotic offenders and family victims in a forensic psychiatry secure unit.' *Proceedings of the 17th International Congress of the International Academy of Law and Mental Health*, 366–380. Leuven, Belgium: International Academy of Law and Mental Health.

Cordess, C. (1992a) 'Pioneers in forensic psychiatry. Edward Glover (1888–1972): psychoanalysis and crime – a fragile legacy.' *The Journal of Forensic Psychiatry 3*, 3, 509–530.

Cordess, C., Riley, W. and Welldon, E. (1994) 'Psychodynamic forensic psychotherapy, an account of a day release course.' *Psychiatric Bulletin 18*, 2, 88–90.

Cordner, S.M., Ranson, D.L. and Singh, B. (1992) 'The practice of forensic medicine in Australasia: review.' *Australian and New Journal of Medicine 22*, 447–486.

Corinder, S. (1991) 'The Royal Commission into aboriginal deaths in custody: aspects of medical interest.' *Medical Journal of Australia 155*, 812–818.

Cornish, D. and Clark, R. (eds) (1986) *The Reasoning Criminal.* New York: Springer-Verlag.

Courtney, R. (1981) 'The universal theatre: background to drama therapy.' In R. Courtney and G. Schattner (eds) *Drama in Therapy Volume Two: Adults.* New York: Drama Book Specialists.

Courtney, R. (1987) 'Dramatherapy and the teacher.' In S. Jennings (ed) *Dramatherapy Theory and Practice 1.* London: Routledge.

Cox, M. (1973a) 'Dynamic psychotherapy and the christian response: areas of congruence.' *Christian I*, 3, 221.

Cox, M. (1973b) 'Group psychotherapy as a redefining process.' *International Journal of Group Psychotherapy 23*, 465.

Cox, M. (1973c) 'I'm dying to live.' *Christian 164–69*.

Cox, M. (1973d) 'Yesterdays.' *Christian*, 221–232.

Cox, M. (1974) 'The psychotherapist's anxiety: liability or asset? with special reference to the offender-patient.' *British Journal of Criminology 14*, 1, 1–17.

Cox, M. (1976) 'Group psychotherapy in a secure setting.' *Proceedings of The Royal Society of Medicine 69*, 215–20.

Cox, M. (1978a) *Coding the Therapeutic Process: Emblems of Encounter.* Reprinted 1988, London: Jessica Kingsley Publishers.

Cox, M. (1978b) *Structuring the Therapeutic Process: Compromise with Chaos.* Reprinted 1988 and 1995. London: Jessica Kingsley Publishers.

Cox, M. (1979) 'Dynamic psychotherapy with sex offenders.' In I. Rosen (ed) *Sexual Deviation.* Second edition. Oxford: Oxford University Press.

Cox, M. (1983) 'The contribution of dynamic psycho-therapy to forensic psychiatry and vice versa.' *International Journal of Law and Psychiatry 6*, 1, 89–99.

Cox, M. (1986) 'The "holding function" of dynamic psychotherapy in a custodial setting: a review.' *Journal of the Royal Society of Medicine 79*, 162–164

Cox, M. (1990a) Foreword. In H. Prins *Bizarre Behaviours: Boundaries of Psychiatric Disorder.* London and New York: Tavistock/Routledge.

Cox, M. (1990b) 'Psychopathology and treatment of psychotic aggression.' In R. Bluglass and P. Bowden (eds) *Principles and Practice of Forensic Psychiatry.* Edinburgh: Churchill Livingstone.

Cox, M. (1992a) (ed) *Shakespeare Comes to Broadmoor: 'The Actors are Come Hither': The Performance of Tragedy in a Secure Psychiatric Hospital.* London: Jessica Kingsley Publishers.

Cox, M. (1992b) 'The place of metaphor in psychotherapy supervision: creative tensions between forensic psychotherapy and dramatherapy.' In S. Jennings (ed) *Dramatherapy: Theory and Practice.* London: Tavistock Routledge.

Cox, M. (1993a) *The Group as Poetic Play-Ground: from Metaphor to Metamorphosis.* The 1990 S.H. Foulkes Annual Lecture. London: Jessica Kingsley Publishers.

Cox, M. (1993b) *Transferring the Untransferable: A Paradox Linking Poetry and Psychosis, Theology and Therapy.* 1991 Frank Lake Memorial Lecture. Oxford: Clinical Theology Association.

Cox, M. (1994) 'Manipulation.' *Journal of Forensic Psychiatry 5*, 1, 9–13.

Cox, M. (1995a) 'The shattered self; psychotherapeutic possibilities.' *British Journal of Psychiatry 167*, 126–29.

Cox, M. (1995b, in press) 'The great feast of languages: passwords to the psychotic's inner world.' In C. Mace and F. Margison (eds) *Psychotherapy of Psychosis.* London: Royal College of Psychiatrists. Gaskell.

Cox, M. and Grounds, A.T. (1991) 'The nearness of the offence: some theological reflections on forensic psychotherapy.' *Theology 94*, 106–115.

Cox, M. and Theilgaard, A. (1987) *Mutative Metaphors in Psychotherapy. The Aeolian Mode.* London: Tavistock.

Cox, M. and Theilgaard, A. (1994) *Shakespeare as Prompter. The Amending Imagination and the Therapeutic Process.* London: Jessica Kingsley Publishers.

Coyle, A.(1992) 'Imprisonment: a challenge for community.' In *Penal Policy: The Way Forward.* Occasional Paper No.27. Edinburgh: Edinburgh Centre for Theology and Public Issues.

Crittenden, P. (1988) 'Family and dyadic patterns of functioning in maltreating families.' In K. Browne., C. Davies. and P. Stratten (eds) *Early Prediction and Prevention Child Abuse.* Chichester: John Wiley and Sons Ltd.

Crittenden, P.M. (1988) 'Relationships at risk.' In J. Belsky and T. Nezworski (eds) *Clinical Implications of Attachment.* Hillsdale, NJ: Lawrence Erlbaum Associates.

Crown, S. (1983) 'Contraindications and dangers of psychotherapy'. *British Journal of Psychiatry 143,* 435–441.

Cullen, E. (1994) 'Grendon: The therapeutic prison that works.' *Therapeutic Communities 15,* 4. Therapeutic Communities for Offenders.

Cullmann, O. (1951) *Christ and Time.* Transl. by F.V. Filson. London: SCM Press.

Cummings, E.M. and Cicchetti, D. (1990) 'Towards a transactional model of relations between attachment and depression.' In M. Greenberg, D. Cicchetti, and E.M. Cummings (eds) *Attachment in the Preschool Years: Theory, Research, and Intervention.* Chicago, IL: The University of Chicago Press.

Cummings, E.M. and Cummings, J. (1956) 'The locus of power in a large mental hospital.' *Psychiatry 19,* 361–370.

Cummings, E.M., Iannotti, R.J. and Zahn-Waxler, C. (1985) 'Influence of conflict between adults on the emotions and aggression of young children.' *Developmental Psychology 21,* 495–507.

Cummings, E.M., Zahn-Waxler, C. and Radke-Yarrow, M. (1981) 'Young children's response to expressions of anger and affection by others in the family.' *Child Development 52,* 1275–1282.

Cummings, E.M., Zahn-Waxler, C. and Radke-Yarrow, M. (1984) 'Developmental changes in children's reactions to anger in the home.' *Journal of Child Psychology and Psychiatry 25,* 63–74.

Curtiz, M. (1942) *Casablanca.* Warner Brothers.

Darwin, C. (1859) *On the Origin of the Species by Means of Natural Selection, or the Preservation of Favoured Races in the Struggle for Life.* London: John Murray.

Darwin, C. (1871) *The Descent of Man, and Selection in Relation to Sex.* London: John Murray.

Darwin, C. (1872) *The Expression of the Emotions in Man and Animals.* Chicago, IL: University of Chicago Press.

Davidow, S. and Bruhn, A.R. (1990) 'Earliest memories and the dynamics of delinquency: A replication study.' *Journal of Personality Assessment 54,* 601–616.

Davidson, D. (1983) *Inquiries into Truth and Interpretation.* Oxford: Oxford University Press.

Davis, K. (1937) 'The sociology of prostitution.' *American Sociological Review 2,* 444–55.

Davis, M. and Dulicai, D. (1992) 'Hitler's movement signature.' *The Drama Review* *36*, 2, 152–172.

Delay, J., Pichot, P., Lemperière, T. and Perse, J. (1955) *Le Test de Rorschach et la Personnalité Epileptique.* Paris: Presses Universitaires de France.

Dell, P. (1989) 'Violence and the systemic view: the problem of power.' *Family Process 28*, 1–14.

Dell, S. (1992) 'Where special means sinister.' *Journal of Forensic Psychiatry 4,* 1, 5–8.

Dell, S. and Robertson, G. (1988) *Sentenced to Hospital: Offenders in Broadmoor.* Maudsley Monograph No. 32. Oxford: Oxford University Press.

Denman, C. (1994) 'Training and supervision in psychotherapy.' *Current Opinion in Psychiatry 7,* 237–240.

Denman, F. (1994) 'Quality in a psychotherapy service. A review of audiotapes of sessions.' *Psychiatric Bulletin 18,* 80–82.

Dennett, D.C. (1978) *Brainstorms.* Cambridge, MA: MIT Press.

Dentler, R.A. and Erikson, K.T. (1959) 'The functions of deviance in groups.' *Social Problems 7,* 102–107.

Department of Health (1989) *Working For Patients.* Cm 555. Working Paper 6, Medical Audit. London: HMSO.

Department of Health (1990) Press Release 90/97, 19 February. Virginia Bottomley outlines radical shifts in the way district health authorities will operate after 1991. London: Department of Health.

Department of Health (1991a) *Contracts for Health Services: Operational Principles* (EL(89)MB/169) London: Department of Health.

Department of Health (1991b) *Health of the Nation.* London: HMSO.

Department of Health (1992a) *Report of the Committee of Inquiry into Complaints about Ashworth Hospital.* 2 vols. Cm 2028-1-2. London: HMSO.

Department of Health (1992b) *The Government's Expenditure Plans 1992–1995.* Department of Health and Office of Population Censuses and Surveys Departmental Report. London: HMSO.

Department of Health (1992c) *Review of Health and Social Services for Mentally Disordered Offenders and Others Requiring Similar Services.* Reed Report Cm 2088. London: HMSO.

Department of Health (1994a) *Report of the Department of Health and Home Office Working Group on Psychopathic Disorder.* London: HMSO.

Department of Health (1994b) 'Draft guidance to arrangements for inter-agency working for the care and protection of severely mentally ill people.' Long Guide. London: HMSO.

Deutsch, H. (1942) 'Some forms of emotional disturbance and their relationship to schizophrenia.' *Psychoanalytic Quarterly 11,* 301–321.

Deutsch, L. and Erickson, M. (1989) 'Early life events as discriminators of socialized and undersocialized delinquents.' *Journal of Abnormal Child Psychology 17*, 541–551.

Dick, B.M. and Woof, K. (1986) 'An evaluation of a time-limited programme of dynamic group psychotherapy.' *British Journal of Psychiatry 148*, 159–164.

Dilts, R., Grinder, J., Bandler, R., Bandler, L. and DeLozier, J. (1980) *Neurolinguistic Programming, Volume I – The Study of Subjective Experience.* Cupertino, CA: Metta Publications.

Dobash, R.E. and Dobash, R. (1979) *Violence Against Wives.* New York: Free Press.

Dolan, B.M. and Coid, J. (1993) *Psychopathic and Antisocial Personality Disorders: Treatment and Research Issues.* London: Royal College of Psychiatrists, Gaskell.

Dolan, B.M. and Norton, K. (1991) 'The predicted impact of the NHS white paper upon the use and funding of a specialist psychiatric service for personality disordered patients.' *Psychiatric Bulletin 15*, 402–404.

Dolan, B.M., Evans, C. and Wilson, J. (1992a) 'Neurotic symptomatology and length of stay in a therapeutic community.' *Therapeutic Communities 13*, 3, 171–177.

Dolan, B.M., Evans, C. and Wilson, J. (1992b) 'Therapeutic community treatment for personality disordered adults: changes in neurotic symptomatology on follow-up.' *International Journal of Social Psychiatry 38*, 4, 243–250.

Dolan, M. (1994) 'Psychopathy – a neurobiological perspective.' *British Journal of Psychiatry 165*, 151–159.

Donabedian, A. (1966) 'Evaluating the quality of medical care.' Millbank Memorial Federation of Quality. Part 3, no 166–203.

Dore, J. (1980) 'The development of conversational competence.' In R. L. Schiefelbusch (ed) *Language Competence: Assessment and Intervention.* London: Taylor and Francis Inc.

Dostoievski, F. (1870) *Crime and Punishment.* Translated by David Magarshack. Harmondsworth: Penguin Books 1963.

Drugs and Therapeutics Bulletin (1993) Leader: 'Psychological treatment for anxiety – an alternative to drugs?' *Drugs and Therapeutics Bulletin 31*, 73–5.

Dumont, F. (1993) 'Inferential heuristics in clinical problem formulation: selective review of their strengths and weaknesses.' *Professional Psychology: Research and Practice 24*, 2, 196–205.

Dunn, J., Bretherton, I. and Munn, P. (1987) 'Conversations about feeling states between mothers and their young children.' *Developmental Psychology 23*, 132–139.

Dunne, J.S. (1973) *Time and Myth: a Meditation of Storytelling as an Exploration of Life and Death.* London: SCM Press.

Dunne, T.P. (1994) 'Challenging behaviour: and there's more...' *Clinical Psychology Forum 67*, 25–27.

Durkheim, E. (1951) *Suicide* (translated by J. Spaulding and G. Simpson). New York: Free Press.

Dutton, D. and Hart, S. (1991) 'Evidence for long-term specific effects of childhood abuse and neglect on criminal behaviour in men.' *International Journal of Offender Therapy and Comparative Criminology 13*, 129–137.

Dye, E. and Roth, S. (1991) 'Psychotherapy with Vietnam veterans and rape and incest survivors.' *Psychotherapy 28*, 103–420.

Eades, J. (1987) 'The management of stress.' *Police Review 95*, 4905, 583–584.

East, W. Norwood (1936) *The Medical Aspects of Crime.* London: J.A. Churchill.

East, W. Norwood and Hubert, W.H. de B. (1939) *Report on the Psychological Treatment of Crime.* London: HMSO.

Eastman, N. (1993) 'Forensic psychiatry going Dutch.' *British Journal of Psychiatry Review of Books.* London: The Royal College of Psychiatrists.

Edelwich, J. and Brodsky, A. (1980) *Burnout: Stages of Disillusionment in the Helping Professions.* New York: Human Sciences Press.

Edgerton, S. (1985) *Pictures and Punishment: Art and Criminal Prosecution during the Florentine Renaissance.* Ithaca, NY: Cornell University Press.

Egeland, B. (1988) 'Breaking the cycle of abuse.' In K. Browne, C. Davies and P. Stratten (eds) *Early Prediction and Prevention of Child Abuse.* Chichester: John Wiley and Sons Ltd.

Egeland, B. and Sroufe, A. (1981) 'Attachment and early maltreatment.' *Child Development 53*, 44–52.

Ehlers, W. (1991) 'Supervision: odyssey or pedagogical experiment.' In I. Szecsödy and K. Gyllensköld (eds) *The Learning Process in Psychotherapy-Supervision and in Psychotherapy: Theories and Applications.* Proceedings of 1st Nordic Symposium for Supervisors. Stockholm: Karolinska Institutet.

Eissler, K.R. (1949) 'Some problems of delinquency.' In K.R. Eissler (eds) *Searchlights on Delinquency: Essays in Honor of August Aichhorn.* New York: International Universities Press.

Eissler, K.R. (1950) 'Ego psychological implications of the psychoanalytic treatment of delinquents.' *Psychoanalytic Study of the Child 6*, 97–121.

Eissler, K.R. (1967) 'Notes on the Problems of Technique in The Psychoanalytic Treatment of Adolescents with some remarks on Perversions'. *Psychoanalytic Study of the Child 13*, 223–254. New York: International Universities Press.

Ekstein, R. and Wallerstein, R.S. (1958) *The Teaching and Learning of Psychotherapy.* New York: Basic Books.

Ellard, J. (1988) 'Some Major Lessons to be Learned from the History of Corrections'. In E. Biles (ed) *Current International Trends in Corrections.* Sydney: Federation Press.

Ellenberger, H. (1966) 'The pathogenic secret and its therapeutics.' In *Beyond the Unconscious. Essays in the History of Psychiatry.* Princeton, NJ: Princeton University Press.

Ellenberger, H. (1970) *The Discovery of the Unconscious.* New York: Basic Books.

Elliott, R. (1991) 'University of Toledo: Investigating significant therapy events.' In L. Beutler and M. Crago (eds) *Psychotherapy Research: An International Review of Programmmatic Studies.* Washington, DC: American Psychiatric Press.

Elliott, R. and Shapiro, D.A. (1988) 'Brief structured recall: a more efficient method for studying significant therapy events.' *British Journal of Medical Psychology 61,* 141–53.

Elliott, R. and Shapiro, D.A. (1992). 'Client and therapist as analysts of significant events.' In S.G. Toukmanian and D.L. Rennie (eds) *Psychotherapy Process Research. Paradigmatic and Narrative Approaches.* Newbury Park: Sage Publications.

Ellis, E.M. (1991) 'Watchers in the Night: An Anthropological Look at Sleep Disorders.' *American Journal of Psychotherapy 45,* 211–220.

Ellsworth, C.P., Muir, D.W. and Hains, S.M.J. (1993) 'Social competence and person-object differentiation: an analysis of the still-face effect.' *Developmental Psychology 29,* 63–73.

Emde, R.N. (1988a) 'Development terminable and interminable. I: Innate and motivational factors from infancy.' *International Journal of Psychoanalysis 69,* 23–42.

Emde, R.N. (1988b) 'Development terminable and interminable. II: Recent psychoanalytic theory and therapeutic considerations.' *International Journal of Psychoanalysis 69,* 283–286.

Epstein, A. (1990) 'Beliefs and symptoms in maladaptive resolutions of the traumatic neurosis.' In D. Ozer, J.M. Healy and A.J. Stewart (eds) *Perspectives in Personality.* London: Jessica Kingsley Publishers.

Erickson, M.F., Sroufe, L.A. and Egeland, B. (1985) 'The relationship between quality of attachment and behavior problems in preschool in a high-risk sample.' In I. Bretherton and E. Waters (eds) 'Growing points of attachment theory and research.' *Monographs of the Society for Research in child development 50,* 1–2, 147–166.

Erikson, E.H. (1956) 'The problem of ego identity.' In E.H. Erikson *Identity and the Life Cycle.* New York: International Universities Press.

Erikson, E.H. (1959a) *Identity and the Life Cycle.* New York: International Universities Press.

Erikson, E.H. (1959b) *Young Man Luther.* London: Faber and Faber.

Erikson, E. H. (1963) *Childhood and Society.* Second edition. New York: W.W. Norton and Co.

Espir, M.E. and Rose, F.C. (1976) *The Basic Neurology of Speech.* Oxford: Blackwell.

Etchegoyen, R.H. (1970) 'Homosexualidad femenina: aspectos dinamicos de la reparacion.' *Revista Uruguaya Psico-Analisis 12*, 431–477.

Eth, S. and Pynoos, R.S. (eds) (1985) *Post Traumatic Stress Disorder in Children.* Los Angeles, CA: American Psychiatric Press.

Etheridge, P. (1994) 'Policing mentally ill people.' *The Metropolitan Journal 11*, 34–36.

Everitt, B. (1987). 'Methodology for investigation: experimental research designs.' In S. Lindsay and G. Powell (eds) *A Handbook of Clinical Adult Psychology.* Aldershot: Gower.

Exner, J.E. (1969) *The Rorschach Systems.* New York: Grune and Stratton.

Exner, J.E. (1974) *The Rorschach: A Comprehensive System.* New York: John Wiley and Sons Ltd.

Eysenck, H.J. (1992) 'The effects of psychotherapy: an evaluation.' *Journal of Consulting and Clinical Psychology 60*, 5, 659–663.

Eysenck, H.J. and Eysenck, S.B.G. (1975) *Manual: Eysenck Personality Questionnaire.* San Diego, CA: Edits.

Fahy, T. (1988) 'The diagnosis of multiple personality disorder: a critical review.' *British Journal of Psychiatry 153*, 597–606.

Fairbairn, W.R.D. (1940) 'Schizoid factors in the personality.' In W.R.D. Fairbairn *An Object-Relations Theory of the Personality.* New York: Basic Books.

Fairbairn, W.R.D. (1944) 'Endopsychic structure considered in terms of object-relationships.' In W.R.D. Fairbairn *Pscyhoanalytic Studies of the Personality.* London: Routledge and Kegan Paul.

Fairbairn, W.R.D. (1951) 'A synopsis of the development of the author's views regarding the structure of the personality.' In W.R.D. Fairbairn *Psychoanalytic Studies of the Personality.* London: Routledge and Kegan Paul.

Fairbairn, W.R.D. (1952a) *An Object-Relations Theory of the Personality.* New York: Basic Books.

Fairbairn, W.R.D. (1952b) *Psychoanalytic Studies of the Personality.* London: Routledge and Kegan Paul.

Farr, R. (1990) 'The social psychology of the prefix "inter": a prologue to the study of dialogue.' In I. Markova and K. Foppa (eds) *The Dynamics of Dialogue.* Sussex: Harvester Wheatsheaf.

Farrenkopf, T. (1992) 'What happens to therapists who work with sex offenders?' *Journal of Offender Rehabilitation 18*, 3/4, 217–223.

Farrington, D.P. (1985) 'Delinquency prevention in the 1980s.' *Journal of Adolescence 8*, 3–16.

Fawcus, M. (1986) 'Causes and classification of voice disorders.' In M. Fawcus (ed) *Voice Disorders and Their Management.* Beckenham: Croom Helm.

Feinstein, A. (1993) 'A prospective study of PTSD.' In J.P. Wilson and B. Raphael (eds) *International Handbook of Traumatic Stress Syndromes.* New York: Plenum Press.

Feldman, M.P. (1977) *Criminal Behaviour: A Psychological Analysis.* Chichester: John Wiley and Sons Ltd.

Felthous, A., Bryant, S.G., Wingerter, C.B. and Barratt, E. (1991) 'The diagnosis of intermittent explosive disorder in violent men.' *Bulletin of the American Academy of Psychiatry and the Law 19,* 71–79.

Fenichel, O. (1945) *The Psychoanalytic Theory of Neurosis.* New York: W.W. Norton and Co.

Ferenczi, S. (1913) 'Stages in the development of the sense of reality.' In S. Ferenczi *First Contributions to Psycho-Analysis.* London: Karnac Books, 1980.

Ferenczi, S. (1931) 'Child analysis in the analysis of adults.' In S. Ferenczi (1955) *Further Contributions to the Problems and Methods of Psychoanalysis.* London: Hogarth Press.

Ferenzi, S. (1932) 'Confusion of tongues between adults and the child.' *Final Contributions 162.*

Ferenczi, S. (1933) 'Confusion of tongues between adults and the child.' In S. Ferenczi *Further Contributions to the Problems and Methods of Psychoanalysis.* London: Hogarth Press.

Fernald, A. (1992) 'Human maternal vocalizations to infants as biologically relevant signals: an evolutionary perspective.' In J.H. Barkow, L. Cosmides, and J. Tooby (eds) *The Adapted Mind: Evolutionary Psychology and the Generation of Culture.* Oxford: Oxford University Press.

Fewtrell, W. and Toms, D. (1985) 'Patterns of discussion in traditional and novel ward round procedures.' *British Journal of Medical Psychology 58,* 57–62.

Fidler, G. and Fidler, J. (1963) *Occupational Therapy: A Communication Process in Psychiatry.* New York: Macmillan.

Field, T. (1989) 'Maternal depression effects on infant interaction and attachment behavior.' In D. Cicchetti (ed) *Rochester Symposium on Developmental Psychopathology, Vol.1: The Emergence of a Discipline.* Hillsdale, NJ: Lawrence Erlbaum Associates.

Field, T., Healy, B., Goldstein, S., Perry, S., Bendell, D., Schanberg, S., Zimmerman, E. and Kuhn, C. (1988) 'Infants of depressed mothers show "depressed" behavior even with nondepressed adults.' *Child Development 59,* 1569–1579.

Fielding, N. and Fielding, J. (1991) 'Police attitudes to crime and punishment.' *British Journal of Criminology 33,* 1.

Finklehor, D. (1984) *Child Sexual Abuse: New Theory and Research.* New York: Free Press.

Finkelhor, D. (ed) (1986) *A Sourcebook on Child Sexual Abuse.* Newbury Park, CA: Sage Publications.

Finklehor, D. (1987) 'The trauma of child sexual abuse: Two models.' *Journal of Interpersonal Violence 2,* 348–366.

Finkelhor, D. (1993) 'Epidemiological factors in the clinical identification of child sexual abuse.' *Child Abuse and Neglect 17*, 67–70.

Firth, J., Shapiro, D.A. and Parry, G. (1986) 'The impact of research on the practice of psychotherapy.' *British Journal of Psychotherapy 2*, 3, 169–179.

Flavell, J.H., Everett, B.A., Croft, K. and Flavell, E.R. (1981) 'Young children's knowledge about visual perception: Further evidence for the Level 1 – Level 2 distinction.' *Developmental Psychology 17*, 99–103.

Fleming, J. and Benedek, T. (1964) 'Supervision: a method of teaching psychoanalysis.' *The Psychanalytic Quarterly 33*, 71–96.

Fletcher and Newland (1989) Hampshire Joint Training for Child Sexual Abuse Investigation. A Joint Evaluation by Hampshire Constabulary and Hampshire Social Services (internal document).

Fónagy, I. and Fonagy, P. (in press) 'Pretend in language, literature and psychoanalysis.' *Psychoanalysis and Contemporary Thought 18.*

Fonagy, P. (1989) 'On tolerating mental states.' *Bulletin of the Anna Freud Centre 12*, 91–115.

Fonagy, P. (1991) 'Thinking about thinking: some clinical and theoretical considerations concerning the treatment of a borderline patient.' *International Journal of Psychoanalysis 72*, 1–18.

Fonagy, P. (1993) 'Psychoanalytic and empirical approaches to developmental psychopathology: can they be usefully integrated?' *Journal of the Royal Society of Medicine 86*, 577.

Fonagy, P., Edgcumbe, R., Moran, G., Kennedy, H. and Target, M. (1993) 'The roles of mental representation and mental processes in therapeutic action.' *Psychoanalytic Study of the Child 48*, 9–47.

Fonagy, P. and Higgit, A. (1990) 'A developmental perspective on borderline personality disorder.' *Revue Internationale de Psychopathologie 1*, 125–159.

Fonagy, P. and Higgit, A. (1992) *British Journal of Psychiatry 161*, 23–43.

Fonagy P. and Moran G. (1991a) 'Understanding psychic change in child psychoanalysis.' *International Journal of Psychoanalysis 72*, 15–22.

Fonagy, P. and Moran, G. (1991b) 'Individual case study.' In L. Luborsky and N. Miller (eds) *Handbook of Psychoanalytic Research.* New York: Basic Books.

Fonagy, P., Steele, M., Moran, G., Steele, H. and Higgitt, A.C. (1991) 'The capacity for understanding mental states: The reflective self in parent and child and its significance for security of attachment.' *Infant Mental Health Journal 13*, 200–216.

Fonagy, P., Steele, H. and Steele, M. (1991) 'Maternal representations of attachment during pregnancy predict the organization of infant–mother attachment at one year of age.' *Child Development 62*, 891–905.

Fonagy, P., Steele, M., Steele, H., Leigh, T., Kennedy, R., Mattoon, G. and Target, M. (in press) 'Attachment, the reflective self and borderline states: The predictive specificity of the Adult Attachment Interview and pathological emotional development.' In S. Goldberg and J. Kerr (eds) *John Bowlby's Attachment Theory: Historical, Clinical and Social Significance.* New York: Analytic Press.

Fonagy, P. and Target, M. (1994) 'The efficacy of psycho-analysis for children with disruptive disorders.' *Journal of the American Academy of Child and Adolescent Psychiatry 33*, 45–55.

Fonagy, P. and Target, M. (in press, a) 'Predictors of outcome in child psychoanalysis: a retrospective study of 763 cases at the Anna Freud Centre.' *Journal of the American Psychiatric Association.*

Fonagy, P. and Target, M. (in press, b) 'Understanding the violent patient.' *International Journal of Psychoanalysis 76.*

Fonagy, P., Target, M. and Moran, G. (1993) 'Aggression and the psychological self.' *International Journal of Psychoanalysis 74*, 471–485.

Ford, M.F., Jones, M., Scannell, T., Powell, A., Coombes, R.C. and Evans, C. (1990) 'Is group psychotherapy feasible for oncology outpatient attenders selected on the basis of psychological morbidity?' *British Journal of Cancer 62*, 624–626.

Forensic Psychiatry Special Advisory Committee to the Joint Committee on Higher Psychiatric Training (1990) *Higher Training in Forensic Psychiatry: Notes of Guidance. Psychotherapy Training for Senior Registrars in Forensic Psychiatry.* London: Royal College of Psychiatrists.

Forensic Psychiatry Specialist Section Executive Committee (1995) *The Role, Responsibilies and Work of the Consultant Forensic Psychiatrist* (draft).

Foss, D.J. and Hakes, D.T. (1978) *Psycholinguistics – Introduction to the Psychology of Language.* Englewood Cliffs, NJ: Prentice Hall.

Foucault, M. (1965) *Madness and Civilization: A History of Insanity in the Age of Reason.* Translated by R. Howard. New York: Random House.

Foucault, M. (1979) *Discipline and Punish. The Birth of the Prison.* Harmondsworth: Peregine Books.

Foucault, M. (1988) 'The dangerous individual.' In J. Kritzman (ed) *Interviews and Other Writing 1977–1984.* London: Routledge.

Foulkes, S.H. (1948) *Introduction to Group-Analytic Psychotherapy.* London: Heinemann.

Foulkes, S.H. (1964) *Therapeutic Group Analysis.* London: George Allen and Unwin Ltd.

Foulkes, S.H. (1975) *Group-Analytic Psychotherapy, Method and Principles.* London: Gordon and Breach. Reprinted Maresfield.

Foulkes, S.H. (1990) *Selected Papers: Psychoanalysis and Group Analysis.* London: Karnac Books.

Foulkes, S.H. and Anthony, E.J. (1965) *Group Psychotherapy.* London: Pelican. Reprinted Maresfield.

Fox, J. (ed) (1987) *The Essential Moreno: Writings on Psychodrama, Group Method and Spontaneity by J.L. Moreno.* New York: Springer.

France, J. (1991) 'Psychoses.' In R. Gravell and J. France (eds) *Speech and Communication Problems in Psychiatry.* London: Chapman and Hall.

Freeman, M. (1982) 'Forensic psychiatry and related topics.' *British Journal of Occupational Therapy 45,* 191–4.

Freud, A. (1936) *The Ego and the Mechanisms of Defence.* London: Hogarth Press.

Freud, A. (1949) 'Certain types and stages of social maladjustment'. In K.R. Eissler (ed) *Searchlights on Delinquency.* New York: New International Press.

Freud, A. (1954) 'The widening scope of indications for psychoanalysis: discussion.' *Journal of the American Psychoanalytical Association 2,* 607–620.

Freud, A. (1966) *Normality and Pathology in Childhood: Assessments of Development.* London: Hogarth Press.

Freud, A. (1974) 'A psychoanalytic view of developmental psychopathology.' In *The Writings of Anna Freud, Vol.8.* New York: International Universities Press.

Freud, A. (1983) 'Problems of pathogenesis: Introduction to the discussion.' *The Psychoanalytic Study of the Child 38,* 383–388.

Freud, S. (1893) 'Preliminary communication.' *The Standard Edition of the Complete Psychological Works of Sigmund Freud, Vol.3.* London: Hogarth Press.

Freud, S. (1894a) Draft E. 'How anxiety originates.' In J. Strachey (ed) *The Standard Edition of the Complete Psychological Works of Sigmund Freud, Vol.1.* London: Hogarth Press.

Freud, S. (1894b) 'The neuro-psychoses of defence.' In J. Strachey (ed) *The Standard Edition of the Complete Psychological Works of Sigmund Freud, Vol.3.* London: Hogarth Press.

Freud, S. (1895) 'Studies in hysteria.' *Standard Edition of the Complete Psychological Works of Sigmund Freud, Vol.2.* London: Hogarth Press.

Freud, S. (1896a) 'The aetiology of hysteria.' In J. Strachey (ed) *The Standard Edition of the Complete Psychological Works of Sigmund Freud, Vol.3.* London: Hogarth Press.

Freud, S. (1896b) 'Further remarks on the neuro-psychoses of defence.' In J. Strachey (ed) *The Standard Edition of the Complete Psychological Works of Sigmund Freud, Vol.3.* London: Hogarth Press.

Freud, S. (1900) 'The interpretation of dreams.' In J. Strachey (ed) *The Standard Edition of the Complete Psychological Works of Sigmund Freud, Vols. 4 and 5.* London: Hogarth Press.

Freud, S. (1901) 'The psychopathology of everyday life.' In J. Strachey (ed) *The Standard Edition of the Complete Psychological Works of Sigmund Freud, Vol.6,* 1–190. London: Hogarth Press.

Freud, S. (1905a) 'Fragment of an analysis of a Case of Hysteria.' In J. Strachey (ed) *The Standard Edition of the Complete Psychological Works of Sigmund Freud, Vol.7.* London: Hogarth Press.

Freud, S. (1905b) 'Jokes and their relation to the unconscious.' In J. Strachey (ed) *The Standard Edition of the Complete Psychological Works of Sigmund Freud, Vol.8.* London: Hogarth Press.

Freud, S. (1905c) 'Three essays on the theory of sexuality'. In J. Strachey (ed) *The Standard Edition of the Complete Psychological Works of Sigmund Freud, Vol.7.* London: Hogarth Press.

Freud, S. (1908a) '"Civilized'" sexual morality and modern nervous illness.' In J. Strachey (ed) *The Standard Edition of the Complete Psychological Works of Sigmund Freud, Vol.9.* London: Hogarth Press.

Freud, S. (1908b) *The Freud/Jung Letters.* Harmondsworth: Penguin Books, 1991.

Freud, S. (1909) 'Notes upon a case of obsessional neurosis.' In J. Strachey (ed) *The Standard Edition of the Complete Psychological Works of Sigmund Freud, Vol.5.* London: Hogarth Press.

Freud, S. (1910a) 'A special type of choice of object made by men (contributions to the psychology of love).' In S. Freud *On sexuality.* Harmondsworth: Penguin Books.

Freud, S. (1910b) 'The future prospect of psychoanalytic therapy.' In J. Strachey (ed) *The Standard Edition of the Complete Psychological Works of Sigmund Freud, Vol.11.* London: Hogarth Press.

Freud, S. (1911a) 'Formulations on the two principles of mental functioning.' In J. Strachey (ed) *The Standard Edition of the Complete Psychological Works of Sigmund Freud, Vol.12.* London: Hogarth Press.

Freud, S. (1911b) 'Psychoanalytic notes on an autobiographical account of a case of paranoia.' In J. Strachey (ed) *The Standard Edition of the Complete Psychological Works of Sigmund Freud, Vol. 12.* London: Hogarth Press.

Freud, S. (1912) 'The dynamics of transference.' In J. Strachey (ed) *The Standard Edition of the Complete Psychological Works of Sigmund Freud, Vol.12.* London: Hogarth Press.

Freud, S. (1913) 'On beginning the treatment.' In J. Strachey (ed) *The Standard Edition of the Complete Psychological Works of Sigmund Freud, Vol.12.* London: Hogarth Press.

Freud, S. (1914a) 'On narcissism: an introduction.' In J. Strachey (ed) *The Standard Edition of the Complete Psychological Works of Sigmund Freud, Vol.14.* London: Hogarth Press.

Freud, S. (1914b) 'Remembering, repeating and working through.' *The Standard Edition of the Complete Psychological Works of Sigmund Freud, Vol.12.* London: Hogarth Press.

Freud, S. (1916a) 'Criminals from a sense of guilt.' *The Standard Edition of the Complete Psychological Works of Sigmund Freud, Vol.14.* London: Hogarth Press.

Freud, S. (1916b) 'The exceptions.' Part II of 'Some character-types met within psycho-analytic work.' *The Standard Edition of the Complete Psychological Works of Sigmund Freud, Vol.14.* London: Hogarth Press.

Freud, S. (1916c) 'Some character-types met with in psychoanalytic work.' In *The Standard Edition of the Complete Psychological Works of Sigmund Freud, Vol.14.* London: Hogarth Press.

Freud, S. (1917) 'Mourning and melancholia.' In J. Strachey (ed) *The Standard Edition of the Complete Psychological Works of Sigmund Freud, Vol.14.* London: Hogarth Press.

Freud, S. (1920) 'Beyond the pleasure principle.' In *The Complete Psychological Works of Sigmund Freud, Vol.18.* London: Hogarth Press.

Freud, S. (1921) 'Group psychology and the analysis of the ego.' *The Standard Edition of the Complete Psychological Works of Sigmund Freud, Vol.18.* London: Hogarth Press.

Freud, S. (1923) 'The ego and the id.' *The Standard Edition of the Complete Psychological Works of Sigmund Freud, Vol.19.* London: Hogarth Press.

Freud, S. (1924) 'The economic problem of masochism.' In *On Meta-Psychology. The Theory of Psychoanalysis.* Harmondsworth: Penguin Books.

Freud, S. (1925a) 'An autobiographical study.' *The Standard Edition of the Complete Psychological Works of Sigmund Freud, Vol.20.* London: Hogarth Press. Cited in S. Grant (1991) Psychotherapy with people who have been sexually abused. In J. Holmes (ed) *Textbook of psychotherapy in psychiatric practice.* London: Churchill Livingstone.

Freud, S. (1925b) Foreword to A. Aichhorn *Wayward Youth.* In *The Standard Edition of the Complete Psychological Works of Sigmund Freud, Vol.19.* London: Hogarth Press.

Freud, S. (1926) 'Inhibitions, symptoms and anxiety.' *The Standard Edition of the Complete Psychological Works of Sigmund Freud, Vol.20.* London: Hogarth Press.

Freud, S. (1933) 'New introductory lectures on psychoanalysis.' *The Standard Edition of the Complete Psychological Works of Sigmund Freud, Vol.22.* London: Hogarth Press.

Freud, S. (1937) 'Analysis terminable and interminable.' *The Standard Edition of the Complete Psychological Works of Sigmund Freud, Vol.23.* London: Hogarth Press.

Freud, S. (1940) 'An outline of psychoanalysis.' In J. Strachey (ed) *The Standard Edition of the Complete Psychological Works of Sigmund Freud, Vol.23.* London: Hogarth Press.

Freudenberger, H.J. (1974) 'Staff burnout.' *Journal of Social Issues 30,* 159–165.

Freudenberger, H.J. (1989) 'Burnout: past, present and future concerns.' *Loss, Grief and Care 3,* 1–10.

Friedlander, K. (1945) 'Formation of the antisocial character.' *Psychoanalytic Study of the Child 1,* 189–203.

Frodi, A. (1985) 'Variations in parental and nonparental response to early infant communication.' In M. Reite and T. Field (eds) *The Psychobiology of Attachment and Separation.* London: Academic Press.

Frosch, J.P. (1983) 'The treatment of antisocial and borderline personality disorders.' *Hospital and Community Psychiatry 34*, 3, 243–248.

Furby, L., Weinrott, M.R. and Blackshaw, L. (1989) 'Sex offender recidivism: a review.' *Psychological Bulletin 105*, 1, 3–20.

Furniss, T. (1983) 'Mutual influence and inter-locking professional family process in the treatment of child sexual abuse.' *Child Abuse and Neglect 7*, 207–223.

Gacono, C.B. and Meloy, J.R. (1992) 'The Rorschach and the DSM-III-R antisocial personality: A tribute to Robert Lindner.' *Journal of Clinical Psychology 48*, 393–406.

Gacono, C.B., Meloy, J.R. and Berg, J.L. (1992) 'Object relations, defensive operations, and affective states in narcissistic, borderline, and antisocial personality disorder.' *Journal of Personality Assessment 59*, 32–49.

Gadamer, H.G. (1985) *Truth and Method.* New York: Crossroad.

Gallwey, P. (1965) 'Prison structure and criminal aggression.' *Sixth International Congress of Psychotherapy, London 1964: Selected Lectures.* New York: Karger.

Gallwey, P. (1985) 'The psychodynamics of borderline personality.' In D. Farrington and J. Gunn (eds) *Aggression and Dangerousness.* London: John Wiley and Sons Ltd.

Gallwey, P. (1991) 'Social maladjustment'. In J. Holmes (ed) *Textbook of Psychotherapy in Psychiatric Practice.* Edinburgh: Churchill Livingstone.

Gallwey, P. (1992) 'The psychotherapy of psychopathic disorder.' *Criminal Behaviour and Mental Health 2*, 159–168.

Gamman, L. and Makinen, M. (1994) *Female Fetishism.* London: Lawrence and Wishart Ltd.

Garfield, S.L. (1990) 'Issues and methods in psychotherapy process research.' *Journal of Consulting and Clinical Psychology 58*, 3, 273–280.

Garfinkel, H. (1956) 'Conditions of successful degradation ceremonies.' *American Journal of Sociology 61*, 420–424.

Garland, C. (1991) 'Trauma and the external world.' In J. Holmes (ed) *Textbook of psychotherapy in psychiatric practice.* London: Churchill Livingstone.

Garland, D. (1994) 'The development of British criminology'. In M. Maguire, R. Morgan and R. Reiner *The Oxford Handbook of Criminology.* Oxford: Oxford University Press.

Gath, K. (1987) 'The social context: communications in families with a handicapped child.' In W. Yule and M. Rutter (eds) *Language Development and Disorders.* Oxford: MacKeith Press.

Geertz, C. (1973) *The Interpretation of Cultures.* New York: Basic Books.

Gelles, R.J. (1987) 'Family violence.' Second edition. London: Sage Publications.

Genders, E. and Player, E. (1995) *Grendon: A Study of a Therapeutic Prison.* Oxford: Oxford University Press.

General Medical Council (1987) *Professional Conduct and Discipline: Fitness to Practise.* London: General Medical Council.

Genet, J. (1990) *Prisoner of Love.* London: Pan Books Limited.

George, C., Kaplan, N. and Main, M. (1984) 'Attachment Interview for Adults.' Unpublished manuscript. University of California, Berkeley.

George, C. and Main, M. (1979) 'Social interactions of young abused children: approach, avoidance and aggression.' *Child Development 50,* 306–318.

Gerstley, L., Mclellan, A.T., Alterman, A.I., Woody, G.E. and Pront, M. (1989) 'Ability to form an alliance with the therapist: a possible marker of prognosis for patients with antisocial personality disorder.' *American Journal of Psychiatry 146,* 4, 508– 512.

Gibbons, R.D., Hedeker, D., Elkin, I., Waternaux, C., Kraemer, H.C., Greenhouse, J.B., Shea, M.T., Imber, S.D., Sotsky, S.M. and Watkins, J.T. (1993) 'Some conceptual and statistical issues in analysis of longitudinal psychiatric data.' *Archives of General Psychiatry 50,* 739–750.

Gibbons, R.D., Hedeker, D., Waternaux, C. and Davis, J.M. (1988) 'Random regression models: a comprehensive approach to the analysis of longitudinal psychiatric data.' *Psychopharmacology Bulletin 24,* 3, 438–442.

Gilkey, L. (1969) *Naming the Whirlwind. The Renewal of God-Language.* New York: The Bobbs-Merrill Company.

Gilkey, L. (1976) *Reaping the Whirlwind: a Christian Interpretation of History.* New York: Seabury Press.

Gilkey, L. (1979) *Message and Existence: an Introduction to Christian Theology.* Minneapolis: Seabury Press.

Gillespie, W.H. (1940) 'A contribution to the study of fetishism.' *International Journal of Psychoanalysis 21,* 401–415.

Gillespie, W.H. (1956) 'The general theory of sexual perversions.' *International Journal of Psychoanalysis 37,* 398–403.

Gillespie, W.H. (1964) 'The psychoanalytic theory of sexual deviation with special reference to fetishism.' In I. Rosen (ed) *Sexual Deviation.* London: Oxford University Press.

Giovacchini, M.D. (1984) *Character Disorders and Adaptative Mechanisms.* New York: Jason Aronson Inc.

Giovacchini, P.L. (1979) *Treatment of Primitive Mental States.* New York: Jason Aronson Inc.

Glancy, J. (1974) *Revised Report of the Working Party on Security in NHS Security Hospitals.* London: Department of Health and Social Security (DHSS).

Glaser, D. and Fry, L.J. (1987) 'Corruption of Prison Staff in Inmate Discipline.' *Journal of Offender Counselling Service and Rehabilitation 12,* 27–38.

Glasser, M. (1979) 'Some aspects of the role of aggression in the perversions'. In I. Rosen (ed) *Sexual Deviation.* Oxford: Oxford University Press.

Glasser, M. (1994) 'Violence: a psychoanalytic research project.' *The Journal of Forensic Psychiatry 5,* 2, 311–320.

Gleason, J.B. (ed) (1992) *Development of Language.* Oxford: Charles E Merrill Publishing Co.

Glover, E. (1933) 'The relation of perversion formation to the development of reality sense.' *International Journal of Psycho-Analysis 241*, 486–503.

Glover, E. (1944) *Mental Abnormality and Crime.* London: Macmillan.

Glover, E. (1960) *The Roots of Crime. Selected Papers on Psychoanalysis.* Volume II. New York: International Universities Press.

Goffman, E. (1961) *Asylums: Essays on the Social Situation of Mental Patients and Other Inmates.* New York: Anchor Books.

Goldner, V., Penn, P., Sheinberg, M. and Walker, G. (1990) 'Love and violence: Gender paradoxes in volatile attachments.' *Family Process 29*, 343–365.

Goldstein, K. (1959) 'The organismic approach.' In S. Arieti (ed) *American Handbook of Psychiatry.* New York: Basic Books.

Gomes-Schwartz, B., Horowitz, T.M. and Carderelli, A. (1990) *Child Sexual Abuse: The Initial Effects.* Beverley Hills, CA: Sage Publications.

Gordon, R. (1978) *Dying and Creating – A Search for Meaning.* London: The Library of Analytical Psychology.

Gordon, R. (1981) 'Humanizing offenders through acting therapy.' In R. Courtney and G. Schattner (eds) *Drama in Therapy.* New York: Drama Book Specialists.

Gorell-Barnes, G. (1994) 'Family therapy.' In M. Rutter, L. Hersov and E. Taylor (eds) *Child and Adolescent Psychiatry.* Third edition.

Gough, H.G. (1948) 'A sociological theory of psychotherapy.' *American Journal of Sociology 53*, 359–366.

Gough, H.G. and Peterson, D.R. (1952) 'The identification measurement of predispositional factors in crime and delinquency'. *Journal of Consultative Psychology 16*, 207–212.

Graff, H. and Mallin, R. (1967) 'The syndrome of the wrist-cutter.' *American Journal of Psychiatry 124*, 36–42.

Graham, D.T. (1967) 'Health, disease, and the mind-body problem: linguistic parallelism.' *Psychosomatic Medicine 29*, 1, 52–71.

Graham, J.R. (1990) *MMPI-2: Assessing Personality and Psychopathology.* Oxford: Oxford University Press.

Grainger, R. (1990) *Drama and Healing: The Roots of Dramatherapy.* London: Jessica Kingsley Publishers.

Gray, W.J. (1973) 'The therapeutic community and the evaluation of results.' *International Journal of Criminology and Penology 1*, 327–334.

Green, B. (1993) 'Identifying survivors at risk.' In J.P. Wilson and B. Raphael (eds) *International Handbook of Traumatic Stress Syndromes.* New York: Plenum Press.

Green, B., Lindy, J., Grace, M., Glesser, G., Leonard, A., Korol, M. and Winget, C. (1990) 'Buffalo Creek survivors in the second decade.' *American Journal of Orthopsychiatry 60*, 43–54.

Greenacre, P. (1945) 'Conscience in the psychopath.' *American Journal of Orthopsychiatry 15*, 495–509.

Greenacre, P. (1968) 'Perversions: general considerations regarding their genetic and dynamic background.' *Psychoanalytic Study of the Child 23*, 47–62.

Greenberg, H.R. (1975) 'The widening gyre: transformations of the quest during adolescence'. *International Review of Psychoanalysis 2*, 231–244.

Greenberg, J.R. and Mitchell, S.A. (1983) *Object Relations in Psychoanalytic Theory.* Cambridge, MA: Harvard University Press.

Greenberg, L.S. (1983) 'Towards a task analysis of conflict resolution.' *Psychotherapy: Theory, Research and Practice 20*, 190–201.

Greenberg, L.S. (1986) 'Research strategies'. In L.S. Greenberg and W.M. Pinsoff (eds) *The Psychotherapeutic Process: A Research Handbook.* New York: Guilford Press.

Greenberg, L.S. (1992) 'Task analysis: Identifying components of intrapersonal conflict resolution.' In S.G. Toukmanian and D.L. Rennie (eds) *Psychotherapy Process Research. Paradigmatic and Narrative Approaches.* Newbury Park, CA: Sage Publications.

Greenberg, L.S. and Pinsoff, W.M. (1986). 'Process research: current trends and future perspectives.' In L.S. Greenberg and W.M. Pinsoff (eds) *The Psychotherapeutic Process: A Research Handbook.* New York: Guilford Press.

Greene, M.C.L. (1975) *The Voice and Its Disorders.* London: Pitman Medical.

Greenson, R.R. (1967) *The Technique and Practice of Psychoanalysis, Vol. I.* New York: International Universities Press.

Griffiths, D., Hingsburger, D. and Christian, R. (1985) 'Treating developmentally handicapped sexual offenders: the York behaviour management services treatment programme.' *Psychiatric Aspects in Mental Retardation Reviews 4*, 49–52.

Grinberg, L. (1962) 'On a specific aspect of countertransference due to the patient's projective identification.' *International Journal of Psychoanalysis 43*, 436–40.

Grinker, R., Werble, B. and Drye, R.C. (1968) *The Borderline Syndrome: A Behavioral Study of Ego Functions.* New York: Basic Books.

Grossmann, K., Grossmann, K.E., Spangler, G., Suess, G. and Unzner, L. (1985) 'Maternal sensitivity and newborns' orientation responses as related to quality of attachment in Northern Germany.' In I. Bretherton and E. Waters (eds) 'Growing Points of Attachment Theory and Research.' *Monographs of the Society for Research in Child Development 50*.

Grounds, A.T., Quayle, M.T., France, J., Brett, T., Cox, M. and Hamilton, J.R. (1987) 'A unit for "psychopathic" disorder patients in Broadmoor Hospital.' *Medicine, Science and the Law 27*, 21–31.

Grundy, K. (1989) *Linguistics in Clinical Practice.* London: Taylor and Francis.

Gudjonsson, G.H. (1994) 'Suspicion and silence: the right to silence in criminal investigations.' In D. Morgan and G. Stephenson (eds) *Psychological Vulnerability.* London: Blackstone Press.

Gudjonsson, G.H., Clare, I., Ruther, S. and Pearse, J. (1993) 'Persons at risk during interviews in police custody: the identification of vulnerabilities.' *Research Study No 12. Royal Commission on Criminal Justice.* London: HMSO.

Gudjonsson, G.H. and Adlam, K.R.C. (1983) 'Personality patterns of British Police officers.' *Personality and Individual Differences 4,* 507–512.

Gunderson, J.G. (1985) *Borderline Personality Disorder.* Washington, DC: American Psychiatric Press.

Gunderson, J. and Sabo, A. (1993) 'The phenomenological and conceptual interface between borderline personality disorder and PTSD.' *American Journal of Psychiatry 150,* 19–27.

Gunn, J. and Taylor, P.J. (eds) (1993) *Forensic Psychiatry: Clinical, Legal, and Ethical Issues.* Oxford: Butterworth-Heinemann.

Gunn, J., Robertson, G., Dell, S. and Way, C. (1978) *Psychiatric Aspects of Imprisonment.* London: Academic Press.

Gurman, A.S. and Kniskern, D.P. (1981) 'Family therapy outcome: research knowns and unknowns.' In A.S. Gurman and D.P. Kniskern (eds) *Handbook of Family Therapy, Vol.1.* New York: Brunnel/Mazel.

Gurman, A.S., Kniskern, D.P. and Prusoff (1986) 'Research on marital and family therapy – progress, perspective and prospects.' In S.L. Garfield and A.E. Bergin (eds) *Handbook of Psychotherapy and Behaviour Change: An Empirical Analysis.* Third edition. New York: John Wiley and Sons Ltd.

Gutheil, T.G. (1982) 'The Psychology of Psychopharmacology.' *Bulletin of the Menninger Clinic 46,* 321–330.

Guy, E. (1985) *Survey of Psychiatric Patients in the Philadelphia County Prisons.* Uunpublished.

Gzudner, G. and Muelle, R. (1987) 'Role of guilt and its implication in the treatment of criminals.' *International Journal of Therapy and Comparative Criminology 31,* 71–78.

Haan, N. (1963) 'Proposed model of ego functioning: coping and defence mechanisms in relationship to IQ change.' *Psychological Monographs 77,* 1–23.

Haley, J. (1963) *Strategies of Psychotherapy.* New York: Grune and Stratton.

Haley, J. (1971) *Changing Families: A Family Therapy Reader.* New York: Grune and Stratton.

Haley, J. (1977) *Problem Solving Therapy.* San Francisco, CA: Jossey-Bass.

Halton, W. (1994) 'Some unconscious aspects of organisational life.' In V. Roberts and A. Obholzer (eds) *The Unconscious at Work.* London: Routledge.

Hamilton, V. (1985) 'John Bowlby: an ethological basis for psychoanalysis.' In J. Reppen (ed) *Beyond Freud: A Study of Modern Psychoanalytic Theorists.* New York: Analytic Press.

Hankins, G.C., Vera, M.I., Barnard, G.W. and Herkov, M.J. (1994) 'Patient–therapist sexual involvement: a review of clinical and research data.' *Bulletin of the American Academy of Psychiatry and Law 22*, 109–126.

Harding, T. (1992) 'Research and evaluation in forensic psychotherapy.' First International Conference of the International Association of Forensic Psychotherapy. London.

Hare, R.D. (1985) *The Psychopathy Check-List.* Vancouver: University of British Columbia.

Hare, R.D. (1991) *The Hare Psychopathy Check-List-Revised.* Toronto: Multi Health Systems.

Hare, R.D., and Cox, D.N. (1987) 'Clinical and empirical conceptions of psychopathy, and the selection of subjects for research.' In R.D. Hare and D. Schalling (eds) *Psychopathic Behavior: Approaches to Research.* Toronto, Ontario: John Wiley and Sons Ltd.

Hare, R.D. and Schalling, D. (1978) *Psychopathic Behaviour. Approaches to Research.* Chichester and New York: John Wiley and Sons Ltd.

Harlow, H.F. and Mears, C. (1979) *Primate Perspectives.* New York: John Wiley and Sons Ltd.

Harris, P.L. (1994) 'The child's understanding of emotion: developmental change and the family environment.' *Journal of Child Psychology and Psychiatry 35*, 3–28.

Hartmann, H. (1939) *Ego Psychology and the Problem of Adaptation.* New York: International Universities Press, 1958.

Hartmann, H. (1950) *Comments on the Psychoanalytic Theory of the Ego.* New York: International Universities Press, 1964.

Hartmann, H. (1955) 'Notes on the theory of sublimation.' In H. Hartmann *Essays on Ego Psychology.* New York: International Universities Press, 1964.

Hartmann, H., Kris, E. and Loewenstein, R. (1946) 'Comments on the formation of psychic structure.' *The Psychoanalytic Study of the Child 2*, 11–38.

Hathaway, S.R. and McKinley, J.C. (1942) *Minnesota Multiphasic Personality Inventory.* Minneapolis, MW: University of Minnesota Press.

Haviland, J.M. and Lelwica, M. (1987) 'The induced affect response: 10-week-old infants' responses to three emotional expressions.' *Developmental Psychology 23*, 97–104.

Hebb, D.O. (1949) *The Organization of Behavior.* New York: John Wiley and Sons.

Heidegger, M. (1962) *Being and Time.* New York and London: Harper and Row.

Heidegger, M. (1971) *Poetry, Language, Thought.* Transl. by Albert Hofstadter. New York: Harper and Row.

Heilbrun, K., Nunez, C.E., Deitchman, M.A., Gustafson, D. and Krull, K. (1992) 'The treatment of mentally disordered offenders: a national survey of psychiatrists.' *Bulletin of the American Academy of Psychiatry and the Law 20,* 4, 475–480.

Heimann, P. (1950) 'On countertransference.' *International Journal of Psychoanalysis 31,* 81–84.

Hendrin, H. (1991) 'Psychodynamics of suicide with particular reference to the young.' *American Journal of Psychiatry 148,* 1150–1158.

Herman, J.L. (1990) 'Sex offenders: a feminist perspective'. In W.L. Marshall, D.R. Laws, and H.E. Barbaree (eds) *Handbook of Sexual Assault.* London: Plenum Press.

Herman, J.L. (1992) 'Complex PTSD: a syndrome in survivors of prolonged and repeated trauma.' *Journal of Traumatic Stress 5,* 377–391.

Herman, J.L., Perry, C. and van der Kolk, B. (1989) 'Childhood trauma in borderline personality disorder.' *American Journal of Psychiatry 146,* 490–495.

Herman, J.L., Russell, D. and Trocki, K. (1986) 'Long term effects of sexual abuse in childhood.' *American Journal of Psychiatry 143,* 1293–1296.

Hermann, I. (1936) 'Clinging-Going in search: a contrasting pair of instincts and their relation to sadism and masochism.' *Psychoanalysis Quarterly 45,* 1.

Hickson, A. (1995) *Creative Action Methods in Groupwork.* Bicester: Winslow Press.

Higgit, A. and Fonagy, P. (1992) 'Psychotherapy in borderline and narcisistic personality disorder.' *British Journal of Psychiatry 161,* 23–43.

Hill, C.E. (1990) 'Exploratory in-session process research in individual psychotherapy: a review.' *Journal of Consulting and Clinical Psychology 58,* 3, 288–294.

Hill, C.E. (1991) 'Almost everything you ever wanted to know about how to do process research on psychotherapy and counselling but didn't know who to ask.' In C.E. Watkins and L.J. Schneider (eds) *Research in Counselling.* Hillsdale, NJ: Lawrence Erlbaum Assocaites.

Hill, D. (1970) 'On the contributions of psychoanalysis to psychiatry: mechanism and meaning.' *British Journal of Psychiatry 117,* 609–615.

Hill, J. (1982) 'Reasons and causes: the nature of explanations in psychology and psychiatry.' *Psychological Medicine 12,* 501–514.

Hill, W.F. and Ottchen, C.J. (1991) *Shakespeare's Insults: Educating Your Wit.* Cambridge: Mainsail Press.

Hinshelwood, R.D. (1987) 'The psychotherapist's role in a large psychiatric institution.' *Psychoanalytic Psychotherapy 2,* 207–15.

Hinshelwood, R.D. (1991) 'Psychodynamic formulation in assessment for psychotherapy.' *British Journal of Psychotherapy 8,* 2, 166–174.

Hinshelwood, R.D. (1993) 'Locked in a role: a psychotherapist within the social defence system of a prison.' *Journal of Forensic Psychiatry 4,* 427–40.

Hinshelwood, R.D. (1994) 'The relevance of psychotherapy.' *Psychoanalytic Psychotherapy 8,* 283–94.

von Hirsch, A. (1976) *Doing Justice: The Choice of Punishments*. New York: Hill and Wang.

Hirschi, T. (1969) *Causes of Delinquency*. Berkeley, CA: University of California Press.

HMSO (1994) *Report of the Inquiry into the Care and Treatment of Christopher Clunis*. London: HMSO.

HMSO (1995) Prison Service Annual Report and Accounts April 1993–March 1994. Hc 185. London: HMSO.

Hobbs, M. (1990) 'The role of the psychotherapist as consultant to in-patient psychiatric units.' *Psychiatric Bulletin 14*, 1, 8–12.

Hodges, G. (1991) 'The use of story stems to assess attachments in children.' Presentation. London: Institute of Child Health.

Hodges, H.A. (1952) *The Philosophy of Wilhelm Dilthey*. London: Routledge and Kegan Paul.

Hodgson, R. and Rollnick, S. (1989) 'More fun, less stress: how to survive in research.' In G. Parry and F. Watts (eds) *Behavioural and Mental Health Research: A Handbook of Skills and Methods*. Hove: Lawrence Erlbaum Associates.

Hofer, M.A. (1984) 'Relationships as regulators: a psychobiologic perspective on bereavement.' *Psychosomatic Medicine 46*, 183–197.

Hoffer, W. (1949) 'Deceiving the deceiver.' In K.R. Eissler (eds) *Searchlights on Delinquency: Essays in Honor of August Aichhorn*. New York: International Universities Press.

Holland, T.R., Heim, R.B. and Holt, N. (1976) 'Personality Patterns among Correctional Officer Applicants.' *Journal of Clinical Psychology 32*, 786–791.

Holmes, J. (1991) 'Psychotherapy 2000. Some predictions for the coming decade.' *British Journal of Psychiatry 159*, 149–155.

Holmes, J. (1993) *John Bowlby and Attachment Theory*. London: Routledge.

Holmes, J. (1994) 'Psychotherapy – a luxury the NHS cannot afford? More expensive not to treat.' *British Medical Journal 309*, 1070–2.

Home Office (1989) *Criminal and Custodial Careers of those Born in 1953, 1958 and 1963*. Home Office Statistical Bulletin, 32/89. London: Home Office.

Home Office (1991) 'Treatment Programmes for Sex Offenders in Custody: A Strategy.' Directorate of Inmate Programmes. HM Prison Service.

Hopper, E. (1991) 'Encapsulation as defence against the fear of annihilation.' *International Journal of Psychoanalysis 72*, 607–624.

Horowitz, M. (1973) 'Phase oriented treatment of stress response syndromes.' *American Journal of Psychotherapy 27*, 506–515.

Horowitz, M. (1990) 'Psychotherapy.' In Bellack and Meisen (eds) *Handbook of Comparative Treatments for Adult Disorders*. New York: John Wiley and Sons Ltd.

Horowitz, M. (1991) 'Emotionality and schematic control processes.' In M. Horowitz (ed) *Person Schemas and Maladaptive Interpersonal Patterns*. Chicago, IL: University of Chicago Press.

Horowitz, M. and Becker, S.S. (1972) 'Cognitive responses to stress: experimental studies of a compulsion to repeat trauma.' *Psychoanalysis and Contemporary Science 1*, 258–261.

Horowitz, M., Markman, M.C., Stinson, C., Fridlander, B. and Ghannam, J.H. (1990) 'A classification theory of defence.' In J.L. Singer (ed) *Repression and Dissociation*. Chicago, IL: University of Chicago Press.

Housman, A.E. (1939) *The Collected Poems*. London: Jonathan Cape.

Howard League Working Party (1985) *Unlawful Sex*. Oxford: Pergamon Press.

Howe, M.C. and Schwartzburg, S. (1986) *Functional Approach to Groupwork in Occupational Therapy*. Philadelphia, PA: J.B. Lippincott.

Hug-Hellmuth, H. (1921) 'On the technique of child analysis.' *International Journal of Psychoanalysis 2*, 287–305.

Hughes, R. (1993) *The Culture of Complaint*. New York: Open University Press.

Hunt, S.J. (1994) *Metropolitan Police Officers' Attitudes to the Causes of Crime*. Unpublished MS, London School of Economics.

The Independent (1994) 'Broadmoor Hospital, where the staff need security.' *The Independent*, 4th April, p.15.

Irving, B.L. and Dunighan, C. (1993) 'Human factors in the quality control of CID investigations.' *Royal Commission on Criminal Procedure Research Study No 21*. London: HMSO.

Isaac, S. (1952) 'The nature and function of fantasy.' In J. Reviere *Developments in Psychoanalysis*. London: Hogarth Press.

Isen, A.M. (1984) 'Toward understanding the role of affect in cognition.' In R.S. Wyer and T.K. Scrull (eds) *Handbook of Social Recognition, Vol. 3*. Hillsdale, NJ: Lawrence Erlbaum Associates.

Jackson, D. and Weakland, J. (1961) 'Conjoint family: some considerations on theory, technique and results.' *Psychiatry 24*, 30–45.

Jackson, M. (1991) 'Psychotic disorders.' In J. Holmes (ed) *Textbook of Psychotherapy in Psychiatric Practice*. London: Churchill Livingstone.

Jackson, M. and Cawley, R. (1992) 'Psychodynamics and *psychotherapy* on an acute psychiatric ward: The story of an experimental unit.' *British Journal of Psychiatry 160*, 41–50.

Jackson, M. and Williams, P. (1994) *Unimaginable Storms. A Search for Meaning in Psychosis*. London: Karnac Books.

Jacobson, E. (1953) 'The affects and their pleasure – unpleasure qualities in relation to the psychic discharge processes.' In R. Loewenstein (eds) *Affects, Drives, Behavior*. New York: International Universities Press.

Jacobson, E. (1954) 'The self and the object world.' *The Psychoanalytic Study of the Child 9*, 75–127.

Jacobson, E. (1964) *The Self and the Object World*. New York: International Universities Press.

Jaques, E. (1955) 'Social systems as a defence against persecutory and depressive anxiety.' In M. Klein, P. Heimann and R.E. Money-Kyrle (eds) *New Directions in Psychoanalysis*. London: Tavistock.

Jehu, D. (1994) *Patients as Victims: Sexual Abuse in Psychotherapy and Counselling*. University of Leicester: John Wiley and Sons Ltd.

Jenkins, A. (1990a) *Invitations to Responsibility*. Adelaide: Dulwich Centre Publications.

Jenkins, J.M. and Astington, J.W. (1993) 'Cognitive, linguistic, and social factors associated with theory of mind development in young children.' Paper presented at the Society for Research in Child Development meeting. New Orleans.

Jenkins, P.L. (1989) *Hazards of Psychiatric Practice: A Clinical and Legal Guide for the Therapist*. Chicago, IL, London, Boca Raton: Year Book Medical Publishers Inc.

Jenkins, R. (1990). Towards a System of Outcome Indicators for Mental Health Care. *British Journal of Psychiatry 157*, 500–514.

Jennings, S. (1990) *Dramatherapy with Families, Groups and Individuals: Waiting in the Wings*. London: Jessica Kingsley Publishers.

Jennings, S. (1992) 'The nature and scope of dramatherapy: theatre of healing.' In M. Cox (ed) *Shakespeare Comes to Broadmoor*. London: Jessica Kingsley Publishers.

Jennings, S. (1993) *Playtherapy with Children: A Practitioners' Guide*. Oxford: Blackwell Scientific.

Jennings, S. (in preparation, a) *The Greek Theatre of Healing*. London: Jessica Kingsley Publishers.

Jennings, S. (in preparation, b) *Shakespeare's Theatre of Healing*. London: Jessica Kingsley Publishers.

Jennings, S. and Minde, A. (1993) *Art Therapy and Dramatherapy: Masks of the Soul*. London: Jessica Kingsley Publishers.

Jennings, S., Orr, M. and McGinley, J. (in preparation) 'Masking and unmasking: *A Midsummer Night's Dream* with offender patients.'

Johns, J. and Quay, H. (1962) 'The effect of social reward on verbal conditioning in psychopathic and neurotic military offenders.' *Journal of Consulting psychology 26*, 217–220.

Johnson, A.M. and Szurek, S.A. (1952) 'The genesis of antisocial acting out in children and adults.' *Psychoanalytic Quarterly 21*, 323–343.

Joint Committee on Accreditation of Fellowship Programs in Forensic Psychiatry (1982) 'Standards for fellowship programs in forensic psychiatry.' *Bulletin of the American Academy of Psychiatry and the Law 10*, 4 285–292.

Joint Committee on Higher Psychiatric Training (JCHPT)(1990) *Handbook*. London: Royal College of Psychiatrists.

Jones, D. (1987) 'Recent development in work with young offenders.' In J. Coleman (ed) *Working with Troubled Adolescents.* London: Academic Press.

Jones, D. and Dean, N. (1992) 'Assessment of need for services for mentally disordered offenders and patients with similar needs.' *Health Trends 24,* 2.

Jones, D. and Franey, A. (in preparation) *A Collaborative Strategy Between Doctors and Managers at Broadmoor Hospital.*

Jones, E.E., Cumming, J.D. and Horowitz, M.J. (1988) 'Another look at the nonspecific hypothesis of therapeutic effectiveness.' *Journal of Consulting and Clinical Psychology 56,* 1, 48–55.

Jones, K. and Fowles, A.J. (1984) *Ideas on Institutions: Analysing the Literature on Long-Term Care and Custody.* London: Routledge and Kegan Paul.

Jones, M. (1952) *Social Psychiatry.* London: Tavistock Books.

Joseph, B. (1985) 'Transference: the total situation.' *International Journal of Psychoanalysis 66,* 47.

Jung, C.G. (1912) *Wandlungen und Symbole der Libido.* Leipzig and Vienna: Deuticke.

Jung, C.G. (1916) *Psychology of the Unconscious.* London: Routledge and Kegan Paul.

Jung, C.G. (1923) *Psychological Types.* London: Routledge and Kegan Paul.

Jung, C.G. (1946) 'The psychology of the transference.' In H. Read *et al.* (eds) *C.G. Jung The Collected Works: Volume 16 The Practice of Psychotherapy.* Second Edition. London: Routledge.

Kagan, J. (1984) *The Nature of the Child.* New York: Basic Books.

Kagan, J. (1994) *Galen's Prophecy.* London: Free Association Books.

Kagan, N. (1975) 'Interpersonal process recall: A method of influencing human interaction.' University of Houston: Educational Psychology Department.

Kalin, N. (1993) 'The neurobiology of fear.' *Scientific American 268,* 54–60.

Kalin, N., Shelton, S. and Takahashi, L. (1991) 'Defensive behaviors in infant rhesus monkeys: ontogeny and context-dependent selective impression.' *Child Development 62,* 1175–1183.

Kaplan, L. (1991a) *Female Perversions Pandora.* New York: Doubleday.

Kaplan L. (1991b) 'Women masquerading as women.' In G. Fogel and W. Myers (eds) *Perversions and Near Perversions.* New Haven, CT: Yale University Press.

Karasu, T. (1981) 'Ethical aspects of psychotherapy.' In S. Bloch and P. Chodoff (eds) *Psychiatric Ethics.* Oxford: Oxford University Press.

Karban, B. and West, A.G. (1994) 'Working as an art therapist in a regional secure unit.' In M. Liebmann (ed) *Art Therapy with Offenders.* London: Jessica Kingsley Publishers.

Kardiner, A. (1941) *The Traumatic Neuroses of War.* New York: Hoeber.

Karterud, S., Vaglum, S., Friis, S., Trion, T., Johns, S. and Vaglum, P. (1992) 'Day hospital therapeutic community treatment for patients with personality disorders. An empirical evaluation of the containment function.' *Journal of Nervous and Mental Disorders 180*, 4, 238–243.

Kehl, M. and Löser, W. (eds) (1982) *The von Balthasar Reader.* Translated by R. Daly and F. Lawrence. Edinburgh: T&T Clark.

Kendall, P.C. and Norton-Ford, J.D. (1982) 'Therapy outcome research methods.' In P.C. Kendall and J.N. Butcher (eds) *Handbook of Research Methods in Clinical Psychology.* New York: John Wiley and Sons Ltd.

Kennard, D. (1993) *Group Therapy at Rampton.* Group Work Co-ordinating Committee, Rampton Hospital.

Kennard, D., Roberts, J. and Winter, D. (1993) *A Workbook of Group-Analytic Interventions.* London: Routledge.

Kennedy, H. and Yorke, C. (1980) 'Childhood neurosis v. developmental deviations: two clinical case histories.' *Dialogue: A Journal of Psychoanalytic Perspectives 4*, 20–33.

Kernberg, O.F. (1967) 'Borderline personality organization.' *Journal of the American Psychoanalytic Association 15*, 641–685.

Kernberg, O.F. (1970) 'A psychoanalytic classification of character pathology.' *Journal of the American Psychoanalytic Association 18*, 800–822.

Kernberg, O.F. (1971) 'Prognostic considerations regarding borderline personality organization.' *Journal of the American Psychoanalytic Association 19*, 595–635.

Kernberg, O.F. (1975) *Borderline Conditions and Pathological Narcissism.* New York: Jason Aronson Inc.

Kernberg, O.F. (1976a) *Object Relations Theory and Clinical Psychoanalysis.* New York: Jason Aronson Inc.

Kernberg, O.F. (1976b) 'Technical considerations in the treatment of borderline personality organisation.' *Journal of the American Psychoanalytic Association 24*, 795–829.

Kernberg, O.F. (1977) 'The structural diagnosis of borderline personality organization.' In P. Hartocollis (eds) *Borderline Personality Disorders: The Concept, the Syndrome, the Patient.* New York: International Universities Press.

Kernberg, O.F. (1980) 'Some implications of object relations theory for psychoanalytic technique.' In H. Blum (eds) *Psychoanalytic Explorations of Technique: Discourse on the Theory of Therapy.* 207–239. New York: International Universities Press.

Kernberg, O.F. (1983) 'Object relations theory and character analysis.' *Journal of the American Psychoanalytic Association 31*, 247–271.

Kernberg, O.F. (1984) *Severe Personality Disorders: Psychotherapeutic Strategies.* New Haven, CT: Yale University Press.

Kernberg, O.F. (1987) 'Borderline personality disorder: A psychodynamic approach.' *Journal of Personality Disorders 1*, 344–346.

Kernberg, O.F. (1989) 'The narcissistic personality disorder and the differential diagnosis of antisocial behavior.' *The Psychiatric Clinics of North America 12,* 553–570.

Kernberg, O.F. (1991) 'Aggression and love in the relationship of the couple.' In G. Fogel and W. Myers (eds) *Perversions and Near Perversions.* New Haven, CT: Yale University Press. 153–175.

Kernberg, O.F. (1992) *Aggression in Personality Disorders and Perversions.* New Haven, CT: Yale University Press.

Kernberg, O.F., Burstein, E.D., Coyne, L., Appelbaum, A., Horwitz, L. and Voth, H. (1972) 'Psychotherapy and psychoanalyses: final report of the Menninger Foundation's psychotherapy research project.' *Bulletin of the Menninger Clinic 36,* 1–275.

Kernberg, O.F., Selzer, M.A., Koenigsberg, H.W., Carr, A.C. and Appelbaum, A.H. (1989) *Psychodynamic Psychotherapy of Borderline Patients.* New York: Basic Books Inc.

Khan, M.M.R. (1979) *Alienation in Perversions.* London: Hogarth Press/Institute of Psycho-Analysis.

Khan, M.M.R. (1986) 'The concept of cumulative trauma.' In G. Kohon (ed) *The British School of Psychoanalysis: The Independent Tradition.* London: Free Association Books.

Kielhofner, G. (1989) 'The model of human occupation: a developing conceptual tool for clinicians.' *British Journal of Occupational Therapy 52,* 6.

Kilpatrick, D., Saunders, B.E., Amick McMullen, A., Best, C., Veronen, L. and Resick, H. (1989) 'Victims and crime factors associated with crime related PTSD.' *Behaviour Therapy 20,* 199–214.

King, P. and Steiner, R. (1991) *The Freud–Klein Controversies 1940–1945.* London/New York: Tavistock/Routledge.

Kinston, W. (1987) *A general theory of symptom formation.* Unpublished.

Kinston, W. and Bentovim, A. (1980) 'Creating a focus for brief marital and family therapy.' In S.H. Budmann (ed) *Forms of Brief Therapy.* New York: Guilford Press.

Kinston, W. and Bentovim, A. (1990) 'A framework for family description.' *Journal of Contemporary Family Therapy 12,* 279–297.

Kinston, W., Loader, P. and Miller, L. (1987) 'Quantifying the clinical assessment of family health.' *Journal of Marital and Family Therapy 13,* 49–67.

Kirby, S. (1994) 'A typical child molester.' *Police Review 102,* 5266, 23–24.

Kirkland Gable, R. (1986) 'Prediction of dangerousness and implications for treatment.' In W.J. Curran, A.L. Mcgarry and S.A. Shah *Forensic Psychiatry and Standards for Interdisciplinary Practice.* Philadelphia: F.A. Davis Company.

Kirkwood, A. (1993) *The Leicestershire Inquiry 1992.* Leicester: Leicester County Council.

Klein, E.D. (1971) *A Comprehensive Etymological Dictionary of the English Language.* Amsterdam and New York: Elsevier Publishing Co.

Klein, M. (1926) 'Notes on some schizoid mechanisms.' In M. Klein *The Writings of Melanie Klein, Vol.3.* London: Hogarth Press.

Klein, M. (1927) 'Criminal tendencies in normal children.' In M. Klein *The Writings of Melanie Klein, Vol.1.* London: Hogarth Press.

Klein, M. (1930) 'The importance of symbol formation in the development of the ego.' In M. Klein *Contributions to Psychoanalysis, 1921–1945.* New York: McGraw-Hill, 1964.

Klein, M. (1932a) *The Psychoanalysis of Children.* London: Hogarth Press 1986.

Klein, M. (1932b) 'The psycho-analysis of children.' In M. Klein *The Writings of Melanie Klein, Vol.2.* London: Hogarth Press.

Klein, M. (1932c) 'The sexual activities of children.' In M. Klein *The Psycho-Analysis of Children.* London: Hogarth Press.

Klein, M. (1934) 'On criminality.' In M. Klein *The Writings of Melanie Klein, Vol.1.* London: Hogarth Press.

Klein, M. (1935) 'A contribution to the psychogenesis of manic depressive states.' In M. Klein *The Writings of Melanie Klein, Vol.1.* London: Hogarth Press.

Klein, M. (1936) 'The psychotherapy of the psychoses.' In M. Klein *Contributions to Psychoanalysis, 1921–1945.* New York: McGraw-Hill, 1964.

Klein, M. (1946) 'Notes on some schizoid mechanisms.' In M. Klein *Envy and Gratitude.* London: Hogarth Press and the Institute of Psychoanalysis.

Klein, M. (1948) 'The development of the child.' In M. Klein *Contributions to Psychoanalysis 1921–1945.* London: Hogarth Press.

Klein, M. (1952) 'The origins of transference.' In M. Klein *The Writings of Melanie Klein, Vol.3.* London: Hogarth Press.

Klein, M. (1957) 'Envy and gratitude.' In M. Klein *The Writings of Melanie Klein, Vol.3.* London: Hogarth Press.

Klein, M. (1975) 'Early stages of the Oedipus Complex.' In M. Klein *Love, Guilt and Reparation.* London: Hogarth Press.

Knight, R. (1953) 'Borderline states.' *Bulletin of the Menninger Clinic 17*, 1–12.

Kobak, R. and Sceery, A. (1988) 'Attachment in late adolescence: Working models, affect regulation and perceptions of self and others.' *Child Development 59*, 135–146.

Kohlberg, L. (1964) 'Development of moral character and moral ideology.' In M.L. Hoffman and L.W. Hoffman (eds) *Review of Child Development Research I.* New York: Russell Sage Foundation.

Kohlberg, L. (1971) 'Stages of moral development as a basis for moral education.' In C.M. Beck, B.S. Crittendon and E.V. Sullivan (eds) *Moral Education: Interdisciplinary approaches.* New York: Newman Press.

Kohut, H. (1959) 'Introspection, empathy and psychoanalysis.' *Journal of American Psychoanalytic Association 7*, 459–483.

Kohut, H. (1968) 'The psychoanalytic treatment of narcissistic personality disorders.' *The Psychoanalytic Study of the Child 23*, 86–113.

Kohut, H. (1971) *The Analysis of the Self.* New York: International Universities Press.

Kohut, H. (1972) 'Thoughts on narcisissm and narcissistic rage'. *The Psychoanalytic Study of the Child 27*, 360–400. New York: International Universities Press.

Kohut, H. (1977) *The Restoration of the Self.* New York: International Universities Press.

Kohut, H. (1984) *How Does Analysis Cure?* Chicago, IL: University of Chicago Press.

van der Kolk, B.A. (1989) 'The compulsion to repeat the trauma: re-enactment, re-victimisation and masochism.' *Psychiatric Clinics of North America 12*, 389–411.

van der Kolk, B.A. (1994) 'The body keeps the score: memory and the evolving psychobiology of post-traumatic stress.' *Harvard Review of Psychiatry 1*, 253–265.

van der Kolk, B.A., Perry, C. and Herman, J.L. (1991) 'Childhood origins of self-destructive behaviour.' *American Journal of Psychiatry 148*, 1665–1671.

Koller, P., Marmar, C. and Kanas, N. (1992) 'Psychodynamic group treatment of PTSD in Vietnam veterans.' *International Journal of Group Psychotherapy 42*, 225–245.

Kolvin, I., Charles, G., Nicholson, R., Fleeting, M. and Fundudis, T. (1990) 'Factors in Prevention in Inner City Deprivation'. In Goldberg and Tantum (eds) *The Public Health Impact of Mental Disorder.* Stuttgart: Hogrete and Huber.

Kornhauser, R. (1978) *Social Sources of Delinquency.* Chicago, IL: University of Chicago Press.

Kotosopoulos, A. and Boodoosingh, L. (1987) 'Language and speech disorders in children attending a day psychiatric programme.' *The British Journal of Disorders of Communication 22*, 3, 227–236.

Kottler, J.A. (1986) *On Being a Therapist.* San Francisco, CA: Jossey-Bass Publishers.

Kraemer, H.C. (1981) 'Coping strategies in psychiatric clinical research.' *Journal of Clinical and Consulting Psychology 49*, 3, 309–319.

Kraemer, S. (1988) 'Splitting and stupidity in child sexual abuse.' *Psychoanalytic Psychotherapy 3*, 3, 247–257.

Kraemer, S. (1992) 'Creating a space to supervise – opportunity or persecution.' *Tavistock Gazette 34*, 1, 1–9.

Krystal, H. (1968) *Massive Psychic Trauma.* New York: International Universities Press.

Krystal, H. (1988) *Integration of Self Healing: Affect, Trauma and Alexithymia.* Hillsdale, NJ: Analytic Press.

Laban, R. (1975) *Laban's Principles of Dance Movement Notation.* Boston: Plays Inc.

Lacan, J. (1977) *Ecrits. A Selection.* London: Tavistock.

Lacan, J. (1986) *The Four Fundamental Concepts of Psychoanalysis.* Harmondsworth: Penguin Books.

Lahad, M. (1992) 'Story-making in assessment method.' In S. Jennings (ed) *Dramatherapy Theory and Practice 2.* London: Routledge.

Laing, R.D. (1967) *The Politics of Experience.* London: Penguin Books.

Lamb, W. (1965) *Posture and Gesture: An Introduction to the Study of Physical Behaviour.* London: Duckworth and Co.

Lambert, M.J. (1989) 'The individual therapist's contribution to psychotherapy process and outcome.' *Clinical Psychology Review 9,* 469–485.

Lampl-de-Groot, J. (1949) 'Neurotics, delinquents and ideal formation.' In K.R. Eissler (eds) *Searchlights on Delinquency.* New York: International Universities Press.

Lampl-de Groot, J. (1975) 'Vicissitudes of narcissism and the problems of civilization.' *Psychoanalytic Studies of the Child 30,* 663–683.

Landy, R. (1986) *Drama Therapy: Theory and Concepts.* New York: Charles Thomas.

Landy, R. (1994) *Persona and Performance: The Meaning of Role in Drama, Therapy and Everyday Life.* London: Jessica Kingsley Publishers.

Landy, R. and Jennings, S. (1995, in press) 'Romeo and Juliet as healing theatre.' *The Arts in Psychotherapy.*

Laplanche, J. and Pontalis, J.B. (1973) *The Language of Psychoanalysis.* London: Hogarth Press.

Laufer, M. and Laufer, M.E. (1984) *Adolescence and Developmental Breakdown.* New Haven, CT: Yale University Press.

Law, J. and Conway, J. (1992) 'Effect of abuse and neglect on the development of children's speech and language.' *Developmental Medicine and Child Neurology 34,* 943–948.

Laws, D.R. (1990) *Relapse Prevention with Sex Offenders.* New York: Guilford Press.

Lazarus, R.S. (1966) *Psychological Stress and the Coping Process.* New York: McGraw-Hill.

Lazarus, R.S., Averill, J.R. and Opton, E.M. (1974) 'The psychology of coping: issues of research and assessment.' In E.G. Coehlo, D. Hamburg and J. Adam (eds) *Copying and Adaptation.* New York: Basic Books.

Leiter, M.P. (1991) 'Coping patterns as predictors of burnout: the function of control and escapist coping patterns.' *Journal of Organizational Behaviour 12,* 123–144.

Lennings, C.J. (1988) 'The effect of court appearance on personality: therapy or torture? A case study.' *International Journal of Offender Therapy and Comparative Criminology 32,* 249–252.

Lerman, H. (1988) 'The psychoanalytic legacy: from whence we come'. In L.E.A. Walker (ed) *Handbook on Sexual Abuse of Children: Assessment and Treatment Issues.* New York: Springer Publishing Company.

Lerner, P.M. (1991) *Psychoanalytic Theory and the Rorschach.* London: The Analytic Press.

Leslie, A.M. (1987) 'Pretense and representation: The origins of "Theory of Mind".' *Psychological Review 94*, 412–426.

Lester, D. and Butler, A. (1978) 'Job satisfaction and cynicism in the Police: a cross-national comparison.' *Psychological Reports 42*, 962.

Levi, P. (1988) *The Drowned and the Saved.* New York: Summit Books.

Lewis, A. (1961) 'Dilemmas in psychiatry.' *Psychological Medicine 1991, 21*, 581–585.

Lewis, G. and Appleby, L. (1988) 'Personality disorder: the patients psychiatrists dislike.' *British Journal of Psychiatry 153*, 44–99.

Lewis, M., Feiring, C., McGuffog, C. and Jaskir, J. (1984) 'Predicting psychopathology in six-year-olds from early social relations.' *Child Development 55*, 123–136.

Lewis, P.S. (1990a) *Attaining the Unattainable (Unsuccessfully).* Special Hospital Conference, Windsor.

Lewis, P.S. (1990b) *Shame and the Therapy Experience.* Lecture to Psychotherapy Department, Lincoln.

Lewis, P.S. (1991) 'Psychodynamics of the dangerous sex offender.' Proceedings of the Pacific Rim Conference in Group Psychotherapy. Melbourne, Australia.

Lewis, P.S., Perkins, D.E., France, J., King, J., Hodge, J. and Orr, M.(1992) *Report of the Working Party on the Assessment and Treatment of Sex Offenders at Broadmoor Hospital.* Internal Document.

Lezak, M.D. (1983) *Neuropsychological Assessment.* Oxford: Oxford University Press.

Li, C.K. and Greenewich, J.A. (1991) 'A view from within: psychotherapy reflections.' *Changes. International Journal of Psychology and Psychotherapy 3*, 201–213.

Lidz, T. (1973) *The Origin and Treatment of Schizophrenic Disorders.* New York: Basic Books.

Lie, N. (1994) 'Offenders tested with projective methods prior to first offence.' *British Journal of Projective Psychology 39*, 1, 23–34.

Lieberman, S. (1980) *Intergenerational Family Therapy.* London: Croom Helm.

Lifton, R.J. (1973) *Home from the War.* New York: Simon and Schuster.

Lillard, A.S. (1993) 'Pretend play skills and the child's theory of mind.' *Child Development 64*, 348–371.

Limentani, A. (1966) 'A re-evaluation of acting out in relation to working through.' *International Journal of Psycho-Analysis 47*, 277.

Limentani, A. (1984) 'Toward a unified conception of the origins of sexual and social deviancy in young persons.' *International Journal of Psychoanalytical Psychotherapy 10*, 383–401.

Lindemann, E. (1944) 'Symptomatology and management of acute grief.' *American Journal of Psychiatry 101*, 141–49.

Lindy, J.D. (1986) 'An outline for the psychoanalytic psychotherapy of PTSD.' In C. Figley (ed) *Trauma and its Wake.* Vol 2. New York: Brunner Mazel.

Lindy, J.D. (1989) 'Transference and PTSD.' *Journal of American Academy of Psychoanalysis 17*, 397–413.

Lindy, J.D. (1993) 'Focal psychoanalytic psychotherapy of PTSD.' In J.P. Wilson and B. Raphael (eds) *International Handbook of Traumatic Stress Syndromes.* New York: Plenum Press.

Lindy, J.D., Green, B. and Grace, M. (1992) 'Somatic reenactments in the treatment of PTSD.' *Psychotherapy and Psychosomatics 57*, 180–186.

Lion, J.R. and Pasternak, S.A. (1973) 'Countertransference reactions to violent patients.' *American Journal of Psychiatry 130*, 207–210.

Litman, R.E. (1989) 'Long-term treatment of chronically suicidal patients.' *Bulletin of the Menninger Clinic 53*, 215–228.

Loader, P., Burck, C., Kinston, W. and Bentovim, A. (1981) 'A method for organising the clinical description of family interaction – the family interaction summary format.' *Australian Journal of Family Therapy 2*, 131–141.

Lonie, I. (1993) 'Borderline disorder and PTSD: an equivalence?' *ANZ Journal of Psychiatry 27*, 233–243.

Lorenz, K. (1966) *On Aggression.* London: Methuen.

Loth, H. (1994) 'Music therapy in forensic psychiatry – choice, denial and the law.' *Journal of British Music Therapy 8*, 2.

Lothstein, L.M. (1979) 'Osyxchodynamics and sociodynamicss of gender-dysphoric states.' *American Journal of Psychotherapy 33*, 21438.

Luborsky, L., Barber, J.P. and Crits-Christoph, P. (1990) 'Theory based research for understanding the process of dynamic psychotherapy.' *Journal of Consulting and Clinical Psychology 58*, 3, 281–287.

Luborsky, L. and Crits-Christoph, P. (1990) *Understanding Transference: The Core Conflictual Relationship Theme Method.* New York: Basic Books.

Lunn, V. and Kramp, P. (1985) 'Retspsykiatri.' In J. Welner (ed) *Psykiatri – En Tekstbog.* Copenhagen: F.A.D.L.'s Forlag.

Luntz, B. and Widom, C. (1994) 'Antisocial personality disorder in abused and neglected children grown up.' *American Journal of Psychiatry 151*, 670–674.

Luria, A.R (1966) *Higher Cortical Functions in Man.* Reprinted 1980. London: Tavistock.

Lyons, S., Tarbuck, P. and Williams, B. (1992) 'Comparative levels of stress within psychiatric nursing.' *Journal for Nurses and other Professionals in Forensic Psychiatry 1*, 16.

Maccoby, E.E. and Martin, J.A. (1983) 'Socialisation in the context of the family: Parent/child interaction.' In E.M. Hetherington (ed) *Handbook of Child Psychology Vol IV.* New York: John Wiley and Sons Ltd.

MacDonald, R. and Grogin, E.R. (1991) 'Personal accounts of satisfying and unsatisfying nursing experiences as a needs assessment strategy.' *The Journal of Continuing Education in Nursing 22,* 1, 11–15.

Macphail, D. and Cox, M. (1973) 'Dynamic psychotherapy with dangerous patients.' *Psychotherapy and Psychosomatics 25,* 13–19.

Macquarrie, J. (1972) *Existentialism.* New York: World Publishing Co.

Madanes, C. (1991) 'Strategic family therapy.' In A.S. Gurman and D.P. Kniskern (eds) *Handbook of Family Therapy 2.* New York: Bruner/Mazel.

Madden, D.J., Lion, J.R. and Penna, M.W. (1976) 'Assaults on psychiatrists.' *American Journal of Psychiatry 133,* 4, 422–426.

Madonna, P., Scoyk, S. and Jones D. T. (1991) 'Family interaction within incest and non incest families.' *American Journal of Psychiatry 5,* 1, 46–49.

Mahler, M.S. (1963) 'Thoughts about development and individuation.' *Psychoanalogical Study of the Child 18,* 307–24.

Mahler, M.S. (1979) *The Selected Papers of Margaret S. Mahler.* New York: Jason Aronson Inc.

Mahler, M.S., Pine, F. and Bergman, A. (1975) *The Psychological Birth of the Human Infant: Symbiosis and Individuation.* New York: Basic Books.

Mahoney, M.J. (1991) *Human Change Processes: The Scientific Foundations of Psychotherapy.* New York: Basic Books.

Main, M. (1991) *A Typology of Human Attachment Organisation, Assessed in Discourse, Drawings and Interviews.* Cambridge: Cambridge University Press.

Main, M. (1993) 'Metacognition.' In C.M. Parkes, J. Stevenson Hinde and P. Marris (eds) *Attachment Across the Life Cycle.* London: Routledge.

Main, M. and George, C. (1985) 'Responses of abused and disadvantaged toddlers to distress in age-mates: a study in a day care setting.' *Developmental Psychology 21,* 407–412.

Main, M., Kaplan, N. and Cassidy, J. (1985) Security in infancy, childhood and adulthood: A move to the level of representation. *Monographs of the Society for Research in Child Development 50,* 1–2, 66–104.

Main, M., Kayman, N. and Cassidy, J. (1985) 'Security in infancy, childhood and adulthood: a move to the level of representation.' In I. Bretherton and E. Waters (eds) *Growing Points in Attachment Theory in Research. Monographs of the Society for Research in Child Development 50,* 1–2. 66–104.

Main, M. and. Main, G.R. (1991) 'An adult attachment classification system.' Unpublished manuscript, University of California, Berkeley.

Main, T.F. (1957) 'The ailment.' *British Journal of Medical Psychology 30,* 129–145.

Main, T.F. (1975) 'Some psychodynamics of large groups.' In L. Kreeger (ed) *The Large Group.* London: Constable.

Main, T.F. (1977) 'Traditional psychiatric defenses against close encounter with patients.' *Canadian Psychiatric Association Journal 12*, 457–466.

Main, T.F. (1981) 'The concept of the therapeutic community.' First S.H Foulkes Memorial lecture. Reprinted in J. Johns (ed) (1989) *The Ailment and Other Psychoanalytic Essays.* London: Free Association Books.

Main, T.F. (1983) 'The concept of the therapeutic community: variations and vicissitudes.' In M. Pines (ed) *The Evolution of Group Analysis.* London: Routledge and Kegan Paul.

Malan, D.H. (1979) *Individual Psychotherapy and the Science of Psychodynamics.* London: Butterworth.

Maloney, C. (ed) (1976) *The Evil Eye.* New York: Columbia University Press.

Managing Public Services. Responsiveness and Results. A Reading Guide (Part B). Open University.

Mancia, M. (1993) 'The absent father: His role in sexual deviations and in transference.' *International Journal of Psychoanalysis 74*, 941–949.

Manning, N. (1989) *The Therapeutic Community Movement: Charisma and Routinisation.* London: Routledge.

Manolias, M. and Hyatt Williams, A. (1986) 'Study of post-shooting experiences in firearms officers.' *Report for the Joint Working Party on Organizational Health and Welfare.* London: HMSO.

Manpower Planning Advisory Group (1990) *Clinical Psychology Project.* London: Department of Health.

Marciniak, R. (1986) 'Implications to forensic psychiatry of PTSD: a review.' *Military Medicine 151*, 434–437.

Marcos, A.C., Bahr, S.J. and Johnson, R.E. (1986) 'Test of a bonding/association theory of adolescent drug use.' *Social Forces 65*, 135–161.

de Maré, P.B. (1972) *Perspectives in Group Psychotherapy.* London: George Allen and Unwin.

Margison, F.R. (1987) 'Stress in psychiatrists.' In R. Payne and J. Firth-Cozens (eds) *Stress in Health Professionals.* Chichester: John Wiley and Sons Ltd.

Mark, P. (1993) *The Day Training Centre: An Applied Group Analytic Therapeutic Community For Offenders – Theory And Practice.* Theoretical Paper, Qualifying Course, Institute of Group Analysis, London.

Marks, I. (1994) 'Psychotherapy – a luxury the NHS cannot afford. Unevaluated or inefficient approaches are hard to justify.' *British Medical Journal 309*, 1070–2.

Marle, H.J.C. van (1986) 'Het voorspellen van gevaarlijk gedrag.' *Tijdschrife Voor Psychiatrie 28*, B2, 1–9.

Marle, H.J.C. van, (1988) 'Klinische Psychotherapie in een Justitiële Inrichting.' ('Clinical Psychotherapy in a Legal Institution.') *Tijdschrift voor psychotherapie 14*, 6.

Marle, H.J.C. van (1992) 'Het voorspellen van gevaarlijk gedrag: consensus gewenst.' *Tijdschrife Voor Psychiatrie 34*, 4, 281–290.

Marle, H.J.C. van (1993) 'Het psychiatrisch deskundigenonderzoek.' In J. Krul-Steketee and M. Zeegers *De Psychiatrie in het Nederlandse Recht.* Second edition. Arnham: Gouda Quint.

Marmar, C.R. (1990) 'Psychotherapy process research: progress, dilemmas, and future directions.' *Journal of Consulting and Clinical Psychology 58*, 3, 265–272.

Marmar, C.R. (1991) 'Brief dynamic psychotherapy of PTSD.' *Psychiatric Annals 21*, 405–414.

Marmar, C.R. and Freeman, M. (1988) 'Brief dynamic psychotherapy of post-traumatic stress disorders: management of narcissistic regression.' *Journal of Traumatic Stress 1*, 323–337.

Marshall, W.L. and. Barbaree, H.E. (1988) 'The long term evaluation of a behavioural treatment program for child molesters.' *Behaviour Research Therapy 26*, 6, 499–511.

Marshall, W.L., Laws, D.R. and Barbaree, H.E. (eds) (1990) *Handbook of Sexual Assault.* London: Plenum Press.

Marshall, W.L., Ward, T., Jones, R., Johnston, P. and Barbaree, H.E. (1991) 'An optimistic evaluation of treatment outcome with sex offenders.' *Violence update 1*, 7.

Martinson, R. (1974) 'What works? – questions and answers about prison reform.' *Public Interest 35*, (Spring), 22.

Maslach, C. (1982) 'Understanding burnout: definitional issues in analyzing a complex phenomenon.' In W. Paine (ed) *Job Stress and Burnout.* Beverly Hills, CA: Sage Publications.

Maslach, C. and Jackson, S.E. (1986) *Maslach Burnout Inventory Manual.* Second edition. Palo Alto, CA: Consulting Psychologists Press.

Maslow, A.H. (1954) *Motivation and Personality.* London: Harper and Row.

Masters, B. (1985) *Killing for Company.* London: Routledge.

Masterson, J.F. (1976) *Psychotherapy of the Borderline Adult: A Developmental Approach.* New York: Brunner/Mazel.

Masterson, J.F. and Rinsley, D.B. (1975) 'The borderline syndrome: the role of the other in the genesis and psychic structure of the borderline personality.' *International Journal of Psychoanalysis 56*, 163–77.

Matthews, J. (1993) 'Working with female sexual abusers.' In M. Eliot (ed) *Sexual Abuse of Children.* London: Longman.

Matza, D. (1969) *Becoming Deviant.* Englewood Cliffs, NJ: Prentice-Hall.

Maxwell, R.J. (1984) 'Quality assessment in health.' *British Medical Journal 288*. 1470–1472.

Mayhew, P., Maung, N.A. and Mirlees-Black, C. (1993) *The 1992 British Crime Survey.* Home Office Research Study no.52. London: HMSO.

McAdam, E.K. (1986) 'Cognitive behaviour therapy and its application with adolescents.' *Journal of Adolescence 9*, 1, 15.

McCord, J. (1984) 'A forty year perspective on effects of child abuse and neglect.' *Child Abuse and Neglect 8*, 203–217.

McDougall, J. (1984) 'Neosexualities: reflections on the role of perversions in the psychic economy.' Reported on in *Bulletin of the Association for Psychoanalytic medicine 24*, 24–29.

McDougall, J. (1992) 'Perversions in psychoanalytic attitude.' In G. Fogel and W. Myers (eds) *Perversions and Near Perversions*. New Haven, CT: Yale University Press.

McFadyen, A. and Altschuler, J. (1990) 'Paediatric liaison research: problems at the clinical-research interface.' *Journal of Family Therapy 14*, 389–397.

McFarlane, A. (1988) 'The longitudinal course of PTSD: the range of outcomes and their predictors.' *Journal of Nervous and Mental Disease 176*, 30–9.

McGinley, J. (1994) 'Evaluation of dramatherapy with mentally disordered offenders.' Preliminary report.

McGoldrick, M., Pearce, J. and Giordano, J. (eds) (1982) *Ethnicity in Family Therapy*. New York: Guilford Press.

McGrath, P.G. (1976) 'Sexual offenders.' In H. Milne and S.J. Hardy (eds) *Psycho-Sexual Problems*. London: Bradford Press.

McNeely, R.L. and Mann, C.R. (1990) 'Domestic violence is a human issue.' *Journal of Interpersonal Violence 5*, 129–132.

Meares, R. (1994) 'Psychotherapeutic treatments of severe personality disorder.' *Current Opinion in Psychiatry 7*, 245–248.

Mechanic, D. (1968) 'Appendix 1.' In D. Mechanic *Medical Sociology: A Selective View*. New York: Free Press.

Meehl, P.E. (1954) *Clinical Versus Statistical Prediction*. Minneapolis: University of Minnesota Press.

Mehlum, L., Friess, S., Irion, T., Johns, S., Karterud, S., Vaglum, P. and Vaglum, S. (1991) 'Personality disorder 2–5 years after treatment: a prospective follow-up study.' *Acta Psychiatrica Scandinavica 84*, 72–77.

Meichenbaum, D. (1977) *Cognitive Behavior Modification: An Integrative Approach*. New York: Plenum Press.

Melden, A.I. (1961) *Free Action*. London: Routledge and Kegan Paul.

Meldrum, B. (1994) 'Historical background and overview of dramatherapy.' In S. Jennings, A. Cattanach, S. Mitchell, A. Chesner and B. Meldrum (eds) *The Handbook of Dramatherapy*. London: Routledge.

Meloy, J.R. (1988a) *The Psychopathic Mind: Origins, Dynamics, and Treatment*. Northvale, NJ: Jason Aronson Inc.

Meloy, J.R. (1988b) 'Violent homicidal behaviour in primitive mental states.' *Journal of the American Academy of Psychoanalysis 16*, 381–394.

Meloy, J.R. (1992) *Violent Attachments*. Northvale, NJ: Jason Aronson Inc.

Meltzer, D. (1968) 'Terror, persecution, dread – a dissection of paranoid anxieties.' *International Journal of Psychoanalysis 49*, 396–400.

Meltzer, D. (1993) *The Claustrum*. Oxford: Clunie Press.

Menninger, K. (1963) *The Vital Process in Mental Health and Illness*. New York: The Viking Press.

Menninger, W.W. (1990) 'Anxiety in the psychotherapist.' *Bulletin of the Menninger Clinic 54*, 232–246.

Menzies, D., Dolan, B. and Norton, K. (1993) 'Are short term savings worth long term costs? Funding psychotherapeutic inpatient treatment of personality disorders.' *Psychiatric Bulletin 17*, 517–19.

Menzies, I. (1959) 'The functioning of social systems as a defence against anxiety: a report on the study of a nursing service of a general hospital.' *Human Relations 13*, 95–121. Republished in I. Menzies *Containing Anxiety in Institutions*. London: Free Association Books.

Menzies, I. (1969) 'The motor-cycle: growing up on two wheels.' In H.S. Klein (ed) *Sexuality and Aggression in Maturation*. London: Balliere Tindall.

Menzies, I. (1960) 'A case study in the functioning of social systems as a defence against anxiety.' *Human Relations 13*, 95–121.

Menzies Lyth, I. (1988a) *Containing Anxiety in Institutions. Selected Essays Volume 1*. London: Free Assocation Books.

Menzies Lyth, I. (1988b) 'A psychoanalytic perspective on social institutions.' In *Melanie Klein Today, Volume 2: Mainly Practice*, 284–99. London: Routledge.

Merskey, H. (1992) 'The manufacture of personalities: the production of multiple personality disorder.' *British Journal of Psychiatry 160*, 327–340.

Merton, R. (1938) 'Social structure and anomie.' *American Sociological Review 3*, 672–82.

Merton, T. (1955) *No Man Is An Island*. Tunbridge Wells: Burns and Dates.

Meyerson, S. (1975) 'Adolescence and delinquency.' In S. Meyerson *Adolescence and Breakdown*. London: George Allen and Unwin Ltd.

Midgely, M. (1992) *Wickedness. A Philosophical Essay*. London: Routledge.

Miles, M.F.R. (1994) 'Art in hospitals: does it work? A survey of evaluation of arts projects in the N.H.S.' *Journal of The Royal Society of Medicine 87*, 161–163.

Miller, A. (1983) *For Your Own Good: The Roots of Violence in Child Rearing*. London: Virago.

Miller, D. (1983) *The Age Between: Adolescence and Therapy*. London: Jason Aronson Inc.

Miller, E.J. (1993) *From Dependency to Autonomy: Studies in Organisation and Change*. London: Free Association Books.

Miller, W. (1958) 'Lower class culture as a generating milieu of gang delinquency.' *Journal of Social Issues 15*, 3, 5–19.

Millon, T. (1981) *Disorders of Personality: DSM-III, Axis II*. New York: John Wiley and Sons Ltd.

Millon, T. and Everly, G.S. (1985) *Personality and its Disorders. A Biosocial Learning Approach.* New York: John Wiley and Sons Ltd.

Milne, D.L. (1985) 'An ecological validation of nurse training in behaviour therapy.' *Behavioural Psychotherapy 13*, 14–28.

Milton, J.J. (1994) 'Abuse and abused: perverse solutions following childhood abuse.' *Psychoanalytic Psychotherapy 8*, 243–255.

Minuchin, S. (1974) *Families and Family Therapy.* London: Tavistock.

Minuchin, S., Baker,. Rosman, B.L., Liebman, R., Milman, L. and Todd, T.C. (1975) 'A conceptual model of psychosomatic illness in children. Family organisation and family therapy.' *Archives of General Psychiatry 32*, 103–8.

Minuchin, S. and Fishman, H.C. (1981) *Family Therapy Techniques.* Cambridge, MA: Harvard University Press.

Mitchell, J. (1983) 'When disaster strikes: the Critical Incident Stress Debriefing Process.' *Journal of Emergency Medical Services 8*, 36–38.

Mitchell, S. (1992) 'Therapeutic theatre: a para-theatrical model of dramatherapy.' In S. Jennings (ed) *Dramatherapy Theory and Practice.* Second edition. London: Routledge.

Mitchell, S. (1994) 'The theatre of self-expression: a therapeutic theatre model of dramatherapy.' In S. Jennings, A. Cattanach, S. Mitchell, A. Chesner and Meldrum (eds) *The Handbook of Dramatherapy.* London: Routledge.

Mittler, P. (1984) 'Quality of life and services for people with disabilities.' *Bulletin of the British Psychological Society 37*, 218–225.

Modell, A.H. (1985) 'Object relations theory.' In A. Rothstein (ed) *Models of the Mind: Their Relationships to Clinical Work.* New York: International Universities Press.

Mohl, P.C., Lomax J., Tasman, A., Chan, C., Sledge, W., Summergrad, P. and Notman, M. (1990) 'Psychotherapy training for the psychiatrist of the future.' *American Journal of Psychiatry 147*, 7–13.

Mollon, P. (1988) 'Oedipus now: the psychoanalytic approach to trauma and child abuse.' *Changes 6*, 1, 17–19.

Mollon, P. (1989) 'Narcissus, Oedipus and the psychologist's fraudulent identity.' *Clinical Psychology Forum 23*, 7–11.

Monahan, J. (1984) 'The prediction of violent behaviour: toward a second generation of theory and policy.' *American Journal of Psychiatry 141*, 1, 10–15.

Monahan, J. (1992) 'Mental disorder and violent behaviour.' *American Psychologist 47*, 511–521.

Monahan, J. and Steadman, H.J. (eds) (1994) *Violence and Mental Disorder. Developments in Risk Assessment.* Chicago, IL: University of Chicago Press.

Monck, E., Bentovim, A., Goodall, G., Hyde, C., Lwin, R. and Sharland, S. (1991) *Child Sexual Abuse: A Descriptive and Treatment Study.* Research Report from Institute of Child Health, Hospitals for Sick Children to the Department of Health.

Money, J. (1986) *Lovemaps. Clinical Concepts of Sexual/Erotic Health and Pathology, Paraphilia, and Gender Transposition in Childhood, Adolescence, and Maturity.* New York: Irvington Publishers.

Montagu, A. (1979) *The Nature of Human Aggression.* London: Oxford University Press.

Montgomery, J,D. and Greif, A.C. (1991) *Masochism, the Treatment of Self-inflicted Suffering.* Madison, CT: International Universities Press.

Mooij, A.W.M. (1991) *Psychoanalysis and the Concept of a Rule.* Berlin, Heidelberg, New York: Springer-Verlag.

Morgan, C. and Murray, H.A. (1935) 'The Thematic Apperception Test.' *Archives of Neurology and Psychiatiatry 34,* 289.

Morris, D. (1969) *The Naked Ape.* New York: Dell.

Morris, P. and Silove, D. (1992) 'Cultural influences in psychotherapy with refugee survivors of torture and trauma.' *Hospital and Community Psychiatry 43,* 820–828.

Mullen, P.E., Martin, J.L., Anderson, J.C., Romans, S.E. and Herbison, G.P. (1993) 'Childhood sexual abuse and mental health in adult life.' *British Journal of Psychiatry 163,* 721–732.

Mullen, P.E., Romans-Clarkson, S., Walton, D.A. and Herbison G.P. (1988) 'Impact of sexual and physical abuse on women's mental health.' *Lancet 1648,* 841–845.

Mumford, P. (1989) 'Doctors in the driving seat.' *Health Service Journal,* May, 612–613.

Murphy. D. (1993) *Heart of Darkness: Observations and Analysis of the Group Psychology of a Special Hospital.* Theoretical Paper, Qualifying Course, Institute of Group Analysis, London.

Murphy, L.B. (1962) *The Widening World of Childhood: Paths Towards Mastery.* New York: Basic Books.

Murray, H.A. (1938) *Explorations in Personality.* New York: Oxford University Press.

Murray, L. and Trevarthen, C. (1985) 'Emotional regulation of interactions between two-month-olds and their mothers.' In T.M. Field and N.A. Fox (eds) *Social Perception in Infants.* Norwood, NJ: Ablex.

Nadelson, T. (1977) 'Borderline rage and the therapist's response.' *American Journal of Psychiatry 134,* 748–751.

Nathanson, D.L. (ed) (1987) *The Many Faces of Shame.* New York: Guilford Press.

National Association for the Care and Resettlement of Offenders (NACRO) (1988) *Diverting Juveniles from Custody.* London: NACRO.

The National Health Service and Community Care Act (1990) London: HMSO.

National Society for the Prevention of Cruelty to Children (1994) *Annual figures.* London: National Society for the Prevention of Cruelty to Children.

Nelson, S.H. and Berger, V.F. (1988) 'Current issues in state mental health forensic programs.' *Bulletin of the American Academy of Psychiatry and the Law 16*, 1, 67–75.

Newham, P. (1993) 'Voice and emotion.' *Open Mind 66*.

NHS Management Executive (1990) EL(90)190 *Services for Mentally Disordered Offenders and Difficult to Manage Patients*. 28 September 1990. London: HMSO.

NHS Management Executive (1991) *Purchasing Intelligence*. London: HMSO.

NHS Management Executive (1992) EL(92)6 *Services for Mentally Disordered Offenders and Patients with Similar Needs*. 5 February 1992. London: HMSO.

NHS Management Executive (1992) EL(92)24 *Assessment of Need for Services for Mentally Disordered Offenders and Patients with Similar Needs*. 8 April 1992. London: HMSO.

NHS Management Executive (1993) *EL(93)10. Managing Activity and Change Through Contracting*. 12 February 1993. London: HMSO.

NHS Management Executive (1994) *EL(92)20. Clinical Audit 1994/95 and Beyond*. 28 February 1994. London: HMSO.

NHS Management Executive (1995) *High Security Psychiatric Services: Changes in Funding and Organisation*. Leeds: NHS Executive.

Nietzsche, F. (1883–91) 'Of the pale criminal.' In F. Nietzsche *Thus Spake Zarathustra*. Translated by R.J. Hollingdale. Harmondsworth: Penguin Books 1961.

Norem-Hebeisen, A., Johnson, D.W., Anderson, D. and Johnson, R. (1984) 'Predictors and concomitants of changes in drug use patterns among teenagers.' *Journal of Social Psychology 124*, 43–50.

Norris, M. (1983) 'Changes in patients during treatment at Henderson Hospital therapeutic community during 1977–1981.' *British Journal of Medical Psychology 56*, 135–143.

North, M. (1975) *Personality Assessment Through Movement*. Boston: Plays Inc.

Norton, K.R.W. (1992) 'A culture of enquiry – its preservation or loss.' *Therapeutic Communities 13*, 1, 3–26.

Notman, M. and Nadelson, C. (1976) 'The rape victim: psychodynamic considerations.' *American Journal of Psychiatry 133*, 408–413.

Novaco, R.W. (1975) *Anger Control: The Development and Evaluation of an Experimental Treatment*. Lexington, Ma: D.C. Heath, Lexington Books.

Novaco, R.W. (1978) 'Anger and coping with stress.' In J.P. Foreyt and D.P. Rathjen (eds) *Cognitive Behaviour Therapy*. New York: Plenum Press.

Østergaard, L., Christensen, A.L., Teasdale, T., Theilgaard, A. (1993) *Undersøgelsesmetoder i Klinisk Psykologi*. Copenhagen: Munksgaard.

O'Brien, L.S. (1994) 'What will be the psychological consequences of the war in Bosnia?' *British Journal of Psychiatry 164*, 443–447.

O'Shaughnessy, E. (1981) 'A clinical study of a defensive organisation.' *International Journal of Psychoanalysis 62*, 359–69.

Obler, L.K. (1992) 'Language through the life-span.' In J.B. Gleason (ed) *The Development of Language.* Oxford: Charles E Merrill Publishing Co.

Open University (1990) *Managing Public Services. Responsiveness and Results. A Reading Guide (Part B).* Milton Keynes: Open University Press.

Oppenheimer, R., Howells, K., Palmer, R.L. and Chaloner, D.A. (1985) 'Adverse sexual experience in childhood and clinical eating disorders: A preliminary description.' *Journal of Psychiatric Research 19* 356–361.

Orlinsky, D.E. (1989) 'Researchers' images of psychotherapy: their origins and influence on research.' *Clinical Psychology Review 9*, 413–442.

Otnow Lewis, D. (1992) 'From abuse to violence.' *Journal of the American Academy of Child and Adolescent Psychiatry 31*, 383–391.

Otswald, P.F. (1963) *Sound Making: The Acoustic Communication of Emotion.* Springfield, IL: Charles C. Thomas.

Padel, R. (1992) *In and Out of the Mind: Greek Images of the Tragic Self.* Princeton, NJ: Princeton University Press.

Pailethorpe, G. W. (1932) *Studies in the Psychology of Delinquency.* London: HMSO.

Palazzoli, M.S., Boscolo, L., Cecchini, G. and Prata, G. (1978) *Paradox and Counter Paradox.* New York: Jason Aronson Inc.

Palazzoli, M.S., Boscolo, L., Cecchini, G, and Prata, G. (1980) 'Hypothesising – circulatory – neutrality: three guidelines for the conductor of the session.' *Family Process 19*, 3–12.

Panksepp, J., Siviy, S.M. and Normansell, L.A. (1985) 'Brain opioids and social emotions.' In M. Reite and T. Field (eds) *The Psychobiology of Attachment and Separation.* London: Academic Press.

Parker, A. (1970) *The Frying Pan.* London: Hutchinson.

Parkes, C.M. (1972) *Bereavement: Studies of Grief in Adult Life.* Harmondsworth: Penguin Books.

Parkes, C.M., Stevenson-Hinde, J. and Marris (eds) (1991) *Attachment Across the Life Cycle.* London: Routledge.

Parry, G. (1992) 'Improving psychotherapy services: applications of research, audit and evaluation.' *British Journal of Clinical Psychology 31*, 3–19.

Parry, G., Shapiro, D.A. and Firth, J. (1986) 'The case of the anxious executive: a study from the research clinic.' *British Journal of Medical Psychology 59*, 221–233.

Partridge, E. (1958) *Origins: A Short Etymological Dictionary of the English Language.* New York: Greenwich House, 1983.

Pastor, D.L. (1981) 'The quality of mother–infant attachment and its relationship to toddlers' initial sociability with peers.' *Developmental Psychology 17*, 326–335.

Patrick, M. (1993) 'Borderline Personality Disorder and the Mental representation of Early Social Experience.' In Contemporary Themes in

Psychoanalytic Research – Public Lectures. 8th May 1993. London: British Psycho-analytic Society.

Paul, R. and Caparulo, B. (1983) 'A longitudinal study of patients with severe developmental disorders and language learning.' *Journal of the American Academy of Child Psychiatry 22.*

Peck, D. (198) 'Small *n* experimental designs in clinical research.' In F. Watts (eds) *New Directions in Clinical Psychology.* Leicester: BPS.

Perkins, D.E. (1991) 'Clinical work with sex offenders in secure settings.' In C. Hollin and K. Howells (eds) *Clinical Approaches to Sex Offenders and Their Victims.* Chichester: John Wiley and Sons Ltd.

Perner, J., Ruffman, T., and Leekam, S.R. (in press) 'Theory of mind is contagious: you catch it from your sibs.' *Child Development 65,* 1224–1234.

Perry, J.C. and Cooper, S. (1989) 'An empirical study of defence mechanisms, I: clinical interviews and life vignette ratings.' *Archives of General Psychiatry 46,* 444–52.

Persaud, R.D. and Meux, C.J. (1994) 'The psychopathology of authority and its loss: The effect on a ward of losing a consultant psychiatrist.' *British Journal of Medical Psychology 67,* 1–11.

Perucci, R. (1974) *Circle of Madness: On Being Insane and Institutionalized in America.* Englewood Cliffs, NJ: Prentice Hall.

Pfäfflin, F. (1994) The Poetic and the Empirical Paradigm. Annotations to Murray Cox: 'The Paradigmatic Challenge "I have thee not and yet I see thee still".' In H. van Marle (ed) *Forensic Psychotherapy.* Proceedings of the Third Annual Meeting of the International Association of Forensic Psychotherapy. Den Haag.

Phillips, G.M. (1984) 'Reticence: a perspective on social withdrawal.' In G. Beeson, J.A. Daly and J.C. McCrosbey (eds) *Avoiding Communication.* London: Sage Publications.

Phillips, W., Baron-Cohen, S. and Rutter, M. (1992) 'The role of eye-contact in goal-detection: evidence from normal toddlers and children with autism or mental handicap.' *Development and Psychopathology 4,* 375–84.

Phillipson, H. (1973) *The Object Relations Technique.* Windsor: NFER Publishing Company.

Piaget, J. (1954) *The Construction of Reality in the Child.* New York: Basic Books.

Piaget, J. (1962) *Plays, Dreams and Imitations in Childhood.* New York: W.W. Norton and Co. Cited in B. van der Kolk (1994) 'The body keeps the score: memory and the evolving psychobiology of PTSD.' *Harvard Review of Psychiatry 1,* 253–265.

Pick, I.B. (1985) 'Working through in the countertransference.' *International Journal of Psychoanalysis 66,* 157–166.

Pilgrim, D. (1987) 'Psychotherapy in British Special Hospitals. A case of failure to thrive.' *Free Associations 11,* 59–72.

Pines, D. (1986) 'Working with women survivors of the Holocaust: affective experiences in the transference and countertransference.' *International Journal of Psychoanalysis 67*, 295–307.

Pines, M. (1981a) 'The fundamentals of group-analytic psychotherapy.' In M. Pines (ed) *The Evolution of Group Analysis*. London: Routledge.

Pines, M. (1981b) 'Introduction to the work of S.H. Foulkes.' In M. Pines (ed) *The Evolution of Group Analysis*. London: Routledge.

Pines, M. (ed) (1985a) *Bion and Group Psychotherapy*. London: Routledge and Kegan Paul.

Pines, M. (1985b) 'Psychic development and the group analytic situation.' *Group 9*, 24–37.

Pines, M. (1987) 'Introduction.' In M. Cox and A. Theilgaard *Mutative Metaphors in Psychotherapy: The Aeolian Mode*. London: Tavistock.

Pines, M. (1992) '"Elaboration of the negative" and other concepts: a tribute to Eduardo Cortesao.' *Group Analysis 25*, 151–169.

Pines, M. Hearst, L. and Behr, H. (1982) 'Group analysis.' In G.M. Gazda (ed) *Basic Approaches to Group Psychotherapy and Group Counselling*. Springfield IL: Charles C. Thomas.

Pinizotto, A.J. and Finkel, N.J. (1990) 'Crime personality profiling: an outcome and process study.' *Law and Human Behaviour 14*, 3, 215–233.

Piontelli, A. (1992) *From Fetus to Child: An Observational and Psychoanalytic Study*. London: Tavistock/Routledge.

Piotrowski, Z.A. (1936–37) 'On the Rorschach method and its application in organic disturbances of the central nervous system.' *Rorschach Research Exchange 1*, 23.

Pithers, W.D. (1990) 'Relapse prevention with sexual aggressors: a method for maintaining therapeutic gain and enhancing external supervision.' In W.L. Marshall, D.R. Laws and H.E. Barbaree (eds) *Handbook of Sexual Assault*. New York: Plenum Press.

Pitman, R.K., Van der Kolk, B.A., Scott, P.O. and Greenberg, M.S. (1990) 'Naloxone-reversible analgesic response to combat-related stimuli in post traumatic stress disorder.' *Archives of General Psychiatry 47*, 540–541.

Plakum, E.M., Burkhardt, P.E. and Muller, J.P. (1985) 'Fourteen-year follow-up of borderline and schizotypal personality disorders.' *Comprehensive Psychiatry 26*, 448–455.

Plato 'Apology' 38a. In *The Last Days of Socrates*. Translated by Hugh Tredennick and Harold Tarrant. Harmondsworth: Penguin Classics, 1993.

Podvoll, M. (1990) *The Seduction of Madness*. New York: Harper Collins.

Police, Drug Misusers and the Community (in press) *Advisory Council on the Misuse of Drugs*. London: HMSO.

Pollack, S. (1974) 'Forensic psychiatry – a specialty.' *Bulletin of the American Academy of Psychiatry and the Law 2*, 1, 1–6.

Poole, R. (1972) *Towards Deep Subjectivity*. London: Allen Lane.

Pope, K.S. and Bouhoutsos, J.C. (1986) *Sexual Intimacy between Therapists and Patients*. New York: Praeger.

Porter, P. (1978) *The Cost of Seriousness*. Oxford: Oxford University Press.

Potter, D. (1994) *Seeing The Blossom: Two Interviews and a Lecture*. London: Faber.

Potter, J. and Wetherell, M. (1987) *Discourse and Social Psychology*. London: Sage Publications.

Power, K.G. and Spencer, A.P. (1987) 'Parasuicidal behaviour of detained Scottish young inmates.' *International Journal of Offender Therapy and Comparative Criminology 31*, 227–235.

Power, M. and Brewin, C. (1991) 'From Freud to cognitive science: a contemporary account of the unconscious.' *British Journal of Clinical Psychology 30*, 289–310.

Price, J. (1992) 'The agonic and hedonic modes: definition, usage, and the promotion of mental health.' *World Futures 35*, 87–113.

Prins, H. (1990) 'Some observations on the supervision of dangerous offender patients.' *British Journal of Psychiatry 156*, 157–162.

Prosser, R., Rasbash, J. and Goldstein, H. (1991) *ML3 Software for Three-Level Analysis: User's Guide for v.2*. London: Institute of Education.

Putnam, F. (1990) 'Dissociation as a response to severe trauma.' In R. Kluft (ed) *Childhood Antecedents of Multiple Personality Disorder*. Washington, DC: American Psychiatric Press.

The Quality of Medical Care (1990) *Report of the Standing Medical Advisory Committee*. London: HMSO.

Quayle, M.T. (1989) *Group Therapy for Personality Disordered Offenders*. Paper presented at Annual Conference of Special Hospital Psychologists, Scarborough.

Quen, J.M. (1974) 'Historical reflections on American legal psychiatry.' *Bulletin of the American Academy of Psychiatry and the Law 2*, 4, 237–241.

Quinsey, V.L. (1988) 'Assessments of the treatability of forensic patients.' *Behavioral Sciences and the Law 6*, 4, 443–452.

Racker, H. (1968) *Transference and Countertransference*. Reprinted 1985. London: Karnac Books.

Raleigh, M., McGuire, M., Brammer, G. and Yuwiler, A. (1984) 'Social and environmental influences on blood serotonin concentrations in monkeys.' *Archives of General Psychiatry 41*, 405–410.

Ramsey, I.T. (1964) *Models and Mystery*. London: Oxford University Press.

Rank, O. (1924) *The Trauma of Birth*. New York: Harcourt, Brace, 1929.

Rapaport, D. (1950) 'On the psychoanalytic theory of thinking.' *International Journal of Psychoanalysis 31*, 161–170.

Rapaport, D., Gill, M. And Schafer, R. (1967) *Diagnostic Psychological Testing*. New York: International Universities Press.

Raphling, D.L. (1989) 'Fetishism in a woman.' *Journal of the American Psychoanalytic Association 37*, 465–491.

Rapoport, R. (1960) *The Community as Doctor.* London: Tavistock.

Rappeport, J.R. (1981) 'Ethics and forensic psychiatry.' In S. Bloch and P. Chodoff (eds) *Psychiatric Ethics.* Oxford: Oxford University Press.

Rappeport, J.R. and Oglesby, T. (1993) 'The Reed Report: a view from Baltimore.' *Journal of Forensic Psychiatry 4*, 2 194–197.

Rascovsky, A. and Rascovsky, M. (1968) 'On the genesis of acting out and psychopathic behaviour in Sophocles' Oedipus.' *International Journal of Psycho-Analysis 53*, 271–6.

Raven, J.C. (1948) *Progressive Matrices.* London: H.K. Lewis and Co.

Ray, I. (1938) *A Treatise on the Medical Jurispudence of Insanity.* Boston: W.H. Freeman and Bolles. Republished 1962, W. Overholsen (ed) Cambridge, MA: Bleknap Press.

Rayner, E. (1991) *The Independent Mind in Psychoanalysis.* London: Free Association Books.

Reed Committee (1992a) *Review of Health and Social Services for Mentally Disordered Offenders and Others Requiring Similar Services.* Staffing and Training Group (June).

Reed Committee. (1992b) *Review of Health and Social Services for Mentally Disordered Offenders and Others Requiring Similar Services.* Final Summary Report DH/DO (November).

Reich, W. (1933) *Character Analysis.* Translated by V.R. Carfagno. Third edition. New York: Farrar, Straus and Giroux.

Reid, W.H. (1985) 'The antisocial personality: a review.' *Hospital and Community Psychiatry 36*, 8, 831–837.

Reilly, M. (1974) *Play as Exploratory Learning.* Beverly Hills, CA: Sage Publications.

Reiman, J. (1979) *The Rich Get Richer and the Poor Get Prison.* New York: John Wiley and Sons Ltd.

Reiner, R. (1992) *Chief Constables.* Oxford: Oxford University Press.

Reusch, J. and Bateson, G. (1987) *Communications in the Social Matrix of Psychiatry, third edition.* London: Norton Lander.

Revitch, E. and Schlesinger, L. (1978) 'Murder: Evaluation, classification, and prediction.' In I. Kutash, S. Kutash, and L. Schlesinger (eds) *Violence: Perspectives on Murder and Aggression.* San Francisco, CA: Jossey Bass.

Revitch, E. and Schlesinger, L. (1981) *Psychopathology of Homicide.* Springfield, IL: Charles C. Thomas.

Rice, A.K. (1969) 'Individual, group and intergroup processes.' *Human Relations 22*, 6, 565–584.

Richards, A. (1989) 'A romance with pain: a telephone perversion in a woman.' *The International Journal of Psychoanalysis 70*, 153–164.

Richards, D. and Rose, J. (1991) 'Therapy for PTSD: four case studies.' *British Journal of Psychiatry 158*, 836–840.

Richman, J. (1932, 1957) *Selected Contributions to Psycho-Analysis.* London: Hogarth Press and the Institute of Psycho-Analysis.

Rickman, J. (1932) 'The psychology of crime.' In *Selected Contributions to Psychoanalysis.* London: Hogarth Press and the Institute of Psychoanalysis.

Rieger, W. (1971) 'Suicide attempts in a federal prison.' *Archives of General Psychiatry 24*, 532–535.

Ristau, C. (ed) (1991) *Cognitive Ethology: The Minds of Other Animals.* Hillsdale, NJ: Lawrence Erlbaum Associates.

Robins, L. (1966) *Deviant Children Grown Up.* Baltimore, MD: Williams and Wilkins.

Robinson, R. and Mitchell, J. (1993) 'Evaluation of psychological debriefing.' *Journal of Traumatic Stress 6*, 367–382.

Rock, P. (1988) 'The present state of criminology in Britain.' *British Journal of Criminology 28*, 2, 188–99.

Rock, P. (1994) 'The social organisation of British criminology.' In M. Maguire, R. Morgan and R. Reiner (eds) *The Oxford Handbook of Criminology.* Oxford: Oxford University Press.

Rodeheffer, M. and Martin, H.P. (1976) 'Special problems in developmental assessments.' In H.P. Martin and C.H. Kemps (eds) *The Abused Child – A Multi-Disciplinary Approach to Developmental Issues and Treatment.* Cambridge, MA: Ballinger.

Rogers, C.R. (1961) *On Becoming a Person.* Boston, MA: Houghton Mifflin.

Rorschach, H. (1921) *Psychodiagnostik.* Bern: Bircher.

Rose, D. (1986) '"Worse than death": psychodynamics of rape victims, and the need for psychotherapy.' *American Journal of Psychotherapy 143*, 817–824.

Rosen, I. (1979) 'The general psychoanalytic theory of perversion: a critical and clinical study.' In I. Rosen (ed) *Sexual Deviation.* Oxford: Oxford University Press.

Rosen, I. (ed) (1979) 'Perversion as a regulator of self-esteem.' In *Sexual Deviation.* Second edition. Oxford: Oxford University Press.

Rosen, S. (ed) (1982) *My Voice Will Go With You: The Teachings of Milton H. Erickson.* New York: W.W.Norton and Co.

Rosenblum, L. and Sunderland, G. (1982) 'Feeding ecology and mother infant relations.' In L.W. Hoffman, R. Gandelmann and H.R. Schiffman (eds) *Biological Basis of Parental Behaviour.* Hillsdale, NJ: Lawrence Erlbaum Associates.

Rosenfeld, H. (1952) 'Notes on the psychoanalysis of the superego conflict of an acute schizophrenic patient.' *The International Journal of Psycho-Analysis 33*, 111–31.

Rosenfeld, H. (1955) 'Notes on the psychoanalysis of the super-ego conflict in an acute schizophrenic patient.' In M. Klein, P. Heimann and R. Money-Kyrie (eds) *New Directions in Psycho-Analysis.* London: Tavistock.

Rosenfeld, H. (1964) 'On the psychotherapy of narcissism: a clinical approach.' *International Journal of Psychoanalysis 45,* 332–7.

Rosenfeld, H. (1971) 'A clinical approach to the psychoanalytic theory of the life and death instincts: an investigation into the aggressive aspects of narcissism.' *International Journal of Psycho-analysis 52,* 169–178.

Rosenfeld, H. (1987) *Impasse and Interpretation.* London: Tavistock.

Rosner, R. (1989) 'Forensic psychiatry: a subspecialty.' *Bulletin of the American Academy of Psychiatry and the Law 17,* 4, 323–333.

Rosner, R. (ed) (1994) *Principles and Practice of Forensic Psychiatry.* New York: Chapman and Hall.

Rosner, R. and Weinstock, R. (1990) *Ethical Practice in Psychiatry and the Law (Vol 7, Critical Issues in American Psychiatry and the Law).* New York: Plenum Press.

Rosser, R.M., Birch, S., Bond, H., Denford, J. and Schuschter, J. (1987) 'Five year follow-up of patients treated with in-patient psychotherapy at the Cassel Hospital for Nervous Diseases.' *Journal of the Royal Society of Medicine 80,* 549–555.

Roth, S., Dye, E. and Lebowitz, L. (1988) 'Group psychotherapy for sexual assault victims.' *Psychotherapy 25,* 82–93.

Rowbottom, R. and Hey, A. (1978) *Organisation of Service for the Mentally Ill.* Working Paper. Brunel Institute of Organisation and Social Studies (B1055).

Royal College of Psychiatrists (1985) *Confidentiality and Forensic Psychiatry.* (EFCC 129/85) Document. London: Royal College of Psychiatrists.

Royal College of Psychiatrists (1991) 'Guidelines for regional advisers on consultant posts in forensic psychiatry.' *Psychiatric Bulletin 15,* 231–232.

Royal College of Psychiatrists (1994) *The Treatment of Perpetrators of Child Sexual Abuse.* (Council report No. CR31). London: Royal College of Psychiatrists.

Royal College of Psychiatrists (1995) *The Responsibilities of Consultants in Psychiatry within the National Health Service and Private Practice* (draft).

Royal Commission (1979) *Royal Commission on the National Health Service.* London: HMSO.

Ruotolo, A. (1968) 'Dynamics of sudden murder.' *American Journal of Psychoanalysis 28,* 162–170.

Rush, B. (1812) *Medical Inquiries and Observations on Diseases of the Mind.* Philadelphia, PA: Kimber and Richardson.

Russell Davis, D. (1992) *Scenes of Madness: A Psychiatrist at the Theatre.* London: Routledge.

Russell, D. (1986) *The Secret Trauma.* New York: Basic Books.

Rutter, M. (1985) 'Resilience in the face of adversity: protective factors and resistance to psychiatric disorder.' *British Journal of Psychiatry 147,* 598–611.

Rutter, M. (1987) 'Psychosocial resilience and protective mechanisms.' *American Journal of Orthopsychiatry 57*, 316–331.

Rycroft, C. (1966) *Psycho-Analysis Observed*. London: Constable.

Rycroft, C. (1979a) *A Critical Dictionary of Psychoanalysis*. Harmondsworth: Penguin Books.

Rycroft, C. (1979b) *The Innocence of Dreams*. London: Hogarth Press.

Ryle, A. (1990) *Cognitive–Analytic Therapy: Active Participation in Change. A New Integration in Brief Psychotherapy*. Chichester: John Wiley and Sons Ltd.

Sacks, H. (1923) 'On the genesis of perversion.' *Psychoanalytical Quarterly 55*, 477–88.

Safran, J.D., Greenberg, L.S. and Rice, L.N. (1988) 'Integrating psychotherapy research and practice: modelling the change process.' *Psychotherapy 25*, 1–17.

Sampson, R.J. and Laub, J.H. (1990) 'Crime and deviance over the life course: The salience of adult social bonds.' *American Sociological Review 55*, 609–627.

Sandler, J. (1983) 'Reflections on some relations between psychoanalytic concepts and psychoanalytic practice.' *International Journal of Psychoanalysis 64*, 35–45.

Sandler, J. (1987) 'The concept of projective identification.' In J. Sandler (ed) *Projection, Identification, Projective Identification*. London: Karnac Books.

Sandler, J. and Dare, C. (1970) 'The psychoanalytic concept of orality.' *Journal of Psychosomatic Research 14*, 211–222.

Sandler, J., Dare, C. and Holder, A. (1982) 'Frames of reference in psychoanalytic psychology: XII. The characteristics of the structural frame of reference.' *British Journal of Medical Psychology 55*, 203–207.

Sandler, J., Dreher, A.U. and Drews, S. (1991) 'An approach to conceptual research in psychoanalysis illustrated by a consideration of psychic trauma.' *International Review of Psychoanalysis 18*, 133–141.

Sandler, J., Holder, A. and Dare, C. (1973) *The Patient and the Analyst. The Basis of the Psychoanalytic Process*. London: George Allen and Unwin Ltd.

Sarbin, T.R. (1954) 'Role theory'. *Handbook of Social Psychology 1*, 22–257. Reading, MA: Addison Wesley Pubs.

Savage, S., Kelly, K., Moon, G. and Bradshaw, Y. (1991) 'The role of the police surgeon.' *Policing 9*, 148–159

Savage, S., Moon, G., Bradshaw, Y. and Twigg, L. (1991) *Forensic Medical Services in the Metropolitan Police Area*. Institute of Police and Criminological Studies/Health Information Research Service, University of Portsmouth.

Saville, E. and Rumney, D. (1992) *The History of the ISTD: A Study of Crime and Delinquency from 1931 to 1992*. London: ISTD.

Scaife, M. and Bruner, J. (1975) 'The capacity for joint visual attention in the infant.' *Nature 253*, 265–6.

Schafer, R. (1983) *The Analytic Attitude*. London: Hogarth Press.

Schaffer, R. (1992) *Retelling a Life: Narration and Dialogue in Psychoanalysis.* New York: Basic Books.

Schank, R.C. (1990) *Tell Me A Story – A New Look at Real and Artificial Memory.* Oxford: Maxwell Macmillan International.

de Shazer, S., Berg, I.K., Lipchik, E., Nunnally, E., Molnor, A., Gingerich, W., Weine, R. and Davis, M. (1986) 'Brief therapy: focused solution development.' *Family Process 25,* 207–222.

Scheffer, J.H. (1984) 'Psychotherapie in de Prof.' Pompe Kliniek Nijmegen (internal publication).

Scheffer, J.H. (1991) 'Intrinsic and extrinsic motivation.' Paper for the Congress on Law and Mental Health in Leuven, Belgium.

Scherer, K.R. and Sherer, U. (1981) 'Speech behaviour in personality.' In J. Darby (ed) *Speech Evaluation in Psychiatry.* New York: Grune and Stratton, Inc.

Schlapobersky, J. (1993) 'The language of the group: monologue, dialogue and discourse in group analysis.' In D. Brown and L. Zinkin (eds) *The Psyche and The Social World.* London: Routledge.

Schlapobersky, J. and Bamber, H. (1988) 'The reclamation of space and time: psychotherapy for the rehabilitation of victims of torture.' In D. Miserere *The Red Cross Handbook on Refugees.* The Hague: Nijhoff.

Schmideberg, M. (1947) 'The treatment of psychopathic and borderline patients.' *American Journal of Psychotherapy 1,* 45–71.

Schmideberg, M. (1949) 'The analytic treatment of major criminals: therapeutic results and technical problems.' In K.R. Eissler (eds) *Searchlights on Delinquency.* New York: International Universities Press.

Schmidt, G. and Schorsch, E. (1981) 'Psychosurgery of sexually deviant patients: review and analysis of new empirical findings.' *Archives of Sexual Behavior 10,* 3, 301–323.

Schneider, C. (1977) *Shame, Exposure and Privacy.* Boston, MA: Beacon Press.

Schorsch, E., Galedary, G., Haag, A., Hauch, M. and Lohse, H. (1990) *Sex Offenders. Dynamics and Psychotherapeutic Strategies.* Berlin: Springer-Verlag.

Schroeder, R.A. (1987) 'Outcome assessment 70 years later: are we ready?' *New England Journal of Medicine,* 160–162.

Schuker, E. (1979) Psychodynamics and treatment of sexual assault victims. *Journal of the American Academy of Psychoanalysis 7,* 553–573.

Schwartz, D.A., Flinn, D.E. and Slawson, P.F (1974) 'The treatment of the suicidal character'. *American Journal of Psychotherapy 28,* 197–207.

Scott, P. (1960) 'The treatment of psychopaths.' *British Medical Journal May 28,* 1641–1646.

Scott, P. (1963) 'Psychopathy.' *Postgraduate Medical Journal 39,* 12.

Scott, P. (1977) 'Assessing dangerousness in criminals.' *British Journal of Psychiatry 131,* 127–42.

Segal, H. (1957) 'Notes on symbol formation.' *International Journal of Psycho-analysis 38,* 391–397.

Segal, H. (1991) *Dream, Phantasy and Art.* London: Routledge.

Seligman, M.E.P. (1975) *Helplessness: On Depression, Development and Death.* San Francisco, CA: W.H. Freeman.

Shadish, W.R.J. and Sweeney, R.B. (1991) 'Mediators and moderators in meta-analysis: there's a reason we don't let dodo birds tell us which psychotherapies should have prizes.' *Journal of Consulting and Clinical Psychology 59,* 6, 883–893.

Shakespeare, W. *Arden Edition.* London: Methuen

Shanfield, S.B., Matthews, K.L. and Hetherly, V. (1993) 'What do excellent psychotherapy supervisors do?' *American Journal of Psychiatry 150,* 1081–1084.

Shapiro, D.A., Barkham, M., Hardy, G.E. and Morrison, L. (1990) 'The second Sheffield psychotherapy project: Rationale, design and preliminary outcome data.' *British Journal of Medical Psychology 63,* 2, 97–108.

Shapiro, D.A. and Shapiro, D. (1977) 'The "double standard" in evaluation of psychotherapies.' *Bulletin of the British Psychological Society 30,* 209–210.

Shapiro, D.A. and Shapiro, D. (1987) 'Change processes in psychotherapy.' *British Journal of Addiction 82,* 431–444.

Shapiro, E.R. (1978) 'The psychodynamics and developmental psychology of the borderline patient: a review of the literature.' *American Journal of Psychiatry 135,* 1305–1315.

Sharpe, M. (ed) (1994) *The Third Eye: Supervision of Analytic Groups.* London: Routledge.

Shaw, C.R. and McKay, H.D. (1942) *Juvenile Delinquency in Urban Areas.* Chicago, IL: Chicago University Press.

Shaw, D., Churchill, C., Noyes, R. and Loeffelholz, P. (1987) 'Criminal behaviour and PTSD in Vietnam veterans.' *Comprehensive Psychiatry 28,* 403–411.

Shaw, D.S. and Vondra, J.I. (1993) 'Chronic family adversity and infant attachment security.' *Journal of Child Psychology and Psychiatry 34,* 1205–1215.

Sheldrick, C. (1985) 'Treatment of delinquents.' In M. Rutter and L. Hersou (eds) *Child and Adolescent Psychiatry. Modern Approaches.* Second edition. Oxford: Blackwell.

Shengold, L. (1988) *Halo in the Sky: Observations on Anality and Defense.* New York: Guilford Press.

Shoham, G.S., Rahav, G., Rubin, R., Buickhuisen, W., Markowski, R., Chard, F., Neuman, F., Ben-Haim, M., Baruch, L., Esformes, Y. and Schwarzman, Z. (1987) 'Family parameters of violent prisoners.' *Journal of Social Psychology 127,* 83–91.

Simon, R.I. (1994a) 'Forensic psychiatry and the perturbation of psychiatrists' attention and neutrality during psychotherapy.' *Bulletin of the American Academy of Psychiatry and the Law 22*, 2, 269–277.

Simon, R.I. (1994b) 'Treatment boundaries in psychiatric practice.' In R. Rosner (ed) *Principles and Practice of Forensic Psychiatry*. New York: Chapman and Hall.

Sinason, V. (1986) 'The relationship of secondary mental handicap to trauma.' *Psychoanalytic Psychotherapy 2*, 2.

Sinason, V. (1988a) 'Sexual abuse.' In H. Wolff, H. Bateman and D.A. Sturgeon (eds) *UCH Handbook of Psychiatry. An Integrated Approach*. London: Duckworth.

Sinason, V. (1988b) 'Smiling, swallowing, sickening and stupefying, the effect of abuse on the child.' *Psychoanalytic Psychotherapy 3*, 2.

Sinason, V. (1988c) 'Dolls and bears. From symbolic equation to symbol. The use of different play material for abused children and others.' *British Journal of Psychotherapy 4*, 4, 349–64.

Sinason, V. (1989) 'The psycholinguistics of discrimination.' In R. Richards (ed) *Crises of the Self, Further Essays on Psychoanalysis and Politics*. London: Free Association Books.

Sinason, V. (1992) *Mental Handicap and the Human Condition*. London: Free Association Books.

Sinason, V. (1993) 'Working with sexually abused individuals who have a learning disability.' In A. Craft (ed) *Practice Issues in Sexuality and Learning Disabilities*. London and New York: Routledge.

Sinclair, I.A.C. and Clarke, R.U.G. (1982) 'Predicting, treating and explaining delinquency: the lessons from research in institutions.' In P. Feldman (ed) *Developments in the Study of Criminal Behaviour, Vol 1. The Prevention and Control of Offending*. Chichester: John Wiley and Sons Ltd.

Singer, M. (1975) 'The borderline delinquent: the interlocking of intrapsychic and interactional determinants.' *International Review of Psycho-Analysis 2*, 429–440.

Slater, R.G. (1986) 'Psychiatric interventions in an atmosphere of terror.' *American Journal of Forensic Psychiatry 7*, 1, 5–12.

Slee, J. (1994) 'Twenty five per cent of prisoners sexually assaulted.' *Sydney Morning Herald* 24 September.

Smialek, J. and Spitz, W. (1978) 'Death behind bars.' *Journal of the American Medical Association 240*, 2563–2564.

de Smit, B. (1992) 'The end of the beginning is the beginning of the end: the structure of the initial interview in forensic psychiatry.' Proceedings of the 17th International Congress of the International Academy of Law and Mental Health. Leuven, Belgium.

Smith, M.H. (1922) *The Psychology of the Criminal*. London: Methuen.

Smith, M.J. (1975) *When I Say No I Feel Guilty*. London: Bantam Books.

Smith, M.L. and Glass, G.V. (1977) 'Meta-analysis of psychotherapy outcome studies.' *American Psychologist*, September, 752–760.

Snowden, P. (1990) 'Regional secure units and forensic services in England and Wales'. In R. Bluglass and P. Bowden (eds) *Principles and Practice of Forensic Psychiatry*. Edinburgh: Churchill Livingstone.

Socarides, C. (1988) *The Preoedipal Origins and Psychoanalytic Therapy of Sexual Perversions*. Maddison, CT: International Universities Press.

Sohn, L. (1985) 'Narcissistic organisation, projective identification, and the formation of the identificate.' *International Journal of Psychoanalysis 66*, 201–13.

Soni, S.D. (1995a) 'Dynamics and dilemmas of multidisciplinary teamwork: a clinician's perspective.' *Shaping British Psychiatry Journal 1*, 2.

Soni, S.D. (1995b) Editorial. *Shaping British Psychiatry Journal 1*, 2.

Sorce, J., Emde, R., Campos, J. and Klinnert, M. (1985) 'Maternal emotional signalling: its effect on the visual cliff behavior of 1 year olds.' *Developmental Psychology 21*, 195–200.

Southwark Arrest Referral Pilot Project Monitoring Group (1988–91) Report to the Home Office on the Southwark Arrest Referral Pilot Project. A study of feasibility of working with people who have been arrested and want help for their problem drug use. January 1988-March 1991. Southwark.

Sparr, L. and Atkinson, R. (1986) 'PTSD as an insanity defence: medico-legal quicksand.' *American Journal of Psychiatry 143*, 608–613.

Spearman, C. (1927) *The Abilities of Man*. New York: Macmillan.

Spence, D.P. (1982) *Narrative Truth and Historical Truth: Meaning and Interpretation in Psychoanalysis*. New York: W. W. Norton and Co.

Spence, D.P. (1994) *The Rhetorical Voice of Psychoanalysis Displacement of Evidence by Theory*. Cambridge, MA: Harvard University Press.

Sperling, M. (1959) 'A study of deviate sexual behaviour in children by the method of simultaneous analysis of mother and child.' In L. Jessner and E. Pavenstedt (eds) *Dynamic Psychopathology in Childhood*. New York: Grune and Stratton.

Spiegel, D. (1990) 'Trauma, dissociation and hypnosis.' In R. Kluft (ed) *Incest Related Syndromes of Adult Psychopathology*. Washington, DC: American Psychiatric Press.

Spillius, E. (1990) 'Asylum and society.' In E. Trist and H. Murray (eds) *The Social Engagement of Social Science: Volume 1 The Socio-Psychological Perspective*. London: Free Association Books.

Spillius, E. (1994) 'Developments on Kleinian thought: overview and personal view.' *Psychoanalytic Inquiry 14*, 324–364.

Sroufe, L.A. (1983) 'Infant–caregiver attachment and patterns of adaptation in preschool: The roots of maladaption and competence.' In M. Perlmutter (ed) *Minnesota Symposium in Child Psychology 16*. Hillsdale, NJ: Lawrence Erlbaum Associates.

Sroufe, L.A. (1985) 'Attachment classifications from the perspective of infant–caregiver relationships and infant temperament.' *Child Development 56*, 1–14.

Sroufe, L.A. (1990) 'An organizational perspective on the self.' In D. Cicchetti and M. Beeghly (eds) *The Self in Transition: Infancy to Childhood.* Chicago, IL: University of Chicago Press.

Sroufe, L.A. and Fleeson, J. (1986) 'Attachment and the construction of relationships.' In W. Hartup and Z. Rubin (eds) *Relationships and Development.* Hillsdale, NJ: Lawrence Erlbaum Associates.

Sroufe, L.A. and Rutter, M. (1984) 'The domain of developmental psychopathology.' *Child Development 83*, 173–189.

Standing Medical Advisory Committee (1990) *The Quality of Medical Care: Report of the Standing Medical Advisory Committee.* London: HMSO.

Stanton, A.H. and Schwartz, M.S. (1954) *The Mental Hospital; A Study of Institutional Participation in Psychiatric Illness and Treatment.* New York: Basic Books.

Staub, E. (1978) *Positive Social Behaviour and Morality, Vol 1: Social and Personal Influences.* New York: Academic Press.

Steele, H., Steele, M. and Fonagy, P. (in preparation) 'A path-analytic model of determinants of infant–parent attachment: limited rather than multiple pathways.'

Steele, H., Steele, M. and Fonagy, P. (in press) 'Associations among attachment classifications of mothers, fathers and their infants.' *Child Development.*

Steiner, J. (1982) 'Perverse relationships between parts of the self: a clinical illustration.' *International Journal of Psychoanalysis 63*, 241–51.

Steiner, J. (1992) 'Psychic retreats.' In E. Spillius (ed) *New Library of Psychoanalysis 19.* London: Routledge.

Steiner, J. (1993a) *Psychic Retreats.* London and New York: Routledge.

Steiner, J. (1993b) 'Two types of pathological organisation in Oedipus the King and Oedipus at Colonus.' *Psychic Retreats. The New Library of Psychoanalysis.*

Steiner, J. (1994) Foreword. In M. Jackson and P. Williams *Unimaginable Storms: A Search for Meaning in Psychosis.* London: Karnac Books.

Stern, A. (1938) 'Psychoanalytic investigation and therapy in borderline group of neuroses.' *Psychoanalytic Quarterly 7*, 467–489.

Stern, D. (1994) 'One way to build a clinically relevant baby.' *Infant Mental Health Journal 15*, 36–54.

Stiles, W.B., Elliott, R., Llewelyn, S., Firth-Cozens, J., Margison, F., Shapiro, D.A. and Hardy, G. (1990) 'Assimilation of problematic experiences by clients in therapy.' *Psychotherapy 27*, 411–420.

Stiles, W.B., Shapiro, D.A. and Firth-Cozens, J.A. (1989) 'Therapist differences in the use of verbal response mode forms and intents.' *Psychotherapy 26*, 3, 314–322.

Stoller, R. (1975) *Perversion: The Erotic Form of Hatred.* New York: Pantheon Books.

Stoller, R. (1976) 'Sexual excitement.' *Archives of General Psychiatry 33,* 899–909.

Stoller, R. (1979) *Sexual Excitement. Dynamics and Erotic Life.* New York: Pantheon Books.

Stoller, R.J. (1991) 'The term perversion.' In G. Fogel and W. Myers (eds) *Perversions and Near Perversions.* New Haven, CT: Yale University Press.

Stone, A.A. (1984) *Law, Psychiatry and Morality: Essays and Analysis.* Washington, DC: American Psychiatric Press.

Stone, A.A. (1994) 'Revisiting the parable: truth without consequences.' *International Journal of Law and Psychiatry 17,* 79–98.

Strachey, J. (1934) 'The nature of the therapeutic action of psycho-analysis.' *International Journal of Psycho-Analysis 15,* 127–159.

Stratton, P. and Swaffer, R. (1988) 'Maternal casual beliefs for abused and handicapped children.' *Journal of Reproductive and Infant Psychology 6,* 201–216.

Strauss, M.A. and Gelles, R.J. (1987) 'Is violence towards children increasing.' In R.J. Gelles (ed) *Family Violence.* Second edition. London: Sage Publications.

Strauss, M.A. and Kantor, G.K. (1987) 'Stress and child abuse.' In R.E. Helfer and R.S. Kemp *The Battered Child.* Fourth edition. Chicago, IL: The University of Chicago Press.

Styron, W. (1991) *Darkness Visible.* London: Jonathan Cape.

Sutherland, E.H. and Cressey, D.R. (1960) *Principles of Criminology.* Philadelphia, PA: J.P. Lippincott,

Suttie, I.D. (1935) *The Origins of Love and Hate.* Harmondsworth: Penguin Books.

Sydney Morning Herald (1994) 'Tough love for young offenders.' *Editorial* 17 August.

Sykes, G.M. (1958) *The Society of Captives: A Study of a Maximum Security Prison.* Princeton: Princeton University Press.

Sylvester, J. (1990) *Attributions of parents who abuse their children.* PhD. Dissertation, University of Leeds.

Symington, N. (1980) 'The response aroused by the psychopath.' *International Review of Psychoanalysis 7,* 291–298.

Szajnberg, N.M. (ed) (1990) 'The individual and society's institutions: Autonomy and integration.' In *Educating the Emotions: Bruno Bettelheim and Psychoanalytic Development.* New York: Plenum Press.

Szecsödy, I. (1990) 'Supervision: a didactic or mutative situation.' *Psychoanalytic Psychotherapy 4,* 245–261.

Tardiff, K. (1994) 'Violence: causes and nonpsychopharmacological treatment.' In R. Rosner (ed) *Principles and Practice of Forensic Psychiatry.* New York: Chapman and Hall.

Target, M. and Fonagy, P. (1994) 'The efficacy of psycho-analysis for children with emotional disorders.' *Journal of the American Academy Child Adolescent Psychiatry 33*, 361–371.

Tarling, R. (1979) *Sentencing Practice in Magistrates' Courts*. Home Office Research Study no.56. London: HMSO.

Tarlov, A., Ware, J.E., Greenfield, S., Nelson, E.C., Perrin, E. and Zubkoff, M. (1989) 'The medical outcomes study: an application of methods for monitoring the results of medical care.' *Journal of the American Medical Association 262*, 925–930.

Taylor, V. (1956) *The Cross of Christ: Eight Public Lectures*. London: Macmillan.

Telch, M.J. (1981) 'The present status of outcome studies: a reply to Frank.' *Journal of Consulting and Clinical Psychology 49*, 3, 472–475.

Terr, L.C. (1991) 'Childhood traumas: an outline and overview.' *American Journal of Psychiatry 148*, 10–20.

Theilgaard, A. (1984) 'A psychological study of the personalities of XYY and XXY men.' *Acta Psychiatrica Scandinavia Sup 315*. Copenhagen: Munksgaard.

Theilgaard, A. (1985) 'Klinisk Psykologi.' In J. Welner (ed) *Psykiatri – en Tekstbog*. Copenhagen: F.A.D.L.'s Forlag.

Theilgaard, A. (1987) 'Brug og misbrug af Rorschachtesten.' In K.V. Mortensen, L. Møller, A. Theilgaard and H. Ziegler (eds) *Rorschach-testning, en Grundbog*. Copenhagen: Dansk Psykologisk Forlag.

Theilgaard, A. (1992) 'Performance and projective possibilities.' In M. Cox (ed) *Shakespeare Comes to Broadmoor – The Actors are Come Hither*. London: Jessica Kingsley Publishers.

Theilgaard, A. (1993) 'Videnskab og klinisk psykologisk forskning.' In N. Rosenberg, K.V. Mortensen, E. Hougaard, S. Lúnn and A. Theilgaard (eds) *Klinisk Psychologisk Forskning*. Copenhagen: Dansk Psykologisk Forlag.

Thomas, B. (1994) 'Teamwork.' In C. Hume and I. Pullen (eds) *Rehabilitation for Mental Health Problems*. London: Churchill Livingstone.

Thompson, S. and Kahn, J.H. (1970) *The Group Processes as a Helping Technique*. Oxford: Pergamon Press.

Tillich, P. (1963) *The Eternal Now*. London: SCM Press.

Toch, H. (1979) *The Psychology of Crime and Criminal Justice*. New York: Holt Rhinehart-Winston.

Tomasello, M. (1988) 'The role of joint-attentional processes in early language acquisition.' *Language Sciences 10*, 69–88.

Totaro, P. (1994) 'Avoid jail – go judge shopping.' *Sydney Morning Herald* 15 June.

Tracy, D. (1981) *The Analogical Imagination: Christian Theology and the Culture of Pluralism*. London: SCM Press.

Traux, C.B. and Carkhoff, R.R. (1967) *Towards Effective Counselling and Psychotherapy; Training and practice*. Chicago, IL: Aldine.

Treurniet, N. (1985) 'Psychoanalyse und Selbstpsychologie. Eine metapsychologische Studie mit Fallbeispiel.' *Psyche 39*, 906–939.

Treurniet, N. (1993) 'What is psychoanalysis now?' *International Journal of Psycho-Analysis 74*, 873–891.

Trevarthen, C. and Logotheti, T. (1989) 'Child in society, and society in children: the nature of basic trust.' In S. Howell and R. Willis (eds) *Societies at Peace: Anthropological Perspectives*. London: Routledge.

Trist, E. and Murray, H. (1990) (eds) *The Social Engagement of Social Science, Volume 1: The Socio-Psychological Perspective*. London: Free Association Books.

Trist, E.L. and Bamforth, K.W. (1951) 'Some social and psychological consequences of the Longwell method of goal-getting.' *Human Relations 4*.

Tronick, E., Als, H., Adamson, L., Wise, S. and Brazelton, T.B. (1978) 'The infant's response to entrapment between contradictory messages in face-to-face interaction.' *Journal of American Academy Child Psychiatry 17*, 1–13.

Trower, P., Bryant, B. and Argyle, M. (1978) *Social Skills and Mental Health*. London: Methuen.

Troy, M. and Sroufe, L.A. (1987) 'Victimisation among preschoolers: role of attachment relationship history.' *Journal of American Academy of Child and Adolescent Psychiatry 26*, 166–172.

Tucker, L., Bauer, S.F., Wagner, S., Harlam, D. and Sher, I. (1987) 'Longterm hospital treatment of borderline patients: a descriptive outcome study.' *American Journal of Psychiatry 144*, 11, 1443–1448.

Tully, B. and Cahill, D. (1984) *Police Interviewing of the Mentally Handicapped: An Experimental Study*. London: The Police Foundation.

Turiel, E. (1983) 'Disruptive school behavior and concepts of social convention in early adolescence.' *Journal of Educational Psychology 75*, 677–685.

Tyrer, P., Casey, P. and Ferguson, B. (1993) 'Personality disorder in perspective.' In P. Tyler and G. Stein (eds) *Personality Disorder Reviewed*. London: Royal College of Psychiatrists.

Tyrer, P. and Stein, G. (eds) *Personality Disorder Reviewed*. London: Royal College of Psychiatrists, Gaskell.

Tyson, P. and Tyson, R.L. (1990) *Psychoanalytic Theories of Development: An Integration*. New Haven, CT: Yale University Press.

Vaglum, P., Friis, S., Irion, T., Johns, S., Karterud, S., Larsen, F. and Vaglum, S. (1990) 'Treatment response of severe and non-severe personality disorders in a therapeutic community day unit.' *Journal of Personality Disorder 4*, 161–172.

Vaihinger, H. (1924) *The Philosophy of 'As If'*. London: Paul, Trench, Trubner.

Vaillant, G.E. (1971) 'Theoretical hierarchy of adaptive ego mechanisms.' *Archives of General Psychiatry 24*, 107–18.

Vaillant, G.E. (1975) 'Sociopathy as a human process.' *Archives of General Psychiatry 32*, 178–183.

Vaillant, G.E. (1977) *Adaptation to Life*. Boston: Little and Brown.

Vaillant, G.E. (1992) *Ego Mechanisms of Defence. A Guide for Clinicians and Researcher.* Washington, DC: American Psychiatric Press.

Vaillant, G.E., Bond, M. and Vaillant, C.O. (1986) 'An empirically validated hierarchy of defence mechanisms.' *Archives of General Psychiatry 43*, 786–94.

Vaillant G.E. and Drake, R.E. (1985) 'Maturity of ego defences in relation to DSM-III axis II personality disorder.' *Archives of General Psychiatry 42*, 59–601.

Vaughan, P. (1983) 'The disordered development of day care in psychiatry.' *Health Trends 15*, 91–94.

van Velsen, C. (1990) 'Working with survivors of torture.' Proceedings of the International Academy of Law and Mental Health, Annual Conference, Toronto, 1990.

Verhage, F. (1994) Paper read to the Dutch Psychoanalytical Society, March 21. *Mededelingenblad ven de Nederlandse Vereniging voor Psychoanalyse 9*, 6, 12–21.

Vidler, A.R. (1950) *Christian Belief.* London: SCM Press.

de Villiers, J. and de Villiers, P. (1978) *Acquisition of Language.* London: Harvard University Press.

Vizard, E. (1987) 'Interviewing young sexually abused children – assessment techniques.' *Family Law 17*, 28–33.

Vizard, E. (1993) 'Interviewing sexually abused children.' In C.J. Hobbs and J.M. Wynne (eds) *Baillieres Clinical Paediatrics: International Practice and Research Child Abuse.* London: Baillière Tyndall.

Vizard, E. and Tranter, M. (1988) 'Interviewing children who may have been sexually abused.' In A. Bentovim, A. Elton, J. Hilderbrand, M. Tranter and E. Vizard (eds) *Child Sexual Abuse Within the Family.* London: Butterworths/Wright.

Vygotsty, L.S. (1962) *Thought and Language.* Cambridge, MA: M.I.T. Press.

Waal, F. de (1989) *Peacemaking Among Primates.* London: Penguin Books.

Wachtel, P.L. (1977) *Psychoanalysis and Behaviour Therapy.* New York: Basic Books.

Waddington, C.H. (1966) *Principles of Development and Differentiation.* New York: Macmillam.

Waelder, R. (1930) 'The principle of multiple function: observations on over-determination.' In S.A. Guttman (eds) *Psychoanalysis: Observation, Theory, Application.* New York: International Universities Press, 1976.

Wagner, R. (1882) *Parsifal.* Libretto translation by I. Salter. Phillips Classics Recording 1962.

Walker, J. (1994) *Remember Walls: A Photographic Study of Berwick upon Tweed.* Berwick upon Tweed: private publication.

Walker, L. (1979) *The Battered Woman.* New York: Harper and Row.

Wallerstein, R.S. (1991). 'Psychoanalytic education and research: a transformative proposal.' *Psychoanalytic Inq. 11*, 196–226.

Watkins, B. and Bentovim, A. (1992) 'The sexual abuse of male children and adolescents: a review of current research.' *Journal of Child Psychiatry and Psychology 33*, 197–249.

Watts, D. and Morgan, G. (1994) 'Malignant alienation: dangers for patients who are hard to like.' *British Journal of Psychiatry 164*, 11–15.

Watts, F. and Bennett, D. (1991) 'Management of the staff team.' In F. Watts and D. Bennett (eds) *Theory and Practice of psychiatric rehabilitation.* Third Edition. Chichester: John Wiley and Sons Ltd.

Watzlawick, P., Beavin, J.H. and Jackson, D.D. (1967) *Pragmatics of Human Communication.* New York: W.W.Norton and Co.

Watzlawick, P., Weakland, J. and Fish, R. (1974) *Change: Principles of Problem Formation and Problem Resolution.* New York: W.W.Norton and Co.

Weber, C.A., Meloy, J.R. and Gacono, C.B. (1992) 'A Rorschach study of attachment and anxiety in inpatient conduct-disordered and dysthymic adolescents.' *Journal of Personality Assessment 58*, 16–26.

Webster, C.D. and Menzies, R.J. (1987) 'The clinical prediction of dangerousness.' In D.N. Weisstub (ed) *Law and Mental Health, International Perspectives, Vol. III.* New York: Pergamon Press.

Wechsler, D. (1939) *The Measurement of Adult Intelligence.* Baltimore: Williams and Wilkins.

Wechsler, D. (1981) *WAIS-R Manual: Wechsler Adult Intelligence Scale – Revised.* San Antonio, CA: The Psychological Corporation.

Weiner, B.A. and Wettstein, R.M. (1993) *Legal Issues in Mental Health Care.* New York: Plenum Press.

Weinryb, R. and Røssel, R. (1991) 'Karolinska Psychodynamic Profile: KAPP.' *Acta Psychiatrica Scandinavia. Sup.363.* Copenhagen: Munksgaard.

Weinstein, H.C. (1989) 'Psychiatric services in gaols and prisons: who cares?' *American Journal of Psychiatry 146*, 1094–1095.

Weinstock, R. (1989) 'Treatment of antisocial and other personality disorders in a correctional setting.' In R. Rosner and R.B. Harmon (eds) *Correctional Psychiatry.* New York: Plenum Press.

Weinstock, R. (1994) 'Utilizing therapists to obtain death penalty verdicts.' *Bulletin of the American Academy of Psychiatry and the Law 22*, 1, 39–52.

Weiss, J., Lamberti, J. and Blackman, N. (1960) 'The sudden murderer: A comparative analysis.' *Archives of General Psychiatry 2*, 669–674.

Weiss, J. and Sampson, H. (1986) *The Psychoanalytic Process.* New York: Guilford Press.

Welldon, E. (1982) 'Eroticization of the group process used by patients suffering from sexual deviations as a resistance against the therapeutic alliance.' *Group Analysis 15*, 1, 22–24.

Welldon, E. (1984) 'The application of group-analytic psychotherapy to those with sexual perversions.' In T. Lear (ed) *Spheres of Group Analysis*. Nass, Co. Kildare: Leicester Leader.

Welldon, E. (1988) *Mother, Madonna, Whore: The Idealization and Denigration of Motherhood*. London: Free Association Books.

Welldon, E. (1993) 'Forensic psychotherapy and group analysis.' *Group Analysis* 26, 4, 487–502.

Welldon, E. (1994) 'Forensic psychotherapy.' In P. Clarkson and M. Pokorny (eds) *Handbook of Psychotherapy*. London: Routledge.

Wellman, H.M. (1990) *The Child's Theory of Mind*. Cambridge, Ma: Bradford Books/MIT Press.

Wellman, H.M. (1993) 'Early understanding of mind: the normal case.' In S. Baron-Cohen, H. Tager-Flusberg, and D.J. Cohen (eds) *Understanding Other Minds: Perspectives from Autism*. New York: Oxford University Press.

Wellman, H.M., Harris, P.L., Banerjee, M. and Sinclair, A. (in preparation) 'Early understandings or emotion: evidence from natural language.' *Cognition and Emotion*.

Werman, D. (1984) *The Practice of Supportive Psychotherapy*. New York: Brunner/Mazel.

Werner, E. (1989) 'High risk children in young adulthood: a longitudinal study from birth to 32 years.' *American Journal of Orthopsychiatry 59*, 72–81.

Wertham, F. (1949) *The Show of Violence*. New York: Doubleday and Company Inc.

Wertham, F. (1966) *A Sign for Cain*. New York: Macmillan.

West, D.J. (1973) *Who Becomes Delinquent?* London: Heinemann.

West, D.J. (1982) *Delinquency: Its Roots, Careers and Prospects*. London: Heinemann.

Westen, D. (1990) 'Towards a revised theory of borderline object relations: contributions of empirical research.' *International Journal of Psycho-Analysis 71*, 661–694.

White, M. (1984) 'Pseudo encopresis: from avalanche to victory, from vicious to virtuous cycle.' *Family Systems Medicine 2*, 15–160.

White, M. (1986) 'Negative explanation, restraint and double description. A template for family therapy.' *Family Process 25*, 169–184.

White, M. (1989) 'The externalising of the problem and the re-authoring of lives and relationship.' *Dulwich Centre Newsletter*. Adelaide: Dulwich Centre Publications.

White, M. and Epston, D. (1989) *Literate Means to Therapeutic Ends*. Adelaide: Dulwich Centre Publications.

Whiteley, J.S. (1970) 'The response of psychopaths to a therapeutic community.' *British Journal of Psychiatry 116*, 517–529.

Whiteley, J.S. (1994) 'Attachment, loss and the space between: personality disorder in the therapeutic community.' 18th Annual S.H. Foulkes Lecture. *Group Analysis 27*, 4, 359–387.

Widom, C. (1989) 'Does violence beget violence?' *Psychological Bulletin 106*, 3–28.

Widom, C. (1991) 'Avoidance of criminality in abused and neglected children.' *Psychiatry 54*, 162–174.

Widom, C. and Ames, M.A. (1994) 'Criminal consequences of childhood victimisation.' *Child Abuse and Neglect 18*, 303–318.

Wilkens, J. and Coid, J. (1991) 'Self mutilation in female remand prisoners I.' *Criminal Behaviour and Mental Health 1*, 247–267.

Wilkinson, G. (1984) 'Day care for patients with psychiatric disorders.' *British Medical Journal 288*, 1710–1711.

Williams, A. (1982) 'Adolescence, violence, and crime.' *Journal of Adolescence 5*, 125–134.

Williams, A. (1989) *The Passionate Technique: Strategic Psychodrama with Individuals, Families, and Groups.* London: Tavistock/Routledge.

Williams, G. (1983) *Textbook of Criminal Law.* Second Edition. London: Stevens and Sons.

Williams, M. (1992) 'What works? Research and rehabilitation.' In HMSO *Perspectives on Prison: A Collection of Views in Prison Life and Running Prisons.* London: HMSO.

Williams, T. (1991) 'Forensic Psychotherapy: symbiosis or impossibility.' Address given at the 17th International Congress of the International Academy of Law and Mental Health. Leuven, Belgium.

Wilson and Kelling (1982) 'The police and neighbourhood safety: broken windows.' *Atlantic Monthly 127*, 28–38.

Wilson, E.O. (1978) *On Human Nature.* Cambridge, MA: Harvard University Press.

Wilson, J.Q. (1985) *Thinking About Crime.* 2nd edition. New York: Vintage Books.

Wilson, J.Q. and Hernstein, R. (1985) *Crime and Human Nature.* New York: Simon and Schuster.

Wilson, P. (1991) 'Psychotherapy with adolescents.' In J. Holmes (ed) *Textbook of Psychotherapy in Psychiatric Practice.* Edinburgh: Churchill Livingstone.

Wimmer, H. and Perner, J. (1983) 'Beliefs about beliefs: representation and constraining function of wrong beliefs in young children's understanding of deception.' *Cognition 13*, 103–128.

Winchel, R.M. and Stanley, M. (1991) 'Self-injurious behaviour: a review of the behaviour and biology of self-mutilation.' *American Journal of Psychiatry 148*, 306–317.

de Wind, E. (1972) 'Persecution, aggression and therapy.' *International Journal of Psychoanalysis 53*, 173–177.

Wing, J.K. (1993) 'Institutionalism revisited.' *Criminal Behaviour and Mental Health 3*, 441–45.

Winnicott, D.W. (1949) 'Hate in countertransference.' *International Journal of Psycho-Analysis 30*, 69–74.

Winnicott, D.W. (1951) 'Transitional objects and transitional phenomena.' In D.W. Winnicott *Collected Papers: Though Paediatrics to Psychoanalysis.* London: Tavistock Publications, 1958. Reprinted 1991, London: Karnac Books.

Winnicott, D.W. (1956) 'The antisocial tendency.' In D.W. Winnicott *Collected Papers: Through Paediatrics to Psycho-analysis.* London: Tavistock, 1958.

Winnicott, D.W. (1958) 'The capacity to be alone.' *International Journal of Psycho-Analysis 39*, 416–20.

Winnicott, D.W. (1960) 'The theory of the parent–infant relationship.' In D.W. Winnicott *The Maturational Processes and the Facilitating Environment.* London: Hogarth Press.

Winnicott, D.W. (1963a) 'Hospital care supplementing intensive psychotherapy in adolescence.' In D.W. Winnicott *The Maturational Processes and the Facilitating Environment.* London: Hogarth Press.

Winnicott, D.W. (1963b) 'The development of the capacity for concern.' *Bulletin of the Menninger Clinic 27*, 16–76.

Winnicott, D.W. (1963c) 'The mentally ill in your case load.' In D.W. Winnicott *The Maturational Processes and the Facilitating Environment.* New York: International Universities Press.

Winnicott, D. (1965) *The Maturational Processes and the Facilitating Environment.* London: Hogarth Press.

Winnicott, D.W. (1966) 'Adolescence: struggling through the doldrums.' In D.W. Winnincott *The Family and Individual Development.* London: Tavistock Publications.

Winnicott, D.W. (1971a) *Playing and Reality.* London: Tavistock Publications.

Winnicott, D.W. (1971b) 'Creativity and its origins.' In D.W. Winnicott *Playing and Reality.* Harmondsworth: Penguin Books.

Winnicott, D.W. (1984) *Deprivation and Delinquency.* London: Tavistock.

Winnicott, D.W. (1986) 'Delinquency as a sign of hope.' In D.W. Winnicott *Home Is Where We Start From.* London: Penguin Books.

Wittgenstein, L. (1953) *Philosophical Investigations.* Oxford: Basil Blackwell.

Wolfe, B.E. and Goldfried, M.R. (1988) 'Research on psychotherapy integration: recommendations and conclusions from an N.I.M.H. workshop.' *Journal of Consulting and Clinical Psychology 56*, 3, 448–451.

Wolff, H.H. (1971) 'The therapeutic and development functions of psychotherapy.' *British Journal of Medical Psychology 44*, 117–130.

Woodhouse, G., Rasbash, J., Goldstein, H. and Yang, M. (1992) *A Guide to ML3 for New Users.* London: Institute of Education, University of London.

Woolf, H. and Tumim, S. (1991) *Prison Disturbances April 1990. Report of an Inquiry by Lord Justice Woolf and Judge Stephen Tumim.* London: HMSO.

World Health Organization (1978) *Mental Disorders: Glossary and Guide to their Classification in Accordance with the Ninth Revision of the International Classification of Diseases.* Geneva: World Health Organisation.

World Health Organization (1981) *Development of Indicators for Monitoring Progress Towards Health for all by the Year 2000.* Geneva: World Health Organisation.

World Health Organization (1989) *Tenth Revision of the International Classification of Disease, Chapter V (F). Mental and Behavioural Disorders (Including Disorders of Psychological Development).* Geneva: World Health Organisation (original classification published 1968).

Wright, A. (in press) *Value Conflicts in Policing: An Empirical Study.* London: The Police Foundation.

Wurmser, L. (1981) *The Mask of Shame.* Baltimore, MD: Johns Hopkins University Press.

Wurmser, L. (1987) 'Shame: the veiled companion of narcissism.' In D.L. Nathanson (ed) *The Many Faces of Shame.* New York: Guilford Press.

Yalom, I.B. (1970) *The Theory and Practice of Group Psychotherapy.* New York: Basic Books.

Yeats, W.B. (1950) *Collected Poems.* Second edition. London: Macmillan.

Yeats, W.B. (1971) *Uncollected Prose 1970–1975.* Edited by J.P. Frayne. London: Macmillan.

Yorke, C., Kennedy, H. and Wiseberg, S. (1981) 'Some clinical and theoretical aspects of two developmental lines.' In S.I. Greenson and H. Pollock (eds) *The Course of Life.* Adelphi, MD: U.S. Department of Health.

Yorke, C., Wiseberg, S. and Freeman, T. (1989) *Development and Psychopathology: Studies in Psychoanalytic Psychiatry.* New Haven, CT and London: Yale University Press.

Young, J. (1988) 'Radical criminology in Britain: the emergence of a competing paradigm.' *British Journal of Criminology 28,* 2, 159–83; and in P. Rock (ed) *The History of British Criminology.* Oxford: Clarendon Press.

Young, J. (1994) 'Incessant chatter: recent paradigms in criminology.' In M. Maguire, R. Morgan and R. Reiner (eds) *The Oxford Handbook of Criminology.* Oxford: Oxford University Press.

Zavitzianos, G. (1971) 'Fetishism and exhibitionism in the female and their relationship to psychopathy and kleptomania.' *International Journal of Psychoanalysis 52,* 297–305.

Zavitzianos, G. (1982) 'The perversion of fetishism in women.' *Psychoanalytical Quarterly 51,* 405–425.

Zilboorg, G. (1955) *The Psychology of the Criminal Act and Punishment.* London: Hogarth Press and Institute of Psycho-Analysis.

Zinner, J. and Shapiro, R. (1974) 'The family group as a single psychic entity, implications for acting out in adolescence.' *International Revenue of Psychoanalysis*

1, 179–86.Zwerling, I. (1979) 'The creative arts therapies as real therapies'. *Hospital and Community Psychiatry 30*, 12.

de Zulueta, F. (1993) *From Pain to Violence: The Traumatic Roots of Destructiveness.* London: Whurr.

The Contributors

Gwen Adshead is Lecturer in Forensic Psychiatry at the Institute of Psychiatry.

Anthony Bateman is Consultant Psychotherapist at the Halliwick Day Unit, St Ann's Hospital.

Arnon Bentovim is Honorary Consultant Child Psychiatrist at Great Ormond Street Hospital for Children and the Tavistock Clinic and Honorary Senior Lecturer at the Institute of Child Health, University of London.

Jacqueline Blatt is Course Co-ordinator for the MA in Dance Movement Therapy at the Laban Centre for Movement and Dance and Associate Professor at Hahnemann University.

Donald Campbell is Principal Psychotherapist and former Chairman of the Portman Clinic, and Member and Training Analyst, The British Psycho-analytic Society.

Jo-anne Carlyle is Clinical Psychologist in Psychoanalytical Psychotherapy at the Tavistock Clinic.

Nick Clark is a Registered Mental Nurse at the Three Bridges Regional Secure Unit, West London Healthcare NHS Trust.

Christopher Cordess is Consultant Forensic Psychiatrist with the North West Thames Forensic Psychiatry Service, London, and Honorary Senior Lecturer in Forensic Psychiatry at Charing Cross and Westminster Medical School. He is a Member of the British Psycho-analytic Society.

Murray Cox was Consultant Psychotherapist at Broadmoor Hospital from 1970 until 1997. He was an Honorary Member of the Institute of Group Analysis, the Danish Society for Psychoanalytic Psychotherapy and an Honorary Research Fellow, The Shakespeare Institute, The University of Birmingham.

Richard Davies is Senior Clinical Lecturer in Social Work and Principal Adult Psychotherapist at the Portman Clinic.

Bridget Dolan is Senior Lecturer in Forensic Psychology and an Honorary Lecturer in the Forensic Psychiatry section at St George's Hospital Medical School and Henderson Hospital.

Chris Evans is Lecturer in Psychotherapy at St George's Hospital.

Graeme Farquharson is Co-ordinator of Training at the Institute of Group Analysis.

Elizabeth Flannigan is Head Occupational Therapist at West London Healthcare Trust.

Peter Fonagy is Director of the sub-department of Clinical Health Psychology and Freud Memorial Professor of Psychoanalysis at University College, London, and is Director of the Anna Freud Centre.

Jennifer France is a Speech and Language Therapist at Broadmoor Hospital.

Stephen Freiberg is Consultant Psychiatrist and Psychotherapist at Wycombe Clinic, Sydney, and Visiting Psychiatrist at Long Bay Correction Centre and Prison Medical Service of New South Wales, Sydney.

Patrick Gallwey is a Psychoanalyst in private practice in Exeter and an Associate Member of the British Psycho-analytic Society.

James Gilligan is the Director of the Centre for the Study of Violence, The Cambridge Hospital, and Lecturer in Psychiatry, Harvard Medical School.

Adrian Grounds is Lecturer in Forensic Psychiatry at the Institute of Criminology and the Department of Psychiatry, University of Cambridge.

John Gunn, CBE, is Professor of Forensic Psychiatry at the Institute of Psychiatry.

Robert M. Hardy is the Bishop of Lincoln and the Anglican Bishop to Prisons.

Harriet Haworth is Clinical Psychologist at the Three Bridges Regional Secure Unit, Ealing Hospital.

Maggie Hilton is Consultant Clinical Psychologist at Henderson Outreach Service, Henderson Hospital.

R.D. Hinshelwood is Clinical Director at Cassel Hospital, and a Member of the British Psycho-analytic Society.

Arthur Hyatt Williams, now a Psychoanalyst in private practice in London, was Head of Adolescent Development at the Tavistock Clinic.

Rein Innes is Senior Art Psychotherapist at the Fromeside Clinic.

Barrie Irving is Director of The Police Foundation.

Jinnie Jefferies is a Psychodramatist and Counselling Psychologist at HM Prison Grendon Underwood.

Sue Jennings is an actress and broadcaster, Senior Research Associate at the University of London, Visiting Professor of Dramatherapy at New York University, and Honorary Consultant Dramatherapist at Broadmoor Hospital.

Dilys Jones is Medical Director, The Special Hospitals Service Authority, and an Honorary Lecturer at the Institute of Psychiatry.

Michael Killian is a Registered Mental Nurse at the Three Bridges Regional Secure Unit, West London Healthcare NHS Trust.

Gabriel Kirtchuk is Consultant Psychotherapist at the Regional Secure Unit, St Bernard's Hospital and an Associate Member of the British Psycho-analytic Society.

Peter Lewis is Director of Clinical Services and Director of Therapy at HM Prison Grendon Underwood.

Helen Loth is Head Music Therapist at Henderson Hospital, Haringey Healthcare.

Hjalmer van Marle is Medical Director at the Pieter Baan Centrum, Utrecht.

Clive Meux is Senior Lecturer in Forensic Psychiatry at The Institute of Psychiatry, University of London, and Honorary Consultant Forensic Psychiatrist at Broadmoor Hospital.

Jeannie Milligan is Clinical Lecturer in Social Work at the Tavistock Clinic.

Anton Mooij is a Member of the Directorate of the Forensic Observation Hospital of the Penitentiary, the Pieter Baan Centrum, Utrecht, and Professor of Forensic Psychiatry, State University of Groningen.

Kingsley Norton is Consultant Psychotherapist at Henderson Hospital and Honorary Senior Lecturer in the Section of Forensic Psychiatry at St George's Hospital.

Derek Perkins is Director of Psychological Services at Broadmoor Hospital.

Friedemann Pfäfflin is Senior Consultant in the Department of Psychotherapy at the University of Ulm.

Elaine Player is a Lecturer in Law at King's College, London.

Marie Quayle is Consultant Clinical Psychologist at Broadmoor Hospital.

J.H.Scheffer is a Psychoanalyst in private practice in Utrecht and is a Member of the Directorate of the Forensic Observation Hospital of the Penitentiary, the Pieter Baan Centrum, Utrecht.

John Schlapobersky is a Group Analyst and Psychotherapist at The Group Analytic Practice.

Valerie Sinason is Principal Child Psychotherapist at the Tavistock Clinic.

Ann Stanley is Senior Registrar in Forensic Psyciatry at the Reaside Clinic, Birmingham.

Deirdre Sutton-Smith is in private practice as a group analyst in Bristol, formerly a Probation Officer with the Inner London Probation Service, a group analyst at the Women's Centre, London and a Member of the Institute of Group Analysis.

Neville Symington is a Psychoanalyst in private practice in Sydney.

Digby Tantam is Professor of Psychotherapy at the University of Warwick.

Mary Target is Lecturer and Senior Research Fellow in Psychology at University College, London and the Anna Freud Centre.

Nicholas Temple is Chairman of the Tavistock Clinic.

Alice Theilgaard is Professor of Medical Psychology at the University of Copenhagen and an Honorary Research Fellow, The Shakespeare Institute, The University of Birmingham.

Nikolaas Treurniet is a Psychoanalyst in private practice in Amsterdam and Training and Supervising Analyst, the Dutch Psychoanalytic Society.

Stephen Tumim is HM Chief Inspector of Prisons.

Cleo van Velsen is Consultant Psychotherapist at The Maudsley Hospital.

Estela V. Welldon is Consultant Psychiatrist at the Portman Clinic and Honorary Senior Lecturer in Forensic Psychotherapy at the University of London.

Richard Wells is Chief Constable of South Yorkshire Police.

Adrian West is Clinical Psychologist at the Personality Disorder Unit, Ashworth Hospital.

J. Stuart Whiteley, now a Consultant Psychotherapist in private practice in Surrey, was Medical Director at Henderson Hospital.

Eric Wilkinson is a Staff Nurse at Broadmoor Hospital.

Peter Wilson is the Director of Young Minds.

Martin Wrench is Senior Social Worker in the Department of Forensic Psychiatry at Shaftsbury Clinic, Springfield Hospital.

John L. Young is Attending Psychiatrist at Yale Medical School and Associate Clinical Professor of Psychiatry at the Whiting Institute.

Felicity de Zulueta is Consultant Psychotherapist at Charing Cross Hospital, Riverside Mental Health Trust, Honorary Senior Lecturer at The University of London, and a qualified Group Analyst.

Subject Index

Author
Index

Abel, G., on effects of
listening to violence
II 236
Abelin, E.L., on role of father
II 350-1
Abraham, K.
on delinquency **I** 122
developmental model **I** 118
Adlam-Hill, S. and Harris,
P.L., on child's
understanding of
emotion **I** 148
Adler, A., on striving for
power **I** 9, 118
Adler, G., on 'clumsy' crime
II 158
Adshead, G.
on development of forensic
psychotherapy **II** 187,
189
on violence to carers **II** 366
Advisory Council on the
Misuse of Drugs **II** 23
Aichhorn, A.
on characteristics of
therapists **II** 322
on delinquency **I** 125
dual deficit model **I** 125-6
on social adaptation **I** 218
Ainsworth, M.D.S., Blehar,
M.C., Waters, E. and
Wall, S., on attachment
I 137-8, 179
Akhtar, S., on anti-social
personality disorder
II 335, 336
Alexander, F.
concept of neurotic
character **I** 126

on superego **I** 129
Alonso, A., *The Quiet
Profession* **II** 204
Alpert, M., on speech **I** 96
Alvarez, A., on defence
mechanisms **I** 41
American Psychiatric
Association, *Diagnostic
and Statistical Manual of
Mental Disorders*
(DSM-II) **II** 334, 356
(DSM-III-R) **II** 275-6,
334-5, 336, 356
DSM-IV **II** 276
Anderson, E., Levine, M.,
Sharma, A., Ferretti, L.,
Steinberg, K. and
Wallach, L., on
mandatory reporting
II 149
Anderson, H., Goolishan, H.
and Windermans, L., on
'problem- determined'
systems **I** 114
Andrews, G., on funding
psychotherapy **II** 166-7
Appelbaum, P.S., on duty to
protect third parties **II** 11
Appelbaum, P.S. and Gutheil,
T.G., on prediction **II** 44
Argyle, M.
on communication skills
I 96
on social skills **II** 453
Aristotle, on shame **II** 482
Arlow, J.A., on perversion
and aggression **II** 274
Arlow, J.A. and Brenner, C.,
on structural frame of
reference **I** 119
Armsden, G.C. and
Greenberg, M.T., on
insecure attachment **I** 138
Aronson, A.E., on voice
disorders **I** 97
Asen, K., George, B., Piper,
R. and Stevens, A., on
rehabilitation **II** 302
Ashurst, N. and Hall, P., on
sexual abuse and
perversion **II** 278

Ashworth, A., on
administrative
criminology **I** 88-9
Auerhahn, N.C. and Laub,
C., on trauma **II** 357
Azima, G. and Azima, J., on
occupational therapy
II 107

Baker, A. and Duncan, S., on
prevalence of abuse
II 368
Balint, M.
on ' Work of Conquest'
II 350
influence of Klein on **I** 157
Bandura, A., on
self-perceptions **I** 59
Bannister, A. and Print, B.,
on police training with
mental health
professionals **II** 23-4
Barch, D. and Berenbaum,
H., on information
processing and language
I 102
Barker, Funk and
Kent-Houston, on
research **II** 523
Baron-Cohen, S.
on child's developing
mental states **I** 144
on gesture **I** 143
Bates, E., Benigni, L.,
Bretherton, I., Camaioni,
L. and Volterra, V., on
infant gestures **I** 143
Bateson, G.
on aesthetics **II** 84, **II** 219
on family patterns **I** 113
Bateson, G., Jackson, D.,
Haley, J. and Weakland,
J., on family **I** 108
Beail, N., on Repertory Grid
Technique **II** 120
Bean, P., Bingley, W., Bynoe,
I., Faulkner, A., Ranaby,
E. and Rogers, A., on
police assessments **II** 22